U0922699

2000 北京统计年鉴

BEIJING STATISTICAL YEARBOOK

北京市统计局编

Compiled by

Beijing Municipal Statistical Bureau

中国统计出版社

China Statistical Publishing House

共和国

▲ 1999年10月1日，走过半个世纪光辉历程的新中国，迎来了她50周年的庆典。首都各界在北京天安门广场举行盛大的阅兵仪式和群众游行，欢庆伟大祖国的这一光辉节日。

① 江泽民主席乘坐国产“红旗检阅车，徐徐向东，检阅由42威武雄壮的人民解放军陆海三军和人民武装警察部队、兵预备役部队组成的地面分队

50周年庆典

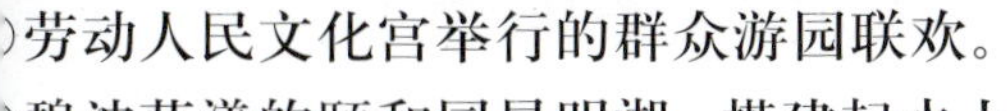

劳动人民文化宫举行的群众游园联欢。

碧波荡漾的颐和园昆明湖，搭建起水上舞台。文艺工作者在精彩表演。

10月1日晚上，天安门广场上空绚丽多彩。

▲ 1999年12月19日晚，首都各界群众在天安门广场举行澳门回归庆祝活动

▶ 2000年中华世纪坛庆典

▲ 中共中央总书记、国家主席江泽民在北京国家图书馆与读者亲切交谈

▶ 北京市政府在各方面的大力支持下，正式申办2008年奥运会

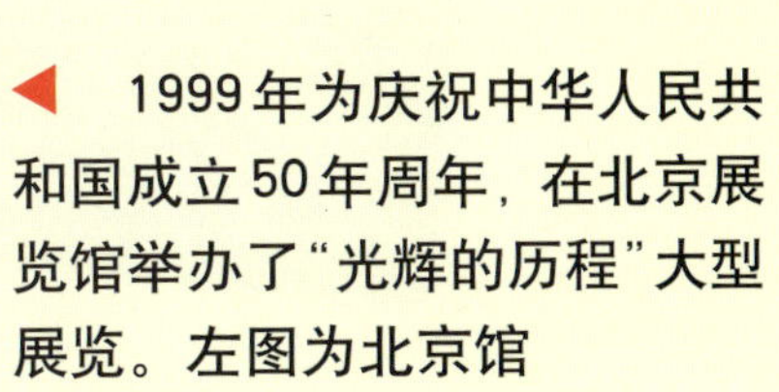

◀ 1999年为庆祝中华人民共和国成立50年周年，在北京展览馆举办了“光辉的历程”大型展览。左图为北京馆

67项重大工程项目扮亮北京

北京市政府为迎接建国50周年确定的67项重大工程项目，经过精心施工，在国庆前夕陆续竣工和外沿亮相，装点了节日的首都。

北京植物园温室

平安大街

菜市口大街

西单文化广场

东方广场

地铁复八线

1999 年北京市统计

1、统计制度方法改革步伐加快。在广泛征求意见的基础上，市统计局推出《北京市1999－2001年统计制度改革方案》。

2、市统计局深入开展“三讲”教育活动。自8月至12月，市统计局先后在局级和处级领导干部中开展了“三讲”教育活动。

3、7月6日，副市长林文漪及市政府有关部门领导到市统计局进行调研。

4、为庆祝建国50周年，市统计局编辑出版大型文献资料集《北京五十年》和《首都经济骨干企业概览》。

5、北京市统计信息工程正式启动。这是首次采用公开招标方式组织建设的政府投资项目。

6、朝阳区举行全市首例统计违法案件听证会。这是政府统计部门依法行政、维护当事人合法权益的行政措施。

7、《北京市统计管理条例》颁布施行五周年。全市各级政府统计部门举行活动，以各种方式纪念《条例》的颁布施行，并加紧实施《行政复议法》。

8、东城区统计信息网络获得好评。经专家鉴定，该系统功能实用，技术先进，在国内同级、同类系统中处于领先水平。

9、我市第五次人口普查前期准备工作全面展开。8月20日，北京市第五次人口普查领导小组第一次扩大会议召开。

10、全市开展了商品交易市场、现有房屋及占用土地情况、城乡和个体工业等多项专项调查。

⑦ A2 专版 中国信息报 1999年11月30日 星期二

纪念《北京市统计管理条例》施行五周年

坚定不移地走依法统计之路

北京市统计局局长 唐龙

依法强化统计　服务社会经济

朝阳区统计局局长 张春秀

完善执法制度是依法行政的重要保证

大兴县统计局局长 汪福祺

大新闻

①
1999年全市统计年报工作会议

②
北京市统计局三讲教育动员大会

③

⑤
北京市统计信息工程开标会

⑥

⑨

⑩
北京市现有房屋及占用土地情况抽样调查工作会议

1999年，全市经济保持了比较活跃和积极的态势，增长率稳中有升。三次产业继续“三二一”格局。

◀ 在保证粮食生产基本稳定的前提下，经济作物比重加大，特菜、特禽、特果逐步加入大众消费市场

北京市国民经济保持良好的发展势头

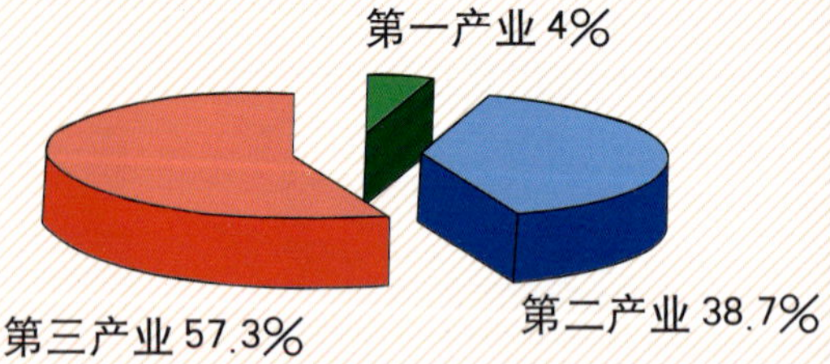

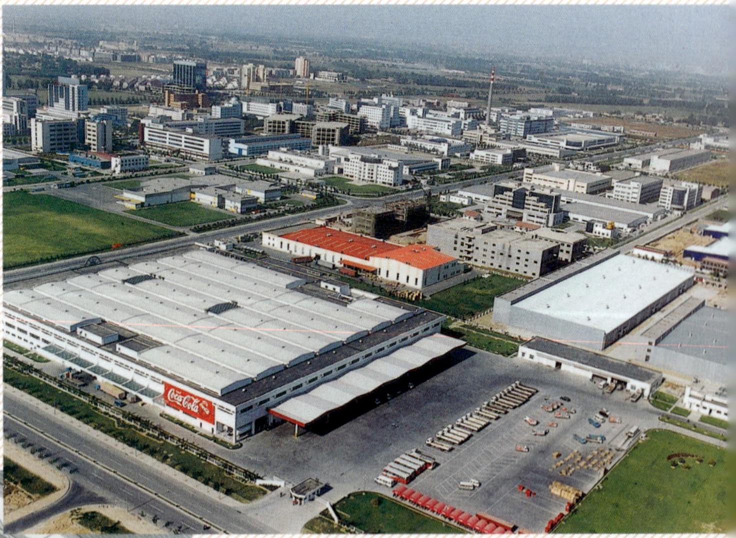

第一产业 4%

第二产业 38.7%

第三产业 57.3%

▲ 高新技术产业为工业发展注入活力，图为北京新技术开发区鸟瞰

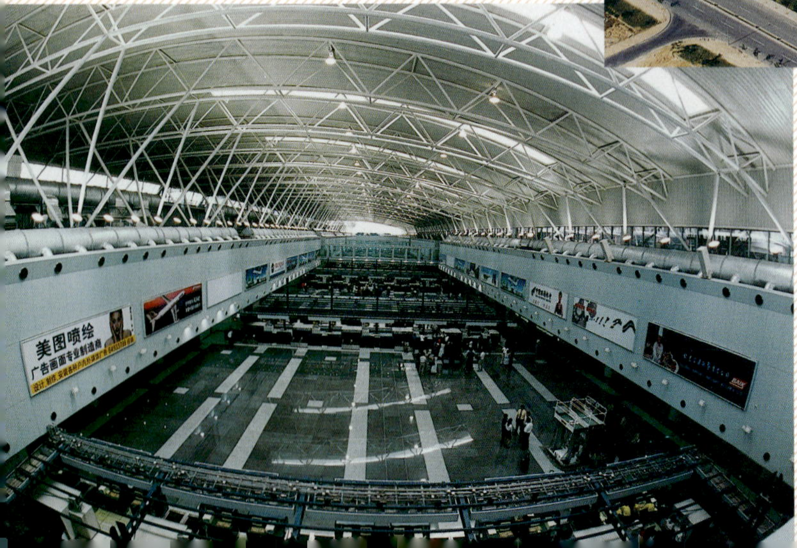

◀ 北京首都国际机场新侯机楼投入使用

北京电视台创建于1979年5月，拥有4个频道，用9种语言播出，日均播出节目75小时，其中自制节目每年生产8000多个小时。第一套节目已于1998年元旦正式通过卫星覆盖全国和亚太38个国家和地区。拥有100余个栏目，在国内外各项评比中，获奖节目逐年增多，仅1997年就获奖318个，其中国际奖4项，国家奖126项。

优秀栏目有《北京新闻》、《今日话题》、《纪实报道》、《东芝动物乐园》、《纪录》、《公益歌曲大擂台》、《荧屏连着我和你》、《同乐园》、《北京您早》、《世界你好》、《双语杂志》、《第7日》、《中国体育报道》、《中国之窗》、《七色光》、《世纪之约》、《电视购物》及影视剧场等。

北京电视台每天播出时间、自制节目数量、技术设备的规模和质量、经济收入总额以及广泛的国际合作关系等方面均在中国地方台中居领先地位。

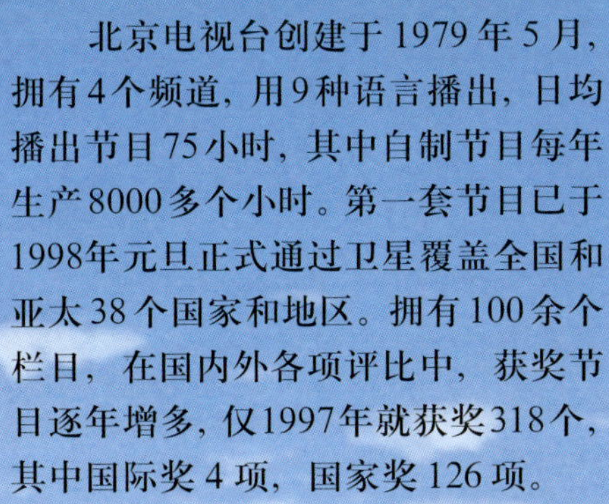

北京电视台与世界上50多个国家和地区的200多个影视机构有着广泛的业务交流与合作，每年5月在北京举办的国际电视周已成为吸引国内外电视同行的盛会。

北京电视台拥有高水平、全功能的技术设备，可以提供安全、可靠、高质量的国际间电视信号传递，现场直播大型文化、体育节目及后期编辑各种特技效果的节目，北京电视台在国内最早播出立体声电视节目。并已实现集团经营、规模发展。

100余个栏目，日均75小时播出

4个频道 9种语言

卫星电视覆盖亚太

北京电视台

地　址：北京市海淀区西三环北路苏洲街3号

邮　编：10089

电　话：68419922　　传　真：68419583　　网　址：WWW.BTV.ORG

BEIJING CITY COMMERCIAL BANK

在创新中求发展 办出地方银行特色

北京市商业银行

北京市商业银行是地方财政和首都众多知名企业参股的新型股份制商业银行，成立于1996年1月8日。四年多来，在北京市委、市政府和中国人民银行的正确领导与关心支持下，坚持稳健经营、规范管理、开拓进取，以实现效益最大化为经营目标，以信誉、服务、管理、科技和业务品种赢得了客户的信任，取得了良好的经营业绩。

截止到1999年末，全行存款余额达到524亿元，比建行初期增加341亿元，在北京银行业中居第三位；贷款余额达到208亿元，比建行初期增加160亿元，累计发放贷款500多亿元，有力地支持了首都经济的发展；资产总额达到608亿元，比建行初期增加390亿元，在全国城市商业银行中居第二位；四年累计实现利润37亿元，在全国银行业中居前列，充分显示了股份制商业银行特有的朝气与活力。

1. 北京市市长刘淇到北京市商业银行调研时与行领导班子合影
2. 北京市商业银行开办国家助学贷款
3. 北京市商业银行与有关单位设立新技术企业担保风险金
4. 北京市商业银行西单支行

北京城市开发集团有限责任公司

BEIJING URBAN DEVELOPMENT GROUP CO.,LTD.

北京城市开发集团有限责任公司（原北京城市建设开发集团总公司），其前身是成立于1980年的北京市城市建设开发总公司，1992年组建为集团，1995年10月，被市政府批准实行国有资产授权经营，1996年改制为有限责任公司。

开发集团是一个以房地产业为主，多元化经营、多成份结构的企业群体，成员企业162家，截止到1998年底，资产总额达131.38亿元；净资产达31.37亿元上缴利税16亿元。核心企业北京城市开发集团有限责任公司为国家资质、资信一级企业。开发集团成立20年来，共开发土地1600余公顷，先后建成了前三门大街、劲松、团结湖、左家庄、方庄（规划建筑面积266万平方米，目前为国内乃至亚洲最大住宅区）、花家地等60余片住宅区及一批道路等市政基础设施，竣工交用各类房屋面积1500万平方米，其中住宅1100万平方米，为首都18万住户、66万余人提供了住房。从1993年以来，向市政府提供安居用房16万平方米。

目前，开发集团正在建设的跨世纪宏伟工程—望京新城，总用地面积约860公顷，规划总建筑面积1400万平方米，包括住宅、公建、商业、仓储及各种配套服务设施，相当于一座总人口25—30万人的中等规模城市，建成后将成为首都北京的副都心，是首都面向21世纪的窗口。望京新城的起步区A 5区商品住宅和K 3、K 4区安居住宅已全部建成，A4区商品住宅也正在建设和销售中。

1992年以来，集团核心企业先后被评为“重合同，守信誉”先进单位和“北京市经济百强”开发类企业第一名；1993年，被国家建设部等有关部门共同评选为中国房地产开发企业百强之首；1993年入选“中国的脊梁”国有企业500强。

法人代表：高久长
总经理：赵康
地址：北京市西城区三里河东路34号
邮编：100045
电话：68031242
传真：68010438
网址：http://www.cbud.com.cn

《北京统计年鉴》编辑委员会

Editorial Board and Staff

编 辑 说 明

1、《北京统计年鉴》是一部按年连续出版的大型统计资料书。本书通过大量的统计数据，真实地记录了北京市一年来社会经济和科技方面的发展变化情况，是国内外各界人士了解北京认识北京的重要资料工具书。

2、《北京统计年鉴——2000》为全部中英文对照版；并配有电子版统计年鉴，具备制图和快速查询的功能，而且可通过转换键实现中英文切换，以增强图书版统计年鉴的功能，满足各方面读者的爱好和习惯，紧跟当前电子信息化的步伐。内容上增加了外来人口及老年人口调查资料，高新技术产业资料、企业集团情况，并完善了重点行业财务状况统计。为了便于读者查阅，每个细目编排了主要指标提要和指标解释。

3、年鉴全书分为两部分——统计公报和统计图表，第一部分登载了北京市 1999 年国民经济和社会发展统计公报；第二部分分综合，人口，劳动力和工资，固定资产投资及房地产，农业和农村经济，工业，能源生产和消费，建筑业，交通运输、邮电通信业，批发零售贸易及餐饮业，对外经济贸易、旅游业，金融、保险，物价，教育，文化，科技，卫生、体育，城市公用事业，人民生活，社会福利、政法及其他，服务业，区县资料等 21 个细目。另外，还在附录部分中分列了北京市自改革开放以来的主要经济数据，各类市场情况，开发区情况，企业及企业集团情况和世界各国及香港、澳门资料等。

4、本年鉴的资料来源大部分来自年度统计报表，部分来自抽样调查；世界各国及香港、澳门资料来自国家统计局

5、本年鉴对以前发表的统计资料重新进行了核实，相应地调整了部分数据。读者在使用历史数据时，如数据有出入，请以本年鉴为准。

6、本年鉴中，顺义县已调整为顺义区，昌平县已调整为昌平区。

7、本年鉴采用的国民经济行业分类是按照中华人民共和国国家标准《国民经济行业分类和代码》划分的；登记注册类型是按照 1998 年 9 月 2 日国家统计局、国家工商行政管理局颁发的《关于划分企业登记注册类型的规定》划分的；使用的度量单位均采用国家统一的标准计量单位。

8、各表分组数相加与总计数略有差额，因四舍五入之故。

9、本年鉴使用的符号说明："…"表示数据不足该表最小单位数；"空格"表示该项指标数据不详或没有数据；"#"表示其中项。

Preface

1. Beijing Statistical Yearbook is a regular large-scale statisical reference book published yearly.With a vast amount of statistical data,the book can keep you abreast of new developments in Beijing on various aspects,including society,science and technology,etc.It is really an important and efficient reference book for people of varous circles in and outside China to know and understand Beijing.

2. Based on the original style,Beijing Staistical Yearbook 2000 is a radical revision of its predecesor.

- To support the opening to outside of Beijing and meet the foreigners' needs for their business and investment in Beijing, Beijing Statistical Yearbook 2000 is published in complete Chinese-English edition.
- To meet various interests and habits of users and reinfoce the functions of the yearbook,Beijing Statistical Yearbook 2000 has its electronic edition published simultaneously,With additional functions like charting,quick search,shift between Chinese and English in search by Shift key,etc.
- The content is enriched by additions on the statistics for nonnatives and old people, high-grade technological industry and enterprise group.
- For the convenience of consulting,outline and explanatory of main indicators are added to every chapter.

3. The yearbook has two parts:Statical Communique and Statistical Graph.The first part consists of Statistical Communique on 1999 Economic and Social Development of Beijing,The second part consists of all the 21 chapters concerning General Survey,Population,Labor Force and Wage,Investment in fixed Assets and Real Estate,Agriculture and Rural Economy,Industry,Energy Production and Consumption, Construction, Transportation, Posts and Communications, Wholesale, Retail and Catering,Foreign Economy,Trade and Tourism,Finance and Insurance,Price,Education and Culture,Technology, Health and Sports,Municipal Pubic Utilities,People's Livelihood,Social Welfare,Politics,Law and Others,Services, General Survey of Districts and Counties,etc.You can find also in the second part as the content of appendix that the economic data from 1978 to 1999, conditions of various markets and Beijing Development Zone, Statistils for enterprise and enterprise group, data of countries and territories .HongKong and Macaom,etc.

4. Most of the data in this yearbook sources are from annual reports,a small part sources from sample survey,data of countries,HongKong and Macao from State Statisical Bureau.

5. Some of the published data are changed in this yearbook according to our checking,therefore,data in this yearbook are reliable whenever you find different data in other publications.

6. Your attention please on that the Shunyi and Changping County in this yearbook have been Changed to Shunyi and Changping District.

7. The classification of national economy in this yearbook is in line with State Standard Classification and Code of National Econmy by Sector of the People's Republic of China.The classification of registered type is in line with The Provisions on Classification of Registered Type of Enterprises issued by State Statistical Bureau and State Administrative Bureau for Industry and Commerce.The units of weights and measures adopted in the yearbook are all international standard units of weights and measures.

8. Sum of numbers of each group may be not equal to the total because of rounding up.

9. Special symbols in this yearbook: “…” indicates the amount is too small to be recorded in the table;“blank space”indicates missing case: “#” indicates an item(indicator)among the previous one.

目　录
CONTENTS

文章选编
ARTICLES

统计图表
STATISTICAL GRAPH AND CHART

综合
GENERAL SURVEY

固定资产投资及房地产业

INVESTMENT IN FLXED ASSETS AND REAL ESTATE

工业

INDUSTRY

能源生产与消费

PRODUCTION AND CONSUMPTION OF ENERGY

批发零售贸易业的餐饮业

WHOLESALE，RETAIL AND CATERING

对外经济贸易、旅游

FORELGN ECONOMY，TRADE AND TOURISM

教育、文化

EDUCATION AND CULTURE

主要统计指标提要及统计图

SUMMARY OF MAIN STATISTICAL INDICATORS AND GRAPH

附录 2：各类开发区资料

APPENDIX 2：VARIOUS DEVELOPMENT ZONES

附录 3：各类市场情况

APPENDIX 3：VARIOUS MARKETS

北京统计年鉴---2000

BEIJING STATISTICAL YEARBOOK

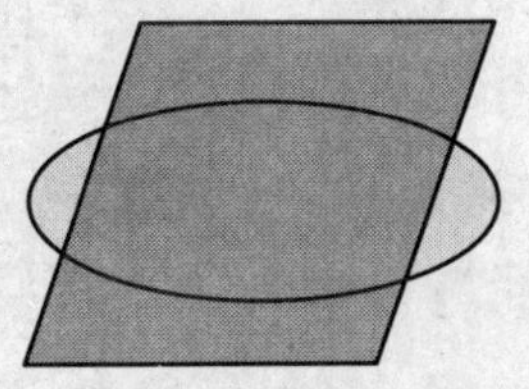

文章选编

ARTICLES

北京市统计局
1999年国民经济和社会发展统计公报

2000年2月2日

1999年，在中共北京市委、北京市人民政府的领导下，全市各族人民深入贯彻党的十五大和十五届三中全会、四中全会精神，紧紧抓住庆祝建国50周年和迎接澳门回归的契机，努力创建良好的经济环境、社会环境和城市环境，国民经济继续保持了良好的发展势头，各项社会事业全面进步，城市环境明显改观，就业形势基本稳定，城乡人民生活水平逐步提高。但进一步启动需求的任务仍很艰巨，经济结构调整的难度不容忽视。

一、综合经济

社会总供给：初步统计，全市实现国内生产总值2169.7亿元，按可比价格计算，比上年同期增长10%，增长速度比年初市人代会通过的9%的预期目标高1个百分点，比上年提高0.2个百分点。1999年我市经济运行中有50年庆典等有利因素的积极影响，更受到物价水平持续下降的制约，在这种形势下，总体经济运行仍保持了比较活跃和积极的态势，经济增长率稳中有升。人均国内生产总值达到19803元，比上年增长9.3%。

三次产业继续保持“三二一”格局，产业发展出现新变化。第三产业实现增加值1238.3亿元，增长8.1%，占国内生产总值的比重为57.1%，比上年提高0.5个百分点。第二产业成为拉动全市经济增长的主要力量。全年第二产业实现增加值843.9亿元，增长12.5%，比全市经济增速高2.5个百分点，对全市经济的贡献率达到59.2%，比上年提高12.9个百分点，这是自1995年以来，第二产业增速和贡献率首次高于第三产业，占国内生产总值的比重为38.9%。第一产业发展保持稳定,全年实现增加值87.5亿元,增长2.5%,占国内生产总值的比重为4%。

国内生产总值构成(%)

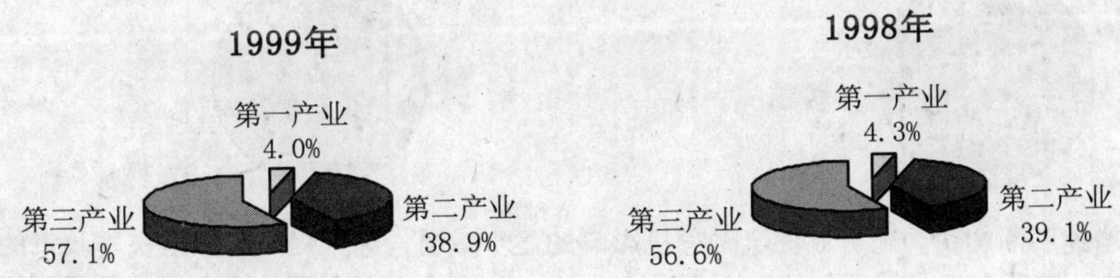

社会总需求：在国家积极的财政政策和适度扩张的货币政策作用下，全市投资需求增长平缓，消费、出口需求增速较快，社会总需求对经济增长的拉动力仍显不足。

投资需求增势减缓。1999年全市投资在67项国庆重大工程的带动下，上半年总体上呈现稳步上升的走势，8月份后，全市投资逐月回落。全年完成全社会固定资产投资1170.6亿元，比上年增长1.3%；其中地方完成投资831.8亿元，增长7.7%，中央完成投资338.8亿元，下降11.5%。

在全市投资中，房地产投资增长最快，全年完成投资 421.5 亿元，增长 11.7 %，基本建设投资完成 432.7 亿元，增长 0.7%，更新改造投资完成 175.2 亿元，呈下降趋势为 -17.1%。全年固定资产投资主要向住宅建设倾斜，其比重达到 30%，比上年提高 4.2 个百分点。

全社会固定资产投资构成（%）

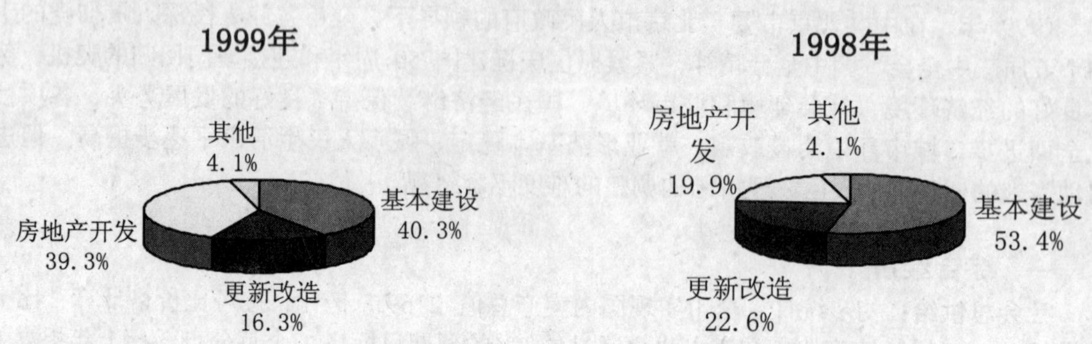

消费需求平稳增长。主要通过消费品零售额指标反映的国内消费，在物价持续走低的形势下，基本延续了上年的走势，全年实现社会消费品零售额 1313.3 亿元，增长 9.9%，扣除价格因素后实际增长 11.2%。积极开拓农村市场的一系列措施初见成效。全年农村实现消费品零售额 191.6 亿元，增长 15.7 %，高于城镇零售额增速 6.7 个百分点；城镇实现零售额 1121.7 亿元，增长 9%。从消费结构看：用类商品保持旺销，全年实现零售额 742.1 亿元，增长 11.6%；吃类商品实现销售额 374.5 亿元，增长 7.7%；穿类商品销售平稳，全年实现销售额 155.6 亿元，增长 7%。

社会消费品零售额的构成（%）

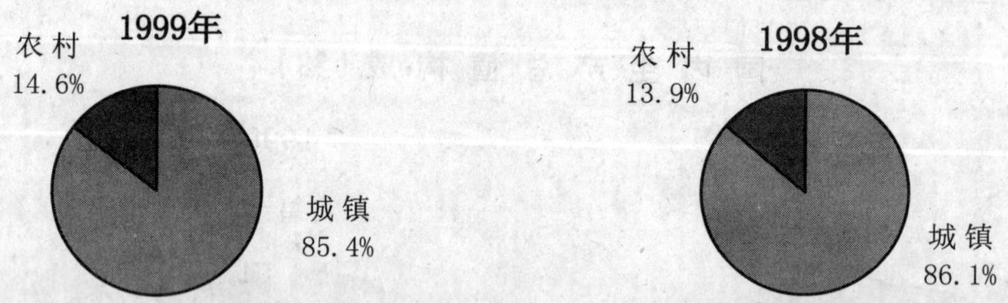

出口增速不断加快。随着亚洲金融危机影响的逐步减弱，国家提高出口退税率政策的效应发挥，全市出口降幅逐月减缓，地方企业累计出口从 8 月份开始转降为升，增速逐月加快。据海关统计，全年全市完成进出口总值 343.9 亿美元，增长 12.7%。其中出口 98.9 亿美元，比上年下降 5.9%。地方完成出口 32.6 亿美元，增长 15.2%。从地方出口产品结构看，工业制成品出口总值 30.1 亿美元，增长 14.2 %，占出口总值的 92.3%，比上年有所下降；初级产品增长较快，增幅达 28.8 %。国有和外商投资企业出口齐头并进，分别完成出口 17.5 亿和 14.7 亿美元，增长 15.0 %和 16.1%。

物价：全年物价总水平继续呈低位运行状态。商品零售价格指数为 98.8%，比上年降幅有所回升；居民消费价格指数为 100.6%，比上年涨幅低了 1.8 个百分点。物价改革稳步推进，年内先后调整了书报杂志、邮政电信、民用燃料、自来水、医疗、公共交通等价格，逐步理顺商品、服务项目的比价关系。

效益：宏观经济效益有所改善。每百元固定资产创造国内生产总值 185.4 元，增长 2.8%。全员劳动生产率 34642 元/人，比上年增长 9.3%。其中，第一产业 12153 元/人，增长 1.8%；第二产业 37929 元/人，增长 14.3%；第三产业 37318 元/人，增长 5.8%

地方财政收入：全年地方财政收入总计 320.5 亿元，比上年增长 22.3%。其中一般预算收入完成 279.1 亿元，增长 22.8%，实现财政收入连续五年增幅在 20%以上；财政支出总计 410.2 亿元，增长 33.2%，其中一般预算支出 367 亿元，增长 30.7%。

二、行业发展

农业：生产结构的调整和优化升级，取得了积极的进展，带动全市农业生产持续增长。从农业内部结构看，养殖业领先于种植业快速发展。全年养殖业产值 88.9 亿元，实际增长 11.6%，高于种植业 9.5 个百分点，占农业总产值的比重上升到 48.2%；比上年提高 0.5 个百分点。从种植业结构看，在保证粮食生产基本稳定的前提下，蔬菜、花卉、牧草等经济作物的比重加大，名、特、优、新品种大幅提高，已达 170 多种，原来仅在宾馆、饭店才得一见的特菜、特禽、特果等已逐步进入大众消费市场。创汇农业迅猛发展，全年出口总值 19.4 亿元，增长 79.6 %。农业机械化水平继续提高，年末农业机械总动力达到 410.4 万千瓦。农村用电量 29.2 亿千瓦小时，比上年增长 6.2 %。

工业：全年实现工业增加值 651 亿元，按可比价格计算，比上年增长 13.1%，为 1995 年以来最高增速，其中规模（年销售收入 500 万元）以上工业实现增加值 589.3 亿元，增长 13.4%。中央工业继续保持高速增长。全年完成增加值 215.6 亿元，比上年增长 20.4%；地方工业完成增加值 373.7 亿元，增长 9.3%。非国有工业率先增长，其中三资工业完成增加值 231.8 亿元，股份制企业完成 61.7 亿元，分别比上年增长 21.4%和 23.9%。重工业发展速度继续快于轻工业，完成增加值 431.8 亿元，增长 16%，增幅快于轻工业 9.7 个百分点；轻工业完成增加值 157.5 亿元。

高新技术产业为工业发展注入活力。全年高新技术产业实现增加值 165 亿元，比上年增长 19.0%；占国内生产总值的比重为 7.6%，占全市工业增加值的比重 25.4%，对全市工业增长的贡献率达到 66.9%，比上年提高 2.3 个百分点。

经济效益明显好转。工业经济效益综合指数为 99.84%，比上年提高 7.74 个百分点；实现利润 63.5 亿元，增长 41.0%，其中盈利企业盈利额为 99.6 亿元，增长 21.6%，亏损企业亏损额 36.1 亿元，比上年下降 2.1%。

建筑业：全年实现增加值 192.9 亿元，比上年增长 9.7%。在全市投资增速减缓的作用下，施工生产增长平稳。全年施工面积 6556.5 万平方米，比上年增长 0.9%，竣工面积 2321.5 万平方米，比上年增长 27.4%。工程质量明显提高。全市工程优良品率达 49.1%，比上年提高 4.1 个百分点。经济效益有所改善。全年实现利润总额 13 亿元，全员劳动生产率达 8.3 万元/人，分别增长 4.8%和 10.7%。

交通运输业：全年实现增加值 60.1 亿元，比上年增长 2.4%。货物运输量 28274.8 万吨，比上年增长 0.8%；旅客运输量 14866.4 万人次，增长 32.4%。公路运输随着道路状况的逐步改善，发挥方便快速的优势，国有运输和社会运力并举，运力运量有所增长；铁路通过调整高低峰谷运力和增设豪华列车等手段，挖掘潜力，满足不同时期、不同消费群体的需要，吸引了大批顾客；航空则以其速度的优势和良好的服务，适应人们不断加快的生活节奏，满足人们高品质的要求。三种运输方式分别占货运量的90.7%、9.1%、0.1%和客运量的66.4%、28.3%、5.3%。

邮电通信业：全年实现增加值110.1亿元，比上年增长14.4%。随着科学技术水平的提高和数字化网络化经济迅速进入中国市场，全市邮电通信业持续高速发展。邮电业务总量达到157.4亿元，增长23.2%。发送报刊14.1亿件，杂志5480万份，特快专递777万件，分别增长0.1%、1.8%和23.3%。全市电话交换机容量达743万门，比上年增长8.2%。电话普及率达到62部/百人，市区电话普及率达到89部/百人；年末移动电话用户达到183.9万户，当年新增67.2万户；新设IC卡公用电话5870部。

国内贸易业：全年批发和零售贸易、餐饮业实现增加值211.2亿元，比上年增长3.1%。全年社会商品购进总值2327.1亿元，增长17.3%；商品销售总值2658.6亿元，增长27.2%。商业经济效益状况有所好转。全年2000余家大中型批发零售贸易业累计实现商品销售收入1673.2亿元，增长8.3%；人均实现销售收入64.5万元，增长15.1%。

金融、保险业：全年实现增加值315亿元，比上年增长13.3%。在国家一系列财政金融措施的影响下，金融机构存款增势明显减缓，货币流动性进一步增强，降低利率、征收利息税的政策显示出一定效果。全市金融机构存款余额8267.2亿元，比年初增加1428.9亿元，比上年增长13.1%，低于上年同期增幅31.9个百分点。全市贷款余额4007.8亿元，比年初增加559.6亿元，受资产管理公司成立及政策性银行贷款管理方式改变等各种因素影响，比上年少增加52亿元。全年累计回笼现金40亿元。

证券市场平稳发展。全年证券交易机构交易额10913.5亿元，比上年增长6.6%;股票交易额5505.7亿元，上升60.7%;全年国债交易额600亿元，下降50.8%。

保险业继续发展。全年完成国内外保险业务收入86.5亿元，比上年增长2.6%；人寿险实现保费收入59.4亿元，下降1.3%；财产险实现保费收入27.1亿元，增长12.4%。全年保险理赔总额17.4亿元，下降3.3%；综合赔付率20.2%，比上年下降1.2个百分点。

房地产业：全年实现增加值69.5亿元，比上年增长1.5%。随着国家房改政策的陆续到位，经济适用房的启动，住房逐步向商品化、市场化发展。全年房地产施工面积3784万平方米，比上年增长8.1%；竣工面积1208.6万平方米，比上年增长43.4%。商品房销售平稳增长。全年销售商品房544.4万平方米，增长33%。其中销售商品住宅484.7万平方米，比上年增长28.6%；商品房销售额307.5亿元，增长42.3%，其中商品住宅销售额232亿元，比上年增长27.9%。

三、城市建设

基础设施建设：全年完成基础设施投资302.7亿元，比上年下降5.5%，占全市固定资产投资的比重为28.2%，比上年下降4个百分点。

重点工程：市政府为迎接建国50周年确定的67项重大工程项目，经过精心施工，在国庆前夕陆续竣工和外沿亮相，装点了节日的首都。到年末，共完成投资174亿元。第九水厂三期25万吨工程、高碑店热电厂、陕甘宁天然气进京市内工程、北京电信工程和有线广播电视网络建设工程等一批项目完工，水、电、气、热、环卫、电信等基础设施供应能力明显提高。中国现代文学馆、北京海洋馆、西单文化广场、国际金融大厦、首都国际机场航站楼等一批文化设施和大型标志性建筑相继建成。全年国家和市重点工程建设共完成投资122.2亿元，占全市投资额的11.4%。

道路建设：平安大街改造、地铁“复八线”、东四环路均已建成通车，昆玉河通航成为北京第一条集旅游、交通、休闲为一体的水上航线；轻轨铁路、南四环路建设已在年底开工，贯穿南北的第三条地下铁路正在筹划之中。

公用事业：公共交通的乘车环境不断改善，运输能力不断增强，运输行为逐步规范。全市公共交通运营车辆达到 1.4 万辆(不含出租车)，其中清洁燃料车 2724 辆、空调车 736 辆。运营线路总长度突破 17000 公里，其中公共交通总公司新辟公共电汽车线路 60 条，调整延长线路 48 条。城市公共交通共运送乘客 49.5 亿人次，其中公共电汽车和小公共汽车运送乘客 38.6 亿人次，占 78%；地铁 4.8 亿人次，占 9.7%；出租汽车 6.1 亿人次，占 12.3%。

全年自来水销售量 7.7 亿吨。集中供热面积突破 4000 万平方米。全年用电量为 297.8 亿千瓦小时。新增燃气用户近 30 万户，为提高燃气质量而置换天然气的用户达到 9.1 万户。

环境保护：市政府将防治大气污染作为工作的重点，采取了一系列有力措施。煤烟型污染得到控制。共有 6700 台茶炉、21000 台大灶、4127 台 1 吨以下和 662 台大吨位燃煤锅炉改用清洁燃料，实现了四环路以内无燃煤大灶，冬季取暖使用低硫煤；取缔露天烧烤 3 万多起。机动车排气污染的加重趋势有所缓解。更换清洁燃料车 2.1 万辆，强制取消“面的”5000 多辆，并采取加强汽车尾气检测等措施。扬尘污染得到防治。全年道路机扫面积扩大到 2019.9 万平方米，喷雾压尘面积扩大到 1380 万平方米。由于采取了综合治理措施，空气质量得到改善。据全年空气质量日报显示，全年空气污染指数 3 级及好于 3 级的天气天数占全年天数的 75%，实现了年初市政府提出的达到 70%以上的目标。

绿化美化：以建国 50 年大庆和澳门回归为契机，城市面貌发生了喜人的变化。全年共拆除各种违章建筑 455 万平方米，恢复绿化面积 130 多万平方米，全年新植树木 224 万株，城近郊区公共绿地面积达 4989 公顷，人均占有公共绿地 8.2 平方米；全市林木覆盖率 42%，市区绿化覆盖率 35.3%。由各级政府和社会共同筹资建设的亮丽工程，共投资 5.9 亿元，使北京的夜晚亮了起来；西单文化广场、建国门街心花园等一批综合性休闲娱乐多功能区域的建成，使北京人在休闲中享受文化。

四、对外开放

利用外资：全市新批外资项目 645 项，合同总金额 30.6 亿美元，合同外资金额 18.2 亿美元，分别比上年下降了 1.4%、51%和 55.6%。实际利用外资全年完成 29.4 亿美元，比上年增长 2.4%。利用外资突破了以往合资、合作、独资的“三资”企业模式，在形式上更加多样化，出现了外资银行和股份制企业。现有“三资”企业增资已成为利用外资的重要方面，全年新增投资 10.1 亿美元，增资额占全部合同外资额的五成以上，其中老企业增资额呈明显上升。全球 500 家跨国公司已有 154 家来京投资，比上年增加 3 家。对外借款增势明显，金额达 9 亿美元，增长 9%。

对外承包工程和劳务合作：全年新签合同额 2.52 亿美元，比上年下降 11.5%；完成营业额 2.62 亿美元，同比下降 42.9%。年末在外人数 3476 人，下降 4.6%。

旅游：建国五十周年和澳门回归使我市旅游业掀起高潮，全年接待海外旅游者 252.4 万人次，比上年增长 14.7%，来京人次与增速均比上年有较大幅度提高，其中亚洲游客增长 28.4%，远远超出平均水平，欧美及大洋洲游客也比上年有不同程度的增长。旅游外汇收入 25 亿美元，比上年增长 4.7%。全市接待国内旅游者 9260 万人次，总花费 450 亿元，分别比上年增长 6.1%和 6%，其中外地来京游客 6130 万人次，增长 6.1%，在京花费 417 亿元，增长 6%。

开发区：全市科技园区、开发区和工业小区发展加快。全年新增建成区土地面积 2.7 平方公里，累计达到 27.2 平方公里。完成招商企业 1112 家，比上年增加 147 家。累计入区企业 10613 家，其中投产企业 9071 家，比上年增加 1522 家。全年共完成固定资产投资 84 亿元，比上年增长 27.5%，实现增加值 265.1 亿元，比上年增长 27.8%，占全市国内生产总值的比重为 12.2%，比上年增加 1.6 个百分点。国务院《关于建设中关村科技园区有关问题的批复》极大地促进了中关村科技园区的发展，全年认定高新技术企业 1227 家，比上年增长 92.9%，区内高新技术企业已达 6690 家；全年完成增加值 226.1 亿元，增长 24.4%；实现技工贸总收入 864 亿元，增长 39.6%。

五、社会事业

科学技术：北京地区拥有科技活动人员 24 万人，约占全国的 18.4%。科技经费筹集总额 230.4 亿元，约占全国的 16.9%，其中科研机构科技活动经费筹集总额 185.3 亿元，约占全国的 30.9%。科技成果 1 万多项，获国家级奖的约占全国的 30%左右，论文产出约占全国的 16%。全市技术市场签定合同 20711 项，合同金额 92.2 亿元，其中技术交易额 88.5 亿元，均位居全国首位。全市有独立科技信息机构 50 多个，首都信息化正在向更加广泛的领域推进。

教育：坚持把教育放在优先发展的战略地位。全年地方财政收入中用于教育事业费的支出为 49.2 亿元，增长 18.7%。高等教育继续贯彻“共建、合并、合作、调整”的方针，进一步加强学校的实力，招生规模扩大。研究生招生人数近两万，比上年增长 19.6%；高等学校招生 7.8 万人，比上年增长 25.8%。成人教育发展迅速，高等教育招收新生 8.8 万人，比上年增长 8.5%，毕业生达到 6.9 万人，比上年增长 15.3%。高等职业教育招生达到 8 千人。继续坚持小学免试就近入学，普通高中扩大招生，招生人数达 5.7 万人，比上年增长 7.6 %，在全国率先普及了高中阶段教育。

文化：文化事业的生机和活力进一步增强。全市共有文化产业单位 3800 多个，创造增加值近 100 亿元，约占国内生产总值的 5%。节庆文化活动和群众文化活动丰富多彩。成功举办了第三届北京新年音乐会、第二届北京国际音乐节；组织了庆祝新中国成立 50 周年大型美术、书法、摄影优秀作品展览；创作了一批优秀剧目和作品，其中有 19 项作品荣获全国“五个一工程”奖。中华世纪坛一期工程、中山公园音乐堂、首都剧场等一批文化设施新建、改建工程相继竣工。全市拥有文艺团体近 40 个，演出近万场次。图书馆 24 个，博物馆 110 家。

卫生：全市共有医疗卫生机构 5990 个，医院床位 6.8 万张，卫生技术人员 11.7 万人。医疗改革成效显著，已有 20 家市级医院通过验收，完成了精简 10%的目标要求。社区卫生服务工作形势喜人，全市 146 家审批合格的社区服务站和社区卫生服务中心加强了社区服务规范化，推进了全科医学人才培训，增设了保健服务项目，取得了较好的社会效益。农村卫生工作取得全面进展，完成卫生“三项建设” (乡镇卫生院、妇幼保健院、卫生防疫站)39 项，其中 98%已完成并交付使用；有 71.5%的行政村开展了合作医疗，比上年提高 2.6 个百分点。

体育：体育事业的社会化、产业化、法制化进程加快。成功举办了第六届全国少数民族传统体育运动会和北京市第四届农民运动会。群众性健身活动呈现新局面。为群众配建了总面积达 12 万多平方米的健身活动场地，开通了全民健身信息台，并隆重举办了第二届北京市全民健身体育节，直接参与人数近 300 万人次。竞技体育取得佳绩，我市共派出运动员 1674 人次参加国际、国内 152 项次比赛，获得金牌 64 枚，银牌 37 枚，铜牌 39 枚。

六、人民生活

人口：根据人口抽样调查统计，年末在北京居住半年以上的常住人口共有 1257.2 万人，比上年增加 11.6 万人。其中外来人口 149.6 万人。全市人口出生率 6.5‰，人口死亡率 5.6‰，人口自然增长率为 0.9‰。公安部门统计的户籍人口为 1099.8 万人。

就业及社会保障：在用工数量无明显变化的情况下，就业形势基本稳定，年末职工人数约454万人。一系列优惠政策的全面落实为下岗职工拓宽了就业渠道，6.09万名下岗职工实现再就业，再就业率达到65.7%。年末城镇实有失业登记2.8万人，登记失业率0.62%，失业人员就业率62.89%，实现了60%的既定目标。随着相关规定的出台，社会保障制度改革取得较大进展。全市参加养老保险的职工及退休人员达379万人，参加失业保险职工306万人，地方企业参加大病统筹职工和退休人员235.1万人，分别比年初增加19.8万人、83.5万人和14.7万人。

居民收入：全市职工平均工资13500元，比上年增长9.9%，扣除价格因素，实际增长9.2%。城镇居民人均可支配收入9182.8元，比上年增长8.4%，扣除价格因素，实际增长7.8%；人均消费性支出为7498.5元，比上年同期增长7.6%。城镇居民恩格尔系数39.5%，首次降到40%以下，显示出人民生活质量的进一步提高。农民收入快速增长，实现了1995年以来的最高增速，全年人均纯收入4316.4元，扣除价格因素，实际增长7.2%，人均生活消费性支出3132.5元，增长6.4%。

居民储蓄：城乡居民储蓄余额2680.7亿元，比年初增加390亿元，其中城镇居民储蓄存款余额2429亿元，比年初增加了362.4亿元；农村居民储蓄存款余额251.7亿元，比年初增加了27.6亿元。

居民住房：住房条件得到明显改善。全市完成住宅投资353.9亿元，比上年增长29.1%，住宅竣工面积1519.9万平方米，比上年增长39%，扣除集体宿舍、高档公寓、别墅后的竣工面积为1393.8万平方米，增长43%。城镇居民人均住房使用面积达到15.44平方米，比上年增长4.1%，农村居民人均生活用房面积28.65平方米，增长3.7%。经济适用房的建设步伐逐步加快。到年末总开复工面积350.3万平方米，完成竣工面积129.1万平方米；截至年底，已预售53.8万平方米，实现销售45.8万平方米。这类住房以其价格较低、贷款方便、利息收取也较低的优势成为居民住房消费的热点。

附1公报注释：

1. 本公报数据为初步统计数。
2. 本公报中所涉及的增加值和全社会劳动生产率，绝对数均按当年价格计算，增长速度均按可比价格计算。

附2统计表：

指标名称	单位	1999年	1999年为1998年%
主要农副产品产量			
粮食总产量	万吨	201.0	84.0
蔬菜总产量	万吨	426.8	105.1
肉类总产量	万吨	49.2	109.6
鲜蛋总产量	万吨	15.8	88.3
牛奶总产量	万吨	24.0	105.7
水产品总产量	万吨	7.5	99.0
出栏猪	万头	400.9	107.0
主要工业产品产量			
钢	万吨	734.5	91.5

指标名称	单位	1999年	1999年为1998年%
成品钢材	万吨	663.8	98.1
原煤	万吨	792.1	84.7
发电量	亿千瓦小时	143.2	105.7
供热量	万百万千焦	3826.0	130.9
液化石油气	万吨	36.6	112.0
化肥（折纯）	万吨	8.8	89.4
水泥	万吨	803.0	109.7
乙烯	万吨	68.0	119.3
载货汽车	辆	91053.0	202.6
传真机	万部	2.3	212.9
移动通信设备	万部（信道）	1249.9	229.4
微型计算机	万部	179.0	158.4
彩电	万部	11.7	93.2
程控交换机	万线	760.6	102.6
房间空调器	万台	28.5	123.0
白酒	万吨	9.9	102.2
啤酒	万吨	138.9	118.6
软饮料	万吨	56.9	126.3
各种运输方式运量:			
货物运输量			
铁路	万吨	2582.8	100.8
公路	万吨	25635.0	93.3
民航	万吨	29.9	133.5
旅客运输量			
铁路	万人次	4200.5	111.7
公路	万人次	9878.0	147.3
民航	万人次	787.7	103.4
商品零售价格指数(以上年为100)		**98.8**	
居民消费价格指数(以上年为100)		**100.6**	
食品类		97.7	
衣着类		99.4	
家庭设备及用品		96.5	
医疗保健		115.8	
交通和通讯工具类		98.3	
娱乐教育文化用品类		98.8	
居住		101.0	
服务项目		107.9	

Statistical Communique on the 1999 National Economic and Social Development of the City of Beijing

February 2, 2000

In 1999, under the leadership of Beijing municipal Party committee of the Communist Party of China and Beijing Municipal Government, people of all nationalities in Beijing implemented the spirit of the 15th National Congress of CPC and the 3rd and 4th Plenary Session of the 15th Central Committee of CPC. Celebrating the 50th anniversary of the founding of PRC and welcoming Macao's return to motherland were taken as opportunities to create good economic environment, social environment and urban environment. The national economy of the city kept growing tendency. Various social works achieved all-round progress. Urban environment was improved distinctively. Employment situation remained stable. Living standards of urban and rural people improved step by step. However, an arduous task was left to stimulate the domestic demand, and the difficulty of economic structure adjustment could not be neglected.

Ⅰ.General

Overall supply: Preliminary statistics indicated that the gross domestic product (GDP) of Beijing was 216.97 billion yuan in 1999, up by 10 percent over the previous year if calculated at comparable price. The growth rate of GDP was 1 percentage point higher than the anticipated target of 9 percent which was approved on the Beijing People's Congress at the beginning of the year, and an increase of 0.2 percentage point over the previous year. In 1999, benefited from such favorable factors as the 50th anniversary ceremony of the founding of PRC, and restricted by the sustained decline of prices, the performance of the national economy in general in Beijing kept relatively active and positive situation. The growth rate of economy rose steadily. The per capita GDP reached 19803 yuan, up 9.3 percent over the previous year.

A pattern of "tertiary, second, primary industry" remained in three industries. New changes took place in the development of industries. The added value of the tertiary industry was 123.83 billion yuan, up by 8.1 percent. The proportion of the tertiary industry in Beijing's GDP was 57.1 percent, 0.5 percentage point higher than the previous year. The secondary industry became the major force to drive the growth of the City's economy. In 1999, the added value of the secondary industry registered 84.39 billion yuan, representing an increase of 12.5 percent, 2.5 percentage points higher than the growth rate of the city's economy. The contribution rate of the secondary industry was 59.2 percent, up 12.9 percentage points over the previous year. This was the first time for the growth rate and contribution rate of the secondary industry exceeding those of the tertiary industry since 1995. The proportion of the secondary industry in Beijing's GDP was 38.9 percent. The primary industry continued to develop steadily. Its added value was 8.75 billion yuan, up by 2.5 percent, taking 4 percent in Beijing's GDP.

Overall demand: Under the effects of active fiscal policies and monetary policy of moderate inflation, the investment demand of the city grew gently, while consumer and export demands grew faster. Overall demand still gave insufficient force to push forward economic growth.

Investment demand rose at a slower speed. In 1999, driven by 67 key projects for the National Day, Beijing's investment in general of the first half of this year tended to rise steadily. After August 1999, the investment of Beijing dropped month by month. The completed investment in fixed assets of the year totaled 117.06 billion yuan, representing an increase of 1.3 percent over the previous year. Of this total, the investment of local units was 83.18 billion yuan, up 7.7 percent; of central units, 33.88 billion yuan, down by 11.5 percent. Among Beijing's total investment, that in real estate sector increased 11.7 percent, the biggest rate, to 42.15 billion yuan; in capital construction, 0.7 percent, to 43.27 billion yuan; in technical updating and transformation, minus 17.1 percent, to 17.52 billion yuan. Preferential policy in investment in fixed assets was mainly given to the construction of houses, of which the proportion in the total investment rose to 30 percent, 4.2 percentage points higher over the previous year.

Consumer demand grew steadily. Under the situation of sustained price reductions, the domestic consumption which was mainly reflected by the retail sales of consumer commodities basically followed the trend of the previous year. The retail sales of consumer commodities of the whole year reached 131.33 billion yuan, up 9.9 percent, a real increase of 11.2 percent if eliminating the price factor. A series of measures to actively open up rural markets achieved preliminary results. The retail sales of consumer commodities in Beijing's rural areas registered 19.16 billion yuan, up 15.7 percent, and 6.7 percentage points higher than the growth rate of retail sales in urban areas. The retail sales in urban areas reached 112.17 billion yuan, up 9 percent. In terms of the structure of consumer commodities, daily use commodities continued to sell well, with 74.21 billion yuan worth of retail sales, up 11.6 percent over the previous year. Retail sales for foodstuffs reached 34.75 billion yuan, an increase of 7.7 percent. Clothes sold steadily, with 15.56 billion yuan worth of sales, up 7 percent.

The growth rate of export continuously increased. Under the gradually weakened influence of the Asian financial crisis, and the effects played by the state's policy to raise the drawback rate for exports, the declining rate of export in Beijing slowed down month by month. Local exports, beginning in August 1999, reversed the decline, and the growth rate was accelerated on a monthly basis. The customs statistics indicated that the total value of import and export completed in the year in Beijing was 34.39 billion US dollars, up by 12.7 percent. Of this total, the export volume was 9.89 billion US dollars, down by 5.9 percent. The export value completed by local units was 3.26 billion US dollars, up 15.2 percent. Analyzed by the structure of export products in local units, the total volume of export of industrial finished products was 3.01 billion US dollars, up 14.2 percent, taking 92.3 percent in the total, dropping a little from the previous year. The export of primary products grew faster at a rate of 28.8 percent. The exports of state-owned enterprises and foreign-funded ones advanced together, rising 15.0 percent and 16.1 percent to 1.75 billion US dollars and 1.47 billion US dollars respectively.

Price: In 1999, the overall level of market prices continued to be at low state. The index for retail prices of commodities was 98.8 percent, representing a little rebound of the falling rate compared with the previous year. The household consumer prices index of the year was 100.6 percent, 1.8 percentage points lower than the growth rate of the previous year. The reform on prices was pushed forward steadily. During the year, the prices of books, newspapers, magazines, posts and telecommunications, civil fuel, tap water, health care and public transportation were successively adjusted. The ratio of prices of commodities to those of service items was gradually rationalized.

Efficiency: The macro economic efficiency improved a little. The GDP created by per 100 yuan fixed assets was 185.4 yuan, up 2.8 percent. The overall production rate was 34642 yuan per person, up 9.3 percent over the previous year, of which, that for the primary industry, 12153 yuan per person, up 1.8 percent, for the secondary industry, 37929 yuan per person, up 14.3 percent, and for the tertiary industry, 37318 yuan per person, up 5.8 percent.

Financial revenue of local governments: In 1999, the financial revenue of local governments of Beijing totaled 32.05 billion yuan, up by 22.3 percent over the previous year. Of the total, the revenues for normal budget registered 27.91 billion yuan, up 22.8 percent, representing a five-consecutive-year growth rate of revenues over 20 percent. The fiscal expenditures amounted to 41.02 billion yuan, up 33.2 percent. Of which, the expenditures for normal budget were 36.7 billion yuan, up 30.7 percent.

Ⅱ.Development of Various Sectors

Agriculture: Active progress was made in the adjustment, optimization and upgrading of the production structure, resulting in sustained growth of agricultural production. In terms of the internal structure of agriculture, the fish-breeding and poultry-raising sector grew faster than the farm production. In 1999, the output value of the fish-breeding and poultry-raising sector was 8.89 billion yuan, a actual increase of 11.6 percent, and 9.5 percentage points higher than that of farm production. Its proportion in the total output value of agriculture went up to 48.2 percent, up 0.5 percentage point over the previous year. In terms of the structure of farm production, proportions of cash crops such as vegetable, flower and grass went up under the precondition that the grain production was ensured to be basically stable. Famous, special, excellent and new varieties increased greatly, up to 170 varieties. Special vegetables, poultry and fruits formerly seen only in hotels had stepped into the market of popular consumers. Foreign exchange-earning agriculture progressed sharply. The export value in 1999 was 1.94 billion yuan, up 79.6 percent. The mechanization level of agriculture continued to rise. By the end of the year, the total power of agricultural machines reached 4.104 million kilowatts. The utilized electricity in rural areas totaled 2.92 billion kilowatt-hours, up 6.2 percent over the previous year.

Industry: In 1999, the total added value of the industrial sector was 65.1 billion yuan, up 13.1 percent over the previous year if calculated at comparable prices, representing the highest growth rate since 1995. The added value created by enterprises with an annual sales income over 5 million yuan totaled 58.93 billion yuan, up 13.4 percent. Central industrial enterprises continued to maintain rapid growth. During the year, the added value completed by central industrial enterprises was 21.56 billion yuan, up 20.4 percent, that by local industrial enterprises was 37.37 billion yuan, up by 9.3 percent. Non-state-owned enterprises took the lead in growing. Among these enterprises, the added value of foreign-funded enterprises was 23.18 billion yuan, that of joint-stock enterprises was 6.17 billion yuan, up by 21.4 percent and 23.9 percent respectively over the previous year. The heavy industry continued to grow faster than light industry. The added value of heavy industry was 43.18 billion yuan, up 16 percent, 9.7 percentage points higher than the growth rate of the light industry. And the added value of light industry was 15.75 billion yuan.

High tech industry added new energy to the industrial development. The added value of high tech industrial enterprises in 1999 was 16.5 billion yuan, up 19.0 percent over the previous year. The added value of high tech industrial enterprises taking 7.6 percent in Beijing's GDP, and 25.4 percent in the total added value of industrial sector of the city. The contribution rate of high tech industry was 66.9 percent, up 2.3 percentage points over the previous year.

The economic efficiency became better clearly. The aggregative index number of the economic efficiency of industrial sector was 99.84 percent, up 7.74 percentage points over the previous year. Total profits achieved in 1999 reached 6.35 billion yuan, up 41.0 percent. Of this total, the profits of profit-making enterprises were 9.96 billion yuan, up 21.6 percent, and the losses of losing enterprises were 3.61 billion yuan, down by 2.1 percent.

Construction: In 1999, the total added value of the construction sector was 19.29 billion yuan, up by 9.7 percent over the previous year. Influenced by the slowed down growth rate of investment of the city, the construction production progressed steadily. The total floor space under construction during the year stood at 65.565 million square meters, up by 0.9 percent over the previous year. The floor space of buildings completed during the year was 23.215 million square meters, an increase of 27.4 percent over the previous year. The quality of projects improved remarkably. Excellent and good projects in the whole city accounted for 49.1 percent of the total, up 4.1 percentage points over the previous year. The economic efficiency was enhanced to some extent. The total profits of the year reached 1.3 billion yuan, and the overall production rate registered 83,000 yuan per person, up by 4.8 percent and 10.7 percent respectively.

Transportation: In 1999, the total added value of the transportation sector was 6.01 billion yuan, up by 2.4 percent over the previous year. The total volume of freight transportation was 282.984 million tons, up by 0.8 percent over the previous year. The total volume of passenger transportation was 148.664 million times person, up by 32.4 percent. For the highway transportation, with the gradual improvement of road conditions, its easy and speedy advantages were exploited to full. State-owned and social transportation operated together, resulting in a little growth of transportation capacity and volume. For the railway transportation, by adjusting the transportation capacity in peak and valley period and offering additional luxury trains, its potential was exploited to meet the requirements of various periods and consumer groups, resulting in a large group of customers attracted. For the civil aviation transportation, with its preponderant speed and good services, it followed the increasingly quickening rhythm of the people's life and met the high-quality requirement of the people. The volume of transportation by these three means accounted for 90.7 percent, 9.1 percent and 0.1 percent of the total of freight transportation respectively and 66.4 percent, 28 percent and 5.3 percent of the total of passenger transportation respectively.

Posts and telecommunications: In 1999, the total added value of the posts and telecommunications sector was 11.01 billion yuan, up by 14.4 percent over the previous year. With the enhancement of the level of science and technology as well as the digital and network economy rapidly stepping into Chinese market, the posts and telecommunications sector of Beijing kept sustained high-speed development. The business transactions of postal and telecommunication service totaled 15.74 billion yuan, up 23.2 percent. Newspapers issued and sent in the year were 1.41 billion copies; magazines, 54.80 million copies; EMS, 7.77 million copies, up 0.1 percent, 1.8 percent and 23.3 percent respectively. The telephone exchanges increased their capacity to 7.43 million gates, up by 8.2 percent over the previous year. There were 62 telephones per 100 population in Beijing and 89 telephones per 100 urban inhabitants. By the end of this year, mobile telephone users reached 1.839 million, a new increase of 672,000 users. In the year, the newly added public telephones using IC cards totaled 5870.

Domestic trade: In 1999, the total added value of the wholesale and retail trades and catering industry was 21.12 billion yuan, up by 3.1 percent over the previous year. The overall value of purchased commodities in the whole year reached 232.71 billion yuan, up 17.3 percent. The gross sales of commodities reached 265.86 billion yuan, up 27.2 percent. The economic benefits of commerce improved a little. The whole-year accumulative sales of about 2000 large- and medium-sized wholesale and retail enterprises reached 167.32 billion yuan, up 8.3 percent, and sales revenue per capita reached 645000 yuan, up 15.1 percent.

Banking and insurance: In 1999, the total added value of the banking and insurance sector was 31.5 billion yuan, up 13.3 percent over the previous year. Affected by a series of fiscal and banking measures of the state, the growth rate of savings deposits in Beijing's banking institutions slowed down evidently. The mobility of currency was further enhanced. Policies for reducing the interest rate and levying personal income tax on the interest of savings deposits brought some certain effects. Savings deposits in Beijing's banking institutions totaled 826.72 billion yuan at the end of the year, 142.89 billion yuan more than that at the beginning of the year, or up 13.1 percent over the previous year, and 31.9 percentage points lower than the growth rate of the previous year. On the other hand, banks issued 400.78 billion yuan worth of net loans, an increase of 55.96 billion yuan over that at the beginning of the year, or 5.2 billion yuan less than the increase of the previous year. Funds returned in the year accumulated to 4.0 billion yuan.

Stock market developed steadily. The transaction volume of all stock institutions totaled 1091.35 billion yuan, up 6.6 percent over the previous year. The transaction volume of stocks was 550.57 billion yuan, up by 60.7 percent, that of treasury bonds was 60.0 billion yuan, down by 50.8 percent.

Continuous progress was made in insurance service. In 1999, the insurance premium in domestic and foreign insurance institutions totaled 8.65 billion yuan, up by 2.6 percent over the previous year. Of the total, the premium of life insurance was 5.94 billion yuan, down by 1.3 percent; of property insurance, 2.71 billion yuan, an increase of 12.4 percent. The insurance companies paid an indemnity of 1.74 billion yuan as reparations in insurance programs, down by 3.3 percent. The overall loss ratio was 20.2 percent, down by 1.2 percentage points over the previous year.

Real estate: In 1999, the total added value of the real estate sector was 6.95 billion yuan, up by 1.5 percent over the previous year. With the successively available policies on housing reform by the state, and with the economic and suitable houses operated, houses developed gradually toward commercialization and marketablization. In 1999, the total floor space under construction reached 37.84 million square meters, up 8.1 percent. Floor space of buildings completed during the year was 12.086 million square meters, up 43.4 percent. Sales of marketable houses grew steadily. The total floor space of marketable houses sold in 1999 was 5.444 million square meters, up 33 percent. Of this total, the floor space of marketable residential houses was 4.847 million square meters, up 28.6 percent over the previous year. The sales of marketable houses reached 30.75 billion yuan, up 42.3 percent, of which the sales of marketable residential houses were 23.2 billion yuan, up 27.9 percent over the previous year.

Ⅲ. Urban Construction

Construction of infrastructure facilities: In 1999, the total investment in infrastructure facilities was 30.27 billion yuan, down 5.5 percent over the previous year, taking 28.2 percent in Beijing's total investment in fixed assets, down 4 percentage points over the previous year.

Key projects: After well-designed construction, the 67 key projects set by the Beijing municipal government aiming at welcoming the 50th anniversary of the founding of PRC were completed one after another before the eve of the National Day and demonstrated to the public to decorate the Capital in festival. By the end of 1999, investment in key projects totaled 17.4 billion yuan. A group of projects, including the Third-phase 250,000-ton Project of the No. 9 Water Plant, Gaobeidian Thermal Power Plant, in-city project of Shaanxi-Gansu-Ningxia natural gas to Beijing, Beijing Telecom project and Cablecasting TV Network project, were completed. The supplying capacity of infrastructure facilities such as water, electricity, gas, thermal, heating, environment sanitation and telecom improved distinctly. A group of cultural facilities and large symbol buildings were built one after another, including China Modern Literature Museum, Beijing Oceanarium, Xidan Culture Square, International Banking Building, Freight Station at Beijing's Capital Int'l Airport, etc.. The investment in national and municipal key construction projects in 1999 totaled 12.22 billion yuan, a proportion of 11.4 percent in Beijing's total investment.

Road construction The rebuilt Ping'an Avenue, "Fuxingmen-Bawangfen" subway line and the East Forth Ring Road had been completed and put into operation. As the first water route in Beijing integrating travel, transportation and relaxation, the Kunminghu Lake-Yuyuantan Lake line was open to navigation. The construction of light-track rails and the South Forth Ring Road had begun at the end of this year. The third subway passing through south to north was under plan.

Urban public utilities: The environment in public transportation vehicles improved unceasingly, with the transportation capacity increased continuously. Operational conducts were standardized step by step. There were 14,000 public transportation vehicles (excluding taxis) in the city, of which, 2724 using LPG (liquefied petroleum gas) and 736 provided with air-conditioners. The total length of public transportation topped 17,000 kilometers. Of the total, 60 lines for public buses and trolley buses were newly added by the Public Transportation Company, 48 lines were adjusted and extended. Urban public transportation vehicles transported passengers of 4.95 billion person-times in the year, of which, 3.86 billion person-times were by buses and mini-buses, accounting for 78 percent of the total; 480 million person-times were by subways, accounting for 9.7 percent; 610 million person-times were by taxis, accounting for 12.3 percent.

There was 770 million tons of tap water sold in 1999. The concentrating heating area topped 40 million square meters. The total utilized electricity was 29.78 billion kilowatt-hours. Fired gas users increased about 300,000 in the year. There were 91,000 users who replaced natural gas to improve the quality of fired gas.

Urban environment protection: The municipal government of Beijing laid the stress on preventing air pollution. A series of forceful measures were adopted. The pollution caused by coal and smoke was controlled. There were 6700 tea stoves, 21000 cooking stoves, 4127 one-ton-below and 662 large tonnage coal-fired boilers changed for LPG fuel. The aim of no coal-fired cooking stoves within the Forth Ring Road was achieved. High-quality coal was used for winter heating. More than 30,000 outdoor barbecue sites were cancelled. The rise of the pollution caused by tail-gas of motor vehicles slowed down a little. There were 21000 motorcars changed for LPG fuel. The operation of more than 5000 minicabs were cancelled compulsively. The pollution caused by raised dust was prevented effectively. The area of roads cleaned by machines increased to 20.199 million square meters; of roads sprayed, 13.80 million square meters. Due to adoption of comprehensive controlling measures, the air quality improved remarkably. Daily report on air quality during the year indicated that days in which the air pollution index was at and above grade 3 shared 75 percent in the total days of the whole year, achieving the target of 70 percent set by the municipal government at the beginning of this year.

Afforestation and beautification: With the opportunity of the 50th anniversary ceremony of PRC and Macao's return to motherland, satisfactory changes took place in Beijing's appearance. There were 4.55 million square meters of unapproved buildings removed. The afforestation area recovered in the year totaled more than 1.30 million square meters. 2.24 million trees were planted in 1999. The public green land in urban and suburban areas covered a totaled area of 4989 hectares, 8.2 square meters per capita. The coverage rate of afforestation in the city reached 42 percent. And 35.3 percent of the urban areas was covered by green land. The investment in bright projects totaled 590 million yuan, jointly funded and built by governments at all levels and social units, resulting in bright nights of Beijing. With the completion of a group of comprehensive multi-purpose regions for relaxation and entertainment including Xidan Culture Square and Jianguomen Street Center Garden, people of Beijing can enjoy culture while relaxation.

Ⅳ.Opening to the Outside World

Use of foreign capitals: The city approved 645 foreign-invested projects in the year, with a total contract value of 3.06 billion US dollars, including 1.82 billion US dollars worth of contract foreign capitals, down by 1.4 percent, 51 percent and 55.6 percent respectively over the previous year. The foreign capitals actually utilized in 1999 stood at 2.94 billion US dollars, up by 2.4 percent over the previous year. There were more diversified forms for use of foreign capitals besides joint venture, cooperation and sole-fund models. Foreign-funded banks and joint-stock enterprises appeared in Beijing. Investment increase in existing foreign-funded enterprises had been an important aspect for the use of foreign capitals. The newly increased investment in the year totaled 1.01 billion US dollars, taking more than 50 percent in the total contract foreign capitals. Of which, the increased investment in old foreign-funded enterprises rose clearly. 154 of the 500 multinational corporations in the world had invested in Beijing, an increase of 3 over the previous year. Foreign borrowings grew distinctly to 900 million US dollars, up 9 percent.

Foreign-contracted construction projects and labor service collaboration: The total value of newly signed contracts in 1999 was 252 million US dollars, down by 11.5 percent over the previous year. The completed turnover totaled 262 million US dollars, down by 42.9 percent. There were 3476 workers in foreign countries by the end of 1999, a decline of 4.6 percent.

Tourism: A tide in the tourism sector was initiated in the year by the 50th anniversary of the founding of PRC and Macao's return to the motherland. The number of foreign tourists for 1999 was 2.524 million, up 14.7 percent over the previous year. The number of tourists to Beijing and the growth rate thereof increased sharply. Of which, tourists from Asian countries increased by 28.4 percent, far more than the average level. Tourists from European, American and Oceanic countries increased to different extents. The foreign exchange incomes from tourism totaled 2.5 billion US dollars, up 4.7 percent over the previous year. Domestic tourists to Beijing in the year totaled 92.60 million, with 45.0 billion yuan worth of total expenses in Beijing, up 6.1 percent and 6.0 percent respectively over the previous year. Tourists to Beijing from other provinces and regions of China reached 61.30 million, up 6.1 percent, with 41.7 billion yuan worth of total expenses in Beijing, up 6 percent.

Development zones: The pace of construction of science & tech parks, development zones and industrial zones accelerated. The newly-built zones in the year covered an area of 2.7 square kilometers, bringing the total area of these zones to 27.2 square kilometers. During the year, 1112 enterprises landed in these zones of the city, 147 more than the previous year, with the total to 10613. Of this total, those had been put into production increased by 1522 to 9071 enterprises. The investment in fixed assets of these zones rose by 27.5 percent to 8.4 billion yuan. The added value realized rose by 27.8 percent to 26.51 billion yuan, a proportion of 12.2 percent in Beijing's GDP, up 1.6 percentage points over the previous year. The State Council's Reply and Ratification on Problems of Building the Zhongguancun High-tech Park greatly promoted the development of the Zhongguancun High-tech Park. 1227 enterprises were recognized as high-tech ones in the year, an increase of 92.9 percent over the previous year. The number of high-tech enterprises in the Park had reached 6690. Their added value in the year totaled 22.61 billion yuan, up 24.4 percent. Their total incomes of technology, industry and trade reached 86.4 billion yuan, up 39.6 percent.

Ⅴ.Social Works

Science and technology: There were 240,000 people engaged in scientific and technological activities in Beijing, accounting for about 18.4 percent of the country's total. Funds raised for scientific and technological activities totaled 23.04 billion yuan, accounting for round 16.9 percent of the country's total. Of which, the funds raised for scientific and technological activities in research and development institutions totaled 18.53 billion yuan, accounting for about 30.9 percent of the country's total. In 1999, the city gained more than 10,000 scientific results, of which, those received prizes from the state accounting for about 30 percent of the country's total; those with thesis, 16 percent of the country's total results. A total of 20,711 contracts were signed on technological markets of the city, with a total contract value of 9.22 billion yuan. Of this total, the amount of technological transactions was 8.85 billion yuan. All of these ranked the first place in the country. There were 50 over independent scientific and technological information institutions. The Capital's informalization was going forward to even wider fields.

Education: The City had adhered to play the education on a strategic position for preferential development. The financial input into education from local fiscal revenues rose 18.7 percent to 4.92 billion yuan. For the higher education, the policy of "joint construction, combination, cooperation and adjustment" was continued to implement. The strength of colleges and universities was further enhanced, and the enrollment was enlarged. There were about 20,000 new entrants of graduate students, up 19.6 percent over the previous year. The number of newly enrolled undergraduate students in general universities rose to 78,000, up 25.8 percent over the previous year. The adult higher education progressed rapidly. There were 88,000 new entrants in the year, up 8.5 percent over the previous year. 69,000 students graduated from adult higher education, up 15.3 percent over the previous year. 8,000 students were enrolled in higher vocational or technical schools. Students graduated from primary school can continue their education in junior high school nearing their homes without entrance examination. New entrants to ordinary senior high school increased to 57000, up 7.6 percent over the previous year. Beijing took the lead in the country in popularizing the education in senior high school

Culture: The vigor of cultural work was further increased. Cultural units in Beijing totaled 3,800, creating 10 billion yuan worth of added value in the year, representing a proportion of 5 percent in Beijing's GDP. There were rich and colorful cultural activities for festival ceremony and mass cultural activities. The Third Beijing New Year Concert and the 2nd Beijing International Music Festival were held successively. Large exhibitions for excellent works of art, calligraphy and photo were organized for celebrating the 50th anniversary of the founding of PRC. A group of programs and works were created, of which, 19 works won prizes of the national "Five-One Project". The new construction and reconstruction projects of a group of cultural facilities such as the first-phase project of China Century Altar, the Music Hall of Zhongshan Park and the Capital Theater were completed one after another. Nearly 40 literary groups in Beijing performed about 10,000 times. There were 24 libraries and 110 museums in Beijing.

Public health: There were 5990 health care institutions in Beijing, with a total of 68,000 beds and 117,000 health workers. Reform on health care system achieved distinct results. 20 hospitals were checked and accepted. The aim of reducing 10 percent hospitals was achieved. Community health care service was on satisfactory. The community service was further standardized in 146 qualified community service stations and community health care centers in the city. Training for medical talents in all departments was promoted. Additional health care items were offered, resulting in better social benefits. All-round progress was made in the health care works in rural areas. 98 percent of 39 construction projects (for town health care institutions, maternity and child care centers, anti-epidemic and sanitation stations) were completed and put into operation. Administrative villages with cooperative medical service made up 71.5 percent of all villages in Beijing, up 2.6 percentage points over the previous year.

Sports: The progress of the socialization, industrialization and legalization of sports was accelerated. The 6th National Traditional Ethnic Minority Sports Meet and the 4th Beijing Farmer Sports Meet were held successively. New situation appeared in public body-building activities. A total area of more than 120,000 square meters for body-building fields was built for the mass. The National Fit-keeping Information Broadcast Station was opened. The 2nd Beijing National Fit-keeping Sport Festival was held ceremoniously in 1999, with 3 million direct participants. Good results were made for athletic sports. A total of 1674 athletes were sent to participant in 152 international and national games., winning 64 gold medals, 37 silver medals and 39 copper medal.

Ⅵ People's Life

Population: The sample population survey indicated that, by the end of 1999, permanent residents having been in Beijing for more than half a year totaled 12.572 million, 116,000 more than that of the previous year. Of the total, 1.496 million were from other provinces, regions and municipalities of China. Beijing's birthrate was 6.5 per thousand, death rate, 5.6 per thousand, the natural population growth rate, 0.9 per thousand. According to statistics from public security department, registered population was 10.998 million.

Employment and social security: Under circumstances of no clear changes in the amount of labor used, the employment had a basically stable situation. By the end of 1999, there were about 4.54 million workers. A series of preferential policies were fully implemented to provide more opportunities for laid-off workers. A total of 60,900 laid-off workers found new jobs. The re-employment rate of laid-off workers was 65.7 percent. By the end of 1999, the number from actual unemployment registration in urban areas was 28000. The registered unemployment rate was 0.62 percent. The employment rate of unemployed workers was 62.89 percent, reaching the set target of 60 percent. With the implementation of relative regulations, larger progress was made in the reform of social security system. There were 3.79 million workers and retired workers participated in the retirement security program, 3.06 million workers participated in the unemployment security program, 2.351 million workers and retired workers of local enterprises participated in the general health care program for major diseases, an increase of 198,000, 835,000 and 147,000 respectively over those at the beginning of this year.

Residents' incomes: In 1999, the annual per capita salary of Beijing's staff and workers was 13,500 yuan, up by 9.9 percent over the previous year, a real increase of 9.2 percent if eliminating the price factor. The annual per capita disposable income of urban households reached 9182.8 yuan, up 8.4 percent over the previous year, a real increase of 7.8 percent if eliminating the price factor. The annual per capita living expenses of Beijing's urban residents reached 7498.5 yuan, up 7.6 percent compared with the corresponding period of the previous year. Among the urban resident's living expenses, those on food dropped below 40 percent to 39.5 percent for the first time, showing the further improvement of the people's living quality. The income of households in rural areas grew rapidly, with the fastest growth rate since 1995. The annual per capita net income of rural households was 4316.4 yuan, a real increase of 7.2 percent if eliminating prices factor. The per capita living expenses of rural households reached 3132.5 yuan, up by 6.4 percent.

Savings of Residents: The savings deposits of urban and rural residents totaled 268.07 billion yuan, 39.0 billion yuan more than that at the beginning of the year. Of the total, those of urban residents were 242.9 billion yuan, 36.24 billion yuan more than that at the beginning of the year; of rural residents, 25.17 billion yuan, 2.76 billion yuan more than that at the beginning of the year.

Houses of Inhabitants Residential conditions improved evidently. In 1999, Beijing's investment in residential buildings totaled 35.39 billion yuan, up 29.1 percent. The floor space of residential buildings completed in the year was 15.199 million square meters, up 39 percent, and 13.938 million square meters excluding that of collective dormitories, high-grade apartments and villas, up by 43 percent. The average per capita usable floor area for urban residents was 15.44 square meters, an increase of 4.1 percent. The average per capita area of rural residents' living houses was 28.65 square meters, an increase of 3.7 percent. The pace of the construction of economic and suitable houses was accelerated step by step. By the end of the year, the total floor space of started and recovered construction of such houses totaled 3.503 million square meters. The floor space of completed houses reached 1.291 million square meters. By the end of the year, a total of 538,000 square meters of buildings were paid in advance, and 458,000 square meters were fully paid. Such houses became the hot spots of people's residential consumption due to their low prices, convenient loans and low interest rate.

Annex 1 Notes:

1. All figures in the Communique are preliminary statistics.
2. Figures in value terms on added value of various sectors and overall production rate are current prices, whereas growth rates are calculated at comparable prices.

Annex 2 Statistical Statements:

Name of Index	Unit	1999	1999 as % of 1998
Output of Major Agricultural Products and Byproducts			
Grain	10,000 tons	201.0	84.0
Vegetable	ditto	426.8	105.1
Meat	ditto	49.2	109.6
Fresh eggs	ditto	15.8	88.3
Milk	ditto	24.0	105.7
Aquatic products	ditto	7.5	99.0
Pigs slaughtered	10,000 heads	400.9	107.0
Output of Major Industrial Products			
Steel	10,000 tons	734.5	91.5
Steel products	ditto	663.8	98.1
Crude coal	ditto	792.1	84.7
Electricity generated	100 million kwhs	143.2	105.7
Heat supplied	10,000 million kjs	3826.0	130.9
LPG	10,000 tons	36.6	112.0
Fertilizer	ditto	8.8	89.4
Cement	ditto	803.0	109.7
Ethylene	ditto	68.0	119.3
Cargo cars	set	91053.0	202.6
Facsimile machines	10,000 sets	2.3	212.9
Mobile communications equipment	10,000 sets(channels)	1249.9	229.4
Micro computers	10,000 sets	179.0	158.4
Color TV set	10,000 sets	11.7	93.2
Program-controlled switchboards	10,000 lines	760.6	102.6
Air-conditioners	10,000 tons	28.5	123.0
Wine	ditto	9.9	102.2
Beer	ditto	138.9	118.6
Soft drinks	ditto	56.9	126.3
Total volume of transportation by various means:			
Volume of cargo transportation			
Railway	10,000 tons	2582.8	100.8

Name of Index	Unit	1999	1999 as % of 1998
Highway	ditto	25635.0	93.3
Airway	ditto	29.9	133.5
Volume of passenger transportation			
Railway	10,000 person-times	4200.5	111.7
Highway	ditto	9878.0	147.3
Civil aviation	ditto	787.7	103.4
Commodity retail price index (previous year=100)	**%**	**98.8**	
Household consumer price index (previous year=100)	**%**	**100.6**	
Foodstuffs		97.7	
Clothing		99.4	
Household equipment and commodities		96.5	
Health care commodities		115.8	
Transportation & communication tools		98.3	
Entertainment, education & cultural commodities		98.8	
Residence		101.0	
Service items		107.9	

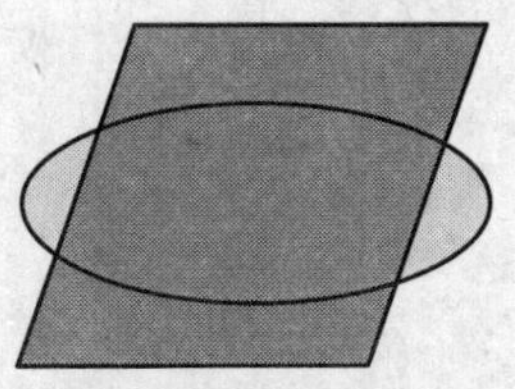

统计图表
STATISICAL GRAPH AND CHART

综　合
GENERAL SURVEY

地方财政收入占国内生产总值比重（1978-1999）

Ratio of Local Financial Revenue to Gross Domestic Product(1978-1999)

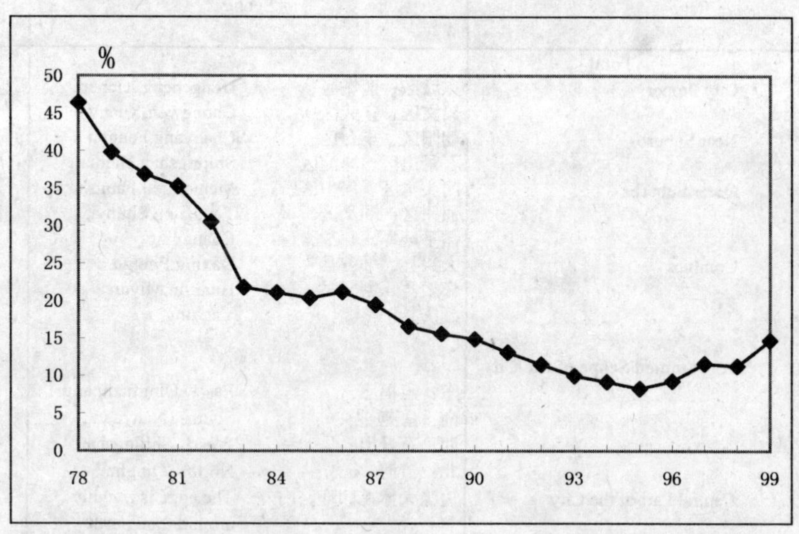

	1999年	1998年	1999年为1998年% 1999 as % of 1998
国内生产总值（亿元） Gross domestic product(100 million yuan)	2174.5	2011.3	110.2
地方财政收入（亿元） Local financial revenue(100 million yuan)	320.5	262.0	122.3

1999年国内生产总值构成（%）

Composition of GDP(%)

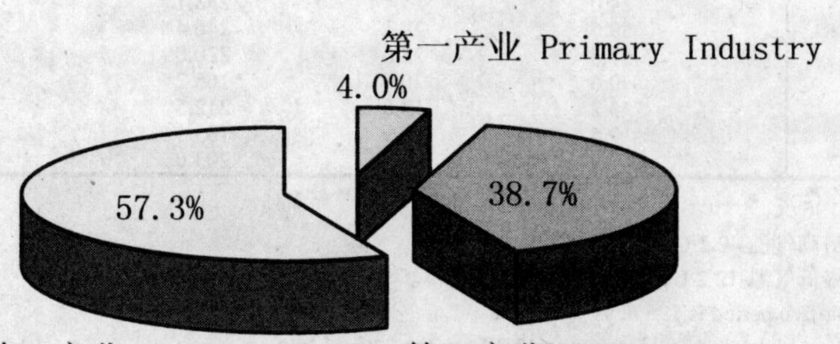

1-1 土 地 面 积
LAND AREA

项 目 Item		范 围 Scope		面积(平方公里) Area (sq.km)	比重(%) Proportion (%)
全 市	**Total**			**16807.8**	**100**
城 区	City Proper	东城区、西城区、崇文区、宣武区	Dongcheng,Xicheng, Chongwen,Xuanwu	87.1	0.5
近郊区	Near Suburbs	朝阳区、丰台区、石景山区、海淀区	Chaoyang,Fengtai, Shijingshan,Haidian	1282.8	7.6
远郊区	Outer Suburbs	门头沟区、房山区 通州区、顺义区、昌平区	Mentougou,Fangshan Tongzhou,Shunyi, Changping	6473.8	38.5
各 县	Counties	大兴县、平谷县 怀柔县、密云县 延庆县	Daxing,Pinggu Huairou,Miyun Yanqing	8964.1	53.4
规划市区	**Programmed Scope of the City**			**1041.0**	**6.2**
		东：定福庄 南：南苑 西：石景山 北：清河	East：Dingfuzhuang South：Nanyuan West：Shijingshan North：Qinghe		
市区中心地区	Central Part of the City	边缘大体在四环路内外	The edge is roughly around the Fourth ring road	289.8	1.7
建成区	Completed Part			490.1	2.9
三环路以内	Within The Third Ring Road			158.0	0.9

附：全市平原面积 6390.3 平方公里，占 38%。山区面积 10417.5 平方公里，占 62%。

Appendix：Area of plain is 6390.3 sq.km,as 38% of total.Area of mountain is 10147.5 sq.km,as 62% of total.

注：1.规划市区、市中心地区面积是 1992 年重新修订北京市城市总体规划后确定的数字。

2.建成区面积是市规划院根据 1989 年航空遥感照射资料重新计算的。

a) Figures on area of programmed scope of the city and central part of the city were in line with revised overall plan of Beijing in 1992.

b) Figure of completed part was recalculated according to data of air remote sensing irradiation by Beijing Planning Institution.

1-2 气 象
METEOROLOGY

月 份 Month	降水量(毫米) Precipitation (mm)	平均气温(℃) Average Temperature (℃)	日照时数(时) Hours of Sunshine (hour)	平均风速(米/秒) Average Wind Speed (mile / second)	平均气压(百帕) Average Pressure (100 pa)	大风日数(日) Days of Strong Wind (day)
全 年 Total	**266.9**	**13.1**	**2594.0**	**2.6**	**1040.8**	**7**
1	0	-1.6	217.1	2.7	1021.5	3
2	0	2.2	225.1	2.6	1021.2	1
3	5.2	4.8	159.5	2.9	1014.1	0
4	33.7	14.4	237.3	2.9	1010.0	0
5	32.4	19.5	264.3	2.5	1006.3	0
6	24.0	25.4	258.1	2.8	1001.7	1
7	59.6	28.1	246.4	2.2	1000.3	0
8	57.0	25.6	220.0	2.1	1003.8	1
9	40.6	20.9	165.2	2.0	1009.8	0
10	4.2	13.0	212.5	2.1	1016.9	1
11	9.5	5.9	185.5	2.2	1359.9	0
12	0.7	-0.6	203.0	2.6	1024.5	1

附：1.无霜期 196 天。

2.年极端最高气温 42.2℃，出现日期 7 月 24 日。

3.年极端最低气温-12.2℃，出现日期 12 月 19 日。

a) Annual forst-free period is 196 days.

b) Annual utmost highest air temperature is 42.2℃,on the 24th of July.

c) Annual utmost lowest air temperature is -12.2℃,on the 19th of December.

1-3 行 政 区 划
ADMINISTRATIVE DIVISIONS

单位：个 (unit)

地 区 Region		镇 Town	乡 Township	街道办事处 Urban Sub-district Office	居民委员会 Neighborhood Committee	村民委员会 Village Committee
全 市	**Total**	**103**	**125**	**124**	**5745**	**4040**
城 区	**City Propers**			**35**	**1503**	
东城区	Dongcheng			10	413	
西城区	Xicheng			10	513	
崇文区	Chongwen			7	235	
宣武区	Xuanwu			8	342	
近郊区	**Near Suburbs**	**1**	**40**	**64**	**3365**	**340**
朝阳区	Chaoyang		24	22	1237	169
丰台区	Fengtai		6	16	769	81
石景山区	Shijingshan			9	271	11
海淀区	Haidian	1	10	17	1088	79
远郊区	**Outer Suburbs**	**53**	**34**	**23**	**667**	**1870**
门头沟区	Mentougou	7	3	5	201	189
房山区	Fangshan	12	12	7	157	463
通州区	Tongzhou	8	12	6	151	480
顺义区	Shunyi	12	7	2	34	425
昌平区	Changping	14		3	124	313
各 县	**Counties**	**49**	**51**	**2**	**210**	**1830**
大兴县	Daxing	9	18		52	547
平谷县	Pinggu	10	11	1	34	273
怀柔县	Huairou	10	5	1	33	287
密云县	Miyun	12	7		61	346
延庆县	Yanqing	8	10		30	377

1-4 全部法人单位数(按所在地分)
TOTAL INSTITUTIONAL UNITS(BY REGION)

单位：个 (unit)

地区	Region	合计 Total	中央单位 Central Entities	市属单位 City Entities	区县属单位 of District and County
全市	**Total**	**93702**	**11052**	**11842**	**18264**
城区	**City Proper**	**24083**	**4320**	**3758**	**4522**
东城区	Dongcheng	8781	1518	1033	1083
西城区	Xicheng	8002	2189	1270	1244
崇文区	Chongwen	3271	220	615	1166
宣武区	Xuanwu	4029	393	840	1029
近郊区	**Near Suburbs**	**43928**	**6099**	**6513**	**6320**
朝阳区	Chaoyang	17224	1666	3201	1467
丰台区	Fengtai	8200	903	1180	947
石景山区	Shijingshan	2476	170	220	1388
海淀区	Haidian	16028	3360	1912	2518
远郊区	**Outer Suburbs**	**15297**	**416**	**1028**	**4261**
门头沟区	Mentougou	1803	36	92	634
房山区	Fangshan	3175	157	169	784
通州区	Tongzhou	4148	94	312	960
顺义区	Shunyi	2940	25	137	974
昌平区	Changping	3231	104	318	909
各县	**Counties**	**10394**	**217**	**543**	**3161**
大兴县	Daxing	4486	119	319	984
平谷县	Pinggu	1377	12	54	480
怀柔县	Huairou	1729	33	54	634
密云县	Miyun	1398	32	48	508
延庆县	Yanqing	1404	21	68	555

1-5 全部法人、产业活动单位数(按所在地分)
TOTAL INSTITUTIONAL UNITS AND ESTABLISHMENTS(BY REGION)

单位：个 (unit)

地区	Region	法人单位数 合计 Institutional Units	单产业法人 Single Sector	多产业法人 Multi-sector	多产业法人单位的产业活动单位数 Establishments of Multi-sector Institutional Units
全市	**Total**	**93702**	**90383**	**3319**	**15907**
城区	**City Proper**	**24083**	**23140**	**943**	**4481**
东城区	Dongcheng	8781	8525	256	1275
西城区	Xicheng	8002	7629	373	1785
崇文区	Chongwen	3271	3154	117	586
宣武区	Xuanwu	4029	3832	197	835
近郊区	**Near Suburbs**	**43928**	**42607**	**1321**	**6579**
朝阳区	Chaoyang	17224	16460	764	3221
丰台区	Fengtai	8200	7980	220	1377
石景山区	Shijingshan	2476	2381	95	536
海淀区	Haidian	16028	15786	242	1445
远郊区	**Outer Suburbs**	**15297**	**14601**	**696**	**3205**
门头沟区	Mentougou	1803	1643	160	767
房山区	Fangshan	3175	3026	149	732
通州区	Tongzhou	4148	3986	162	744
顺义区	Shunyi	2940	2886	54	168
昌平区	Changping	3231	3060	171	794
各县	**Counties**	**10394**	**10035**	**359**	**1642**
大兴县	Daxing	4486	4368	118	501
平谷县	Pinggu	1377	1324	53	300
怀柔县	Huairou	1729	1639	90	427
密云县	Miyun	1398	1358	40	127
延庆县	Yanqing	1404	1346	58	287

注：多产业法人单位的产业活动单位在本市有 15907 个,有 45 个在外省市。

Note：Establishments of multi-sector institutional units of city totaled 15907 , because 45 are out of districts and counties.

1-6 全部法人、产业活动单位数
TOTAL INSTITUTIONAL UNITS AND ESTABLISHMENTS

单位：个 (unit)

项目	Item	法人单位数 合计 Institutional Units	单产业法人 Single Sector	多产业法人 Multi-sector	多产业法人单位的产业活动单位数 Establishments of Multi-sector Institutional Units
总计	**Total**	**93702**	**90383**	**3319**	**15952**
按登记注册类型分	**Grouped by Registered Type**				
内资经济	Domestic Investment Economy	88178	84898	3280	15732
国有经济	State-owned	26225	24384	1841	9516
集体经济	Collective-owned	29741	28902	839	5463
股份合作企业	Share Holding Cooperative	4409	4373	36	123
联营经济	Joint-owned	988	963	25	94
国有独资公司	State-owned Funded Company	222	209	13	61
其他有限责任公司	Other Limited-Liability Company	7431	7389	42	160
股份有限公司	Share Holding Company	1320	1289	31	176
私营经济	Private-owned	11218	11187	31	131
其他	Others	6624	6202	422	8
港澳台商投资经济	Hongkong,Macao and Taiwan Funded	2308	2291	17	63
与港澳台商合资经营	Joint Venture with Hongkong, Macao and Taiwan	1600	1588	12	38
与港澳台商合作经营	Cooperative with Hongkong, Macao and Taiwan	230	228	2	8
港、澳、台商独资经济	Hongkong,Macao and Taiwan Funded	453	451	2	6
港澳台商投资股份有限公司	Hongkong,Macao and Taiwan Share Holding Company	25	24	1	11
外商投资经济	Foreign Funded	3216	3194	22	157
中外合资经营	Chinese-Foreign Joint Venture	1968	1951	17	141
中外合作经营	Chinese-Foreign Cooperative	240	239	1	4
外资(独资)经济	Foreign Funded	987	984	3	11
外商投资股份有限公司	Foreign Share Holding Company	21	20	1	1
按单位类别分	**Grouped by Type of Units**				
农业	Agriculture	743	707	36	178
工业	Industry	19692	19309	383	1499
建筑业	Construction	3385	3241	144	611
运输邮电业	Transportation,Posts and Telecommunications	534	489	45	298
批发零售贸易及餐饮业	Wholesale, Retail and Catering	26101	25096	1005	7151
服务业	Services	24430	23821	609	3738
行政事业及其他	Administrative Units, Institutions and Others	18817	17720	1097	2477
按隶属关系分	**Grouped by Administrative Relationship**				
中央属	Central	11052	10614	438	2037
市属	City	11842	11004	838	3751
区县属	Districts and Counties	18264	17097	1167	6540
街道属	Subdistrict	4579	4433	146	1145
镇属	Town	3774	3690	84	348
乡属	Township	3630	3538	92	320
居委会属	Neighborhood Committee	3543	3234	309	684
村委会属	Village Committee	11842	11718	124	676
其他	Others	25176	25055	121	451
按地理位置分	**Grouped by Geographic Position**				
二环路以内	Within the Second Ring	16615	15953	662	3237
二环路至三环路	the Second-third Ring Road	18989	18345	644	2968
三环路至四环路	the Third-Fourth Ring Road	16393	15924	469	2196
四环路以外	Beyond the Fourth Ring Road	41705	40161	1544	7551
按执行会计制度分	**Grouped by Accounting System Executed**				
企业	Enterprises	75361	73110	2251	11953
事业	Institutions	7967	7448	519	2426
机关	Organizations	1569	1497	72	212
其他	Others	8805	8328	477	1361

1-7 企业法人单位数
ENTERPRISE INSTITUTIONAL UNITS

单位：个 (unit)

项目	Item	法人单位 合计 Institutional Unit
总计	**Total**	**75361**
城区	**City Proper**	**20019**
东城区	Dongcheng	7516
西城区	Xicheng	6322
崇文区	Chongwen	2651
宣武区	Xuanwu	3530
近郊区	**Near Suburbs**	**37443**
朝阳区	Chaoyang	14795
丰台区	Fengtai	6971
石景山区	Shijingshan	1906
海淀区	Haidian	13771
远郊区	**Outer Suburbs**	**10989**
门头沟区	Mentougou	1141
房山区	Fangshan	2117
通州区	Tongzhou	3207
顺义区	Shunyi	2142
昌平区	Changping	2382
各县	**Counties**	**6910**
大兴县	Daxing	3460
平谷县	Pinggu	805
怀柔县	Huairou	1181
密云县	Miyun	751
延庆县	Yanqing	713
按营业状况分	**Grouped by Business**	
营业	Going on	67745
停业	Closed	3218
筹建	Preparation	1692
当年撤销	Recall in this Year	1441
其他	Others	1265
按开业时间分	**Grouped by Set up Time**	
1949年以前	Before 1949	219
1950-1965		2001
1966-1979		2147
1980-1989		11633
1990年以后	After 1990	59361
按企业规模分	**Grouped by Size**	
大型	Large	683
中型	Medium	2390
小型	Small	45485
按登记注册类型分	**Grouped by Type of Enterprises Registered**	

项目	Item	法人单位 合计 Institutional Unit
内资企业	Domestic Investment Enterprises	69847
国有企业	State-owned	16538
集体企业	Collective-owned	27739
股份合作企业	Share Holding Cooperative	4400
联营企业	Joint-owned	983
国有独资公司	State-owned Funded Company	220
其他有限责任公司	Other Limited-Liability Company	7431
股份有限公司	Share Holding Company	1320
私营企业	Private	11137
其他内资企业	Others	79
港澳台商投资企业	Hongkong,Macao and Taiwan Funded	2305
与港澳台商合资经营企业	Joint Venture with Hongkong,Maocao and Taiwan	1600
与港澳台商合作经营企业	Cooperative with Hongkong,Macao and Taiwan	229
港、澳、台商独资企业	Hongkong,Macao and Taiwan Funded	451
港澳台商投资股份有限公司	Hongkong,Macao and Taiwan Share Holding Company	25
外商投资企业	Foreign Funded	3209
中外合资经营企业	Chinese-Foreign Joint Venture	1967
中外合作经营企业	Chinese-Foreign Cooperative	237
外资(独资)企业	Foreign Funded	984
外商投资股份有限公司	Foreign Share Holding Company	21
按地理位置分	**Grouped by Location**	
二环路以内	Within the Second Ring Road	13833
二环路至三环路	Between the Second-third Ring Road	15966
三环路至四环路	Between the Third-Fourth Ring Road	14151
四环路以外	Beyond the Fourth Ring Road the Three-Four Ring Road	31411
按控股情况分	**Grouped by Share Holding Conditions**	
# 国有绝对控股	State-owned Relative Holding	17369
# 国有相对控股	State-owned Absolute Holding	1352

1-8 国民经济各行业法人和产业活动单位数(按行业分)
INSTITUTIONAL UNITS AND ESTABLISHMENTS(BY SECTOR)

单位：个 (unit)

行业	Sector	法人单位数 合计 Institutional Units	单产业法人 Single Sector	多产业法人 Multi-sector	多产业法人单位的产业活动单位数 Establishments of Multi-sector Institutional Units
合计	**Total**	**93702**	**90383**	**3319**	**15952**
农业	Agriculture	368	354	14	75
林业	Forestry	61	48	13	27
畜牧业	Animal Husbandry	341	320	21	79
渔业	Fishery	48	47	1	12
农、林、牧、渔服务业	FFAF Services	529	503	26	102
煤炭采选业	Coal Mining and Dressing	195	192	3	67
石油和天然气开采业	Petroleum and Natural Gas Extraction	1	1		
黑色金属矿采选业	Ferrous Metals Mining and Dressing	19	19		2
有色金属矿采选业	Nonferrous Metals Mining and Dressing	15	15		3
非金属矿采选业	Nonmetal Minerals Mining and Dressing	273	271	2	18
其他矿采选业	Other Minerals Mining and Dressing	2	2		
食品加工业	Food Processing	576	565	11	54
食品制造业	Food Making	674	666	8	57
饮料制造业	Beverage Production	273	271	2	8
烟草制造业	Tobacco Processing	4	4		
纺织业	Textile Industry	512	496	16	54
服装及其他纤维制品制造业	Garments and Other Fiber Products	988	964	24	80
皮革、毛皮、羽绒及其制品业	Leather,Furs,Down and Related Products	171	167	4	12
木材加工及竹、藤、棕、革制品业	Timber Processing,Bamboo,Cane,Palm Fiber and Straw Products	246	244	2	21
家具制造业	Furniture Manufacturing	545	540	5	20
造纸及纸制品业	Papermaking and Paper Products	525	524	1	10
印刷业、记录媒介的复制	Printing and Record Medium Reproduced	1016	991	25	65
文教体育用品制造业	Stationery,Education and Sports Goods	242	237	5	10
石油加工及炼焦业	Petroleum Processing and Coking Products	109	106	3	6
化学原料及化学制品制造业	Raw Chemical Materials and Chemical Products	1359	1344	15	69
医药制造业	Medical and Pharmaceutical Products	256	252	4	19
化学纤维制造业	Chemical Fibers	44	44		

1-8 续表 1 continued

单位：个 (unit)

行业	Sector	法人单位数 合计 Institutional Units	单产业法人 Single Sector	多产业法人 Multi-sector	多产业法人单位的产业活动单位数 Establishments of Multi-sector Institutional Units
橡胶制品业	Rubber Products	139	130	9	16
塑料制品业	Plastic Products	742	733	9	40
非金属矿物制品业	Nonmetal Mineral Products	1777	1754	23	106
黑色金属冶炼及压延加工业	Smelting and Processing of Ferrous Metals	78	72	6	29
有色金属冶炼及压延加工业	Smelting and Processing of Nonferrous Metals	148	144	4	8
金属制品业	Metal Products	2281	2261	20	117
普通机械制造业	Ordinary Machinery	1251	1226	25	92
专业设备制造业	Special Purpose Equipment	1005	969	36	108
交通运输设备制造业	Transportation Equipment	1348	1303	45	196
武器弹药制造业	Weapons and Ammunition	8	4	4	4
电气机械及器材制造业	Electric Equipment and Machinery	927	901	26	62
电子及通信设备制造业	Electronic and Telecommunication	764	751	13	29
仪器仪表及文化办公用机械制造业	Instruments,Meters,Cultural and Official Machinery	486	481	5	21
其他制造业	Other Manufacturing	606	584	22	77
电力、蒸汽、热水的生产和供应业	Electricity,Steam,Hot Water Production and Supply	64	60	4	17
煤气生产和供应业	Gas Production and Supply	10	9	1	1
自来水的生产和供应业	Tap Water Production and Supply	13	12	1	1
土木工程建筑业	Civil Engineering	1444	1337	107	430
线路、管道和设备安装业	Circuit,Pipelines and Equipment Installation	767	739	28	101
装修装饰业	Buildings Decoration	1174	1165	9	80
地质勘查业	Geological Prospecting	58	55	3	3
水利管理业	Water Conservancy	197	178	19	27
铁路运输业	Railway Transport	23	21	2	81
公路运输业	Highway Transport	406	369	37	151
管道运输业	Pipeline Transport	1	1		
水上运输业	Water Way Transport	2	2		
航空运输业	Air Transport	12	12		
交通运输辅助业	Transport Supporting and Auxiliary Services	268	266	2	25
其他交通运输业	Other Transport	16	15	1	5
仓储业	Storage	232	226	6	21
邮电通信业	Posts and Telecommunications	87	82	5	63
食品、饮料、烟草和家庭用品批发业	Wholesale of Food, Beverage,Tabacoo and Household Goods	5284	5076	208	635

1-8 续表 2 continued

单位：个 (unit)

行业	Sector	法人单位数 合计 Institutional Units	单产业法人 Single Sector	多产业法人 Multi-sector	多产业法人单位的产业活动单位数 Establishments of Multi-sector Institutional Units
能源、材料和机械电子设备批发业	Wholesale of Energy, Materials and Electronic Equipment	5032	4914	118	490
其他批发业	Other Wholesale	841	823	18	65
零售业	Retail	12113	11539	574	4839
商业经纪与代理业	Commercial Brokerage and Agencies	77	74	3	7
餐饮业	Catering	2831	2744	87	1122
金融业	Banking	1032	754	278	1597
保险业	Insurance	57	57		
房地产开发与经营业	Real Estate Development and Operation	704	685	19	75
房地产管理业	Real Estate Management	1011	981	30	73
房地产代理与经纪业	Real Estate Brokerage and Agency	104	104		2
公共服务业	Public Services	1373	1313	60	182
居民服务业	Resident Services	1764	1687	77	839
旅馆业	Hotels	1726	1675	51	420
租赁服务业	Leasing	367	363	4	45
旅游业	Tourism	344	339	5	30
娱乐服务业	Recreation	342	335	7	47
信息、咨询服务业	Information and Consultancy Services	5638	5612	26	116
计算机应用服务业	Computer Application Services	1954	1949	5	16
其他社会服务业	Other Social Services	1334	1303	31	118
卫　生	Health	680	666	14	49
体　育	Sports	111	105	6	16
社会福利保障业	Social Welfare	180	177	3	18
教　育	Education	2959	2696	263	1407
文化艺术业	Culture and Arts	1149	1104	45	82
广播电影电视业	Radio,Film,Television	173	167	6	10
科学研究业	Scientific Research	560	530	30	55
综合技术服务业	Polytechnical Services	6067	6031	36	104
国家机关	Government Organs	1664	1580	84	111
政党机关	Party Organs	110	110		
社会团体	Social Bodies	488	476	12	17
基层群众自治组织	Masses Autonomous Body	8692	8210	482	483
其他行业	Other Sectors	1215	1155	60	101

1-9 国民经济主要指标
MAJOR INDICATORS FOR NATIONAL ECONOMY

项目		Item		1999	1998	1999年为1998年% 1999 as % of 1998
人口		**Population**				
年底常住人口	(万人)	Year-end Permanent Residents	(10000 persons)	1099.8	1091.5	100.8
劳动力		**Labor Force**	**(10000 persons)**			
从业人员	(万人)	Employment	(10000 persons)	618.6	622.2	99.4
#职工人数	(万人)	Staff and Workers	(10000 persons)	438.0	450.1	97.3
国内生产总值	**(亿元)**	**Gross Domestic Product (100 million yuan)**		**2174.5**	**2011.3**	**110.2**
工农业总产值 (1990年不变价,亿元)		**Gross Output Value of Industry and Agriculture(at 1990 constant prices, 100 million yuan)**		**2224.9**	**2054.2**	**108.3**
全社会固定资产投资	**(亿元)**	**Total Investment in Fixed Assets (100 million yuan)**		**1170.6**	**1155.6**	**101.3**
#固定资产投资	(亿元)	Investment in Fixed Assets		1072.9	1060.3	101.2
#基本建设投资	(亿元)	Capital Construction		432.7	429.6	100.7
更新改造投资	(亿元)	Innovation		175.2	211.4	82.9
房地产开发投资	(亿元)	Real Estate Development		421.5	377.4	111.7
财政		**Finance**				
财政收入	(亿元)	Revenue	(100 million yuan)	320.5	262.0	122.3
财政支出	(亿元)	Expenditures	(100 million yuan)	410.2	307.8	133.2
物价		**Price Indices**				
居民消费价格总指数	(%)	Consumer Price Index	(%)	100.6	102.4	
商品零售价格总指数	(%)	Retail Price Index	(%)	98.8	98.3	
职工工资		**Wages of Staff and Workers**				
职工工资总额	(亿元)	Total Wages	(100 million yuan)	614.5	558.2	110.1
职工平均工资	(元)	Average Wage	(yuan)	13778.0	12285.0	112.2
居民消费水平	**(元)**	**Per Capita Consumption**	**(yuan)**	**5784.0**	**5178.0**	**110.8**
非农业居民	(元)	Non-Agricultural	(yuan)	7040.0	6240.0	111.8
农业居民	(元)	Agricultural	(yuan)	3168.0	3032.0	104.9
农村经济		**Rural Economy**				
农林牧渔业总产值 (1990年不变价,亿元)		Gross Output Value of Farming,Forestry,Animal Husbandry and Fishery (at 1990 constant prices,100 million yuan)		99.6	93.5	106.5
乡镇集体企业数	(个)	Number of Township and Village Enterprises	(unit)	13428.0	15711.0	85.5
乡镇企业从业人数	(万人)	Employment of Township and Village Enterprises	(10000 persons)	69.3	73.7	94.0
乡镇企业总收入	(亿元)	Total Revenue of Township and Village Enterprises	(100 million yuan)	589.2	574.7	102.5
工业		**Industry**				
工业总产值(1990年不变价，不含个体工业，亿元)		Gross Output Value (at 1990 constant prices,excluding individual industry, 100 million yuan)		2081.0	1926.7	108.0
轻工业	(亿元)	Light Industry	(100 million yuan)	556.1	539.4	103.1
重工业	(亿元)	Heavy Industry	(100 million yuan)	1524.9	1387.4	109.9
独立核算工业企业全员劳动生产率(按增加值计算,元/人)		Overall Labor Productivity of Enterprises with Independent Accounting System (according to added value,yuan/person)		36347.0	35130.0	103.5

注：本表的发展速度按可比口径计算。(续表同)

Note: Development indices are calculated at constant prices.(the continued tables are the same)

1-9 续表 1 continued

项 目 Item		1999	1998	1999 年为 1998 年% 1999 as % of 1998
独立核算工业企业主要财务指标	Major Financial Indicators for Enterprises with Independent Accounting System			
固定资产原价 (亿元)	Original Value of Fixed Assets (100 million yuan)	2312.1	2221.3	104.1
利税总额 (亿元)	Total Pre-tax Profits (100 million yuan)	184.6	161.7	114.2
运输邮电	**Transportation,Posts and Telecommunications**			
货物周转量 (亿吨公里)	Freight Ton-Kilometers (100 million ton-km)	538.8	540.1	99.8
铁路	Railways	447.9	450.7	99.4
公路	Highways	75.4	78.3	96.3
民航	Civil Aviation	15.5	11.0	140.5
管道	Pipelines	0.02	0.03	44.5
旅客周转量 (亿人公里)	Passenger-Kilometers (100 million passenger-km)	331.7	298.5	111.1
铁路	Railways	119.6	107.1	111.6
公路	Highways	40.1	30.5	131.5
民航	Civil Aviation	172.1	161.0	106.9
邮电业务总量 (亿元)	Business Volume of Posts and Telecommunication Services (100 million yuan)	156.6	129.1	121.3
全市电话交换机总容量 (万门)	Total Capacity of Telephone Exchanges (10000 lines)	743.0	686.8	108.3
商 业	**Commerce**			
社会消费品零售额 (亿元)	Total Retail Sales of Consumer Goods (100 million yuan)	1313.3	1195.2	109.9
批发零售贸易业	Wholesale and Retail	926.2	865.7	107.0
餐饮业	Catering	81.3	81.8	99.3
其他	Others	305.8	247.7	123.5
商业、饮食业、服务业营业网点 (万个)	Outlets of Commerce,Catering and Services (10000)	24.4	24.1	101.2
# 商业	Commerce	17.7	18.1	97.8
饮食业	Catering	3.2	2.9	110.3
服务业	Services	3.5	3.2	109.4
对外经济贸易和旅游	**Foreign Economy,Trade and Tourism**			
进出口总额 (亿美元)	Total Import and Export (USD100million)	84.4	65.1	129.7
进口额	Total Imports	51.8	36.8	140.9
出口额	Total Exports	32.6	28.3	115.2
新批三资企业数 (个)	Number of Foreign-funded Enterprises	647.0	656.0	98.6

1-9 续表 2 continued

项目	Item	1999	1998	1999年为1998年% 1999 as % of 1998
协议外资金额 (亿美元)	Total Amount of Foreign Capital in the Signed Agreements (USD 100 million)	18.3	41.1	44.5
实际利用外资 (亿美元)	Total Amount of Foreign Capital Actually Used (USD 100 million)	29.4	28.7	102.4
# 外商直接投资	Foreign Direct Investments	22.3	20.6	108.3
接待入境旅游人数 (万人)	Number of International Tourists (10000 persons)	252.4	220.1	114.7
金融保险	**Banking and Insurance**			
银行贷款增加额 (亿元)	Adding Deposits of Banks (100 million yuan)	513.4	610.8	84.1
城乡居民储蓄存款余额 (亿元)	Saving Deposits of Urban and Rural Residents (100 million yuan)	2680.7	2287.2	117.2
城镇 (亿元)	Urban (100 million yuan)	2429.0	2063.2	117.7
农村 (亿元)	Rural (100 million yuan)	251.6	224.0	112.3
保险公司保险费收入 (亿元)	Premiums Income of Insurance Com- panies (100 million yuan)	86.5	82.6	104.7
教　育	**Education**			
毕业生数 (万人)	Number of Graduates (10000 persons)	50.1	49.3	101.6
研究生 (人)	Postgraduates (person)	12241	11045.0	110.8
高等学校 (万人)	Institutions of Higher Education (10000 persons)	5.0	4.9	102.0
中等职业技术教育 (万人)	Secondary Vocational Technical Education (10000 persons)	7.9	7.2	109.7
普通中学 (万人)	Regular Secondary School (10000 persons)	19.4	21.3	91.1
小学 (万人)	Primary Schools (10000 persons)	17.6	15.6	112.8
文　化	**Culture**			
公共图书馆藏书 (万册)	Collection of Public Libraries (10000 copies)	2934.0	2848.0	103.0
艺术剧团国内演出场次 (场)	Times of Domestic Performance of Art Troupes (time)	8564.0	8105.0	105.7
科　技	**Science and Technology**			
科技人员 (万人)	Personnel (10000 persons)	136.1	132.2	103.0
卫　生	**Health**			
医院病床数 (万张)	Hospitals Beds (10000)	6.4	6.3	101.6
卫生技术人员数 (万人)	Medical Technical Personnel (10000 persons)	11.7	11.6	100.9
# 医生 (万人)	Doctors (10000 persons)	5.3	5.2	101.9
护师(士) (万人)	Senior and Junior Nurses (10000 persons)	4.0	3.9	102.6
城市公用事业	**Urban Public Utilities**			
用电量 (亿千瓦时)	Electricity Consumption (100 million kwh)	297.3	276.2	107.6
自来水销售量 (亿吨)	Sales of Tap Water (100 million tons)	7.8	7.6	102.6
居民燃气用户 (万户)	Households of Access to Gas (10000)	259.8	247.3	105.1
城市公共交通客运量 (亿人次)	Passengers Carried of City Public Transport (100 million person.times)	42.7	41.9	101.9
城市大型立交桥 (座)	Large Flyovers (unit)	141.0	138.0	102.2
城市绿化覆盖率 (%)	Coverage Rate of Urban Green Area (%)	36.3	35.6	
城市居民人均住房使用面积 (平方米)	Per Capita Using Space of Rooms of Urban Residents (sq.m)	15.88	14.96	106.1
农村居民人均住房面积 (平方米)	Per Capita Floor Space of Rooms of Rural Residents (sq.m)	28.6	27.6	103.6

1-10 国民经济主要指标比例关系
PERCENTAGE OF MAIN NATIONAL ECONOMIC INDICATORS

项　　目	Item	绝对值(万元) Value(10000 yuan)		构　成(%) Composition(%)	
		1999	1998	1999	1998
全市从业人员　(人)	**Total Employment　(person)**	**6185812**	**6221565**	**100**	**100**
第一产业	Primary Industry	745270	714503	12.0	11.5
第二产业	Secondary Industry	2161961	2259949	35.0	36.3
第三产业	Tertiary Industry	3278581	3247113	53.0	52.2
国内生产总值	**Gross Domestic Product**	**21744600**	**20113100**	**100**	**100**
第一产业	Primary Industry	874800	865600	4.0	4.3
第二产业	Secondary Industry	8402300	7868500	38.7	39.1
第三产业	Tertiary Industry	12467500	11379000	57.3	56.6
固定资产投资	**Investment in Fixed Assets**	**6513968**	**6829237**	**100**	**100**
第一产业	Primary Industry	16647	15226	0.3	0.2
第二产业	Secondary Industry	1793558	2017281	27.5	29.5
第三产业	Tertiary Industry	4703763	4796730	72.2	70.3
固定资产投资拨贷款	**Allocations and Loans on Investment in Fixed Assets**	**6575841**	**6693722**	**100**	**100**
国家预算内资金	State Budgetary Appropriation	1356504	938629	20.6	14.0
国内贷款	Domestic Loans	969362	1084327	14.7	16.2
利用外资	Foreign Capital	344867	412267	5.2	6.2
债　券	Bonds		158300		2.4
自筹资金	Self-raised Funds	3590697	3829243	54.7	57.2
#股　票	Stocks	35411	33445	0.5	0.5
其他资金	Other Capital	314411	270956	4.8	4.0
工农业总产值(现价)	**Gross Output Value of Industry and Agriculture(at current prices)**	**23746033**	**22036374**	**100**	**100**
工　业	Industry	21902616	20270235	92.2	92.0
农　业	Agriculture	1843427	1766139	7.8	8.0
工业总产值 (不含个体工业，现价)	**Gross Output Value of Industry (excluding individual industry, at current prices)**	**21446119**	**19919611**	**100**	**100**
轻工业	Light Indutry	6106775	6120157	28.5	30.7
重工业	Heavy Industry	15339344	13799453	71.5	69.3
农业总产值(现价)	**Gross Output Value of Agriculture (at current prices)**	**1843426.7**	**1766138.8**	**100**	**100**
种植业	Farming	911918.7	891629.8	49.4	50.5
林　业	Forestry	41868.4	32302.2	2.3	1.8
牧　业	Animal Husbandry	810859.3	766338.4	44.0	43.4
渔　业	Fishery	78779.6	75868.4	4.3	4.3
货运量　(万吨)	**Freight Traffic　(10000 tons)**	**45589.3**	**48017.4**	**100**	**100**
铁　路	Railways	19897.3	20453.4	43.6	42.6
公　路	Highways	25635.0	27490.0	56.2	57.3
民　航	Civil Aviation	29.9	22.4	0.1	…
管　道	Pipelines	27.1	51.6	0.1	0.1
客运量　(万人)	**Passenger Traffic　(10000 persons)**	**20322.4**	**16171.2**	**100**	**100**
铁　路	Railways	9656.6	8705.1	47.5	53.8
公　路	Highways	9878.0	6704.0	48.6	41.5
民　航	Civil Aviation	787.9	762.1	3.9	4.7
社会消费品零售总额	**Retail Sales of Consumer Goods**	**13133233**	**11952118**	**100**	**100**
批发零售贸易业	Wholesale and Retail	9261776	8657131	70.5	72.4
餐饮业	Catering	812690	818162	6.2	6.8
制造业	Manufacturing	798169	637469	6.1	5.3
其　他	Others	2260598	1839356	17.2	15.4
农民对非农民	Peasants Saling to Non-Peasants	76180	89463	0.6	0.7
地方财政收入相当于国内生产总值的比例 (%)	The Proportion of Local Financial Revenue in Gross Domestic Product (%)	14.7	13.0		
地方基建支出占地方财政收入的比例 (%)	The Proportion of Local Capital Construction Expenditures in Local Financial Revenue (%)	18.2	12.4		

1-11 按登记注册类型分国民经济主要指标比例关系
PERCENTAGE OF MAIN NATIONAL ECONOMIC INDICATORS BY REGISTERED TYPE

项目	Item	绝对值 Value 1999	1998	构成(%) Composition(%) 1999	1998
全市从业人员 (人)	**Total Employment (person)**	**6185812**	**6221565**	**100**	**100**
国有	State-Owned	2876190	3080645	46.5	49.5
集体	Collective Owned	496790	509986	8.0	8.2
其他	Others	950148	840916	15.4	13.5
城镇个体、私营	Urban Individuals	237293	200722	3.8	3.2
农村劳动者	Rural Labor Force	1625391	1589296	26.3	25.6
固定资产投资 (万元)	**Investment in Fixed Assets (10000 yuan)**	**6513968**	**6829237**	**100**	**100**
国有	State-Owned	5840694	5955574	89.6	87.1
集体	Collective Owned	129955	119613	2.0	1.8
联营	Joint Owned	3531	13542	0.1	0.2
股份合作企业	Share Holding Enterprises	17477	9008	0.3	0.1
股份有限公司	Share Holding Company	75301	54083	1.2	0.8
有限责任公司	Limited-liability Company	24492	26543	0.4	0.4
其他内资企业	Others		4482		0.1
中外合资经营	Chinese-foreign Joint Venture	157469	289371	2.4	4.2
中外合作经营	Chinses-foreign Cooperative	4787	33138	0.1	0.5
外商(独资)企业	Foreign Enterprises	15580	10703	0.2	0.2
外商投资股份有限公司	Foreign Funded Share Holding Company	1126	90	…	…
港澳台合资经营	Joint Venture with HongKong, Macao and Taiwan	93003	196402	1.4	2.9
港澳台合作经营	Cooperative from HongKong,Macao and Taiwan	138083	108825	2.1	1.6
港澳台商独资	HongKong,Macao and Taiwan Enterprises	10470	7863	0.2	0.1
港澳台商投资股份有限责任公司	Hongkong,Macao and Taiwan Funded Share Holding Company	2000		…	
工业总产值 (不含个体工业,现价,万元)	**Gross Output Value of Industry (excluding individual industry, at current prices,10000 yuan)**	**21446119**	**19919611**	**100**	**100**
国有	State-Owned	7695460	8634587	35.9	43.4
集体	Collective Owned	2631668	2752170	12.3	13.8
私营	Private	371298	199641	1.7	1.0
联营	Joint Owned	285789	274056	1.3	1.4
股份合作企业	Share Holding Enterprises	243651	259183	1.1	1.3
股份有限公司	Share Holding Company	918343	652427	4.3	3.3
有限责任公司	Limited-liability Company	1278151	1033833	6.0	5.2
其他内资企业	Others	428	208	…	…

1-11 续表 continued

项目	Item	绝对值 Value 1999	1998	构成(%) Composition(%) 1999	1998
中外合资经营	Chinese-foreign Joint Venture	5186351	4441395	24.2	22.3
中外合作经营	Chinses-foreign Cooperative	145261	68663	0.7	0.3
外商(独资)企业	Foreign Enterprises	431159	286846	2.0	1.4
外商投资股份有限公司	Foreign Funded Share Holding Company	151826	59352	0.7	0.3
港澳台合资经营	Joint Venture with HongKong, Macao and Taiwan	1198653	1092185	5.6	5.5
港澳台合作经营	Cooperative from HongKong,Macao and Taiwan	36024	25593	0.2	0.1
港澳台商独资	HongKong,Macao and Taiwan Enterprises	861265	128992	4.0	0.6
港澳台商投资股份有限责任公司	Hongkong,Macao and Taiwan Funded Share Holding Company	10792	10481	0.1	0.1
建筑业总产值 (万元)	**Gross Output Value of Construction (10000 yuan)**	**6814102.3**	**6246617.6**	**100**	**100**
国有	State-Owned	3529404.9	3323585.9	51.9	53.3
集体	Collective Owned	1536494.5	1390341.7	22.5	22.3
私营	Private	54127.0	26873.0	0.8	0.4
联营	Joint Owned	20733.4	26560.8	0.3	0.4
股份合作企业	Share Holding Enterprises	176854.1	152567.7	2.6	2.4
股份有限公司	Share Holding Company	688383.0	572431.1	10.1	9.2
有限责任公司	Limited-liability Company	567656.5	524404.2	8.3	8.4
其他内资企业	Others	8158.2	2858.8	0.1	…
外商投资企业	Foreign Funded Enterprises	131615.7	131916.2	1.9	2.1
港澳台商投资企业	Hongkong,Macao and Taiwan Funded Enterprises	100675.0	95078.2	1.5	1.5
大中型批发零售贸易业消费品零售额 (万元)	**Retail Sales Consumer Goods of Large and medium Wholesale and Retail Sales (10000 yuan)**	**5554995**	**5628046**	**100**	**100**
国有	State-Owned	2551678	2671500	45.8	47.4
集体	Collective Owned	792314	825893	14.3	14.7
股份有限公司	Share Holding Company	727343	702305	13.1	12.5
其他内资企业	Other Domestic Investment Enterprises	1027252	1028591	18.5	18.3
外商投资企业	Foreign Funded Enterprises	413869	349787	7.5	6.2
港澳台商投资企业	Hongkong,Macao and Taiwan Funded Enterprises	42539	49970	0.8	0.9

1-12 北 京 一 日
A DAY IN BEIJING

项 目	Item		1999	1998
生产量	**Output**			
国内生产总值(当年价格)(万元)	Gross Domestic Product	(at current prices) (10000 yuan)	59574.2	55104.4
工业总产值(当年价格) (万元)	Gross Output Value of Industry(at current prices)	(10000 yuan)	60007.2	55534.9
原 煤 (吨)	Coal	(ton)	21700.2	27108.5
发电量 (万千瓦时)	Electricity	(10000 kwh)	3922.7	4292.1
钢 (吨)	Steel	(ton)	20122.3	22006.1
农业总产值(当年价格)(万元)	Gross Output Value of Agriculture (at current prices)	(10000 yuan)	5050.5	4838.7
建筑业总产值 (万元)	Gross Output Value of Construction	(10000 yuan)	18668.8	17114.0
新建住宅竣工面积(万平方米)	Floor Space of New Residence Completed	(10000 sq.m)	4.2	3.0
货运量(包括管道) (万吨)	Freight Traffic(including pipelines)	(10000 tons)	77.5	82.5
客运量 (万人)	Passenger Traffic	(10000 persons)	40.0	30.8
社会消费品零售总额 (万元)	Retail Sales of Consumer Goods	(10000 yuan)	35981.5	32745.5
海关出口额 （地方，万美元)	Exports	(Local, USD 10000)	893.4	775.0
财政收入 (万元)	Financial Revenue	(10000 yuan)	8779.5	7178.3
旅游收入 (万美元)	Tourism Revenue	(USD 10000)	683.8	653.2
消费量	**Consumption**			
粮 食 (吨)	Grain	(ton)	4765.5	4963.5
猪 肉 (吨)	Pork	(ton)	878.2	672.2
牛羊肉 (吨)	Beef and Mutton	(ton)	558.1	278.7
鲜 蛋 (吨)	FreshEggs	(ton)	322.0	260.3
水产品 (吨)	Aquatic Products	(ton)	625.1	738.2
食用植物油 (吨)	Edible Vegetable Oil	(ton)	937.2	807.8
鲜 菜 (吨)	Fresh Vegetable	(ton)	10105.9	11932.3
生活用水(自来水厂)(万吨)	Residential Use of Tap Water	(10000 tons)	165.1	156.3
其 他	**Others**			
市内公共交通客运量 (万人次)	Urban Passenger Traffic	(10000 person.times)	1169.1	1147.5
接待旅游人数 (人次)	Tourists Received	(person.time)	6914.9	6030.0
邮寄函件 (万件)	Mail Delivery	(10000)	150.9	139.1
拍发公众电报 (万份)	Telegrams	(10000)	0.2	0.2
城乡居民储蓄存款 (万元)	Saving Deposit of Urban and Rural Residents	(10000 yuan)	10780.2	8545.9
出生人口 (人)	Birth Population	(person)	172.0	183.0
死亡人口 (人)	Death Population	(person)	169.0	206.0
结婚对数 (对)	Marriage	(couple)	226.0	232.0
离婚对数 (对)	Divorce	(couple)	65.4	65.0

1-13 平均每人主要社会经济活动
MAJOR ECONOMIC INDICATORS PER CAPITA

项目		Item		1999	1998	1999年为1998年% 1999 as % of 1998
国内生产总值(当年价格)	(元)	**Gross Domestic Product (at current prices)**	**(yuan)**	**19846.0**	**18478.0**	**109.5**
工农业总产值(1990年不变价)	(元)	**Gross Output Value of Industry and Agriculture(at 1990 constant prices)**	**(yuan)**	**20306.0**	**18871.9**	**107.6**
财政收入	(元)	**FinancialRevenue**	**(yuan)**	**2924.6**	**2407.0**	**121.5**
房屋建筑竣工面积	(平方米)	**Floor Space of Building Completed**	**(sq.m)**	**2.1**	**1.7**	**123.5**
# 新建住宅	(平方米)	NewResidence	(sq.m)	1.4	1.0	140.0
工　业		**Industry**				
工业总产值(1990年不变价)	(元)	Gross Output Value of Industry (at 1990 constant prices,yuan)		19396.7	18012.8	107.7
主要工业产品产量		Output of Major Products				
布	(米)	Cloth	(meter)	13.5	19.6	68.9
彩色电视机(百人)	(台)	ColorTelevision(100persons)	(unit)	1.1	1.1	100.0
原　煤	(千克)	Coal	(kg)	722.9	909.0	79.5
发电量	(千瓦时)	Electricity	(kwh)	1306.7	1439.2	90.8
钢	(千克)	Steel	(kg)	670.3	737.9	90.8
农　业		**Agriculture**				
农业总产值(1990年不变价)	(元)	Gross Output Value of Agriculture (at 1990 constant prices,yuan)		909.2	859.1	105.8
主要农产品产量		Output of Major Products				
粮　食	(千克)	Grain	(kg)	183.4	219.8	83.4
肉　类	(千克)	Meat	(kg)	45.2	41.3	109.4
鲜　蛋	(千克)	FreshEggs	(kg)	14.4	16.4	87.8
鲜　菜	(千克)	FreshVegetable	(kg)	389.5	373.1	104.4
水产品	(千克)	AquaticProducts	(kg)	6.9	7.0	98.6
牛　奶	(千克)	Milk	(kg)	21.9	20.9	104.8
干鲜果	(千克)	DryandFreshFruit	(kg)	51.5	51.6	99.8
商　业		**Commerce**				
社会消费品零售总额	(元)	Retail Sales of Consumer Goods	(yuan)	11986.2	10980.4	109.2
# 吃的商品		Food		3417.9	3196.0	106.9
穿的商品		Clothing		1420.5	1336.7	106.3
用的商品		Daily Used Articles		6772.9	6108.2	110.9
主要消费品零售量		Retail Sales of Major Consumer Goods in Quantity				
粮　食	(千克)	Grain	(kg)	115.3	109.8	105.0
食用植物油	(千克)	EdibleVegetableOil	(kg)	29.3	25.1	117.0
猪　肉	(千克)	Pork	(kg)	24.2	20.2	119.8
鲜　蛋	(千克)	FreshEggs	(kg)	10.5	8.7	120.7
水产品	(千克)	AquaticProducts	(kg)	20.8	15.4	135.1
邮　电		**Posts and Telecommunications**				
邮寄函件	(件)	MailDelivery	(unit)	50.3	46.6	107.9
城市公用事业		**Urban Public Utilities**				
日生活用水量	(千克)	DailyResidentialUseofWater	(kg)	250.1	238.2	105.0
城市居民居住面积	(平方米)	Living Space of Urban Residents	(sq.m)	10.63	10.03	106.0
平均每千人拥有公共交通车辆	(辆)	Possession of Public Traffic VehiclesPer1000Persons	(unit)	1.14	0.99	115.2
乘坐公共电汽车次数	(人次)	Times of Riding in Bus or Trolley	(person.time)	345.4	342.2	100.9
公共绿地面积	(平方米)	PublicGreenAreas	(sq.m)	9.1	9.0	101.4
卫　生		**Health**				
平均每千人拥有医生	(人)	Number of Doctors Per 1000 Persons	(person)	4.79	4.76	100.6
平均每千人拥有医院床位	(张)	Number of Beds Per 1000 Persons	(unit)	6.15	6.13	100.3
人民生活		**Pepople's Livelihood**				
职工年平均工资	(元)	AnnualAverageWage	(yuan)	13778.0	12285.0	112.2
居民家庭可支配收入	(元)	Annual Discretionary Income of Urban Residence	(yuan)	9182.8	8472.0	108.4
农民家庭纯收入	(元)	Annual Net Income of Rural Residence	(yuan)	4316.4	4028.9	107.1
城乡居民储蓄存款余额	(元)	Savings Deposit of Urban and Rural Residents	(yuan)	24374.1	20954.5	116.3
城镇居民		Urban		32508.4	28120.3	115.6
农村居民		Rural		7136.5	6260.5	114.0

1-14 总　产　出
TOTAL OUTPUT

单位：万元　　(10000 yuan)

项　目 Item		1999	1998	1999年为1998年% 1999 as % of 1998
总　计	**Total**	**72338300**	**65985000**	**113.4**
第一产业	Primary Industry	1843400	1766100	106.5
第二产业	Secondary Industry	33691000	30757600	116.0
工　业	Industry	26284500	24197500	116.8
建筑业	Construction	7406500	6560100	112.3
第三产业	Tertiary Industry	36803900	33461300	109.8
# 交通运输、仓储及邮电业	Transportation,Storage, Posts and Telecommunications	4649300	4442500	105.0
批发和零售贸易、餐饮业	Wholesale,Retail and Catering	3980300	3910300	103.3

注：绝对数按现价计算，发展速度按可比价格计算(下同)。

Note: The data in terms of value are calculated at current prices,while the related indices are calculated at comparable prices. (The followings are the same)

1-15 国民生产总值
GROSS NATIONAL PRODUCT

单位：万元　　(10000 yuan)

项　目 Item		1999	1998	1999年为1998年% 1999 as % of 1998	构成(%) Composition(%)	
					1999	1998
国民生产总值	**Gross National Product**	**21749700**	**20117700**	**110.2**		
国内生产总值	**Gross Domestic Product**	**21744600**	**20113100**	**110.2**	**100**	**100**
第一产业	**Primary Industry**	**874800**	**865600**	**102.5**	**4.0**	**4.3**
第二产业	**Secondary Industry**	**8402300**	**7868500**	**112.0**	**38.7**	**39.1**
工　业	Industry	6493400	6106600	112.8	29.9	30.4
建筑业	Construction	1908900	1761900	108.0	8.8	8.7
第三产业	**Tertiary Industry**	**12467500**	**11379000**	**109.1**	**57.3**	**56.6**
农林牧渔服务业	FFAF Services	22700	19400	116.5	0.1	0.1
地质勘探业、水利管理业	Geological Prospecting and Water Conservancy	46000	45000	103.4	0.2	0.2
交通运输、仓储及邮电业	Transportation,Storage, Posts and Telecommunications	1675400	1544500	108.9	7.7	7.7
批发和零售贸易、餐饮业	Wholesale,Retail and Catering	2104300	2073300	102.7	9.7	10.3
金融保险业	Banking and Insurance	3163700	2776400	113.7	14.5	13.8
房地产业	Real Estate	694500	682500	101.7	3.2	3.4
社会服务业	Social Services	1477400	1357900	103.0	6.8	6.8
卫生、体育、社会福利事业	Health,Sports and Social Welfare	335900	305800	110.9	1.5	1.5
教育、文艺、广播电影电视事业	Education,Culture,Art,Radio,Film and Television	1199500	1106700	109.7	5.5	5.5
科学研究和综合技术服务业	Scientific Research and Polytechnical Services	1011700	808300	124.9	4.7	4.0
国家政党机关、社会团体	Government Organs,Party Organs and Social Bodies	579100	518300	113.1	2.7	2.6
其他	Others	157300	140900	111.9	0.7	0.7
国外(地区)净要素收入	**Net Income of Essential Factor from Foreign Country(Territory)**	**5100**	**4600**	**109.5**		
人均国内生产总值(元)	**Per Capita Gross Domestic Products (yuan)**	**19846**	**18478**	**109.5**		

1-16 国内生产总值构成项目
COMPOSITION OF GROSS DOMESTIC PRODUCT

单位：万元 (10000 yuan)

项目	Item	增加值 Added Value	劳动者报酬 Remuneration for Labors	固定资产折旧 Depreciation of Fixed Asset	生产税净额 Net Taxes on Production	营业盈余 Operating Surplus
国内生产总值	**Gross Domestic Product**	**21744600**	**10530900**	**4005300**	**2949100**	**4259300**
第一产业	**Primary Industry**	**874800**	**544600**	**70900**	**100**	**259200**
第二产业	**Secondary Industry**	**8402300**	**4352300**	**1610000**	**1792800**	**647200**
工　业	Industry	6493400	3136900	1467400	1479000	410100
建筑业	Construction	1908900	1215400	142600	313800	237100
第三产业	**Tertiary Industry**	**12467500**	**5634000**	**2324400**	**1156200**	**3352900**
农林牧渔服务业	FFAF Services	22700	18300	3400	500	500
地质勘探业、水利管理业	Geological Prospecting and Water Conservancy	46000	24400	19500	4200	-2100
交通运输、仓储及邮电业	Transportation,Storage, Posts and Telecommunications	1675400	515500	632300	157400	370200
批发和零售贸易、餐饮业	Wholesale,Retail and Catering	2104300	1297600	325900	265100	215700
金融保险业	Banking and Insurance	3163700	220700	124300	288000	2530700
房地产业	Real Estate	694500	235900	294100	214600	-50100
社会服务业	Social Services	1477400	1068400	389200	74900	-55100
卫生、体育、社会福利事业	Health,Sports and Social Welfare	335900	270900	50800	2900	11300
教育、文艺、广播电影电视事业	Education,Culture,Art,Radio,Film and Television	1199500	817200	167800	60900	153600
科学研究和综合技术服务业	Scientific Research and Polytechnical Services	1011700	634000	176300	71600	129800
国家政党机关、社会团体	Government Organs,Party Organs and Social Bodies	579100	450700	113200	5900	9300
其他	Others	157300	80400	27600	10200	39100

1-17 按支出法计算的国内生产总值
GROSS DOMESTIC PRODUCTS CALCULATED WITH EXPENDITURE APPROACH

单位：万元 (10000 yuan)

项目	Item	1999	1998	1999年为1998年% 1999 as % of 1998
国内生产总值	**Gross Domestic Product**	**21744600**	**20463100**	**110.4**
最终消费	Final Consumption	9541400	8098200	118.8
居民总消费	Residential Consumption	6337600	5636200	112.6
农业居民	Agricultural	1125200	1092600	105.0
非农业居民	Non-Agricultural	5212400	4543600	114.7
政府消费	Government Consumption	3203800	2462000	131.4
资本形成总额	Total Capital Formation	15261600	13964000	112.2
固定资产形成总额	Completed Fixed Assets	12334600	11719000	106.8
存货增加	Changes in Stock	2927000	2245000	134.9
货物和服务净出口	Net Export of Products and Services	-3058400	-1599100	

1-18 居 民 总 消 费 水 平
CONSUMPTION LEVEL OF RESIDENTS

单位：元 (yuan)

项 目	Item	1999	1998	1999年为1998年% 1999 as % of 1998
全市居民总消费水平	**Consumption Level of all Residents**	**5784**	**5178**	**110.8**
农业居民	Agricultural	3168	3032	104.9
非农业居民	Non-Agricultural	7040	6240	111.8
农业居民与非农业居民对比 (以农业居民为100)	**Ratio of Consumption of Agricultural to Non-Agricultural (Agricultural=100)**	**1:2.2**	**1:2.1**	

1-19 最 终 消 费
FINAL CONSUMPTION

单位：万元 (10000 yuan)

项 目	Item	1999	1998	1999年为1998年% 1999 as % of 1998
最终消费	**Final Consumption**	**9541400**	**8098200**	**118.8**
居民消费	**Resident Consumption**	**6337600**	**5636200**	**112.6**
农业居民	Agricultural	1125200	1092600	105.0
自给性消费	Self-sufficiency	68300	61500	116.9
商品性消费	Commodity	675000	657600	104.7
文化生活及服务性消费	Culture and Services	234100	230000	101.8
住房及水电消费	Residence,Water and Electricity	147800	143500	102.9
# 住房消费	Residence	80400	77800	103.2
非农业居民	Non-Agricultural	5212400	4543600	114.7
商品性消费	Commodity	3107200	2774300	112.5
文化生活及服务性消费	Culture and Services	1732600	1458800	117.5
住房及水电消费	Residence,Water and Electricity	372600	310500	119.9
# 住房消费	Residence	269400	201200	133.8
政府消费	**Government Consumption**	**3203800**	**2462000**	**131.4**

1-20 主要社会经济效益指标
MAJOR ECONOMIC EFFICIENCY INDICATORS

项目		Item		1999	1998
社会劳动生产率(当年价格)		**Overall Labor Productivity (at current prices)**		**35152.0**	**32328.0**
	(元/人)		**(yuan/person)**		
第一产业	(元/人)	Primary Industry	(yuan/person)	11738.0	12106.0
第二产业	(元/人)	Secondary Industry	(yuan/person)	38864.0	34816.0
第三产业	(元/人)	Tertiary Industry	(yuan/person)	38027.0	35045.0
每百元总投资新增国内生产总值		**Incremental GDP Per 100 yuan Investment**		**10.7**	**14.4**
	(元)		**(yuan)**		
总产出中间投入率	(%)	**IntermediateInput/TotalOutput**	**(%)**	**69.9**	**69.5**
第一产业	(%)	PrimaryIndustry	(%)	52.2	51.0
第二产业	(%)	SecondaryIndustry	(%)	75.1	74.4
第三产业	(%)	TertiaryIndustry	(%)	66.1	66.0
增加值率	(%)	**GDP/TotalOutput**	**(%)**	**30.1**	**30.5**
第一产业	(%)	PrimaryIndustry	(%)	47.5	49.0
第二产业	(%)	SecondaryIndustry	(%)	24.9	25.6
第三产业	(%)	TertiaryIndustry	(%)	33.9	34.0

1-21 1998 年 国 民 经 济 总 体 帐 户
OVERALL ACCOUNT OF NATIONAL ECONOMY OF 1998

1-21-1 生　产　帐　户
PRODUCTION ACCOUNT

单位：亿元 (100 million yuan)

劳动者报酬	Remuneration for Labors	979.9	总产出	Total Output	6598.5
工资及工资性收入	Wages	847.5	减：中间消耗	Substract：Intermediate Consumption	4587.2
单位社会保险付款	Organization Insurance	132.4			
生产税净额	Net Taxes on Production	274.1			
生产税	Production Tax	393.9			
减：生产补贴	Substract：Production Subsidy	119.8			
亏损补贴	Lossing Subsidy	98.2			
价格补贴	Price Subsidy	21.6			
固定资产折旧	Depreciation of Fixed Assets	384.9			
营业盈余	Earnings Surplus	372.4			
增加值分配	**Distribution of Value Added**	**2011.3**	**增加值**	**Value Added**	**2011.3**

1-21-2 收入分配及支出帐户
INCOME DISTRIBUTION AND EXPENDITURE ACCOUNT

单位：亿元 (100 million yuan)

财产收入支付	Payment for Property Right	1518.4	营业盈余	Earnings Surplus	372.4
利息支出	Interest	379.9	固定资产折旧	Depreciation of Fixed Asset	384.9
红利支出	Dividend Payment	7.4	财产收入	Property Income	1604.2
土地租金支出	Land Rental		利息收入	Interest Income	379.9
其他支出	Other Expenditures	1131.1	红利收入	Dividend Income	94.7
经常转移支出	Current Payment	402.8	土地租金收入	Land Rental Income	
收入税支出	Income Taxes	90.2	其他收入	Other Income	1129.6
财政经常性拨款支出	Fiscal Current Allocation		劳动者报酬	Remuneration for Labors	979.9
社会保险付款支出	Social Insurance Payment	132.4	工资及工资性收入	Wages	847.5
社会补助支出	Social Subsidy	8.5	单位社会保险付款	Organization Insurance	132.4
其他经常转移支出	Other Current Expenditure	171.7	生产税净额	Net Taxes on Production	274.1
可支配总收入	Total Disposable Income	2167.8	生产税	Production Tax	393.9
最终消费	Final Consumption	809.8	减：生产补贴	Substract：Production Subsidy	119.8
居民消费	Private Consumption	563.6			
政府消费	Government Consumption	246.2	亏损补贴	Lossing Subsidy	98.2
总储蓄	Total Savings	1358.0	价格补贴	Price Subsidy	21.6
			经常转移收入	Current Income	473.5
			收入税收入	Income Tax	90.2
			财政经常性拨款收入	Fiscal Current Allocation	
			社会保险付款收入	Social Insurance Payment	132.4
			社会补助收入	Social Subsidy Income	8.5
			其他经常转移收入	Other Current Income	242.4
支出和总储蓄	**Expenditure and Total Savings**	**4089.0**	**收入**	**Income**	**4089.0**

1-21-3 资 本 帐 户
CAPITAL ACCOUNT

单位：亿元 (100 million yuan)

固定资产形成总额	Fixed Asset Formation	1171.9	总储蓄	Total Savings	1358.0
存货增加	Changes of Inventory	224.5	资本转移收入净额	Net Flow of Capital	
其他非金融资产获得减处置	Net Incremental Non-financial Assets		资本转移收入	Inflow of Capital	60.9
			投资性补助收入	Investment-subsidy	60.9
资金余缺	Surplus or Shortage of Capital	156.5	其他资本转移收入	Other Capital	
			减：资本转移支出	Substract: Capital-change Expenditure	60.9
统计误差	Statistical Error	-194.9			
			投资性补助支出	Investment-subsidy	60.9
			其他资本转移支出	Other Capital-change Expenditure	
资本运用	**Capital Use**	**1358.0**	**资本筹集**	**Capital Source**	**1358.0**

1-21-4 金 融 帐 户
BANKING ACCOUNT

单位：亿元 (100 million yuan)

国内金融交易	Domestic Banking Business	2669.1	国内金融交易	Domestic Banking Business	2435.9
通货	Currency	126.5	通货	Currency	
存款	Deposits	1270.9	存款	Deposits	1354.7
短期存款	Short-term	786.7	短期存款	Short-term	852.9
长期存款	Long-term	484.2	长期存款	Long-term	501.8
贷款	Loans	942.8	贷款	Loans	942.8
短期贷款	Short-term	540.9	短期贷款	Short-term	540.9
长期贷款	Long-term	401.9	长期贷款	Long-term	401.9
证券(不含股票)	Securities(excluding stock)	81.8	证券(不含股票)	Securities(excluding stock)	81.8
短期证券	Short-term		短期证券	Short-term	
长期证券	Long-term	81.8	长期证券	Long-term	81.8
股票及其他股权	Stock and Other Stock Ownership	43.7	股票及其他股权	Stock and Other Stock Ownership	43.7
保险准备金	Premium Reserve	12.9	保险准备金	Premium Reserve	12.9
其他金融资产	Other Financial Assets	190.5	其他负债	Other Liabilities	
国际资本往来	International Capital Movement	-74.2	国际资本往来	International Capital Movement	2.5
短期资本	Short-term	-71.5			
长期资本	Long-term	-2.7	短期资本	Short-term	2.3
国际储备资产	International Reserves		长期资本	Long-term	0.2
			资金余缺	Surplus or Shortage of Capital	156.5
金融资产净增额	**Net Increase of Banking Capital**	**2594.9**	**负债净增额与资金余缺**	**Net Increase of Liability and Surplus or Shortage of Capital**	**2594.9**

1-21-5 期 末资产负债帐户
YEAR-END BALANCE ACCOUNT

单位：亿元 (100 million yuan)

非金融资产	Non-financial Assets	10909.3	负债	Liabilities	13688.5
固定资产	Fixed Assets	8041.0	国内金融资产	Domestic Financial Assets	13353.4
存货	Inventories	2325.0		and Liabilities	
其他非金融资产	Others	543.3	通货	Currency	
金融资产	Financial Assets	14705.6	存款	Deposits	7196.4
国内金融资产	Domestic Financial Assets	14705.6	短期存款	Short-term	3649.1
	and Liabilities		长期存款	Long-term	3547.3
通货	Currency	240.7	贷款	Loans	3400.4
存款	Deposits	7196.4	短期贷款	Short-term	2513.4
短期存款	Short-term	3649.1	长期贷款	Long-term	887.0
长期存款	Long-term	3547.3	证券(不含股票)	Securities(excluding stock)	7.5
贷款	Loans	3400.4	短期证券	Short-term	
短期贷款	Short-term	2513.4	长期证券	Long-term	7.5
长期贷款	Long-term	887.0	股票及其他股权	Stock and Other Stock	2667.7
证券(不含股票)	Securities(excluding stock)	1119.1		Ownership	
短期证券	Short-term	147.3	保险准备金	Premium Reserve	81.3
长期证券	Long-term	971.8	其他负债	Other Liabilities	
股票及其他股权	Stock and Other Stock	2667.7	国外金融负债	Foreign Financial Liabi-	335.2
	Ownership			lities	
保险准备金	Premium Reserve	81.3	短期负债	Short-term	
其他金融资产	Other Financial Assets		长期负债	Long-term	335.2
国外金融资产	Foreign Financial Assets		资产负债差额	Balance of Assets and Lia-	11926.4
短期资本	Short-term Capital			bilities	
长期资本	Long-term Capital				
储备资产	Reserves				
资　产	**Assets**	**25614.9**	**负债与资产负债**	**Liabilities and Balance of**	**25614.9**
			差额	**Assets and Liabilities**	

1-22 1998 年资产负债表

单位：亿元

项目	Item	非金融部门 Non-banking 使用 Use	来源 Source	金融部门 Banking 使用 Use	来源 Source
非金融资产	**Non-financial Assets**	**6138.45**		**291.66**	
固定资产	Fixed Assets	3445.03		194.97	
固定资产净值	Net Value	3354.61		122.83	
固定资产原值	Original Value	4869.52		162.55	
减：累计折旧	Substract：Accumulative Depreciation	1514.91		39.72	
在建工程	Projects under Construction	90.42		72.14	
固定资产清理	Liquidation Fixed Assets				
待处理固定资产净损失	Net Lossing of Fixed Assets Unsettled				
存货	Inventories	2233.30		17.44	
产成品和商品库存	Finished Products and Commodity Stock	249.84			
其他资产	Others	460.12		79.25	
无形资产	Intangible Assets	235.42		39.28	
金融资产与负债	**Financial Assets and Liabilities**	**5356.67**	**6370.87**	**3967.31**	**7277.72**
国内金融资产与负债	Domestic Financial Assets and Liabilities	5356.67	6035.70	3967.31	7277.72
通　货	Currency	41.39		0.85	
存　款	Deposits	4013.75			7196.39
短期存款	Short-term	2559.27			3649.09
#财政存款	Financial				95.16
长期存款	Long-term	1454.48			3547.30
贷　款	Loans		3360.44	3400.37	
短期贷款	Short-term		2510.2	2513.41	
#财政借款	Financial				
长期贷款	Long-term		850.24	886.96	
股票及其他股权	Stock and Other Stock Ownership	1051.79	2667.76	29.95	
证　券(不含股票)	Securities(excluding stock)	228.08	7.50	536.14	
短期证券	Short-term	23.27		53.15	
#政府债券	Government	23.27		45.52	
长期证券	Long-term	204.81	7.50	482.99	
#政府债券	Government	187.56		284.42	
保险准备金	Premium Reserve	21.66			81.33
其　他	Others				
国外金融资产与负债	Foreign Financial Assets and Liabilities		335.17		
短期资本	Short-term Capital				
长期资本	Long-term Capital		335.17		
资产负债差额	**Balance of Assets and Liabilities**		**5124.25**		**-3018.75**

1998 BALANCE SHEET

(100 million yuan)

政府部门 Government		住户部门 Private		国外 Foreign		合计 Total	
使用 Use	来源 Source	使用 Use	来源 Source	使用 Use	来源 Source	使用 Use	来源 Source
1719.55		**2759.59**				**10909.25**	
1696.05		2704.93				8040.98	
1696.05		2704.93				7878.42	
1843.73		3646.35				10522.15	
147.68		941.42				2643.73	
						162.56	
19.63		54.66				2325.03	
						249.84	
3.87						543.24	
						274.70	
2201.89	**22.51**	**3179.81**	**17.42**	**335.17**		**15040.85**	**15040.85**
2201.89	22.51	3179.81	17.42			14705.68	14705.68
12.27		186.21				240.72	240.72
889.99		2292.65				7196.39	7196.39
650.51		439.31				3649.09	3649.09
95.16						95.16	95.16
239.48		1853.34				3547.3	3547.3
	22.51		17.42			3400.37	3400.37
			3.21			2513.41	2513.41
	22.51		14.21			886.96	886.96
1299.63		286.39				2667.76	2667.76
		354.89				1119.11	1119.11
		70.85				147.27	147.27
		70.85				139.64	139.64
		284.04				971.84	971.84
		237.51				709.49	709.49
		59.67				81.33	81.33
				335.17		335.17	335.17
				335.17		335.17	335.17
	3898.93		**5921.98**		**335.17**		**10909.25**

1-23 地 方 财 政 收 入
LOCAL FINANCIAL REVENUE

项 目	Item	绝 对 数(万元) Value(10000 yuan)		1999 年为 1998 年% 1999 as % of 1998	构 成(%) Composition(%)	
		1999	1998		1999	1998
总 计	**Total**	**3204514**	**2620068**	**122.3**	**100**	**100**
一般预算财政收入合计	**General Budgetary Financial Revenue**	**2790863**	**2273313**	**122.8**	**87.1**	**86.8**
#增值税	Increased Value Tax	397303	375807	105.7	12.4	14.3
营业税	Operating Tax	1288568	1129996	114.0	40.2	43.1
个人所得税	Private Income Tax	458824	364938	125.7	14.3	13.9
城市维护建设税	City Maintenance Tax	129817	120054	108.1	4.1	4.6
固定资产投资方向调节税	Adjusting Tax of Investment in Fixed Assets	69530	51374	135.3	2.2	2.0
农牧业税和耕地占用税类	Tax for Farming and Animal Husbandry and Cultivated Land Occupation	94224	45187	208.5	2.9	1.7
企业所得税	Enterprise Income Tax	530717	480483	110.5	16.6	18.3
国有资产经营收益	Operating Income of State-owned Assets	1992	611	326.0	0.1	0.0
国有企业计划亏损补贴类	Losing Subsidies of Planning of State-owned Enterprises	-570790	-631097	90.4	-17.8	-24.1
企业所得税退税	Returned Tax of Income Tax of Enterprises	-70788	-66276	106.8	-2.2	-2.5
罚没收入、行政性收费	Forfeit and Administrative Fee	110043	91825	119.8	3.4	3.5
基金预算收入合计	**Total Fund Budgetary Income**	**413651**	**346755**	**119.3**	**12.9**	**13.2**

1-24 地 方 财 政 支 出
LOCAL FINANCIAL EXPENDITURE

项 目	Item	绝 对 数(万元) Value(10000 yuan)		1999 年为 1998 年% 1999 as % of 1998	构 成(%) Composition(%)	
		1999	1998		1999	1998
总 计	**Total**	**4101873**	**3078329**	**133.2**	**100**	**100.0**
一般预算财政支出	**General Budgetary Financial Expenditure**	**3670316**	**2810718**	**130.6**	**89.5**	**91.3**
#基本建设支出	Capital Construction	583720	326077	179.0	14.2	10.6
企业挖潜改造资金	Innovation Funds of Enterprises	313357	193348	162.1	7.6	6.3
科技三项费用	Science and Technology Promotion	38838	22105	175.7	0.9	0.7
流动资金	Circulating Funds	15917	9889	161.0	0.4	0.3
农林水气等部门事业费	Agriculture,Forestry, Water Conservancy and Meteorology	36788	33129	111.0	0.9	1.1
支援农村生产支出	Supporting Agricultural Production	78463	57680	136.0	1.9	1.9
城市维护费	City Maintenance	170930	129914	131.6	4.2	4.2
工业交通等部门的事业费	Fees of Industrial and Transportation Departments	14474	12120	119.4	0.4	0.4
文化事业费	Fees of Culture	23481	21294	110.3	0.6	0.7
教育事业费	Fees of Education	492356	414950	118.7	12.0	13.5
卫生经费	Funds of Health	228670	204056	112.1	5.6	6.6
科学事业费	Science	49074	41118	119.3	1.2	1.3
行政管理费	Government Administration	177440	137347	129.2	4.3	4.5
公检法司支出	Public Security Agency,Procuratorial Agency and Court of Justice	263704	218024	121.0	6.4	7.1
抚恤和社会福利救济费	Pensions and Relief Funds for Social Welfare	80038	65477	122.2	2.0	2.1
政策性补贴支出	Policy Subsidies	100521	139032	72.3	2.5	4.5
基金支出合计	**Funds Expenditure**	**431557**	**267611**	**161.3**	**10.5**	**8.7**

主要统计指标解释

国内生产总值 是按市场价格计算的国内生产总值的简称。它是一个国家（地区）所有常住单位在一定时期内生产活动的最终成果。国内生产总值有三种表现形式，即价值形态、收入形态和产品形态。从价值形态看，它是所有常住单位在一定时期内所生产的全部货物和服务价值超过同期投入的全部非固定资产货物和服务价值的差额，即所有常住单位的增加值之和；从收入形态看，它是所有常住单位在一定时期内所创造并分配给常住单位和非常住单位的初次分配收入之和；从产品形态看，它是最终使用的货物和服务减去进口货物和服务。在实际核算中，国内生产总值的三种表现形态表现为三种计算方法，即生产法、收入法和支出法。三种方法分别从不同的方面反映国内生产总值及其构成。

三次产业 根据社会生产活动历史发展的顺序对产业结构的划分，产品直接取自自然界的部门称为第一产业，对初级产品进行再加工的部门成为第二产业。为生产和消费提供各种服务的部门称为第三产业。它是世界上通用的产业结构分类，但各国的划分不尽一致。我国的三次产业划分是：

第一产业：农业（包括种植业、林业和渔业）。

第二产业：工业（包括采掘工业、制造业、自来水、电力、蒸汽、热水、煤气）和建筑业。

第三产业：除第一、第二产业以外的其他各业。由于第三产业包括的行业多、范围广，根据我国的实际情况第三产业可分为两大部门：一是流通部门，二是服务部门。具体又可分为四个层次：

第一层次：流通部门，包括交通运输业、邮电通讯业、商业、饮食业、物资供销业和仓储业。

第二层次：为生产和生活服务的部门，包括金融、保险业、地质普查业、房地产业、公用事业，居民服务业，咨询服务业和综合技术服务业，农、林、牧、渔、服务业和水利业，公路、内河（湖）航道养护业等。

第三层次：为提高科学文化水平和居民素质服务的部门，包括教育、文化、广播电视，科学研究、卫生、体育和社会福利事业。

第四层次：为社会公共需要服务的部门，包括国家机关、社会团体，以及军队和警察等。

可比价格 指在不同时期的价值指标对比时，扣除了价格变动的因素，以确切反映物量的变化。按可比价格计算有两种方法：一种是直接用产量乘某一年的不变价格计算；另一种是用价格指数换算。

不变价格 指用同类产品的年平均价格作为固定价格，来计算各年产品价值。按不变价格计算的产品价值消除了价格变动因素，不同时期对比可以反映生产的发展速度。新中国成立后，随着工农业产品价格水平的变化，国家统计局先后五次制定了全国统一的工业产品不变价格和农业产品不变价格，从1949年到1952年使用1952年工（农）业产品不变价格，从1957年到1971年使用1957年不变价格，从1971年到1981年使用1970年不变价格，从1981年到1990年使用1980年不变价格，从1990年开始使用1990年不变价格。

支出法国内生产总值 指一个国家（或地区）所有常住单位在一定时期内用于最终消费、资本形成总额，以及货物和服务的净出口总额，它反映本期生产的国内生产总值的使用构成。

最终消费 指常住单位在一定时期内对于货物和服务的全部最终消费支出，也就是常住单位为满足物质、文化和精神生活的需要，从本国经济领土和国外购买的货物和服务的支出。它不包括非常住单位在本国经济领土内的消费支出。最终消费分为居民消费和政府消费。

（一）居民消费：指常住住户在一定时期内对于货物和服务的全部最终消费支出。居民关于货物的最终消费支出在货物的所有权发生变化时记录，关于服务的最终支出在服务提供的时候记录。居民消费支出按市场价格计算，即按居民支付的购买者价格计算，货物的购买价格是购买者取得交货所支付的价格，它包括购买者支付的运输和商业费用。居民支出除了直接以货币形式购买的货物和服务的消费支出外，还包括以其他方式获得的货物和服务的消费支出，即所谓的虚拟消费支出。居民虚拟消费支出包括如下几种类型：单位以实物报酬及实物转移的形式提供给劳动者的货物和服务；住户生产并由本住户消费了的货物和服务，其中自有住房服务；金融机构提供的金融媒介服务；保险公司提供的保险服务。

（二）政府消费　指政府部门为全社会提供的公共服务的消费支出和免费或以较低的价格向居民住户提供的货物和服务的净支出，前者等于政府服务的产出价值减去政府单位所获得的经营收入的价值，政府服务的产出价值等于它的经常性业务支出加上固定资产折旧；后者等于政府部门向居民住户提供的货物和服务的市场价值减去向居民住户收取的价值。

资本形成总额　指常住单位在一定时期内获得减去处置的固定资产和存货的净值，包括固定资产形成总额和存货增加两项。

（一）固定资产形成总额　指常住单位在一定时期内购置、转入和自产自用的固定资产价值，扣除固定资产的销售和转出后的价值 。可分为有形固定资产形成总额和无形固定资产形成总额。有形固定资产形成总额包括一定时期内完成的建筑工程、安装工程和设备工器具购置（减处置）价值，以及土地改良、新增役、种、奶、毛、娱乐用牲畜和新增经济林木价值。无形固定资产形成总额包括矿藏的勘探、计算机软件、娱乐和文学艺术品原件等获得价值。

（二）存货增加　指常住单位在一定时期内存货实物量变动的市场价值即期末价值减期初价值的差额。存货增加可以是正值，也可以是负值，正值表示存货上升，负值表示存货下降。它包括生产单位购进的原材料、燃料和储备物资等存货，以及生产单位生产的产成品、在制品和半成品等存货等。

货物和服务净出口　指货物和服务出口减货物和服务进口的差额。出口包括常住单位向非常住单位出售或无偿转让的各种货物和服务的价值；进口包括常住单位从非常住单位购买或无偿得到的各种货物和服务的价值。由于服务活动的提供与使用同时发生，因此服务的进出口业务并不发生出入境现象，一般把常住单位从国外得到的服务作为进口，非常住单位从本国得到的服务作为出口。货物的出口和进口都按离岸价格计算。

净出口　指出口与进口的差额。出口包括常住单位向非常住单位出售或无偿转让的各种货物和服务的总值；进口包括常住单位从非常住单位购买或无偿得到的各种货物和服务的总值。由于服务活动提供与使用同时发生，因此服务的进出口业务并不发生出入境现象，应把常住单位从国外得到的服务作为进口，反之，非常住单位从我国得到的服务作为出口。

劳动者报酬　劳动者报酬是指劳动者因从事生产活动所获得的全部报酬。它包括劳动者获得的各种形式工资、奖金和津贴，既包括货币形式的，也包括实物形式的，它还包括劳动者所享受的公费医疗和医药卫生费、上下班交通补贴和单位支付的社会保险费等。单位支付的社会保险费，就是单位直接支付给负责社会保险的政府单位（一般指劳动部门）的社会保险金或为本单位职工离退休、发生死亡、伤残、医疗保险等而支付的保险费。对于个体经济来说，其所有者所获得的劳动报酬和经营利润不易区分，这两部分统一作为劳动者报酬处理。

生产税净额　指生产税减生产补贴后的差额。生产税指政府对生产单位生产、销售和从事经营活动以及因从事生产活动使用某些生产要素，如固定资产、土地、劳动力所征收的各种税、附加费和规费。具体包括销售税金及附加、增值税、管理费中开支的各种税、应交纳的养路费、排污费和水电费附加、烟酒专卖上缴政府的专项收入等。生产补贴与生产税相反，是政府对生产单位的单方面收入转移，因此视为负生产税处理，包括政策亏损补贴、粮食系统价格补贴、外贸企业出口退税收入等。

固定资产折旧 指一定时期内为弥补固定资产损耗按照核定的固定资产折旧率提取的固定资产折旧，或按国民经济核算统一规定的折旧率虚拟计算的固定资产折旧。它反映了固定资产在当期生产中的转移价值。各种类型企业和企业化管理的事业单位的固定资产折旧指实际计提并计入成本费用中的折旧费；不计提折旧的单位，如政府机关、非企业化管理的事业单位和居民住房的固定资产折旧则是按照统一规定的折旧率和固定资产原值计算的虚拟折旧。原则上，固定资产折旧应按固定资产的重置价值来计算，但是我国目前尚不具备对全社会固定资产进行重估价的基础，所以暂时只能采用上述方法来计算。

营业盈余 指常住单位创造的增加值扣除劳动者报酬、生产税净额和固定资产折旧后的余额。它相当于企业的经营利润加上生产补贴，但要扣除从利润中开支的工资和福利以及从税后利润中提取的公益金等。

登记注册类型 以在工商行政管理机关登记注册的各类企业为划分对象。行政机关、事业单位和社会团体及其他经济组织参照执行。

国有企业 指企业全部资产归国家所有，并按国家有关法律规定登记注册的非公司制的经济组织。不包括有限责任公司中的国有独资公司。

集体企业 指企业资产归集体所有，并按国家有关法律规定登记注册的经济组织。

股份合作企业 以合作制为基础，由企业职工共同出资入股，吸收一定比例的社会资产投资组建，实行自主经营、自负盈亏，共同劳动，民主管理，按劳分配与按股分红相结合的一种集体经济组织。

联营企业 指两个及两个以上相同或不同所有制的企业法人或事业单位法人，按自愿、平等、互利的原则，共同投资组成的经济组织。包括国有联营、集体联营、国有与集体联营和其他联营企业。

有限责任公司 指根据国家有关法律规定登记注册，由两个以上，五十个以下的股东共同出资，公司以其全部资产对其债务承担责任的经济组织。包括国有独资公司以及其他有限责任公司。

股份有限公司 指根据国家有关法律规定登记注册，其全部注册资本由等额股份构成并通过发行股票筹集资本的经济组织。

私营企业 指由自然人投资设立或由自然人控股，以雇佣劳动为基础的盈利性经济组织。包括按照有关法律、条例规定登记注册的私营独资企业、私营合伙企业、私营有限责任公司和私营股份有限公司。

其他企业 指上述单位之外的其他内资经济组织。

港、澳、台商投资企业 指港澳台地区投资者依照中华人民共和国有关涉外经济的法律、法规，以合资、合作、独资、股份有限公司的形式在内地设立的企业。凡其中港澳台股本占公司注册资本比例小于25%的，属于内资企业中的股份有限公司。

外商投资企业 指外国企业或外国人依照中华人民共和国有关涉外经济的法律、法规，以合资、合作、独资、股份有限公司的形式在中国内地投资设立的企业。凡其中外资股本占公司注册资本比例小于25%的，属于内资企业中的股份有限公司。

Explanatory Notes On Main Statistical Indicators

Gross Domestic Product refers to gross domestic product calculated at market prices, which is the final products of all resident units in a country （or region）during a certain period of time. Gross domestic product is expressed in three different forms, i. e. value added, income, and products respectively. The form of value added refers to the total value of all products and services produced by all resident units during a certain period of time minus total value of input of non-fixed assets materials and services, or the summation of the value added by each of the resident units; the form of income refers to the total income created by each resident unit and distributed Primarily to all resident and non-resident units; the form of products refers to the total of final goods and services minus imports of goods and services. In the practice of national accounting, gross domestic product is calculated with three approaches, i. e. product approach, income approach, and expenditure approach respectively to reflect gross domestic product and its composition from different aspects.

Three Industries An industry structure classified according to the historical evolution of economic activity. Primary industry refers to extraction of natural resources ; secondary industry involves processing of primary products; and tertiary industry provides various kinds of services for production and consumption. The classification is universal although it varies to some extent form country to country. Each industry in China comprises:

Primary industry: Agriculture（including farming, forestry, animal husbandry, and fishery）.

Secondary industry: Industry（including mining and quarrying, manufacturing , water supply, electricity generation and supply, steam, hot water, gas）and Construction .

Tertiary industry: all other industries not included in primary or secondary industry.

Due to the fact that tertiary industry involves in a large variety of industries in China, it is divided into two groups: circulation groups, and service groups and further into four levels:

The first level: Circulation department, including transportation, posts and telecommunications, commerce, catering, material distribution, and storage.

The second level: Service department providing production and consumption services, including banking, insurance, geological survey, real estates, public utilities, service for residents, consulting service, and comprehensive technical services, and service for agriculture, forestry, animal husbandry, fishery, water conservancy, and maintenance of roads and inland water ways, etc.

The third level: Service department for upgrading scientific, educational and cultural level of the people, including education , culture, broadcasting , television, scientific research, public health, sports, and social welfare, etc.

The fourth level: Department providing public goods, including government organs, social organizations, armies, and policemen.

Comparable Prices are applied when comparing indicators of value over time to reflect accurately the changes in real term. Two methods are used for calculating comparable price indicators: 1. Multiplying the output of products by their constant prices of a certain year; 2. Conversion of the data in current prices by relevant price index.

Constant Prices refers to the average price of a given product in a certain year, which is used for comparison of output value over time. As the output value at constant prices removes the factor of price changes, it reflects the trend of production development over time. Since 1949, with the changes in general price level, the State Statistical Bureau has issued nationally unified constant prices five times: the 1952 constant prices for 1949-1957; the 1957 constant prices for 1958-1970; the 1970 constant prices for 1971-1981; the 1980 constant prices for 1981-1990; and the 1990 constant prices have been used since 1991.

GDP Calculated with Expenditure Approach refers to total expenditure on final consumption, total capital formation and net export of goods and services by resident units of a country in a certain period of time. It reflects the composition of GDP by its uses.

Final Consumption refers to the total expenditure of resident units on final consumption of goods and services in a certain period, namely the expenditure of the resident units on goods and services from domestic economic territory and abroad to meet the needs of material, cultural and spiritual life. It excludes the consumption expenditure of non-resident units in the economic territory of the country. The final consumption is classified into private consumption and government consumption.

（1）Private consumption refers to the total expenditure of households on the final consumption of goods and services in a certain period of time. The expenditure of households on final consumption of goods is recorded when the change of the ownership of goods happens. The expenditure of residents on the final consumption of services is recorded when the services is provided. The expenditure of private consumption is calculated at market prices, namely the purchasers' prices which the households pay; the purchasers' prices of goods are the prices the households pay when they obtain the goods, including the transport and commercial expenses paid by the households. In addition to the expenditure on consumption of goods and services with cash, there are other expenditures on goods and services obtained in other ways, i. e. the so-called fictitious expenditure on consumption, is also included in the expenditure of private consumption. The fictitious expenditure of private consumption includes the following cases: （a）the goods and services provided to private by the units as remuneration or benefit; （b）consumption of self-produced goods and services, in which the services refer only to the services provided by the residential buildings owned by the households; （c）the financial intermediary services provided by the financial institutions; （d）the insurance services provided by the insurance companies.

（2）Government consumption refers to the expenditure on the consumption of the public services provided by the government to the whole society and the net expenditure on the goods and services provided by the government to the households free charge or at lower prices. The former equals to the actual output value of the government services minus the value of operating income obtained by the government department. （The output value of the government services equals to its current operating expenditure plus the depreciation of its fixed assets）. The latter equals to the market value of the goods and services provided by the government to the households minus the value received by the government from the households.

Total Capital Formation refers to the net amount of that the fixed assets and inventory acquired minus those disposed, including the net incremental fixed assets and the net incremental inventory.

（1）Net incremental fixed assets refers to the value of fixed assets purchased, transferred in and self-produced by the resident units deducting the value of fixed assets sold and transferred out in a certain period. It can be classified into net incremental tangible assets and net incremental intangible assets. The net incremental tangible assets include the value of the construction projects, installation projects completed and the equipment, apparatus and instruments purchased as well as the value of land improved, the incremental value of draught animals, breeding stock, milk, wool and recreational animals and the economic forest in a certain period. The net incremental intangible assets includes the prospecting of minerals, the acquisition of computer softwares, the originals of recreational, literary and art works.

（2）Net incremental inventory refers to the market value of the change in inventory in a certain period, i.e, the difference of inventory value between the beginning and the end of the period . The net incremental inventory can be positive or negative. A positive value indicates the net increase in inventory while a negative value indicates the net decrease in inventory. The inventory includes the raw materials, fuels and reserve materials purchased by the production units as well as the inventory of finished products, semi-finished products, work-in-progress, etc.

Net Export of Goods and Services refers to the difference between the exports and the imports of goods and services. The exports include the value of various goods and services sold or voluntary transferred by the resident units to the non-resident units. The imports include the value of various goods and services purchased or gratuitously acquired by the resident units from the non-resident units. Because the provision and the use of services happen simultaneously, the import and export of services are not necessarily to cross the border of a country. The services received by the resident units from abroad are usually regarded as imports while the services received by non-resident units are usually regarded as exports . The exports and imports of goods are calculated at FOB.

Laborers' Remuneration refers to all the incomes earned by the laborers from their productive activities, which include wages, bonuses and allowances the laborers received in various forms, including incomes in money and in kind . It also includes the free medical services and the medicine subsidies provided to the laborers as well as traffic subsidies and social insurance fee paid by the laborers' working units for them. The social insurance fee paid by the laborers' working units refers to the social insurance fee paid directly by the working units to the government department （usually the department of labor ）or the insurance fee paid by the enterprises and institutions for the retirement, death, and medical injury treatment of the staff and workers. For the individual economy, since the laborers' remuneration is not easily distinguished from the operating profit , both are treated as laborers' remuneration.

Net Taxes on Production refers to the difference between the taxes and the subsidies on production. The taxes on production refers to the various taxes, extra charges and fees levied on the production units on their production, sale and business activities as well as on some factors in production, such as fixed assets, land and labor force. In detail,, they include sales tax and extra charges, value added tax, various taxes paid from overhead, road toll, sewage charges, extra charges on water and electric power consumed, special revenue turned over to the government by the monopolized trade of tobacco and liquor, etc. In contrast to the taxes on production , the subsidies on production is an unilateral revenue transfer from the government to the production units and is therefore treated as the negative taxes on production. They include subsidies on the loss due to implementation of government policies, price subsidies to the grain institutions, foreign trade corporations' export rebates, etc.

Depreciation of Fixed Assets refers to the depreciation of fixed assets drawn in accordance with the stipulated depreciation rate for the purpose of compensating the wear loss of the fixed assets, or the depreciation of fixed assets calculated in a fictitious way in accordance with the stipulated unified depreciation rate in the national economic accounting system. It reflects the transferred value of the fixed assets in the production of the current period. The depreciation of fixed assets in various enterprises and institutions managed as enterprises refers to the depreciation expenses actually drawn and recorded as cost. In the units which do not draw the depreciation expenses, such as government organs, institutions not managed as enterprises as well as the houses of residents, the depreciation of fixed assets is the fictitious depreciation, which is calculated in accordance with the stipulated unified depreciation rate. In principle, the depreciation of fixed assets should be calculated on the basis of the re-purchased value of the fixed assets. However, it is not feasible to re-evaluate all the fixed assets in China. Therefore, the above-mentioned methods are temporarily adopted at present.

Operating Surplus refers to the net value of that the value added created by the resident units deducting the laborers' remuneration, net taxes on production and the depreciation of fixed assets. It is equivalent to the business profit of the enterprises plus subsidies on production , but the wages and welfare expenses paid from the profits and the public welfare fund drawn from the post-tax profits should be deducted.

Registered Type refers to type that all kinds of enterprises registered in administrative organ of industry and commerce. And registered type of government organs, party organs, institutions, social bodies and other economic organizations will be in light of the above.

State-owned Enterprises refers to non-company economic organizations with enterprises' assets owned by the state and registered according to related laws of the state, exclude state-owned sole-funds company of limited-liability company.

Collective-owned Enterprises refers to economic organizations with enterprises' assets owned by collectives and registered according to related laws of the state.

Share Holding Cooperative Enterprises refers to collective-owned economic organizations founded on bases of cooperative system and funded by shares of staff and workers and social assets in a certain proportion. They carry out rules of voluntary, equality, personal responsibility for profit and loss, working together, democratic management, combine distribution according to work with sharing profits according to shares.

Joint Enterprises refers to economic organizations funded by two or above institutional units with same or different ownership on the basis of voluntary, equality and mutual benefit , include state-owned joint, collective-owned joint, state-collective joint and other joint enterprises.

Limited-liability Company refers to economic organizations funded by two-fifty shareholders and registered according to related laws of the state, include state-owned sole-funds company and other limited-liability companies.

Share Holding Company refers to economic organizations registered according to related laws of the state and their total capital composed with same quota shares and collected by issuing shares.

Private Owned Enterprises refers to profit-making economic organizations founded on bases of wage labor and funded or share held by personnel, include sole-funded enterprises, cooperative enterprises, limited-liability company and share holding company registered according to related laws of the state.

Other Enterprises refers to other domestic investment economic organizations excluding the above.

Hongkong,Macao and Taiwan Funded Enterprises refers to enterprises established by entrepreneurs from Hongkong, Macao and Taiwan within the territory of mainland China according to related economic laws and regulations of the People's Republic of China in forms of joint ventures, cooperative sole-funded and share holding company. And those proportion of shares capital of Hongkong, Macao and Taiwan in registered capital less than 25% will be part of share holding company of domestic invested enterprises.

Foreign Funded Enterprises refers to enterprises established by foreign entrepreneurs within the territory of mainland China according to related economic laws and regulations of the People's Republic of China in forms of joint ventures, cooperative sole-funded and share holding company. And those proportion of foreign shares capital in registered capital less than 25% will be part of share holding company of domestic invested enterprises.

人　口
POPULATION

人口自然增长率(1978-1999年)
Natural Growth Rate of Population

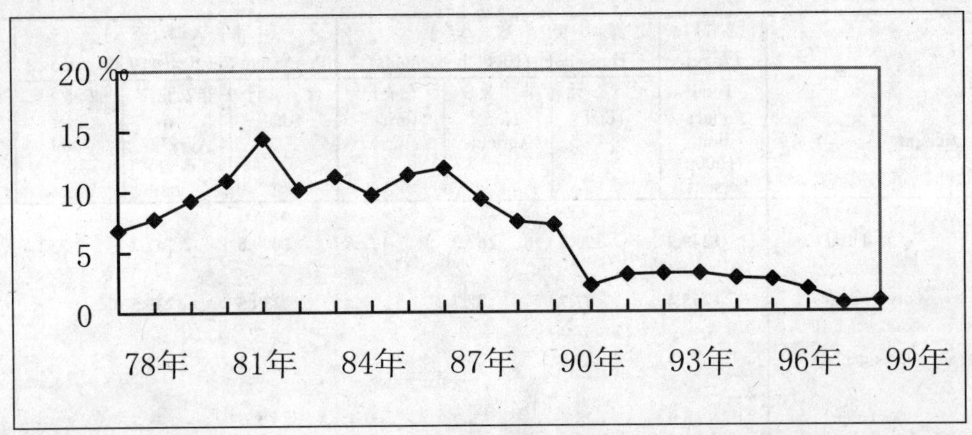

	1999	1998	1999年为1998年% 1999 as % of 1998
常住人口（万人） Permanent Residents(10000 persons)	1099.8	1091.5	100.8
人口密度（人/平方公里） Population Density(person/sq.km)	654.0	647.0	101.1
暂住人口（万人） Temporary Residents(10000 persons)	150.1	131.9	113.8

总人口　Total Population

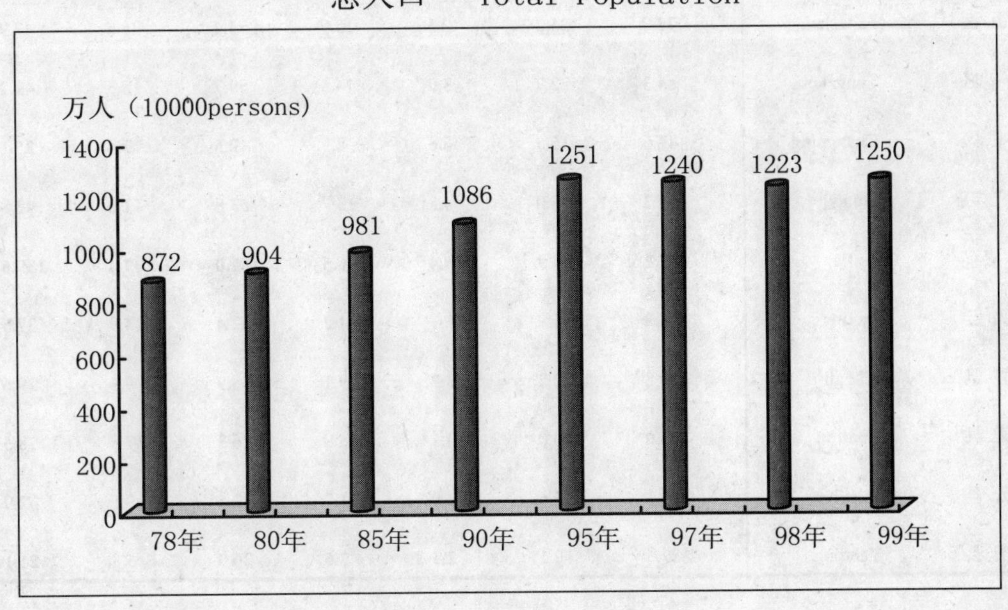

2-1 户 数 及 人 口 数(户籍统计)
NUMBER OF HOUSEHOLDS AND POPULATION(REGISTERED STATISTICS)

地 区 Region		总人口(万人) Total Population (10000 persons)	户 数 (万户) Households(10000 households)			常住人口 (万人) Permanent Residents(10000 persons)			暂住人口 (万人) Temporary Residents (10000 persons)
			合 计 Total	非农业户 Non-Agricultural	农业户 Agricultural	合 计 Total	非农业户 Non-Agricultural	农业户 Agricultural	
全 市	**Total**	**1249.9**	**390.3**	**267.5**	**122.8**	**1099.8**	**747.2**	**352.6**	**150.1**
城 区	**City Proper**	**265.4**	**87.7**	**87.7**	**...**	**239.5**	**239.5**	**...**	**25.9**
东城区	Dongcheng	71.0	23.5	23.5		62.9	62.9		8.1
西城区	Xicheng	85.9	28.2	28.2	...	78.7	78.7	...	7.2
崇文区	Chongwen	46.3	15.8	15.8	...	41.7	41.7	...	4.6
宣武区	Xuanwu	62.2	20.2	20.2	...	56.2	56.2	...	6.0
近郊区	**Near Suburbs**	**514.6**	**147.4**	**127.3**	**20.1**	**419.4**	**371.7**	**47.7**	**95.2**
朝阳区	Chaoyang	181.5	55.1	46.9	8.2	148.8	130.1	18.7	32.7
丰台区	Fengtai	106.3	30.5	24.5	6.0	80.9	66.2	14.7	25.4
石景山区	Shijingshan	40.4	11.2	10.5	0.7	32.7	31.1	1.6	7.7
海淀区	Haidian	186.4	50.6	45.4	5.2	157.0	144.3	12.7	29.4
远郊区	**Outer Suburbs**	**272.7**	**90.3**	**34.1**	**56.2**	**253.9**	**88.6**	**165.3**	**18.8**
门头沟区	Mentougou	25.6	8.9	5.7	3.2	23.5	15.2	8.3	2.1
房山区	Fangshan	78.0	25.2	9.3	15.9	74.4	26.5	47.9	3.6
通州区	Tongzhou	64.3	22.7	8.2	14.5	59.7	18.5	41.2	4.6
昌平区	Changping	47.6	15.5	6.6	8.9	42.5	17.4	25.1	5.1
顺义区	Shunyi	57.2	18.0	4.3	13.7	53.8	11.0	42.8	3.4
各 县	**Counties**	**197.2**	**64.9**	**18.4**	**46.5**	**187.0**	**47.4**	**139.6**	**10.2**
大兴县	Daxing	58.8	16.9	5.7	11.2	52.4	14.9	37.5	6.4
平谷县	Pinggu	39.8	12.3	3.2	9.1	38.9	9.3	29.6	0.9
怀柔县	Huairou	28.0	10.0	3.1	6.9	26.3	7.8	18.5	1.7
密云县	Miyun	43.1	15.6	3.9	11.7	42.5	9.6	32.9	0.6
延庆县	Yanqing	27.5	10.1	2.5	7.6	26.9	5.8	21.1	0.6

2-2 人 口 密 度(户籍统计)
POPULATION DENSITY(REGISTERED STATISTICS)

地 区 Region		常住人口 (万人) Permanent (10000 persons)	土地面积 (平方公里) Land Area (sq.km)	人口密度 (人/平方公里) Population Density (person/sq.km)
全 市	**Total**	**1099.8**	**16807.8**	**654**
城 区	**City Proper**	**239.5**	**87.1**	**27478**
市中心最稠密街道	The Densest Streets			
天坛街道	Tiantan Street	6.9	1.3	52908
椿树街道	Chunshu Street	4.9	1.0	49494
前门街道	Qianmen Street	4.8	1.1	43814
崇文门街道	Chongwenmen Street	4.7	1.1	42503
大栅栏街道	Dashanlan Street	5.4	1.3	41878
东城区	Dongcheng	62.9	24.7	25452
西城区	Xicheng	78.7	30.0	26242
崇文区	Chongwen	41.7	15.9	26242
宣武区	Xuanwu	56.2	16.5	33949
近郊区	**Near Suburbs**	**419.4**	**1282.8**	**3261**
朝阳区	Chaoyang	148.8	470.8	3160
丰台区	Fengtai	80.9	304.2	2661
石景山区	Shijingshan	32.7	81.8	3867
海淀区	Haidian	157.0	426.0	3686
远郊区	**Outer Suburbs**	**253.9**	**6478.0**	**392**
门头沟区	Mentougou	23.5	1331.3	177
房山区	Fangshan	74.4	1866.7	399
通州区	Tongzhou	59.7	870.0	686
昌平区	Changping	42.5	1430.0	297
顺义区	Shunyi	53.8	980.0	548
各 县	**Counties**	**187.0**	**8959.9**	**209**
大兴县	Daxing	52.4	1012.0	518
平谷县	Pinggu	38.9	1075.0	362
怀柔县	Huairou	26.3	2557.3	103
密云县	Miyun	42.5	2335.6	182
延庆县	Yanqing	26.9	1980.0	136

2-3 常住人口性别构成及性别比(户籍统计)

SEX COMPOSITION AND SEX RATIO OF PERMANENT RESIDENTS (REGISTERED STATISTICS)

地区	Region	常住人口(万人) Permanent Residents(10000 persons) 合计 Total	男 Male	女 Female	性别比(女=100) Sex Ratio (female=100)
全市	**Total**	**1099.8**	**556.7**	**543.1**	**102.5**
城区	**City Proper**	**239.5**	**120.8**	**118.7**	**101.8**
东城区	Dongcheng	62.9	31.4	31.5	99.4
西城区	Xicheng	78.7	39.4	39.3	100.4
崇文区	Chongwen	41.7	20.8	20.9	100.0
宣武区	Xuanwu	56.2	29.2	27.0	108.2
近郊区	**Near Suburbs**	**419.4**	**215.0**	**204.4**	**105.2**
朝阳区	Chaoyang	148.8	75.8	73.0	103.8
丰台区	Fengtai	80.9	41.2	39.7	103.9
石景山区	Shijingshan	32.7	17.3	15.4	111.5
海淀区	Haidian	157.0	80.7	76.3	105.8
远郊区	**Outer Suburbs**	**253.9**	**126.8**	**127.1**	**99.8**
门头沟区	Mentougou	23.5	12.3	11.2	109.2
房山区	Fangshan	74.4	37.4	37.0	101.3
通州区	Tongzhou	59.7	29.4	30.3	97.1
昌平区	Changping	42.5	21.2	21.3	99.4
顺义区	Shunyi	53.8	26.5	27.3	97.0
各县	**Counties**	**187.0**	**94.1**	**92.9**	**101.2**
大兴县	Daxing	52.4	26.2	26.2	100.1
平谷县	Pinggu	38.9	19.4	19.5	99.9
怀柔县	Huairou	26.3	13.4	12.9	102.9
密云县	Miyun	42.5	21.4	21.1	101.4
延庆县	Yanqing	26.9	13.7	13.2	103.1

2-4 户籍人口自然变动人数(户籍统计)
NATURAL CHANGE OF OF REGISTERED POPULATION(REGISTERED STATISTICS)

单位:人 (person)

地区	Region	出生人数 Number of Birth		死亡人数 Number of Death		自然增加人数 Number of Natural Growth	
		1999	1998	1999	1998	1999	1998
全市	**Total**	**62757**	**66892**	**61598**	**75247**	**1159**	**-8355**
城区	**City Proper**	**9213**	**8838**	**14594**	**19148**	**-5381**	**-10310**
东城区	Dongcheng	2588	2472	3786	4538	-1198	-2066
西城区	Xicheng	3270	3085	4378	5687	-1108	-2602
崇文区	Chongwen	1391	1326	2628	3897	-1237	-2571
宣武区	Xuanwu	1964	1955	3802	5026	-1838	-3071
近郊区	**Near Suburbs**	**21161**	**20042**	**20417**	**25184**	**744**	**-5142**
朝阳区	Chaoyang	7525	6911	7886	8652	-361	-1741
丰台区	Fengtai	4213	4146	4654	6678	-441	-2532
石景山区	Shijingshan	1512	1522	1578	2239	-66	-717
海淀区	Haidian	7911	7463	6299	7615	1612	-152
远郊区	**Outer Suburbs**	**17349**	**20296**	**17048**	**19475**	**301**	**821**
门头沟区	Mentougou	1483	1590	1670	2431	-187	-841
房山区	Fangshan	5730	6345	4846	5064	884	1281
通州区	Tongzhou	3650	5195	4166	3937	-516	1258
昌平区	Changping	3098	2969	2241	3670	857	-701
顺义区	Shunyi	3388	4197	4125	4373	-737	-176
各县	**Counties**	**15034**	**17716**	**9539**	**11440**	**5495**	**6276**
大兴县	Daxing	4497	5510	2842	3387	1655	2123
平谷县	Pinggu	2906	3462	1870	2162	1036	1300
怀柔县	Huairou	1926	2739	1618	2239	308	500
密云县	Miyun	3271	3561	1286	1739	1985	1822
延庆县	Yanqing	2434	2444	1923	1913	511	531

2-5 人 口 变 动(户籍统计)
POPULATION CHANGE(REGISTERED STATISTICS)

单位:人 (person)

项目 Item		1999	1998
自然变动	**Natural Change**		
自然增加	Natural Increase	1159	-8355
非农业人口	Non-agricultural Population	-1418	-12121
农业人口	Agricultural Population	2577	3766
出　生	Birth	62757	66892
非农业人口	Non-agricultural Population	35251	33542
农业人口	Agricultural Population	27506	33350
死　亡	Death	61598	75247
非农业人口	Non-agricultural Population	36669	45663
农业人口	Agricultural Population	24929	29584
机械变动	**Non-natural Change**		
机械增加	Non-natural Increase	68845	57609
非农业人口	Non-agricultural Population	63083	49817
农业人口	Agricultural Population	5762	7792
市外迁入	Move in from outside	113369	102840
非农业人口	Non-agricultural Population	103450	90648
农业人口	Agricultural Population	9919	12192
迁往市外	Move out	44524	45231
非农业人口	Non-agricultural Population	40367	40831
农业人口	Agricultural Population	4157	4400

2-6 1999 年人口实际自然变动情况
ACTUAL NATURAL CHANGE OF POPULATION IN 1999

项目 Item			常住人口 Permanent Residents
自然变动人数(人)	**Natural Change of Population**	**(person)**	
出生人数	Number of Birth		81341
死亡人数	Number of Death		70078
自然增加人数	Natural Increase of Population		11263
自然变动率 (‰)	**Natural Growth Rate**	**(‰)**	
出生率	Birth Rate		6.5
死亡率	Death Rate		5.6
自然增长率	Natural Growth Rate		0.9

注：本表"常住人口"栏中数字为 1999 年人口变动情况抽样调查推算数字。

Note：Data in column"Permanent Residents" are estimated through sample survey on population change in 1999.

2-7 家 庭 户 规 模(人口变动情况抽样调查资料)
FAMILY SIZE(DATA FROM SAMPLE SURVEY ON POPULATION CHANGE)

地 区	Region	家庭总户数(户) Total Number of Households (household)	家庭户规模所占比重(%) Percentage of Various Sized Family(%)				
			一人户 One Person	二人户 Two Persons	三人户 Three Persons	四人户 Four Persons	五人及以上户 Five Persons and above
全 市	**Total**	**12797**	**9.9**	**21.8**	**40.0**	**16.8**	**11.6**
城 区	**City Proper**	**2711**	**11.7**	**22.9**	**42.3**	**14.6**	**8.5**
东城区	Dongcheng	529	17.2	23.6	36.3	14.0	8.9
西城区	Xicheng	1151	10.5	23.2	40.4	17.6	8.3
崇文区	Chongwen	332	13.5	21.1	46.7	11.2	7.5
宣武区	Xuanwu	699	8.7	22.9	47.7	12.0	8.7
近郊区	**Near Suburbs**	**5094**	**11.0**	**23.1**	**42.2**	**13.3**	**10.4**
朝阳区	Chaoyang	1856	9.7	19.1	44.4	13.5	13.3
丰台区	Fengtai	1037	14.5	27.8	38.8	12.0	6.9
石景山区	Shijingshan	357	5.3	17.7	48.4	18.2	10.4
海淀区	Haidian	1844	11.4	25.7	40.7	12.9	9.3
远郊区	**Outer Suburbs**	**2854**	**7.0**	**20.6**	**40.1**	**19.1**	**13.2**
门头沟区	Mentougou	364	9.6	24.2	42.6	16.5	7.1
房山区	Fangshan	622	6.1	20.4	41.8	17.7	14.0
通州区	Tongzhou	826	9.0	20.1	42.0	19.7	9.2
昌平区	Changping	528	6.3	25.2	42.2	14.8	11.5
顺义区	Shunyi	514	3.9	14.2	31.1	25.9	24.9
各 县	**Counties**	**2138**	**8.5**	**18.9**	**31.5**	**25.0**	**16.1**
大兴县	Daxing	529	9.6	17.8	24.6	25.3	22.7
平谷县	Pinggu	542	5.9	16.6	22.7	32.7	22.1
怀柔县	Huairou	332	6.9	20.8	47.0	16.6	8.7
密云县	Miyun	369	11.6	21.7	38.5	16.8	11.4
延庆县	Yanqing	366	9.0	19.7	33.3	29.0	9.0

2-8 年 龄 组 人 口 数(人口变动情况抽样调查资料)
POPULATION GROUP BY AGE(DATA FROM SAMPLE SURVEY ON POPULATION CHANGE)

项　　目	Item	1999 年被抽样人口 Sample Data of 1999		1998 年人口抽样调查各年龄组占总人口比　重 (%) Percentage of Each Groupe in Total of 1998 (%)
		抽样人口数(人) Number of Persons Sampled (person)	年龄组人口占总人口比重(%) Percentage (%)	
总　　计	**Total**	**39838**	**100**	**100**
# 法定婚龄 男(22 岁以上)	Legal Marry Age: Male (age 22 and above)	14588	36.6	37.6
女(20 岁以上)	Female (age 20 and above)	15657	39.3	37.9
育龄妇女(15-49 岁)	Women of Child-bearing Age (age15-49)	11771	29.5	29.8
不满周岁婴儿(0 岁)	Below Age 1	259	0.7	0.5
学龄前儿童(1-6 岁)	Age 1-6	1705	4.3	4.4
小学学龄组(7-12 岁)	Age 7-12	2878	7.2	8.2
初中学龄组(13-15 岁)	Age 13-15	1680	4.2	4.1
劳动年龄组	Of Labor Age	26326	66.1	66.6
男(16-59 岁)	Male(age 16-59)	13661	34.3	35.2
女(16-54 岁)	Female(age 16-54)	12665	31.8	31.4
超过劳动年龄组	Over Labor Age	6990	17.5	16.2
男(60 岁以上)	Male(age 60 and above)	2850	7.2	6.9
女(55 岁以上)	Female(age 55 and above)	4140	10.4	9.3

2-9 人口年龄构成及性别比(人口变动情况抽样调查资料)
AGE COMPOSITION AND SEX RATIO OF POPULATION(DATA FROM SAMPLE SURVEY ON POPULATION CHANGE)

年　龄　组 Age Group	抽样人口数(人) Number of Persons Sampled (person)			占抽样人口数的比重(%) Percentage(%)			性 别 比 (女=100) Sex Ratio (female=100)
	合 计 Total	男 Male	女 Female	合 计 Total	男 Male	女 Female	
总　计　Total	**39838**	**19936**	**19902**	**100**	**50.04**	**49.96**	**100.2**
0-4	1338	710	628	3.36	1.78	1.58	113.1
5-9	1812	983	829	4.55	2.47	2.08	118.6
10-14	2811	1442	1369	7.06	3.62	3.44	105.3
15-19	2902	1483	1419	7.28	3.72	3.56	104.5
20-24	2831	1442	1389	7.11	3.62	3.49	103.8
25-29	3394	1709	1685	8.52	4.29	4.23	101.4
30-34	3382	1756	1626	8.49	4.41	4.08	108.0
35-39	4078	2103	1975	10.24	5.28	4.96	106.5
40-44	3824	1903	1921	9.60	4.78	4.82	99.1
45-49	3462	1706	1756	8.69	4.28	4.41	97.2
50-54	2154	989	1165	5.41	2.48	2.92	84.9
55-59	1886	860	1026	4.73	2.16	2.58	83.8
60-64	1876	895	981	4.71	2.25	2.46	91.2
65-69	1815	905	910	4.56	2.27	2.28	99.5
70-74	1139	534	605	2.86	1.34	1.52	88.3
75-79	688	326	362	1.73	0.82	0.91	90.1
80-84	281	127	154	0.71	0.32	0.39	82.5
85-89	125	44	81	0.31	0.11	0.20	54.3
90 岁及以上　90 and above	40	19	21	0.10	0.05	0.05	90.5

2-10 劳动年龄人口抚养系数(人口变动抽样调查资料)
DEPENDENCY RATIO(DATA FROM SAMPLE SURVEY ON POPULATION CHANGE)

单位：% (%)

地区 Region		总抚养系数 Total Dependency Ratio	抚养老年人口系数 Of the Old	抚养少儿人口系数 Of Children
全市	**Total**	**33.7**	**13.7**	**20.0**
城区	City Proper	37.8	20.6	17.2
近郊区	Near Suburbs	29.6	12.6	17.1
远郊区	Outer Suburbs	30.3	10.1	20.1
各县	Counties	44.1	14.0	30.1

2-11 育龄妇女分年龄、孩次的生育状况(人口变动情况抽样调查资料)
FERTILITY OF WOMEN ON CHILDBEARING AGE BY AGE OF MOTHER AND BIRTH ORDER (DATA FROM SAMPLE SURVEY ON POPULATION CHANGE)

单位：人，‰ (person, ‰)

年龄 Age	平均育龄妇女人数 Average Number of Women on Childbearing Age	出生人数 Number of Birth	生育率 Fertility Rate	第一孩 1st Birth		第二孩 2nd Birth		第三孩及以上 3rd Birth and over	
				出生数 Birth	生育率 Fertility	出生数 Birth	生育率 Fertility	出生数 Birth	生育率 Fertility
总计 Total	**11597**	**259**	**22.3**	**249**	**21.5**	**10**	**0.9**		
15-19	1506								
20-24	1293	39	30.2	38	29.4	1	0.8		
25-29	1748	154	88.1	152	87.0	2	1.1		
30-34	1635	46	28.1	42	25.7	4	2.5		
35-39	1962	16	8.2	13	6.6	3	1.5		
40-44	1916	4	2.1	4	2.1				
45-49	1539								

2-12 计 划 生 育 状 况
FAMILY PLANNING

项目		Item		1999	1998	1999年比1998年增、减 1999 compared with 1998
全 市		**Total**				
计划生育状况		Family Planning Status				
计划内生育	(人)	Within Plan	(person)	70727	74193	-3466
计划生育率	(%)	Family Planning Rate	(%)	98.4	98.7	-0.3
已婚育龄妇女人数	(人)	Number of Married Women of Childbearing Age	(person)	2298077	2260899	37178
实际采取节育措施人数	(人)	Number of Women Controlled Birth	(person)	2042666	2018799	23867
独生子女领证率	(%)	Acceptance Rate of Only-child Certificate	(%)	64.7	64.8	-0.1
城 市		**City**				
计划生育率	(%)	Planned Birth Rate	(%)	99.7	99.8	-0.1
已婚育龄妇女人数	(人)	Number of Married Women of Childbearing Age	(person)	1420880	1370604	50276
实际采取节育措施人数	(人)	Number of Women Controlled Birth	(person)	1232457	1200284	32173
独生子女领证率	(%)	Acceptance Rate of Only-child Certificate	(%)	78.3	79.4	-1.1
农 村		**Rural**				
计划生育率	(%)	Planned Birth Rate	(%)	96.8	97.4	-0.6
已婚育龄妇女人数	(人)	Number of Married Women of Childbearing Age	(person)	877197	890295	-13098
实际采取节育措施人数	(人)	Number of Women Controlled Birth	(person)	810209	818515	-8306
独生子女领证率	(%)	Acceptance Rate of Only-child Certificate	(%)	42.8	42.3	0.4

资料来源：北京市计划生育委员会。

Data source：Beijing Birth Control Committee.

2-13 外来人口户口所在地
RESIDENCE CARD LOCATION OF NONNATIVES

户口所在地 Residence Card Location		人口数（人） Population (person)			占总人口的百分比（%） Percentage in Total Population(%)		
		合 计 Total	男 Male	女 Female	合 计 Total	男 Male	女 Female
总　　计	**Total**	**112452**	**69775**	**42677**	**100**	**62.05**	**37.95**
天　津	Tianjin	634	417	217	0.56	0.37	0.19
河　北	Hebei	25918	16358	9560	23.05	14.55	8.50
山　西	Shanxi	3182	1997	1185	2.83	1.78	1.05
内蒙古	Neimenggu	2783	1533	1250	2.47	1.36	1.11
辽　宁	Liaoning	2407	1290	1117	2.14	1.15	0.99
吉　林	Jilin	2064	1067	997	1.84	0.95	0.89
黑龙江	Heilongjiang	3799	1896	1903	3.38	1.69	1.69
上　海	Shanghai	157	114	43	0.14	0.10	0.04
江　苏	Jiangsu	5712	4322	1390	5.08	3.84	1.24
浙　江	Zhejiang	3827	2236	1591	3.40	1.99	1.41
安　徽	Anhui	10468	6263	4205	9.31	5.57	3.74
福　建	Fujian	1936	1285	651	1.72	1.14	0.58
江　西	Jiangxi	1495	947	548	1.33	0.84	0.49
山　东	Shandong	8966	5598	3368	7.97	4.98	3.00
河　南	Henan	18035	11420	6615	16.04	10.16	5.88
湖　北	Hubei	4280	2693	1587	3.81	2.39	1.41
湖　南	Hunan	1483	841	642	1.32	0.75	0.57
广　东	Guangdong	959	693	266	0.85	0.62	0.24
广　西	Guangxi	241	135	106	0.21	0.12	0.09
海　南	Hainan	87	56	31	0.08	0.05	0.03
重　庆	Chongqing	961	571	390	0.85	0.51	0.35
四　川	Sichuan	8239	5140	3099	7.33	4.57	2.76
贵　州	Guizhou	430	239	191	0.38	0.21	0.17
云　南	Yunnan	205	95	110	0.18	0.08	0.10
西　藏	Xizang	11	3	8	0.01	0.00	0.01
陕　西	Shanxi	2358	1492	866	2.10	1.33	0.77
甘　肃	Gansu	1197	702	495	1.06	0.62	0.44
青　海	Qinghai	112	71	41	0.10	0.06	0.04
宁　夏	Ningxia	203	133	70	0.18	0.12	0.06
新　疆	Xinjiang	303	168	135	0.27	0.15	0.12

资料来源：1999 年北京市外来人口动态监测资料。（表 2-14 至表 2-20 同）
Source: 1999 Nonnatives Dynamic Control Data of Beijing(2-14 to 2-20 are the same).

2-14 外来人口的户数和人数

NUMBER OF HOUSEHOLDS AND PERSONS OF NONNATIVES

地区 Region		户数(户) Number of Households(household)				人口数(人) Number of Persons(person)			
		合计 Total	有外来人口的本市家庭户 Households having Nonnatives	纯外来人口的家庭户 Households of Nonnatives	有外来人口的集体户 Collective Households having Nonnatives	合计 Total	有外来人口的本市家庭户 Households having Nonnatives	纯外来人口的家庭户 Households of Nonnatives	有外来人口的集体户 Collective Households having Nonnatives
全市	**Total**	**13153**	**1469**	**8387**	**3297**	**112452**	**5855**	**52830**	**53767**
城区	**City Propers**	**1627**	**389**	**768**	**470**	**18988**	**1928**	**6724**	**10336**
东城区	Dongcheng	336	103	124	109	5638	585	1915	3138
西城区	Xicheng	432	138	154	140	6205	764	1823	3618
崇文区	Chongwen	553	62	353	138	3834	259	2030	1545
宣武区	Xuanwu	306	86	137	83	3311	320	956	2035
近郊区	**Near Suburbs**	**7898**	**609**	**5244**	**2045**	**65684**	**2408**	**34144**	**29132**
朝阳区	Chaoyang	2022	58	1361	603	17710	470	8273	8967
丰台区	Fengtai	1787	110	1143	534	15598	338	8647	6613
石景山区	Shijingshan	1064	104	742	218	7919	361	4053	3505
海淀区	Haidian	3025	337	1998	690	24457	1239	13171	10047
远郊区	**Outer Suburbs**	**2214**	**329**	**1481**	**404**	**16601**	**1164**	**6859**	**8578**
门头沟区	Mentougou	236	77	127	32	1824	450	946	428
房山区	Fangshan	246	88	102	56	3244	346	713	2185
通州区	Tongzhou	413	13	351	49	2285	48	1198	1039
顺义区	Shunyi	522	68	341	113	3505	183	1531	1791
昌平区	Changping	797	83	560	154	5743	137	2471	3135
各县	**Counties**	**1414**	**142**	**894**	**378**	**11179**	**355**	**5103**	**5721**
大兴县	Daxing	697	49	442	206	5756	84	2896	2776
平谷县	Pinggu	39	7	14	18	1093	28	133	932
怀柔县	Huairou	341	47	225	69	2407	156	1025	1226
密云县	Miyuan	185	19	116	50	1084	55	573	456
延庆县	Yanqing	152	20	97	35	839	32	476	331

2-15 外来人口的受教育状况 EDUCATIONAL LEVEL OF NONNATIVES

受教育程度 Educational Level		人口数（人） Population (person)			占6岁及以上人口的百分比（%） Percentage in Population at six-year-old and above(%)		
		合计 Total	男 Male	女 Female	合计 Total	男 Male	女 Female
6岁及以上人口合计	**Population of and above 6-year-old**	**107132**	**66810**	**40322**	**100**	**62.36**	**37.64**
不识字或识字很少	Illiterate or Semi-illiterate	2911	831	2080	2.72	0.78	1.94
小学	Primary School	16805	9005	7800	15.69	8.41	7.28
初中	Junior Middle School	64603	42623	21980	60.30	39.79	20.52
高中	Senior Middle School	15136	9639	5497	14.13	9.00	5.13
大学专科	Undergraduate	5961	3590	2371	5.56	3.35	2.21
大学本科及以上	College Level and above	1716	1122	594	1.60	1.05	0.55

2-16 外来人口的来京时间分布 PERIOD IN BEIJING OF NONATIVES

来京时间 Period in Beijing		人口数（人） Population(person)			占总人口的百分比（%） Percentage in Total Population(%)		
		合计 Total	男 Male	女 Female	合计 Total	男 Male	女 Female
总计	**Total**	**112452**	**69775**	**42677**	**100**	**62.05**	**37.95**
一个月以下	below One Month	8982	5868	3114	7.99	5.22	2.77
一个月至三个月以下	One Month-Three Months	14101	9178	4923	12.54	8.16	4.38
三个月至半年以下	Three Months-Half a Year	11325	7048	4277	10.07	6.27	3.80
半年至一年以下	Half a Year-One Year	23517	15670	7847	20.91	13.93	6.98
一年至三年以下	One Year-Three Years	35510	20519	14991	31.58	18.25	13.33
三年至五年以下	Three-Five Years	8397	4953	3444	7.47	4.40	3.06
五年及以上	Five Years and above	10620	6539	4081	9.44	5.81	3.63

2-17 外来人口年龄构成
AGE COMPOSITION OF NONNATIVES

年龄组 Age Group	人口数（人） Population(person)			占总人口的百分比（%） Percentage in Total Population(%)		
	合计 Total	男 Male	女 Female	合计 Total	男 Male	女 Female
总计 Total	**112452**	**69775**	**42677**	**100**	**62.05**	**37.95**
0 – 4	4561	2543	2018	4.06	2.26	1.79
5 – 9	2707	1526	1181	2.41	1.36	1.05
10 – 14	1361	802	559	1.21	0.71	0.50
15 – 19	14741	8033	6708	13.11	7.14	5.97
20 – 24	26443	15500	10943	23.51	13.78	9.73
25 – 29	23503	14756	8747	20.9	13.12	7.78
30 – 34	16725	11142	5583	14.87	9.91	4.96
35 – 39	9184	6475	2709	8.17	5.76	2.41
40 – 44	4886	3614	1272	4.34	3.21	1.13
45 – 49	3550	2503	1047	3.16	2.23	0.93
50 – 54	1982	1346	636	1.76	1.20	0.57
55 – 59	1079	640	439	0.96	0.57	0.39
60 – 64	848	471	377	0.75	0.42	0.34
65岁及以上 65 years old and above	882	424	458	0.78	0.38	0.41

2-18 外来人口的职业分布
VOCATION DISTRIBUTION OF NANNATIVES

职业 Vocation		就业人口数（人） Employment Population(person)			占就业人口的百分比（%） Percentage in Employment Population(%)		
		合计 Total	男 Male	女 Female	合计 Total	男 Male	女 Female
总计	**Total**	**88358**	**59629**	**28729**	**100**	**67.49**	**32.51**
各类专业技术人员	Professional Technical Personnel	1359	950	409	1.54	1.08	0.46
国家机关，党群组织企事业单位负责人	Chairman of Government Organs,Party,Mass Organizations,Enterprises and Institutions	151	126	25	0.17	0.14	0.03
办事人员和有关人员	Office Workers and Related Personnel	3364	2677	687	3.81	3.03	0.78
商业工作人员	Commerce	17828	11121	6707	20.18	12.59	7.59
废旧物资回收人员	Waste Recovery	1127	805	322	1.28	0.91	0.36
餐饮服务工作人员	Catering	12666	6651	6015	14.33	7.53	6.81
修理服务工作人员	Repairs Services	3032	2647	385	3.43	3.00	0.44
其他服务性工作人员	Other Services	15378	8207	7171	17.40	9.29	8.12
农林牧渔劳动者	Farming,Forestry,animal Husbandry and Fishery	3294	1934	1360	3.73	2.19	1.54
工业劳动者	Industry	12343	7536	4807	13.97	8.53	5.44
建筑业劳动者	Construction	15445	14876	569	17.48	16.84	0.64
运输业劳动者	TRsportation	1944	1823	121	2.20	2.06	0.14
不便分类的劳动者	No Classfied Labor	427	276	151	0.48	0.31	0.17

2-19 外来人口的在京状况
STATISTICS FOR NONNATIVES IN BEIJING

单位：人 (person)

地　区 Region		合 计 Total	务工经商 in Work or Business	从事其它工作 Engaged in Other Work	暂无工作 Having no Job Currently	随亲家属 Famliy Member	探亲访友 Visiting Relatives and Friends
全　市	**Total**	**112452**	**88045**	**313**	**1974**	**13677**	**1469**
城　区	City Propers	18988	14783	89	157	2036	422
近郊区	Near Suburbs	65684	51518	108	1549	7691	894
远郊区	Outer Suburbs	16601	12615	51	142	2181	118
各　县	Counties	11179	9129	65	126	1769	35

地　区 Region		因公出差 on Business Trip	学习培训 for Study and Training	旅游购物 Tourism and Purchasing	治病疗养 under Treatment and Recuperation	旅途中转 Transfer During Trip	其　他 Others
全　市	**Total**	**910**	**4394**	**262**	**1032**	**128**	**248**
城　区	City Propers	666	219	226	308	66	16
近郊区	Near Suburbs	238	2841	31	585	61	168
远郊区	Outer Suburbs	5	1323	2	105	1	58
各　县	Counties	1	11	3	34		6

2-20 外来人口的住所形式
HOUSING OF NONNATIVES

单位：人 (person)

地　区 Region		合 计 Total	租住房屋 Rent	自建房屋 Self-building	自购房屋 Purchase	单位宿舍 Living Quarters	工作场所 Working Place
全　市	**Total**	**112452**	**61568**	**3634**	**715**	**22510**	**9076**
城　区	City Propers	18988	7403	20	27	2412	3365
近郊区	Near Suburbs	65684	40400	2609	139	10992	4654
远郊区	Outer Suburbs	16601	7772	633	220	5874	391
各　县	Counties	11179	5993	372	329	3232	666

地　区 Region		工　棚 Builder's Temporary Shed	雇主房屋 House of Employer	亲友房屋 House of Relatives	旅馆饭店 Hotels	医院 Ward of Hospitals	其　他 Others
全　市	**Total**	**5167**	**2369**	**3601**	**3205**	**571**	**36**
城　区	City Propers	1156	816	1624	2141	11	13
近郊区	Near Suburbs	3055	746	1654	980	437	18
远郊区	Outer Suburbs	735	596	229	57	94	
各　县	Counties	221	211	94	27	29	5

2-21 老年人的婚姻状况
MARRIAGE STATUS OF OLD PEOPLE

单位：% (%)

婚姻状况 Marriage Status		合 计 Total	男 Male	女 Female
总 计	**Total**	**100**	**48.21**	**51.79**
未 婚	Unmarried	0.64	0.53	0.11
有配偶	Married	74.55	40.59	33.96
丧 偶	Widowed	24.08	6.69	17.39
离 婚	Divorced	0.73	0.40	0.33

资料来源：1999 年北京市老年人抽样调查。（以下各表同）
Source: 1999 sample survey on old people of Beijing(the followings are the same).

2-22 老年人的受教育程度
EDUCATIONAL LEVEL OF OLD PEOPLE

单位：% (%)

受教育程度 Educational Level		合 计 Total	男 Male	女 Female
总 计	**Total**	**100**	**48.21**	**51.79**
文盲、半文盲	Illiterate or Semi-illiterate	30.03	6.74	23.29
小 学	Primary School	30.71	16.68	14.03
初 中	Junior Middle School	14.89	9.12	5.77
高 中	Senior Middle School	9.81	6.12	3.69
大 专	Undergraduate	6.30	3.85	2.40
大学本科	College Level	8.26	5.70	2.56

2-23 老年人的户内活动自理情况
STATISTICS FOR TAKING CARE OF ONESELF DURING INDOOR ACTIVES OF OLD PEOPLE

单位：% (%)

项 目 Item		合 计 Total	男 Male	女 Female
总 计	**Total**	**100**	**48.21**	**51.79**
完全能自理	Partial Taking Care of Oneself	89.09	43.09	46.00
部分能自理	Complete Taking Care of Oneself	8.79	3.95	4.84
完全不能自理	Not Taking Care of Oneself Completely	2.12	1.17	0.95

2-24 老年人最希望解决的问题
MATTERS MOST CONCERNED FOR OLD PEOPLE

单位：% (%)

项目	Item	合计 Total	男 Male	女 Female
总计	**Total**	**100**	**48.21**	**51.79**
生活有人照料	be Taken Care of	18.05	7.69	10.36
经济上有人帮助	Get Financial Help	9.92	4.09	5.83
有宽敞的住房	Having Commodious House	12.68	6.34	6.34
出行方便	Having a good Transport	1.30	0.90	0.40
看病就医方便	Receiving Medical Convenient	9.88	4.80	5.08
增加服务社区	Adding Social Services	8.66	4.42	4.24
找到合适的养老机构	Get Suitable Home for Destitute Old People	3.58	1.92	1.66
合法权益受到保护	Legitimate Rights and Interests be Protected	5.92	3.31	2.61
开发老年生活用品	Developing Daily Necessities for Old People	1.15	0.57	0.58
其他	Others	6.43	3.16	3.27
没有问题	No Problem	22.43	11.01	11.42

2-25 老年人的经济来源
ECONOMIC RESOURCE OF OLD PEOPLE

单位：% (%)

项目	Item	合计 Total	男 Male	女 Female
总计	**Total**	**100**	**48.21**	**51.79**
工作收入	Wages	5.39	4.31	1.08
离退休金	Pensions for VCSR	62.44	34.95	27.49
子女供给	Supply from Children	23.88	7.76	16.12
配偶供给	Supply from Spouse	5.55	0.09	5.46
其他亲属供给	Supply from Other Relatives	0.42	0.15	0.27
社会救济金	Relief Pensions	0.84	0.42	0.42
以前的积蓄	Previous Savings	0.82	0.42	0.40
其他	Others	0.66	0.11	0.55

2-26 老年人是否愿意与子女居住在一起
STATISTICS FOR WHETHER OLD PEOPLE LIKE LIVE WITH CHILDREN TOGETHER

单位：% (%)

项目	Item	合计 Total	男 Male	女 Female
总计	**Total**	**100**	**48.21**	**51.79**
无子女	Having no Children	1.48	0.91	0.57
愿意与子女居住在一起	Like	59.08	27.11	31.97
不愿意与子女居住在一起	Not Like	35.93	18.32	17.61
说不清	No Answer	3.51	1.87	1.64

2-27 老年人愿意与子女居住在一起的原因
STATISTICS FOR REASON OF OLD PEOPLE LIKE LIVE WITH CHILDREN TOGETHER

单位：% (%)

项目	Item	愿意与子女居住在一起的老人 Old People Like Live with Children	男 Male	女 Female
总计	**Total**	**100**	**45.89**	**54.11**
可以互相照应	Taking Care of Each Other	87.66	39.57	48.09
精神充实不寂寞	Not Lonely	10.55	5.50	5.05
其他	Others	1.79	0.82	0.97

2-28 老年人不愿意与子女居住在一起的原因
STATISTICS FOR REASON OF OLD PEOPLE NOT LIKE LIVE WITH CHILDREN TOGETHER

单位：% (%)

项目	Item	不愿意与子女居住在一起的老人 Old People not Like Live with Children	男 Male	女 Female
总计	**Total**	**100**	**50.98**	**49.02**
居住在一起会产生家庭矛盾	Family Contradiction	25.28	12.06	13.22
与子女的生活方式不同	Different Life Style from Children	52.89	27.61	25.28
居住条件会变差	Living Conditions Changed Worse	13.65	7.13	6.52
怕受累	Afraid of	3.01	1.47	1.54
其他	Others	5.17	2.71	2.46

2-29 老年人的养老意愿
WISHES FOR WAYS OF TAKEN CARE OF CHOSEN BY OLD PEOPLE

单位：% (%)

项目	Item	合计 Total	男 Male	女 Female
总计	**Total**	**100**	**48.21**	**51.79**
家庭养老	Family	84.91	40.15	44.76
养老院养老	Home for Destitute Old People	7.64	3.77	3.87
老年公寓养老	Department for Old People	4.84	2.83	2.01
托老所养老	Old People-Care Center	0.80	0.49	0.31
其他方式养老	Others	1.81	0.97	0.84

主 要 统 计 指 标 解 释

人口数 指一定时点、一定地区范围内有生命的个人的总和。年度统计的年末人口数是指每年12月31日24时的人口数。

出生率 指在一定时期内（通常为一年）出生人数与同期平均人数(或期中之数)的比率，一般用千分率表示。计算公式：

$$出生率=\frac{年出生人数}{年平均人数}\times 100‰$$

出生人数是指活产，即脱离母体时（不管怀孕月数），有过呼吸或其他生命现象的活婴儿总和。

年平均人数是年初、年底人口数的平均数，也可用年中人口数代替。

死亡率 指在一定时期内（通常为一年）一定地区的死亡人数与同期平均人数（或期中人数）之比，一般用千分率表示。计算公式：

$$死亡率=\frac{年死亡人数}{年平均人数}\times 100‰$$

人口自然增长率 指在一定时期内（通常为一年）人口自然增加数（出生人数减死亡人数）与该时期内平均人数（或期中人数）之比，一般用千分率表示。计算公式：

$$人口自然增长率=\frac{本年出生人数-本年死亡人数}{年平均人数}\times 1000‰$$

人口自然增长率=人口出生率—人口死亡率

Explanatory Notes On Main Statistical Indicators

Total Population refers to the total number of people alive at a certain point of time within a given area. Year-end total population is that at 24:00 on 31st of December.

Birth Rate refers to the ratio of the number of births to the average population during a certion period of time (usually a year), which is often expressed in ‰. The following formula is used:

$$\text{Birth Rate}=\frac{\text{Number of Birth}}{\text{Average Population}}\times 1000‰$$

Number of Birth refers to live births, i. e. the births when babies had showed any vital phenomena regardless of the length of pregnancy.

Average Population is the average of population at the beginning of a year and that at the end of the year. Sometimes it is substituted for with the mid-year population.

Death Rate refers to the ratio of the number of deaths to the average population （or mid-year population）during a certain period of time (usually one year), which is often expressed in ‰. The following formula is used:

$$\text{Death Rate}=\frac{\text{Number of Deaths}}{\text{Average Population}}\times 1000‰$$

Natural Growth Rate of Population refers to the ratio of the natural increase in population

(number of births minus number of deaths)in a certain period of time (usually a year)to the average population (or mid-year population)of the same period, which is often expressed in ‰. The following formulas are applied:

$$\text{Natural Growth Rate of Population} = \frac{\text{Number of Births - Number of Deaths}}{\text{Average Population}} \times 1000‰$$

Natural Growth Rate of Population = Birth Rate – Death Rate

劳动力和工资
LABOR FORCE AND WAGE

职工平均工资（1978-1999）
Average Wage for Staff and Workers(1978-1999)

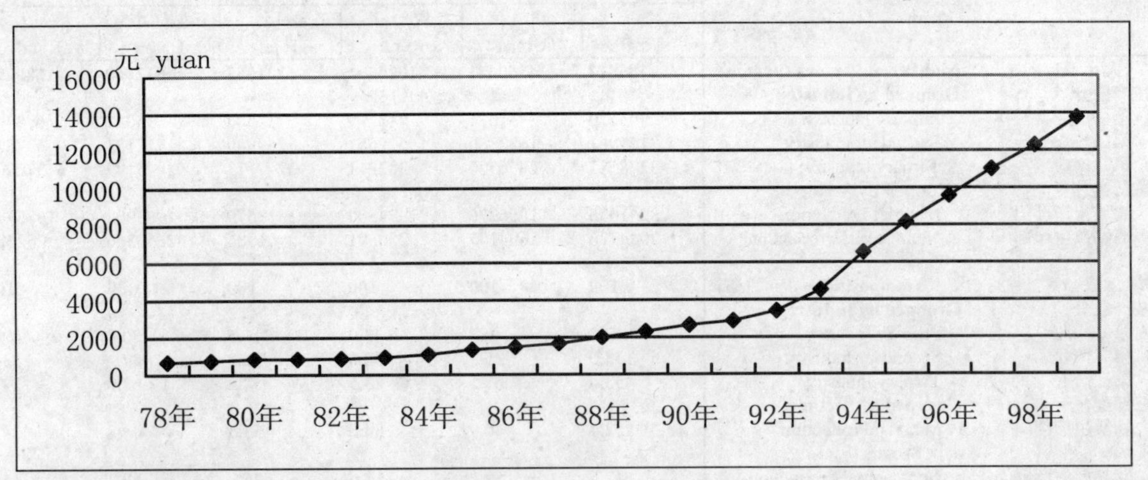

	1999	1998
职工人数（万人） Number of Staff and Workers(10000 persons)	438	450.1
职工工资总额（亿元） Total Wages of Staff and Workers(100 million yuan)	614.5	558.2
职工平均工资（元） Average Wage for Staff and Workres(yuan)	13778	12285

职工平均工资（按经济类型分）

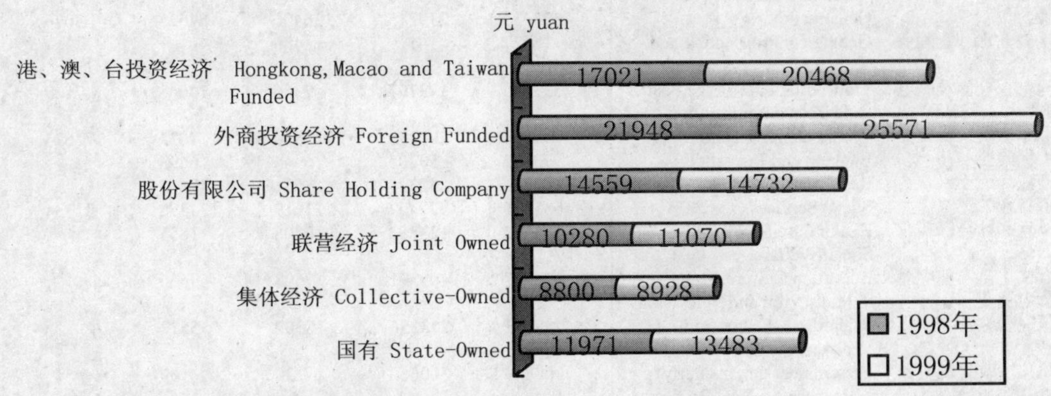

3-1 全市从业人员(产业、部类分)
EMPLOYMENT BY INDUSTRY AND SECTOR

项目	Item	1999 合计 Total	1999 城市 Urban	1999 农村 Rural	1998 合计 Total	1998 城市 Urban	1998 农村 Rural
人数 (人)	**Number of Persons (person)**	**6185812**	**4560421**	**1625391**	**6221565**	**4632269**	**1589296**
按产业分	**Grouped by Industry**						
第一产业	Primary Industry	745270	31671	713599	714503	35037	679466
第二产业	Secondary Industry	2161961	1632380	529581	2259949	1722123	537826
第三产业	Tertiary Industry	3278581	2896370	382211	3247113	2875109	372004
按部类分	**Grouped by Sector**						
物质生产部门	Material Production	3241076	1866276	1374800	3318679	1981903	1336776
非物质生产部门	Nonmaterial Production	2944736	2694145	250591	2902886	2650366	252520
构成 (%)	**Composition (%)**	**100**	**100**	**100**	**100**	**100**	**100**
按产业分	**Grouped by Industry**						
第一产业	Primary Industry	12.0	0.7	43.9	11.5	0.8	42.8
第二产业	Secondary Industry	35.0	35.8	32.6	36.3	37.2	33.8
第三产业	Tertiary Industry	53.0	63.5	23.5	52.2	62.0	23.4
按部类分	**Grouped by Sector**						
物质生产部门	Material Production Sectors	52.4	40.9	84.6	53.3	42.8	84.1
非物质生产部门	Nonmaterial Production Sectors	47.6	59.1	15.4	46.7	57.2	15.9

注：根据国家统计局的规定，1998 年对从业人员进行口径调整。（下同）

Note: According to the rules of State Statistical Bureau, standard counted of employment is adjusted from 1998. (the followings are the same)

3-2 全市从业人员(按登记注册类型分)
EMPLOYMENT BY REGISTERED TYPE

单位：人 (person)

行业	Sector	合计 Total	国有经济 State-Owned	集体经济 Collective-Owned	其他经济 Others	城镇个体私营劳动者 Urban Individuals and Private Owned	农村劳动者 Rural Labors
总计	**Total**	**6185812**	**2876190**	**496790**	**950148**	**237293**	**1625391**
农、林、牧、渔业	Farming,Forestry,Animal Husbandry and Fishery	745270	25219	1692	4241	519	713599
采掘业	Excavation	34775	28283	353	182	24	5933
制造业	Manufacturing	1434574	561356	109988	351230	20101	391899
电力、煤气及水的生产和供应业	Electricity,Gas,Water Production and Supply	42350	39469	641	1834		406
建筑业	Construction	633435	279215	136406	84623	2076	131115
地质勘查业水利管理业	Geological Prospecting and Water Conservancy	16827	16119	480			228
交通运输、仓储及邮电通信业	Transportation,Storage,Post and Telecommunication	333845	173707	7366	14043	7109	131620
批发和零售贸易餐饮业	Wholesale,Retail and Catering	907214	228180	112840	177035	172624	216535
金融、保险业	Banking and Insurance	73842	50205	6944	16693		
房地产业	Real Estate	106306	52377	3551	48463		1915
社会服务业	Social Services	631946	327407	71619	173378	31334	28208
卫生体育和社会福利业	Health Care,Sports and Social Welfare	135522	123382	10008	1855		277
教育、文化艺术和广播电影电视业	Education,Culture,Art, Radio,Film and Television	426417	408391	7608	9566		852
科学研究和综合技术服务业	Scientific Research and Polytechnical Services	288071	213896	18302	55512		361
国家机关、政党机关和社会团体	Government Organs,Party Organs and Social Bodies	300849	300660	120	69		
其他行业	Others	74569	48324	8872	11424	3506	2443

3-3 城镇单位从业人员年末人数
YEAR-END EMPLOYMENT IN URBAN UNITS

单位：人 (person)

项目	Item	从业人员 Total Employees	在岗职工 Staff and Workers at their Posts	聘用留用的离退休人员 Retired and VCSR Engaged and Kept on	聘用的外籍及港澳台方人员 Personnel of Foreign,Hong-kong,Macao and Taiwan	人事档案关系保留在原单位人员 Personnel Organization-al Affiliation Reserved
总计	**Total**	**4323128**	**4029540**	**114848**	**4648**	**174092**
按登记注册类型分	**Grouped by Registered Type**					
内资经济	Domestic Investment Economy	3981842	3731661	103805	654	145722
国有经济	State-owned	2876190	2767126	51146	442	57476
集体经济	Collective-owned	496790	444223	24883	23	27661
联营经济	Joint-owned	47608	42849	1419	10	3330
股份有限公司	Share Holding Company	248746	214186	11717	95	22748
有限责任公司	Limited-Liability Company	239714	201873	9798	34	28009
股份合作企业	Share Holding Cooperative	70721	59971	4478	46	6226
其他经济	Others	2073	1433	364	4	272
外商投资经济	Foreign Funded	205999	184316	4862	2753	14068
港、澳、台商投资经济	Hongkong,Macao and Taiwan Funded	135287	113563	6181	1241	14302
按隶属关系分	**Grouped by Administrative Relationship**					
# 中央	Central	1256823	1179115	31830	1024	44854
地方	Local	2620058	2473089	61203	1904	83862
按行业分	**Grouped by Sector**					
农、林、牧、渔业	Farming,Forestry,Animal Husbandry and Fishery	31152	30721	173	20	238
# 农业	Farming	4234	4117	31	5	81
采掘业	Excavation	28818	28751	64	1	2
制造业	Manufacturing	1022574	975104	17704	1253	28513
电力、煤气及水的生产和供应业	Electricity,Gas,Water Production and Supply	41944	41149	355		440
建筑业	Construction	500244	470119	13096	90	16939
地质勘查业水利管理业	Geological Prospecting and Water Conservancy	16599	16461	131		7
交通运输、仓储及邮电通信业	Transportation,Storage,Posts and Telecommunications Services	195116	186792	1330	59	6935
# 交通运输业	Transportation	132121	128600	455	50	3016
邮电通信业	Posts and Telecommunications Services	49279	44719	767	3	3790
批发和零售贸易餐饮业	Wholesale, Retail and Catering	518055	468200	16024	338	33493
# 批发业	Wholesale	188123	166903	7194	86	13940
零售业	Retail	257939	235072	7623	70	15174
餐饮业	Catering	66775	61233	1130	177	4235
金融、保险业	Banking and Insurance	73842	72174	815	182	671
房地产业	Real Estate	104391	89821	6740	342	7488
社会服务业	Social Services	572404	502383	22730	1303	45988
# 公共服务业	Public Services	172397	157244	3066	7	12080
居民服务业	Residents Services	46482	42454	1636	31	2361
旅馆业	Hotels	120855	106845	5023	399	8588
卫生体育和社会福利业	Health Care,Sports and Social Welfare	135245	131871	2415	74	885
# 卫生	Health Care	122633	119793	2163	30	647
体育	Sports	7991	7687	161	5	138
教育、文化艺术和广播电影电视业	Education,Culture,Art, Radio,Film and Television	425565	406804	10908	511	7342
教育	Education	332682	320688	7975	393	3626
文化艺术业	Culture and Art	73231	68748	2285	65	2133
广播电影电视业	Radio,Film and Television	19652	17368	648	53	1583
科学研究和综合技术服务业	Scientific Research and Polytechnical Services	287710	252338	17441	237	17694
科学研究业	Scientific Research	136675	131756	4442	6	471
综合技术服务业	Polytechnical Services	151035	120582	12999	231	17223
国家机关、政党机关和社会团体	Government Organs,Party Organs and Social Bodies	300849	295817	2983	1	2048
其他行业	Others	68620	61035	1939	237	5409

注：城镇单位从业人员年末人数与报国家统计局劳动工资年报口径一致，不含城镇个体、私营企业、农村从业人员。

Note:Data in this table is in accordance to the annual bulletin of labors and wages reported to state statistical bureau, not include urban individuals,private and rural employees.

3-4 职 工 人 数

NUMBER OF STAFF AND WORKERS

单位：人 (person)

项 目	Item	1999	1998	1999 年为 1998 年% 1999 as % of 1998
总 计	**Total**	**4379854**	**4500635**	**97.3**
按登记注册类型分	**Grouped by Registered Type**			
内资经济	Domestic Investment Economy	4071320	4186395	97.3
国有经济	State-owned	3029773	3216576	94.2
集体经济	Collective-owned	496005	508146	97.6
联营经济	Joint-owned	51806	57379	90.3
股份有限公司	Share Holding Company	220136	169231	130.1
有限责任公司	Limited-Liability Company	210413	172839	121.7
股份合作企业	Share Holding Cooperative	61712	60860	101.4
其他经济	Others	1475	1364	108.1
外商投资经济	Foreign Funded	191480	198379	96.5
港、澳、台商投资经济	Hongkong,Macao and Taiwan Funded	117054	115861	101.0
按隶属关系分	**Grouped by Administrative Relationship**			
# 中央	Central	1223360	1322242	92.5
地方	Local	2775852	2911922	95.3
按行业分	**Grouped by Sector**			
农、林、牧、渔业	Farming,Forestry,Animal Husbandry and Fishery	33677	37302	90.3
# 农业	Farming	4755	5122	92.8
采掘业	Excavation	30895	36030	85.7
制造业	Manufacturing	1154474	1215468	95.0
电力、煤气及水的生产和供应业	Electricity,Gas,Water Production and Supply	41752	41697	100.1
建筑业	Construction	514461	561489	91.6
地质勘查业水利管理业	Geological Prospecting and Water Conservancy	16958	16743	101.3
交通运输、仓储及邮电通信业	Transportation,Storage,Posts and Telecommunications Services	196556	200397	98.1
# 交通运输业	Transportation	135400	144469	93.7
邮电通信业	Posts and Telecommunications Services	44786	43456	103.1
批发和零售贸易餐饮业	Wholesale, Retail and Catering	524923	531295	98.8
# 批发业	Wholesale	188593	205731	91.7
零售业	Retail	266686	260898	102.2
餐饮业	Catering	64230	61266	104.8
金融、保险业	Banking and Insurance	72295	71650	100.9
房地产业	Real Estate	92148	85530	107.7
社会服务业	Social Services	528425	504239	104.8
# 公共服务业	Public Services	163069	160148	101.8
居民服务业	Residents Services	44599	25573	174.4
旅馆业	Hotels	111180	113701	97.8
卫生体育和社会福利业	Health Care,Sports and Social Welfare	133016	135152	98.4
# 卫生	Health Care	120619	122825	98.2
体育	Sports	7977	8021	99.5
教育、文化艺术和广播电影电视业	Education,Culture,Art, Radio,Film and Television	411604	418926	98.3
教育	Education	324070	332246	97.5
文化艺术业	Culture and Art	70073	69238	101.2
广播电影电视业	Radio,Film and Television	17461	17442	100.1
科学研究和综合技术服务业	Scientific Research and Polytechnical Services	258752	272683	94.9
科学研究业	Scientific Research	135602	138213	98.1
综合技术服务业	Polytechnical Services	123150	134470	91.6
国家机关、政党机关和社会团体	Government Organs,Party Organs and Social Bodies	304918	313810	97.2
其他行业	Others	65000	58224	111.6

3-5 职 工 人 数 增 减 情 况
CHANGES IN NUMBER OF STAFF AND WORKERS

单位：人 (person)

项目	Item	1999 合计 Total	1999 #中央单位 Central	1999 #地方单位 Local	1998 合计 Total	1998 #中央单位 Central	1998 #地方单位 Local
净增人数	**Net Increase**	**-191459**	**-46261**	**-144793**	**-157026**	**-44497**	**-140890**
增加人数	**Number of Persons Increased**	**587689**	**120473**	**352019**	**641668**	**185011**	**357327**
从农村招收	Recruited from Rural Area	211348	39438	124414	249624	72837	144126
从城镇招收	Recruited from Urban Area	64597	9685	28024	62693	13248	27110
录用的退伍军人	Employment of Demobilized Soldiers	5018	1373	3205	4827	1335	3040
录用大中专技校毕业生	Employment of Graduate	61239	19700	35411	69095	22398	40953
不在岗职工重新上岗	Personnel Rework after off their posts	25742	2374	22674	10009	2073	6902
调入人数	Job Changes	115535	24549	73933	123659	36387	74759
# 市外调入	from Outside Beijing	8658	2436	3138	14306	8380	3745
其他	Others	104210	23354	64358	121761	36733	60437
减少人数	**Number of Persons Decreased**	**779148**	**166734**	**496812**	**798694**	**229508**	**498217**
离休退休退职	Retire and Quit	78223	24261	52510	98920	38362	58540
开除除名辞退	Discharge	71545	24357	32100	126105	65588	45843
终止解除合同	Contract Expiration	277914	40088	186080	232259	33634	168397
在岗职工无岗	Personnel at their posts but have no work	54867	6865	47052	88643	14699	73332
调出人数	Job Changes	145232	38164	86692	137912	39042	85368
# 调往市外	to Outside Beijing	12815	2692	2328	11411	2238	2950
其他	Others	151367	32999	92378	114855	38183	66737

3-6 城镇新增就业人数
INCREMENTAL IN URBAN AREA

单位：人 (person)

项目	Item	1999	1998	1999年为1998年% 1999 as % of 1998
总计	**Total**	**116841**	**105270**	**111.0**
国有经济	State-Owned Economy	52766	59604	88.5
集体经济	Collective-Owned Economy	6340	8455	75.0
个体经济	Individual Economy	18285		
其他经济	Other	39450	37211	106.0

3-7 国民经济各行业职工人数(按隶属关系、登记注册类型分)

单位：人

行业	Sector	全市 Total	# 在岗职工中女性 Female at their Posts	比重(%) Proportion(%)
总计	**Total**	**4379854**	**1541733**	**35.2**
农、林、牧、渔业	**Farming,Forestry,Animal Husbandry and Fishery**	**33677**	**11200**	**33.3**
# 农、林、牧、渔服务业	FFAF Services	9680	3122	32.3
采掘业	**Excavation**	**30895**	**6185**	**20.0**
制造业	**Manufacturing**	**1154474**	**380954**	**33.0**
食品加工业	Food Processing	23066	7097	30.8
食品制造业	Food Making	35190	16205	46.1
饮料制造业	Beverage Manufacturing	26506	9040	34.1
烟草制造业	Tobacco Processing	1018	428	42.0
纺织业	Textile Industry	54047	27995	51.8
服装及其他纤维制品制造业	Garments and Other Fiber Products	40739	23772	58.4
皮革、毛皮、羽绒及其制品业	Leather,Furs,Down and Related Products	8863	3012	34.0
木材加工及竹、藤、棕、革制品业	Timber Processing,Bamboo,Cane, Palm Fiber and Straw Products	3949	1151	29.1
家具制造业	Furniture Manufacturing	8102	2091	25.8
造纸及纸制品业	Papermaking and Paper Products	11403	4218	37.0
印刷业、记录媒介的复制	Printing and Record Medium Reproduced	43347	19272	44.5
文教体育用品制造业	Stationery,Education and Sports Goods	10296	4224	41.0
石油加工及炼焦业	Petroleum Processing and Coking Products	53513	14288	26.7
化学原料及化学制品制造业	Raw Chemical Materials and Chemical Products	48572	15705	32.3
医药制造业	Medical and Pharmaceutical Products	26896	12563	46.7
化学纤维制造业	Chemical Fibers	6970	2211	31.7
橡胶制品业	Rubber Products	11882	4210	35.4
塑料制品业	Plastic Products	20420	6407	31.4
非金属矿物制品业	Nonmetal Mineral Products	70461	19432	27.6
黑色金属冶炼及压延加工业	Smelting and Pressing Ferrous Metals	162517	35712	22.0
有色金属冶炼及压延加工业	Smelting and Pressing of Nonferrous Metals	4286	1023	23.9
金属制品业	Metal Products	37034	8955	24.2
普通机械制造业	Ordinary Machinery	71398	20153	28.2
专业设备制造业	Special Purpose Equipment	68349	18131	26.5
交通运输设备制造业	Transportation Equipment	116120	33926	29.2
武器弹药制造业	Weapons and Ammunition	12318	3522	28.6
电气机械及器材制造业	Electric Equipment and Machine	52535	18501	35.2
电子及通信设备制造业	Electronic and Telecommunication	77991	29889	38.3
仪器仪表及文化办公用机械制造业	Instruments,Meters,Cultural and Official Machinery	27974	10343	37.0
其他制造业	Other Manufacturing	18712	7478	40.0
电力、煤气及水的生产和供应业	**Electricity,Gas and Water Production and Supply**	**41752**	**14309**	**34.3**
电力、蒸气、热水的生产和供应业	Electricity,Steam and Hot Water Production and Supply	26922	8600	31.9
煤气生产和供应业	Gas Production and Supply	8495	3374	39.7
自来水的生产和供应业	Water Production and Supply	6335	2335	36.9
建筑业	**Construction**	**514461**	**68537**	**13.3**
土木工程建筑业	Civil Engineering	415097	54291	13.1
线路、管道和设备安装业	Pipeline and Equipment Installation	66140	10171	15.4
建筑物的装修装饰业	Building Completion	33224	4075	12.3
地质勘查业、水利管理业	**Geological Prospecting and Water Conservancy**	**16958**	**3400**	**20.0**
地质勘查业	Geological Prospecting	5913	1343	22.7
水利管理业	Water Conservancy	11045	2057	18.6

NUMBER OF STAFF AND WORKERS BY SECTOR (BY ADMINISTRATIVE RELATIONSHIP AND REGISTERED TYPE)

(person)

# 中 央 Central	# 地 方 Local	国有经济 State-Owned	# 中 央 Central	# 地 方 Local	集体经济 Collective-Owned	其他经济 Others
1223360	**2775852**	**3029773**	**1082948**	**1903428**	**496005**	**854076**
1556	**31867**	**27988**	**820**	**27168**	**1640**	**4049**
672	8921	7928	672	7256	1122	630
151	**30744**	**30356**	**151**	**30205**	**353**	**186**
184489	**926830**	**672604**	**157427**	**514484**	**133892**	**347978**
534	21264	14306	44	14262	688	8072
1841	29773	15949	189	15760	1936	17305
178	25403	13166	71	13095	1621	11719
15	1003	75		75	15	928
109	53441	30103	22	30081	5449	18495
1666	33536	8673	1558	7115	10499	21567
56	8133	4392		4392	2804	1667
717	2782	2484	639	1845	612	853
742	4513	1790	326	1464	1563	4749
276	10560	6523	227	6296	1252	3628
24054	18114	31656	22386	9270	5804	5887
237	9094	5300	33	5267	2134	2862
44965	8404	45310	44766	544	398	7805
1191	45373	21459	449	21001	2937	24176
2399	23304	16985	2267	14711	1472	8439
	6891	4257		4257	893	1820
255	11560	8310	110	8200	2657	915
850	18052	7922	446	7056	3745	8753
2433	65936	26300	1802	24498	10707	33454
95	162380	155727		155727	967	5823
23	4188	2408	23	2385	698	1180
2740	30877	14486	1125	13290	10961	11587
10317	59576	44381	4819	39533	11214	15803
13273	52365	36458	12060	24358	5537	26354
48735	64836	67495	43459	23966	14236	34389
12318		12318	12318			
1037	49736	28835	124	28711	12614	11086
7873	67190	24956	3919	20990	6360	46675
4666	22450	16333	4210	12123	4399	7242
894	16096	4247	35	4212	9720	4745
12711	**29041**	**39431**	**10831**	**28600**	**550**	**1771**
12711	14211	24657	10831	13826	550	1715
	8495	8439		8439		56
	6335	6335		6335		
124655	**300761**	**308806**	**100572**	**181593**	**125405**	**80250**
93389	259203	269600	82942	160407	92081	53416
28223	29878	34225	16402	17643	21991	9924
3043	11680	4981	1228	3543	11333	16910
5681	**11277**	**16483**	**5681**	**10802**	**475**	
5207	706	5913	5207	706		
474	10571	10570	474	10096	475	

3-7 续表 1 continued

单位：人

行业	Sector	全市 Total	# 在岗职工中女性 Female at their Posts	比重(%) Proportion(%)
交通运输、仓储及邮电通信业	**Transportation,Storage,Posts and Telecommunications**	**196556**	**58660**	**29.8**
铁路运输业	Railway	63083	12669	20.1
公路运输业	Highway	29249	7221	24.7
管道运输业	Pipeline	88	21	23.9
航空运输业	Airway	10969	4078	37.2
交通运输辅助业	Transportation Subsidiary	32011	9423	29.4
仓储业	Storage	16370	4555	27.8
邮电通信业	Posts and Telecommunications	44786	20693	46.2
批发和零售贸易餐饮业	**Wholesale,Retail and Catering**	**524923**	**235794**	**44.9**
批发业	Wholesale	188593	66438	35.2
零售业	Retail	266686	136549	51.2
商业经纪与代理业	Commercial Management and Agency	5414	1700	31.4
餐饮业	Catering	64230	31107	48.4
金融、保险业	**Banking and Insurance**	**72295**	**37415**	**51.8**
金融业	Banking	67106	35067	52.3
保险业	Insurance	5189	2348	45.2
房地产业	**Real Estate**	**92148**	**33005**	**35.8**
房地产开发与经营业	Real Estate Development	25080	8166	32.6
房地产管理业	Real Estate Management	65958	24388	37.0
房地产代理与经纪业	Real Estate Brokerage and Agency	1110	451	40.6
社会服务业	**Social Services**	**528425**	**189832**	**35.9**
公共设施服务业	Public Utilities	163069	61426	37.7
# 市内公共交通业	Public Transportation in City	103187	38526	37.3
# 市内公共汽电车业	Public Bus and Trolleybus	56983	28815	50.6
园林绿化业	Gardens Afforest	18359	7791	42.4
环境卫生业	Environmental Sanitation	24304	9416	38.7
市政工程管理业	Municipal Engineering Management	8049	2233	27.7
居民服务业	Residential Services	44599	17223	38.6
旅馆业	Hotels	111180	52928	47.6
租赁服务业	Leasing	5610	1885	33.6
旅游业	Tourism	9146	3810	41.7
娱乐服务业	Recreation	8567	4049	47.3
信息、咨询服务业	Information and Consultancy Services	56812	21842	38.4
# 广告业	Advertisement	9746	3941	40.4
咨询服务业	Consultancy Services	8606	3839	44.6
计算机应用服务业	Computer Application Services	36750	12596	34.3
其他社会服务业	Other Social Services	92692	14073	15.2
# 市场管理服务业	Market Management Services	19156	4273	22.3
卫生、体育和社会福利业	**Health Care,Sports and Social Welfare**	**133016**	**80130**	**60.2**
卫生	Health Care	120619	74630	61.9
体育	Sports	7977	3084	38.7
社会福利	Social Welfare	4420	2416	54.7
教育、文化艺术及广播电影电视业	**Education,Culture and Arts, Radio, Film and Television**	**411604**	**216100**	**52.5**
教育	Education	324070	179840	55.5
高等教育	Higher Education	110633	49435	44.7
普通高等教育	Ordinary Higher Education	98136	43603	44.4
成人高等教育	Adult Higher Education	12497	5832	46.7

3-7 续表 2 continued

(person)

		国有经济			集体经济	其他经济
# 中 央 Central	# 地 方 Local	State-Owned	# 中 央 Central	# 地 方 Local	Collective-Owned	Others
130295	**62973**	**175904**	**124508**	**51252**	**7606**	**13046**
62866	217	63083	62866	217		
2089	26785	22991	1748	21243	5242	1016
88						88
10969		9810	9810			1159
11472	19575	25324	9328	15862	1001	5686
1513	14629	14869	1397	13472	977	524
41298	1767	39827	39359	458	386	4573
67203	**351842**	**255526**	**51142**	**201132**	**115143**	**154254**
43538	112489	103971	36401	65744	37587	47035
15413	205157	125872	8735	116442	62772	78042
4236	1029	5059	4031	1028		355
4016	33167	20624	1975	17918	14784	28822
67082	**3465**	**49733**	**48429**	**1199**	**6970**	**15592**
62504	2870	46544	45240	1199	6970	13592
4578	595	3189	3189			2000
14772	**59464**	**49852**	**7619**	**41938**	**3328**	**38968**
2163	18708	13513	1443	11983	799	10768
12557	40130	35708	6124	29376	2493	27757
52	626	631	52	579	36	443
97787	**337302**	**324404**	**67921**	**246283**	**64485**	**139536**
6675	150872	141150	4051	136914	8743	13176
4201	95958	89300	2748	86385	5998	7889
	56866	56860		56860	6	117
368	17932	17084	314	16770	140	1135
132	23675	22171	49	22122	480	1653
44	7554	7083		7083	251	715
3519	15794	10162	1485	8660	26498	7939
41433	54704	58618	26899	24303	8371	44191
1755	2454	2858	1439	1409	1057	1695
3224	5434	7035	3054	3848	443	1668
1119	3952	1941	213	1719	472	6154
17561	15133	17641	12041	5187	6053	33118
2822	2147	2936	1871	1052	1329	5481
1904	4913	2073	1271	710	211	6322
6103	22152	9792	5006	4756	3646	23312
16398	66807	75207	13733	59487	9202	8283
464	18265	17314	179	17135	661	1181
40307	**92080**	**122142**	**39923**	**82212**	**9750**	**1124**
37327	82905	110681	36943	73738	9435	503
2813	5000	7448	2813	4635	77	452
167	4175	4013	167	3839	238	169
158006	**248563**	**399426**	**156701**	**242584**	**6153**	**6025**
94330	227314	315589	93752	221696	5758	2723
83431	26686	109934	83153	26667	292	407
76241	21781	98136	76241	21781		
7190	4905	11798	6912	4886	292	407

3-7 续表 3 continued

单位：人

行业	Sector	全市 Total	# 在岗职工中女性 Female at their Posts	比重 (%) Proportion(%)
中等教育	Secondary School Education	108884	61245	56.2
中等专业学校	Specialized Secondary Schools	14153	7200	50.9
普通中学	Regular Secondary Schools	76532	44126	57.7
农业、职业中学	Agricultural and Vocational Schools	11643	6760	58.1
技工学校	Technical Schools	2623	1247	47.5
成人中等学校	Adult Secondary Schools	3513	1757	50.0
工读学校	Schools for Juvenile Delinquents	420	155	36.9
初等教育	Primary Education	76344	52564	68.9
小学校	Primary Schools	76244	52472	68.8
成人初等学校	Adult Primary Schools	100	92	92.0
学前教育	Preschool Education	11612	10016	86.3
特殊教育	Special Education	943	670	71.0
其他教育	Other Education	15654	5910	37.8
文化艺术业	Culture and Arts	70073	29408	42.0
艺术	Arts	9246	3356	36.3
出版	Publication	38683	16600	42.9
文物保护	Protection of Historical Relics	4590	1675	36.5
图书馆	Library	3027	1799	59.4
档案馆	Archives	1054	525	49.8
群众文化	Mass Culture	4429	1987	44.9
新闻	News	4339	1555	35.8
文化艺术经纪与代理业	Cultural Art Brokerage	2072	848	40.9
其他文化艺术业	Other Cultural Art	2633	1063	40.4
广播电影电视业	Radio,Film and Television	17461	6852	39.2
广播	Radio	5044	2088	41.4
电影	Film	5604	2062	36.8
电视	Television	6813	2702	39.7
科学研究和综合技术服务	**Scientific Research and Polytechical Services**	**258752**	**90650**	**35.0**
科学研究业	Scientific Research	135602	48867	36.0
自然科学研究	Natural Science Research	83453	30912	37.0
社会科学研究	Social Science Research	8821	3425	38.8
其他科学研究	Other Scientific Research	43328	14530	33.5
综合技术服务业	Polytechnical Services	123150	41783	33.9
气象	Atmospheric	2611	1134	43.4
地震	Seismology	1216	355	29.2
测绘	Surveying and Mapping	2139	799	37.4
技术监督	Technology Supervisor	8674	3192	36.8
海洋环境	Sea and Ocean Environments	314	97	30.9
环境保护	Environmental Protection	1535	451	29.4
技术推广和科技交流服务业	Technology Promotion and Exchange Services	12630	4312	34.1
工程设计业	Engineering Design	26565	10429	39.3
其他综合技术服务业	Other Polytechnical Services	67466	21014	31.1
国家机关、政党机关和社会团体	**Government Organs,Party Organs and Social Bodies**	**304918**	**94220**	**30.9**
国家机关	Government Organs	284843	86841	30.5
政党机关	Party Organs	10105	3279	32.4
社会团体	Social Bodies	9970	4100	41.1
其他行业	**Other Sectors**	**65000**	**21342**	**32.8**

3-7 续表 4 continued

(person)

		国有经济			集体经济	其他经济
# 中 央 Central	# 地 方 Local	State-Owned	# 中 央 Central	# 地 方 Local	Collective- Owned	Others
3870	104530	106469	3772	102697	1553	862
1155	12961	13860	1155	12705	256	37
2396	73691	74708	2298	72410	1008	816
4	11639	11643	4	11639		
93	2530	2353	93	2260	270	
177	3334	3485	177	3308	19	9
45	375	420	45	375		
889	75349	76238	889	75349		106
889	75276	76165	889	75276		79
	73	73		73		27
1640	9942	9200	1640	7560	2412	
148	777	925	148	777	18	
4352	10030	12823	4150	8646	1483	1348
51726	16027	66938	51162	15776	304	2831
5847	3376	9068	5756	3312	59	119
34344	4202	38285	34094	4191	148	250
3125	1403	4528	3125	1403		62
1975	1052	3027	1975	1052		
685	369	1054	685	369		
325	3955	4277	325	3952	3	149
4294	45	4339	4294	45		
579	938	1169	378	791	43	860
552	687	1191	530	661	51	1391
11950	5222	16899	11787	5112	91	471
3943	1101	5044	3943	1101		
3585	1778	5224	3529	1695	55	325
4422	2343	6631	4315	2316	36	146
168804	**75472**	**203292**	**164097**	**38245**	**14029**	**41431**
121985	12790	135239	121985	12498	186	177
74333	9049	83186	74333	8830	161	106
8350	471	8821	8350	471		
39302	3270	43232	39302	3197	25	71
46819	62682	68053	42112	25747	13843	41254
2593	18	2611	2593	18		
1152	64	1216	1152	64		
1158	981	2066	1158	908	73	
4615	3751	7933	4490	3443	208	533
314		314	314			
222	1077	772	222	550	288	475
3336	5788	5457	2459	2970	1697	5476
17903	7486	23111	17036	6041	1121	2333
15526	43517	24573	12688	11753	10456	32437
123180	**181030**	**304782**	**123092**	**180995**	**95**	**41**
108408	175740	284843	108408	175740		
7145	2960	10105	7145	2960		
7627	2330	9834	7539	2295	95	41
26681	**33141**	**49044**	**24034**	**24736**	**6131**	**9825**

3-8 国民经济各行业在岗职工人数(按用工期限分)

单位：人

行业	Sector	全市 Total	长期职工 Permanent Workers	临时职工 Temporary Workers
总计	**Total**	**4029540**	**3476156**	**553384**
农、林、牧、渔业	**Farming,Forestry,Animal Husbandry and Fishery**	**30721**	**24382**	**6339**
# 农、林、牧、渔服务业	FFAF Services	9348	8489	859
采掘业	**Excavation**	**28751**	**28267**	**484**
制造业	**Manufacturing**	**975104**	**898382**	**76722**
食品加工业	Food Processing	18622	16022	2600
食品制造业	Food Making	30914	24793	6121
饮料制造业	Beverage Manufacturing	24851	21958	2893
烟草制造业	Tobacco Processing	1005	994	11
纺织业	Textile Industry	42264	40047	2217
服装及其他纤维制品制造业	Garments and Other Fiber Products	33909	27101	6808
皮革、毛皮、羽绒及其制品业	Leather,Furs,Down and Related Products	5422	5020	402
木材加工及竹、藤、棕、革制品业	Timber Processing,Bamboo,Cane, Palm Fiber and Straw Products	3090	2702	388
家具制造业	Furniture Manufacturing	7752	5827	1925
造纸及纸制品业	Papermaking and Paper Products	9428	8111	1317
印刷业、记录媒介的复制	Printing and Record Medium Reproduced	39647	36228	3419
文教体育用品制造业	Stationery,Education and Sports Goods	8706	7328	1378
石油加工及炼焦业	Petroleum Processing and Coking Products	43421	43146	275
化学原料及化学制品制造业	Raw Chemical Materials and Chemical Products	41175	37959	3216
医药制造业	Medical and Pharmaceutical Products	25216	23907	1309
化学纤维制造业	Chemical Fibers	4669	4560	109
橡胶制品业	Rubber Products	9615	7962	1653
塑料制品业	Plastic Products	15198	12520	2678
非金属矿物制品业	Nonmetal Mineral Products	62969	54757	8212
黑色金属冶炼及压延加工业	Smelting and Pressing Ferrous Metals	137588	137022	566
有色金属冶炼及压延加工业	Smelting and Pressing of Nonferrous Metals	3582	3243	339
金属制品业	Metal Products	30434	25753	4681
普通机械制造业	Ordinary Machinery	58492	56312	2180
专业设备制造业	Special Purpose Equipment	59960	56191	3769
交通运输设备制造业	Transportation Equipment	98297	93471	4826
武器弹药制造业	Weapons and Ammunition	10933	10883	50
电气机械及器材制造业	Electric Equipment and Machine	42928	38425	4503
电子及通信设备制造业	Electronic and Telecommunication	67783	62314	5469
仪器仪表及文化办公用机械制造业	Instruments,Meters,Cultural and Official Machinery	23691	22123	1568
其他制造业	Other Manufacturing	13543	11703	1840
电力、煤气及水的生产和供应业	**Electricity,Gas and Water Production and Supply**	**41149**	**40027**	**1122**
电力、蒸气、热水的生产和供应业	Electricity,Steam and Hot Water Production and Supply	26494	25605	889
煤气生产和供应业	Gas Production and Supply	8486	8456	30
自来水的生产和供应业	Water Production and Supply	6169	5966	203
建筑业	**Construction**	**470119**	**304200**	**165919**
土木工程建筑业	Civil Engineering	373265	244917	128348
线路、管道和设备安装业	Pipeline and Equipment Installation	64561	44504	20057
建筑物的装修装饰业	Building Completion	32293	14779	17514
地质勘查业、水利管理业	**Geological Prospecting and Water Conservancy**	**16461**	**12847**	**3614**

STAFF AND WORKERS AT THEIR POSTS IN DIFFERENT TRADES (BY TYPE OF STAFF AND WORKERS)

(person)

# 全市国有经济 Total State-Owned Economy	长期职工 Permanent Workers	临时职工 Temporary Workers	# 地方国有经济 Local State-Owned Economy	长期职工 Permanent Workers	临时职工 Temporary Workers
2767126	**2521335**	**245791**	**1683158**	**1558032**	**125126**
25058	**20826**	**4232**	**24250**	**20065**	**4185**
7605	7064	541	6938	6404	534
28218	**28127**	**91**	**28067**	**27976**	**91**
549534	**530014**	**19520**	**413302**	**397448**	**15854**
10430	9574	856	10386	9549	837
12058	10666	1392	11872	10628	1244
12588	11631	957	12519	11591	928
75	65	10	75	65	10
23225	23070	155	23203	23063	140
6728	5727	1001	5496	4756	740
2109	1969	140	2109	1969	140
1838	1766	72	1465	1393	72
1523	1294	229	1279	1080	199
4816	4603	213	4589	4433	156
28828	27276	1552	8676	8055	621
4249	4051	198	4216	4018	198
35485	35467	18	448	441	7
17318	16202	1116	16872	15858	1014
15748	15159	589	13531	13334	197
2389	2360	29	2389	2360	29
6343	5887	456	6234	5780	454
4711	4254	457	4115	3734	381
22874	20182	2692	21090	18746	2344
131559	131359	200	131559	131359	200
1790	1739	51	1767	1723	44
11317	10215	1102	10294	9336	958
35055	34520	535	30726	30240	486
29991	29351	640	19218	18652	566
58303	56917	1386	19065	18389	676
10933	10883	50			
22153	20429	1724	22029	20358	1671
18987	18032	955	15397	14553	844
13229	12654	575	9836	9305	531
2882	2712	170	2847	2680	167
38828	**37855**	**973**	**28006**	**27142**	**864**
24229	23459	770	13407	12746	661
8430	8430		8430	8430	
6169	5966	203	6169	5966	203
267653	**207443**	**60210**	**145592**	**127497**	**18095**
230082	177275	52807	125708	110151	15557
32912	27151	5761	16618	15271	1347
4659	3017	1642	3266	2075	1191
15987	**12404**	**3583**	**10688**	**7367**	**3321**

3-8 续表 1 continued

单位：人

行业	Sector	全市 Total	长期职工 Permanent Workers	临时职工 Temporary Workers
地质勘查业	Geological Prospecting	5508	5257	251
水利管理业	Water Conservancy	10953	7590	3363
交通运输、仓储及邮电通信业	**Transportation,Storage,Posts and Telecommunications**	**186792**	**168345**	**18447**
铁路运输业	Railway	61172	60850	322
公路运输业	Highway	24496	21006	3490
管道运输业	Pipeline	88	88	
航空运输业	Airway	10968	10847	121
交通运输辅助业	Transportation Subsidiary	31876	21135	10741
仓储业	Storage	13473	12402	1071
邮电通信业	Posts and Telecommunications	44719	42017	2702
批发和零售贸易餐饮业	**Wholesale,Retail and Catering**	**468200**	**392423**	**75777**
批发业	Wholesale	166903	149256	17647
零售业	Retail	235072	204496	30576
商业经纪与代理业	Commercial Management and Agency	4992	4877	115
餐饮业	Catering	61233	33794	27439
金融、保险业	**Banking and Insurance**	**72174**	**69597**	**2577**
金融业	Banking	66996	64720	2276
保险业	Insurance	5178	4877	301
房地产业	**Real Estate**	**89821**	**71822**	**17999**
房地产开发与经营业	Real Estate Development	24712	21581	3131
房地产管理业	Real Estate Management	64005	49272	14733
房地产代理与经纪业	Real Estate Brokerage and Agency	1104	969	135
社会服务业	**Social Services**	**502383**	**408833**	**93550**
公共设施服务业	Public Utilities	157244	143195	14049
# 市内公共交通业	Public Transportation in City	98039	94961	3078
# 市内公共汽电车业	Public Bus and Trolleybus	53624	53129	495
园林绿化业	Gardens Afforest	18014	15726	2288
环境卫生业	Environmental Sanitation	24205	19378	4827
市政工程管理业	Municipal Engineering Management	7932	6910	1022
居民服务业	Residential Services	42454	16731	25723
旅馆业	Hotels	106845	86775	20070
租赁服务业	Leasing	4906	4115	791
旅游业	Tourism	8909	7865	1044
娱乐服务业	Recreation	8473	5561	2912
信息、咨询服务业	Information and Consultancy Services	55430	46801	8629
# 广告业	Advertisement	9663	7909	1754
咨询服务业	Consultancy Services	8526	7967	559
计算机应用服务业	Computer Application Services	36350	32334	4016
其他社会服务业	Other Social Services	81772	65456	16316
# 市场管理服务业	Market Management Services	9460	7817	1643
卫生、体育和社会福利业	**Health Care,Sports and Social Welfare**	**131871**	**122656**	**9215**
卫生	Health Care	119793	112202	7591
体育	Sports	7687	6754	933
社会福利保障业	Social Welfare	4391	3700	691
教育、文化艺术及广播电影电视业	**Education,Culture and Arts, Radio, Film and Television**	**406804**	**376553**	**30251**
教育	Education	320688	298249	22439
高等教育	Higher Education	109854	98928	10926
普通高等教育	Ordinary Higher Education	97512	88084	9428
成人高等教育	Adult Higher Education	12342	10844	1498

3-8 续表 2 continued

(person)

# 全市国有经济 Total State-Owned Economy	长期职工 Permanent Workers	临时职工 Temporary Workers	# 地方国有经济 Local State-Owned Economy	长期职工 Permanent Workers	临时职工 Temporary Workers
5508	5257	251	683	671	12
10479	7147	3332	10005	6696	3309
167337	**152425**	**14912**	**44938**	**34107**	**10831**
61172	60850	322	217	217	
19148	16285	2863	17516	14723	2793
9810	9810				
25226	16312	8914	15826	8667	7159
12220	11461	759	10925	10264	661
39761	37707	2054	454	236	218
217720	**199827**	**17893**	**165879**	**152740**	**13139**
89850	84402	5448	53851	50461	3390
105052	97477	7575	95839	89603	6236
4637	4534	103	710	672	38
18181	13414	4767	15479	12004	3475
49653	**47498**	**2155**	**1193**	**1134**	**59**
46475	44493	1982	1193	1134	59
3178	3005	173			
48557	**39636**	**8921**	**40730**	**34631**	**6099**
13237	11817	1420	11739	10393	1346
34693	27210	7483	28416	23681	4735
627	609	18	575	557	18
303278	**266949**	**36329**	**226401**	**206641**	**19760**
135707	126554	9153	131496	123070	8426
84402	82594	1808	81491	80060	1431
53501	53013	488	53501	53013	488
16752	14722	2030	16449	14493	1956
22072	18832	3240	22023	18783	3240
7014	6263	751	7014	6263	751
8979	7521	1458	7484	6330	1154
55850	42714	13136	22031	18803	3228
2279	2106	173	831	725	106
6804	5994	810	3694	3106	588
1904	1341	563	1682	1226	456
16951	15128	1823	4711	4088	623
2882	2449	433	1025	804	221
2040	1915	125	687	618	69
9516	8759	757	4705	4125	580
65288	56832	8456	49767	45168	4599
7727	6639	1088	7551	6522	1029
121174	**112958**	**8216**	**81586**	**76051**	**5535**
110027	103073	6954	73193	68624	4569
7158	6471	687	4574	4147	427
3989	3414	575	3819	3280	539
394999	**366583**	**28416**	**239416**	**225273**	**14143**
312548	291431	21117	219295	207306	11989
109155	98262	10893	26490	23779	2711
97512	88084	9428	21652	19447	2205
11643	10178	1465	4838	4332	506

3-8 续表 3 continued

单位：人

行业	Sector	全市 Total	长期职工 Permanent Workers	临时职工 Temporary Workers
中等教育	Secondary School Education	107685	102709	4976
中等专业学校	Specialized Secondary Schools	14038	13025	1013
普通中学	Regular Secondary Schools	75733	72729	3004
农业、职业中学	Agricultural and Vocational Schools	11419	10961	458
技工学校	Technical Schools	2613	2331	282
成人中等学校	Adult Secondary Schools	3486	3269	217
工读学校	Schools for Juvenile Delinquents	396	394	2
初等教育	Primary Education	75528	72698	2830
小学校	Primary Schools	75428	72598	2830
成人初等学校	Adult Primary Schools	100	100	
学前教育	Preschool Education	11237	10391	846
特殊教育	Special Education	939	868	71
其他教育	Other Education	15445	12655	2790
文化艺术业	Culture and Arts	68748	62839	5909
艺术	Arts	8877	8310	567
出版	Publication	38206	34966	3240
文物保护	Protection of Historical Relic7s	4540	3936	604
图书馆	Library	2982	2880	102
档案馆	Archives	1050	997	53
群众文化	Mass Culture	4118	3610	508
新闻	News	4339	4047	292
文化艺术经纪与代理业	Cultural Art Brokerage	2035	1850	185
其他文化艺术业	Other Cultural Art	2601	2243	358
广播电影电视业	Radio,Film and Television	17368	15465	1903
广播	Radio	5043	4772	271
电影	Film	5512	4969	543
电视	Television	6813	5724	1089
科学研究和综合技术服务	**Scientific Research and Polytechnical Services**	**252338**	**233439**	**18899**
科学研究业	Scientific Research	131756	126973	4783
自然科学研究	Natural Science Research	80584	77702	2882
社会科学研究	Social Science Research	8791	8467	324
其他科学研究	Other Scientific Research	42381	40804	1577
综合技术服务业	Polytechnical Services	120582	106466	14116
气象	Atmospheric	2594	2406	188
地震	Seismology	1194	1159	35
测绘	Surveying and Mapping	1896	1884	12
技术监督	Technology Supervisor	8522	7929	593
海洋环境	Sea and Ocean Environments	309	308	1
环境保护	Environmental Protection	1519	1362	157
技术推广和科技交流服务业	Technology Promotion and Exchange Services	12111	10443	1668
工程设计业	Engineering Design	26134	25124	1010
其他综合技术服务业	Other Polytechnical Services	66303	55851	10452
国家机关、政党机关和社会团体	**Government Organs,Party Organs and Social Bodies**	**295817**	**268720**	**27097**
国家机关	Government Organs	275855	249869	25986
政党机关	Party Organs	10099	9382	717
社会团体	Social Bodies	9863	9469	394
其他行业	**Other Sectors**	**61035**	**55663**	**5372**

3-8 续表 4 continued

(person)

# 全市国有经济 Total State-Owned Economy	长期职工 Permanent Workers	临时职工 Temporary Workers	# 地方国有经济 Local State-Owned Economy	长期职工 Permanent Workers	临时职工 Temporary Workers
105283	100592	4691	101524	97088	4436
13757	12744	1013	12602	11653	949
73909	71079	2830	71618	68966	2652
11419	10961	458	11415	10957	458
2343	2169	174	2252	2083	169
3459	3245	214	3286	3080	206
396	394	2	351	349	2
75422	72594	2828	74545	71737	2808
75349	72521	2828	74472	71664	2808
73	73		73	73	
9097	8452	645	7461	6864	597
921	850	71	776	705	71
12670	10681	1989	8499	7133	1366
65645	60191	5454	15081	13563	1518
8716	8161	555	3093	2899	194
37808	34594	3214	4120	3717	403
4478	3883	595	1355	1127	228
2982	2880	102	1040	952	88
1050	997	53	369	357	12
3968	3477	491	3643	3155	488
4339	4047	292	45	44	1
1134	1043	91	774	716	58
1170	1109	61	642	596	46
16806	14961	1845	5040	4404	636
5043	4772	271	1101	948	153
5132	4634	498	1623	1422	201
6631	5555	1076	2316	2034	282
197589	**188544**	**9045**	**36478**	**33030**	**3448**
131438	126702	4736	11417	10831	586
80359	77521	2838	8016	7519	497
8791	8467	324	453	439	14
42288	40714	1574	2948	2873	75
66151	61842	4309	25061	22199	2862
2594	2406	188	18	12	6
1194	1159	35	64	63	1
1823	1811	12	885	873	12
7804	7257	547	3383	3031	352
309	308	1			
762	719	43	544	505	39
5146	4592	554	2767	2340	427
22690	22227	463	5990	5774	216
23829	21363	2466	11410	9601	1809
295693	**268598**	**27095**	**174516**	**167175**	**7341**
275855	249869	25986	169284	162178	7106
10099	9382	717	2955	2871	84
9739	9347	392	2277	2126	151
45848	**41648**	**4200**	**22116**	**19755**	**2361**

3-9 职 工 工 资 总 额
TOTAL WAGES OF STAFF AND WORKERS

单位：万元 (10000 yuan)

项　目	Item	1999	1998	1999 年为 1998 年% 1999 as % of 1998
总　计	**Total**	**6144815**	**5581851**	**110.1**
按登记注册类型分	**Grouped by Registered Type**			
内资经济	Domestic Investment Economy	5413102	4947772	109.4
国有经济	State-owned	4200008	3919010	107.2
集体经济	Collective-owned	447507	450010	99.4
联营经济	Joint-owned	58615	59308	98.8
股份有限公司	Share Holding Company	310687	234898	132.3
有限责任公司	Limited-Liability Company	329420	229306	143.7
股份合作企业	Share Holding Cooperative	64890	53703	120.8
其他经济	Others	1975	1537	128.5
外商投资经济	Foreign Funded	491122	434192	113.1
港、澳、台商投资经济	Hongkong,Macao and Taiwan Funded	240590	199885	120.4
按隶属关系分	**Grouped by Administrative Relationship**			
# 中央	Central	2021963	1830990	110.4
地方	Local	3584429	3367399	106.4
按行业分	**Grouped by Sector**			
农、林、牧、渔业	Farming,Forestry,Animal Husbandry and Fishery	33176	31434	105.5
# 农业	Farming	4023	3533	113.9
采掘业	Excavation	31586	36945	85.5
制造业	Manufacturing	1391474	1316529	105.7
电力、煤气及水的生产和供应业	Electricity,Gas,Water Production and Supply	75340	63888	117.9
建筑业	Construction	636356	619696	102.7
地质勘查业水利管理业	Geological Prospecting and Water Conservancy	20947	19407	107.9
交通运输、仓储及邮电通信业	Transportation,Storage,Posts and Telecommunications Services	310646	265270	117.1
# 交通运输业	Transportation	199018	180924	110.0
邮电通信业	Posts and Telecommunications Services	92562	71188	130.0
批发和零售贸易餐饮业	Wholesale, Retail and Catering	654041	609684	107.3
# 批发业	Wholesale	271636	259880	104.5
零售业	Retail	296538	271635	109.2
餐饮业	Catering	70712	71228	99.3
金融、保险业	Banking and Insurance	171295	152731	112.2
房地产业	Real Estate	162611	132545	122.7
社会服务业	Social Services	787261	717604	109.7
居民服务业	Residents Services	37359	25463	146.7
旅馆业	Hotels	163319	159184	102.6
卫生体育和社会福利业	Health Care,Sports and Social Welfare	236459	197004	120.0
# 卫生	Health Care	218039	179542	121.4
体育	Sports	12204	12379	98.6
教育、文化艺术和广播电影电视业	Education,Culture,Art, Radio,Film and Television	631553	542418	116.4
教育	Education	471097	405330	116.2
文化艺术业	Culture and Art	123041	101611	121.1
广播电影电视业	Radio,Film and Television	37414	35476	105.5
科学研究和综合技术服务业	Scientific Research and Polytechnical Services	435699	384399	113.3
科学研究业	Scientific Research	214128	184310	116.2
综合技术服务业	Polytechnical Services	221571	200089	110.7
国家机关、政党机关和社会团体	Government Organs,Party Organs and Social Bodies	426797	387520	110.1
其他行业	Others	139574	104779	133.2

3-10 职 工 平 均 工 资
AVERAGE WAGE OF STAFF AND WORKERS

单位：元 (yuan)

项 目	Item	1999	1998	1999 年为 1998 年% 19998 as % of 1998
总 计	**Total**	**13778**	**12285**	**112.2**
按登记注册类型分	**Grouped by Registered Type**			
内资经济	Domestic Investment Economy	13043	11701	111.5
国有经济	State-owned	13483	11971	112.6
集体经济	Collective-owned	8928	8800	101.5
联营经济	Joint-owned	11070	10280	107.7
股份有限公司	Share Holding Company	14732	14559	101.2
有限责任公司	Limited-Liability Company	15870	13873	114.4
股份合作企业	Share Holding Cooperative	10600	9336	113.5
其他经济	Others	14045	10773	130.4
外商投资经济	Foreign Funded	25571	21948	116.5
港、澳、台商投资经济	Hongkong,Macao and Taiwan Funded	20468	17021	120.3
按隶属关系分	**Grouped by Administrative Relationship**			
# 中央	Central	16132	13671	118.0
地方	Local	12650	11441	110.6
按行业分	**Grouped by Sector**			
农、林、牧、渔业	Farming,Forestry,Animal Husbandry and Fishery	9127	8254	110.6
# 农业	Farming	8116	7054	115.1
采掘业	Excavation	9476	9714	97.5
制造业	Manufacturing	11759	10602	110.9
电力、煤气及水的生产和供应业	Electricity,Gas,Water Production and Supply	16510	15076	109.5
建筑业	Construction	11644	10777	108.0
地质勘查业水利管理业	Geological Prospecting and Water Conservancy	13079	11668	112.1
交通运输、仓储及邮电通信业	Transportation,Storage,Posts and Telecommunications Services	15328	13183	116.3
# 交通运输业	Transportation	14134	12443	113.6
邮电通信业	Posts and Telecommunications Services	20635	16639	124.0
批发和零售贸易餐饮业	Wholesale, Retail and Catering	12273	11329	108.3
# 批发业	Wholesale	14208	12462	114.0
零售业	Retail	10888	10260	106.1
餐饮业	Catering	11058	11618	95.2
金融、保险业	Banking and Insurance	24450	21718	112.6
房地产业	Real Estate	18012	16311	110.4
社会服务业	Social Services	14880	14280	104.2
居民服务业	Residents Services	8403	10058	83.5
旅馆业	Hotels	14329	13750	104.2
卫生体育和社会福利业	Health Care,Sports and Social Welfare	17832	14616	122.0
# 卫生	Health Care	18112	14654	123.6
体育	Sports	15527	15412	100.7
教育、文化艺术和广播电影电视业	Education,Culture,Art, Radio,Film and Television	15365	12959	118.6
教育	Education	14553	12207	119.2
文化艺术业	Culture and Art	17623	14720	119.7
广播电影电视业	Radio,Film and Television	21396	20262	105.6
科学研究和综合技术服务业	Scientific Research and Polytechnical Services	16582	14133	117.3
科学研究业	Scientific Research	15439	13052	118.3
综合技术服务业	Polytechnical Services	17860	15300	116.7
国家机关、政党机关和社会团体	Government Organs,Party Organs and Social Bodies	14078	12301	114.4
其他行业	Others	21726	18073	120.2

3-11 国民经济各行业职工工资总额及平均工资

行业	Sector	工资总额 (万元) Total Wages (10000 yuan)	# 中央 Central	# 地方 Local	国有经济 State-Owned
总计	**Total**	**6144815**	**2021963**	**3584429**	**4200008**
农、林、牧、渔业	**Farming,Forestry,Animal Husbandry and Fishery**	**33176**	**1834**	**31019**	**27410**
# 农、林、牧、渔服务业	FFAF Services	11670	1106	10424	9805
采掘业	**Excavation**	**31586**	**414**	**31172**	**31045**
制造业	**Manufacturing**	**1391474**	**260691**	**1073629**	**741365**
食品加工业	Food Processing	23108	669	20361	11645
食品制造业	Food Making	46096	4557	37324	14954
饮料制造业	Beverage Manufacturing	32742	192	30994	15246
烟草制造业	Tobacco Processing	2509	18	2491	69
纺织业	Textile Industry	47086	105	46507	27322
服装及其他纤维制品制造业	Garments and Other Fiber Products	33384	1750	25661	7398
皮革、毛皮、羽绒及其制品业	Leather,Furs,Down and Related Products	6285	194	5388	2762
木材加工及竹、藤、棕、革制品业	Timber Processing,Bamboo,Cane, Palm Fiber and Straw Products	3466	621	2424	2093
家具制造业	Furniture Manufacturing	7911	745	4267	1676
造纸及纸制品业	Papermaking and Paper Products	12252	399	11167	5544
印刷业、记录媒介的复制	Printing and Record Medium Reproduced	56439	34368	20444	41500
文教体育用品制造业	Stationery,Education and Sports Goods	10836	540	9306	5627
石油加工及炼焦业	Petroleum Processing and Coking Products	84877	72111	12656	72047
化学原料及化学制品制造业	Raw Chemical Materials and Chemical Products	59671	2040	55184	19824
医药制造业	Medical and Pharmaceutical Products	40495	3316	35009	22598
化学纤维制造业	Chemical Fibers	4775	11	4717	2371
橡胶制品业	Rubber Products	10578	288	10230	7658
塑料制品业	Plastic Products	17911	980	15804	5945
非金属矿物制品业	Nonmetal Mineral Products	78861	2981	73117	25408
黑色金属冶炼及压延加工业	Smelting and Pressing Ferrous Metals	195668	59	195577	187599
有色金属冶炼及压延加工业	Smelting and Pressing of Non-ferrous Metals	4587	26	4500	2191
金属制品业	Metal Products	34785	2649	28846	14353
普通机械制造业	Ordinary Machinery	70016	14943	52628	38759
专业设备制造业	Special Purpose Equipment	77829	15923	55980	37305
交通运输设备制造业	Transportation Equipment	128679	59834	66222	74336
武器弹药制造业	Weapons and Ammunition	13868	13868		13868
电气机械及器材制造业	Electric Equipment and Machine	56307	1397	52730	30065
电子及通信设备制造业	Electronic and Telecommunication	157973	18055	133546	29105
仪器仪表及文化办公用机械制造业	Instruments,Meters,Cultural and Official Machinery	54482	6701	45887	18333
其他制造业	Other Manufacturing	18000	1352	14661	3765
电力、煤气及水的生产和供应业	**Electricity,Gas and Water Production and Supply**	**75340**	**29851**	**45489**	**71929**
电力、蒸气、热水的生产和供应业	Electricity,Steam and Hot Water Production and Supply	54064	29851	24213	50705
煤气生产和供应业	Gas Production and Supply	11975		11975	11923
自来水的生产和供应业	Water Production and Supply	9301		9301	9301
建筑业	**Construction**	**636356**	**178748**	**367216**	**404001**
土木工程建筑业	Civil Engineering	494179	122843	305408	334923
线路、管道和设备安装业	Pipeline and Equipment Installation	108788	51056	49478	62924
建筑物的装修装饰业	Building Completion	33390	4850	12329	6153
地质勘查业、水利管理业	**Geological Prospecting and Water Conservancy**	**20947**	**6781**	**14166**	**20525**
地质勘查业	Geological Prospecting	7683	6004	1679	7683
水利管理业	Water Conservancy	13264	777	12487	12842

TOTAL WAGES AND AVERAGE WAGE OF STAFF AND WORKERS BY DIFFERENT TRADES OF NATIONAL ECONOMY

				平均工资			
# 中 央 Central	# 地 方 Local	集体经济 Collective-Owned	其他经济 Others	(元) Average Wage (yuan)	国有经济 State-Owned	集体经济 Collective-Owned	其他经济 Others
1735986	**2411423**	**447507**	**1497300**	**13778**	**13483**	**8928**	**17748**
1223	**26187**	**1461**	**4305**	**9127**	**9220**	**8814**	**8674**
1106	8699	1095	771	11729	11993	9640	12061
414	**30631**	**261**	**280**	**9476**	**9444**	**8992**	**16490**
207843	**533099**	**101348**	**548762**	**11759**	**10656**	**7302**	**15731**
43	11602	457	11007	9614	7673	8916	13187
143	14811	1328	29814	12792	9005	6418	17175
61	15184	1558	15939	12209	11381	9902	13452
	69	18	2422	24010	7866	9778	25796
17	27306	2936	16828	8294	8472	5160	8934
1644	5754	5685	20301	7973	8065	5114	9408
	2762	1743	1780	6428	5366	5921	10555
532	1560	304	1069	8186	7741	5187	11317
354	1322	1136	5099	9230	8012	7259	10376
295	5250	948	5760	10346	8062	7060	15900
31604	9895	4865	10075	12911	12993	8104	17460
61	5566	1494	3715	10475	10661	7006	12659
71655	392	556	12275	15530	15580	13329	15353
527	19290	2791	37056	11834	8722	9254	15015
3191	19404	1376	16521	14973	13002	9483	20113
11	2360	466	1937	6568	5302	5028	10354
175	7483	1786	1134	8295	8423	6532	12247
369	5400	2791	9175	8520	7210	7093	10376
2258	23150	7997	45455	10542	9067	7145	12772
	187599	958	7112	11933	11957	9654	11686
26	2164	886	1510	10153	8710	11146	12503
1199	13094	7631	12800	9065	9261	6771	11031
5229	33498	8868	22389	9451	8348	7732	13831
13776	23489	4745	35779	11496	10000	8369	14471
49084	25198	10238	44106	10885	10837	6941	12650
13868				11024	11024		
312	29744	9811	16431	10375	9844	7551	15303
5791	23272	5745	123123	20416	10940	8657	27895
5582	12752	4450	31698	18491	10553	9779	42040
35	3729	7783	6452	9101	8406	7450	13300
27233	**44696**	**830**	**2581**	**16510**	**16596**	**15572**	**14663**
27233	23472	830	2529	17494	17688	15572	14842
	11923		52	14237	14271		9204
	9301			14719	14719		
143407	**225785**	**118428**	**113928**	**11644**	**11579**	**9884**	**14647**
111083	189795	76573	82683	11252	11131	8918	15765
30360	32237	32130	13733	14463	14799	14384	13251
1964	3753	9725	17512	10406	11181	8372	11698
6781	**13744**	**422**		**13079**	**13210**	**8830**	
6004	1679			12877	12877		
777	12065	422		13199	13418	8830	

3-11 续表 1 continued

行 业	Sector	工资总额 (万元) Total Wages (10000 yuan)	# 中央 Central	# 地方 Local	国有经济 State-Owned
交通运输、仓储及邮电通信业	**Transportation,Storage,Posts and Telecommunications**	**310646**	**218051**	**79182**	**265772**
铁路运输业	Railway	86201	85999	202	86201
公路运输业	Highway	26809	3339	22825	20151
管道运输业	Pipeline	165	165		
航空运输业	Airway	24703	24703		21706
交通运输辅助业	Transportation Subsidiary	61139	22556	36704	46781
仓储业	Storage	19066	2477	16141	16896
邮电通信业	Posts and Telecommunications	92562	78812	3310	74036
批发和零售贸易餐饮业	**Wholesale,Retail and Catering**	**654041**	**150842**	**388498**	**342000**
批发业	Wholesale	271636	106122	124741	168127
零售业	Retail	296538	25913	223114	138876
商业经纪与代理业	Commercial Management and Agency	15155	13444	1360	13903
餐饮业	Catering	70712	5363	39283	21093
金融、保险业	**Banking and Insurance**	**171295**	**146431**	**9718**	**100765**
金融业	Banking	158695	135695	8125	94566
保险业	Insurance	12600	10735	1593	6198
房地产业	**Real Estate**	**162611**	**27457**	**101796**	**77598**
房地产开发与经营业	Real Estate Development	60342	4831	43632	26936
房地产管理业	Real Estate Management	100092	22552	56773	49309
房地产代理与经纪业	Real Estate Brokerage and Agency	2177	74	1390	1353
社会服务业	**Social Services**	**787261**	**169264**	**470147**	**438400**
公共设施服务业	Public Utilities	232709	8459	219132	209705
# 市内公共交通业	Public Transportation in City	135751	3757	129446	124018
# 市内公共汽电车业	Public Bus and Trolleybus	86398		86126	86120
园林绿化业	Gardens Afforest	31345	428	30864	29439
环境卫生业	Environmental Sanitation	38681	408	37997	36697
市政工程管理业	Municipal Engineering Management	14210	114	13386	12141
居民服务业	Residential Services	37359	4654	16534	11944
旅馆业	Hotels	163319	64553	81392	71829
租赁服务业	Leasing	8194	4011	2140	4408
旅游业	Tourism	15311	7455	7047	12111
娱乐服务业	Recreation	13791	2192	6284	2337
信息、咨询服务业	Information and Consultancy Services	131168	38436	26392	33183
# 广告业	Advertisement	19219	7897	2837	5973
咨询服务业	Consultancy Services	22295	6546	11483	5747
计算机应用服务业	Computer Application Services	89782	12207	53221	17744
其他社会服务业	Other Social Services	95629	27298	58003	75140
# 市场管理服务业	Market Management Services	26304	510	25168	24578
卫生、体育和社会福利业	**Health Care,Sports and Social Welfare**	**236459**	**79641**	**155528**	**220916**
卫生	Health Care	218039	74250	142712	203728
体育	Sports	12204	5148	6899	11649
社会服务保障业	Social Welfare	6215	244	5917	5540
教育、文化艺术及广播电影电视业	**Education,Culture and Arts, Radio, Film and Television**	**631553**	**257055**	**366836**	**613667**
教育	Education	471097	140478	326336	458875
高等教育	Higher Education	164539	122871	40676	163486
普通高等教育	Ordinary Higher Education	146169	112962	33071	146169
成人高等教育	Adult Higher Education	18370	9909	7606	17318

3-11 续表 2 continued

# 中 央 Central	# 地 方 Local	集体经济 Collective-Owned	其他经济 Others	平均工资 (元) Average Wage (yuan)	国有经济 State-Owned	集体经济 Collective-Owned	其他经济 Others
202009	**63484**	**7510**	**37365**	**15328**	**14597**	**9653**	**29150**
85999	202			13640	13640		
1927	18224	5066	1592	8941	8499	9498	16899
			165	18770			18770
21706			2997	22783	22292		27100
16718	29802	1020	13338	16663	15575	10340	23532
2230	14666	922	1248	11213	10896	9222	25054
73430	589	502	18024	20635	18564	10906	39912
122621	**215980**	**99589**	**212453**	**12273**	**13013**	**8403**	**14015**
92755	73323	36052	67457	14208	15595	9267	15165
14911	123294	52060	105602	10888	10748	8028	13489
12560	1343		1252	27961	27498		34386
2395	18020	11477	38142	11058	10175	7776	13403
98269	**2140**	**7290**	**63240**	**24450**	**21020**	**10459**	**41740**
92071	2140	7290	56839	24455	21114	10459	43276
6198			6402	24390	19684		31738
11514	**65305**	**4268**	**80744**	**18012**	**15658**	**12617**	**21626**
3089	23542	1276	32130	24263	19770	17132	30600
8351	40483	2907	47876	15569	13967	11182	18143
74	1279	85	739	19487	21480	22303	16452
107212	**321438**	**56454**	**292407**	**14880**	**13457**	**8623**	**21218**
4285	205270	8332	14673	14133	14649	9509	11513
2391	121514	4423	7309	13171	13833	7356	9871
	86120	5	273	15077	15059	8810	24558
364	29076	117	1790	15736	15775	8111	16064
73	36624	370	1615	15831	16470	7766	9635
	12141	492	1577	17395	17014	19163	20317
1954	9972	17165	8250	8403	11737	6405	11022
33975	30121	7855	83636	14329	11990	9112	18402
3401	987	948	2838	14882	15158	9990	17211
7109	4871	428	2772	16506	16863	9430	16901
188	2133	418	11035	15186	11451	8139	16909
24048	8467	7605	90380	24139	19163	12957	29012
4558	1403	1946	11300	20041	21777	14318	20590
3486	2098	547	16001	27648	27845	25685	27650
9591	8115	4301	67737	25421	17731	12177	31102
22660	51503	9403	11086	10345	10282	9428	11808
294	24284	488	1238	14366	14930	8029	9981
79385	**141520**	**13290**	**2253**	**17832**	**18124**	**13618**	**23541**
73994	129733	13054	1257	18112	18424	13824	34450
5148	6501	61	495	15527	15846	7798	11486
244	5285	175	500	14248	13979	7341	31083
254410	**359089**	**7847**	**10038**	**15365**	**15371**	**12606**	**18010**
139569	319138	7307	4915	14553	14554	12550	18905
122712	40638	802	251	14826	14825	26923	6187
112962	33071			14851	14851		
9750	7567	802	251	14626	14605	26923	6187

3-11 续表 3 continued

行业 Sector		工资总额 (万元) Total Wages (10000 yuan)	# 中央 Central	# 地方 Local	国有企业 State-Owned
中等教育	Secondary School Education	164622	7043	156667	160450
中等专业学校	Specialized Secondary Schools	19938	1571	18328	19507
普通中学	Regular Secondary Schools	116367	5032	110468	113045
农业、职业中学	Agricultural and Vocational Schools	18299	6	18293	18299
技工学校	Technical Schools	4095	120	3975	3711
成人中等学校	Adult Secondary Schools	5227	230	4990	5193
工读学校	Schools for Juvenile Delinquents	696	83	613	696
初等教育	Primary Education	102516	1639	100632	102270
小学校	Primary Schools	102411	1639	100547	102186
成人初等学校	Adult Primary Schools	104		84	84
学前教育	Preschool Education	15447	2385	13007	13023
特殊教育	Special Education	1262	150	1094	1245
其他教育	Other Education	22712	6391	14260	18401
文化艺术业	Culture and Arts	123041	90403	29718	118399
艺术	Arts	13063	8201	4830	12909
出版	Publication	78740	65922	12561	77688
文物保护	Protection of Historical Relics	6634	4499	1961	6461
图书馆	Library	4370	3040	1330	4370
档案馆	Archives	1602	916	686	1602
群众文化	Mass Culture	5919	423	5326	5748
新闻	News	4982	4914	68	4982
文化艺术经纪与代理业	Cultural Art Brokerage	3731	1534	1478	2252
其他文化艺术业	Other Cultural Art	4000	953	1476	2386
广播电影电视业	Radio,Film and Television	37414	26174	10782	36393
广播	Radio	7934	5998	1936	7934
电影	Film	7846	5588	1933	7372
电视	Television	21634	14588	6912	21087
科学研究和综合技术服务	**Scientific Research and Polytechical Services**	**435699**	**281486**	**134814**	**334670**
科学研究业	Scientific Research	214128	193617	19395	213695
自然科学研究	Natural Science Research	133749	120169	13495	133419
社会科学研究	Social Science Research	11514	10675	839	11514
其他科学研究	Other Scientific Research	68866	62773	5061	68762
综合技术服务业	Polytechnical Services	221571	87869	115419	120976
气象	Atmospheric	4371	4051	320	4371
地震	Seismology	1513	1420	92	1513
测绘	Surveying and Mapping	3689	1333	2355	3540
技术监督	Technology Supervisor	14077	7313	6262	12890
海洋环境	Sea and Ocean Environments	541	541		541
环境保护	Environmental Protection	2019	354	1417	1126
技术推广和科技交流服务业	Technology Promotion and Exchange Services	23221	5028	13679	7183
工程设计业	Engineering Design	53202	34479	16681	45554
其他综合技术服务业	Other Polytechnical Services	118938	33350	74613	44258
国家机关、政党机关和社会团体	**Government Organs,Party Organs and Social Bodies**	**426797**	**157050**	**268734**	**426621**
国家机关	Government Organs	398552	136579	261023	398552
政党机关	Party Organs	12840	8595	4245	12840
社会团体	Social Bodies	15404	11876	3465	15228
其他行业	**Other Sectors**	**139574**	**56367**	**46485**	**83324**

3-11 续表 4 continued

				平均工资			
# 中 央 Central	# 地 方 Local	集体企业 Collective-Owned	其他企业 Others	(元) Average Wage (yuan)	国有企业 State-Owned	集体企业 Collective-Owned	其他企业 Others
6875	153575	2111	2061	15330	15272	13428	27437
1571	17935	393	39	13993	13982	15118	10153
4864	108181	1311	2011	15496	15410	12678	28559
6	18293			15861	15861		
120	3591	384		15859	15973	14833	
230	4963	23	11	14916	14938	12017	12616
83	613			16690	16690		
1639	100632		245	13309	13296		22311
1639	100547		225	13311	13297		25614
	84		20	11322	12021		9095
2385	10638	2424		13291	14100	10160	
150	1094	17		13437	13513	9570	
5809	12561	1952	2359	14411	14289	12611	17682
89048	29351	389	4253	17623	17679	12420	16784
8137	4773	49	104	13969	14069	8008	9154
65142	12546	242	809	20402	20336	16239	33304
4499	1961		173	14438	14271		25514
3040	1330			14268	14268		
916	686			15102	15102		
423	5325	2	170	13502	13405	5400	18236
4914	68			11504	11504		
1037	1215	51	1427	18560	20091	11676	16887
938	1448	45	1569	16461	19830	8025	13403
25793	10599	152	870	21396	21462	16841	19773
5998	1936			15708	15708		
5517	1855	54	421	13843	13923	9939	13182
14278	6809	98	450	31966	31897	27194	37151
267976	**65386**	**17336**	**83693**	**16582**	**16131**	**11389**	**20891**
193617	19049	239	194	15439	15450	12027	10856
120169	13229	212	118	15647	15659	12180	11127
10675	839			12943	12943		
62773	4982	27	76	15539	15550	10963	10464
74360	46336	17096	83499	17860	17494	11380	20936
4051	320			16702	16702		
1420	92			12082	12082		
1333	2207	148		16836	16715	20342	
7015	5874	232	956	16201	16078	11494	20333
541				17287	17287		
336	790	269	624	13294	14508	9316	13750
3279	3855	1925	14112	19040	12945	11543	28344
31746	13774	1581	6067	19339	18984	12332	27182
24639	19423	12940	61739	17550	18053	11244	19447
156912	**268709**	**110**	**66**	**14078**	**14078**	**11739**	**17362**
136579	261023			14083	14083		
8595	4245			12505	12505		
11738	3440	110	66	15579	15609	11739	17362
48777	**34231**	**11064**	**45186**	**21726**	**16929**	**17744**	**51418**

3-12 分地区职工人数、平均工资
NUMBER OF STAFF AND WORKERS,AVERAGE WAGE BY REGION

地区	Region	职工人数(人) Staff and Workers (person) 1999	1998	平均工资(元) Average Wage (yuan) 1999	1998
全市	**Total**	**4379854**	**4500635**	**13778**	**12285**
城区	**City Proper**	**1438411**	**1440433**	**14371**	**13155**
东城区	Dongcheng	420837	437364	15410	13462
西城区	Xicheng	589542	580036	15490	13970
崇文区	Chongwen	143293	142699	12698	11432
宣武区	Xuanwu	284739	280334	11492	11908
近郊区	**Near Suburbs**	**2181546**	**2289480**	**14431**	**12523**
朝阳区	Chaoyang	834011	874995	15309	13203
丰台区	Fengtai	334082	382792	11711	10074
石景山区	Shijingshan	290592	296310	11077	10380
海淀区	Haidian	722861	735383	16061	13840
远郊区	**Outer Suburbs**	**482485**	**483070**	**11285**	**10223**
门头沟区	Mentougou	66826	74420	9905	9329
房山区	Fangshan	134203	130831	12922	11764
通州区	Tongzhou	89869	85180	9859	8644
昌平区	Changping	112996	116822	10494	8549
顺义区	Shunyi	78591	75817	9730	9274
各县	**Counties**	**275207**	**285831**	**10892**	**9202**
大兴县	Daxing	109476	108901	11592	10459
平谷县	Pinggu	47726	49464	8937	8027
怀柔县	Huairou	37411	42445	11575	9770
密云县	Miyun	47392	49014	9946	8823
延庆县	Yanqing	33202	36007	10293	8867
外地	**Nonlocal**	**2205**	**1821**	**9656**	**11702**

主要统计指标解释

从业人员 指从事一定社会劳动并取得劳动报酬或经营收入的人员。包括：（1）全部在岗职工（2）再就业的离退休人员（3）私营业主（4）个体户主（5）私营和个体从业人员（6）乡镇企业从业人员（7）农村从业人员（8）其他从业人员（包括民办教师、宗教职业者、现役军人等人事档案关系保留在原单位的人员）

这一指标反映了一定时期内全部劳动力资源的实际利用情况，是研究我国基本国情国力的重要指标。

职工 指在国有经济、城镇集体经济、联营经济、股份合作经济、股份有限公司、有限责任公司、外商和港、澳、台商投资经济、其他经济及其附属机构工作，并由其支付工资或生活费的各类人员。

职工工资总额 指各单位在一定时期内直接支付给本单位全部在岗职工劳动报酬总额和不在岗职工的生活费。

工资总额的计算原则应以直接支付给职工的全部劳动报酬为根据。各单位支付给职工的劳动报酬以及其他根据有关规定支付的工资，不论是计入成本的还是不计入成本的，不论是按国家规定列入计征奖金税项目的，还是未列入计征奖金税项目的，不论是以货币形式支付的还是以实物形式支付的，均包括在工资总额内。

职工平均工资 指企业、事业、机关单位的职工在一定时期内平均每人所得的货币工资额。它表明一定时期职工工资收入的高低程度，是反映职工工资水平的主要指标。计算公式为：

$$\text{职工平均工资}=\frac{\text{报告期实际支付的全部职工工资总额}}{\text{报告期全部职工平均人数}}$$

Explanatory Notes On Main Statistical Indicators

Employment refers to the persons who are engaged in social labor and receive payment or earn business income, including: (1) all staff and workers, (2) re-employed retirees , (3) owners of private enterprises,(4)owners of individual business,(5)employed persons in private enterprises and individual business, (6) employed persons in the township and village enterprises, (7) employed persons in agriculture, (8) other employed persons (including teachers in the schools run by the local people , people engaged in religious profession and the servicemen, etc.) .

This indicator reflects the actual utilization of total labor force during a certain period of time and is often used for the research on China's economic affairs and national power.

Staff and Workers refer to the persons who work in (and receive payment therefrom)enterprises and institutions of state-owned,collective-owned,share holding cooperative,share holding company,limited-liability company, and foreign, Hongkong, Macao, Taiwan funded, and other types of ownership and their affiliated units.

Total Wages of Staff and Workers refer to the total remuneration payment to staff and workers in various units during a certain period of time.

The calculation of total wages is based on the total remuneration payment to the staff and workers. Therefore, all the wages and salaries and other payments to staff and workers are included in the total wages regardless of their sources, categories, and forms (in kind or cash) .

Average Wage of Staff and Workers refers to the average wage in money terms per employed person during a certain period of time for staff and workers in enterprises, institutions and government agencies, which reflects the general level of wage income during a certain period of time, and is calculated as follows:

$$\text{Average Wage of Staff and Workers}=\frac{\text{Total Wages of Staff and Workers}}{\text{Average Number of Staff and Workers}}$$

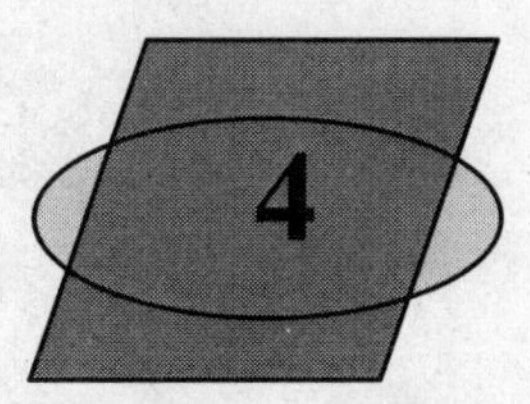

固定资产投资及房地产业
INVESTMENT IN FIXED ASSETS AND REAL ESTATE

城市基础设施投资占全社会固定资产投资比重(1978-1999年)

Ratio of Municipal Infrastructure Investment to Total Investment in Fixed Assets

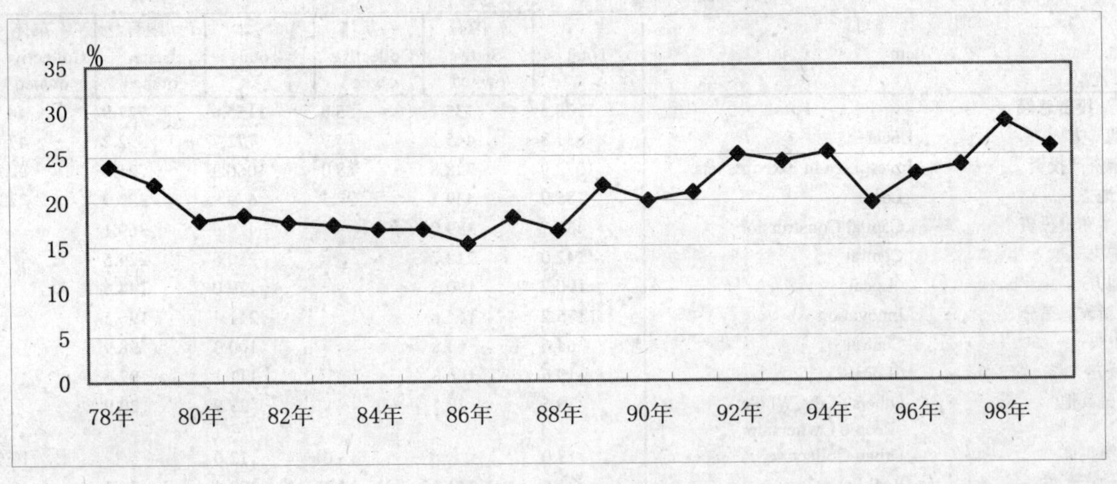

单位:亿元(100 million yuan)

	1999	1998
全社会固定资产投资额 Investment in Fixed Assets	1170.6	1155.6
基本建设 Capital Construction	432.7	429.6
更新改造 Innovation	175.2	211.4
房地产开发 Real Estate Development	421.5	377.4

房屋建筑每平方米造价(元)

Cost Per SQ.M OF Buildings(yuan)

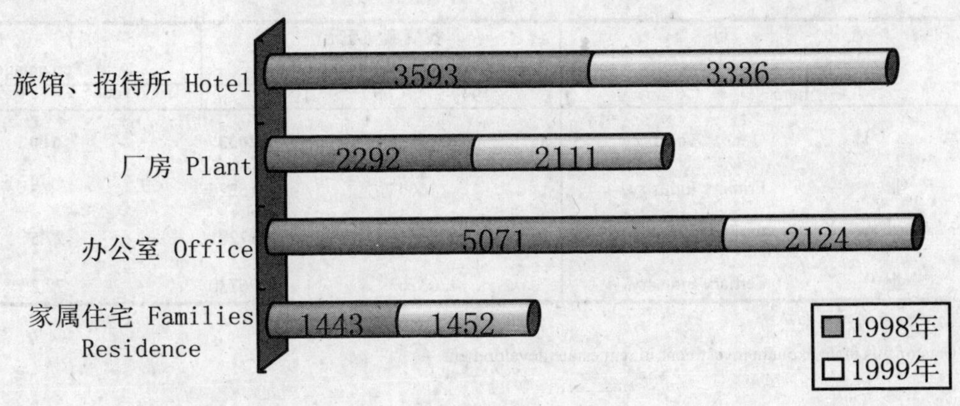

4-1 全社会固定资产投资额
TOTAL INVESTMENT IN FIXED ASSETS

单位: 亿元 (100 million yuan)

项目	Item	1999 合计 Total	1999 # 国有 State-owned	1999 # 集体 Collective-owned	1998 合计 Total	1998 #国有 State-owned	1998 # 集体 Collective-owned
投资总额	**Total**	**1170.6**	**735.7**	**55.8**	**1155.6**	**727.9**	**48.7**
# 地　方	Local	831.8	445.2	54.9	772.7	392.2	47.7
固定资产投资	Investment in Fixed Assets	1072.9	728.8	28.0	1060.3	721.8	22.6
# 地方	Local	735.9	439.7	27.5	679.8	387.9	22.2
基本建设投资	Capital Construction	432.7	389.0		429.6	369.1	
中央	Central	242.0	218.7		250.6	224.5	
地方	Local	190.7	170.3		179.0	144.6	
更新改造措施	Innovation	175.2	164.6		211.4	196.5	
中央	Central	64.6	63.8		100.3	98.9	
地方	Local	110.6	100.8		111.1	97.6	
全民其他	Others of the Whole People Ownership	30.5	30.5		29.9	29.9	
城镇集体	Urban Collective	13.0		13.0	12.0		12.0
房地产开发	Real Estate	421.5	144.7	15.0	377.4	126.3	10.6
# 地方	Local	391.1	138.1	14.5	347.8	115.8	10.2
零星固定资产建造及购置	Building and Purchasse of Odd Fixed Assets	9.0	6.9	2.1	7.9	6.1	1.8
中央	Central	1.8	1.4	0.4	2.4	1.8	0.6
地方	Local	7.2	5.5	1.7	5.5	4.3	1.2
城镇私营、个体投资	Urban Private and Individual	8.2			9.3		
城镇私人建房投资	Urban Personnal House	2.3			2.3		
农村固定资产投资	Rural Investment in Fixed Assets	78.2		25.7	75.8		24.3
非农户固定资产投资	Investment in Fixed Assets Non-agriculture Households	54.8		25.7	58.3		24.3
农户固定资产投资	Investment in Fixed Assets of Agriculture Household	23.4			17.5		
# 私人建房	Individual House	12.5			11.6		

注：1999 年年报国家统计制度对固定资产投资统计范围进行了调整，增加城镇私营、个体投资统计，调整扩大农村固定资产投资统计范围。根据国家统计制度规定，对 1998 年同期数据做相应调整。

Note: According to state statistical rules, statistical range of investment in fixed assets has been adjusted-adding data of urban private and individual units, expanding the range of rural investment and data of 1998 has been made corresponding changes.

4-2 产业投资及比重
INVESTMENT AND PERCENTAGE BY INDUSTRY

项目	Item	投资额（万元） Investment(10000 yuan) 1999	1998	比重（%） Percentage(%) 1999	1998
总　　计	**Total**	**6513968**	**6829237**	**100**	**100**
第一产业	Primary Industry	16647	15226	0.3	0.2
第二产业	Secondary Industry	1793558	2017281	27.5	29.5
第三产业	Tertiary Industry	4703763	4796730	72.2	70.3

注：本表不含房地产开发投资。

Note：Data of this table exclude investment in real estate development.

4-3 全市固定资产投资额
INVESTMENT IN FIXED ASSETS OF THE CITY

单位：万元 (10000 yuan)

项目 Item		1999 合计 Total	1999 # 基本建设 Capital Construction	1999 # 更新改造 Technical Updating and Transformation	1998 合计 Total	1998 # 基本建设 Capital Construction	1998 # 更新改造 Technical Updating and Transformation
投资额	**Total**	**6513968**	**4327251**	**1752093**	**6829237**	**4295514**	**2114549**
按构成分	**Grouped by Use of Fund**						
建筑安装工程	Construction and Installation	4005057	2914124	761921	3761993	2659633	841515
设备工器具购置	Purchases of Equipments and Instrument	1281769	560222	705686	1576605	718836	837479
其他	Others	1227142	852905	284486	1490639	917045	435555
按用途分	**Grouped by User**						
农林牧渔业用	Farming,Forestry, Animal Husbandry and Fishery	6953	6451	502	2037	1435	602
工业、建筑业用	Industry,Construction	1480297	1022237	427910	1682749	1011303	632775
商业、运输邮电业用	Commerce,Transportation,Posts and Tele communications	1268980	419591	546617	1955743	824870	834212
住宅	Residence	1173016	1040232	58954	1060692	843968	162075
其他	Others	2584722	1838740	718110	2128016	1613938	484885
更新改造投资按用途分	**Grouped by Effect of Investment in Innovation**						
增产	Increase Production	126065		126065	206871		206871
节约能源	Economize on Energy	12668		12668	21062		21062
其他节约	Other Economy	2070		2070	933		933
增加品种	Increase Varieties	40554		40554	67400		67400
提高产品质量	Improve Quality of Products	36506		36506	36358		36358
三废治理	Deal with the Three Wastes	139807		139807	51681		51681
其他	Others	1394423		1394423	1730244		1730244
按建设性质分	**Grouped by Feature of Construction**						
新建	New Construction	1596842	1294950	10618	1638524	1337033	27792
改建和扩建	Replacement and Expanding	4093048	2481402	1536248	4483048	2559533	1822482
单纯建造生活设施	Living Installation	573259	480117	36560	535909	363517	131870
迁建和恢复	Movement and Recovery	103995	65063	34830	103155	32235	67990
单纯购置设备	Purchase of Equipment	146824	5719	133837	68601	3196	64415

4-3 续表 continued

单位：万元 (10000 yuan)

项目	Item	1999			1998		
		合计 Total	# 基本建设 Capital Construction	# 更新改造 Technical Updating and Transformation	合计 Total	# 基本建设 Capital Construction	# 更新改造 Technical Updating and Transformation
按建设项目规模分	**Grouped by Size of Construction Projects**						
基本建设大中型项目	Large and Medium Projects of Capital Construction	774239	774239		966960	966960	
基本建设小型项目	Small Projects of Capital Construction	3547293	3547293		3325358	3325358	
更新改造限额以上项目	Projects of Technical Updating and Transformation above the Limits	744704		744704	871472		871472
更新改造限额以下项目	Projects of Technical Updating and Transformation below the Limits	873552		873552	1178662		1178662
其他	Others	574180	5719	133837	486785	3196	64415
按企业登记注册类型分	**Grouped by Type of Enterprises Registered**						
内资企业	Domestic Investment Enterprises	6091450	3945320	1711506	6182845	3753087	2010584
国有企业	State-Owned	5840694	3890475	1645550	5955574	3690991	1965022
集体企业	Collective Owned	129955			119613		
联营企业	Joint Owned	3531	3531		13542	9519	4023
股份合作企业	Share Holding Cooperative	17477	9951	7526	9008	9008	
股份有限公司	Share Holding Company	75301	27384	47917	54083	29250	24833
有限责任公司	Limited-Liability Company	24492	13979	10513	26543	14099	12444
其他企业	Others				4482	220	4262
港澳台商投资企业	Hongkong,Macao and Taiwan Funded Enterprises	243556	235279	8277	313090	282522	30568
港澳台合资经营	Joint Venture	93003	86806	6197	196402	168139	28263
港澳台合作经营	Cooperative	138083	138003	80	108825	106520	2305
港澳台商独资企业	Hongkong, Macao and Taiwan Enterprises	10470	10470		7863	7863	
港澳台商投资股份有限公司	Hongkong,Macao and Taiwan Funded Share Holing Company	2000		2000			
外商投资企业	Foreign Funded Enterprises	178962	146652	32310	333302	259905	73397
中外合资经营	Joint Venture	157469	125257	32212	289371	215974	73397
中外合作经营	Cooperative	4787	4787		33138	33138	
外资(独资)企业	Foreign Enterprises	15580	15580		10703	10703	
外商投资股份有限公司	Foreign Funded Share Holding Company	1126	1028	98	90	90	

注：本表及以下各表包括基本建设、更新改造和其他投资，不含房地产开发投资。

Note: This table and its followings include capital constrution,technical updating and transformation and other investment, exclude real estate development investment.

4-4 地方固定资产投资额
LOCAL INVESTMENT IN FIXED ASSETS

单位：万元 (10000 yuan)

项目 Item		1999 合计 Total	1999 #基本建设 Capital Construction	1999 #更新改造 Technical Updating and Transformation	1998 合计 Total	1998 #基本建设 Capital Construction	1998 #更新改造 Technical Updating and Transformation
投资额	**Total**	**3447454**	**1907191**	**1105639**	**3319283**	**1788958**	**1111151**
按构成分	**Grouped by Use of Fund**						
建筑安装工程	Construction and Installation	2207536	1311404	567120	1922198	1092767	568586
设备工器具购置	Purchases of Equipments and Instrument	485490	166200	303429	404721	182455	201976
其他	Others	754428	429587	235090	992364	513736	340589
按用途分	**Grouped by User**						
农林牧渔业用	Farming,Forestry, Animal Husbandry and Fishery	6953	6451	502	2037	1435	602
工业、建筑业用	Industry,Construction	732267	396362	305755	879966	462130	379165
商业、运输邮电业用	Commerce,Transportation,Posts and Tele communications	574675	198463	73440	683937	256032	131244
住宅	Residence	436896	323831	39235	486580	289902	142029
其他	Others	1696663	982084	686707	1266763	779459	458111
更新改造投资按用途分	**Grouped by Effect of Investment in Innovation**						
增产	Increase Production	98680		98680	144143		144143
节约能源	Economize on Energy	10495		10495	17690		17690
其他节约	Other Economy	2056		2056	883		883
增加品种	Increase Varieties	35595		35595	38037		38037
提高产品质量	Improve Quality of Products	27802		27802	27850		27850
三废治理	Deal with the Three Wastes	112456		112456	39129		39129
其他	Others	818555		818555	843419		843419
按建设性质分	**Grouped by Feature of Construction**						
新建	New Construction	1264448	963044	10130	1150287	848896	27692
改建和扩建	Replacement and Expanding	1719280	713070	930812	1712959	759073	852853
单纯建造生活设施	Living Installation	298943	209992	32369	332444	163757	128165
迁建和恢复	Movement and Recovery	58090	19158	34830	88027	17107	67990
单纯购置设备	Purchase of Equipment	106693	1927	97498	35566	125	34451

4-4 续表 continued

单位：万元 (10000 yuan)

项目	Item	1999 合计 Total	1999 # 基本建设 Capital Construction	1999 # 更新改造 Technical Updating and Transformation	1998 合计 Total	1998 # 基本建设 Capital Construction	1998 # 更新改造 Technical Updating and Transformation
按建设项目规模分	**Grouped by Size of Construction Projects**						
基本建设大中型项目	Large and Medium Projects of Capital Construction	403065	403065		403688	403688	
基本建设小型项目	Small Projects of Capital Construction	1502199	1502199		1385145	1385145	
更新改造限额以上项目	Projects of Technical Updating and Transformation above the Limits	664089		664089	683723		683723
更新改造限额以下项目	Projects of Technical Updating and Transformation below the Limits	344052		344052	392977		392977
其他	Others	534049	1927	97498	453750	125	34451
按企业登记注册类型分	**Grouped by Type of Enterprises Registered**						
内资企业	Domestic Investment Enterprises	3258035	1757424	1065987	2938224	1507189	1011861
国有企业	State-Owned	3015453	1703227	1007557	2720959	1445603	975795
集体企业	Collective Owned	129955			119613		
联营企业	Joint Owned	3531	3531		13542	9519	4023
股份合作企业	Share Holding Cooperative	9951	9951		9008	9008	
股份有限公司	Share Holding Company	75301	27384	47917	48719	29250	19469
有限责任公司	Limited-Liability Company	23844	13331	10513	21901	13589	8312
其他企业	Others				4482	220	4262
港澳台商投资企业	Hongkong,Macao and Taiwan Funded Enterprises	95655	87378	8277	192595	162027	30568
港澳台合资经营	Joint Venture	36197	30000	6197	158858	130595	28263
港澳台合作经营	Cooperative	46988	46908	80	25874	23569	2305
港澳台商独资企业	Hongkong,Macao and Taiwan Enterprises	10470	10470		7863	7863	
港澳台商投资股份有限公司	Hongkong,Macao and Taiwan Funded Share Holing Company	2000		2000			
外商投资企业	Foreign Funded Enterprises	93764	62389	31375	188464	119742	68722
中外合资经营	Joint Venture	73501	42224	31277	164196	95474	68722
中外合作经营	Cooperative	4057	4057		13475	13475	
外资(独资)企业	Foreign Enterprises	15580	15580		10703	10703	
外商投资股份有限公司	Foreign Funded Share Holding Company	626	528	98	90	90	

4-5 固定资产投资财务拨贷款额
FINANCIAL ALLOCATIONS AND LOANS FOR INVESTMENT IN FIXED ASSETS

单位：万元 (10000 yuan)

项目	Item	1999 合计 Total	1999 # 基本建设 Capital Construction	1999 # 更新改造 Technical Updating and Transformation	1998 合计 Total	1998 # 基本建设 Capital Construction	1998 # 更新改造 Technical Updating and Transformation
上年末结余资金	**Balance of Last Year-end**	**1015427**	**837265**	**150039**	**870327**	**630079**	**223560**
本年拨款贷款	**Allocations and Loans in this Year**	**6575841**	**4488073**	**1712951**	**6693722**	**4379728**	**1900022**
国家预算内资金	State Budgetary Appropriation	1356504	1175077	170927	938629	866744	61885
国内贷款	Domestic Loans	969362	650658	161034	1084327	634527	282266
债　券	Bonds				158300	58500	92100
利用外资	Foreign Capital	344867	239544	105323	412267	368558	43709
自筹资金	Self-raised Funds	3590697	2148398	1248068	3829243	2263449	1349604
# 股票	Stocks	35411	3533	31878	33445	10555	22890
其他资金	Others	314411	274396	27599	270956	187950	70458

4-6 地方固定资产投资财务拨贷款额
FINANCIAL ALLOCATIONS AND LOANS FOR LOCAL INVESTMENT IN FIXED ASSETS

单位：万元 (10000 yuan)

项目	Item	1999 合计 Total	1999 # 基本建设 Capital Construction	1999 # 更新改造 Technical Updating and Transformation	1998 合计 Total	1998 # 基本建设 Capital Construction	1998 # 更新改造 Technical Updating and Transformation
上年末结余资金	**Balance of Last Year-end**	**507037**	**350408**	**128506**	**507213**	**281241**	**209284**
本年拨款贷款	**Allocations and Loans in this Year**	**3485301**	**1971159**	**1139325**	**3125718**	**1713441**	**998305**
国家预算内资金	State Budgetary Appropriation	468305	301639	156166	150522	81055	59467
国内贷款	Domestic Loans	585946	302769	125507	699271	376889	154848
债　券	Bonds				144300	44500	92100
利用外资	Foreign Capital	220315	131487	88828	202024	172457	29567
自筹资金	Self-raised Funds	1957320	1020147	742942	1708746	897246	595310
# 股票	Stocks	33555	3130	30425	33445	10555	22890
其他资金	Others	253415	215117	25882	220855	141294	67013

4-7 城市基础设施投资额
MUNICIPAL INFRASTRUCTURE INVESTMENT

项目	Item	投资额（万元）Investment(10000 yuan) 全市 Total	# 地方 Local	比重(%) Proportion(%) 全市 Total	# 地方 Local
全市总计	**Total**	**3027479**	**1819276**	**100**	**100**
能源	**Energy**	**902759**	**335301**	**29.8**	**18.4**
电力	Electricity	586213	18755	19.3	1.0
供热	Heat	111455	111455	3.7	6.1
供气	Gas	102815	102815	3.4	5.7
供水	Water	102276	102276	3.4	5.6
公共服务业	**Public Services**	**928195**	**928195**	**30.7**	**51.0**
市内公共交通	Public Traffic	207461	207461	6.9	11.4
# 市内公交电汽车	Buses and Trolleys	76792	76792	2.5	4.2
出租汽车	Taxies	387	387	…	…
园林绿化	Parks and Green Areas	54300	54300	1.8	3.0
环境卫生	Environmental Sanitation	19884	19884	0.7	1.1
市政工程管理	Municipal Construction	646550	646550	21.4	35.5
其他公共服务业	Others				
交通运输	**Transportation**	**422583**	**321376**	**14.0**	**17.7**
铁路	Railway				
公路	Highway	300771	300771	9.9	16.5
管道运输	Pipeline				
航空	Aviation	800	800	…	…
其他	Others	121012	19805	4.0	1.1
邮政电信	**PostsandTelecommunications**	**539616**	**190**	**17.8**	**…**
邮政	Posts	3603		0.1	
电信	Telecommunications	536013	190	17.7	…
其他	**Others**	**234326**	**234214**	**7.7**	**12.9**
水利	Water Conservancy	117270	117270	3.9	6.4
环境保护	Environmental Protection	88524	88524	2.9	4.9
其他	Others	28532	28420	0.9	1.6

4-8 能源及交通投资额
INVESTMENT IN ENERGY AND TRANSPORTATION

单位：万元 (10000 yuan)

项目	Item	全市 Total 1999	1998	# 地方 Local 1999	1998
全市固定资产投资总额	**Investment in Fixed Assets of the City**	**6513968**	**6829237**	**3447454**	**3319283**
# 能源、交通投资额	Investment in Energy and Transportation	2041641	2660138	637311	711610
占全市投资额比重 (%)	Proportion (%)	31.3	39.0	18.5	21.4
能源投资额	Investment in Energy	959216	961932	275314	256810
占全市投资额比重 (%)	Proportion (%)	14.7	14.1	8.0	7.7
运输、邮电投资额	Investment in Transportation, Posts and Telecommunications	1082425	1698206	361997	454800
占全市投资额比重 (%)	Proportion (%)	16.6	24.9	10.5	13.7
在能源投资中	Of the Investment in Energy				
煤(国家统配煤矿)	Coal(State Collieries)	4113	5197	4113	5197
电(公用电厂及小水电)	Electricity(Public Power Plants and Hydropower Stations)	599915	577305	19713	30762
油品(炼油厂原油加工)	Oil Products(Crude Oil Processing of Refinery)	108708	162485	5008	3906
燃料气(液化石油气、焦炉煤气)	Fuel Gas(Liquefied Petroleum Gas,Gas)	101718	72200	101718	72200
热气(公用局)	Heat(Public Utilities Bureau)	144762	144745	144762	144745
在运输投资中	**Of Investment in Transportation**				
铁路	Railway	35472	107309		
公路	Highway	332676	432313	332676	432043
航空	Aviation	15339	20649	850	
邮政、电信	Posts and Telecommunications	568966	827231	4696	3703
交通运输辅助业	Logistic Support for Transportation	129972	310704	23775	19054

4-9 施工及投入生产(或交付使用)的项目数
NUMBER OF PROJECTS UNDER CONSTRUCTION AND PRODUCTION (OR PUT INTO OPERATION)

单位：个 (unit)

项目	Item	全市 Total 1999	1998	#地方 Local 1999	1998
全市施工项目	**Total Projects under Construction**	**2878**	**3213**	**1596**	**1675**
# 本年新开工	Begin Construction this Year	1406	1658	809	779
全部竣工投产项目	Total Projects Completed	1474	1607	852	801
建设项目投产率（%）	the Projects under Construction as a Percentage of Total Projects (%)	51.2	50.0	53.4	47.8
基本建设施工项目	**Capital Construction Projects**	**1194**	**1261**	**729**	**714**
# 本年新开工	Begin Construction this Year	426	457	327	320
全部竣工投产项目	Total Projects Completed	438	415	315	294
建设项目投产率（%）	the Projects under Construction as a Percentage of Total Projects (%)	36.7	32.9	43.2	41.2
更新改造措施施工项目	**Projects of Innovation and Replacement**	**1558**	**1806**	**741**	**815**
# 本年新开工	Begin Construction this Year	927	1131	429	389
全部竣工投产项目	Total Projects Completed	965	1108	466	423
建设项目投产率（%）	the Projects under Construction as a Percentage of Total Projects (%)	61.9	61.4	62.9	51.9
其他投资施工项目	**Other Projects under Construction**	**126**	**146**	**126**	**146**
# 本年新开工	Begin Construction this Year	53	70	53	70
全部竣工投产项目	Total Projects Completed	71	84	71	84
建设项目投产率（%）	the Projects under Construction as a Percentage of Total Projects (%)	56.3	57.5	56.3	57.5

4-10 全市固定资产投资额及新增固定资产(按行业分)

TOTAL INVESTMENT IN FIXED ASSETS AND INCREMENTAL FIXED ASSETS (BY SECTOR)

单位：万元 (10000 yuan)

行业	Item	投资额 Investment			新增固定资产 Incremental Fixed Assets		
		合计 Total	中央 Central	地方 Local	合计 Total	中央 Central	地方 Local
总计	**Total**	**6513968**	**3066514**	**3447454**	**5697763**	**2833733**	**2864030**
农、林、牧、渔业	**Farming,Forestry,AnimalHusbandry and Fishery**	**24399**	**1651**	**22748**	**19737**		**19737**
农业	Farming	13156		13156	12423		12423
林业	Forestry	3389		3389	1123		1123
渔业	Fishery	102		102	140		140
淡水渔业	Freshwater Fishery	102		102	140		140
农、林、牧、渔服务业	FFAF Services	7752	1651	6101	6051		6051
采掘业	**Excavation**	**23734**		**23734**	**16860**		**16860**
煤炭采选业	Coal Mining and Dressing	4113		4113	2936		2936
黑色金属矿采选业	Ferrous Metals Mining and Dressing	19153		19153	13694		13694
铁矿采选业	Iron Mining and Dressing	19153		19153	13694		13694
非金属矿采选业	Nonmetal Minerals Mining and Dressing	468		468	230		230
土砂石开采业	Sand and Stone Mining and Dressing	468		468	230		230
制造业	**Manufacturing**	**697814**	**270905**	**426909**	**807702**	**244088**	**563614**
食品加工业	Food Processing	7102		7102	8480		8480
粮食及饲料加工业	Grain and Feed	3514		3514	3713		3713
植物油加工业	Vegetable Oil	333		333	312		312
屠宰及肉类蛋类加工业	Butcher, Meat and Egg	3255		3255	4455		4455
食品制造业	Food Making	6442		6442	9660		9660
糕点、糖果制造业	Pastry and Candy	200		200	200		200
乳制品制造业	Dairy Products	2996		2996	8272		8272
调味品制造业	Flavorings	2678		2678	700		700
其他食品制造业	Other Foods	568		568	488		488
饮料制造业	Beverage Production	6900		6900	21988		21988
酒精及饮料酒制造业	Alcohol and Beverage Wine	6900		6900	21988		21988
纺织业	Textile Industry	11607		11607	10658		10658
棉纺织业	Cotton Textile	6622		6622	9267		9267
毛纺织业	Woolen Textile	379		379			
针织品业	Knitting Textile	4513		4513	1298		1298
其他纺织业	Others	93		93	93		93
服装及其他纤维制品制造业	Garments and Other Fiber Products	3058		3058	1819		1819
服装制造业	Garment Industry	2857		2857	1618		1618
制鞋业	Shoes Making	201		201	201		201
皮革、毛皮、羽绒及其制品业	Leather,Furs,Down and Related Products	3574		3574	1591		1591
制革业	Leather Making	713		713			
皮革制品制造业	Leathers and Related Products	2861		2861	1591		1591
木材加工及竹、藤、棕、草制品业	Timber Processing,Bamboo, Cane,Palm Fiber and Straw Products	1924		1924	1159		1159
人造板制造业	Artificial Board Manufacturing	1924		1924	1159		1159

4-10 续表 1 continued

单位：万元 (10000 yuan)

行业	Item	投资额 Investment 合计 Total	中央 Central	地方 Local	新增固定资产 Incremental Fixed Assets 合计 Total	中央 Central	地方 Local
家具制造业	Furniture Industry	8164		8164	15715		15715
木制家具制造业	Wooden Furniture	5639		5639	15715		15715
其他家具制造业	Other Furniture	2525		2525			
造纸及纸制品业	Papermaking and Paper Products	2228		2228	14685		14685
纸浆制造业	Paper Pulp	900		900	300		300
纸制品业	Paper Products	1328		1328	14385		14385
印刷业、记录媒介的复制	Printing and Record Medium Reproduced	25475	14174	11301	15542	13305	2237
印刷业	Printing	24888	13587	11301	15542	13305	2237
记录媒介的复制	Record Medium Reproduced	587	587				
文教体育用品制造业	Stationery,Education and Sports Goods	6405		6405	6620		6620
文化用品制造业	Stationery	5318		5318			
乐器及其他文娱用品制造业	Music Instruments and Other Stationery Goods	1087		1087	6620		6620
石油加工及炼焦业	Petroleum Processing and Coking Products	108708	103700	5008	143889	140452	3437
原油加工业	Petroleum Processing	101597	101597		139840	139840	
石油制品业	Petroleum Products	2160	2103	57	1222	612	610
炼焦业	Coking Products	4951		4951	2827		2827
化学原料及化学制品制造业	Raw Chemical Materials and Chemical Products	104688	80485	24203	123673	22144	101529
基本化学原料制造业	Elementary Raw Chemical Materials	2350		2350	666		666
化学肥料制造业	Chemical Fertilizer	326		326	2198		2198
有机化学产品制造业	Organic Chemical Products	20752	12984	7768	85779	13464	72315
合成材料制造业	Synthetic Materials	68231	67501	730	9920	8680	1240
专用化学产品制造业	Special Purpose Chemical Products	7109		7109	23710		23710
日用化学产品制造业	Daily Use Chemical Products	5920		5920	1400		1400
医药制造业	Medical and Pharmaceutical Products	30301	2699	27602	9933	3414	6519
化学药品制剂制造业	Original Chemical Medicine	22794	730	22064	6369		6369
中药材及中成药加工	Raw Material and Products of Chinese Medicine	3381		3381			
生物制品业	Biological Products	4126	1969	2157	3564	3414	150
化学纤维制造业	Chemical Fiber Manufacturing	140	140		140	140	
合成纤维制造业	Synthetic Fibers	140	140		140	140	
橡胶制品业	Rubber Products	2609		2609	1994		1994
轮胎制造业	Tire Manufacturing	2066		2066	1451		1451
日用橡胶制品业	Daily-use Products	543		543	543		543
塑料制品业	Plastic Products	7665		7665	4680		4680
塑料薄膜制造业	Plastic Film	1872		1872	85		85
泡沫塑料及人造革、合成革制造业	Foamed Plastics,Imitation Leather and Synthetic Leather	4920		4920	2683		2683
其他塑料制品业	Other Plastic Products	873		873	1912		1912
非金属矿物制品业	Nonmetal Mineral Products	37174	3026	34148	30986	1220	29766
水泥制造业	Cement Manufacturing	5954	1112	4842	4895	1112	3783

4-10 续表 2 continued

单位：万元 (10000 yuan)

行业	Item	投资额 Investment 合计 Total	中央 Central	地方 Local	新增固定资产 Incremental Fixed Assets 合计 Total	中央 Central	地方 Local
水泥制品和石棉水泥制品业	Cement and Asbestos Products	5864	158	5706	5137	108	5029
砖瓦、石灰和轻质建筑材料制造业	Brick,Tile and Light Construction Material	16412	1756	14656	10155		10155
玻璃及玻璃制品业	Glass and Glass Products	8744		8744	10616		10616
陶瓷制品业	Ceramics Products	85		85	85		85
耐火材料制品业	Refractory Products	115		115	98		98
黑色金属冶炼及压延加工业	Smelting and Pressing Ferrous Metals	39189		39189	26060		26060
炼铁业	Iron-smelting	1246		1246	8421		8421
钢压延加工业	Steel Pressing	37615		37615	17536		17536
铁合金冶炼业	Alloy Iron Smelting	328		328	103		103
有色金属冶炼及压延加工业	Smelting and Pressing of Nonferrous Metals	2466		2466	120		120
有色金属压延加工业	Nonferrous Metals Pressing	2466		2466	120		120
金属制品业	Metal Products	7367		7367	9516		9516
金属结构制造业	Metal Structure	528		528	618		618
铸铁管制造业	Tube of Cast Iron	149		149	149		149
工具制造业	Tools Manufacturing	300		300	300		300
集装箱和金属包装物品制造业	Container and Metal Cover Manufacturing	352		352			
建筑用金属制品业	Products for Construct Use	5758		5758	8169		8169
日用金属制品业	Daily Metal Products	280		280	280		280
普通机械制造业	Ordinary Machine-building	23469	1770	21699	11739	2550	9189
锅炉及原动机制造业	Boiler and Motive Machine	11796	1770	10026	3460	2550	910
金属加工机械制造业	Metal Processing Machine	5521		5521	3237		3237
通用设备制造业	Universal Equipment	464		464			
其他通用零部件制造业	Other Universal Components and Parts	5688		5688	5042		5042
专用设备制造业	Special Purpose Equipment Building	42746	5343	37403	52214	12049	40165
机电工业专用设备制造业	Equipment for Engine and Electricity	3228	2337	891	8996	8873	123
石化及其他工业专用设备制造业	Equipment for Petroleum and Other Sector of Industry	14314	2636	11678	10396	2636	7760
农、林、牧、渔,水利业机械制造业	Machines for Farming,Forestry,Animal Husbandry,Fishing and Irrigation	11708		11708	24511		24511
医疗器械制造业	Medical Machines	6651		6651	4727		4727
其他专用设备制造业	Other Special Purpose Equipment	6845	370	6475	3584	540	3044
交通运输设备制造业	Transportation Equipment Manufacturing	75583	45228	30355	143412	41175	102237
铁路运输设备制造业	Railway Transportation Equipment	9633	8401	1232	8870	7638	1232
汽车制造业	Motor Vehicles	26626		26626	98731		98731
航空航天器制造业	Aviation and Spaceflight Equipment	35892	35892		32945	32945	
交通运输设备修理业	Transportation Equipment Repairing	2916	935	1981	2350	592	1758

4-10 续表 3 continued

单位：万元 (10000 yuan)

行业	Item	投资额 Investment 合计 Total	中央 Central	地方 Local	新增固定资产 Incremental Fixed Assets 合计 Total	中央 Central	地方 Local
其他交通运输设备制造业	Other Transportation Equipment Manufacturing	516		516	516		516
武器弹药制造业	Weapon and Ammunition Manufacturing	3550	3550		970	970	
电气机械及器材制造业	Electric Equipment and Appliances Manufacturing	18235		18235	14704		14704
电机制造业	Generator	1170		1170	1145		1145
输配电及控制设备制造业	Electricity Transmit,Distribution and Control Equipment	5374		5374	1845		1845
电工器材制造业	Electrical Appliances	328		328	273		273
日用电器制造业	Daily Use Electrical Appliances	11363		11363	11441		11441
电子及通信设备制造业	Electronic and Telecommunication Equipment	83344	10220	73124	69772	6501	63271
通信设备制造业	Telecommunication Equipment	25310	5474	19836	28677	6381	22296
广播电视设备制造业	Radio and Television Equipment	1246		1246	469		469
电子计算机制造业	Computer	18949	4626	14323	11605		11605
电子器件制造业	Electronic Device	16746		16746	5575		5575
电子元件制造业	Electronic Cell	15026		15026	19873		19873
日用电子器具制造业	Daily Use Electronic Appliances	3015		3015	3043		3043
其他电子设备制造业	Other Electronic Machines	3052	120	2932	530	120	410
仪器仪表及文化、办公用机械制造业	Instruments,Meters,Cultural and Official Machinery	22810	570	22240	44815	168	44647
通用仪器仪表制造	General Instruments and Meters	14329	570	13759	22237	168	22069
电子测量仪器制造业	Electronic Survey Instrument	1253		1253	2118		2118
其他仪器仪表制造业	Other Instruments and Meters	1382		1382	150		150
计量器具制造业	Measuring Implements	5846		5846	20310		20310
其他制造业	Other Manufacturing	4891		4891	11168		11168
工艺美术品制造业	Art Products Manufacturing	488		488			
其他生产、生活用品制造业	Others	4403		4403	11168		11168
电力、煤气及水的生产和供应业	**Electricity,Gas and Water Production and Supply**	**944524**	**580202**	**364322**	**874369**	**644655**	**229714**
电力、蒸气、热水的生产和供应业	Electricity,Steam and Hot Water Production and Supply	744677	580202	164475	802432	644655	157777
电力生产业	Electricity Production	147824	146163	1661	395362	394351	1011
电力供应业	Electricity Supply	452091	434039	18052	257811	250304	7507
蒸气、热水生产和供应业	Steam and Hot Water Production and Supply	144762		144762	149259		149259
煤气生产和供应业	Gas Production and Supply	101718		101718	45866		45866
煤气生产业	Gas Production	1		1	6000		6000
煤气供应业	Gas Supply	101717		101717	39866		39866
自来水的生产和供应业	Water Production and Supply	98129		98129	26071		26071
自来水生产业	Water Production	94760		94760	23510		23510
自来水供应业	Water Supply	3369		3369	2561		2561
建筑业	**Construction**	**127486**	**54375**	**73111**	**92808**	**36179**	**56629**
土木工程建筑业	Civil Engineering Construct	121826	49275	72551	88668	32079	56589
房屋建筑业	Building Construction	111719	40072	71647	77317	22312	55005
铁路、公路、遂道、桥梁建筑业	Railways,Highways,Tunnels and Bridges Construction	9375	9063	312	9819	9507	312
堤坝、电站、码头建筑业	Dikes and Dams,Power Station and Wharves	592		592	1272		1272
其他土木工程建筑业	Other Civil Engineering Construction	140	140		260	260	
线路、管道和设备安装业	Line and Equipments Installation	5660	5100	560	4140	4100	40

4-10 续表 4 continued

单位：万元 (10000 yuan)

行业	Item	投资额 Investment 合计 Total	中央 Central	地方 Local	新增固定资产 Incremental Fixed Assets 合计 Total	中央 Central	地方 Local
线路、管道安装业	Line Installation	3300	3300		4100	4100	
设备安装业	Equipment Installation	2360	1800	560	40		40
地质勘查业、水利管理业	**Geological Prospecting and Water Conservancy**	**133460**	**1544**	**131916**	**28628**	**1540**	**27088**
地质勘查业	Geological Prospecting	949	949		1540	1540	
海洋地质勘察业	Sea Prospecting	200	200				
矿产地质勘查业	Minerals Prospecting	360	360		830	830	
地球物理和地球化学勘察业	Geophysical and Geochemical Prospecting	389	389		710	710	
水利管理业	Water Conservancy	132511	595	131916	27088		27088
交通运输、仓储及邮电通信业	**Transportation,Storage,Posts and Telecommunications**	**1123333**	**730929**	**392404**	**790490**	**668889**	**121601**
铁路运输业	Railways	35472	35472		30536	30536	
公路运输业	Highways	332676		332676	61595		61595
汽车运输业	Motor Vehicles	332676		332676	61595		61595
航空运输业	Aviations	15339	14489	850	12987	12987	
航空客货运输业	Passenger and Freight Transportation	14489	14489		12987	12987	
通用航空业	Universal Aviation	850		850			
交通运输辅助业	Logistic Support for Transportation	129972	106197	23775	29877	9680	20197
公路管理及养护业	Highway Management and Maintenance	20635		20635	14057		14057
机场及航空运输辅助业	Airport and Logistics of Aviation	109337	106197	3140	15820	9680	6140
仓储业	Storage	40908	10501	30407	33992	1430	32562
邮电通信业	Posts and Telecommunications	568966	564270	4696	621503	614256	7247
邮政业	Posts	8457	8457		7005	7005	
电信业	Telecommunications	556121	555813	308	608173	607251	922
邮电业	Posts and Telecommunications	4388		4388	6325		6325
批发和零售贸易餐饮业	**Wholesale,Retail and Catering**	**109081**	**16438**	**92643**	**100314**	**15353**	**84961**
食品、饮料、烟草和家庭用品批发业	Wholesale of Food,Beverage, Tabacco and Family Use Goods	33827	5959	27868	22780	7263	15517
食品、饮料、烟草批发业	Food,Beverage and Tabacco	14922	4167	10755	7893		7893
棉麻土畜产品批发业	Cotton,Fiber,Local and Animal Products	67		67	335		335
纺织品、服装和鞋帽批发业	Textile,Garments,Shoes and Hats	4005		4005	3880		3880
日用百货批发业	Daily Use Goods	9064		9064	311		311
五金交电化工批发业	Hardware,Electrical Appliance and Chemical	5669	1792	3877	10095	7263	2832
药品及医疗器械批发业	Medicine and Medical Appliance	100		100	266		266
能源、材料、机械和电子设备批发业	Wholesale of Energy,Materials Machine and Electronic Equipment	15099	903	14196	15986	1305	14681
能源批发业	Energy	7562	50	7512	8502		8502
化工材料批发业	Chemical Materials	590		590			
建筑材料批发业	Building Materials	3005		3005	3093		3093
金属材料批发业	Ferrous Materials	465		465	402		402
机械、电子设备批发业	Machine and Electronic Equipment	2193	853	1340	1305	1305	
汽车、摩托车及零配件批发业	Automobile,Motorcycle and Spares and Fittings	184		184	184		184
再生物资回收批发业	Recovery of Reclaimed Materials	1100		1100	2500		2500
其他批发业	Other Wholesales	8176	5016	3160	6785	6785	
图书报刊批发业	Books,Newspaper and Magazines	316	316				

4-10 续表 5 continued

单位：万元 (10000 yuan)

行业	Item	投资额 Investment			新增固定资产 Incremental Fixed Assets		
		合计 Total	中央 Central	地方 Local	合计 Total	中央 Central	地方 Local
农业生产资料批发业	Agricultural Capital Goods	3160		3160			
其他类未包括的批发	Others	4700	4700		6785	6785	
零售业	Retail	38729	560	38169	47753		47753
食品、饮料和烟草零售业	Food,Beverage and Tabacco	3760		3760	1871		1871
日用百货零售业	Daily Use Goods	27012	560	26452	38308		38308
纺织品、服装和鞋帽零售业	Textile,Garments,Shoes and Hats	991		991	930		930
五金交电化工零售业	Hardware,Electrical Appliance and Chemical	517		517	900		900
图书报刊零售业	Books,Newspaper and Magazines	252		252	252		252
其他零售业	Others	6197		6197	5492		5492
商业经纪与代理业	Business Agencies	7942	4000	3942	6300		6300
餐饮业	Catering	5308		5308	710		710
正餐	Dinner	5308		5308	710		710
金融、保险业	**Banking and Insurance**	**89370**	**88503**	**867**	**9590**	**8173**	**1417**
金融业	Banking	89254	88387	867	9590	8173	1417
中央银行	Central Bank	1183	1183		1263	1263	
商业银行	Commercial Bank	78041	78041				
其他银行	Other Banks	4910	4910		6910	6910	
信用合作社	Credit Cooperative	867		867	1417		1417
其他非银行金融业	Other Non-bank Banking	4253	4253				
保险业	Insurance	116	116				
房地产业	**Real Estate**	**22748**	**1000**	**21748**	**27961**		**27961**
房地产管理业	Management	22748	1000	21748	27961		27961
社会服务业	**Social Services**	**1234254**	**81167**	**1153087**	**1181631**	**177982**	**1003649**
公共服务业	Public Services	1034637		1034637	922793		922793
市内公共交通业	Urban Public Traffic	233625		233625	96378		96378
园林绿化业	Gardens Afforest	99258		99258	47753		47753
环境卫生业	Environmental Sanitation	25495		25495	26746		26746
市政工程管理业	Municipal Engineering Management	676259		676259	751916		751916
居民服务业	Personal Services	21881		21881	7967		7967
沐浴业	Bath	3410		3410			
殡葬业	Funeral and Interment Services	6471		6471	1967		1967
其他居民服务业	Others	12000		12000	6000		6000
旅馆业	Hotels	71075	8164	62911	65866	14348	51518
租赁服务业	Rentals	2532	2332	200	22133	22133	
旅游业	Tourism	10174	107	10067	850		850
娱乐服务业	Recreation	18643	13054	5589	38346	35535	2811
信息、咨询服务业	Information and Consultancy	4689		4689	1855		1855
咨询服务业	Consultancy Services	1474		1474			
其他类未包括的信息咨询服务业	Others	3215		3215	1855		1855
计算机应用服务业	Computer Application	13779	2673	11106	17134	2166	14968
软件开发咨询业	Software Development Consultancy	13779	2673	11106	17134	2166	14968
其他社会服务业	Other Social Services	56844	54837	2007	104687	103800	887
市场管理服务业	Market Management	2007		2007	887		887
其他类未包括的社会服务业	Others	54837	54837		103800	103800	
卫生体育和社会福利业	**Health Care,Sports and Social Welfare**	**86503**	**37383**	**49120**	**98897**	**64107**	**34790**
卫生	Health Care	72882	35491	37391	94141	64107	30034

4-10 续表 6 continued

单位：万元 (10000 yuan)

行业	Item	投资额 Investment			新增固定资产 Incremental Fixed Assets		
		合计 Total	中央 Central	地方 Local	合计 Total	中央 Central	地方 Local
医院	Hospitals	69345	35491	33854	92001	64107	27894
卫生防疫站	Sanitation and Antiepidemic Stations	1284		1284	580		580
妇幼保健所(站)	Maternity and Child Care Institutions	732		732	1560		1560
其他医院	Other Hospitals	1521		1521			
体育	Sports	10710	1892	8818	2901		2901
社会福利保障业	Social Welfare and Securation	2911		2911	1855		1855
社会福利业	Social Welfare	2741		2741	1855		1855
其他类未包括的社会福利保障业	Others	170		170			
教育、文化艺术及广播电影电视业	**Education,Culture and Arts, Radio,Film and Television**	**633609**	**459198**	**174411**	**449310**	**288417**	**160893**
教育	Education	442035	325086	116949	295612	167327	128285
高等教育	Higher Education	354244	311088	43156	195133	158596	36537
中等教育	Secondary School Education	56075	8221	47854	58151	1688	56463
初等教育	Primary Education	4357		4357	3301		3301
学前教育	Preschool Education	436		436	436		436
特殊教育	Special Education	1748		1748	311		311
其他教育	Other Education	25175	5777	19398	38280	7043	31237
文化艺术业	Culture and Arts	146854	97859	48995	72485	42334	30151
艺术	Arts	41899	37796	4103	13806	3575	10231
出版	Publication	28214	28214		27510	27510	
文物保护	Preservation of Culture Relics	510		510	152		152
图书馆	Libraries	10281	4170	6111	282	282	
群众文化	Mass Culture	10170	6000	4170	7453		7453
新闻	News	9890	9890				
其他文化艺术业	Others	45890	11789	34101	23282	10967	12315
广播电影电视业	Radio,Film and Television	44720	36253	8467	81213	78756	2457
广播	Radio	21551	15947	5604	74752	73772	980
电影	Film	7187	5788	1399	2295	2295	
电视	Television	15982	14518	1464	4166	2689	1477
科学研究和综合技术服务业	**Scientific Research and Polytechnical Services**	**351769**	**203427**	**148342**	**342034**	**203858**	**138176**
科学研究业	Scientific Research	182611	173840	8771	192859	185693	7166
自然科学研究	Natural Science	160534	154849	5685	145690	142616	3074
社会科学研究	Social Science	7687	7687		18270	18270	
其他科学研究	Others	14390	11304	3086	28899	24807	4092
综合技术服务业	Polytechnical Services	169158	29587	139571	149175	18165	131010
气象	Meteorology	2706	2706		2635	2635	
地震	Earthquake	256	56	200			
技术监督	Technology Control	3029	2812	217	3029	2812	217
海洋环境	Sea Environment	1596	1596		1770	1770	
环境保护	Environment Protection	126007	3575	122432	121026		121026
技术推广和科技交流服务业	Technology Spreading and Scientific Technical Exchanges	869	430	439	321	321	
工程设计业	Engineering Design	25234	13624	11610	9085	8627	458
其他综合技术服务业	Others	9461	4788	4673	11309	2000	9309
国家机关、政党机关和社会团体	**Government Agencies,Party Agencies and Social Organizations**	**774029**	**506806**	**267223**	**729207**	**462312**	**266895**
国家机关	Government Agencies	662600	402990	259610	623974	357326	266648
政党机关	Party Agencies	86712	86465	247	95795	95548	247
社会团体	Social Organizations	24717	17351	7366	9438	9438	
其他行业	**Other Sectors**	**137855**	**32986**	**104869**	**128225**	**18180**	**110045**
企业管理机构	Administrative Organs of Enterprises	81056	25645	55411	97655	16927	80728
其他类未包括的行业	Others	56799	7341	49458	30570	1253	29317

4-11 全市基本建设投资额及新增固定资产(按行业分)

TOTAL INVESTMENT IN CAPITAL CONSTRUCTION AND INCREMENTAL FIXED ASSETS (BY SECTOR)

单位：万元 (10000 yuan)

行业	Item	投资额 Investment 合计 Total	中央 Central	地方 Local	新增固定资产 Incremental Fixed Assets 合计 Total	中央 Central	地方 Local
总计	**Total**	**4327251**	**2420060**	**1907191**	**3569318**	**2080568**	**1488750**
农、林、牧、渔业	**Farming,Forestry,Animal Husbandry and Fishery**	**23797**	**1651**	**22146**	**19397**		**19397**
农业	Farming	13056		13056	12223		12223
林业	Forestry	2989		2989	1123		1123
农、林、牧、渔服务业	FFAF Services	7752	1651	6101	6051		6051
采掘业	**Excavation**	**3376**		**3376**	**9022**		**9022**
黑色金属矿采选业	Ferrous Metals Mining and Dressing	3376		3376	9022		9022
铁矿采选业	Iron Mining and Dressing	3376		3376	9022		9022
制造业	**Manufacturing**	**353128**	**217836**	**135292**	**301968**	**200737**	**101231**
食品加工业	Food Processing	6219		6219	3951		3951
粮食及饲料加工业	Grain and Feed	3468		3468			
屠宰及肉类蛋类加工业	Butcher, Meat and Egg	2751		2751	3951		3951
食品制造业	Food Making	910		910	830		830
乳制品制造业	Dairy Products	830		830	830		830
其他食品制造业	Others	80		80			
纺织业	Textile Industry	5502		5502	5801		5801
棉纺织业	Cotton Textile	3865		3865	5708		5708
针织品业	Knitting Textile	1544		1544			
其他纺织业	Others	93		93	93		93
服装及其他纤维制品制造业	Garments and Other Fiber Products	3058		3058	1819		1819
服装制造业	Garment Industry	2857		2857	1618		1618
制鞋业	Shoes Making	201		201	201		201
皮革、毛皮、羽绒及其制品业	Leather,Furs,Eider Down and Related Products	822		822	371		371
皮革制品制造业	Leather Products	822		822	371		371
木材加工及竹、藤、棕、草制品业	Timber Processing,Bamboo, Cane,Palm Fiber and Straw Products	1736		1736			
人造板制造业	Artificial Board Manufacturing	1736		1736			
家具制造业	Furniture Industry	5885		5885	13156		13156
木制家具制造业	Wooden Furniture	3360		3360	13156		13156
其他家具制造业	Other Furniture	2525		2525			
造纸及纸制品业	Papermaking and Paper Products	1100		1100	300		300
纸浆制造业	Paper Pulp	900		900	300		300
纸制品业	Paper Products	200		200			
印刷业、记录媒介的复制	Printing and Record Medium Reproduced	12994	6206	6788	7304	6566	738
印刷业	Printing	12407	5619	6788	7304	6566	738
记录媒介的复制	Record Medium Reproduced	587	587				
文教体育用品制造业	Stationery,Education and Sports Goods	1239		1239	1222		1222

4-11 续表 1 continued

单位：万元 (10000 yuan)

行业	Item	投资额 Investment 合计 Total	中央 Central	地方 Local	新增固定资产 Incremental Fixed Assets 合计 Total	中央 Central	地方 Local
文化用品制造业	Stationery	627		627			
乐器及其他文娱用品制造业	Music Instruments and Other Stationery Goods	612		612	1222		1222
石油加工及炼焦业	Petroleum Processing and Coking Products	89841	89841		134605	134605	
原油加工业	Petroleum Processing	89841	89841		134605	134605	
化学原料及化学制品制造业	Raw Chemical Materials and Chemical Products	68352	60847	7505	6801	2706	4095
有机化学产品制造业	Organic Chemical Products	1325	370	955	2305	850	1455
合成材料制造业	Synthetic Materials	60967	60477	490	3096	1856	1240
专用化学产品制造业	Special Use Chemical Products	200		200			
日用化学产品制造业	Daily Use Chemical Products	5860		5860	1400		1400
医药制造业	Medical and Pharmaceutical Products	17958	1026	16932	450		450
化学药品制剂制造业	Original Chemical Medicine	15920	730	15190	450		450
中药材及中成药加工	Raw Material and Products of Chinese Medicine	577		577			
生物制品业	Biological Products	1461	296	1165			
塑料制品业	Plastic Products	400		400			
其他塑料制品业	Other Plastic Products	400		400			
非金属矿物制品业	Nonmetal Mineral Products	11137	150	10987	6700		6700
水泥制造业	Cement Making	384		384			
水泥制品和石棉水泥制品业	Cement and Asbestos Products	5756	50	5706	5029		5029
砖瓦、石灰和轻质建筑材料制造业	Brick,Tile and Light Construction Material	4807	100	4707	1586		1586
玻璃及玻璃制品业	Glass and Glass Products	105		105			
陶瓷制品业	Pottery and porcelain	85		85	85		85
黑色金属冶炼及压延加工业	Smelting and Pressing Ferrous Metals	1246		1246	8421		8421
炼铁业	Iron-smelting	1246		1246	8421		8421
有色金属冶炼及压延加工业	Smelting and Pressing of Nonferrous Metals	1450		1450			
有色金属压延加工业	Pressing of Nonferrous Metals	1450		1450			
金属制品业	Metal Products	1316		1316	1406		1406
金属结构制造业	Metal Structure	528		528	618		618
工具制造业	Tools	300		300	300		300
建筑用金属制品业	Products for Construct Use	208		208	208		208
日用金属制品业	Daily Metal Products	280		280	280		280
普通机械制造业	Ordinary Machine-building	9670	1770	7900	6524	2550	3974
锅炉及原动机制造业	Boiler and Motive Machine	4834	1770	3064	3231	2550	681
金属加工机械制造业	Metal Processing Machine	71		71	351		351
通用设备制造业	Universal Equipments	133		133			
其他通用零部件制造业	Other Universal Components and Parts	4632		4632	2942		2942
专用设备制造业	Special Purpose Equipment Building	11702	2031	9671	9856	8681	1175
冶金、矿山、机电专用设备设备制造业	Equipmentfor Metallurgy,Mining,Machine and Electronic	1497	1497		7977	7977	
石化及其他专用设备制造业	Equipment for Petroleum and Other Sector of Industry	1446	164	1282	164	164	

4-11 续表 2 continued

单位：万元 (10000 yuan)

行业	Item	投资额 Investment			新增固定资产 Incremental Fixed Assets		
		合计 Total	中央 Central	地方 Local	合计 Total	中央 Central	地方 Local
农、林、牧、渔,水利业机械制造业	Machines for Farming,Forestry,Animal Husbandry,Fishing and Irrigation	1880		1880			
医疗器械制造业	Medical Machines	1154		1154			
其他专用设备制造业	Other Special Purpose Equipment	5725	370	5355	1715	540	1175
交通运输设备制造业	Transportation Equipment Manufacturing	43395	41774	1621	39274	38158	1116
铁路运输设备制造业	Railway Transportation Equipment	5882	5882		5213	5213	
汽车制造业	Motor Vehicles	505		505			
航空航天器制造业	Aviation and Spaceflight Equipment	35892	35892		32945	32945	
交通运输设备修理业	Transportation Equipment Repairing	600		600	600		600
其他交通运输设备制造业	Other Transportation Equipment Manufacturing	516		516	516		516
武器弹药制造业	Weapon and Ammunition	3550	3550		970	970	
电气机械及器材制造业	Electric Equipment and Appliances Manufacturing	4069		4069	2121		2121
电机制造业	Electrical Machinery	260		260	235		235
输配电及控制设备制造业	Electricity Transmit,Distribution and Control Equipment	3023		3023	1100		1100
日用电器制造业	Daily Use Electrical Appliance	786		786	786		786
电子及通信设备制造业	Electronic and Telecommunication Equipment	43135	10220	32915	29596	6501	23095
通信设备制造业	Telecommunication Equipment	9813	5474	4339	12724	6381	6343
电子计算机制造业	Computer	17629	4626	13003	9355		9355
电子器件制造业	Electronic Device	8112		8112			
电子元件制造业	Electronic Cell	4551		4551	7397		7397
其他电子设备制造业	Other Electronic Machines	3030	120	2910	120	120	
仪器仪表及文化、办公用机械制造业	Instruments,Meters,Cultural and Official Machinery	6317	421	5896	20310		20310
通用仪器仪表制造	General Instruments and Meters	471	421	50			
计量器具制造业	Measuring Implements	5846		5846	20310		20310
其他制造业	Other Manufacturing	125		125	180		180
工艺美术品制造业	Art Products	55		55			
其他生产、生活用品制造业	Others	70		70	180		180
电力、煤气及水的生产和供应业	**Electricity,Gas and Water Production and Supply**	**811627**	**509595**	**302032**	**619559**	**452601**	**166958**
电力、蒸气、热水的生产和供应业	Electricity,Steam and Hot Water Production and Supply	641898	509595	132303	569195	452601	116594
电力生产业	Electricity Production	81233	81233		207974	207974	
电力供应业	Electricity Supply	442193	428362	13831	252134	244627	7507
蒸气、热水生产和供应业	Steam and Hot Water Production and Supply	118472		118472	109087		109087
煤气生产和供应业	Gas Production and Supply	75587		75587	35684		35684
煤气生产业	Gas Production	1		1	6000		6000
煤气供应业	Gas Supply	75586		75586	29684		29684
自来水的生产和供应业	Water Production and Supply	94142		94142	14680		14680
自来水生产业	Water Production	91266		91266	12145		12145
自来水供应业	Water Supply	2876		2876	2535		2535

4-11 续表 3 continued

单位：万元 (10000 yuan)

行业	Item	投资额 Investment			新增固定资产 Incremental Fixed Assets		
		合计 Total	中央 Central	地方 Local	合计 Total	中央 Central	地方 Local
建筑业	**Construction**	**109482**	**49848**	**59634**	**73315**	**34179**	**39136**
土木工程建筑业	Civil Engineering Construct	103822	44748	59074	69175	30079	39096
房屋建筑业	Building Construction	93715	35545	58170	57824	20312	37512
铁路、公路、遂道、桥梁建筑业	Railways,Highways,Tunnels and Bridges Construction	9375	9063	312	9819	9507	312
堤坝、电站码头建筑业	Dikes and Dams,Power Station and Wharves	592		592	1272		1272
其他土木工程建筑业	Others	140	140		260	260	
线路、管道和设备安装业	Line and Equipments Installation	5660	5100	560	4140	4100	40
线路、管道安装业	Line Installation	3300	3300		4100	4100	
设备安装业	Equipment Installation	2360	1800	560	40		40
地质勘查业、水利管理业	**Geological Prospecting and Water Conservancy**	**8079**	**1544**	**6535**	**1990**	**1540**	**450**
地质勘查业	Geological Prospecting	949	949		1540	1540	
海洋地质勘察业	Sea Prospecting	200	200				
矿产地质勘查业	Minerals Prospecting	360	360		830	830	
地球物理和地球化学勘察业	Geophysical and Geochemical Prospecting	389	389		710	710	
水利管理业	Water Conservancy	7130	595	6535	450		450
交通运输、仓储及邮电通信业	**Transportation,Storage,Posts and Telecommunications**	**307614**	**245953**	**61661**	**226218**	**171821**	**54397**
铁路运输业	Railways	15328	15328		5415	5415	
公路运输业	Highways	18759		18759	8631		8631
汽车运输业	Motor Vehicles	18759		18759	8631		8631
航空运输业	Aviations	10039	9189	850	7687	7687	
航空客货运输业	Passenger and Freight Transportation	9189	9189		7687	7687	
通用航空业	Universal Aviation	850		850			
交通运输辅助业	Logistic Support for Transportation	110027	102917	7110	12698	6400	6298
公路管理及养护业	Highway Management and Main tenance	3970		3970	158		158
机场及航空运输辅助业	Airport and Logistics of Aviation	106057	102917	3140	12540	6400	6140
仓储业	Storage	39467	9221	30246	33281	1060	32221
邮电通信业	**Posts and Telecommunications**	**113994**	**109298**	**4696**	**158506**	**151259**	**7247**
邮政业	Posts	8457	8457		7005	7005	
电信业	Telecommunications	101149	100841	308	145176	144254	922
邮电业	Posts and Telecommunications	4388		4388	6325		6325
批发和零售贸易餐饮业	**Wholesale,Retail and Catering**	**75986**	**16438**	**59548**	**41923**	**15353**	**26570**
食品、饮料、烟草和家庭用品批发业	Wholesale of Food,Beverage, Tabacco and Family Use Goods	28322	5959	22363	18613	7263	11350
食品、饮料、烟草批发业	Food,Beverage and Tabacco	11646	4167	7479	4417		4417
棉麻土畜产品批发业	Cotton,Fiber,Local and Animal Products	67		67	335		335
纺织品、服装和鞋帽批发业	Textile,Garments,Shoes and Hats	3500		3500	3500		3500
日用百货批发业	Daily Use Goods	7340		7340			
五金交电化工批发业	Hardware,Electrical Appliance and Chemical	5669	1792	3877	10095	7263	2832
药品及医疗器械批发业	Medicine and Medical Appliance	100		100	266		266
能源、材料、机械和电子设备批发业	Wholesale of Energy,Materials Machine and Electronic Equipment	7855	903	6952	4156	1305	2851
能源批发业	Energy	5718	50	5668	2332		2332
化工材料批发业	Chemical Materials	590		590			
建筑材料批发业	Building Materials	112		112			
金属材料批发业	Ferrous Materials	398		398	335		335
机械、电子设备批发业	Machine and Electronic Equipment	853	853		1305	1305	

4-11 续表 4 continued

单位：万元 (10000 yuan)

行业	Item	投资额 Investment 合计 Total	中央 Central	地方 Local	新增固定资产 Incremental Fixed Assets 合计 Total	中央 Central	地方 Local
汽车、摩托车及零配件批发业	Automobile,Motorcycle and Spares and Fittings	184		184	184		184
其他批发业	Others	5016	5016		6785	6785	
图书报刊批发业	Books,Newspaper and Magazines	316	316				
其他类未包括的批发	Others	4700	4700		6785	6785	
零售业	Retail	25585	560	25025	11809		11809
食品、饮料和烟草零售业	Food,Beverage and Tabacco	3760		3760	1871		1871
日用百货零售业	Daily Use Goods	15896	560	15336	4194		4194
图书报刊零售业	Books,Newspaper and Magazines	252		252	252		252
其他零售业	Others	5677		5677	5492		5492
商业经纪与代理业	Business Agencies	4000	4000				
餐饮业	Catering	5208		5208	560		560
正餐	Dinner	5208		5208	560		560
金融、保险业	**Banking and Insurance**	**88503**	**88503**		**8173**	**8173**	
金融业	Banking	88387	88387		8173	8173	
中央银行	Central Bank	1183	1183		1263	1263	
商业银行	Commercial Bank	78041	78041				
其他银行	Other Banks	4910	4910		6910	6910	
其他非银行金融业	Other Non-bank Banking	4253	4253				
保险业	Insurance	116	116				
房地产业	**Real Estate**	**14279**	**1000**	**13279**	**10879**		**10879**
房地产管理业	Management	14279	1000	13279	10879		10879
社会服务业	**Social Services**	**824410**	**78701**	**745709**	**743002**	**175516**	**567486**
公共服务业	Public Services	679196		679196	509404		509404
市内公共交通业	Urban Public Traffic	144403		144403	18736		18736
园林绿化业	Gardens Afforest	92964		92964	43939		43939
环境卫生业	Environmental Sanitation	24073		24073	25590		25590
市政工程管理业	Municipal Engineering Management	417756		417756	421139		421139
居民服务业	Personal Services	10181		10181	7967		7967
沐浴业	Bath	3410		3410			
殡葬业	Funeral and Interment Services	3771		3771	1967		1967
其他居民服务业	Others	3000		3000	6000		6000
旅馆业	Hotels	33057	8164	24893	44331	14348	29983
租赁服务业	Rentals	2332	2332		22133	22133	
旅游业	Tourism	9324	107	9217			
娱乐服务业	Recreation	18363	13054	5309	38346	35535	2811
信息、咨询服务业	Information and Consultancy	4300		4300	1466		1466
咨询服务业	Consultancy Services	1474		1474			
其他类未包括的信息咨询服务业	Others	2826		2826	1466		1466
计算机应用服务业	Computer Application	11613	507	11106	14968		14968
软件开发咨询业	Software Development Consultancy	11613	507	11106	14968		14968
其他社会服务业	Other Social Services	56044	54537	1507	104387	103500	887
市场管理服务业	Market Management	1507		1507	887		887
其他类未包括的社会服务业	Others	54537	54537		103500	103500	
卫生体育和社会福利业	**Health Care,Sports and Social Welfare**	**75508**	**32358**	**43150**	**97227**	**63817**	**33410**
卫生	Health Care	65058	30466	34592	92671	63817	28854
医院	Hospitals	61521	30466	31055	90531	63817	26714

4-11 续表 5 continued

单位：万元 (10000 yuan)

行 业	Item	投资额 Investment 合计 Total	中央 Central	地方 Local	新增固定资产 Incremental Fixed Assets 合计 Total	中央 Central	地方 Local
卫生防疫站	Sanitation and Antiepidemic Stations	1284		1284	580		580
妇幼保健所(站)	Maternity and Child Care Institutions	732		732	1560		1560
其他医院	Other Hospitals	1521		1521			
体育	Sports	7793	1892	5901	2901		2901
社会福利保障业	Social Welfare and Securation	2657		2657	1655		1655
社会福利业	Social Welfare	2487		2487	1655		1655
其他类未包括的社会服务业	Others	170		170			
教育、文化艺术及广播电影电视业	**Education,Culture and Arts, Radio,Film and Television**	**617666**	**452986**	**164680**	**442268**	**288095**	**154173**
教育	Education	435718	325086	110632	289576	167327	122249
高等教育	Higher Education	354244	311088	43156	195133	158596	36537
中等教育	Secondary School Education	50817	8221	42596	53316	1688	51628
初等教育	Primary Education	4291		4291	3223		3223
学前教育	Preschool Education	436		436	436		436
特殊教育	Special Education	1748		1748	311		311
其他教育	Other Education	24182	5777	18405	37157	7043	30114
文化艺术业	Culture and Arts	137228	91647	45581	71479	42012	29467
艺术	Arts	41787	37684	4103	13694	3463	10231
出版	Publication	28114	28114		27300	27300	
文物保护	Preservation of Cultureb Relics	510		510	152		152
图书馆	Libiaries	9454	4170	5284	282	282	
群众文化	Mass Culture	4170		4170	7453		7453
新闻	News	9890	9890				
其他文化艺术业	Others	43303	11789	31514	22598	10967	11631
广播电影电视业	Radio,Film and Television	44720	36253	8467	81213	78756	2457
广播	Radio	21551	15947	5604	74752	73772	980
电影	Film	7187	5788	1399	2295	2295	
电视	Television	15982	14518	1464	4166	2689	1477
科学研究和综合技术服务业	**Scientific Research and Polytechnical Services**	**223464**	**199936**	**23528**	**218914**	**199620**	**19294**
科学研究业	Scientific Research	175180	170349	4831	188402	181455	6947
自然科学研究	Natural Science	153307	151498	1809	141360	138378	2982
社会科学研究	Social Science	7687	7687		18270	18270	
其他科学研究	Others	14186	11164	3022	28772	24807	3965
综合技术服务业	Polytechnical Services	48284	29587	18697	30512	18165	12347
气象	Meteorologe	2706	2706		2635	2635	
地震	Earthquake	256	56	200			
技术监督	Technology Control	2812	2812		2812	2812	
海洋环境	Sea Environment	1596	1596		1770	1770	
环境保护	Environment Protection	7012	3575	3437	2980		2980
技术推广和科技交流服务业	Technology Spreading and Scientific Technical Exchanges	869	430	439	321	321	
工程设计业	Engineering Design	24382	13624	10758	8745	8627	118
其他综合技术服务业	Others	8651	4788	3863	11249	2000	9249
国家机关、政党机关和社会团体	**Government Agencies,Party Agencies and Social Organizations**	**709833**	**504742**	**205091**	**670916**	**461990**	**208926**
国家机关	Government Agencies	602693	400926	201767	565930	357004	208926
政党机关	Party Agencies	86465	86465		95548	95548	
社会团体	Social Organizations	20675	17351	3324	9438	9438	
其他行业	**Other Sectors**	**80499**	**18969**	**61530**	**84547**	**7126**	**77421**
企业管理机构	Administrative Organs of Enterprises	59913	11628	48285	83144	5873	77271
其他类未包括的行业	Others	20586	7341	13245	1403	1253	150

4-12 全市更新改造投资额及新增固定资产(按行业分)

TOTAL INVESTMENT IN INNOVATION AND INCREMENTAL FIXED ASSETS (BY SECTOR)

单位：万元 (10000 yuan)

行业	Item	投资额 Investment 合计 Total	中央 Central	地方 Local	新增固定资产 Incremental Fixed Assets 合计 Total	中央 Central	地方 Local
总计	**Total**	**1752093**	**646454**	**1105639**	**1990395**	**753165**	**1237230**
农、林、牧、渔业	**Farming,Forestry,Animal Husbandry and Fishery**	**602**		**602**	**340**		**340**
农业	Farming	100		100	200		200
林业	Forestry	400		400			
渔业	Fishery	102		102	140		140
淡水渔业	Freshwater Fishery	102		102	140		140
采掘业	**Excavation**	**3909**		**3909**	**2949**		**2949**
煤炭采选业	Coal Mining and Dressing	3373		3373	2719		2719
黑色金属矿采选业	Ferrous Metals Mining and Dressing	68		68			
铁矿采选业	Iron Mining and Dressing	68		68			
非金属矿采选业	Nonmetal Minerals Mining and Dressing	468		468	230		230
土沙石开采业	Sand and Stone Mining and Dressing	468		468	230		230
制造业	**Manufacturing**	**309809**	**53069**	**256740**	**468245**	**43351**	**424894**
食品加工业	Food Processing	883		883	4529		4529
粮食及饲料加工业	Grain and Feed	46		46	3713		3713
植物油加工业	Vegetable Oil	333		333	312		312
屠宰及肉类蛋类加工业	Butcher, Meat and Egg	504		504	504		504
食品制造业	Food Making	5532		5532	8830		8830
糕点、糖果制造业	Pastry and Candy	200		200	200		200
乳制品制造业	Dairy Products	2166		2166	7442		7442
调味品制造业	Flavorings	2678		2678	700		700
其他食品制造业	Others	488		488	488		488
饮料制造业	Beverage Production	6900		6900	21988		21988
酒精及饮料酒制造业	Alcohol and Beverage Wine	6900		6900	21988		21988
纺织业	Textile Industry	3746		3746	1980		1980
棉纺织业	Cotton Textile	777		777	682		682
针织品业	Knitting Textile	2969		2969	1298		1298
皮革、毛皮、羽绒及其制品业	Leather,Furs,Eider Down and Related Products	1733		1733	690		690
制革业	Leather Making	713		713			
皮革制品制造业	Leather Products	1020		1020	690		690
木材加工及竹、藤、棕、草制品业	Timber Processing,Bamboo, Cane,Palm Fiber and Straw Products	188		188	1159		1159
人造板制造业	Artificial Board	188		188	1159		1159
家具制造业	Furniture Industry	1329		1329	1329		1329
木制家具制造业	Wood Furniture	1329		1329	1329		1329
造纸及纸制品业	Papermaking and Paper Products	1128		1128	14385		14385
纸制品业	Paper Products	1128		1128	14385		14385

4-12 续表 1 continued

单位：万元 (10000 yuan)

行业	Item	投资额 Investment			新增固定资产 Incremental Fixed Assets		
		合计 Total	中央 Central	地方 Local	合计 Total	中央 Central	地方 Local
印刷业、记录媒介的复制	Printing and Record Medium Reproduced	9411	7968	1443	8054	6739	1315
印刷业	Printing	9411	7968	1443	8054	6739	1315
文教体育用品制造业	Stationery,Education and Sports Goods	5166		5166	5398		5398
文化用品制造业	Stationery	4691		4691			
乐器及其他文娱用品制造业	Music Instruments and Other Stationery Goods	475		475	5398		5398
石油加工及炼焦业	Petroleum Processing and Coking Products	18867	13859	5008	9284	5847	3437
原油加工业	Petroleum Processing	11756	11756		5235	5235	
石油制品业	Petroleum Products	2160	2103	57	1222	612	610
炼焦业	Coking Products	4951		4951	2827		2827
化学原料及化学制品制造业	Raw Chemical Materials and Chemical Products	35636	19638	15998	116872	19438	97434
基本化学原料制造业	Elementary Raw Chemical Materials	2350		2350	666		666
化学肥料制造业	Chemical Fertilizer	326		326	2198		2198
有机化学产品制造业	Organic Chemical Products	19427	12614	6813	83474	12614	70860
合成材料制造业	Synthetic Materials	7264	7024	240	6824	6824	
专用化学产品制造业	Special Purpose Chemical Products	6209		6209	23710		23710
日用化学产品制造业	Daily Use Chemical Products	60		60			
医药制造业	Medical and Pharmaceutical Products	11401	1673	9728	9483	3414	6069
化学药品制剂制造业	Original Chemical Medicine	6874		6874	5919		5919
中药材及中成药加工	Raw Material and Products of Chinese Medicine	2804		2804			
生物制品业	Biological Products	1723	1673	50	3564	3414	150
化学纤维制造业	Chemical Fiber Manufacturing	140	140		140	140	
合成纤维制造业	Synthetic Fibers	140	140		140	140	
橡胶制品业	Rubber Products	2066		2066	1451		1451
轮胎制造业	Tire Manufacturing	2066		2066	1451		1451
塑料制品业	Plastic Products	7265		7265	4680		4680
塑料薄膜制造业	Plastic Film	1872		1872	85		85
泡沫塑料及人造革合成革	Foamed Plastics,Imitation Leatherand Synthetic Leather	4920		4920	2683		2683
其他塑料制品业	Other Plastic Products	473		473	1912		1912
非金属矿物制品业	Nonmetal Mineral Products	24327	2876	21451	20037	1220	18817
水泥制造业	Cement Manufacturing	4770	1112	3658	4070	1112	2958
水泥制品和石棉水泥制品业	Cement Products and Asbestos Cement Products	108	108		108	108	
砖瓦、石灰和轻质建筑材料制造业	Brick,Tile and Light Construction Material	11605	1656	9949	8569		8569
玻璃及玻璃制品业	Glass and Glass Products	7729		7729	7192		7192
耐火材料制品业	Refractory Products	115		115	98		98
黑色金属冶炼及压延加工业	Smelting and Pressing of Ferrous Metals	36523		36523	16350		16350
钢压延加工业	Steel Pressing	36195		36195	16247		16247
铁合金冶炼业	Alloy Iron Smelting	328		328	103		103
有色金属冶炼及压延加工业	Smelting and Pressing of Nonferrous Metals	1016		1016	120		120
有色金属压延加工业	Nonferrous Metals Pressing	1016		1016	120		120
金属制品业	Metal Products	6051		6051	8110		8110

4-12 续表 2 continued

单位：万元 (10000 yuan)

行业	Item	投资额 Investment 合计 Total	中央 Central	地方 Local	新增固定资产 Incremental Fixed Assets 合计 Total	中央 Central	地方 Local
铸铁管制造业	Tube of Cast Iron	149		149	149		149
集装箱和金属包装物品制造业	Container and Metal Cover Manufacturing	352		352			
建筑用金属制品业	Products for Construct Use	5550		5550	7961		7961
普通机械制造业	Ordinary Machine-building	7465		7465	5215		5215
锅炉及原动机制造业	Boiler and Motive Machine	628		628	229		229
金属加工机械制造业	Metal Processing Machine	5450		5450	2886		2886
通用设备制造业	Universal Equipment	331		331			
其他通用零部件制造业	Other Universal Components and Parts	1056		1056	2100		2100
专用设备制造业	Special Purpose Equipment Building	28261	3312	24949	36355	3368	32987
机电工业专用设备制造业	Equipment for Engine and Electricity	1731	840	891	1019	896	123
石化及其他工业专用设备制造业	Equipment for Petroleum and Other Sector of Industry	10085	2472	7613	4229	2472	1757
农、林、牧、渔,水利业机械制造业	Machines for Farming,Forestry,Animal Husbandry,Fishing and Irrigation	9828		9828	24511		24511
医疗器械制造业	Medical Machines	5497		5497	4727		4727
其他专用设备制造业	Other Special Purpose Equipment	1120		1120	1869		1869
交通运输设备制造业	Transportation Equipment Manufacturing	32188	3454	28734	104138	3017	101121
铁路运输设备制造业	Railway Transportation Equipment	3751	2519	1232	3657	2425	1232
汽车制造业	Motor Vehicles	26121		26121	98731		98731
交通运输设备修理业	Transportation Equipment Repairing	2316	935	1381	1750	592	1158
电气机械及器材制造业	Electric Equipment and Appliances Manufacturing	12828		12828	11300		11300
输配电及控制设备制造业	Electricity Transmit,Distribution and Control Equipment	2351		2351	745		745
日用电器制造业	Daily Use Electrical Appliances	10477		10477	10555		10555
电子及通信设备制造业	Electronic and Telecommunication Equipment	39483		39483	37903		37903

4-12 续表 3 continued

单位：万元 (10000 yuan)

行业	Item	投资额 Investment 合计 Total	中央 Central	地方 Local	新增固定资产 Incremental Fixed Assets 合计 Total	中央 Central	地方 Local
通信设备制造业	Telecommunication Equipment	15497		15497	15953		15953
广播电视设备制造业	Radio and Television Equipment	1246		1246	469		469
电子计算机制造业	Computer	1320		1320	2250		2250
电子器件制造业	Electronic Device	8134		8134	5251		5251
电子元件制造业	Electronic Cell	10249		10249	10527		10527
日用电子器具制造业	Daily Use Electronic Appliance	3015		3015	3043		3043
其他电子设备制造业	Other Electronic Appliance	22		22	410		410
仪器仪表及文化、办公用机械制造业	Instruments,Meters,Cultural and Official Machinery	5943	149	5794	7477	168	7309
通用仪器仪表制造	General Instruments and Meters	4898	149	4749	7327	168	7159
电子测量仪器制造业	Electronic Survey Instrument	463		463			
其他仪器仪表制造业	Other Instruments and Meters	582		582	150		150
其他制造业	Other Manufacturing	4333		4333	10988		10988
其他生产、生活用品制造	Other Goods for Production and Life	4333		4333	10988		10988
电力、煤气及水的生产和供应业	**Electricity,Gas and Water Production and Supply**	**132897**	**70607**	**62290**	**254810**	**192054**	**62756**
电力、蒸气、热水的生产和供应业	Electricity,Steam and Hot Water Production and Supply	102779	70607	32172	233237	192054	41183
电力生产业	Electricity Production	66591	64930	1661	187388	186377	1011
电力供应业	Electricity Supply	9898	5677	4221	5677	5677	
蒸气、热水生产和供应业	Steam and Hot Water Production and Supply	26290		26290	40172		40172
煤气生产和供应业	Gas Production and Supply	26131		26131	10182		10182
煤气供应业	Gas Supply	26131		26131	10182		10182
自来水的生产和供应业	Water Production and Supply	3987		3987	11391		11391
自来水生产业	Water Production	3494		3494	11365		11365
自来水供应业	Water Supply	493		493	26		26
建筑业	**Construction**	**6820**	**4527**	**2293**	**4293**	**2000**	**2293**
土木工程建筑业	Civil Engineering Construct	6820	4527	2293	4293	2000	2293
房屋建筑业	Building Construction	6820	4527	2293	4293	2000	2293
地质勘查业、水利管理业	**Geological Prospecting and Water Conservancy**	**125381**		**125381**	**26638**		**26638**
水利管理业	Water Conservancy	125381		125381	26638		26638
交通运输、仓储及邮电通信业	**Transportation,Storage,Posts and Telecommunications**	**520001**	**484976**	**35025**	**534627**	**497068**	**37559**
铁路运输业	Railways	20144	20144		25121	25121	
公路运输业	Highways	21893		21893	26633		26633
汽车运输业	Motor Vehicles	21893		21893	26633		26633

4-12 续表 4 continued

单位：万元 (10000 yuan)

行业	Item	投资额 Investment 合计 Total	中央 Central	地方 Local	新增固定资产 Incremental Fixed Assets 合计 Total	中央 Central	地方 Local
航空运输业	Aviations	5300	5300		5300	5300	
航空客货运输业	Passenger and Freight Transportation	5300	5300		5300	5300	
交通运输辅助业	Logistic Support for Transportation	16291	3280	13011	13905	3280	10625
公路管理及养护业	Highway Management and Maintenance	13011		13011	10625		10625
机场及航空运输辅助业	Airport and Logistics of Aviation	3280	3280		3280	3280	
仓储业	Storage	1401	1280	121	671	370	301
邮电通信业	Posts and Telecommunications	454972	454972		462997	462997	
电信业	Telecommunications	454972	454972		462997	462997	
批发和零售贸易餐饮业	**Wholesale,Retail and Catering**	**13589**		**13589**	**41721**		**41721**
食品、饮料、烟草和家庭用品批发业	Wholesale of Food,Beverage, Tabacco and Family Use Goods	986		986	986		986
食品、饮料、烟草批发业	Food,Beverage and Tabacco	986		986	986		986
能源、材料、机械和电子设备批发业	Wholesale of Energy,Materials Machine and Electronic Equipment	5311		5311	8297		8297
能源批发业	Energy	1844		1844	6170		6170
建筑材料批发业	Building Materials	2060		2060	2060		2060
金属材料批发业	Metal Materials	67		67	67		67
机械电子设备批发业	Machine and Electronic Equipments	1340		1340			
零售业	Retail	7292		7292	32438		32438
日用百货零售业	Daily Use Goods	7231		7231	32438		32438
纺织品、服装和鞋帽零售业	Textile,Garments,Shoes and Hats	61		61			
房地产业	**Real Estate**	**3091**		**3091**	**3091**		**3091**
房地产管理业	Management	3091		3091	3091		3091

4-12 续表 5 continued

单位：万元 (10000 yuan)

行业	Item	投资额 Investment			新增固定资产 Incremental Fixed Assets		
		合计 Total	中央 Central	地方 Local	合计 Total	中央 Central	地方 Local
社会服务业	**Social Services**	**395799**	**2466**	**393333**	**436767**	**2466**	**434301**
公共服务业	Public Services	355441		355441	413389		413389
市内公共交通业	Urban Public Traffic	89222		89222	77642		77642
园林绿化业	Gardens Afforest	6294		6294	3814		3814
环境卫生业	Environmental Sanitation	1422		1422	1156		1156
市政工程管理业	Municipal Engineering Management	258503		258503	330777		330777
旅馆业	Hotels	37692		37692	20912		20912
租赁服务业	Rentals	200		200			
计算机应用服务业	Computer Application	2166	2166		2166	2166	
软件开发咨询业	Software Development Consultancy	2166	2166		2166	2166	
其他社会服务业	Others	300	300		300	300	
其他类未包括的社会服务业	Others	300	300		300	300	
卫生体育和社会福利业	**Health Care,Sports and Social Welfare**	**10950**	**5025**	**5925**	**1670**	**290**	**1380**
卫生	Health Care	7779	5025	2754	1470	290	1180
医院	Hospitals	7779	5025	2754	1470	290	1180
体育	Sports	2917		2917			
社会福利保障业	Social Welfare and Securation	254		254	200		200
社会福利业	Social Welfare	254		254	200		200
教育、文化艺术及广播电影电视业	**Education,Culture and Arts, Radio,Film and Television**	**13063**	**6212**	**6851**	**6632**	**322**	**6310**
教育	Education	3437		3437	5626		5626
中等教育	Secondary Education	2758		2758	4835		4835
初等教育	Primary Education	66		66	78		78
其他教育	Other Education	613		613	713		713
文化艺术业	Culture and Arts	9626	6212	3414	1006	322	684
艺术	Arts	112	112		112	112	
出版	Publication	100	100		210	210	
图书馆	Libraries	827		827			
群众文化	Mass Culture	6000	6000				
其他文化艺术业	Others	2587		2587	684		684
科学研究和综合技术服务业	**Scientific Research and Polytechnical Services**	**126460**	**3491**	**122969**	**123120**	**4238**	**118882**
科学研究业	Scientific Research	5586	3491	2095	4457	4238	219
自然科学研究	Natural Science	5382	3351	2031	4330	4238	92
其他科学研究	Others	204	140	64	127		127
综合技术服务业	Polytechnical Services	120874		120874	118663		118663
技术监督	Technology Control	217		217	217		217
环境保护	Environment Protection	118995		118995	118046		118046
工程设计业	Engineering Design	852		852	340		340
其他综合技术服务业	Others	810		810	60		60
国家机关、政党机关和社会团体	**GovernmentAgencies,PartyAgencies and Social Organizations**	**60154**	**2064**	**58090**	**58291**	**322**	**57969**
国家机关	Government Agencies	59907	2064	57843	58044	322	57722
政党机关	Party Agencies	247		247	247		247
其他行业	**Other Sectors**	**29568**	**14017**	**15551**	**27201**	**11054**	**16147**
企业管理机构	Administrative Organs of Enterprises	15507	14017	1490	11054	11054	
其他类未包括的行业	Others	14061		14061	16147		16147

4-13 新增生产能力(或效益)
INCREMENTAL PRODUCTION CAPACITY(OR BENEFIT)

能力名称		Production Capacity		合计 Total	国有 State-Owned	集体 Collective Owned
天然气管输	(公里)	Natural Gas Pipeline Carrying	(km)	53.0	53.0	
	(亿立方米／年)		(100 million cu.m/year)	6.0	6.0	
人造富铁矿	(万吨／年)	Artificial Rich Iron Ore	(10000 tons/year)	6.2	6.2	
球团铁矿	(万吨／年)	Spherical Iron Ore		6.2	6.2	
铜材加工	(吨／年)	Copper Products Processing	(ton/year)	1000.0	1000.0	
铜带材	(吨／年)	Copper Band Products	(ton/year)	1000.0	1000.0	
火力发电	(万千瓦)	Thermal Power	(10000 kw)	18.5		
输电线路长度		Length of Transmit Electricity		11.2	11.2	
	(11 万伏及以上,公里)	Line	(over11,0000 volts,km)			
水泥	(万吨／年)	Cement	(10000 tons/year)	8.0	8.0	
卫生陶瓷	(万件／年)	Sanitary Pottery and Porcelain	(10000/year)	3.6		
家具	(万件／年)	Furniture	(10000/year)	5.4	5.4	
氮肥	(吨／年)	Nitrogenous Fertilizer	(ton/year)	20000.0	20000.0	
丙　烯	(吨／年)	Propylene	(ton/year)	30000.0	30000.0	
塑料树脂及共聚物	(吨／年)	Plastic Resin and Copolymer	(ton/year)	200000.0	200000.0	
化学原料药	(吨／年)	Chemical Raw Medicine	(ton/year)	30.0		
片剂	(万片/年)	Tablet	(10000 tables/year)	250000.0		
金属切削机床制造	(台／年)	Metal-cutting Machine	(unit/year)	110.0	110.0	
建筑机械制造	(台／年)	Construction Machinery	(unit/year)	200.0	200.0	
# 挖掘机	(台／年)	Excavator	(unit/year)	200.0	200.0	
医疗器械制造	(台／年)	Medical Appliances	(unit/year)	260.0		
铁路客车制造	(辆／年)	Passenger Train	(unit/year)	50.0	50.0	
客车制造	(辆／年)	Coach	(unit/year)	500.0	500.0	
摩托车制造	(辆／年)	Motorcycle	(unit/year)	30000.0		
肉加工品	(吨／年)	Meat Products	(ton/year)	6079.0	6079.0	
# 熟肉加工		Cooked Meat		6000.0	6000.0	
其他乳制品	(吨／年)	Other Dairy Products	(ton/year)	19000.0	19000.0	
啤　酒	(万吨／年)	Beer	(10000 tons/year)	12.0	10.0	
合成洗涤剂原料	(吨/年)	Synthetic Detergents	(ton/year)	52500.0		
服　装	(万件／年)	Garments	(10000/year)	8.0		
塑料制品	(万吨/年)	Plastic Products	(10000 tons/year)	0.9	0.9	
日用玻璃制品	(万吨/年)	Daily Use Glass Products	(10000 tons/year)	0.4	0.4	
家用洗衣机	(万台／年)	Household Washing Machines	(10000/year)	20.0	20.0	
房间空气调节器	(万台／年)	House Air Conditioner	(10000/year)	8.0	8.0	
移动电话机（手持机）	(部／年)	Mobilphone	(unit/year)	200.0	200.0	
程控交换机	(万线／年)	ProgramcontrolTelephoneExchange	(10000 lines/year)	50.0		
新建公路	(公里)	Highway New Built	(km)	4.4	4.4	

4-13 续表 continued

能力名称 Production Capacity				合计 Total	国有 State-Owned	集体 Collective Owned
一级公路	(公里)	First-grade Highways	(km)	4.4	4.4	
改建公路	(公里)	Reconstructed Highways	(km)	55.0	55.0	
新建独立公路桥梁	(延长米)	Absolute Highway and Bridge	(extension mile)	399.0	399.0	
	(座)	New Built	(unit)	1.0	1.0	
造林面积	(万亩)	Afforestation Area	(10000 mu)	9.0	9.0	
粮食仓库	(万公斤)	Grain Storehouse	(10000 kg)	38900.0	38900.0	
	(平方米)		(sq.m)	74913.0	74913.0	
高等院校：学生席位	(个)	Institutions of Higher Education: Student Seats	(unit)	4400.0	4400.0	
建筑面积	(平方米)	Floor Space	(sq.m)	60856.0	60856.0	
中等院校：学生席位	(个)	Secondary Schools: Student Seats	(unit)	4265.0	4265.0	
建筑面积	(平方米)	Floor Space	(sq.m)	52393.0	52393.0	
小学校： 学生席位	(个)	Primary Schools: Student Seats	(unit)	615.0	615.0	
建筑面积	(平方米)	Floor Space	(sq.m)	5353.0	5353.0	
其他学校：学生席位	(个)	Other Schools: Student Seats	(unit)	1899.0	1899.0	
建筑面积	(平方米)	Floor Space	(sq.m)	32626.0	32626.0	
文化馆	(平方米)	Cultural Center	(sq.m)	9745.0	9745.0	
医院病床	(张)	Hospitaleds	(unit)	2151.0	2151.0	
宾馆旅馆招待所客房数	(间)	Guest Rooms of Hotels	(room)	459.0	375.0	34.0
	(平方米)		(sq.m)	28984.0	24784.0	1500.0
城市自来水供水能力	(万吨/日)	Urban Tap Water Supplying Capacity	(10000 tons/day)	30.0	30.0	
城市自来水管道长度	(公里)	Length of City Tap Water Pipelines	(km)	68.1	68.1	
城市供热能力:蒸气	(吨/小时)	Heat Supply Capacity: Vapor	(ton/hour)	535.0	535.0	
热水	(兆瓦/小时)	Heat Water	(megaw/hour)	379.0	379.0	
城市公共交通车辆购置	(辆)	Purchase of Public Traffic Vehicles	(unit)	2543.0	2543.0	
城市道路扩建长度	(公里)	Expanded Length of Highways	(km)	80.1	74.7	
城市道路扩建面积	(万平方米)	Expanded Area of Highways	(10000 sq.m)	294.5	280.5	
城市排水管道铺设长度	(公里)	Length of Paved Drainage Pipeline	(km)	55.0	55.0	
城市永久性桥梁	(座)	Perpetual Bridges	(unit)	33.0	33.0	

4-14 房屋建筑施工及竣工面积
FLOOR SPACE OF BUILDINGS UNDER CONSTRUCTION AND COMPLETED

单位：万平方米 (10000 sq.m)

项目	Item	1999	1998	占竣工面积(%) Proportion in Floor Space Completed(%) 1999	1998
施工总面积	**Floor Space of Buildings under Construction**	**6556.5**	**6496.1**		
竣工总面积	**Floor Space of Buildings Completed**	**2321.4**	**1821.5**	**100**	**100**
在竣工总面积中：	**Of the Floor Space Completed:**				
按用途分	**Grouped by Use**				
#厂房	Plant	72.4	97.0	3.1	5.3
仓库	Storehouse	19.1	17.4	0.8	1.0
办公室	Office	42.3	103.2	1.8	5.7
家属住宅	Families Residence	1375.1	974.7	59.2	53.5
单身宿舍	Benchelor Quarters	25.7	27.0	1.1	1.5
教育用房	Education	68.8	71.4	3.0	3.9
科研用房	Scientific Research	36.5	25.7	1.6	1.4
医疗用房	Medical	27.0	17.4	1.2	1.0
商业营业用房	Commerce	86.6	122.7	3.7	6.7
礼堂、俱乐部	Assembly Hall and Club	3.6	3.0	0.2	0.2
影剧院	Theater and Cinema	2.0	1.2	0.1	0.1
托儿所、幼儿园	Nursery and Kindergarten	9.0	4.0	0.4	0.2
旅馆、招待所	Hotel	16.6	5.5	0.7	0.3
按隶属关系分	**Grouped by Administrative Relationship**				
中央	Central	572.0	439.7	24.6	24.1
地方	Local	540.9	539.0	23.3	29.6
#国有	State-Owned	414.3	412.0	17.8	22.6
集体	Collective Owned	63.2	59.1	2.7	3.2
房地产开发企业	Comprehensive Development	1208.5	842.8	52.1	46.3
按地区分	**Grouped by Region**				
城区	City Propers	430.7	367.3	18.6	20.2
近郊区	Near Suburbs	1357.7	1087.6	58.5	59.7
远郊区	Outer Suburbs	533.0	366.6	22.9	20.1

4-15 房屋建筑每平方米造价
COST PER SQ.M OF BUILDINGS

单位：元 (yuan)

项目	Item	1999	1998	1999年比1998年增(+)减(-) Increase or Decrease
平均造价	**Average Cost**	**1929**	**2126**	**-197**
#厂房	Plant	2111	2292	-181
仓库	Storehouse	1614	1353	261
办公室	Office	2124	5071	-2947
家属住宅	Families Residence	1452	1443	9
单身宿舍	Benchelor Quarters	1488	1392	96
教育用房	Education	2051	1955	96
科研用房	Scientific Research	2105	1997	108
医疗用房	Medical	2577	2157	420
商业营业用房	Commerce	2299	3182	-883
礼堂、俱乐部	Assembly Hall and Club	4528	2578	1950
影剧院	Theater and Cinema	3566	2792	774
托儿所、幼儿园	Nursery and Kindergarten	1548	1634	-86
旅馆、招待所	Hotel	3336	3593	-257

4-16 基本建设大中型项目一览表

单位：万元

建设项目名称 Construction Project	建设地址 Address	国民经济行业 Sector	隶属关系 Administrative Relationship	建设性质 Type of Construction	建设阶段 Stage	开工年月 Beginning Time	投产年月 Operating Time	计划总投资 Total Investment
总　　计								**4455616**
对外经济贸易大学211工程	北京	普通高等教育	中央	单纯建造	施工	199806		12400
中国农业大学211工程	北京	普通高等教育	中央	扩建	施工	199612		18700
北京林业大学211工程	北京	普通高等教育	中央	扩建	施工	199701		6748
中央美术学院学院迁建	北京	普通高等教育	中央	迁建	施工	199812		45911
北方交通大学211工程	北京	普通高等教育	中央	扩建	施工	199806		25520
北京邮电大学211工程	北京	普通高等教育	中央	扩建	筹建			25000
文化部文化设施建设管理中心天桥剧场	北京	艺术	中央	扩建	施工	199611		19800
文化部文化设施建设管理中心戏曲学院	北京	普通高等教育	中央	迁建	施工	199804		37489
中央电台业务楼	北京	广播	中央	新建	施工	199212	199910	46222
北京科技大学211工程	北京	普通高等教育	中央	扩建	施工	199706		9000
清华大学211工程	北京	普通高等教育	中央	扩建	施工	199611		48825
北京大学211工程	北京	普通高等教育	中央	扩建	施工	199510		61149
中国人民大学211工程	北京	普通高等教育	中央	扩建	施工	199406		14084
北京师范大学211工程	北京	普通高等教育	中央	扩建	施工	199611		4700
北京医科大学211工程	北京	普通高等教育	中央	扩建	施工	199609		12500
国家教委电化教育大楼	北京	国家机关	中央	新建	施工	199009		20342
中国地质大学211工程	北京	普通高等教育	中央	扩建	施工	199812		14000
石油大学(北京)211工程	北京	普通高等教育	中央	扩建	施工	199601		8454
理工大学 211工程	北京	普通高等教育	中央	扩建	施工	199612		51901
北京航空航天大学211工程	北京	普通高等教育	中央	扩建	施工	199703		10100
中国现代文学馆	北京	其他文化艺术业	中央	新建	施工	199801		15000
中国科技馆二期工程	北京	其他文化艺术业	中央	扩建	施工	199802	199910	12367
北京燕山石油化工丁基橡胶装置	北京	合成橡胶制造业	中央	扩建	施工	199711		109977
顺义50万变电站	北京	电力供应业	中央	新建	施工	199812		44065
首都机场航站区扩建工程	北京	机场及航空运输辅助业	中央	扩建	施工	199510		872041
首钢水厂铁矿扩建	北京	铁矿采选业	地方	扩建	施工	198612		299406
首钢日电电子NEC技术升级	北京	集成电路制造业	地方	扩建	施工	199606		105000
高碑店污水处理厂二期工程	北京	市政工程管理业	地方	扩建	施工	199711		112000
北京粮食销区中心库一期工程	北京	仓储业	地方	新建	施工	199410	199912	15000
东四环改造	北京	市政工程管理业	地方	新建	施工	199805	199911	279400
北京地铁复兴门--八王坟	北京	轨道交通业	地方	新建	施工	198805		757174
陕北天然气进京市内工程	北京	煤气供应业	地方	新建	施工	199604		355439
第九水厂扩建(三期)	北京	自来水生产业	地方	扩建	施工	199712		251278
密云水库安全加固工程	北京	水利管理业	地方	改建	施工	199707		45270
中央音乐学院附中迁建工程	北京	中等专业学校	中央	迁建	施工	199812		26233
华能北京热电厂	北京	火力发电业	中央	新建	施工	199404		663121

LARGE AND MEDIUM PROJECTS OF CAPITAL CONSTRUCTION

(10000 yuan)

本年计划投资 Planning Investment of this Year	自年初累计完成投资 Accumulative Investment Since Year-Beginning	建筑工程 Construction	安装工程 Installation	设备购置 Purchase of Equipments	本年新增固定资产 Incremental Fixed Assets	年初累计资金来源合计 Accumulative Fund Source Since Year-Beginning	建筑规模和新增生产能力(或效益) Construction Size and Incremental Productive Capital(or Benefit): 名称 Item	计算单位 Counting Unit	建设规模 Size	新增能力累计 Accumulative Incremental Capacity	# 本年 of this Year
1009742	774239	356319	56791	165061	568729	873233					
2710	163	56									
2720	1022			1022	1022	170					
1798	900			900	900	900					
12715	12715	11542	88	200	468	3146					
8447	8448	3123		5255	8278	8448					
40	40					40					
8000	8020	6281		1280		8000					
25000	24330	10916		2824		25000					
2276	4674	2628	249	1695	46222	2276					
4822	4212	4200				4012					
5387	5387	3397		1990	2130	6832					
10160	9459	8008		1400	1400	10009					
4470	2367	2334				3240					
1380	1360			1360	1360	1360					
2400	620			620	620	620					
1094	273	239				195					
3550	642			449	642	1028					
3350	3350			3350	3350	3350					
17312	17656	12015		3811	15312	17656	高等院校:学生席位	个	2000.0	2000.0	2000.0
							建筑面积	平方米	38130.0	38130.0	38130.0
1715	4000	1290		2695	2695	2914					
8054	5236	5114		3		2000					
6553	6553	4155	382	1900	10967	4367					
60000	60477	2133	14399	25819	1856	53893	合成橡胶	吨/年	30000.0		
23020	10020	4000	1000	5000		22000					
106141	95148	56516	5883	5174		101596	侯机楼	座	1.0		
								平方米	326500		
7000	3376	194		116	9022	3376	铁矿开采	万吨/年	1050.0		
							铁矿石成品矿	万吨/年	305.0		
28511	8112		210	7902		8112	集成电路	万块/年	3000.0	3000.0	
20750	14250	3438	700	8810		15490	城市污水处理能力	万吨/日	50.0		
357	357	30				132	粮食仓库	万公斤	7400.0	7400.0	
								平方米	16868.0	16868.0	
116000	94821	90791			235153	115604	城市道路扩建长度	公里	15.8	15.8	15.8
							城市道路扩建面积	万平方米	110.0	110.0	110.0
							城市永久性桥梁	座	31.0	31.0	31.0
136744	129001	54399	18128	22744		165657					
146000	60460	9011	1266	8337	19358	94024	天然气管输	公里	204.0	53.0	53.0
								亿立方米/年	10.0	6.0	6.0
107518	86268	49120	4900	13530		102915	城市自来水供水能力	万吨/日	50.0	25.0	25.0
							城市自来水管道长度	公里	89.0	52.0	52.0
25270	6420	5807				21000					
7312	2869	1618		3		7312	中等学校:学生席位	个	100.0		
							建筑面积	平方米	29345.0		
91166	81233	3964	9586	36872	207974	56559	火力发电	万千瓦	65.0	65.0	18.5

4-17 国家及北京市重点工程一览表

单位：万元

建设项目名称 Construction Project	国民经济行业 Sector	隶属关系 Administrative Relationship	建设性质 Type of Construction	建设阶段 Stage	开工年月 Beginning Time	投产年月 Operating Time	计划总投资 Total Investment
一.重大项目							10426809
1.市政基础设施项目							4691492
地铁"复---八"线工程	轨道交通	市属	新建	施工	8805		757174
八达岭高速公路二期工程	汽车运输	市属	新建	收尾	9701	9812	200000
东四环(高速公路联络线)	市政管理	市属	新建	施工	9805	9911	279400
平安大街建设工程	市政管理	市属	扩建	施工	9802		280366
菜市口南大街道路工程	市政管理	区属	扩建	施工	9807	9909	145164
南闹市口打通工程	市政管理	市属	新建	施工	9805	9909	76000
陕甘宁天然气进京市内工程	煤气供应	市属	新建	施工	9604		355439
高碑店热电厂市内供热管网工程	蒸气热水	市属	新建	施工	9404		372383
双榆树供热厂及供热管网工程	蒸气热水	市属	新建	施工	9412		134440
第九水厂三期及分钟寺调蓄水厂工程	自来水生产	市属	扩建	施工	9604		268978
高碑店北京热电厂（华能）	火力发电	中央	新建	施工	9404		663121
北京供电城网"9950"工程	电力供应	市属	扩建	施工	9512		780000
电信及广播通讯工程	电信业	中央	扩建	施工	9505		72127
高碑店污水处理厂二期工程	市政管理	市属	扩建	施工	9711		112000
水系综合整治及故宫护城河改造工程	水利管理	市属	改建	施工	9804		170000
北京市垃圾处理工程	环境卫生业	区属	新建	施工	9804		24900
2.大型公建和社会事业及公用设施项目							4506115
首都机场航站区扩建	航空运输	中央	扩建	施工	9510		872041
北京公共交通运营调度指挥中心	市内公共交通	市属	新建	施工	9802	9909	18000
"八一"大楼	国家机关	中央	新建	施工	9703	9909	45300
东方广场	房地产开发	区属	新建	施工	9409		1618500
首都时代广场	房地产开发	区属	新建	施工	9511		190270
国际金融大厦	金融业	市属	新建	施工	9612	9912	160000
航华科贸中心	房地产开发	中央	新建	施工	9505		240345
国贸中心二期工程	旅馆业	中央	扩建	施工	9612	9912	81430
中国银行总行大厦	金融业	中央	新建	施工	9608		230000
北京站改造	市政管理	区属	改建	施工	9808	9909	17000
北京远洋大厦	房地产开发	市属	新建	施工	9708		193221
北京饭店改造	旅馆业	市属	改建	施工	9808		38800
嘉里中心	房地产开发	市属	新建	施工	9510		193672
华润大厦	房地产开发	市属	新建	施工	9705	9912	86103
中国评剧院剧场	艺术	市属	新建	施工	9703	9905	5487
北京戏曲学校排演场综合楼	中等专业学校	市属	扩建	施工	9711		19942
中国建筑文化中心	其它文化艺术	中央	新建	施工	9705		36800
中国现代文学馆一期工程	其它文化艺术	中央	新建	施工	9801		15000
首都图书大厦	图书报刊零售	市属	新建	收尾	9312	9808	32000
首都图书馆新馆	图书馆	市属	新建	施工	9712		20000
中国紫檀博物馆	文物保护	中央	新建	施工	9803	9912	15200
西单文化广场	房地产开发	区属	新建	施工	9804		54000
玉渊潭南门广场	房地产开发	区属	新建	施工	9903		21377
朝阳公园	园林绿化业	区属	扩建	施工	9803	9912	18000
中华民族园二期工程	旅游业	区属	扩建	施工	9712		30000
北京海洋馆	园林绿化业	市属	新建	施工	9510		77190
北京植物园展览温室	园林绿化业	市属	扩建	施工	9806		22000
北京大学理科群楼 1#、2#	普通高教	中央	扩建	施工	9710		61149
首都经贸大学图书馆	普通高教	市属	扩建	施工	9712	9910	3798
北京工业大学信息工程楼、经管楼	普通高教	市属	扩建	施工	9502		2310
首都师范大学文科教学楼	普通高教	市属	扩建	施工	9610		4312
北京联合大学图书馆	普通高教	市属	扩建	施工	9712	9912	2600
首都医科大学科研楼	普通高教	市属	扩建	收尾	9308	9812	13332
中国戏曲学院迁建工程	普通高教	中央	迁建	施工	9804		37489
中国科技馆二期工程	其它文化艺术	中央	扩建	施工	9802	9910	12367
妇婴保健中心	妇婴保健	市属	新建	施工	9509		9580
佑安医院病房手术楼	专科医院	市属	扩建	施工	9610		7500
3.住宅开发项目							1229202
望京 A5 住宅区	房地产开发	市属	单建	施工	9503		358357
小营世纪住宅村	房地产开发	市属	单建	收尾	9512	9806	95400
育新花园住宅区二期工程	房地产开发	市属	单建	施工	9709	9912	35000
梅源住宅小区	科学研究	中央	单建	施工	9711		36000
力鸿花园住宅区	房地产开发	市属	单建	施工	9512		45498
燕化星城	企业管理机构	中央	单建	施工	9503		150000
牛街危改住宅区一期工程	房地产开发	市属	单建	施工	9804		200000
平渊里危改住宅区	房地产开发	市属	单建	施工	9512		56000
东花市二期危改住宅区工程	房地产开发	市属	单建	施工	9207	9909	83700

MAJOR PROJECTS OF STATE AND BEIJING

(10000 yuan)

本年计划投资 Planning Investment of this Year	自年初累计完成投资 Accumulative Investment Since Year-Beginning	建筑工程 Construction	安装工程 Installation	设备、工器具购置 Purchase of Equipments and Implements	本年新增固定资产 Incremental Fixed Assets	本年资金来源 Fund Source of this Year	建筑规模和新增生产能力(或效益) Construction Size and Incremental Productive Capital(or Benefit)				
							名称 Item	计算单位 Counting Unit	建设规模 Size	累计新增能力 Accumulative Incremental Capacity	# 本年 of this Year
2324404	1740425	989538	99873	190482	1697220	1889083					
1138175	789547	396902	45772	102896	813045	901578					
136744	129001	54399	18128	22744		165657	地铁	公里	13.5	1.8	
							高速路	公里	30.7	30.7	
116000	94821	90791			235153	115604	城市道路	公里	15.0	15.0	15.0
41100	47828	38982			77391	109000	城市道路	公里	7.0	7.0	7.0
40000	39592	10000			145164	18374	城市道路	公里	2.0	2.0	2.0
6500	3221	1995			4691	3221	城市道路	公里	0.9	0.9	0.9
146000	60460	9011	1266	8337	19358	94024	天然气管	公里	204.0		
69000	78290	41784			103414	70615	供热	兆瓦/小时	500.0	500.0	500.0
22000	35889	14673	1025	2464		36438	供热水	兆瓦/小时	348.0		
110518	86504	49120	4900	13530		105715	自来水	万吨/日	50.0	50.0	
91166	81233	3964	9586	36872	207974	56559	火力发电	万千瓦	65.0	65.0	18.5
230000	29974	10900	9307	7492		29974	变电设备	万千伏安	165.8	63.0	
22197	21454	16709	80	150		9981	交换机	万门	160.0		
20750	14250	3438	700	8810		15490	污水处理	万吨/日	50.0		
75000	53247	43002	42	313		64000					
11200	13783	8134	738	2184	19900	6926					
1038340	822135	490550	53422	84649	756517	852692					
106141	95148	56516	5174	5883		101956	候机楼	平方米	326500		
12500	11944	8474	1000	1916	18000	3100					
					45300						
269517	240589	152286	1862	4345	94	224814					
21029	21029	19801				26098					
5000	2866				139580	2689					
80000	10971	10438	55	117	103611	18767					
40524	51037	45842	590	4605	103500	51037					
110000	78041	20721	24223	27838		52978					
10000	10000	9980			17000	11000					
110000	23325	16826				38219					
30000	17262	16031				40975	客房间数	间	79.0		
54983	54983	24213	5475	13948	126116	107639					
1998	16007	15750			135700	16699					
					6261						
10466	10466	5900	1160	3406		22295					
8054	5236	5114		3		2000					
6000	5284	4999		372		6900					
1500	1500	1010	140	350	3669	1500					
20000	7045	4098	253	1336							
10800	15993	14842	35	197		15812					
18000	40705	8264	1423	3488	39804	37953					
14000	9217	9044				5209					
35000	33849	2749	11000	982		9002					
10198	10354	6810	570	1200		8198					
12927	9459	8008		1400	1400	10009					
1148	1909	1888			2895	1239					
552	720	720				730					
550	1272	661	50	497	2620	907					
							席位	个	3400.0	3400.0	
25000	24339	10916		10599		25000					
6553	6553	4155	382	1900	10967	4367					
3000	2765	2386	30	267		2800	病床	张	300.0		
2900	2267	2108				2800	病床	张	700.0		
147889	128743	102086	679	2937	127658	134813					
4180	5225	5225			34412	30077					
19289	15937	7708			32077	16084					
5395	5395	5395			2090	5395					
17000	4544	3209	524	280		12725					
39000	39750	37453		1815	42688	29750					
36313	36185	25179	100	520		27267					
9672	6227	4339	55	315		2207					
3000	5451	4075				719					

4-17 续表

单位：万元

建设项目名称 Construction Project	国民经济行业 Sector	隶属关系 Administrative Relationship	建设性质 Type of Construction	建设阶段 Stage	开工年月 Beginning Time	投产年月 Operating Time	计划总投资 Total Investment
小黄庄危改住宅区	房地产开发	市属	单建	施工	8810		39247
沙子口危改住宅小区	房地产开发	市属	单建	施工	9612		41000
马家堡安居小区	房地产开发	市属	单建	施工	9511	9901	16000
采石路安居小区东区	房地产开发	市属	单建	施工	9511		23000
望京 K4 区安居小区	房地产开发	市属	单建	施工	9512		50000
二.国家及北京市重点工程							3273649
1.国家重点							1217168
北京大学"211"工程	普通高教	中央	扩建	施工	9510		61149
清华大学"211"工程	普通高教	中央	扩建	施工	9611		48825
中国人民大学"211"工程	普通高教	中央	扩建	施工	9406		14084
北京航空航天大学"211"工程	普通高教	中央	扩建	施工	9703		10100
北京理工大学"211"工程	普通高教	中央	扩建	施工	9612		51901
中国农业大学"211"工程	普通高教	中央	扩建	施工	9612		18700
北京医科大学"211"工程	普通高教	中央	扩建	施工	9609		12500
中国地质大学"211"工程	普通高教	中央	扩建	施工	9812		14000
北京科技大学"211"工程	普通高教	中央	扩建	施工	9706		9000
北京师范大学"211"工程	普通高教	中央	扩建	施工	9611		4700
北方交通大学"211"工程	普通高教	中央	扩建	施工	9806		25520
北京邮电大学"211"工程	普通高教	中央	扩建	筹建			25000
北京林业大学"211"工程	普通高教	中央	扩建	施工	9701		6748
对外经济贸易大学"211"工程	普通高教	中央	单建	施工	9806		12400
首都机场航站区扩建	航空运输	中央	扩建	施工	9510		872041
2.北京市重点工程							2056481
经济适用房							
松下彩管三期工程	电真空器件	市属	扩建	施工	9610		287400
化工三厂搬迁	化学试剂	市属	迁建	筹建			46253
门头沟门矸石空心砖项目	砖瓦制造业	区属	新建	筹建			11000
电子城	其他行业	市属	新建	施工	9801		17336
丰台公安分局看守所	国家机关	区属	扩建	施工	9708		8100
顺义公安分局看守所	国家机关	区属	扩建	筹建			1920
第二中级人民法院	国家机关	市属	新建	施工	9812		8500
北京六里桥长途客运主枢纽	汽车运输	市属	新建	筹建			20000
中华社会大学	高等教育	市属	新建	筹建			15000
大石桥大学生公寓	房地产开发	区属	单建	筹建			20000
北京农产品中央批发市场	零售批发贸易	市属	新建	施工	9410		49500
粮库建设	仓储业	市属	扩建	施工	9809		37548
电话局工程	电信业	中央	新建	施工	9511		80072
农村电网改造	电力供应	中央	改建	施工	9806		92860
天安门广场改造	市政管理	市属	改建	施工	9810	9909	15651
长安街整治工程	市政管理	市属	改建	施工	9901	9912	36700
公路二环（通州至马驹桥段，顺义至西沙屯）	汽车运输	市属	新建	施工	9812		146676
二三环路改造（含西直门立交桥改造）	市政管理	市属	扩建	施工	9901	9909	58330
西便门至莱园街道路	市政管理	市属	新建	施工	9712		900
顺平路改扩建工程	汽车运输	市属	新建	施工	9801		67000
香山道路工程	市政管理	市属	新建	施工	9907	9912	88037
京沈高速公路（北京段）	汽车运输	市属	新建	施工	9808		349582
京开高速公路工程（含玉泉营立交）	汽车运输	市属	新建	施工	9903		240000
石景山给水厂	自来水生产	区属	新建	施工	9805		12000
密云水厂	自来水生产	县属	新建	施工	9905		4500
南口水厂	自来水生产	市属	新建	筹建			
酒仙桥污水处理厂	市政管理	市属	新建	施工	9905		57000
亮马河北岸污水截流管线	市政管理	市属	扩建	施工	9905		15000
永定河芦沟桥以下险工治理	水利管理	市属	改建	施工	9811	9912	12000
密云水库加固工程	水利管理	市属	改建	施工	9707		45270
通惠河整治工程	水利管理	市属	扩建	施工	9702		100000
小清河行滞洪区建设	水利管理	区属	扩建	施工	9812	9907	7325
密云水库上游水土保持工程	水利管理	市属	改建	施工	9812	9908	3928
节水增效灌溉示范项目	水利管理	市属	扩建	施工	9805		250
潮白河灌区	水利管理	市属	改建	施工	9812		2680
海子灌区	水利管理	市属	改建	施工	9811		8500
怀柔国家生态环境综合治理示范区	环境保护	县属	新建	施工	9808		2980
昌平国家生态环境建设重点工程	环境保护	县属	新建	施工	9808		4379
生态防护林工程	林业	市属	新建	施工	9808		2600
北京经济技术开发区基础设施	房地产开发	市属	新建	施工	9204		42693
郊区河道整治	水利管理	市属	改建	施工	9510		34211
西五环（杏石口路至香泉路段）	汽车运输	市属	扩建	施工	9906	9912	2800
抗日战争纪念碑和雕塑园工程	房地产开发	区属	新建	施工	9907		30500

continued

(10000 yuan)

本年计划投资 Planning Investment of this Year	自年初累计完成投资 Accumulative Investment Since Year-Beginning	建筑工程 Construction	安装工程 Installation	设备、工器具购置 Purchase of Equipments and Implements	本年新增固定资产 Incremental Fixed Assets	本年资金来源 Fund Source of this Year	建筑规模和新增生产能力(或效益) Construction Size and Incremental Productive Capital(or Benefit)				
							名称 Item	计算单位 Counting Unit	建设规模 Size	累计新增能力 Accumulative Incremental Capacity	# 本年 of this Year
600	941	941				89					
3390	3180	3180				3170					
2000	612	612			4421	585					
1700	1856	1849		7	11970	1370					
6350	3440	2921				5375					
1013065	1221791	559298	11575	41119	228948	680828					
179752	153115	92670	5174	25385	34359	160516					
10160	9459	8008		1400	1400	10009					
5387	5387	3397		1990	2130	6832					
4470	2367	2334				3240					
1715	4000	1290		2695	2695	2914					
17312	17656	12015		3811	15312	17656	席位	个	2000.0	2000.0	2000.0
2720	1022			1022	1022	170					
2400	620			620	620	620					
3550	642			449	642	1028					
4822	4212	4200				4012					
1380	1360			1360	1360	1360					
8447	8448	3123		5255	8278	8448					
40	40	40				40					
1798	900			900	900	900					
2710	163	56									
106141	95148	56516	5174	5883		101596	候机楼	平方米	326500.0		
833313	1068676	466628	6401	15734	194589	520312					
	375770						面积	万平方米	350.3		6.9
50000							彩管	万只	380.0	90.0	
9100	400					600					
8356	9113	5399	591	2292	13083	9088					
4320	4843	4843				3814					
800											
1600	1319	907				800					
5200											
3000	1900					1900					
8005	10181	2638	448	607		6280					
4137	15691	11612	814	2330	19036	10049	粮食仓库	万公斤	44900.0	7400.0	
24364	24364	20515			2734	20984					
42976	30077	14075	4100	9695		30077					
10651	14642	14100									
36700	36700	22800			36700	36700					
69000	63992	49182			13236	38600	高速公路	公里	26.0		
40897	68745	41959			69245	33897					
							城市道路	公里	0.9		
32000	41232	39232				32000	一级公路	公里	30.0		
72030	68554	15888				32900	城市道路	公里	26.4	26.4	26.4
155000	149410	125817				108400	高速公路	公里	40.0		
90000	24295	11293				13150	高速公路	公里	41.0		
10853	4997	3578		277	9546	4065	供水	万吨/日	5.0	5.0	5.0
1500	1200	910			395	930					
28358	26566	11888				33382	污水处理	万吨/日	20.0		
10000	5017	3209				10000					
5800	5800	4424	400	200	12000	3000					
25270	6420	5807				21000					
26500	31402	16698				26500					
3605	3605	3599				3605					
2598	2598	2598			2598	2598					
209	150	150				209					
							有效灌溉	万亩	33.6		
3500	3500	3378				3500	有效灌溉	万亩	33.6		
2980	2980	2980			2980	2980					
1358	1358	1206		152	2229	851					
2534	2534	402		1	533	2534					
20143	5755	5755				6000					
17969	17969	14692	48	180	4677	17369					
2000	5597	5094			5597	2550	一级公路	公里	4.4	4.4	4.4
6700	1691	1691				1691					

4-18 新建住宅竣工面积
FLOOR SPACE OF NEW RESIDENCE COMPLETED

单位：万平方米 (10000 sq.m)

项　目 Item		1949-1999 合计 Total	1999	占新建住宅面积(%) Proportion in Floor Space of New Residence(%) 合计 Total	1999
总　计	**Total**	**16951.7**	**1519.9**	**100**	**100**
平　房	Singal-storey House	814.1	7.3	4.8	0.5
楼　房	Storied Building	16137.6	1512.6	95.2	99.5
二～三层	2-3 Stories	916.2	39.1	5.4	2.6
四～五层	4-5 Stories	3182.3	62.3	18.8	4.1
六～八层	6-8 Stories	7390.6	681.1	43.6	44.8
九层以上	Over 9 Stories	4648.5	730.1	27.4	48.0
在总计中	**Of Total**				
城　区	City Proper	2809.6	208.1	16.6	13.7
近郊区	Near Suburb	11121.2	884.9	65.6	58.2
远郊区	Outer Suburb	3020.9	426.9	17.8	28.1

4-19 农村集体及城乡私人建房面积
FLOOR SPACE OF BUILDINGS CONSTRUCTED BY RURAL COLLECTED-OWNED UNITS,URBAN AND RURAL INDIVIDUALS

单位：万平方米、间 (10000 sq.m,room)

项　目 Item		1999年 建成房屋面积 Floor Space of Buildings in 1999	#住宅面积 Floor Space of Residence	#住宅间数 Rooms of Residence	1998年 建成房屋面积 Floor Space of Buildings in 1998	#住宅面积 Floor Space of Residence	#住宅间数 Rooms of Residence
总　计	**Total**	**742.6**	**471.6**	**393000.0**	**680.3**	**391.5**	**326250.0**
城镇私人建房	Urban Individuals	35.6	31.6	26333.0	35.2	31.3	26083.0
农村集体建房	Rural Collective-Owned Units	707.0	440.0	366667.0	645.1	360.2	300167.0
非农户	Agriculture	365.0	131.0	109167.0	340.5	68.4	57000.0
农　户	Non-agriculture	342.0	309.0	257500.0	304.6	291.8	243167.0

注：根据国家统计制度规定，1999年年报调整和扩大农村固定资产投资统计范围,因此对1998年同期数据做了相应调整。

Note: According to state statistical rules, statistical range of rural investment in fixed assets is adjusted and expanded in 1999, and the data of 1998 has been made corresponding changes.

4-20 房地产开发企业基本情况
BASIC INFORMATION OF REAL ESTATE COMPANIES

项目	Item	企业单位个数 (个) Number of Companies (unit)	资本金合计 (万元) Total Capital (10000 yuan)	资产总计 (万元) Total Assets (10000 yuan)	年末职工人数 (人) Staff and Workers (year-end) (person)
总计	**Total**	**716**	**5032845**	**29145663**	**36722**
按企业登记注册类型分	**Grouped by Type of Enterprises Registered**				
内资企业	Domestic Investment Enterprises	459	1730605	16027984	25086
国有企业	State-Owned	248	786469	11097712	14813
集体企业	Collective Owned	29	38231	553393	2182
联营企业	Joint Owned	2	1672	33092	62
股份合作企业	Share Holding Cooperative	8	19584	134524	409
股份有限公司	Share Holding Company	34	395179	954901	2025
有限责任公司	Limited-Liability Company	129	374683	2965391	5219
其他企业	Others	9	114787	288971	376
港澳台商投资企业	Hongkong,Macao and Taiwan Funded Enterprises	179	2425207	9347631	7550
港澳台合资经营	Joint Venture	82	730861	3278467	2942
港澳台合作经营	Cooperative	91	1654205	5822398	4336
港澳台商独资企业	Hongkong,Macao and Taiwan Enterprises	3	29859	142786	234
港澳台商投资股份有限公司	Hongkong,Macao and Taiwan Funded Share Holing Company	3	10282	103980	38
外商投资企业	Foreign Funded Enterprises	78	877033	3770048	4086
中外合资经营	Joint Venture	28	314410	1268964	1704
中外合作经营	Cooperative	48	431623	1870599	2119
外资(独资)企业	Foreign Enterprises				
外商投资股份有限公司	Foreign Funded Share Holding Company	2	131000	630485	263
按隶属关系分	**Grouped by Administrative Relationship**				
中央单位	Central	90	509777	2766145	3918
地方单位	Local	626	4523068	26379518	32804
按资质等级分	**Grouped by Grade**				
一级	First-grade	37	470712	6771981	6202
二级	Second-grade	71	300688	2732600	3999
三级	Third-grade	22	133208	817336	1275
四级	Fourth-grade				
五级	Fifth-grade				
无级	No-grade	581	4100334	18665052	24782
兼营	Part-time Operating	5	27903	158694	464
按营业状况分	**Grouped by Business Condition**				
营业	Going on	630	4647582	27874841	34888
停业	Closed down	13	95933	321263	268
筹建	Preparing to Establish	46	227323	693159	965
当年撤消	Cancel in this Year	1			17
其他	Others	26	62007	256400	584

4-21 房地产开发企业开发情况
BUSINESS OF REAL ESTATE DEVELOPMENT ENTERPRISES

单位：万元,平方米 (10000 yuan,sq.m)

项目	Item	全市 合计 Total	# 国有企业 State-Owned	# 三资企业 Foreign Funded	按隶属关系分 Grouped by Administrative Relationship 中央单位 Central Unit	地方单位 Local Unit
计划总投资	Total Planned Investment	31590667	12997913	11999944	2083301	29507366
自开始建设至本年度累计完成投资	Accumulative Investment up to the End of This Year	17114632	5723584	8197999	1321711	15792921
本年完成投资合计	Investment in This Year	4214591	1447175	1557946	303389	3911202
# 商品房建设投资	Commercial House	3094375	980360	1287682	193676	2900699
土地开发投资	Land Development	246465	97654	57381	11910	234555
土地购置费	Purchase of Land	366247	107835	105910	80341	285906
本年完成投资按用途分	Grouped by Purpose of Investment in This Year					
住宅	Residence	2365641	842794	600705	167460	2198181
办公楼	Office	525079	86458	391422	51769	473310
商业营业用房	Commerce	302018	55607	179048	24821	277197
其他	Others	1021853	462316	386771	59339	962514
本年土地开发	Land Development in The Year					
完成开发土地面积	Area of Development Completed	1871817	769288	273647	111800	1760017
开发土地面积	Area of Land Development	3172452	1419605	326072		3172452
购置土地面积	Area of Land Purchasing	4460456	2761563	648727	418630	4041826
房屋建筑施工和竣工面积	Floor Space of Buildings under Construction or Completed					
施工面积	Floor Space of Buildings under Construction	37839569	15828245	11469732	2570355	35269214
# 住宅	Residence	24479002	11381085	4758996	1307399	23171603
竣工面积	Floor Space of Buildings Completed	12085468	5579953	2611071	833241	11252227
# 住宅	Residence	9082634	4376838	1204587	524965	8557669
销售面积	Floor Space of Buildings Sold	5444403	2270149	1159036	341985	5102418
# 住宅	Residence	4847144	2135549	747789	242945	4604199
销售额	Sales Valne	3074693	853787	1367501	304210	2770483
# 住宅	Residence	2320213	785818	735496	137968	2182245

主要统计指标解释

全社会固定资产投资　固定资产投资是全社会固定资产再生产的主要手段。通过建造和购置固定资产的活动，国民经济不断采用先进技术装备，建立新兴部门，进一步调整经济结构和生产力的地区分布，增强经济实力，为改善人民物质文化生活创造物质条件。这对我国的社会主义现代化建设具有重要意义。全社会固定资产投资包括基本建设项目、更新改造项目、国有单位其他投资、城镇集体经济、联营经济、股份制经济、城镇私营经济、城镇个体经济、外商投资经济、港澳台投资经济及其他经济类型投资单位，各种经济类型的房地产开发企业、城镇和工矿区私人建房、农村投资。

基本建设项目　是指批准包括在一个总体设计范围内进行建设，由一个或若干个设计文件规定的有内在联系的单项工程所组成。经济上实行统一核算，行政上有独立组织形式，实行统一管理的基本建设单位。通常以一个企业、事业、行政单位或独立工程作为一个基本建设项目。包括（1）列入中央和各级地方本年基本建设计划的建设项目，以及虽未列入本年基本建设计划，但使用以前年度基本建设结转资金（包括基建库存设备和材料）在本年继续施工的建设项目；（2）本年基本建设计划内投资与更新改造计划内投资结合安排的新建项目和新增生产能力（或工程效益）达到大中型项目标准的扩建项目，以及为改变生产力布局而进行的全厂性迁建项目；（3）国有单位既未列入基建计划，也未列入更新改造计划的总投资在 50 万元及以上的新建、扩建、恢复项目和为改变生产力布局而进行的全厂性迁建项目，以及行政、事业单位增建业务用房和生活福利设施的项目。

更新改造项目　是指经有权单位批准，具有独立的设计文件或项目建议书，能独立发挥效益的工程。更新改造项目大体上相当于基本建设项目的单项工程。包括：（1）列入中央和各级地方本年更新改造计划的项目和虽未列入本年更新改造计划，但使用上年更新改造结转资金（包括库存设备和材料）；（2）本年更新改造计划内投资与基本建设计划内投资结合安排的对企、事业单位原有设施进行技术改造或更新的项目，和增建主要生产车间、分厂等其新增生产能力（或工程效益）未达到大中型项目标准的项目，以及由于城市环境保护和安全生产的需要而进行的迁建项目；（3）国有企、事业单位既未列入基建计划也未列入更新改造计划，总投资在 50 万元及以上的属于改建或更新改造性质的项目，以及由于城市环境保护和安全生产的需要而进行的迁建工程。

国有单位其他投资　是指国有单位按规定不列入基本建设计划和更新改造计划管理的，总投资在 50 万元及以上的投资。包括（1）用油田维护费和石油开发基金进行的油田维护和开发工程；（2）煤炭、铁矿、森工等采掘采伐业用维简费进行的开拓延伸工程；（3）交通部门用公路养路费对原有公路、桥梁进行的改造工程；（4）商业部门用简易建筑费建造的仓库工程。

城镇集体经济投资　是指包括县及县以上人民政府所在地建制镇地域内的城镇集体经济单位，总投资在 50 万元及以上建造和购置固定资产的投资。

房地产开发　包括各种经济类型的房地产开发公司、商品房建设公司及其他房地产开发单位统一开发的包括统建、代建、拆迁、还建的住宅、厂房、仓库、饭店、宾馆、度假村、写字楼、办公楼等房屋建筑物和配套的服务设施、土地开发工程，如道路、给水、排水、供电、供热、通讯、平整场地等基础设施工程的投资。包括非房地产企业实际从事房地产开发或经营活动，不包括单纯的土地交易活动。

城镇私营、个体经济投资　是指包括县及县以上人民政府所在地建制镇地域内的全部城镇私营、个体经济的固定资产投资。城镇私营经济投资包括总投资2万元及以上建造和购置固定资产的投资；城镇个体经济投资包括总投资2000元及以上建造和购置固定资产的投资。

零星固定资产投资 是指包括除基本建设项目、更新改造项目、国有单位其他投资、城镇集体经济投资以外的，总投资在50万元及以下建造和购置固定资产的投资。

城镇和工矿区私人建房投资 是指包括市、县城、镇、工矿区所辖范围内的全部私人建房投资，不论其房主是否系本地常住户口均应包括。

农村投资 是指县及县以上人民政府所在地建制镇地域以外的全部农村固定资产投资。包括非农户投资和农户投资。非农户投资包括使用年限一年以上、单位价值200元以上建造和购置固定资产的投资；农户投资包括使用年限一年以上，单位价值50元以上建造和购置固定资产的投资。

固定资产投资的资金来源 根据固定资产投资的资金来源不同，分为上年末结余资金、本年资金来源和各项应付款。本年资金来源包括国家预算内资金、国内贷款、债券、利用外资、自筹资金和其他资金来源六种。

国家预算内资金 分为财政拨款和财政安排的贷款两部分。包括中央财政的基本建设基金、专项支出、收回再贷、贴息资金，财政安排的挖潜革新改造和新产品试制支出、城建支出、商业部门简易建筑支出、不发达地区发展基金等基金中用于固定资产投资的自决；地方财政中由国家统筹安排的资金等。

国内贷款 指报告期企、事业单位向银行及非银行金融机构借入的用于固定资产投资的各种国内借款。国内贷款包括：银行利用自有资金及吸收的存款发放的贷款、上级主管部门拨入的国内贷款、国家专项贷款（包括煤代油贷款、劳改煤矿专项贷款等），地方财政专项资金安排的贷款、国内储备贷款、周转贷款等。

债券 是企业（公司）或金融机构通过发行各种证券筹集到的用于固定资产投资的资金，包括由银行代理国家专业投资公司发行的重点企业证券和重点建设证券。

利用外资 指报告期收到的用于固定资产建造和购置的境外资金。包括外商直接投资、对外借款（外国政府贷款、国际金融组织贷款、出口信贷、外国银行商业贷款、对外发行债券和股票）及外商其他投资（包括补偿贸易和加工装配中由外商提供的设备价款、国际租赁）。不包括我国自有外汇资金。国家统借统还的外资，是指由我国政府出面同外国政府、团体或金融组织签定贷款协议、并负责偿还本息的国外贷款。

自筹资金 指建设单位报告期收到的，由各地区、各部门及企事业单位筹集用于固定资产投资的预算外资金。包括中央各部门、各级地方和企事业单位的自有资金。股票是指股份制企业通过发行股票筹集到的用于固定资产投资的资金。

其他资金来源 指报告期收到的除以上各种资金之外其他用于固定资产投资的资金。包括社会集资、个人资金、无偿捐赠的资金及其他单位拨入的资金等。

固定资产投资按国民经济行业分 根据现有企业、事业、行政单位和基本建设项目建成投产后的主要产品或主要用途及社会经济活动性质来确定。基本建设按建设项目划分国民经济行业，一般情况下，一个基本建设项目只能属于一种国民经济行业；更新改造、国有经济单位其他投资、城镇集体、城镇私营、城镇个体经济根据整个企业、事业单位所属的行业来划分，一个企业、事业单位只能属于一种国民经济行业。

固定资产投资按建设性质分 建设项目的建设性质一般分为新建、扩建、改建、单纯建造生活设施、迁建、恢复、单纯购置。基本建设按建设项目划分建设性质，更新改造、国有单位其他投资、城镇集体、城镇私营、城镇个体按整个企业、事业单位的建设情况确定建设性质。

新建　一般是指从无到有、“平地起家”开始建设的单位或独立工程。有的单位原有基础很小，经过建设后其新增加的固定资产价值超过原有固定资产价值（原值）三倍以上的也算新建。

扩建　是指为扩大原有产品的生产能力（或效益）或增加新的产品生产能力，而增建主要生产车间（或主要工程）、独立的生产线、分厂的企业；行政、事业单位在原单位增建业务用房（如学校增建教学用房、医院增建门诊部或病房、行政机关增建办公楼等）也作为扩建。

改建　是指现有企业、事业单位不增建主要生产车间、分厂等，而对原有设施进行技术改造或更新为了技术进步（包括相应配套的辅助性生产、生活福利设施）的作为改建；为适应市场变化的需要，而改变企业的主要产品种类，或原有产品生产作业线由于各工序之间能力不平衡，为填平补齐充分发挥原有生产能力而增建不增加本单位主要产品设计能力的车间，也作为改建。

单纯建造生活设施　是指在不扩建、改建生产性工程和业务用房的情况下，单纯建造职工住宅、托儿所、子弟学校、医务室、浴室、食堂等生活福利设施。

固定资产投资按用途分　固定资产投资按用途分为农林牧渔业用、工业建筑业用、商业运输邮电业用、住宅和其他五部分，是研究不同用途的固定资产投资之间比例关系的重要指标。基本建设项目、更新改造限额以上项目、国有单位其他投资、城镇集体、城镇私营、城镇个体投资按单项工程确定，更新改造限额以下投资单位按项目确定。

固定资产投资按构成分　固定资产投资活动按其工作内容和实现方式分为建筑安装工程，设备、工具、器具购置，其他费用三个部分。

建筑安装工程（建安工作量）　指各种房屋、建筑物的建造工程和各种设备、装置的安装工程。包括各种房屋建造工程，各种用途设备基础和各种工业窑炉的砌筑工程；为施工而进行的各种准备工作和临时工程以及完工后的清理工作等；铁路、道路的铺设，矿井的开凿及石油管道的架设等；水利工程；防空地下建筑等特殊工程；以及各种机械设备的安装工程；为测定安装工程质量，对设备进行的试行工作。在安装工程中，不包括被安装设备本身的价值。

设备、工具、器具购置　指购置或自制达到固定资产标准的设备、工具、器具的价值，固定资产的标准按财务部门规定。新建及扩建单位的新建车间按照设计和计划要求购置或自制的全部设备、工具、器具，不论是否达到固定资产标准均计入“设备、工具、器具购置”中。

其他费用　指在固定资产建造和购置过程中发生的，除上述几项以外的各种应摊入固定资产的费用。它包括两种性质的费用，一种是属于增加固定资产的费用，主要有：建设单位管理费，土地、青苗等补偿费和安置补助费、勘察设计费，研究试验费、农林单位牲畜购置费、各种经济林木的营造费、办公和生活家具、器具购置费、引进技术和进口设备项目的其他费用、联合试运转费等；一种是属于不增加固定资产的费用，主要有：施工机械转移费、生产职工培训费、农业开荒费用及报废工程损失费等。

施工项目　指报告期内曾进行建筑或安装工程施工活动的建设项目。施工项目分为报告期正式施工项目、报告期收尾项目和以前年度全部停缓建项目。正式施工项目包括报告期内新开工项目、报告期以前开工跨入报告期继续施工的项目以及报告期施工过并在报告期内全部建成投产或停缓建的项目。

新增生产能力或工程效益　指通过固定资产投资活动而增加的设计能力或工程效益，它是用实物形态表示的固定资产投资的成果。新增生产能力的计算，是以能独立发挥生产能力或效益的单项工程　（或项目）为对象。当建设项目（或单项工程）建成，经有关部门鉴定合格，正式移交投入生产，即可计算新增生产能力或工程效益。计算新增生产能力或工程效益有以下几种表现形式：1. 以建设项目（单位工程）建成投产后的年产能力表示。如煤炭开采、石油开采等；2. 以建设项目（单项工程）建成投产后处理原料的能力表示。如选矿工程的处理矿石能力，洗煤厂年洗原煤能力等；3. 以新增的主要设备数量或容量表示。如棉纺锭数，发电机组容量等。4. 以建筑物容积、容量、面积或长度表示。如水库容量、铁路公路里程等。

新增生产能力的数量一般按设计能力计算。设计能力是指设计文件中规定的在正常情况下能够达到的生产能力，而不论投产后的实际产量如何。以设备数量、建筑物容积、面积、长度等表示的新增生产能力（或工程效益），则按建成的实际数量计算。

城市基础设施投资 城市基础设施包括第二产业中的电力、煤气及水的生产和供应业；第三产业中的水利业、铁路运输、公路运输、管道运输、航空运输、邮电通信、公共服务和环境保护等。

房屋施工面积 是指报告期内施工的全部房屋建筑面积。包括报告期新开工的面积、报告期施工过并在报告期竣工的面积，以及以前年度已停建在报告期继续施工的面积。房屋建筑面积是从房屋外墙线算起的各层平面面积的总和，包括房屋结构（如柱、墙）占用的面积和地下室面积。多层建筑按各自然层面积总和计算，包括房屋内的楼隔层，突出墙面的眺望间、门斗、有柱雨罩的面积。不包括突出墙面结构的构件、艺术装饰等所占的面积，如台阶等。凹阳台、挑阳台按其水平投影面积一半计算建筑面积。

房屋竣工面积 指在报告期内房屋建筑按照设计要求已全部完工，达到住人和使用条件，经验收鉴定合格（或达到竣工验收标准），正式移交使用单位的建筑面积。

房屋面积竣工率 指一定时期内房屋竣工面积占同期房屋施工面积的比率。它是从房屋建筑施工速度的角度反映投资效果和建筑业经济效益的指标。

新增固定资产 指通过投资活动所形成的新的固定资产价值。包括已经建成投入生产或交付使用的工程价值和达到固定资产标准的设备、工具、器具的价值及有关应摊入的费用。它是以价值形式表示的固定资产投资成果的综合性指标，可以综合反映不同时期、不同部门、不同地区的固定资产投资成果。

建设项目投产率 指一定时期内全部建成投产项目个数占同期正式施工项目个数的比率。它是从建设项目建设速度的角度反映投资效果的指标。

Explanatory Notes On Main Statistical Indicators

Total Investment in Fixed Assets Investment in fixed assets is essential for reproduction of fixed assets. By means of construction and purchase of fixed assets, more advanced technologies and equipments are adopted in the national economy, and new sectors are established, which promote the adjustment of economic structure and the regional distribution of production and enhance the economic strengths so as to provide the material conditions for improving people's livelihood. This is significant for speeding up the socialist modernization in China.Total investment in fixed assets includes projects of capital construction, replacement & innovation, other investment by the state-owned units, the investment by the urban collective units, the investment by the joint-owned units, the share holding units, urban private and individual units, the investment by the foreign funds and Hongkong, Macao and Taiwan units and other investment units, the investment of real estate development enterprises, personal house building in urban areas and the jurisdiction of city, and rural investment.

Investment in Capital Construction Capital construction refers to the new construction projects or extension projects and the related work of the enterprises, institutions or administrative units mainly for the purpose of expanding production capacity or improving project efficiency. It includes: （1）

Projects listed in the capital construction plan of the central government and the local governments at various levels in current year as well as the on-going projects from previous years' plan of capital construction and carried forward the investment to this year (including the equipments and materials kept in stock of the capital construction) ; (2) New construction projects arranged in both the plan of capital construction and the plan of replacement & innovation; Extension projects with the newly increased production capacity (or project efficiency) up to the standard of a large and medium-sized project; and the projects of moving the whole factory to a new site so as to improve the distribution of productive forces; (3) New construction projects, extension projects or restoration projects with the total investment at and above 500 thousand RMB by the state-owned units, though listed neither in the plan of capital construction nor in the plan of replacement & innovation; the projects in the state-owned units of moving the whole factory to a new site so as to improve the distribution of productive forces; and the projects of additional business houses by the administrative units and institutions and welfare facilities by the administrative units.

Investment in Replacement & Innovation: Replacement & innovation refers to the renewal or technological upgrade of the original fixed assets by the enterprises and institutions as well as the corresponding supplementary projects and works (excluding major overhaul and maintenance) . It includes: (1) Projects listed in the replacement & innovation plan of the central government and the local governments at various levels in current year as well as the on-going projects from previous years, replacement & innovation plan with the investment carried forward to this year; (2) Replacement or innovation projects arranged both in the plan of replacement & innovation and in the plan of capital construction; Extension projects (main workshops or a branch of the factory) with the newly increased production capacity (or project efficiency) below the standard of a large and medium-sized project; and the projects of moving the whole factory to a new site so as to meet the requirements of urban environmental protection or safe production; (3) Replacement or innovation projects with the total investment at and above 500 thousand RMB by the state-owned units, though listed neither in the plan of capital construction nor in the plan of replacement & innovation; Projects in state-owned units of moving a whole factory to new site so as to meet the requirements of urban environmental protection or safe production.

Other Investment by State-owned Units refers to investment by stated-owned units at and above 500 thousand RMB which not listed in capital construction and replacement & innovation plan. It includes: (1) Projects of oil fields maintenance and exploitation with the oil fields maintenance funds and petroleum development funds; (2) Opening and extending projects with the maintenance funds in coal, ore and other mining enterprises and logging enterprises; (3) Reconstruction of the original highways and bridges with the highway maintenance funds in the department of communications; (4) Construction of warehouses with the funds of simple construction in the commercial department.

Investment by Urban Collective Units refers to investment by urban collective units at and above 500 thousand RMB on building and purchasing fixed assets.

Investment in Real Estate Development includes the investment by the real estate development companies, commercial buildings construction companies and other real estate development units of various types of ownership in the construction of buildings, such as residential buildings, factory buildings, warehouses, hotels, guesthouses, holiday villages, office buildings, and the complementary service facilities and land development projects, such as road, water supply, water drainage, power supply, heating, telecommunications, land leveling and other infrastructures. It covers the activities of the non-real estate companies in real estate development or management, but excludes the activities in simple land transactions.

Investment by Urban Private and Individual Units refers to investment by all urban private and individual units. Investment by urban private units includes that at and above 20 thousand RMB on building and purchasing fixed assets and investment by urban individual units includes that at and above

2000 RMB on building and purchasing fixed assets.

Odd Investment in Fixed Assets refer to investment above 20 thousand RMB and below 500 thousand RMB on building and purchasing fixed assets except investment in capital construction, replacement & innovation, investment by state-owned units and urban collective units.

Investment in Personal House in Urban Area, Industrial and Mining Area refers to investment in personal house of city, county,town, industrial and mining area.

Rural Investment It includes investment by agricultural and non-agricultural households. Investment by non-agricultural households includes that on building and purchasing fixed assets which unit value at 200 RMB, using limits above one year. Investment by agricultural households includes that on building and purchasing fixed assets which unit value above 50 RMB, using limits above one year.

Sources of Funds for Investment in Fixed Assets are classified into: (a) balance of funds brought forward from the previous year, （b）subtotaled sources of funds in this year and （c）various payable funds. The subtotaled sources of funds in this year is further divided into six categories: state budgetary appropriation, domestic loans, bonds, foreign investment, self-raised funds, and others.

State Budgetary Appropriation are classified into financial allocations and loans, includes the central capital construction fund, special expenditure, reloans after drawn back, discount fund, funds from finance on innovation, new products development, city construction, simply construction of commercial department and development fund of developing area, funds overall arranged by state of local finance.

Domestic Loans refer to various funds borrowed by enterprises and institutions from banks and non-bank financial institutions during the reference period for the purpose of investment in fixed assets. Domestic loans include loans issued by bands from their self-owned funds and deposit, loans appropriated by higher responsible authorities, special loans by government（including loan for replacing petroleum with coal, special loan for reform-through-labor coal mines ）, loans arranged by local government from special funds, domestic reserve loan, and working loan, etc..

Bonds refer to funds raised by enterprises（companies ）or financial institutions through issuing various bonds for the purpose of investment in fixed assets, The bonds include Key Enterprise Bond and Key Construction Program Bonds issued by the banks on behalf of the state specialized investment companies.

Foreign Investment refers to foreign funds received during the reference period for the purpose of building and purchasing fixed assets, including direct investment, loans and other foreign investment, excluding self-owned foreign exchange. Foreign funds borrowed and managed by the government refer to foreign loan borrowed by the government from foreign government, organizations, or financial institutions under official agreements and the government is responsible for the repayment of the principal and the interests.

Self-raised Funds refer to extra-budgetary funds received by each region, department, enterprise and institution on investment in fixed assets, including self-owned funds of central departments, local enterprises and institutions. Stocks refer to funds raised by share holding enterprises through issuing stocks for the purpose of investment in fixed assets.

Other Funds Sources refer to funds received during the reference period which are not included in the above-mentioned source, including social fund raising, individual funds, contribution gratis and funds allocated by other units..

Investment in Fixed Assets by Sector The classification of construction projects by sector is determined by the major products or the purpose of the projects when they are put into use, and by the nature of their social economic activities. The investment in capital construction is classified according to construction projects, In general, one project only belong to one sector. While investment in replacement & innovation, other investment by state-owned units and urban collective, private and individual units are classified according to the sector which the whole enterprise or institution belongs to. In general, one enterprise or institution can only belong to one sector.

Investment in Fixed Assets by Type of Construction The investment projects in general can be classified into new construction, expansion, reconstruction, building living construction, moving away, purchasing and restoration. For capital construction the type of construction is determined by the project. For investment in replacement & innovation and for other investment by state-owned and collective-owned units, urban private and individual units, the type of construction is determined by the enterprise or the institution.

New construction in general refers to newly constructed units or independent projects; some of expansions are also considered as new constructions in the case that the value of the original fixed assets is quite small, and the value of increased fixed assets exceeds the original ones over three times,.

Expansion refers to construction of new major production workshop or projects, independent production line, or construction branch of a factory so as to increase the production capacity and efficiency of the original products. Newly constructed business houses in institutions and administrative organizations (such as the newly constructed teaching buildings in schools, clinics or bed building in hospitals, and office buildings in administrative organizations, etc.) are classified as expansions.

Reconstruction refers to technical upgrade and renewal of the existing equipment and technical conditions undertaken by enterprises and institutions for the purposes of technological advancement, improvement in product quality, enlarging variety of products, promoting new generation of products, reducing productive consumption and cost, promoting comprehensive utilization of resources, strengthening treatment of waste gas, wastewater and solid wastes, and safety in production, etc. through application of new technologies and techniques, use of new equipment and new materials (including accessory facilities for production or for living and welfare purposes). Construction of new workshops for easing the bottleneck limits rather than increasing production capacity is also considered as reconstruction.

Building living construction refers to Building welfare constructions such as residence,kingdergarden,schools,clinics,canteens and so on for staff and workers with no expansion,reconstruting productive projects and business buildings.

Investment in Fixed Assets by Industry can be classified into five fields, i. e. construction for FFAF; industry and construction; commerce,transportation,posts and telecommunications; residence and others, which reflects important proportions of investment among different industries. The industry of the investment in capital construction, replacement & innovation above quota, other investment in fixed assets by state-owned units, urban collective units, urban private and individual units is determined according to the individual projects. The industry of the investment in replacement & innovation below quota is determined according to the relevant projects.

Investment in Fixed Assets by Composition refers to the three major parts of investment activities, i. e. construction and installation, purchase of equipment and instrument, and other expenses.

Construction and installation (work load of construction and installation) refers to the construction of various houses and buildings and installation of various kinds of equipment and instruments, including construction of various houses, equipment foundations and industrial kilns and stoves, preparation in advance and clearing up afterwards for project construction, pavement of railways and roads, drilling of mines and putting up of oil pipes, construction for water conservancy, underground constructions for air defense and other special projects, installation of various machinery equipment, trial running for testing the quality of installation. The value of equipment installed is not included in the value of installation projects.

Purchase of equipment and instruments refers to the total value of equipment, tools, and vessels purchased or self-produced which come up to standards for fixed assets. Equipment, tools and vessels purchased or self-produced for new workshops by newly established or expanded units are categorized as "purchase of equipment and instruments" no matter whether they come up to the standards for fixed assets or not.

Other expenses refers to expenses on building and purchasing fixed assets except the above items, which consist of two categories: one results in the increase of fixed assets, including administration expenses of construction units, compensation for the loss of land and young crops, subsidies for moving, and expenses on geological prospecting and designing, research and testing, purchase of animals by agricultural and forestry units, planting and operating of various economic forest, purchase of office and home furniture, purchase of instruments and vessels, introduction of technology and imports of equipment, and joint trial running; the other does not result in the increase of fixed assets, including expenses on transportation of construction machines, training of staff and workers , opening up waste land, and loss of discarded projects.

Projects under Construction refer to projects having construction and installation activities undertaken in the reference period, including projects under construction or winding up in the reference period, stop or delayed from previous period. Projects under construction including those started in the reference period, or continued from previous period, or completed and put into production or suspended in the reference period.

Newly Increased Production Capacity or Project Efficiency refers to the increase of designed capacity and project efficiency through investment in fixed assets, which reflects the accomplishment of investment in fixed assets in kind. The statistics of newly increased production capacity is based on individual project with possibility of operating independently. A project is counted as newly increased production capacity when it is completed and checked and accepted and put into use. The newly increased production capacity and project efficiency are usually expressed in one of the following terms: (1) annual production capacity , such as extraction of coal and petroleum; (2) raw material processing capacity, such as ore dressing capacity of ore dressing projects, the dressing, capacity of a coal washer; (3) number or capacity of major equipment increased, such as the number of cotton spindles increased and the capacity of generating sets increased; (4) physical measures of construction, such as volume, capacity, area, and length, for instance, the capacity of reservoirs, the length of railways or highways.

Newly increased production capacity in terms of quantity is calculated at designed capacity in general, which refers to the production capacity or project efficiency of a project under normal conditions supposed in construction documents regardless of the actual output.

Investment in urban infrastructure facilities include the production and supply of electricity, gas and tap water in the secondary industry and water conservancy, railway transportation, highway transportation, pipeline transportation, air transportation, posts and telecommunications, public services, environmental protection in the tertiary industry.

Floor Space of Buildings under Construction refers to total floor of buildings under construction, including those of buildings started in the reference period, or continued from previous period, constructed and completed in the reference period and reconstruction in the reference period. It is total of each story of buildings calculated from the outside line of building walls, including the space occupied by constructions like pillars or walls and basements. The floor space of space of multi-story building is the totaled floor space of each story, including area occupied by separating walls, watching rooms, doorways, and pillars, excluding protruding wall structures, artistic decoration, etc.(for example, flight of steps) . The space of porch and balcony is counted by half of the projection area.

Floor Space of Buildings Completed refers to the total floor space of the completed buildings, which have met the designed using or living conditions, passed the check and accepted by the users in the reference period.

Percentage of Floor Space of Buildings Completed refers to the ratio of the floor space of buildings completed to the floor space of buildings under construction in the same period, which reflects the investment result and economic efficiency of the construction industry from the point of the construction speed.

Incremental Fixed Assets refer to the newly increased value of fixed assets through investment, including the value of projects completed and put into use, the value of equipment, tool and vessels considered as fixed assets as well as the relevant expenses accounted as investment in fixed assets. This is a comprehensive indicator of investment in fixed assets, reflecting the achievements of investment in fixed assets in given periods, given sectors or given regions.

Rate of Construction Projects Put into Use refers to the ratio of the number of construction projects completed and put into use to the number of projects under construction in the same period, which reflects the investment efficiency from the point of the construction speed.

农业及农村经济
AGRICULTURE AND RURAL ECONOMY

1999年主要农作物、农产品产量(万吨)

Yield of Major Farm Crops and Farm Products (10000ton)

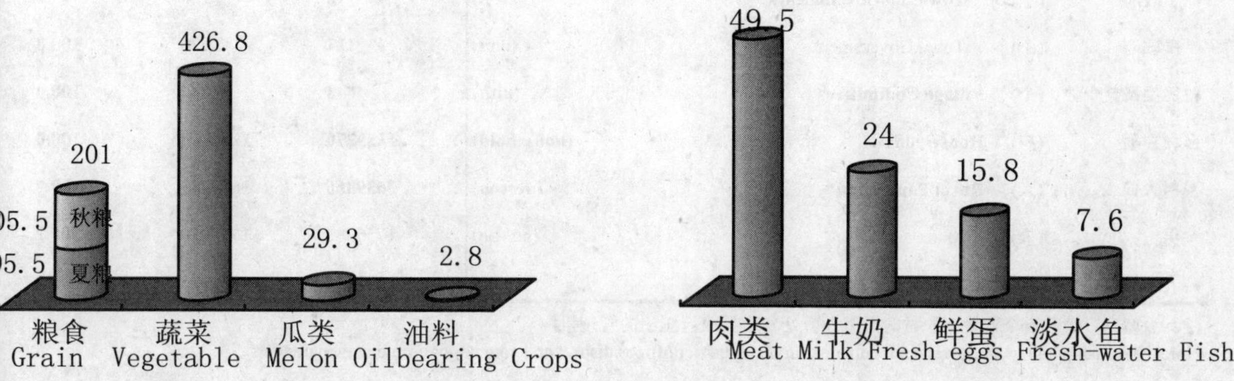

1999年乡镇企业主要产品产量占全市的比重

Major Products Output of Town and Township Enterprises and Their Proportion in Total of the City

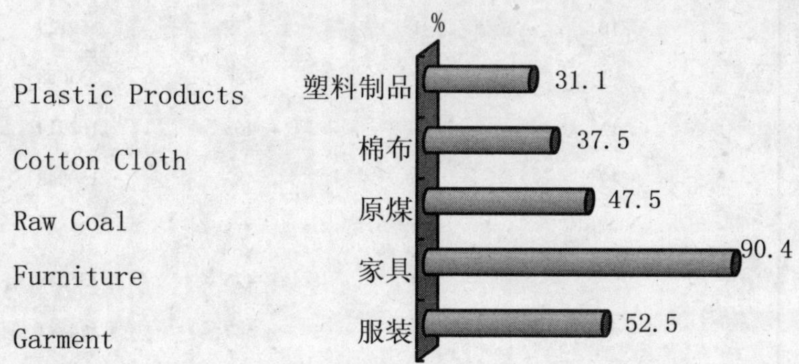

5-1 农村基层组织情况
BASIC RURAL UNITS

项目 Item				1999	1998	1999年为1998年% 1999 as % of 1998
乡镇政府个数	**(个)**	**Number of Township and Town Government**	**(unit)**	**239**	**246**	**97.2**
乡政府	(个)	Township Government	(unit)	118	126	93.7
镇政府	(个)	Town Government	(unit)	121	120	100.8
村民委员会个数	**(个)**	**Village Committees**	**(unit)**	**4043**	**4044**	**100.0**
乡村户数	**(户)**	**Households**	**(household)**	**1259270**	**1259368**	**100.0**
乡村人口	**(人)**	**Rural Population**	**(person)**	**3639366**	**3644265**	**99.9**
男	(人)	Male	(person)	1755986	1753050	100.2
女	(人)	Female	(person)	1883380	1891215	99.6

注：乡政府、镇政府个数含有农村的街道办事处和区县政府派出的管理机构。

Note：Township and town government contains rural subdistrict offices,district and county government agencies.

5-2 郊区县基层组织情况
BASIC UNITS IN SUBURBS AND COUNTIES

单位：个 (unit)

项目	Item	乡政府 Township Government	镇政府 Town Government	村民委员会 Village Committee	乡村户数(户) Rural Household (household)	乡村人口(人) Rural Population (person)
全市	**Total**	**118**	**121**	**4043**	**1259270**	**3639366**
朝阳区	Chaoyang	24		170	84260	203131
丰台区	Fengtai	6		81	59417	152647
石景山区	Shijingshan			12	7215	15821
海淀区	Haidian	10	1	79	59125	149505
门头沟区	Mentougou	3	9	186	35068	96495
房山区	Fangshan	12	16	463	162914	488993
通州区	Tongzhou	12	10	483	150048	419657
昌平区	Changping		17	313	91601	258169
顺义区	Shunyi		19	426	135589	432523
大兴县	Daxing	18	9	547	114841	382131
平谷县	Pinggu	11	10	275	97828	314140
怀柔县	Huairou	5	10	287	70257	188445
密云县	Miyun	7	12	347	115517	324170
延庆县	Yanqing	10	8	374	75590	213539

5-3 乡 村 从 业 人 员
RURAL EMPLOYMENT

单位：人 (person)

项目	Item	1999	1998	构成(%) Composition(%) 1999	构成(%) Composition(%) 1998
乡村从业人员	**Rural Employment**	**1652709**	**1610221**	**100**	**100**
# 种植业	Planting	572041	564893	34.6	35.1
林业	Forestry	48984	40783	3.0	2.5
牧业	Animal Husbandry	77777	60951	4.7	3.8
渔业	Fishery	12032	10658	0.7	0.7
农村工业	Industry	348580	366347	21.1	22.8
乡镇工业	Township and Town Industry	132736	144573	8.0	9.0
村及村以下工业	Industry at Village Level and Below	215844	221774	13.1	13.8
农村建筑业	Construction	127270	117744	7.7	7.3
农村运输业	Transportation	118797	101562	7.2	6.3
农村商业、饮食业	Commerce and Catering	102991	87219	6.2	5.4

5-4 郊 区 县 乡 村 从 业 人 员
RURAL EMPLOYMENT IN SUBURBS AND COUNTIES

单位：人 (person)

项目	Item	从业人员 Employment 1999	从业人员 Employment 1998	# 种植业从业人员 Employment of Planting 1999	# 种植业从业人员 Employment of Planting 1998
全市	**Total**	**1652709**	**1610221**	**710834**	**564893**
朝阳区	Chaoyang	90957	92615	18432	15629
丰台区	Fengtai	71394	70258	18303	15603
石景山区	Shijingshan	7638	7729	1281	736
海淀区	Haidian	61383	57154	15299	9375
门头沟区	Mentougou	43210	45530	11729	10237
房山区	Fangshan	213154	217501	78131	68081
通州区	Tongzhou	184599	183317	82852	70083
昌平区	Changping	118142	102781	47761	32798
顺义区	Shunyi	189018	1873978	62788	45238
大兴县	Daxing	191692	179112	127421	114804
平谷县	Pinggu	149169	139513	79235	62818
怀柔县	Huairou	81752	81135	36330	24636
密云县	Miyun	156813	156927	78604	54679
延庆县	Yanqing	93788	88671	52668	40176

5-5 郊区国内生产总值
GROSS DOMESTIC PRODUCT OF SUBURBS

单位：万元 (10000 yuan)

项目	Item	1999	1998	1999年为1998年% 1999 as % of 1998	构成(%) Composition(%) 1999	1998
总计	**Total**	**4869831.5**	**4466070.5**	**109.0**	**100**	**100**
第一产业	**Primary Industry**	**874786.3**	**865618.7**	**101.1**	**18.0**	**19.4**
第二产业	**Secondary Industry**	**1943080.2**	**1809374.5**	**107.4**	**39.9**	**40.5**
# 工业	Industry	1486978.1	1374344.9	108.2	30.5	30.8
第三产业	**Tertiary Industry**	**2051965.0**	**1791077.3**	**114.6**	**42.1**	**40.1**
农林牧渔服务业	Services of FFAF	19525.0	18677.3	104.5	0.4	0.4
地质勘查及水利管理业	Geographic Prospect and Water Conservancy	4687.9	5307.5	88.3	0.1	0.1
交通运输、仓储及邮电通信业	Transportation,Storge, Posts and Telecommunications	304261.9	246807.7	123.3	6.2	5.5
批发零售贸易及餐饮业	Wholesales,Retail Sales and Catering	409050.9	363963.8	112.4	8.4	8.1
金融保险业	Banking and Insurance	216089.0	244422.8	88.4	4.4	5.5
房地产业	Real Estate	241247.3	191272.9	126.1	5.0	4.3
社会服务业	Social Services	354346.4	332543.5	106.6	7.3	7.4
卫生、体育及社会福利事业	Health,Sports and Social Welfares	58941.6	44666.5	132.0	1.2	1.0
教育、文化及广播电影电视业	Education,Culture, Radio,Film and Television	145764.1	119626.3	121.8	3.0	2.7
科学研究及综合技术服务业	Scientific Research and Polytechnic Services	22996.0	19256.1	119.4	0.5	0.4
国家机关、党政机关及社会团体	Government Organs, Party Organs and Social Bodies	134040.7	110233.9	121.6	2.8	2.5
其他行业	Others	141014.2	94299.0	149.5	2.9	2.1

注：“郊区国内生产总值”统计口径：近郊区为乡及乡以下农村部分；远郊区（县）为县及县以下所属部分。(下表同)

Note: Gross domestic product of near suburbs is that produced by units of rural area at townships level and below,and that of outer suburbs and counties is produced by units at counties level and below.(the following is the same)

5-6 郊区国内生产总值构成项目
COMPOSITION OF GROSS DOMESTIC PRODUCT OF SUBURBS

单位：万元 (10000 yuan)

项目	Item	增加值 Added Value	劳动者报酬 Remuneration for Labors	固定资产折旧 Depreciation on Fixed Assets	生产税净额 Net Taxes on Production	营业盈余 Operating Surplus
总计	**Total**	**4869831.5**	**2394296.9**	**817786.2**	**494580.3**	**1163168.1**
第一产业	**Primary Industry**	**874786.3**	**544639.6**	**70835.7**	**135.6**	**259175.4**
第二产业	**Secondary Industry**	**1943080.2**	**926043.3**	**315167.0**	**349807.9**	**352062.0**
# 工业	Industry	1486978.1	651113.0	274132.0	294363.4	267369.7
第三产业	**Tertiary Industry**	**2051965.0**	**923614.0**	**431783.5**	**144636.8**	**551930.7**
农林牧渔服务业	Services of FFAF	19525.0	12850.1	2935.0	799.9	2940.0
地质勘查及水利管理业	Geographic Prospect and Water Conservancy	4687.9	4483.0	1621.9	281.6	-1698.6
交通运输、仓储及邮电通信业	Transportation,Storge, Posts and Telecommunications	304261.9	137877.0	65743.4	24330.8	76310.7
批发零售贸易及餐饮业	Wholesales,Retail Sales and Catering	409050.9	215477.2	51326.6	43900.9	98346.2
金融保险业	Banking and Insurance	216089.0	26637.5	11264.2	16868.4	161318.9
房地产业	Real Estate	241247.3	21577.6	166853.7	16769.5	36046.5
社会服务业	Social Services	354346.4	153527.1	71000.3	32269.3	97549.7
卫生、体育及社会福利事业	Health,Sports and Social Welfares	58941.6	47212.5	5966.7	724.0	5038.4
教育、文化及广播电影电视业	Education,Culture, Radio,Film and Television	145764.1	121115.6	20581.4	1294.8	2772.3
科学研究及综合技术服务业	Scientific Research and Polytechnic Services	22996.0	10168.1	6070.6	1330.2	5427.1
国家机关、党政机关及社会团体	Government Organs, Party Organs and Social Bodies	134040.7	1039479.0	16378.0	874.5	12840.3
其他行业	Others	141014.2	68740.4	12041.7	5192.9	55039.2

5-7 农业总产值
GROSS OUTPUT VALUE OF AGRICULTURE

单位：万元 (10000 yuan)

项目	Item	总产值（1990年不变价格） Gross Output Value(at 1990 constant prices)		1999年为1998年% 1999 as % of 1998	总产值（现价） Gross Output Value (at current prices)		1999年为1998年% 1999 as % of 1998
		1999	1998		1999	1998	
总计	**Total**	**996231.2**	**935164.4**	**106.5**	**1843426.7**	**1766138.8**	**104.4**
种植业	**Planting**	**492854.1**	**484585.7**	**101.7**	**911918.7**	**891629.8**	**102.3**
谷物	Cereal	106059.8	123353	86.0	263270.8	302562.5	87.0
豆类	Soybeans	2825.5	3599	78.5	6422.3	8778.8	73.2
经济作物	Cash Crops	9974.3	5864.9	170.1	15385.5	11405.1	134.9
蔬菜、瓜类	Vegetable and Melon	236078	220061.4	107.3	450075.4	412014.3	109.2
桑、水果	Mulberry and Fruit	95109.7	82906.9	114.7	120034.9	102787.6	116.8
其他	Others	42806.8	48800.5	87.7	56729.8	54081.5	104.9
林业	**Forestry**	**18127.5**	**15880.7**	**114.1**	**41868.4**	**32302.2**	**129.6**
牧业	**Animal Husbandry**	**434137.3**	**395030.4**	**109.9**	**810859.3**	**766338.4**	**105.8**
家畜繁殖增重	Weight Increase of Domestic Animals Breeding	201134	178598.2	112.6	416181.3	410361.8	101.4
# 养猪	Hogs	146503.3	147947.8	99.0	312604.6	341258	91.6
家禽饲养	Poultry Raising	125294.5	99813.7	125.5	230150.6	169778.6	135.6
活的畜禽产品	Live Animal and Poultry Production	104513.3	111262.6	93.9	157746.5	168175.3	93.8
# 鲜蛋	Fresh Eggs	70284.7	80471	87.3	79319.2	100528.7	78.9
其他	Others	3195.5	5355.9	59.7	6780.9	18022.7	37.6
渔业	**Fishery**	**51112.3**	**39667.6**	**128.9**	**78779.6**	**75868.4**	**103.8**

5-8 农林牧渔业中间消耗

INTERMEDIATE INPUT OF FARMING,FORESTRY,HUSBANDRY AND FISHERY

单位：万元 (10000 yuan)

项　　目	Item	1999	1998	1999 年为 1998 年% 1999 as % of 1998
农林牧渔业生产中间消耗总计	**Total**	**968640.4**	**900520.1**	**107.6**
农业中间消耗合计	**Farming**	**409487.8**	**376133.0**	**108.9**
种植业中间消耗	Planting	398638.3	368679.1	108.1
中间物质消耗	Intermediate Material Input	346489.8	335218.5	103.4
# 用种量	Seeds	42857.3	44948.1	95.3
肥　料	Fertilizer	118560.1	103300.8	114.8
农　药	Farm Chemical	15069.6	13132.2	114.8
对非物质生产部门劳务支出	Services Expenditure to Non-material Production Departments	52148.5	33460.6	155.9
其他农业中间消耗	Others	10849.5	7453.9	145.6
中间物质消耗	Intermediate Material Input	10411.9	6790.1	153.3
对非物质生产部门劳务支出	Services Expenditure to Non-material Production Departments	437.6	663.8	65.9
林业中间消耗合计	**Forestry**	**14156.9**	**12013.7**	**117.8**
中间物质消耗	Intermediate Material Input	12629.5	11231	112.5
# 农　药	Farm Chemical	835.4	757.1	110.3
对非物质生产部门劳务支出	Services Expenditure to Non-material Production Departments	1527.4	782.7	195.1
牧业中间消耗合计	**Animal Husbandry**	**497373.5**	**469476.0**	**105.9**
中间物质消耗	Intermediate Material Input	473748.3	455783.2	103.9
# 饲料、饲草	Forage and Forage Grass	408246.4	411404.3	99.2
对非物质生产部门劳务支出	Services Expenditure to Non-material Production Departments	23625.2	13692.8	172.5
渔业中间消耗合计	**Fishery**	**47622.2**	**42897.4**	**111.0**
中间物质消耗	Intermediate Material Input	44255	41197.1	107.4
# 饲　料	Forage	29616.7	30721.7	96.4
对非物质生产部门劳务支出	Services Expenditure to Non-material Production Departments	3367.2	1700.3	198.0

5-9 耕 地 面 积
AREA UNDER CULTIVATION

项 目 Item		面 积 (公顷) Area (hectare)		构 成 (%) Composition(%)	
		1999	1998	1999	1998
合 计	**Total**	**338384.4**	**341056.7**	**100**	**100**
按水利状况分	**Grouped by Irrigation Conditions**				
水 田	Irrigated Field	29536.7	31091.4	8.7	9.1
旱 地	Non-irrigated Farmland	308847.7	309965.3	91.3	90.9
# 水浇地	Irrigated Land	246524.9	253494.1	72.9	74.3
# 菜 地	Vegetable Plot		...		...
按当年使用分	**Grouped by Using in this Year**				
粮食作物	Grain Crops	240510.2	249346.5	71.1	73.1
经济作物	Cash Crops	11876.1	11634.9	3.5	3.4
蔬 菜	Vegetable	43157.7	42679.1	12.8	12.5
其 他	Others	42840.4	37396.2	12.6	11.0

注：本表数字由市土地局提供。

Note：Data of this table are provided by Beijing Municipal Land Bureau.

5-10 国有农场基本情况
BASIC STATISTICS ON STATE-OWNED FARMS

项 目 Item				1999	1998	1999 年为 1998 年% 1999 as % of 1998
农场数	(个)	Number of Farms	(unit)	15	15	100.0
年末固定职工	(人)	Number of Full-time Staff(year-end)	(person)	38719	41734	92.8
耕地面积	(公倾)	Cultivated Land	(hectare)	2752	3003	91.6
农业总产值 (1990 年不变价,万元)		Gross Output Value of Agriculture	(at 1990 constant prices,10000 yuan)	26102	25910	100.7
工业总产值 (1990 年不变价,万元)		Gross Output Value of Industry	(at 1990 constant prices,10000 yuan)	121288	115183	105.3
主要农产品产量		Yield of Major Farm Products				
粮 食	(吨)	Grain	(ton)	6840	7664	89.2
蔬 菜	(吨)	Vegetable	(ton)	1295	1787	72.5
牛 奶	(吨)	Milk	(ton)	126000	122662	102.7
# 商品量	(吨)	Commodity	(ton)	122336	119070	102.7
干鲜果品	(吨)	Dry and Fresh Fruit	(ton)	3421	5012	68.3
大中型拖拉机	(台)	Large and Medium Tractors	(unit)	155	169	91.7
小型拖拉机	(台)	Mini-Tractors	(unit)	41	72	56.9
载重汽车	(辆)	Trucks	(unit)	252	301	83.7
销售收入	(万元)	Sales Revenue	(10000 yuan)	299017	369963	80.8
利 润	(万元)	Profits	(10000 yuan)	3339	3238	103.1
税 金	(万元)	Taxes	(10000 yuan)	10662	8568	124.4

注：本表数据由市农场局提供。

Note：Data of this table are provided by Beijing Municipal Farm Bureau.

5-11 主要农作物播种面积及产量
SOWN AREAS AND YIELD OF MAJOR FARM CROPS

项目 Item		1999 播种面积(公顷) Sown Areas (hectare)	1999 单产(公斤/公顷) Unit Yield (kg/hectare)	1999 总产量(吨) Total Yield (ton)	1998 播种面积(公顷) Sown Areas (hectare)	1998 单产(公斤/公顷) Unit Yield (kg/hectare)	1998 总产量(吨) Total Yield (ton)
粮食	**Grain**	**409708.0**	**4905.4**	**2009793.0**	**422659.1**	**5660.6**	**2392472.0**
按季节分	Grouped by Season						
夏粮	Summer Grain	168195.4	5680.1	955362.0	171275.9	5648.9	967507.0
秋粮	Autumn Grain	241512.6	4365.9	1054431.0	251383.1	5668.5	1424965.0
按品种分	Grouped by Variety						
稻谷	Rice	19152.7	6755	129377.0	19430.0	6847.5	133055.0
冬小麦	Winter Wheat	168039.7	5683.2	955003.0	171154.6	5651.1	967212.0
玉米	Corn	198111.3	4374.0	866539.0	207722.7	5904.0	1226395.0
薯类	Tubers	5222.2	4591.9	23980.0	4955.1	4686.0	23216.0
大豆	Soybean	10376.4	1948.5	20218.0	10237.7	2445.0	25031.0
棉花	**Cotton**	**1857.9**	**1016.2**	**1888.0**	**2103.0**	**854.4**	**1797.0**
油料	**Oil-bearing Crops**	**10427.1**	**2647.0**	**27601.0**	**9652.2**	**2941.4**	**28391.0**
#花生	Peanuts	9859.4	2736.9	26984.0	9227.5	3010.9	27783.0
蔬菜	**Vegetable**	**93517.9**	**45635.3**	**4267718.0**	**90177.7**	**45036.2**	**4061261.5**
瓜类	**Melon**	**5457.3**	**53775.9**	**293471.0**	**5405.7**	**54494.9**	**294581.0**
#西瓜	Watermelon	5032.9	54911.3	276363.0	5122.9	55197.0	282767.0

5-12 郊区县粮食、油料占耕地面积
THE PROPORTION OF GRAIN,OIL-BEARING CROPS IN CULTIVATED AREA OF SUBURBS AND COUNTIES

单位：公顷 (hectare)

地区	Region	粮食 Grain 1999	粮食 Grain 1998	粮食 Grain 1999年为1998年% 1999 as % of 1998	油料 Oil-bearing Crops 1999	油料 Oil-bearing Crops 1998	油料 Oil-bearing Crops 1999年为1998年% 1999 as % of 1998
全市	**Total**	**240510.2**	**249346.5**	**96.5**	**9723.4**	**9093.5**	**106.9**
朝阳区	Chaoyang	6872.1	7150.2	96.1			
丰台区	Fengtai	2191.1	2293.2	95.5		2.7	
海淀区	Haidian	5037.8	5116.3	98.5			
门头沟区	Mentougou	2482.7	3638.3	68.2			
房山区	Fangshan	31593.1	32038.4	98.6	683.0	679.0	100.6
通州区	Tongzhou	37115.4	39564.2	93.8	634.7	449.0	141.4
昌平区	Changping	18789.4	19859.9	94.6	12.2	15.2	80.3
顺义区	Shunyi	40119.9	40309.2	99.5	339.3	311.3	109.0
大兴县	Daxing	29962.9	31485	95.2	3582.2	3242.7	110.5
平谷县	Pinggu	13661.6	14270.8	95.7	254.5	244.6	104.0
怀柔县	Huairou	12463.9	12917.2	96.5	672.8	642.7	104.7
密云县	Miyun	16075.4	16436.3	97.8	3477.5	3439.7	101.1
延庆县	Yanqing	23444.5	24267.5	96.6	67.2	66.6	100.9
农场局	Municipal Farm Bureau	700.4					

5-13 郊区县蔬菜、西瓜占耕地面积
THE PROPORTION OF VEGETABLE,WATERMELON IN CULTIVATED AREA OF SUBURBS AND COUNTIES

单位：公顷　(hectare)

地　区 Region		蔬　菜 Vegetable 1999	1998	1999年为1998年% 1999 as % of 1998	西　瓜 Watermelon 1999	1998	1999年为1998年% 1999 as % of 1998
全　市	**Total**	**43157.7**	**42679.0**	**101.1**	**3399.8**	**3515.0**	**96.7**
朝阳区	Chaoyang	2209.9	2315.0	95.5	0.3		
丰台区	Fengtai	1982.7	2178.0	91.0			
石景山区	Shijingshan	113.3	126.7	89.4			
海淀区	Haidian	1424.5	1854.0	76.8			
门头沟区	Mentougou	430.7	436.9	98.6			
房山区	Fangshan	2113.1	2341.5	90.3	68.9	62.3	110.6
通州区	Tongzhou	6764.1	6118.9	110.5	212.5	252.7	84.1
昌平区	Changping	1554.5	1447.5	107.4		36.4	
顺义区	Shunyi	7069.9	7164.0	98.7	437.3	348.7	125.4
大兴县	Daxing	9765.3	9257.8	105.5	2549.8	2606.9	97.8
平谷县	Pinggu	2958.8	2807.0	105.4	108.2	174.3	62.1
怀柔县	Huairou	781.8	871.6	89.7	1.3	1.0	130.0
密云县	Miyun	1320.9	1350.5	97.8	16.9	24.9	67.9
延庆县	Yanqing	4630.1	4408.8	105.0	4.6	7.8	59.0
农场局	Municipal Farm Bureau	38.1					

5-14 郊区县粮食、油料播种面积
SOWN AREAS OF GRAIN,OIL-BEARING CROPS IN SUBURBS AND COUNTIES

单位：公顷　(hectare)

地　区 Region		粮　食 Grain 1999	1998	1999年为1998年% 1999 as % of 1998	油　料 Oil-bearing Crops 1999	1998	1999年为1998年% 1999 as % of 1998
全　市	**Total**	**409708.0**	**422659.1**	**96.9**	**10427.0**	**9652.2**	**108.0**
朝阳区	Chaoyang	11808.3	12144.9	97.2			
丰台区	Fengtai	3202.3	3417.4	93.7		2.7	
海淀区	Haidian	5505.9	5341.2	103.1			
门头沟区	Mentougou	3959.6	4009.1	98.8			
房山区	Fangshan	52813.1	53724.7	98.3	705.6	680.8	103.6
通州区	Tongzhou	72695.4	77477.6	93.8	653.5	449	145.5
昌平区	Changping	32169.7	33813.1	95.1	18.5	19.1	96.9
顺义区	Shunyi	77087.7	77827.9	99.0	348.0	321.3	108.3
大兴县	Daxing	54235.7	56892.2	95.3	3996.3	3647.6	109.6
平谷县	Pinggu	25724.6	26912.7	95.6	276.1	261.3	105.7
怀柔县	Huairou	19859.1	20856.5	95.2	679.5	646.4	105.1
密云县	Miyun	25172.2	25445.3	98.9	3678.3	3547.5	103.7
延庆县	Yanqing	24191.1	24796.0	97.6	71.2	76.5	93.1
农场局	Municipal Farm Bureau	1283.3					

5-15 郊区县蔬菜、西瓜播种面积
SOWN AREAS OF VEGETABLE,WATERMELON IN SUBURBS AND COUNTIES

单位：公顷 (hectare)

地 区 Region		蔬 菜 Vegetable			西 瓜 Watermelon	
	1999	1998	1999年为1998年% 1999 as % of 1998	1999	1998	1999年为1998年% 1999 as % of 1998
全 市 Total	**93517.9**	**90177.7**	**103.7**	**5032.8**	**5122.9**	**98.2**
朝阳区 Chaoyang	4713.1	4720.0	99.9	0.7		
丰台区 Fengtai	3894.9	4474.0	87.1			
石景山区 Shijingshan	241.2	258.0	93.5			
海淀区 Haidian	3326.5	3556.6	93.5			
门头沟区 Mentougou	822.1	871.6	94.3			
房山区 Fangshan	4994.3	4686.2	106.6	80.3	62.3	128.9
通州区 Tongzhou	15607.7	15257.0	102.3	425.1	505.5	84.1
昌平区 Changping	3046.5	2985.8	102.0		38.5	
顺义区 Shunyi	14800.8	14485.0	102.2	874.6	697.3	125.4
大兴县 Daxing	22007.5	20775.0	105.9	3390.7	3477.8	97.5
平谷县 Pinggu	7108.5	6747.5	105.4	216.3	278.3	77.7
怀柔县 Huairou	1746.6	1878.0	93.0	2.7	1.9	142.1
密云县 Miyun	3102.3	3212.0	96.6	33.9	48.3	70.2
延庆县 Yanqing	8048.1	6271.0	128.3	8.5	13.0	65.4
农场局 Municipal Farm Bureau	57.8					

5-16 郊区县粮食、油料总产量
TOTAL YIELD OF GRAIN,OIL-BEARING CROPS IN SUBURBS AND COUNTIES

单位：吨 (ton)

地 区 Region	粮 食 Grain			油 料 Oil-bearing Crops		
	1999	1998	1999年为1998年% 1999 as % of 1998	1999	1998	1999年为1998年% 1998 as % of 1998
全 市 Total	**2009793**	**2392472**	**84.0**	**27601**	**28391**	**97.2**
朝阳区 Chaoyang	65881	75726	87.0			
丰台区 Fengtai	10872	15289	71.1		3	
海淀区 Haidian	36288	34819	104.2			
门头沟区 Mentougou	8386	8784	95.5			
房山区 Fangshan	271848	298006	91.2	1485	1444	102.8
通州区 Tongzhou	382884	500344	76.5	1579	1190	132.7
昌平区 Changping	162680	170506	95.4	75	78	96.2
顺义区 Shunyi	377797	443929	85.1	1316	1280	102.8
大兴县 Daxing	282632	332873	84.9	11367	11512	98.7
平谷县 Pinggu	108511	156311	69.4	518	579	89.5
怀柔县 Huairou	112824	133264	84.7	2635	2616	100.7
密云县 Miyun	94459	129593	72.9	8548	9585	89.2
延庆县 Yanqing	140166	176539	79.4	78	104	75.0
农场局 Municipal Farm Bureau	6884					

注：各区县粮食总产量之和不等于全市合计数。

Note: The sum of output of grain of suburbs and counties is not equal to the total.

5-17 郊区县蔬菜、西瓜总产量
TOTAL YIELD OF VEGETABLE,WATERMELON IN SUBURBS AND COUNTIES

单位：吨 (ton)

地区	Region	蔬菜 Vegetable 1999	1998	1999年为1998年% 1999 as % of 1998	西瓜 Watermelon 1999	1998	1999年为1998年% 1999 as % of 1998
全市	**Total**	**4267718**	**4061261.5**	**105.1**	**276363.0**	**282767.0**	**97.7**
朝阳区	Chaoyang	176573	182846.0	96.6	30.0		
丰台区	Fengtai	155205	190516.2	81.5			
石景山区	Shijingshan	8825	9653.0	91.4			
海淀区	Haidian	139312	157836.0	88.3			
门头沟区	Mentougou	22989	21293.8	108.0			
房山区	Fangshan	206200	202449.0	101.9	3585.0	3657.0	98.0
通州区	Tongzhou	756107	753073.3	100.4	27919.0	30781.0	90.7
昌平区	Changping	122148	104995.0	116.3		981.0	
顺义区	Shunyi	850208	839945.7	101.2	44855.0	37633.0	119.2
大兴县	Daxing	984891	929425.2	106.0	186253.0	194146.0	95.9
平谷县	Pinggu	330697	296576.0	111.5	11880.0	14502.0	81.9
怀柔县	Huairou	51183	50341.3	101.7	140.0	114.0	122.8
密云县	Miyun	159061	161349.0	98.6	1286.0	386.0	333.2
延庆县	Yanqing	423024	360962.0	117.2	415.0	567.0	73.2
农场局	Municipal Farm Bureau	1295					

注：各区县蔬菜总产量之和不等于全市合计数。
Note: The sum of output of vegetable of suburbs and counties is not equal to the total.

5-18 蔬菜播种面积及产量
SOWN AREAS AND YIELD OF VEGETABLE

项目	Item	播种面积（公顷） Sown Areas(hectare) 1999	1998	总产量（吨） Total Yield(ton) 1999	1998
合计	**Total**	**93517.9**	**90177.7**	**4267718.0**	**4061261.5**
冬季生产	**Produced in Winter**	**7494.7**	**6678.3**	**366853.0**	**297935.6**
越冬根茬菜小计	**Winter Stubble Vegetable**	**6741.1**	**6475.6**	**178036.0**	**200403.3**
# 菠菜	Spinach	2058.2	1905.3	60746.0	42876.4
芹菜	Celery				
早春风障菜小计	**Early Spring Windbreak Vegetable**	**4358.5**	**4346.6**	**160290.0**	**143208.7**
# 小萝卜	Radish	996.4	935.9	35550.0	37395.1
小白菜	Chinese Cabbage	508.5	470.3	19294.0	18965.0
小油菜	Rape	876.4	864.4	33988.0	33703.1
春播露地菜小计	**Spring-sown Open-land Vegetable**	**30703.7**	**30724.1**	**1329216.0**	**1362358.2**
# 黄瓜	Cucumber	3508.3	3625.7	179258.0	182194.3
茄子	Aggplant	2744.3	2758.6	126611.0	124221.2
大椒	Chili	1712.9	1741.5	75730.0	78076.9
冬瓜	Wax Guard	759.4	743.9	51626.0	52281.5
西红柿	Tomato	3391.7	3430.0	186281.0	192417.4
元白菜	Cabbage	2911.7	3042.7	134317.0	143903.7
云架豆	Beans round Trellis	1073.1	1276.2	34769.0	39412.6
老葱	Overgrown Onion	1128.8	1208.5	45266.0	49239.6
大蒜	Garlic	624.7	746.3	20998.0	27499.6
夏播菜小计	**Summer-sown Vegetable**	**15774.1**	**14726.9**	**576838.0**	**568769.2**
# 黄瓜	Cucumber	2711.9	2840.5	113605.0	119156.8
茄子	Aggplant	1645.0	1472.5	74637.0	71729.1
冬瓜	Wax Guard	854.2	796.5	51347.0	50575.8
元白菜	Cabbage	977.3	999.3	49085.0	50934.0
云架豆	Beans round Trellis	2115.8	1930.2	73135.0	60972.5
秋播菜小计	**Autumn-sown Vegetable**	**28419.1**	**27204.1**	**1647834.0**	**1485516.7**
# 窖白菜	Chinese Cabbage Stored	12920.5	12550.2	925771.0	806258.5
贩白菜	ChineseCabbagefoSelling	2661.5	2511.9	137932.0	128387.7
菜花	Cauliflower	1206.1	1190.9	53519.0	44588.1
各种萝卜	Radish	3768.3	3447.4	195954.0	156444.2
芹菜	Celery	1237.1	1073.8	81184.0	66583.6

5-19 郊区县粮食耕地面积单位产量
UNIT YIELD OF GRAIN CULTIVATED AREA IN SUBURBS AND COUNTIES

地区 Region		1999			1998		
		耕地面积 (公顷) Cultivated Areas (hectare)	单产 (公斤/公顷) Unit Yield (kg/hectare)	总产量 (吨) Total Yield (ton)	耕地面积 (公顷) Cultivated Areas (hectare)	单产 (公斤/公顷) Unit Yield (kg/hectare)	总产量 (吨) Total Yield (ton)
全市	Total	240510	8356.4	2009793	249347	9595.0	2392472
朝阳区	Chaoyang	6872	9586.9	65881	7150	10590.1	75726
丰台区	Fengtai	2191	4962.1	10872	2293	6667.1	15289
海淀区	Haidian	5038	7202.9	36288	5116	6806.0	34819
门头沟区	Mentougou	2483	3377.4	8386	3638	2414.3	8784
房山区	Fangshan	31593	8604.7	271848	32038.4	9301.5	298006
通州区	Tongzhou	37115	10316.2	382884	39564	12646.0	500344
昌平区	Changping	18789	8658.3	162680	19860	8585.4	170506
顺义区	Shunyi	40120	9416.7	377797	40309	11013.0	443929
大兴县	Daxing	29963	9432.7	282632	31485	10572.4	332873
平谷县	Pinggu	13662	7942.5	108511	14271	10953.2	156311
怀柔县	Huairou	12464	9052.0	112824	12917	10316.8	133264
密云县	Miyun	16075	5876.1	94459	16436	7884.6	129593
延庆县	Yanqing	23445	5978.5	140166	24268	7274.7	176539
农场局	Municipal Farm Bureau	700	9834.3	6884			

5-20 郊区县蔬菜耕地面积单位产量
UNIT YIELD OF VEGETABLE CULTIVATED AREA IN SUBURBS AND COUNTIES

地区 Region		1999			1998		
		耕地面积 (公顷) Cultivated Areas (hectare)	单产 (公斤/公顷) Unit Yield (kg/hectare)	总产量 (吨) Total Yield (ton)	耕地面积 (公顷) Cultivated Areas (hectare)	单产 (公斤/公顷) Unit Yield (kg/hectare)	总产量 (吨) Total Yield (ton)
全市	**Total**	**43157.7**	**98886.6**	**4267718.0**	**42679.1**	**95158.1**	**4061261.5**
朝阳区	Chaoyang	2209.9	79900.9	176573.0	2315.1	78979.7	182846.0
丰台区	Fengtai	1982.7	78279.6	155205.0	2178.3	87461.0	190516.2
石景山区	Shijingshan	113.3	77890.6	8825.0	126.7	76187.8	9653.0
海淀区	Haidian	1424.5	97797.1	139312.0	1854.1	85128.1	157836.0
门头沟区	Mentougou	430.7	53375.9	22989.0	436.9	48738.4	21293.8
房山区	Fangshan	2113.1	97581.8	206200.0	2341.5	86461.2	202449.0
通州区	Tongzhou	6764.1	111782.4	756107.0	6118.9	123073.3	753073.3
昌平区	Changping	1554.5	78577.0	122148.0	1447.5	72535.4	104995.0
顺义区	Shunyi	7069.9	120257.4	850208.0	7164.3	117240.4	839945.7
大兴县	Daxing	9765.3	100856.2	984891.0	9257.8	100393.7	929425.2
平谷县	Pinggu	2958.8	111767.3	330697.0	2807.0	105655.9	296576.0
怀柔县	Huairou	781.8	65468.2	51183.0	871.6	57757.3	50341.3
密云县	Miyun	1320.9	120418.7	159061.0	1350.5	119473.5	161349.0
延庆县	Yanqing	4630.1	91363.9	423024.0	4408.9	81871.2	360962.0
农场局	Municipal Farm Bureau	38.1	33989.5	1295.0			

5-21 畜 牧 业 生 产
ANIMALS HUSBANDRY

项目 Item		1999 合计 Total	1999 #国有集体 State-Owned and Collective-Owned	1998 合计 Total	1998 #国有集体 State-Owned and Collective-Owned	1999年为1998年% 1999 as % of 1998 合计 Total	1999年为1998年% 1999 as % of 1998 #国有集体 State-Owned and Collective-Owned
大牲畜	**Large Animals**						
年末总头数 (万头)	Total(year-end) (10000 heads)	19.0		18.5		102.7	
#役畜	Draught Animals	4.1		7.4		55.4	
牛	Cattle and Buffaloes	13.6		12.5		108.8	
马	Horses	0.7		0.9		77.8	
骡	Mules	1.8		2.1		85.7	
驴	Donkeys	2.9		3.1		93.5	
乳牛	**Cows**						
年末总头数 (头)	Total(year-end) (head)	64411.0	39638.0	54514.0	31240.0	118.2	126.9
#成乳牛	Adult Cows	42716.0		35949.0		118.8	
牛奶总产量 (万吨)	Cow Milk (10000 tons)	24.0	16.7	22.7	18.4	105.7	90.8
肉牛	**Beef Cattle**						
全年出栏 (头)	Slaughtered Cattle (head)	134899.0		116127.0		116.2	
折净肉 (吨)	Converted into Beef (ton)	23905.0		20618.9		115.9	
羊	**Sheep and Goats**						
全年出栏羊 (万只)	Slaughtered Sheep and Goats (10000 heads)	88.2		80.0		110.3	
折净肉 (吨)	Converted into Mutton (ton)	13462.0		12191.0		110.4	
年末存栏 (万只)	Livestock on Hand (year-end) (10000 heads)	103.1		95.8		107.6	
山羊 (万只)	Goats (10000 heads)	47.9		45.2		106.0	
绵羊 (万只)	Sheep (10000 heads)	55.2		50.6		109.1	
猪	**Hogs**						
全年出栏肥猪 (万头)	Slaughtered Fattened Hogs (10000 heads)	400.9	198.1	374.8	165.8	107.0	119.5
折带骨肉 (万吨)	Converted into Pork with Bone (10000tons)	28.6		27.9		102.5	
年末存栏 (万头)	Livestock on Hand (year-end) (10000 heads)	248.3	116.8	254.5	105.7	97.6	110.5
家禽	**Poultry**						
年末存栏 (万只)	Livestock on Hand (year-end) (10000 heads)	3135.1		2810.2		111.6	
鸭	Ducks	364.8		260.7		139.9	
肉鸡	Chickens	1349.5	564.5	1118.2	527.3	120.7	107.1
产蛋鸡	Hens	1420.8	512.1	1431.3	460.0	99.3	111.3
产蛋量 (万吨)	Poultry Eggs (10000 tons)			17.9			
#鸡蛋 (万吨)	Eggs (10000 tons)	15.5		17.6		88.1	
年末养兔 (万只)	**Rabbits (year-end)** (10000 heads)	35.0		34.6		101.2	
养蜂	**Bees**						
年末养蜂 (万箱)	Bees (year-end) (10000 boxes)	6.9		4.5		153.3	
蜂蜜产量 (吨)	Honey (ton)	1838.9		1779.5		103.3	

5-22 林业及干鲜果品生产
FORESTRY,DRY AND FRESH FRUIT PRODUCTION

项 目 Item				1999	1998	1999年为1998年% 1999 as % of 1998
林业生产		**Forestry**				
本年造林面积	(公顷)	Afforestation Area this Year	(hectare)	30198.1	36874.0	81.9
育苗面积	(公顷)	Nursery Garden Area	(hectare)	4920.2	4410.1	111.6
# 本年新育	(公顷)	New Growing this Year	(hectare)	1462.0	1311.4	111.5
果类生产		**Fruit**				
干鲜果总产量	(吨)	Output of Dry and Fresh Fruit	(ton)	564301.0	561782.0	100.4
干 果	(吨)	Dry Fruit	(ton)	23724.0	20725.0	114.5
# 核 桃	(吨)	Walnut	(ton)	8030.0	7364.0	109.0
板 栗	(吨)	Chinese Chestnut	(ton)	10578.0	8917.0	118.6
鲜 果	(吨)	Fresh Fruit	(ton)	540577.0	541057.0	99.9
# 苹 果	(吨)	Apple	(ton)	151717.0	162930.0	93.1
梨	(吨)	Pear	(ton)	98705.0	105436.0	93.6
葡 萄	(吨)	Grape	(ton)	179614.0	20318.0	884.0
柿 子	(吨)	Persimmon	(ton)	48979.0	40781.0	120.1
桃	(吨)	Peach	(ton)	179614.0	174066.0	103.2
年末实有果园面积	**(公顷)**	**Orchard Area(year-end)**	**(hectare)**	**64008.1**	**60223.5**	**106.3**

5-23 水 产 品 生 产
AQUATIC PRODUCTS

项 目 Item				1999	1998	1999年为1998年% 1999 as _% of 1998
现有水面面积	**(公顷)**	**Area of Water Surface**	**(hectare)**	**24451.1**	**24391.6**	**100.2**
# 已利用水面面积	(公顷)	Utilized Area	(hectare)	23605.4	23385.6	100.9
大水库	(公顷)	Large Reservoir	(hectare)	13853.3	13853.3	100.0
中、小水库	(公顷)	Medium and Small Reservoirs	(hectare)	1931.0	1631.9	118.3
坑 塘	(公顷)	Puddle and Pond	(hectare)	7777.9	7878.8	98.7
# 鱼种池	(公顷)	Fish Fry Pond	(hectare)	1011.6	1033.9	97.8
鱼种生产量	**(万尾)**	**Output of Fish Fry**	**(10000 piece)**	**13873.4**	**12887.2**	**107.7**
放养鱼种	**(万尾)**	**Breeding Fish Fry**	**(10000 piece)**	**16213.7**	**15342.7**	**105.7**
成鱼捕捞量	**(吨)**	**Fish Catched**	**(ton)**	**75555.5**	**76366.4**	**98.9**
# 大水库	(吨)	Large Reservoir	(ton)	4178.6	3709.0	112.7
中、小水库	(吨)	Medium and Small Reservoirs	(ton)	837.3	864.4	96.9
坑 塘	(吨)	Puddle and Pond	(ton)	68479.8	71290.8	96.1
# 鱼类商品量	(吨)	Commodity Fish	(ton)	66265.5	63626.2	104.1

5-24 主要农产品产量
OUTPUT OF MAJOR FARM PRODUCTS

项目 Item				1999	1998	1999年为1998年% 1999 as % of 1998
蔬菜产量	**(吨)**	**Yield of Vegetable**	**(ton)**	**4267718.0**	**4061261.5**	**105.1**
#特菜	(吨)	Special Vegetable	(ton)	199340.0	128241.4	155.4
干鲜果品产量	**(吨)**	**Yield of Dry and Fresh Fruit**	**(ton)**	**564301.0**	**561782.0**	**100.4**
#干果产量	(吨)	Dry Fruit	(ton)	23724.0	20725.0	114.5
鲜果产量	(吨)	Fresh Fruit	(ton)	540577.0	541057.0	99.9
肉类总产量	**(吨)**	**Output of Meat**	**(ton)**	**494879.0**	**449063.0**	**110.2**
#猪肉	(吨)	Pork	(ton)	285509.0	279283.0	102.2
牛肉	(吨)	Beef	(ton)	23905.0	20618.9	115.9
羊肉	(吨)	Mutton	(ton)	13462.0	12191.0	110.4
牛奶产量	**(吨)**	**Output of Cow Milk**	**(ton)**	**240112.0**	**227073.0**	**105.7**
鲜蛋产量	**(吨)**	**Output of Fresh Eggs**	**(ton)**	**157902.0**	**178833.4**	**88.3**
#鸡蛋	(吨)	Eggs	(ton)	155213.0	175861.0	88.3
鸭蛋	(吨)	Duck's Eggs	(ton)	2669.0	2925.4	91.2
淡水鱼产量	**(吨)**	**Output of Fresh-water Fish**	**(ton)**	**75555.5**	**76366.4**	**98.9**

5-25 郊区县副食品产量
OUTPUT OF NON-STAPLE FOOD IN SUBURBS AND COUNTIES

地区	Region	蔬菜 (吨) Vegetable (ton)	鲜蛋 (吨) Fresh Eggs (ton)	牛奶 (吨) Cow Milk (ton)	干鲜果 (吨) Dry and Fresh Fruit (ton)	成鱼捕捞量 (吨) Adult Fish Catched (ton)	肥猪出栏量 (头) Slaughtered Fattened Hog (head)	蛋鸡存栏量 (万只) Hens on Hand (10000 head)
全市	**Total**	**4267718**	**157902**	**240112**	**564301**	**75555**	**4008657**	**14207958**
朝阳区	Chaoyang	176573	753	7383	770	6340	262005	59252
丰台区	Fengtai	155205	5181	3220	4926	404	86574	452343
石景山区	Shijingshan	8825	1540	1983	770	40	37687	142000
海淀区	Haidian	139312	2861	1511	11112	2750	111613	224610
门头沟区	Mentougou	22989	1339	3575	5442	400	37959	133252
房山区	Fangshan	206200	13645	7601	51413	2054	314223	1696652
通州区	Tongzhou	756107	14795	13789	33065	11460	426598	1174481
昌平区	Changping	122148	8122	15791	52805	8046	250817	745430
顺义区	Shunyi	850208	22408	7524	41968	16037	1340344	1947545
大兴县	Daxing	984891	28419	21577	85106	5181	382075	2472055
平谷县	Pinggu	330697	20953	503	146911	13997	248650	2101899
怀柔县	Huairou	51183	6749	13071	47915	2004	192760	630583
密云县	Miyun	159061	16653	2529	38000	4126	308285	1404237
延庆县	Yanqing	423024	12198	18089	40677	2716	146492	841941
农场局	Municipal Farm Bureau	1295	2286	125966	3421		67549	181678

5-26 设施农业面积及产量
AREAS AND OUTPUT OF FACILITY-AGRICULTURE

项目 Item		设施农业面积（亩） Areas of Facility-agriculture (mu)	设施农业产量（吨） Output of Facility-agriculture (ton)
合计	**Total**	**226086**	
按类型划分	Grouped by Type		
#温室	Hothouse	34214	
日光温室	Sunshine-hothouse	32337	
大棚	Large Shed	57941	
中、小棚	Medium and Small Shed	85998	
阳畦	Sunshine Bed	15596	
按品种划分	Grouped by Variety		
#蔬菜	Vegetable	172956	995179
花卉	Flowers	5133	
瓜类	Melon	37675	136771
果类	Fruits	4986	4141

5-27 农村劳动生产率
RURAL LABOR PRODUCTIVITY

项目 Item			1999	1998	1999年为1998年% 1999 as % of 1998
每一农村从业人员创造产值（按各业从业人员分别计算）		**Output Value Per Employment (calculated separately by sectors)**			
每一农村从业人员创造农村社会总产值	(元)	Rural Gross Output Value Per Employment (yuan)	55907	51737	108.1
每一农村从业人员创造农业总产值	(元)	Gross Output Value of Agriculture Per Employment (yuan)	25919	26077	99.4
每一农村从业人员创造工业总产值	(元)	Gross Output Value of Industry Per Employment (yuan)	123107	104979	117.3
每一农村从业人员创造建筑业总产值	(元)	Gross Output Value of Construction Per Employment (yuan)	109783	98608	111.3
每一农村从业人员创造运输业总产值	(元)	Gross Output Value of Transportation Per Employment (yuan)	63818	66913	95.4
每一农村从业人员创造商业、饮食业总产值	(元)	Gross Output Value of Commerce and Catering Per Employment (yuan)	92213	100686	91.6
每一农业从业人员生产的农产品产量 (按农林牧渔从业人员合计计算)		**Yield of Farm Products Per Employment (calculated by total employment of farming,forestry,animal husbandry and fishery)**			
粮食	(公斤)	Grain (kg)	2827	3532	80.0
油料	(公斤)	Oil-bearing Crops (kg)	39	42	92.9
蔬菜	(公斤)	Vegetable (kg)	6004	5996	100.1
水果	(公斤)	Fruit (kg)	761	799	95.2
猪牛羊肉	(公斤)	Pork,Beef and Mutton (kg)	454	461	98.5
牛奶	(公斤)	CowMilk (kg)	338	335	100.9
鲜蛋	(公斤)	FreshEggs (kg)	222	264	84.1
淡水鱼	(公斤)	Fresh-water Fish (kg)	106	113	93.8

5-28 农 业 生 产 条 件
PRODUCTIVE CONDITIONS OF AGRICULTURE

项 目		Item		1999	1998	1999年为1998年% 1999 as % of 1998
主要农业机械拥有量		**Possession of Agricultural Machinery**				
农业机械总动力	(万千瓦)	Total Power of Agricultural Machinery	(10000 kw)	410.4	415.5	98.8
大中型拖拉机	(混合台)	Large and Medium Tractors	(unit)	11852.0	12032.0	98.5
小型拖拉机	(台)	Mini-Tractors	(unit)	27295.0	30000.0	91.0
机引农具	(台)	Towing Farm Machinery	(unit)		36800.0	
机动喷雾器	(部)	Motorized Sprayer	(unit)	128470.0	127700.0	100.6
机动插秧机	(台)	Motorized Rice Transplanter	(unit)	317.0	378.0	83.9
联合收割机	(台)	Combine Harvester	(unit)	4528.0	4445.0	101.9
机动脱粒机	(台)	MotorizedSheller	(unit)	13324.0	12174.0	109.4
米面加工机	(台)	Processing Machine of Rice and Flour	(unit)	9549.0	10586.0	90.2
机动挤奶器	(台)	Motorized Milker	(unit)	185.0	104.0	177.9
饲料粉碎机	(台)	Fodder Grinder	(unit)	4957.0	5100.0	97.2
载重汽车	(辆)	Truck	(unit)	16884.0	18147.0	93.0
农业机械作业面积		**Operation Area of Agricultural Machinery**				
机耕面积	(公顷)	Cultivated Area by Machine	(hectare)	258867.0	263570.0	98.2
占全部耕地面积比重	(%)	As Percentage of Total	(%)	76.5	77.3	99.0
机播面积	(公顷)	Sown Area by Machine	(hectare)	293687.0	339430.0	86.5
占播种面积比重	(%)	As Percentage of Sown Area	(%)	55.7	63.4	87.9
机收面积	(公顷)	Harvest Area by Machine	(hectare)	245827.0	254620.0	96.5
占播种面积比重	(%)	As Percentage of Harvest Area	(%)	46.6	47.6	97.9
农村用电量及小水电		**Rural Electricity Consumption and Small Hydropower Station**				
农村用电量	(万千瓦小时)	Rural Electricity Consumption	(10000 kwh)	330069.0	290859.0	113.5
# 农业生产用	(万千瓦小时)	For Agricultural Productive Use	(10000 kwh)	125650.0	107992.0	116.4
乡镇、村办企业用	(万千瓦小时)	For Township and Village Enterprises Use	(10000 kwh)	94226.0	82831.0	113.8
农村小水电站	(处)	Rural Small Hydropower Station		43.0	40.0	107.5
发电量	(万千瓦小时)	Generated Energy	(10000 kwh)	1633.2	2573.3	63.5
农田水利		Irrigation and Water Conservancy				
排灌用动力机械	(台)	Power-driven Irrigation Machinery	(unit)	62900.0	63200.0	99.5
	(万千瓦)		(10000 kwh)	68.4	68.4	100.0
机(电)井	(眼)	Motor-pumped Well	(unit)	44505.0	49385.0	90.1
# 已配套	(眼)	Completed Set	(unit)			
扬水站(固定机电排灌站)	(处)	Pumping Station	(unit)	4861.0	4815.0	101.0
有效灌溉面积	(公顷)	Irrigated Areas	(hectare)	322120.0	323000.0	99.7
占耕地面积		As Percentage of Cultivated Areas	(%)	95.3	94.7	100.6
化肥施用量(折纯)		**Consumption of Chemical Fertilizers (converted into Pure)**				
化肥施用量	(吨)	Consumption of Chemical Fertilizers	(ton)	190291.0	192870.9	98.7
氮 肥	(吨)	Nitrogenous Fertilizer	(ton)	115940.0	119056.9	97.4
磷 肥	(吨)	Phosphate Fertilizer	(ton)	10851.0	10181.1	106.6
钾 肥	(吨)	Potash Fertilizer	(ton)	3922.0	3803.0	103.1
每公顷耕地施用量	(公斤)	Consumption Per Hectare Cultivated Areas	(kg)	562.0	566.0	99.3

注：农村小水电站是指乡村两级小水电实有数。农村用电量为市供电局提供。

Note：Data of rural small hydropower station refer to actual number of small hydropower at township and Village level.Data on consumption of electricity are provided by Beijing Municipal Power Supply Bureau.

5-29 乡镇集体企业各业基本情况
BASIC STATISTICS ON SECTORS OF TOWN AND TOWNSHIP ENTERPRISES

行业 Sector	企业个数（个） Number of Enterprises (unit)		从业人员（人） Employment (person)		总收入（万元） Total Revenue (10000 yuan)		利润总额（万元） Total Profits (10000 yuan)		税金（万元） Taxes (10000 yuan)
	数量 Number	占% Proportion	数量 Number	占% Proportion	数量 Number	占% Proportion	数量 Number	占% Proportion	
合计 Total	**13428**	**100**	**693013**	**100**	**5891870**	**100**	**315986**	**100**	**222693**
农业 Agriculture	584	4.3	11750	1.7	165926	2.8	22166	7.0	2374
工业 Industry	8801	65.5	451071	65.1	3338554	56.7	155734	49.3	142260
交通运输业 Transportation	366	2.7	11393	1.6	83562	1.4	4138	1.3	2459
施工建筑业 Construction	840	6.3	133468	19.3	928721	15.8	51895	16.4	36059
商品流通业 Commerce	1581	11.8	30569	4.4	858926	14.6	28192	8.9	20295
旅游饮服业 Tourism,Catering and Services	1073	8.0	45723	6.6	352496	6.0	30325	9.6	13066
其他 Others	183	1.4	9039	1.3	163685	2.7	23536	7.5	6180

5-30 乡镇集体企业出口供货情况
GOODS SUPPLIES FOR EXPORT OF TOWN AND TOWNSHIP ENTERPRISES

单位：万元 (10000 yuan)

行业	Sector	出口产品交货总额 Total Amount on Delivery of Exports		直接出口 Direct Export		间接出口 Indirect Export	
		1999	1998	1999	1998	1999	1998
合计	**Total**	**453277**	**405727**	**311906**	**284529**	**141371**	**121198**
化工	Chemical Products	3424	5620	2354	2722	1070	2898
机械	Machinery	18833	13945	15230	10180	3603	3765
矿产	Mineral Products	1731	5574	712	3291	1019	2283
轻工	Light Industry	84620	60262	48900	35095	35720	25167
食品	Food	6880	8362	1041	2255	5839	6107
土产	Local Products	4435	1213	4266	1181	169	32
畜产	Livestock Products	5642	3751	5617	3615	25	136
纺织	Textile	39954	52093	27752	41183	12202	10910
服装	Garment	194290	162969	143384	118336	50906	44633
工艺品	Handicraft	29923	45692	22038	37885	7885	7807
其他	Others	63545	46246	40612	28786	22933	17460

5-31 乡镇企业主要产品产量及占全市的比重

MAJOR PRODUCTS OUTPUT OF TOWN AND TOWNSHIP ENTERPRISES AND THEIR PROPORTION IN TOTAL OF THE CITY

产品名称 Products				1999		1998	
				数量 Output	占全市比重(%) Proportion(%)	数量 Output	占全市比重(%) Proportion(%)
发电量	(万千瓦时)	Generated Energy	(10000 kwh)	4328.0	0.3	3874.0	0.3
原煤	(万吨)	Raw Coal	(10000 tons)	376.6	47.5	529.0	53.5
塑料制品	(吨)	Plastic Products	(ton)	48161.0	31.1	44049.0	44.9
泵	(台)	Pump	(unit)	10109.0	11.4	22020.0	79.7
暖气片	(万片)	Heating Radiator	(10000 pieces)				
水泥	(万吨)	Cement	(10000 tons)	255.0	31.8	229.0	30.1
砖	(亿块)	Brick	(100 million pieces)	49.9	98.8	53.5	100.0
石灰	(万吨)	Lime	(10000 tons)	152.7		119.7	...
水磨石	(万平方米)	Terrazzo	(10000 sq.m)	52.2		49.3	...
水泥预制构件	(万立方米)	Cement Prefabricated Components	(10000 sq.m)	166.9		92.8	82.5
棉布	(万米)	Cotton Cloth	(10000 meters)	8250.0	37.5	7223.0	50.6
服装	(万件)	Garment	(10000)	6664.0	52.5	7051.0	64.8
布鞋	(万双)	Cloth Shoes	(10000 pairs)	265.0		298.0	55.8
白酒	(吨)	White Sprite	(ton)	1995.0	2.0	4344.0	4.4
家具	(万件)	Furniture	(10000)	349.0	90.4	464.0	...

5-32 郊区县乡镇集体企业主要经济指标

MAIN ECONOMIC INDICATORS FOR TOWN AND TOWNSHIP ENTERPRISES IN SUBURBS AND COUNTIES

地区 Region		企业个数 (个) Number of Enterprises (unit)	从业人员 (人) Employment (person)	总收入 (万元) Total Revenue (10000 yuan)	利润总额 (万元) Total Profits (10000 yuan)	人均利润 (元) Profit Per Capita (yuan)	税金 (万元) Taxes (10000 yuan)	# 所得税 (万元) Income Tax (10000 yuan)
全市	**Total**	**13428**	**693013**	**5891870**	**315986**	**4560**	**222693**	**52513**
朝阳区	Chaoyang	1710	84425	687661	22891	2711	25719	5498
丰台区	Fengtai	1378	61276	642999	54574	8906	19074	4893
石景山区	Shijingshan	239	7975	109651	2222	2786	2752	358
海淀区	Haidian	1001	42514	535968	20161	4742	16911	2900
门头沟区	Mentougou	557	16101	121117	7005	4351	4576	893
房山区	Fangshan	1369	89920	606838	31304	3481	19044	4290
通州区	Tongzhou	1811	75409	505620	28638	3798	22863	5701
昌平区	Changping	1078	43862	335332	20888	4762	14782	6062
顺义区	Shunyi	922	82396	548210	25890	3142	21276	3693
大兴县	Daxing	1291	55177	532779	32891	5961	17565	3836
平谷县	Pinggu	844	49634	427565	30507	6146	24982	5290
怀柔县	Huairou	590	32633	516943	28079	8604	19623	5892
密云县	Miyun	334	29720	144338	2893	973	6531	1168
延庆县	Yanqing	304	21971	176849	8043	3661	6995	2039

5-33 郊区县农村个体、联合体企业主要经济指标

MAIN ECONOMIC INDICATORS FOR RURAL PRIVATE AND JOINT ENTERPRISES IN SUBURBS AND COUNTIES

地　区	Region	企业个数 (个) Number of Enterprises (unit)	从业人员 (人) Employment (person)	总收入 (万元) Total Revenue (10000 yuan)	利润总额 (万元) Total Profits (10000 yuan)	人均利润 (元) Profit Per Capita (yuan)	税金 (万元) Taxes (10000 yuan)	# 所得税 (万元) Income Tax (10000 yuan)
全　市	**Total**	**89020**	**266703**	**2299839**	**202780**	**7603**	**44536**	**7126**
朝阳区	Chaoyang	50	1566	109375	258	1648	278	55
丰台区	Fengtai	1027	3283	18538	2753	8385	1153	275
石景山区	Shijingshan	420	1558	24274	1336	8575	741	30
海淀区	Haidian	1259	4223	54506	1872	4433	1697	90
门头沟区	Mentougou	7396	15272	99468	12542	8212	1917	241
房山区	Fangshan	28902	82995	898467	76057	9164	9202	1152
通州区	Tongzhou	110005	34243	204768	34137	9969	5635	1140
昌平区	Changping	1854	4273	19340	1928	4512	532	32
顺义区	Shunyi	9660	40026	236783	24190	6043	5103	994
大兴县	Daxing	10180	22398	181592	14617	6526	5839	755
平谷县	Pinggu	2391	8036	21087	1856	2310	501	81
怀柔县	Huairou	1849	9570	190496	15428	16121	4356	1362
密云县	Miyun	9210	27029	171887	12874	4763	5526	674
延庆县	Yanqing	3817	12231	69258	2932	2397	2056	245

5-34 8 县 75 乡农村劳动力转移情况
STATISTICS ON RURAL LABOR FORCE TRANSFERRING OF THE 75 TOWNSHIPS IN 8 COUNTIES

项目	Item	合计 Total		平原 Plain		山区 Mountain Area	
		数量（人） Number (person)	构成（%） Composition (%)	数量（人） Number (person)	构成（%） Composition (%)	数量（人） Number (person)	构成（%） Composition (%)
调查户劳动力转移人数	**Labor Force Transferring of Household in Surveyed**	**1736**	**100**	**1346**	**100**	**390**	**100**
当年转移的劳动力	**Labor Force Transferred in This Year**	**220**	**12.7**	**157**	**11.7**	**63**	**16.2**
转移劳动力素质情况	**Quality Level of Labor Force Transferring**						
性别构成	Sex Composition						
男劳动力	Male	1064	61.3	825	61.3	239	61.3
# 整劳动力	Full Labor Force	878	50.6	680	50.5	198	50.8
女劳动力	Female	672	38.7	521	38.7	151	38.7
# 整劳动力	Full Labor Force	519	29.9	402	29.9	117	30.0
文化程度	Educational Level						
小学以下文化程度	at Primary School Level and below	102	5.9	79	5.9	23	5.9
初中文化程度	at Junior Middle School Level	962	55.4	746	55.4	216	55.4
中专以上文化程度	at Specialized Secondary School Level and above	601	34.6	466	34.6	135	34.6
大专及以上文化程度	at Junior College Level	71	4.1	55	4.1	16	4.1
接受专业培训情况	Taking Professional Training						
接受专业培训	Trained	920	53.0	713	53.0	207	53.1
未接受专业培训	No Trained	816	47.0	633	47.0	183	46.9
转移劳动力行业分布	**Sector Transfer to**						
农牧渔业	Farming,Animal Husbandry and Fishery	6	0.4	5	0.4	1	0.3
工业	Industry	576	33.2	447	33.2	129	33.1
建筑业	Construction	142	8.2	110	8.2	32	8.2
交通运输业	Transportations,	190	10.9	147	10.9	43	11.0
邮电通讯业	Posts and Telecommunications	14	0.8	11	0.8	3	0.8
商业饮食业	Commerce and Catering	148	8.5	115	8.5	33	8.5
服务业	Services	292	16.8	226	16.8	66	16.9
文教卫生	Culture,Education and Health	121	7.0	94	7.0	27	6.9
其他	Others	247	14.2	191	14.2	56	14.3
转移地域	**Region Transfer To**						
本市内转移	Within Local City	1728	99.5	1340	99.6	388	99.5
转向外省市	To Nonlocal	8	0.5	6	0.4	2	0.5
调查户当年返回农业的劳动力	**Labor Force Back to Agriculture in This Year of Households in Survey**						

注：本表是在 8 个被调查县抽选 75 个乡(镇)，每个乡(镇)抽选 3 个村，每村调查 1 个村民小组。

Note：Sampling of the survey is as following--select 75 townships from 8 counties,select 3 villages from those of townships, and select a villager group from those of villages.

5-35 8县75乡劳动力构成
COMPOSITION OF LABOR FORCE OF THE 75 TOWNSHIPS IN 8 COUNTIES

项目	Item	合计 Total		平原 Plain		山区 Mountain Area	
		数量（人）Number (person)	构成（%）Composition (%)	数量（人）Number (person)	构成（%）Composition (%)	数量（人）Number (person)	构成（%）Composition (%)
调查村整半劳动力	**Full and Half Labor Force in Village Surveyed**	**3714**	**100**	**2782**	**100**	**932**	**100**
按性别分	Grouped by Sex						
男劳动力	Male	1890	50.9	1416	50.9	474	50.9
# 整劳动力	Full Labor Force	1436	38.7	1076	38.7	360	38.6
女劳动力	Female	1834	49.1	1366	49.1	458	49.1
# 整劳动力	Full Labor Force	1223	32.9	916	32.9	307	32.9
按文化程度分	Grouped by Educational Level						
文盲或半文盲	Illiteracy and Half-illiteracy	53	1.4	40	1.4	13	1.4
小学程度	at Primary School Level	447	12.0	335	12.0	112	12.0
初中程度	at Junior Middle School Level	2123	57.2	1590	57.2	533	57.2
中专程度	at Specialized Secondary School	1013	27.3	759	27.3	254	27.3
大专及以上程度	at Junior College Level	78	2.1	58	2.1	20	2.1
按是否接受过专业培训分	Grouped by Whether Received Specialized Training						
受过各种专业培训	Received All Kinds of Specialized Training	1438	38.7	1077	38.7	361	38.7
未接受专业培训	Never Received Specializedraining	2276	61.3	1705	61.3	571	61.3

注：本表是在8个被调查县抽选75个乡(镇)，每个乡(镇)抽选3个村，每村调查1个村民小组。

Note：Sampling of the survey is as following--select 75 townships from 8 counties,select 3 villages from those of townships, and select a villager group from those of villages.

5-36 8县75乡平均每人拥有固定资产投资情况
FIXED ASSETS AND INVESTMENT PER CAPITA OF THE 75 TOWNSHIPS IN 8 COUNTIES

单位：元，平方米 (yuan sqm)

项目	Item	合计 Total	乡(镇)所有 Of Township	村组所有 Of Village	农户所有 Of Household
本年新增固定资产原值	**Original Value of Incremental Fixed Assets**	**1894.4**	**801.9**	**511.0**	**581.5**
本年固定资产投资完成额	**Investment in Fixed Assets Completed in this year**	**2102.9**	**789.5**	**668.1**	**645.3**
按资金来源分	Grouped by Source of Funds				
自筹资金	One's Own	1635.2	581.6	459.1	594.5
银行信用社贷款	Loan from Bank and Credit Cooperative	263.7	181.2	76.8	5.7
其他来源	Others	204.0	26.7	132.2	45.1
按资金投向分	Grouped by Use of Funds				
农业	Agriculture	224.9	28.4	73.2	123.3
工业	Industry	371.4	177.9	183.2	10.3
建筑业	Construction	293.7	95.7	154.6	43.4
交通运输业	Transportation	181.4	35.0	19.9	126.5
邮电通讯业	Posts and Telecommunications	0.5	0.3	0.2	
批发零售贸易业	Wholesale and Retail Trade	45.3	7.0	35.6	2.7
社会服务业	Social Services	239.5	217.7	21.1	0.7
文化教育事业	Culture and Education	42.4	20.8	5.5	16.1
卫生体育社会福利业	Health,Sports and Social Welfare	62.8	18.3	16.9	27.6
其他	Others	640.9	188.4	157.9	294.6
本年施工房屋面积	**Floor space of Buildings under Construction in this Year**	**2.5**	**0.9**	**0.6**	**1.0**
# 住宅	Residence	1.4	0.2	0.3	0.9
本年竣工房屋面积	**Floor space of Buildings Completed in this Year**	**2.1**	**0.5**	**0.6**	**0.9**
# 住宅	Residence	1.2	0.2	0.2	0.8
本年竣工房屋投资完成额	**Investment of Buildings Completed in this Year**	**1149.1**	**461.5**	**254.2**	**433.4**
# 住宅	Residence	612.0	79.1	128.6	404.3

5-37 农村经济收入与分配
INCOME AND DISTRIBUTION OF RURAL ECONOMY

单位：万元 (10000 yuan)

项 目 Item		1999	1998	1999 年为 1998 年% 1999 as % of 1998
营业收入	**Operation Income**	**11188467.2**	**10115280.6**	**110.6**
农 业	Agriculture	663178.8	705823.1	94.0
# 粮食	Grain	249007.7	316289.4	78.7
林 业	Forestry	99695.5	91350.1	109.1
牧 业	Animal Husbandry	562019.7	531826.9	105.7
渔 业	Fishery	58158.0	60441.8	96.2
工 业	Industry	3899783.2	3588332.7	108.7
交通运输业	Transportation	989193.5	895605.8	110.4
建筑业	Construction	1430955.1	1241911.0	115.2
商业、饮食业	Commerce and Catering	1950388.5	1701188.3	114.6
服务业	Services	844027.9	700346.4	120.5
其 他	Others	691067.0	598454.3	115.5
营业成本	**Operation Cost**	**9903286.7**	**8971404.6**	**110.4**
农 业	Agriculture	589759.7	611777.2	96.4
# 粮食	Grain	187476.4	217502.5	86.2
林 业	Forestry	86991.3	82513.8	105.4
牧 业	Animal Husbandry	540204.0	504887.0	107.0
渔 业	Fishery	60937.9	55608.5	109.6
工 业	Industry	3413093.5	3138350.2	108.8
交通运输业	Transportation	956514.7	819376.2	116.7
建筑业	Construction	1246755.4	1101346.4	113.2
商业、饮食业	Commerce and Catering	1766741.9	1574650.3	112.2
服务业	Services	704861.9	587546.9	120.0
其 他	Others	537424.4	495347.9	108.5
营业利润	**Operation Profits**	**583410.5**	**495906.1**	**117.6**
利润总额	**Total Profits**	**661737.8**	**582196.5**	**113.7**
税后利润	**Net Profits**	**602434.1**	**529998.2**	**113.7**
可供分配的利润	**Profit to be Divided**	**560407.5**	**476848.5**	**117.5**
未分配利润	**Retained Profits**	**73334.8**	**55159.7**	**132.9**

5-38 郊区规模乡镇发展情况
STATISTICS FOR LARGE SCALE TOWN AND TOWNSHIPS IN SUBURBS AND COUNTIES

乡镇名称 Name	总人口 (人) Population (person)	总劳动力 (人) Labor Force (person)	农村社会总产值 (万元) Rural Gross Output Value (10000 yuan)	乡镇企业个数 (个) Town and Township Enterprises (unit)	乡镇企业总收入 (万元) Total Revenue of Town and Township Enterprises (10000 yuan)	乡镇企业利润总额 (万元) Total Profits of Town and Township Enterprises (10000 yuan)
南磨房地区	5022	2786	94968.8	46	151633.0	8000.0
高碑店地区	28934	6560	81836.0	111	80230.0	9052.0
小红门乡	18003	8383	105486.5	256	95560.0	3177.0
十八里店乡	22753	11424	68763.2	106	30347.0	1284.0
洼里乡	8539	3789	53335.3	87	68186.0	1211.0
来广营乡	8375	3987	60657.4	117	52000.0	986.0
卢沟桥乡	38279	19960	119321.8	309	225037.0	17745.0
花乡	38433	20807	118217.0	348	244697.0	18479.0
南苑乡	26637	15510	53595.0	355	142109.0	6203.0
长辛店乡	19434	6235	51963.1	380	29571.0	-465.0
石景山乡	16441	8025	59861.4	239	109723.0	1864.0
四季青乡	48666	17872	72540.5	317	98865.0	264.0
永定镇	14439	6962	58422.4	106	37272.0	1664.0
房山街道	30508	13487	160058.3	173	278810.8	6788.0
良乡地区	72718	10069	114258.6	2671	162629.6	1957.0
周口店地区	27658	9502	125107.0	129	148880.0	11203.0
琉璃河地区	24334	11288	98995.5	515	65409.8	2161.2
阎村镇	28374	9044	102997.2	2644	110911.0	8329.0
交道镇	17945	6470	78776.0	55	72924.0	3292.0
窦店镇	20020	7430	132155.6	1330	143198.0	3989.0
石楼镇	27913	12016	68377.4	65	21545.0	244.0
东营乡	16380	7115	171265.4	1250	140818.0	8042.0
永顺地区	34281	12954	125002.0	2405	140213.0	20033.0
犁园地区	25992	6525	88809.0	1242	77640.0	6204.0
宋庄镇	28580	23111	119416.0	1332	96141.0	6673.0
张家湾镇	26396	10513	88771.0	330	75665.0	1800.0
牛堡屯镇	24739	12054	59799.8	640	40187.0	972.0
仁和地区	37562	16231	127922.0	2135	118257.0	2706.0
后沙峪地区	15495	6500	58117.3	70	30996.0	2336.0
天竺地区	14632	6794	59042.1	56	34285.0	2144.0
杨镇地区	42004	17696	89052.6	1006	37020.0	1788.0
南法信地区	12107	6205	50580.2	342	41717.0	3917.0
马坡地区	18269	7671	58146.8	159	49018.0	3557.0
高丽营镇	19407	8571	64714.5	1000	49392.0	924.0
李桥镇	30689	12235	99749.3	218	41345.0	3124.2
南彩镇	31128	15396	79347.5	602	46478.0	2307.0
大孙各庄镇	26150	11992	102350.2	73	42024.0	5276.0
张镇	21877	10115	72023.3	136	21666.3	975.3
龙湾屯镇	16184	7966	52262.7	20	23646.0	784.0
木林镇	34225	13065	64603.0	130	13500.0	630.0
北小营镇	28478	11786	92223.6	12	24102.0	1424.0
赵全营镇	22739	9676	82688.9	108	32800.0	2480.0
沙河镇	20214	8262	58353.0	139	8661.0	140.0
北七家镇	21917	7424	62385.4	72	24122.0	1423.5
黄村镇	17085	9024	85309.0	116	75376.0	4147.0
西红门镇	20785	10421	74133.4	209	123919.0	12905.0
旧宫镇	45545	8464	59511.6	134	44241.0	2140.0
榆垡镇	25982	14206	58345.6	312	46696.0	1043.0
庞各庄镇	21199	10483	53248.1	54	38629.0	652.0
马坊镇	10333	5133	82177.8	350	83714.0	10900.0
马昌营镇	15342	7365	56968.2	53	40649.0	3629.0
怀柔镇	23335	10104	212879.0	149	124260.0	4980.0
北房镇	17042	7903	63315.0	182	42123.0	2334.0
杨宋镇	14466	4597	64423.6	190	64731.0	3814.0
庙城镇	15827	5770	79585.3	158	69803.4	3386.4
桥梓镇	18206	7388	86453.4	53	68413.0	2876.0
太师屯镇	38716	16941	63404.2	667	33559.0	1215.0
延庆镇	33896	15758	141879.8	15	18365.0	140.0
旧县镇	22673	11113	62076.7	20	42030.0	1309.0

注：规模乡镇是指农村社会总产值达到 5 亿元的乡镇。

Note：Town and townships refer to those their rural gross output value amount to 500 million yuan.

主要统计指标解释

农业总产值 是以货币表现的农、林、牧、渔业全部产品的总量，它反映一定时期内农业生产总规模和总成果。

农、林、牧、渔业的统计范围包括国有经济各种专业农（农、林、牧、渔）场以及国家各级机关团体学校、部队；集体所有制的乡、镇、村各级办农场；工矿企业经营的农、林、牧、渔业，农村各种经济组织和农户经营的农林牧渔业和农民家庭兼营的商品性工业等。

（1）农业 包括种植业和其他农业。

种植业 包括谷物、豆类、薯类、棉、油料、糖料、麻类、烟叶、蔬菜、药材、瓜类和其他农作物的种植，以及茶园、桑园、果园的生产经营。

其他农业 包括采集野生植物的果实、纤维、树胶、树脂、油料以及柴草、野生药材、菌类等及农民家庭兼营的商品性工业。

（2）林业 包括林木的栽培（不包括茶园、桑园和果园的栽培、管理和收获等活动）、林产品的采集和村及村以下合作经济组织和农户的竹木采伐。

（3）牧业 包括除渔业养殖以外的一切动物饲养和放牧以及野生动物的捕猎和饲养。

（4）渔业 包括水生动物和海藻类植物的养殖和捕捞。

农业总产值的计算方法通常是按农林牧渔业产品及其副产品的产量分别乘以各自单位产品价格求得，少数生产周期较长，当年没有产品或产品产量不易统计的，则采用间接方法匡算其产值，然后将四业产品产值相加即为农业总产值。

1957 年以前的农业总产值中包括了厩肥和农民自给性手工业（如农民自制衣服、鞋、袜，自己从事粮食初步加工等）。1958 年及以后的农业总产值，林业中增加了村及村以下竹木采伐产值；牧业中取消费厩肥产值；副业中取消了农民自给性手工业产值；渔业中增加了海洋捕捞水产品产值。1980 年及以后的农业总产值，在副业中增加了农民家庭兼营工业商品部分的产值。从 1984 年起村及村以下办工业产值划归工业。从 1993 年起，取消副业。将野生动物的捕猎划入牧业，野生植物采集和农民家庭兼营商品性工业划归农业。

耕地面积 指年初可以用来种植农作物、经常进行耕锄的田地，除包括熟地、当年新开荒地、连续撂荒未满三年的耕地和当年的休闲地（轮歇地）外，还包括以种植农作物为主并附带种植桑树、茶树、果树和其他林木的土地，以及沿海、沿湖地区已围垦利用的“海涂”、“湖田 ”等面积。但不包括属于专业性的桑园、茶园、果园、果木苗圃、林地、芦苇地、天然或人工草地面积。

农作物播种面积 指实际播种或移植有农作物的面积。凡是实际种植有农作物的面积，不论种植在耕地上还是种植在非耕地上，均包括在农作物播种面积中。在播种季节基本结束后，因遭灾而重新改种和补种的农作物面积，也包括在内。

有效灌溉面积 指具有一定的水源，地块比较平整，灌溉工程或设备已经配套，在一般年景下当年能够进行正常灌溉的耕地面积。

农业机械总动力 指主要用于农、林、牧、渔业的各种动力机械的动力总和。包括耕作机械、排灌机械、收获机械、农用运输机械、植物保护机械、牧业机械、渔业机械和其他农用机械[内燃机按引擎马力折成瓦（特）计算，电动机按功率折成瓦（特）计算]。不包括专门用于乡、镇、村、组办工业、基本建设、非农业运输、科学实验和教学等非农业生产方面用的动力机械与作业机械。

乡村从业人员 指乡村人口中 16 岁以上实际参加生产经营活动并取得实物或货币收入的人员，既包括劳动年龄内经常参加劳动的人员，也包括超过劳动年龄但经常参加劳动的人员。但不包括户口在家的在外学生、现役军人和丧失劳动能力的人，也不包括待业人员和家务劳动者。从业人员年龄为 16 岁以上。从业人员按从事主业时间最长（时间相同按收入）分为农业从业人员、工业从业人员、建筑业从业人员、交运仓储及邮电通讯业从业人员、批零贸易及餐饮业从业人员、其它从业人员人员。

期初（末）畜禽存栏头（只）数 指本期期初（末）农村各种合作经济组织和国营农场、农民个人、机关、团体、学校、工矿企业、部队等单位以及城镇居民饲养的大牲畜、猪、羊、家禽等禽畜的存栏头（只）数。

乡镇企业 即原来农村人民公社和生产大队两级集体经济举办的社队企业。在农村政社组织管理体制分设以后，除了乡、村合作经济组织办企业外，又出现了部分农民联营或其他形式的合作企业和个体企业。1984 年 3 月确定将这类企业统称“乡镇企业”。

乡镇企业单位一般应拥有固定的组织、生产场所、生产设备和从业人员；有核算制度，承担经济责任和纳税义务；是一个比较稳定的经济实体。

Explanatory Notes On Main Statistical Indicators

Gross Output of Agriculture refers to the total volume of products of farming, forestry, animal husbandry and fishery in value terms, which reflects the total scale and total result of agricultural production during a given period of time.

The statistical coverage of farming, forestry, animal husbandry and fishery are as follows:

In terms of ownership, China's agriculture includes specialized state farms（farming, forestry, animal husbandry and fishery), farms managed by various government organs, organizations, schools, research institutions, and army; farms managed by rural collective organizations at levels of township, town, and village; farming, forestry, animal husbandry, fishery run by mining and industrial enterprises; farming, forestry, animal husbandry and fishery and some commodity industries run by individual farmers.

（1）Farming includes cultivation of farm crops and other agricultural activities .

Cultivation includes the cultivation of grain crops, beans, tubers, cotton, oil-bearing crops, sugar crops, fiber crops, tobacco, vegetables, medicinal herbs, melons and gourds, and cultivation and management of tea plantations, mulberry fields and orchards.

Other agricultural activities includes gathering fruits, fiber, oil, gum and resin of wild plants, firewood and firegrass, wild medicinal herbs, fungus plants, and commodity industries of the rural households.

（2）Forestry refers to planting various kinds of trees（excluding tea plantations, mulberry fields and orchards）, gathering of forest products, and felling of bamboo and trees by villages and other cooperative organizations under villages.

（3）Animal husbandry refers to raising and grazing of all animals except fishery and aquaculture, and hunting and raising of wild animals.

（4）Fishery refers to cultivation and catching of fish and other aquatic animals and cultivation and collection of seaweed and other aquatic plants.

Gross output value of agriculture is obtained by first multiplying the output of each product or by-product by its price, resulting in the output value of each single item. For a small number of products, annual output of which is not available or difficult to get due to the long production/ growing process involved, the output value is estimated through an indirect approach. The sum of output value of all products of farming, forestry, animal husbandry, and fishery is then equal to the gross output value of agriculture.

Prior to 1957, China's gross agricultural output value included barnyard manure and handicraft products for self-consumption (clothes, shoes, stockings, and initial grain processing undertaken by peasants). Since 1958, felling of bamboo and trees by villages and other cooperative organizations under villages had been added to forestry; value of barnyard manure had been removed from animal husbandry; self-consumed handicrafts had been removed from sideline productions; while the output value of industries run by villages and cooperative organizations under village had been added in sideline productions and the output value of fish catches by motor fishing boats had been added to fishery. Since 1980, the value of handicraft products made for sale by households had been added to sideline productions. Since 1984, industry run by villages and cooperative organizations under villages has been put in the sector of industry. Since 1993, the subdivision of sideline productions has been canceled, and the hunting of wild animals has been classified into animal husbandry, and the gathering of wild plants and commodity industry run by rural households has been put in farming.

Cultivated Area (Area under cultivation) refers to farmland which is plowed constantly for growing crops, including cultivated land, newly cultivated land in the current year, farmland left without cultivation for less than three years and fallow land in the current year, rotation land, farmland for crops but growing also a few fruit trees, mulberry trees and other trees and cultivated seashore land and lake land, etc. The land of mulberry fields, tea plantations, orchards, nurseries of young plants, forestland, reed land, natural and man-made grassland are not included in cultivated land.

Sown Area of Crops refers to area of land sown or transplanted with crops regardless of being in cultivated area or non-cultivated area. Area of land resown after natural disasters is also included in.

Irrigated Area refers to areas that are effectively irrigated, i. e. level land which has water source and complete sets of irrigation facilities and is able to provide adequate water for irrigation under normal conditions.

Total Power of Farm Machinery refers to total mechanical power of machinery used in farming, forestry, animal husbandry, and fishery, including plow, irrigation and drainage, harvesting, transport, plant protection, stock breeding, forestry and fishery. The horsepower of internal combustion engines is converted into watts and the power of electric motors is converted into watts. Machinery employed for non-agricultural industry, construction, transportation, scientific experiments and teaching is excluded.

Employment Engaged in Farming, Forestry, Animal Husbandry and Fishery refers to the total labors who are directly engaged in production of farming, forestry, animal husbandry and fishery.

Number of Livestock or Poultry on Hand at the Beginning (or End) of the reference Period refers to the total number of big animals, pigs, sheep, fowls, etc. raised by rural cooperative organizations, army, and urban residents at the beginning (or end) of the reference period.

Township Enterprises refer to enterprises originally run by the collective economies at the people's commune and the production brigade levels. After the rural administrative system reform, besides the enterprises run by townships and villages, farmers' cooperative or other types of cooperative enterprises and private enterprises had appeared in the rural areas. In March 1984, all the aforesaid enterprises were defined as the "township enterprises."

Township Enterprises should have fixed organization, production sites, production equipment and employees, and also have accounting systems, undertake economic responsibilities and pay taxes. So, they are relatively stable economic entities.

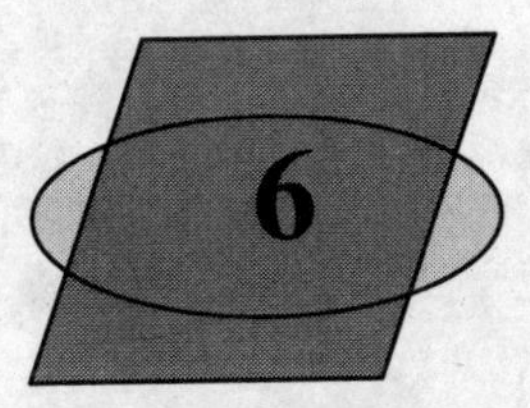

工　业
INDUSTRY

	1999年	1998年
企业单位数(个) Number of Enterprises(unit)	32870	30160
工业总产值(亿元) Gross Output Value of Industry(100 million yuan)	2125.3	1960.7

1999年按注册类型分构成%（不含个体工业）
Composition of Grouped by Registered Type % (exclude Individual Industry)

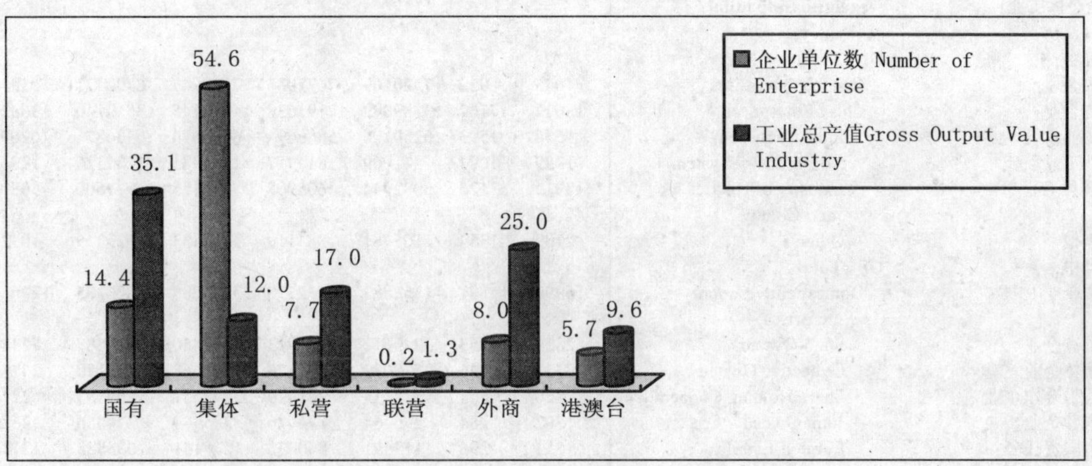

1999年部分工业产品产量
Output of Industry Product

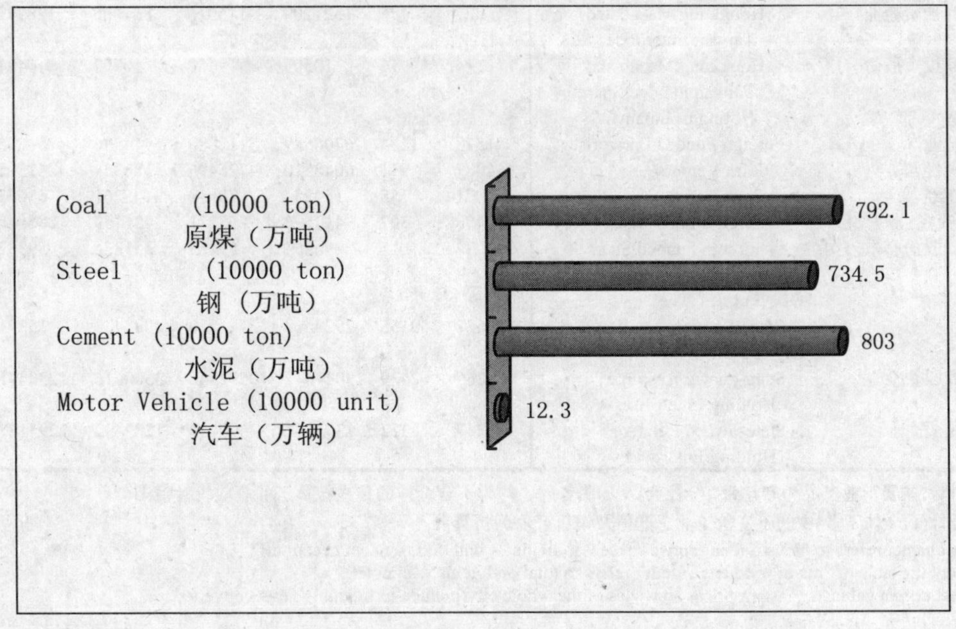

6-1 工业企业单位数和工业总产值、销售产值

NUMBER OF INDUSTRIAL ENTERPRISES，GROSS OUTPUT VALUE AND SALES

单位：万元 (10000 yuan)

项目	Item	企业单位数(个) Number of Enterprises (unit) 1999	1998	工业总产值 Gross Output Value of Industry 1990年不变价 at 1990 constant prices 1999	1998	当年价格 at current prices 1999	1998	销售产值(当年价格) Sales (at current prices)
全市合计(含个体工业)	**The Whole City (include Individual Industry)**	**32870**	**30160**	**21253006**	**19606882**	**21902616**	**20270235**	**21260783**
总　计(不含个体工业)	**Total (exclude Individual Industry)**	**19682**	**18089**	**20810067**	**19267723**	**21446119**	**19919611**	**20817981**
在总计中：	**Of Total:**							
中央企业	Central Enterprises	1045	922	7520169	7072085	7190947	6400471	7135166
地方企业	Local Enterprises	18637	17167	13289899	12195638	14255145	13519140	13682815
工业系统	Industry System	1554	1593	6260106	5886694	6446674	6386871	6269997
非工业系统	Non-Industry System	1059	1094	841069	819917	1316985	1225320	1291311
区县工业	Industry of District and County	13915	13126	5082944	4605908	5376153	4977600	5089004
其他	Others	2109	1354	1105781	883119	1115333	929349	1032503
在总计中：	**Of Total:**							
内资企业	Domestic Investment Enterprises	16990	15891	11352883	13032570	13424788	13806105	12968075
国有企业	State-Owned	2829	3253	5920611	8205913	7695460	8634587	7548563
集体企业	Collective Owned	10738	10446	2510989	2595723	2631668	2752170	2478980
股份合作企业	Share Holding Cooperative	826	603	228015	241410	243651	259183	224914
联营企业	Joint Owned	302	284	296764	274976	285789	274056	267448
有限责任公司	Limited-Liability Company	553	295	1113691	850832	1278151	1033833	1211228
股份有限公司	Share Holding Company	206	157	927143	679439	918343	652427	895368
私营企业	Private Owned	1524	849	355227	184157	371298	199641	341202
其他企业	Others	12	4	445	121	428	208	372
港澳台商投资企业	Hongkong,Macao and Taiwan Funded Enterprises	1114	914	2750595	1122273	2106734	1257251	2061291
港澳台合资经营	Joint Venture	821	686	1185884	974073	1198653	1092185	1150929
港澳台合作经营	Cooperative	52	37	32999	22532	36024	25593	37610
港澳台商独资企业	Hongkong,Macao and Taiwan Enterprises	227	175	1521209	116016	861265	128992	863116
港澳台商投资股份有限公司	Hongkong,Macao and Taiwan Funded Share Holing Company	14	16	10503	9652	10792	10481	9635
外商投资企业	Foreign Funded Enterprises	1578	1284	6706589	5112880	5914596	4856255	5788616
中外合资经营	Joint Venture	1087	911	6048510	4725495	5186351	4441395	5089648
中外合作经营	Cooperative	71	55	144254	70632	145261	68663	130380
外资(独资)企业	Foreign Enterprises	408	307	417572	257271	431159	286846	418154
外商投资股份有限公司	Foreign Funded Share Holding Company	12	11	96253	59483	151826	59352	150434
在总计中：	**Of Total:**							
农村企业	Rural Enterprises	9627	9155	2924508	2741020	3083423	2915391	2869051
在总计中：	**Of Total:**							
国有绝对控股企业	State-owned Absolute Holding Enterprises	4266	2639	13029642	10592340	13500616	11230475	13135576
国有相对控股企业	State-owned Relative Holding Enterpeises	247	312	1301641	2690140	1282492	2295182	1356715

注：1.本资料除"主要工业产品生产总量"(全社会)及标明者外，均为不含个体的独立核算工业企业统计范围。

2.全市合计(含个体工业)中的不变价工业总产值及销售产值为折算数。

a) Data of this chapter refers to industrial enterprises except individuals with independent accounting system,except the table of "major products output"(refers to total)and items with note.

b) Data of gross output value at constant prices and sales of the whole city(include individual)is that converted.

6-1 续表 1 continued

单位：万元 (10000 yuan)

项目	Item	企业单位数(个) Number of Enterprises (unit) 1999	1998	工业总产值 Gross Output Value of Industry 1990年不变价 at 1990 constant prices 1999	1998	当年价格 at current prices 1999	1998	销售产值(当年价格) Sales (at current prices)
在总计中：	Of Total:							
轻工业	Light Industry	9559	8837	5560892	5393576	6106775	6120157	5868560
以农产品为原料	Using Farm Products as Raw Material	5713	5327	3261405	3209874	3934752	4019696	3776773
以非农产品为原料	Using Non-Farm Products as Raw Material	3846	3510	2299486	2183702	2172023	2100461	2091787
重工业	Heavy Industry	10123	9252	15249176	13874148	15339344	13799453	14949421
采掘工业	Excavation	502	497	114320	122113	191301	199917	179699
原料工业	Raw Material	1277	1162	3379893	3104281	4920776	4591597	4839864
加工工业	Processing	8344	7593	11754963	10647755	10227267	9007939	9929858
在总计中：	Of Total:							
大型企业	Large Enterprises	217	266	7705996	9312944	8266005	9659578	8007348
中型企业	Medium Enterprises	292	268	2441733	945904	2448433	1182932	2405108
小型企业	Small Enterprises	19173	17555	10662339	9008876	10731681	9077101	10405524
在总计中：	Of Total:							
煤炭采选业	Coal Mining and Dressing	194	203	57035	59908	125320	125821	120343
石油和天然气开采业	Petroleum and Natural Gas Extraction	1	1	138	155	138	155	138
黑色金属矿采选业	Ferrous Metals Mining and Dressing	19	26	10985	13888	17541	22220	17299
有色金属矿采选业	Nonferrous Metals Mining and Dressing	16	19	4213	6082	4284	6259	4041
非金属矿采选业	Nonmetal Minerals Mining and Dressing	271	247	42089	41867	44210	45253	38047
其他矿采选业	Other Minerals Mining and Dressing	2	1	291	213	270	211	253
食品加工业	Food Processing	573	558	447626	571689	629688	819264	620803
食品制造业	Food Making	668	641	421002	333086	547637	464351	526031
饮料制造业	Beverage Production	271	230	556623	484259	634867	603891	614141
烟草加工业	Tobacco Processing	4	4	45142	46449	70101	68203	71921
纺织业	Textile Industry	516	469	380403	411755	403711	470389	394547
服装及其他纤维制品制造业	Garments and Other Fiber Products	985	876	426799	435354	491168	509911	469502
皮革、毛皮、羽绒及其制品业	Leather,Furs,Down and Related Products	174	164	45513	48443	56009	58672	54638
木材加工及竹藤、棕、草制品业	Timber Processing,Bamboo Cane,Palm Fiber and Straw Products	247	233	45373	41774	53141	46660	50509
家具制造业	Furniture Manufacturing	547	514	146877	142930	152044	148018	147713
造纸及纸制品业	Papermaking and Paper Products	525	489	186889	180851	200846	201040	195931
印刷业，记录媒介的复制	Printing and Record Medium Reproduced	1011	980	352979	324648	468519	422291	423950

6-1 续表 2 continued

单位：万元 (10000 yuan)

项目	Item	企业单位数（个）Number of Enterprises (unit)		工业总产值 Gross Output Value of Industry				销售产值（当年价格）Sales (at current prices)
				1990年不变价 at 1990 constant prices		当年价格 at current prices		
		1999	1998	1999	1998	1999	1998	
文教体育用品制造业	Stationery,Educational and Sports Goods	242	214	96264	89792	114157	107609	106345
石油加工及炼焦业	Petroleum Processing and Coking Products	110	97	898414	750125	1445224	1142289	1427331
化学原料及化学制品	Raw Chemical Materials and Chemical Product	1358	1196	1179687	1005914	1177497	1022599	1138663
医药制造业	Medical and Pharmaceutical Products	254	220	496184	428956	450470	397817	426935
化学纤维制造业	Chemical Fibers	45	37	59162	61158	41838	50169	39622
橡胶制品业	Rubber Products	139	133	153245	143788	135539	122422	132043
塑料制品业	Plastic Products	736	689	271760	280883	268703	279258	258287
非金属矿物制品	Nonmetal Mineral Products	1780	1674	872528	784915	1042200	948051	988496
黑色金属冶炼及压延加工业	Smelting and Pressing of Ferrous Metals	79	100	1041863	1113519	1494973	1680659	1471573
有色金属冶炼及压延加工业	Smelting and Pressing of Nonferrous Metals	151	134	95351	92763	98028	88103	96527
金属制品业	Metal Products	2282	2130	639080	604608	638648	614993	601241
普通机械制造业	Ordinary Machinery Manufacturing	1247	1145	464901	501321	489141	546997	481973
专用设备制造业	Special Purposes Equipment Manufacturing	1007	897	944247	810186	973475	827211	956504
交通运输设备制造业	Transportation Equipment Manufacturing	1344	1296	1053515	1050675	1186733	1161437	1137387
武器弹药制造业	Weapon and Ammunition Manufacturing	9	10	54806	47628	70696	62344	69221
电气机械及器材制造	Electric Equipment and Machinery	930	848	914764	720118	867126	710585	836233
电子及通信设备制造	Electronic and Telecommunications	763	568	7551449	6800618	5643635	4780540	5547920
仪器仪表及文化、办公用机械制造	Instruments,Meters, Cultural and official Machine	486	376	369142	347974	366497	339448	319194
其他制造业	Other Manufacturing	605	574	158902	179297	153180	185864	150191
电力、蒸汽、热水的生产和供应业	Electricity,Steam and Hot Water Production and Supply	66	77	233833	252298	688150	726370	687390
煤气生产和供应	Gas Production and Supply	12	8	39131	32132	75521	37750	75500
自来水的生产和供应	Tap Water Production and Supply	13	11	51862	25708	125230	74489	119597

6-2 主 要 工 业 产 品 生 产 总 量
OUTPUT OF MAIN INDUSTRIAL PRODUCTS

主要工业产品名称		Products		本年生产量 Output in this Year
原　煤	(吨)	Coal	(ton)	7920578
铁矿石成品矿	(吨)	Iron Ore Products	(ton)	5154481
发电量	(万千瓦小时)	Electricity	(10000 kwh)	1431772
火　电	(万千瓦小时)	Thermal Power	(10000 kwh)	1344407
供热量	(万百万千焦)	Heating Supply	(10 billion kilo-joule)	3826
自来水生产量	(万吨)	Tap Water Production	(10000 tons)	81146
大　米	(吨)	Rice	(ton)	13973
小麦粉	(万吨)	Wheat Flour	(10000 tons)	35
食用植物油	(吨)	Edible Vegetable Oil	(ton)	139304
配混合饲料	(吨)	Mixed Feed	(ton)	725067
乳制品	(吨)	Dairy Products	(ton)	14255
方便主食品	(吨)	Convenient Staple Food	(ton)	67769
罐　头	(吨)	Canned Food	(ton)	1559
白　酒	(吨)	Liquor	(ton)	98910
啤　酒	(吨)	Beer	(ton)	1388582
软饮料	(吨)	Soft Drink	(ton)	568520
冷冻饮品	(吨)	Frozen Drink	(ton)	18698
卷　烟	(箱)	Cigarettes	(case)	164316
合成纤维	(吨)	Synthetic Fiber	(ton)	24107
纱	(吨)	Yarn	(ton)	46813
布	(万米)	Cloth	(10000 m)	14753
#棉　布	(万米)	Cotton Cloth	(10000 m)	9425
混纺交织布	(万米)	Blend Cloth	(10000 m)	5251
纯化纤布	(万米)	Pure Chemical Fiber Cloth	(10000 m)	77
绒线(毛线)	(吨)	Knitting Wool	(ton)	2761
呢　绒	(万米)	Woolen Piece Goods	(10000 m)	894
丝织品	(万米)	Silk Fabrics	(10000 m)	749
服　装	(万件)	Garments	(10000)	12672
锯　材	(立方米)	Sawn Timber	(cu.m)	15398
家具	(件)	Furniture	(unit)	3861528
人造板	(立方米)	Artificial Wooden Board	(cu.m)	113501
机制纸	(吨)	Machine-made Paper	(ton)	52391
机制纸板	(吨)	Machine-made Paperboard	(ton)	77294
体育用品及用具	(千元)	Sports Goods and Appliance	(1000 yuan)	128384
工艺美术制品	(千元)	Handicrafits	(1000 yuan)	393168
汽　油	(吨)	Gasoline	(ton)	1242719
煤　油	(吨)	Kerosene	(ton)	318

6-2 续表 1 continued

主要工业产品名称		Products		本年生产量 Output in this Year
柴　油	(吨)	Diesel Oil	(ton)	1700699
润滑油	(吨)	Lubricating Oil	(ton)	373035
燃料油	(吨)	Fuel Oil	(ton)	808685
焦　炭	(吨)	Coke	(ton)	3959342
硫酸(折 100%)	(吨)	Sulphuric Acid(100%)	(ton)	84217
氢氧化钠(烧碱)(折 100%)	(吨)	Caustic Soda(100%)	(ton)	117392
碳化钙(电石)(折 300 升／千克)	(吨)	Calcium Carbide(300 liters/kg)	(ton)	9896
合成氨	(吨)	Synthetic Ammonia	(ton)	97203
农用氮、磷、钾化学肥料(折纯)	(吨)	Chemical Fertilizer(pure)	(ton)	87850
乙　烯	(吨)	Ethylene	(ton)	679780
纯　苯	(吨)	Pure Benzene	(ton)	109204
冰醋酸	(吨)	Glacial Acetic Acid	(ton)	5028
油　漆	(吨)	Paint	(ton)	9841
染　料	(吨)	Dyestuff	(ton)	3581
塑料树脂及共聚物	(吨)	Plastic Resin and Copolymer	(ton)	890016
合成橡胶	(吨)	Synthetic Rubber	(ton)	121907
合成纤维单体	(吨)	Synthetic Fiber(Monomer)	(ton)	71962
合成纤维聚合物	(吨)	Synthetic Fiber(Polymerizate)	(ton)	10586
合成洗涤剂	(吨)	Synthetic Detergents	(ton)	57616
化学原料药	(吨)	Chemical Raw Medicine	(ton)	4166
轮胎外胎	(条)	Tires	(unit)	3040305
塑料制品	(吨)	Plastic Products	(ton)	154007
# 农业用薄膜	(吨)	Film for Farm Use	(ton)	17776
水　泥	(万吨)	Cement	(10000 tons)	803
平板玻璃	(重量箱)	Plate Glass	(wt.case)	4742892
生　铁	(吨)	Pig Iron	(ton)	7175578
钢	(吨)	Steel	(ton)	7344643
成品钢材	(吨)	Steel Products	(ton)	6638138
# 普通中型钢材	(吨)	Ordinary Rolled-Steel,Medium	(ton)	164004
普通小型钢材	(吨)	Ordinary Rolled-Steel,Small	(ton)	2518725
优质钢型钢材	(吨)	High Quality Section Steel	(ton)	283951
线　材	(吨)	Wire Rod	(ton)	2729698
中厚钢板	(吨)	Medium Steel Plate	(ton)	492540
钢　带	(吨)	Steel Band	(ton)	310408
无缝钢管	(吨)	Seamless Steel Pipe	(ton)	38
焊接钢管	(吨)	Welded Steel Pipe	(ton)	134040
铁合金	(吨)	Ferroalloy	(ton)	38332
铜	(吨)	Copper	(ton)	125

6-2 续表 2 continued

主要工业产品名称		Products		本年生产量 Output in this Year
铜加工材	(吨)	Copper Products	(ton)	11904
铝 材	(吨)	Aluminum Products	(ton)	19030
日用精铝制品	(吨)	Daily-use Refined Aluminum Products	(ton)	14
工业锅炉	(台)	Boiler for Industrial Use	(ton)	1477
金属切削机床	(台)	Metal-Cutting Machine	(unit)	1761
# 高精度机床	(台)	High-Precision Machine Tools	(unit)	34
数控机床	(台)	Numerical Control Machine Tools	(unit)	481
大型机床	(台)	Large Machine Tools	(unit)	24
印刷机	(台)	Priting Machine	(unit)	14426
小型拖拉机	(台)	Mini-tractor	(unit)	2885
汽 车	(辆)	Motor Vehicle	(unit)	122707
# 载货汽车	(辆)	Trucks	(unit)	91053
公路汽车	(辆)	Highway Motor Vehicle	(unit)	21688
轿车	(辆)	Cars	(unit)	9505
摩托车	(辆)	Motorcycle	(unit)	6204
发电设备	(千瓦)	Generating Equipment	(kw)	37000
绝缘制品	(吨)	Insulating Products	(ton)	5141
交流电动机	(台)	Alternating Current Electric Motor	(unit)	1420188
家用洗衣机	(台)	Household Washing Machines	(unit)	200000
家用电冰箱	(台)	Household Refrigerators	(unit)	58182
家用冷冻箱	(台)	Household Freezer	(unit)	569
电风扇	(台)	Electric Fan	(unit)	24369
房间空气调节器	(台)	House Air Conditioner	(unit)	284733
排油烟机	(台)	Smoke Absorber	(unit)	386
家用电热烘烤器具	(个)	Electric Toast Appliance	(unit)	54989
程控交换机	(线)	Program Control Telephone Exchange	(line)	7605691
电子计算机	(部)	Computer	(unit)	459
微型电子计算机	(部)	Micro-computer	(unit)	1789872
彩色显象管	(只)	Tricolor Tube	(unit)	4594556
半导体集成电路	(万块)	Semiconductor Integrated Circuit	(10000)	12605
电子元件	(万只)	Electronic Cell	(10000)	979367
彩色电视机	(部)	Color TV Set	(unit)	117218
录相机	(部)	Videocorder	(unit)	937366
收录放机	(部)	Recorder	(unit)	310732
自动化仪表及系统	(台)	Automatic Meters and System	(unit)	1164571
光学仪器	(台)	Optical Instrument	(unit)	68096
照相机	(台)	Camera	(unit)	816319
表	(只)	Clock	(unit)	1167702

6-3 全部独立核算工业企业主要经济指标

单位：万元

项目	Item	企业单位个数(个) Number of Enterprises (unit)	#亏损企业 Loss-making Enterprises	工业总产值(当年价格) Gross Output Value of Industry (at current price)	新产品产值 Value of New Products	工业总产值(1990年不变价格) Gross Output Value of Industry (at 1990 constant prices)	工业增加值(生产法) Added Value of Industry (with production method)
总　计	**Total**	**19682**	**3995**	**21446119**	**3538698**	**20810067**	**6352167**
在总计中:	**Of Total:**						
中央企业	Central Enterprises	1045	285	7190974	2226404	7520169	2161913
地方企业	Local Enterprises	18637	3710	14255145	1312293	13289899	4190254
工业系统	Industry System	1554	340	6446674	910177	6260106	1798115
非工业系统	Non-Industry System	1059	272	1316985	2866	841069	406457
区县工业	Industry of District and County	13915	2227	5376153	150487	5082944	1656610
其他	Others	2109	871	1115333	248764	1105781	329072
在总计中:	**Of Total:**						
内资企业	Domestic Investment Enterprises	16990	2922	13424788	2269835	11352883	4124532
国有企业	State-Owned	2829	634	7695460	1557770	5920611	2473369
集体企业	Collective Owned	10738	1537	2631668	90511	2510989	834618
股份合作企业	Share Holding Cooperative	826	144	243651	15416	228015	81207
联营企业	Joint Owned	302	61	285789	10320	296764	77243
有限责任公司	Limited-Liability Company	553	154	1278151	209774	1113691	318233
股份有限公司	Share Holding Company	206	43	918343	353768	927143	251850
私营企业	Private Owned	1524	345	371299	32277	355227	87931
其他企业	Others	12	4	428		445	84
港澳台商投资企业	Hongkong,Macao and Taiwan Funded Enterprises	1114	450	2106734	305827	2750595	454025
港澳台合资经营	Joint Venture	821	312	1198653	48041	1185884	295165
港澳台合作经营	Cooperative	52	16	36024	797	32999	8985
港澳台商独资企业	Hongkong,Macao and Taiwan Enterprises	227	114	861265	256989	1521209	145685
港澳台商投资股份有限公司	Hongkong,Macao and Taiwan Funded Share Holing Company	14	8	10792		10503	4191
外商投资企业	Foreign Funded Enterprises	1578	623	5914596	963035	6706589	1773608
中外合资经营	Joint Venture	1087	402	5186351	829873	6048510	1536750
中外合作经营	Cooperative	71	17	145261	1264	144254	43537
外资(独资)企业	Foreign Enterprises	408	201	431159	120521	417572	131638
外商投资股份有限公司	Foreign Funded Share Holding Company	12	3	151826	11377	96253	61684
在总计中:	**Of Total:**						
农村企业	Rural Enterprises	9627	1051	3083432	11960	2924508	1018194
在总计中:	**Of Total:**						
国有绝对控股企业	State-owned Absolute Holding Enterprises	4266	1034	13500616	2715639	13029642	3889406
国有相对控股企业	State-owned Relative Holding Enterprises	247	77	1282492	71601	1301641	407639
在总计中:	**Of Total:**						
轻工业	Light Industry	9559	2157	6106775	293879	5560892	2002287
以农产品为原料	Using Farm Products as Raw Material	5713	1345	3934752	115179	3261405	1274781
以非农产品为原料	Using Non-Farm Products as Raw Material	3846	812	2172023	178700	2299486	727506
重工业	Heavy Industry	10123	1838	15339344	3244818	15249176	4349880
采掘工业	Excavation	502	37	191301		114320	103875
原料工业	Raw Material	1277	246	4920776	278896	3379893	1513174
加工工业	Processing	8344	1555	10227267	2965923	11754963	2732831
在总计中:	**Of Total:**						
大型企业	Large Enterprises	217	63	8266005	1439000	7705996	2197270
中型企业	Medium Enterprises	292	63	2448433	1098392	2441733	688640
小型企业	Small Enterprises	19173	3869	10731681	1001306	10662339	3466257

MAIN INDICATORS FOR INDUSTRIAL ENTERPRISES WITH INDEPENDENT ACCOUNTING SYSTEM

(10000 yuan)

工业销售产值(当年价格) Sales Value of Industry (at current price)	出口交货值 Delivery Value of Exports	全部从业人员年平均人数(人) Average Number of Employment (person)	资产负债 Assets and Liabilities 流动资产合计 Circulating Assets	应收帐款净额 Accounts Receivable	存货 Stock	产成品 Finished Products	流动资产平均余额 Average Balance of Circulating Assets	长期投资 Long-time Investment	固定资产合计 Fixed Assets
20817981	**1387039**	**1610811**	**19169496**	**5517631**	**6112953**	**2310044**	**18090799**	**3157131**	**18180562**
7135166	325739	219725	4885484	1398503	1337117	330308	4573230	603351	5503937
13682815	1061300	1391086	14284012	4119128	4775836	1979736	13517568	2553780	12676625
6269997	583424	506555	7304670	2747730	2245990	863803	7173490	2099404	7068584
1291311	17518	98306	1158743	286197	308897	116753	1038569	64823	2036023
5089004	394286	668533	4194492	829942	1773224	825208	3893183	298903	3024309
1032503	66072	117692	1626107	255260	447724	173973	1412327	90650	547709
12968075	563545	1315898	13002028	3361217	4277986	1740239	12287658	3077421	14815638
7548563	255597	623881	7656586	2123585	2305341	799990	7348071	2084431	10286243
2478980	141640	449493	2300958	452576	1009674	516092	2115264	205449	1386608
224914	8018	33814	223939	39802	92458	47223	200146	15637	119849
267448	30333	34918	336145	106857	127746	53940	331981	62288	247682
1211228	105822	97915	1477838	427223	422036	185746	1412403	542612	2248158
895368	18658	39875	767326	169830	220506	92505	680631	160466	406017
341202	3477	35803	238603	41252	99977	44579	198623	6538	120478
372	0	199	633	93	248	165	539		603
2061291	162940	139197	1591641	386448	597393	247533	1566073	35091	785156
1150929	128914	70038	1140955	248462	426521	188770	1072078	28543	681199
37610	5380	55305	37269	7097	12715	5950	34836	905	38227
863116	28646	13036	403813	128744	154083	51490	449869	5214	60442
9635		818	9605	2146	4073	1323	9289	429	5288
5788616	660555	155716	4575827	1769966	1237574	322272	4237068	44618	2579768
5089648	557967	122836	4016083	1598912	1063512	259004	3755299	40586	2144121
130380	13679	4735	92725	20177	40449	17107	76638	205	76199
418154	64135	19077	392763	125424	105067	35214	328670	1727	182932
150434	24774	9068	74256	25453	28547	10947	76462	2100	176517
2869051	264760	429219	1990850	405458	969360	513556	1858384	82828	1329820
13135576	763725	851556	12256177	3807750	3701065	1252747	11857506	2856788	14265195
1356715	112180	83237	947550	407457	221469	64765	814587	17759	546950
5868560	615930	639586	5977329	1233104	2119179	1009827	5620437	673137	4860225
3776773	422706	426952	3640376	717298	1283795	611922	3437222	368462	2885567
2091787	193224	212634	2336952	515806	835384	397905	2183215	304675	1974658
14949421	771110	971225	13192167	4284528	3993774	1300217	12470361	2483994	13320337
179699	34633	53394	213532	131169	42257	26374	215121	19326	183575
4839864	144265	233217	3844640	1215355	892360	296758	3817715	1418088	8450214
9929858	592211	684614	9133995	2938004	3059157	977085	8437526	1046580	4686548
8007348	344810	503699	8142899	2645018	2371245	813779	7990090	2132198	11269093
2405108	180099	140435	2028331	471604	618190	202857	1874668	399107	1259819
10405524	862130	966677	8998266	2401010	3123518	1293408	8226041	625826	5651651

6-3 续表 1 continued

单位：万元

项目	Item	资产负债 固定资产原价合计 Original Value of Fixed Assets	# 生产经营用 For Productive Use	累计折旧 Accumulative Depreciation	#本年折旧 Depreciation in this Year	固定资产净值年平均余额 Average Net Value of Fixed Assets	无形资产及递延资产 Intangible and Deferred Assets
总 计	**Total**	**23121446**	**18914254**	**7544038**	**1094740**	**14607244**	**1819669**
在总计中：	**Of Total:**						
中央企业	Central Enterprises	6843879	5458752	2418563	344801	4044449	216454
地方企业	Local Enterprises	16277567	13455502	5125475	749939	10562796	1603215
工业系统	Industry System	9338828	7920899	3297424	404247	5972624	973460
非工业系统	Non-Industry System	2557547	2305303	632204	117893	1682927	65432
区县工业	Industry of District and County	3684513	2810671	1025873	185722	2490778	323904
其他	Others	696679	418630	169973	42078	416467	240420
在总计中：	**Of Total:**						
内资企业	Domestic Investment Enterprises	18776839	15447184	6246223	808785	11710680	1246342
国有企业	State-Owned	13276604	11302671	4751187	603382	8329982	578752
集体企业	Collective Owned	1766186	1238575	562449	81791	1095026	113988
股份合作企业	Share Holding Cooperative	146717	104200	39556	8507	88258	12886
联营企业	Joint Owned	337945	233046	99757	13022	219222	27975
有限责任公司	Limited-Liability Company	2640429	2044629	619871	64699	1607195	434459
股份有限公司	Share Holding Company	476393	435579	148583	28377	277197	65241
私营企业	Private Owned	131932	88051	24654	8978	93346	13034
其他企业	Others	634	433	166	29	455	9
港澳台商投资企业	Hongkong,Macao and Taiwan Funded Enterprises	949327	759625	259682	64254	661197	252530
港澳台合资经营	Joint Venture	829572	667744	230462	56871	577772	97566
港澳台合作经营	Cooperative	38985	31096	8618	3131	27972	1503
港澳台商独资企业	Hongkong,Macao and Taiwan Enterprises	74158	55281	19135	3812	50258	152601
港澳台商投资股份有限公司	Hongkong,Macao and Taiwan Funded Share Holing Company	6612	5504	1469	441	5196	860
外商投资企业	Foreign Funded Enterprises	3395280	2707444	1038132	221701	2235367	320797
中外合资经营	Joint Venture	2847800	2240335	908089	191221	1843436	257839
中外合作经营	Cooperative	77337	59161	20059	6573	55681	8669
外资(独资)企业	Foreign Enterprises	260418	206015	50957	13375	188639	28988
外商投资股份有限公司	Foreign Funded Share Holding Company	209724	201934	59028	10532	147611	25301
在总计中：	**Of Total:**						
农村企业	Rural Enterprises	1684765	1238562	480747	83216	1139765	101979
在总计中：	**Of Total:**						
国有绝对控股企业	State-owned Absolute Holding Enterprises	18153614	15187055	6123387	804215	11321550	1152033
国有相对控股企业	State-owned Relative Holding Enterprises	770068	683715	266435	61587	477705	61977
在总计中：	**Of Total:**						
轻工业	Light Industry	6181665	4814232	1804303	313152	4003586	707595
以农产品为原料	Using Farm Products as Raw Material	3655065	2790793	1099343	193305	2399702	295126
以非农产品为原料	Using Non-Farm Products as Raw Material	2526600	2023439	704960	119846	1603883	412469
重工业	Heavy Industry	16939780	14100022	5739735	781588	10603659	1112075
采掘工业	Excavation	250801	170608	85621	7353	166520	10878
原料工业	Raw Material	10640689	9505821	3543439	467995	6679526	623518
加工工业	Processing	6048290	4423592	2110674	306240	3757613	477678
在总计中：	**Of Total:**						
大型企业	Large Enterprises	14386420	12310758	4877320	646820	9176618	890462
中型企业	Medium Enterprises	1534164	1204888	515802	80964	948177	180996
小型企业	Small Enterprises	7200862	5398608	2150915	366956	4482450	748211

6-3 续表 2 continued

(10000 yuan)

Assets and Liabilities										
	其他资产	资产总计	流动负债合计		长期负债合计		负债合计	所有者权益	实收资本	
#无形资产 Intangible Assets	Other Assets	Total Assets	Liquid Liabilities	短期借款 Short-time Loans	Long-term Liabilities	长期借款 Long-time Loans	Total Liabilities	Ownership Interest	Contributed Capital	国家资本 State
828602	**214001**	**42540707**	**17907812**	**6585529**	**7680039**	**5000059**	**25863159**	**16677549**	**11351465**	**4488061**
161371	21326	11230552	4013093	1127761	3139903	1074266	7351053	3879500	2193215	1257575
667231	192675	31310155	13894719	5457769	4540136	3925793	18512106	12798049	9158250	3230486
236578	78395	17524567	7367616	3273168	3357558	2904922	10745197	6779370	3982791	1389920
41240	18979	3343864	1017981	287977	286436	251606	1321859	2022005	1704938	1334963
171962	61884	7903493	4218148	1515384	727351	614790	4979472	2924021	2517596	414009
217450	33418	2538231	1290974	381240	168792	154475	1465578	1072654	952925	91594
341559	66871	32208165	12386674	4655553	6885628	4264808	19510997	12697168	7419620	3840093
186232	48139	20654016	7163693	2868767	4800566	2389889	12183698	8470319	4455038	3325376
43592	12994	4019996	2308703	749624	415621	353882	2736852	1283144	1007077	41485
9098	2211	374523	206938	83079	29968	24741	239365	135158	108960	6953
6467	744	674833	392820	143482	91416	61450	484659	190174	160048	23283
39364	-1165	4701902	1629874	580884	1467628	1372186	3098731	1603171	1162722	373314
46687	1300	1400350	485451	175120	65612	49968	551136	849214	389406	68190
10112	2645	381298	198622	54571	14817	12691	215979	165320	135572	1059
9	2	1246	573	27			578	668	797	434
215192	48532	2712880	1624395	551855	201408	185057	1839336	873544	897576	166371
67396	43713	1991975	1194807	453239	95888	84337	1303723	688252	765180	163277
538	2423	80328	37575	6748	12471	12471	50047	30281	36762	1730
146614	2318	624317	384364	90997	89929	87956	474796	149521	89499	
645	78	16260	7650	871	3120	293	10770	5490	6135	1364
271850	98598	7619663	3896742	1378122	593003	550194	4512826	3106837	3034269	481597
219104	79349	6538033	3388023	1266183	524826	490509	3933597	2604436	2451256	426367
7026	2388	180185	76521	18763	7612	7611	84689	95496	83773	8859
22296	15425	621835	344883	60803	54654	49250	401298	220536	360271	
23424	1436	279610	87316	32373	5912	2824	93242	186368	138969	46371
53471	26477	3531954	1902022	748597	283994	235113	2202728	1329227	1112462	46933
323459	79058	30609116	11435262	4416062	6680949	4137719	18357926	12251190	7003142	4131528
50646	24128	1598365	858703	294451	167090	157726	1032160	566205	593497	138451
411369	121208	12339413	5761708	2290255	1355419	1092745	7158146	5181267	4308108	1487159
168601	58659	7248190	3419990	1352258	668838	513116	4125595	3122595	2641612	769644
242768	62549	5091223	2341718	937997	686581	579629	3032551	2058672	1666496	717515
417233	92793	30201294	12146103	4295275	6324620	3907314	18705013	11496282	7043357	3000902
807	258	427570	177798	63981	62343	48828	241268	186301	109450	69127
175591	-2853	14333608	3757873	1756128	4753033	2633743	8706992	5626615	3087251	2146293
240836	95388	15440117	8210432	2475166	1509244	1224744	9756752	5683365	3846656	785482
284953	57193	22491845	7726303	3528660	5768966	3407718	13702853	8788992	4971917	2912481
76873	17725	3885977	1716264	505921	391024	294214	2122384	1763593	1005934	393377
466776	139084	16162885	8465244	2550949	1520049	1298127	10037922	6124963	5373614	1182202

6-3 续表 3 continued

单位：万元

项目	Item	资产负债 Assets and Liabilities 集体资本 Collective	法人资本 Institutional Units	个人资本 Individuals	港澳台资本 Hongkong, Macao and Taiwan	外商资本 Foreign
总计	**Total**	**986157**	**3132574**	**310565**	**578996**	**1855113**
在总计中：	**Of Total:**					
中央企业	Central Enterprises	21706	668447	29291	39435	176761
地方企业	Local Enterprises	964451	2464127	281274	539561	1678352
工业系统	Industry System	140433	1594541	64298	107207	686394
非工业系统	Non-Industry System	10146	102107	23152	92558	142011
区县工业	Industry of District and County	791110	592382	135303	226040	358752
其他	Others	22762	175097	58522	113756	491194
在总计中：	**Of Total:**					
内资企业	Domestic Investment Enterprises	844204	2391451	288957	10493	44423
国有企业	State-Owned	31856	1069588	25246	1931	1041
集体企业	Collective Owned	707613	181182	42107	7644	27047
股份合作企业	Share Holding Cooperative	25452	55146	20978	431	
联营企业	Joint Owned	48418	85130	2073	107	1037
有限责任公司	Limited-Liability Company	16566	723342	49062	91	347
股份有限公司	Share Holding Company	10363	211736	84167		14950
私营企业	Private Owned	3936	65294	65118	165	
其他企业	Others		33	205	125	
港澳台商投资企业	Hongkong,Macao and Taiwan Funded Enterprises	56880	204601	7721	433595	28408
港澳台合资经营	Joint Venture	55072	193643	5537	331520	16133
港澳台合作经营	Cooperative	638	6983	270	22818	4322
港澳台商独资企业	Hongkong,Macao and Taiwan Enterprises	40	3292	1040	77542	7586
港澳台商投资股份有限公司	Hongkong,Macao and Taiwan Funded Share Holing Company	1130	684	874	1715	368
外商投资企业	Foreign Funded Enterprises	85073	536522	13888	134908	1782282
中外合资经营	Joint Venture	76648	484959	5614	87586	1370083
中外合作经营	Cooperative	5119	9258	2500	19112	38926
外资(独资)企业	Foreign Enterprises	578	8312	34	28210	323136
外商投资股份有限公司	Foreign Funded Share Holding Company	2728	33994	5740		50136
在总计中：	**Of Total:**					
农村企业	Rural Enterprises	537911	279599	73845	62659	111516
在总计中：	**Of Total:**					
国有绝对控股企业	State-owned Absolute Holding Enterprises	74947	2236601	127645	113958	318463
国有相对控股企业	State-owned Relative Holding Enterprises	15614	92175	2253	94033	250972
在总计中：	**Of Total:**					
轻工业	Light Industry	471596	887231	127896	404499	929727
以农产品为原料	Using Farm Products as Raw Material	292814	517440	80336	314893	666485
以非农产品为原料	Using Non-Farm Products as Raw Material	178782	369791	47559	89606	263243
重工业	Heavy Industry	514561	2245343	182669	174497	925386
采掘工业	Excavation	17941	18415	3561	23	384
原料工业	Raw Material	60515	720266	46778	7257	106142
加工工业	Processing	436104	1506663	132330	167217	818860
在总计中：	**Of Total:**					
大型企业	Large Enterprises	76011	1171966	48405	91823	671231
中型企业	Medium Enterprises	66623	402521	52882	16935	73597
小型企业	Small Enterprises	843523	1558087	209278	470239	1110285

6-3 续表 4 continued

(10000 yuan)

损 益 及 分 配 Profits,Loss and Distribution										
产品销售收入 Sales Revenue	产品销售成本 Cost of Sales	产品销售费用 Expenses of Sales	产品销售税金及附加 Sales Tax and Extra Charges	产品销售利润 Sales Profits	管理费用 Overhead Cost	税金 Taxes	财产保险费 Premium of Property	劳动待业保险费 Premium for Employment Insurance	财务费用 Financial Expenses	利息支出 Expenses of Interest
22186280	**18246619**	**1060545**	**239887**	**2639229**	**2068988**	**66706**	**27634**	**280932**	**626745**	**597837**
7671893	6450868	219809	86943	914272	503550	10391	9333	64017	145336	136996
14514388	11795750	840736	152944	1724957	1565438	56316	18302	216915	481410	460841
6890818	5740109	279245	48940	822524	809842	32173	10104	173645	322913	328475
1432387	1137886	168430	37395	88676	162426	5858	1852	19006	19381	22066
4971406	4002228	266409	62797	639972	434567	16369	4509	22117	116150	92725
1219776	915527	126652	3812	173785	158603	1916	1837	2148	22965	17575
13932918	11493180	530363	204101	1705275	1463319	51721	20667	269738	474515	453044
8423097	6902460	314101	168013	1038523	932238	30499	13664	201084	324186	317186
2442090	2053384	85289	18650	284767	230323	7923	2322	16880	61306	45760
225013	183236	12823	1349	27606	20241	879	220	889	5497	4502
286279	243841	11421	2045	28972	40733	2039	402	7466	11180	10662
1317787	1124017	53069	5620	135081	147110	5725	3300	36291	55777	57867
900826	718920	34010	5732	142163	65862	3804	544	6936	12844	14161
337349	266855	19620	2687	48186	26744	851	215	194	3724	2906
478	468	29	5	-23	68	1			1	1
2180981	1814915	131348	2938	231780	170502	2161	1411	1898	36040	34755
1189350	993373	62908	2668	130401	102943	1831	1123	1697	26545	25319
34078	25721	2824	27	5507	4639	55	63	47	276	302
945402	785515	64826	229	94832	61557	266	205	147	9010	8988
12151	10306	790	14	1041	1363	8	20	7	210	147
6072381	4938523	398834	32849	702175	435167	12825	5556	9296	116191	110038
5248085	4339574	296099	30978	581435	344695	11639	4882	7694	107618	101749
128012	92534	12586	294	22598	8859	158	74	29	1261	907
545536	399269	78494	448	67325	71450	778	405	750	3707	4064
150747	107146	11655	1129	30817	10163	250	195	824	3604	3318
2735324	2286405	104548	16042	328329	175509	7496	1997	1494	54346	39343
14266364	11849477	541113	193001	1682773	1354452	43213	19622	252954	451255	453057
1428753	1228901	57787	7844	134221	87131	5094	1346	4677	31764	30533
6099702	4744913	468709	105675	780406	738033	24263	8804	79563	178415	164081
3946901	3050866	296976	91305	507754	453202	16779	5991	46861	93222	85799
2152801	1694047	171733	14370	272651	284830	7485	2813	32702	85193	78281
16086578	13501706	591836	134212	1858824	1330955	42443	18830	201369	448331	433756
172077	116811	15420	1967	37879	31784	1077	36	16119	4288	4428
5185481	4346910	147150	84684	606737	378094	15156	10677	71651	224992	218685
10729020	9037986	429266	47561	1214208	921077	26210	8118	113599	219051	210643
9204047	7562031	375485	143763	1122769	889625	30565	15797	179952	346362	332242
2414959	1955215	106882	44671	308191	253349	7842	2361	33920	51115	53077
10567274	8729373	578179	51453	1208269	926014	28299	9476	67060	229268	212517

6-3 续表 5 continued

单位：万元

项目	Item	营业利润 Operating Profits	投资收益 Investment Income	补贴收入 Subsidy Income	营业外收入 Out-business Income	营业外支出 Out-business Expenditure	利润总额 Total Profits
		损益及分配 Profits,Loss and Distribution					
总计	**Total**	**237992**	**129594**	**140972**	**338633**	**156687**	**697807**
在总计中:	**Of Total:**						
中央企业	Central Enterprises	336849	31460	3252	31087	34754	383161
地方企业	Local Enterprises	-98857	98134	137721	307546	121933	314646
工业系统	Industry System	-175761	80952	55853	226916	77846	104763
非工业系统	Non-Industry System	-76977	5291	72278	25114	18043	8572
区县工业	Industry of District and County	134185	10346	9978	45261	20622	176584
其他	Others	19697	1545	-388	10256	5422	24728
在总计中:	**Of Total:**						
内资企业	Domestic Investment Enterprises	6162	128986	141043	284203	125223	440712
国有企业	State-Owned	-67538	110416	104603	190880	83658	261557
集体企业	Collective Owned	30000	5042	3932	28862	11649	52310
股份合作企业	Share Holding Cooperative	3921	1039	834	3423	812	8254
联营企业	Joint Owned	-14149	2376	601	10911	1944	-1697
有限责任公司	Limited-Liability Company	-39835	2626	24423	45287	24286	11098
股份有限公司	Share Holding Company	75473	7435	5384	2360	2200	88481
私营企业	Private Owned	18383	51	1266	2481	675	20803
其他企业	Others	-93					-93
港澳台商投资企业	Hongkong,Macao and Taiwan Funded Enterprises	52701	399	1107	9431	5598	58048
港澳台合资经营	Joint Venture	6320	448	1024	6520	4246	9829
港澳台合作经营	Cooperative	1675	15	24	34	132	1668
港澳台商独资企业	Hongkong,Macao and Taiwan Enterprises	45225	-64	59	2857	1218	47052
港澳台商投资股份有限公司	Hongkong,Macao and Taiwan Funded Share Holing Company	-519			20	1	-500
外商投资企业	Foreign Funded Enterprises	179130	209	-1178	44999	25867	199046
中外合资经营	Joint Venture	144415	200	77	38169	21672	163674
中外合作经营	Cooperative	12665		300	1677	230	13106
外资(独资)企业	Foreign Enterprises	4837	-1	-1555	4900	3627	2740
外商投资股份有限公司	Foreign Funded Share Holding Company	17213	10		253	338	19527
在总计中:	**Of Total:**						
农村企业	Rural Enterprises	107883	936	2890	19566	7104	119801
在总计中:	**Of Total:**						
国有绝对控股企业	State-owned Absolute Holding Enterprises	96764	123078	134197	273611	117241	523092
国有相对控股企业	State-owned Relative Holding Enterprises	24148	242	1259	4574	7273	24112
在总计中:	**Of Total:**						
轻工业	Light Industry	-21876	35567	44931	137325	59710	137562
以农产品为原料	Using Farm Products as Raw Material	23669	17042	7684	77285	45869	81543
以非农产品为原料	Using Non-Farm Products as Raw Material	-45545	18525	37248	60041	13841	56019
重工业	Heavy Industry	259868	94027	96041	201307	96977	560245
采掘工业	Excavation	3044	589	11804	958	5277	12764
原料工业	Raw Material	37168	25820	67801	40586	36062	147202
加工工业	Processing	219656	67619	16436	159764	55638	400279
在总计中:	**Of Total:**						
大型企业	Large Enterprises	21737	100163	107776	144017	68123	307555
中型企业	Medium Enterprises	53756	18836	4866	40054	21147	102566
小型企业	Small Enterprises	162500	10595	28331	154562	67418	287687

6-3 续表 6 continued

(10000 yuan)

				工资，福利费，增值税 Wages,Welfares and Added Value Tax					
应交所得税 Income Tax Payable	应付利润 Profits Payable	亏损企业亏损额 Total Loss-ing of Loss-making Enterprises	利税总额 Total Pre-tax Profits	本年应付工资总额 Total Wags Payable	本年应付福利费总额 Total Welfares Payable	本年应交增值税 Added Value Tax	本年进项税额 Tax In-clude in Purchas-ing Cost	本年销项税额 Tax In-clude in Sales Cost	工业中间投入合计 Intermediate Input of Industry
175886	**275919**	**501386**	**1846310**	**1703845**	**282056**	**908616**	**2789682**	**3602247**	**16002568**
66539	51690	56609	726712	353945	52932	256608	1165767	1370164	5285669
109346	224229	444778	1119598	1349900	229124	652008	1623915	2232083	10716899
42388	136649	176481	483855	637926	117992	330152	862332	1170491	4978711
9696	5924	47765	113277	128759	23036	67310	132209	198055	977838
50005	67293	143771	444609	485096	69341	205228	491556	680879	3924771
7257	14362	76762	77858	98119	18755	49318	137818	182658	835579
131246	93795	251290	1297524	1273839	173381	652711	1711925	2325236	9952967
76039	46348	123376	873620	738329	105900	444050	1066494	1488907	5666141
21399	21042	63747	160396	281856	35597	89436	247778	329691	1886486
2496	1964	4413	17778	24880	2847	8175	22456	29461	170619
2126	2685	9796	9417	31113	4096	9069	36310	45543	217615
5681	4626	38981	69797	119986	15539	53079	152260	202373	1012997
19033	11485	4847	133447	51468	6995	39234	152226	186663	705727
4471	5646	6035	33136	26043	2319	9646	34374	42548	293014
		95	-64	165	89	24	28	51	368
9498	16602	64108	134155	128214	21828	73169	377347	404454	1725878
8351	15750	52975	56112	90240	18388	43615	131488	172337	947103
20	-725	1710	3586	3566	580	1891	3511	5197	28930
1107	1565	8839	74350	33465	2634	27069	241612	225572	742649
19	11	585	109	944	226	595	736	1349	7196
35142	165522	185988	414630	301791	86847	182735	700410	872557	4323723
30054	151395	137254	341726	241107	71659	147074	611026	750931	3796675
3918	2774	3690	18013	6543	1571	4613	13797	18337	106337
863	8803	39614	28140	41768	10646	24952	67566	89379	324473
308	2550	5430	26752	12373	2971	6096	8021	13911	96238
25882	31475	36547	225610	262536	35471	89767	241580	322122	2155005
118431	189450	208066	1356929	1076054	170433	640836	1927773	2490541	10252046
7797	14752	33386	49336	62234	16499	17380	160016	173108	892233
66167	81720	244802	526974	597705	103950	283737	587082	853904	4388225
44076	60120	168041	363128	389655	69033	190280	370741	550047	2850251
22092	21600	76761	163846	208050	34917	93457	216341	303857	1537974
109719	194199	256585	1319336	1106140	178106	624879	2202599	2748343	11614343
1291	2031	836	22289	38747	8993	7558	15023	22063	94984
37300	14060	59183	552998	337847	48497	321112	664179	977414	3728714
71128	178109	196566	744050	729547	120615	296210	1523397	1748866	7790646
68768	142949	132005	929561	688672	116458	478243	1325576	1743281	6546978
25831	11994	37207	228809	168250	23798	81572	288917	362513	1841365
81287	120976	332174	687941	846922	141800	348801	1175189	1496453	7614225

6-4 全部独立核算工业企业主要经济指标(按行业分)

单位：万元

项目	Item	企业单位个数(个) Number of Enterprises (unit)	#亏损企业 Loss-making Enterprises	工业总产值(当年价格) Gross Output Value of Industry (at current price)	新产品产值 Value of New Products	工业总产值(1990年不变价格) Gross Output Value of Industry (at 1990 constant prices)	工业增加值(生产法) Added Value of Industry (with production method)
煤炭采选业	Coal Mining and Dressing	194	15	125320		57035	78357
石油和天然气开采业	Petroleum and Natural Gas Extraction	1		138		138	42
黑色金属矿采选业	Ferrous Metals Mining and Processing	19	1	17541		10985	6714
有色金属矿采选业	Nonferrous Metals Mining and Processing	16		3822		4213	584
非金属矿采选业	Nonmetal Minerals Mining and Processing	271	21	43792		42089	17652
其他矿采选业	Other Minerals Mining and Processing	2		270		291	109
食品加工业	Food Processing	573	154	621052	38523	447626	107178
食品制造业	Food Making	668	189	544439	14618	421002	155599
饮料制造业	Beverage Production	271	85	632753	4210	556623	233200
烟草加工业	Tobacco Processing	4		70101	1547	45142	45482
纺织业	Textile Industry	516	120	399365	19833	380403	122961
服装及其他纤维制品制造业	Garments and Other Fiber Products	985	270	482708	3565	426799	147718
皮革、毛皮、羽绒及其制品业	Leather,Furs,Down and Related Products	174	44	54794		45513	11888
木材加工及竹、藤、棕、草制品业	Timber Processing,Bamboo,Cane, Palm Fiber and Straw Products	247	44	52854		45373	573
家具制造业	Furniture Manufacturing	547	99	149481	245	146877	6947
造纸及纸制品业	Papermaking and Paper Products	525	91	200318		186889	64639
印刷业、记录煤介的复制	Printing and Record Medium Reproduced	1011	204	467508	1274	352979	214205
文教、体育用品制造	Stationery,Educational and Sports Goods	242	60	113256	15068	96264	34192
石油加工及炼焦业	Petroleum Processing and Coking Products	110	24	1444424	174767	898414	395811
化学原料及化学制品制造业	Raw Chemical Materials and Chemical Products	1358	263	1168666	51225	1179687	320310
医药制造业	Medical and Pharmaceutical Product	254	46	443397	55405	496184	219535
化学纤维制造业	Chemical Fibers	45	16	41838	233	59162	6151
橡胶制品业	Rubber Products	139	26	134800	8670	153245	25503
塑料制品业	Plastic Products	736	169	266121	4603	271760	22605
非金属矿物制品业	Nonmetal Mineral Products	1780	248	1016528	65805	872528	325902
黑色金属冶炼及压延加工业	Smelting and Pressing of Ferrous Metals	79	16	1494937	57634	1041863	335068
有色金属冶炼及压延加工业	Smelting and Pressing of Nonferrous Metals	151	29	94998	11718	95351	16549
金属制品业	Metal Products	2282	402	627229	5524	639080	192059
普通机械制造业	Ordinary Machinery Manufacturing	1247	209	479267	41653	464904	157467
专用设备制造业	Special Purposes Equipment Manufacturing	1007	235	961850	284143	944247	255056
交通运输设备制造业	Transportation Equipment Manufacturing	1344	291	1181668	338220	1053515	301840
武器弹药制造业	Weapon and Ammunition Manufacture	9	4	70696	17336	54806	19054
电气机械及器材制造	Electric Equipment and Machinery	930	197	859190	188119	914764	231113
电子及通信设备制造	Electronic and Telecommunications	763	176	5636748	2009074	7551449	1445948
仪器仪表及文化、办公用机械制造业	Instruments,Meters,Cultural and Official Machine Manufacturing	486	96	365658	111739	369142	128370
其他制造业	Other Manufacturing	605	134	152542	2372	158902	57287
电力、蒸汽、热水的生产和供应业	Electricity,Steam and Hot Water Production and Supply	66	12	328254	2580	233833	58038
煤气生产和供应业	Gas Production and Supply	12	1	75272		39131	61852
自来水的生产和供应	Water Production and Supply	13	4	125230		51862	31315

MAIN INDICATORS FOR INDUSTRIAL ENTERPRISES WITH INDEPENDENT ACCOUNTING SYSTEM(BY SECTOR)

(10000 yuan)

工业销售产值(当年价格) Sales Value of Industry (at current price)	出口交货值 Delivery Value of Exports	全部从业人员年平均人数(人) Average Number of Employment (person)	资产负债 Assets and Liabilities						
			流动资产合计 Circulating Assets	应收帐款净额 Accounts Receivable	存货 Stock	产成品 Finished Products	流动资产平均余额 Average Balance of Circulating Assets	长期投资 Long-time Investment	固定资产合计 Fixed Assets
120343	34447	42518	157535	112199	26887	17000	162124	11660	129100
138		2	47	42			47		49
17299		3064	24373	12263	8594	4250	24681	2171	25408
4041		539	9956	435	637	279	7570	3470	966
38047	186	7232	21322	6126	6049	4772	20348	2026	27955
253		39	299	104	91	73	351		97
620803	4681	28074	594094	68402	120650	35108	616669	17755	267777
526031	16367	47206	445675	80554	117456	42299	370543	42345	412200
614141	6926	35402	500105	99709	176596	45845	508895	102053	588717
71921	1686	964	19948	4286	5461	339	23482	2746	34237
394547	149512	72360	500045	168902	199712	116761	444058	43927	385871
469502	181607	89577	433602	77423	211024	123228	407891	25506	236773
54638	11659	11568	99588	13050	32925	17049	97417	9692	50144
50509	1382	8042	57055	10464	34239	19708	48329	2855	64433
147713	16152	22218	128604	19460	71832	35330	120712	2108	63897
195931	5847	26981	182246	48658	58713	29078	181777	10387	164425
423950	405	64451	335272	57239	111014	47016	299752	33342	473103
106345	17581	15417	118601	28418	54244	24072	117019	6906	64722
1427331	12570	42849	744239	151830	223973	69013	736566	76484	1295130
1138663	98845	123843	822511	269619	297936	144419	827356	144020	1520777
426935	29084	32417	621663	124502	213664	140782	586082	124794	293215
39622	62	6807	34421	7112	17192	6977	37426	1165	68686
132043	6340	15532	107665	31070	50354	27861	127238	8310	150239
258287	10776	32203	253733	52833	94086	45722	242828	39506	289869
988496	25542	146925	1014222	275190	384812	222308	944297	260805	1073097
1471573	31887	64418	1322766	520706	317978	57098	1297236	836671	1677032
96527	3746	8136	88994	27248	32347	14720	82634	13749	58105
601241	28306	86161	555595	122350	248294	130668	519576	23722	386577
481973	32578	88255	855087	195557	377777	128579	838776	57823	559365
956504	8603	86015	1077408	256980	439663	176342	1016932	169336	590371
1137387	18900	127313	1224134	335894	491380	119504	1245145	301170	928675
69221	2951	11980	94704	33639	40439	8672	91936	15786	121355
836233	22799	74692	1046552	307807	375450	146602	983091	87071	516005
5547920	559973	84264	4135187	1623306	1012203	219392	3618119	399480	1191241
319194	23393	31465	414691	85859	157670	54380	339390	47636	151646
150191	14625	26684	155138	42534	63112	30586	147473	9930	80468
687390		30218	759447	198877	21847	406	788976	208830	3234727
75500		8435	87826	32344	8519	15	59837	7801	401184
119597		6545	125147	14642	8135	3794	108219	4096	602927

6-4 续表 1 continued

单位：万元

项目	Item	资产负债 固定资产原价合计 Original Value of Fixed Assets	#生产经营用 For Productive Use	累计折旧 Accumulative Depreciation	#本年折旧 Depreciation in this Year	固定资产净值年平均余额 Average Net Value of Fixed Assets	无形资产及递延资产 Intangible and Deferred Assets
煤炭采选业	Coal Mining and Dressing	188081	118738	66560	4551	123382	5137
石油和天然气开采业	Petroleum and Natural Gas Extraction	183	183	134	16	49	
黑色金属矿采选业	Ferrous Metals Mining and Processing	25633	22037	7825	1116	16641	2286
有色金属矿采选业	Nonferrous Metals Mining and Processing	1137	1135	213	36	967	144
非金属矿采选业	Nonmetal Minerals Mining and Processing	35632	28382	10851	1627	25380	3259
其他矿采选业	Other Minerals Mining and Processing	135	134	38	9	102	52
食品加工业	Food Processing	343836	273213	105142	18842	234605	26308
食品制造业	Food Making	520000	371501	147740	39189	349355	44062
饮料制造业	Beverage Production	689951	615905	158868	32372	499483	65566
烟草加工业	Tobacco Processing	41058	38062	13855	2926	28414	791
纺织业	Textile Industry	536969	427549	195809	21638	334607	51849
服装及其他纤维制品制造业	Garments and Other Fiber Products	307822	209708	94780	15204	201995	26593
皮革、毛皮、羽绒及其制品业	Leather,Furs,Down and Related Products	61184	51343	16971	1899	36848	9668
木材加工及竹、藤、棕、草制品业	Timber Processing,Bamboo,Cane, Palm Fiber and Straw Products	73029	61898	11408	1964	27497	1974
家具制造业	Furniture Manufacturing	83739	60378	22869	4713	53292	4561
造纸及纸制品业	Papermaking and Paper Products	186773	133367	45535	7424	124995	23240
印刷业、记录煤介的复制	Printing and Record Medium Reproduced	660509	445842	225811	38350	393406	9046
文教、体育用品制造	Stationery,Educational and Sports Goods	81692	68774	24875	3454	48890	6314
石油加工及炼焦业	Petroleum Processing and Coking Products	2089604	1764187	1095708	121145	1029049	84877
化学原料及化学制品制造业	Raw Chemical Materials and Chemical Products	1911998	1718462	470432	64254	1253473	423525
医药制造业	Medical and Pharmaceutical Product	348446	253622	103192	20062	235086	49943
化学纤维制造业	Chemical Fibers	104078	85095	37867	2542	67223	38553
橡胶制品业	Rubber Products	155645	125667	50607	15283	92509	15964
塑料制品业	Plastic Products	370017	264367	99472	16904	275534	48161
非金属矿物制品业	Nonmetal Mineral Products	1293352	1021668	407485	61339	809376	147868
黑色金属冶炼及压延加工业	Smelting and Pressing of Ferrous Metals	2213833	2072275	914646	100954	1593607	53054
有色金属冶炼及压延加工业	Smelting and Pressing of Nonferrous Metals	80147	64573	29587	2289	47655	31505
金属制品业	Metal Products	496617	371224	152978	25498	323905	35645
普通机械制造业	Ordinary Machinery Manufacturing	711729	548762	240488	26753	448704	60895
专用设备制造业	Special Purposes Equipment Manufacturing	742173	402056	276567	26284	447809	42669
交通运输设备制造业	Transportation Equipment Manufacturing	1191385	844674	453271	50840	727815	34168
武器弹药制造业	Weapon and Ammunition Manufacture	154276	126123	43811	2132	112640	3796
电气机械及器材制造	Electric Equipment and Machinery	686443	473082	210543	29616	406257	69577
电子及通信设备制造	Electronic and Telecommunications	1589405	1248950	544849	116158	969716	186439
仪器仪表及文化、办公用机械制造业	Instruments,Meters,Cultural and Official Machine Manufacturing	211914	144021	78645	8270	130498	17984
其他制造业	Other Manufacturing	111563	82033	40935	5032	73123	13732
电力、蒸汽、热水的生产和供应业	Electricity,Steam and Hot Water Production and Supply	3542056	3128728	846333	145137	2214976	36137
煤气生产和供应业	Gas Production and Supply	521283	505924	128567	24050	354222	
自来水的生产和供应	Water Production and Supply	758120	740614	168771	34874	494164	144330

6-4 续表 2 continued

(10000 yuan)

Assets and Liabilities										
#无形资产 Intangible Assets	其他资产 Other Assets	资产总计 Total Assets	流动负债合计 Liquid Liabilities	短期借款 Short-time Loans	长期负债合计 Long-term Liabilities	长期借款 Long-time Loans	负债合计 Total Liabilities	所有者权益 Ownership Interest	实收资本 Contributed Capital	国家资本 State
284	91	303523	129396	44039	43397	37895	173249	130274	71106	60091
		96	26				26	70	121	
		54238	25819	14861	10331	5351	36150	18088	9875	7841
30		14536	2019	333	1097	1097	3116	11420	10783	458
440	153	54715	20306	4748	7518	4484	28494	26221	17267	657
52	14	462	234				234	228	298	80
20385	14211	920145	447239	154727	44814	37556	496770	423375	272653	110285
20079	10534	954816	469216	195055	106389	97445	578345	376471	568022	77999
52143	8067	1264508	458958	224761	89155	74843	566772	697736	473360	177525
544		57722	-649	103	7475	7527	6826	50896	40241	40211
11649	3305	984996	605554	278254	145113	116219	751247	233749	258599	40188
14698	7606	730079	418177	151211	52434	33333	474348	255732	266120	28564
1047	483	169574	106714	35042	13721	10671	121110	48464	43177	3374
1137	2456	128773	80647	12082	6120	2719	86853	41919	45500	12494
2327	2527	201696	118860	29654	13809	10541	134640	67056	73778	4046
10990	3261	383559	196652	81970	44360	28909	242686	140873	117442	21423
4112	1419	852181	278659	64174	116730	80156	395776	456406	334246	187009
2459	2618	199160	116433	46708	11477	9540	128023	71137	56348	21352
83829	104	2200835	737484	404322	263444	229658	1195514	1005321	533150	526394
55573	7672	2918504	1004345	424371	1087065	1014183	2093063	825441	522863	267621
41918	46580	1136249	474955	217665	63448	44668	539037	597212	315727	102855
649	11	142835	50800	25777	85799	84772	136727	6109	30473	1383
12493	156	282333	170090	63091	66955	60283	237055	45278	47627	9896
11165	3190	634459	327727	130565	108506	96098	436922	197538	198419	23762
46258	19528	2515520	1081420	341120	419270	352832	1514169	1001351	730911	223697
44055	-12654	3876869	1254127	785475	625670	568066	1880066	1996804	655959	542701
751	227	192581	81393	30897	49374	43450	130951	61630	42840	12579
25742	9856	1011258	601608	205436	82475	76240	686884	324374	343960	37048
33384	4444	1537543	812005	273281	203306	170491	1019109	518434	468255	113463
21186	5506	1885290	1022435	280073	95420	59949	1119409	765882	421272	82652
19491	8313	2496460	1143997	339605	329204	255508	1476768	1019692	809168	184112
3463		235640	86064	43930	24406	14810	110470	125170	46655	19659
19901	17562	1736767	1078573	460769	139873	114077	1220636	516130	410634	59801
96453	40714	5953061	3368335	1019564	486835	379927	3866102	2086959	1176262	210953
10816	3056	635014	311561	80904	45603	28943	357715	277299	199534	58455
4364	2438	261706	147861	36461	23358	15189	173034	88673	93429	19389
11671	554	4239694	569941	62134	2555696	637168	3125637	1114057	878722	432874
		496811	23326	187	15132	2131	38458	458354	309890	309543
143064		876499	85508	22181	195263	193334	280771	595729	456782	455628

6-4 续表 3 continued

单位：万元

项目	Item	资产负债 Assets and Liabilities 集体资本 Collective	法人资本 Institutional Units	个人资本 Individuals	港澳台资本 Hongkong, Macao and Taiwan	外商资本 Foreign
煤炭采选业	Coal Mining and Dressing	8218	1127	1670		
石油和天然气开采业	Petroleum and Natural Gas Extraction	121				
黑色金属矿采选业	Ferrous Metals Mining and Processing	1910	38	86		
有色金属矿采选业	Nonferrous Metals Mining and Processing	280	10002	44		
非金属矿采选业	Nonmetal Minerals Mining and Processing	7401	7248	1762	23	176
其他矿采选业	Other Minerals Mining and Processing	11				208
食品加工业	Food Processing	18996	40401	6443	36013	60515
食品制造业	Food Making	18877	80490	6944	112709	271003
饮料制造业	Beverage Production	18011	65805	18485	41077	152456
烟草加工业	Tobacco Processing	31				
纺织业	Textile Industry	51634	110934	4696	35654	15492
服装及其他纤维制品制造业	Garments and Other Fiber Products	81587	67002	12630	27518	48820
皮革、毛皮、羽绒及其制品业	Leather,Furs,Down and Related Products	15894	14914	1919	1357	5720
木材加工及竹、藤、棕、草制品业	Timber Processing,Bamboo,Cane, Palm Fiber and Straw Products	5805	13673	1398	1878	10252
家具制造业	Furniture Manufacturing	16218	30663	7870	7437	7544
造纸及纸制品业	Papermaking and Paper Products	20827	23137	1590	18141	32325
印刷业、记录媒介的复制	Printing and Record Medium Reproduced	37207	46919	3949	17737	41423
文教、体育用品制造	Stationery,Educational and Sports Goods	14917	7178	1572	4636	6693
石油加工及炼焦业	Petroleum Processing and Coking Products	2935	1429	1111	150	1131
化学原料及化学制品制造业	Raw Chemical Materials and Chemical Products	39204	117693	18722	11259	68364
医药制造业	Medical and Pharmaceutical Product	10179	90351	29163	19421	63760
化学纤维制造业	Chemical Fibers	1587	25223	554	397	1330
橡胶制品业	Rubber Products	6433	22274	167	1540	7317
塑料制品业	Plastic Products	40886	74372	4504	13760	41136
非金属矿物制品业	Nonmetal Mineral Products	102697	244078	11697	13608	135135
黑色金属冶炼及压延加工业	Smelting and Pressing of Ferrous Metals	13067	97870	1867	358	98
有色金属冶炼及压延加工业	Smelting and Pressing of Nonferrous Metals	5594	15768	6584	304	2011
金属制品业	Metal Products	90130	88870	19927	49186	58801
普通机械制造业	Ordinary Machinery Manufacturing	66684	127806	7356	5125	147820
专用设备制造业	Special Purposes Equipment Manufacturing	31911	216800	33909	15512	40490
交通运输设备制造业	Transportation Equipment Manufacturing	79437	418660	13079	25153	88726
武器弹药制造业	Weapon and Ammunition Manufacture	6	26990			
电气机械及器材制造	Electric Equipment and Machinery	74590	155009	12873	19238	89124
电子及通信设备制造	Electronic and Telecommunications	54361	401253	48439	67122	394135
仪器仪表及文化、办公用机械制造业	Instruments,Meters,Cultural and Official Machine Manufacturing	18493	67496	6617	26729	21745
其他制造业	Other Manufacturing	26685	18437	1167	4078	23674
电力、蒸汽、热水的生产和供应业	Electricity,Steam and Hot Water Production and Supply	3254	402159	21690	1050	17694
煤气生产和供应业	Gas Production and Supply	80	184	83		
自来水的生产和供应	Water Production and Supply		324		830	

6-4 续表 4 continued

(10000 yuan)

损益及分配 Profits,Loss and Distribution										
产品销售收入 Sales Revenue	产品销售成本 Cost of Sales	产品销售费用 Expenses of Sales	产品销售税金及附加 Sales Tax and Extra Charges	产品销售利润 Sales Profits	管理费用 Overhead Cost	税金 Taxes	财产保险费 Premium of Property	劳动待业保险费 Premium for Employment Insurance	财务费用 Financial Expenses	利息支出 Expenses of Interest
110883	67907	13299	1160	28517	27059	817	4	15710	2724	2926
138	135			3	16	12	1			
16549	12073	491	355	3630	963	76	6	227	1289	1285
3810	3065	37	1	706	453	2		15	-162	1
40442	33428	1580	451	4983	3276	172	25	167	435	216
256	203	12		40	18		1		1	
618122	551987	24698	626	40811	39396	1532	617	2403	12759	12575
542198	384701	94132	1149	62215	79846	1620	764	5227	14058	10374
634758	421493	66044	50404	96817	54014	1460	822	2493	10062	10343
71794	33806	756	30280	6953	5410	70	226	712	209	271
392910	340080	11822	1085	39922	50237	1953	864	9235	21256	21233
440296	371299	29497	1361	38139	47846	1418	664	4142	10723	8861
49103	41045	3453	140	4465	11680	336	224	2431	3674	3457
50008	42447	1660	219	5681	7034	211	37	464	1132	957
141453	119632	6571	839	14413	12125	389	209	626	2107	1729
196582	155737	12117	654	28074	23556	904	144	2450	5710	4083
437227	329511	11439	2576	93701	75613	2989	789	12077	4846	4735
118600	94838	6071	392	17299	15731	438	171	2241	3178	3110
1481825	1199886	20626	61466	199847	144775	3823	7087	20502	31287	32749
1093802	900234	44554	10314	138701	111231	5763	3168	15664	39721	41361
610703	398293	94066	3032	115313	83988	2064	1100	7494	27932	30716
42695	40235	638	141	1681	6148	231	71	1913	2348	2347
138198	114868	3592	3829	15910	13650	335	277	2473	17057	12348
257748	218561	9722	764	28701	31093	977	491	3291	11548	8891
952474	775733	35952	5942	134848	113655	3929	967	17961	31894	28643
1494263	1315687	10669	9706	158200	83898	5657	175	26763	84815	90123
94029	79508	2556	295	11669	7996	191	100	861	2115	1836
598537	503672	22387	2666	69812	61778	1935	508	4575	16383	13845
505883	418122	22600	1809	63351	90709	2921	827	14982	12047	14692
976895	793923	44601	4049	134323	128629	5746	812	24413	18880	19830
1259910	1068778	28820	16087	146226	161072	4458	1014	26229	33689	33823
73427	60411	1017	68	11932	15528	258	82	3198	3052	3096
816522	657719	49897	2430	106477	102119	2515	1199	14594	24698	20270
6274066	5365972	261743	14036	632316	324413	6561	2832	18641	102658	97356
352279	280299	23543	977	47460	51129	1247	878	7122	4493	4880
150528	111193	15723	1160	22452	32646	993	230	3037	5089	4196
860162	642657	83938	8313	125254	19872	1394	39	2888	57676	45369
179554	191959	23	696	-13124	12305	517	213	1479	228	250
107652	105522	200	416	1514	18082	795	2233		5136	5058

6-4 续表 5 continued

单位：万元

项目	Item	损益及分配 Profits,Loss and Distribution					
		营业利润 Operating Profits	投资收益 Investment Income	补贴收入 Subsidy Income	营业外收入 Out-business Income	营业外支出 Out-business Expenditure	利润总额 Total Profits
煤炭采选业	Coal Mining and Dressing	357	228	11733	432	4472	9730
石油和天然气开采业	Petroleum and Natural Gas Extraction	-13					
黑色金属矿采选业	Ferrous Metals Mining and Processing	862	1		59	643	394
有色金属矿采选业	Nonferrous Metals Mining and Processing	413	256		14	3	680
非金属矿采选业	Nonmetal Minerals Mining and Processing	1403	103	71	452	156	1940
其他矿采选业	Other Minerals Mining and Processing	22			2	4	20
食品加工业	Food Processing	-9306	240	3975	1838	1474	-4409
食品制造业	Food Making	-26080	852	501	4287	4519	-22525
饮料制造业	Beverage Production	36438	4985	1030	13206	8770	49013
烟草加工业	Tobacco Processing	1532	1253		3	2	2614
纺织业	Textile Industry	-25280	471	504	30540	20084	-11755
服装及其他纤维制品制造业	Garments and Other Fiber Products	-8946	233	437	4838	2070	-6604
皮革、毛皮、羽绒及其制品业	Leather,Furs,Down and Related Products	-3200	-352	27	3741	411	-143
木材加工及竹、藤、棕、草制品业	Timber Processing,Bamboo,Cane, Palm Fiber and Straw Products	-2204	92	105	702	139	-1538
家具制造业	Furniture Manufacturing	1530	145	39	2162	438	2403
造纸及纸制品业	Papermaking and Paper Products	763	4669	275	4699	747	9167
印刷业、记录媒介的复制	Printing and Record Medium Reproduced	29828	1400	410	7900	3089	36099
文教、体育用品制造	Stationery,Educational and Sports Goods	1375	854	1	1977	548	3359
石油加工及炼焦业	Petroleum Processing and Coking Products	33975	128	30	7018	6707	45119
化学原料及化学制品制造业	Raw Chemical Materials and Chemical Products	-3164	5323	24329	6706	7715	26344
医药制造业	Medical and Pharmaceutical Product	8884	8842	2295	28753	3108	45236
化学纤维制造业	Chemical Fibers	-5795	-29	107	1391	491	-4816
橡胶制品业	Rubber Products	-11930	113	1509	1312	1034	-26508
塑料制品业	Plastic Products	-9927	276	285	9965	2074	-2183
非金属矿物制品业	Nonmetal Mineral Products	-3486	3462	5835	8417	4332	11085
黑色金属冶炼及压延加工业	Smelting and Pressing of Ferrous Metals	-3686	27094	1	19966	7548	37397
有色金属冶炼及压延加工业	Smelting and Pressing of Nonferrous Metals	6021	46	594	722	244	6756
金属制品业	Metal Products	-1530	679	665	6527	3042	2673
普通机械制造业	Ordinary Machinery Manufacturing	-25494	340	912	38948	8663	575
专用设备制造业	Special Purposes Equipment Manufacturing	4553	9491	5487	53705	19696	53121
交通运输设备制造业	Transportation Equipment Manufacturing	-36814	8456	1154	27293	5202	-2862
武器弹药制造业	Weapon and Ammunition Manufacture	-2446	13	1271	352	1004	-1797
电气机械及器材制造	Electric Equipment and Machinery	-3880	2351	1496	24674	5181	29207
电子及通信设备制造	Electronic and Telecommunications	279032	49245	133	12844	11060	331957
仪器仪表及文化、办公用机械制造业	Instruments,Meters,Cultural and Official Machine Manufacturing	12651	2218	217	5256	2793	16745
其他制造业	Other Manufacturing	-6050	-428	1909	3374	1171	-3028
电力、蒸汽、热水的生产和供应业	Electricity,Steam and Hot Water Production and Supply	51453	-3869	18837	4388	17616	53266
煤气生产和供应业	Gas Production and Supply	-23542	215	25410	94	76	2101
自来水的生产和供应	Water Production and Supply	-20328	195	29390	81	360	8978

6-4 续表 6 continued

(10000 yuan)

应交所得税 Income Tax Payable	应付利润 Profits Payable	亏损企业亏损额 Total Lossing of Loss-making Enterprises	利税总额 Total Pre-tax Profits	工资，福利费，增值税 Wages,Welfares and Added Value Tax 本年应付工资总额 Total Wags Payable	本年应付福利费总额 Total Welfares Payable	本年应交增值税 Added Value Tax	本年进项税额 Tax Include in Purchasing Cost	本年销项税额 Tax Include in Sales Cost	工业中间投入合计 Intermediate Input of Industry
735	1491	257	16338	31589	8233	5448	12507	18297	52411
			12	1		12	12	24	108
76	35	29	1255	2346	167	506	2134	2572	11333
137	40		701	324	17	20	73	93	3258
338	465	550	3949	4463	574	1558	274	1045	27698
5			35	23	3	15	23	32	176
3490	5015	22454	7807	27047	5143	11590	41525	51672	525464
5136	9138	53591	15395	57388	12402	36771	52100	86912	425611
9643	19760	24236	142485	39937	9114	43068	62045	103986	442621
653	2		40990	2317	186	8096	5153	13239	32715
1630	1976	22169	3787	55424	9073	14457	42221	55015	290861
1749	1095	17648	6928	64253	11638	12171	41334	52525	347161
581	257	2911	811	8071	1677	814	4153	4688	43720
172	373	2695	72	6076	955	1391	5348	6649	53672
993	1858	4100	7935	17670	2064	4693	13080	17139	147227
3630	1519	8180	19470	19297	3221	9649	21878	31045	145328
10837	12370	9594	69163	66679	9365	30488	43082	72689	283791
1071	1357	3447	8383	14115	2318	4632	13426	17726	83696
26424	1026	1118	177085	77369	10936	70500	273014	342300	1119113
8534	8571	17201	87294	80596	12589	50636	130511	178272	898992
9674	5309	5418	82395	41700	8917	34127	60404	91708	257989
75	25	5121	-3318	4956	768	1357	5588	7091	37044
469	405	31168	-13799	13155	2131	8880	13693	22272	118177
1578	2688	15506	14654	41987	3885	16073	34297	49164	259589
6806	5492	29046	66202	130290	18672	49175	88322	134346	739801
-494	151	10940	145507	110392	14418	98404	167150	261332	1258273
1597	348	1206	8832	6632	702	1781	10400	11593	80230
4164	5283	25105	26733	65018	9198	21394	68209	85240	456564
1901	7234	18125	23719	80293	12633	21335	62495	81253	343135
15535	12127	14110	99524	95212	14706	42354	182600	223507	749148
6341	13256	37999	51052	138890	27066	37827	133516	171917	917655
984		2076	-1458	13858	1792	271	7715	7203	51913
6751	9557	19755	62278	72526	12537	30641	98931	129717	658718
32321	131268	48264	456556	190862	34374	110563	959965	1011649	4301363
4427	3297	7681	31599	36261	6168	13877	35286	47187	251165
1597	3820	12239	6214	23289	4144	8082	12894	21694	103337
6268	9002	27011	155033	43636	7027	93454	63993	157232	363670
1	314	53	8928	10724	1647	6131	18633	25037	19551
55		385	15770	9183	1601	6376	1702	7189	100291

6-5 全部独立核算工业企业主要经济分析指标

单位：%

项目 Item		企业亏损面 Loss-making Enterprises as % of Total	总资产贡献率 Contribution Rate of Total Assets	资产保值增值率 Changing Rate of Net Assets
总计（不含个体工业）	**Total (exclude individual industry)**	**27.77**	**5.91**	**109.08**
在总计中：	Of Total:			
中央企业	Central Enterprises	39.36	7.98	109.84
地方企业	Local Enterprises	27.16	5.18	108.85
工业系统	Industry System	36.44	4.74	106.76
非工业系统	Non-Industry System	48.48	4.04	111.41
区县工业	Industry of District and County	20.92	7.04	111.67
其他	Others	57.23	3.97	110.09
在总计中：	Of Total:			
内资企业	Domestic Investment Enterprises	23.57	9.92	109.34
国有企业	State-Owned	32.28	5.71	103.76
集体企业	Collective Owned	19.19	5.03	95.32
股份合作企业	Share Holding Cooperative	23.65	5.84	142.63
联营企业	Joint Owned	29.05	2.85	85.16
有限责任公司	Limited-Liability Company	40.53	3.27	1046.93
股份有限公司	Share Holding Company	29.05	11.80	119.19
私营企业	Private Owned	32.12	12.35	17.98
其他企业	Others	66.67	-8.51	484.06
港澳台商投资企业	Hongkong,Macao and Taiwan Funded Enterprises	54.48	6.88	119.96
港澳台合资经营	Joint Venture	51.32	4.16	104.9
港澳台合作经营	Cooperative	47.06	5.69	198.52
港澳台商独资企业	Hongkong,Macao and Taiwan Enterprises	66.67	20.45	301.72
港澳台商投资股份有限公司	Hongkong,Macao and Taiwan Funded Share Holing Company	61.54	1.31	75.43
外商投资企业	Foreign Funded Enterprises	53.71	7.10	105.35
中外合资经营	Joint Venture	49.69	6.90	97.78
中外合作经营	Cooperative	37.78	11.70	136.84
外资(独资)企业	Foreign Enterprises	67.68	5.69	165.32
外商投资股份有限公司	Foreign Funded Share Holding Company	33.33	13.10	226.36
在总计中：	Of Total:			
农村企业	Rural Enterprises	13.98	7.57	106.32
在总计中：	Of Total:			
国有绝对控股企业	State-owned Absolute Holding Enterprises	35.35	6.30	118.65
国有相对控股企业	State-owned Relative Holding Enterpeises	45.03	3.77	487.55
在总计中：	Of Total:			
轻工业	Light Industry	30.38	5.75	112.06
以农产品为原料	Using Farm Products as Raw Material	31.28	6.24	109.3
以非农产品为原料	Using Non-Farm Pro ducts as Raw Material	29.00	5.02	117.12
重工业	Heavy Industry	25.23	5.98	107.78
采掘工业	Excavation	10.48	6.17	100.05
原料工业	Raw Material	26.54	5.58	113.87
加工工业	Processing	25.9	6.35	102.61
在总计中：	Of Total:			
大型企业	Large Enterprises	30.00	5.34	92.45
中型企业	Medium Enterprises	23.25	8.69	177.11
小型企业	Small Enterprises	27.83	6.23	127.93

注：全员劳动生产率按现价增加值计算。（6-7 表同）

MAIN INDICATORS ON ECONOMIC BENIFIT OF INDUSTRIAL ENTERPRISES WITH INDEPENDENT ACCOUNTING SYSTEM

(%)

资产负债率 Liabilities/ Total Assets	流动资产周转率(次) Turnover Rate of Circulating Assets (time)	成本费用利润率 Total Profits/Total Costs and Expenses	全员劳动生产率(元) Overall Labor Productivity (yuan)	产品销售率 Sales Value/ Gross Output Value	增加值率 Value Added/ Gross Output Value	人均销售收入(元) Sales Revenue Per Capita	流动比率 Circulating Assets/ Liquid Liabilities	速动比率 Quick-circulating Assets/ Liquid Liabilities
60.80	**1.23**	**3.17**	**36347**	**97.05**	**25.26**	**137734**	**107.05**	**72.91**
65.46	1.68	5.23	81611	99.18	24.61	349159	121.74	88.42
59.12	1.07	2.14	29198	96.02	25.51	104339	102.8	68.43
61.32	0.96	1.46	35082	97.25	25.09	136033	99.15	68.66
39.53	1.38	0.58	39828	98.19	28.71	145707	113.83	83.48
63.00	1.28	3.66	23696	94.68	24.81	74363	99.44	57.40
57.74	0.86	2.02	26244	92.65	26.92	103641	125.96	91.28
60.58	1.13	3.16	27753	96.55	25.71	105881	104.97	70.43
58.99	1.15	3.09	33567	98.02	27.38	135011	106.88	74.70
68.08	1.15	2.15	17301	94.23	25.40	54330	99.66	55.93
63.91	1.12	3.72	22811	92.22	26.93	66544	108.22	63.54
71.82	0.86	-0.55	20809	93.67	22.64	81986	85.57	53.05
65.90	0.93	0.80	31538	94.86	21.80	134585	90.67	64.78
39.36	1.32	10.64	60763	97.52	21.92	225912	158.06	112.64
56.64	1.70	6.56	22117	91.75	18.19	94224	120.13	69.79
46.39	0.89	-16.43	4221	86.92	19.59	24020	110.47	67.19
67.80	1.39	2.70	31966	97.86	18.49	156683	97.98	61.21
65.45	1.11	0.83	40965	96.03	21.04	169815	95.49	59.79
62.30	0.98	4.99	1612	104.44	20.53	6162	99.19	65.35
76.05	2.10	5.11	111179	100.23	14.66	725224	105.06	64.97
66.24	1.31	-3.95	51222	89.28	38.86	148545	125.56	72.31
59.23	1.43	3.38	112892	97.86	26.72	389965	117.43	85.67
60.16	1.40	3.22	124084	98.13	26.10	427243	118.54	87.15
47.00	1.67	11.37	89723	89.59	23.20	270353	121.18	68.32
64.53	1.66	0.50	67906	96.96	31.77	285965	113.88	83.42
33.35	1.97	14.73	68024	99.08	36.95	166241	85.04	52.35
62.37	1.47	4.57	22353	93.06	25.92	63728	104.67	53.71
59.98	1.20	3.68	40992	97.23	24.38	167533	107.18	74.81
64.58	1.75	1.72	48599	105.81	31.10	171649	110.35	84.56
58.01	1.09	2.24	30356	96.11	28.39	95370	103.74	66.96
56.92	1.15	2.09	29035	96.00	28.20	92444	106.44	68.91
59.56	0.99	2.51	33008	96.30	28.73	101244	99.80	64.12
61.93	1.29	3.53	40293	97.43	23.93	165632	108.61	75.73
56.43	0.80	7.58	19376	93.99	43.80	32228	120.10	96.33
60.75	1.36	2.89	48796	98.22	23.51	222346	102.31	78.56
63.19	1.27	3.77	39028	97.14	23.67	156716	111.25	73.99
60.92	1.15	3.35	43623	96.87	24.44	182729	105.39	74.70
54.62	1.29	4.33	49001	98.23	24.16	171963	118.18	82.16
62.10	1.28	2.75	30718	96.91	26.13	109315	106.30	69.40

Note:Overall labor Productivity is calculated by adeled value at cunewt prices. (table 6-7 is the same)

6-6 全部独立核算国有工业企业主要经济指标

单位：万元

项目	Item	企业单位个数(个) Number of Enterprises (unit)	#亏损企业 Loss-making Enterprises	工业总产值(当年价格) Gross Output Value of Industry (at current price)	新产品产值 Value of New Products	工业总产值(1990年不变价格) Gross Output Value of Industry (at 1990 constant prices)	工业增加值(生产法) Added Value of Industry (with production method)
总计	**Total**	**2829**	**634**	**7695460**	**1557770**	**5920611**	**2473369**
在总计中：	**Of Total:**						
中央企业	Central Enterprises	531	127	3732658	1275120	2805254	1255238
地方企业	Local Enterprises	2298	507	3962802	282650	3115357	1218131
工业系统	Industry System	488	80	2622794	271632	2136276	733498
非工业系统	Non-Industry System	546	143	707338	2795	430623	288841
区县工业	Industry of District and County	1255	283	628219	8223	536837	194320
其他	Others	9	1	4451		11621	1472
在总计中：	**Of Total:**						
轻工业	Light Industry	1350	340	1638826	79791	1266634	653064
以农产品为原料	Using Farm Products as Raw Material	869	221	1118467	25861	777489	465608
以非农产品为原料	Using Non-Farm Products as Raw Material	481	119	520360	53930	489145	187457
重工业	Heavy Industry	1479	294	6056633	1477979	4653977	1820303
采掘工业	Excavation	18	1	99473		39383	65020
原料工业	Raw Material	203	29	3493489	240209	2163423	1177849
加工工业	Processing	1258	264	2463672	1237770	2451171	577435
在总计中：	**Of Total:**						
大型企业	Large Enterprises	140	30	4756893	531313	3361340	1313466
中型企业	Medium Enterprises	177	28	1552972	923936	1551163	457407
小型企业	Small Enterprises	2512	576	1385595	102522	1008108	702495

MAIN INDICATORS FOR STATE-OWNED INDUSTRIAL ENTERPRISES WITH INDEPENDENT ACCOUNTING SYSTEM

(10000 yuan)

工业销售产值(当年价格) Sales Value of Industry (at current price)	出口交货值 Delivery Value of Exports	全部从业人员年平均人数(人) Average Number of Employment (person)	资产负债 Assets and Liabilities						
			流动资产合计 Circulating Assets	应收帐款净额 Accounts Receivable	存货 Stock	产成品 Finished Products	流动资产平均余额 Average Balance of Circulating Assets	长期投资 Long-time Investment	固定资产合计 Fixed Assets
7548563	**255597**	**623881**	**7656586**	**2123585**	**2305341**	**799990**	**7348071**	**2084431**	**10286243**
3643980	40386	175605	2699726	538600	798686	223300	2585436	335162	4501628
3904583	215212	448276	4956860	1584985	1506655	576689	4762636	1749269	5784615
2599766	196101	299998	3734420	1317995	1134222	432216	3653554	1598894	3528713
688294	6973	69438	717809	180935	171775	69494	598225	48210	1683196
612662	12138	78470	498920	85936	197667	74721	508426	102013	571906
3861		370	5712	118	2992	259	2431	152	802
1589528	115176	208739	1932687	425680	662435	335777	1815661	425897	2240304
1082617	72040	139461	1138559	267548	417764	222536	1067187	255879	1177424
506911	43136	69278	794128	158133	244671	113241	748473	170018	1062879
5959035	140422	415142	5723899	1697904	1642906	464213	5532411	1658535	8045939
95456	33964	32265	163594	116398	26281	14025	169737	17930	136741
3453755	44080	137476	2562156	847581	524458	112918	2523892	967036	6131776
2409824	62378	245401	2998149	733926	1092167	337270	2838781	673568	1777422
4661143	198953	385180	5209814	1517703	1544165	523358	5112627	1614769	8284387
1554746	50970	91051	1250835	275152	386108	110190	1127542	306925	746606
1332674	5675	147650	1195937	330729	375068	166441	1107903	162737	1255251

6-6 续表 1 continued

单位：万元

项目	Item	固定资产原价合计 Original Value of Fixed Assets	# 生产经营用 For Productive Use	累计折旧 Accumulative Depreciation	#本年折旧 Depreciation in this Year	固定资产净值年平均余额 Average Net Value of Fixed Assets	无形资产及递延资产 Intangible and Deferred Assets
		资产负债					
总计	**Total**	**13276604**	**11302671**	**4751187**	**603382**	**8329982**	**578752**
在总计中：	**Of Total:**						
中央企业	Central Enterprises	5674969	4646020	2125672	288418	3450709	124733
地方企业	Local Enterprises	7601635	6656652	2625515	314965	4879273	454019
工业系统	Industry System	4813861	4162964	1926199	195139	3082153	387698
非工业系统	Non-Industry System	2110852	1942602	511670	91085	1353085	18528
区县工业	Industry of District and County	675763	551019	187270	28713	443513	47732
其他	Others	1160	67	377	27	522	61
在总计中：	**Of Total:**						
轻工业	Light Industry	2878040	2340705	891829	125438	1792791	222294
以农产品为原料	Using Farm Products as Raw Material	1485138	1129832	496592	67582	935835	85197
以非农产品为原料	Using Non-Farm Products as Raw Material	1392901	1210872	395237	57856	856956	137097
重工业	Heavy Industry	10398564	8961967	3859359	477945	6537191	356458
采掘工业	Excavation	194772	127752	71482	5001	124982	7381
原料工业	Raw Material	7915127	7152176	2921161	382719	5067884	174117
加工工业	Processing	2288665	1682039	866715	90225	1344325	174961
在总计中：	**Of Total:**						
大型企业	Large Enterprises	10675771	9242513	3902480	493504	6703488	330147
中型企业	Medium Enterprises	908419	658818	299963	41855	579373	116700
小型企业	Small Enterprises	1692414	1401340	548744	68023	1047120	131905

6-6 续表 2 continued

(10000 yuan)

Assets and Liabilities										
#无形资产 Intangible Assets	其他资产 Other Assets	资产总计 Total Assets	流动负债合计 Liquid Liabilities	短期借款 Short-time Loans	长期负债合计 Long-term Liabilities	长期借款 Long-time Loans	负债合计 Total Liabilities	所有者权益 Ownership Interest	实收资本 Contributed Capital	国家资本 State
186232	**48139**	**20654016**	**7163693**	**2868767**	**4800566**	**2389889**	**12183698**	**8470319**	**4455038**	**3325376**
103911	9551	7670801	2255879	671882	2776238	713978	5227057	2443744	1232844	1016964
82321	38588	12983216	4907814	2196885	2024328	1675911	6956641	6026575	3222194	2308412
66788	30819	9280543	3819195	1871838	1696842	1397842	5526106	3754438	1637161	852676
7297	7026	2474634	573516	124738	216478	186949	792830	1681804	1260024	1230335
8236	733	1221303	510049	200306	110400	90523	632044	589259	324118	224560
	10	6736	5054	4	608	598	5662	1074	891	841
30839	45351	4866397	1937846	785533	749350	579013	2699037	2167360	1339931	1012344
15050	1945	2659004	1109871	423285	327527	234375	1448618	1210385	658482	450325
15789	43406	2207393	827975	362248	421823	344638	1250419	956974	681449	562019
155393	2788	15787620	5225848	2083234	4051215	1810876	9484660	6302959	3115108	2313033
375		325646	131526	51631	56201	43125	187728	137918	82897	68019
106716	-11230	9823856	2251909	1174611	3301544	1251501	5747616	4076240	1874458	1805111
48302	14018	5638118	2842412	856992	693470	516250	3549317	2088801	1157753	439903
147938	31469	15470586	4860705	2257102	4193805	1925373	9254118	6216469	3111635	2436651
24803	11703	2432768	1089908	289093	272258	202552	1367707	1065061	553184	312813
13491	4968	2750662	1213080	322571	334502	261964	1561873	1188789	790219	575913

6-6 续表 3 continued

单位：万元

项 目 Item		资产负债 Assets and Liabilities				
		集体资本 Collective	法人资本 Institutional Units	个人资本 Individuals	港澳台资本 Hongkong, Macao and Taiwan	外商资本 Foreign
总 计	**Total**	**31856**	**1069588**	**25246**	**1931**	**1041**
在总计中：	**Of Total:**					
中央企业	Central Enterprises	703	212446	2304	104	323
地方企业	Local Enterprises	31153	857142	22942	1827	718
工业系统	Industry System	23528	753749	6615		594
非工业系统	Non-Industry System	1119	28062	298	210	
区县工业	Industry of District and County	6506	75281	16030	1617	124
其他	Others		50			
在总计中：	**Of Total:**					
轻工业	Light Industry	17817	286849	21060	1737	124
以农产品为原料	Using Farm Products as Raw Material	10494	175110	20902	1527	124
以非农产品为原料	Using Non-Farm Products as Raw Material	7323	111740	158	210	
重工业	Heavy Industry	14039	782739	4186	194	917
采掘工业	Excavation	500	14378			
原料工业	Raw Material	405	68596	257	90	
加工工业	Processing	13134	699766	3930	104	917
在总计中：	**Of Total:**					
大型企业	Large Enterprises	14961	638990	20440		594
中型企业	Medium Enterprises	6408	229887	2402	1527	148
小型企业	Small Enterprises	10487	200712	2405	404	299

6-6 续表 4 continued

(10000 yuan)

损益及分配 Profits,Loss and Distribution										
产品销售收入 Sales Revenue	产品销售成本 Cost of Sales	产品销售费用 Expenses of Sales	产品销售税金及附加 Sales Tax and Extra Charges	产品销售利润 Sales Profits	管理费用 Overhead Cost	税金 Taxes	财产保险费 Premium of Property	劳动待业保险费 Premium for Employment Insurance	财务费用 Financial Expenses	利息支出 Expenses of Interest
8423097	**6902460**	**314101**	**168013**	**1038523**	**932238**	**30499**	**13664**	**201084**	**324186**	**317186**
4010442	3281593	85447	73173	570229	364490	7498	7901	58863	112214	100134
4412656	3620867	228654	94840	468294	567748	23001	5763	142221	211972	217052
3041581	2574142	92325	25961	349153	406013	17503	3657	119434	193277	195335
761109	600644	103621	35621	21224	95275	3733	1096	14617	8586	9427
605734	442132	32648	33213	97742	66145	1760	1010	8168	10138	12289
4232	3950	60	46	176	315	5	1	1	-29	
1827475	1409859	100777	77185	239654	288877	9531	4051	58511	70309	74201
1247784	920781	61586	71891	193526	183623	6089	2969	36230	26193	30194
579691	489077	39191	5294	46129	105254	3441	1082	22281	44116	44007
6595622	5492601	213324	90828	798869	643361	20968	9613	142572	253877	242985
82873	47268	13118	672	21816	25924	658	9	16086	3099	3517
3800328	3137244	112420	79278	471387	260238	11959	7476	49640	168896	160977
2712420	2308089	87786	10879	305666	357200	8351	2128	76847	81881	78491
5656982	4618835	191767	119160	727220	597501	21664	10848	148025	248737	239211
1556719	1246982	70982	40841	197914	167094	3192	1595	27038	30433	32436
1209396	1036643	51352	8012	113389	167643	5642	1221	26021	45016	45539

6-6 续表 5 continued

单位：万元

项目	Item	营业利润 Operating Profits	投资收益 Investment Income	补贴收入 Subsidy Income	营业外收入 Out-business Income	营业外支出 Out-business Expenditure	利润总额 Total Profits
		损益及分配 Profits,Loss and Distribution					
总计	**Total**	**-67538**	**110416**	**104603**	**190880**	**83658**	**261557**
在总计中：	**Of Total:**						
中央企业	Central Enterprises	131824	34923	2608	22807	17032	188772
地方企业	Local Enterprises	-199362	75493	101995	168073	66625	72785
工业系统	Industry System	-163869	64776	29462	143619	48128	14815
非工业系统	Non-Industry System	-69260	4794	70888	19561	14834	13053
区县工业	Industry of District and County	33575	5902	1644	4832	3641	44664
其他	Others	193	22		61	23	253
在总计中：	**Of Total:**						
轻工业	Light Industry	-48285	30580	36759	84091	33865	76170
以农产品为原料	Using Farm Products as Raw Material	23356	16806	3656	48975	29431	70305
以非农产品为原料	Using Non-Farm Products as Raw Material	-71641	13774	33103	35116	4435	5865
重工业	Heavy Industry	-19253	79837	67843	106789	49792	185387
采掘工业	Excavation	-6099	577	11733	731	4880	2366
原料工业	Raw Material	62462	30309	44486	18814	17377	149932
加工工业	Processing	-75616	48951	11624	87244	27536	33089
在总计中：	**Of Total:**						
大型企业	Large Enterprises	-26906	81102	82364	114904	60493	190979
中型企业	Medium Enterprises	27178	15709	2152	31735	17370	65037
小型企业	Small Enterprises	-67810	13605	20087	44242	5794	5540

6-6 续表 6 continued

(10000 yuan)

应 交 所得税 Income Tax Payable	应 付 利 润 Profits Payable	亏损企业 亏损额 Total Loss-ing of Loss-making Enterprises	利 税 总 额 Total Pre-tax Profits	工资，福利费，增值税 Wages,Welfares and Added Value Tax 本年应付 工资总额 Total Wags Payable	本年应付 福利费 总额 Total Welfares Payable	本年应交 增值税 Added Value Tax	本 年 进项税额 Tax In-clude in Purchas-ing Cost	本 年 销项税额 Tax In-clude in Sales Cost	工业中间 投入合计 Intermediate Input of Industry
76039	**46348**	**123376**	**873620**	**738329**	**105900**	**444050**	**1066494**	**1488907**	**5666141**
50082	21272	16937	461465	244902	34389	199520	563022	756912	2676940
25957	25076	106439	412155	493428	71511	244530	503472	731995	2989201
10179	3521	76039	200324	335133	51747	159548	376305	524416	2048844
5932	522	13349	86506	78988	11238	37832	66461	102335	456329
9817	20835	16940	124923	78640	8475	47046	59888	104525	480945
29	197	114	404	666	51	105	819	720	3084
27607	31187	44628	256394	209639	29781	103039	187845	280512	1088801
20703	28585	24934	216259	138710	19599	74063	126266	197111	726922
6904	2602	19694	40135	70929	10182	28976	61579	83401	361879
48432	15161	78749	617226	528691	76119	341011	878649	1208395	4577341
91		8	7313	23523	6957	4275	13078	17787	38728
32500	11001	7817	496743	226632	32678	267533	495592	757356	2583173
15841	4160	70923	113171	278535	36484	69203	369980	433252	1955440
47399	26238	59192	645169	487108	74203	335030	707909	1031645	3778457
15340	6981	10317	155001	99747	12997	49123	215058	258720	1144688
13300	13129	53868	73449	151474	18700	59897	143527	198542	742997

6-7 全部独立核算国有工业企业主要经济分析指标

单位：%

项　　目	Item	企业亏损面 Loss-making Enterprises as % of Total	总资产贡献率 Contribution Rate of Total Assets	资产保值增值率 Changing Rate of Net Assets
总　计	**Total**	**32.28**	**5.93**	**112.42**
在总计中：	**Of Total:**			
中央企业	Central Enterprises	33.87	7.48	112.38
地方企业	Local Enterprises	31.91	5.00	112.44
工业系统	Industry System	27.49	4.33	109.46
非工业系统	Non-Industry System	43.87	4.22	122.52
区县工业	Industry of District and County	29.33	11.75	105.88
其他	Others	14.29	8.53	135.50
在总计中：	**Of Total:**			
轻工业	Light Industry	34.73	7.20	115.07
以农产品为原料	Using Farm Products as Raw Material	34.48	9.74	111.48
以非农产品为原料	Using Non-Farm Products as Raw Material	35.21	4.08	119.95
重工业	Heavy Industry	29.85	5.55	111.53
采掘工业	Excavation	7.14	3.32	103.81
原料工业	Raw Material	22.48	6.69	110.20
加工工业	Processing	31.35	3.59	114.82
在总计中：	**Of Total:**			
大型企业	Large Enterprises	21.43	5.76	107.86
中型企业	Medium Enterprises	16.67	8.34	123.60
小型企业	Small Enterprises	34.78	4.79	130.72

MAIN INDICATORS ON ECONOMIC BENEFIT OF STATE-OWNED INDUSTRIAL ENTERPRISES WITH INDEPENDENT ACCOUNTING SYSTEM

(%)

资产负债率 Liabilities/Total Assets	流动资产周转率(次) Turnover Rate of Circulating Assets (time)	成本费用利润率 Total Profits/Total Costs and Expenses	全员劳动生产率(元) Overall Labor Productivity (yuan)	产品销售率 Sales Value/Gross Output Value	增加值率 Value Added/Gross Output Value	人均销售收入(元) Sales Revenue Per Capita	流动比率 Circulating Assets/Liquid Liabilities	速动比率 Quick-circulating Assets/Liquid Liabilities
58.99	**1.15**	**3.09**	**33567**	**98.02**	**27.38**	**135011**	**106.88**	**74.70**
68.14	1.55	4.91	50807	97.37	25.73	228379	119.68	84.27
53.58	0.93	1.57	26814	98.58	28.72	98436	101.00	70.30
59.55	0.83	0.45	24225	99.14	26.91	101387	97.78	68.08
32.04	1.27	1.62	40535	97.52	38.15	109610	125.16	95.21
51.75	1.19	8.11	24508	97.52	25.46	77193	97.82	59.06
84.06	1.74	5.89	39786	86.73	27.07	114370	113.02	53.82
55.46	1.01	4.07	30762	97.07	37.77	87548	99.73	65.55
54.48	1.17	5.90	32899	96.89	39.35	89472	102.58	64.94
56.65	0.77	0.87	26462	97.44	34.33	83676	95.91	66.36
60.08	1.19	2.81	34978	98.3	24.41	158876	109.53	78.09
57.65	0.49	2.65	20151	95.96	46.20	25685	124.38	104.4
58.51	1.51	4.08	59503	98.73	25.50	276436	113.78	90.49
62.95	0.96	1.17	23188	97.84	21.76	110530	105.48	67.06
59.82	1.11	3.38	34100	97.99	26.98	146866	107.18	75.41
56.22	1.38	4.29	50236	100.11	25.31	170972	114.77	79.34
56.78	1.09	0.43	21899	94.98	32.24	81910	98.59	67.67

6-8 全部独立核算集体工业企业主要经济指标

单位：万元

项　目 Item		企业单位个数（个） Number of Enterprises (unit)	#亏损企业 Loss-making Enterprises	工业总产值（当年价格） Gross Output Value of Industry (at current price)	新产品产值 Value of New Products	工业总产值（1990年不变价格） Gross Output Value of Industry (at 1990 constant prices)	工业增加值（生产法） Added Value of Industry (with production method)
总　计	**Total**	**10738**	**1537**	**2631668**	**90511**	**2510989**	**834618**
在总计中：	**Of Total:**						
中央企业	Central Enterprises	263	60	61467	3003	55814	30442
地方企业	Local Enterprises	10475	1477	2570201	87509	2455175	804176
工业系统	Industry System	540	116	116774	5632	120669	38248
非工业系统	Non-Industry System	240	35	16739		14551	9873
区县工业	Industry of District and County	9551	1273	2387356	68321	2257888	749575
其他	Others	144	53	49332	13555	62037	6480
在总计中：	**Of Total:**						
街镇农村企业	Rural Enterprises of Subdistricts and Towns	7981	809	1930687	6963	2510989	660409
在总计中：	**Of Total:**						
轻工业	Light Industry	4842	733	1122535	20725	1088657	335262
以农产品为原料	Using Farm Products as Raw Material	2800	417	734271	2913	680079	217167
以非农产品为原料	Using Non-Farm Products as Raw Material	2042	316	388264	17812	408577	118096
重工业	Heavy Industry	5896	804	1509133	69787	1422332	499356
采掘工业	Excavation	438	34	78439		61393	33461
原料工业	Raw Material	696	122	241657	152	225582	89153
加工工业	Processing	4762	648	1189038	69635	1135358	376738
在总计中：	**Of Total:**						
大型企业	Large Enterprises	9	5	139131	42356	150277	9167
中型企业	Medium Enterprises	45	17	74575	1205	76837	17858
小型企业	Small Enterprises	10684	1515	2417962	46951	2283875	807594

MAIN INDICATORS FOR COLLECTIVE-OWNED INDUSTRIAL ENTERPRISES WITH INDEPENDENT ACCOUNTING SYSTEM

(10000 yuan)

工 业 销售产值 (当年价格) Sales Value of Industry (at current price)	出口交货值 Delivery Value of Exports	全部从业人员年平均人数(人) Average Number of Employment (person)	资产负债 Assets and Liabilities: 流动资产合计 Circulating Assets	应收帐款净额 Accounts Receivable	存货 Stock	产成品 Finished Products	流动资产平均余额 Average Balance of Circulating Assets	长期投资 Long-time Investment	固定资产合计 Fixed Assets
2478980	**141640**	**449493**	**2300958**	**452576**	**1009674**	**516092**	**2115264**	**205449**	**1386608**
57521		8952	49501	9303	17152	4547	43041	6675	20042
2421459	140614	440541	2251457	443273	992522	511545	2072223	198774	1366566
121154	3172	27338	169895	44547	74744	41054	167995	30428	117853
16449		3042	12664	2713	6179	2250	10444	1059	4615
2239120	138465	405255	1932916	373201	866287	438432	1758520	134064	1183715
44735	4	4906	135981	22811	45313	29809	135263	33223	60383
1809210	113245	321491	1220175	245502	618008	339585	1138982	55798	776960
1061069	101369	201426	925696	187772	421808	224081	872758	88446	583483
694092	87436	130429	504809	108124	232597	120117	477315	38217	357638
366977	13933	70997	420887	79648	189211	103964	395443	50229	225845
1417911	40271	248067	1375261	264804	587866	292011	1242506	117003	803125
71606	669	20000	44378	13499	14398	10931	42359	1305	41611
224253	1829	25276	170484	35328	74258	42171	161574	9665	165664
1122051	37772	202791	1160400	215977	499211	238909	1038572	106033	595849
126925	17139	11380	392997	61592	104796	32957	320903	75078	205908
69545	9053	15440	99080	17634	46692	26009	100186	12672	99980
2282510	115448	422673	1808880	373350	858186	457126	1694175	117700	1080721

6-8 续表 1 continued

单位：万元

项目	Item	资产负债：固定资产原价合计 Original Value of Fixed Assets	#生产经营用 For Productive Use	累计折旧 Accumulative Depreciation	#本年折旧 Depreciation in this Year	固定资产净值年平均余额 Average Net Value of Fixed Assets	无形资产及递延资产 Intangible and Deferred Assets
总　计	**Total**	**1766186**	**1238575**	**562449**	**81791**	**1095026**	**113988**
在总计中：	**Of Total:**						
中央企业	Central Enterprises	30642	19132	13110	2275	17370	440
地方企业	Local Enterprises	1735544	1219443	549340	79516	1077656	113548
工业系统	Industry System	145067	103349	52635	6126	82457	13844
非工业系统	Non-Industry System	6312	2333	2302	272	3229	192
区县工业	Industry of District and County	1518831	1106135	486003	72408	973915	96258
其他	Others	65334	7626	8400	710	18055	3255
在总计中：	**Of Total:**						
街镇农村企业	Rural Enterprises of Subdistricts and Towns	1032064	762441	328453	49483	664306	32204
在总计中：	**Of Total:**						
轻工业	Light Industry	746187	509122	230677	31641	442795	35869
以农产品为原料	Using Farm Products as Raw Material	464419	348143	148298	21440	288199	21196
以非农产品为原料	Using Non-Farm Products as Raw Material	281768	160980	82378	10201	154596	14674
重工业	Heavy Industry	1019999	729452	331773	50150	652231	78119
采掘工业	Excavation	51183	38399	12911	1972	37799	1998
原料工业	Raw Material	173921	144354	45102	7155	110273	12543
加工工业	Processing	794896	546699	273760	41023	504159	63577
在总计中：	**Of Total:**						
大型企业	Large Enterprises	241058	100610	51644	10038	141063	47994
中型企业	Medium Enterprises	126429	104481	44319	4585	75727	3994
小型企业	Small Enterprises	1398699	1033484	466486	67168	878236	62000

6-8 续表 2 continued

(10000 yuan)

Assets and Liabilities										
#无形资产 Intangible Assets	其他资产 Other Assets	资产总计 Total Assets	流动负债合计 Liquid Liabilities	短期借款 Short-time Loans	长期负债合计 Long-term Liabilities	长期借款 Long-time Loans	负债合计 Total Liabilities	所有者权益 Ownership Interest	实收资本 Contributed Capital	国家资本 State
43592	**12994**	**4019996**	**2308703**	**749624**	**415621**	**353882**	**2736852**	**1283144**	**1007077**	**41485**
136	237	76895	39190	3962	3580	2017	44491	32405	20840	2950
43455	12757	3943101	2269513	745662	412041	351865	2692361	1250739	986237	38535
2073	80	332099	176100	42671	31367	19380	207558	124541	86388	540
46	40	18570	11545	589	362	61	11947	6622	4782	768
39996	12625	3359578	1921235	630642	373409	325656	2305319	1054259	881415	36797
1340	12	232854	160632	71760	6902	6769	167538	65316	13652	430
16128	6664	2091802	1134149	428733	200249	168315	1343692	748110	596990	25813
12453	2723	1636217	941399	374909	136901	110542	1081622	554596	416300	17514
7513	2006	923865	500021	198018	93229	74903	596141	327725	258597	12045
4940	717	712352	441378	176891	43672	35639	485481	226871	157704	5468
31139	10271	2383779	1367304	374715	278720	243340	1655231	728549	590777	23971
321	181	89474	41767	10883	5164	4726	47982	41492	20461	252
10921	525	358881	199267	70451	74218	66466	274720	84161	66137	8133
19896	9565	1935424	1126270	293381	199338	172148	1332528	602896	504178	15587
20912	5147	727123	454731	128780	98017	94641	552748	174376	107678	3310
872	613	216338	115541	48020	22738	19952	138279	78059	59703	1304
21808	7234	3076535	1738432	572825	294866	239289	2045825	1030709	839696	36871

6-8 续表 3 continued

单位：万元

项目 Item		资产负债 Assets and Liabilities				
		集体资本 Collective	法人资本 Institutional Units	个人资本 Individuals	港澳台资本 Hongkong, Macao and Taiwan	外商资本 Foreign
总计	**Total**	**707613**	**181182**	**42107**	**7644**	**27047**
在总计中：	Of Total:					
中央企业	Central Enterprises	15077	2710	103		
地方企业	Local Enterprises	692537	178471	42004	7644	27047
工业系统	Industry System	73553	11155	1141		
非工业系统	Non-Industry System	3559	448	7		
区县工业	Industry of District and County	607698	164582	37647	7644	27047
其他	Others	7728	2286	3208		
在总计中：	Of Total:					
街镇农村企业	Rural Enterprises of Subdistricts and Towns	413469	119805	31814	2000	4088
在总计中：	Of Total:					
轻工业	Light Industry	301915	74391	19896	863	1722
以农产品为原料	Using Farm Products as Raw Material	178310	53526	12578	600	1538
以非农产品为原料	Using Non-Farm Products as Raw Material	123606	20865	7318	263	184
重工业	Heavy Industry	405698	106791	22211	6781	25325
采掘工业	Excavation	16519	2110	1581		
原料工业	Raw Material	44975	9438	3234	358	
加工工业	Processing	344204	95243	17396	6423	25325
在总计中：	Of Total:					
大型企业	Large Enterprises	50905	23332	1720	5643	22768
中型企业	Medium Enterprises	49014	8314	714	358	
小型企业	Small Enterprises	607694	149536	39673	1643	4279

6-8 续表 4 continued

(10000 yuan)

损益及分配 Profits,Loss and Distribution										
产品销售收入 Sales Revenue	产品销售成本 Cost of Sales	产品销售费用 Expenses of Sales	产品销售税金及附加 Sales Tax and Extra Charges	产品销售利润 Sales Profits	管理费用 Overhead Cost	税金 Taxes	财产保险费 Premium of Property	劳动待业保险费 Premium for Employment Insurance	财务费用 Financial Expenses	利息支出 Expenses of Interest
2442090	**2053384**	**85289**	**18650**	**284767**	**230323**	**7923**	**2322**	**16880**	**61306**	**45760**
70335	57199	3336	477	9322	8137	97	260	590	-27	93
2371755	1996185	81953	18173	275445	222187	7827	2062	16289	61333	45666
123375	101891	4283	719	16482	30312	869	339	5698	2587	2592
11304	9570	420	86	1229	2151	48	10	354	23	41
2189419	1846444	73921	17135	251919	184162	6884	1692	10141	57844	42904
47657	38279	3330	234	5815	5561	26	21	97	879	130
1718811	1455346	50567	11150	201749	104759	4817	1058	786	34673	24914
1052778	886814	42724	9779	113461	97878	3719	1099	7747	24668	18823
688093	581919	29156	7348	69669	54793	2460	644	4309	15119	11632
364685	304895	13568	2431	43792	43086	1259	455	3438	9550	7191
1389312	1166570	42566	8871	171306	132445	4205	1224	9132	36638	26936
76466	59239	1811	1112	14305	5105	411	24	19	1070	882
207581	177921	6379	956	22326	16052	426	397	477	6916	5172
1105265	929411	34376	6804	134675	111289	3368	803	8637	28652	20883
135901	118627	4147	295	12832	16620	165	89	662	11522	5966
71406	59731	2746	418	8511	17346	536	258	3050	3774	3435
2234783	1875026	78396	17937	263425	196357	7223	1975	13167	46010	36359

6-8 续表 5 continued

单位：万元

项 目 Item		损益及分配 Profits,Loss and Distribution 营业利润 Operating Profits	投资收益 Investment Income	补贴收入 Subsidy Income	营业外收入 Out-business Income	营业外支出 Out-business Expenditure	利润总额 Total Profits
总 计	**Total**	**30000**	**5042**	**3932**	**28862**	**11649**	**52310**
在总计中：	**Of Total:**						
中央企业	Central Enterprises	2109	245	-43	252	260	2287
地方企业	Local Enterprises	27891	4797	3975	28610	11389	50023
工业系统	Industry System	-8240	830	20	6874	2701	-3516
非工业系统	Non-Industry System	-525	70	393	56	117	-119
区县工业	Industry of District and County	36158	3896	3551	21442	8504	52959
其他	Others	497	1	11	239	67	699
在总计中：	**Of Total:**						
街镇农村企业	Rural Enterprises of Subdistricts and Towns	68649	633	1986	11709	4413	76384
在总计中：	**Of Total:**						
轻工业	Light Industry	11091	685	2168	13903	5428	19566
以农产品为原料	Using Farm Products as Raw Material	13167	-563	1583	7215	2637	16437
以非农产品为原料	Using Non-Farm Products as Raw Material	-2076	1248	585	6688	2791	3129
重工业	Heavy Industry	18909	4357	1764	14959	6221	32744
采掘工业	Excavation	8259	12	71	211	340	9513
原料工业	Raw Material	219	123	29	1381	445	568
加工工业	Processing	10431	4223	1664	13367	5436	22663
在总计中：	**Of Total:**						
大型企业	Large Enterprises	-10815	2960	5	246	298	-7904
中型企业	Medium Enterprises	-6718	573		3780	1133	-3496
小型企业	Small Enterprises	47533	1510	3927	24836	10218	63709

6-8 续表 6 continued

(10000 yuan)

				工资，福利费，增值税 Wages,Welfares and Added Value Tax					
应交所得税 Income Tax Payable	应付利润 Profits Payable	亏损企业亏损额 Total Lossing of Loss-making Enterprises	利税总额 Total Pre-tax Profits	本年应付工资总额 Total Wags Payable	本年应付福利费总额 Total Welfares Payable	本年应交增值税 Added Value Tax	本年进项税额 Tax Include in Purchasing Cost	本年销项税额 Tax Include in Sales Cost	工业中间投入合计 Intermediate Input of Industry
21399	**21042**	**63747**	**160396**	**281856**	**35597**	**89436**	**247778**	**329691**	**1886486**
936	198	1075	5894	8968	1940	3130	8574	11499	34155
20464	20845	62672	154502	272888	33657	86306	239204	318192	1852331
558	489	5326	3008	23664	3094	5805	14777	20079	84331
92	9	726	663	2269	281	696	1060	1657	7562
19648	20257	56202	147920	243647	29922	77826	215683	286914	1715607
166	90	419	2912	3308	360	1979	7686	9542	44831
15828	21715	19647	148501	181801	21384	60967	153024	208557	1331245
8896	8542	28123	65930	119392	14460	36585	103160	137826	823858
6065	5219	14093	47952	75941	9461	24167	67392	90896	541271
2832	3323	14030	17979	43451	4999	12419	35768	46930	282587
12503	12500	35624	94466	162464	21137	52851	144618	191865	1062628
996	1957	758	13603	14258	1828	2978	1876	4148	47956
1472	-452	5471	8534	18089	2447	7010	25640	31493	159514
10035	10995	29395	72330	130118	16862	42863	117102	156224	855158
583	-463	8260	-4154	12434	1551	3455	26393	28627	133419
298	747	5132	-19	11797	1724	3059	8293	11370	59776
20518	20758	50355	164569	257624	32322	82923	213092	289693	1693291

6-9 全部独立核算"三资"工业企业主要经济指标

单位：万元

项　目 Item		企业单位个数(个) Number of Enterprises (unit)	#亏损企业 Loss-making Enterprises	工业总产值(当年价格) Gross Output Value of Industry (at current price)	新产品产值 Value of New Products	工业总产值(1990年不变价格) Gross Output Value of Industry (at 1990 constant prices)	工业增加值(生产法) Added Value of Industry (with production method)
总　计	**Total**	**2692**	**1073**	**8021331**	**1268862**	**9457184**	**2227635**
在总计中：	**Of Total:**						
中央企业	Central Enterprises	188	79	3083741	716362	4365264	759771
地方企业	Local Enterprises	2504	994	4937590	552500	5091920	1467865
工业系统	Industry System	374	115	2286935	366496	2630687	716186
非工业系统	Non-Industry System	212	75	464461	71	323486	83901
区县工业	Industry of District and County	1158	392	1462645	45741	1431887	416083
其他	Others	760	412	723549	140193	705860	251696
在总计中：	**Of Total:**						
轻工业	Light Industry	1661	696	2509197	115459	2331807	764772
以农产品为原料	Using Farm Products as Raw Material	1089	474	1631325	52340	1380871	482675
以非农产品为原料	Using Non-Farm Products as Raw Material	572	222	877872	63119	950937	282097
重工业	Heavy Industry	1031	377	5512134	1153403	7125377	1462863
采掘工业	Excavation	5		1281		2233	364
原料工业	Raw Material	131	40	299957	1115	243111	83071
加工工业	Processing	895	337	5210896	1152288	6880033	1379428
在总计中：	**Of Total:**						
大型企业	Large Enterprises	43	22	2174506	556682	3079004	627184
中型企业	Medium Enterprises	41	13	374506	7177	348814	79474
小型企业	Small Enterprises	2608	1038	5472319	705003	6029366	1520977

MAIN INDICATORS FOR FOREIGN INDUSTRIAL ENTERPRISES WITH INDEPENDENT ACCOUNTING SYSTEM

(10000 yuan)

工业销售产值(当年价格) Sales Value of Industry (at current price)	出口交货值 Delivery Value of Exports	全部从业人员年平均人数(人) Average Number of Employment (person)	资产负债 Assets and Liabilities						
			流动资产合计 Circulating Assets	应收帐款净额 Accounts Receivable	存货 Stock	产成品 Finished Products	流动资产平均余额 Average Balance of Circulating Assets	长期投资 Long-time Investment	固定资产合计 Fixed Assets
7849906	**823494**	**294913**	**6167468**	**2156415**	**1834967**	**569805**	**5803141**	**79710**	**3364924**
3160339	277726	23619	1632424	785341	438770	77348	1496572	7859	488348
4689567	545768	271294	4535044	1371074	1396197	492456	4306568	71850	2876576
2146219	249106	71784	1913596	867971	565284	170107	1889912	16092	1332863
470730	10545	17700	328611	76380	90507	34893	334190	13372	297950
1388943	223368	100036	1165283	248893	470369	200782	1104128	25318	906781
683675	62749	81774	1127554	177830	270037	86675	978338	17068	338982
2429779	362570	144706	2330640	455355	734943	302064	2222088	51767	1563328
1576093	231533	110896	1648526	261539	500696	200608	1580538	46806	1116371
853686	131037	33810	682114	193816	234247	101456	641551	4961	446957
5420127	460925	150207	3836828	1701059	1100024	267741	3581053	27942	1801596
1277		140	712	403	66	16	645		937
292907	9316	12474	193197	64608	58815	21126	198761	5354	319357
5125944	451609	137593	3642918	1636048	1041144	246599	3381647	22589	1481302
2056982	16105	38912	1423402	689376	365015	84787	1447749	8554	1022733
364698	109294	16492	306374	112038	93876	33237	323118	9253	185194
5428227	698069	239509	4437692	1355001	1376076	451781	4032273	61903	2156997

6-9 续表 1 continued

单位：万元

项目 Item		资产负债 固定资产原价合计 Original Value of Fixed Assets	# 生产经营用 For Productive Use	累计折旧 Accumulative Depreciation	#本年折旧 Depreciation in this Year	固定资产净值年平均余额 Average Net Value of Fixed Assets	无形资产及递延资产 Intangible and Deferred Assets
总计	**Total**	**4344606**	**3467070**	**1297815**	**285955**	**2896565**	**573327**
在总计中：	**Of Total:**						
中央企业	Central Enterprises	629706	372867	176260	44901	444409	45090
地方企业	Local Enterprises	3714901	3094202	1121555	241054	2452155	528237
工业系统	Industry System	1803635	1653914	638430	124385	1099951	152352
非工业系统	Non-Industry System	375521	305074	102193	23097	288062	43702
区县工业	Industry of District and County	1067108	839778	255250	62941	777716	134952
其他	Others	468636	295435	125682	30632	286427	197231
在总计中：	**Of Total:**						
轻工业	Light Industry	1999729	1516601	546115	127890	1390851	371181
以农产品为原料	Using Farm Products as Raw Material	1428219	1096973	389421	90426	985913	164501
以非农产品为原料	Using Non-Farm Products as Raw Material	571510	419628	156694	37465	404938	206681
重工业	Heavy Industry	2344877	1950469	751700	158065	1505714	202146
采掘工业	Excavation	787	759	278	62	520	226
原料工业	Raw Material	359036	342334	85573	20319	213502	44516
加工工业	Processing	1985055	1607376	665849	137684	1291691	157404
在总计中：	**Of Total:**						
大型企业	Large Enterprises	1373636	1157628	444831	82109	877218	102869
中型企业	Medium Enterprises	223231	182443	73823	16262	162948	31663
小型企业	Small Enterprises	2747739	2126999	779161	187585	1856399	438795

6-9 续表 2 continued

(10000 yuan)

Assets and Liabilities										
#无形资产 Intangible Assets	其他资产 Other Assets	资产总计 Total Assets	流动负债合计 Liquid Liabilities	短期借款 Short-time Loans	长期负债合计 Long-term Liabilities	长期借款 Long-time Loans	负债合计 Total Liabilities	所有者权益 Ownership Interest	实收资本 Contributed Capital	国家资本 State
487042	**147131**	**10332542**	**5521138**	**1929977**	**794411**	**735251**	**6352162**	**3980380**	**3931845**	**647968**
38057	11241	2184962	1389183	351394	104039	105699	1494618	690344	426579	159644
448986	135890	8147580	4131954	1578583	690372	629552	4857544	3290036	3505266	488324
136397	48587	3463543	1694915	710253	336581	307428	2041171	1422372	1443779	267616
32966	11862	695497	333922	149881	64226	61896	412518	282979	404763	93832
95413	45375	2277709	1251380	493360	164753	143368	1423574	854135	947814	105419
184210	30067	1710831	851738	225089	124812	116861	980281	730550	708909	21458
328197	69616	4386587	2193870	853062	347577	311533	2563815	1822773	2068293	318259
133393	52148	3028352	1471744	588381	209013	176287	1700335	1328017	1491694	255545
194804	17468	1358235	722126	264681	138564	135246	863480	494756	576599	62714
158846	77515	5945955	3327268	1076915	446834	423718	3788347	2157608	1863552	329709
110	14	1890	536	172	200	200	809	1081	852	80
42027	7790	570214	251342	82478	14367	17231	265865	304349	267744	76094
116709	69710	5373851	3075390	994265	432267	406288	3521674	1852177	1594957	253535
92913	20507	2578066	1190355	604158	216866	218296	1415173	1162893	1126458	184402
30028	4804	537288	301653	102473	36272	24121	346399	190889	203557	35848
364102	121819	7217189	4029130	1223346	541273	492835	4590591	2626598	2601831	427718

6-9 续表 3 continued

单位：万元

项目	Item	集体资本 Collective	法人资本 Institutional Units	个人资本 Individuals	港澳台资本 Hongkong, Macao and Taiwan	外商资本 Foreign
		资产负债 Assets and Liabilities				
总　计	**Total**	**141953**	**741123**	**21608**	**568503**	**1810690**
在总计中：	**Of Total:**					
中央企业	Central Enterprises	3042	48125		39331	176438
地方企业	Local Enterprises	138911	692999	21608	529172	1634252
工业系统	Industry System	10897	381995	5340	107082	670850
非工业系统	Non-Industry System	3595	72968	8	92348	142011
区县工业	Industry of District and County	114725	167274	13938	216262	330196
其他	Others	9694	70762	2322	113480	491194
在总计中：	Of Total:					
轻工业	Light Industry	99560	312692	9377	401412	926994
以农产品为原料	Using Farm Products as Raw Material	71642	179878	7399	312409	664822
以非农产品为原料	Using Non-Farm Products as Raw Material	27918	132814	1978	89004	262172
重工业	Heavy Industry	42393	428431	12232	167091	883696
采掘工业	Excavation	328		37	23	384
原料工业	Raw Material	6924	71907	38	6638	106142
加工工业	Processing	35142	356524	12156	160430	777170
在总计中：	Of Total:					
大型企业	Large Enterprises		222958		86179	632919
中型企业	Medium Enterprises	4732	69177	5299	15050	73450
小型企业	Small Enterprises	137221	448988	16309	467274	1104321

6-9 续表 4 continued

(10000 yuan)

损益及分配 Profits,Loss and Distribution										
产品销售收入 Sales Revenue	产品销售成本 Cost of Sales	产品销售费用 Expenses of Sales	产品销售税金及附加 Sales Tax and Extra Charges	产品销售利润 Sales Profits	管理费用 Overhead Cost	税金 Taxes	财产保险费 Premium of Property	劳动待业保险费 Premium for Employment Insurance	财务费用 Financial Expenses	利息支出 Expenses of Interest
8253362	**6753438**	**530182**	**35786**	**933955**	**605669**	**14986**	**6967**	**11194**	**152231**	**144793**
3302059	2885285	116957	10495	289322	105379	2465	1132	1897	28649	29777
4951303	3868154	413225	25291	644633	500290	12521	5834	9297	123582	115016
2222168	1786891	133189	15947	286141	204398	6838	2785	5055	63987	65053
514631	396341	60531	413	57346	54659	1844	702	1736	9723	11490
1368490	1053555	122905	7682	184349	128257	2392	1274	1206	32489	24755
846014	631367	96600	1250	116797	112976	1447	1073	1300	17383	13718
2445354	1847231	273023	13772	311329	274262	8317	2898	5443	64049	54336
1598209	1217754	175701	10104	194649	180351	6482	2003	3523	40354	34087
847146	629476	97322	3668	116680	93911	1835	895	1920	23695	20249
5808007	4906208	257159	22015	622626	331406	6669	4069	5751	88182	90457
1287	915	175		197	144		2		18	14
290415	244467	8495	990	36463	22779	336	248	545	4438	4549
5516305	4660825	248490	21025	585966	308483	6332	3819	5206	83726	85894
2153752	1765879	139736	18097	230040	148287	2908	1915	1520	38862	38472
374580	318595	21030	405	34550	35664	645	297	766	8382	8916
5725031	4668965	369416	17284	669365	421718	11433	4755	8908	104987	97405

6-9 续表 5 continued

单位：万元

项目	Item	营业利润 Operating Profits	投资收益 Investment Income	补贴收入 Subsidy Income	营业外收入 Out-business Income	营业外支出 Out-business Expenditure	利润总额 Total Profits
		损益及分配 Profits,Loss and Distribution					
总 计	**Total**	**231831**	**608**	**-71**	**54429**	**31464**	**257095**
在总计中：	**Of Total:**						
中央企业	Central Enterprises	177823	275	41	7083	4625	182679
地方企业	Local Enterprises	54008	333	-112	47347	26840	74416
工业系统	Industry System	28608	123	56	21680	13635	40469
非工业系统	Non-Industry System	-4943	166	4	4017	2782	-4552
区县工业	Industry of District and County	26808	122	1324	14183	6120	34288
其他	Others	3534	-78	-1496	7468	4303	4211
在总计中：	**Of Total:**						
轻工业	Light Industry	-14642	526	922	26939	16857	-6473
以农产品为原料	Using Farm Products as Raw Material	-21484	414	606	16028	12665	-21062
以非农产品为原料	Using Non-Farm Products as Raw Material	6842	112	316	10912	4192	14589
重工业	Heavy Industry	246473	83	-993	27490	14608	263568
采掘工业	Excavation	35			5	14	27
原料工业	Raw Material	12423			625	467	12557
加工工业	Processing	234014	83	-993	26860	14127	250984
在总计中：	**Of Total:**						
大型企业	Large Enterprises	65873	-14	40	15351	4408	78587
中型企业	Medium Enterprises	-4874	178		1046	1018	-4114
小型企业	Small Enterprises	170832	444	-111	38033	26038	182621

6-9 续表 6 continued

(10000 yuan)

				工资，福利费，增值税 Wages,Welfares and Added Value Tax					
应交所得税 Income Tax Payable	应付利润 Profits Payable	亏损企业亏损额 Total Lossing of Loss-making Enterprises	利税总额 Total Pre-tax Profits	本年应付工资总额 Total Wags Payable	本年应付福利费总额 Total Welfares Payable	本年应交增值税 Added Value Tax	本年进项税额 Tax Include in Purchasing Cost	本年销项税额 Tax Include in Sales Cost	工业中间投入合计 Intermediate Input of Industry
44640	**182124**	**250097**	**548786**	**430006**	**108675**	**255905**	**1077757**	**1277011**	**6049601**
12624	28595	13414	238430	81730	13887	45256	579622	579568	2369226
32016	153529	236682	310356	348275	94788	210649	498135	697443	3680374
16530	121606	82885	153796	147937	45357	97380	223282	316046	1668129
3082	4981	32005	19905	34444	10569	24044	46880	71285	404604
9591	14810	57283	96376	101531	24056	54406	136491	186975	1100968
2813	12133	64509	40281	64363	14806	34820	91482	123138	506673
16951	32111	153425	123449	199925	50894	116150	221686	333633	1860575
12413	23362	118386	68299	140471	35929	79257	142636	215855	1227907
4538	8750	35039	55150	59455	14965	36893	79050	117779	632668
27689	150013	96672	425338	230080	57781	139755	856071	943378	4189026
7			41	167	76	14		10	931
394	3133	15132	23840	20050	4392	10293	31472	41019	227179
27288	146880	81541	401457	209863	53313	129448	824598	902349	3960916
8978	106624	59073	181127	97638	28295	84443	378247	418981	1631765
2662	4385	20733	9221	31689	5660	12930	31462	43828	307962
33000	71115	170291	358437	300679	74720	158532	668048	814202	4109874

6-10 地方独立核算大中型工业企业主要经济指标

单位：万元

项目	Item	企业单位个数(个) Number of Enterprises (unit)	#亏损企业 Loss-making Enterprises	工业总产值(当年价格) Gross Output Value of Industry (at current price)	新产品产值 Value of New Products	工业总产值(1990年不变价格) Gross Output Value of Industry (at 1990 constant prices)	工业增加值(生产法) Added Value of Industry (with production method)
总计	**Total**	**365**	**103**	**6500858**	**869201**	**5975752**	**6837840**
在总计中：	**Of Total:**						
工业系统	Industry System	217	42	4986369	815476	4731871	5247008
非工业系统	Non-Industry System	39	11	565249	1547	345077	591702
区县工业	Industry of District and County	89	38	795422	35243	746112	837773
其他	Others	20	12	153818	16936	152692	161358
在总计中：	**Of Total:**						
内资企业	Domestic Investment Enterprises	295	70	4819319	564616	4032368	5088209
国有企业	State-Owned	210	39	3209397	264166	2462229	3405574
集体企业	Collective Owned	46	21	213705	43561	227113	219974
股份合作企业	Share Holding Cooperative	2		12369	7977	12025	12848
联营企业	Joint Owned	13	3	142645	1266	156614	147916
有限责任公司	Limited-Liability Company	11	5	615445	26231	537904	644943
股份有限公司	Share Holding Company	10		615766	221416	627157	646863
私营企业	Private Owned	3	2	9992		9327	10092
港澳台商投资企业	Hongkong,Macao and Taiwan Funded Enterprises	22	9	210451	10937	208611	217625
港澳台合资经营	Joint Venture	19	9	199516	10937	197675	206317
港澳台合作经营	Cooperative	1		8734		8734	8962
港澳台商独资企业	Hongkong,Macao and Taiwan Enterprises	1		1601		1601	1723
港澳台商投资股份有限公司	Hongkong,Macao and Taiwan Funded Share Holing Company	1		600		600	624
外商投资企业	Foreign Funded Enterprises	48	24	1471089	293648	1734774	1532007
中外合资经营	Joint Venture	38	17	1383379	291190	1658806	1440041
中外合作经营	Cooperative	1		15790	1264	14445	16260
外资(独资)企业	Foreign Enterprises	7	5	39527		36211	42018
外商投资股份有限公司	Foreign Funded Share Holding Company	2	2	32392	1194	25312	33686
在总计中：	**Of Total:**						
农村企业	Rural Enterprises	19	6	86351	300	76263	89730
在总计中：	**Of Total:**						
轻工业	Light Industry	170	52	1691277	127565	1562888	1789038
以农产品为原料	Using Farm Products as Raw Material	100	30	972592	23297	759435	1037476
以非农产品为原料	Using Non-Farm Products as Raw Material	70	22	718684	104268	803453	751561
重工业	Heavy Industry	195	51	4809582	741636	4412864	5048803
采掘工业	Excavation	4		98111		38174	102308
原料工业	Raw Material	29	8	2209614	88672	1667253	2347905
加工工业	Processing	162	43	2501857	652964	2707436	2598590
在总计中：	**Of Total:**						
大型企业	Large Enterprises	160	50	5293054	839152	4860865	5572232
中型企业	Medium Enterprises	205	53	1207805	30049	1114887	1265608

MAIN INDICATORS FOR LOCAL LARGE AND MEDIUM INDUSTRIAL ENTERPRISES WITH INDEPENDENT ACCOUNTING SYSTEM

(10000 yuan)

工业销售产值(当年价格) Sales Value of Industry (at current price)	出口交货值 Delivery Value of Exports	全部从业人员年平均人数(人) Average Number of Employment (person)	资产负债 Assets and Liabilities: 流动资产合计 Circulating Assets	应收帐款净额 Accounts Receivable	存货 Stock	产成品 Finished Products	流动资产平均余额 Average Balance of Circulating Assets	长期投资 Long-time Investment	固定资产合计 Fixed Assets
6300409	**477850**	**475563**	**7200380**	**2472008**	**2093648**	**765263**	**6945014**	**2175242**	**7835526**
4836247	403976	370269	5620496	2209083	1627749	612549	5552202	1965592	5612645
558872	11790	37952	509755	105652	136526	46286	456905	28917	1292964
769433	61992	62397	728592	112413	261411	75749	668304	143335	698998
135857	92	4945	341537	44861	67962	30680	267603	37399	230920
4744690	353478	428337	5762492	1784981	1742293	679889	5539244	2161229	6822734
3178625	210415	324492	4055611	1309884	1209506	434926	3916586	1629400	4686359
196459	26192	26783	491921	79210	151343	58965	420926	87749	305879
11849	92	907	54601	6314	11245	5793	52012	6704	20234
133433	7601	13497	180878	65258	71139	29171	180309	50100	130005
593654	102764	40391	521836	203890	168828	94846	582333	264578	1397154
621530	6415	21692	452053	120073	126051	54570	381486	121872	279338
9139		575	5593	352	4180	1619	5593	827	3766
196806	14366	10968	256253	85213	67353	23728	266634	7973	153787
185647	9916	10315	250646	84648	65087	22062	261775	7973	150167
8882	4450	571	3140	394	2045	1666	3143		1919
1601		52	2397	141	211		1646		1481
675		30	70	30	10		70		219
1358914	110006	36258	1181636	601814	284002	61647	1139137	6040	859005
1267521	86041	29795	1083077	579813	246814	47621	1045495	5518	761601
14997	5177	911	12318	3917	6259	3844	10861		9444
40442		1474	55481	11649	15300	3159	48045		64532
35955	18788	4078	30760	6436	15629	7022	34736	522	23429
85540	31096	8787	79041	15283	35701	23498	80917	4467	46707
1675430	236352	159587	2148703	480796	705587	346347	1977430	414667	2234542
963123	117428	95643	1099600	270167	389360	195316	995496	215376	1054470
712307	118924	63944	1049103	210629	316227	151032	981933	199292	1180072
4624979	241498	315976	5051678	1991212	1388061	418915	4967585	1760575	5600985
94225	33964	31784	151286	115400	25027	12841	159737	13407	132768
2173549	119193	104127	1850079	728613	438559	130154	1859148	1086551	3475246
2357205	88341	180065	3050313	1147199	924476	275920	2948699	660618	1992971
5108949	325918	366979	5980558	2113650	1713044	605021	5745922	1896879	6874063
1191461	151932	108584	1219822	358358	380604	160242	1199093	278364	961463

6-10 续表 1 continued

单位：万元

项目	Item	资产负债 固定资产原价合计 Original Value of Fixed Assets	# 生产经营用 For Productive Use	累计折旧 Accumulative Depreciation	#本年折旧 Depreciation in this Year	固定资产净值年平均余额 Average Net Value of Fixed Assets	无形资产及递延资产 Intangible and Deferred Assets
总 计	**Total**	**10044958**	**8686202**	**3194724**	**426232**	**6551094**	**912175**
在总计中：	**Of Total:**						
工业系统	Industry System	7301759	6440673	2548462	309518	4793670	771451
非工业系统	Non-Industry System	1590485	1451290	363012	66079	1023789	23853
区县工业	Industry of District and County	831940	657661	217677	38669	555521	89370
其他	Others	320775	136579	65573	11966	178114	27501
在总计中：	**Of Total:**						
内资企业	Domestic Investment Enterprises	8683583	7536975	2741379	342537	5677238	799115
国有企业	State-Owned	6087798	5361168	2122844	254920	3954986	328500
集体企业	Collective Owned	367458	205062	95943	14623	216781	51988
股份合作企业	Share Holding Cooperative	22643	13641	3269	1074	10046	4130
联营企业	Joint Owned	186356	121775	57153	6907	116718	16891
有限责任公司	Limited-Liability Company	1659133	1499309	344395	42612	1182466	378007
股份有限公司	Share Holding Company	353506	330882	114493	22245	192038	19128
私营企业	Private Owned	6689	5138	3283	156	4205	473
港澳台商投资企业	Hongkong,Macao and Taiwan Funded Enterprises	171049	150544	50376	11025	108186	18708
港澳台合资经营	Joint Venture	167650	149164	49810	10671	106957	18471
港澳台合作经营	Cooperative	1788	1200	49	43		
港澳台商独资企业	Hongkong,Macao and Taiwan Enterprises	1391		517	311	1010	236
港澳台商投资股份有限公司	Hongkong,Macao and Taiwan Funded Share Holing Company	220	180	1	1	219	
外商投资企业	Foreign Funded Enterprises	1190326	998684	402969	72669	765670	94352
中外合资经营	Joint Venture	1029465	871575	371566	67936	640874	77380
中外合作经营	Cooperative	12608	12123	4890	1074	7897	2218
外资(独资)企业	Foreign Enterprises	112196	82374	13739	2357	93014	13129
外商投资股份有限公司	Foreign Funded Share Holding Company	36057	32612	12773	1303	23886	1624
在总计中：	**Of Total:**						
农村企业	Rural Enterprises	60281	51754	16683	3073	41831	1969
在总计中：	**Of Total:**						
轻工业	Light Industry	2874549	2345335	819933	121987	1788838	242542
以农产品为原料	Using Farm Products as Raw Material	1357176	1083993	408197	58978	841435	100145
以非农产品为原料	Using Non-Farm Products as Raw Material	1517373	1261341	411736	63009	947403	142397
重工业	Heavy Industry	7170409	6340868	2374791	304245	4762256	669633
采掘工业	Excavation	188663	125878	68886	4793	121103	5504
原料工业	Raw Material	4465697	4194355	1405122	175140	3086184	467091
加工工业	Processing	2516050	2020635	900783	124312	1554969	197037
在总计中：	**Of Total:**						
大型企业	Large Enterprises	8861756	7705233	2802540	370911	5813150	771276
中型企业	Medium Enterprises	1183203	980969	392184	55321	737944	140899

6-10 续表 2 continued

(10000 yuan)

Assets and Liabilities										
#无形资产 Intangible Assets	其他资产 Other Assets	资产总计 Total Assets	流动负债合计 Liquid Liabilities	短期借款 Short-time Loans	长期负债合计 Long-term Liabilities	长期借款 Long-time Loans	负债合计 Total Liabilities	所有者权益 Ownership Interest	实收资本 Contributed Capital	国家资本 State
228935	**65534**	**18188858**	**6989895**	**3255105**	**3353704**	**2932748**	**10371423**	**7817435**	**4656515**	**2265609**
148534	45179	14015362	5558419	2736986	2921227	2539154	8487696	5527666	2803809	1193073
15925	6845	1862334	402337	94475	187456	175281	597755	1264580	1034512	909428
39173	8550	1668844	721441	227486	206582	180384	938753	730091	452975	160410
25303	4961	642318	307698	196158	38439	37930	347219	295099	365219	2697
125190	41894	15587465	5753251	2638963	3127570	2724491	8892218	6695246	3452297	2104127
72567	35461	10735330	3916483	1912271	1726750	1431588	5653524	5081805	2567079	1834723
21784	5760	943297	570149	176799	120750	114588	690899	252397	167349	4613
4100		85668	52748	32424	5039	4800	57787	27881	17576	
664		377874	217415	67485	64870	41646	282285	95589	70749	9243
14040		2561574	713251	340354	1158036	1092653	1871288	690287	416096	255358
11570	668	873057	279720	108963	49897	37109	329641	543416	210981	95
467	6	10665	3484	669	2228	2106	6793	3872	2467	95
17247	7035	443755	272329	126866	25670	24629	298459	145296	157887	49595
17011	6897	434154	269703	126266	23889	22848	294052	140101	153584	49595
	138	5198	2347	600	281	281	2628	2570	1764	
236		4115	129		1500	1500	1629	2485	2400	
		289	150				150	139	139	
86498	16605	2157638	964315	489275	200464	183628	1180745	976893	1046331	111887
69815	13301	1940877	874528	455915	175136	168501	1065629	875248	883322	105492
2218		23981	10965	6060	3092	3092	14057	9924	9815	6185
12942	2751	135892	41293	11732	10405	10259	51697	84195	131952	
1524	553	56888	37530	15568	11832	1777	49362	7526	21243	210
1164	1455	133638	55228	24476	15214	8783	70442	63196	51010	2634
93446	51873	5092327	2098208	1022817	649571	501921	2767152	2325174	1739952	783635
56915	6885	2476476	1059757	488677	244156	179941	1323259	1153217	924168	276612
36531	44987	2615850	1038451	534141	405415	321980	1443894	1171957	815785	507023
135489	13662	13096532	4891687	2232288	2704133	2430828	7604271	5492261	2916563	1481973
		302964	124747	50319	52812	40650	177558	125406	70791	67864
54574	-13649	6865317	1857493	1091429	1855604	1726801	3713122	3152195	1442819	1220038
80915	27311	5928250	2909448	1090539	795717	663377	3713590	2214660	1402953	194072
174595	53838	15576614	5810253	2834883	3022757	2667360	8846298	6730316	3883684	2037397
54340	11697	2612244	1179643	420222	330947	265388	1525125	1087119	772831	228212

6-10 续表 3 continued

单位：万元

项目 Item		资产负债 Assets and Liabilities 集体资本 Collective	法人资本 Institutional Units	个人资本 Individuals	港澳台资本 Hongkong, Macao and Taiwan	外商资本 Foreign
总计	**Total**	**141324**	**1379069**	**79232**	**93748**	**697535**
在总计中:	**Of Total:**					
工业系统	Industry System	57689	1155915	62560	39825	294746
非工业系统	Non-Industry System	1975	64274	110	1492	57233
区县工业	Industry of District and County	78055	118030	16494	24080	55906
其他	Others	3604	40850	68	28351	289650
在总计中:	**Of Total:**					
内资企业	Domestic Investment Enterprises	136591	1091806	73933	7528	38312
国有企业	State-Owned	21289	688330	20617	1527	594
集体企业	Collective Owned	99887	31646	2434	6001	22768
股份合作企业	Share Holding Cooperative	1707	15840	30		
联营企业	Joint Owned	13645	47861			
有限责任公司	Limited-Liability Company		160738			
股份有限公司	Share Holding Company	60	145091	50785		14950
私营企业	Private Owned	4	2300	68		
港澳台商投资企业	Hongkong,Macao and Taiwan Funded Enterprises	270	44569		62758	696
港澳台合资经营	Joint Venture		40536		62758	696
港澳台合作经营	Cooperative	160	1604			
港澳台商独资企业	Hongkong,Macao and Taiwan Enterprises		2400			
港澳台商投资股份有限公司	Hongkong,Macao and Taiwan Funded Share Holing Company	110	29			
外商投资企业	Foreign Funded Enterprises	4463	242694	5299	23463	658527
中外合资经营	Joint Venture	2107	236197		11463	528064
中外合作经营	Cooperative					3630
外资(独资)企业	Foreign Enterprises				12000	119952
外商投资股份有限公司	Foreign Funded Share Holding Company	2356	6497	5299		6881
在总计中:	**Of Total:**					
农村企业	Rural Enterprises	17476	23831	129	664	6277
在总计中:	**Of Total:**					
轻工业	Light Industry	62021	388896	38251	58952	408196
以农产品为原料	Using Farm Products as Raw Material	30707	231730	20851	48587	315680
以非农产品为原料	Using Non-Farm Products as Raw Material	31314	157166	17400	10366	92516
重工业	Heavy Industry	79302	990172	40981	34796	289339
采掘工业	Excavation		2927			
原料工业	Raw Material	4338	189890	12334	358	15862
加工工业	Processing	74964	797356	28647	34438	273476
在总计中:	**Of Total:**					
大型企业	Large Enterprises	76011	1019789	48405	76947	625136
中型企业	Medium Enterprises	65312	359280	30828	16801	72399

6-10 续表 4 continued

(10000 yuan)

损益及分配 Profits,Loss and Distribution										
产品销售收入 Sales Revenue	产品销售成本 Cost of Sales	产品销售费用 Expenses of Sales	产品销售税金及附加 Sales Tax and Extra Charges	产品销售利润 Sales Profits	管理费用 Overhead Cost	税金 Taxes	财产保险费 Premium of Property	劳动待业保险费 Premium for Employment Insurance	财务费用 Financial Expenses	利息支出 Expenses of Interest
6748734	**5525118**	**332981**	**114165**	**776470**	**748185**	**31015**	**10304**	**154563**	**278116**	**277865**
5244665	4397364	165121	42559	639622	590129	23384	8027	137992	244480	251744
570968	414132	107784	34705	14347	66944	2724	818	10831	5428	6680
779631	595278	39367	36799	108188	69402	4327	1045	5618	19563	16370
153470	118345	20709	102	14314	21710	580	414	121	8645	3072
5156036	4224582	233886	96611	600956	608202	27705	8229	152475	236040	236489
3492825	2821572	186597	89053	395604	432673	18023	4745	118596	169624	174790
207302	178355	6894	713	21340	33926	701	348	3713	15296	9400
11953	9280	1439	47	1187	1709	257	15	231	1460	875
160840	139496	5206	1494	14644	22544	707	193	4847	4314	4215
620397	534368	16836	2653	66541	73531	4472	2488	19104	37140	37854
654592	534306	16450	2644	101193	43287	3546	441	5985	7962	9311
8127	7206	465	9	447	533				244	44
193407	169780	7784	787	15056	19254	411	136	121	7565	7658
186136	164957	6871	763	13547	18605	410	133	118	7437	7632
4830	2960	786		1084	385				100	
1765	1279	56	12	418	262	1	4	3	26	26
676	584	72	12	8	2				2	
1399291	1130755	91311	16767	160458	120728	2899	1939	1967	34512	33719
1296587	1050220	79291	16586	150490	107096	2542	1835	1510	32891	31771
15027	12288	1151		1588	1184	5	2		331	326
51067	37068	5817		8182	8061	262	17	143	-437	267
36610	31179	5052	180	199	4387	90	84	314	1727	1354
81629	65091	6713	291	9534	6470	206	85	82	1979	1210
1903681	1477769	124176	81342	220393	252580	7694	3901	40954	63955	59743
1126742	824867	79695	76149	146031	147564	4477	2632	21496	32002	30169
776939	652902	44481	5193	74363	105016	3216	1269	19458	31953	29575
4845053	4047349	208805	32822	556077	495605	23321	6403	113609	214161	218122
81023	45814	13033	652	21525	25253	632	8	16033	3217	3475
2244381	1885626	110693	13093	234969	164564	8879	2810	41256	118604	125279
2519650	2115909	85080	19077	299583	305788	13811	3585	56320	92340	89369
5572642	4593470	285040	73006	621126	588796	24069	8255	128635	241460	239729
1176092	931648	47941	41159	155344	159389	6946	2049	25929	36656	38136

6-10 续表 5 continued

单位：万元

项 目	Item	营业利润 Operating Profits	投资收益 Investment Income	补贴收入 Subsidy Income	营业外收入 Out-business Income	营业外支出 Out-business Expenditure	利润总额 Total Profits
		损益及分配 Profits,Loss and Distribution					
总 计	**Total**	**-125041**	**85568**	**109517**	**165786**	**72525**	**156697**
在总计中：	**Of Total:**						
工业系统	Industry System	-88468	72015	55361	136848	53919	111167
非工业系统	Non-Industry System	-51191	4502	52614	20349	14618	13228
区县工业	Industry of District and County	29507	8487	1541	6929	3483	45178
其他	Others	-14888	565	1	1659	504	-12876
在总计中：	**Of Total:**						
内资企业	Domestic Investment Enterprises	-124778	85390	109477	150492	67762	145234
国有企业	State-Owned	-118317	65848	82037	130154	62163	89733
集体企业	Collective Owned	-17502	3533	5	3996	1431	-11399
股份合作企业	Share Holding Cooperative	-1625	581		2119	322	754
联营企业	Joint Owned	-9094	2290		7709	633	275
有限责任公司	Limited-Liability Company	-28541	7053	22740	5700	1989	4953
股份有限公司	Share Holding Company	50630	6086	4694	803	1216	61244
私营企业	Private Owned	-329		1	11	7	-325
港澳台商投资企业	Hongkong,Macao and Taiwan Funded Enterprises	-10006	88	40	508	424	-9923
港澳台合资经营	Joint Venture	-10739	88	40	508	411	-10643
港澳台合作经营	Cooperative	600				13	586
港澳台商独资企业	Hongkong,Macao and Taiwan Enterprises	129					129
港澳台商投资股份有限公司	Hongkong,Macao and Taiwan Funded Share Holing Company	4					4
外商投资企业	Foreign Funded Enterprises	9742	90		14786	4339	21386
中外合资经营	Joint Venture	15009	80		13924	3872	25547
中外合作经营	Cooperative	108			1		109
外资(独资)企业	Foreign Enterprises	658			735	299	1155
外商投资股份有限公司	Foreign Funded Share Holding Company	-6033	10		126	168	-5425
在总计中：	**Of Total:**						
农村企业	Rural Enterprises	1048		1	339	343	1045
在总计中：	**Of Total:**						
轻工业	Light Industry	-44916	24789	33467	62013	33905	47611
以农产品为原料	Using Farm Products as Raw Material	-8131	12463	1390	47525	29104	29965
以非农产品为原料	Using Non-Farm Products as Raw Material	-36785	12326	32076	14488	4801	17646
重工业	Heavy Industry	-80125	60779	76051	103773	38620	109087
采掘工业	Excavation	-5910	240	11733	595	4869	2092
原料工业	Raw Material	-37589	29330	53356	11021	8372	48178
加工工业	Processing	-36626	31209	10962	92157	25378	58817
在总计中：	**Of Total:**						
大型企业	Large Enterprises	-122159	73653	105060	128543	53765	121112
中型企业	Medium Enterprises	-2882	11915	4458	37242	18760	35585

6-10 续表 6 continued

(10000 yuan)

应交所得税 Income Tax Payable	应付利润 Profits Payable	亏损企业亏损额 Total Loss-ing of Loss-making Enterprises	利税总额 Total Pre-tax Profits	工资，福利费，增值税 Wages,Welfares and Added Value Tax 本年应付工资总额 Total Wags Payable	本年应付福利费总额 Total Welfares Payable	本年应交增值税 Added Value Tax	本年进项税额 Tax In-clude in Purchas-ing Cost	本年销项税额 Tax In-clude in Sales Cost	工业中间投入合计 Intermediate Input of Industry
47082	**145003**	**153098**	**608952**	**594439**	**106008**	**338090**	**837962**	**1156915**	**1108**
30043	121131	95879	415208	465278	86147	261482	684088	928331	843
5272	629	10566	74407	57422	8407	26474	49099	76417	21
11716	18797	21004	124571	60338	9403	42594	88005	127935	243
50	4446	25650	-5234	11402	2051	7540	16771	24233	
37619	32691	76707	511836	495956	73615	269991	669557	921365	1101
19992	21976	57905	375612		56542	196826	394583	579477	649
882	284	13392	-4174	24217	3273	6512	34686	39995	243
39			1280	1131	106	479	1966	2445	
394	324	1610	7040	15751	1806	5271	23853	28205	
1283	-269	3464	37298	55515	7685	29692	74881	104185	194
15029	10376		95000	29496	4177	31112	138205	165685	15
		336	-216	385	27	100	1382	1372	
746	1827	16027	-1962	17677	2116	7174	23609	30917	
715	1827	16027	-3079	16927	2101	6801	22787	29706	
			814	617		228	593	821	
31			263	113	15	122	178	300	
			40	20		24	50	90	
8718	110485	60364	99078	80807	30277	60925	144796	204634	7
8718	105705	47976	98795	70615	26543	56662	136670	192240	
			579	1566	515	470	1851	2321	
	4715	6963	3646	4244	1854	2491	4703	7180	
	65	5425	-3944	4382	1365	1301	1572	2892	7
458	810	1822	4715	7982	1826	3379	5802	9129	
23488	23125	68314	226902	184975	30631	97949	191316	282849	188
14343	22149	48452	171042	105419	18598	64928	115748	177606	44
9146	976	19862	55860	79555	12034	33021	75569	105244	144
23594	121878	84784	382050	409465	75377	240141	646646	874066	920
17			6941	23114	6908	4197	13007	17641	
531	2621	8909	199756	164986	22341	138485	252098	386037	194
23046	119258	75876	175353	221365	46128	97459	381541	470388	726
31876	133893	118708	474311	473344	88450	280193	713383	978495	1015
15206	11110	34390	134640	121095	17558	57896	124579	178420	93

6-11 地方独立核算大中型工业企业主要经济指标(按行业分)

单位：万元

项目	Item	企业单位个数(个) Number of Enterprises (unit)	#亏损企业 Loss-making Enterprises	工业总产值(当年价格) Gross Output Value of Industry (at current price)	新产品产值 Value of New Products	工业总产值(1990年不变价格) Gross Output Value of Industry (at 1990 constant prices)	工业增加值(生产法) Added Value of Industry (with production method)
煤炭采选业	Coal Mining and Dressing	1		86765		32242	60412
黑色金属矿采选业	Ferrous Metals Mining and Processing	1		9512		5009	3475
非金属矿采选业	Nonmetal Minerals Mining and Processing	2		1833		923	789
食品加工业	Food Processing	11	3	85807		49966	10513
食品制造业	Food Making	11	7	79050	190	63411	29911
饮料制造业	Beverage Production	12	5	344667	2201	261976	145355
烟草加工业	Tabacco Processing	1		69931	1547	45010	45436
纺织业	Textile Industry	17	4	143539	15816	129798	43361
服装及其他纤维制品制造业	Garments and Other Fiber Products	12	3	57902		43999	14522
皮革、毛皮、羽绒及其制品业	Leather,Furs,Down and Related Products	5	1	3124		2437	-1357
木材加工及竹、藤、棕、草制品业	Timber Processing,Bamboo,Cane, Palm Fiber and Straw Products	1	1	4509		2675	1435
家具制造业	Furniture Manufacturing	2		4722		5752	1172
造纸及纸制品业	Papermaking and Paper Products	6	2	34737		33189	3873
印刷业、记录煤介的复制	Printing and Record Medium Reproduced	17	3	66031		54897	36288
文教、体育用品制造	Stationery,Educational and Sports Goods	6	2	35065	6411	24360	12229
化学原料及化学制品制造业	Raw Chemical Materials and Chemical Products	21	7	686492	32071	656828	149515
医药制造业	Medical and Pharmaceutical Product	11	2	164762	13805	196623	69337
化学纤维制造业	Chemical Fibers	1	1	15007		19026	2576
橡胶制品业	Rubber Products	8	5	70904	2378	93789	8854
塑料制品业	Plastic Products	11	3	48563	1290	49552	7291
非金属矿物制品业	Nonmetal Mineral Products	28	6	351661	8091	297406	106620
黑色金属冶炼及压延加工业	Smelting and Pressing of Ferrous Metals	4	2	1356602	57634	938245	322946
有色金属冶炼及压延加工业	Smelting and Pressing of Nonferrous Metals	3		19211	4693	20124	3306
金属制品业	Metal Products	15	7	59821	1530	67537	15240
普通机械制造业	Ordinary Machinery Manufacturing	25	4	134862	23392	122704	41100
专用设备制造业	Special Purposes Equipment Manufacturing	22	4	518898	222393	501165	100472
交通运输设备制造业	Transportation Equipment Manufacturing	21	9	495920	231568	428189	105098
电气机械及器材制造	Electric Equipment and Machinery	25	4	294195	123697	345272	58927
电子及通信设备制造	Electronic and Telecommunications	33	10	1011009	112033	1352521	371755
仪器仪表及文化、办公用机械制造业	Instruments,Meters,Cultural and Official Machine Manufacturing	18	5	62004	8462	62679	21167
其他制造业	Other Manufacturing	9	3	12628		12006	4198
电力、蒸汽、热水的生产和供应业	Electricity,Steam and Hot Water Production and Supply	3		64150		27024	24868
煤气生产和供应业	Gas Production and Supply	1		17805		7216	12850
自来水的生产和供应	Water Production and Supply	1		89169		22203	17118

MAIN INDICATORS FOR LOCAL LARGE AND MEDIUM INDUSTRIAL ENTERPRISES WITH INDEPENDENT ACCOUNTING SYSTEM(BY SECTOR)

(10000 yuan)

工业销售产值(当年价格) Sales Value of Industry (at current price)	出口交货值 Delivery Value of Exports	全部从业人员年平均人数(人) Average Number of Employment (person)	资产负债 Assets and Liabilities						
			流动资产合计 Circulating Assets	应收帐款净额 Accounts Receivable	存货 Stock	产成品 Finished Products	流动资产平均余额 Average Balance of Circulating Assets	长期投资 Long-time Investment	固定资产合计 Fixed Assets
82656	33964	29709	134345	107512	20005	11025	141227	10630	102289
9221		1420	12528	6412	4244	1166	14206	2171	20379
2349		655	4413	1477	778	651	4305	606	10100
86314		2795	30886	4084	5603	2595	35419	1051	36792
66278		5825	104347	15361	14192	4360	41108	4607	119681
342481	6334	20948	247181	42363	99615	13877	258659	92765	397687
71763	1686	939	19686	4129	5362	281	23223	2746	34164
145098	66249	28967	240139	108537	77178	47059	193585	26403	190682
62351	36740	9359	74840	21980	30409	20947	79318	7221	30252
2621	291	4027	42467	4244	7106	2853	41336	6957	26262
3862		1662	14030	2224	9997	7867	1169	1607	4917
5976		639	4399	2103	1370	951	4575	290	3205
37656		6534	76150	12336	19884	11404	73919	9558	73747
62222		6215	63935	20829	15049	3829	61693	9395	62547
35065	7469	4978	46306	16594	17773	8451	49389	4727	38389
671911	95492	33679	483651	182344	161905	86897	509182	96673	1218188
168732	12595	13174	306576	48429	128967	93532	287247	68862	125377
14909		1519	13976	2829	8491	4895	17050		22212
68512		7837	71804	20025	36480	21269	93007	7829	116888
48215		6646	71607	12157	23279	7689	72275	24167	105342
337616	6905	45010	436701	130253	139068	71081	426924	218314	503772
1339621	30978	47537	1132014	459882	251645	27790	1114380	832233	1521837
19234	39	1366	12998	5839	4616	1549	15725	1139	19635
53071	6729	6919	85879	20364	26069	13151	82177	2332	64549
137008	5078	32745	434862	101020	150321	44250	431834	45235	312231
520353	2317	27971	369507	67801	149722	58384	343993	133921	271158
472064	12922	32862	497220	207797	165052	41169	513941	216587	383881
287914	13488	27222	526032	171946	165781	60175	520102	58685	252764
903860	131729	36987	1294563	600548	278762	67488	1169606	254170	623674
62865	5547	11394	124366	27425	50634	19148	119898	23337	62479
12698	1300	2909	16235	1177	11095	5466	17484	2805	19664
64130		6730	97457	34277	2571	406	89956	3397	443584
17805		3264	10454		3233		12416	1407	53734
83980		5120	98827	7713	7395	3608	84688	3415	563466

6-11 续表 1 continued

单位：万元

项目	Item	资产		负		债	
		固定资产原价合计 Original Value of Fixed Assets	# 生产经营用 For Productive Use	累计折旧 Accumulative Depreciation	#本年折旧 Depreciation in this Year	固定资产净值年平均余额 Average Net Value of Fixed Assets	无形资产及递延资产 Intangible and Deferred Assets
煤炭采选业	Coal Mining and Dressing	159544	97807	61348	3766	99625	2683
黑色金属矿采选业	Ferrous Metals Mining and Processing	17781	17781	4860	820	12152	2236
非金属矿采选业	Nonmetal Minerals Mining and Processing	11338	10290	2678	207	9326	585
食品加工业	Food Processing	37366	31349	11431	1037	27629	788
食品制造业	Food Making	158554	78085	40753	8543	81377	18806
饮料制造业	Beverage Production	469742	438285	114391	22193	322469	34663
烟草加工业	Tabacco Processing	40947	37964	13817	2922	28414	791
纺织业	Textile Industry	283769	218399	117523	11664	167907	16704
服装及其他纤维制品制造业	Garments and Other Fiber Products	41851	35638	15991	1893	24574	2285
皮革、毛皮、羽绒及其制品业	Leather,Furs,Down and Related Products	30774	26814	7858	608	16017	2751
木材加工及竹、藤、棕、草制品业	Timber Processing,Bamboo,Cane, Palm Fiber and Straw Products	7864	5474	3417	332	371	9
家具制造业	Furniture Manufacturing	3951	3210	1836	184	2145	17
造纸及纸制品业	Papermaking and Paper Products	75487	48465	17387	2096	44857	17201
印刷业、记录煤介的复制	Printing and Record Medium Reproduced	116992	90961	31236	3491	67257	2796
文教、体育用品制造	Stationery,Educational and Sports Goods	47177	43136	15099	1772	26620	3070
化学原料及化学制品制造业	Raw Chemical Materials and Chemical Products	1526443	1413047	355578	45913	1029980	376269
医药制造业	Medical and Pharmaceutical Product	165925	106446	48072	7929	120566	14702
化学纤维制造业	Chemical Fibers	27080	25935	5195	339	22045	8764
橡胶制品业	Rubber Products	112847	91116	40799	13158	64613	14334
塑料制品业	Plastic Products	136462	89480	36161	3745	100354	14534
非金属矿物制品业	Nonmetal Mineral Products	624024	487310	197803	26197	420696	103241
黑色金属冶炼及压延加工业	Smelting and Pressing of Ferrous Metals	2028271	2026018	839714	96269	1479694	46031
有色金属冶炼及压延加工业	Smelting and Pressing of Nonferrous Metals	27249	21964	10803	779	16174	28015
金属制品业	Metal Products	75197	62352	25447	4750	49348	5670
普通机械制造业	Ordinary Machinery Manufacturing	380762	290624	129745	12312	243281	33549
专用设备制造业	Special Purposes Equipment Manufacturing	281754	212806	82353	9586	184696	17131
交通运输设备制造业	Transportation Equipment Manufacturing	474259	428228	201296	25528	260847	10618
电气机械及器材制造	Electric Equipment and Machinery	361787	221227	125343	11399	175956	28191
电子及通信设备制造	Electronic and Telecommunications	859492	689673	292729	49651	527255	94505
仪器仪表及文化、办公用机械制造业	Instruments,Meters,Cultural and Official Machine Manufacturing	90370	66403	36944	2338	55384	5300
其他制造业	Other Manufacturing	25944	23088	7477	849	18844	3817
电力、蒸汽、热水的生产和供应业	Electricity,Steam and Hot Water Production and Supply	556651	478747	116330	18409	332972	1286
煤气生产和供应业	Gas Production and Supply	73563	67794	23472	2717	47947	
自来水的生产和供应	Water Production and Supply	713744	700288	159839	32836	469705	834

6-11 续表 2 continued

(10000 yuan)

Assets and Liabilities										
#无形资产 Intangible Assets	其他资产 Other Assets	资产总计 Total Assets	流动负债合计 Liquid Liabilities	短期借款 Short-time Loans	长期负债合计 Long-term Liabilities	长期借款 Long-time Loans	负债合计 Total Liabilities	所有者权益 Ownership Interest	实收资本 Contributed Capital	国家资本 State
		249946	108274	39938	40907	35550	149181	100765	60025	60025
		37314	12849	9438	9883	5000	22732	14582	7839	7839
		15704	3624	943	2021	100	5645	10059	2927	
366	317	69833	38098	14157	4465	4129	42563	27270	24803	16907
7096	1234	248674	90926	58042	19922	18658	110847	137827	241336	19062
29894	1641	773936	222600	108686	45878	36400	286709	487227	302803	134238
544		57386	-793		7414	7466	6621	50765	40211	40211
3453		473927	294667	119489	82272	62249	376939	96988	91093	12090
1767	691	115289	50260	21301	14646	6020	64907	50382	38992	5065
		78436	47439	16956	6014	5123	53453	24983	13655	
		20563	16190	370	700	30	16890	3673	2941	
		7911	3815	2101	1743		5558	2353	1573	
8308	1649	178304	95677	48225	34084	19400	129762	48542	54415	10940
2351	528	139201	57429	15855	23042	18939	80471	58731	60360	10465
1641	166	92658	56983	32686	7357	7100	64340	28318	16463	11031
18180	66	2174847	667271	323748	1008816	957508	1676112	498735	274760	179736
11944	43688	559205	224711	143429	40769	25689	265480	293725	106920	22280
		44951	17505	8554	24007	24021	41511	3440	5607	
11508		210856	135538	50229	58836	54366	194374	16483	21708	
1594	-21	215629	110155	41538	38232	36559	148387	67242	51446	2100
15676	4638	1266666	481050	152965	280610	234844	761687	504979	330068	154722
37267	-13649	3518467	1026782	709332	608606	558041	1635388	1883079	569457	541669
17		61787	15679	7314	40751	38525	56431	5357	4339	4339
3841	717	159147	109536	50983	13004	11961	122969	36178	46714	12434
13800	639	826516	405590	144691	160830	136198	566420	260095	196839	63979
4193	2991	794709	334322	111755	48856	30899	383203	411506	139121	12700
5513	2456	1110762	476721	188737	146563	133021	623284	487478	357950	37411
7947	1113	866784	521618	262807	84816	63494	606433	260351	171682	17388
35319	15112	2282025	1172623	520297	315364	232871	1495959	786066	483773	30739
2480	647	216128	93698	31334	25284	12789	118982	97146	77193	36172
2611	914	43435	18202	6903	6282	5194	25597	17838	14308	4795
1077		545724	50541	12300	31271	30294	81812	463912	369930	342005
		65596	8056		145		8202	57394	52209	52209
548		666542	22261		120314	120314	142575	523967	423055	423055

6-11 续表 3 continued

单位：万元

项目	Item	资产负债 Assets and Liabilities 集体资本 Collective	法人资本 Institutional Units	个人资本 Individuals	港澳台资本 Hongkong, Macao and Taiwan	外商资本 Foreign
煤炭采选业	Coal Mining and Dressing					
黑色金属矿采选业	Ferrous Metals Mining and Processing					
非金属矿采选业	Nonmetal Minerals Mining and Processing		2927			
食品加工业	Food Processing	266	3826			3804
食品制造业	Food Making	64	43627	88	13527	164969
饮料制造业	Beverage Production		44160	14400	19446	90561
烟草加工业	Tabacco Processing					
纺织业	Textile Industry	7076	69231		2361	335
服装及其他纤维制品制造业	Garments and Other Fiber Products	8693	22022	333		2879
皮革、毛皮、羽绒及其制品业	Leather,Furs,Down and Related Products	6426	7230			
木材加工及竹、藤、棕、草制品业	Timber Processing,Bamboo,Cane, Palm Fiber and Straw Products		2941			
家具制造业	Furniture Manufacturing		1333		240	
造纸及纸制品业	Papermaking and Paper Products	3101	5464	30	10458	24423
印刷业、记录媒介的复制	Printing and Record Medium Reproduced	3251	15871		2062	28710
文教、体育用品制造	Stationery,Educational and Sports Goods	3654	1471		306	
化学原料及化学制品制造业	Raw Chemical Materials and Chemical Products	3899	64646	10617		15862
医药制造业	Medical and Pharmaceutical Product	340	38489	19460		26351
化学纤维制造业	Chemical Fibers		5607			
橡胶制品业	Rubber Products	1407	20300			
塑料制品业	Plastic Products	3218	37449			8679
非金属矿物制品业	Nonmetal Mineral Products	11970	134869	23	1041	27444
黑色金属冶炼及压延加工业	Smelting and Pressing of Ferrous Metals	4338	21335	1757	358	
有色金属冶炼及压延加工业	Smelting and Pressing of Nonferrous Metals					
金属制品业	Metal Products	8207	11144		10550	4378
普通机械制造业	Ordinary Machinery Manufacturing	6312	62698	320		63530
专用设备制造业	Special Purposes Equipment Manufacturing	16	100431	25400		573
交通运输设备制造业	Transportation Equipment Manufacturing	13315	249060	5299	11463	41403
电气机械及器材制造	Electric Equipment and Machinery	22635	85936			45723
电子及通信设备制造	Electronic and Telecommunications	28749	273656	845	6106	143677
仪器仪表及文化、办公用机械制造业	Instruments,Meters,Cultural and Official Machine Manufacturing	474	24221	660	15338	328
其他制造业	Other Manufacturing	3914	1200		493	3907
电力、蒸汽、热水的生产和供应业	Electricity,Steam and Hot Water Production and Supply		27925			
煤气生产和供应业	Gas Production and Supply					
自来水的生产和供应	Water Production and Supply					

6-11 续表 4 continued

(10000 yuan)

损益及分配 Profits,Loss and Distribution										
产品销售收入 Sales Revenue	产品销售成本 Cost of Sales	产品销售费用 Expenses of Sales	产品销售税金及附加 Sales Tax and Extra Charges	产品销售利润 Sales Profits	管理费用 Overhead Cost	税金 Taxes	财产保险费 Premium of Property	劳动待业保险费 Premium for Employment Insurance	财务费用 Financial Expenses	利息支出 Expenses of Interest
68905	36902	12839	542	18622	24243	557		15692	2346	2626
9640	6857	185	87	2511	533	61	6	227	809	809
2478	2054	9	23	392	476	14	3	113	62	40
86628	78728	1322	50	6528	3602	190	73	461	872	878
66430	50954	16145	159	-829	15699	414	70	1669	5428	1697
353173	223936	30000	43840	55397	32247	792	631	1813	2549	5430
71613	33652	753	30279	6929	5397	70	226	712	199	261
138887	115361	3286	446	19794	25450	1295	410	6561	9896	10377
59122	47298	7089	75	4661	6528	181	282	1090	1393	919
2414	2657	311	2	-556	5933	158	169	1751	2556	2537
2848	2198		11	640	1337	58	4	241	464	464
6093	5007	106	23	957	1029	14	16	272	109	113
40202	34582	4693	23	904	11478	432	24	2068	2517	1616
64642	46998	957	230	16457	12303	308	174	1311	1542	947
44044	35472	1665	171	6735	6772	245	84	1487	2066	2121
647096	552213	15264	4979	74639	64286	2064	2503	12753	32530	33919
330286	240296	30878	1561	57550	39917	648	855	4791	7350	8950
16420	14843	343	91	1142	1450	31	-6	498	1123	1121
74243	63362	2159	3365	5357	8294	218	140	2309	15588	10833
50624	41894	2338	73	6319	10712	486	225	2204	2863	3042
352138	287014	14503	1563	49058	49107	1699	416	12495	15833	15851
1352099	1177527	8296	9491	156786	69893	5379	41	21155	77168	82608
18986	16571	202	28	2185	1943	76	33	558	558	562
55490	47269	2621	35	5565	9061	277	51	1297	2551	2546
172975	148573	5860	617	17926	41796	1660	354	11126	2423	5171
493271	408060	16233	1917	67060	45655	4040	446	10745	6927	7648
526710	474793	12573	11658	27686	55399	1740	675	8701	15391	15178
291573	238989	17029	559	34996	45961	1322	736	8593	14022	10879
1084823	888028	37196	1032	158568	108165	4271	1305	13950	48896	46296
63913	53866	3975	129	5943	14668	449	137	2940	1451	2058
13147	10699	950	269	1229	4855	118	74	1011	1002	462
92163	14602	83202	462	-6103	11082	780	10	1610	123	493
23458	30996			-7538	4497	188	140	244	-74	
72201	92865		375	-21039	8418	781		2120	-416	-582

6-11 续表 5 continued

单位：万元

项 目	Item	损益及分配 Profits,Loss and Distribution 营业利润 Operating Profits	投资收益 Investment Income	补贴收入 Subsidy Income	营业外收入 Out-business Income	营业外支出 Out-business Expenditure	利润总额 Total Profits
煤炭采选业	Coal Mining and Dressing	-6351	228	11733	414	4298	2029
黑色金属矿采选业	Ferrous Metals Mining and Processing	569	1		54	561	63
非金属矿采选业	Nonmetal Minerals Mining and Processing	-128	11		127	11	
食品加工业	Food Processing	2060	106	900	184	91	3168
食品制造业	Food Making	-20335	344	61	1077	764	-19175
饮料制造业	Beverage Production	23043	4996		10635	7116	33649
烟草加工业	Tabacco Processing	1530	1253		3	2	2612
纺织业	Textile Industry	-11102	276	344	24639	18725	-1357
服装及其他纤维制品制造业	Garments and Other Fiber Products	-299	3	45	396	229	-83
皮革、毛皮、羽绒及其制品业	Leather,Furs,Down and Related Products	-2614	-376		3360	293	110
木材加工及竹、藤、棕、草制品业	Timber Processing,Bamboo,Cane, Palm Fiber and Straw Products	-1105	85		308	1	-713
家具制造业	Furniture Manufacturing	176	54			32	198
造纸及纸制品业	Papermaking and Paper Products	-11505	4661		3343	317	-3633
印刷业、记录煤介的复制	Printing and Record Medium Reproduced	4194	767	40	3313	1113	7200
文教、体育用品制造	Stationery,Educational and Sports Goods	-387	897		918	182	1246
化学原料及化学制品制造业	Raw Chemical Materials and Chemical Products	-17983	4902	22660	3392	2567	11123
医药制造业	Medical and Pharmaceutical Product	12582	1256	1656	2017	1209	16451
化学纤维制造业	Chemical Fibers	-1196			17	41	-1220
橡胶制品业	Rubber Products	-15807	78	1333	286	71	-30612
塑料制品业	Plastic Products	-5327	90	235	7428	969	1505
非金属矿物制品业	Nonmetal Mineral Products	-10721	2816	4635	5408	2067	438
黑色金属冶炼及压延加工业	Smelting and Pressing of Ferrous Metals	14048	27219		4200	3254	42224
有色金属冶炼及压延加工业		38	80	50	95	1	261
金属制品业	Metal Products	-3752	-14	5	335	481	-3906
普通机械制造业	Ordinary Machinery Manufacturing	-16723	45	746	34928	6570	3384
专用设备制造业	Special Purposes Equipment Manufacturing	19032	4948	5016	22564	12984	38970
交通运输设备制造业	Transportation Equipment Manufacturing	-35718	7047	211	18642	1303	-9410
电气机械及器材制造	Electric Equipment and Machinery	-15267	737	112	8976	1677	2756
电子及通信设备制造	Electronic and Telecommunications	33235	21895	221	6221	2434	58136
仪器仪表及文化、办公用机械制造业	Instruments,Meters,Cultural and Official Machine Manufacturing	-1265	907		1326	877	100
其他制造业	Other Manufacturing	-2341			1009	237	-1510
电力、蒸汽、热水的生产和供应业	Electricity,Steam and Hot Water Production and Supply	-16065	40	18690	58	1866	1278
煤气生产和供应业	Gas Production and Supply	-11591	58	11810	40	71	246
自来水的生产和供应	Water Production and Supply	-27965	157	29015	73	111	1168

6-11 续表 6 continued

(10000 yuan)

				工资，福利费，增值税 Wages,Welfares and Added Value Tax					
应交所得税 Income Tax Payable	应付利润 Profits Payable	亏损企业亏损额 Total Lossing of Loss-making Enterprises	利税总额 Total Pre-tax Profits	本年应付工资总额 Total Wags Payable	本年应付福利费总额 Total Welfares Payable	本年应交增值税 Added Value Tax	本年进项税额 Tax Include in Purchasing Cost	本年销项税额 Tax Include in Sales Cost	工业中间投入合计 Intermediate Input of Industry
			6375	21488	6716	3804	11429	15717	30157
17			407	1154	126	257	1578	1787	6294
			159	471	66	136		136	1180
1139	2371	603	4564	3403	425	1346	4783	6055	76640
609	8	20936	-14075	9425	1043	4941	6253	11208	54080
6813	16159	14036	106064	25763	5961	28575	32228	59589	227887
652			40978	2294	183	8087	5121	13208	32582
813	2147	5379	5014	25415	3902	5925	16202	21462	106103
178	163	1258	1934	8442	1638	1942	4229	6178	45322
6		54	72	2736	354	-40	686	486	4441
		713	-619	938	131	83	411	494	3157
35	167		595	933	242	374	678	1052	3924
43		3735	-2186	6388	1222	1424	5505	6967	32288
1198	1134	1684	12539	8805	1590	5109	8005	13002	34852
517	586	325	3335	5524	853	1918	6810	8469	24754
3490	2659	5110	46448	44221	6475	30346	80910	110274	567323
5690	-269	2177	31200	19655	3927	13188	37757	49939	108613
		1220	-216	1655	232	913	2324	3224	13344
		30612	-22968	8159	1190	4279	9274	13486	66329
170	3	720	3542	6047	965	1964	6956	8481	43236
1789	1015	7421	21862	51387	7610	19861	38379	58797	264902
-963	54	4423	147892	90628	12180	96177	144676	236680	1129833
			653	947	-167	364	3190	3544	16269
259	-12	4913	-1927	6662	1050	1944	7192	9074	46525
364	5238	2989	9884	32716	5542	5883	25061	30220	99645
11166	6056	1615	62714	30800	4664	21827	130117	148954	440253
986	-199	15207	19771	44397	13005	17523	68792	86862	408345
1229	630	5272	13068	32998	4946	9753	39259	48981	245021
9873	106215	18530	97436	66066	14986	38268	117361	149100	677522
925	776	2378	2978	11701	1683	2749	6749	9262	43586
46		1789	-799	2884	428	442	1881	2212	8872
38	103		6166	8394	1173	4426	9172	13397	43708
			302	4283	600	56	3299	3354	5011
			5791	7659	1067	4248	1697	5263	76299

6-12 规模以上工业企业主要经济指标

单位：万元

项　目 Item		企业单位个数（个） Number of Enterprises (unit)	工业总产值（当年价格） Gross Output Value of Industry (at current prices)	# 新产品产值 Value of New Products
总　计	**Total**	**5225**	**19999706**	**3523503**
在总计中：	**Of Total:**			
中央企业	Central Enterprises	662	7161195	2225932
地方企业	Local Enterprises	4563	12838511	1297570
工业系统	Industry System	782	6373820	908336
非工业系统	Non-Industry System	643	1291738	2866
区县工业	Industry of District and County	2798	4207226	144614
其　他	Others	340	965727	241755
在总计中：	**Of Total:**			
内资企业	Domestic Investment Enterprises	4285	12178080	2257959
国有企业	State-Owned	2829	7692409	1557770
集体企业	Collective Owned	955	1681801	87358
股份合作企业	Share Holding Cooperative	102	178993	13750
联营企业	Joint Owned	71	256378	10051
有限责任公司	Limited-Liability Company	149	1235075	204937
股份有限公司	Share Holding Company	64	894203	353047
私营企业	Private Owned	115	239222	31053
港澳台商投资企业	Hongkong,Macao and Taiwan Funded Enterprises	372	2022787	304659
港澳台合资经营	Joint Venture	293	1136066	47378
港澳台合作经营	Cooperative	16	33663	797
港澳台商独资企业	Hongkong,Macao and Taiwan Enterprises	59	844749	256483
港澳台商投资股份有限公司	Hongkong,Macao and Taiwan Funded Share Holing Company	4	8309	
外商投资企业	Foreign Funded Enterprises	568	5795789	960879
中外合资经营	Joint Venture	434	5101961	827844
中外合作经营	Cooperative	23	140675	1264
外资(独资)企业	Foreign Enterprises	104	402086	120395
外商投资股份有限公司	Foreign Funded Share Holding Company	7	151066	11377
在总计中：	**Of Total:**			
农村企业	Rural Enterprises	1162	2155506	10816
在总计中：	**Of Total:**			
国有绝对控股企业	State-owned Absolute Holding Enterprises	3212	13393357	2713173
国有相对控股企业	State-owned Relative Holding Enterpeises	97	1262859	71203

注：规模以上工业企业是指年销售收入在 500 万元及以上的工业企业。

MAIN INDICATORS FOR INDUSTRIAL ENTERPRISES IN SCALE

(10000 yuan)

工业总产值 (1990 年不变价格) Gross Output Value of Industry (at 1990 constant prices)	工业销售产值 Sales Value of Industry	# 出口交货值 Delivery Value of Exports	从业人员平均人数(人) Average Number of employment (person)	工业增加值 Added Value of Industry
19420577	**19458384**	**1346811**	**1242186**	**5822116**
7491800	7104889	324127	211493	2149996
11928777	12353495	1022684	1030693	3672120
6188344	6196480	581819	486970	1763112
817032	1268699	16644	90025	392537
3960035	3996914	365246	364640	1246076
963367	891402	58975	89058	270394
10160065	11798264	542176	987345	3657385
5917619	7546001	255597	615095	2470318
1610120	1581734	124186	187026	479311
164252	164395	7415	18097	59688
267495	239933	29449	28247	65132
1070642	1173621	105506	90182	300850
902975	874273	18658	36741	237566
226962	218308	1366	11957	44521
2665003	1982431	159047	120859	425191
1120992	1091604	125590	56452	273429
31014	35002	5380	54620	9385
1504912	848601	28077	9365	139006
8085	7224		422	3370
6592517	5675122	645588	133787	1736489
5967095	5009902	548726	107244	1507407
139909	125977	13679	3597	41794
389977	389593	58688	14023	125937
95537	149650	24495	8923	61350
2037072	2004060	240219	199532	676942
12923906	13034089	759443	820988	3845213
1282755	1337842	110480	80224	401060

Note: Industrial enterprises in scale refer to the enterprises which sales revenue at 5 million yuan and above.

6-12 续表 1 continued

单位：万元

项目	Item	企业单位个数（个） Number of Enterprises (unit)	工业总产值（当年价格） Gross Output Value of Industry (at current prices)	# 新产品产值 Value of New Products
在总计中：	**Of Total:**			
轻工业	Light Industry	2555	5409486	290584
以农产品为原料	Using Farm Products as Raw Material	1684	3510961	113770
以非农产品为原料	Using Non-Farm Products as Raw Material	871	1898524	176813
重工业	Heavy Industry	2670	14590220	3232919
采掘工业	Excavation	54	152816	
原料工业	Raw Material	386	4802882	278270
加工工业	Processing	2230	9634523	2954649
在总计中：	**Of Total:**			
大型企业	Large Enterprises	206	8265181	1439000
中型企业	Medium Enterprises	266	2445509	1098120
小型企业	Small Enterprises	4753	9289016	986383
在总计中：	**Of Total:**			
煤炭采选业	Coal Mining and Dressing	16	111760	
黑色金属矿采选业	Ferrous Metals Mining and Dressing	6	15823	
有色金属矿采选业	Nonferrous Metals Mining and Dressing	3	1937	
非金属矿采选业	Nonmetal Minerals Mining and Dressing	29	23296	
食品加工业	Food Processing	251	593310	38523
食品制造业	Food Making	229	502302	14602
饮料制造业	Beverage Production	87	617756	4210
烟草加工业	Tobacco Processing	3	69931	1547
纺织业	Textile Industry	150	362660	19621
服装及其他纤维制品制造业	Garments and Other Fiber Products	246	422293	3495
皮革、毛皮、羽绒及其制品业	Leather,Furs,Down and Related Products	40	46314	
木材加工及竹藤、棕、草制品业	Timber Processing,Bamboo Cane,Palm Fiber and Straw Products	44	37423	
家具制造业	Furniture Manufacturing	102	104389	
造纸及纸制品业	Papermaking and Paper Products	101	150784	
印刷业，记录媒介的复制	Printing and Record Medium Reproduced	355	392196	1072

6-12 续表 2 continued

(10000 yuan)

工业总产值（1990 年不变价格） Gross Output Value of Industry (at 1990 constant prices)	工业销售产值 Sales Value of Industry	# 出口交货值 Delivery Value of Exports	从业人员平均人数（人） Average Number of employment (person)	工业增加值 Added Value of Industry
4887190	5213181	583843	454267	1765099
2857574	3379350	399432	309575	1127343
2029616	1833831	184411	144692	637755
14533387	14245203	762968	787919	4057016
82311	144481	34164	40466	87470
3265252	4727429	141927	215734	1459001
11185824	9373293	586877	531719	2510548
7705206	8006489	344755	501358	2198357
2438283	2402455	179695	136074	688878
9277089	9049441	822361	604754	2934880
48823	107910	34164	36263	64797
8899	15767		2322	4996
1937	1907		136	-1301
22653	18897		1942	-2844
413705	585761	3833	23822	79436
378706	482653	16188	37943	113462
539262	598841	6891	31192	218203
45010	71763	1686	939	45312
340494	355804	143493	58110	86256
359703	404861	174396	63077	87303
36786	45255	10546	8057	3408
30024	35718	1250	4684	-14858
101375	103651	16013	11746	-38145
140524	149685	5071	15937	15105
281302	352603	397	43232	138893

6-12 续表 3 continued

单位：万元

项 目	Item	企业单位个数（个） Number of Enterprises (unit)	工业总产值（当年价格） Gross Output Value of Industry (at current prices)	# 新产品产值 Value of New Products
文教体育用品制造业	Stationery,Educational and Sports Goods	60	98362	14826
石油加工及炼焦业	Petroleum Processing and Coking Products	30	1435685	174767
化学原料及化学制品	Raw Chemical Materials and Chemical Product	353	1067765	50576
医药制造业	Medical and Pharmaceutical Products	117	431695	54963
化学纤维制造业	Chemical Fibers	16	37406	233
橡胶制品业	Rubber Products	42	126823	8670
塑料制品业	Plastic Products	185	207067	4603
非金属矿物制品	Nonmetal Mineral Products	338	869918	65071
黑色金属冶炼及压延加工业	Smelting and Pressing of Ferrous Metals	27	1483601	57634
有色金属冶炼及压延加工业	Smelting and Pressing of Nonferrous Metals	46	83403	11718
金属制品业	Metal Products	395	457991	3897
普通机械制造业	Ordinary Machinery Manufacturing	315	397072	40964
专用设备制造业	Special Purposes Equipment Manufacturing	310	915955	285843
交通运输设备制造业	Transportation Equipment Manufacturing	403	1114203	337728
武器弹药制造业	Weapon and Ammunition Manufacturing	6	70661	17336
电气机械及器材制造	Electric Equipment and Machinery	286	801486	187662
电子及通信设备制造	Electronic and Telecommunications	311	5603997	2008558
仪器仪表及文化、办公用机械制造	Instruments,Meters, Cultural and official Machine	163	338842	110442
其他制造业	Other Manufacturing	107	120091	2360
电力、蒸汽、热水的生产和供应业	Electricity,Steam and Hot Water Production and Supply	36	685535	2580
煤气生产和供应	Gas Production and Supply	6	74746	
自来水的生产和供应	Tap Water Production and Supply	11	125230	

6-12 续表 4 continued

(10000 yuan)

工业总产值(1990年不变价格) Gross Output Value of Industry (at 1990 constant prices)	工业销售产值 Sales Value of Industry	# 出口交货值 Delivery Value of Exports	从业人员平均人数(人) Average Number of employment (person)	工业增加值 Added Value of Industry
81416	91262	16630	10471	19298
889095	1418314	12570	41501	387072
1071446	1036814	97715	107624	219409
476375	409703	28882	28848	207833
54644	35397	62	6024	1719
144760	123537	6142	12941	17526
212423	200407	10493	18536	-36449
712141	829493	23532	101655	179292
1030877	1461214	31878	63157	323732
80916	82304	3746	6282	4954
461868	429139	25170	42226	22821
377007	395195	30191	65325	75272
888369	904667	8123	72497	209161
982558	1067525	18498	103707	234375
54770	69185	2951	11959	19019
849797	773259	22699	58659	173409
7511702	5510728	559719	77428	1413197
342966	291920	23083	26078	101554
126223	118186	10800	13278	24579
231808	684717		29585	415319
38356	74746		8386	61326
51862	119597		6545	31315

6-13 个体经营工业主要指标
MAIN INDICATORS ON INDIVIDUAL ENTERPRISES

单位：万元 (10000 yuan)

项　　目	Item	企　业 单位数 (个) Number of Enterprise (unit)	从业人员 年末人数 (人) Employment (year-end) (person)	工业总产值 (当年价格) Gross Output Value of Industry (at current prices)	上缴税金 Taxes Turned Over	自有资金 Self-own Capital
总　　计	**Total**	**13188**	**76485**	**456497**	**12850**	**83593**
在总计中：	**Of Total:**					
轻 工 业	Light Industry	10122	55532	310327	9742	57585
重 工 业	Heavy Industry	3066	20953	146170	3108	26008
在总计中：	**Of Total:**					
城镇个体工业	UrbanIndividualEnterprises	2437	7297	42376	1967	6024
农村个体工业	RuralIndividualEnterprises	10751	69188	414120	10883	77569

6-14 大中型工业企业按销售收入排序
ARRANGING IN SALES REVENUE ORDER OF LARGE AND MEDIUM INDUSTRIAL ENTERPRISES

单位：万元 (10000 yuan)

企业名称	Enterprise	序号 No.	销售收入 Sales Revenue
中国石化集团北京燕山石油化工有限公司	Beijing Yanshan Petrochemical Group Co.,Ltd	1	1308625.7
首钢总公司	Shougang Group	2	1264766.9
北京北大方正集团公司	Beijing Peking University Founder Group Crop.	3	841416.6
联想（北京）有限公司	LEGEND(Beijing) Group Co.,Ltd	4	767228.9
中国华北电力集团公司(在京单位)	NORTH China Power Group Co.	5	406766.3
北京化学工业集团有限责任公司	Beijing Chemical Industry Group Corp.	6	376463.8
北京松下彩色显像管有限公司	Beijing National Color Kinescope Co.,Ltd	7	307356.0
北汽福田车辆股份有限公司	Beiqifutian Auto Corp.	8	284434.5
北京国际交换系统有限公司	Beijing International Switching Corp.	9	255380.9
中国北京同仁堂集团公司	Tongrentang Group Co.	10	220170.4
北京吉普汽车有限公司	Beijing Jeep Corp.	11	200143.9
北京燕京啤酒集团公司	Beijing Yanjing Beer Group Corp.	12	184450.4
北京建筑材料集团有限责任公司	Beijing Building Materials Group Corp.	13	179520.9
北京邮电通信设备厂	Beijing Post&Telecom Equipment Factory	14	173027
中国石化长城高级润滑油公司	China Petrochemical Great Wall Hi-Grade Lubricant Co.	15	118240.4
北京化二股份有限公司	Beijing Huaer Co.,Ltd	16	95385.9
北京牡丹电子集团公司	Beijing Peony Electronics Group Co.	17	93579.7
长峰科技工业集团公司	CHINA ChangFeng Science Technology Industry Group Corp.	18	85353.1
北京福田车辆股份有限公司怀柔车辆厂	Beijing Futian Auto Corp.Huairou Auto Factory	19	84522.9
北京汽车摩托车联合制造公司	Beijing Automobile & Motorcycle Union Manufacturing Co.	20	84455.4
清华同方股份有限公司	Tsinghua TongFang CO.,LTD	21	84194.7
北京市热力公司	Beijing Thermal Power Corp.	22	80172.7
北京东方电子集团股份有限公司	Beijing Orient Electronics Group CO.,LTD.	23	78512.3
北京大唐发电股份有限公司	Beijing Datang Electric Power Co.,Ltd	24	74316.6
北京市自来水集团有限责任公司	Beijing Running Water Group Corp.	25	72201.1
北京市客车总厂	Beijing Coach General Factory	26	71805.1
北京卷烟厂	Beijing Tobacco Factory	27	71613.2
北京四通集团公司	Beijing Stone Group Co.	28	68906.0
北京矿务局	Beijing Mining Ministry	29	68904.6
北京ＪＶＣ电子产业有限公司	Beijng JVC Electronics Industrial Co.,Ltd.	30	68200.2
北京轻型汽车有限公司	Beijing Light Automobile Co., Ltd	31	67928.6
北京京棉集团有限责任公司	Beijing jingmian Group Corp.	32	64824.2
北京市石景山热电厂	Beijing Shijingshan Thermal Power Supply Factory	33	62667.6
北京松下电子部品有限公司	Beijing Matsushita Electronics Components Co.,Ltd.	34	62438.9
北京首钢宝生带钢厂	Beijing Shougang Posheng Strip Co.,Ltd.	35	61114.3
北京可口可乐饮料有限公司	Beijing Coca-Cola Beverage Co.,Ltd.	36	60682.3
北京印钞厂	Beijing Printing Bill Factory.	37	55955.9
首都航天机械公司	Capital Aviation Machinery Co.	38	55333
北新建材（集团）有限公司	Beijing New Building Materials Co.,Ltd	39	54007.9
北内集团总公司	Beinei Group Corp.	40	53745.3
北京二七车辆厂	Beijing Erqi Auto Factory.	41	50277
北京市顺义区肉类联合加工厂	Beijing Shunyi District Meat United Processing Factory.	42	47946.8
中国大恒（集团）公司	China Daheng (Group) Corp.	43	47201.1
北京北方车辆制造厂	Beijing North Auto Factory.	44	43796.8
北人印刷机械股份有限公司	Beiren Printing mechanic Corp.	45	42722.6
北京开关厂	Beijing Switching Factory.	46	42011.6
北京市汽车修理公司	Beijing Automobile Repair Company	47	41276.7
北京恩布拉科雪花压缩机有限公司	Beijing Embraco Snowflake Compressor Company Led.	48	40470.7
清华紫光（集团）总公司	Tsinghua ZiGuang (Group) Corp.	49	39878.2
北京轮胎厂(北京首创轮胎有限责任公司)	Beijing Tire Factory(Beijing Capital Tire CO.,Ltd.)	50	37425.6

6-14 续表 continued

单位：万元 (10000 yuan)

企 业 名 称	Enterprise	序号 No.	销售收入 Sales Revenue
北京星海乐器有限责任公司	Beijing XingHai Musical Instruments Company Ltd.	51	36567.4
北京市牛栏山酒厂	Beijing Niulanshan Wine Factory.	52	34641.2
北京红星酿酒集团公司	Beijing Red Star Wine-Marking Group Company.	53	32515.8
北京二七机车厂	Beijing Erqi Auto Factory.	54	31508.0
北京电力设备总厂	Beijing Power Equipment Group.	55	31241.5
北京四通松下电工有限公司	Beijing STONE Matsushita Electric Works Ltd.	56	31171.2
北京双鹤药业股份有限公司	Beijing Double-crane Medicine CO.,LTD	57	30794.2
北京煤矿机械厂	Beijing Coal Mining Machinery Factory.	58	29319.0
北京顺美服装股份有限公司	Beijing Smart Garments CO.,LTD.	59	28969.0
北京市顺义宏利钢管有限公司	Beijing Shunyi Hongli Steel Tube Ltd.	60	25523.3
北京玻璃集团公司	Beijing Glass Group Co.	61	24833.8
北京古桥电器公司	Beijing GuQiao Electric Co.	62	24266.2
北京亚洲双合盛五星啤酒有限公司	Beijing Asia ShuangHeSheng Five Star Beer CO.,LTD.	63	24139.3
北京市三露厂	CHINA Beijing Sanlu Factory	64	23925.5
北京市液化石油气公司	Beijing Liquefied Petroleum Gas Company	65	23458.0
拜耳医药保健有限公司	Bayer Healthcare Company LTD.	66	22353.0
北京化工实验厂	Beijing Chemical Engineering Experimental Plant	67	22044.9
北京兆维电子(集团)有限责任公司	Beijing C&W Electronics(Group) CO.,LTD.	68	21830.8
北京健力宝太平洋包装制品有限公司	Beijing Jianlibao Pacific	69	21504.8
北京北化精细化学品有限责任公司	Beijing Beihua Fine Chemicals CO.,Ltd.	70	21358.0
北京电视配件三厂	Beijing 3RD TV Parts Factory.	71	20394.6
北京第一机床厂	Beijing 1ST Machine Tool Factory.	72	20261.9
北京爱立信通信系统有限公司	Beijing Ericsson Communication System CO.,Ltd.	73	20233.7
北京万东医疗装备股份有限公司	Beijing Wandong Medical Equipment CO.,Ltd	74	19688.0
北京三环亚太啤酒有限公司	Beijing Three Ring Asia Pacific Beer CO.,LTD.	75	19567.9
北京敬业电工集团	Beijing JingYe Electric Group.	76	19278.1
北京雪莲羊绒有限公司	Beijing Snow_Lotus Cashmere Co.,Ltd.	77	19017.3
北京邮电电话设备厂	Beijing P&T Telephone Equipment Factory	78	18971.9
北京起重机器厂	Beijing Crane Factory.	79	18865.9
北京市电机总厂	Beijing General Electrical Machinery Factory.	80	18601.4
邮电部北京邮票厂	Beijing Postage Stamp Printing Flouse.	81	17833.4
丰台桥梁工厂	Fengtai Bridge Factory	82	17555.0
北京京海集团公司	Beijing Jinghai Group Corp.	83	17309.9
北京第三制药厂	Beijing 3RD Pharmaceutical Factory.	84	17299.8
北京市东方罗门哈斯有限公司	Beijing Eastern Tohm&Haas CO.,Ltd.	85	17222.2
北京重型电机厂	Beijing Heavy-duty Electrical Machinery Factory.	86	17079.6
北京市造纸包装工业公司	Beijing Paper&Package Industry Corp.	87	16554.3
北京合成纤维实验厂(北京华英纶化纤公司)	Beijing Systhetic Fibre Experimental Factory.	88	16419.7
北京广东健力宝饮料有限公司	Beijing Guangdong Jianlibao Beverage CO.,Ltd	89	16301.7
北京 ABB 电气传动系统有限公司	ABB Beijing Drive Systems Co.,Ltd.	90	16081.3
北京雪花电器集团公司	Beijing Snowflake Electric Appliance Group Corp.	91	15700.5
北人集团公司	Beiren Group Corp.	92	15549.9
北京电研高技术实业总公司	Beijing Electric Power Technology Corp.	93	15493.0
中国迅达电梯有限公司	CHINA-Schindler Elevator Co.,Ltd	94	15433.2
北京染料厂	Beijing Dyestuffs Plant	95	15260.5
国营华北光学仪器厂	North CHINA Optical Instrument Factory.	96	15076.0
北京天海工业有限公司	Beijing Tianhai Industry CO.,Ltd	97	15026.8
SMC(中国)有限公司	SMC(China) CO.,Ltd	98	14386.5
北京保温瓶工业公司	Beijing Vacuum Bottle Industry Corp.	99	14341.4
北京平谷县化工总厂	PingGu General Chemical Factory Of Beijing	100	13980.1

6-15 大中型工业企业按利税总额排序

ARRANGING IN TOTAL PRE-TAX PROFITS OF LARGE AND MEDIUM INDUSTRIAL ENTERPRISES

单位：万元 (10000 yuan)

企业名称	Enterprise	序号 No.	利税总额 Pre-tax Profits
中国石化集团北京燕山石油化工有限公司	Beijing Yanshan Petrochemical Group Co.,Ltd	1	167669.6
首钢总公司	Shougang Group	2	150106.2
中国华北电力集团公司(在京单位)	NORTH China Power Group Co.	3	115906.6
北京燕京啤酒集团公司	Beijing Yanjing Beer Group Corp.	4	77000.0
北京国际交换系统有限公司	Beijing International Switching Corp.	5	59603.0
联想（北京）有限公司	LEGEND(Beijing) Group Co.,Ltd	6	58788.3
北京卷烟厂	Beijing Tobacco Factory	7	40977.9
北汽福田车辆股份有限公司	Beiqifutian Auto Corp.	8	27988.8
北京大唐发电股份有限公司	Beijing Datang Electric Power Co.,Ltd	9	22856.8
北京松下彩色显像管有限公司	Beijing Matsushita Electronics Components Co.,Ltd.	10	22614.4
北京邮电通信设备厂	Beijing Post&Telecom Equipment Factory	11	22451.9
北京北大方正集团公司	Beijing Peking University Founder Group Crop.	12	21853.1
北京化学工业集团有限责任公司	Beijing Chemical Industry Group Corp.	13	18297.7
北京印钞厂	Beijing Printing Bill Factory.	14	16258.6
清华同方股份有限公司	Tsinghua TongFang CO.,LTD	15	16235.3
北京市牛栏山酒厂	Beijing Niulanshan Wine Factory.	16	15442.2
中国北京同仁堂集团公司	Tongrentang Group Co.	17	14410.4
北京双鹤药业股份有限公司	Beijing Double-crane Pharmaceutical CO.,Ltd	18	14336.1
北京建筑材料集团有限责任公司	Beijing Building Materials Group Corp.	19	13429.1
北京东方电子集团股份有限公司	Beijing Orient Electronics Group CO.,LTD.	20	13325.1
北京市三露厂	CHINA Beijing Sanlu Factory	21	13140.6
北京福田车辆股份有限公司怀柔车辆厂	Beijing Futian Auto Corp.Huairou Auto Factory	22	12279.6
长峰科技工业集团公司	CHINA ChangFeng Science Technology Industry Group Corp.	23	11638.6
北人印刷机械股份有限公司	Beiren Printing mechanic Corp.	24	11064.2
北京红星酿酒集团公司	Beijing Red Star Wine-Marking Group Company.	25	10910.7
清华紫光（集团）总公司	Tsinghua ZiGuang (Group) Co.	26	10289.1
北京吉普汽车有限公司	Beijing Jeep Corp.	27	9520.0
北京可口可乐饮料有限公司	Beijing Coca-Cola Beverage Co.,Ltd.	28	8327.8
中国石化长城高级润滑油公司	China Petrochemical Great Wall Hi-Grade Lubricant Co.	29	7676.0
北京化二股份有限公司	Beijing Huaer Co.,Ltd	30	6847.9
北京三环亚太啤酒有限公司	Beijing Three Ring Asia Pacific Beer CO.,LTD.	31	6509.3
北京矿务局	Beijing Mining Ministry	32	6375.1
北京万东医疗装备股份有限公司	Beijing Wandong Medical Equipment CO.,Ltd	33	6091.4
北京兆维电子(集团)有限责任公司	Beijing C&W electronics(Group) CO.,LTD.	34	5923.7
北京天坛生物制品股份有限公司	Beijing Tiantan Biological Product CO.,LTD	35	5830.6
北京市自来水集团有限责任公司	Beijing Running Water Group Corp.	36	5790.9
北京市石景山热电厂	Beijing Shijingshan Thermal Power Supply Factory	37	5732.1
北京汽车摩托车联合制造公司	Beijing Automobile & Motorcycle Union Manufacturing Co.	38	5412.9
北京市热力公司	Beijing Thermal Power Corp.	39	5408.2
北新建材（集团）有限公司	Beijing New Building Materials Co.,Ltd.	40	4963.1
SMC(中国)有限公司	SMC(China) CO.,Ltd	41	4886.3
北京日邦印刷有限公司	Beijing Ribang Printing CO.,Ltd	42	4433.3
北京京棉集团有限责任公司	Beijing jingmian Group Corp.	43	4389.0
中国大恒（集团）公司	China Daheng (Group) Corp.	44	4278.4
北京四环制药厂	Beijing Sihuan Pharmaceutical Factory.	45	4266.4
北京市顺义区肉类联合加工厂	Beijing Shunyi District Meat United Processing Factory.	46	3535.3
北京电研高技术实业总公司	Beijing Electric Power Technology Corp.	47	3458.6
北京普莱克斯实用气体有限公司	Beijing Pulaikesi Practical Gas CO.,Ltd	48	3456.7
北京开关厂	Beijing Switching Factory.	49	3304.8
北京市汽车修理公司	Beijing Automobile Repair Company	50	3290.7

6-15 续 表 continued

单位：万元 (10000 yuan)

企业名称	Enterprise	序号 No.	利税总额 Pre-tax Profits
北京星海乐器有限责任公司	Beijing XingHai Musical Instruments Company Ltd.	51	3219.8
北京恩布拉科雪花压缩机有限公司	Beijing Embraco Snowflake Compressor Company Led.	52	3125.9
北京煤矿机械厂	Beijing Coal Mining Machinery Factory.	53	2836.0
北京中融安全印务公司	Beijing Zhongrong Safety Printing Corp.	54	2831.8
北京 ABB 电气传动系统有限公司	ABB Beijing Drive Systems Co.,Ltd.	55	2712.7
北京市客车总厂	Beijing Coach General Factory	56	2685.8
北京电视配件三厂	Beijing 3RD TV Parts Factory.	57	2607.7
北京二七车辆厂	Beijing Erqi Auto Factory.	58	2554.0
北京松下电子部品有限公司	Beijing Matsushita Electronics Components Co.,Ltd.	59	2519.5
美航快速彩色印刷公司	Meihang Quick Color Printing Corp.	60	2477.1
北人集团公司	Beiren Printing Group Corp.	61	2419.0
北京晓星容器有限公司	Beijing Xiaoxing Container CO.,Ltd	62	2405.9
北京中医药大学药厂	Beijing Traditional Chinese Medicine College Pharmaceutical Factory	63	2363.8
中科实业集团（控股）公司	Zhongke Industry Group(Holding) Corp.	64	2248.8
北京丽都亚洲啤酒有限公司	Beijing Lidu Asia Beer CO.,Ltd	65	2098.4
北京市东方罗门哈斯有限公司	Beijing Eastern Tohm&Haas CO.,Ltd.	66	2093.6
北京玻璃集团公司	Beijing Glass Group Co.	67	2019.5
北京双燕商标彩印厂	Beijing Double-swallow Trademark Color Printing Factory.	68	2018.7
北京华环电子有限公司	Beijing Huahuan Electron CO.,Ltd	69	1863.6
北京日用化学二厂	Beijing 2ND Daily Chemistry Factory.	70	1830.6
邮电部北京邮票厂	Beijing Postage Stamp Printing Flouse.	71	1820.6
北京宝岛包装印刷有限公司	Beijing Baodao Packing & Printing CO.,Ltd	72	1768.4
北京电力设备总厂	Beijing Power Equipment Group.	73	1731.7
北京市王致和腐乳厂	Beijing Wangzhihe Fermented Bean Curd Factory.	74	1708.7
北京ＪＶＣ电子产业有限公司	Beijng JVC Electronics Industrial Co.,Ltd.	75	1689.3
北京豪特耐集中供热设备有限公司	Beijing Haotenai Central Heat Supply Equipment CO.,Ltd	76	1682.7
新华通讯社印刷厂	The Xinhua News Agency Printing Factory.	77	1659.1
北京平谷县化工总厂	PingGu General Chemical Factory Of Beijing	78	1586.0
北京康达电器控制设备集团公司	Beijing Kangda Electric Appliances Control Equipment Group Co.	79	1583.6
北京第一机床厂	Beijing 1ST Machine Tool Factory.	80	1556.9
北京雪莲羊绒有限公司	Beijing Snow_Lotus Cashmere Co.,Ltd.	81	1542.1
北京云岗热电厂	Beijing Yungang Heat and Power Plant	82	1522.4
北京轻联包装印刷集团公司	Beijing Light Industry Federation Packing & Printing Group Co.	83	1520.4
北京轻型汽车有限公司	Beijing Light Automobile Co., Ltd	84	1513.8
北京清华阳光能源开发有限责任公司	Beijing Tsinghua Sunshine Energy Development CO.,Ltd	85	1470.7
北京正元保健品厂	Beijing Zhengyuan Health Articles Factory	86	1467.0
北京中生生物工程高技术公司	Beijing Zhongsheng Biological Project High Technology Co.	87	1440.6
北京博飞仪器股份有限公司	Beijing Bofei Instrument CO.,Ltd	88	1403.0
北京航天石化技术装备工程公司	Beijing Hangtian Petrochemical Technological Equipment Engineering Co.	89	1375.0
北京贝利控制有限公司	Beijing Beili Control CO.,Ltd	90	1373.6
北京二七机车厂	Beijing Erqi Auto Factory.	91	1330.0
北京南常肉食机械有限公司	Beijing Nanchang Meat Machinery CO.,Ltd	92	1288.4
丰台桥梁工厂	Fengtai Bridge Factory	93	1276.0
北京铁路信号工厂	Beijing Railway Signal Factory	94	1253.0
国营华北光学仪器厂	North CHINA Optical Instrument Factory.	95	1237.6
北京精工华晖凹印制板有限公司	Beijing Jinggong Huahui Gravure Plate-making CO.,Ltd	96	1235.5
北京市机电研究院机床实验工厂	Beijing Mechanical & Electrical Research Institute Laboratory Factory	97	1210.3
北京万辉药业集团	Beijing Wanhui Pharmaceutical Group	98	1205.8
北京市紫微星实业总公司	Beijing Ziweixing Industry Corp.	99	1150.0
北京照明器材公司	Beijing Lighting Equipment Corp.	100	1148.5

6-16 大中型工业企业按总资产贡献率排序
ARRANGING IN RATIO OF PRE-TAX PROFITS TO TOTAL CAPITAL ORDER OF LARGE AND MEDIUM ENTERPRISES

单位：%　　　　(%)

企业名称	Enterprise	序号 No.	总资产贡献率 Contribution Rate of Total Assets
北京卷烟厂	Beijing Tobacco Factory	1	73.97
美航快速彩色印刷公司	Meihang Quick Color Printing Corp.	2	70.06
北京南常肉食机械有限公司	Beijing Nanchang Meat Machinery CO.,Ltd	3	63.33
北京正元保健品厂	Beijing Zhengyuan Health Articles Factory	4	57.30
联想（北京）有限公司	LEGEND(Beijing) Group Co.,Ltd	5	48.88
北京福田车辆股份有限公司怀柔车辆厂	Beijing Futian Auto Corp.Huairou Auto Factory	6	45.16
北京宝岛包装印刷有限公司	Beijing Baodao Packing & Printing CO.,Ltd	7	39.89
北京市牛栏山酒厂	Beijing NiuLanshan Wine Factory.	8	38.86
北京天坛京伟家具有限公司	Beijing Tiantan Jingwei Furniture CO.,Ltd	9	38.07
北京中生生物工程高技术公司	Beijing Zhongsheng Biological Project High Technology Co.	10	37.59
北京市三露厂	CHINA Beijing Sanlu Factory	11	35.55
北京双燕商标彩印厂	Beijing Double-swallow Trademark Color Printing Factory.	12	32.10
北京四环生物工程制品厂	Beijing Sihuan Pharmaceutical Factory.	13	32.08
北京维根制衣有限公司	Beijing Weigen Garment CO.,Ltd	14	31.33
北京华环电子有限公司	Beijing Huahuan Electron CO.,Ltd	15	31.13
北京邮电通信设备厂	Beijing Post&Telecom Equipment Factory	16	30.96
北京万东医疗装备股份有限公司	Beijing Wandong Medical Equipment CO.,Ltd	17	28.32
北京日邦印刷有限公司	Beijing Ribang Printing CO.,Ltd	18	28.04
北京中医药大学药厂	Beijing Traditional Chinese Medicine College Pharmaceutical Factory	19	26.59
北京首安工业消防工程有限公司	Beijing Shouan Industrial Fire Engineering CO.,Ltd	20	26.42
北京航天石化技术装备工程公司	Beijing Hangtian Petrochemical Technological Equipment Engineering Co.	21	26.20
北京 ABB 电气传动系统有限公司	ABB Beijing Drive Systems Co.,Ltd.	22	26.04
北京康达电器控制设备集团公司	Beijing Kangda Electric Appliances Control Equipment Group Co.	23	25.54
北京红星酿酒集团公司	Beijing Red Star Wine-Marking Group Company.	24	25.27
北京协和制药二厂	Beijing Xiehe 2ND Pharmaceutical Factory	25	23.71
北京市王致和腐乳厂	Beijing Wangzhihe Fermented Bean Curd Factory.	26	23.34
北京科化化学新技术公司	Beijing Kehua Chemical New Technology Corp.	27	22.83
中国大恒（集团）公司	China Daheng (Group) Corp.	28	22.63
北京中融安全印务公司	Beijing Zhongrong Safety Printing Corp.	29	21.44
北汽福田车辆股份有限公司	Beiqifutian Auto Corp.	30	21.16
北京双鹤药业股份有限公司	Beijing Double-crane Medicine CO.,LTD	31	20.94
北京北方生物技术研究所	Beijing North Biological Technology Research Institute	32	20.74
北京大唐发电股份有限公司	Beijing Datang Electric Power Co.,Ltd	33	20.59
北京燕京啤酒集团公司	Beijing Yanjing Beer Group Corp.	34	20.34
北京燕达皇冠盖有限公司	Beijing Yanda Huangguangai CO.,Ltd	35	20.07
北京四环制药厂	Beijing Sihuan Pharmaceutical Factory.	36	19.54
北京印钞厂	Beijing Printing Bill Factory.	37	19.10
北京照明器材公司	Beijing Lighting Equipment Corp.	38	18.60
中国中医研究院实验药厂	China Traditional Chinese Medicine Research Institute Laboratory Pharmaceutical Factory.	39	18.59
北京晓星容器有限公司	Beijing Xiaoxing Container CO.,Ltd	40	18.58
长峰科技工业集团公司	CHINA ChangFeng Science Technology Industry Group Corp.	41	17.68
北京路桥机械厂	Beijing Luqiao Machinery Factory.	42	17.65
北京市紫微星实业总公司	Beijing Ziweixing Industry Corp.	43	17.53
北京国际交换系统有限公司	Beijing International Switching Corp.	44	17.53
北京博飞仪器股份有限公司	Beijing Bofei Instrument CO.,Ltd	45	17.45
北京富通高压管件技术开发公司	Beijing Futong High-pressure Pipe Technology Development Co.	46	17.25
北京豪特耐集中供热设备有限公司	Beijing Haotenai Central Heat Supply Equipment CO.,Ltd	47	16.61
北京三环亚太啤酒有限公司	Beijing Three Ring Asia Pacific Beer CO.,LTD.	48	15.83
北京市东方罗门哈斯有限公司	Beijing Eastern Tohm&Haas CO.,Ltd.	49	15.74
北京天坛生物制品股份有限公司	Beijing Tiantan Biological Product CO.,LTD	50	15.71

6-16 续 表 continued

单位：%　　　　(%)

企 业 名 称	Enterprise	序 号 No.	总资产贡献率 Contribution Rate of Total Assets
北京精工华晖凹印制板有限公司	Beijing Jinggong Huahui Gravure Plate-making CO.,Ltd	51	15.50
北京市顺义区肉类联合加工厂	Beijing Shunyi District Meat United Processing Factory.	52	15.16
北京汇能亚澳通讯设备厂	Beijing Huineng Yaao Communication Equipment Factory	53	15.16
北京可口可乐饮料有限公司	Beijing Coca-Cola Beverage Co.,Ltd.	54	14.65
清华紫光（集团）总公司	Tsinghua ZiGuang (Group) Corp.	55	14.01
北京国际气雾剂有限公司	Beijing International Aerosol CO.,Ltd	56	13.84
经济日报印刷厂	Economic Daily Printing Factory.	57	13.54
北京清华阳光能源开发有限责任公司	Beijing Tsinghua Sunshine Energy Development CO.,Ltd	58	13.43
北京云岗热电厂	Beijing Yungang Heat and Power Plant	59	13.28
新华通讯社印刷厂	The Xinhua News Agency Printing Factory.	60	13.13
北京市礼花厂	Beijing Fireworks Display Factory	61	12.40
北京贝利控制有限公司	Beijing Beili Control CO.,Ltd	62	12.07
清华同方股份有限公司	Tsinghua TongFang CO.,LTD	63	11.93
北京市华都酿酒食品工业公司	Beijing Huadu Winery food Industry Corp.	64	11.92
北京华藤示范米厂有限公司	Beijing Huateng Demonstration Rice CO.,Ltd	65	11.52
解放军报社印刷厂	The PLA News Agency Printing Factory	66	11.48
北京普莱克斯实用气体有限公司	Beijing Pulaikesi Practical Gas CO.,Ltd	67	11.37
北京印刷二厂	Beijing 2ND Printing Factory	68	11.22
房山区双山水泥集团	Fangshan Shuangshan Cement Group	69	10.90
北京万辉药业集团第四制药厂	Beijing Wanhui Pharmaceutical Group 4TH Factory	70	10.80
北京威顿玻璃制品有限公司	Beijing Weidun Glass Products CO.,Ltd	71	10.62
北京埃姆毛纺有限公司	Beijing Aimu Woolen CO.,Ltd	72	10.46
北京电研高技术实业总公司	Beijing Electric Power Technology Corp.	73	10.40
北京平谷县化工总厂	PingGu General Chemical Factory Of Beijing	74	10.37
房山区水泥一厂	Fangshan 1ST Cement Factory	75	10.26
北京电子管厂	Beijing Electron Tube Factory	76	9.95
北京鹏翼包装制品公司	Beijing Pengyi Packing Products Corp.	77	9.90
北京中科科仪科学仪器厂	Beijing Zhongke Keyi Scientific Instrument Factory	78	9.89
北人印刷机械股份有限公司	Beiren Printing Mechanic Corp.	79	9.89
北京三联混凝土联营公司	Beijing Sanlian Concrete Joint Operation Corp.	80	9.82
中国石化集团北京燕山石油化工有限公司	Beijing Yangshan Petrochemical Group Co.,Ltd	81	9.80
密云县粮食局加工厂	Miyun County Grain Bureau Processing Plant	82	9.79
北京星海乐器有限责任公司	Beijing XinHai Musical Instruments Company Ltd.	83	9.75
北京希望电脑公司	Beijing Hope Computer Corp.	84	9.66
北京华颐中药制药厂	Beijing Huayi Traditional Chinese Medicine Factory	85	9.63
北京电视配件三厂	Beijing 3RD TV Parts Factory.	86	9.48
北京北大方正集团公司	Beijing Peking University Founder Group Crop.	87	9.47
北京铁路信号工厂	Beijing Railway Signal Factory	88	9.36
北京丽都亚洲啤酒有限公司	Beijing Lidu Asia Beer CO.,Ltd	89	9.31
北京市顺义牛栏山水泥厂	Shunyi Niulanshan Cement Factory	90	9.28
北京光华染织厂	Beijing Guanghua Dope Dyeing Factory	91	9.12
北京胶印厂	Beijing Offset Printing Factory	92	9.01
北京市顺义飞达玻璃厂	Beijing Shunyi Feida Glass Factory	93	9.00
北京维宝光盘有限公司	Beijing Weibao Disc CO.,Ltd	94	8.99
北京京城汽车车厢总厂	Beijing Jingcheng Auto Carriage General Factory	95	8.97
北京印刷三厂	Beijing 3RD Printing Factory.	96	8.94
北京市石景山热电厂	Beijing Shijingshan Thermal Power Supply Factory	97	8.86
北京煤矿机械厂	Beijing Coal Mining Machinery Factory.	98	8.79
北京制呢厂	Beijing Woolen Cloth Factory	99	8.66
北京松下彩色显像管有限公司	Beijing National Color Kinescope Co.,Ltd	100	8.47

6-17 大中型工业企业按资产总额排序
ARRANGING IN TOTAL ASSETS OF LARGE AND MEDIUM INDUSTRIAL ENTERPRISES

单位：万元 (10000 yuan)

企业名称	Enterprise	序号 No.	资产总额 Total Assets
首钢总公司	Shougang Group	1	3344132.6
中国华北电力集团公司(在京单位)	NORTH China Power Group Co.	2	2481192.2
中国石化集团北京燕山石油化工有	Beijing Yangshan Petrochemical Group Co.,Ltd	3	2030896.6
北京化学工业集团有限责任公司	Beijing Chemical Industry Group Corp.	4	1542244.9
北京建筑材料集团有限责任公司	Beijing Building Materials Group Corp.	5	715446.7
北京市自来水集团有限责任公司	Beijing Running Water Group Corp.	6	666542.0
北京市热力公司	Beijing Thermal Power Corp.	7	498502.9
北京燕京啤酒集团公司	Beijing Yanjing Beer Group Corp.	8	426526.2
北京国际交换系统有限公司	Beijing International Switching Corp.	9	414895.9
北京北大方正集团公司	Beijing Peking University Founder Group Crop.	10	381612.0
北京四通集团公司	Beijing Stone Group Co.	11	352614.5
北京松下彩色显像管有限公司	Beijing National Color Kinescope Co.,Ltd	12	288835.9
北内集团总公司	Beinei Group Corp.	13	273976.8
中国北京同仁堂集团公司	Tongrentang Group Co.	14	272880.5
联想（北京）有限公司	LEGEND(Beijing) Group Co.,Ltd	15	251429.7
北京矿务局	Beijing Mining Ministry	16	249946.3
北京吉普汽车有限公司	Beijing Jeep Corp.	17	233542.1
北京东方电子集团股份有限公司	Beijing East Electronics Group Corp.	18	230677.9
北京牡丹电子集团公司	Beijing Peony Electronics Group Co.	19	218384.8
北京京棉集团有限责任公司	Beijing jingmian Group Corp.	20	194052.5
北京汽车工业集团总公司	Beijing Automobile Industry Group Co.	21	189347.1
北京汽车摩托车联合制造公司	Beijing Automobile & Motorcycle Union Manufacturing Co.	22	187233.1
清华同方股份有限公司	Tsinghua TongFang CO.,LTD	23	185592.1
北京轻型汽车有限公司	Beijing Light Automobile Co., Ltd	24	184834.0
北新建材（集团）有限公司	Beijing New Building Materials Co.,Ltd.	25	180236.0
北京京海集团公司	Beijing Jinghai Group Corp.	26	177482.6
北京兆维电子(集团)有限责任公司	Beijing C&W electronics(Group) CO.,LTD.	27	174302.6
北京化二股份有限公司	Beijing Huaer Co.,Ltd	28	171197.7
北汽福田车辆股份有限公司	Beiqifutian Auto Corp.	29	162033.9
北京重型电机厂	Beijing Heavy-duty Electrical Machinery Factory.	30	154822.5
北京玻璃集团公司	Beijing Glass Group Co.	31	150462.5
北京市石景山热电厂	Beijing Shijingshan Thermal Power Supply Factory	32	145822.9
首都航天机械公司	Capital Aviation Machinery Co.	33	145108.0
北人集团公司	Beiren Group Corp.	34	144179.2
中国石化长城高级润滑油公司	China Petrochemical Great Wall Hi-Grade Lubricant Co.	35	122844.6
清华紫光（集团）总公司	Tsinghua ZiGuang (Group) Corp.	36	113663.1
北人印刷机械股份有限公司	Beiren Printing mechanic Corp.	37	112628.4
北京大唐发电股份有限公司	Beijing Datang Electric Power Co.,Ltd	38	111067.0
北京轮胎厂	Beijing Tire Factory(Beijing Capital Tire CO.,Ltd.)	39	109942.4
和路雪(中国)有限公司	Walls(China) CO.,Ltd	40	109250.7
北京雪花电器集团公司	Beijing Snowflake Electric Appliance Group Corp.	41	101130.3
北京首钢宝生带钢厂	Beijing Shougang Posheng Strip Co.,Ltd.	42	99053.9
北京电力设备总厂	Beijing Power Equipment Group.	43	95512.6
北京北方车辆制造厂	Beijing North Auto Factory.	44	93074.7
北京市造纸包装工业公司	Beijing Paper&Package Industry Corp.	45	92795.6
北京印钞厂	Beijing Printing Bill Factory.	46	90469.5
北京亚洲双合盛五星啤酒有限公司	Beijing Asia ShuangHeSheng Five Star Beer CO.,LTD.	47	89508.3
北京第一机床厂	Beijing 1ST Machine Tool Factory.	48	82918.8
北京双鹤药业股份有限公司	Beijing Double-crane Medicine CO.,LTD	49	81890.1
长峰科技工业集团公司	CHINA ChangFeng Science Technology Industry Group Corp.	50	81482.6

6-17 续 表 continued

单位：万元 (10000 yuan)

企业名称	Enterprise	序号 No.	资产总额 Total Assets
北京航星机器制造公司	Beijing Hangxing Machine Building Corp.	51	79093.1
北京市平板玻璃集团公司	Beijing Plate-glass Group Corp.	52	78759.5
北京开关厂	Beijing Switching Factory.	53	78250.4
北京邮电通信设备厂	Beijing Post&Telecom Equipment Factory	54	70695.7
邮电部北京邮票厂	Beijing Postage Stamp Printing Flouse.	55	70566.3
北京华德液压工业集团有限责任公司	Beijing Huade Hydraulic Industry CO.,Ltd	56	70113.0
北京亚都科技股份有限公司	Beijing Yadu Science Technology CO.,Ltd	57	68259.1
北京可口可乐饮料有限公司	Beijing Coca-Cola Beverage Co.,Ltd.	58	67753.1
北京市汽车修理公司	Beijing Automobile Repair Company	59	66388.9
北京市液化石油气公司	Beijing Liquefied Petroleum Gas Company	60	65595.5
北京市顺义宏利钢管有限公司	Shunyi Hongli Steel Tube CO.,Ltd	61	65500.8
北京第三制药厂	Beijing 3RD Pharmaceutical Factory	62	64702.5
北京拖拉机公司	Beijing Tractor Corp.	63	64559.9
SMC(中国)有限公司	SMC(China) CO.,Ltd	64	64402.8
北京市客车总厂	Beijing Coach General Factory	65	62016.8
北京广播器材厂(七六一厂)	Beijing Broadcast Equipment Factory	66	59239.2
北京卷烟厂	Beijing Tobacco Factory	67	57386.0
北京电视设备厂	Beijing Television Equipment Factory	68	56538.0
北京二七机车厂	Beijing Erqi Auto Factory.	69	56063.0
北京星海乐器有限责任公司	Beijing XinHai Musical Instruments Company Ltd.	70	55239.8
北京恩布拉科雪花压缩机有限公司	Beijing Embraco Snowflake Compressor Company Led.	71	55119.2
北京化工实验厂	Beijing Chemical Engineering Experimental Plant	72	54289.2
北京雪莲羊绒有限公司	Beijing Snow_Lotus Cashmere Co.,Ltd.	73	54252.0
北京电子管厂	Beijing Electron Tube Factory	74	53158.3
北京中策北京啤酒有限公司	Beijing Zhongce Beijing Beer CO.,Ltd	75	52576.8
北京松下电子部品有限公司	Beijing Matsushita Electronics Components Co.,Ltd.	76	51913.9
北京白菊电器集团	Beijing Baiju Electric Appliance Group	77	50796.1
北京齿轮总厂	Beijing Gear General Factory	78	50593.4
北京万辉药业集团	Beijing Wanhui Pharmaceutical Group	79	49546.1
北京市机电研究院机床实验工厂	Beijing Mechanical & Electrical Research Institute Laboratory Factory	80	49054.9
北京煤矿机械厂	Beijing Coal Mining Machinery Factory.	81	47410.0
北京万东医疗装备股份有限公司	Beijing Wandong Medical Equipment CO.,Ltd	82	46438.5
北京起重机器厂	Beijing Crane Factory.	83	46269.4
北京市三露厂	CHINA Beijing Sanlu Factory	84	45934.0
北京二毛纺织集团	Beijing 2ND Woolen Group	85	45871.6
北京三环亚太啤酒有限公司	Beijing Three Ring Asia Pacific Beer CO.,LTD.	86	45850.0
北京北化精细化学品有限责任公司	Beijing Beihua Fine Chemicals CO.,Ltd.	87	45012.9
北京合成纤维实验厂(北京华英纶	Beijing Synthetic Fiber Experimental Factory.	88	44951.2
北京化工三厂	Beijing 3RD Chemical Plant	89	44517.0
北京红星酿酒集团公司	Beijing Red Star Wine-Marking Group Company.	90	44272.6
北京四通松下电工有限公司	Beijing STONE Matsushita Electric Works Ltd.	91	44208.3
中国大恒（集团）公司	China Daheng (Group) Corp.	92	43435.4
北京丽源公司	Beijing Liyuan Corp.	93	43219.3
北京南口机车车辆工厂	Beijing Nankou Rolling stock Plant	94	42967.0
北京天坛生物制品股份有限公司	Beijing Tiantan Biological Product CO.,LTD	95	42484.3
北京青云航空仪表有限公司	Beijing Qingyun Air Meter CO.,Ltd	96	42109.3
拜耳医药保健有限公司	Bayer Healthcare Company LTD.	97	41538.5
国营北京电子动力公司	Beijing Electron Power Corp.	98	41176.7
北京长空机械公司	Beijing Changkong Machinery Corp.	99	40907.8
北京铜材厂	Beijing Copper Products Factory	100	39880.8

主要统计指标解释

工业 指从事自然资源的开采，对采掘品和农产品进行加工和再加工的物质生产部门。具体包括：（1）对自然资源的开采，如采矿、晒盐、森林采伐等（但不包括禽兽捕猎和水产捕捞）；（2）对农副产品的加工、再加工，如粮油加工、食品加工、扎花、纺织、制革等；（3）对采掘品的加工、再加工，如炼铁、炼钢、化工生产、石油加工、机器制造、木材加工等，以及电力、自来水、煤气的生产和供应等；（4）对工业品的修理、翻新，如机器设备的修理、交通运输工具（包括小卧车）的修理等。

1984 年以前农村的村及村以下办工业归属农业，1984 年以后划归工业。

独立核算工业企业 非独立核算工业生产单位 工业企业按其行政和财务是否独立，分为核算工业企业和非独立核算工业生产单位。

独立核算工业企业应同时具备下列三个条件：（1）行政上有独立的组织形式；（2）经济上独立核算、自负盈亏、编制独立的资金平衡表；（3）有权与其他单位签订合同，并在银行社有独立帐户。独立核算工业企业不论是单一性生产或联合性生产的企业，均以整个企业作为一个基层单位进行统计，而不按分厂、车间统计。

非独立核算工业生产单位是指不同时具备独立核算工业企业三个条件，附设与其他企业、事业、机关、团体、学校、科研机构、部队等单位的工业生产单位。非独立核算工业生产单位必须同时具备下列三个条件，才能列入工业统计范围，即：（1）有固定的生产场所和生产设备；（2）有固定的生产工人和学徒在十人以上；（3）一般单位常年生产，季节性生产的单位全年开工时间在三个月以上。

轻工业 指主要提供生活消费品和制作手工工具的工业。按其所使用的原料不同，可分为两大类：（1）以农业为原料的轻工业，是指直接或间接以农产品为基本原料的轻工业。主要包括食品制造、饮料制造、烟草加工、纺织、缝纫、皮革和毛皮制作、造纸以及印刷等工业；（2）以非农产品为原料的轻工业，是指以工业品为原料的轻工业。主要包括文教体育用品、化学药品制造、合成纤维制造、日用化学制品、日用玻璃制品、日用金属制品、手工工具制造、医疗器械制造、文化和办公用机械制造等工业。

重工业 是指为国民经济各部门提供物质技术基础的主要生产资料的工业。按其生产性质和产品用途，可以分为下列三类：（1）采掘（伐）工业，是指对自然资源的开采，包括石油开采、煤炭开采、金属矿开采、非金属矿开采和木材采伐等工业；（2）原材料工业，指向国民经济各部门提供基本材料、动力和燃料的工业。包括金属冶炼及加工、炼焦及焦炭化学、化工原料、水泥、人造板以及电力、石油和煤炭加工等工业；（3）加工工业，是指对工业原材料进行再加工制造的工业。包括装备国民经济各部门的机械设备制造工业、金属结构、水泥制品等工业，以及为农业提供的生产资料如化肥、农药等工业。

根据上述划分原则，修理业中以重工业产品为修理作业对象的划为重工业，反之划为轻工业。

工业总产值 是以货币表现的工业在一定时期内生产的已出售或可供出售工业产品总量，它反映一定时期内工业生产的总规模和总水平。它包括：在本企业内不再进行加工，经检验、包装入库（规定不需包装的产品除外）的成品价值，工业性作业价值，自制半成品、在产品期末初差额价值。工业总产值采用“工厂法”计算，即以工业作业为一个整体，按企业生产活动的最终成果来计算，企业内部不允许重复计算，不能把企业内部各个车间（分厂）生产的成果相加。但在企业之间、行业之间、地区之间存在着重复计算。

轻重工业总产值的划分也是按“工厂法”计算的，即一个工业企业在正常情况下生产的主要产品的性质属于轻工业，则该企业的全部总产值作为轻工业总产值；一个工业企业生产的主要产品的性质属于重工业，则该企业的全部总产值作为重工业总产值。

工业增加值 是指工业行业在报告期内以货币表现的工业生产活动的最终成果。

工业销售产值 是以货币表现的工业企业在一定时期内销售的本企业生产的工业产品产量。包括已销售的成品、半成品价值，对外提供的工业性作业价值和对本单位基本建设部门、生活福利部门等提供的产品和工业性作业及自制设备的价值。已销售的成品、半成品不论是本期生产的、还是上期生产的，只要是本期销售出去的均包括在内。对外提供的工业性作业是指企业按合同对外提供的工业性劳务。企业为本单位基本建设部门、生活福利部门等提供的产品和工业性作业及自制设备也应视同销售，这部分也应作为销售统计。

工业销售产值的计算范围、计算价格和计算方法与工业总产值一致，但两者计算的基础不同，工业销售产值计算的基础是产品销售总量，工业总产值计算的基础是工业产品生产总量。

固定资产原价 指企业在建造、购置、安装、改建、扩建、技术改造某项固定资产时所支出的全部货币总额。它一般包括买价、包装费、运杂费和安装费等。

固定资产净值 是指固定资产原价减去历年已提折旧额后的净值。

新产品 指采用新技术原理、新设计构思、生产的全新产品或在结构、材质、工艺等某一方面比老产品有明显改进，从而显著提高了生产性能或扩大了使用功能的产品。

出口交货值 指工业企业交给外贸部门或自营（委托）出口（包括销往香港、澳门、台湾），用外汇价格结算的批量销售，在国内或边境批量出口的产品价值，还包括外商来样、来料加工、来件装配和补偿贸易等生产的产品价值。

工业品自销零售额 指各种经济类型的制造业生产单位，将本单位生产的产品直接售给居民（包括本企业职工）和社会集团取得的零售额。

工业企业主要财务指标和经济效益指标

1. 资本金合计 是企业在工商行政管理部门登记的注册资金。资本金合计包括国家资本金、法人资本金、个人资本金、外商资本金和集体资本金等。

（1）国家资本金 是指有权代表国家投资的政府部门或者机构以国有资产投入企业形成的资本金。不论企业的资本金是哪个政府部门或机构投入的，只要是以国家资金进行投资的，均作为国家资本金。

（2）法人资本金 是指其他法人单位以其依法可以支配的资产投入企业形成的资本金。

（3）个人资本金 是指社会个人或者企业内部职工以个人合法财产投入企业形成的资本金。

（4）外商资本金 是指外国投资者以及香港、澳门、台湾地区投资者投入企业形成的资本金。

（5）集体资本金 是指集体所有制企业投入企业形成的资本金。

2. 资产合计 指企业拥有或控制的全部资产。包括流动资产、长期投资、固定资产、无形及递延资产、其他长期资产、递延税项等，即为企业资产负债表的资产总计项。

（1）流动资产 指企业可以在一年内或者超过一年的一个生产周期内变现或耗用的资产合计。包括现金及各种存款、短期投资、应收及预付款项、存货等。

（2）固定资产 指企业固定资产净值、固定资产清理、在建工程、待处理固定资产损失所占用的资金合计。

（3）无形资产　指企业长期使用而没有实物形态的资产。包括专利权、非专利技术、商标权、著作权、土地使用权、商誉等。

3. 负债合计　指企业承担并需要偿还的全部债务。包括流动负债和长期负债、递延税项等，即为企业资产负债表的负债合计项。

（1）流动负债　指企业在一年内或者超过一年的营业周期内需要偿还的债务合计，其中包括短期借款、应付及预收款项、应付工资、应交税金和应交利润等。

（2）长期负债　指企业在一年以上或者超过一年的生产周期以上需要偿还的债务合计，其中包括长期借款、应付债务、长期应付款项等。

4. 利税总额　指企业利润总额、产品销售税金及附加和应交增值税之和。

5. 产品销售收入　指企业销售产品的销售收入和提供劳务等主要经营业务取得的业务总额。

6. 产品销售成本　指企业销售产品和提供劳务等主要经营业务的实际成本。

7. 产品销售税金及附加　指企业销售产品和提供工业性劳务等主要经营业务应负担的城市维护建设税、消费税、资源税和教育费附加。

8. 产品销售利润　指企业销售产品和提供工业性劳务等主要经营业务收入扣除其成本、费用、税金后的利润。

9. 利润总额　指企业实现的利润。

10. 所有制者权益　指企业投资人对企业净资产的所有权。企业净资产等于企业全部资产减去全部负债后余额，其中包括投资者对企业的最初投入，以及资本公积金、盈余公积金和未分配利润，对股份制企业即为股东权益。

11. 工业经济效益综合指数　是综合衡量工业经济效益各方面在数量上总体水平的一种特殊相对数，是反映工业经济运行质量的总量指数，是以各项工业经济效益指数实际数值分别除以该项指标的全国标准值并乘以各自权数求得。计算公式：

$$\text{工业经济效益综合指数}=\frac{\text{某项经济效益指标报告期数值}}{\text{该项指标全国标准值}}\times(\text{权数})\div\text{总权数}$$

计算工业经济效益综合指数时，各项经济效益指标的分子、分母应按报告期止累计数（如产品销售收入为报告期止累计产品销售收入）或序时平均数（如平均流动资产为报告期止各月平均流动资产之和除以累计月数）计算。

全国的标准值：是根据“八五”期间全国乡及乡以上工业企业每项指标实际完成数值加权平均计算出来的。

权数：是根据上述各项工业经济效益指标在综合经济效益中的重要程度，由专家调查法确定的。

12. 工业产品销售率　指报告期工业销售产值与同期全部工业总产值之比。计算公式：

$$\text{工业产品销售率}(\%)=\frac{\text{报告期现价工业销售产值}}{\text{报告期现价工业总产值}}\times 100\%$$

13. 工业资金利税率　指报告期已实现的利润、税金总额与同期的资产（流动资产和固定资产净值）之比，反映每单位（通常是每万元）资金所提供的利润税金额。它是考察和评价部门或企业资金运用的经济效益，分析资金投入效果的主要分析指标。计算公式：

$$工业资金利税率(\%)=\frac{报告期累计实现利税总额}{流动资产平均余额+固定资产净值平均余额}\times 100\%$$

14. 工业增加值率　指报告期工业增加值占工业总产值的比重，反映降低中间消耗的经济效益。计算公式：

$$工业增加值率(\%)=\frac{报告期现价工业增加值}{报告期现价工业总产值}\times 100\%$$

15. 工业成本费用利润率　指在一定时期内实现的利润与成本费用之比，是反映工业生产成本及费用投入的经济效益指标，同时也是反映降低成本的经济效益的指标。计算公式：

$$工业成本费用利润率(\%)=\frac{利润总额}{成本费用总额}\times 100\%$$

16. 工业全员劳动生产率　指根据产品的价值量指标计算的平均每一个职工在单位时间内的产品生产量。是考核企业经济活动的重要指标，是企业生产技术水平、经济管理水平、职工技术熟练程度和劳动积极性的综合表现。目前我国的全员劳动生产率是将工业企业的工业增加值除以同一时期全部职工的平均人数来计算的。计算公式：

$$工业全员劳动生产率(元/人)=\frac{工业增加值(现价)}{全部职工平均人数}$$

17. 流动资产周转次数　指在一定时期内流动资产完成的周转次数，反映流动资产的周转速度。计算公式：

$$流动资产周转次数(次)=\frac{产品销售收入}{流动资产平均余额}$$

18. 销售收入利税率　指报告期已实现的利润、税金总额（包括利润总额、产品销售税金及附加和应交增值税）占同期全部销售收入的百分比。计算公式：

$$销售收入利税率(\%)=\frac{利润总额}{销售收入}\times 100\%$$

19. 流动比率　是反映企业每百元流动负债中，有多少元流动资产作后盾。计算公式：

$$流动比率=\frac{流动资产总额}{流动负债总额}$$

20. 速动比率　是衡量企业流动资产中可以立即用于偿付流动负债的能力。计算公式：

$$速动比率=\frac{速动资产}{流动负债}$$

注：速动资产是流动资产中流动性相对更强的部分，通常等于现金，短期有价证券与应收款之和。

21. 资产负债率　是反映在企业资产总额中有多少资产是通过借债而得的，也可以用于衡量企业利用债权人提供资金进行经营活动的能力以及企业在清算时保护债权人利益的程度。计算公式：

$$资产负债率=\frac{负债总额}{资产总额}\times 100\%$$

22. 总资产贡献率　反映企业全部资产的获利能力，是企业经营业绩和管理水平的集中体现，是评价和考核企业盈利能力的核心指标。计算公式为：

$$总资产贡献率=(利润总额+税金总额+利息支出)\div 平均资产总额\times\frac{12}{累计月数}$$

其中：税金总额为产品销售税金及附加与应交增值税之和；平均资产总额为期初期末资产总计的算术平均值。

23. 资本保值增值率　反映企业净资产的变动状况，是企业发展能力的集中体现。计算公式为：

资本保值增值率 = 报告期期末所有者权益/上年同期期末所有者权益

Explanatory Notes On Main Statistical Indicators

Industry refers to the physical production concerning extraction of natural resources, processing and reprocessing of minerals and agricultural products: (1) extraction of natural resources, such as mining, salt production, logging (but excluding hunting and fishing); (2) processing and reprocessing of farm and sideline products, such as rice husking, flour milling, wine making, oil pressing, cotton ginning, silk reeling, spinning and weaving, and leather making; (3) manufacturing of industrial products, such as steel making, iron smelting, chemicals production, petroleum processing, machine building, timber processing; production and supply of water, gas and electricity; (4) repairing of industrial products such as the repairing of machine and vehicles for transportation (including cars).

Prior to 1984, the rural industrial run by villages and cooperative organizations under village was classified into agriculture. Since 1984, it has been grouped into industry.

Independent Accounting Industrial Enterprises and Non-Independent Accounting Industrial Production Units are distinct by whether they have independent administration and accounting system.

An independent accounting industrial enterprises should satisfy all the following three conditions: (1)having an independent organization for administration; (2)having independent accounting system and filling independent balance sheets, being responsible for its own profits and losses; (3)being able to sign contracts with outside units and having independent bank accounts. An independent accounting industrial enterprise, no matter it is a single-business company or multi-business corporation, is counted as a basic statistical unit and its branch factories and workshops are no longer counted separately.

A non-independent accounting industrial production units is an industrial production unit with one or more of the three conditions unsatisfied. They usually attach to some enterprises, institutions, government departments, organizations, schools , scientific research institutions, or army units. A non-independent accounting industrial production units become a basic units of industrial statistics only when it can satisfy all the following three conditions: (1) having stable production sites and production equipment; (2) having more than 10 permanent workers and apprentices; (3) operating all-year-round for normal production or more than three months a year for seasonal production.

Light Industry refers to the industry that produces consumer goods and hand tools. Depending on the materials used, it is classified into two categories:

(1) <u>Industries using farm products as raw materials</u> directly or indirectly input farm products as basic raw materials, including the production of foods and beverages, tobacco processing, textile, clothing, fur and leather manufacturing, paper making, printing, etc..

(2) Industries using non-farm products as raw materials input manufactured goods as raw materials, including the manufacture of cultural, educational articles and sports goods, chemicals, synthetic fiber, daily use chemical products, glass products, metal products, hand tools, medical apparatus and instruments, and the manufacturing of cultural and office equipment.

Heavy Industry refers to the industry that produces capital goods. It provides various sectors of the national economy with necessary material and technical basis. According to the nature of production and the use of products, it is classified into three groups:

(1) Mining, quarrying and logging industry refers to the extraction of natural resources, including petroleum, coal, metal and non-metal ores and logging.

(2) Raw materials industry refers to the industry that provides various sectors of the national economy with raw materials, fuels and power. It includes smelting and processing of metals, coke and coke chemistry, chemical materials and building materials such as cement, plywood, power, petroleum refining and coal dressing, etc..

(3) Manufacturing industry refers to the industry that processes raw materials. It includes machine-building industry that equips sectors of the national economy, industries of metal structure and cement products, industries producing means of agricultural production, such as chemical fertilizers and pesticides.

According to the above principle of classification, the repairing mainly for heavy industry products are classified into heavy industry while these mainly for light industry products are put into light industry.

Gross Industrial Output Value is the total volume of industrial products sold or available for sale in value terms which reflects the total achievements and overall scale of industrial production during a given period. It includes the value of the finished products, which are not to be further processed in the enterprises and have been inspected, packed and put in storage, the value of industrial services rendered to other units and the differences in the value of the semi-finished products and products in process between the beginning and closing of the period. The gross industrial output value is calculated with "factory method". Based on the final products of every enterprise, there is no double calculation within every enterprise. However, double calculation does occur among different enterprises as well as different sectors and different regions.

Gross output value of light and heavy industries is also classified with the "factory" method. Under normal conditions, if the major products of an industrial enterprise belong to light industry products, the gross output value of the enterprise is put into light industry; the same principle apples to the contrary case.

Value Added of Industry refers to the final results of industrial production in money terms during the reference period.

Sales Value of Industry refers to total sales value of products produced by industrial enterprises during a given period, including sales of finished goods, semi-finished products, value of industrial services provided to outside units, value of products, industrial services and self-produced equipment provided for internal capital construction and welfare. Sales of finished goods and semi-finished products in current period are taken into account regardless whether the production is in the same period. Gross output value of industry is based on output of products while sales value of industry is based on sales of products.

Original Value of Fixed Assets refers to the total value of fixed assets calculated at the cost paid for purchase, installation, reconstruction, expansion, innovation and replacement of the fixed assets, which is normally classified into expenses on purchase, package, transportation, and installation.

Net Value of Fixed Assets is obtained by deducting cumulative depreciation over years from the original value of fixed assets.

New Products refers to new products using new technological principal, new designing ideas or be improved than old products in structure, materials or technology, and so improve production performance or exploited using function.

Delivery Value of Exports refers to value of products which delivered to foreign trade department or self exported(including selled to Hongkong, Macao and Taiwan) by industrial enterprises, and batch selled at exchange prices, batch exported within country or at border, also including value of sample from foreigners, materials received processing, scripts received assembling and compensation trade.

Retail Sales of Self-selling Industrial Products refers to retails sales of products which directly selled to residents(including staff and workers of enterprises) and social groups by manufacturing production units of various ownership.

The Main Financial Indexes and Economic Efficiency Indexes of Industrial Enterprises

1. Total Equity Capital refers to capital of an enterprise registered in Administrative Bureau for Industry and Commerce, which includes the state equity capital, the legal entity equity capital, individuals equity capital, foreign equity capital and collective equity capital.

State equity capital refers to the equity capital formed with the state-owned assets input by government departments or organizations that have the right to invest on behalf of the state. As long as the equity capital formed with the state-owned assets, it belongs to state equity capital, regardless which government department or organization the investor is.

Legal entity equity capital refers to the equity capital formed with the legal assets of a company or organization.

Individual equity capital is the equity capital formed with the legal individual assets from outside persons or internal employees.

Foreign equity capital is the equity capital formed with the legal assets from foreign parties, including parties or investors from Hong Kong, Macao and Taiwan.

Collective equity capital is the equity capital formed with the legal assets from collective enterprises.

2. Total Assets refers to all assets owned or controlled by an enterprises, including current assets, long-term investment, fixed assets, intangible assets and deferred assets, other long-term assets, and deferred taxes, etc. The summation of above items is equal to total assets shown in the balance sheet of the enterprise.

(1) current assets (working capital) refer to assets which can be cashed in or consumed in one year or an operating cycle over one year, including cash, all kinds of deposits, short term investment, receivable, advance payment, inventory, etc.

(2) Fixed assets refer to the total net value of fixed assets, clearance of fixed assets, project under construction, fixed assets losses in suspense. These are corporations' fund holdings.

(3)Intangible assets refer to the assets without physical form used by enterprises over a long time, such as patents, know-how, trade marks, copyright, usufruct of land, good-will, etc.

3. Total Liabilities refers to the debts that enterprises are responsible for repayment, including liquid liabilities, long-term liabilities and deferred taxes, etc. Total liabilities correspond to the summation item of liabilities shown in the balance sheets of the enterprises.

(1) Current liabilities refer to enterprises total debt payable within one year or an operating cycle over one year, including short term loans, payables and advance receipts, wages payable, taxes payable and profit payable, etc.

(2) Long-term liabilities refers to total debt payable within an operating cycle of one year or over one year, including long-term loans, long-term debts, long-term payables, etc.

4. Total Value of Profit and Tax (Pre-tax Profits) refers to the sum of the total net profits, products sales tax and surcharges and the value added tax payable of industrial enterprises, namely pre-tax profits.

5. Product Sales Income refers to the total income obtained by an enterprise via selling its products and providing industrial services.

6. Sales Cost of Industrial Products refers to actual cost of the products sold and the industrial services provided, etc.

7. Sales Tax and surcharges of Products refer to the tax of city maintenance and construction, consumption tax, resources tax and extra charges for education, which levied on enterprises providing products and industrial services.

8. Sales Profit of Products refers to the profit earned by the enterprises after deducting cost, charges and taxes from the business income with selling products and providing industrial services.

9. Total Profits refer to the total profits gained by the enterprises.

10. Owners' Equity refers to investors' claim for net assets of the enterprise, which equals to the total assets of the enterprise minus its total liabilities, including the initial capital from investors, capital accumulation fund, surplus accumulation fund and undistributed profit. It is the share holders' equity in share holding companies.

11. Aggregate Index of Industrial Economic Efficiency is a special relative value for comprehensively measuring the overall levels in quantitative terms of the industrial economic efficiency from various aspects. It is also a total quantity index reflecting the economic performance quality of the industry. It is the result of the actual value of the industrial economic efficiency index divided by the national standard value in the same field and then multiplied by the weight. The formula is as follows:

Aggregate index of industrial economic deficiency (%)

$$=\left(\frac{\text{Value of an economic deficiency index}}{\text{National stndard value in the same field}}\times \text{weight}\right)(\text{overall weight})$$

12. Sales Rate of Industrial Products refers to the ratio of the sales value of industry to the gross industrial output value in the same period. The formula is as follows:

$$\text{Sales Rate of Industrial Products}(\%)=\frac{\text{Sales value of industry}}{\text{Gross industrial output value}}\times 100\%$$

13. Ratio of Profit and Tax to Capital in Industry refers to the ratio of the total realized profits and taxes to total assets (net fixed assets plus working capital), often expressed as pre-tax profit earned per 10000 yuan capital, which reflects the utilization efficiency of the assets and is calculated as follows:

Ratio of Profit and Tax to Capital in Industry (%)

$$=\frac{\text{Total realized pre - tax profit}}{\text{Average current assets + Average net value of fixed assets}}\times 100\%$$

14. Value Added Rate of industry refers to the ratio of value added of industry to the gross output value in the same period, which reflects the economic efficiency of productive consumption and is calculated as follows:

$$\text{Value Added Rate of industry}(\%)=\frac{\text{Value Added of Industry}}{\text{Gross industrial Output Value}}\times 100\%$$

15. Ratio of Profits to Total Industrial Costs refers to the ratio of profits realized to the total costs occurred in the same period, which reflects the economic efficiency of input in costs and expenses and is calculated as follows:

$$\text{Ratio of Profits to Total Industrial Costs}(\%)=\frac{\text{Total Profits}}{\text{Total Costs}}\times 100\%$$

16. Overall Labor Productivity of Industrial Enterprises refers to the average output per staff and worker in industrial enterprises in value terms within a given period, which reflects comprehensively the technological level, the management level, the skills and initiatives of the staff or workers. At present, the overall labor productivity is gotten via dividing the value added by the average number of staff and workers of an industrial enterprises in a given period. The formula:

$$\text{Overall Labor Productivity (yuan/person)} = \frac{\text{Value Added of industry (at current prices)}}{\text{Average Number of Staff and Workers}}$$

17. Current Assets Turnover refers to times of the current assets turnover in a given period, which reflects the speed of the turnover of current assets and is calculated as follows:

$$\text{Current Assets Turnover (time)} = \frac{\text{Product Sales Income}}{\text{Average Balance of Circulating Assets}}$$

18. Ratio of Pre-tax Profits to Sales Revenue refers to the ratio of the total amount of pre-tax profits (including total profits, products sales tax and surcharges as well as the value added tax payable) to the total sales revenue in the same period. The formula is as follows:

$$\text{Ratio of Pre - tax Profits to Sales Revenue (\%)} = \frac{\text{Total Pre - tax Profits}}{\text{Total Sales Revenue}} \times 100\%$$

19. Current Ratio refers to how many times of the current assets can cover the current liabilities. The formula is as follows:

$$\text{Current Ratio} = \frac{\text{Total Current Assets}}{\text{Total Current Liabilities}}$$

20. Quick Ratio reflects to the capability of an enterprise to repay its current liabilities immediately. The equation is as follows:

$$\text{Quick Ratio} = \frac{\text{Total Quick Assets}}{\text{Total Current Liabilities}}$$

Note: Quick Assets is the more liquid part of current assets, usually equals to the sum of cash, short-term securities and receivable.

21. Debt - Asset Ratio refers to the proportion of debts as an enterprise's total assets, which reflects the enterprise's capability in utilizing debts for operation and also to what extent the interest of the creditors be protected at the expiration. The formula:

$$\text{Debt - Asset Ratio} = \frac{\text{Total Debt}}{\text{Total Assets}} \times 100\%$$

22. EBIT to Total Assets reflects the profitability of total assets, depending on performance in various aspects of an enterprise, therefore, became a central indicators for evaluate an enterprise. The formula:

$$\text{EBIT to Total Assets} = \frac{\text{Net profit + Total tax + Inerest payment}}{\text{Average total Assets}} \times 100\%$$

23. Ratio of Capital Increment and Preservation refers to the change of owner’s net assets,and presents corporations’ strength.The formula:

$$\text{Capital Increment and Preservation Ratio} = \frac{\text{Owner' Capital of the end of Reference Period}}{\text{Owner's Capital of the previous end of Reference Period}}$$

能源生产与消费
PRODUCTION AND CONSUMPTION OF ENERGY

7-1 能 源 消 费 总 量
TOTAL CONSUMPTION OF ENERGY

单位：万吨标准煤 (10000 tons standard-coal)

项 目	Item	1999 数量 Quantity	1999 构成(%) Composition(%)	1998 数量 Quantity	1998 构成(%) Composition(%)
合 计	**Total**	**3985.6**	**100**	**3913.3**	**100**
第一产业	Primary Industry	86.9	2.2	96.2	2.5
第二产业	Secondary Industry	2498.4	64.1	2543.5	65.0
# 工业	Industry	2436.2	62.5	2486.1	63.5
第三产业	Tertiary Industry	923.1	23.7	818.6	20.9
# 交通邮电	Transportation,Posts and Telecommunications	283	7.3	233.5	6.0
生活消费	Living consumption	477.2	12.2	455.0	11.6
城 镇	Urban	330.5	8.5	303.2	7.7
农 村	Rural	146.6	3.8	151.8	3.9

注：电力按当年平均火力发电煤耗折算标准煤，其他能源品种均按其当量热值折算标准煤，以下各表同。

Note: Electricity conversed to ton-standard-coal according to average coal consumption from thermal power, other energy other energy conversed to tsd according to calorific value.(the followings are the same.)

7-2 能 源 生 产 量
PRODUCTION VOLUME OF ENERGY

项 目		Item		1999	1998	1999 年为 1998 年% 1999 as % of 1998
一次能源	**(吨标煤)**	**Directly Used Energy**	**(ton-standard-coal)**	**595.6**	**738.0**	**80.7**
原 煤	(万吨)	Coal	(10000 tons)	792.1	989.5	80.1
水 电	(亿千瓦时)	Water and Electricity	(100 million kwh)	9.4	9.2	101.8
二次能源	**(吨标煤)**	**Indirectly Used Energy**	**(ton-standard-coal)**	**2156.8**	**2183.3**	**98.8**
洗精煤	(万吨)	Clean Coal	(10000 tons)	25.8	42.8	60.3
其他洗煤	(万吨)	Other Clean Coal	(10000 tons)	3.8	9.9	38.5
煤制品	(万吨)	Coal Products	(10000 tons)	10.4	28.8	36.1
焦 碳	(万吨)	Coke	(10000 tons)	395.7	406.2	97.4
焦炉煤气	(亿立方米)	Coking Gas	(100 million cu.m)	17.3	18.4	94.2
其他煤气	(亿立方米)	Other Gas	(100 million cu.m)	3.0	3.8	78.7
汽 油	(万吨)	Gasoline	(10000 tons)	124.3	118.1	105.3
柴 油	(万吨)	Diesel Oil	(10000 tons)	170.1	117.1	145.2
燃料油	(万吨)	Fuel Oil	(10000 tons)	75.5	120.8	62.5
液化石油气	(万吨)	Liquefied Petroleum	(10000 tons)	35.6	32.7	109.0
炼厂干气	(万吨)	Gas of Plant	(10000 tons)	18.1	7.4	243.9
其他石油制品	(万吨)	Other Petroleum Products	(10000 tons)	223.3	194.6	114.8
其他焦化产品	(万吨)	Other Coking Products	(10000 tons)	21.0	19.7	106.8
热 力	(万百万千焦)	Heat	(1 billion kilo-joules)	7885.4	7789.2	101.2
电 力	(亿千瓦时)	Electricity	(100 million kwh)	164.9	147.2	112.0

7-3 工业分行业能源终端消费量(实物量)

项目	Item	原煤(万吨) Coal (10000 tons)	洗精煤(万吨) Clean Coal (10000 tons)	其他洗煤(万吨) Other Clean Coal (10000 tons)	焦炭(万吨) Coke (10000 tons)	焦炉煤气(亿立方米) Coking Gas (100 million cu.m)	其他煤气(亿立方米) Other Gas (100 million cu.m)	原油(万吨) Crude Oil (10000 tons)
工 业	**Industry**	**738.04**	**4.95**	**2.99**	**433.69**	**9.80**	**2.45**	**47.48**
轻工业	Light Industry	128.35			0.14	0.10		0.10
重工业	High Industry	609.69	4.95	2.99	433.55	9.70	2.45	47.38
采掘业	**Excavation**	9.92			0.04			
煤炭采选业	Coal Mining and Dressing	8.29						
石油和天然气开采	Petroleum and Natural Gas Extraction							
黑色金属矿采选业	Ferrous Metals Mining and Dressing	0.10						
有色金属矿采选业	Nonferrous Metals Mining and Dressing							
非金属矿采选业	Nonmetal Minerals Mining and Dressing	1.53						
其他矿采选业	Other Minerals Mining and Dressing				0.04			
木材及竹材采运业	Timber and Bamboo Cutting and Shipping							
制造业	**Manufacturing**	**708.52**	**4.95**	**2.99**	**433.65**	**9.75**	**2.45**	**47.37**
食品加工业	Food Processing	9.36						
食品制造业	Food Making	17.39			0.08	0.05		0.10
饮料制造业	Beverage Production	31.23						
烟草加工业	Tobacco Processing	1.31						
纺织业	Textile Industry	18.05				0.02		
服装及其他纤维制品制造业	Garments and Other Fiber Products	9.75			0.01			
皮革、毛皮、羽绒及其制品业	Leather,Furs,Down and Related Products	1.84						
木材加工及竹、藤、棕、草制品业	Timber Processing,Bamboo,Cane,Palm Fiber and Straw Products	2.63						
家具制造业	Furniture Manufacturing	2.89			0.02			
造纸及纸制品业	Papermaking and Paper Products	10.06						
印刷业、记录媒介的复制	Printing and Record Medium Reproduced	8.39				0.03		
文教体育用品制造业	Stationery,Educational and Sports Goods	1.20			0.01			
石油加工及炼焦业	Petroleum Processing and Coking Products	2.24						
化学原料及化学制品制造业	Raw Chemical Materials and Chemical Products	28.22	4.95	2.55	15.76	3.56	2.43	47.26
医药制造业	Medical and Pharmaceutical Products	10.81						
化学纤维制造业	Chemical Fibers	1.80						
橡胶制品业	Rubber Products	11.56						
塑料制品业	Plastic Products	8.09			0.05			
非金属矿物制品业	Nonmetal Mineral Products	268.08		0.44	1.41	0.29		
黑色金属冶炼及压延加工业	Smelting and Pressing of Ferrous Metals	174.50	4.95		409.35	5.57		
有色金属冶炼及压延加工业	Smelting and Pressing of Nonferrous Metals	1.60			0.35			
金属制品业	Metal Products	8.09			2.25	0.07		
普通机械制造业	Ordinary Machinery	11.68			3.46	0.06		0.01
专用设备制造业	Special Purpose Equipment	11.28			0.27	0.01		
交通运输设备制造业	Transportation Equipment	27.49			0.43	0.04	0.02	
武器弹药制造业	Weapon and Ammunition	3.67						
电气机械及器材制造	Electric Equipment and Machinery	10.54			0.14	0.02		
电子及通信设备制造	Electronic and Telecommunications	8.40			0.03	0.03		
仪器仪表及文化、办公用机械制造业	Instruments,Meters,Cultural and Official Machinery	3.04			0.01			
其他制造业	Other Manufacturing	3.33			0.02			
电力、煤气及水的生产和供应业	**Electricity,Gas and Water Production and Supply**	**19.60**				**0.05**		**0.11**
电力、蒸汽、热水的生产和供应业	Electricity,Steam and Hot Water Production and Supply	18.63						0.11
煤气生产和供应业	Gas Production and Supply	0.03				0.05		
自来水的生产和供应	Water Production and Supply	0.94						

ENERGY TERMINAL CONSUMPTION IN KIND OF INDUSTRY BY SECTOR

汽油 (万吨) Gasoline (10000 tons)	煤油 (万吨) Kerosene (10000 tons)	柴油 (万吨) Diesel Fuel Oil (10000 tons)	燃料油 (万吨) Fuel Oil (10000 tons)	液化石油气 (万吨) Liquefied Petroleum (10000ton)	炼厂干气 (万吨) Net Gas of Plant (10000 tons)	天然气 (亿立方米) Natural Gas (100 million cu.m)	其他石油制品 (万吨) Other Petroleum Products (10000 tons)	其他焦化产品 (万吨) Other Coking Product (10000 tons)	热力 (万百万千焦) Heat (10 billion kilo-joule)	电力 (亿千瓦时) Electricity (100 million kwh)	能源合计 (万吨标准煤) Total (10000 standard-coal)
12.97	**0.27**	**14.48**	**37.92**	**6.89**	**4.93**	**0.41**	**175.76**	**20.10**	**4843.28**	**155.31**	**2306.92**
3.92	0.04	2.21	0.25	0.17		0.09	0.06		406.77	17.76	180.98
9.05	0.23	12.27	37.67	6.72	4.93	0.32	175.70	20.10	4436.51	137.55	2125.96
0.33	0.01	1.09								2.56	17.73
0.22		0.20								1.75	12.40
0.02		0.16								0.52	1.99
										0.02	0.05
0.09	0.01	0.73								0.27	3.20
											0.04
12.15	**0.26**	**12.79**	**36.69**	**6.69**	**4.93**	**0.41**	**175.76**	**20.10**	**4708.96**	**125.39**	**2178.26**
0.39		0.40		0.01		0.01	0.04		0.07	1.40	12.85
0.58		0.98	0.23	0.13		0.02			36.30	1.84	23.97
0.66		0.22							19.21	2.17	32.45
										0.04	1.12
0.28	0.01	0.14		0.01					212.23	3.19	32.78
0.37		0.10		0.01					8.36	1.01	11.62
0.04									0.85	0.18	2.09
0.07		0.02							2.65	0.18	2.79
0.18	0.01	0.03							0.88	0.36	3.72
0.34		0.17		0.01			0.02		5.30	1.13	12.17
0.50	0.02	0.06				0.06			17.67	1.90	14.98
0.14		0.02							8.44	0.17	2.03
1.00	0.01	1.03	7.80	6.07	4.93		175.27		2425.39	15.01	427.06
0.86	0.01	0.36	5.18			0.04	0.41	10.10	771.02	15.22	232.31
0.21		0.04	0.02						46.73	0.77	12.82
0.03									49.19	0.92	6.24
0.17		0.03	0.18						0.25	0.93	12.20
0.32		0.16		0.01					1.24	1.65	12.16
1.43	0.07	2.94	4.25	0.11		0.15	0.01	0.13	67.96	13.51	265.84
0.56	0.01	3.85	18.26					9.75	709.14	46.63	898.77
0.07		0.13								0.64	3.87
0.93	0.03	0.38	0.11	0.26			0.01	0.12	2.80	2.59	19.78
0.61	0.03	0.30							69.64	2.50	24.54
0.44	0.01	0.52		0.02		0.03			36.28	1.68	17.46
0.93	0.05	0.52	0.57	0.01		0.01			147.38	3.51	43.99
0.03		0.08	0.06			0.05			11.71	0.45	5.55
0.49		0.19		0.03					34.69	1.65	15.84
0.27		0.07	0.03	0.01		0.03			13.02	3.38	18.92
0.11		0.02				0.01			9.02	0.49	4.53
0.14		0.03							1.54	0.29	3.78
0.49		**0.60**	**1.23**	**0.20**					**134.32**	**27.36**	**110.95**
0.28		0.57	1.23						134.32	24.83	101.21
0.15		0.01		0.20						0.14	1.32
0.06		0.02								2.39	8.42

7-4 分品种能源消费量
ENERGY CONSUMPTION BY CATEGORY

项目 Item		1999	1998	1999年为1998年% 1999 as % of 1998
煤炭 (万吨) Coal	(10000 tons)	2650.7	2677.7	99.0
焦碳 (万吨) Coke	(10000 tons)	441.3	482.5	91.5
焦炉煤气 (亿立方米) Coking Gas	(100 million cu.m)	14.6	16.6	87.8
其他煤气 (亿立方米) Other Gas	(100 million cu.m)	2.5	3.0	84.2
原油 (万吨) Crude Oil	(10000 tons)	719.8	643.0	111.9
汽油 (万吨) Gasoline	(10000 tons)	92.3	82.3	112.2
煤油 (万吨) Kerosene	(10000 tons)	110.4	91.3	120.9
柴油 (万吨) Diesel Oil	(10000 tons)	70.0	64.5	108.5
燃料油 (万吨) Fuel Oil	(10000 tons)	113.7	154.7	73.5
液化石油气 (万吨) Liquefied Petroleum	(10000 tons)	30.2	25.9	116.5
炼厂干气 (万吨) Gas of Plant	(10000 tons)	18.1	7.4	243.9
天然气 (亿立方米) Natural Gas	(100 million cu.m)	6.5	3.2	203.1
其他石油制品 (万吨) Other Petroleum Products	(10000 tons)	190.3	185.9	102.4
其他焦化产品 (万吨) Other Coking Products	(10000 tons)	20.1	20.5	98.1
热力 (万百万千焦) Heat	(1billion kilo-joules)	7670.6	7789.2	98.5
电力 (亿千瓦时) Electricity	(100 million kwh)	314.7	291.5	108.0

7-5 平均每万元国内生产总值能源消费量
ENERGY CONSUMPTION PER 10000 YUAN GROSS DOMESTIC PRODUCT

项目 Item		1999	1998
能源总消费量 (吨标煤/万元) Total	**(ton standard-coal/10000 yuan)**	**1.83**	**1.95**
煤炭 (吨/万元) Coal	(ton/10000 yuan)	1.22	1.33
电力 (万千瓦时/万元) Electricity	(10000 kwh/10000 yuan)	0.14	0.15
石油 (吨/万元) Petroleum	(ton/10000 yuan)	0.31	0.32

7-6 人均生活用能量
LIVING CONSUMPTION OF ENERGY PER CAPITA

项目 Item		1999	1998
人均生活用能量 (千克标准煤) Living Consumption Per Capita	**(kg standard-coal)**	**433.8**	**416.8**
煤炭 (千克) Coal	(kg)	254.6	289.3
电力 (千瓦时) Electricity	(kwh)	324.2	269.4
液化石油气 (千克) Liquefied Petroleum	(kg)	16.8	14.1
天然气 (立方米) Natural Gas	(cu.m)	16.3	11.4
煤气 (立方米) Gas	(cu.m)	19.1	25.3

主要统计指标解释

能源总消费量 指报告期内社会各行业和居民生活所消费的各种能源数量，是观察本地区能源消费水平、构成和发展速度的总量指标，能源总消费量包括终端能源消费量、加工转换损失量和损失量三部分。

一次能源生产量 指报告期内生产一次能源的企业将自然界现存的能源资源经过开采而产出的合格产品，主要包括原煤、原油、天然气、水电等。

二次能源生产量 指报告期内将一次能源经过各种加工转换设备生产出的另一种形式的各种合格的能源产品。如火电、热力、洗煤、焦碳、各种石油制品、焦炉煤气、城市煤气等。

工业终端消费量 又称最终消费量。它反映报告期内工业企业作为原料、燃料和动力消费的能源及其去向。它们的消费过程体现了能源消费的终止。不包括用于加工转换投入量、加工转换损失量和损失量。

平均每万元国内生产总值能源消费量 能源总消费量或分品种能源消费量与国内生产总值之比。

人均生活用能量 指用于生活消费的各种能源数量与人口总数之比。

Explanatory Notes On Main Statistical Indicators

Total Energy Consumption refers to the total consumption of all sectors and households in a given period. It is a comprehensive indicator to show the scale, composition and trend of energy consumption of some region. The total energy consumption can be divided into three parts: Final Energy Consumption, Loss During the Process of Energy Conversion and Loss.

Production Volume of Directly-use Energy refers to qualified products through excavation and production from energy source in stock of nature , mainly include coal, crude oil, natural gas, water and electricity and so on.

Production Volume of Indirectly-use Energy refers to qualified energy products in another form through pressing and changing-over from directly-use energy, such as thermal power, heat, clean coal, coke, petroleum products, coking gas, city gas and so on.

Terminal Consumption of Industry named final consumption, too. It reports energy consumped as raw materials, fuels and power by industrial enterprises and the direction that has gone. The process of consumption reflects the end of energy consumption, exclude input in pressing and changing-over, loss in pressing and changing-over and loss.

Energy Consumption Per 10000 yuan GDP refers to ratio of total consumption or consumption put into different categories to Gross Domestic Product(GDP).

Living Consumption of Energy Per Capita refers to ratio of living consumption to total population.

建筑业
CONSTRUCTION

全市建筑施工企业主要经济指标
Main Economic Indicators on Construction Enterprises

	1999年	1998年
企业单位数（个） Number of Enterprises(unit)	1606	1511
建筑业总产值（万元） Gross Output Value of Construction(10000 yuan)	6823119	6268097
年末从业人员（人） Number of Employment(year-end person)	620391	758438
劳动生产率（元/人） Overall Labor Productivity(yuan/person)	82412	73620

1999年独立核算建筑施工企业工程质量
Projects Quality of Construction Enterprises with Independent Accounting System

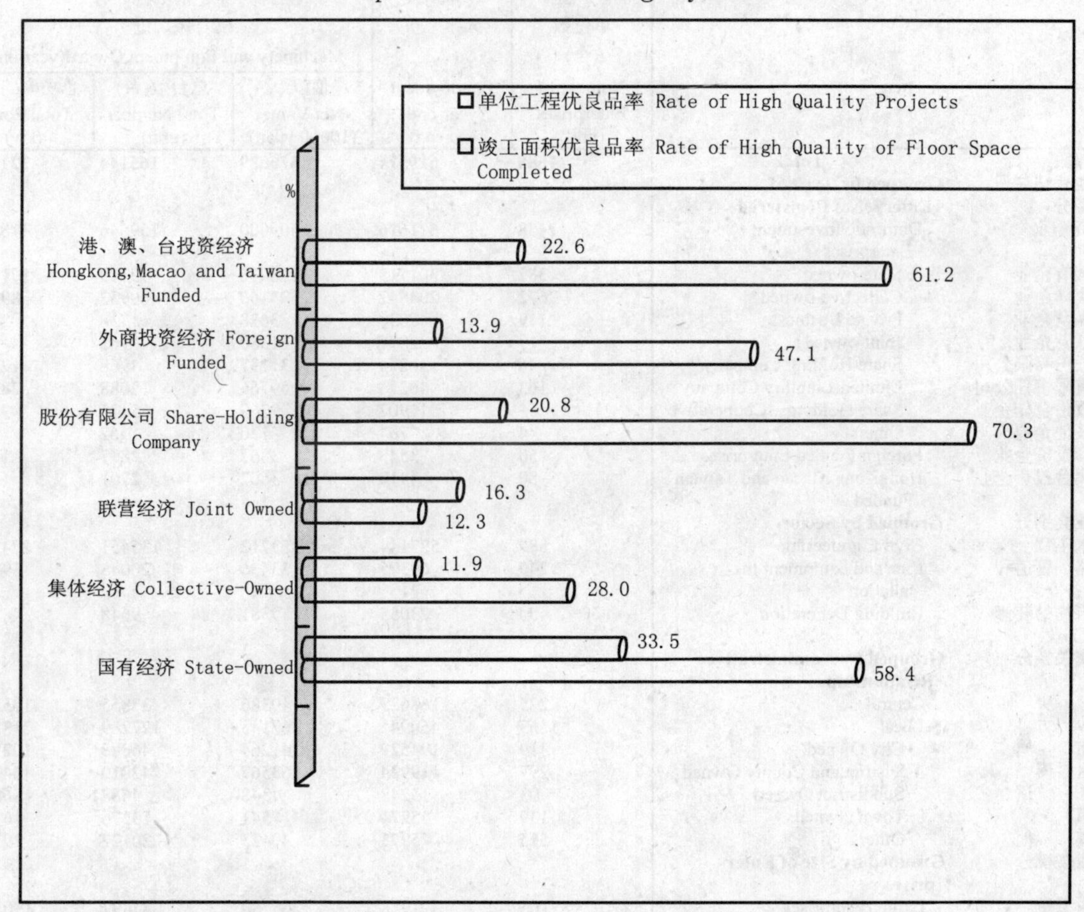

8-1 全市建筑施工企业主要经济指标
MAIN ECONOMIC INDICATORS ON CONSTRUCTION ENTERPRISES

项目 Item				全市总计 Total	独立核算建筑施工企业 Construction Enterprises with Independent Accounting System	#大中型企业 Large and Medium Enterprises	建筑业活动单位 Construction Units
企业单位数	(个)	Number of Enterprises	(unit)	1606	1588	243	18
建筑业总产值	(万元)	Gross Output Value of Construction	(10000 yuan)	6823119	6814102	5169144	9017
自有机械设备年末总台数	(台)	Number of Machinery and Equipment Owned(year-end)	(unit)	165442	165144	104978	298
自有机械设备年末总功率	(千瓦)	Total Power of Machinery and Equipment Owned(year-end)	(kw)	3224221	3217276	2398138	6945
年末从业人数	(人)	Number of Employment(year-end)	(person)	620391	619574	416800	817
劳动生产率	(元/人)	Overall Labor Productivity	(yuan/person)	82412	82465	89505	55524

8-2 独立核算建筑施工企业基本情况
BASIC STATISTICS FOR CONSTRUCTION ENTERPRISES WITH INDEPENDENT ACCOUNTING SYSTEM

项目	Item	企业单位数(个) Number of Enterprises (unit)	年末从业人员(人) Employment (year-end) (person)	年末自有机械设备 Machinery and Equipment Owned(year-end)		
				净值(万元) Net Value (10000 yuan)	总台数(台) Total Number (unit)	总功率(千瓦) Total Power (kw)
总计	**Total**	**1588**	**619574**	**416529**	**165144**	**3217276**
按企业登记注册类型分	**Grouped by Type of Enterprises Registered**					
内资企业	Domestic Investment Enterprises	1458	611616	409000	159546	3188241
国有企业	State-owned	382	301718	228930	73319	1716745
集体企业	Collective-owned	672	204842	94160	60932	892045
私营企业	Private Business	119	7038	3638	1738	20742
联营企业	Joint-owned	17	2877	1380	963	9704
股份有限公司	Share Holding Company	46	36254	31737	4968	173734
有限责任公司	Limited-Liability Company	163	46276	39766	12088	283941
股份合作企业	Share Holding Cooperative	55	11907	9269	5476	90828
其他企业	Others	4	704	120	62	502
外商投资企业	Foreign Funded Enterprises	50	3548	3867	2897	14251
港澳台投资企业	HongKong,Macao and Taiwan Funded	80	4410	3662	2701	14784
按行业类别分	**Grouped by Sector**					
土木工程	Civil Engineering	889	527144	353712	135451	2743816
线路、管道和设备安装	Line and equipment Installation	249	69375	53436	20045	390657
建筑物的装修装饰业	Building Decoration	450	23055	9381	9648	82803
按隶属关系分	**Grouped by Administrative Relationship**					
中央	Central	225	168629	149386	37855	1033283
地方	Local	1363	450945	267143	127289	2183993
市属	City Owned	319	194529	141264	46888	1027942
区县属	District and County Owned	297	119924	63567	42010	640183
街道	Subdistrict Owned	93	15248	4348	4688	60175
镇	Town Owned	139	45271	17541	13576	161854
其他	Others	515	75973	40423	20127	293839
按企业规模分	**Grouped by Size of Enterprises**					
大型	Large Enterprises	105	321988	268780	77497	1908777
中型	Medium Enterprises	138	94812	59814	27481	489361
小型	Small Enterprises	1345	202774	87935	60166	819138

8-3 独立核算建筑施工企业总产值和劳动生产率
GROSS OUTPUT VALUE AND LABOR PRODUCTIVITY OF CONSTRUCTION ENTERPRISES WITH INDEPENDENT ACCOUNTING SYSTEM

项 目	Item	总产值(万元) Gross Output Value (10000 yuan)		劳动生产率(元/人) Overall Labor Productivity (yuan/person)	
		1999	1998	1999	1998
总 计	**Total**	**6814102.3**	**6246617.6**	**82465**	**73644**
按企业登记注册类型分	**Grouped by Type of Enterprises Registered**				
内资企业	Domestic Investment Enterprises	6581811.6	6019623.2	81553	75341
国有企业	State-Owned	3529404.9	3323585.9	85286	56730
集体企业	Collective Owned	1536494.5	1390341.7	62612	69897
私营企业	Private	54127.0	26873.0	64452	100501
联营企业	Joint Owned	20733.4	26560.8	59854	122508
股份有限公司	Share Holding Company	688383.0	572431.1	127750	93969
有限责任公司	Limited-Liability Company	567656.5	524404.2	85908	28906
股份合作企业	Share Holding Cooperative	176854.1	152567.7	118186	71716
其他企业	Others	8158.2	2858.8	78520	86928
外商投资企业	Foreign Funded	131615.7	131916.2	123944	78695
港、澳、台商投资企业	Hongkong,Macao and Taiwan Funded	100675.0	95078.2	116671	85446
按行业类别分	**Grouped by Sector**				
土木工程	Civil Engineering	5575647.0	5178611.8	79339	71716
线路、管道和设备安装	Line and Equipment Installation	896373.2	797516.8	103853	86928
建筑物的装修装饰业	Building Decoration	342082.1	270489.0	91879	78695
按隶属关系分	**Grouped by Administrative Relationship**				
中 央	Central	2067213.8	2049461.7	96993	85446
地 方	Local	4746888.5	4197155.9	77415	68992
市 属	City Owned	2588927.3	2396764.9	89130	80003
区县属	District and County Owned	1055741.5	944131.8	66063	59598
街 道	Subdistrict Owned	71444.5	73282.1	43310	42579
镇	Town Owned	342141.3	248300.7	62881	49671
其 他	Others	688633.9	534676.4	74854	64297
按企业规模分	**Grouped by Size of Enterprises**				
大 型	Large Enterprises	4249405.5	4053311.8	94327	86107
中 型	Medium Enterprises	919738.9	816465.6	72406	68508
小 型	Small Enterprises	1644957.9	1376840.2	66120	53303

8-4 独立核算建筑施工企业竣工率
RATIO OF COMPLETED OF CONSTRUCTION INDEPENDENT ACCOUNTING SYSTEM

单位：% (%)

项目	Item	产值竣工率 Ratio of Output Value Completed to Total		面积竣工率 Ratio of Floor Space of Building Completed	
		1999	1998	1999	1998
总计	**Total**	**69.0**	**67.7**	**38.6**	**34.1**
按企业登记注册类型分	**Grouped by Type of Enterprises Registered**				
内资企业	Domestic Investment Enterprises	69.3	67.5	38.5	33.9
国有企业	State-Owned	71.7	71.1	38.7	32.4
集体企业	Collective Owned	70.4	68.8	49.2	43.7
私营企业	Private	63.0	88.3	54.1	47.6
联营企业	Joint Owned	67.8	58.2	45.3	56.1
股份有限公司	Share Holding Company	66.2	48.3	27.0	21.7
有限责任公司	Limited-Liability Company	60.1	63.6	23.2	25.4
股份合作企业	Share Holding Cooperative	55.2	57.8	41.0	37.0
其他企业	Others	99.4	98.9	100.0	100.0
外商投资企业	Foreign Funded	59.5	87.5	38.6	62.6
港、澳、台商投资企业	Hongkong,Macao and Taiwan Funded	62.3	56.7	71.1	19.3
按行业类别分	**Grouped by Sector**				
土木工程	Civil Engineering	69.9	66.8	38.5	34.0
线路、管道和设备安装	Line and Equipment Installation	68.5	73.4	41.1	54.1
建筑物的装修装饰业	Building Decoration	56.1	67.9	55.6	
按隶属关系分	**Grouped by Administrative Relationship**				
中央	Central	71.4	69.2	37.2	32.5
地方	Local	68.0	67.0	39.0	34.7
市属	City Owned	67.9	68.1	31.0	27.7
区县属	District and County Owned	68.1	60.4	46.6	40.0
街道	Subdistrict Owned	79.5	67.1	63.2	45.2
镇	Town Owned	65.4	67.4	49.0	48.4
其他	Others	68.1	73.5	51.6	48.4
按企业规模分	**Grouped by Size of Enterprises**				
大型	Large Enterprises	65.7	66.8	34.6	30.0
中型	Medium Enterprises	68.0	65.9	39.6	37.2
小型	Small Enterprises	78.2	71.6	52.0	49.5

8-5 独立核算建筑施工企业工程质量
PROJECTS QUALITY OF CONSTRUCTION ENTERPRISES WITH INDEPENDENT ACCOUNTING SYSTEM

单位：% (%)

项目	Item	单位工程优良品率 Rate of High Quality Project		竣工面积优良品率 Rate of High Quality of Floor Space Completed	
		1999	1998	1999	1998
总计	**Total**	**18.7**	**21.4**	**49.2**	**48.9**
按企业登记注册类型分	**Grouped by Type of Enterprises Registered**				
内资企业	Domestic Investment Enterprises	18.7	21.6	49.1	48.6
国有企业	State-Owned	33.5	38.6	58.4	56.2
集体企业	Collective Owned	11.9	13.6	28.0	36.8
私营企业	Private	8.9	28.1	0.3	23.8
联营企业	Joint Owned	16.3	24.0	12.3	18.2
股份有限公司	Share Holding Company	20.8	13.8	70.3	55.1
有限责任公司	Limited-Liability Company	30.6	34.9	60.5	54.8
股份合作企业	Share Holding Cooperative	13.1	10.0	65.2	40.6
其他企业	Others				
外商投资企业	Foreign Funded	13.9	6.8	47.1	63.4
港、澳、台商投资企业	Hongkong,Macao and Taiwan Funded	22.6	13.0	61.2	32.7
按行业类别分	**Grouped by Sector**				
土木工程	Civil Engineering	26.7	26.7	49.2	49.1
线路、管道和设备安装	Line and Equipment Installation	12.1	16.1	35.2	13.7
建筑物的装修装饰业	Building Decoration	6.8		48.3	
按隶属关系分	**Grouped by Administrative Relationship**				
中央	Central	39.4	43.3	62.5	62.3
地方	Local	14.0	14.3	44.8	44.3
市属	City Owned	20.4	26.0	66.9	57.5
区县属	District and County Owned	14.7	14.9	29.0	33.1
街道	Subdistrict Owned	10.5	11.4	37.6	27.3
镇	Town Owned	13.0	14.5	21.6	22.1
其他	Others	10.6	7.5	31.2	47.1
按企业规模分	**Grouped by Size of Enterprises**				
大型	Large Enterprises	46.6	41.1	62.0	62.2
中型	Medium Enterprises	18.6	21.0	41.2	47.1
小型	Small Enterprises	9.4	14.3	22.8	14.2

8-6 独立核算建筑施工企业主要财务指标

单位：万元

项目	Item	资产总计 Total Assets	流动资产 合计 Total Circulating Assets	# 货币资金 Cash	# 应收帐款 Accounts Receivable	# 存货 Stock
总计	**Total**	**10329718**	**8351692**	**1059760**	**2721985**	**2302821**
按企业登记注册类型分	**Grouped by Type of Enterprises Registered**					
内资企业	Domestic Investment	10050269	8104906	1006468	2678712	2225824
国有企业	State-Owned	6776162	5474341	663103	1750649	1416602
集体企业	Collective Owned	1450389	1133456	215466	288761	443487
私营企业	Private	56409	41033	7223	15030	12336
联营企业	Joint Owned	27437	22787	4622	6669	5898
股份有限公司	Share Holding Company	583741	530899	32256	254392	152157
有限责任公司	Limited-Liability Company	959015	742977	57592	323227	133234
股份合作企业	Share Holding Cooperative	162727	125980	17519	39061	39072
其他企业	Others	34389	33433	8687	923	23038
外商投资企业	Foreign Funded	145713	127638	33835	22015	42582
港、澳、台商投资企业	Hongkong,Macao and Taiwan Funded	133736	119148	19457	21258	34415
按行业类别分	**Grouped by Sector**					
土木工程	Civil Engineering	8455162	6796761	752341	2412531	1818860
线路、管道和设备安装	Line and Equipment Installation	1468517	1222618	247857	235493	381513
建筑物的装修装饰业	Building Decoration	406039	332313	59562	73961	102448
按隶属关系分	**Grouped by Administrative Relationship**					
中央	Central	3222665	2503500	394128	795169	469440
地方	Local	7107053	5848192	665632	1926816	1833381
市属	City Owned	4976576	4177338	371468	1485324	1187756
区县属	District and County Owned	967530	740177	106046	210027	279546
街道	Subdistrict Owned	91045	76955	12390	13998	39289
镇	Town Owned	279375	202544	20604	92969	63001
其他	Others	792527	651178	155124	124498	263789
按企业规模分	**Grouped by Size of Enterprises**					
大型	Large Enterprises	7165513	5764738	618606	2013921	1451819
中型	Medium Enterprises	1205813	984254	135186	349813	281181
小型	Small Enterprises	1958392	1602700	305968	358251	569821

注：本表中的建筑施工企业为四级及四级以上施工企业。

MAIN FINANCIAL INDICATORS ON CONSTRUCTION ENTERPRISES WITH INDEPENDENT ACCOUNTING SYSTEM

(10000 yuan)

#在建工程 under Construction	长期投资 Long-term Investment	固定资产合计 Total Fixed Assets	固定资产原价合计 Original Value of Fixed Assets	#生产经营用 for Production Use	累计折旧 Accumulative Depreciation	#本年折旧 of this Year	专项工程 Special Projects	无形及递延资产合计 Intangible and Deffered Assets	#无形资产 Intangible
999174	**495322**	**1129944**	**1735675**	**1151012**	**619613**	**106388**	**193527**	**75261**	**44124**
965574	492695	1110462	1702738	1129479	606143	103326	193078	70564	40460
603154	353545	721617	1124795	744627	411349	68777	149027	37976	27020
161127	43795	218341	311339	191503	94706	16733	15036	17478	5529
3326	1244	12759	15705	9509	2967	1207	749	343	70
781	160	4168	5640	2038	1472	323	243	78	53
95985	4180	41825	76316	71986	34515	6394	1636	1330	160
71566	83539	85298	134591	93959	53186	8319	24123	10813	5466
29635	6069	25696	33122	15559	7476	1534	2264	2510	2162
	163	758	1230	298	472	39		36	
12094	976	11023	17497	10661	6485	1755	160	1079	839
21506	1651	8459	15440	10872	6985	1307	289	3618	2825
758188	442807	924902	1414543	939957	501258	84450	162132	60899	34817
192777	42342	158797	257677	170902	100961	17063	28944	7856	5146
48209	10173	46245	63455	40153	17394	4875	2451	6506	4161
315710	169705	436334	685885	473071	253538	44010	66359	21814	12490
683464	325617	693610	1049790	677941	366075	62378	127168	53447	31634
431590	265819	385855	621175	413728	243131	37962	93510	23397	19562
129599	26761	154952	214606	126674	61201	11295	22075	15801	9276
20783	1933	10216	17170	11754	7037	1189	1079	556	290
10244	6881	45276	61193	41650	16076	2592	3709	9854	1553
91248	24223	97311	135646	84135	38630	9340	6795	3839	953
598378	420482	738319	1160442	774160	432291	72116	150656	44826	33241
152640	24977	141501	209458	143448	69300	12023	26783	8126	4228
248156	49863	250124	365775	233404	118022	22249	16088	22309	6655

Note: Construction enterprises of this table are those at and above forth grade.

8-6 续表 1 continued

单位：万元

项目	Item	其他资产合计 Other Assets	负债合计 Total Liability	流动负债合计 Total Circulating Liability	#短期借款 Short-term Loans	#应付帐款 Accounts Payable
总计	**Total**	**83972**	**8182804**	**7859340**	**1103780**	**1975851**
按企业登记注册类型分	**Grouped by Type of Enterprises Registered**					
内资企业	Domestic Investment	78564	8015707	7694505	1086299	1932043
国有企业	State-Owned	39657	5596781	5328762	700305	1282351
集体企业	Collective Owned	22282	983830	966271	122475	250705
私营企业	Private Owned	282	28955	28833	4616	12372
联营企业	Joint Owned	1	20256	19780	4556	6810
股份有限公司	Share Holding Company	3871	487975	485335	101141	148398
有限责任公司	Limited-Liability Company	12264	741642	710434	130095	202515
股份合作企业	Share Holding Cooperative	207	124144	122959	23091	28839
其他企业	Others		32124	32131	20	53
外商投资企业	Foreign Funded	4836	96640	95470	11429	31867
港、澳、台商投资企业	Hongkong,Macao and Taiwan Funded	572	70457	69365	6052	11941
按行业类别分	**Grouped by Sector**					
土木工程	Civil Engineering	67663	6746006	6486707	1026749	1730197
线路、管道和设备安装	Line and Equipment Installation	7961	1190531	1130421	49191	194759
建筑物的装修装饰业	Building Decoration	8348	246267	242212	27840	50895
按隶属关系分	**Grouped by Administrative Relationship**					
中央	Central	24953	2585183	2427712	295531	577917
地方	Local	59019	5597621	5431628	808249	1397934
市属	City Owned	30656	4153545	4017495	607081	1023996
区县属	District and County Owned	7764	691169	676018	104879	198344
街道	Subdistrict Owned	306	65028	64302	671	21906
镇	Town Owned	11111	162390	159044	40170	70517
其他	Others	9182	525489	514769	55448	83171
按企业规模分	**Grouped by Size of Enterprises**					
大型	Large Enterprises	46493	5918129	5647767	846786	1369913
中型	Medium Enterprises	20173	920444	896937	81097	251706
小型	Small Enterprises	17306	1344231	1314636	175897	354232

8-6 续表 2 continued

(10000 yuan)

长期负债合计 Total Long-term Liability	#长期借款 Long-term Loans	所有者权益合计 Ownership Interest	实收资本 Contributed Capital	国家资本 State	集体资本 Collective	法人资本 Institutionnai Units	个人资本 Individuals	港澳台资本 Hongkong, Macao and Taiwan	外商资本 Foreign	工程结算收入 Revenue of Settlement of Projects
323464	**99019**	**2146914**	**1377914**	**608967**	**276778**	**384801**	**47583**	**29960**	**29824**	**6457642**
321202	97861	2034563	1263271	592730	271478	353795	45006	263		6226854
268020	71966	1179381	680813	510734	1093	166814	2172			3583912
17559	13189	466559	280599	148	241930	38016	505			1263186
122	121	27454	25860			10903	14957			37495
476	280	7182	10682	4659	4670	1276	77			16776
2640	1458	95766	74708	43274	4330	21618	5224	263		673150
31208	9860	217373	158248	33912	7440	103614	13283			524057
1185	995	38582	30168	3	11015	10361	8788			121019
-8	-8	2266	2193		1000	1193				7259
1170	405	49073	52056	4770	1792	13159	2512	239	29585	128512
1092	753	63278	62587	11467	3508	17847	65	29458	239	102276
259299	75558	1709156	1054603	528565	221735	275980	14662	7453	6209	5233738
60111	22517	277986	156712	45810	37901	60190	7903	3638	1269	884897
4054	944	159772	166599	34592	17142	48631	25018	18869	22346	339007
157471	44006	637482	375071	229516	10142	121319	2105	8134	3855	2169361
165993	55013	1509432	1002843	379451	266636	263482	45478	21826	25969	4288281
136050	34160	823031	531401	314463	32202	159290	6722	9746	8978	2533708
15151	10149	276361	200021	58148	95291	32854	8903	2253	2572	787838
726	446	26017	19998		18075	1176	276	156	315	72252
3346	2206	116985	64671	200	45865	16832	805	99	870	289167
10720	8052	267038	186752	6640	75203	53330	28772	9572	13234	605316
270362	78228	1247383	713994	427608	73889	206592	2421	960	2523	4055342
23506	7887	285369	184385	67314	54707	50987	7102	2456	1818	859746
29596	12904	614162	479535	114045	148182	127222	38060	26544	25483	1542554

8-6 续表 3 continued

单位：万元

项目	Item	工程结算成本 Cost of Settlement of Projects	工程结算税金及附加 Tax and Extra Charges of Settlement of Projects	工程结算利润 Profits of Settlement of Projects	其他业务收入 Revenue of Other Business	其他业务利润 Profits of Other Business
总计	**Total**	**5576656**	**197296**	**683690**	**433650**	**72913**
按企业登记注册类型分	**Grouped by Type of Enterprises Registered**					
内资企业	Domestic Investment	5379429	191354	656072	430893	72319
国有企业	State-Owned	3119430	109730	354752	366258	55117
集体企业	Collective Owned	1087496	41441	134249	22950	10305
私营企业	Private Owned	31715	1161	4620	856	183
联营企业	Joint Owned	14568	581	1627	227	166
股份有限公司	Share Holding Company	572702	19609	80840	1804	211
有限责任公司	Limited-Liability Company	444987	15405	63665	38136	6249
股份合作企业	Share Holding Cooperative	102296	3187	15535	662	88
其他企业	Others	6235	240	784		
外商投资企业	Foreign Funded	107569	3098	17845	1039	258
港、澳、台商投资企业	Hongkong,Macao and Taiwan Funded	89658	2844	9773	1718	336
按行业类别分	**Grouped by Sector**					
土木工程	Civil Engineering	4538208	157926	537605	386446	64953
线路、管道和设备安装	Line and Equipment Installation	750860	29470	104566	42770	6888
建筑物的装修装饰业	Building Decoration	287588	9900	41519	4434	1072
按隶属关系分	**Grouped by Administrative Relationship**					
中央	Central	1904309	65457	199595	131012	12417
地方	Local	3672347	131839	484095	302638	60496
市属	City Owned	2165683	76349	291676	269654	47380
区县属	District and County Owned	682521	24110	81207	13660	4422
街道	Subdistrict Owned	62111	2409	7732	858	409
镇	Town Owned	243659	10186	35322	2779	388
其他	Others	518373	18785	68158	15687	7897
按企业规模分	**Grouped by Size of Enterprises**					
大型	Large Enterprises	3510710	122872	421760	374050	57184
中型	Medium Enterprises	741897	26353	91496	23908	8835
小型	Small Enterprises	1324049	48071	170434	35692	6894

8-6 续表 4 continued

(10000 yuan)

管理费用 Overhead Cost	税金 Taxes	财产保险费 Premium of Property	劳动待业保险费 Premium for Employment	财务费用 Financial Expense	#利息支出 Interest Expenditure	营业利润 Operating Profits	投资收益 Investment Income	营业外收入 Out-business Income	营业外支出 Out-business Expenditure	利润总额 Total Profits
573312	**8449**	**2592**	**75438**	**52272**	**41728**	**131019**	**6741**	**26313**	**13745**	**135595**
548580	7868	2458	75157	51926	41560	127885	6729	25894	13605	131950
337248	3953	1493	54506	31182	25112	41439	5369	22759	8678	47376
89655	2785	683	1892	3622	1029	51277	734	2060	3272	51535
5854	97	49	49	-5	-19	-1047	17	8	51	-1510
1631	33	5	218	32	26	130	1	87	8	268
50305	204	77	6644	9345	8551	21401	287	328	493	21478
53787	678	120	11760	6961	6740	9166	276	275	923	7312
9688	118	31	87	937	269	4999	45	377	122	5029
412			1	-148	-148	520			58	462
13029	506	82	129	368	295	4705	12	257	56	4959
11703	75	52	152	-22	-127	-1571		162	84	-1314
445671	6409	2104	60108	50615	41329	106271	3674	24912	11627	113075
89085	1291	296	14798	589	-486	21781	2893	765	1787	19368
38556	749	192	532	1068	885	2967	174	636	331	3152
172824	1667	478	24448	13934	8957	25253	2143	2880	4013	24013
400488	6782	2114	50990	38338	32771	105766	4598	23433	9732	111582
264516	3398	995	47236	31950	30091	42589	3673	20219	5500	48113
62585	1678	577	3030	4105	2351	18939	103	1691	2402	18937
7056	180	26	137	-15	-81	1101	16	190	231	1042
16194	889	103	35	3071	1958	16445	2	432	290	16824
50137	637	413	552	-773	-1548	26692	804	901	1309	26666
362470	4785	1347	62175	44559	36943	71915	5148	21364	9468	75314
71945	785	493	8191	3366	2216	25021	549	856	1325	24160
138897	2879	752	5072	4347	2569	34083	1044	4093	2952	36121

8-6 续表 5 continued

单位：万元

项目	Item	应交所得税 Income Tax Payable	转作奖金的利润 Profits Distributed as Bonus	提取盈余公积 Surplus Accumulation Funds Drawn	应付利润 Profits Payable	# 已分配股利 Divided Payment
总计	**Total**	**49908**	**3529**	**39928**	**16354**	**2893**
按企业登记注册类型分	**Grouped by Type of Enterprises Registered**					
内资企业	Domestic Investment	48480	3524	39561	14594	1433
国有企业	State-Owned	19784	1717	22166	2820	452
集体企业	Collective Owned	15769	1639	13927	8052	225
私营企业	Private Owned	316	3	49	89	3
联营企业	Joint Owned	125		188	45	
股份有限公司	Share Holding Company	6632	138	1572	1129	433
有限责任公司	Limited-Liability Company	3887	27	1152	1827	31
股份合作企业	Share Holding Cooperative	1786		480	498	289
其他企业	Others	181		27	134	
外商投资企业	Foreign Funded	1080	1	316	1302	1187
港、澳、台商投资企业	Hongkong,Macao and Taiwan Funded	348	4	51	458	273
按行业类别分	**Grouped by Sector**					
土木工程	Civil Engineering	39441	2912	35954	11558	1364
线路、管道和设备安装	Line and Equipment Installation	7793	531	3123	3147	655
建筑物的装修装饰业	Building Decoration	2674	86	851	1649	874
按隶属关系分	**Grouped by Administrative Relationship**					
中央	Central	9900	218	8488	2077	830
地方	Local	40008	3311	31440	14277	2063
市属	City Owned	20512	1459	16105	3377	432
区县属	District and County Owned	6473	412	4621	2656	7
街道	Subdistrict Owned	468	60	236	103	14
镇	Town Owned	5179	198	2094	2646	68
其他	Others	7376	1182	8384	5495	1542
按企业规模分	**Grouped by Size of Enterprises**					
大型	Large Enterprises	27295	1411	28940	4321	804
中型	Medium Enterprises	6982	450	3747	4803	1351
小型	Small Enterprises	15631	1668	7241	7230	738

8-6 续表 6 continued

(10000 yuan)

未分配利润 Profits Undistributed	本年应付工资总额 Total Wages Payable in the Year	# 主营业务应付工资 Wage Payable of Major Business	本年应付福利费总额 Welfares Payable in the Year	# 主营业务应付福利费 of Major Business	建筑业增加值 Value Added of Construction	流动比率 (%) Circulating Assets /Liquid Liabilities(%)	速动比率(%) Quick-circulating Assets /Liquid Lia-bilities(%)	资产负债率 (%) Liabilities/ Total Assets(%)	存货周转率 (%) Turn-over Rate of Stock(%)	资本金利润率 (%) Profits/ Capital (%)
78021	**717783**	**660669**	**85099**	**77700**	**1806102**	**1.06**	**0.77**	**0.79**	**2.52**	**0.10**
77898	704763	647833	82623	75230	1753314	1.05	0.76	0.80	2.50	0.10
11919	403160	359055	50670	45184	994239	1.03	0.76	0.83	2.24	0.07
49296	176713	170422	16367	15614	381498	1.17	0.71	0.68	2.56	0.18
-489	5186	5050	346	325	12505	1.42	1.00	0.51	3.03	-0.06
-410	1670	1609	194	188	4579	1.15	0.85	0.74	3.53	0.03
11609	49703	48338	7487	7383	169274	1.09	0.78	0.84	4.13	0.29
5065	51193	46467	6083	5065	151332	1.05	0.86	0.77	3.52	0.05
887	16294	16051	1371	1366	37877	1.03	0.71	0.76	2.95	0.17
21	844	841	105	105	2010	1.04	0.32	0.93	0.31	0.21
1682	7168	6997	1305	1305	31636	1.34	0.89	0.66	3.05	0.10
-1559	5852	5839	1171	1165	21152	1.72	1.22	0.53	3.12	-0.02
74414	581031	527249	67399	60697	1431532	1.05	0.77	0.80	2.58	0.11
8507	111235	108396	14646	13986	289039	1.08	0.74	0.81	2.12	0.12
-4900	25517	25024	3054	3017	85531	1.37	0.95	0.61	2.92	0.02
6100	199827	179835	25303	22163	536958	1.03	0.84	0.80	4.24	0.06
71921	517956	480834	59796	55537	1269144	1.08	0.74	0.79	2.08	0.11
15320	288627	260367	37270	34103	749631	1.04	0.74	0.84	1.86	0.09
16745	113813	110119	11876	11403	242430	1.10	0.68	0.71	2.66	0.10
266	12950	12713	1134	1109	25409	1.20	0.59	0.71	1.81	0.05
8693	32208	29161	2990	2600	80587	1.27	0.88	0.58	4.01	0.26
30897	70358	68474	6526	6322	171087	1.27	0.75	0.66	2.07	0.14
48821	455942	412575	56229	50894	1145765	1.02	0.76	0.83	2.46	0.11
13679	89864	82286	10343	9039	229724	1.10	0.78	0.76	2.66	0.13
15521	171977	165808	18527	17767	430613	1.22	0.79	0.69	2.60	0.08

8-7 全市建筑施工企业利税总额前50名
THE FIRST FIFTY PLACES OF TOTAL PRE-TAX PROFITS OF CONSTRUCTION ENTERPRISES

单位：万元 (10000 yuan)

名次 No.	企业名称	Enterprise	利税总额 Total Pre-tax Profits
1	北京韩村河建筑集团总公司	Beijing Hancunhe Construction Engineering Group Co.	10126.0
2	北京城建集团二公司	Beijing No.2 Urban Construction Company	8365.0
3	中国建筑第一工程局第四建筑公司	China Construction First Division 4th Construction Co.	8036.9
4	北京市第五城市建设工程公司	Beijing No.5 Urban Construction Company	7465.4
5	北京市第四城市建设工程公司	Beijing No.4 Urban Construction Company	7363.1
6	铁道部第十六工程局	16th Engineering Bureau of Ministry of Railways	6727.4
7	中国电子系统工程总公司	China Electronic Systems Engineering Corporation	5469.0
8	北京中铁建筑工程公司	Beijing Zhong-Tie Construction Engineering Group	5465.8
9	交通部第一公路工程总公司	Ministry of Communication 1th Highway engineering Co.	5163.5
10	北京市市政工程总公司	Beijing Municipal Engineering Corporation	5099.3
11	北京市第一城市建设工程公司	Beijing No.1 Urban Construction Company	4919.4
12	北京住总集团有限责任公司	Beijing Residential House Development &Construction Group Co.	4773.0
13	中国人民解放军总后工程总队	CPLA General Logistics Department Head Engineering Team	4578.5
14	北京市第五建筑工程公司	Beijing No.5 Construction Engineering Company	4453.6
15	北京市城建道桥工程公司	Beijing Urban Construction & Road Bridge Engineering Company	4359.9
16	北京市第六建筑工程公司	Beijing No.6 Construction Engineering Company	4092.0
17	北京市第二住宅建筑工程公司	Beijing 2th Residential Construction Engineering Co.	3754.5
18	北京市房山区建筑企业集团总公司	Beijing Fangshan Construction General Company (Group) Corp	3603.4
19	北京建雄建筑集团	Beijing Jianxiong Construction Group	3581.5
20	北京市第三城市建设工程公司	Beijing No.3 Urban Construction Company	3362.8
21	北京市第一建筑工程公司	Beijing No.1 Construction Engineering Company	3232.4
22	北京市第三建筑工程公司	Beijing No.3 Construction Engineering Company	3176.7
23	中建第一工程局第五建筑公司	China Construction First Division 5th Construction Co.	3092.8
24	中国四海工程公司	China Si Hai Engineering Corporation	3019.7
25	中建建筑承包公司	CSCEC Construction Co.,Ltd	2992.7
26	北京城建亚泰工程公司	Beijing Urban Construction Yatai Engineering Company	2941.5
27	北京市第五住宅建筑工程公司	Beijing 5th Residential Construction Engineering Co.	2918.9
28	北京市朝阳田华建筑集团公司	Beijing Chaoyang Tianhua Construction Group Co.	2911.0
29	中国对外建设总公司	China Construction International Corp	2878.5
30	北京市第三住宅建筑工程公司	Beijing 3th Residential Construction Engineering Co.	2731.2
31	北京市城市建设工程安装公司	Beijing Urban Construction Engineering Installation Company	2721.8
32	房山建工企业集团总公司	Fangshan Construction & Industry Enterprise (FCIE) Group Corp	2718.9
33	中国建筑第一工程局第三建筑公司	China Construction First Division 3th Construction Co.	2687.4
34	光大国际交通工程总公司	Everbringht International Construction Corporation	2659.6
35	北京市平谷县建筑工程总公司	Beijing Pinggu Construction Engineering Co.	2605.4
36	北京市房山城乡建筑企业集团总公司	Beijing Fangshan Urban & Rural Construction Group Co.	2507.0
37	中国建筑第二局第一建筑工程公司	China Construction 2th Bureau 1th Construction Company	2463.4
38	北京电力建设公司	Beijing Electric Power Construction Company	2458.8
39	北京城乡建设集团有限责任公司	Beijing Urban & Rural Construction Group Co., Ltd	2456.8
40	北京市第六住宅建筑工程公司	Beijing 6th Residential Construction Engineering Co.	2336.8
41	北京市第七建筑工程公司	Beijing No.7 Construction Engineering Company	2322.6
42	北京铁路工程总公司	Beijing Ralway Construction Engineering Co.	2265.1
43	北京市设备安装工程公司	Beijing Machinery Equipment & Installation Engineering Company	2257.2
44	北京华威建筑工程有限公司	Beijing Huawei Construction Limited Company	2186.9
45	北京市第三市政工程公司	Beijing 3th Municpal Engineering Corp	2139.3
46	北京顺义建筑企业集团公司	Beijing Shunyi Construction Group Corp	2078.9
47	北京市第二建筑工程公司	Beijing No.2 Construction Engineering Company	1969.8
48	北京市第二市政工程公司	Beijing 2th Municpal Engineering Corp	1908.3
49	北京市第七城市建设工程公司	Beijing No.7 Urban Construction Company	1849.5
50	北京怀柔建筑企业集团总公司	Beijing Huairou Construction Group Corp	1835.9

8-8 外埠进京施工单位主要指标
MAIN INDICATORS ON NON-LOCAL CONSTRUCTION UNITS IN BEIJING

项　　目 Item			1999	1998
单位个数	(个) Number of Units	(unit)	216.0	187.0
职工人数	(万人) Number of Staff and Workers	(10000 persons)	6.4	5.1
施工产值	(亿元) Output Value of Construction	(100 million yuan)	51.8	25.9
施工面积	(万平方米) Floor Space of Buildings under Construction	(10000 sq.m)	528.8	349.1
竣工面积	(万平方米) Floor Space of Buildings Completed	(10000 sq.m)	234.6	120.8

8-9 经济适用房
ECONOMIC AND SUITABLE HOUSES

项　　目 Item			合　计 Total	#住　宅 Residence
完成投资	(万元) Investment Completed	(10000 yuan)	371009	280415
施工面积	(万平方米) Floor Space of Buildings under Construction	(10000 sq.m)	3503173	3101764
竣工面积	(万平方米) Floor Space of Buildings Completed	(10000 sq.m)	1291155	1228972
竣工套数	(套) Suites of Rooms Completed	(suite)	12901	12901
销售面积	(万平方米) Floor Space of Buildings Sold	(10000 sq.m)	457711	
销售套数	(套) Suites of Rooms Sold	(suite)	4995	4995
预售面积	(万平方米) Floors Space of Buildings Sold in advance	(10000 sq.m)	537917	
预售套数	(套) Suites of Rooms Sold in advance	(suite)	5101	5101

主要统计指标解释

建筑业统计单位 是指从事房屋、构筑物建造和设备安装活动的生产单位。根据不同的组织方式，建筑业统计的调查单位可分为法人建筑业企业和附营建筑施工单位。法人建筑业企业是指专门组织的独立核算的法人建筑业企业。它应同时具备的条件是：（1）依法成立，有自己的名称、组织机构和场所，能够承担民事责任；（2）独立拥有和使用资产，承担负债，有权与其他单位签订合同；（3）独立核算盈亏，能够编制资产负债表。附营建筑施工单位是指建筑业以外行业的企业、事业单位为完成本单位固定资产建造任务而自行组织的建筑施工单位。它应同时具备的条件是：（1）具有一个场所，从事或主要从事建筑安装活动；（2）单独组织生产经营活动；（3）在企业内部单独核算收支。

建筑业总产值（即自行完成施工产值） 是指建筑业企业或附营建筑施工单位自行完成的按工程进度计算的建筑安装生产总值。建筑业产值包括：

（1）建筑工程产值 指列入建筑工程预算内的各种工程价值。

（2）设备安装工程产值 指设备安装工程价值。

（3）房屋、构筑物修理产值 是指房屋构筑物修理所完成的价值，但不包括被修理房屋、构筑物本身的价值和生产设备的修理价值。

（4）非标准设备制造产值 是指加工制造没有定型的、非标准的生产设备的加工费和原材料价值，不论是现场还是附属加工厂为本单位承建工程制造的非标准设备的价值，都应计算产值。

自有机械设备年末总台数 是指归本企业（或单位）所有，属于本企业固定资产的生产性机械设备年末总台数。包括施工机械、生产设备、运输设备以及其他设备。

自有机械设备年末总功率 是指本企业（或单位）自有施工机械、生产设备、运输设备以及其他设备等列为在册固定资产的生产性机械设备年末总功率，按设定能力或查定能力计算。包括机械本身的动力和为该机械服务的单独动力设备，如电动机等。计算单位用千瓦，动力换算可按 1 马力=0.735 千瓦折合成千瓦数。电焊机、变压器、锅炉不计算动力。

企业总收入 是指与企业生产经营直接有关的各项收入，包括工程结算收入和其他业务收入，即：

企业总收入=工程结算收入+其他业务收入

Explanatory Notes On Main Statistical Indicators

Statistical Unit of Construction refers to the establishment engaged in the construction of buildings and structures or the installation of equipment. Depending upon the way of organization, they can be divided into two categories: corporate construction enterprises and affiliated construction units,. A corporate construction enterprise is a legal entity with independent accounting system, especially set up to undertake construction activities. It should meet the following three conditions: (1) being set up in line with relevant legal basis, having its full name, organization and location, and capable of taking civil liabilities; (2) independently possessing and using its assets and assuming its liabilities, and entitled to sign contracts with other institutions; and (3) making independent accounts of its profits and losses, and capable of compiling its own balance sheet. On the other hand, the affiliated construction units are subsidiary constructing units that are established by enterprises or institutions in other industries to take construction projects to build up their fixed assets. They should also meet three conditions: (1) engaged exclusively or mainly in construction and installation activities with a stable sits; (2) organizing independently their production/management; and (3) with independent accounting capability in the enterprises to which they are attached.

Gross Output Value of Construction (Output Value of Projects Under Construction) refers to the gross output value of construction and installation projects that are undertaken by construction enterprises or affiliated constructing units, calculated in line with the planned schedule. It includes:

(1) Output value of construction projects, which is the value of projects covered by the project budgets;

(2) Output value of installation projects, which is the value of the installation of equipment;

(3) Output value of repair of buildings and structures, which is the value created through the repairs, exclude the value of buildings or structures being repaired or the value of the repair of production equipment;

(4) Output value of manufactured non-standard equipment, that is the value of non-standard production equipment (including raw materials and manufacturing cost) made for the construction project, irrespective of whether the equipment is manufactured on the construction site or in subsidiary workshops.

Total Number of Self-Owned Machinery at Year End refers to the number of machines and equipment owned by the enterprises (or units), and listed as the fixed assets of the enterprises (or units) by the end of the year, including machinery and equipment for construction, production, transportation and other purposes.

Total Power of Self-Owned Machinery at Year End refers to the total power of machines and equipment owned by the enterprises (or units), and listed as the fixed assets of the enterprises (or units) by the end of the year, including machines and equipment for construction, production, transportation and other purposes. The power of the machinery is calculated on basis of the designed or verified capacity, covering the power of the machinery/equipment and the separate power equipment serving the machinery/equipment (such as electric motors), but excluding welders, transformers and boilers. The unit used for the calculation of power is kilowatt, with horsepower converted to kilowatt by 1 horsepower = 0.735 kilowatt.

Total Revenue of Enterprises refers to the sum of income from production and operation of enterprises, including income from settlement of projects and other operational income, namely:

Total Revenue of Enterprises = Income from Settlement of Projects + Other Operation Income

交通运输、邮电通信业

TRANSPORTATION，POSTS AND TELECOMMUNICATIONS

社会客货运总量（换算周转量）
Passenger and Freight Traffic(converted into turnover volume)

万吨公里 10000 tn-km

	1999年	1998年	1999年为1998年% 1999 as % of 1998
铁路 Railway	2509028	2458156	102.1
公路 Highway	794324	813696	97.6
民航 Civil Aviation	294080	230364	127.7
管道 Pipeline	152.5	342.7	44.5

邮电业务总量
Posts and Telecommunications Services

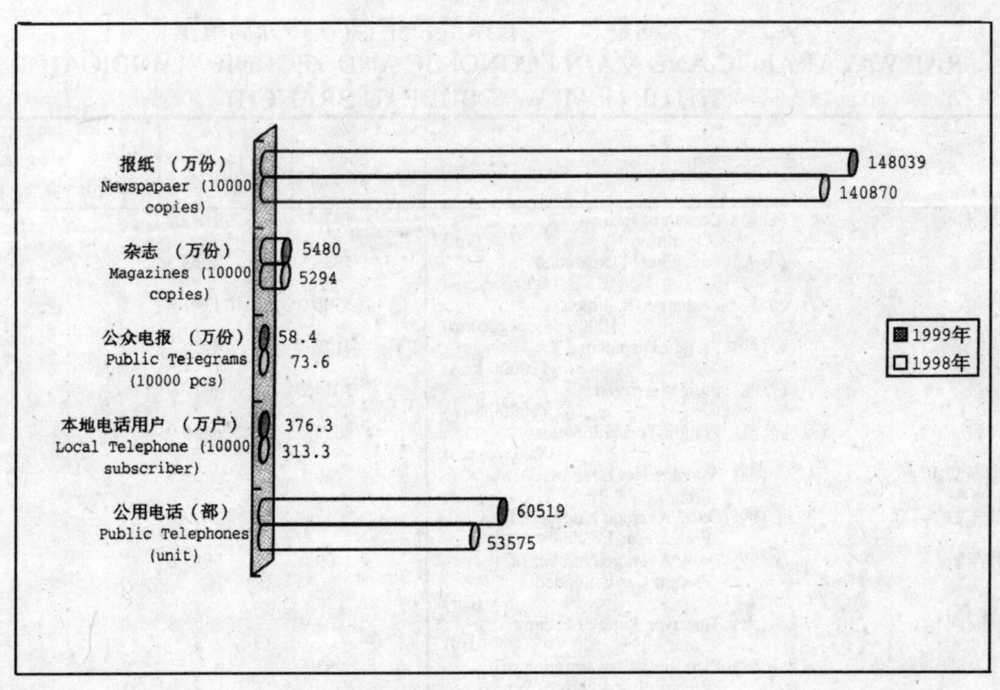

9-1 社 会 客 货 运 总 量 (换算周转量)
PASSENGER AND FREIGHT TRAFFIC(CONVERTED INTO TURNOVER VOLUME)

项 目	Item	1999	1998	1999年为1998年% 1999 as % of 1998	构 成(%) Composition(%) 1999	1998
运输总量 (万吨公里)	**Total (10000 tn-km)**	**3597584.6**	**3502558.7**	**102.7**	**100**	**100**
铁路	Railway	2509028.0	2458156.0	102.1	69.7	70.2
公路	Highway	794323.7	813696.0	97.6	22.1	23.2
# 交通运输系统	Transportation System	53515.1	52009.9	102.9		
民航	Civil Aviation	294080.4	230364.0	127.7	8.2	6.6
# 国航	Air China	269960.0	217547.5	124.1		
新华	Xinhua	24120.4	12816.5	188.2		
管道	Pipeline	152.5	342.7	44.5	…	…

9-2 运 输 线 路
TRANSPORTATION ROUTES

项 目	Item	条 数 (条) Routes(unit) 1999	1998	长 度 (公里) Length(km) 1999	1998
铁 路	Railway	26	26	1879.7	1817.2
公 路	Highway	2685	2647	12825	12498.0
民 航	Civil Aviation	173	168		
# 国航	Air China	133	134		
新华	Xinhua	40	34		
管 道	Pipeline	8	8	28.8	28.8

注：民航包括国际航空公司,新华航空公司。

Note：Data of civil aviation include those of Air China and China Xinhua Airlines.

9-3 铁路运输量及主要技术经济指标(铁路分局范围)
RAILWAY TRAFFIC AND MAIN ECONOMIC AND TECHNICAL INDICATORS (WITHIN RAILWAY BUREAU BRANCH)

项 目	Item	1999	1998	1999年为1998年% 1999 as % of 1998
营业里程 (公里)	Length of Railways in Operation (km)	1879.7	1817.2	103.4
旅客发送量 (万人)	Passengers Dispatched (10000 persons)	5335.5	4953.3	107.7
旅客周转量 (万人公里)	Passenger-Kilometers (10000 passenger-km)	1195566.0	1071241.0	111.6
货物发送量 (万吨)	Freight Dispatched (10000 tons)	4122.4	4256.3	96.9
货物到达量 (万吨)	Freight Arrived (10000 tons)	7014.2	7216.9	97.2
货物周转量 (万吨公里)	Freight Ton-Kilometers (10000 ton-km)	4478635.0	4506860.0	99.4
货物平均净载重 (吨)	Average Net Load of Freight (ton)	56.1	55.8	100.5
平均日装车数 (辆)	Daily Average Number of Freight Car Loaded	2013.0	2089.0	96.4
平均日卸车数 (辆)	Daily Average Number of Freight Car Unloaded (car)	3409.0	3553.0	95.9
货车周转时间 (天)	Turnover Time of Freight Train (day)	1.9	1.8	107.4
电力机车万吨公里耗电 (千瓦时)	Electricity Consumption of Electric Locomotives Per 10000 Ton-km (kwh)	93.5		
内燃机万吨公里耗油 (公斤)	Oil Consumption of Diesel Locomotives Per 10000 Ton-km (kg)	28.7	29.2	98.3

9-4 全社会客、货运输量及周转量
PASSENGER AND FREIGHT TRAFFIC AND TURNOVER VOLUME

项　目 Item		1999	1998	1999年为1998年% 1999 as % of 1998	构　成(%) Composition(%)	
					1999	1998
旅客运输量	**(万人次) Passenger Traffic (10000 person.times)**	**14866.4**	**11227.7**	**132.4**	**100**	**100**
铁路	Railway	4200.5	3761.6	111.7	28.3	33.5
公路	Highway	9878.0	6704.0	147.3	66.4	59.7
交通运输系统	Transportation System	8541.6	5945.0	143.7		
非交通运输系统	Non-transportation System	1336.4	759.0	176.1		
民航	Civil Aviation	787.9	762.1	103.4	5.3	6.8
旅客周转量	**(万人公里) Passenger-Kilometers (10000 passenger-km)**	**2701470.8**	**2419786.9**	**111.6**	**100**	**100**
铁路	Railway	579759	505553.8	114.7	21.5	20.9
公路	Highway	400597.0	304592.0	131.5	14.8	12.6
交通运输系统	Transportation System	36079.6	199249.0	18.1		
非交通运输系统	Non-transportation System	364517.4	105343.0			
民航	Civil Aviation	1721114.8	1609641.1	106.9	63.7	66.5
货物运输量	**(万吨) Freight Traffic (10000 tons)**	**28274.8**	**30126.5**	**93.9**	**100**	**100**
铁路	Railway	2582.8	2562.5	100.8	9.1	8.5
公路	Highway	25635.0	27490.0	93.3	90.7	91.2
交通运输系统	Transportation System	539.2	688.0	78.4		
非交通运输系统	Non-transportation System	25095.8	26802.0	93.6		
民航	Civil Aviation	29.9	22.4	133.7	0.1	0.1
管道	Pipeline	27.1	51.6	52.5	0.1	0.2
货物周转量	**(万吨公里) Freight Ton-Kilometers (10000 ton-km)**	**2838856.6**	**2846652.2**	**99.7**	**100**	**100**
铁路	Railway	1929269	1952602	98.8	68	68.6
公路	Highway	754264.0	783237.0	96.3	26.6	27.5
交通运输系统	Transportation System	26723.4	32085.0	83.3		
非交通运输系统	Non-transportation System	727540.6	751152.0	96.9		
民航	Civil Aviation	155171.1	110470.5	140.5	5.4	3.9
管道	Pipeline	152.5	342.7	44.5	…	…

9-5 公路、民航、邮电主要技术经济指标
MAIN TECHNICAL AND ECONOMIC INDICATORS OF HIGHWAY,CIVIL AVIATION, POSTS AND TELECOMMUNICATIONS

项目		Item		1999	1998	1999年为1998年% 1999 as % of 1998
公路货运		**Highway Freight Traffic**				
货车百吨公里耗汽油	(升)	Petroleum Consumption of Trucks Per 100 Ton-km	(liter)	6.7	6.7	100.0
货车百吨公里耗柴油	(升)	Diesel Consumption of Trucks Per 100 Ton-km	(liter)	4.5	4.5	100.0
货车车吨日产量	(吨公里)	Average Daily Tonnage of Trucks	(ton-km)	44.3	46.8	94.7
货车完好率	(%)	Intact Rate of Trucks	(%)	90.0	89.2	
民　航		**Civil Aviation**				
每吨公里耗航空油	(公斤)	Aviation-oil Consumption Per Kilometer	(kg)			
# 国航		Air China		0.34	0.37	91.9
新华		Xinhua		0.53	0.54	98.1
邮　电		**Posts and Telecommunications**				
总包邮件损失	(个)	Loss of Parcels	(piece)	1.0	126.0	0.8
邮件全程时限延误率	(%)	Lossing Rate of Time Limit of Postal Matter Mailed during Whole Course	(%)	0.02	0.03	

注：民航包括国际航空公司,新华航空公司。

Note：Data of civil aviation include those of Air China and China Xinhua Airlines.

9-6 邮 电 业 务 总 量
POSTS AND TELECOMMUNICATIONS SERVICES

项目		Item		1999	1998	1999年为1998年% 1999 as % of 1998
邮电业务量	**(万元)**	**Sales Revenue of Posts and Telecommunications**	**(10000 yuan)**	**1566110.3**	**1290966.5**	**121.3**
邮电业务总量		**Sales Volume of Posts and Telecommunications**				
函件	(万件)	Letters	(10000 pcs)	55071.0	50762.0	108.5
包件	(万件)	Parcels	(10000 pcs)	445.0	438.0	101.6
汇票	(万件)	Postal Money Order	(10000)	888.0	869.0	102.2
报纸累计	(万份)	Newspaper	(10000 copies)	148039.0	140870.0	105.1
杂志累计	(万份)	Magazines	(10000 copies)	5480.0	5294.0	103.5
公众电报	(万份)	Public Telegrams	(10000 pcs)	58.4	73.6	79.4
用户电报	(万次)	Telex	(10000 times)	88.4	125.0	70.7
长途电话	(万次)	Long-Distance Calls	(10000 times)	70849.1	70375.8	100.7
本地电话用户	(户)	Local Telephone Subscribers	(subscriber)	3763224.0	3132642.0	120.1
公用电话	(部)	Public Telephone	(unit)	60519.0	53575.0	113.0

注：本地电话用户包括市内电话用户和农村电话用户，以后农村电话指标不再单独反映。

Note：Data of local telephone subscribers included urban and rural areas,and rural telephones won't be reported separately any more.

9-7 邮电局、所及邮路

POSTS AND TELECOMMUNICATIONS OFFICES AND POSTAL ROUTES

单位：公里 (km)

项目	Item	1999	1998	1999年为1998年% 1999 as % of 1998	构成(%) Composition(%) 1999	1998
邮电局所 (处)	**Number of Posts and Telecommunications Offices (unit)**	**750**	**728**	**103.0**		
邮路单程总长度	**Length of Postal Route**	**109838**	**101715**	**108.0**	**100**	**100**
航空邮路	Air Routes	47029	48987	96.0	42.8	48.1
铁路邮路	Railway Routes	20789	19844	104.8	18.9	19.5
自办汽车邮路	Highway Routes	40232	31094	129.4	36.6	30.6
其　他	Others	1788	1790	99.9	1.7	1.8

9-8 邮电局、所地区分布

POSTS AND TELECOMMUNICATIONS OFFICES BY REGION

地区	Region	邮电局、所 Posts and Telecommunications Offices 1999	1998	# 设在农村 In Rural Areas 1999	1998
全　市	**Total**	**750**	**728**	**276**	**265**
城　区	**City Proper**	**104**	**110**		
东城区	Dongcheng	37	38		
西城区	Xicheng	38	42		
崇文区	Chongwen	10	10		
宣武区	Xuanwu	19	20		
近郊区	**Near Suburbs**	**286**	**276**		
朝阳区	Chaoyang	112	116		
丰台区	Fengtai	51	40		
石景山区	Shijingshan	13	13		
海淀区	Haidian	110	107		
远郊区	**Outer Suburbs**	**218**	**206**	**170**	**162**
门头沟区	Mentougou	22	20	15	13
房山区	Fangshan	68	68	56	56
通州区	Tongzhou	49	47	35	35
昌平区	Changping	41	40	36	35
顺义区	Shunyi	38	31	28	23
各　县	**Counties**	**142**	**136**	**106**	**103**
大兴县	Daxing	43	40	32	30
平谷县	Pinggu	23	23	16	16
怀柔县	Huairou	26	25	21	21
密云县	Miyun	25	25	19	19
延庆县	Yanqing	25	23	18	17

9-9 各 种 车 辆
VARIOUS VEHICLES

单位：辆 (unit)

项 目 Item		1999	1998	1999年为1998年% 1999 as % of 1998	构 成(%) Composition(%) 1999	1998
机动车	**Motor Vehicles**	**1241719**	**1163338**	**106.7**	**100**	**100**
汽 车	Automobiles	948506	890141	106.6	76.4	76.5
货 车	Trucks	202195	196068	103.1	21.3	16.9
#大 货	Heavy Trucks	57932	56550	102.4	28.7	28.8
客 车	Coaches	742299	690344	107.5	59.8	59.3
#小客车	Small Coaches	719837	670217	107.4	97.0	97.1
特种车	Special Purpose Vehicles	4012	3729	107.6	0.4	0.3
机动脚踏车(摩托车)	Motorcycles	292621	272612	107.3	23.6	23.4
#轻 便	Light	121676	115992	104.9	41.6	42.6
电 车	Trolleys	592	585	101.2	0.1	0.1
私人机动车	**Private Automobiles**	**762361**	**697707**	**109.3**	**100**	**100**
#小轿车	cars	206152	177466	116.2	27.0	25.44
非机动车	**Nonmotor Vehicles**	**10308466**	**10002620**	**103.1**	**100**	**100**
自行车	Bicycles	9678544	9404252	102.9	93.9	94.0
三轮车	Tricycles	629922	598368	105.3	6.1	6.0

主要统计指标解释

铁路营业里程 又称营业长度，指办理客货运输业务的铁路正线总长度。凡是全线或部分建成双线及以上的线路，以第一线的实际长度计算；复线、站线、段管线、岔线和特殊用途线以及不计算运费的联络线都不计算营业里程。铁路营业里程是反映铁路运输业基础设施发展水平的重要指标，也是计算客货周转量、运输密度和机车车辆运用效率等指标的基础资料。

货（客）运量 指在一定时期内，各种运输工具实际运送的货物（旅客）数量。是反映运输业为国民经济和人民生活服务的数量指标，也是制定和检查运输生产计划，研究运输发展规模和速度的重要指标。货运按吨计算，客运按人计算。货物不论运输距离长短，货物类别，均按实际重量统计；旅客不论行程远近或票价多少，均按一人一次作为客运量统计。半价票、小孩票也按一人统计。

货物（旅客）周转量 指在一定时期内，由各种运输工具运送的货物（旅客）数量与其相应运输距离的乘积之总和，是反映运输业生产总成果的重要指标，也是编制和检查运输生产计划，计算运输效率、劳动生产率以及核算运输单位主要基础资料。通常以吨公里和人公里为计算单位。计算货物周转量通常按发出站与到达站之间的最短距离，也就是计费距离计算。

邮电业务总量 指以货币表现的邮电部门用于传递信息和提供其他邮电服务的总数量。它综合反映了一定时期邮电工作的总成果，是研究邮电业务量构成和发展趋势的重要指标。根据邮电管理体制不同，分为中央国营业务总量和地方国营业务总量。它用各种邮电分类业务量，如函件件数、电报份数、长话张数、市内电话和农村电话的年均户数、订销报刊累计份数等，分别乘以相应的平均单价（不变价），加总后再加上出租电路和设备的收入、代用户维护电话交换机和线路等设备的收入、其他业务收入求得。

Explanatory Notes On Main Statistical Indicators

Length of Railways in Operation refers to the total length of the trunk line for passenger and freight transportation. The calculation is based on the actual length of the first line if the line has a full or partial double track or more tracks, excluding double tracks, station sidings, tracks under the charge of stations, branch lines, specialpurpose lines and the non-payable connecting lines. The length of railways in operation is an important indicator to show the development of the infrastructure for the railway transport, and also the essential data to calculate volume of passenger freight , traffic density and utilization of the locomotives and carriages.

Freight （Passenger)Traffic refers to the volume of freight （passenger)transported with various means. Freight transport is calculated in tons and passenger traffic is calculated in the number of persons. Despite the type of freight and traveling distance, the freight traffic is calculated by weight. Similarly, the passenger traffic is calculated by person regardless he/she travels with a half-price ticket or a child ticket or an adults ticket or how long his/her trip is. The freight(passenger)traffic provides a quantitative measure to show how the transport industry serves the national economy and people, and is also an important indicator for planning the transport industry and for studying the development scale and speed of the transport industry.

Freight Ton-kilometers(Passenger -kilometers)refer to the sum of the products of the volume of transported cargo（passengers）multiplying by the transport distance, usually using ton-kilometer and passenger-kilometers as units for measurement. Normally , the shortest distance between the departure station and the destination station（I. e., the payable distance）is the bases to calculate the freight ton-kilometers. This is an important indicator to show the total results of the transport industry, to prepare and examine the transport plan and to measure the efficiency, the labour productivity and the unit cost of transport.

Business Volume of Posts and Telecommunications refers to the total value of the information delivered and other posts and telecommunications services provided by the posts and telecommunications departments for the customers. It is derived by first multiplying the business volume of different types, such as number of letters, telegrams, long distance calls., city and rural telephone subscribers and accumulated number of newspapers and journals subscribed and sold, etc. by their respective average unit price（fixed price）, and then adding these products together, and then plus the income from the rent of line and equipment, the income from maintenance of telephone exchanges and lines, and the income from other business operations. The business volume of posts and telecommunication indicates the total achievements made by the posts and telecommunications department during a given period of time in a comprehensive way, and is an important indicator to study the composition and development of the posts and telecommunications business.

批发零售贸易业和餐饮业

WHOLESALE，RETAIL AND CATERING

社会消费品零售额（1978-1999年）
Total Retail Sales of Consumer Goods(year 1978-1999)

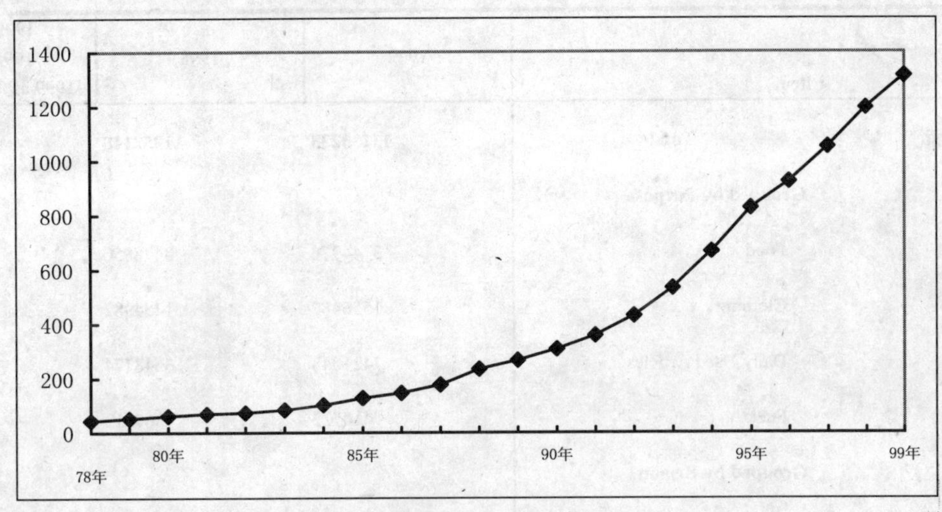

	1999	1998	1999年为1998年% 1999 as % of 1998
社会消费品零售额(亿元) Total Retail Sales of Consumer Goods (100 million yuan)	1313.3	1195.2	109.9

构成(%) Composition(%)

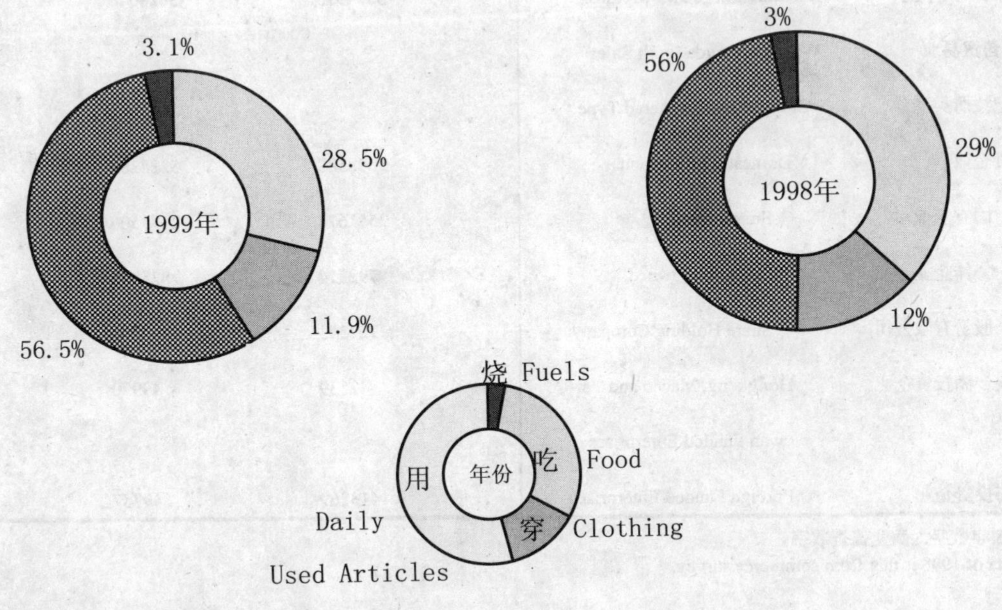

10-1 社会消费品零售额
TOTAL RETAIL SALES OF CONSUMER GOODS

单位：万元 (10000 yuan)

项目	Item	1999	1998	1999年为1998年% 1999 as % of 1998
总计	**Total**	**13133233**	**11952118**	**109.9**
按用途分	**Grouped by Purpose**			
吃的商品	Food	3744976	3478850	107.6
穿的商品	Clothing	1556487	1454982	107.0
用的商品	Daily Used Articles	7421048	6648774	111.6
烧的商品	Fuels	410722	369512	111.2
按地区分	**Grouped by Region**			
城镇零售额	City Ang Counties	11216745	10295606	108.9
农村零售额	Below County Level	1916488	1656512	115.7
按行业分	**Grouped by Sectors**			
批发零售贸易业	Wholesale and Retail Trade	9261776	8657131	107.0
餐饮业	Catering	812690	818162	99.3
制造业	Manufacturing	798169	637469	125.2
其他	Others	2260598	1839356	122.9
# 农民对非农民	Peasant to Non-peasant	76180	89463	85.2
在总计中：大中型	**Of Total: Large and Medium**	**5554995**	**5628046**	**98.7**
批发零售贸易业	**Wholesale and Retail Sales**			
按登记注册类型分	Grouped by Registered Type			
内资企业	Domestic Investment	5098587	5228289	97.5
# 国有企业	State-owned	2551678	2671500	95.5
集体企业	Collective-owned	792314	825893	95.9
股份有限公司	Share Holding Company	727343	702305	103.6
港澳台商投资企业	Hongkong, Macao and Taiwan Funded Enterprises	42539	49970	85.1
外商投资企业	Foreign Funded Enterprises	413869	349787	118.3

注：1998年数字为商业普查数字。

Note: Data of 1998 is that from commerce survey.

10-2 各区县消费品零售额
RETAIL SALES OF CONSUMER GOODS IN DISTRICTS AND COUNTIES

单位：万元 (10000 yuan)

地区	Region	合计 Total	按用途分 Grouped by Purpose			
			吃的商品 Food	穿的商品 Clothing	用的商品 Daily Used Articles	烧的商品 Fuels
全市	**Total**	**9995218**	**3185064**	**1148246**	**5326488**	**335420**
城区	**City Proper**	**2620881**	**871342**	**419763**	**1312477**	**17299**
东城区	Dongcheng	744669	278820	126227	330374	9248
西城区	Xicheng	985838	263848	182059	536977	2954
崇文区	Chongwen	418983	171532	66921	179073	1457
宣武区	Xuanwu	471391	157142	44556	266053	3640
近郊区	**Near Suburbs**	**5070302**	**1388150**	**411324**	**3101422**	**169406**
朝阳区	Chaoyang	1642919	540520	225080	754100	123219
丰台区	Fengtai	613137	283987	64920	241656	22574
石景山区	Shijingshan	319603	178753	14076	121800	4974
海淀区	Haidian	2494643	384890	107248	1983866	18639
远郊区	**Outer Suburbs**	**1449722**	**557276**	**184382**	**609007**	**99057**
门头沟区	Mentougou	161721	74627	10972	70976	5146
房山区	Fangshan	454008	124578	79059	205149	45222
通州区	Tongzhou	330069	166025	23765	134008	6271
昌平区	Changping	180521	74798	17871	76334	11518
顺义区	Shunyi	323403	117248	52715	122540	30900
各县	**Counties**	**854313**	**368296**	**132777**	**303582**	**49658**
大兴县	Daxing	256166	122959	27666	86329	19212
平谷县	Pinggu	128418	44004	23629	49099	11686
怀柔县	Huairou	137223	42241	24915	66265	3802
密云县	Miyun	146712	80692	16138	41079	8803
延庆县	Yanqing	185794	78400	40429	60810	6155

注：本表中区县商业企业为中央属及区县属口径。
Note: Data of this table refers to that of central units,districts and counties.

10-3 社会批发零售贸易业商品购、销、存总值
TOTAL PURCHASES,SALES AND INVENTORY IN WHOLESALE AND RETAIL

单位：万元 (10000 yuan)

项目	Item	1999	1998	1999年为1998年% 1999 as % of 1998
商品购进总额	**Total Purchases of Goods**	**23271293**	**26521113**	**87.7**
市内纯购进	In the City	11603478	11577465	100.2
市外购进	From Outside	7404008	10084294	73.4
进　口	Import	4263807	4859354	87.7
商品销售总额	**Total Sales**	**26585799**	**27239511**	**97.6**
市内纯销售	In the City	17914608	16793976	106.7
市外销售	To Outside	3324421	3575296	93.0
出　口	Export	5346770	6870239	77.8
年末库存	**Inventory (year-end)**	**5207716**	**5729750**	**90.9**

注：1998 年数字为商业普查数字。
Note: Data of 1998 is that from commerce survey.

10-4 批发零售贸易业商品购、销、存总值
PURCHASES,SALES AND INVENTORY IN WHOLESALE AND RETAIL

单位：万元 (10000 yuan)

项目	Item	1999	1998	1999年为1998年% 1999 as % of 1998
商品购进总额	**Total Purchases of Goods**	**20193079**	**21904768**	**92.2**
市内纯购进	In the City	8399383	8656702	97.0
市外购进	From Outside	7372452	8388712	87.9
进　口	Import	4421244	4859354	91.0
商品销售总额	**Total Sales**	**21575476**	**22623166**	**95.4**
市内纯销售	In the City	13064834	12177631	107.3
市外销售	To Outside	3292687	3575296	92.1
出　口	Export	5217955	6870239	76.0
年末库存	**Inventory (year-end)**	**5496141**	**5729750**	**95.9**

10-5 商委各局大中型批发零售贸易业商品购、销、存总值
PURCHASES,SALES AND INVENTORY OF LARGE AND MEDIUM WHOLESALE AND RETAIL TRADES OF COMMERCIAL COMMITTEE

单位：万元 (10000 yuan)

项目	Item	北京一商集团有限责任公司 Beijing Yishang Group CO.,LTD	北京二商集团有限责任公司 Beijing Ershang (Group) CO.,LTD	北京粮食集团有限责任公司 Beijing Grain Group CO.,LTD	北京石油集团有限责任公司 Beijing Petrol Group CO.,LTD	北京市供销合作社 The Supply And Marketing Cooperatives In Beijing	北京燕莎集团有限责任公司 Beijing Yansha Group CO.,LTD
商品购进总额	**Total Purchases**	**257673**	**250591**	**123190**	**381610**	**191483**	**142454**
从生产者购进	From Producers	127372	104220	-1	200603	119287	68200
# 农副产品	Farm and Sideline Products	22	3717			35768	8
市外购进	From Outside	83359	70586		1031	79126	20446
从批发零售贸易业购进	From Wholesalers and Retailers	129796	112388	78768	181008	51782	74110
# 市外购进	From Outside	54428	39043	15149	51214	5011	4522
进口额	Import		209	44423		20357	207
其他	Others	506	33773	1		58	-63
商品销售总额	**Total Sales**	**280202**	**274914**	**149413**	**427631**	**208488**	**193781**
对生产经营单位销售额	To Producers	23909	21212	4494	164894	34805	
# 生产资料销售	Capital Goods	7			2129	932	
市外销售	To Outside	3255	2803		294	3102	
对批发零售贸易业批发	To Wholesalers and Retailers	189270	222572	133228	237726	116909	26114
# 市外批发	From Outside	28398	13183	2326	5438	27583	
出口额	Export		91				60
对居民的商品零售额	To Residents	52090	30016	6887	3895	46229	153831
对集团的商品零售额	To Organizations	14933	1023	4803	21117	10545	13777
年末库存	**Inventory(year-end)**	45933	51257	243572	-758	29909	20350

项目	Item	中国烟草总公司北京市公司 China National Tobacco Corp., Beijing Corp.,	北京王府井百货(集团)股份有限公司 Beijing Wangfujing Department Store (Group) CO.,LTD	北京西单商场股份有限公司 Beijing Xidan Shopping CO.,LTD	北京东安集团公司 Beijing Dongan Group CO.,LTD	北京友谊商店股份有限公司 Beijing Friendship Store CO.,LTD	中盐北京市盐业公司 Beijing Salt Corp., China General industry Corp.,
商品购进总额	**Total Purchases**	**451195**	**65381**	**133455**	**179354**	**14557**	**3552**
从生产者购进	From Producers	82350	28503	58211	117468	7743	3552
# 农副产品	Farm and Sideline Products						
市外购进	From Outside	272	15134	22879	57880	3332	3551
从批发零售贸易业购进	From Wholesalers and Retailers	368238	34964	75237	61886	6815	
# 市外购进	From Outside	178304	3279	11562	10717	1075	
进口额	Import		1896				
其他	Others	607	19	7			
商品销售总额	**Total Sales**	**486646**	**89977**	**172301**	**206454**	**20549**	**7245**
对生产经营单位销售额	To Producers		3313	6721			2265
# 生产资料销售	Capital Goods						
市外销售	To Outside		2832	1423			
对批发零售贸易业批发	To Wholesalers and Retailers	475209	18972	23420	359	2336	4882
# 市外批发	From Outside	60951	68	8	59	220	
出口额	Export		2914				
对居民的商品零售额	To Residents		59902	140219	193398	17535	37
对集团的商品零售额	To Organizations	11437	4876	1941	12696	678	61
年末库存	**Inventory (year-end)**	**31646**	**5451**	**14172**	**10539**	**3796**	**419**

10-6 大中型批发零售贸易业商品购、销、存总值(按行政区划分)

PURCHASES,SALES AND INVENTORY LARGE AND MEDIUM WHOLESALE AND RETAIL TRADES(BY ADMINISTRATIVE REGION)

单位：万元 (10000 yuan)

项目	Item	东城 Dong-cheng	西城 Xicheng	崇文 Chongwen	宣武 Xuanwu	朝阳 Chaoyang	丰台 Fengtai	石景山 Shijing-shan	海淀 Haidia
商品购进总额	**Total Purchases**	**4135156**	**5645412**	**1047004**	**1988702**	**4353949**	**1289912**	**328456**	**2128838**
从生产者购进	From Producers	2690589	1650907	637297	1460315	2536258	979963	208579	1189156
# 农副产品	Farm and Sideline Products	131038	27301	1013	12158	10595	17121	8	25370
市外购进	From Outside	1564732	606886	246678	973816	1082912	122393	13406	398629
从批发零售贸易业购进	From Wholesalers and Retailers	771011	1238318	310537	396711	1237296	289552	118550	599848
# 市外购进	From Outside	229002	461038	69400	119968	425565	63856	10390	74598
进口额	Import	668259	2698043	87954	124529	504028	16123		322192
其他	Others	5297	58144	11216	7147	76367	4274	1328	17642
商品销售总额	**Total Sales**	**4271924**	**5350882**	**1172332**	**2288438**	**4949541**	**1435384**	**331098**	**2215191**
对生产经营单位销售额	To Producers	1151939	1227801	132419	796214	1337431	761102	115012	693494
# 生产资料销售	Capital Goods		13443	1	861	2456	405		2868
市外销售	To Outside	618446	287016	8371	361167	465107	20775	7502	106870
对批发零售贸易业批发	To Wholesalers and Retailers	638895	1610401	589856	890420	1211636	210759	48206	468558
# 市外批发	From Outside	163773	438845	88321	422354	186256	17535	6678	62653
出口额	Export	1938916	1538880	66878	166019	1276492	31664		170674
对居民的商品零售额	To Residents	411283	842676	213813	323627	826402	275815	128864	701114
对集团的商品零售额	To Organizations	130892	131124	169366	112158	297581	156044	39015	181351
年末库存	**Inventory(year-end)**	**497545**	**1994099**	**215770**	**518141**	**738813**	**105188**	**30110**	**298260**

项目	Item	门头沟 Mentou-gou	房山 Fang-shan	昌平 Chang-ping	顺义 Shunyi	通州 Tong-zhou	大兴 Daxing	平谷 Pinggu	怀柔 Huairou	密云 Miyun	延庆 Yanqing
商品购进总额	**Total Purchases**	**43258**	**263391**	**124286**	**224731**	**135549**	**159995**	**50952**	**97515**	**59245**	**33640**
从生产者购进	From Producers	17034	180341	46573	109635	55762	99275	38032	35033	24121	15107
# 农副产品	Farm and Sideline Products	127	5357	512	9565	99	8605		1698	1487	57
市外购进	From Outside	1235	3485	7243	19637	13100	25332	2140	12474	12542	4522
从批发零售贸易业购进	From Wholesalers and Retailers	25142	80985	55686	113091	79746	60493	12753	62235	34675	18533
# 市外购进	From Outside	665	4343	8629	8846	13409	8208	299	2018	2875	1490
进口额	Import				118						
其他	Others	1081	2065	22027	1888	41	227	168	247	449	
商品销售总额	**Total Sales**	**54157**	**280197**	**138304**	**256694**	**163361**	**203750**	**55105**	**124456**	**63606**	**39171**
对生产经营单位销售额	To Producers	13970	85364	23650	60696	45190	65853	4671	26919	15016	4226
# 生产资料销售	Capital Goods	91	4966	3086	6509	4689	10991	1876	2769	6896	2278
市外销售	To Outside	3132	1198	25	2378	272	3416	36	25	613	18
对批发零售贸易业批发	To Wholesalers and Retailers	7033	107047	23831	61825	40667	52787	29737	31663	24622	11734
# 市外批发	From Outside	44	6671	1476	4496	1291	3391	150	1932	147	309
出口额	Export			25268		27	38			3100	
对居民的商品零售额	To Residents	31292	69910	50506	114097	66861	67299	14646	56999	15709	20568
对集团的商品零售额	To Organizations	1863	17877	15049	20076	10618	17774	6052	8875	5160	2642
年末库存	**Inventory(year-end)**	**4473**	**21622**	**45060**	**31585**	**16322**	**25561**	**4002**	**13507**	**10536**	**5534**

10-7 批发零售贸易企业商品分类销售库存

SALES AND INVENTORY BY CATEGORY IN WHOLESALE AND RETAIL TRADES

单位：万元 (10000 yuan)

项目	Item	合计 Total 商品总销售 Total Sales	# 零售额 Retail	年末库存 Inventory (year-end)	# 大型企业 Large Enterprises 商品总销售 Total Sales	# 零售额 Retail	年末库存 Inventory (year-end)
合 计	**Total**	**27369954**	**7070247**	**5496141**	**13747898**	**3414996**	**3198140**
食品类	Food	2735961	896394	555371	1546652	484325	352930
# 肉禽蛋类	Meat,Poultry and Eggs	303946	127711	34896	173649	76312	9804
饮料类	Beverage	270861	131126	22015	92188	68841	8670
烟酒类	Tabacco and Liquor	884806	161996	126239	262799	83877	53812
服装、鞋帽类	Garments,Shoes and Hats	1328384	854293	143750	933610	676131	75093
针、纺织品类	Knitwear	898654	196416	114897	491682	116094	38726
化妆品类	Cosmetics	277837	136889	25863	201868	107635	12501
金银珠宝类	Jewelry	354211	176434	118086	194348	132886	38714
日用品类	Articles for Daily Use	766424	462731	113764	384842	286722	34877
# 洗涤用品类	Detergents	131389	70393	12198	68250	44496	4960
五金、电工器具类	Hardware and Electrical Appliances	448385	167753	78366	51826	33674	5767
体育、娱乐用品类	Recreation and Sports Articles	192787	100933	18281	66345	55717	4804
书报、杂志类	Book and Newspaper	359755	155108	106776	191276	56531	36919
电子出版物及音像制品类	Electronic Publication and Sound-video Products	42933	29657	9339	19540	16179	3748
家用电器和音像器材类	Household Appliances and Sound-video Equipments	1147985	778865	157005	730461	543009	79698
中西药品类	Medicines	1088044	545256	199904	433429	258399	82200
文化、办公用品类	Culture and Office Articles	480965	214488	73525	87133	72525	4792
家具类	Furniture	108710	78486	15741	25956	20581	3058
通讯器材类	Communication Equipments	936906	79149	33870	709119	10829	14970
煤炭及制品类	Coal and Coal Products	1004201	35033	18644	896519	7	298
木材及制品类	Timber and Related Products	253942	15499	45746	142827	4	9861
石油及制品类	Petroleum and Related Products	1962987	423554	70968	958990	18950	5104
化工材料及制品类	Chemical Materials and Products	1697507	48215	219357	914897	1748	118402
黑色金属材料类	Ferrous Metal Materials	1916544	28638	224488	748747	510	98896
有色金属材料类	Nonferrous Metal Materials	700637	4242	79344	261359		52224
建筑及装潢材料类	Building Materials	387897	116076	118548	18631	4148	2380
机电设备及零件类	Mechanical and Electrical Instruments	3813561	557634	877919	2094324	184150	455652
# 农机类	Agricultural Machinery	52842	3338	11976	9958	29	1291
种子饲料类	Seeds and Forage	237300	994	120781	181847	35	110400
棉麻、土畜产品类	Cotton,Flax,Local and Animal Products	352134	4333	1337305	126394	637	1300398
其他类	Others	2719636	670058	470250	980292	180851	193249
# 生活消费品	Consumer Goods	134074	101509	16240	43104	36088	3364

10-7 续表 continued

单位：万元 (10000 yuan)

项目	Item	# 中型企业 Medium Enterprises 商品总销售 Total Sales	# 零售额 Retail	年末库存 Inventory (year-end)	# 小型企业 Small Enterprises 商品总销售 Total Sales	# 零售额 Retail	年末库存 Inventory (year-end)
合计	**Total**	**9645693**	**2139999**	**1377987**	**3976364**	**1515252**	**920014**
食品类	Food	922366	324246	166600	266943	87823	35841
# 肉禽蛋类	Meat,Poultry and Eggs	70804	42260	18218	59494	9139	6874
饮料类	Beverage	114453	49151	10165	64221	13133	3180
烟酒类	Tabacco and Liquor	561893	62180	56326	60114	15939	16102
服装、鞋帽类	Garments,Shoes and Hats	322595	144035	43614	72179	34127	25044
针、纺织品类	Knitwear	299990	42700	46692	106982	37622	29479
化妆品类	Cosmetics	63079	24274	12511	12891	4980	851
金银珠宝类	Jewelry	140359	30383	32727	19504	13165	46645
日用品类	Articles for Daily Use	251328	124711	43602	130254	51298	35285
# 洗涤用品类	Detergents	52408	21378	6638	10731	4520	600
五金、电工器具类	Hardware and Electrical Appliances	196303	39206	23760	200256	94873	48839
体育、娱乐用品类	Recreation and Sports Articles	99433	31319	9839	27009	13896	3639
书报、杂志类	Book and Newspaper	128001	81873	51841	40478	16704	18016
电子出版物及音像制品类	Electronic Publication and Sound-video Products	12860	7551	5052	10533	5926	539
家用电器和音像器材类	Household Appliances and Sound-video Equipments	311786	155221	53072	105738	80635	24235
中西药品类	Medicines	550009	251714	101576	104607	35142	16128
文化、办公用品类	Culture and Office Articles	280190	90541	50551	113642	51422	18182
家具类	Furniture	61565	36634	8560	21189	21272	4123
通讯器材类	Communication Equipments	122620	12449	11328	105167	55871	7572
煤炭及制品类	Coal and Coal Products	99744	30181	16628	7939	4845	1718
木材及制品类	Timber and Related Products	85417	1252	18621	25698	14243	17263
石油及制品类	Petroleum and Related Products	573282	136181	23505	430715	268422	42359
化工材料及制品类	Chemical Materials and Products	568752	5917	69539	213858	40550	31417
黑色金属材料类	Ferrous Metal Materials	879771	11325	82539	288026	16803	43053
有色金属材料类	Nonferrous Metal Materials	384761	215	21508	54517	4027	5613
建筑及装潢材料类	Building Materials	136504	22451	27171	232762	89477	88998
机电设备及零件类	Mechanical and Electrical Instruments	1055913	161373	191145	663325	212111	231121
# 农机类	Agricultural Machinery	38574	3309	10685	4310		
种子饲料类	Seeds and Forage	55019	735	10271	434	224	110
棉麻、土畜产品类	Cotton,Flax,Local and Animal Products	204089	396	36907	21652	3300	
其他类	Others	1163613	261785	152339	575731	227422	124662
# 生活消费品	Consumer Goods	56459	32451	7196	34512	32969	5680

10-8 社会农副产品购进、销售、库存数量
PURCHASES,SALES AND INVENTORY OF FARM AND SIDELINE PRODUCTS

单位：百公斤 (100 kg)

项目	Item	从生产者购进 Purchase from Producers	市外购进 Purchase from Outside	商品总销售 Total Sales	# 对生产经营单位销售 To Producer	# 出口 Export	# 零售量 Retail Sales	年末库存 Inventory (year-end)
粮食	Grain	19111049	11231750	48197860	4758758	2323105	12635442	41346529
食用植物油	Edible Vegetable Oil	3359339	4634218	14027513	202642	59740	3218277	1318449
猪和猪肉	Hog and Pork	4108527	2034679	8578800	556156	3797525	2649246	1555479
牛和牛肉	Oxes and Beef	1830084	2031110	1861105	355670	785842	652238	7187188
羊和羊肉	Goat,Sheep and Mutton	2452626	636798	2081861	11723	953930	1017343	205865
家禽	Poultry	2363362	582470	2581337	562877	293492	1191341	183066
鲜蛋	Fresh Eggs	1178130	348738	1187739	25212	67	1150087	13950
鲜菜	Fresh Vegetable	36652026	11943517	37063896	4681	2810	36881972	25863
鲜瓜果	Fresh Melon and Fruit	14606719	5095467	14858664	1078	1600	13742298	15139
水产品	Aquatic Products	2243854	793856	2479492	2835	3940	2278941	42248

10-9 大中型批发零售贸易企业商品购进、销售、库存数量
PURCHASES,SALES AND INVENTORY VOLUME BY LARGE AND MEDIUM WHOLESALERS AND RETAILERS

项目	Item	从生产者购进 Purchase from Producers	市外购进 Purchase from Outside	商品总销售 Total Sales	# 对生产经营单位销售 To Producer	# 出口 Export	# 零售量 Retail Sales	年末库存 Inventory (year-end)
粮食 (百公斤)	Grain (100 kg)	1164378	6105113	17775999	1033078	2323105	1737131	20125579
食用植物油 (百公斤)	Edible Vegetable Oil (100 kg)	718330	2631076	9882634	83802		464918	939709
猪和猪肉 (百公斤)	Hog and Pork (100 kg)	553153	424507	1077556	370032	15690	306430	141554
牛和牛肉 (百公斤)	Cattle and Beef (100 kg)	44647	35856	67659	1260	15334	33237	29394
羊和羊肉 (百公斤)	Goat,Sheep and Mutton (100 kg)	16992	49721	80336	387	1522	42151	46298
家禽 (百公斤)	Poultry (100 kg)	226969	142368	289700	992	191968	91880	26154
鲜蛋 (百公斤)	Fresh Eggs (100 kg)	16469	836	24596	319		22030	357
鲜菜 (百公斤)	Fresh Vegetable (100 kg)	396001	171332	556993	18903	43686	258715	25013
鲜瓜果 (百公斤)	Fresh Melon and Fruit (100 kg)	1373371	1059848	1411814	16421	24612	93261	17089
水产品 (百公斤)	Aquatic Product (100 kg)	695991	390592	901481	593361	5143	54955	124870
盐 (百公斤)	Salt (100 kg)	1004655	982973	1229038	486180		132402	100292
食糖 (百公斤)	Sugar (100 kg)	1362798	1368750	5600641	321456	3795215	97027	1466009
卷烟 (箱)	Cigarettes (case)	1107773	1688605	4714547	3950	208027	177926	250620
酒 (百公斤)	Alcoholic Beverage (100 kg)	686645	190747	1032739	7256	38965	337180	125171
茶叶 (百公斤)	Tea (100 kg)	284917	259352	261576	3630	207765	34035	19751
棉花 (百公斤)	Cotton (100 kg)	1189895	1830001	1186146	353860	785692	819	7157508
布 (百米)	Cloth (100 m)	3369886	2902196	3245283	484518	2630810	77240	419570
# 棉布	Cotton Cloth	1489789	1231878	1562479	315935	1185708	32693	208144
呢绒 (百米)	Wool Fabric (100 m)	45929	4306	60674	3503	36457	12342	22883
绸缎 (百米)	Silk and Satin (100 m)	76094	77477	90840	742	64655	22563	19326
各种服装 (百件)	All Garments (100 pieces)	1909094	462230	1498689	11413	953930	461931	160115
# 针织内衣裤	Knitted Underwear	384720	110264	438573	1636	283666	135934	53216

10-9 续表 1 continued

项目 Item	从生产者购进 Purchase from Producers	市外购进 Purchase from Outside	商品总销售 Total Sales	# 对生产经营单位销售 To Producer	# 出口 Export	# 零售量 Retail Sales	年末库存 Inventory (year-end)
鞋 (百双) Shoe (100 pairs)	162232	68131	319268	467	140687	138010	62226
# 皮　鞋 Leather Shoe	54338	16860	87148	58	2379	65772	29592
毛　线 (百公斤) Knitting Wool (100 kg)	14992	2560	20527	12247	1548	6167	8301
手　表 (百个) Watches (100)	4771	6572	14036			12473	4505
黄金饰品 (千元) Gold Ornament (1000 yuan)	1281101	645788	1902479	211091	500473	1059687	438898
照相机 (台) Cameras (set)	271212	202985	617282	33550		309595	79545
自行车 (辆) Bicycle (unit)	169382	92114	268121	11223	22691	207947	30476
电视机 (台) TV Sets (set)	863484	451826	1235029	17197	68232	681933	137856
# 彩色电视机 Color TV Set	838543	419779	1130707	12635		655366	134586
# 25 寸及以上 25 inches and above	573278	262878	734793	7300		438051	78741
录音机 (台) Recorders (set)	106463	85451	313776	82	88046	215198	32376
# 组合音响 Hi-Fi	31577	15072	53596	252	67	45044	12600
摄像机 (架) Pickup Camera (set)	8247	8303	21377	171		17903	2273
录相机 (台) Video-corders (set)	13645	8855	22910	1078		14354	10389
影碟机 (台) Video CD (set)	250724	162657	430672	1935	3690	302971	41348
# 进口影碟机 Import	4031	32089	38181	3		13004	7928
家用电风扇 (台) Electrical Fans (unit)	160914	45620	452963	4369	44522	332914	94778
家用电冰箱 (台) Refrigerators (unit)	242167	184603	347495	1722		286492	48308
家用洗衣机 (台) Washing Machine (unit)	279231	209764	424508	3071	1152	278933	85729
房间空调器 (台) Air Conditioners (unit)	330516	202928	452561	29200		242538	48553
微波炉 (台) Microwave Oven (unit)	209635	131410	302842	1933		201621	40973
热水淋浴器 (台) Showers (unit)	171889	99227	242992	502		219934	36262
冰　柜 (台) Ice Cabinet (unit)	33489	24325	56836	254		44173	8446
吸尘器 (台) Dust Catcher (unit)	59763	50353	103228	101	24269	67437	11471
抽油烟机 (台) Range Hoods (unit)	165670	62296	238035	39676		171722	13015
电饭锅 (个) Electric Rice Cooker (unit)	316813	172765	482498	2062	10	298541	92093

10-9 续表 2 continued

项目 Item	从生产者购进 Purchase from Producers	市外购进 Purchase from Outside	商品总销售 Total Sales	# 对生产经营单位销售 To Producer	# 出口 Export	# 零售量 Retail Sales	年末库存 Inventory (year-end)
微型计算机 (台) Micro Computers (unit)	71842	30721	112059	22573	14709	46852	5188
普通电话机 (部) Telephones (unit)	419262	109500	620958	209969	15197	321788	47823
移动电话机 (部) Mobilphone (unit)	3626393	2221214	3894471	1411557		45991	183507
寻呼机 (部) BP (unit)	308368	59706	440705	272080		72299	35755
煤　炭 (吨) Coal (ton)	35214677	25202774	36982638	3655327	31169330	1589939	669551
木　材 (立方米) Timber (cu.m)	611217	465496	568149	301958	203627	13245	265471
汽　油 (吨) Gasoline (ton)	1370220	551577	2794063	791948	550692	422346	21518
柴　油 (吨) Diesel Oil (ton)	1019861	316416	1519505	786053	96328	114204	42974
煤　油 (吨) Kerosene (ton)	858955	855426	917239	907578		855	48930
硫　酸 (吨) Sulphuric Acid (ton)	3847	3829	3258	2940			761
纯　碱 (吨) Soda (ton)	1216	1104	1433	1182	60	130	70
烧　碱 (吨) Ashcaustic Soda (ton)	694	692	2673	656	1324	517	134
橡胶 (吨) Rubber (ton)	55783	52020	59667	50232	3073	32	14043
化学肥料 (吨) Chemical Fertilizer (ton)	364715	252174	1485606	887755	1404	4375	179341
农用塑料薄膜 (吨) Agricultural Plastic Film (ton)	186707	174467	127665	115614		25	4213
化学农药 (吨) Farm Chemical (ton)	147879	146026	70380	50827	16018	66	3426
钢　材 (吨) Steel Products (ton)	4049163	3058361	5397659	3594771	8030	80196	512706
铜 (吨) Copper (ton)	41332	27376	55944	38247	285		1754
铝 (吨) Aluminum (ton)	24045	17208	53429	35354		342	5337
铅 (吨) Lead (ton)	4221	3223	1815	1472			525
锌 (吨) Zinc (ton)	26897	24131	24540	3071	20176	136	5743
锡 (吨) Tin (ton)	2010	1970	1825	287	1224		21
铜　材 (吨) Copper Products (ton)	5679	2970	6906	3530	79	1	343
铝　材 (吨) Aluminum Products (ton)	9463	6584	9725	8936		500	1760
水　泥 (吨) Cement (ton)	1398905	675970	1415153	1206574	28408	38908	343074
汽　车 (辆) Automobile (unit)	57096	48337	130235	17101	1124	66889	9336
# 小轿车 Cars	33980	37584	83013	4177	683	44099	4910
摩托车 (辆) Motorcycle (unit)	70114	23249	78349	5674	1248	42212	11902
拖拉机 (台) Tractors (unit)	384	280	630	380		160	231

10-10 重点零售商业企业主要经济指标

单位：万元

商业企业	Enterprise	商品销售收入 Sales Revenue 1999	1998
百货类	**Department Store**		
城乡贸易中心股份有限公司	Beijing Urban-Rural Trade Center CO.,LTD	69529	112308
北京百盛轻工发展有限公司	Beijing Parkson Light Industry Development CO.,LTD	68420	47274
北京燕莎友谊商城	YouYI Shopping City CO.,LTD	88488	89820
赛特购物中心	Scitech Plaza Scitech Group CO.,LTD	67852	66667
北京北辰购物中心	Beijing North Star Shopping Center	81051	60819
西单商场股份有限公司	Beijing Xidan Shopping CO.,LTD	125980	147317
北京双安商场	Shuangan Department Store CO.,LTD	87544	84271
北京蓝岛大厦	Blue island Mansion	97094	99846
北京市复兴商业城	Fuxing Shopping City	43730	43297
北京市西单购物中心	Xidan Shopping Center	34112	45478
中贸联万客隆商业有限公司	CTA Makro Commercial CO.,LTD	84012	56770
北京翠微集团	Cuiwei Tower	79083	61274
菜市口百货有限责任公司	Caishikou Department Store CO.,LTD	36063	33212
北京贵友大厦有限公司	Beijing Mansion Guiyou CO.,LTD	39117	46235
北京东安集团公司长安商场	Changan Market	55347	43558
西单赛特商城有限责任公司	Xidan Scitech Shopping City	27277	26096
王府井百货大楼	Beijing Wangfujing Department Store (Group) CO.,LTD	77138	113935
北京东安集团公司	Beijing Sun Dong An CO.,LTD	36460	34480
国华商场有限责任公司	Guohua Department Store CO.,LTD	17112	15882
亿客隆商业股份有限公司	Beijing Yikelong Commercial Limited Company	48389	37515
北京市星座商厦	Beijing Constellation Market CO.,LTD	15677	19790
北京燕莎望京购物中心	Beijing Yansha Wangjing Wholesale Warehouse	31639	26677
北京华联商厦有限公司	Hualian Mansion CO.,LTD	37637	57174
白广路百货有限责任公司	Baiguang Road Department Store CO.,LTD	11217	11267
北京市超音波总公司	Super Wave Chain	27764	24089
北京友谊商店股份有限公司	Beijing Friendship Store CO.,LTD	17232	14365
方庄购物中心股份有限公司	Fangzhuang Shopping Center CO.,LTD	14231	14017
北京锐步体育用品中心	Beijing Reebok Sporting Goods Center	6079	6638
华奥商厦有限责任公司	Huaao Department Store	13618	14768
北京兴城商厦	Xingcheng Market	22063	21033
西城区新街口百货商场	Xinjiekou Department Store	11402	12798
北京创益佳商场	Carrefour	46293	34008
北京市天桥百货商场	Tianqiao Department Store	15408	18340
万方西单商场有限责任公司	Beijing Wanfang Xidan Shopping CO.,LTD	12454	10867
北京天元和平商业大厦	Beijing Tianyuan Heping Commercial House	12864	23044
北京金伦股份有限公司	Beijing Jinlun CO.,LTD	22011	22680
北京当代商城实业公司	Modern Plaza	36116	44613
北京市成文厚帐簿卡片公司	Chengwenhou Account Book Paper Company	4759	4653
北京庄胜崇光百货商场	Beijing Junefield Sogo Department Store	41893	15559
北京中旭三利百货公司	Beijing Zhongxu Sunry Shopping Center	24117	22514

MAIN ECONOMIC INDICATORS FOR MAJOR RETAIL ENTERPRISES

(10000 yuan)

利税总额 Total Profits		人均销售额 Sales Value Per Capita		人均创利税 Pre-tax Per Capita		销售利税率(%) Ratio of Pre-tax to Sales Revenue(%)		存货周转率(%) Turnover Rate of Stock(%)	
1999	1998	1999	1998	1999	1998	1999	1998	1999	1998
20250	16114	36.7	55.2	10.7	7.9	29.1	14.3	685.4	981.2
5928	6135	94.5	54.8	8.2	7.1	8.7	13.0	2243.5	1455.7
12609	11479	49.0	46.0	7.0	5.9	14.2	12.8	745.5	790.9
7180	8723	70.3	62.4	7.4	8.2	10.6	13.1	1107.9	844.6
5360	4652	83.6	72.6	5.5	5.6	6.6	7.6	1151.2	1519.6
12358	17662	38.3	46.3	3.8	5.5	9.8	12.0	618.6	2036.7
4207	3965	44.5	40.6	2.1	1.9	4.8	4.7	1283.2	1254.4
6360	7563	35.2	32.5	2.3	2.5	6.6	7.6	550.1	529.4
3402	3437	50.3	48.3	3.9	3.8	7.8	7.9	1311.0	2917.0
4074	4746	43.2	45.0	5.2	4.7	11.9	10.4	1977.0	1360.8
1623	130	113.8	77.2	2.2	0.2	1.9	0.2	1671.8	1876.9
3852	2668	32.9	22.4	1.6	1.0	4.9	4.4	753.2	649.1
3916	3838	82.7	77.8	9.0	9.0	10.9	11.6	468.6	1427.2
2394	4000	48.5	56.0	3.0	4.8	6.1	8.7	1023.0	1178.8
2095	1717	28.8	21.6	1.1	0.9	3.8	3.9	1230.0	3868.3
1405	1714	64.2	52.5	3.3	3.4	5.2	6.6	2470.2	2438.5
1679	10729	22.5	32.8	0.5	3.1	2.2	9.4	1158.3	1329.7
1283	1399	25.2	28.0	0.9	1.1	3.5	4.1	2686.4	2282.6
1580	1613	47.5	43.2	4.4	4.4	9.2	10.2	835.2	652.3
1117	1276	25.8	19.1	0.6	0.7	2.3	3.4	684.3	649.6
758	739	23.8	19.4	1.2	0.7	4.8	3.7	1386.5	681.1
655	156	39.2	31.9	0.8	0.2	2.1	0.6	1150.5	1555.2
590		59.2	77.0	0.9		1.6		310.4	546.1
547	761	51.9	49.2	2.5	3.3	4.9	6.8	1425.5	1917.2
572	826	67.6	70.4	1.4	2.4	2.1	3.4	327.7	339.8
1597	1144	14.9	10.6	1.4	0.8	9.3	8.0	206.5	265.5
1207	1344	26.6	23.2	2.3	2.2	8.5	9.6		
1037		184.2	184.3	31.4		17.1		521.5	623.5
739	1019	19.6	20.4	1.1	1.4	5.4	6.9	772.1	743.3
416	686	35.7	17.8	0.7	0.6	1.9	3.3	1366.9	984.2
585	436	24.5	25.5	1.3	0.9	5.1	3.4	1539.1	982.6
98	1265	68.6	52.3	0.1	1.9	0.2	3.7	1818.0	1710.2
518	4543	21.6	15.6	0.7	3.9	3.4	24.8	580.5	488.1
492	24	24.6	17.5	1.0		4.0	0.2	1275.5	804.4
1179	2193	18.6	20.2	1.7	1.9	9.2	9.5		
718	745	20.9	19.7	0.7	0.6	3.3	3.3	547.5	508.3
450		31.5	27.1	0.4		1.2		294.9	252.8
742	495	43.7	41.9	6.8	4.5	15.6	10.6	342.9	217.6
		61.7	11.7					1229.9	344.6
173		46.6	29.7	0.3		0.7		981.8	745.1

10-10 续表 1 continued

单位：万元

商业企业	Enterprise	商品销售收入 Sales Revenue 1999	1998
北京市朝阳商业大楼	Chaoyang Commercial Mansion	10281	10062
北京大百商贸集团	Beijing DaBai Commodity Trading Group	23140	22773
北京市隆福大厦	Beijing Longfu Department Store	49751	19704
北京绿屋百货有限责任公司	Green House Department Store CO.,LTD	2782	2790
北京市昌平新世纪商城	Beijing Changping New Century Business city	12162	11662
北京市西四电器公司	Xisi Elctrical Appliance Company	3044	3050
西城区西直门外百货商场	Outside-Xizhimen Department Store	8187	20250
华普朝阳商业贸易有限公司	Huapu Chaoyang Commerce and Trading CO.,LTD	30273	17723
北京利生体育商厦	Beijing Tianyuan Lisheng Sports Trade Tower	9439	12635
北京地百商贸股份有限公司	Beijing Dibai Commerce And Trading CO.,LTD	8172	13082
北京世都百货有限责任公司	Beijing World Department Store CO.,LTD	27183	21092
北京市丰台百货商场	Fengtai Department Store	8894	10498
北京市顺义国泰商业大厦	Beijing Shunyi Guotai Trade Building	10408	12157
怀柔百货大楼股份有限公司	Department Store CO.,LTD Huairou Beijing	12324	8688
华光商厦有限责任公司	Huaguang Department Store	5971	6968
北京银岛商厦有限责任公司	Silver Island Commercial House CO.,LTD	4842	3882
北京市劲松商场	Jinsong Department Store	6106	8178
北京麒麟大厦	Beijing Kyin-Plaza	10746	11471
北京中商西友大厦有限公司	Beijing Zhongshang Seiyu Mansion CO.,LTD	12865	12535
北京市京北大世界商贸集团	Beijing Jingbei Great World Commercial Trade Group	12917	14309
北京顺义隆华购物中心	Beijing Shunyi Longhua Shopping Center	13101	13572
京西旅游公司百货商场	Department Store Of Beijing Jingxi Tourism Development CO.,LTD	3168	2877
光明百货市场	The Bright Department Store	6092	6467
北京市东高地百货商场	Donggaodi Department Store	3027	3528
百盛购物中心百盛商场	Parkson Shopping Center, Parkson Department Store	10901	10289
北京天元安定门百货商场	Beijing Tianyuan Andingmen Department Store	2282	4063
北京市昌平商业大厦	Beijing Changping Commercial Building	7029	6075
北京燕京前门商厦	Yanjing Qianmen Commercial company	9607	9911
北京雪银大厦	Xueyin Mansion	9049	14658
北京市鼓楼电器公司	Gulou Electrical Appliance Company	3288	3761
朝阳区团结湖百货商场	Tuanjie Lake Department Store	2608	4105
北京市房山商业大楼	Fangshan Commercial Building	2223	2518
北京工美艺术世界大厦	Beijing Arts & Crafts World	4714	2095
北京市西直门五金批发商店	Xizhimen Hardware Wholesale Store	2069	2045
北京市东门仓第一百货商场	Dongcangmen No.1 Department Store	2811	3253
北京市宣武区内联升鞋店	Neiliansheng Shoes Store	1558	1473
北京丝绸商店	Beijing Silk Store	1390	1365
北京三里河百货商场	Sanlihe Department Store	1100	1189
北京正阳商城	Zhengyang Shopping City	1825	1191
元隆丝绸股份有限公司	Yuanlong Silk CO.,LTD	1280	1258

10-10 续表 2 continued

(10000 yuan)

利税总额 Total Profits		人均销售额 Sales Value Per Capita		人均创利税 Pre-tax Per Capita		销售利税率(%) Ratio of Pre-tax to Sales Revenue(%)		存货周转率(%) Turnover Rate of Stock(%)	
1999	1998	1999	1998	1999	1998	1999	1998	1999	1998
350	486	33.6	32.3	1.1	1.6	3.4	4.8	1051.4	1116.3
750	774	14.0	12.3	0.5	0.4	3.2	3.4	264.4	303.2
		22.1	8.8					1269.8	509.5
437	3310	15.9	14.7	2.5	17.4	15.7	118.6	214600.0	207400.0
558	501	19.3	18.8	0.9	0.8	4.6	4.3	298.6	278.2
347	274	35.0	32.1	4.0	2.9	11.4	9.0	856.2	1507.5
340	509	22.3	36.0	0.9	0.9	4.2	2.5	610.6	1219.7
	670	25.2	25.0		0.9		3.8	899.9	658.1
728	965	11.3	15.7	0.9	1.2	7.7	7.6		
278	683	15.8	24.5	0.5	1.3	3.4	5.2	11058.1	738.5
		32.5	31.9					652.3	447.0
216	332	12.8	14.2	0.3	0.4	2.4	3.2	2795.5	1863.9
331	249	19.1	19.9	0.6	0.4	3.2	2.0	278.0	559.4
50	94	41.1	27.4	0.2	0.3	0.4	1.1	1015.1	649.3
263	423	15.3	17.4	0.7	1.1	4.4	6.1	785.9	573.1
263	292	13.6	9.9	0.7	0.7	5.4	7.5	692.6	401.6
287	346	12.5	16.4	0.6	0.7	4.7	4.2	692.8	709.0
370	356	10.7	9.6	0.4	0.3	3.4	3.1	292.5	310.7
5		20.1	18.2					1184.9	1144.0
122		18.3	18.3	0.2		0.9		421.5	634.2
54	1	25.7	29.3	0.1		0.4		554.8	270.2
313	366	9.7	8.6	1.0	1.1	9.9	127.7	379.8	1079.7
150	227	16.9	15.0	0.4	0.5	2.5	3.5	818.9	581.8
193	182	13.5	15.6	0.9	0.8	6.4	5.2	613.2	574.0
		42.7	37.6					657.1	568.4
376	608	6.4	8.8	1.1	1.3	16.5	15.0		1629.4
166	200	15.4	16.3	0.4	0.5	2.4	3.3	419.2	540.0
135	195	16.0	14.5	0.2	0.3	1.4	2.0	364.4	288.7
311	432	8.5	16.0	0.3	0.5	3.4	2.9		
57	27	17.6	18.9	0.3	0.1	1.7	0.7	3137.1	670.2
92	106	11.5	18.8	0.4	0.5	3.5	2.6	3374.1	716.8
106	100	14.1	14.9	0.7	0.6	4.8	4.0	907.8	998.2
310		5.8	2.6	0.4		6.6		117.7	41.8
110	65	17.1	15.4	0.9	0.5	5.3	3.2	494.9	413.2
65	56	13.1	14.6	0.3	0.3	2.3	1.7	2049.2	1911.2
149	108	9.0	7.9	0.9	0.6	9.6	7.3	308.0	224.3
133	65	11.5	12.0	1.1	0.6	9.6	4.8	247.0	258.5
90	75	5.4	5.6	0.4	0.4	8.2	6.3	1170.7	1813.0
77	42	11.4	6.6	0.5	0.2	4.2	3.5	609.0	445.7
102	90	8.8	8.4	0.7	0.6	8.0	7.2	122.6	106.3

10-10 续表 3 continued

单位：万元

商业企业	Enterprise	商品销售收入 Sales Revenue 1999	1998
前门文化体育用品公司	Qianmen Culture & Sport Branch Company of Beijing Yilong Commercial CO.,LTD	1740	1910
三环毛纺织集团三友商场	Beijing Sanyou Market CO.,LTD	4169	4501
八角西单商场有限责任公司	Bajiao Xidan Shopping CO.,LTD	1990	2667
北京亿客发商贸集团	Yikefa Commerce and Trading Group	3344	4495
北京密云燕赛购物中心	Beijing Yansai Shopping Center	2033	1918
北京市西四商场	Xisi Department Store	1939	1274
房山区良乡商场	Liangxiang Market	1618	2127
北京天元商业大楼	Beijing Tianyuan Commercial House	518	1158
延庆县百货大楼	Yanqing Department Store	995	1361
北京市新汇奥尼尔百货商场	Xinhui Oneal Department Store	1699	219
宣武菜市口文化用品商店	Caishikou Stationery Store	833	1101
北京市金源商城	Jinyuan Shopping City	396	2016
北京市宣武和平门百货商场	Hepingmen Department Store	592	777
北京市怀柔商业大厦	Commercial Edifice Huairou Beijing	191	568
新时代妇女儿童用品公司	Newtime Articles for Women and Childre	154	560
北京市平谷银座购物中心	Pinggu Yinzuo Shopping Center	26	244
副食类	**Grocery**		
北京稻香村食品集团	Beijing Daoxiangcun Food Group	38090	48113
北太平庄商场有限责任公司	Beitaipingzhuang Department Store	9001	9180
北京市崇文门菜市场	Chongwenmen Food Market of Beijing	23927	23053
奥士凯集团公司朝内菜市场	Inside-Chaoyangmen Food Market	6552	2396
北京吴裕泰茶叶公司	Wuyutai Tea Company	3954	3272
北京市朝阳区燕丰商场	Yanfeng Department Store	11192	11195
北京京客隆商厦	Jingkelong Market	70069	37579
北京市西城和平门菜市场	Hepingmen Food Market	2610	2819
北京市朝阳区万惠商场	Wanghui Department Store	8898	8915
北京市新街口购物中心	Xinjiekou Shopping Center	2167	2321
西城区地安门副食商场	Di'anmen Food Store	4235	6099
宣武西珠市口副食商店	Zhushikou Food Store	1831	1013
北京市老白广路商场	Old Baiguang Road Department Store	2404	3312
东城区奥之光银龙商贸公司	Yinlong Commerce and Trading Company	1831	2488
北京博兰特北大地副食商场	Beidadi Food Store	1390	1523
北京市海淀区海淀菜市场	Haidian Super Market	2314	3126
北京桂香村食品中心	Fragrant Village Food Shop	1334	2710
北京市宣武宣武门副食商场	Xuanwumen Food Store	1491	1284
东城区奥之光宝龙商贸公司	Baolong Commerce and Trading Company	1172	1534

10-10 续表 4 continued

(10000 yuan)

利税总额 Total Profits		人均销售额 Sales Value Per Capita		人均创利税 Pre-tax Per Capita		销售利税率(%) Ratio of Pre-tax to Sales Revenuc(%)		存货周转率(%) Turnover Rate of Stock(%)	
1999	1998	1999	1998	1999	1998	1999	1998	1999	1998
89	107	9.7	9.1	0.5	0.5	5.1	5.6	249.4	3997.3
	126	6.7	10.2		0.3		2.8	406.4	327.6
		5.8	7.3					1613.3	1932
		4.7	5.9					441.4	381.7
		7.0	6.2					1011.2	744.5
		8.6	6.0					842.3	6362.5
60	83	7.0	8.0	0.3	0.3	3.7	3.9	283.6	359.6
52		4.0	3.6	0.4		10.0			212.9
36	41	6.0	7.9	0.2	0.2	3.6	3.0	505.2	492.3
	39	11.0	11.5		2.1		17.8	335.4	571.9
	118	9.4	11.6		1.2		10.7	504.8	625.4
		2.0	7.5					923.1	2340.8
	25	6.4	8.0		0.3		3.2	474.3	802.6
		1.1	3.0					75.6	168.9
		1.6	2.6					31.8	834.0
		0.1	0.7					8.0	58.2
3933	7692	50.3	39.9	5.2	6.4	10.3	16.0	1972.3	2578.4
528	528	25.1	21.9	1.5	1.3	5.9	5.8	2007.9	1257.3
1398	1567	17.0	15.6	1.0	1.1	5.8	6.8	1343.5	
410	123	27.3	11.0	1.7	0.6	6.3	5.1	1419.3	574.2
730	566	25.8	26.0	4.8	4.5	18.5	17.3	641.0	812.6
449	487	22.3	29.5	0.9	1.3	4.0	4.4	922.6	817.9
1616	1148	11.8	23.3	0.3	0.7	2.3	3.1	436.6	574.0
148	211	17.9	18.9	1.0	1.4	5.7	7.5	1542.3	1269.2
206	297	20.6	15.8	0.5	0.5	2.3	3.3	1230.4	802.6
170	97	7.6	9.1	0.6	0.4	7.8	4.2	3503.9	7219.2
94	174	11.7	15.9	0.3	0.5	2.2	2.9	2437.6	3416.3
74	61	16.6	8.0	0.7	0.5	4.0	6.0	2695.0	1163.2
63	213	24.3	23.7	0.6	1.5	2.6	6.4	1154.0	1627.4
139	225	4.1	5.4	0.3	0.5	7.6	9.0	1572.8	2679.7
73	84	11.4	10.7	0.6	0.6	5.3	5.5	11350.0	6961.1
69	112	8.9	11.6	0.3	0.4	3.0	3.6	1148.8	1708.6
146	177	4.3	6.4	0.5	0.4	10.9	6.5		71033.3
39	5	19.4	15.5	0.5	0.1	2.6	0.4	1548.1	9750.0
75	124	4.4	5.6	0.3	0.5	6.4	8.1	514.4	625.1

10-11 商委各局大中型批发零售贸易业财务状况

单位：万元

企业名称	Enterprise	商品销售收入 Sales Revenue
北京一商集团有限责任公司	Beijing Yishang Group CO.,LTD	237490
北京二商集团有限责任公司	Beijing Ershang(Group) CO.,LTD	285862
北京粮食集团有限责任公司	Beijing Grain Group CO.,LTD	131279
北京石油集团有限责任公司	Beijing Petrol Group CO.,LTD	342002
北京市供销合作社	The Supply And Marketing Cooperatives In Beijing	156552
北京燕莎集团有限责任公司	Beijing Yansha Group CO.,LTD	168615
中国烟草总公司北京市公司	China National Tobacco Corp., Beijing Corp.,	434999
北京王府井百货(集团)股份有限公司	Beijing Wangfujing Department Store (Group) CO.,LTD	77138
北京西单友谊集团	Beijing Xidan Friendship Group	170450
北京东安集团公司	Beijing Dongan Group CO.,LTD	180945
中盐北京市盐业公司	Beijing Salt Corp., China General industry Corp.,	6179

企业名称	Enterprise	财务费用 Finan-cial Expense
北京一商集团有限责任公司	Beijing Yishang Group CO.,LTD	2912
北京二商集团有限责任公司	Beijing Ershang(Group) CO.,LTD	4432
北京粮食集团有限责任公司	Beijing Grain Group CO.,LTD	49296
北京石油集团有限责任公司	Beijing Petrol Group CO.,LTD	3176
北京市供销合作社	The Supply And Marketing Cooperatives In Beijing	2302
北京燕莎集团有限责任公司	Beijing Yansha Group CO.,LTD	847
中国烟草总公司北京市公司	China National Tobacco Corp., Beijing Corp.,	3340
北京王府井百货(集团)股份有限公司	Beijing Wangfujing Department Store (Group) CO.,LTD	-3108
北京西单友谊集团	Beijing Xidan Friendship Group	2799
北京东安集团公司	Beijing Dongan Group CO.,LTD	1150
中盐北京市盐业公司	Beijing Salt Corp., China General industry Corp.,	181

FINANCIAL INDICATORS FOR LARGE AND MEDIUM WHOLESALERS AND RETAILERS OF COMMERCIAL COMMISSION

(10000 yuan)

商品销售收入净额 Net Value of Sales Revenue	商品销售成本 Sales Cost	经营费用 Operating Expense	商品销售税金及附加 Sales Tax and Extra Charges	商品销售利润 After-tax Profits	主营业务利润 Profits from Major Business	其他业务利润 Profits from Other Business	管理费用 Overhead Cost
237490	217401	10302	539	9248	9248	5166	12891
285832	262732	17280	660	5160	5163	6140	12859
130131	133245	16646	63	-19823	-19823	773	3283
342002	310800	8994	495	21713	21713	711	13803
156344	143766	8580	208	3791	3791	6402	8746
166005	133664	17724	217	14400	14403	368	12492
434999	407351	5993	369	21286	21286	228	8202
77138	67334	3935	344	5524	5524	480	8916
170450	141591	8005	547	20306	20306	3880	19741
180945	148042	15603	1004	16298	16298	1933	15664
6179	3718	927	50	1484	1484	170	1406

利润总额 Total Profits	应付工资 Wages Payable	资产总计 Total Assets	流动资产合计 Total Circulating Assets	固定资产合计 Total Fixed Assets	流动负债合计 Total Liquid Liability	长期负债合计 Total Long-term Liability	实收资本 Total Capital
561	7779	200212	102956	76197	123581	27459	36124
275	8027	246978	184187	49730	188689	20628	39043
-858	716	840560	802868	9096	759179	51145	17903
5404	3123	131361	46600	34416	59144	7391	40959
370	6042	98972	60928	29677	73378	3968	17891
2236	7777	61837	44386	12771	38700	4116	19594
10374	1899	167206	88482	61524	71489	-118	10956
1362	4596	244933	155850	34776	82064	6429	35725
6580	1278	234953	102304	124656	114469	2900	24100
950	10473	141989	46616	35079	72001	5473	40621
136	556	12133	4519	7024	-32784	1595	2746

10-12 大中型批发零售贸易业财务状况

单位：万元

项目	Item	流动资产 合计 Total Circulating Assets	#货币资金 Cash	#应收帐款 Accounts Receivable	#存货 Stock	长期投资 Long-term Investment
合计	**Total**	**17912807**	**2447513**	**4018082**	**4956293**	**3418365**
按企业登记注册类型分	**Grouped by Type of Enterprises Registered**					
内资企业	Domestic Investment	17784578	2403630	4001927	4923559	3415403
国有企业	State-Owned	13516054	1882645	3505251	3014303	2944363
集体企业	Collective Owned	1967447	119556	130243	1354959	47602
私营企业	Private Owned	130585	24617	17767	60659	1928
联营企业	Joint Owned	298137	20293	19658	124562	7405
股份合作企业	Share Holding Cooperative	124525	12645	8775	44949	13257
股份有限公司	Share Holding Company	680581	171353	69844	136728	177510
有限责任公司	Limited-Liability Company	1067250	172520	250389	187399	223339
其他企业	Others					
港澳台商投资企业	Hongkong,Macao and Taiwan Funded Enterprises	13678	4868	831	5318	485
外商投资企业	Foreign Funded Enterprises	114551	39016	15325	27416	2477
按国民经济行业分	**Grouped by Sectors**					
批发业	Wholesale	15952022	2083784	3900538	4354731	3153244
食品饮料烟草和家庭用品批发业	Food,Beverage,Tabacoo and Family Use Goods	5502589	504141	740997	2709854	875326
食品饮料烟草批发业	Food,Beverage and Tabacco	2341212	278611	309227	1081226	593723
棉麻、土畜产品批发业	Cotton,Flax,Local and Animal Products	1693899	65832	90433	1187296	134807
纺织品、服装和鞋帽批发业	Textile,Garments,Shoes and Hats	597277	57798	164707	181510	55164
日用百货批发业	Daily Use Goods	187657	17746	32652	57603	11110
日用杂品批发业	Grocery	15899	4868	1676	4897	259
五金交电化工批发业	Hardware,Electrical Appliance and Chemic	264103	25178	48498	50662	28579
药品及医疗器械批发业	Medicine and Medical Appliance	402543	54110	93804	146660	51684
能源、材料和机械电子设备批发业	Energy,Materials,Machinery and Electronic Equipments	6907562	1141608	2141974	972692	1705685
能源批发业	Energy	933376	160760	433178	89185	152070
化工材料批发业	Chemical Materials	635101	176089	150490	95956	178384
木材批发业	Timbers	87924	11001	20362	20715	26593
建筑材料批发业	Building Materials	174312	26379	55613	27783	19557
矿产品批发业	Mineral Products	91029	14429	27831	24617	4138
金属材料批发业	Metal Materials	2657191	293922	760249	281026	972194
机械、电子设备批发业	Machinery and Electronic Equipments	1879670	386930	595594	309409	264499
汽车摩托车及零配件批发业	Spares and Fittings of Automobile and Motorcycle	398125	63181	90777	115346	73621
再生物资回收批发业	Recovery of Reclaimed Materials	50834	8917	7882	8655	14630
其他批发业	Others	3541872	438035	1017567	672186	572233
工艺美术品批发业	Handicrafts	318646	25939	105412	27430	150989
图书报刊批发业	Books,Newspaper and Magazines	145534	34356	30542	35162	35540
农业生产资料批发业	Agricultural Capital Goods	655664	58698	69884	223055	58755
其他类未包括的批发	Others	2422029	319042	811729	386539	326949
零售业	Retail	1960785	363729	117544	601562	265121
食品、饮料和烟草零售业	Food,Beverage and Tabacco	280436	59941	7292	81569	7287
日用百货零售业	Daily Use Goods	1023334	177276	38229	264300	189573
纺织品、服装和鞋帽零售业	Textile,Garments,Shoes and Hats	69463	4366	3885	27734	3795
日用杂品零售业	Grocery	10519	2025	698	5616	454
五金交电化工零售业	Hardware,Electrical Appliance and Chemical	154204	26058	18147	63227	5070
药品及医疗器械零售业	Medicine and Medical Appliance	44621	10801	6027	18128	5896
图书报刊零售业	Books,Newspaper and Magazines	52122	13764	5910	28155	11783
其他零售业	Others	326087	69500	37357	112835	41264
按规模划分	**Grouped by Size**					
大型企业	Large Enterprises	11422297	1398195	2489413	3633086	2304396
中型企业	Medium Enterprises	6490509	1049318	1528670	1323207	1113969

FINANCIAL INDICATORS FOR LARGE AND MEDIUM WHOLESALERS AND RETAILERS

(10000 yuan)

固定资产合计 Total Fixed Assets	固定资产原价合计 Original Value of Fixed Assets	#生产经营用 for Production Use	累计折旧 Accumulative Depreciation	#本年折旧 of this Year	无形及递延资产合计 Intangible and Deffered Assets	#无形资产 Intangible	其他资产合计 Other Assets	资产合计 Total Assets	流动负债合计 Total Circulating Liability
3115766	**3121154**	**2211192**	**668651**	**139047**	**415327**	**194894**	**2058442**	**26922420**	**15798361**
3007110	2999543	2103060	649374	131545	347512	136018	2054831	26611131	15642391
2179271	2141044	1452098	472693	89169	187720	75749	51180	18879542	11795821
270860	292352	198908	61121	12425	33940	7558	2000296	4320145	1754871
12574	13510	9638	3096	990	2758	150	1453	149297	117074
72863	95355	77605	29006	6226	37365	29867		415769	317350
32105	35867	31507	6183	1547	7334	5490	710	177931	110432
275611	258136	246198	45975	13383	52109	12150	623	1186434	465907
163828	163279	87104	31302	7806	26286	5054	569	1482013	1080935
8333	12805	4589	5443	772	2419	864	102	25017	14178
100322	108806	103543	13834	6730	65396	58012	3509	286272	141793
1942993	1927044	1245798	421329	77250	148315	79322	2050878	23248424	13680974
535301	511023	346832	137029	24802	34044	17167	2021125	8968384	4865945
262552	230410	136906	73863	11642	13945	6157	14151	3225583	2048078
81241	80876	73486	13995	4201	4920	2165	1999357	3914224	1464989
57692	41660	26226	10082	1759	2094	1470		712227	584782
19155	24176	20422	8386	1635	2620	1320	4	220546	190977
4434	6181	2161	1762	147			212	20804	20569
37547	44885	35210	8721	1884	6927	3035	132	337286	233481
72679	82835	52421	20221	3534	3540	3020	7269	537714	323070
935822	922014	569679	200118	35550	74947	44579	29538	9654526	6132937
208697	249690	185362	58685	8972	22917	8604	1487	1318547	872452
55580	53267	29799	13778	2722	2877	1102	1	871941	518133
4340	5240	2982	949	225	948	595		119804	80807
59695	64389	19195	12793	2643	3362	1505	20	256947	189095
2291	1651	1427	712	199	177			97635	74190
327912	263606	200310	54665	8147	18330	12281	12250	3988834	2483047
232960	228960	96861	44119	9701	14597	10973	15629	2407372	1502469
38031	46741	29840	11564	2586	10144	8018	151	520071	364525
6317	8470	3903	2853	357	1595	1502		73376	48218
471870	494008	329288	84182	16897	39324	17576	215	4625514	2682093
56323	64696	14712	9714	1923	6687	6262		532645	365258
44728	48075	25742	11975	1884	1585	1340	160	227547	118281
47938	52816	34797	13581	3966	8040	7736		770397	611231
322881	328420	254038	48913	9125	23011	2239	55	3094926	1587323
1172772	1194110	965393	247322	61797	267012	115572	7564	3673996	2117387
180394	190168	142764	45869	9897	34047	23743	29	502191	306072
795707	782924	664679	146117	39425	210279	87192	4604	2224239	1200640
24365	22767	12545	6210	1045	2349	364	1	99973	62332
3096	3643	1542	1234	206	233			14302	8254
22078	28337	22032	9521	1918	2637	731	361	184350	136690
13238	14187	12919	4095	1149	2961	1093	6	66723	41165
18865	21676	19747	6057	1359	1433	504	227	84430	50556
115029	130409	89165	28220	6799	13073	1946	2336	497788	311677
1773950	1735991	1336520	348186	80819	288708	135536	2020161	17810467	9716584
1341816	1385163	874672	320465	58228	126619	59357	38281	9111953	6081778

10-12 续表 1 continued

单位：万元

项目	Item	# 短期借款 Short-term Loans	# 应付帐款 Accounts Payable	长期负债合计 Total Long-term Liability	# 长期借款 Long-term Loans	负债合计 Total Liabilities
合计	**Total**	**6972163**	**3685136**	**4414001**	**1790042**	**20212363**
按企业登记注册类型分	**Grouped by Type of Enterprises Registered**					
内资企业	Domestic Investment	6938207	3615569	4391955	1769459	20034346
国有企业	State-Owned	4753404	3014792	1960566	1652019	13756387
集体企业	Collective Owned	1543978	142611	2299204	24819	4054074
私营企业	Private Owned	11625	32792	5851	5076	122926
联营企业	Joint Owned	57517	101794	5052	4576	322402
股份合作企业	Share Holding Cooperative	19686	20636	13780	7357	124212
股份有限公司	Share Holding Company	181175	80802	32990	24833	498898
有限责任公司	Limited-Liability Company	370822	222142	74512	50780	1155447
其他企业	Others					
港澳台商投资企业	Hongkong,Macao and Taiwan Funded Enterprises	7800	2433	725		14903
外商投资企业	Foreign Funded Enterprises	26157	67135	21321	20583	163114
按国民经济行业分	**Grouped by Sectors**					
批发业	Wholesale	6377459	3190055	4191547	1650338	17872521
食品饮料烟草和家庭用品批发业	Food,Beverage,Tabacoo and Family Use Goods	3178403	592395	2600336	208215	7466281
食品饮料烟草批发业	Food,Beverage and Tabacco	1156005	217736	288546	189170	2336624
棉麻、土畜产品批发业	Cotton,Flax,Local and Animal Products	1537156	39736	2238818	2438	3703807
纺织品、服装和鞋帽批发业	Textile,Garments,Shoes and Hats	221842	109393	5887	3852	590668
日用百货批发业	Daily Use Goods	85237	48046	9245	2317	200222
日用杂品批发业	Grocery	9748	6041	317		20885
五金交电化工批发业	Hardware,Electrical Appliance and Chemic	93698	42401	9112	7816	242593
药品及医疗器械批发业	Medicine and Medical Appliance	74718	129042	48411	2622	371481
能源、材料和机械电子设备批发业	Energy,Materials,Machinery and Electronic Equipments	2143756	2266066	809900	666925	6942837
能源批发业	Energy	203514	1346468	68548	17546	941000
化工材料批发业	Chemical Materials	224352	82223	23735	18061	541868
木材批发业	Timbers	38522	4926	10171	10049	90978
建筑材料批发业	Building Materials	59413	46625	8623	5042	197719
矿产品批发业	Mineral Products	42259	10634	23208	22290	97398
金属材料批发业	Metal Materials	919537	383335	181379	125327	2664426
机械、电子设备批发业	Machinery and Electronic Equipments	474427	299048	453112	439958	1955581
汽车摩托车及零配件批发业	Spares and Fittings of Automobile and Motorcycle	155364	87997	40658	28644	405184
再生物资回收批发业	Recovery of Reclaimed Materials	26368	4811	466	8	48685
其他批发业	Others	1055300	331594	781310	775198	3463403
工艺美术品批发业	Handicrafts	228561	26051	13595	13592	378853
图书报刊批发业	Books,Newspaper and Magazines	18714	26012	4910		123190
农业生产资料批发业	Agricultural Capital Goods	251203	119028	26081	21677	637311
其他类未包括的批发	Others	556823	160503	736725	739929	2324048
零售业	Retail	594704	495081	222455	139703	2339842
食品、饮料和烟草零售业	Food,Beverage and Tabacco	61374	72895	49769	23456	355842
日用百货零售业	Daily Use Goods	409737	253914	127009	94531	1327649
纺织品、服装和鞋帽零售业	Textile,Garments,Shoes and Hats	17731	22142	3645	2663	65977
日用杂品零售业	Grocery	1083	4563	402	118	8657
五金交电化工零售业	Hardware,Electrical Appliance and Chemical	26709	30506	6461	2495	143152
药品及医疗器械零售业	Medicine and Medical Appliance	5271	19953	5633	1716	46799
图书报刊零售业	Books,Newspaper and Magazines	5559	25518	225	42	50780
其他零售业	Others	67240	65590	29310	14684	340988
按规模划分	**Grouped by Size**					
大型企业	Large Enterprises	4790127	2583311	3738658	1295774	13455241
中型企业	Medium Enterprises	2182037	1101825	675344	494267	6757122

10-12 续表 2 continued

(10000 yuan)

所有者权益合计 Ownership Interest	# 实收资本 Proceeds of Capital	#国家资本 State	#集体资本 Collective	#法人资本 Institutional Units	#个人资本 Individual	#港澳台资本 Hongkong, Macao and Taiwan	#外商资本 Foreign	商品销售收入 Sales Revenue
6710057	**3917056**	**2227911**	**175276**	**1293970**	**151737**	**6328**	**61835**	**20028931**
6576785	3784190	2217871	174836	1237547	151607	1300	1028	19623909
5123155	2851526	2101562	7868	735360	6736			14172850
266071	224362	24326	143863	26947	29225			1474032
26371	29555	555	747	11372	16881			436782
93368	90326	16537	7424	63123	2293		950	521558
53719	54782	657	1544	38929	13453	200		229230
687536	262869	25137	10555	160523	66355	300		1044465
326566	270771	49098	2835	201294	16666	800	78	1744991
10114	9569	3682	255	701		4751	180	57649
123158	123297	6359	185	55722	129	276	60626	347372
5375903	3023108	1962828	86943	933240	38257	651	1189	15270169
1502103	744999	534148	37990	163590	8281	30	960	4967289
888958	401129	331486	12434	56686	513		10	2370441
210417	90036	76810	5	13221				380065
121559	98017	27968	15586	51535	1978		950	824820
20324	26952	11910	1198	11177	2638	30		313156
-81	3346	1389	1739	73	145			32887
94694	60155	42198	3979	11379	2599			337641
166233	65365	42388	3050	19520	407			708278
2711689	1609734	823637	31654	725309	28530	375	229	8179075
377547	182245	93173	7178	80562	1103	175	55	1839376
330074	187690	133038	4312	38340	12000			765217
28826	23889	18474		2914	2500			105833
59228	33376	12223	3150	15431	2573			162725
237	5399	924	4474					52871
1324408	830638	360908	5770	461019	2741	200		2812007
451791	243526	165619	2366	72027	3340		174	1701226
114888	92652	32117	1861	54704	3970			680728
24691	10320	7160	2544	312	304			59093
1162111	668375	605043	17299	44341	1446	246		2123805
153792	78090	70490		7000	600			248213
104356	41310	40407		902				211637
133085	67609	39759	15801	11875	174			501190
770878	481366	454387	1497	24564	672	246		1162766
1334155	893948	265084	88333	360730	113480	5676	60645	4758762
146350	103196	40552	12191	34677	4808		10968	763039
896590	573037	145820	33557	260298	83012	1594	48756	2365510
33997	22597	5889	4062	11071	1575			96022
5645	3126	84	2830	90	122			20097
41198	37197	3976	14619	8660	9864		78	399003
19925	9028	6370	924	640	412	683		156254
33650	26095	4980	390	20716	10			88455
156800	119672	57413	19760	24579	13677	3400	843	870384
4355226	2405435	1429552	31415	794689	89567	764	59449	12116588
2354832	1511621	798360	143861	499281	62169	5564	2386	7912343

10-12 续表 3 continued

单位：万元

项目	Item	商品销售收入净额 Net Value of Sales Revenue	商品销售成本 Sales Cost	经营费用 Operating Expense	# 运杂及装卸费 Traffic Related Expense	商品销售税金及附加 Sales Tax and Extra Charges
合计	**Total**	**19949203**	**18218978**	**894717**	**122207**	**34691**
按企业登记注册类型分	**Grouped by Type of Enterprises Registered**					
内资企业	Domestic Investment	19546774	17888486	846780	121647	34236
国有企业	State-Owned	14118539	12954450	594255	96666	22458
集体企业	Collective Owned	1467097	1333844	77118	6398	3609
私营企业	Private Owned	436510	394947	23802	1145	752
联营企业	Joint Owned	520841	472650	16746	1747	1093
股份合作企业	Share Holding Cooperative	229219	207817	15466	1052	521
股份有限公司	Share Holding Company	1039872	910854	51785	7304	3600
有限责任公司	Limited-Liability Company	1592431	1470283	70048	6326	2328
其他企业	Others					
港澳台商投资企业	Hongkong,Macao and Taiwan Funded Enterprises	57550	48604	3566	55	123
外商投资企业	Foreign Funded Enterprises	344880	281888	44371	505	332
按国民经济行业分	**Grouped by Sectors**					
批发业	Wholesale	15215872	14101797	546278	111958	18743
食品饮料烟草和家庭用品批发业	Food,Beverage,Tabacoo and Family Use Goods	4961369	4617968	183802	31091	4910
食品饮料烟草批发业	Food,Beverage and Tabacco	2369110	2255809	68317	15615	2299
棉麻、土畜产品批发业	Cotton,Flax,Local and Animal Products	380065	371677	13285	4347	183
纺织品、服装和鞋帽批发业	Textile,Garments,Shoes and Hats	824820	745541	32958	6313	268
日用百货批发业	Daily Use Goods	313024	272145	22283	1040	736
日用杂品批发业	Grocery	32887	26280	4533	1194	25
五金交电化工批发业	Hardware,Electrical Appliance and Chemic	336673	314770	9970	985	444
药品及医疗器械批发业	Medicine and Medical Appliance	704791	631745	32456	1597	956
能源、材料和机械电子设备批发业	Energy,Materials,Machinery and Electronic Equipments	8172508	7671765	241097	66062	9876
能源批发业	Energy	1838201	1654380	83618	19059	3314
化工材料批发业	Chemical Materials	765194	719950	20963	10448	427
木材批发业	Timbers	105825	93290	8538	2411	8
建筑材料批发业	Building Materials	160941	149458	7646	1837	328
矿产品批发业	Mineral Products	52871	44370	7804	5316	76
金属材料批发业	Metal Materials	2811932	2690607	62964	17254	4030
机械、电子设备批发业	Machinery and Electronic Equipments	1697901	1608247	34033	7949	1144
汽车摩托车及零配件批发业	Spares and Fittings of Automobile and Motorcycle	680551	656098	13555	1181	456
再生物资回收批发业	Recovery of Reclaimed Materials	59093	55367	1976	607	94
其他批发业	Others	2081995	1812064	121379	14806	3957
工艺美术品批发业	Handicrafts	248213	218762	12725	3118	119
图书报刊批发业	Books,Newspaper and Magazines	169838	136076	15138	1691	233
农业生产资料批发业	Agricultural Capital Goods	501190	470591	18506	2267	422
其他类未包括的批发	Others	1162756	986636	75010	7729	3183
零售业	Retail	4733331	4117181	348439	10249	15948
食品、饮料和烟草零售业	Food,Beverage and Tabacco	761712	672469	73470	1869	2053
日用百货零售业	Daily Use Goods	2360095	1987178	186955	3311	10138
纺织品、服装和鞋帽零售业	Textile,Garments,Shoes and Hats	96022	78180	11216	179	459
日用杂品零售业	Grocery	20074	16831	1766	235	92
五金交电化工零售业	Hardware,Electrical Appliance and Chemical	398819	369092	18046	1328	692
药品及医疗器械零售业	Medicine and Medical Appliance	153741	129871	10143	246	517
图书报刊零售业	Books,Newspaper and Magazines	82077	61026	10767	209	266
其他零售业	Others	860792	802534	36076	2874	1733
按规模划分	**Grouped by Size**					
大型企业	Large Enterprises	12069356	10960032	527137	69757	21944
中型企业	Medium Enterprises	7879848	7258946	367580	52450	12747

10-12 续表 4 continued

(10000 yuan)

商品销售利润 Sales Profits	代购代销收入 Revenue from Agency Activity	主营业务利润 Profits of Major Business	其他业务利润 Profits of Other Business	管理费用 Overhead Expense	# 税金 Taxes	#财产保险费 Premium of Property	# 劳动待业保险 Premium for Employment	财务费用 Financial Expense	# 利息支出 Interest Expenditure	营业利润 Operating Profits
800817	**113816**	**914633**	**244341**	**837450**	**20090**	**8870**	**67828**	**298814**	**366675**	**46228**
777272	113812	891084	238846	806076	19387	8632	66654	295954	363423	51624
547377	105761	653138	170668	547405	13514	5799	49309	253364	304639	30033
52526	350	52876	23392	72428	2098	860	6111	15373	14183	-7377
17009	53	17062	2574	23574	120	134	88	430	545	-3901
30352	12	30364	2537	26637	273	210	1616	5238	5885	1343
5415		5415	3758	11261	257	148	1060	2623	2542	-4545
73632	3268	76900	15439	61306	1317	1194	5937	284	13093	30844
49772	1727	51499	17543	70527	1525	281	1528	11612	11767	-1504
5257		5257	9	4061	79	7	551	240	557	973
18289	3	18292	5487	27313	624	232	623	2620	2696	-6370
549055	113257	662311	143783	511354	13223	4782	31170	269570	324643	36287
154690	10994	165684	45950	164786	4432	1956	10851	108292	114765	-57529
42685	2075	44760	32815	60377	1592	1026	4624	65369	70640	-45093
-5080	4502	-578	2464	15690	979	121	757	8913	9651	-22674
46053	2820	48872	2564	30020	381	248	1595	18381	17862	3856
17861	746	18607	2321	13021	182	204	614	5672	6341	2005
2049	6	2054	168	2332	24	11	113	1249	1286	-1249
11489	264	11753	2714	10195	257	55	741	3417	3595	1112
39634	583	40217	2905	33151	1019	291	2407	5290	5389	4513
249769	53681	303450	73190	251207	5390	2078	14505	105205	136117	25687
96889	13580	110469	19881	62474	995	842	3222	7183	11402	60054
23854	6848	30702	6702	15305	384	121	814	11478	10916	10625
3989	298	4287	616	2287	34	13	232	3080	3166	104
3509	1237	4746	7374	13221	235	103	551	3061	3274	-2203
621	1642	2263	512	1732	28		182	1238	535	-195
54332	11553	65885	22301	78684	1532	428	5173	50679	62331	-38219
54477	17130	71608	11374	64383	1875	334	3321	19786	34568	-917
10441	1394	11836	3419	10628	234	142	398	7081	8325	-2363
1656		1656	1012	2494	74	95	612	1619	1600	-1198
144596	48582	193177	24643	95361	3401	748	5814	56073	73761	68129
16607	673	17281	2969	12707	364	356	1075	9362	10267	-1187
18391	874	19265	1895	12454	236	95	1484	95	828	8767
11671	6716	18387	5385	14072	274	90	770	9295	11490	411
97927	40318	138245	14393	56128	2527	207	2485	37321	51176	60139
251763	559	252322	100558	326095	6867	4088	36658	29244	42033	9941
13721	3	13723	27672	38108	1409	627	10065	3197	3878	1228
175824	270	176095	48643	207211	3531	2618	19279	18605	30104	348
6166	84	6250	3626	8066	105	74	913	580	745	671
1385		1385	1162	2307	86	20	298	44	22	183
10989	84	11073	3122	13490	647	110	1082	1251	1283	636
13211	107	13318	700	10615	97	135	1222	332	445	3141
10018		10019	899	9501	178	164	1363	36	202	1412
20449	11	20459	14734	36797	813	340	2437	5199	5353	2323
560243	56098	616342	110864	429594	9354	4948	32515	177311	225275	121054
240574	57717	298291	133477	407856	10735	3922	35313	121504	141401	-74827

10-12 续表 5 continued

单位：万元

项　　目	Item	投资收益 Investment Income	补贴收入 Subsidy Income	营业外收入 Out-business Income	营业外支出 Out-business Expenditure	利润总额 Total Profits	应交所得税 Income Tax Payable
合　　计	**Total**	**88569**	**153254**	**49699**	**26062**	**303696**	**126480**
按企业登记注册类型分	**Grouped by Type of Enterprises Registered**						
内资企业	Domestic Investment	88289	153254	49120	25544	308361	124459
国有企业	State-Owned	74442	139738	37274	20200	252099	91974
集体企业	Collective Owned	1512	11570	5308	1827	9627	6722
私营企业	Private Owned	-206		370	310	-4331	-40
联营企业	Joint Owned	234	16	599	875	2377	2601
股份合作企业	Share Holding Cooperative	59	8	840	132	-3976	403
股份有限公司	Share Holding Company	7815	65	2573	885	42877	10946
有限责任公司	Limited-Liability Company	1979	936	1897	1290	-522	7305
其他企业	Others						
港澳台商投资企业	Hongkong,Macao and Taiwan Funded Enterprises	190		134	37	1260	439
外商投资企业	Foreign Funded Enterprises	90		445	481	-5925	1582
按国民经济行业分	**Grouped by Sectors**						
批发业	Wholesale	81045	146035	31901	17491	268316	101003
食品饮料烟草和家庭用品批发业	Food,Beverage,Tabacoo and Family Use Goods	29750	114665	8499	3760	85698	30922
食品饮料烟草批发业	Food,Beverage and Tabacco	18934	87255	3568	1588	57055	14934
棉麻、土畜产品批发业	Cotton,Flax,Local and Animal Products	854	25633	942	-268	4847	1157
纺织品、服装和鞋帽批发业	Textile,Garments,Shoes and Hats	481	1440	569	899	4411	4748
日用百货批发业	Daily Use Goods	1029	5	656	455	3479	3043
日用杂品批发业	Grocery			176	101	-1175	163
五金交电化工批发业	Hardware,Electrical Appliance and Chemic	1199		1595	516	3136	3595
药品及医疗器械批发业	Medicine and Medical Appliance	7253	332	994	469	13945	3282
能源、材料和机械电子设备批发业	Energy,Materials,Machinery and Electronic Equipments	38700	23549	17147	11071	90493	47847
能源批发业	Energy	6363	8386	2854	2683	78991	22794
化工材料批发业	Chemical Materials	3258	3183	896	1151	15618	5138
木材批发业	Timbers	187	30	1	400	-638	524
建筑材料批发业	Building Materials	48		741	599	-2589	596
矿产品批发业	Mineral Products	373	20	4	21	180	53
金属材料批发业	Metal Materials	9451	10420	3443	4291	-18700	7379
机械、电子设备批发业	Machinery and Electronic Equipmenst	15661	1386	7205	1455	16646	9896
汽车摩托车及零配件批发业	Spares and Fittings of Automobile and Motorcycle	2471	76	1746	429	989	1461
再生物资回收批发业	Recovery of Reclaimed Materials	889	49	258	42	-3	6
其他批发业	Others	12595	7821	6255	2661	92125	22235
工艺美术品批发业	Handicrafts	697	816	430	142	988	3108
图书报刊批发业	Books,Newspaper and Magazines	356	1861	915	403	11809	5225
农业生产资料批发业	Agricultural Capital Goods	2585	2966	2315	252	8015	3321
其他类未包括的批发	Others	8957	2178	2595	1865	71313	10581
零售业	Retail	7525	7219	17798	8571	35380	25477
食品、饮料和烟草零售业	Food,Beverage and Tabacco	383	5481	3205	993	9314	4300
日用百货零售业	Daily Use Goods	6231	48	8140	3202	12986	13252
纺织品、服装和鞋帽零售业	Textile,Garments,Shoes and Hats	526		648	837	1107	524
日用杂品零售业	Grocery	22	3	98	43	220	100
五金交电化工零售业	Hardware,Electrical Appliance and Chemical	422		1054	614	1418	1544
药品及医疗器械零售业	Medicine and Medical Appliance	54		2572	1983	3665	1180
图书报刊零售业	Books,Newspaper and Magazines	212	30	46	98	1570	867
其他零售业	Others	-326	1657	2035	801	5100	3710
按规模划分	**Grouped by Size**						
大型企业	Large Enterprises	46228	100114	20450	11019	269789	79248
中型企业	Medium Enterprises	42342	53140	29248	15043	33907	47233

10-12 续表 6 continued

(10000 yuan)

转作奖金的利润 Profits Distributed as Bonus	应付利润 Profits Payable	本年应付工资总额 Total Wages Payable in the Year	#主营业务应付工资 Wage Payable of Major Business	本年应付福利费总额 Welfares Payable in the Year	#主营业务应付福利费 of Major Business	本年应交增值税 Value Added Payable in the Year	本年进项税额 Tax included in Purchasing Cost	本年销项税额 Tax included in Sales Value
966	**186380**	**370628**	**331609**	**53864**	**48192**	**142688**	**2593421**	**2457386**
966	184709	356858	318350	49315	43666	131439	2537610	2390683
308	163140	233985	212134	32609	29395	85116	1749448	1583984
456	1874	37664	31859	4703	3917	8765	204546	211860
82	4301	7332	5442	790	510	5789	69681	75217
46	2402	10239	9428	2342	2244	7301	70397	77215
75	113	7444	6970	996	953	2509	35308	37529
	6813	29041	26584	4141	3645	13071	157049	157634
82	9388	32530	26317	3852	2992	10770	242019	247590
	1503	1759	1666	461	438	1302	8399	9652
	168	12011	11593	4088	4088	9947	47412	57052
380	166549	161144	137114	23328	19920	46659	1919325	1691714
182	18530	57286	50141	8173	7215	10948	639074	541633
17	7056	21856	19518	3226	2914	14393	272648	251204
	993	3261	3254	447	447	-10292	42488	20729
10	6970	8393	6244	1063	772	-8914	117852	53417
3	167	5339	4715	733	613	6333	47291	52084
4	183	1055	959	-57	-61	-1063	3746	1863
1	1090	4437	3792	650	525	2420	50710	52277
146	2070	12946	11660	2112	2005	8070	104340	110060
198	89841	72702	60388	10957	9196	28273	1089275	1027131
	79978	13840	12789	2135	1964	15616	143584	162812
	292	4294	3677	691	594	-7767	81986	67085
	10	654	648	86	86	48	11832	10159
23	170	4523	2986	547	347	4370	69372	74033
		1047	1047	108	108	-26	3868	3239
161	1031	21820	16044	3189	2393	8107	422643	380704
4	6728	20944	18496	3458	3163	3041	232726	206331
11	1630	4281	3761	562	457	4242	113856	112759
	2	1299	939	181	85	643	9408	10011
	58178	31155	26585	4199	3508	7439	190977	122950
	1903	5235	4631	740	644	565	33151	5914
	2564	8794	7539	954	738	1588	15826	17466
	5050	4215	4089	500	487	128	11028	10691
	48661	12912	10326	2004	1640	5158	130971	88879
586	19831	209484	194494	30536	28272	96029	674096	765672
301	1242	46766	44513	6146	5946	13612	101175	113146
	14871	115553	106655	18281	16598	60826	333857	393003
	34	6216	5644	747	683	2631	10880	13277
	3	1319	916	162	90	551	2836	3381
37	493	7327	6808	929	883	3295	60582	63220
10	297	8275	8153	933	929	4016	21344	25453
	611	6812	6738	955	952	2384	8220	10591
239	2280	17216	15068	2383	2192	8716	135203	143603
201	166708	178357	163520	27765	25141	94262	1497067	1432695
765	19673	192270	168089	26099	23051	48426	1096354	1024692

10-13 大中型餐饮业财务状况

单位：万元

项目 Item		合计 Total	按登记注册类型分 国有企业 State-Owned	集体企业 Collective Owned	私营企业 Private Owned	联营企业 Joint-Owned	股份合作企业 Share Holding Cooperative
流动资产合计	Total Circulating Assets	193592	48496	13789	5108	3568	6862
# 货币资金	Cash	59473	23198	3237	455	876	652
应收帐款	Accounts Receivable	18305	2288	4391	391	544	2019
存　货	Inventory	20111	3476	1473	954	505	1030
长期投资	Long-term Investment	41959	10111	1910		26	593
固定资产合计	Total Fixed Assets	190752	50210	9031	9531	3667	3873
固定资产原价合计	Total Original Value of Fixed Assets	240521	58841	12251	9801	4476	4970
# 生产经营用	For Production and Business Use	212422	44287	9396	8601	2723	3891
累计折旧	Accumulative Depreciation	70272	16490	4468	815	837	1400
# 本年折旧	of this Year	14630	2984	1063	301	116	280
无形及递延资产合计	Total Intangible and Deffered Assets	61173	11560	5070	5322	1098	2473
# 无形资产	Intangible Assets	13041	2359	263	3	4	755
其他资产合计	Other Assets	20484	309	48			
资产合计	Total Assets	507959	120686	29847	19961	8359	13802
流动负债合计	Total Liquid Liabilities	283129	55161	18352	14916	4882	8859
# 短期借款	Short-term Loans	54716	6132	3029	2702	1460	3155
应付帐款	Payment Payable	44727	4668	5580	3942	1281	1846
长期负债合计	Total Long-term Liabilities	46396	4696	2003			387
# 长期借款	Long-term Loans	19988	2850	430			139
负债合计	Total Liabilities	329525	59858	20355	14916	4882	9246
所有者权益合计	Total Ownership Interest	178434	60828	9493	5045	3477	4556
# 实收资本	Capital Stock	211611	32105	16491	10199	2790	4639
# 国家资本	State	45730	24753	244		428	
集体资本	Collective	20928	746	11757	3249	714	201
法人资本	Institutional Units	61142	6366	4166	1160	1646	2791
个人资本	Individual	17478	240	324	5790	3	1647
港澳台资本	Honkong,Macao and Taiwan	34277					
外商资本	Foreign	32057					
营业收入	Business Revenue	407746	85526	33491	11395	5254	12467
营业成本	Business Cost	194033	42839	18851	5737	2557	7594
营业费用	Business Expenses	143387	29087	10229	5045	2044	3056
营业税金及附加	Business Tax and Extra Charges	20258	4300	1786	633	260	461
主营业务利润	Profits of Major Business	50068	9299	2625	-20	392	1356
其他业务利润	Profits of Other Business	230	230				
管理费用	Overhead Expenses	53734	10712	3764	1946	546	1566
# 税　金	Taxes	2630	521	185	59	39	289
财产保险费	Premium of Property	547	123	35	14	4	1
劳动待业保险费	Premium for Employment	5332	3852	114	18	125	
财务费用	Financial Expenses	7987	-559	62	202	9	202
# 利息支出	Interest Expenditure	8159	207	130	195	23	91
营业利润	Operating Profits	-11424	-624	-1201	-2168	-163	-413
投资收益	Investment Income	982	369	12			
补贴收入	Subsidy Income	34	34				
营业外收入	Out-business Income	2955	1440	111	377	7	1
营业外支出	Out-business Expenditure	2534	439	75	43	6	1
利润总额	Total Profits	-9843	793	-1176	-1832	42	-413
应交所得税	Income Tax Payable	6728	1144	855	32	66	63
应付利润	Profits Payable	3219	216	-136		115	1
转作奖金的利润	Profits Distributed as Bonus	123		1	7	1	57
本年应付工资总额	Total Wages Payable of this Year	53992	15621	4242	1747	848	1087
# 主营业务应付工资	of Major Business	50219	14572	3940	1524	669	975
本年应付福利费总额	Total Welfares Payable of this Year	9323	2041	541	125	86	90
# 主营业务应付福利费	of Major Business	8316	1934	383	-153	78	89

FINANCIAL INDICATORS FOR LARGE AND MEDIUM CATERING TRADES

(10000 yuan)

By Registered Type					按行业划分 By Sectors			按规模划分 By Size	
股份有限公司 Share Holding Company	有限责任公司 Limited-liabilities	其他企业 Others	港澳台商投资企业 Hongkon,Macao, Taiwan Funded	外商投资企业 Foreign Funded	正餐 Dinner	快餐 Fast Food	其他餐饮业 Others	大型企业 Large	中型企业 Medium
278	24618	165	40142	50569	155840	34705	3046	117182	76409
37	6257	2	6083	18678	46438	12392	642	39422	20051
129	2952	1	2510	3081	17213	1031	60	7704	10600
110	2856	108	2989	6609	14212	5504	396	10433	9678
	12973		9242	7105	41635	324		35275	6684
178	21706	71	24115	68371	132415	56423	1913	126389	64363
205	25597	74	34720	89586	166449	71714	2357	156174	84347
205	25198	29	30998	87095	139547	70580	2295	146275	66147
27	5823	3	12673	27737	49916	19889	467	43100	27172
26	1596	3	2439	5823	9807	4780	43	9188	5443
1170	5891		15037	13552	44270	16324	579	29936	31237
	1101		7051	1507	6055	6985		10409	2632
	80		3669	16378	10033	10357	93	18139	2345
1625	65267	235	92204	155974	384194	118133	5631	326921	181038
1517	29914	227	62281	87019	221489	59917	1724	182223	100905
	5068		1677	31492	32550	21984	182	37852	16864
118	4152	226	5377	17538	33666	10444	617	24273	20454
	8106		4494	26710	38409	7888	100	19884	26513
	5643		2884	8042	12495	7394	100	15449	4539
1517	38020	227	66775	113729	259897	67804	1824	202107	127418
108	27247	8	25429	42245	124297	50329	3808	124814	53620
126	20127	38	58601	66496	152859	53440	5313	121432	90179
	3512		4974	11818	35913	9617	200	25080	20649
	312	38	2843	1067	20620	177	130	6292	14635
110	12347		19187	13369	43991	16904	246	42198	18944
16	3956		5017	488	11767	5712		9019	8459
			26160	8118	24909	4632	4736	15603	18674
			420	31637	15659	16399		23239	8818
2469	46054	123	45357	165610	279399	126163	2185	272449	135297
1058	21973	86	19396	73941	133542	59462	1029	125166	68867
852	15400	29	20426	57219	97539	44653	1195	92757	50630
136	2253	7	2080	8343	14011	6156	91	13407	6851
423	6428	2	3455	26107	34307	15892	-130	41120	8949
					230				230
122	5159	32	9173	20715	42478	10271	985	31400	22334
108	215		622	592	2134	496	1	1439	1191
	47		37	288	315	232		409	138
7	831		87	299	5042	281	9	3484	1848
78	605		3431	3957	6345	1660	-17	5791	2196
77	714		2813	3909	6399	1761		5788	2371
223	665	-30	-9148	1435	-14287	3961	-1098	3928	-15352
	563			38	944	38	-1	517	465
					34				34
	96		437	486	2311	636	8	2091	864
2	86		1005	877	1386	1142	7	2237	297
-9	1206	-30	-10760	2336	-13031	4185	-997	4166	-14008
	1013		193	3361	4625	2099	4	5601	1127
	401		69	2553	1657	1560	2	3205	14
	48		3	6	123			54	68
205	6262	25	6906	17049	42936	10506	550	31986	22005
205	6259	25	6469	15581	40170	9505	544	30356	19863
26	745		1323	4348	7466	1847	9	6300	3023
26	745		1257	3958	6743	1564	9	5858	2458

10-14 商业、饮食业、服务业经营机构及人员
OPERATING UNITS AND PERSONNEL OF COMMERCE,CATERING AND SERVICES

项 目 Item		经营机构(个) Operating Units (unit)		人 员(人) Personnel (person)	
		1999	1998	1999	1998
总 计	**Total**	**255900**	**252618**	**1231619**	**1250212**
商 业	Commerce	188809	191867	828393	827218
批 发	Wholesale	11949	11357	282723	269237
零 售	Retail	176860	180510	545670	557981
饮食业	Catering	32120	28754	166031	192694
服务业	Services	34971	31997	237195	230300

10-15 商业、饮食业、服务业营业网点及人员(按所有制形式分)
OUTLETS AND PERSONNEL OF COMMERCE,CATERING AND SERVICES (BY OWNERSHIP)

单位：个、人 (unit,person)

项 目 Item		合计 Total	国有 State-owned	集体 Collective-owned	个体 Individuals	其他 Others
营业网点	**Outlets**	**243951**	**7723**	**9616**	**219234**	**7378**
人 员	**Personnel**	**948896**	**266170**	**152003**	**299434**	**231289**
商 业	Commerce					
零售网点	Retail Outlets	176860	5019	6090	160547	5204
人 员	Personnel	545670	143157	88345	199414	114754
饮食业	Catering					
营业网点	Outlets	32120	959	1657	28276	1228
人 员	Personnel	166031	28256	27430	60440	49905
服务业	Services					
营业网点	Outlets	34971	1745	1869	30411	946
人 员	Personnel	237195	94757	36228	39580	66630

10-16 批发业网点及人员
OUTLETS AND PERSONNEL OF WHOLESALE

单位：个、人 (unit,person)

项目	Item	网点 Outlets	人员 Personnel
总计	**Total**	**11949**	**282723**
食品、饮料、烟草批发业	Food,Beverage and Tabacco	1487	46942
棉、麻、土畜产品批发业	Cotton,Fiber,Local and Livestock Products	58	2638
纺织品、服装和鞋帽批发业	Textile Products,Garments,Shoes and Hats	713	14930
日用百货批发业	Daily Use Goods	1134	21344
日用杂品批发业	Daily Use Groceries	127	2770
五金、交电、化工批发业	Hardware,Electrical Appliances and Chemical	1769	28689
药品及医疗器械批发业	Medicines and Medical Appliances	407	15918
工艺美术品批发业	Handicraft Articles	121	3112
图书报刊批发业	Books,Newspapers and Magazines	70	2783
农业生产资料批发业	Agricultural Capital Goods	181	5406
其他批发业	Others	5882	138191

10-17 商业零售网点及人员
OUTLETS AND PERSONNEL OF RETAIL

单位：个、人 (unit,person)

项目	Item	网点 Outlets	人员 Personnel
总计	**Total**	**176860**	**545670**
食品、饮料、烟草零售业	Food,Beverage and Tabacco	41914	114990
日用百货零售业	Daily Use Goods	28232	201648
纺织品、服装和鞋帽零售业	Textile Products,Garments,Shoes and Hats	17004	26884
日用杂品零售业	Daily Use Groceries	3296	7670
五金、交电、化工零售业	Hardware,Electrical Appliances and Chemical	28889	72588
药品及医疗器械零售业	Medicines and Medical Appliances	5865	15906
图书报刊零售业	Books,Newspapers and Magazines	4738	11145
其他零售业	Others	46922	94839

10-18 饮食业营业网点及人员
OUTLETS AND PERSONNEL OF CATERING

单位：个、人 (unit,person)

项目	Item	网点 Outlets	人员 Personnel
总计	**Total**	**32120**	**166031**
正餐	Dinner	26555	139879
快餐	Fast Food	2891	22234
其他	Others	2674	3918

10-19 服务业营业网点及人员
OUTLETS AND PERSONNEL OF SERVICES

单位：个、人 (unit,person)

项目	Item	网点 Outlets	人员 Personnel
总计	**Total**	**34971**	**237195**
理发及美容化妆业	Services of Haircut,Beauty and Making-up	7025	13491
沐浴业	Bath Service	414	4805
洗染业	Cleaning and Dyeing	1281	3369
摄影及扩印业	Photography and Large-printing	2055	5797
日用品修理业	Repairs of Daily Use Articles	12437	20822
其他居民服务业	Other Residential Services	9235	35804
旅馆业	Hotels	2524	153107

10-20 个体工商业户数及人数
OUTLETS AND PERSONNEL OF SELF-EMPLOYMENT BUSINESS

单位：个、人 (unit,person)

项目 Item			1999 全市 Total	1999 城镇 Urban	1999 农村 Rural	1998 全市 Total	1998 城镇 Urban	1998 农村 Rural
总户数	**Total Outlets**		**257416**	**141551**	**115865**	**246294**	**108329**	**137965**
总人数	**Total Persons**		**359077**	**199253**	**159824**	**346550**	**155037**	**191513**
农林牧渔业								
Farming,Forestry,Animal	户数	Units	1436	164	1272	1131	36	1095
Husbandry and Fishery	人数	Persons	2110	212	1898	1519	60	1459
工业	户数	Units	16831	6838	9993	16254	4513	11741
Industry	人数	Persons	33719	11298	22421	33339	7018	26321
建筑业	户数	Units	592	246	346	700	220	480
Construction	人数	Persons	1956	701	1255	2272	500	1772
交通运输业	户数	Units	17330	6119	11211	20594	4939	15655
Transportation	人数	Persons	19151	6750	12401	22690	5419	17271
商业	户数	Units	160547	91230	69317	154214	73046	81168
Commerce	人数	Persons	199414	111847	87567	188288	91188	97100
饮食业	户数	Units	28276	17750	10526	24263	12411	11852
Catering	人数	Persons	60440	42934	17506	60328	33377	26951
服务业	户数	Units	18990	12485	6505	15222	6962	8260
Services	人数	Persons	25351	16802	8549	21416	10637	10779
修理业	户数	Units	12066	6333	5733	12557	5953	6604
Repairs	人数	Persons	15146	8193	6953	14876	6515	8361
其他行业	户数	Units	1348	386	962	1359	249	1110
Others	人数	Persons	1790	516	1274	1822	323	1499

主要统计指标解释

社会消费品零售额 指各种经济类型的批发零售贸易业、餐饮业、制造业及其他业对城乡居民、社会集团的消费品零售额。这个指标反映通过各种商品流通渠道向居民和社会集团供应的生活消费品以满足他们生活需要，是研究人民生活、社会消费品购买力、货币流通等问题的重要指标。社会消费品零售额包括：（1）售给城乡居民作为生活用的商品和修建房屋用的建筑材料；（2）售给机关、团体、学校、部队、企业、事业单位的职工食堂和旅店（招待所）附设专门供本店旅客食用、不对外营业的食堂的各种食品、饮料；企业、单位和国营农场直接售给本单位职工和职工食堂的自己生产的产品；（3）售给部队、战士生活用的粮食、副食品、衣着品、日用品、燃料；（4）售给来华的外国人、华侨、港澳台同胞的消费品；（5）居民自费购买的中、西药品、中药材及医疗用品；（6）报社、出版社直接给居民和社会集团的报纸、图书、杂志、集邮公司出售的新、旧纪念邮票、特种邮票、首日封、集邮册、集邮工具等；（7）旧货寄售商店自购、自销部分的商品；（8）煤气公司、液化石油气站售给居民和社会团体的煤气灶具和罐装液化石油气；（9）农民售给非农业居民和社会团体的商品。不包括售给国民经济各部门企业、事业单位（包括国有经济的农场）生产经营用的各种原材料、燃料、设备、工具等和售给批发零售贸易业、餐饮业作为转卖用的商品、旧货寄售商店受托寄售卖出的商品、服务业的营业收入、邮局出售邮票的收入、自来水、电力、煤气生产（供应）单位的产品供应收入，也不包括农民之间的商品销售。

批发零售贸易业商品购、销、存总额 指以各种经济类型的批发、零售贸易业（不包括个体）为总体的商品购、销、存。

商品购进总额 指从本企业（单位）以外的单位和个人购进（包括从国外直接购进）作为转卖或加工后转卖的商品。这个指标反映批发零售贸易业从国内、国外市场上购进商品的总量。商品购进总额包括：（1）从工农业生产者购进的商品；（2）从出版社、报社的发行部门购进的图书、杂志和报纸；（3）从各种经济类型的批发零售贸易企业（单位）购进的商品，如从机关、团体、企业、单位购进的剩余物资，从餐饮业、服务业购进的商品，从海关、市场管理部门购进的缉私和没收的商品，从居民收购的废旧商品等；（5）从国（境）外直接进口的商品。不包括企业（单位）为自身经营用，和未通过买卖行为而收入的商品以及销售退回、商品升溢等。

商品销售总额 指对本企业（单位）以外的单位和个人出售（包括对国（境）外直接出口）的商品。这个指标反映批发零售贸易业在国内市场上销售商品以及出口商品的总量。商品销售总额包括：（1）售给城乡居民和社会集团消费用的商品；（2）售给工业、农业、建筑业、运输邮电业、批发零售贸易业、餐饮业、服务业等作为生产、经营使用的商品；（3）售给批发零售贸易业作为转卖或加工后转卖的商品；（4）对国（境）外直接出口的商品。不包括：出售本企业（单位）自用的废旧包装用品，为通过买卖行为付出的商品，经本单位介绍，由买卖双方直接结算，本单位只收取手续费的业务，购货退出的商品以及商品损耗和损失等。

批发零售贸易业年末库存 指年末各种经济类型的批发零售贸易企业（单位）已取得所有权的商品。它反映各地区、各批发零售企业（单位）的库存情况，和对市场商品供应的保证程度。年末库存包括：（1）存放在批发零售贸易经营单位（如门市部、批发站、经营处）仓库、货场、货柜和货架中的商品；（2）挑选、整理、包装中的商品；（3）已计入购进而尚未运到本单位的商品，即发货单或银行承兑凭证已到而货未到部分；（4）寄放他处的商品，如因购货方拒绝承付而暂时存放在购货方的商品和已办完加工成品收回手续而未提回的商品；（5）委托其他单位代销（未作销售或调出）尚未售出的商品；（6）代其他单位购进尚未交付的商品。不包括所有权不属于本单位的商品、拨付除批发零售贸易业以外的其他行业所属独立核算加工等加工生产尚未收回成品的商品、代国家物资储备部门保管的商品等。年末库存总额计算方法是：农副产品采购单位按购进价计算，批发单位按进货价计算，零售单位按什么价格核算就按什么价格计算。

网点 指本批发零售贸易企业（单位）设立的从事批发、零售贸易业务的自然单位[包括本企业（单位）自身]，具有独立固定的营业场所，配备一定的业务人员，不论单位大小，不论是否单独核算，均按自然网点计算，即有一个点就算一个网点。不包括同一营业场所内各柜组以及派出的流动推销小组，流动售货车等。

人员 指在批发、零售贸易网点工作并取得劳动报酬的从业人员。包括职工、聘请的离退休人员等。

Explanatory Notes On Main Statistical Indicators

Total Retail Sales of Consumer Goods refer to the sum of retail sales of consumer goods to urban and rural residents and social groups by the establishments in wholesale, retail, catering, manufacturing and other industries of various ownerships. This indicator is used to show the supply of consumers goods through various channels to households and institutions to meet their demands, and is therefore very important for the study of the issues on people's livelihood , on the purchasing power of consumer goods and on the circulation of money. The retail sales of consumer goods include: （1）commodities sold to urban and rural residents for residential use and building materials sold to them for the construction or repair of houses; （2）food and Beverage sold to canteens of institutions, enterprises, schools, military units and to canteens of hotels that only serve their guests, and commodities produced by enterprises, institutions or state farms and sold directly to their employees or their canteens; （3）grain and non-staple food, clothing, daily articles and fuels sold to military and soldiers; （4）consumer goods sold to foreigners, overseas Chinese and Chinese compatriots from Taiwan, Hong Kong and Macao during their stay in the mainland of China; （5）Chinese and western medicines, herbs and medical facilities purchased by residents; （6）newspapers, books and magazines directly sold to residents and social groups by publishers, new and old commemorative stamps, special stamps, first-day envelope, stamp albums and other stamp-collection articles sold by stamp companies; （7）consumer goods purchased and then sold by second-hand shops; （8）stoves and other heating facilities and liquefied gas sold by gas companies to households and institutions; and （9）commodities sold by farmers to non-agricultural residents and social groups. But sales like followings are not included in total retail sales of consumer goods: (1) raw materials, fuels, equipment, tools sold to enterprises, institutions and state farms for production purpose; (2) commodities sold to trade establishments for re-selling; (3) commissioned sales at second-hand shops; (4) operational income of various services; (5) stamps sold at post offices; (6) income of water, power, gas production and supply establishments from the supply of their products; (7) and sales of commodities among farmers.

Purchase, Sales and Stock of Commodities by Wholesalers and Retailers refer to the purchase, sales and stock of commodities by wholesale and retail establishments of different ownership（excluding individual sellers）.

Total Purchases of Commodities refer to the purchases of commodities by the establishments from other establishments or individuals（including direct import from abroad）for the purpose of re-selling, with or without further processing of the commodities purchased. This indicator is used to show the total value of purchases of commodities by wholesale and retail establishments from domestic and overseas markets. The total purchases include: （1）agricultural and industrial products purchased from producers; （2）books, magazines and newspapers purchased from distribution departments of the publishers; （3）commodities purchased from wholesale and retail establishments of various ownership; （4）commodities purchased from other units, such as surplus materials purchased from government agencies, enterprises or institutions, commodities purchased from catering and service establishments, confiscated goods purchased from customs authorities or market management agencies, second-hand goods and wastes purchased from residents; and（5）commodities directly imported from abroad. Excluded are commodities purchased by establishments（units）for use in their own business operation, commodities obtained without buying or selling procedures, rejected commodities, etc.

Total Sales of Commodities refer to selling of commodities by the establishments to other establishments and individuals(including direct export). This indicator is used to show the total value of sales of commodities at domestic markets and export, The total sales include: （1）commodities sold to urban and rural residents and social groups for final consumption; （2）commodities sold to establishments in industry, agriculture, construction, transportation, post and telecommunications, wholesale and retail trades, catering and public utility for productive consumption; （3）commodities sold to wholesale and retail establishments for re-selling, with or without further processing; and （4）commodities for direct export to other countries. Excluded are sales of self-used waste packaging materials, commodities transferred without buying or selling procedures, commission income from brokerage in transactions whose settlement is directly handled by buyers and sellers, rejected commodities in the purchase, loss in commodities, etc.

Commodity Stock of Wholesale and Retail Enterprises at Year-end refers to total commodities possessed by wholesale and retail enterprises（units）of various ownership, which reflects the inventory level of various wholesale and retail enterprises and the potential for market supply. It includes: （1）Commodities put in storage, garages, counters, and shelves of operating units（such as stores, wholesale centers, and operating offices）of wholesale and retail enterprises; （2）commodities in the process of selecting, sorting, and packing ; （3）commodities not arrived but recorded as purchase in the account, i. e. Commodities not arrived but payment receipts for the commodities from the sellers or the banks arrived; （4） specially deposited commodities, for instance, commodities in the hold of purchasers temporarily due to the refusal of payment and commodities not taken back after going through the formalities; （5）commodities entrusted to other units to sell but not sold yet; （6）commodities purchased for other units but not delivered yet. Commodities not included as stock are those not owned by the enterprise（units）, those allocated to financially independent factories rather than wholesale and retail enterprises for processing but not taken back yet, and finally those put in stock by wholesale and retail enterprises on behalf of the state material reserves units. In the calculation of the value of commodities stock at the end of period, the value is calculated at purchasing prices for agricultural goods purchasing units and wholesale units, and at the market prices for retail units.

Commercial Front Site refers to the operating site (shop, store or supply center) of the wholesale or retail sale enterprise engaged in the wholesaling or retailing, including the enterprise itself. Every front site has its own independent location and a number of personnel for commercial operation, regardless of the size and with or without independent accounting system. But the different counters in a front site, the mobile selling groups of a front site no longer counted as a front site.

Personnel refers to the persons who are employed in wholesale or retail front sites and receive remuneration payments, including staff and workers as well as the retires invited to work in wholesale or retail front sites.

北京统计年鉴---2000
BEIJING STATISTICAL YEARBOOK

对外经济贸易、旅游
FOREIGN ECONOMY，TRADE AND TOURISM

1999年地方进出口构成（%）

Compsition of Imports and Exports of Local(%)

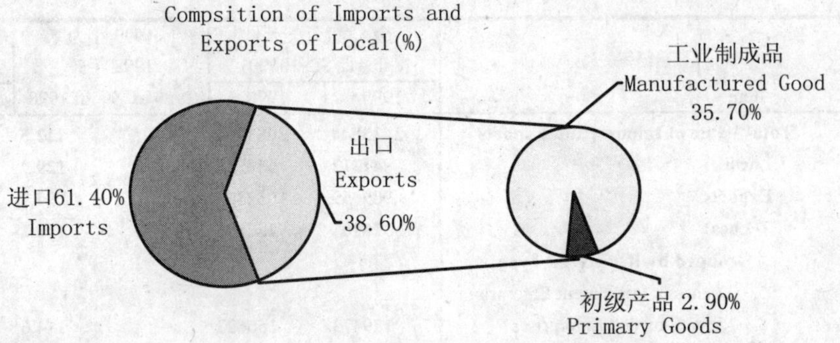

亿美元(100 million USD)	1999	1998	1999年为1998年% 1999 as % of 1998
进出口总额（地方） Total Value of Imports and Exports (Local)	84.4	65.1	129.7
出口 Exports	32.6	28.3	115.2
进口 Imports	51.8	36.8	140.9

接待外国旅游人数(1978-1999年） Foreign Tourists

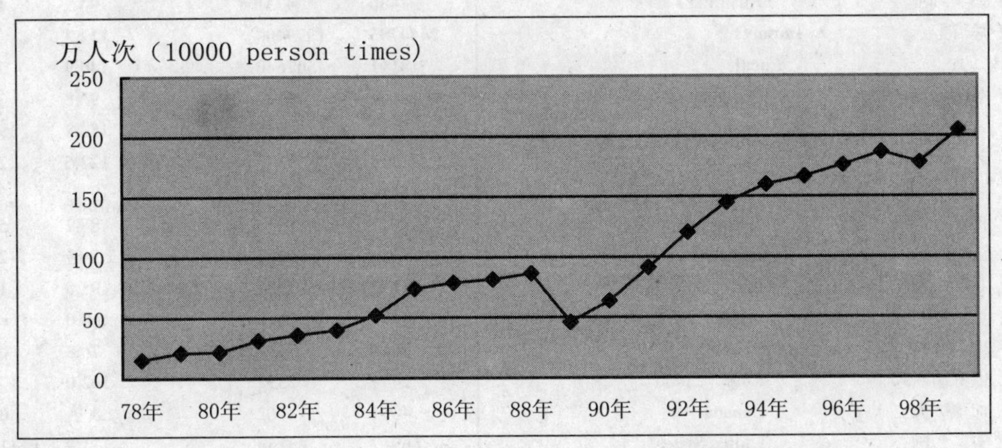

11-1 海关进出口贸易总额
TOTAL VALUE OF IMPORTS AND EXPORTS AT CUSTOMS

项目	Item	金额(万美元) Value (USD 10000) 1999	1998	1999年为1998年% 1999 as % of 1998	构成(%) Composition(%) 1999	1998
进出口总额	**Total Value of Imports and Exports**	**3433844**	**3051738**	**112.5**		
#地方	**Local**	**844212**	**650536**	**129.7**		
出口总额	**Exports**	**989059**	**1052334**	**94.1**		
#地方	**Local**	**326101**	**282896**	**115.2**	**100**	**100**
按登记注册类型分	**Grouped by Registered Type**					
内资企业	Domestic Investment Enterprises					
国有企业	State-owned Enterprises	179473	156623	114.6	55.0	55.4
集体企业	Collective-owned Enterprises	3916	4116	95.2	1.2	1.5
其他	Others	200	105	190.7	…	…
外商投资企业	Foreign Funded Enterprises	146628	126273	116.1	45.0	44.6
中外合资	Joint Venture	120223	105989	113.4	36.9	37.4
中外合作	Cooperative	3164	2203	143.5	1.0	0.8
外商独资	Foreign Enterprises	23241	18081	128.5	7.1	6.4
外商投资股份有限公司	Foreign Funded Share Holding Company					
按国别(地区)分	**Grouped by Country (Region)**					
#香港地区	Hongkong	41721	49131	85.0	12.8	17.4
澳门地区	Macao	172	63	2.7倍	…	…
日本	Japan	72643	67337	107.8	22.3	23.8
新加坡	Singapore	4263	6343	67.3	1.3	2.2
英国	United Kingdom	7169	4190	171.1	2.2	1.5
德国	Germany	13491	10363	130.1	4.1	3.7
法国	France	2506	2658	94.3	0.8	0.9
意大利	Italy	4569	4012	113.8	1.4	1.4
瑞士	Switzerland	1529	923	165.6	0.5	0.3
波兰	Poland	3064	1760	174.0	0.9	0.6
俄罗斯联邦	Russia Union	40836	20975	194.6	12.5	7.4
埃及	Egypt	782	498	157.0	0.2	0.2
加拿大	Canada	3104	3161	98.2	1.0	1.1
美国	United States	47033	39491	119.1	14.4	14.0
澳大利亚	Australia	4480	4731	94.7	1.4	1.7
进口总额	**Imports**	**2444785**	**1999404**	**122.3**		
#地方	**Local**	**518111**	**367640**	**140.9**	**100**	**100**
#香港地区	Hongkong	18161	19172	94.8	3.5	5.2
日本	Japan	99713	64656	154.2	19.2	17.6
新加坡	Singapore	11314	9147	123.6	2.2	2.5
英国	United Kingdom	10116	5232	193.3	2.0	1.4
德国	Germany	29047	32938	88.2	5.6	9.0
法国	France	11071	5081	2.2倍	2.1	1.4
意大利	Italy	5192	5586	93.0	1.0	1.5
瑞士	Switzerland	4179	2612	160.0	0.8	0.7
比利时	Belgium	2614	3407	76.8	0.5	0.9
俄罗斯联邦	Russia Union	2441	2392	102.0	0.5	0.7
加拿大	Canada	4093	1762	2.3倍	0.8	0.5
美国	United States	56947	43154	131.9	11.0	11.7
澳大利亚	Australia	8873	9725	91.3	1.7	2.6

11-2 海关进出口商品类别及构成(地方企业)
VALUE AND COMPOSITION OF IMPORTS AND EXPORTS AT CUSTOMS BY CATEGORY OF COMMODITIES(LOCAL)

项目	Item	金额(万美元) Value (USD 10000) 1999	1998	构成(%) Composition(%) 1999	1998
出口总额	**Exports**	**326101**	**282896**	**100**	**100**
初级产品	Primary Goods	24871	19302	7.6	6.8
食品及主要供食用的活动物	Food and Lively Animals Chiefly for Food	15968	12416	4.9	4.4
饮料及烟草	Beverage and Tabacco	523	599	0.2	0.2
非食用原料（燃料除外）	Non-edible Raw Materials(excluding Fuel)	4802	3838	1.5	1.4
矿物燃料、润滑油及有关原料	Mineral Fuels,Lubricants and Related Materials	3449	2318	1.0	0.8
动植物油、脂及蜡	Animal and Vegetable Oils,Fats and Waxes	129	131	…	…
工业制成品	Manufactured Goods	301230	263594	92.4	93.2
化学品及有关产品	Chemicals and Related Products	9841	9446	3.0	3.3
按原料分类的制成品	Finished Products Grouped by Materials	39529	50822	12.1	18.0
机械及运输设备	Machinery and Transport Equipment	110863	86890	34.0	30.7
杂项制品	Miscellaneous Products	140963	116380	43.3	41.2
未分类商品	Products Not Classified	34	56	…	…
进口总额	**Imports**	**518111**	**367640**	**100**	**100**
初级产品	Primary Goods	35471	43161	6.8	11.7
食品及主要供食用的活动物	Food and Lively Animals Chiefly for Food	9769	10913	1.9	3.0
饮料及烟草	Beverage and Tabacco	1259	864	0.2	0.2
非食用原料（燃料除外）	Non-edible Raw Materials(excluding Fuel)	20961	23872	4.0	6.5
矿物燃料、润滑油及有关原料	Mineral Fuels,Lubricants and Related Materials	518	769	0.1	0.2
动植物油、脂及蜡	Animal and Vegetable Oils,Fats and Waxes	2964	6743	0.6	1.8
工业制成品	Manufactured Goods	482640	324479	93.2	88.3
化学品及有关产品	Chemicals and Related Products	26274	19028	5.1	5.2
按原料分类的制成品	Finished Products Grouped by Materials	51490	45418	9.9	12.4
机械及运输设备	Machinery and Transport Equipment	367840	235271	71.0	64.0
杂项制品	Miscellaneous Products	36635	24451	7.1	6.7
未分类商品	Products Not Classified	401	311	0.1	

11-3 进出口商品检验
TEST OF IMPORTS AND EXPORTS COMMODITIES

项目	Item	1999	1998	1999年为1998年% 1999 as % of 1998
进口商品检验	**Imports Test**			
批数 (批)	Batches (batch)	2789	2058	135.5
金额 (万美元)	Value (USD 10000)	69840	70105	99.6
# 不合格商品	Substandard			
批数 (批)	Batches (batch)	517	396	130.6
金额 (万美元)	Value (USD 10000)	1723	1523	113.1
出口商品检验	**Exports Test**			
批数 (批)	Batches (batch)	36762	33718	109.0
金额 (万美元)	Value (USD 10000)	102467	93235	109.9
# 不合格商品	Substandard			
批数 (批)	Batches (batch)	180	107	168.2

11-4 海关主要商品出口量
MAJOR EXPORTS COMMODITIES IN VOLUME(CUSTOMS STATISTICS)

品名 Item	1999	1998
食用油籽 (万吨) Edible Oil Seeds (10000 tons)		1
冻鸡 (吨) Frozen Chicken (ton)	24445	18917
蔬菜 (万吨) Vegetable (10000 tons)	1	1
干鲜果 (万吨) Dry and Fresh Fruit (10000tons)	1	
栗子 (吨) Chestnuts (ton)	4281	4414
啤酒 (万升) Beer (10000 liters)	170	592
中成药 (万美元) Chinese Medicines (USD 10000)	737	762
真丝绸缎 (万米) Silk and Satins (10000 m)	760	1070
手表 (万只) Watches (10000)	178	64
服装及衣着附件 (万美元) Garments (USD 10000)	90537	75787
皮鞋 (万双) Leather Shoes (10000 pairs)	1628	384
胶或塑料底布鞋 (万双) Cloth Shoes with Outer Soles of Rubber or Artificial Plastic Materials (10000 pairs)	1303	887

品名 Item	1999	1998
棉纱 (吨) Cotton Yarn (ton)	4273	5310
棉布 (万米) Cotton Cloth (10000 m)	8122	10510
铅笔 (吨) (Pencils) (ton)	993	660
洗衣粉 (吨) Detergents (ton)	122	53
彩色电视机 (万美元) Color TV Sets (USD 10000)	11	22
收录机 (万台) Recorders (10000)	14	17
照相机 (万架) Cameras (10000)	75	94
自行车 (万辆) Bicycle (10000)		80
地毯 (万平方米) Carpets (10000 sq.m)	54	68
首饰 (万美元) Jewelry (USD10000)	5478	8045
玻璃制品 (万美元) Glass Ware (USD 10000)	1092	752
石蜡 (万美元) Paraffin Wax (USD 10000)	651	635
钢材 (万美元) Rolled-steel (USD 10000)	1965	3620
铜材 (吨) Copper Products (ton)	337	586
铝材 (吨) Aluminum Products (ton)	133	182
机床 (万台) Machine Tools (10000)	184	256
汽车 (辆) Motor Vehicle (unit)	365	363

11-5 海关主要商品进口量
MAJOR IMPORTS COMMODITIES IN VOLUME(CUSTOMS STATISTICS)

品名	Item	1999	1998	品名	Item	1999	1998
食糖 (万吨)	Sugar (10000 tons)	1	1	复印机 (台)	Duplicators (unit)	555	109
谷物及谷物粉 (万吨)	Cereal and Cereal Powder (10000 tons)	10	1	食品加工机械 (万美元)	Food Processing Machine (USD 10000)	1009	1011
纺织用合成纤维 (万吨)	Synthetic Fibers Suitable for Spin-ning (10000 tons)	1	2	聚乙烯 (吨)	Polyethylene (ton)	13606	14408
合成纤维纱线 (吨)	Synthetic Fibers, Continuous Filament and Yarn (ton)	849	338	聚丙烯 (吨)	Polypropylene (ton)	2372	1491
羊毛及羊毛条 (吨)	Wool and Wool Top (ton)	3514	15056	聚苯乙烯及共聚物 (吨)	Polystyrene and Copolymer (ton)	6981	3557
纸及纸板 (万吨)	Paper and Paper-board (10000 tons)	5	3	钢材 (万吨)	Rolled-steel (10000 tons)	8	5
空气调节器 (台)	Air Conditioners (unit)	833	293	铝材 (吨)	Aluminum Products (ton)	20543	12741
家用电冰箱 (台)	Refrigerator (unit)		28	机床 (台)	Machine Tools (unit)	1751	477
彩色电视机 (台)	Color TV Set (unit)	3422	1937	汽车 (辆)	Motor Vehicle (unit)	445	1008
收录机 (万台)	Recorders (10000)			成套数字式数据处理设备 (台)	Complete Sets of Digital Data Process-ing Equipment (unit)	7757	5208
电视摄像机 (台)	Television Camera (unit)	8681	127	成套数字式中央处理机 (台)	Complete Sets of Digital Central Processing (unit)	1692	3960

11-6 利用外资签约情况
UTILIZATION OF FOREIGN CAPITAL

项目	Item	合同数(个) Number of Contracts (unit)		合同外资金额(万美元) Contracted Foreign Capital(USD 10000)	
		1999	1998	1999	1998
合计	**Total**	**647**	**656**	**182648.6**	**410567.2**
对外借款	Foreign Loans	2	5	964.0	890.0
外商直接投资	Direct Foreign Investments	645	651	181684.6	409677.2
合资经营	Joint Venture	336	344	54613.1	61426.3
合作经营	Cooperative Operation	96	104	63013.4	232524.0
独资经营	Foreign Enterprises	210	201	57337.3	105952.1
股份制	Share Holding	3	2	6720.8	9774.9

注：1.外商投资企业投资性借款作为外商直接投资统计，对外借款中不再重复统计。

2.合资经营项目合同外资金额为项目注册资本乘以外商出资比例。

a) Loans for investment of foreign funded enterprises are counted as foreign direct investment and not counted in foreign loans any more.

b) Contracted foreign capital of joint venture projects are counted from registered capital multiplied proportion of foreign investment.

11-7 外商投资企业签约情况
STATISTICS ON CONTRACTS OF FOREIGN FUNDED ENTERPRISES

项目 Item		项目数（个） Number of Contracts (unit)		合同总金额（万美元） Total Value of Contracts(USD 10000)		# 外资金额 Foreign Capital	
		1999	1998	1999	1998	1999	1998
合　计	**Total**	**645**	**651**	**307120.0**	**624008.2**	**181684.6**	**409677.2**
按登记注册类型分	**Grouped by Investment Manner**						
合资经营	Joint Venture	336	344	133359.9	173877.7	55022.3	61426.3
合作经营	Cooperative Operation	96	104	99507.0	307899.1	62208.4	232524.0
独资经营	Foreign Funded Enterprises	210	201	62711.9	115756.6	57733.2	105952.0
股份制	Share Holding		2	7833.2	26474.9	3012.7	9774.9
外资银行	Foreign Banks	3		3708.0		3708.0	
按三次产业分	**Grouped by Three Industry**						
第一产业	Primary Industry	16	23	6966.4	5171.6	3026.3	2885.0
第二产业	Secondary Industry	372	332	129468.9	185433.7	88565.9	119086.9
第三产业	Tertiary Industry	257	296	170684.7	433402.9	90092.4	287705.3
按客商国别(地区)分	**Grouped by Country(Region) of Foreign Partner**						
# 日　本	Japan	39	53	16809.6	28529.4	10304.1	21066.7
美　国	United States	130	120	50470.1	86139.2	27955.0	41297.2
香港地区	Hongkong	154	176	82282.4	345262.8	45860.5	250018.6
澳大利亚	Australia	20	15	5445.3	7344.4	1991.0	3247.2
法　国	France	11	16	8654.6	14173.0	7602.1	11705.5
新加坡	Singapore	15	23	4918.0	6778.7	2151.9	5005.5
加拿大	Canada	24	15	2090.7	3770.8	850.1	2801.0
德　国	Germany	16	15	15251.2	28988.7	12086.5	24989.3
西班牙	Spain	2	1	1075.6	192.2	479.7	113.7
台　湾	Taiwan	58	55	9068.8	6763.9	3586.9	4063.9
瑞　典	Sweden	2	4	3227.5	5361.9	3220.0	1915.6
泰　国	Thailand	2	3	32.0	4383.0	17.8	2105.1
比利时	Belgium	0	4	25.0	290.0	25.0	119.3
丹　麦	Denmark	3	1	116.1	235.0	79.5	180.0
韩　国	Korea	45	40	4417.8	2290.7	3160.4	1492.8
俄罗斯	Russia	3	1	159.9	100.0	42.0	49.0

注：合资企业外资金额是以项目注册资本乘以外商出资比例。

Note：Foreign capital of joint venture are counted from registered capital multiplied proportion of foreign investment.

11-8 外商投资企业生产经营情况
STATISTICS ON PRODUCTION AND BUSINESS OF FOREIGN ENTERPRISES

单位：万元 (10000 yuan)

项目	Item	销售营业收入 Business Revenue 1999	1998	利润总额 Total Profits 1999	1998	交纳税金总额 Taxes 1999	1998
合计	**Total**	**13515429**	**9525702**	**148830**	**-52193**	**938605**	**728355**
按登记注册类型分	**Grouped by Registered Type**						
外商投资企业	Foreign Funded Enterprises	8695071	6337389	224875	118874	681634	540795
中外合资	Joint Venture	6929639	5146287	186957	96084	517456	426752
中外合作	Cooperative	297588	204087	-7004	272	22846	19350
外商独资	Foreign Enterprises	1436437	872810	46506	-7229	126114	82094
外商投资股份有限公司	Foreign Funded Share Holding Company	31407	114205	-1584	29747	15218	12599
港澳台商投资企业	Hongkong,Macao and Taiwan Funded Enterprises	4820358	3188313	-76045	-171067	256971	187560
港澳台合资	Joint Venture	2803554	2695134	-118471	-134071	183633	147653
港澳台合作	Cooperative	331774	231807	15751	-24837	29446	30466
港澳台商独资	Hongkong,Macao and Taiwan Enterprises	1629489	261372	20402	-12159	38168	9441
港澳台商投资股份有限公司	Hongkong,Macao and Taiwan Funded Share Holding Company	55541		6273		5724	
按行业分	**Grouped by Sector**						
农林牧渔水利业	Farming,Forestry,Animal Husbandry,Fishery and Water Conservancy	131375	99215	-1184	-5322	267	321
工业	Industry	9157936	6447493	190420	-9084	599824	484156
运输邮电业	Transportation,Post and Telecommunications	35746	18626	1507	-2947	1012	510
商业饮食业	Commerce and Catering Services	639512	499544	-33802	-20338	32817	29936
居民服务业	Residential Services	960410	759498	-30351	-71500	81398	67628
其他行业	Others	2590450	1701326	22240	56998	223287	145804
按客商国别(地区)分	**Grouped by Country(Region) of Foreign Partner**						
# 香港地区	Hongkong	4378955	2837814	-68438	-152596	233153	171687
澳门地区	Macao	34773	30780	1007	-804	999	476
台湾地区	Taiwan	406630	319719	-8614	-17667	22819	15397
朝鲜民主主义人民共和国	Democratic People's Republic of Korea	11859	9964	1096	-1260	329	116
日本	Japan	1826234	1241620	31711	-39789	101118	79532
泰国	Thailand	223817	216399	6905	2392	5442	4671
新加坡	Singapore	306356	307989	28137	52936	21035	17730
印度尼西亚	Indonesia	869	960	-331	-955	62	98
法国	France	196457	111314	13893	-3845	16483	7580
意大利	Italy	17844	13594	-1488	-742	677	307
荷兰	The Holland	209521	161135	-36627	-19446	9178	8951
瑞典	Sweden	849447	501222	28584	25684	52280	58419
西班牙	Spain	9598	1874	-2092	-1523	1052	81
美国	United States	2108890	1705231	35058	-36215	181881	148400
德国	Germany	706031	563668	80054	100326	124545	94329
丹麦	Denmark	16785	6987	-6127	-2567	2227	1259
菲律宾	Philippines	17829	24149	-5964	-11223	2781	4076
澳大利亚	Australia	60571	44238	-9490	-14535	3396	1647
新西兰	New Zealand	3754	4217	-918	-688	101	95
韩国	Korea	132905	122329	-3654	-11730	7612	5998
英国	United Kingdom	95908	151987	-5287	31604	18835	14866
瑞士	Switzerland	162567	85634	18	-4218	11240	7888
奥地利	Austria	6995	2949	-203	-234	100	136
加拿大	Canada	73613	50254	5425	-6905	2786	2686

注：1997 年以前，外商投资企业经营情况不包括中央在京企业，1998 年起将中央在京外商投资企业纳入统计范围。

Note: Data of foreign funded enterprises exclude that of central enterprises in Beijing before 1997,and statistics include that of foreign enterprises of central in Beijing from 1998.

11-9 外商投资企业利用外资情况
UTILIZATION OF FOREIGN CAPITAL OF FOREIGN FUNDED ENTERPRISES

单位：万美元 (USD 10000)

项目	Item	实际利用外资额 Amount of Foreign Capital Actually Used	客商实际投资 Auctual Foreign Investment	企业对外借款投资 Foreign Loans for Investment
合计	**Total**	**223123.8**	**178191.4**	**44932.4**
按登记注册类型分	**Grouped by Investment Manner**			
合资经营	Joint Venture	53477.4	43405.2	10072.2
合作经营	Cooperative Operation	81938.9	47078.7	34860.2
独资经营	Foreign Funded Enterprises	58385.5	58385.5	
股份制	Share Holding	25644.0	25644.0	
其他	Others	3678.0	3678.0	
按行业分	**Grouped by Sector**			
工业	Industry	46918.8	44705.9	2212.9
建筑业	Construction	2429.2	2429.2	
商业饮食业	Commerce and Catering	578.2	578.2	
居民服务业	Residential Services	158635.0	115945.5	42689.5
# 房地产业	Real Estate	103750.7	62977.4	40773.3
其他行业	Others	14562.6	14532.6	30.0
按客商国别(地区)分	**Grouped by Country(Region) of Foreign Partner**			
香港地区	Hongkong	54345.6	52096.0	2249.6
台湾地区	Taiwan	3721.0	3721.0	
日本	Japan	14732.6	14434.7	297.9
泰国	Thailand	200.0	200.0	
新加坡	Singapore	2476.3	2476.3	
法国	France	9427.6	9427.6	
美国	United States	24027.2	23678.8	348.4
德国	Germany	15432.5	15187.8	244.7
新西兰	New Zealand	20.0	20.0	
韩国	Korea	5594.7	4397.8	1196.9
英国	United Kingdom	33123.0	32723.0	400.0
奥地利	Austria			
加拿大	Canada	554.0	554.0	
其他	Others	59469.3	19274.4	40194.9

注：包括对外借款及其他形式，全年实际利用外资 29.4 亿美元。

Note：Including foreign loans and other investments,amount of foreign capital actually used is 29.4 USD 100 million.

11-10 外商投资企业投产开业情况
STATISTICS FOR OPENING OF FOREIGN FUNDED ENTERPRISES

项目	Item	企业单位数（个） Number of Enterprises (unit) 1999	1998	企业职工人数(人) Number of Staff and Workers (person) 1999	1998
合计	**Total**	**5118**	**5419**	**436316**	**425980**
按登记注册类型分	**Grouped by Registered Type**				
外商投资企业	Foreign Funded Enterprises	2596	2628	229565	225342
中外合资	Joint Venture	1814	1925	183651	186478
中外合作	Cooperative	138	129	11630	9109
外商独资	Foreign Enterprises	642	572	32254	26981
外商投资股份有限公司	Foreign Funded Share Holding Company	2	2	2030	2774
港澳台商投资企业	Hongkong,Macao and Taiwan Funded Enterprises	2522	2791	206751	200638
港澳台合资	Joint Venture	1909	2184	172116	174383
港澳台合作	Cooperative	185	171	10723	11908
港澳台商独资	Hongkong,Macao and Taiwan Enterprises	427	436	20653	14347
港澳台商投资股份有限公司	Hongkong,Macao and Taiwan Funded Share Holding Company	1		3259	
按行业分	**Grouped by Sector**				
农林牧渔水利业	Farming,Forestry,Animal Husbandry,Fishery and Water Conservancy	40	51	3347	4478
工　业	Industry	3231	3685	282532	298825
运输邮电业	Transportation,Posts and Telecommunications	26	20	1943	867
商业饮食业	Commerce and Catering	293	304	27774	28617
居民服务业	Residential Services	254	256	60810	48539
其他行业	Others	1274	1103	59910	44654
按客商国别(地区)分	**Grouped by Country (Region) of Foreign Partner**				
# 香港地区	Hongkong	1999	2223	177971	171450
澳门地区	Macao	36	46	2668	2704
台湾地区	Taiwan	487	522	26112	26484
朝鲜民主主义人民共和国	Democratic People's Republic of Korea	8	11	411	291
日　本	Japan	576	620	61978	67690
泰　国	Thailand	47	51	4036	5573
新加坡	Singapore	189	191	13972	13968
印度尼西亚	Indinesia	8	9	329	388
法　国	France	77	68	5735	4975
意大利	Italy	22	22	1658	1423
荷　兰	The Holland	36	26	4461	3711
瑞　典	Sweden	22	23	3308	3403
西班牙	Spain	14	12	652	366
美　国	United States	797	813	66597	67066
德　国	Germany	110	82	14242	10176
丹　麦	Denmark	9	9	880	867
菲律宾	Philippines	10	16	1621	1416
澳大利亚	Australia	67	75	3037	3366
新西兰	New Zealand	16	18	515	486
韩　国	Korea	145	146	11090	11506
英　国	United Kingdom	77	55	5673	4277
瑞　士	Switzerland	27	23	5112	4479
奥地利	Austria	11	13	310	394
加拿大	Canada	100	105	3852	4325

11-11 对外承包工程和劳务合作
CONTRACTED PROJECTS AND LABOR SERVICES COOPERATION WITH FOREIGN COUNTRIES

地区	Region	签定合同份数(份) Number of Contracts (unit)		签定合同金额(万美元) Contracted Value (USD 10000)		营业额(万美元) Fulfilled Value (USD 10000)	
		1999	1998	1999	1998	1999	1998
合　计	**Total**	**90**	**184**	**25229**	**28520**	**26165**	**45812**
对外承包工程	**Constructed Projects**	**17**	**37**	**18404**	**21789**	**19342**	**39207**
# 斯里兰卡	Sri Lanka		2		2670	1483	1440
马来西亚	Malaysia		3		2374		2504
美　国	United States						
巴基斯坦	Pakistan		2		470	2248	3189
新加坡	Singapore	5	2	7393	5801	7292	6461
对外劳务合作	**Labor Services**	**62**	**136**	**6516**	**6234**	**6477**	**6077**
# 日　本	Japan	23	21	401	186	223	241
香港地区	Hongkong	2	3	140	146	72	132
马来西亚	Malaysia					2	5
新加坡	Singapore	1	7	6	139	8	57
韩　国	Korea						1
埃　及	Egypt		2		4	1	1
美　国	United States		13		27	4	3
德　国	Germany	1	3	4	9		
塞浦路斯	Cyprus	1	5	2	34	3	5
尼日利亚	Nigeria	8	9	8	15	15	20
泰　国	Thailand	3	4	3	1	1	7
巴　林	Bahrain		1		14	1	
澳门地区	Macao		5		17	90	212
沙特阿拉伯	Saudi Arabia	3	1	75	6	5	
斯里兰卡	Sri Lanka		2		123	126	102
以色列	Israel						
波　兰	Poland						
设计咨询	**Consulting Services for Designing**	**11**	**11**	**309**	**497**	**346**	**528**

11-12 海外企业审批情况
STATISTICS ON EXAMINING AND APPROVING OF CONTRACTS OF OVERSEAS ENTERPRISES

项目	Item	审批项目数(个) Number of Projects Examined and Approved (unit)		# 中方投资金额(万美元) Investment by Chinese Partner(USD 10000)	
		1999	1998	1999	1998
合计	**Total**	**13**	**21**	**395.0**	**550.7**
按登记注册类型分	**Grouped by Investment Manner**				
合资经营	Joint Venture	4	6	119.2	78.5
合作经营	Cooperative Operation				
独资经营	Foreign Enterprises	9	15	275.8	472.3
按生产性、非生产性分	**Grouped by Production and Non-production**				
生产性企业	Productive Enterprises	1	1	13.0	9.0
非生产性企业	Non-productive Enterprises	12	20	382.0	541.7
按投资国别(地区)分	**Grouped by Country(Region) of Investment**				
美国	United States	3	4	133.0	160.8
澳大利亚	Australia	1	1	96.0	10.5
日本	Japan		1		
巴基斯坦	Pakistan		1		
蒙古	Mongolia		1		9.0
印度尼西亚	Indonesia		1		12.3
俄罗斯	Russia	2	2	1.8	1.3
德国	Germany	1	2	8.4	38.5
英属百慕大	Bumerda of United Kingdom		1		52.0
荷兰	Holland		2		89.4
罗马尼亚	Romania	1	2	0.1	16.0
匈牙利	Hungary		2		151.0
南非	the South Africa Republic		1		10.0
秘鲁	Peru	1		50.0	
阿尔及利亚	Algeria	1			
波兰	Poland	1		0.3	
新加坡	Singapore	1		95.0	
多米尼克	Dominica	1		10.0	

11-13 外国企业及华侨、港澳地区企业驻京代表机构
REPRESENTATIVE OFFICES IN BEIJING OF FOREIGN,OVERSEAS CHINESE HONGKONG AND MACAO ENTERPRISES

项目	Item	数量(个) Number(unit) 1999	1998	构成(%) Composition(%) 1999	1998
总计	**Total**	**6107**	**7083**	**100**	**100**
#日本	Japan	593	720	9.7	10.2
港澳地区	Hongkong and Macao	1698	2192	27.8	31.0
美国	United States	1152	1322	18.9	18.7
德国	Germany	345	343	5.6	4.8
法国	France	185	199	3.0	2.8
英国	United Kingdom	181	188	3.0	2.7
意大利	Italy	146	144	2.4	2.0
瑞士	Switzerland	94	96	1.5	1.4
瑞典	Sweden	55	49	0.9	0.7
加拿大	Canada	176	184	2.9	2.6
澳大利亚	Australia	128	134	2.1	1.9
比利时	Belgium	38	43	0.6	0.6
新加坡	Singapore	232	287	3.8	4.1
荷兰	The Holland	89	85	1.5	1.2
奥地利	Austria	41	44	0.7	0.6

11-14 区县对外经济基本情况
FOREIGN ECONOMY OF DISTRICTS AND COUNTIES

项目	Item	合计 Total	城区 City Proper	近郊区 Near Suburbs	远郊区 Outer Suburbs	各县 Counties
利用外资	**Utilization of Foreign Capital**					
签约项目 (个)	Projects Signed (unit)	541.0	101.0	244.0	93.0	103.0
合同外资金额 (万美元)	Contracted Foreign Capital (USD 10000)	74085.9	29481.7	26671.7	8767.1	9165.4
外商实际投资额 (万美元)	Foreign Actual Investment (USD 10000)	141968.0	96939.5	21641.6	17480.9	5906.0
出口商品交货	**Export Delivery**					
交货总额 (万元)	Total Value (10000 yuan)	428821.3	1616.1	32263.8	191309.7	203631.7
直接交货 (万元)	Direct Delivery (10000 yuan)	301747.7	1616.1	22597.3	132444.6	145089.7
# 交本市外贸收购 (万元)	Purchased by Local Foreign Trade (10000 yuan)	144285.7	1616.1	21315.5	74606.0	46748.1
间接交货 (万元)	Indirect Delivery (10000 yuan)	127073.6		9666.5	58865.1	58542.0
旅游业	**Tourism**					
接待海外游客 (人次)	Foreign Tourists (person.time)	185770.0	71133.0	84014.0	29782.0	841.0

11-15 接待旅游人数 TOURISTS

单位：人次 (person.time)

项目	Item	1999	1998	项目	Item	1999	1998
合计	**Total**	**2523943**	**2200947**	法国	France	78772	69413
外国人	**Foreigner**	**2050159**	**1781800**	德国	Germany	105305	112580
#日本	Japan	456451	435156	意大利	Italy	39178	43579
菲律宾	Philippines	11760	9698	瑞典	Sweden	29458	25074
新加坡	Singapore	72824	68228	瑞士	Switzerland	25302	18597
泰国	Thailand	41113	25542	俄罗斯	Russia	45763	61555
印度尼西亚	Indonesia	20774	10429	澳大利亚	Australia	48537	46473
马来西亚	Malaysia	109546	74084	新西兰	New Zealand	10046	8142
蒙古	Mongolia	21817	20223	荷兰	The Holland	30496	27775
韩国	Korea	191539	81825	西班牙	Spain	14992	12542
印度	India	7018	5696	**华侨**	**Overseas Chinese**	**33216**	**28352**
美国	United States	240924	231662	**港澳台胞**	**Hongkong,Macao and Taiwan Chinese**	**440568**	**390795**
加拿大	Canada	54498	47874				
英国	United Kingdom	88148	88054				
				#台胞	Taiwan Chinese	175318	141292

11-16 旅游外汇收入 FOREIGN EXCHANGE EARNING FROM INTERNATIONAL TOURISM

单位：亿美元 (USD 100 million)

项目	Item	1999	1998	1999年为1998年% 1999 as % of 1998	项目	Item	1999	1998	1999年为1998年% 1999 as % of 1998
合计	**Total**	**25.0**	**23.8**	**105.0**	住宿	Accommodation	3.5	3.5	100.0
长途交通费	Long-distance Transportation Expenses	8.2	8.0	102.5	餐饮	Catering Service	2.1	2.1	100.0
					商品	Commodity	4.6	4.0	115.0
					邮政电讯	Posts and Telecommunications	0.5	1.1	45.5
#民航	Civil Aviation	7.3	7.3	100.0					
铁路	Railway	0.4	0.2	200.0	景点门票	Tickets of Tourism Spots	1.2	0.6	200.0
汽车	Motor Vehicles	0.4	0.1	400.0					
					文化娱乐	Culture and Entertainment	1.3	1.2	108.3
市内交通费	Local Transportation Expense	1.2	0.5	240.0					
					其他	Others	2.4	2.8	85.7

11-17 生产型“三资”企业按销售收入排序
ARRANGING IN SALES REVENUE OF PRODUCTIVE FOREIGN FUNDED ENTERPRISES

排名 No.	单位名称	Enterprise
1	联想(北京)有限公司	LEGEND(BEIJING)LIMITED
2	北京诺基亚移动通信有限公司	BEIJING NOKIA MOBILE TELECOMMUNICATIONS LTD
3	北京爱立信移动通信有限公司	BEIJING ERICSSON MOBILE COMMUNICATIONS CO., LTD.
4	北京诺基亚航星通讯系统有限公司	BEIJING NOKIA HANGXING TELECOMMUNICATIONS SYSTEMS CO.,LTD.
5	北京·松下彩色显象管有限公司	BEIJING·MATSUSHITA COLOR CRT,CO.,LTD
6	北京国际交换系统有限公司	BEIJING INTERNATIONAL SWITCHING SYSTEM CORPORATION LTD.
7	北京吉普汽车有限公司	BEIJING JEEP CORPORATION,LTD.
8	中国惠普有限公司	CHINA HEWLETT – PACKART
9	UT 斯达康（中国）有限公司	UTSTARCOM （CHINA）CO.,LTD.
10	北京大发正大有限公司	BEIJING DAFA CHIA TAI CO.,LTD.
11	北京飞机维修工程有限公司	AIRCRAFT MAINTENANCE AND ENGINEERING CORPORATION，BEIJING
12	北京松下通信设备有限公司	BEIJING MATSUSHITA COMMUNICATION EQUIPMENT CO.,LTD.
13	北京北大方正电子有限公司	BEIJING FOUNDER ELECTRONICS CO.,LTD.
14	首钢日电电子有限公司	SHOUGANG NEC ELECTRONICS CO., LTD.
15	北京 JVC 电子产业有限公司	JVC BEIJING ELECTRONIC INDUSTRIES CO., LTD.
16	北京轻型汽车有限公司	BEIJING LIGHT AUTOBILE CO.LTD
17	北京恒基伟业电子产品有限公司	BEIJING HI-TECH WEALTH ELECTRONIC PRODUCT CO.,LTD
18	北京.松下电子部品有限公司	BEIJING MATSUSHITA ELECTRONIC COMPONENTS CO.,LTD.
19	北京首钢宝生带钢有限公司	BEIJING SHOUGANG-POHSENG STRIP STEEL CO.,LTD.
20	北京可口可乐饮料有限公司	BEIJING COCA-COLA BEVERAGE CO., LTD.
21	爱芬食品（北京）有限公司	EFFEM FOODS (BEIJING) CO., LTD.
22	北京三元食品有限公司	BEIJING SANYUAN FOOD CO., LTD.
23	北京朗讯科技光缆有限公司	LUCENT TECHNOLOGIES FIBER OPTIC CABLE CO.LTD.,BEIJING
24	北京飞利浦有限公司	BEIJING PHILIPS AUDIO & VIDEO CO.,LTD.
25	红牛维他命饮料有限公司	RED BULL VITAMIN DRINK CO.,LTD.

11-17 续表 continued

排 名 No.	单位名称	Enterprise
26	北京村田电子有限公司	BEIJING MURATA EIECTRONICS CO., LTD.
27	北京东方冠捷电子有限公司	BEIJING ORIENT TOP VICTORY ELECTRONICS CO.,LTD.
28	北京恩布拉科雪花压缩机有限公司	BEIJING EMBRACO SNOWFLAKE COMPRESSOR CO.,LTD.
29	北京富特波尔容器有限公司	BEIJING FTB PACKAGING LTD.
30	和德(集团)有限公司	HARMONY HOLDING(GROUP) CORPORATION
31	三菱四通集成电路有限公司	MITSUBISHI STONE SEMICONDUCTOR CO.,LTD.
32	施耐德（北京）中压电器有限公司	SCHNEIDER (BEIJING) MEDIUM VOLTAGE CO.,LTD.
33	三伍电子系统(北京)有限公司	THREE – FIVE SYSTEMS (BEIJING) CO.,LTD.
34	北京四通松下电工有限公司	BEIJING STONE MATSUSHITA ELECTRIC WORKS LTD.
35	航卫通用电气医疗系统有限公司	GE HANGWEI MEDICAL SYSTEMS CO.LTD
36	北京协兴建筑工程有限公司	BEIJING HIP HING CONSTRUCTION &ENGINEERING CO.,LTD.
37	北京顺美服装股份有限公司	BEIJING SMART GARMENTS CO.LTD
38	北京诺华制药有限公司	BEIJING NOVARTIS PHARMA CO.,LTD.
39	北京佳顺制油有限公司	BEIJING JIA SHUN EDIBLE OIL LIMITED
40	北京博士伦眼睛护理公司	BEIJING BAUSCH & LOMB EYECARE CO.LTD
41	北京地杰通信设备有限公司	BEIJNG D&G TELECOMMUNICATION EQUIPMENT CO.,LTD.
42	北京北控制水有限公司	BEIJING BEIKONG WATER PRODUCTION CO.,LTD.
43	北京航空食品有限公司	BEIJING AIR CATERING CO., LTD.
44	北京利乐包包装有限公司	BEIJING TETRA PAK PACKAGING CO.,LTD.
45	北京统一食品有限公司	BEIJING PRESIDENT FOOD CO.,LTD.
46	北京艾森绿宝油脂有限公司	BEIJING EISEN-LUBAO OIL CO.,LTD.
47	北京 ABB 高压开关设备有限公司	ABB HIGH VOLTAGE SWITCHGEAR CO., LTD. BEIJING
48	北京亚洲双合盛五星啤酒有限公司	BEIJING ASIA SHUANG HE SHENG FIVE STAR BEER CO.,LTD.
49	北京天纬油泵油嘴股份有限公司	BEIJING TIANWEI FUEL INJECTION EQUIPMENT INC
50	北京索鸿电子有限公司	BEIJING SUOHONG ELECTRONICS CO.,LTD.

11-18 非生产型"三资"企业按销售收入排序
ARRANGING IN SALES REVENUE OF NON-PRODUCTIVE FOREIGN FUNDED ENTERPRISES

排名 No.	单位名称	Enterprise
1	松下电器（中国）有限公司	MATSUSHITA ELECTRIC （CHINA）CO., LTD.
2	国际商业机器中国有限公司	IBM CHINA COMPANY LTD.
3	爱立信（中国）有限公司	ERICSSON （CHINA）COMPANY LIMITED
4	西门子（中国）有限公司	SIEMENS LTD., CHINA
5	朗讯科技(中国)有限公司	LUCENT TECHNOLOGIES (CHINA) CO.,LTD.
6	赛特集团有限公司	SCITECH GROUP COMPANY LIMITED'
7	北京燕莎友谊商城有限公司	BEIJING YOU YI SHOPPING CITY CO., LTD. BEIJING LUFTHANSA CENTER
8	中贸联万客隆商业有限公司	CTA MAKRO COMMERCIAL CO.,LTD.
9	北京春苑房地产开发有限公司	BEIJING CHUN YUAN REAL ESTATE DEVELOPMENT CO.,LTD
10	北京百盛轻工发展有限公司	BEIJING PARKSON LIGHT INDUSTRY DEVELOPMENT COMPANY LIMITED
11	北京北辰实业股份有限公司	BEIJING NORTH STAR COMPANY LIMITED
12	北京麦当劳食品有限公司	BEIJING MCDONALD'S FOOD CO.,LTD.
13	中国国际贸易中心有限公司	CHINA WORLD TRADE CENTER LTD.
14	丽都饭店有限公司	LIDO HOTEL CO.,LTD.
15	东陶机器(中国)有限公司	TOTO (CHINA) CO., LTD.
16	北京肯德基有限公司	BEIJING KENTUCKY CO.,LTD.
17	精信广告有限公司	GREY CHINA ADVERTISING CO.,LTD.
18	北京金远见电脑技术有限公司	BEIJING GOLDEN GLOBAL VIEW COMPUTER TECHNOLOGY CO.,LTD
19	北京燕莎中心有限公司	BEIJING LUFTHANSA CENTER CO.,LTD.
20	北京贵友大厦有限公司	BEIJING MANSION GUIYOU CO.,LTD.
21	华糖洋华堂商业有限公司	HUA TANG YOKADO COMMERCIAL CO., LTD.
22	北京万泉花园物业开发有限公司	BEIJING WAN QUAN GARDEN REAL ESTATE DEVELOPMENT CO.,LTD.
23	北京南湖花园公寓有限公司	BEIJING NANHU HWAYUAN APARTMENT CO.,LTD.
24	北京甲骨文软件系统有限公司	BEIJING ORACLE SOFTWARE SYSTEM CO.,LTD.
25	微软（中国）有限公司	MICROSOFT (CHINA) CO.,LTD.

11-18 续表 continued

排 名 No.	单 位 名 称	Enterprise
26	通标标准技术服务有限公司	SGS – CSTC STANDARDS TECHNICAL SERVICES CO.,LTD.
27	北京香江花园别墅房产开发有限公司	BEIJING RIVIERA ESTATE MANAGEMENT OFFICE
28	北京名都房地产开发有限公司	BEIJING CAPITAL PROPERTY DEVELOPMENT COMPANY LIMITED
29	北京市长城饭店公司	GREAT WALL HOTEL JOINT VENTURE OF BEIJING
30	北京冠海房地产有限公司	BEIJING GUANHAI REAL ESTATE CO.,LTD.
31	北京市华远房地产股份有限公司	BEIJING HUAYUAN PROPERTY COMPANY LIMITED
32	王府饭店有限公司	THE PALACE HOTEL CO.,LTD
33	北京昆仑饭店有限公司	BEIJING KUNLUN HOTEL COMPANY LIMITED
34	北京香格里拉饭店有限公司	BEIJING SHANGRI – LA HOTEL CO.,LTD.
35	中国国际金融有限公司	CHINA INTERNATIONAL CAPITAL CORPORATION LIMITED
36	北京京广中心有限公司	BEIJING JING GUANG CENTRE CO., LTD.
37	三井物产(中国)有限公司	MITSUI & CO. (CHINA) LTD.
38	北京中粮广场	BEIJING COFCO PLAZA DEVELOPMENT CO.,LTD
39	智威汤逊 – 中乔广告有限公司	J.WALTER THOMPSON – BRIDGE ADVERTISING CO.,LTD.
40	北京国际俱乐部有限公司	BEIJING INTERNATIONAL CLUB CORPORATION LTD.
41	北京市长富宫中心有限责任公司	BEIJING CHANG FU GONG CENTRE CO.,LTD.
42	北京亮马河大厦有限公司	BEIJING LANDMARK TOWERS COMPANY LIMITED
43	新世纪国际租赁有限公司	NEW CENTURY INTERNATIONAL LEASING CO., LTD.
44	港澳中心有限公司	HONG KONG MACAU CENTER LTD.
45	北京昌信回龙园别墅有限公司	BEIJING CHANGXIN HUILONGYUAN VILLA REBSORT CO.,LTD.
46	雀巢（中国）有限公司	NESTLE （CHINA）LTD.
47	北京新东安有限公司	BEIJING SUN DONG AN CO., LTD.
48	北京南天信息工程有限公司	BEIJING NANTIAN INFORMIATION ENGINEERING CO.,LTD.
49	中航狮威国际货运代理有限公司	ZHONG HANG SCANWELL INTERNATIONAL FREIGHT AGENT CO., LTD.
50	赫斯特（中国）投资有限公司	HOECIIST (CHINA) INVESTMENT CO.,LTD

11-19 北京市三星级及以上涉外饭店一览表
LIST OF HOTELS OF 3-STAR GRADE AND ABOVE GRADE

星 级 Star Grade	饭 店 名 称 Hotel	地 址 Address	邮政编码 Postcode	电 话 Telephone
5	北京饭店	北京市东城区东长安街 33 号	100004	65137766
5	长城饭店	北京市朝阳区东三环北路 10 号	100026	65905566
5	长富宫中心	北京市朝阳区建国门外大街 26 号	100022	65125555
5	钓鱼台宾馆	北京市阜成路 2 号	100830	68591188
5	港澳中心瑞士酒店	北京市东城区朝阳门北大街 2 号	100027	65012288
5	贵宾楼饭店	北京市东城区东长安街 35 号	100006	65137788
5	华侨大厦	北京市东城区王府井大街 2 号	100006	65136666
5	皇冠假日饭店	北京市东城区王府井大街 48 号	100006	65133388
5	京广中心	北京市朝阳区呼家楼	100020	65978888
5	凯宾斯基饭店	北京市朝阳区亮马桥路 50 号	100016	64653388
5	昆仑饭店	北京市朝阳区新源南路 2 号	100004	65903388
5	王府饭店	北京市东城区金鱼胡同 8 号	100006	65128899
5	希尔顿酒店	北京市朝阳区东三环北路东方路 1 号	100027	64662288
5	香格里拉饭店	北京市海淀区紫竹院路 29 号	100081	68412211
5	新世纪饭店	北京市海淀区首体南路 6 号	100044	68492001
5	中国大饭店	北京市建外大街 1 号	100004	65052266
4	大观园酒店	北京市宣武区南菜园 88 号	100054	63538899
4	德宝饭店	北京市西城德宝新园 22 号	100044	68318866
4	国都大饭店	北京市朝阳区首都机场南小天竺村	100621	64565588
4	国际饭店	北京市东城区建国门内大街 9 号	100005	65126688
4	国贸饭店	北京市建外大街 1 号	100004	65052277
4	海逸酒店	北京市朝阳区将台西路 8 号	100016	64362288
4	和平宾馆	北京市东城区金鱼胡同 3 号	100004	65128833
4	河南大厦	北京市朝阳区潘家园华威里 28 号	100021	67751188
4	华润饭店	北京市朝阳区建国路 35 号	100025	65572233
4	皇家大饭店	北京市朝阳区北三环东路甲 6 号	100028	64663388
4	建国饭店	北京市朝阳区建国门外大街 5 号	100020	65002233
4	金都假日饭店	北京市西城区阜外北礼士路 98 号	100037	68338822
4	金台饭店	北京市东城区地安门西大街 38 号	100035	63099111
4	京都信苑宾馆	北京市海淀区什坊院 6 号	100036	63901166
4	京伦饭店	北京市朝阳区建国门外大街 3 号	100020	65002266
4	凯莱大酒店	北京市朝阳区建国门南大街 2 号	100022	65158855
4	丽都假日饭店	北京市朝阳区首都机场路将台路口	100004	64376688
4	亮马河大厦	北京市朝阳区东三环北路 8 号	100004	65906688
4	民族饭店	北京市西城区复兴门内大街 51 号	100046	66014466
4	赛特饭店	北京市朝阳区建国门外大街 22 号	100004	65123388
4	首都大酒店	北京市东城区前门东大街 3 号	100006	65129988
4	天伦王朝饭店	北京市东城区王府井大街 50 号	100006	65138888
4	五洲大酒店	北京市朝阳区北四环东路 8 号	100101	64915588
4	西苑饭店	北京市海淀区三里河路 1 号	100044	68313388
4	香山饭店	北京市海淀区香山公园内	100093	62591166
4	新大都饭店	北京市西城区车公庄 21 号	100044	68319988
4	燕山大酒店	北京市海淀区海淀路甲 138 号	100086	62563388
4	友谊宾馆	北京市海淀区白石桥路 3 号	100873	68498888
4	渔阳饭店	北京市朝阳区新源西里中街 18 号	100027	64669988
4	兆龙饭店	北京市朝阳区工体北路 2 号	100027	65972299
4	中旅大厦	北京市朝阳区北三环东路 2 号	100028	64622288
4	中苑宾馆	北京市海淀区高梁桥斜街 18 号	100081	62178888
3	奥林匹克饭店	北京市海淀区白石桥 52 号	100081	62176688
3	保利大厦	北京市东城区东直门南大街 14 号	100027	65001188
3	宝灵城饭店	北京市海淀区志新路 16 号	100083	62326655
3	北人大酒店	北京市东三环南路 48 号	100022	67716600
3	北展宾馆	北京市西城区西直门外大街 135 号	100044	68316633
3	碧湖宾馆	北京市怀柔县湖光小区 37 号	101400	69625088
3	城市宾馆	北京市朝阳区工体东路 4 号	100027	65007799
3	崇文门饭店	北京市崇文区崇文门西大街 2 号	100062	65122211
3	大雁楼供电培训中心	北京市怀柔雁栖湖南岸西端	101407	69662569
3	东方饭店	北京市宣武区万明路 11 号	100050	63014466
3	二十一世纪饭店	北京市朝阳区亮马桥路 40 号	100016	64663311

注：北京旅游涉外饭店住宿设施共 308 家，其中五星级 16 家，四星级 32 家，三星级 66 家，二星级 112 家，一星级 36 家。

Note: There are 308 foreign hotels ,including 16 5-grade hotels,32 4-grade hotels,66 3-grade hotels, 112 2-grade hotels, 36 1-grade 46 hotels and hotels with no grade.

11-19 续表 continued

星 级 Star Grade	饭 店 名 称 Hotel	地 址 Address	邮政编码 Postcode	电 话 Telephone
3	方舟宾馆	北京市朝阳区枣营路甲 3 号	100026	65947733
3	丰泽园饭店	北京市宣武珠市口西大街 83 号	100050	63186688
3	光明饭店	北京市朝阳区小亮马桥路	100016	64678822
3	国门路大饭店	北京市朝阳区和平路 2 号	100015	64378866
3	和平里大酒店	北京市和平里北街 16 号	100013	64221866
3	鸿翔大厦	北京市海淀区龙翔路 15 号	100083	62013355
3	华北大酒店	北京市朝阳区鼓楼外大街 19 号	100011	62028888
3	华都饭店	北京市朝阳区新源南路 8 号	100027	65971166
3	华风宾馆	北京市前门东大街 5 号	100006	65247311
3	黄河京都大酒店	北京市崇文区夕照寺中街 29 号	100061	67135588
3	皇苑大酒店	北京市海淀区西三环北路厂洼 19 号	100081	68413388
3	回龙观饭店	北京市昌平县回龙观	102208	62913931
3	建银大厦	北京市丰台区太平桥东里九号	100073	63266633
3	金朗大酒店	北京市东城区崇内大街 75 号	100005	65136688
3	金世纪大酒店	北京市朝阳东三环南路 1 号	100022	67782255
3	金叶大厦	北京市朝阳水碓子东里 26 号	100026	65013322
3	京都苑宾馆	北京市建国门南大街 8 号	100022	65291166
3	京闽饭店	北京市朝阳区十八里店周庄	100023	67326699
3	凯迪克大酒店	北京市朝阳北辰东路 18 号	100101	64921188
3	空港花园酒店	北京市首都机杨道口	100621	64563388
3	龙泉宾馆	北京市门头沟区水闸北路 21 号	102300	69843366
3	梅地亚中心	北京市海淀区复兴路乙 11 号	100038	68514422
3	栖湖饭店	北京市怀柔雁栖湖北岸	101408	69661188
3	奇然大酒店	北京市宣武区陶然亭路 2 号	100050	63532288
3	前门饭店	北京市宣武区永安路 75 号	100050	63016688
3	日坛宾馆	北京市朝阳区日坛路 1 号	100020	65125588
3	商务会馆	北京市丰台右安门外玉林里一号楼	100054	63292244
3	神路圆大酒店	北京市朝外大街甲 77 号	100020	65041188
3	顺成饭店	北京市西城区金融大街甲 16 号	100032	66216688
3	四环宾馆	北京市海淀区永定路 100 号	100039	68185599
3	松鹤大酒店	北京市东城区灯市口大街 88 号	100006	65138822
3	苏源锦江大厦	北京市宣武区广安门外大街 3 号	100055	63267788
3	台湾饭店	北京市东城区王府井金鱼胡同 5 号	100006	65136688
3	泰山饭店	北京市海淀区西三旗安宁北里 8 号	100085	62919988
3	天龙宾馆	北京市顺义县天竺镇龙山村	101300	64591331
3	天桥宾馆	北京市宣武区西经路 11 号	100050	63012266
3	天坛饭店	北京市崇文区体育馆路 1 号	100061	67112277
3	天兆大饭店	北京市朝阳区工体东路 18 号	100020	65080088
3	铁道大厦	北京市海淀区北蜂窝甲 102 号	100083	63229199
3	锡华海体酒店	北京市海淀区西苑操场 15 号	100080	62646688
3	新侨饭店	北京市东城区东交民巷 2 号	100004	65133366
3	新兴宾馆	北京市海淀区西三环中路 17 号	100036	68166688
3	亚洲大酒店	北京市东城区新中西街 8 号	100027	65007788
3	燕京饭店	北京市西城区复外大街 19 号	100045	68536688
3	燕翔饭店	北京市朝阳区将台路甲 2 号	100016	64376666
3	裕龙大酒店	北京市海淀区阜成路 40 号	100046	68415588
3	圆山大酒店	北京市西城区德外裕民东里 20 号	100029	62010033
3	越秀大饭店	北京市宣武区宣武门东大街 24 号	100051	63014499
3	云湖度假村	北京市密云水库内湖	101512	61021982
3	云岫山庄	北京市怀柔雁栖湖东侧	101408	69962338
3	职工之家	北京市西城区真武庙路一号	100045	68566688
3	中粮龙泉山庄	北京市门头沟区龙家雾山	102300	60811616
3	中土大厦	北京市海淀区北蜂窝 6 号	100038	63246666
3	重庆饭店	北京市朝阳区光熙门北里 15 号	100028	64228888
3	竹园宾馆	北京市西城区旧鼓楼大街小石桥 24 号	100009	64032229

主要统计指标解释

进出口总额　海关进出口总额指实际进、出我国关境并能引起我国境内物质资源增加或减少的进出口货物总金额。包括我国境内法人和其他组织以一般贸易、易货贸易、加工贸易、补偿贸易、寄售代销贸易等方式进出口的货物、租赁期一年及以上的租赁进出口货物、边境小额贸易货物、国际援助物资或捐赠品、保税区和保税仓库进出口货物等的金额合计。进出口总额用以观察一个国家在对外贸易方面的总规模。我国规定出口货物按离岸价格统计，进口货物按到岸价格统计。

利用外资　指我国各级政府、部门、企业和其他经济组织通过对外借款、吸收外商直接投资以及用其他方式筹措的境外现汇、设备、技术等。

对外借款　是我国利用外资的主要部分。包括我国通过外国政府贷款，国际金融组织贷款，外国银行商业贷款，出口信贷以及对外发行债券，股票等方式，从境外筹措的资金。

外商直接投资　是指外国企业和经济组织或个人（包括华侨、港澳台同胞以及我国在境外注册的企业）按我国有关政策、法规,用现汇、实物、技术等在我国境内开办外商独资企业、与我国境内的企业或经济组织共同举办中外合资经营企业、合作经营企业或合作开发资源的投资（包括外商投资收益的再投资）以及经政府有关部门批准的项目投资总额内，企业从境外借入的资金。

对外承包工程　包括各对外承包公司以招标议标承包方式承揽的下列业务（1）承包国外工程建设项目；（2）承包我国对外经援项目；（3）承包我国驻外机构的工程建设项目；（4）承包我国境内利用外资进行建设的工程项目；（5）与外国承包公司合营或联合承包工程项目时我国公司分包部分；（6）以服务成果向业主收费的技术服务项目（包括承担地形地貌测绘；地质资源勘探与普查；建设区域规划；提供设计文件、图纸、生产工艺技术资料和工程技术经济咨询；工程项目的可行性考察、研究和评估；进行技术指导和培训人员等）；（7）对外承包兼营的房屋开发业务。对外承包工程的营业额是以货币表现的本期内完成的对外承包工程的工作量，包括以前年度签定的合同和本年度新签定的合同在报告期完成的工作量。

对外劳务合作　指以收取工资的形式向业主承包商提供技术和劳动服务的活动。我国对外承包公司在境外开办的合营企业，中国公司同时又提供劳务的，其劳务部分也纳入劳务合作统计。劳务合作营业额按报告期内向雇主提交的结算数（包括工资、加班费和奖金等）统计。

海外旅游者　指来华入境的海外游客中，在我国旅游住宿设施内至少停留一夜的外国人、港澳台同胞。海外旅游者不包括以下人员：（1）应邀来华访问的政府部长以上官员及其随行人员；（2）外国驻华使领馆官员、外交人员以及随行人员；（3）常驻我国一年以上的外国专家，留学生、记者、商务机构人员等；（4）乘坐国际航班过境不需要通过护照检查进入我国口岸的中转旅客；（5）边境地区往来的边民；（6）回大陆定居的港澳台同胞；（7）已在我国定居的外国人和原已出境又返回在我国定居的外国侨民；（8）归国的我国出国人员。

国际旅游（外汇）收入　海外旅游者在中国（大陆）境内旅行、浏览过程中用于交通、参观浏览、住宿、餐饮、购物、娱乐等全部花费。

Explanatory Notes On Main Statistical Indicators

Total Imports and Exports at Customs refer to the value of commodities imported and exported across the boundary of China and cause increase or decrease of material resource within the boundaries of our country. It includes imports and exports in manner of general trade, barter trade, processing trade, compensation trade, consignment and commission agent trade, leasing commodities with renting period in one year and above, imports and exports in border trade, donations and gifts between governments, imported and exported goods in China from bonded warehouses. The indicator of the total imports and exports at customs can be used to observe the total size of external trade in a country . In accordance with the stipulation of the Chinese government, imports are calculated at CIF, while exports are calculated at FOB.

Utilization of Foreign Capital refers to foreign exchange, equipment and technology financed with foreign loans, foreign direct investment and other ways undertaken by the Chinese governments at all levels, by various departments, enterprises and other economic units.

Foreign Loans refers to funds borrowed from abroad, including loans of foreign governments, loans of international financial institutions, commercial loans of foreign banks, export credit, and funds raised via bonds and shares issued abroad. It is a major part of China's utilization of foreign capital.

Direct Investment by Foreign Enterprises refers to the investments in foreign enterprises, Sino-foreign joint ventures and Sino-foreign cooperative enterprises in China and in Sino-foreign co-operative exploration of resources in China by foreign enterprises, economic organizations or individuals(including overseas Chinese, compatriots from Hong Kong, Taiwan and Macao, and Chinese enterprises registered abroad) , following the relevant policies and laws of China. It includes the re-investment of the foreign parties with the return of the investment and the funds that enterprises borrow from abroad for the investment of projects approved by the relevant government department.

Overseas Projects Contracted refer to projects undertaken by Chinese contractors (project contracting companies) through bidding process, which include:

(1) overseas civil engineering construction projects financed by foreign investor;

(2) overseas projects financed by the Chinese government foreign-aid programs;

(3) construction projects of Chinese institutions functioning abroad;

(4) construction projects in China financed by foreign investment;

(5) sub-contracted projects to be taken by Chinese contractors through a joint umbrella project with foreign contractors;

(6) technical assistance projects charged from the foreign owners according to service results (such as topographic surveying, geological prospecting, development zone programming, provision of designing documents, blueprint, materials on production process, technical consultation, project feasibility studies and evaluation, personnel training , etc.) ;

(7) house development projects.

The business income from overseas projects contracted is the work volume of contracted projects completed in the reference period, including completed projects signed contracts in previous years.

Overseas Labor Service Co-operation refers to the activities of providing technology and labor services to employers or contractors and getting salaries and wages in return. Labor services providing by contractual joint ventures of Chinese international contracting corporations should be included in the statistics of overseas labor service co-operation. The business income of labor service co-operation is the total income of wages, salaries, over-time pay, bonuses and other remuneration received from the employers during the reference period.

Number of Tourists refers to the number of foreigners, overseas Chinese, and compatriots from Hong Kong, Macao and Taiwan coming to China for sightseeing, visits, tours, family reunions, vacations, international meetings and other activities concerning business, science and technology, culture, education, physical culture and religious, which does not include the number of employees of foreign institutions in China such as embassies, consulates, news agencies, the offices of corporations and enterprises and foreign experts and students residing in China, or the persons without staying over night in China.

Foreign Exchange Receipt from International Tourism refers to the total expenditures of the foreigners, overseas Chinese, compatriots from Hong Kong , Macao and Taiwan during their staying in the mainland of China.

金融、保险
BANKING AND INSURANCE

城乡居民储蓄存款余额
Saving Deposit Balance in Urban and Rural Areas

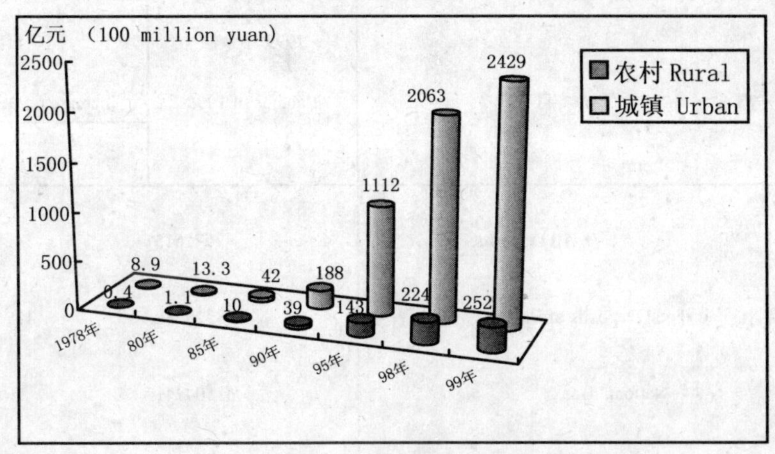

单位：万元 (10000 yuan)	1999年	比年初增加额 Increase than Year-beginning 1999年	1998年
地区金融机构存款余额 Deposits of Financial Institutions	8267.2	1428.9	1263.2
地区金融机构贷款余额 Loans of Financial Institutions	4007.8	559.6	611.6

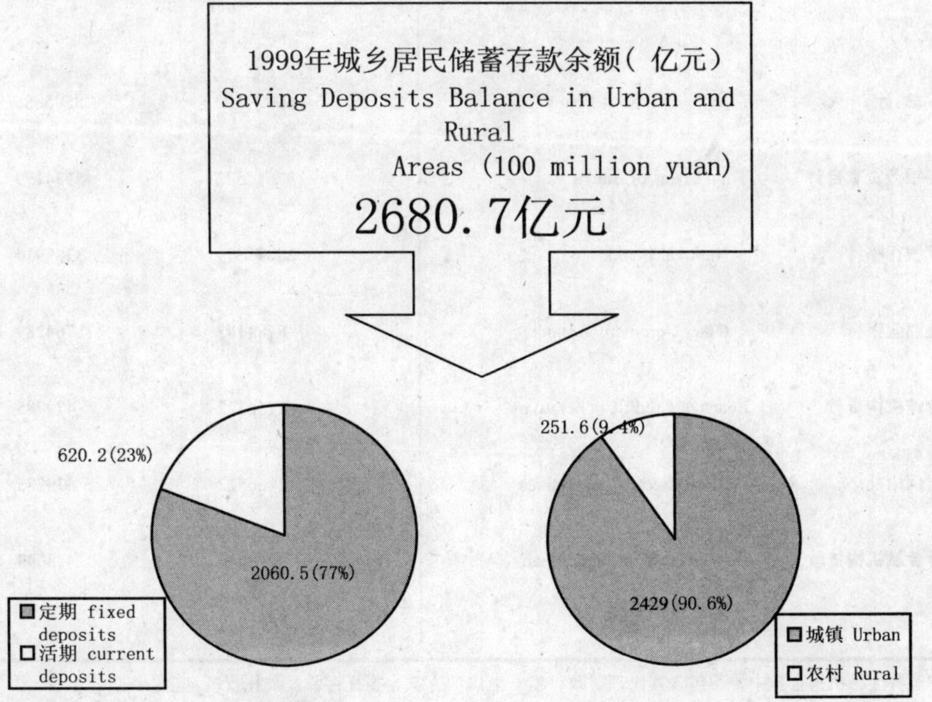

12-1 北京地区金融机构存贷款
DEPOSITS AND LOANS OF FINANCIAL INSTITUTIONS IN BEIJING

单位：万元 (10000 yuan)

项 目	Item	1999 年余额 Balance of 1998	比年初增减额(+、-) Increase or Decrease than Year-beginning	
			1999	1998
存 款 总 计	All Deposits	82671615	14289313	12631644
全市各银行存款合计	Total Deposits of Banks	78223288	13769050	12067272
国家银行小计	National Banks	61504241	9951854	10266014
其他商业银行	Other Commercial Banks	16719047	3817196	1801258
信用合作机构存款	Deposits of Credit Cooperatives	4197648	597212	482072
农村信用社	Rural Credit Cooperatives	4197648	597212	482072
非银行金融机构存款	Deposits of Non-bank Financial Institutions	250679	-76949	82300
贷 款 总 计	All Loans	40077590	5595885	6116200
全市各银行贷款合计	Total Loans of Banks	37612522	5134199	5868702
国家银行小计	National Banks	28831379	3369910	4728931
其他商业银行	Other Commercial Banks	8781143	1764289	1139771
信用合作机构贷款	Loans of Credit Cooperatives	2166522	479785	257854
农村信用社	Rural Credit Cooperatives	2166522	479785	257854
非银行金融机构贷款	Deposits of Non-bank Financial Institutions	298546	-18099	-10356

注：本表各金融机构存款中，不包含其代理财政存款、汇出汇入款、委托存款及委托投资基金。
Note: All deposits exclude agent financial deposits, remittance, trust deposits and trust investment-fund.

12-2 银行存款及贷款余额
DEPOSITS AND LOANS OF BANKS

项目	Item	绝对数(万元) Amount (10000 yuan) 1999	1998	1999年为1998年% 1999 as % of 1998	构成(%) Composition (%) 1999	1998
年末各项存款合计	**Deposits Balance (year-end)**	**78223288**	**62740154**	**124.7**	**100**	**100**
#地方存款	Local Deposits	59892419	49606422	120.7	76.6	79.1
# 地方工业企业存款	Industrial Enterprise	3116038	2887912	107.9	4.0	4.6
地方商业企业存款	Commercial Enterprise	3541272	2604718	136.0	4.5	4.2
#企业存款	Enterprise Deposits	44475637	36289291	122.6	56.9	57.8
# 工业存款	Industry	6081437	5646250	107.7	7.8	9.0
商业存款	Commerce	4027515	3262666	123.4	5.1	5.2
建筑业存款	Construction	2792950	2171962	128.6	3.6	3.5
城镇储蓄存款	Urban Savings Deposits	24290306	20631876	117.7	31.1	32.9
农业存款	Agricultural Deposits	271969	266550	102.0	0.3	0.4
信托存款	Trust Deposits	507	1731	29.3		
机关团体存款	Deposits of Government Organs and Bodies	2997893	2139696	140.1	3.8	3.4
年末各项贷款合计	**Loans Balance (year-end)**	**37612521**	**31269744**	**120.3**	**100**	**100**
#地方贷款	Local Loans	30850111	25721221	119.9	82.0	82.3
# 地方工业贷款	Industrial Enterprise	6916918	6309327	109.6	18.4	20.2
地方商业贷款	Commercial Enterprise	6119240	5433193	112.6	16.3	17.4
#短期贷款	Short-term Loans	25601364	20993880	121.9	68.1	67.1
# 工业贷款	Industry	9917578	8919232	111.2	26.4	28.5
商业贷款	Commerce	6722679	5892568	114.1	17.9	18.8
建筑业企业贷款	Construction	1967942	1383505	142.2	5.2	4.4
农业贷款	Agriculture	505578	530789	95.3	1.3	1.7
中长期贷款	Mid-term and Long-term Loans	8229492	7281840	113.0	21.9	23.3
# 基本建设贷款	Capital Construction	3195413	3001495	106.5	8.5	9.6
技术改造贷款	Technical Updates and Transformation	4533975	3844921	117.9	12.1	12.3
信托贷款	Trust Loans	1020	1020	100.0		

12-3 城乡居民储蓄存款余额
SAVINGS DEPOSIT BALANCE IN URBAN AND RURAL AREAS

项目 Item		绝对数(万元) Amount(10000 yuan) 1999	1998	1999年为1998年% 1999 as % of 1998	构成(%) Composition(%) 1999	1998
年末储蓄存款余额	**Savings Deposit Balance**	**26806646**	**22871883**	**117.2**	**100**	**100**
定　期	Fixed Deposits	20604805	18516975	111.3	76.9	81.0
活　期	Current Deposits	6201841	4354908	142.4	23.1	19.0
城镇居民存款	Urban Savings Deposit	24290306	20631876	117.7	90.6	90.2
农民存款	Rural Savings Deposit	2516340	2240007	112.3	9.4	9.8

12-4 银行、保险系统机构及人员
INSTITUTIONS AND PERSONNEL OF BANK AND INSURANCE SYSTEM

项目 Item		银行系统 Bank System		保险系统 Insurance System	
		机构(个) Institution(unit)	人员(人) Personnel(person)	机构(个) Institution(unit)	人员(人) Personnel(person)
全　市	**Total**	**2574**	**51017**	**125**	**4570**
城　区	City Propers	587	19292	38	2290
郊　区	Suburbs	1549	26148	69	1881
各　县	Counties	438	5577	18	399

12-5 保险费收入 PREMIUMS INCOME

项目	Item	绝对数(万元) Amount (10000 yuan) 1999	1998	1999年为1998年% 1999 as % of 1998	构成(%) Composition(%) 1999	1998
国内保费总计	**Domestic Premiums**	**856247**	**815584**	**105.0**	**100**	**100**
财产险小计	**Property Insurance**	**262256**	**230555**	**113.7**	**30.6**	**28.3**
企业财产险	Enterprise Property	33271	31957	104.1	3.9	3.9
家庭财产险	Family Property	7665	2924	262.1	0.9	0.4
运输工具及责任险	Transportation Equipment and Responsibility	192882	160665	120.1	22.5	19.7
货物运输险	Freight Transport	12763	15286	83.5	1.5	1.9
农业险	Agricultural Insurance	79	153	51.6		
其他财产险	Other Property	15596	19570	79.7	1.8	2.4
人身险小计	**Personal Insurance**	**593991**	**585029**	**101.5**	**69.4**	**71.7**
短期人身险	Short-term Insurance	32055	36457	87.9	3.7	4.5
中长期人寿险	Long Term and Medium Term Insurame	561936	548572	102.4	65.6	67.3
国外保费总计	**Oversease Premiums**	**8730**	**10520**	**83.0**	**100**	**100**
# 货物运输险	Freight Tranport Insurance	2923	3790	77.1	33.5	36.0
船舶险	Ship Insurance	114	560	20.4	1.3	5.3
各种非水险	Non-water Insurance	5065	5534	91.5	58.0	52.6
飞机险	Airplane Insurance	246	342	71.9	2.8	3.3
其他险		382	294	129.9	4.4	2.8

12-6 金融市场交易量 FINANCIAL MARKET TRANSACTIONS

单位：万元 (10000 yuan)

项目	Item	1999	1998	1999年为1998年% 1999 as % of 1998
合计	**Total**	**106944575**	**102415000**	**104.4**
国家债券	Treasury Bonds	5936815	12197900	48.7
股票交易	Stock Transactions	52681881	34263700	153.8
国债回购	Repurchase of Treasury Bonds	44118337	52156400	84.6
基金	Funds	3417393	1870200	182.7
其他	Others	790149	1926800	41.0

主要统计指标解释

信贷资金 国家银行用于发放贷款的资金叫信贷资金。中国人民银行信贷资金的来源有各项存款、对国际金融机构负债、流通中货币、银行自有资金及当年结益等。信贷资金的运用有各项贷款、黄金占款、外汇占款、财政借款及在国际金融机构中的资产等。

存款 企业、机关、团体或居民根据可以收回的原则，把货币资金存入银行或其他信用机构保管并取得一定利息的一种信用活动形式。根据存款对象的不同可划分为企业存款、财政存款、机关团体存款、城镇储蓄存款、农村存款等科目。它是银行信贷资金的主要来源。

贷款 银行或其他信用机构根据必须归还的原则，按一定利率，为企业、个人等提供资金的一种信用活动形式。我国银行贷款分为流动资金贷款、固定资产贷款、城乡个体工商户贷款以及农业贷款等科目。

保费 又叫保险费。是保险人根据保险合同的有关规定，为被保险人取得因约定危险事故发生所造成的经济损失补偿（或给付）权利，付给保险人的代价。包括财产险和人身险收入。

Explanatory Notes On Main Statistical Indicators

Credit Funds refer to the funds issued as loans by state banks. The sources of credit funds of the People's Bank of China included deposits, liabilities to international financial institutions, currency in circulation, self-owned funds and current retained profits, etc. The credit funds can be used in forms of loan, gold, foreign exchange, government debt and assets in the international financial institutions.

Deposit is a form of credit by which enterprises, institutions, organizations or residents can put money into banks and other credit institutions for safekeeping and interest earning under the principle of free withdrawal. According to different depositors, deposits are divided into enterprise deposits, treasury deposits, deposits of government organs and institutions,urban savings deposits, rural deposits and other deposits. Deposits are major sources of the credit funds of banks.

Loan is a form of credit by which banks and other credit institutions provide funds at certain interest rate to enterprises and individuals in the light of the principle of unconditional repayment. Loans from Chinese banks include circulating capital loans, fixed assets loans, loans to urban and rural individuals engaged in industrial and commercial business and agricultural loans.

Premium is the fee paid by the insured based on a proportion of the benefit he or she may get from the insurance plus the insurance value. It includes the income from property insurance and personal insurance.

物　价
PRICE INDEX

物 价 指 数（上年=100）
Price Index (preceding year=100)

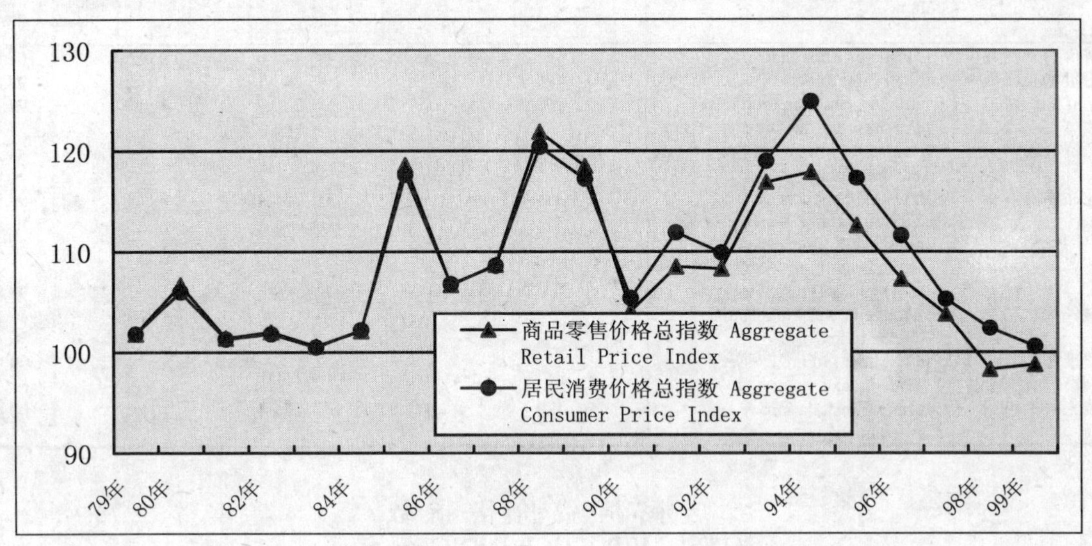

1999年居民消费价格指数（上年=100）
Residence Consumer Price Index (preceding year=100)

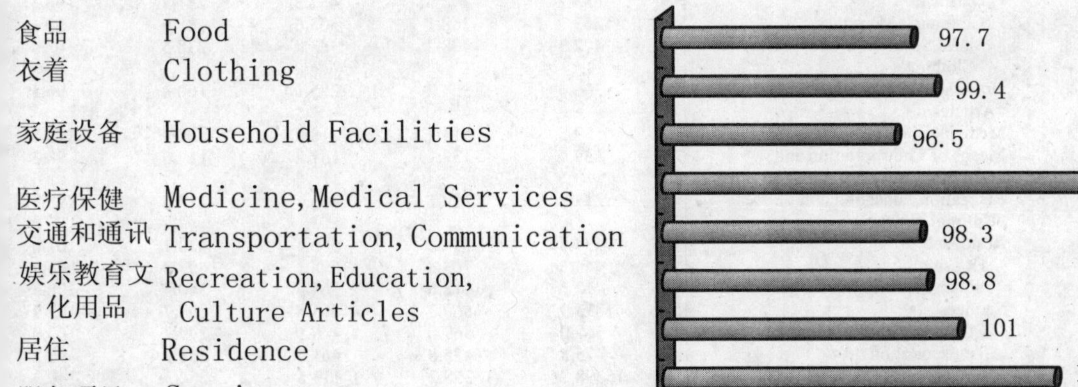

13-1 各种物价总指数
OVERALL PRICE INDICES

单位：% （%）

项　　目 Item		1978=100	1980=100	1985=100	1990=100	1998=100
居民消费价格总指数	Consumer Price Index	601.8	557.5	447.6	259.5	100.6
商品零售价格总指数	Retail Price Index	470.7	433.0	344.1	197.2	98.8
农副产品收购价格总指数	Farm and Sideline Products Purchasing Price Index	442.1	382.7	280.7	166.8	97.5
农业生产资料价格总指数	Means of Agricultural Production Price Index	359.7		318.8	192.1	94.2
郊区工业品零售价格总指数	Industrial Products of Suburb Retail Price Ixndex	365.4	361.6	330.4	194.1	99.9
工业品出厂价格总指数	Industrial Products Producer Price Index					97.7
原材料、燃料、动力购进价格指数	Raw Material,Fuels and Motive Power Purchasing Price Index					95.8
固定资产投资额价格指数	Investment in Fixed Assets Price Index					99.9
建筑安装工程价格指数	Building Installation Price Index	478.1	342.1	276.4	101.8	100.4

13-2 居民消费价格指数
CONSUMER PRICE INDICES

单位：% （%）

项　　目 Item		1978=100	1980=100	1985=100	1990=100	1998=100
总　指　数	**Aggregate Index**	**601.8**	**557.5**	**447.6**	**259.5**	**100.6**
食品类	Food	661.4	598.9	423.1	239.8	97.7
# 粮　食	Grain	703.9	703.9	676.7	477.0	97.9
油脂类	Oil	594.4	594.4	508.0	233.3	99.4
肉禽及其制品	Meat,Poultry and Related Products	635.4	514.2	378.2	220.7	92.3
水产品	Aquatic Products	1473.3	1046.7	417.5	164.5	95.5
菜　类	Vegetable	1165.6	1031.1	534.9	283.8	106.4
# 鲜　菜	Fresh Vegetable	1233.4	1079.5	509.4	268.4	106.2
干　菜	Dried Vegetable	508.1	489.4	426.0	235.3	98.0
调味品	Flavoring	703.3	724.1	658.8	356.7	95.9
干鲜瓜果类	Dried and Fresh Melon and Fruits	704.4	658.3	361.7	180.6	99.6
衣着类	Clothing	369.6	378.0	399.6	226.2	99.4
服　装	Garments	383.2	395.5	437.3	231.7	96.3
衣着材料	Clothing Material	267.1	268.1	303.6	188.9	99.6
鞋袜帽及其他衣着	Shoes,Socks,Hats and Other Clothing	402.3	408.2	383.9	238.5	107.5
家庭设备及用品	Household Facilities and Articles	306.4	304.7	285.1	160.4	96.5
医疗保健	Medicine and Medical Services	559.5	514.4	418.2	228.1	115.8
交通和通讯工具	Means of Transportation and Communications	139.4	139.4	157.2	117.6	98.3
娱乐教育文化用品	Recreation,Education and Cultural Articles	214.8	209.1	203.4	110.5	98.8
居　住	Residence	434.5	584.2	560.4	428.1	101.0
住　房	Housing	445.3	703.8	698.1	493.8	95.4
水电燃料	Water,Electricity and Fuels	412.6	412.6	364.5	340.4	108.7
服务项目	Services	1873.9	1869.3	1663.8	804.7	107.9
# 电讯费	Communication	569.0	569.0	440.5	299.7	100.0
交通费	Transportation	475.8	475.8	461.5	338.9	96.8
文娱费	Recreation	15398.2	15398.2	14113.5	6264.3	140.3
学杂保育费	Education and Nursery	1486.4	1486.4	1486.4	860.4	100.5
修理及其他服务费	Repair and Other Services	1160.7	1146.3	776.7	411.3	109.8
医疗保健服务	Medicine and Medical Service	1110.4	1110.4	1110.4	616.8	110.1

13-3 商品零售价格指数
RETAIL PRICE INDICES

单位：%　　　　　　　　　　　　　　　　　　　　　　　　　　　　（%）

项目	Item	1998=100	项目	Item	1998=100
商品零售价格指数	**Aggregate Index**	**98.8**	其他纺织品	Other Textiles	100.5
食品类	Food	97.7	中西药品类	Traditional Chinese and Western Medicines	115.6
粮　食	Grain	98.2	中　药	Traditional Chinese Medicines	141.3
油脂类	Oil	99.4	西　药	Western Medicine	98.2
肉蛋禽	Meat,Egg and Poultry	92.1	医疗用品	Medicine and Medical Articles	103.9
水产品	Aquatic Products	95.5	化妆品类	Cosmetics	98.1
鲜　菜	Fresh Vegetable	106	书报杂志类	Book,Newspaper and Magazine	105.5
干　菜	Dried Vegetable	100.9	文化体育用品	Stationery and Sports Goods	108.2
鲜　果	Fresh Fruit	101.4	文化用品	Stationery	108.5
干　果	Nuts	93.8	体育用品	Sports Goods	101.4
其他食品类	Other Foods	99.5	日用品类	Daily Use Articles	96.0
饮食业	Catering	98.7	一般日用品	Ordinary Daily Use Articles	95.2
饮料烟酒类	Beverage,Tobacco and Liquor	96.4	家具类	Furnitures	96.7
饮　料	Beverage	97.9	日用杂品	Daily Use Sundiries	98.9
烟　酒	Tobacco and Liquor	95.5	家用电器类	Household Appliances	94.8
服装鞋帽类	Garments,Shoes,Hats	99.8	首饰类	Jewelry	92.2
服　装	Garments	96.8	燃料类	Fuels	114.5
鞋	Shoes	107.6	建筑装潢材料类	Building Decoration Materials	102.2
其他衣着	Other Clothing	107.7	机电产品类	Mechanical and Electrical Products	93.8
纺织品类	Textile	100.1			
棉　布	Cotton Cloth	99.3			
棉花化纤混纺布	Blend Cloth	106.3			
化纤布	Chemical Fiber Cloth	99.9			
呢　绒	Woolen Fabric	95.9			
绸　缎	Silk	104.7			

13-4 居民货币购买力指数
MONETARY PURCHASING POWER OF RESIDENTS

单位：%　　　　　　　　　　　　　　　　　　　　　　　　　　　　（%）

基期 Base Period	1999	1998
1957=100	16.2	16.3
1965=100	16.8	16.9
1970=100	16.5	16.6
1975=100	16.5	16.6
1978=100	16.6	16.7
1980=100	18.0	18.1
1985=100	22.4	22.5
1990=100	38.6	38.8
以上年为100 Preceding Year=100	99.4	97.7

13-5 鲜菜零售价格指数
RETAIL PRICE INDICES OF FRESH VEGETABLE

单位：% (%)

项目	Item	1985=100	1990=100	1998=100
总指数	**Aggregate Index**	**509.4**	**268.4**	**106.2**
大白菜	Chinese Cabbage	1133.6	975.7	139.2
元白菜	Cabbage	590.6	422.9	114.0
菠菜	Spinach	996.3	408.5	110.1
油菜	Rape	637.5	317.8	96.4
芹菜	Celery	506.4	274.1	95.0
韭菜	Chinese Chives	324.3	187.2	111.7
菜花	Cauliflower	340.5	178.9	107.9
生笋	Bamboo Shoot	545.2	355.4	113.9
黄瓜	Cucumber	514.9	224.2	106.1
冬瓜	Wax Gourd	809.2	333.1	102.8
西红柿	Tomato	547.4	221.4	107.8
茄子	Eggplant	449.9	226.5	109.9
青椒	Green Pepper	753.4	244.5	100.4
豆角	Fresh Kidney Beans	422.0	228.3	108.5
大葱	Scallion	802.4	479.5	157.3
大蒜	Garlic	436.1	319.5	93.8
萝卜	Radish	1537.4	553.3	130.5
胡萝卜	Carrot	1034.0	382.9	95.9

13-6 农副产品收购价格总指数
PURCHASING PRICE INDICES FOR FARM AND SIDELINES PRODUCTS

单位：% (%)

项目	Item	1978=100	1985=100	1990=100	1998=100
总指数	**Aggregate Index**	**442.1**	**280.7**	**166.8**	**97.5**
粮食类	Grain	306.3	210.3	134.4	91.9
经济作物类	Industrial Crops	525.9	314.4	135.1	93.1
畜禽产品类	Livestock Products,Poultry and Eggs	486.5	330.5	190.9	104.7
生猪	Pigs	532.1	362.1	183.2	86.1
鸡蛋	Chicken Eggs	344.6	238.9	144.1	107.4
干鲜果类	Dried and Fresh Fruits	475.1	267.2	171.5	88.0
鲜瓜果	Fresh Melons and Fruits	456.6	287.6	199.3	101.5
鲜果	Fresh Fruits	388.9	211.9	155.2	83.0
西瓜	Water Melon	311.1	226.8	144.1	101.5
鲜菜类	Fresh Vegetable	696.3	343.8	194.7	98.3
水产品类	Aquatic Products	738.5	259.7	166.7	127.0

13-7 郊区工业品零售价格指数
RETAIL PRICE INDICES OF INDUSTRIAL PRODUCTS IN SUBURBS

单位：% (%)

项目	Item	1978=100	1985=100	1990=100	1998=100
总指数	**Aggregate Index**	**365.4**	**330.4**	**194.1**	**99.9**
日用消费品	**Daily Use Articles**	**359.0**	**332.5**	**192.8**	**100.7**
食品类	Food	463.9	383.0	228.4	97.7
衣着类	Clothing	306.3	322.0	175.1	99.4
日用杂品类	Daily Use Sundries	266.8	254.7	155.6	103.2
农业生产资料	**Agricultural Capital Goods**	**359.7**	**318.8**	**192.1**	**94.2**
农业机械	Agricultural Machinery	310.9	297.9	187.2	103.8
化学肥料	Chemical Fertilizer	446.4	373.4	243.6	91.1
化学农药	Agricultural Chemicals	217.7	207.4	86.7	108.2
农机用油	Oil for Agricultural Machinery		401.4	326.8	107.9
种子	Seed		229.0	142.2	94.9
饲料	Forage		492.7	257.9	93.8

13-8 工农业产品综合比价指数
AGGREGATE PRICE PARITY INDEX OF INDUSTRIAL AND AGRICULTURAL PRODUCTS

单位：% (%)

基期 Base Period	农副产品收购价格总指数 Purchasing Price Indices of Farm and Sidelining Products	农村工业品零售价格总指数 Retail Price Index of Industrial Products in in Rural Area	工农业产品综合比价指数 Aggregate Parity Index of Industrial and Agricultural Products	
			以农产品指数为100 Agricultural Products Index=100	以工业品指数为100 Industrial Products Index=100
1957=100	542.7	349.2	64.5	155.0
1965=100	487.6	339.2	69.8	143.3
1970=100	486.8	360.2	74.2	134.7
1975=100	453.0	370.6	81.9	121.9
1978=100	442.1	365.4	83.0	120.6
1980=100	382.7	361.6	94.8	105.5
1985=100	280.7	330.4	118.1	84.7
1990=100	166.8	194.1	116.7	85.7
1995=100	86.0	103.5	120.8	82.8
1998=100	97.5	97.4	107.0	93.4

13-9 固定资产投资额价格指数
PRICE INDICES OF INVESTMENT IN FIXED ASSETS

单位：% (%)

项目	Item	1992=100	1993=100	1994=100	1998=100
总指数	**Aggregate Index**	**187.5**	**148.2**	**127.4**	**99.9**
建筑安装工程	Building Installation	211.6	161.4	134.7	100.4
设备、工器具购置	Purchase of Equipment, Tools and Instruments	145.7	126.8	124.2	98.8
其他费用	Others	158.4	129.8	105.0	99.0

注：按国家统计局的有关规定，固定资产投资额价格指数从 1992 年开始计算。

Note: According to rules of State Statistical Bureau, price indices of investment in fixed assets are counted from 1992.

13-10 建筑安装工程价格指数
PRICE INDICES OF BUILDING INSTALLATION

单位：%　　　　(%)

项　目	Item	1978=100	1985=100	1990=100	1998=100
总　指　数	**Aggregate Index**	**478.1**	**342.1**	**276.4**	**100.4**
直接费用价格指数	**Price Index of Direct Cost**	**599.6**	**379.0**	**307.0**	**100.1**
人 工 费	Labor Cost	972.7	668.8	717.7	107.6
材料费用	Material Cost	510.8	360.2	259.7	98.5
其他费用价格指数	**Price Index of Other Cost**	**328.7**	**236.9**	**188.1**	**101.3**

13-11 建筑安装工程中主要材料费用价格指数
PRICE INDICES OF MAJOR MATERIALS IN BUILDING INSTALLATION

单位：%　　　　(%)

项　目	Item	1978=100	1985=100	1990=100	1998=100
总 指 数	**Aggregate Index**	**510.8**	**360.2**	**259.7**	**98.5**
钢　材	Rolled-steel Products	456.0	361.3	323.7	96.6
木　材	Timber	830.7	428.1	312.8	99.2
水　泥	Cement	701.2	499.0	318.0	99.3
地方材料	Local Materials	512.0	345.3	232.5	100.2
其他材料	Other Materials	536.7	381.1	268.4	100.2

13-12 房地产价格指数(以上年为100)
PRICE INDICES OF REAL ESTATE(PRECEDING YEAR=100)

单位：%　　　　(%)

项　目	Item	1998	1999
土地交易价格指数	**Price Indices of Land Transaction**	**104.6**	**100.2**
居民住宅用地	Residential Building	102.0	100.2
工业用地	Industry	103.7	100.1
商业旅游娱乐用地	Commerce,Tourism and Recreation	109.1	100.3
其他用地	Others	105.3	100.3
房地产销售价格指数	**Price Indices of Real Estate Sales**	**101.1**	**100.1**
商品房	Commodity Building	99.0	98.7
住宅	Residence	102.2	98.3
非住宅	Non-residence	93.1	100.6
旧房交易	Transaction of Old Residence	99.8	99.2
公有住房	Public Residence	109.2	101.8
房地产租赁价格指数	**Price Indices of Real Estate Rent**	**100.0**	**98.5**
住宅	Residence	100.0	100.4
公房	Public	100.0	100.0
私房	Private	100.3	103.8
办公用房	Office	99.9	87.3
商业用房	Commerce	99.8	95.8
厂房仓库	Plant	100.0	100.0
旅店饭店客房	Guest Room of Hotel	96.3	91.9

主要统计指标解释

零售价格指数 是反映城乡商品零售价格变动趋势的一种经济指数。零售价格的调整变动直接影响到城乡居民的生活支出和国家的财政收入，影响居民购买力和市场供需平衡，影响消费与积累的比例。因此，计算零售价格指数，可以从一个侧面对上述经济活动进行观察和分析。

居民消费价格指数 是反映一定时期内城乡居民所购买的生活消费品价格和服务项目价格变动趋势和程度的相对数。是综合了城市居民消费价格指数和农民消费价格指数计算取得。利用居民消费价格指数，可以观察和分析消费品的零售价格和服务价格变动对城乡居民实际生活费支出的影响程度。

农产品收购价格指数 是反映国有商业、集体商业、个体商业、外贸部门、国家机关、社会团体等各种经济类型的商业企业和有关部门收购农产品价格的变动趋势和程度的相对数。农产品收购价格指数可以观察和研究农产品价格总水平的变化情况，以及对农民货币收入的影响，作为制定和检查农产品价格政策的依据。计算指数所选的商品有 11 各大类、包括 276 种农副土特产品。采用加权倒数平均公式（即按报告期实际收购金额加权综合法）计算。

工业产品出厂价格指数 是反映全部工业产品出厂价格总水平的变动趋势和程度的相对数。其中包括工业企业售给商业、外贸、物资部门的产品外，还包括售给工业和其他部门的生产资料以及直接售给居民的生活消费品。通过工业生产价格指数能观察出厂价格变动对工业总产值的影响。

原材料、燃料、动力购进价格指数 是反映全部工业原材料、燃料、动力购进价格总水平的变动趋势和程度的相对数。用其可以观察和研究工业企业原材料价格变动对生产的影响，以及企业对原材料涨价的消化能力和承受能力，为制订价格政策提供依据。

固定资产投资价格指数 是反映固定资产投资额价格变动趋势和程度的相对数。固定资产投资额是由建筑安装工程投资完成额、设备、工器具购置投资完成额和其他费用投资完成额三部分组成的。编制固定资产投资价格指数应首先分别编制上述三部分投资的价格指数，然后采用加权算术平均法求出固定资产投资价格总指数。

编制固定资产投资价格指数可以准确地反映固定资产投资中涉及的各类商品和取费项目价格变动趋势和变动幅度，消除按现价计算的固定资产投资指标中的价格变动因素，真实地反映固定资产投资的规模、速度、结构和效益，为国家科学地制定，检查固定资产投资计划并提高宏观调控水平，为完善国民经济核算体系提供科学的，可靠的依据。

房地产价格指数 是反映全部房地产价格总水平的变动趋势和程度的相对数。包括土地出让价格指数、房地产销售价格指数、房地产租赁价格指数。

土地交易价格指数 是指房地产开发商或其他建设单位在进行商品房开发前为取得土地使用权而实际支付的价格的变动趋势和程度的相对数。

房地产销售价格指数 是指房地产销售价格总水平变动趋势和程度的相对数。

房地产租赁价格指数 是指房地产租赁价格总水平变动趋势和程度的相对数。

Explanatory Notes On Main Statistical Indicators

Retail Price Index reflects the general trend in retail prices of commodities. The change and adjustment in retail prices directly affect the living expenditure of urban and rural residents, government revenue, purchasing power of residents and the equilibrium of market supply and demand, and the ratio of consumption to accumulation. Therefore, the calculation of retail price index is useful to analyze the relevant economic activities.

Consumer Price Index reflects the relative change in prices of consumer goods and services purchased by urban and rural residents, and is a composite index derived from the urban consumer price index and the rural consumer price index. Consumer price index can be used to analyze the impact of consumer price change on actual living expenditures of urban and rural residents.

Purchasing Price Index of Farm Products reflects the relative change in purchasing prices of farm products purchased by state-owned, collective-owned, and individual commercial enterprises, foreign trade sectors, government agencies, social organizations and other units of various types of ownership. It is used to observe the impact of change in purchasing prices of farm products on money income of peasants and is calculated with the method of weighted harmonic mean, taking the amount of purchases during a given period as the weight. Number of products involved in the current calculation totaled 276 in 11 categories.

Ex-factory Price Index of Industrial Products reflects the relative change in general ex-factory prices of all industrial products, including sales of industrial products to commercial enterprises, foreign trade sectors , materials supplying and distributing sectors as well as sales of production means to industry and other sectors and sales of consumer goods to residents. It can be used to analyze the impact of ex-factory prices on gross industrial output value.

Purchase Price Index of Raw Materials, Fuel and Power reflects relative changes in the general purchase price of all industrial raw materials, fuel and power. The index can be used to study and analyze the impact of price changes of industrial raw materials of the production and enterprises capability to bear and digest the price increase of raw materials, so as to provide basis for the government to formulate price policies.

Price Index of Investment in Fixed Asses reflects the change in prices of investment in fixed assets. The investment in fixed assets consists of three components, namely the investment in construction and installation, the investment in purchases of equipment and instrument, and the investment in other items. Price index of investment in fixed assets is calculated as the weighted arithmetic mean of the price indices of the three components.

Price index of investment in fixed asses reflects the change of price in various goods and services involved in investment in fixed assets and therefore can be used to observe the actual size, speed, structure, and efficiency of investment in fixed assets and provides reliable and rational data for government planning, management, decision making, and further improving the current national accounting system.

Price Indices of Real Estate reflects the trend and extent of price changes of real estate, including price indices of land sale, price indices of real estate sale and price indices of real estate rent.

Price Indices of Land Transaction reflects the changing trend and extent of price which paid actually by developing enterprises or construction units to get land use rights before development of commodity buildings.

Price Indices of Real Estate Sale reflects the trend and extent of price changes of real estate sale.

Price Indices of Real Estate Rent reflects the trend and extent of price changes of real estate rent.

教育、文化
EDUCATION AND CULTURE

1999年平均每万人口在校学生数(人)
Average Number of Student Enrollment per 10000 Population (person)

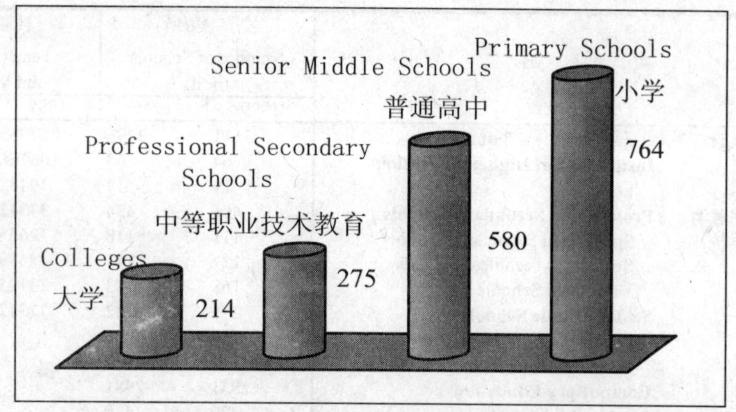

1999年	学校数（所） Number of Schools(unit)	在校学生数（人） Students Enrollment (person)
高等学校 Institutions of Higher Education	64	234033
中等职业技术教育 Professional Secondary Schools	406	301199
普通高中 Senior Middle Schools	275	161473
小学 Primary Schools	2352	836655

广播、电视、图书馆
Broadcasting,Television and Library

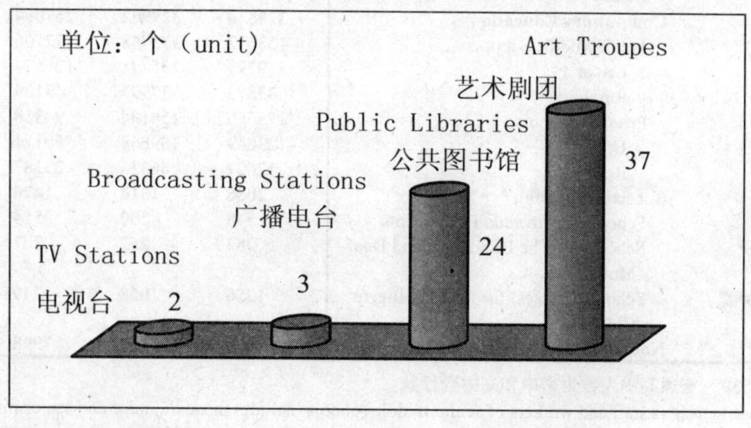

14-1 各类学校基本情况
BASIC STATISTICS FOR EDUCATION

单位：人 (person)

类别	Item	校数(所) Number of Schools (unit)		教职工数 Teachers;Staff and Workers		# 专任教师 Full-time Teachers	
		1999	1998	1999	1998	1999	1998
总计	**Total**	**3611**	**3796**	**287935**	**284674**	**162363**	**164491**
高等学校	**Institutions of Higher Education**	**64**	**63**	**106766**	**101442**	**34976**	**36559**
# 地方	Local	19	19	19482	19956	7261	7618
中等职业技术教育	**Professional Secondary Schools**	**406**	**434**	**33312**	**35128**	**17175**	**17649**
中等专业学校	Specialized Secondary Schools	111	118	12658	14253	5780	6334
技工学校	Secondary Technical Schools	127	143	7459	7900	3704	3711
职业学校	Vocational Schools	168	173	13195	12975	7691	7604
普通高中	**Senior Middle Schools**	**275**	**282**	**72312**	**71849**	**12023**	**11412**
城镇	Urban	258	265			11507	10882
农村	Rural	17	17			516	530
义务教育	**Compulsory Education**	**2831**	**2981**			**97263**	**98044**
初中	Junior Middle Schools	479	470			36142	36242
城镇	Urban	304	290			27343	27512
农村	Rural	175	180			8799	8730
小学	Primary Schools	2352	2511	74114	74916	61121	61802
城镇	Urban	1231	1306	51855	52509	41941	42583
农村	Rural	1121	1205	22259	22407	19180	19219
特殊教育	**Special Education**	**35**	**36**	**1431**	**1339**	**926**	**827**
工读学校	Schools for Juvenile Delinquents	6	6	422	414	197	183
盲聋哑学校	Schools for The Blind,Deaf and Deaf-Mutes	7	7	440	420	287	274
弱智儿童辅读学校(班)	Schools(Classes) for Less Intelligent Children	22	23	569	505	442	370
民办学校	**Non-state Owned Schools**	**59**	**83**	**3439**	**4022**	**2106**	**2442**

类别	Item	毕业生数 Graduates		招生数 New Students Enrollment		在校学生数 Students Enrollment	
		1999	1998	1999	1998	1999	1998
总计	**Total**	**500762**	**492531**	**494699**	**473882**	**2015940**	**2046766**
高等学校	**Institutions of Higher Education**	**49936**	**49322**	**78354**	**62264**	**234033**	**212984**
# 地方	Local	15989	15230	27028	21449	76496	67342
外国留学生	Foreign Students	3945	5462	4198	6441	8203	9314
中等职业技术教育	**Professional Secondary Schools**	**79252**	**71734**	**90813**	**102808**	**301199**	**295892**
中等专业学校	Specialized Secondary Schools	27266	23078	34294	38003	123379	117965
技工学校	Secondary Technical Schools	17512	15491	25515	25215	70856	64879
职业学校	Vocational Schools	34474	33165	31004	39590	106964	113048
普通高中	**Senior Middle Schools**	**40660**	**39683**	**56998**	**52956**	**161473**	**145966**
城镇	Urban	38793	37703	54880	50898	155309	139886
农村	Rural	1867	1980	2118	2058	6164	6080
义务教育	**Compulsory Education**	**328828**	**329982**	**267064**	**254551**	**1310077**	**1383468**
初中	Junior Middle Schools	153172	173788	172706	154136	473422	463937
城镇	Urban	119299	135791	129577	115390	360427	354282
农村	Rural	33873	37997	43129	38746	112995	109655
小学	Primary Schools	175656	156194	94358	100415	836655	919531
城镇	Urban	123049	109868	69171	71134	578595	625668
农村	Rural	52607	46326	25187	29281	258060	293863
特殊教育	**Special Education**	**2086**	**1810**	**1470**	**1303**	**9158**	**8456**
工读学校	Schools for Juvenile Delinquents	548	500	514	445	912	889
盲聋哑学校	Schools for The Blind,Deaf and Deaf-Mutes	282	252	207	273	1412	1442
弱智儿童辅读学校(班)	Schools(Classes) for Less Intelligent Children	1256	1058	749	585	6834	6125
民办学校	**Non-state Owned Schools**	**3890**	**6553**	**7998**	**17278**	**24035**	**38295**

注：教职工数中，普通高中人数为初中和高中合计数。

Note: Number of teachers,staff and workers of senior middle schools includes those of junior and senior middle schools.

14-2 高等学校基本情况
BASIC STATISTICS FOR INSTITUTION OF HIGHER EDUCATION

单位：人 (person)

类别	Item	校数(所) Number of Schools (unit)	毕业生数 Graduates	招生数 New Students Enrollment	在校学生数 Students Enrollment	教职工数 Teachers, Staff and Workers	#专任教师 Full-time Teachers
总计	**Total**	**64**	**49936**	**78354**	**234033**	**106766**	**34976**
综合大学	Comprehensive Universities	3	5885	9971	29647	13178	4435
理工院校	Science and Engineering	20	23301	35309	106216	36977	12976
农业院校	Agriculture	2	2215	3381	9882	3459	1263
林业院校	Forestry	1	814	1840	4529	1283	439
医药院校	Medicine	6	2100	2482	9612	24506	5140
师范院校	Teacher Training	3	3186	4617	14850	6269	2470
语文院校	Literature	7	2948	5535	13766	5629	2338
财经院校	Economics and Finance	5	3819	5187	17026	5172	1979
政法院校	Politics and Law	4	2481	4019	12364	3798	1223
体育院校	Physical Culture	1	512	810	2634	919	367
艺术院校	Art	7	695	1119	3381	2618	1082
民族院校	National Colleges	1	999	969	3799	1763	722
职业技术学院	Professional Institute	4	981	3115	6327	1195	542
在总计中：	**Of Total:**						
市属院校	Municipal	19	15989	27028	76496	19482	7261
综合大学	Comprehensive Universities	1	2283	5413	13992	3196	1226
理工院校	Science and Engineering	7	7281	10268	32121	7809	2798
农业院校	Agriculture	1	459	847	2073	495	194
医药院校	Medicine	2	776	1015	3256	1392	461
师范院校	Teacher Training	2	1884	2932	8901	2940	1167
语文院校	Literature	1	517	542	1299	278	120
财经院校	Economics and Finance	2	1808	2746	8611	2565	915
政法院校	Politics and Law			348	971		
艺术院校	Art						
职业技术学院	Professional Institute	3	981	2917	5272	807	380

14-3 高等学校分科学生数
NUMBER OF STUDENTS BY DEPARTMENTS IN INSTITUTIONS OF HIGHER EDUCATION

单位：人 (person)

学科	Item	毕业生数 Graduates	招生数 New Students Enrollment	在校学生数 Students Enrollment
总计	**Total**	**49936**	**78354**	**234033**
哲学	Philosophy	183	158	526
经济学	Economics	9252	13042	39842
法学	Law	3436	6918	18414
教育学	Education	2054	2695	8430
文学	Literature	6424	10681	30269
历史学	History	399	596	2246
理学	Science	3186	5038	15573
工学	Engineering	21733	34565	103396
农学	Agriculture	883	1902	5047
医学	Medicine	2386	2759	10290

14-4 高等学校及科研机构分科研究生数
NUMBER OF POSRGRADUATE BY FIELD OF STUDY IN INSTITUTIONS OF HIGHER EDUCATION AND SCIENTIFIC RESEARCH INSTITUTIONS

单位：人 (person)

学科	Item	攻读博士学位研究生 Postgraduate for Doctor Degree			攻读硕士学位研究生 Postgraduate for Master Degree			研究生班研究生数 Postgraduates in Class
		毕业生数 Graduates	招生数 New Students Enrollment	在学研究生数 Postgraduates Enrollment	毕业生数 Graduates	招生数 New Students Enrollment	在学研究生数 Postgraduate Enrollment	
总计	**Total**	**3114**	**5451**	**14935**	**9127**	**13994**	**35612**	**108**
# 市属院校	Municipal	42	108	247	727	1064	2687	
哲学	Philosophy	83	118	324	89	140	376	
经济学	Economics	258	518	1237	1240	2081	5320	
法学	Law	217	486	1179	992	1373	4050	
教育学	Education	67	123	314	204	354	884	
# 体育学	Physical Culture	16	27	72	76	88	229	
文学	Literature	124	232	621	585	977	2422	108
# 艺术	Art	18	44	112	102	203	437	108
历史学	History	58	113	291	129	174	481	
理学	Science	749	1057	2933	1175	1646	4247	
工学	Engineering	1037	2087	6143	4022	6196	15017	
# 力学	Mechanics	64	92	324	129	147	406	
农学	Agriculture	133	211	536	206	307	816	
# 林学	Forestry	22	49	124	47	65	178	
医学	Medicine	388	506	1357	485	746	1999	

14-5 高等学校专任教师学历情况
EDUCATIONAL BACKGROUND OF FULL-TIME TEACHERS IN INSTITUTIONS OF HIGHER EDUCATION

单位：人 (person)

学历	Educational Background	总计 Total	正高级 Senior Title	副高级 Asso. Senior Title	中级 Middle Title	初级 Junior Title	无职称 No Title
合计	**Total**	**34976**	**5772**	**11451**	**12008**	**4560**	**1185**
研究生毕业	Postgraduate						
博士	Doctor Degree	4761	1164	2147	1297	77	76
硕士	Master Degree	11220	950	3190	4785	1785	510
未获博士硕士学位	Not Obtained Degrees	1065	333	355	334	33	10
本科毕业	Undergraduate						
学士	Bachelor	12383	1172	3459	4817	2423	512
研究生肄业	Not Pass the Postgraduate Study	97	17	33	27	8	12
未获学士学位	Not Obtained Degree	4397	2057	1874	357	60	49
专科毕业及本专科肄业两年及以上	Graduate from College for Professional Training and Undergraduate Study for Two Years above	849	47	345	323	120	14
本专科肄业未满两年	Undergraduate Study for Less than Two Years	204	32	48	68	54	2

14-6 中等专业学校基本情况
BASIC STATISTICS ON SPECIALIZED SECONDARY SCHOOLS

单位：人 (person)

类别 Item		校数(所) Number of Schools (unit)	毕业生数 Graduates	招生数 New Students Enrollment	在校学生数 Students Enrollment	教职工数 Teachers, Staff and Workers	#专任教师 Full-time Teachers
总计	**Total**	**111**	**27266**	**34294**	**123379**	**12658**	**5780**
中等技术学校	**Secondary Technical Schools**	**93**	**23640**	**33744**	**119267**	**10610**	**4850**
工业学校	Industry	29	14711	22126	78067	5059	2252
农业学校	Agriculture	1	875	1204	3456	336	128
林业学校	Forestry	1	173	183	622	95	36
医药学校	Medicine	36	2985	1858	9203	1764	835
财经学校	Economics and Finance	8	2863	5484	16785	1330	587
政法学校	Politics and Law	4	852	801	4001	301	122
体育学校	Physical Culture	7	263	625	1601	616	234
艺术学校	Art	6	654	1045	3810	1034	597
其他学校	Others	1	264	418	1722	75	59
中等师范学校	**Teacher Training School**	**18**	**3626**	**550**	**4112**	**2048**	**930**
# 幼儿师范	Kindergarten	1	214	94	493	135	55

14-7 中等专业学校专任教师学历
EDUCATIONAL BACKGROUND OF FULL-TIME TEACHERS IN SPECIALIZED SECONDARY SCHOOLS

单位：人 (person)

学历 Educational Background		中等专业学校 Secondary Specialized Schools		#中等专业技术学校 Secondary Technical Schools		# 中等专业师范学校 Teacher Training Schools	
		人数 Number of Persons	构成(%) Composition(%)	人数 Number of Persons	构成(%) Composition(%)	人数 Number of Persons	构成(%) Composition(%)
合计	**Total**	**5780**	**100**	**4850**	**100**	**930**	**100**
本科毕业及以上	Undergraduate and the Level above	4359	75.4	3538	72.9	821	88.3
专科毕业和本专科肄业两年及以上	College for Professional Training and Undergraduate Study for Two Years above	1017	17.6	922	19.0	95	10.2
本专科肄业未满两年	Undergraduate Study for Less than Two Years	38	0.7	38	0.8		
中专、高中毕业及以下	Specialized Secondary School,Senior Middle School and the Level Below	366	6.3	352	7.3	14	1.5

14-8 中等专业学校分学科学生数
NUMBER OF STUDENTS IN SPECIALIZED SECONDARY SCHOOLS BY FIELD OF STUDY

单位：人 (person)

学科	Item	毕业生数 Graduates 1999	1998	招生数 New Students Enrollment 1999	1998	在校学生数 Students Enrollment 1999	1998
总计	**Total**	**27266**	**23078**	**34294**	**38003**	**123379**	**117965**
工科	Engineering	10471	8738	16710	17409	57931	52998
农科	Agriculture	411	248	537	410	1625	1426
林科	Forestry	61	109	155	226	632	544
医药卫生	Medicine	2985	2630	1858	2766	9088	10300
财经	Economics and Finance	4155	2848	3256	4128	14668	15670
管理	Administration	3458	2402	7736	8272	22918	18740
政法	Politics and Law	952	722	937	1530	4236	4249
艺术	Art	864	563	1862	1374	6329	5437
体育	Physical Culture	263	294	660	432	1720	1267
师范	Teacher Training	3646	4524	583	1456	4232	7334
# 幼儿师范专业	Kindergarten	339	422	94	208	580	825
特教师范专业	Special Education	157	38	181		431	41

14-9 普通中学分课程专任教师数
NUMBER OF FULL-TIME TEACHERS BY SUBJECTS OF REGULAR SECONDARY SCHOOLS

单位：人 (person)

学科	Item	合计 Total 1999	1998	高中 Senior Middle School 1999	1998	初中 Junior Middle School 1999	1998
总计	**Total**	**48165**	**47654**	**12023**	**11412**	**36142**	**36242**
政治	Politics	3241	3296	871	792	2370	2504
语文	Chinese	7663	7493	1746	1670	5917	5823
数学	Math	7818	7688	1809	1742	6009	5946
物理	Physics	3869	3889	1320	1262	2546	2627
化学	Chemical	2795	2854	1302	1230	1493	1624
生物	Biology	1813	1777	352	333	1461	1444
地理	Geography	1735	1710	359	324	1376	1386
历史	History	2277	2257	687	658	1590	1599
英语	English	7328	7141	1711	1596	5617	5545
俄语	Russian		1		1		
日语	Japanese	13	17	8	11	5	6
体育	Physical Education	2920	2913	729	708	2191	2205
生理卫生	Physiology	94	73	1	2	93	71
音乐	Music	1038	1018	135	120	903	898
美术	Art	974	939	111	95	863	844
计算机	Computer	864	725	312	279	552	446
职业劳动	Vocational Labor	650	594	43	49	607	545
其他	Others	406	405	80	70	326	335

14-10 职业高中分科学生数
NUMBER OF STUDENTS BY FIELD OF STUDY IN VOCATIONAL SCHOOLS

单位：人　　　　(person)

学科 Item		毕业生数 Graduates 1999	1998	招生数 New Students Enrollment 1999	1998	在校学生数 Students Enrollment 1999	1998
总计	**Total**	**34380**	**33005**	**31004**	**39590**	**106941**	**112954**
工科	Engineering	9784	8839	8685	9526	30019	25537
农科	Agriculture	105	194	100	132	230	299
林科	Forestry	352	213	487	474	1426	1254
医药卫生	Medical Health	889	684	897	1328	3968	4025
财经	Economics and Finance	6090	5514	4469	4980	17053	17443
管理	Administration	13618	13860	11621	18238	40609	51125
政法	Politics and Law	216	94	214	229	615	622
艺术	Art	2285	2573	3332	3489	9655	8992
体育	Physical Culture	254	175	455	359	1026	968
师范	Teacher Training	787	859	744	835	2340	2689

14-11 普通中学、职业中学、小学校舍情况
STATISTICS FOR SCHOOLHOUSES OF REGULAR SECONDARY SCHOOLS, VOCATIONAL SCHOOLS AND PRIMARY SCHOOLS

单位：万平方米　　　　(10000 sq.m)

类别 Item		学校占地面积 Areas of Schools	校舍建筑面积 Floor Space of School-houses	教学及辅助用房 Teaching and Auxiliary Houses	行政办公用房 Administrative Houses	生活福利用房 Houses for Welfare and Life
合计	**Total**	**4064.5**	**1168.3**	**627.6**	**206.9**	**333.9**
城市	Urban	1217.8	640.7	336.5	117.0	187.1
县镇	Towns	1344.6	307.4	160.4	50.0	97.1
农村	Rural	1502.1	220.2	130.7	39.8	49.7
普通中学	**Regular Secondary Schools**	**1830.0**	**567.5**	**274.7**	**102.8**	**190.1**
城市	Urban	634.5	327.2	159.5	59.7	107.9
县镇	Towns	709.6	164.1	74.1	27.6	62.4
农村	Rural	485.9	76.2	41.1	15.4	19.7
职业中学	**Vocational Schools**	**318.7**	**123.7**	**60.8**	**23.3**	**39.6**
城市	Urban	152.3	88.9	44.1	18.9	25.9
县镇	Towns	101.0	24.7	10.9	3.3	10.6
农村	Rural	65.4	10.1	5.8	1.1	3.2
小学	**Primary Schools**	**1915.8**	**477.1**	**292.1**	**80.8**	**104.2**
城市	Urban	431.0	224.6	132.9	38.4	53.3
县镇	Towns	534.0	118.6	75.4	19.1	24.1
农村	Rural	950.8	133.9	83.8	23.3	26.8

14-12 普通中小学专任教师学历
EDUCATIONAL BACK OF FULL-TIME TEACHERS IN PRIMARY AND SECONDARY SCHOOLS

单位：人 (person)

学历	Educational Background	高中 Senior Middle Schools		初中 Junior Middle School		小学 Primary School	
		人数 Number of Persons	构成(%) Composi-tion(%)	人数 Number of Persons	构成(%) Composi-tion(%)	人数 Number of Persons	构成(%) Composi-tion(%)
总计	**Total**	**12023**	**100**	**36142**	**100**	**61121**	**100**
本科毕业及以上	Undergraduate and The Level above	10203	84.9	14671	40.6	1118	1.8
大专毕业	College for Professional Training	1722	14.3	18316	50.7	15626	25.6
中专毕业	Specialized Secondary School	63	0.5	2218	6.1	37422	61.2
高中及以下	Senior Middle School and the Level below	35	0.3	937	2.6	6955	11.4

14-13 平均每万人口在校学生数
AVERAGE NUMBER OF STUDENT ENROLLMENT PER 10000 POPULATION

单位：人 (person)

类别	Item	1999	1998
大学	Colleges	213.6	195.6
中等职业教育	Professional Secondary Schools	274.9	271.7
普通中学	Regular Secondary Schools	579.5	560.0
小学	Primary Schools	763.7	844.3

14-14 平均每一专任教师负担学生数
AVERAGE NUMBER OF STUDENTS INSTRUCTED BY A FULL-TIME TEACHER

单位：人 (person)

类别	Item	1999	1998
大学	Colleges	6.7	5.4
中等职业教育	Professional Secondary Schools	17.5	15.5
普通中学	Regular Secondary Schools	13.2	13.2
小学	Primary Schools	13.7	15.7

14-15 小学学龄儿童入学率
ENROLLMENT RATE OF CHILDREN AT SCHOOL-AGE

单位：人 (person)

项目	Item	校内外学龄人口总数 Number of Children at School-age	#女 Female	在校学龄人口总数 Number of Children at School-age in Schools	#女 Female	入学率(%) Enrollment Rate(%)	#女 Female
合计	**Total**	**791848**	**383214**	**791425**	**382984**	**99.95**	**99.94**
城市	Urban	347819	169241	347796	169232	99.99	100.00
县镇	Towns	204392	98879	204158	98756	99.89	99.88
农村	Rural	239637	115094	239471	114993	99.93	99.91

14-16 中、小学校外教育
AFTER-SCHOOL EDUCATION OF SECONDARY AND PRIMARY SCHOOLS

单位：人 (person)

项目	Item	单位数(个) Number of Units(unit)	活动小组数(个) Activities Groups(unit)	参加小组学生数 Students Join Groups	教职工人数 Staff and Workers	# 辅导员 Counselors	兼职辅导员 Part-time Counselors
总计	**Total**	**1594**	**6628**	**112775**	**2685**	**1946**	**3024**
少年宫	Children's Palace	17	2104	42982	978	526	251
少年科技馆(站)	Children's Scientific Museums (Centers)	9	560	10382	264	158	29
少年之家	Children's Home	37	891	15085	446	265	114
少年活动站	Children's Club	1531	3073	44326	997	997	2630

14-17 幼儿园基本情况
STATISTICS FOR KINDERGARTENS

单位：人 (person)

项目	Item	总计 Total	# 女 Female	城市 Urban	县镇 Towns	农村 Rural
园数 (所)	Number of Kindergartens (unit)	2180		700	420	1060
班数 (个)	Number of Classes (unit)	8708		4489	1670	2549
# 学前班	Preschool Classes	1028		304	253	471
在园幼儿数	Children Enrollment	237055	111691	129416	48089	59550
# 学前班	Preschool Classes	31261	14812	9583	8224	13454
教职工数	Teachers,Staff and Workers	29367	27706	21193	4936	3238
# 园长	Headmaster	2058	2000	1278	414	366
教师	Teachers	13216	13126	9079	2575	1562
保健员	Health Workers	1117	1048	848	167	102

14-18 各类成人教育毕业生、招生、在校学生数
NUMBER OF GRADUATES NEW STUDENTS ENROLLMENT AND STUDENTS ENROLLMENT OF ADULT EDUCATION

单位：人 (person)

类别	Item	校数(教学点)(所) Number of Schools(unit)	毕(结)业生数 Graduates	招生数 New Students Enrollment	在校学生数 Students Enrollment
高等教育	**Higher Education**		**68916**	**88169**	**237787**
广播电视大学	Radio and TV Universities	2	1586	1705	5262
职工高等学校	Schools for Staff and Workers	36	10395	9491	30529
管理干部学院	Management Colleges	28	9105	12443	26467
教育学院	Pedagogical Colleges	1	1634	2630	6641
独立函授学院	Independent Correspondence Colleges	2	865	599	2134
普通高校函授部	Correspondence Department Run by Institutions of Higher Education		25803	33738	96657
普通高校夜大学	Evening Universities Run by Institutions of Higher Education		12836	16988	48766
普通高校成人脱产班	Full Time Adult Class Run by Institutions of Higher Education		6692	10575	21331
中等专业教育	**Specialized Secondary Education**	**106**	**25169**	**16388**	**60919**
广播电视中专	Radio and TV Specialized Secondary Schools	1	7832	5015	15645
职工中专学校	Specialized Secondary Schools for Staff and Workers	61	9064	6480	25539
干部中专学校	Specialized Secondary School for Cadres	8	1035	262	2061
农民中专学校	Specialized Secondary School for Peasants	16	4929	2325	10696
函授中专学校	Specialized Correspondence Secondary Schools	1	1463	1923	5337
教师进修学校	Teacher Training Schools	19	846	383	1641
中等文化教育	**Secondary Education**	**25**	**3650**	**3981**	**5977**
职工中学	Middle Schools for Staff and Workers	24	3564	3859	5617
农民中学	Middle Schools for Peasants	1	86	122	360

14-19 各类成人教育教职工数

NUMBER OF TEACHERS,STAFF AND WORKERS IN ADULT EDUCATION

单位：人 (person)

类别	Item	合计 Total		# 专任教师 Full-time Teachers		# 兼任教师 Part-time Teachers	
		1999	1998	1999	1998	1999	1998
高等教育	**Higher Education**	**16952**	**20645**	**7281**	**8665**	**3873**	**4877**
广播电视大学	Radio and TV Universities	1121	1121	392	363	809	471
职工高等学校	School of Higher Education for Staff and Workers	9793	10020	4510	4558	2442	2336
管理干部学院	Management Colleges	5406	6436	2103	2405	622	292
教育学院	Pedagogical Colleges	530	566	213	231		
独立函授学院	Independent Correspondence Colleges	102	763	63	338		24
普通高校函授部、夜大学	Correspondence Department or Evening Universities Run by Institutions of Higher Education		1739		770		1754
中等专业教育	**Specialized Secondary Education**	**7133**	**7069**	**3277**	**3188**	**1787**	**1922**
广播电视中专	Radio and TV Specialized Secondary Schools	823	823	450	450	746	746
职工中专学校	Specialized Secondary Schools for Staff and Workers	2899	2824	1176	1120	564	675
干部中专学校	Specialized Secondary Schools for Cadres	458	474	146	120	87	96
农民中专学校	Specialized Secondary Schools for Peasants	913	878	432	403	362	384
函授中专学校	Specialized Correspondence Secondary Schools	205	204	98	97	14	14
教师进修学校	Teacher Training Schools	1835	1866	975	998	14	7

14-20 民办学校基本情况
STATISTICS FOR NON-STATE OWNED SCHOOLS

单位：人 (person)

类别	Item		1999	1998
普通中学	**Regular Secondary Schools**			
校　数　(个)	Number of Schools	(unit)	42	65
毕业生数	Number of Graduates		2770	5486
高　中	Senior Middle Schools		1662	1813
招生人数	New Students Enrollment		6479	15419
高　中	Senior Middle Schools		3883	6038
在校学生数	Students Enrollment		17213	30788
高　中	Senior Middle Schools		11622	13005
专任教师数	Full-time Teachers		1379	1790
职业中学	**Vocational Secondary Schools**			
校　数　(个)	Number of Schools	(unit)	14	13
毕业生数	Number of Graduates		462	626
招生人数	New Students Enrollment		985	1241
在校学生数	Students Enrollment		2595	2775
专任教师数	Full-time Teachers		146	137
小　学	**Primary Schools**			
校　数　(个)	Number of Schools	(unit)	3	5
毕业生数	Number of Graduates		658	441
招生人数	New Students Enrollment		534	618
在校学生数	Students Enrollment		4227	4732
专任教师数	Full-time Teachers		581	515

14-21 公 共 图 书 馆
PUBLIC LIBRARIES

项目 Item		总计 Total	中央属 Central	市属 Municipal	区县属 District and County
个数 (个) Number	(unit)	24	1	2	21
从业人员 (人) Employment	(person)	2493	1440	269	784
总藏数 (万册、件) Total Collections	(10000 volumes)	2934	2194	313	427
# 图书 (万册、件) Books	(10000 volumes)	1288	649	241	398
建筑面积 (平方米) Floor Space of Building	(sq.m)	264185	163537	10492	90156
阅览座席 (个) Seats for Reading	(unit)	10133	2600	330	7203
外借人次 (万人次) Person-times of Lending	(10000)	607	298	25	284
外借册次 (万册次) Volume-times Lending	(10000)	371	163	15	193

14-22 艺 术 剧 团
ART TROUPES

项目	Item	个数 (个) Number (unit)	从业人员 (人) Employment (person)	国内演出场次 (场) Domestic Performances	#农村 In Rural Areas	国内观众人数 (万人次) Domestic Spectator (10000 person.time)	总收入 (千元) Total Revenue (1000 yuan)	# 演出收入 from Performances
总计	**Total**	**37**	**6959**	**8564**	**714**	**1275**	**284097**	**70346**
按隶属关系分组	**Grouped by Administrative Relationship**							
中央属	Central	17	4562	2715	412	378	178148	47852
市属	Municipal	11	2037	4633	281	876	98434	20035
区县属	District and County	9	360	1216	21	21	7515	2459
按剧种分	**Grouped by Art Troupes**							
话剧、儿童剧团	Drama,Children's Play	5	965	539		56	46780	7679
歌剧、舞剧、歌舞剧团	Opera,Dance Drama and Song and Dance Troupe	2	640	457	27	24	19480	5991
歌舞团、轻音乐团	Song and Dance Ensembles and Light Music Troupes	5	1336	1211	115	607	61569	25123
乐团	Philharmonic Troupes	4	742	369	81	33	43969	12399
文工团	Cultural Troupes	4	1125	755	367	92	27502	2913
戏曲剧团	Local Opera Troupes	12	1745	3233	124	290	66845	10304
# 京剧团	Local Beijing Opera Troupes	3	1003	1233	25	91	39310	6764
曲、杂、木、皮影剧团	Recitation and Ballad Troupe,Acrobatics and Circus Troupe,Puppet Show Troupe and Shadow Puppet Troupe	5	406	2000		173	17952	5937

14-23 电影摄制情况
STATISTICS FOR FILM PRODUCTION

类别 Item		合计 Total		#长片 Long Film		#短片 Short Film	
		部 Film	本 Reel	部 Film	本 Reel	部 Film	本 Reel
合计	**Total**	**38**	**289**	**26**	**256**	**12**	**33**
故事片	Feature Film	21	208	21	208		
舞台艺术片	Stagecraft Film						
纪录片	Documentary Film	2	18	2	18		
科教片	Popular Science Film	11	24			11	24
译制片	Dubbed Film	3	30	3	30		
美术片	Puppet Film	1	9			1	9

14-24 报纸出版情况
NEWSPAPER PUBLICATION

门类 Item		种数 (种) Number of Publications (kind)	平均期印数 (万份) Average Printed Copies Per Issue (10000)	总印数 (万份) Total Printed Copies (10000)	总印张 (千印张) Total Signature (1000)
总计	**Total**	**247**	**3520**	**716453**	**14465182**
综合报	Comprehensive	50	1536	396775	8210258
专业报	Professional	197	1984	319678	6254924

14-25 杂志出版情况
MAGAZINES PUBLICATION

门类 Item		种数 (种) Number of Publications (kind)	平均期印数 (万册) Average Copies Per Issue (10000)	总印数 (万册) Total Copies (10000)	总印张 (千印张) Total Signatures (1000)
总计	**Total**	**2273**	**6116**	**80428**	**3517893**
综合	Comprehensive	133	1021	12264	496641
哲学、社会科学	Philosophy and Social Sciences	543	2368	36865	1236743
自然科学技术	Natural Sciences and Technology	1243	1631	17828	830715
文化、教育	Culture and Education	197	598	7737	333120
文学、艺术	Literature and Art	107	239	2601	531568
少年儿童读物	Juvenile and Children's Books	15	191	2281	53239
画刊	Pictorial	35	68	852	35867

14-26 图书出版情况
BOOKS PUBLICATION

门类 Item		出版图书种数 合计 (种) umber of Publications (kind)	# 新书 New Publications	总印数 (万册、张) Total Copies (10000)	总印张 (千印张) Total Signatures (1000)
总计	**Total**	**54797**	**35710**	**113352**	**9303096**
书籍合计	**Books**	**54048**	**35312**	**111067**	**9261138**
马列主义、毛泽东思想	Maxism-Leninism-Mao Zedong Thought	56	49	143	12777
哲学	Philosophy	593	445	491	54580
社会科学总论	General Social Sciences	810	703	635	84787
政治、法律	Politics and Law	3794	3025	6132	690863
军事	Military	281	264	282	32608
经济	Economics	4681	3580	4620	660681
文化、科学、教育、体育	Culture,Science,Education and Sports	15182	8136	69059	3721641
语言、文字	Languages	2349	1335	5895	796952
文学	Literature	3013	2392	2887	387023
艺术	Art	1825	1234	1707	138956
历史、地理	History and Geography	1616	1332	2253	213950
自然科学总论	General Natural Sciences	105	70	102	12656
数学科学、化学	Mathematics and Chemistry	1027	463	1649	202744
天文学、物理科学	Astronomy and Physics	452	411	102	12669
生物科学	Biology	286	173	131	22299
医药、卫生	Medicine and Health Care	2950	2002	2563	423354
农业科学	Agricultural Science	1760	1109	1792	133329
工业技术	Industrial Technology	10280	6367	7811	1336004
交通运输	Transportation	980	602	903	106252
航空、航天	Aeronautics and Aerospace	67	66	19	2698
环境科学	Environmental Science	240	192	255	15030
综合性图书	General Books	1701	1362	1636	199285
图片合计	**Pictures**	**749**	**398**	**2285**	**41958**

14-27 电视台情况
BASIC STATISTICS ON TELEVISION STATIONS

项目		Item		1999 中央 Central	1999 地方 Local	1998 中央 Central	1998 地方 Local
基本情况		**Basic Statistics**					
电视台	(座)	Television Stations	(unit)	1	1	1	1
电视发射台、转播台	(座)	Transmission Stations and Relay Stations	(unit)	1	10	1	10
电视差转台	(座)	Transformation Stations	(unit)		62		
节目套数	(套)	Programs	(set)	8	12	8	12
平均每周播出时间 (按12月份第三周计算)	(时：分)	Program Hours Per Week (according to the third week of December)	(hour:minute)	1020:54	828:30	1020:54	774:46
播放节目情况		**Shows of TV Programs**					
自办节目时间	(时：分)	Self-Produced Programs	(hour:minute)	1021:54	716:25	1021:54	673:46
新闻节目	(时：分)	News Programs	(hour:minute)	177:10	81:11	177:10	103:05
专题节目	(时：分)	Special Topic Programs	(hour:minute)	317:59	163:31	317:59	104:46
教育节目	(时：分)	Educational Programs	(hour:minute)	28:45	29:00	28:45	47:14
文艺节目	(时：分)	Entertainment Programs	(hour:minute)	419:45	350:24	419:45	347:14
服务性节目	(时：分)	Service Programs	(hour:minute)	78:15	92:19	78:15	71:27

注：电视台数不包括区县电视台。

Note: Number of television stations excludes those of districts and counties.

14-28 广播电台情况
BASIC STATISTICS ON BROADCASTING STATIONS

项目		Item	1999 中央 Central	1999 地方 Local	1998 中央 Central	1998 地方 Local
基本情况		**Basic Statistics**				
电台	(座)	Broadcasting Stations (unit)	2	1	2	1
发射台、转播台	(座)	Transmission Stations and Relay Stations (unit)	5	10	5	10
节目套数	(套)	Programs (set)	7	16	7	16
平均每日播音时间 (按12月份计算)	(时：分)	Program Hours Per Week (according to December) (hour:minute)	320:00	178:12	320:00	174:40
播放节目情况		**Shows of TV Programs**				
自办节目时间	(时：分)	Self-Produced Programs (hour:minute)	310:15	164:32	310:15	158:08
新闻节目	(时：分)	News Programs (hour:minute)	85:10	12:45	85:10	14
专题节目	(时：分)	Special Topic Programs (hour:minute)	89:05	28:15	89:05	28:15
教育节目	(时：分)	Educational Programs (hour:minute)	26:30	17:15	26:30	19:05
文艺节目	(时：分)	Entertainment Programs (hour:minute)	85:55	83:15	85:55	74:03
服务性节目	(时：分)	Service Programs (hour:minute)	23:35	23:02	23:35	22:45

注：广播电台数不包括区县电台。

Note: Number of broadcasting stations excludes those of districts and counties.

14-29 文化产业活动单位情况
STATISTICS OF CULTURAL INDUSTRIAL UNITS

单位：个 (unit)

行业类别	Sector	合计 Total	按隶属关系分 Grouped by Administrative Relationship 地方属 Local	中央属 Central
合计	**Total**	**3804**	**2758**	**1046**
出版业	Publication	454	55	399
印刷业	Printing	430	353	77
图书报刊批发、零售业	Wholesale and Retail of Books and Newspapers	509	355	154
文化体育用品制造业	Stationery,Educational and Sports Goods Making	307	300	7
文化体育用品零售业	Retail of Stationery,Educational and Sports Goods	545	476	69
艺术业	Arts	86	46	40
文物保护业	Protection of Historical Relics	71	54	17
图书馆、档案馆	Libraries and Archives	41	28	13
群众文化业及其他文化业	Mass Culture and Others	208	178	30
广播电影电视业（含新闻）	Radio,Film and Television (including News)	129	80	49
体育	Sports	81	56	25
娱乐服务业	Recreational Services	170	150	20
摄影及扩印业	Photography and Large-printing	97	86	11
园林业	Parks	157	148	9
广告业	Advertisement	519	393	126

14-30 文化产业活动单位从业人员
EMPLOYMENT OF CULTURAL INDUSTRIAL UNITS

单位：人 (person)

行业类别 Sector		合计 Total	按隶属关系分 Grouped by Administrative Relationship	
			地方属 Local	中央属 Central
合　计	**Total**	**224459**	**126207**	**98252**
出版业	Publication	37748	4000	33748
印刷业	Printing	41079	23415	17664
图书报刊批发、零售业	Wholesale and Retail of Books and Newspapers	11687	7525	4162
文化体育用品制造业	Stationery,Educational and Sports Goods Making	21683	21436	247
文化体育用品零售业	Retail of Stationery,Educational and Sports Goods	7049	6287	762
艺术业	Arts	8428	3303	5125
文物保护业	Protection of Historical Relics	6893	3629	3264
图书馆、档案馆	Libraries and Archives	3841	1474	2367
群众文化业及其他文化业	Mass Culture and Others	8610	4633	3977
广播电影电视业（含新闻）	Radio,Film and Television (including News)	23518	4799	18719
体育	Sports	7718	4736	2982
娱乐服务业	Recreational Services	11902	10614	1288
摄影及扩印业	Photography and Large-printing	3328	2785	543
园林业	Parks	21214	20826	388
广告业	Advertisement	9761	6745	3016

14-31 文化产业活动单位资产情况
ASSETS OF CULTURAL INDUSTRIAL UNITS

单位：万元 (10000 yuan)

行业类别 Sector		合计 Total	按隶属关系分 Grouped by Administrative Relationship	
			地方属 Local	中央属 Central
合　计	**Total**	**5065038**	**2101290**	**2963748**
出版业	Publication	1442475	271996	1170478
印刷业	Printing	427814	195709	232105
图书报刊批发、零售业	Wholesale and Retail of Books and Newspapers	311977	111171	200806
文化体育用品制造业	Stationery,Educational and Sports Goods Making	223234	212557	10678
文化体育用品零售业	Retail of Stationery,Educational and Sports Goods	52172	44733	7439
艺术业	Arts	82638	21898	60740
文物保护业	Protection of Historical Relics	45419	27728	17691
图书馆、档案馆	Libraries and Archives	106652	16325	90327
群众文化业及其他文化业	Mass Culture and Others	88576	75507	13069
广播电影电视业（含新闻）	Radio,Film and Television (including News)	887735	167267	720467
体育	Sports	181059	87304	93755
娱乐服务业	Recreational Services	468986	440854	28132
摄影及扩印业	Photography and Large-printing	25489	15094	10406
园林业	Parks	239818	233071	6748
广告业	Advertisement	480994	180087	300908

14-32 文化产业活动单位创造增加值情况
VALUE ADDED OF CULTURAL INDUSTRIAL UNITS

行业类别	Sector	合计 (万元) Total (10000 yuan)	人均增加值 (元/人) Value Added Per Capita (yuan/person)
合　计	**Total**	**1153636**	**51396**
出版业	Publication	389197	103104
印刷业	Printing	9928	24169
图书报刊批发、零售业	Wholesale and Retail of Books and Newspapers	4329	38895
文化体育用品制造业	Stationery,Educational and Sports Goods Making	38249	17640
文化体育用品零售业	Retail of Stationery,Educational and Sports Goods	1016	15126
艺术业	Arts	21667	25708
文物保护业	Protection of Historical Relics	12946	18781
图书馆、档案馆	Libraries and Archives	15439	40194
群众文化业及其他文化业	Mass Culture and Others	21156	24572
广播电影电视业（含新闻）	Radio,Film and Television (including News)	227246	96627
体育	Sports	26497	34331
娱乐服务业	Recreational Services	69163	58110
摄影及扩印业	Photography and Large-printing	8428	25324
园林业	Parks	67667	31897
广告业	Advertisement	108162	110810

14-33 文化产业活动单位经营收入情况
OPERATING REVENUE OF CULTURAL INDUSTRIAL UNITS

单位：万元　　(10000 yuan)

行业类别	Sector	合计 Total	按隶属关系分 Grouped by Administrative Relationship	
			地方属 Local	中央属 Central
合　计	**Total**	**2900170**	**1026659**	**1873511**
出版业	Publication	965594	134205	831389
印刷业	Printing	212416	119195	93221
图书报刊批发、零售业	Wholesale and Retail of Books and Newspapers	36592	23804	12788
文化体育用品制造业	Stationery,Educational and Sports Goods Making	126865	122013	4852
文化体育用品零售业	Retail of Stationery,Educational and Sports Goods	23652	21286	2365
艺术业	Arts	43610	20464	23146
文物保护业	Protection of Historical Relics	45792	14247	31545
图书馆、档案馆	Libraries and Archives	34219	10155	24064
群众文化业及其他文化业	Mass Culture and Others	37894	20187	17707
广播电影电视业（含新闻）	Radio,Film and Television (including News)	767745	128598	639147
体育	Sports	78063	27079	50984
娱乐服务业	Recreational Services	88005	75262	12743
摄影及扩印业	Photography and Large-printing	21336	17154	4182
园林业	Parks	145034	142430	2603
广告业	Advertisement	273354	150580	122774

14-34 文化产业活动单位人均营业收入情况
BUSINESS REVENUE PER CAPITA OF CULTURAL INDUSTRIAL UNITS

单位：元/人 (yuan/person)

行业类别	Sector	合 计 Total	按隶属关系分 Grouped by Administrative Relationship	
			地方属 Local	中央属 Central
合　计	**Total**	**129207**	**81347**	**190684**
出版业	Publication	255800	335512	246352
印刷业	Printing	51709	50905	52774
图书报刊批发、零售业	Wholesale and Retail of Books and Newspapers	31310	31633	30726
文化体育用品制造业	Stationery,Educational and Sports Goods Making	58509	56920	196437
文化体育用品零售业	Retail of Stationery,Educational and Sports Goods	33553	33858	31039
艺术业	Arts	51744	61956	45162
文物保护业	Protection of Historical Relics	66433	39259	96645
图书馆、档案馆	Libraries and Archives	89089	68896	101663
群众文化业及其他文化业	Mass Culture and Others	44012	43571	44525
广播电影电视业（含新闻）	Radio,Film and Television (including News)	326450	267968	341443
体育	Sports	101145	57177	170974
娱乐服务业	Recreational Services	73941	70908	98939
摄影及扩印业	Photography and Large-printing	64112	61596	77017
园林业	Parks	68367	68391	67095
广告业	Advertisement	280047	223247	407074

主 要 统 计 指 标 解 释

普通高等学校 指按照国家规定的设置标准和审批程序批准举办， 通过国家统一招生考试， 招收高中毕业生为主要培养对象， 实施高等教育的全日制大学、独立设置的学院和高等专科学校、短期职业大学。

成人高等学校 指按照国家有关规定审批， 招收通过全国成人高教统一招生考试的具有高中毕业或同等学历的在职从业人员，利用脱产、半脱产、业余或函授等多种形式对其实施高等学历教育， 培养高等教育专科或本科毕业水平的专门人才， 修业年限、课程设置和总学时数均按高等学历教育要求付诸实施的学校。包括广播电视大学、职工高等学校、农民高等学校、管理干部学院、教育学院、独立设置的函授学院等。

小学学龄儿童入学率 指调查范围内已入小学学习的学龄儿童占校内外学龄儿童总数（包括弱智儿童在内，但不包括聋哑儿童）的比重。计算公式：

$$\text{小学学龄儿童入学率} = \frac{\text{已入学的小学学龄儿童数}}{\text{校内外小学学龄儿童总数}} \times 100\%$$

艺术剧团 指从事戏曲、音乐、舞蹈、杂技等专业艺术表演，有独立帐户、实行独立核算的团体。不包括半工半艺和民间职业剧团。

艺术表演观众人数（人次） 指售票、包场演出或民族地区免费演出的艺术表演观众人次数。不包括彩排审查和内部观摩演出的观众人次数。

Explanatory Notes On Main Statistical Indicators

Regular Institutions of Higher Education refer to full-time universities, colleges, high professional schools and short-term professional universities set up according to the government standards and approval procedures, enrolling graduates from senior secondary schools through nation-wide unified examination and providing higher education courses and training.

Institutions of Higher Education for Adults refer to Radio and TV universities, staff colleges, peasants colleges, colleges for management cadres, educational colleges and independent correspondence colleges set up in line with relevant government policies, enrolling staff and workers with senior secondary school or equivalent education, and providing higher education courses in various forms of full-time, part-time, spare-time, or correspondence for adults. There are government regulations on various aspects for institutions of higher education for adults, such as the courses and total learning hours.

Enrollment Rate of School-Age Children refers to the proportion of primary school-age children enrolled at primary schools to the total number of primary school-age children both in and outside primary schools （including retarded children, but excluding blind, deaf and mute children）. The formula is:

$$\text{Enrollment Rate of School - age Children} = \frac{\text{Total school - age children in schools}}{\text{Total school - age children in and outside schools}} \times 100\%$$

Art Troupe refers to the troupe which is engaged in drama, opera, music, dance, acrobatics or other art performance, opens independent accounts in banks and has independent accounting system; excluding the troupes which are engaged partly in industrial or agricultural activities, partly in art performance or the non-governmental troupes.

Number of Spectators at Art Performance refers to the number of attendants at commercial shows, completely booked shows or free shows given in minority national areas, and does not include the number of spectators at rehearsals and internal shows.

科 技
SCIENCE AND TECHNOLOGY

1999年专利申请及授权情况(项)
Patent Applications Examined and Certified(item 1999)

外观设计
Designs
1616 1308
实用新型
Utilities Models
4045 3948
发明
Creations and Inventions
2055 573
□ 申请量
■ 批准量

每万从业人员拥有专业技术人员(人)
Number of Scientific and Technical Personnel per 10000 Employment (person)

		1999	1998
全 市	Total	3149	2982
中 央	Central	4237	3813
地 方	Local	2756	2616

市属国有企事业单位专业技术人员（人）
Number of Scientific and Technical Personnel in Local State-owend Enterprises and Institutions (person)

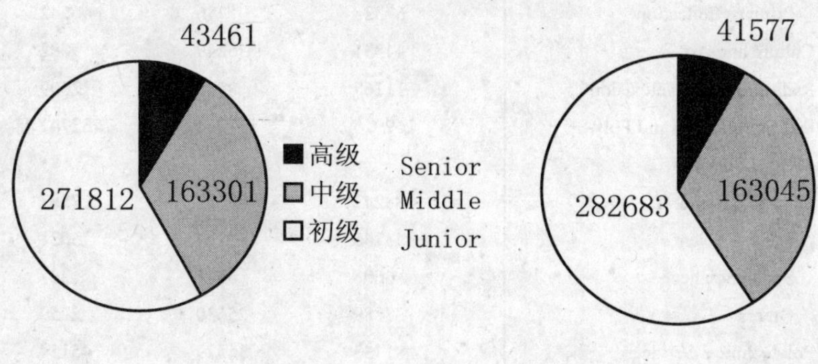

1999年

1998年

15-1 国民经济各行业专业技术人员
NUMBER OF PROFESSIONAL TECHNICAL PERSONNEL BY SECTORS OF NATIONAL ECONOMY

单位：人 (person)

项目	Item	1999 全市 Total	1999 中央 Central	1999 地方 Local	1998 全市 Total
合计	**Total**	**1361168**	**532533**	**828635**	**1321559**
农、林、牧、渔业	Farming,Forestry,Animals Husbandry and Fishery	8202	723	7479	8337
采掘业	Excavation	4114	147	3967	3232
制造业	Manufacturing	219042	46243	172799	224448
电力、煤气及水的生产和供应业	Electricity,Gas and Water Production and Supply	10713	4671	6042	8797
建筑业	Construction	112203	31714	80489	111948
地质勘查业、水利管理业	Geological Prospecting and Water Conservancy	5173	2893	2280	5608
交通运输、仓储及邮电通讯业	Transportation,Storage,Posts and Telecommunications	37026	28600	8426	37054
批发和零售贸易、餐饮业	Wholesale,Retail and Catering	111092	32919	78173	108146
金融、保险业	Banking and Insurance	58910	54845	4065	49347
房地产业	Real Estate	24466	4087	20379	21630
社会服务业	Social Services	120629	33548	87081	112580
卫生、体育和社会福利业	Health Care,Sports and Social Welfare	94995	28713	66282	92451
卫生	Health Care	92296	28266	64030	89959
体育	Sports	1449	406	1043	1362
社会福利保障业	Social Welfare	1250	41	1209	1130
教育、文化艺术和广播电影电视业	Education,Culture and Arts and Radio,Film and Television	291663	102158	189505	287586
教育	Education	236165	58351	177814	233776
高等教育	Higher Education	69979	51948	18031	67032
中等教育	Secondary Education	84557	2663	81894	84227
初等教育	Primary Education	67328	786	66542	68524
文化艺术	Culture and Art	44331	35249	9082	42379
广播电影电视	Radio,Film and Television	11167	8558	2609	11431
科学研究和综合技术服务业	Scientific Research and Polytechnical Services	169975	117234	52741	167807
科学研究	Scientific Research	88242	80655	7587	86837
自然科学研究	Natural Science	53745	48724	5021	56318
社会科学研究	Social Science	6608	6301	307	5788
其他科学研究	Others	27889	25630	2259	24731
综合技术服务	Polytechnical Services	81733	36579	45154	80970
国家机关、政党机关和社会团体	Government Organs,Party Organs and Social Bodies	68041	29324	38717	63544
其他行业	Others	24924	14714	10210	19044

15-2 国民经济各行业每万从业人员拥有专业技术人员
NUMBER OF SCIENTIFIC AND TECHNICAL PERSONNEL PER 10000 EMPLOYMENT BY SECTORS OF NATIONAL ECONOMY

单位：人 (person)

项目	Item	1999 全市 Total	1999 中央 Central	1999 地方 Local	1998 全市 Total
合计	**Total**	**3149**	**4237**	**2756**	**2982**
农、林、牧、渔业	Farming,Forestry,Animals Husbandry and Fishery	2633	4620	2527	2406
采掘业	Excavation	1428	9484	1384	965
制造业	Manufacturing	2142	2750	2014	2083
电力、煤气及水的生产和供应业	Electricity,Gas and Water Production and Supply	2554	3651	2073	2093
建筑业	Construction	2243	2412	2365	2038
地质勘查业、水利管理业	Geological Prospecting and Water Conservancy	3116	5382	2031	3351
交通运输、仓储及邮电通讯业	Transportation,Storage,Posts and Telecommunications	1898	2130	1296	1831
批发和零售贸易、餐饮业	Wholesale,Retail and Catering	2144	4708	1589	2069
金融、保险业	Banking and Insurance	7978	8070	7375	6720
房地产业	Real Estate	2344	2284	2329	2306
社会服务业	Social Services	2107	2980	1620	2075
卫生、体育和社会福利业	Health Care,Sports and Social Welfare	7024	7055	7073	6723
卫生	Health Care	7526	7474	7609	7210
体育	Sports	1813	1498	1990	1632
社会福利保障业	Social Welfare	2705	2398	2754	2571
教育、文化艺术和广播电影电视业	Education,Culture and Arts and Radio,Film and Television	6854	6192	7382	6666
教育	Education	7099	5999	7640	6898
高等教育	Higher Education	6090	6042	6239	5646
中等教育	Secondary Education	7579	6541	7645	7592
初等教育	Primary Education	8862	8851	8880	8689
文化艺术	Culture and Art	6054	6567	4649	5797
广播电影电视	Radio,Film and Television	5682	6101	4693	5883
科学研究和综合技术服务业	Scientific Research and Polytechnical Services	5908	6664	4629	5529
科学研究	Scientific Research	6456	6535	5677	6184
自然科学研究	Natural Science	6417	6509	5635	6134
社会科学研究	Social Science	7281	7322	6518	7142
其他科学研究	Others	6362	6416	5669	6105
综合技术服务	Polytechnical Services	5412	6967	4466	4966
国家机关、政党机关和社会团体	Government Organs,Party Organs and Social Bodies	2262	2375	2181	2053
其他行业	Others	3632	4971	2917	3119

15-3 市属国有企事业单位专业技术人员

NUMBER OF SCIENTIFIC AND TECHNICAL PERSONNEL IN LOCAL STATE-OWNED ENTERPRISES AND INSTITUTIONS

单位：人 (person)

项　目	Item	总　计 Total	# 高 级 Senior	# 中 级 Middle	# 初 级 Junior
总　　计	**Total**	**515699**	**43461**	**163301**	**271812**
工程技术人员	Engineering	120100	11380	37876	62203
农业技术人员	Agriculture	5267	258	1488	3210
科研实验人员	Scientific Research and Experimentation	3560	1087	1661	524
卫生技术人员	Health Care	68581	5419	17972	42946
教学人员	Teaching	165847	19999	66820	66886
高等教育	Higher Education	10160	3879	4257	1610
中　　专	Specialized Secondary Schools	10571	1965	3924	3399
中　　学	Secondary Schools	71709	14155	24996	25798
小　　学	Primary Schools	73407		33643	36079
民航人员	Aviation	8	1	4	3
船舶人员	Ship	3			2
经济人员	Economy	54887	1412	11581	35132
会计人员	Accountant	46320	645	6566	35204
统计人员	Statistician	8908	85	1891	6439
翻译人员	Translator	1348	65	662	543
图书档案人员	Librarian and Archvist	6281	266	2264	3388
新闻出版人员	News Publisher	3378	535	1336	1148
律师公证人员	Law and Notarization	323	15	102	132
播音人员	Broadcasting	183	14	49	93
工艺美术人员	Industrial Art	742	44	194	482
体育人员	Sports	872	151	338	324
艺术人员	Art	2423	477	1269	589
政工人员	Political Staff	26668	1608	11228	12564

15-4 科学研究机构及人员
SCIENTIFIC RESEARCH INSTITUTIONS AND PERSONNEL

项目	Item	机构（个）Institution (unit)	职工人数（人）Staff and Workers (person)	从事科技活动人员（人）Personnel Engaged in Scientific and Technological Activity (person)	# 大学毕业以上及具有高中级职称人员 Personnel at or above Undergraduate Level and Having Senior or Middle Title
合　计	**Total**	**432**	**121152**	**74800**	**54841**
自然科学	**Natural Science**	**338**	**108443**	**65555**	**47205**
中　央	Central	233	87565	56225	41004
地　方	Local	105	20878	9330	6201
在自然科学研究机构中:	**Of Natural Scientific Research Institutions**				
农、林、牧、渔业	Farming,Forestry,Animals Husbandry and Fishery	25	4232	3081	2229
采掘业	Excavation	4	4777	2624	2065
制造业	Manufacturing	95	38750	21245	13552
电力、煤气及水的生产和供应业	Electricity,Gas and Water Production and Supply	3	1524	1095	787
建筑业	Construction	13	4908	3224	2515
地质勘查业、水利管理业	Geological Prospecting and Water Conservancy	12	2595	1893	1598
交通运输、仓储及邮电通信业	Transportation,Stock,Posts and Telecommunications	17	5661	3735	2831
房地产业	Real Estate	1	101	70	46
社会服务业	Social Services	15	2183	1187	973
卫生、体育和社会福利业	Health Care,Sports and Social Welfare	43	16141	8046	5284
教育、文化艺术及广播电影电视业	Education,Culture,Art and Radio,Film and Television	8	618	445	321
科学研究和综合技术服务业	Scientific Research and Polytechnical Services	92	25811	18033	14330
国家机关、政党机关和社会团体	Government Organs,Party Organs and Social Bodies	7	595	478	394
其他行业	Others	3	547	399	280
社会科学	**Social Science**	**62**	**5120**	**4389**	**3906**
中　央	Central	58	4458	3904	3495
地　方	Local	4	662	485	411
在社会科学研究机构中:	**Of Social Scientific Research Institutions**				
管理学	Administration	2	152	134	110
马克思主义	Marxism	2	72	68	64
哲　学	Philosophy	1	143	131	125
宗教学	Religion	1	81	77	69
语言学	Language	1	87	78	73
文学	Literature	3	282	256	240
艺术学	Art	1	571	451	393
历史学	History	4	396	361	331
考古学	Archeology	2	185	159	143
经济学	Economics	24	1472	1282	1138
政治学	Politics	3	123	110	97
法　学	Law	3	191	165	143
社会学	Sociology	8	403	352	321
民族学	Ethnology	1	154	149	124
新闻学与传播学	News and Propagation	2	101	67	59
教育学	Education	3	669	513	445
统计学	Statistics	1	38	36	31
情报科学	**Intelligence Science**	**32**	**7589**	**4856**	**3730**

15-5 大中型工业企业技术开发机构和人员情况
INSTITUTIONS AND PERSONNEL OF TECHNOLOGICAL DEVELOPMENT IN LARGE AND MEDIUM INDUSTRIAL ENTERPRISES

项目	Item	企业数(个) Enterprises (unit)	技术开发机构数(个) Technological Development Institutions (unit)	企业从事技术开发人员(人) Personnel Engaged in Technological Development(person)	# 科学家和工程师 Scientist and Engineer
合计	**Total**	**472**	**277**	**38259**	**22225**
采掘业	**Excavation**	**4**	**3**	**716**	**307**
制造业	**Manufaturing**	**456**	**266**	**37111**	**21590**
食品加工业	Food Processing	12	4	78	30
食品制造业	Food Making	11	3	229	74
饮料制造业	Beverage Production	13	7	637	452
烟草加工业	Tobacco Processing	1	1	26	9
纺织业	Textile Industry	13	9	685	283
服装及其他纤维制品制造业	Garments and Other Fiber Products	12	3	107	21
皮革、毛皮、羽绒及其制品业	Leather,Furs,Down and Related Products	4	2	51	17
木材加工及竹、藤棕、草制品业	Timber Processing,Bamboo, Cane,Palm Fiber and Straw Products	2			
家具制造业	Furniture Industry	2	1	52	37
造纸及纸制品业	Papermaking and Paper Products	6		510	242
印刷业、记录媒介的复制	Printing and Record Pressing	49	5	194	78
文教体育用品制造业	Stationery,Educational and Sports Goods	5	3	206	83
石油加工及炼焦业	Petroleum Processing and Coking Products	2	2	2807	1202
化学原料及化学制品制造业	Raw Chemical Materials and Chemical Products	26	18	2582	954
医药制造业	Medical and Pharmaceutical Products	20	11	549	218
化学纤维制造业	Chemical Fibers	1	1	17	17
橡胶制品业	Rubber Products	8	5	322	114
塑料制品业	Plastic Products	12	6	507	247
非金属矿物制品业	Nonmetal Mineral Products	33	16	2026	889
黑色金属冶炼及压延加工业	Smelting and Pressing of Ferrous Metals	4	2	2031	1595
有色金属冶炼及压延压延加工业	Smelting and Pressing of Nonferrous Metals	4	3	115	74
金属制品业	Metal Products	13	7	187	111
普通机械制造业	Ordinary Machinery	30	24	3540	1985
专用设备制造业	Special Purposes Equipment	29	21	2885	2047
交通运输设备制造业	Transportation Equipment	39	30	3946	1928
武器弹药制造业	Weapon and Ammunition	6	6	777	443
电气机械及器材制造业	Electric Equipment and Machinery	24	17	2059	1397
电子及通迅设备制造业	Electronic and Telecommunications	42	34	8097	5797
仪器仪表及文化、办公用机械制造业	Instrument,Meters,Cultural and Official Machinery	26	22	1834	1236
其他制造业	Other Manufacturing	7	3	55	10
电力、煤气及水的生产和供应业	**Electricity,Gas and Water Production and Supply**	**12**	**8**	**432**	**328**
电力、蒸汽、热水的生产和供应业	Electricity,Steam and Hot Water Production and Supply	9	6	347	243
煤气生产和供应业	Gas Production and Supply	2	1	25	25
自来水的生产和供应业	Tap Water Production and Supply	1	1	60	60

15-6 大中型工业企业技术开发经费情况
FUND RAISING FOR TECHNOLOGICAL DEVELOPMENT IN LARGE AND MEDIUM INDUSTRIAL ENTERPRISES

单位：万元 (10000 yuan)

项目	Item	技术开发经费筹集 Funds of Technological Development	# 企业自筹 Self-raising	技术开发经费支出 Expenses of Technological Development	# 用于开发新产品 New Products Development
合计	Total	**270483**	**219540**	**254545**	**150245**
采掘业	**Excavation**	**1561**	**1561**	**1107**	**350**
制造业	**Manufaturing**	**267832**	**216889**	**251104**	**149831**
食品加工业	Food Processing	88	88	87	1
食品制造业	Food Making	385	365	171	66
饮料制造业	Beverage Production	4595	4106	4481	136
烟草加工业	Tobacco Processing	154	154	154	138
纺织业	Textile Industry	3233	3182	3343	780
服装及其他纤维制品制造业	Garments and Other Fiber Products	113	113	167	109
皮革、毛皮、羽绒及其制品业	Leather,Furs,Down and Related Products	39	39	46	17
木材加工及竹、藤棕、草制品业	Timber Processing,Bamboo, Cane,Palm Fiber and Straw Products				
家具制造业	Furniture Industry	117	117	117	
造纸及纸制品业	Papermaking and Paper Products			29	
印刷业、记录媒介的复制	Printing and Record Pressing	752	634	843	4
文教体育用品制造业	Stationery,Educational and Sports Goods	667	602	703	368
石油加工及炼焦业	Petroleum Processing and Coking Products	17076	8700	15427	1206
化学原料及化学制品制造业	Raw Chemical Materials and Chemical Products	10412	9270	10435	2831
医药制造业	Medical and Pharmaceutical Products	4371	3037	3376	515
化学纤维制造业	Chemical Fibers	10	10	10	5
橡胶制品业	Rubber Products	651	626	651	435
塑料制品业	Plastic Products	1467	1040	1485	921
非金属矿物制品业	Nonmetal Mineral Products	6900	5154	7465	3872
黑色金属冶炼及压延加工业	Smelting and Pressing of Ferrous Metals	11799	11114	11685	1817
有色金属冶炼及压延加工业	Smelting and Pressing of Nonferrous Metals	1848	1218	1514	1252
金属制品业	Metal Products	715	705	753	473
普通机械制造业	Ordinary Machinery	4981	4521	4363	3221
专用设备制造业	Special Purposes Equipment	10706	7196	9901	3122
交通运输设备制造业	Transportation Equipment	10886	7963	9422	5408
武器弹药制造业	Weapon and Ammunition	2252	979	1921	1475
电气机械及器材制造业	Electric Equipment and Machinery	11948	6797	9878	5129
电子及通迅设备制造业	Electronic and Telecommunications	150926	135837	143224	108915
仪器仪表及文化、办公用机械制造业	Instrument,Meters,Cultural and Official Machinery	10646	3235	9328	7490
其他制造业	Other Manufacturing	95	87	125	125
电力、煤气及水的生产和供应业	**Electricity,Gas and Water Production and Supply**	**1090**	**1090**	**2334**	**64**
电力、蒸汽、热水的生产和供应业	Electricity,Steam and Hot Water Production and Supply	643	643	2163	64
煤气生产和供应业	Gas Production and Supply	116	116	125	
自来水的生产和供应业	Tap Water Production and Supply	331	331	46	

15-7 技术合同签定及执行情况
CONCLUSION AND IMPLEMENTATION OF TECHNICAL CONTRACTS

项目	Item	签定合同数(项) Contracts Concluded (item)		合同金额(万元) Amount of Contracts (10000 yuan)	
		1999	1998	1999	1998
合计	**Total**	**20711**	**20724**	**921889.4**	**815591.2**
按合同类别分类	**Grouped by Type**				
技术开发合同	Technological Development	3750	3609	386291.1	250149.9
技术转让合同	Technology Transfer	4469	3753	129643.8	158530.5
技术咨询合同	Technical Consultation	1931	1850	34721.4	36335.7
技术服务合同	Technical Service	10561	11512	371233.1	370575.1
按合同卖方类别分类	**Grouped by Type of Seller**				
科研机构	Scientific Research Institutions	11865	12647	363760.8	416830.4
高等院校	Institutions of Higher Education	1227	1911	31924.9	49872.7
工业企业	Industrial Enterprises	1265	337	124774.6	46862.1
技术贸易机构	Technology Trade Institutions	1897	1839	37012.1	48734.1
个人及个人合伙	Individual and Individual Partnership	48	88	2703.9	2530.1
其他	Others	4409	3902	361713.1	250761.8
按合同买方类别分类	**Grouped by Type of Buyer**				
工业企业	Industrial Enterprises	12360	11067	620899.5	463984.4
科研机构	Scientific Research Institutions	4132	2533	70671.9	92689.7
各级管理部门	Management Departments	1796	1452	127165.0	86538.7
技术贸易机构	Technology Trade Institutions	860	1137	53018.4	58441.8
个人及个人合伙	Individual and Individual Partnership	246	734	1387.8	1380.9
其他	Others	1317	3801	48746.8	112555.7
按服务社会经济目标分类	**Grouped by Social and Economic Service Objection**				
陆地、海洋和大气的开发与估价	Development and Appraisal of Lands,Seas and Atmosphere	65	62	2399.2	9012.0
民用宇宙空间	Civil Universal Space	337	278	18600.7	7694.1
农业、林业和渔业的发展	Development of Agriculture, Forestry and Fishery	225	694	12726.5	27070.8
促进工业的发展	Promoting Industrial Development	4199	6607	192502.4	235423.7
能源的生产、储存和分配	Production,Stockpile and Distribution of Energy	1479	1566	77254.4	68960.5
交通、通讯事业的发展	Development of Transportation and Telecommunication	2401	2131	163804.8	123677.3
教育事业的发展	Development of Education	132	102	7549.8	8236.1
卫生事业的发展	Development of Health Care	916	957	22718.9	21279.1
社会发展和社会经济服务	Social Development and Economic Service	6132	5493	246500.4	179582.6
环境保护	Environmental Protextion	1091	846	23369.7	10010.6
知识的全面发展	All-round Development of Knowledge	110	85	2736.6	4258.5
其他目标	Others	3427	1689	128539.3	86485.2
国防	National Defence	197	214	23186.7	33900.7
按技术流向分类	**Grouped by Spread Area**				
北京	Beijing	8963	8684	426543.5	338420.6
外地	Outside Beijing	11748	12040	495345.9	477170.6

15-8 科学技术协会及所属学会工作情况
BASIC STATISTICS OF SCIENCE AND TECHNOLOGY ASSOCIATION AND SUBORDINATE INSTITUTES

项 目	Item	合 计 Total	市 科 协 Municipal Science and Technology Association	市级学会 Institutes at Municipal Level
机构与人员	**Institutions and Personnel**	□	□	□
机 构 (个)	Institutions (unit)	146	1	145
人 员 (人)	Personnel (person)	242749	56	242693
学术交流	**Academic Exchange**			
国内学术会议 (次)	Domestic Academic Meeting (time)	470	3	467
参加人数 (人次)	Participants (person.time)	33839	230	33609
交流论文 (篇)	Papers Presented (article)	6927	96	6831
国际学术会议 (次)	International Academic Meeting (time)	51		51
参加人数 (人次)	Participants (person.time)	12158		12158
交流论文 (篇)	Papers Presented (article)	646		646
民间科技交流	**Non-governmental Scientific and Technological Exchange**			
出国科学考察 (人次)	Scientific Visit abroad (person.time)	293	187	106
出国参加国际会议 (人次)	Scientific Meeting abroad (person.time)	105		105
出国参加技贸活动 (人次)	Technology Trade abroad (person.time)	26		26
外派科技研修生 (人次)	Study abroad (person) (person.time)	22	19	3
接待海外科技团组 (个)	Foreign Scientic and Technology Visit (unit)	86	14	72
接待人次 (人次)	Participants (person.time)	788	89	699
举办国际学术报告 (场)	International Academic Meeting (unit)	47		47
听报告人次 (人次)	Participants (person.time)	3876		3876
科学普及	**Scientific Promoting**			
科普讲座 (次)	Lectures (time)	420	74	346
参加人次 (人次)	Participants (person.time)	159149	11550	147599
科普展览 (次)	Exhibitions (time)	79	23	56
参观人次 (人次)	Participants (person.time)	844370	428000	416370
科技培训	**Training Program**			
培训班数 (个)	Classes (time)	463	131	332
培训人数 (人次)	Participants (person.time)	41752	14612	27140
科技咨询服务	**Consultative Services**			
完成咨询合同 (项)	Contracts Completed (item)	885	761	124
咨询合同实现金额 (万元)	Contracts Revenue (10000 yuan)	44800	44505	295
无偿咨询项目 (项)	Free Consultative Project (item)	1390	10	1380
决策合同 (项)	Contracts of Concluded (item)	56	1	55
青少年科技活动	**Activity of Teenagers Science-Technology**			
科技夏(冬)令营 (个)	Summer/Winter Science and Technology Camp (time)	26	7	19
参加人数 (人次)	Participants (person.time)	8674	2250	6424
青少年科技竞赛 (个)	Science and Technology Competetions (unit)	54	18	36
参加人数 (人次)	Participants (person.time)	378146	120200	257946

15-9 专 利 申 请 及 授 权 情 况
PATENT APPLICATIONS EXAMINED AND CERTIFIED

单位：项 (item)

项 目 Item		申请量 Total Applications Examined		批准量 Total Applications Certified	
		1999	1998	1999	1998
合 计	**Total**	**7716**	**6321**	**5829**	**3800**
按种类分	**Grouped by Type**				
发 明	Creations and Inventions	2055	1754	573	309
实用新型	Utility Models	4045	3444	3948	2522
外观设计	Designs	1616	1123	1308	969
按对象分	**Grouped by Applicator**				
工矿企业	Industrial and Mineral Enterprises	1850	1252	1339	749
大专院校	Universities and Colleges	288	263	227	141
科研单位	Scientific Research Institution	726	547	549	373
机关团体	Government Organs and Associations	39	31	82	80
个 人	Individuals	4813	4228	3632	2457

15-10 计量器具检定情况
STATISTICS FOR MEASURING IMPLEMENTS TEST

单位：台、件、套 (unit)

地区 Region		合计 Total	长度 Length	温度 Temperature	力学 Mechanics	#衡器 Weighing Apparatus	电学 Electricity	光学 Optics	声学 Acoustics	化学 Chemistry	电离辐射 Ionization Radiation	无线电 Radio	时间频率 Time Frequency	其他 Other
总计	**Total**	**675258**	**114098**	**25830**	**408862**	**85445**	**56071**	**2418**	**252**	**38181**	**1001**	**2003**	**886**	**60019**
市属小计	**Municipal**	**185712**	**27203**	**2390**	**144374**	**662**	**4042**	**1354**	**200**	**3044**	**1001**	**1218**	**886**	
区县属小计	**District and County**	**489546**	**86895**	**23440**	**264488**	**84783**	**52029**	**1064**	**52**	**774**		**785**		**60019**
东城区	Dongcheng	41772	20678	59	20209	4884	826							
西城区	Xicheng	50354	24494	407	22464	5158	2172			200		617		
崇文区	Chongwen	33523	2823	396	11857	1361	1273			61		106		
宣武区	Xuanwu	16516	8227	10368	12046	3423	2882							
朝阳区	Chaoyang	80086	6659	2636	32994	12281	6462							31335
丰台区	Fengtai	22422	2287	1026	19109	3786								
石景山区	Shijingshan	11941	1174	1673	7838	908	271	932		53				
海淀区	Haidian	22867	300		20994	13463	768	12		287		38		468
门头沟区	Mentougou	7719	802		6743	811	71							103
房山区	Fangshan	58041	4034	1506	17492	7607	23672							11337
通州区	Tongzhou	36617	4819	2393	23028	11149	6175							202
昌平区	Changping	24082	15	102	13657	3155				133				10175
顺义区	Shunyi	23765	5155	1464	9313	1920	2033							5800
大兴县	Daxing	14693	920	428	12980	2086	79	66						220
平谷县	Pinggu	9925	1028	450	7999	4624	330	26	52	40				
怀柔县	Huairou	11977	613		10300	3682	739	28						297
密云县	Miyun	13002	2196	406	10318	3299								82
延庆县	Yanqing	10244	671	126	5147	1186	4276					24		

15-11 高新技术产业情况
STATISTICS ON HIGH-GRADE TECHNOLOGICAL INDUSTRY

单位：亿元 (100 million yuan)

项目	Item	工业总产值(现价) Gross Output Value of Industry (at constant prices)		1999年为1998年% 1999 as % of 1998
		1999	1998	
合　计	**Total**	**610.8**	**538.1**	**113.5**
按登记注册类型分	**Grouped by Registered Type**			
国有企业	State-owned	219.1	192.2	113.9
集体企业	Collective-owned	26.8	22.3	120.2
中外合资、合作企业	Chinese-foreign Joint Venture and Cooperative	339.7	305.2	111.3
股份制企业	Share Holding	25.2	18.4	136.9
按行业类别分	**Grouped by Sectors**			
医药制造业	Medicine and Pharmaceutical Products	31.1	29.5	105.4
专用设备制造业	Special Purpose Equipment	7.8	6.9	113
交通运输设备制造业	Transportation Equipment	21.6	17.3	124.9
电气机械及器材制造业	Electric Equipment and Machine	24.2	22.4	108
电子及通讯设备制造业	Electronic and Telecommunication	437.2	380.5	114.9
仪器仪表制造业	Instruments and Meters	28.1	25.9	108.5
其　他	Others	60.8	55.6	109.4
按技术领域分	**Grouped by the Field of Technology**			
电子与信息	Electron and Information	433.9	364.0	119.2
生物及医药制品	Biological and Pharmaceutical Products	57.5	63.0	91.3
新材料	New Materials	25	23.2	107.8
光机电一体化	Organic Whole of Light, Machine	77.1	72.8	105.9
	and Electricity	2.0	1.4	142.8
新能源	New Energy			
环保设备	Equipment for Environmental Protection	1.7	1.6	106.2
航空航天及地球空间技术	Technology on Aerospace and Earth Space	13.6	12.1	112.4

主 要 统 计 指 标 解 释

专业技术人员 指已取得专业技术职称，或大学、中专毕业，以及从工作实践中提拔，从事研究、教学、生产的专业人员和在机关、企业、事业中从事管理工作的专业人员。

工程技术人员 指从事工程技术工作的专业技术人员，包括：高级工程师、工程师、助理工程师、技术员和未评定职称的技术人员。

农业技术人员 指从事农业技术工作的专业技术人员，包括：高级农艺师、农艺师、助理农艺师、技术员和未评定职称的技术人员。

发明 指专利法及其实施细则所称的发明，指对有关产品、方法或其改进所提出的新的技术方案。

实用新型 指专利法及其实施细则所称的实用新型，指对产品的形状、构造或者其结合所提出的适于实用的新的技术方案。

外观设计 指专利法及其实施细则所称的外观设计，指对产品的形状、图案、色彩或者其结合所作出的富有美感并适于工业上应用的新设计。

Explanatory Notes On Main Statistical Indicators

Professional and Technical Personnel refers to those professionals with technical titles, or those being graduated from colleges and specialized secondary schools, or those being promoted in practice and working on research, teaching and production , or the professionals doing administrative work in government agencies, enterprises and institutions.

Engineering Professionals refer to the persons who are engaged in engineering science and technology, including senior engineers, engineers, assistant engineers, technicians and technical personnel without professional titles.

Agricultural Professionals refer to the persons who are working on the science of agriculture, including senior agronomists, agronomists, assistant agronomists, technicians and technical personnel without professional titles.

Inventions refer to the inventions as specified by the patent law and its detailed rules and regulations for implementation, including the new technical proposals or modifications for products or the methods.

Utility Models refer to the utility models as specified by the patent law and its detailed rules and regulations for implementation, including the practical and new technical proposals on the shape and structure of the product or the combination of both .

External Form Design refer to the external form design specified by the patent law and its detailed rules and regulations for implementation, including the practical and new technical proposals on the structure, shape and color of the product or the combination of them.

[illegible]

[illegible]

Explanatory Notes on Main Statistical Indicators

Professional and Technical Personnel refer to those professional or technical titles, or those having graduated from colleges and technical secondary schools, or those [illegible] [illegible] [illegible] [illegible] production [illegible] [illegible] [illegible] [illegible] [illegible]

Engineering Professionals are persons who are engaged in engineering, [illegible] technology, [illegible] [illegible] [illegible] [illegible] [illegible] [illegible] technicians, and [illegible] [illegible]

Agricultural Professionals refer to persons who are taking [illegible] [illegible] [illegible] [illegible] [illegible] [illegible] [illegible] [illegible] [illegible] [illegible]

Development [illegible] [illegible] [illegible] [illegible] [illegible] [illegible] [illegible] [illegible] [illegible] [illegible]

Utility Models refer to [illegible] [illegible] [illegible] [illegible] [illegible] [illegible] [illegible] [illegible] [illegible] [illegible] [illegible] [illegible] [illegible] [illegible]

External Design [illegible] [illegible] [illegible] [illegible] [illegible] [illegible] [illegible] [illegible] [illegible] [illegible] [illegible] [illegible] [illegible] [illegible] [illegible] [illegible] [illegible]

卫生、体育
HEALTH AND SPORTS

卫　　生　Health

	1999年	1998年
卫生事业机构（个） Health Care Institutions(unit)	5990	5723
床位（张） Beds(unit)	69465	69095
卫生技术人员（人） Medical Technivcal Personnel(person)	116597	115976
平均每千人拥有医生（人） Doctors per 1000 persons(person)	4.79	4.76

体　育　Sports

1999年

运动员获奖牌情况（块）

Statistics on Medals Won(piece)

金牌	银牌	铜牌
83	41	41

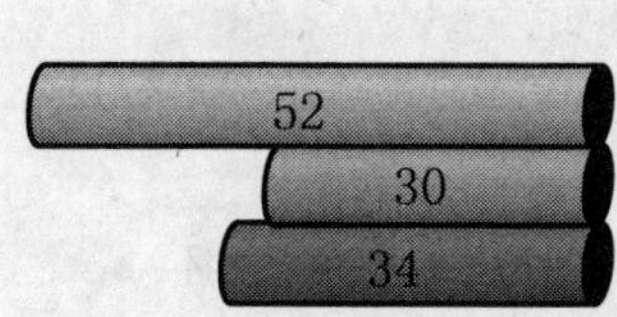

金牌 Gold Medal
银牌 Silver Medal
铜牌 Bronze Medal

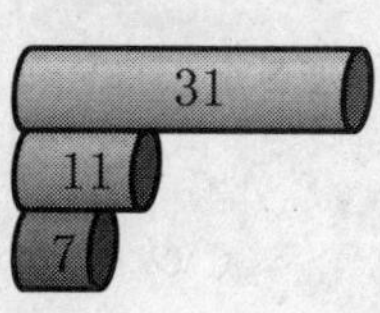

国内比赛 Domestic Competitions　　国际比赛 International Competitions

16-1 医疗卫生机构基本情况
BASIC STATISTICS FOR INSTITUTIONS OF PUBLIC HEALTH

项　目		Item		1999	1998	构　成(%) Composition(%)	
						1999	1998
卫生事业机构	(个)	**Health Care Institutions**	**(unit)**	**5990**	**5723**	**100**	**100**
# 医　院	(个)	Hospitals	(unit)	460	449	7.7	7.8
门诊部	(个)	Clinics	(unit)	210	194	3.5	3.4
诊所、卫生保健所、医务室	(个)	Clinics and Health Stations	(unit)	4859	4613	81.1	80.6
疗养院	(个)	Sanatoriums	(unit)	5	7	0.1	0.1
卫生防疫站	(个)	Sanitation and Antiepidemic Stations	(unit)	22	22	0.4	0.4
妇幼保健所、站	(个)	Maternity and Child Care Centers	(unit)	8	11	0.1	0.2
专科防治所、站	(个)	Specialized Stations	(unit)	41	42	0.7	0.7
床　位	(张)	**Beds**	**(unit)**	**69465**	**69095**	**100**	**100**
# 医　院	(张)	Hospitals	(unit)	63660	63144	91.6	91.4
门诊部	(张)	Clinics	(unit)	186	96	0.3	0.1
疗养院、所	(张)	Sanatoriums	(unit)	1000	1219	1.4	1.8
平均每千人拥有医院床位	(张)	Hospital Beds per 1000 Population	(unit)	6.15	6.13		
卫生技术人员	(人)	**Medical Technical Personnel**	**(person)**	**116597**	**115976**		**100**
# 医　生	(人)	Doctors	(person)	52646	51902	45.2	44.8
护师(士)	(人)	Senior and Junior Nurses	(person)	39625	38883	34.0	33.5
平均每千人拥有医生	(人)	Doctors per 1000 Population	(person)	4.79	4.76		
平均每千人拥有护士	(人)	Nurses per 1000 Population	(person)	3.60	3.56		

注：按卫生部指标解释,1996 年始医院数仅包括县及县以上医院和其他医院,乡镇卫生院不再作为医院统计。(下同)

Note：According to the explanation of health department,number of hospitals of 1996 included hospitals at county level and above and other hospitals,township hospitals were no longer taken into account.(the following as the same)

16-2 农村医疗卫生机构基本情况
HEALTH INSTITUTIONS IN RURAL AREA

项目 Item				1999	1998	构成(%) Composition(%) 1999	1998
卫生事业机构	(个)	**Health Care Institutions**	**(unit)**	**861**	**1107**	**100**	**100**
# 医　院	(个)	Hospitals	(unit)	63	84	7.3	7.6
乡(镇)卫生院	(个)	Township Hospitals	(unit)	116	157	13.5	14.2
床　位	(张)	**Beds**	**(unit)**	**10385**	**13845**	**100**	**100**
# 医　院	(张)	Hospitals	(unit)	8413	11066	81.0	79.9
乡(镇)卫生院	(张)	Township Hospitals	(unit)	1609	2229	15.5	16.1
卫生技术人员	(人)	**Medical Technical Personnel**	**(person)**	**13733**	**19001**	**100**	**100**
# 医　生	(人)	Doctors	(person)	6931	9534	50.5	50.2
护师(士)	(人)	Senior and Junior Nurses	(person)	3836	5293	27.9	27.9
乡村医生和卫生员	(人)	**Doctors and Health Workers**	**(person)**	**5705**	**5972**	**100**	**100**
# 会接生的	(人)	Midwife	(person)	221	604	3.9	10.1
乡村医生	(人)	Doctors	(person)	5391	5480	94.5	91.8
卫生员	(人)	Health Workers	(person)	314	492	5.5	8.2

16-3 全市各饮食单位食品卫生合格率情况
FOOD QUALIFIED RATE OF FOOD AND BEVERAGE DEALERS

单位：%　　(%)

地区	Region	合计 Total	生产加工业 Processing	批发零售业 Wholesale and Retail	饮食服务业 Catering Services	集体食堂 Canteen	食品摊贩 Food Street Pedlar
合计	**Total**	**83.4**	**88.0**	**91.3**	**74.3**	**86.5**	**85.7**
东城区	Dongcheng	84.5	83.8	92.4	76.4	96.6	93.6
西城区	Xicheng	62.4	100.0	81.4	52.8	83.2	61.9
崇文区	Chongwen	96.9	93.0	94.2	95.0	96.1	99.7
宣武区	Xuanwu	86.1	90.7	80.8	82.3	78.3	93.0
朝阳区	Chaoyang	93.3	73.0	92.0	81.9	90.3	96.6
海淀区	Haidian	69.1	81.3	75.8	46.1	79.0	73.5
丰台区	Fengtai	72.6	89.5	79.6	65.2	74.0	75.9
石景山区	Shijingshan	80.9	81.8	91.7	75.2	94.0	80.0
门头沟区	Mentougou	98.9	94.5	99.6	99.2	99.8	97.9
房山区	Fangshan	98.3	97.3	99.6	98.1	98.5	97.2
通州区	Changping	90.7	91.9	93.7	85.8	98.0	92.8
顺义区	Daxing	92.3	92.2	95.1	86.1	93.1	92.6
昌平区	Tongzhou	88.5	85.0	96.7	92.6	97.4	82.2
大兴县	Shunyi	96.5	94.1	98.6	93.9	96.7	87.5
怀柔县	Huairou	92.7	94.1	93.5	91.9	90.4	93.0
密云县	Miyun	83.2	84.7	87.3	78.9	88.1	81.8
延庆县	Yanqing	91.9	80.8	95.7	92.6	87.0	85.9
平谷县	Pinggu	97.9	99.3	96.4	99.0	98.5	98.4

16-4 全市医院基本情况
BASIC STATISTICS FOR HOSPITALS

项目	Item	医院数 (个) Hospitals (unit)	床位数 (张) Beds (unit)	职工人数 (人) Staff and Workers (person)	#卫生技术人员 Medical Technical Personnel	中医师 Doctors of Chinese Medicine	西医师 Junior of Western Medicine	中医士 Junior Doctors of Chinese Medicine
总计	**Total**	**460**	**63660**	**116337**	**87547**	**4170**	**28163**	**221**
县及县以上医院	**Hospitals at and above County Level**	**278**	**56574**	**104861**	**78754**	**3538**	**25487**	**131**
城市	Urban	226	48477	94310	70682	3110	22758	99
农村	Rural	52	8097	10551	8072	428	2729	32
其他医院	**Others**	**182**	**7086**	**11476**	**8793**	**632**	**2676**	**90**
在县及县以上医院中	**Of Hospitals at and above County Level**							
综合医院	Comprehensive Hospitals	195	35334	67013	50550	1214	17896	45
中医医院	Hospitals of Chinese Medicine	23	4081	8170	6240	1669	867	64
医学院校附属医院	Hospitals Attached to Medical College	9	5060	10939	8542	450	2485	1
传染病院	Infectious Disease Hospitals	3	1034	1512	1126	12	303	
精神病院	Mental Hospitals	9	3725	2762	1923	23	442	9
结核病院	Tuberculosis Hospitals	1	533	594	423	1	114	
妇幼保健院	Hospitals for Maternity and Child Care	11	592	1704	1351	16	617	2
妇产医院	Hospitals for Gynecology and Obstetrics	2	439	1063	726	7	221	
儿童医院	Children's Hospitals	4	1030	2616	2007	29	636	
职业病院	Hospitals for Occupational Diseases	1	175	267	146	3	51	
肿瘤医院	Tumor Hospitals	3	1299	2270	1629	3	455	
康复医院	Recovery Hospital	6	961	1332	735	28	189	2
口腔医院	Stomatological Hospitals	1	80	621	426		207	
骨科医院	Hospitals of Orthopedics	2	360	720	524	25	165	3
整形医院	Plastically Hospitals	1	328	444	264	2	84	
中西医结合医院	Hospitals Which Integrate Traditional Chinese Therapeutics with tics in Practices	2	306	579	487	41	164	2
其他专科医院	Other Specialized Hospitals	5	1237	2255	1655	15	591	3

16-4 续表 continued

项目 Item		西医士 Junior Doctors of Western Medicine	中西医结合医师 Doctors Who Integrate Traditional Chinese Therapeutics with Western Therapeutics in Practice	其他中医 Other Doctors of Chinese Medicine	药师 Pharmacists	检验师 Laboratory Technicians	助产士 Midwives	护师(士) Senior and Junior Nurses
总计	**Total**	**2146**	**328**	**84**	**4989**	**2783**	**236**	**35262**
县及县以上医院	**Hospitals at and above County Level**	**1473**	**289**	**48**	**4363**	**2504**	**230**	**32745**
城市	Urban	1208	280	43	3887	2263	206	29534
农村	Rural	265	9	5	476	241	24	3211
其他医院	**Others**	**673**	**39**	**36**	**626**	**279**	**6**	**2517**
在县及县以上医院中	**Of Hospitals at and above County Level**							
综合医院	Comprehensive Hospitals	971	51	14	2803	1721	115	21377
中医医院	Hospitals of Chinese Medicine	81	146	17	620	154	19	2001
医学院校附属医院	Hospitals Attached to Medical College	129	59	6	380	196	4	3489
传染病院	Infectious Disease Hospitals	7	1	9	59	99	13	501
精神病院	Mental Hospitals	44			72	33		1132
结核病院	Tuberculosis Hospitals				16	21		241
妇幼保健院	Hospitals for Maternity and Child Care	70			57	51	21	457
妇产医院	Hospitals for Gynecology and Obstetrics	20	11	1	28	16	58	292
儿童医院	Children's Hospitals	10	11		129	77		947
职业病院	Hospitals for Occupational Diseases				8	9		57
肿瘤医院	Tumor Hospitals	7	5		40	25		645
康复医院	Recovery Hospital	7	3		37	21		329
口腔医院	Stomatological Hospitals				12	8		118
骨科医院	Hospitals of Orthopedics	51		1	29	15		151
整形医院	Plastically Hospitals				6	5		145
中西医结合医院	Hospitals Which Integrate Traditional Chinese Therapeutics with tics in Practices	62	2		28	15		156
其他专科医院	Other Specialized Hospitals	14			43	38		707

16-5 医院、卫生院工作情况
WORKS OF HOSPITALS

项目	Item	机构数 (个) Institutions (unit)	诊疗人次数 (人次) Patients Treated (person.time)	#门诊 (人次) Out-patients (person.time)	健康检查人数 (人) Health Check (person)	平均开放病床数 (张) Beds in Use (unit)	入院人数 (人) In-patients (person)
合　　计	**Total**	**670**	**51887822**	**45762628**	**1841586**	**63470**	**778460**
县及县以上医院合计	**Hospitals at and above County Level**	**276**	**42196837**	**37009069**	**1196693**	**53266**	**679966**
卫生部门医院合计	Hospitals of Health Care Department	116	28640430	25706313	556386	35092	518139
综合医院	Comprehensive Hospitals	49	15705743	13634594	306271	17138	300083
# 县医院	Countyship Hospitals	12	2108451	1566536	35698	2490	52642
中医医院	Hospitals of Chinese Medicine	19	3301142	3100919	41693	3347	35406
医学院校附属医院	Hospitals Attached to Medical College	9	5397656	4934967	33928	5110	89038
传染病院	Infectious Disease Hospitals	3	148437	141037	1480	1034	7492
精神病院	Mental Hospitals	7	270241	259689	7230	2596	4974
结核病院	Tuberculosis Hospitals	1	37828	37056		476	2863
妇幼保健院	Hospitals for Maternity and Child Care	10	628349	608749	111721	447	15589
妇产医院	Hospitals for Gynecology and Obstetrics	2	264442	257347	3787	439	9756
儿童医院	Children's Hospitals	4	1686406	1583543	6606	1030	20692
肿瘤医院	Tumor Hospitals	2	301384	297121	9905	1191	12242
康复医院	Recovery Hospitals	2	38339	33557	6000	416	677
口腔医院	Stomatological Hospitals	1	310615	298641	5262	80	611
整形医院	Plastically Hospitals	1	21301	21009	57	328	3197
中西医结合医院	Hospitals Which Integrate Traditional Chinese Therapeutics with Western Therapeutics in Practices	1	288849	271152	11206	208	3515
其他专科医院	Other Specialized Hospitals	5	239698	226932	11240	1251	12004
工业及其他部门医院	Hospitals of Industry and Other Departments	152	12649438	10472731	582926	16748	149747
集体所有制医院	Collective-Owned Hospitals	8	906969	830025	57381	1426	12080
其他医院合计	**Other Hospitals**	**174**	**4602807**	**4049334**	**305753**	**6657**	**34533**
卫生院合计	**Total Township Hospitals**	**220**	**5088178**	**4704225**	**339140**	**3547**	**63961**

16-5 续表 continued

项　　目	Item	出院人数（人）Leaving Hospital (person)	治愈率（%）Recovering Rate (%)	好转率（%）Mending Rate (%)	病死率（%）Rate of Death of Illness (%)	病床周转次数（次）Turnover Beds (times)	病床使用率（%）Utilization Rate (%)	出院者平均住院日（日）Average Hospitalization Period (day)
合　　计	**Total**	**781225**	**59.4**	**34.2**	**2.5**	**12.3**	**68.0**	**20.4**
县及县以上医院合计	**Hospitals at and above County Level**	**684512**	**58.4**	**34.8**	**2.6**	**12.9**	**72.8**	**21.5**
卫生部门医院合计	Hospitals of Health Care Department	522340	58.2	34.9	2.4	14.9	81.0	20.0
综合医院	Comprehensive Hospitals	303486	58.2	35.1	2.5	17.7	82.7	16.9
# 县医院	Countyship Hospitals	56315	58.4	36.2	1.5	22.6	73.2	12.5
中医医院	Hospitals of Chinese Medicine	35656	43.0	49.8	3.4	10.7	68.3	23.6
医学院校附属医院	Hospitals Attached to Medical College	89151	59.5	32.8	2.1	17.5	86.3	21.1
传染病院	Infectious Disease Hospitals	7412	56.6	32.2	5.0	7.2	57.0	28.0
精神病院	Mental Hospitals	4883	40.1	55.4	1.2	1.9	100.3	172.6
结核病院	Tuberculosis Hospitals	2894	23.6	51.8	5.5	6.1	79.4	47.8
妇幼保健院	Hospitals for Maternity and Child Care	16165	95.9	3.3	0.1	36.2	72.4	7.0
妇产医院	Hospitals for Gynecology and Obstetrics	9767	85.7	12.1	0.2	22.3	83.4	12.6
儿童医院	Children's Hospitals	20650	63.7	31.1	0.9	20.1	75.5	13.1
肿瘤医院	Tumor Hospitals	12093	52.1	37.4	3.3	10.2	93.6	32.4
康复医院	Recovery Hospitals	737	58.6	35.6	2.4	1.8	23.4	53.5
口腔医院	Stomatological Hospitals	615	90.1	9.9		7.7	40.4	19.0
整形医院	Plastically Hospitals	3167	92.5	6.8		9.7	62.7	24.1
中西医结合医院	Hospitals Which Integrate Traditional Chinese Therapeutics with Western Therapeutics in Practices	3553	51.2	42.9	2.9	17.1	84.0	17.9
其他专科医院	Other Specialized Hospitals	12111	43.7	47.4	2.7	9.7	69.5	25.7
工业及其他部门医院	Hospitals of Industry and Other Departments	149920	59.0	34.6	3.2	9.0	56.9	26.8
集体所有制医院	Collective-Owned Hospitals	12252	61.5	33.5	3.0	8.6	58.4	21.7
其他医院合计	**Other Hospitals**	**33071**	**48.2**	**42.1**	**4.8**	**5.0**	**47.3**	**25.8**
卫生院合计	**Total Township Hospitals**	**63642**	**75.1**	**23.3**	**0.4**	**17.9**	**35.9**	**6.2**

16-6 全市居民前十位死因顺位、死亡率及构成
DEATH RATE AND COMPOSITION OF 10 MAJOR DISEASE

顺位 No.	死因名称	Cause of Death	死亡率 (1/10万) Death Rate (1/100 thousand)	构成 (%) Composition (%)
	全　　市	**Total**	**535.6**	**93.5**
1	脑血管病	Cerebrovasular Disease	154.7	27.0
2	心脏病	Heart Trouble	125.0	21.8
3	恶性肿瘤	Malignant Tumour	106.2	18.5
4	呼吸系病	Respiratory Disease	68.1	11.9
5	损伤和中毒	Trauma and Toxicosis	33.6	5.9
6	内分泌、营养、代谢及免疫病	Internal System,Nutrition,Metabolite and Immunity Disease	17.2	3.0
7	消化系病	Gigestive Disease	13.1	2.3
8	泌尿生殖系病	Urinary Disease	8.8	1.5
9	神经系病	Neuropathy	5.0	0.9
10	传染病	Infection Disease	3.8	0.7
	市	**Districts**	**517.9**	**94.3**
1	脑血管病	Cerebrovasular Disease	132.7	24.2
2	心脏病	Heart Trouble	127.0	23.1
3	恶性肿瘤	Malignant Tumour	114.7	20.9
4	呼吸系病	Respiratory Disease	64.4	11.7
5	损伤和中毒	Trauma and Toxicosis	25.9	4.7
6	内分泌、营养、代谢及免疫病	Internal System,Nutrition,Metabolite and Immunity Disease	19.6	3.6
7	消化系病	Gigestive Disease	14.3	2.6
8	泌尿生殖系病	Urinary Disease	9.6	1.7
9	神经系病	Neuropathy	5.8	1.1
10	传染病	Infection Disease	4.1	0.8
	县	**Counties**	**574.7**	**91.9**
1	脑血管病	Cerebrovasular Disease	203.1	32.5
2	心脏病	Heart Trouble	120.8	19.3
3	呼吸系病	Respiratory Disease	87.7	14.0
4	恶性肿瘤	Malignant Tumour	76.3	12.2
5	损伤和中毒	Trauma and Toxicosis	50.6	8.1
6	内分泌、营养、代谢及免疫病	Internal System,Nutrition,Metabolite and Immunity Disease	11.9	1.9
7	消化系病	Gigestive Disease	10.5	1.7
8	泌尿生殖系病	Urinary Disease	7.1	1.1
9	神经系病	Neuropathy	3.4	0.6
10	传染病	Infection Disease	3.2	0.5

16-7 全市0-6岁儿童系统管理情况
STATISTICS FOR SYSTEMATIC CARE OF CHILDREN AT AGE 0-6

地区 Region		0-6岁儿童数(人) Number of Children at Age 0-6 (person)	系统管理人数(人) Children under Systematic Care (person)	体检人数(人) Children Having Health Check (person)	0~2岁儿童佝偻病患病率(%) Suffering Rate from Rickets of Children at Age 0-2 (%)	0~2岁儿童贫血患病率(%) Suffering Rate from Amenia of Children at Age 0-2 (%)	3~6岁儿童贫血患病率(%) Suffering Rate from Amenia of Children at Age 3-6 (%)	0~6岁儿童系统管理覆盖率(%) Covering Rate of Systematic Care of Children at Age 0-6 (%)
合计	**Total**	**476142**	**436778**	**431024**	**0.76**	**4.78**	**1.64**	**96.11**
东城区	Dongcheng	19340	16846	16794	0.15	4.32	0.66	100.00
西城区	Xicheng	23694	20093	20026	0.03	6.39	0.66	100.00
崇文区	Chongwen	10059	13428	13315	0.00	8.12	1.16	100.00
宣武区	Xuanwu	10368	11868	11858	0.02	2.17	0.27	100.00
朝阳区	Chaoyang	50186	53942	53848	0.24	3.85	0.90	98.10
海淀区	Haidian	101998	60777	60177	0.69	4.21	1.17	98.53
丰台区	Fengtai	23392	31525	29852	1.54	5.93	1.59	98.31
石景山区	Shijingshan	11431	12412	12121	0.26	5.52	0.67	97.74
门头沟区	Mentougou	9651	9663	9626	1.79	8.20	2.64	91.53
房山区	Fangshan	40842	37956	37905	1.44	6.64	3.32	92.43
通州区	Tongzhou	26055	27894	25350	0.64	6.28	3.15	91.65
昌平区	Changping	20831	18190	18190	0.80	5.30	1.66	100.00
大兴县	Daxing	25463	27493	26859	0.76	2.00	0.87	99.01
顺义区	Shunyi	20735	21675	21714	0.43	4.51	2.38	99.96
怀柔县	Huairou	15459	14141	14024	0.22	5.82	2.49	97.04
密云县	Miyun	28175	23377	25331	1.30	2.29	1.05	82.97
延庆县	Yanqing	14003	13714	12874	1.12	4.64	1.85	88.55
平谷县	Pinggu	24460	21784	21160	1.55	4.00	3.58	90.64

16-8 全市婴儿、新生儿死亡率
DEATH RATE OF INFANT AND NEWBORN BABY

单位：‰ (‰)

地区 Region		婴儿死亡率 Death Rate of Infant		新生儿死亡率 Death Rate of Newborn Baby	
		1999	1998	1999	1998
合计	**Total**	**7.95**	**7.58**	**5.94**	**5.53**
区	District	7.78	9.07	5.74	6.46
县	County	8.38	5.75	6.45	4.39

16-9 农 村 改 水 情 况
STATISTICS FOR WATER-CHANG IN RURAL AREA

项目		Item		1999	1998
农村总人口	(万人)	Total Rural Population	(10000 persons)	373.4	373.4
# 女 性	(万人)	Female	(10000 persons)		
已改水累计受益人口	(万人)	Accumulative Population Benefited from Water-changing	(10000 persons)	372.8	372.5
# 女 性	(万人)	Female	(10000 persons)		
饮用自来水		Using Tap Water			
现有水厂	(万座)	Water Plants	(10000)	3839.0	3828.0
累计受益人口	(万人)	Accumulative Benefited Population	(10000 persons)	365.9	365.3
饮用水压机井水		Using Motor-Pumped Water			
现有机井	(万台)	Motor-Pumped Wells	(10000)	1.6	1.7
累计受益人口	(万人)	Accumulative Benefited Population	(10000 persons)	5.0	5.4
其他形式		Others			
累计受益人口	(万人)	Accumulative Benefited Population	(10000 persons)	1.9	1.9

16-10 举 办 运 动 会 情 况
SPORTS MEETINGS

项目		Item		1999	1998
举办县以上运动会次数	(次)	Sports Meetings above County Level	(time)	3497	2417
体委系统		Physical Culture and Sports Commissions		261	221
其他系统		Other Departments		3236	2196
参加县以上运动会运动员人数	(人次)	Athletes Attending Sports Meetings above County Level	(person.time)	3481313	1009434
体委系统		Physical Culture and Sports Commissions		801271	240766
其他系统		Other Departments		2680042	768668
举办乡镇运动会次数	(次)	Sports Meetings at Town and Township Level	(time)	413	572
参加乡镇运动会运动员人数	(人次)	Athletes Attending Sports Meetings at Town and Township Level	(person.time)	116709	107649

16-11 分等级运动员发展人数情况
NUMBER OF CERTIFIED ATHLETES ADMITTED

单位：人 (person)

项 目 Item	合 计 Total	国家级健将 National Master Athletes	运动健将 Master Athletes	一 级 First Grade Athletes	二 级 Second Grade Athletes	三 级 Third Grade Athletes	少年级 Juvenile Grade Athletes
总 计 Total	**2213**	**7**	**28**	**216**	**986**	**584**	**302**
# 女 性 Female	925	6	16	98	347	237	221

16-12 专职教练员获职称人数情况
NUMBER OF PROFESSIONAL TRAINERS GAINED TITLE

单位：人 (person)

项 目 Item	合 计 Total	高级职称 Senior	中级职称 Middle	初级职称 Junior
总 计 Total	**565**	**105**	**229**	**231**
# 女 性 Female	169	19	64	86

16-13 分等级裁判员发展人数情况
NUMBER OF CERTIFIED REFEREES ADMITTED

单位：人 (person)

项 目 Item	合 计 Total	国家级 National Referees	一 级 First Grade Referees	二 级 Second Grade Referees	三 级 Third Grade Referees
总 计 Total	**1199**	**27**	**173**	**351**	**648**
# 女 性 Female	301	6	39	90	166

16-14 运动员获奖牌情况
STATISTICS ON MEDALS WON

单位：块 (piece)

项 目 Item	金 牌 Gold	银 牌 Silver	铜 牌 Bronze
合 计 Total	**83**	**41**	**41**
国际比赛 International Competitions	31	11	7
国内比赛 Domestic Competitions	52	30	34

16-15 北京市运动员获全国冠军名单
LIST OF NATIONAL CHAMPIONSHIPS WON BY ATHLETES OF BEIJING

比赛名称	Matches	大项名称	Item	小项名称 Item	姓名 Name
全国锦标赛	The National Championships	射箭	Archery	女子淘汰赛团体	
全国锦标赛	The National Championships	田径	Track and Field	男子马拉松	战东林
全国锦标赛	The National Championships	田径	Track and Field	女子跳高	景雪竹
全国锦标赛	The National Championships	羽毛球	Badminton	男子单打	董炯
全国锦标赛	The National Championships	自行车	Cycling	男子凯林赛	龚玉岩
全国锦标赛	The National Championships	自行车	Cycling	男子公路个人计时赛 40km	汤学忠
全国锦标赛	The National Championships	体操	Gymnastics	男子个人全能	张津京
全国锦标赛	The National Championships	体操	Gymnastics	男子单杠	张津京
全国锦标赛	The National Championships	柔道	Judo	男子 60 公斤级	李燕豫
全国锦标赛	The National Championships	柔道	Judo	男子 73 公斤级	张海峰
全国锦标赛	The National Championships	柔道	Judo	女子 52 公斤级	刘玉香
全国锦标赛	The National Championships	赛艇	Rowing	女子单人双浆	杨立梅
全国锦标赛	The National Championships	赛艇	Rowing	女子八人单浆有舵手	
全国锦标赛	The National Championships	射击	Shooting	男子 10 米移动靶 30+30 个人	牛志远
全国锦标赛	The National Championships	射击	Shooting	女子飞碟双多向	李清念
全国锦标赛	The National Championships	射击	Shooting	女子 10 米移动靶个人（20+20）	张怡
全国锦标赛	The National Championships	游泳	Swimming	女子 100 米自由泳	韩雪
全国锦标赛	The National Championships	游泳	Swimming	女子 200 米碟泳	庞然
全国锦标赛	The National Championships	游泳	Swimming	女子 4*100 米自由泳接力	
全国锦标赛	The National Championships	跳水	Diving	女子十米跳台	李娜
全国锦标赛	The National Championships	跳水	Diving	女子双人三米跳板	
全国锦标赛	The National Championships	跳水	Diving	女子双人十米跳台	
全国锦标赛	The National Championships	乒乓球	Table Tennis	女子团体	
全国锦标赛	The National Championships	网球	Tennis	男子团体	
全国锦标赛	The National Championships	网球	Tennis	男子双打	
全国锦标赛	The National Championships	摔跤	Wrestling	自由式 54 公斤级	蒙海波
全国锦标赛	The National Championships	摔跤	Wrestling	自由式 58 公斤级	张帆
全国锦标赛	The National Championships	摔跤	Wrestling	自由式 76 公斤级	张文岩
全国锦标赛	The National Championships	武术	Wushu	散手 85、90 公斤级团体	
全国锦标赛	The National Championships	武术	Wushu	女子长拳全能	王晓娜
全国锦标赛	The National Championships	武术	Wushu	女子刀棍全能	刘晓雷
全国锦标赛	The National Championships	跆拳道	Taiquan	男子 54 公斤级	张后军
全国锦标赛	The National Championships	速度赛马	Speed Horse Race	5000 米个人	段志珍
全国甲级联赛	The National Grade A League Matches	棒球	Baseball	男子	
全国甲级联赛	The National Grade A League Matches	足球	Football	女子	
全国甲级联赛	The National Grade A League Matches	垒球	Softball	女子	
全国冠军赛	The National Tournament	射箭	Archery	女子淘汰赛团体	
全国冠军赛	The National Tournament	射击	Shooting	男子 10 米移动靶 30+30 个人	牛志远
全国冠军赛	The National Tournament	射击	Shooting	女子飞碟双多向	李清念
全国冠军赛	The National Tournament	射击	Shooting	女子 10 米移动靶个人（20+20）	张怡
全国冠军赛	The National Tournament	游泳	Swimming	女子 100 米自由泳	韩雪
全国冠军赛	The National Tournament	游泳	Swimming	女子 100 米碟泳	庞然
全国冠军赛	The National Tournament	游泳	Swimming	女子 4*100 米自由泳接力	
全国冠军赛	The National Tournament	跳水	Diving	女子三米跳板	梁小桥
全国冠军赛	The National Tournament	跳水	Diving	女子双人十米跳台	
全国冠军赛	The National Tournament	花样游泳	Figure Swimming	双人	
全国冠军赛	The National Tournament	花样游泳	Figure Swimming	集体	
全国冠军赛	The National Tournament	摔跤	Wrestling	古典式 58 公斤级	张洋
全国冠军赛	The National Tournament	跆拳道	Taiquan	女子 51 公斤级	杨娜

主要统计指标解释

等级运动员人数 指经考核正式批准授予等级运动员称号的人数。运动员等级分为国际级运动健将、运动健将、一级运动员、二级运动员、三级运动员、少年级运动员。

等级裁判员人数 指经考核正式批准授予等级裁判员称号的人数。裁判员等级分为国际级裁判、国家级裁判、一级裁判、二级裁判、三级裁判。

卫生技术人员 指卫生机构支付工资的全部固定职工和合同制职工中现任职务为卫生技术工作的专业人员。包括中医师、西医师、中西医结合医师、护师、中药师、西药师、检验师、其他技师、中医士、西医士、护士、助产士、中药剂士、西药剂士、检验士、其他技士、其他中医、护理员、中药剂员、西药剂员、检验员，其他初级卫生技术人员。

Explanatory Notes On Main Statistical Indicators

Number of Athletes in Grades refers to the number of athletes who have been given titles through examination. The titles of athletes include international masters of sports, masters of sports, first-grade, second-grade and third-grade sportsmen and young athletes.

Number of Referees in Grades refers to the number of referees who have been given titles through examination. They are classified as international referees, national referees and referees of the first, second and third grades.

Medical Technical Personnel refers to all permanent medical staff and workers employed by medical institutions, including doctors of Chinese and Western medicine, doctors who integrate traditional Chinese therapeutics with Western therapeutics in practice, senior nurses, pharmacists of Chinese and Western medicine, laboratory specialists, other specialists, paramedics of Chinese and Western medicine, nurses, midwives, druggists in Chinese and Western medicine, laboratory technicians, other technicians, other practitioners of Chinese medicine , nursing attendants, pharmacological workers of Chinese and Western medicine, laboratory workers, and other primary medical personnel.

城市公用事业
URBAN PUBLIC UTILITIES

		1999年	1998年
	用电量（万千瓦小时） Electricity Consumption(10000 kwh)	2972629	2762080
	年末运营车辆（辆） Operating Vehicles(unit year-end)	12509	10819
	桥梁（座） Bridges(unit)	787	715

城 市 公 用 事 业

URBAN PUBLIC UTILITIES

1999年

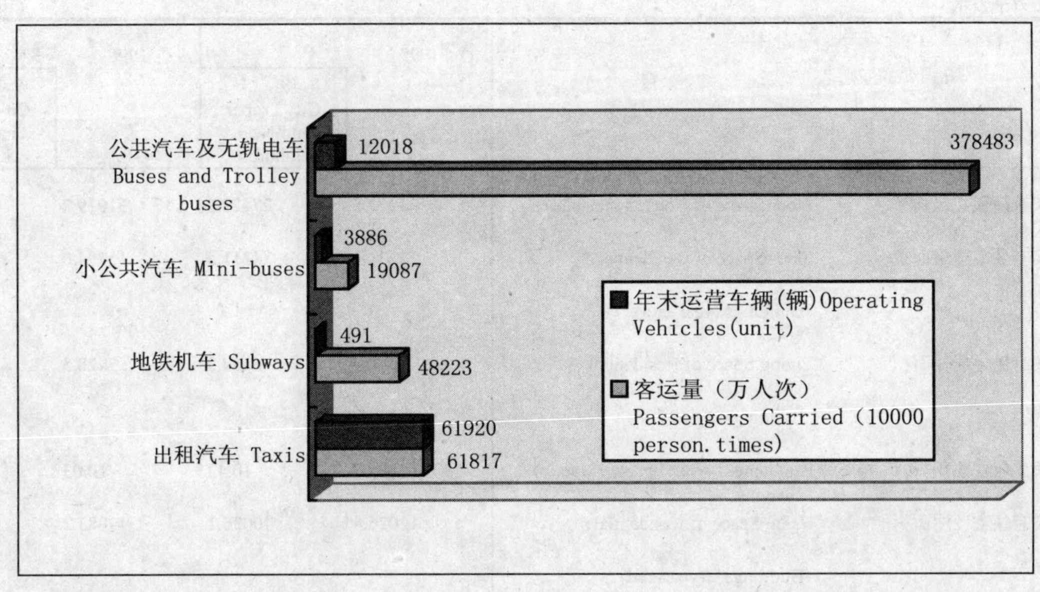

17-1 城镇建设用地
URBAN CONSTRUCTION LAND

单位：公顷 (hectare)

项目	Item	全市 Total	城近郊区 City Proper and Near Suburbs	远郊区 Outer Suburbs	各县 Counties
合计	**Total**	**288.1**	**183.2**		**104.9**
商业服务业用地	Commerce and Services	1.9			1.9
工业用地	Industry	8.4	8.4		
仓储用地	Stock				
交通用地	Transportation				
市政公用设施及绿化用地	Municipal Public Facilities and Green Areas	159.5	56.5		103.0
公共建筑用地	Public Construction	26.4	26.4		
住宅用地	Residential Buildings	91.9	91.9		
特殊用地	Special Purposes				
其他用地	Others				

17-2 城市居民居住水平
RESIDENTIAL CONDITIONS OF URBAN RESIDENTS

单位：万平方米 (10000 sq.m)

项目	Item	1999	#市区 City Proper and Near Suburbs	1998	#市区 City Proper and Near Suburbs
年末实有房屋建筑面积	Floor Space of Houses(year-end)	33272.5	27429.8	31019.2	25686.3
年末实有住宅建筑面积	Floor Space of Residential Buildings (year-end)	17234.4	14211.5	15794.0	13184.5
年末实有住宅居住面积	Living Space of Residential Building (year-end)	8046.9	6669.9	7428.5	6226.7
平均每人居住面积（平方米）	Per Capita Living Space (sq.m)	10.63	10.43	10.03	9.87
年末实有住宅使用面积	Using Space of Residential Buildings (year-end)	12026.4	10036.1	11083.2	9356.1
平均每人使用面积（平方米）	Per Capita Using Space (sq.m)	15.88	15.69	14.96	14.83

17-3 用　电　量(北京地区)
ELECTRICITY CONSUMPTION(BEIJING AREA)

单位：万千瓦小时　　(10000 kwh)

项目	Item	1999	1998	1999年为1998年% 1999 as % of 1998
合计	**Total**	**2972629**	**2762080**	**107.6**
农、林、牧、渔、水利业	Farming,Forestry,Animals Husbandry, Fishery and Water Conservancy	121242	108267	112.0
# 排灌	Irrigation and Drainage	71635	62356	114.9
工业	Industry	1478523	1457149	80.9
按轻重工业分	Grouped by Heavy and Light Industry			
轻工业	Light Industry	282405	278785	101.3
重工业	Heavy Industry	1196118	1178364	101.5
按行业分	Grouped by Sectors			
采掘业	Excavation	73236	72226	101.4
采矿业	Minerals Mining	47584	47164	100.9
制造业	Manufacturing	1405287	1384923	101.5
食品、饮料和烟草制造业	Food,Beverage and Tobacco Production	62677	60802	103.1
纺织业	Textile Industry	37832	40751	92.8
石油加工业	Petroleum Processing	132866	104149	127.6
炼焦、煤气及煤制品业	Coking,Gas and Coal Products	16226	17438	93.0
化学工业	Chemical Industry	169310	170914	99.1
建筑材料及其他非金属矿制品业	Construction Materials and Other Nonmetal Minerals Products	152980	143981	106.3
黑色金属冶练及压延加工业	Smelting and Pressing of Ferrous Metals	374178	403551	92.7
金属制品业	Metal Products	32866	31506	104.3
机械工业	Machinery Manufacturing	48726	48938	99.6
交通运输、电气、电子设备制造业	Transportations,Electric and Electronic Equipment Manufacturing	108403	104749	103.5
电力、蒸汽热水生产和供应业	Electricity,Steam and Hot Water Production and Supply	108283	108073	100.2
自来水生产和供应	Tap Water Production and Supply	25596	25062	102.1
建筑业	Construction	103454	91336	113.3
地质普查和勘探业	Geological Survey and Prospecting	1383	1258	109.9
交通运输、邮电通信业	Transportations,Posts and Telecommunications	98521	90080	109.4
商业、公共饮食业、物资供销和仓储业	Commerce,Catering,Capital Goods Distribution and Storage	266741	237079	112.5
其他事业	Others	546189	482866	113.1
# 市内公共交通业	Municipal Public Transportation	8667	5485	158.0
# 路灯业	Road Lamps	7964	7067	112.7
城乡居民生活用电	Electricity Consumption by Urban and Rural Households	356576	294045	121.3
乡　村	Rural	79934	73502	108.8
城　市	Urban	276642	220543	125.4

17-4 供　热
HEAT SUPPLY

项　目	Item	1999	1998	1999年为1998年% 1999 as % of 1998
全市采暖面积合计 (万平方米)	**Total Heating Area (10000 sq.m)**	**9991.7**	**9102.1**	**109.8**
集中供热	Central Heat Supply			
热力供应能力 (百万千焦/小时)	Supply Capacity (10^9 joule/hour)	15198.0	9315.0	163.2
采暖单位 (户)	Heat Users (unit)	3142	2868	109.6
采暖面积(万平方米)	Heating Area (10000sq.m)	4145.4	3645.8	113.7
热力供应单位 (户)	Heat Suppler (unit)	981	897	109.4
管道长度 (公里)	Length of Pipeline (km)	242.0	227.0	106.6
销售量 (万百万千焦)	Volume Supplied (10^13 joule)	1986.5	1859.2	106.8
小区集中供热	Central Heat Supply in Residential Districts			
采暖面积 (万平方米)	Heating Area (10000 sq.m)	5622.9	5232.9	107.5
余热供热	Surplus Heat Supply			
采暖面积 (万平方米)	Heating Area (10000 sq.m)	223.4	223.4	100.0

注：小区集中供热、联片供热、余热供热统计范围为市区10万平米以上的供热面积。
Note: Figures for central heat supply in residential districts,joint heat supply and surplus heat supply only include those who heating areas are more than 100000 sq.m.

17-5 供　气
STEAM SUPPLY

项　目	Item	1999	1998	1999年为1998年% 1999 as % of 1998
蒸气供应能力 (吨／小时)	Supply Capacity (ton/hour)	1350	850	158.8
用气单位 (个)	Steam Users (unit)	119	105	113.3
#工　业 (个)	Industry (unit)	119	98	121.4
管道长度 (公里)	Length of Pipeline (km)	42.0	41.8	100.5
销售量 (万吨)	Volume Supplied (10000 tons)	352.2	330.3	106.6
#工　业 (万吨)	Industry (10000 tons)	352.2	330.3	106.6

17-6 煤气、液化石油气及天然气
GAS,LIQUEFIED PETROLEUM GAS AND NATURAL GAS

项目		Item		1999	1998	1999年为1998年% 1999 as % of 1998
煤 气		**Gas**				
管道长度	(公里)	Length of Pipeline	(km)	1217.7	1494.8	81.5
供应量	(万立方米)	Gas Supply	(10000 cu.m)	74682.2	84130.0	88.8
# 燃气集团	(万立方米)	Gas Group	(10000 cu.m)	71599.6	81355.0	88.0
销售量	(万立方米)	Gas Sale	(10000 cu.m)	61845.6	68998.0	89.6
# 工业用	(万立方米)	for Industrial Use	(10000 cu.m)	9581.1	9994.0	95.9
# 生活用	(万立方米)	for Living Use	(10000 cu.m)	47385.3	58114.0	81.5
# 燃气集团	(万立方米)	Gas Group	(10000 cu.m)	44454.8	55359.0	80.3
用 户	(万户)	Consumer	(10000 households)	48.9	57.4	85.2
# 家庭用户	(万户)	Household	(10000 households)	46.9	57.1	82.1
液化石油气		**Liquefied Petroleum Gas**				
储气能力	(吨/罐)	Storage Capability	(ton/tank)	21803/81	20905/81	
# 燃气集团	(吨/罐)	Gas Group	(ton/tank)	18000/49	18000/49	
供应站	(个)	Supply Units	(unit)	216	154	140.3
# 燃气集团	(个)	Gas Group	(unit)	80	80	100.0
液化气钢瓶	(万个)	Tanks	(10000)	142.9	126.0	113.4
销售量	(吨)	Gas Sales	(ton)	188450	174464.0	108.0
# 工业用	(吨)	for Industrial Use	(ton)	2458.5	2899.0	84.8
# 生活用	(吨)	for Living Use	(ton)	185959.0	168516.0	110.4
# 燃气集团	(吨)	Gas Group	(ton)	147578.0	142957.0	103.2
用 户	(万户)	Consumer	(10000 households)	113.9	118.4	96.2
# 家庭用户	(万户)	Household	(10000 households)	109.5	115.9	94.5
天然气		**Natural Gas**				
管道长度	(公里)	Length of Pipeline	(km)	3277.3	2182.0	150.2
供应量	(万立方米)	Gas Supply	(10000 cu.m)	75833.7	37969.0	199.7
# 燃气集团	(万立方米)	Gas Group	(10000 cu.m)	75833.7	37969.0	199.7
销售量	(万立方米)	Gas Sales	(10000 cu.m)	64833.0	32619.0	198.8
# 工业用	(万立方米)	for Industrial Use	(10000 cu.m)	3759.0	1876.0	200.4
# 生活用	(万立方米)	for Living Use	(10000 cu.m)	61040.4	29453.0	207.2
# 燃气集团	(万立方米)	Gas Group	(10000 cu.m)	61040.4	29453.0	207.2
用 户	(万户)	Consumer	(10000 households)	105.0	81.9	128.2
# 家庭用户	(万户)	Household	(10000 households)	103.4	81.4	127.0
居民燃气用户	**(万户)**	**Household with Access to Gas**	**(10000 households)**	**259.8**	**247.3**	**105.1**
气化率	(%)	Percentage of Population Using Gas	(%)	97.1	95.4	

注：本表燃气气化率数字为年末燃气家庭用户占全部城市户数的百分比。

Note:Figure for percentage of population using gas refers to proportion of households using gas in total urban households.

17-7 自来水及自备水源
TAP WATER AND SELF-PROVIDED SOURCE OF WATER

项目	Item	1999	# 城近郊区 City Propers and Near Suburbs	1998	# 城近郊区 City Propers and Near Suburbs
自来水	**Tap Water**				
水厂 (个)	Water Plants (unit)	20.0	10.0	24.0	13.0
生产能力 (万吨/日)	Production Capacity (10000 tons/day)	356.6	304.6	330.3	266.0
管线长度 (公里)	Length of Pipelines (km)	7178.5	5741.3	6989.3	5383.8
供水面积 (平方公里)	Area of Water Supply (sq.km)	722.9	549.9	703.6	515.6
售水量 (万吨)	Sales in Volume (10000 tons)	78098.0	68619.5	75968.5	65790.0
# 工业用 (万吨)	for Industrial Use (10000 tons)	13432.9	11102.3	13944.9	11729.4
生活用 (万吨)	for Living Use (10000 tons)	60243.2	54001.1	57032.0	50089.6
平均每人每日生活用水 (公斤)	Living Consumption Per Day (kg)	250.1	266.8	238.2	256.2
自来水普及率 (%)	Percentage of Population Using Tap Water (%)	100.0	100.0	100.0	100.0
自备水源	**Self-provided Source of Water**				
生产能力 (万吨/日)	Production Capacity (10000 tons/day)	291.7	202.7	290.5	201.9
用水量 (万吨)	Consumption (10000 tons)	46426.4	36251.2	47243.5	36050.8
生产用 (万吨)	Production (10000 tons)	23922.1	16760.7	25543.5	17573.6
生活用 (万吨)	Living (10000 tons)	22472.3	19458.4	21699.9	18477.2

17-8 节　水
WATER SAVING

项目	Item	1999	1998	1999年为1998年% 1999 as % of 1998
节水量 (万吨)	Volume Saved (10000 tons)	2051.0	2107.0	97.3
自来水 (万吨)	Tap Water (10000 tons)	1469.0	1555.0	94.5
自备水井 (万吨)	Self-Provided Well (10000 tons)	582.0	552.0	105.4
完成节水措施 (项)	Save Measures Completed (item)	141.0	160.0	88.1

注：节水量中未包括河水节水量。

Note:Volume saved excluded river water.

17-9 公 共 交 通
PUBLIC TRAFFIC

项目		Item		1999	# 城近郊区 City Propers and Near Suburbs	1998	# 城近郊区 City Propers and Near Suburbs
年末营运车辆	**(辆)**	**Operating Vehicles (year-end)**	**(unit)**	**12509**	**11029**	**10819**	**9267**
公共汽车	(辆)	Buses	(unit)	11472	9992	9844	8292
# 小公共汽车	(辆)	Mini-Buses	(unit)	3886	2721	4102	2856
无轨电车	(辆)	Trolley Buses	(unit)	546	546	538	538
地铁机车	(辆)	Subways	(unit)	491	491	437	437
营运线路		**Operating Routes**					
条　数	(条)	Number	(line)	750	602	690	542
公共汽车	(条)	Buses	(line)	735	587	674	526
# 小公共汽车	(条)	Mini-Buses	(line)	340	200	340	200
无轨电车	(条)	Trolley Buses	(line)	13	13	14	14
地　铁	(条)	Subways	(line)	2	2	2	2
长　度	(公里)	Length	(km)	16566.2	12641.6	14929.2	11004.6
公共汽车	(公里)	Buses	(km)	16354.5	12429.9	14719.6	10795.0
# 小公共汽车	(公里)	Mini-Buses	(km)	6800.0	3000.0	6800.0	3000.0
无轨电车	(公里)	Trolley Buses	(km)	158.0	158.0	168.0	168.0
地　铁	(公里)	Subways	(km)	53.7	53.7	41.6	41.6
里程利用率		**Utilization Rate of Mileage**					
公共汽车	(%)	Buses	(%)	93.6	93.9	93.1	93.6
# 小公共汽车	(%)	Mini-Buses	(%)	89.4	89.1	87.9	86.7
无轨电车	(%)	Trolley Buses	(%)	99.8	99.8	99.6	99.6
地　铁	(%)	Subways	(%)	99.8	99.8	99.8	99.8
客运量	**(万人次)**	**Passengers Carried**	**(10000 person.times)**	**426705.6**	**415919.2**	**418824.9**	**408773.9**
按车种分		By Type of Vehicles					
公共汽车及无轨电车	(万人次)	Buses and Trolley Buses	(10000 person.times)	378482.7	367696.3	372494.2	362443.2
# 小公共汽车	(万人次)	Light Buses	(10000 person.times)	19087.2	15157.6	19100.0	15500.0
地　铁	万人次)	Subways	(10000 person.times)	48222.9	48222.9	46330.7	46330.7
按购票方式分		By Ways of Payment					
普　票	(万人次)	Common	(10000 person.times)	116188.5	111631.8	122174.3	102967.6
月　票	(万人次)	Monthly	(10000 person.times)	305569.6	299894.7	305538.1	301266.1
包　车	(万人次)	Hire	(10000 person.times)	3287.2	2802.9	2931.0	2460.0
旅　游	(万人次)	Tourism	(10000 person.times)	381.1	358.3	863.0	849.0
免　费	(万人次)	Free of Charge	(10000 person.times)	1279.2	1231.4	1275.0	1231.0
售出月票	**(万张)**	**Monthly Ticket Sales**	**(10000)**	**1969.4**	**1931.3**	**1974.9**	**1974.9**
客运收入	**(万元)**	**Revenue of Passengers Traffic**	**(10000 yuan)**	**182704.2**	**172586.0**	**159542.1**	**150100.1**

17-10 客运出租汽车
TAXIS SERVICE

项目		Item		1999	1998	1999年为1998年% 1999 as % of 1998
出租汽车营运单位		**Operating Units**		**2185**	**2175**	**100.5**
国有单位	(个)	State-Owned	(unit)	398	381	104.5
集体单位	(个)	Collective-Owned	(unit)	469	542	86.5
个体户	(个)	Individuals	(unit)	1164	1167	99.7
中外合资	(个)	Joint Venture	(unit)	4	4	100.0
其　他	(个)	Others	(unit)	150	81	185.2
营运车辆	**(辆)**	**Operating Vehicles**	**(unit)**	**61920**	**61301**	**101.0**
小轿车	(辆)	Cars	(unit)	59485	54128	109.9
微型面包车	(辆)	Minicoaches	(unit)		5152	
旅行车	(辆)	Wagon Cars	(unit)	1162	968	120.0
大轿车	(辆)	Coaches	(unit)	1273	1053	120.9
客运量		**Passengers Carried**		**61817**	**63817**	**96.9**
小轿车	(万人次)	Cars	(10000 person.times)	59111	54717	108.0
微型面包车	(万人次)	Minicoaches	(10000 person.times)		6855	
旅行车	(万人次)	Wagon Cars	(10000 person.times)	1145	996	115.0
大轿车	(万人次)	Coaches	(10000 person.times)	1561	1249	125.0
里程利用率		**Utilization Rate of Mileage**				
小轿车	(%)	Cars	(%)	67	67	100.0
微型面包车	(%)	Minicoaches	(%)		85	
旅行车	(%)	Wagon Cars	(%)	85	85	100.0
大轿车	(%)	Coaches	(%)	87	87	100.0

17-11 交通管理设施
UTILITIES OF TRANSPORTATION ADMINISTRATION

项目		Item		1999	1998	1999年为1998年% 1999 as % of 1998
交通警岗	(个)	Police Boxes	(unit)	2760	1089	253.4
灯　岗	(个)	Lamp Posts	(unit)	940	208	451.9
巡逻岗	(个)	Patrol Posts	(unit)	1820	881	206.6
信号灯	(座)	Traffic Lights	(unit)	940	482	195.0
# 自动信号灯	(座)	Automatic	(unit)	940	482	195.0
安全示意线	(公里)	Signal Lines for Safety	(km)	7469	6463	115.6
交通标志	(面)	Transportation Signal	(unit)	46289	42784	108.2
隔离墩	(套)	Separate Blocks	(set)	8453	24732	34.2
护　栏	(米)	Protective Fences	(m)	204403	168541	121.3

17-12 道路及桥梁
ROADS AND BRIDGES

项目		Item		1999	# 城近郊区 City Proper and and Near Suburb	1998	# 城近郊区 City Proper and and Near Suburb
道路		**Roads**					
道路长度	(公里)	Length	(km)	3753.2	3277.3	3720.9	3255.1
按质量分		By Quality					
# 高级	(公里)	Senior	(km)	1777.4	1616.2	1667.8	1510.9
次高级	(公里)	Secondary Senior	(km)	1481.9	1170.2	1446.5	1123.7
按车辆运行方式分		By Operating Ways of Vehicles					
# 快慢车分行路	(公里)	Separate Routes of Quick and Slow Vehicles	(km)	417.7	276.0	381.1	267.0
道路面积	(万平方米)	Areas of Roads	(10000 sq.m)	4353.0	3654.4	4214.2	3590.2
按质量分		By Quality					
# 高级	(万平方米)	Senior	(10000 sq.m)	2864.1	2592.3	2680.3	2680.3
次高级	(万平方米)	Secondary Senior	(10000 sq.m)	1288.9	867.1	1248.0	1258.9
按车辆运行方式分		By Operating Ways of Vehicles					
# 快慢车分行路	(万平方米)	Separate Routes of Quick and Slow	(10000 sq.m)	1196.4	878.0	1113.9	848.0
铺装步路	(万平方米)	Paved Roads	(10000 sq.m)	628.6	486.9	574.9	444.3
桥梁		**Bridges**					
城市桥梁	(座)	City Bridges	(unit)	787	665	715	602
# 大型道路立交桥	(座)	Large Flyovers	(unit)	141	113	138	113
行人过街天桥	(座)	Overpass	(unit)	149	147	125	123
地下通道	**(座/处)**	**Underpass**	**(unit/place)**	**174/131**	**149/106**	**167/126**	**141/100**

17-13 城市路灯设施
STREET LAMPS

项目		Item		1999	# 城近郊区 City Proper and and Near Suburb	1998	# 城近郊区 City Proper and and Near Suburb
路灯盏数	**(盏)**	**Number of Road Lamps**	**(unit)**	**183576**	**148143**	**114917**	**89499**
# 白炽灯	(盏)	Incandescent Lamps	(unit)	20129	16548	7932	5507
# 汞灯	(盏)	Mercury Lamps	(unit)	79793	67818	57839	49164
# 钠灯	(盏)	Sodium Lamps	(unit)	81618	63149	49146	34828
线路长度	**(公里)**	**Length of Lines**	**(km)**	**4952.4**	**3560.2**	**6414.9**	**3312.6**

17-14 城市园林绿化
GARDENS AND PLANTED AREAS

项目	Item	1999	# 城近郊区 City Proper and and Near Suburb	1998	# 城近郊区 City Proper and and Near Suburb
年末公共绿地面积 (公顷)	Public Green Areas(year-end) (hectare)	6457.0	4989.0	6351.0	4945.0
平均每人占有公共绿地面积 (包括水面) (平方米)	PerCapita Public Green Areas (including water surface) (sq.m)	9.1	8.2	9.0	8.2
城市绿化覆盖率 (%)	Coverage of City Green Areas (%)	36.3	35.3	35.6	34.9
道路绿化总长度 (公里)	Total Length of Green Roads (km)	2600.0	2115.0	2307.0	1844.0
年末实有树木 (万株)	Trees(year-end) (10000)	4865.0	3758.0	4613.0	3590.0
# 本年新植 (万株)	Newly Planted (10000)	309.0	224.0	257.0	207.0
全年出圃苗木 (万株)	Total Nursery Stage (10000)	118.0	118.0	188.0	188.0
苗圃面积 (公顷)	Areas of Nursery (hectare)	651.0	651.0	648.0	648.0
草坪面积 (万平方米)	Areas of Lawn (10000 sq.m)	4602.0	3526.0	4219.0	3280.0
# 本年新植 (万平方米)	Newly Planted (10000 sq.m)	565.0	427.0	272.0	216.0
公园个数 (个)	Parks (unit)	117	95	116	94
公园面积 (公顷)	Areas of Parks (hectare)	4320.0	3856.0	4183.0	3847.0
全年游园人数 (万人次)	Visitors to Parks and Zoos (10000 person.times)	8756.0	8284.0	9164.0	8707.0

注：公园面积包括风景区、游乐园、动物园面积。

Note: Area of parks includes those of scenic spots, amusement parks and zoos.

17-15 城市排水
DRAINAGE

项目	Item	1999	# 城近郊区 City Proper and and Near Suburb	1998	# 城近郊区 City Proper and and Near Suburb
下水道长度 (公里)	**Length of Sewer (km)**	**4737.1**	**4067.2**	**4645.6**	**3898.9**
雨水管 (公里)	Rain Pipes (km)	1391.0	1273.8	1346.5	1222.9
污水管 (公里)	Sewage Pipes (km)	1753.7	1631.9	1712.4	1557.1
雨污合流管 (公里)	Rain and Sewage Pipes (km)	1592.4	1161.5	1586.7	1118.9
污水处理	**Dispose of Sewage**				
处理厂 (个)	Disposal Plants (unit)	4.0	4.0	4.0	4.0
处理能力 (万吨／日)	Disposal Capability (10000 tons/day)	58.5	58.5	58.5	58.5
处理量 (万吨)	Disposed Volume (10000 tons)	25440.5	23725.0	22702.0	21170.0
处理率 (%)	Disposal Rate (%)	25.0	25.0	22.5	22.5
平均每日污水量 (万吨)	Daily Sewage (10000 tons)	278.8	260.0	276.4	258.2

17-16 城市环境卫生
MUNICIPAL ENVIRONMENT AND SANITATION

项目	Item	1999	# 城近郊区 City Proper and and Near Suburb	1998	# 城近郊区 City Proper and and Near Suburb
工作量	**Work Load**				
清扫街道面积 (万平方米／日)	Area Cleaned (10000 sq.m/day)	5574.0	4705	5168.0	4308.0
清运垃圾 (万吨)	Garbage Disposal (10000 tons)	505.0	449.5	495.1	431.6
清运粪便 (万吨)	Night Soil Disposal (10000 tons)	298.0	273.5	295.6	269.9
环卫机械数量 (辆)	**Number of Environmental Sanitation Equipment (unit)**	**3184**	**2868**	**3120**	**2733**
大中型扫尘车 (辆)	Large and Medium Road Sweepers (unit)	170	151	163	142
大中型洒水车 (辆)	Large and Medium Watering Cars (unit)	136	125	101	90
大中型垃圾车 (辆)	Large and Medium Dustcarts (unit)	1892	1671	1944	1681
真空吸粪车 (辆)	Vacuum Dung-drawer Carts (unit)	497	444	449	392
其他环卫车辆 (辆)	Others (unit)	489	477	463	428
环卫设施	**Environmental Sanitation Facilities**				
垃圾桶 (个)	Garbage Cans (unit)	12327	5092	11453	4655
果皮箱 (个)	Dustbins (unit)	12643	10877	10569	9087
公共厕所 (座)	Lavatories (unit)	6535	5900	6556	5825
密闭式集装箱垃圾站 (座)	Airtight Container Caerbage Stations (unit)	791	757	745	709

主要统计指标解释

年底自来水生产能力 是指城市供水设施取水、净水、送水、出厂输水干管等环节的综合生产能力，按设计能力（以四个环节中最薄弱环节为主）计算。在设计生产能力的基础上，经挖、革、改增加的生产能力，应按一次或数次增加的设计生产能力总和加原设计生产能力求得。

气化率 是指使用燃气（包括人工煤气、液化石油气、天然气）的城市非农业人口数（不包括临时人口和流动人口）与城市非农业人口总数之比。计算公式：

$$气化率=\frac{城市非农业用气人口数}{城市非农业人口总数}\times 100\%$$

城市桥梁 是指城市范围内，修建在河道上的桥梁和道路与道路立交、道路跨越铁路的立交桥，以及人行天桥。包括永久性桥和半永久性桥，不包括临时性桥、铁路桥、涵洞。

城市下水道总长度 是指汇集和排放污水、废水和雨水的管渠及其附属设施所组成的系统。长度按所有排水总管、干管、支管及检查井，联接井进出水口等长度之和计算，不包括雨水口至排水管道间的联接管、进户管及明渠。

城市污水日处理能力 是指污水处理厂每昼夜处理污水量的设计能力。

营运线路长度 是指公共交通全部运营线路的长度之和。

公共绿地 是指向公众开放的各级各类公园，小游园、街头绿地等，包括其范围内的水域。

Explanatory Notes On Main Statistical Indicators

Production Capacity of Tap Water at Year-end refers to the comprehensive production capacity such as water inflow, purification, conveyance and outflow of the trunk pipelines into account of the urban water-suppling construction, counted according to designed capacity(taking the weakest link of the above four as the principal one). The incremental capacity through innovation and reproduction on the bases of designed capacity, will be the sum of original designed capacity and incremental ones through one time or several times.

Percentage of Urban Gas Users refers to the ratio of the urban non-agricultural population using gas（including gas, liquefied petroleum gas and natural gas ）to the total of urban non-agricultural population （excluding temporary and mobile population）. The formula is:

$$\text{Percentage of Urban Gas Users}=\frac{\text{Urban Non - agricultural gas users}}{\text{Urban Non - agricultural Population}}\times 100\%$$

Urban Bridges refer to bridges over river courses, great separated junctions and overpasses in urban areas, including permanent bridges and semi-permanent bridges, excluding temporary bridges, railway bridges and culverts.

Length of Urban Sewage Pipes refers to the total length of general drainage, trunks, branches and blind drainage, inspection wells, connection wells, inlets and outlets, etc.

Daily Disposal Capacity of Urban Sewage refers to the designed 24-hour capacity of sewage disposal at the sewage works.

Length of Routes in Operation refers to the sum length of all routes in operation of public traffic.

Public Green Area refers to green areas of various parks, amusement parks and green-land streets opened to the public, including waters within the above region.

人民生活
PEOPLES LIVELIHOOD

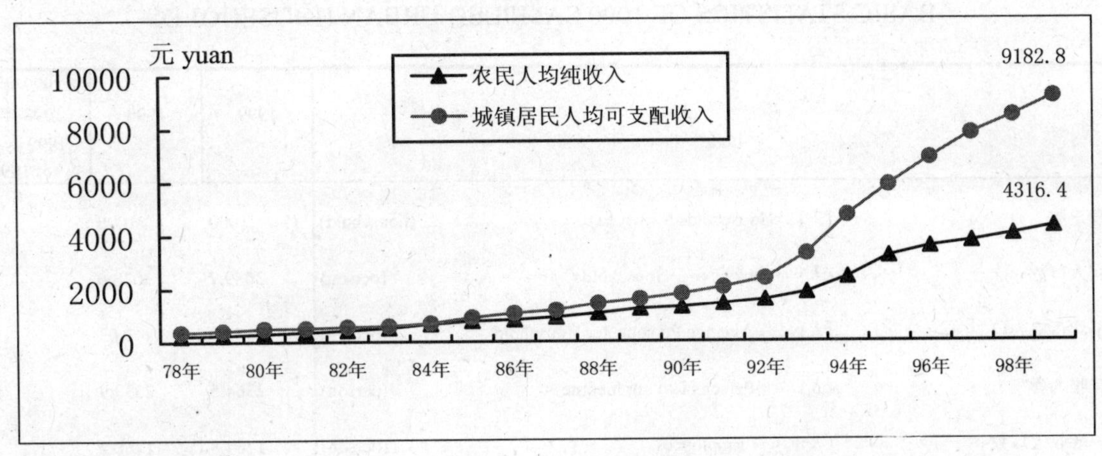

人均居住面积（平方米）
Per Capita Living Space(sq. m)

	1999	1998	1999年为1998年% 1999 as % of 1998
城镇(Urban)	10.63	10.03	106.0
农村(Rural)	28.6	27.6	103.6

1000户居民家庭平均每百户耐用消费品年末拥有量（1999年）
Per 100 Households year-end Possession of Durable Consumer Goods of 1000 Urban Households(1999)

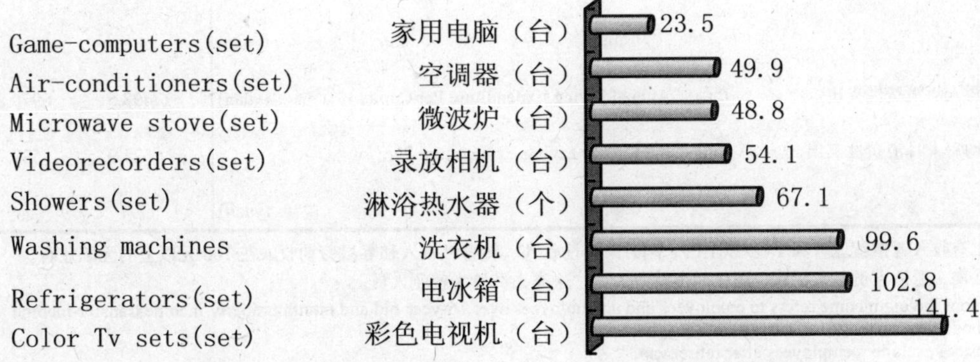

18-1 1000户居民家庭基本情况
BASIC STATISTICS OF 1000 SAMPLED URBAN HOUSEHOLDS

项　　目 Item				1999	1998	1999年为1998年% 1999 as % of 1998
调查户数	(户)	Households Surveyed	(household)	1000	1000	
家庭人口数	(人)	Persons of Households	(person)	3089.7	3028.6	102.0
平均每户人口	(人)	Average Persons Per Household	(person)	3.09	3.03	102.0
有收入者	(人)	Persons Having Income	(person)	2364.5	2337.9	101.1
就业人口数	(人)	Employees	(person)	1764.8	1768.2	99.8
平均每户就业人口数	(人)	Average Employees Per Household	(person)	1.76	1.77	99.4
国有经济单位职工人数	(人)	in State-owned Units	(person)	1317.8	1289.3	102.2
集体经济单位职工人数	(人)	in Collective-owned Units	(person)	111.3	126.5	87.9
其他所有制单位职工人数	(人)	in Other Units	(person)	140.6	96.0	146.5
个体经营者人数	(人)	Individual Employer	(person)	16.8	20.2	83.1
个体被雇者人数	(人)	Individual Employee	(person)	9.7	2.3	416.8
离、退休再就业人数	(人)	Reemployees after retirement	(person)	159.9	227.0	70.5
其他就业者人数	(人)	Others	(person)	8.8	7.0	126.1
离退休人员数	(人)	Retirees	(person)	594.7	550.5	108.0
其他有收入者人数	(人)	Others	(person)	4.9	19.2	25.6
无收入者人数	(人)	Persons having no Income	(person)	725.2	690.7	105.0
平均每一就业者负担人数	(人)	Dependents Per Employee	(person)	1.4	1.4	100.0
平均每人年可支配收入	(元)	Annual Discretionary Income Per Capita	(yuan)	9182.8	8472.0	108.4
平均每人月可支配收入	(元)	Monthly Discretionary Income Per Capita	(yuan)	765.2	706.0	108.4
平均每人年消费性支出	(元)	Annual Living Expenditure Per Capita	(yuan)	7498.5	6970.8	107.6
平均每人月消费性支出	(元)	Monthly Living Expenditure Per Capita	(yuan)	624.9	580.9	107.6

注：1.有收入者指就业者和16岁以上的、当月财产性收入、转移性收入和零星劳动收入在100元以上的无职业者。

2.离、退休人员不包括离、退休后再就业人员，这类人员计为就业人员。

a) Persons having income refers to employees and unemployees over 16-year-old and month property-income,transfer-income and odd income totaled to more than 100 yuan.

b) Retirees exclude reemployees after retirement.

18-2 1000户居民家庭基本情况(按收入水平分)
BASIC STATISTICS OF 1000 SAMPLED URBAN HOUSEHOLDS(BY INCOME LEVEL)

项目		Item		全市合计 Total	低收入户 Low Income	中等偏下收入户 Medium-Low Income	中等收入户 Medium Income	中等偏上高收入户 Medium-High Income	高收入户 High Income
调查户数	(户)	Households Surveyed	(household)	1000	200	200	200	200	200
家庭人口数	(人)	Persons of Households	(person)	3089.7	664.2	645.8	623.9	589.0	567.1
平均每户人口	(人)	Average Persons Per Household	(person)	3.1	3.3	3.2	3.1	3.0	2.8
有收入者	(人)	Persons Having Income	(person)	2364.5	452.8	474.1	471.8	479.3	483.8
就业人口数	(人)	Employees	(person)	1764.8	338.3	342.5	356.8	353.1	370.8
平均每户就业人口数	(人)	Average Employees Per Household	(person)	1.8	1.7	1.7	1.8	1.8	1.9
国有经济单位职工人数	(人)	in State-owned Units	(person)	1317.8	253.3	269.1	285.7	265.9	241.7
集体经济单位职工人数	(人)	in Collective-owned Units	(person)	111.3	39.0	26.2	18.2	13.8	15.1
其他所有制单位职工人数	(人)	in Other Units	(person)	140.6	20.1	19.8	26.8	27.2	45.9
个体经营者人数	(人)	Individual Employer	(person)	16.8	6.3		2.5	2.8	5.3
个体被雇者人数	(人)	Individual Employee	(person)	9.7	2.0		0.4	4.5	2.8
离、退休再就业人数	(人)	Reemployees after retirement	(person)	159.9	13.7	23.4	23.2	38.9	59.3
其他就业者人数	(人)	Others	(person)	8.8	4.0	4.0			0.8
离退休人员数	(人)	Retirees	(person)	594.7	110.3	131.6	115.0	126.1	112.6
其他有收入者人数	(人)	Others	(person)	4.9	4.3			0.1	0.5
无收入者人数	(人)	Persons having no Income	(person)	725.2	211.3	171.7	152.2	109.8	83.3
平均每一就业者负担人数	(人)	Dependents Per Employee	(person)	1.4	1.6	1.5	1.4	1.3	1.2
平均每人年可支配收入	(元)	Annual Discretionary Income Per Capita	(yuan)	9182.8	5310.5	7167.5	8577.6	10516.0	15200.8
平均每人月可支配收入	(元)	Monthly Discretionary Income Per Capita	(yuan)	765.2	442.5	597.3	714.8	876.3	1266.7
平均每人年消费性支出	(元)	Annual Living Expenditure Per Capita	(yuan)	7498.5	4873.9	5973.1	7079.0	8676.2	11456.3
平均每人月消费性支出	(元)	Monthly Living Expenditure Per Capita	(yuan)	624.9	406.2	497.8	589.9	723.0	954.7

18-3 1000户居民家庭每人每年现金收入
ANNUAL CASH INCOME PER CAPITA OF THE 1000 URBAN HOUSEHOLDS

单位：元 (yuan)

项目	Item	总平均 Average	低收入户 Low Income	中等偏下收入户 Medium-Low Income	中等收入户 Medium Income	中等偏上收入户 Medium-High Income	高收入户 High Income	1999年为1998年% 1999 as % of 1998
现金收入	**Cash Income**	**10654.84**	**6342.89**	**8031.19**	**9939.69**	**12213.11**	**17767.51**	**105.5**
实际收入	Real Income	9238.80	5358.09	7218.59	8630.23	10572.90	15275.20	108.4
# 可支配收入	Discretionary Income	9182.76	5310.48	7167.53	8577.56	10515.90	15200.82	108.4
职工收入	Staff and Workers	6179.73	3488.15	4810.31	6118.60	7072.70	9953.34	111.9
个体经营劳动者收入	Individuals	65.63	29.70		44.68	110.70	158.69	114.7
离退休再就业者收入	Reemployee after Retirement	237.58	84.62	140.23	148.00	269.70	577.16	80.4
其他就业者收入	Other Employee	5.19	12.62	5.69			7.02	68.9
其他劳动收入	Other Income from Work	191.49	131.17	129.52	100.62	191.20	433.07	91.3
财产性收入	Property Income	91.91	39.09	31.19	66.38	111.30	230.51	84.7
转移性收入	Transfer Income	2467.26	1572.74	2101.66	2151.94	2817.20	3915.41	106.4
#离退休金	Pension	2075.82	1348.26	1842.50	1742.06	2477.90	3142.77	107.8
赡养收入	Maintenance Income	93.55	56.36	52.98	120.00	76.90	172.45	101.3
赠送收入	Gift Income	120.17	56.93	100.09	157.25	82.80	215.25	98.9
亲友搭伙费	Poor Funds	53.97	34.16	19.81	31.81	66.90	126.91	82.8
记帐补贴	Subsidies of Account	48.93	46.84	49.04	45.61	49.30	54.61	112.9
出售财物收入	Proceeds from Sales of Belongings	12.94	0.90	0.32	3.02	3.70	61.83	268.5
其　他	Others	57.50	24.06	32.97	51.33	54.50	134.59	117.4
借贷收入	Credit Income	1416.04	984.80	812.60	1309.46	1640.20	2492.31	89.8

18-4 1000户居民家庭每人每年现金支出
ANNUAL CASH EXPENDITURES PER CAPITA OF THE 1000 URBAN HOUSEHOLDS

单位：元 (yuan)

项目	Item	总平均 Average	低收入户 Low Income	中等偏下收入户 Medium-Low Income	中等收入户 Medium Income	中等偏上收入户 Medium-High Income	高收入户 High Income	1999年为1998年% 1999 as % of 1998
现金支出合计	**Total**	**9893.62**	**5906.97**	**7375.16**	**9243.27**	**11304.60**	**16583.44**	**101.9**
实际支出	**Actual Expenditures**	**8453.58**	**5485.89**	**6624.98**	**8048.30**	**9730.10**	**13023.61**	**102.9**
消费性支出	Living Expenditures	7498.48	4873.89	5973.05	7079.03	8676.20	11456.33	107.6
非消费支出	Non-Living Expenditures	955.10	612.00	651.93	969.27	1053.80	1567.28	76.7
贷款利息	Loan Interets	0.15			0.61		0.18	
个人所得税	IndividualIncome-tax	7.11	0.77	2.01	7.06	7.70	19.77	134.9
各种税金	Taxes	11.16	1.90	3.03	4.31	3.10	28.13	121.7
非储蓄性保险	Non-saving-deposits Insurance	36.42	19.75	21.07	47.89	50.50	45.47	359.5
赡养支出	Support Expenditures	158.93	80.03	120.99	130.55	133.30	340.29	107.4
赠送支出	Gift Expenditures	329.53	145.57	198.29	273.64	355.30	727.26	101.5
购房与建房支出	Expenditures on Purchasing and Building Houses	332.64	329.65	262.91	383.91	432.00	255.13	46.3
其他非消费性支出	Others	86.30	34.31	43.63	121.31	71.90	170.82	237.0
借贷支出	**Credit Expenditures**	**1440.04**	**421.09**	**750.18**	**1194.97**	**1574.50**	**3559.83**	**96.5**
存入储蓄款	Saving Deposits	1085.05	263.09	479.53	921.27	1149.20	2861.29	95.3
存入储金会款	Reserve Fund	5.63	0.49	0.48	1.60	15.60	11.66	67.4
归还借款	Returning Loans	39.88	32.63	21.68	30.45	35.10	84.38	95.2
其他	Others	105.64	64.24	87.25	107.13	124.90	156.00	32.5

18-5 1000户居民家庭平均每人年消费性支出
ANNUAL LIVING EXPENDITURE PER CAPITA OF THE 1000 URBAN HOUSEHOLDS

单位：元 (yuan)

项目	Item	总平均 Average	低收入户 Low Income	中等偏下收入户 Medium-Low Income	中等收入户 Medium Income	中等偏上收入户 Medium-High Income	高收入户 High Income	1999年为1998年% 1999 as % of 1998
消费性支出	**Living Expenditures**	**7498.48**	**4873.89**	**5973.05**	**7079.03**	**8676.24**	**11456.33**	**107.57**
食　品	Food	2959.19	2302.76	2676.60	2871.94	3338.31	3719.99	103.26
衣　着	Clothing	730.79	375.95	554.32	666.57	857.75	1277.61	102.40
家庭设备用品及服务	Household Facilities, Articles and Services	749.41	378.88	476.39	636.16	831.94	1517.43	94.37
医疗保健	Medicine and Medical Services	513.34	357.56	409.52	488.78	458.20	895.45	147.56
交通通讯	Transportation and Communication	467.87	215.97	298.90	396.97	632.13	855.87	126.61
娱乐、教育文化服务	Recreation,Education and Culture Services	1141.82	674.53	912.26	1111.62	1427.26	1678.91	118.42
居住	Residence	478.42	364.87	360.74	489.36	551.94	654.34	90.60
杂项	Miscellaneous	457.64	203.37	284.32	417.63	578.70	856.73	118.13

18-6 1000户居民家庭平均每人年消费性支出比重
COMPOSITION OF ANNUAL LIVING EXPENDITURE PER CAPITA OF THE 1000 URBAN HOUSEHOLDS

单位：%

项目	Item	1999	1998	1999年比1998年增减百分点 Inerease or Decrense
消费性支出	**Living Expenditures**	**100**	**100**	
食　品	Food	39.46	41.11	-1.65
衣　着	Clothing	9.75	10.24	-0.49
家庭设备用品及服务	Household Facilities, Articles and Services	9.99	11.39	-1.40
医疗保健	Medicine and Medical Services	6.85	4.99	1.86
交通通讯	Transportation and Communication	6.24	5.30	0.94
娱乐、教育文化服务	Recreation,Education and Culture Services	15.23	13.83	1.40
居住	Residence	6.38	7.58	-1.20
杂项	Miscellaneous	6.10	5.56	0.54

18-7 1000户居民家庭平均每人年购买食品支出
ANNUAL EXPENDITURE OF FOOD PER CAPITA OF THE 1000 URBAN HOUSEHOLDS

单位：元 (yuan)

项目	Item	总平均 Average	低收入户 Low Income	中等偏下收入户 Medium-Low Income	中等收入户 Medium Income	中等偏上收入户 Medium-High Income	高收入户 High Income	1999年为1998年% 1999 as % of 1998
食品	**Food**	**2959.19**	**2302.76**	**2676.60**	**2871.94**	**3338.31**	**3719.99**	**103.3**
粮食	Grain	244.13	239.03	247.63	241.75	241.99	249.90	95.0
淀粉及薯类	Starches and Tuber	24.31	22.54	23.20	25.70	24.53	25.74	102.9
干豆类及豆制品	Bean and Bean Products	41.43	34.88	39.31	41.70	46.32	46.32	100.7
油脂类	Oil	73.04	85.32	71.79	70.67	65.44	70.38	100.8
肉禽及制品	Meat,Poultry and Related Products	540.40	473.00	512.48	530.62	84.83	623.09	91.5
蛋类	Eggs	78.06	71.43	73.94	79.72	158.51	81.30	99.5
水产品类	Aquatic Products	131.01	93.25	116.88	120.00	270.01	172.62	102.2
菜类	Vegetable	248.03	218.56	232.15	247.18	62.44	277.47	106.2
调味品	Flavorings	56.82	48.72	54.59	56.13	51.77	63.14	99.8
糖类	Sugar	43.08	31.42	35.48	43.41	101.37	56.40	100.6
烟草类	Tabacco	96.14	76.64	98.59	94.81	199.62	113.43	105.7
酒和饮料	Liquor and Beverage	189.74	150.91	175.24	196.54	251.25	232.54	105.3
干鲜瓜果类	Dried and Fresh Melon and Fruits	223.53	174.24	205.46	220.86	55.00	276.24	109.4
坚果和果仁	Nuts and Kernel	51.24	37.17	49.76	50.70	116.88	65.67	97.6
糕点类	Cake	99.56	73.13	92.66	102.45	172.72	116.91	99.1
奶及奶制品	Milk and Dairy Products	142.52	103.55	130.17	132.52	133.14	182.28	125.8
其他食品	Others	103.60	60.92	86.98	91.32	726.40	156.59	102.9
在外用餐	Dinning Out	572.32	307.87	430.02	525.74	0.27	909.71	114.9
食品加工费	Food Processing Service	0.23	0.18	0.27	0.13	575.87	0.26	48.9

18-8 1000户居民家庭平均每人年购买主要食品支出
ANNUAL PURCHASES OF MAJOR FOOD PER CAPITA OF THE 1000 URBAN HPUSEHOLDS

单位：元 (yuan)

项目	Item	总平均 Average	低收入户 Low Income	中等偏下收入户 Medium-Low Income	中等收入户 Medium Income	中等偏上收入户 Medium-High Income	高收入户 High Income	1999年为1998年% 1999 as % of 1998
粮食	Food	319.67	294.82	325.17	311.15	331.06	333.98	97.9
植物油	Edible Vegetable Oil	107.55	108.43	97.86	100.00	101.14	118.92	106.4
鲜菜	Fresh Vegetable	334.71	257.90	288.04	329.69	381.33	424.87	112.0
猪肉	Pork	443.46	344.15	384.04	426.88	489.43	592.28	94.7
牛羊肉	Beef and Mutton	196.01	148.28	175.65	190.24	222.97	242.81	94.5
家禽	Poultry	156.24	108.67	134.88	148.12	182.46	217.74	105.5
鲜蛋	Fresh Eggs	101.66	82.49	88.70	101.28	116.04	116.76	104.7
水产品	Aquatic Products	192.90	118.51	158.33	170.70	249.44	291.68	107.9
食糖	Sugar	15.67	14.45	13.44	15.43	16.54	17.65	103.0
卷烟	Cigarettes	96.05	76.63	97.72	95.19	102.97	113.39	105.8
酒	Wine	74.63	61.66	70.63	79.65	76.34	81.88	97.0
茶叶	Tea	44.04	36.03	40.64	41.76	43.00	59.88	110.5
鲜瓜果	Fresh Melons and Fruits	158.79	130.30	145.96	156.43	178.85	187.95	104.8
糖果	Candy	18.81	11.67	15.44	18.22	22.06	29.08	121.8
糕点	Cake	99.56	73.13	92.89	104.09	118.90	116.91	99.1
鲜奶	Fresh Milk	71.68	51.79	66.56	64.59	83.32	97.15	123.5
调味品	Flavorings	56.82	48.72	54.55	55.94	62.17	63.14	99.8
饮料	Beverage	71.06	53.22	62.34	70.76	79.68	90.78	112.1

18-9 1000户居民家庭平均每人年购买衣着、家庭设备用品及服务、医疗保健支出
ANNUAL PURCHASES OF CLOTHING,HOUSEHOLDS ARTICLES AND SERVICES, MEDICINE AND MEDICAL SERVICES PER CAPITA OF THE 1000 URBAN HOUSEHOLDS

单位：元 (yuan)

项目	Item	总平均 Average	低收入户 Low Income	中等偏下收入户 Medium-Low Income	中等收入户 Medium Income	中等偏上收入户 Medium-High Income	高收入户 High Income	1999年为1998年% 1999 as % of 1998
衣着	**Clothing**	**730.79**	**375.95**	**554.32**	**666.57**	**857.75**	**1277.61**	**102.4**
服装	Garments	480.80	222.85	351.74	432.57	559.72	896.66	105.5
衣着材料	Clothing Materials	44.03	31.32	33.49	35.52	55.44	68.80	79.8
棉布	Cotton Cloth	8.26	5.30	5.22	7.95	10.21	13.55	103.5
棉化纤混纺布	Cotton/Chemical Fabric Blend Cloth	4.12	2.50	3.73	4.58	4.33	5.98	100.0
化纤布	Chemical Fabric Cloth	10.86	6.63	8.85	6.84	13.59	19.83	69.6
呢绒	Woolen Fabric	6.45	4.16	2.29	5.31	11.54	9.72	58.9
绸缎	Silk and Stain	3.12	1.94	3.51	1.60	2.78	6.08	99.7
毛线	Knitting Wool	6.90	6.67	6.78	5.66	8.14	7.42	88.1
其他	Others	4.32	4.11	3.10	3.58	4.86	6.22	78.0
鞋袜帽及其他	Shoes,Socks,Hats and Others	185.79	110.11	152.14	177.37	218.32	283.76	104.3
衣着加工费	Clothing Processing	20.17	11.67	16.95	21.10	24.27	28.39	82.2
家庭设备用品及服务	**Households Articles and Services**	**749.41**	**378.88**	**476.39**	**636.16**	**831.94**	**1517.43**	**94.4**
耐用消费品	Durable Consumer Goods	460.60	212.83	250.20	389.65	496.32	1018.78	89.0
家具	Furniture	120.93	29.47	42.34	65.16	147.77	347.57	112.0
住房装饰	House Decorate	64.72	63.75	37.59	15.08	36.19	180.97	47.3
家庭设备	Households Facility	274.94	119.60	170.27	309.42	312.35	490.25	101.1
室内装饰品	Room Ornament	22.49	8.33	8.95	13.50	16.90	69.05	105.4
床上用品	Articles for Bed	29.53	14.36	21.94	28.39	30.13	56.14	113.4
家庭日用杂品	Groceries for Households Daily Use	168.27	114.28	146.43	170.80	198.35	220.39	97.0
家具材料	Furniture Materials	2.76	0.08	1.66	0.87	5.58	6.27	336.6
家庭服务	Households Services	65.76	29.00	47.22	32.94	84.66	146.80	120.2
医疗保健	**Medicine and Medical Services**	**513.34**	**357.56**	**409.52**	**488.78**	**458.20**	**895.45**	**147.6**
医疗器具	Medical Implements	7.59	3.50	5.67	10.92	4.90	13.70	112.0
保健用品	Health Appliance	14.19	5.25	19.24	10.27	16.86	20.46	103.2
医药费	Medicine Expenses	339.63	246.28	272.22	337.65	310.61	556.78	133.3
补药品	Tonic	43.90	18.63	43.00	33.31	48.30	80.38	180.5
医疗保健服务	Medical Services	94.71	76.15	60.06	87.69	65.15	193.55	205.9
其他	Others	13.31	7.76	9.33	8.94	12.38	30.58	616.2

18-10 1000 户居民家庭平均每人年交通通讯、娱乐文教服务支出
ANNUAL EXPENDITURE OF TRANSPORTATION,COMMUNICATION, RECREATION,CULTURE AND EDUCATION SERVICES PER CAPITA OF THE 1000 URBAN HOUSEHOLDS

单位：元 (yuan)

项目	Item	总平均 Average	低收入户 Low Income	中等偏下收入户 Medium-Low Income	中等收入户 Medium Income	中等偏上收入户 Medium-High Income	高收入户 High Income	1999年为1998年% 1999 as % of 1998
交通和通讯	**Transportation and Communication**	**467.87**	**215.97**	**298.89**	**396.97**	**632.13**	**855.87**	**126.6**
交　通	Transportation	204.72	86.57	106.55	149.89	318.95	393.78	127.1
# 家庭交通工具	Means of Transport for Households	60.73	11.42	17.01	20.89	147.6	121.83	240.5
交通费	Transport Fare	118.29	62.95	75.16	104.53	142.26	219.94	103.4
维修服务费	Fare for Repair	23.89	11.7	13.46	24.38	26.63	46.42	120.3
通　讯	Communication	263.15	129.4	192.35	247.08	313.18	462.09	126.3
# 通讯工具	Means	57.04	16.1	18.69	32.27	79.23	152.47	175.1
电讯费	Telecommunication Fare	195.28	110.81	160.41	202.02	220.91	296.65	129.4
邮　费	Post Fare	5.8	0.87	4.14	8.57	6.56	9.64	145.7
其　他	Others	5.03	1.61	9.11	4.22	6.48	3.33	24.0
娱乐文教服务	**Recreation,Culture and Education services**	**1141.82**	**674.53**	**912.26**	**1111.62**	**1427.26**	**1678.91**	**118.4**
耐用消费品	Durable Consumer Goods	375.28	122.06	287.35	326.64	526.78	661.57	141.8
# 彩　电	Color TV	119.94	64.56	65.96	81.21	196.97	202.90	112.2
影碟机	Video CD	26.53	13.19	28.07	21.28	31.01	41.53	87.1
录放象机	Video-corder	0.25		1.2				5.0
家用电脑	Game-computer	134.15	7.53	136.27	141.35	176.28	228.3	196.2
录音机	Recorder	7.02	4.68	3.72	8.16	6.36	12.97	111.8
组合音响	Hi-Fi System	17.36	2.79	7.45	11.73	26.81	42.08	683.5
摄象机	Pickup Camera	9.17	7.57			25.26	14.87	100.0
照相机	Camera	7.38		4.42	7.46	5.83	20.89	159.7
照相器材	Photographic Equipment	0.09	0.73	0.09	0.24			34.6
钢　琴	Piano							
中高档乐器	Secondary and Top Grade Musical Instrument	5.92	1.34	11.66	3.89	3.74	9.23	485.3
其　他	Others	31.79	7.23	13.67	35.89	38.5	69.72	105.5
修理服务费	Fare for Repairs	14.29	12.36	14.05	13.75	14.29	16.96	191.8
教　育	Education	493.19	414.98	411.21	492.23	589.17	586.00	107.3
# 教学参考书	Teaching Reference Book	39.76	32.83	37.43	39.81	38.61	51.11	132.5
学杂费	Tuition and Incidentals	302.45	285.3	259.11	329.18	344.68	311.42	104.8
托幼费	Child-care Fare	32.90	24.23	24.31	25.59	40.85	52.60	90.1
成人教育	Adult Education	23.58	4.73	11.39	13.12	37.61	53.28	110.7
其　他	Others	94.51	67.89	78.97	84.53	127.41	117.59	113.5
文化娱乐	Culture and Recreation	273.35	137.48	213.71	292.76	311.31	431.33	114.0
# 文娱用品	Appliance	87.07	34.82	62.26	93.55	114.46	137.97	114.5
书报杂志	Book,Newspaper and Magazine	76.19	35.31	67.39	81.15	82.48	120.29	107.8
文娱费	Fare	110.09	67.35	84.06	118.06	114.37	173.07	118.2

18-11 1000户居民家庭平均每人年居住、杂项商品和服务支出
ANNUAL EXPENDITURE OF RESIDENCE,MISCELLANEOUS COMMODITIES AND SERVICES PER CAPITA OF THE 1000 URBAN HOUSEHOLDS

单位：元 (yuan)

项 目	Item	总平均 Average	低收入户 Low Income	中等偏下收入户 Medium-Low Income	中 等收入户 Medium Income	中等偏上收入户 Medium-High Income	高收入户 High Income	1999年为1998年% 1999 as % of 1998
居 住	**Residence**	**478.42**	**364.87**	**360.74**	**489.36**	**551.94**	**654.34**	**90.6**
住 房	House	199.23	132.74	106.34	218.14	230.32	327.94	72.5
# 建筑材料	Construction Materials	78.36	55.80	42.39	87.21	101.29	112.39	91.0
房 租	Rent	59.29	47.96	51.74	49.40	78.42	70.20	51.2
维修服务	Repairs	61.58	28.98	12.21	81.52	50.61	145.35	84.7
水电燃料	Fare for Water, Electricity and Fuel	279.20	232.13	254.40	271.23	321.62	326.40	110.1
# 水 费	Water	36.87	30.34	33.33	36.26	41.24	44.28	141.2
电 费	Electricity	125.03	101.42	107.79	117.81	153.06	151.52	127.3
燃 料	Fuel	102.41	91.95	97.41	100.83	112.86	110.25	91.9
煤 炭	Coal	25.56	30.65	25.84	25.97	27.02	17.00	105.2
液化石油气	Liquefied Petroleum Gas	23.84	25.68	24.16	23.48	24.66	21.20	109.4
管道煤气	Pipeline Gas	49.56	34.19	46.80	44.44	59.09	65.42	122.2
其 他	Others	3.45	1.43	0.61	6.94	2.08	6.63	13.9
其 他	Others	14.82	8.42	15.64	16.32	14.36	20.36	84.3
杂项商品和服务	**Miscellaneous Commodities and Services**	**457.64**	**203.37**	**284.76**	**417.63**	**578.70**	**856.73**	**118.1**
个人消费	Personal Consumption	411.69	182.96	255.94	367.19	526.24	780.25	120.5
个人用品	Personal Articles	132.06	64.57	110.77	117.98	164.46	213.78	101.7
# 金银珠宝饰品	Golden,Silver and Jewelry Ornament	25.40	6.35	15.20	19.65	38.65	51.17	96.0
纸张文具	Paper and Stationery	18.20	12.56	18.37	17.87	17.24	26.14	101.4
其他日用品	Other Articles for Daily Use	83.14	43.52	72.66	78.14	102.48	124.78	103.6
理发、美容用品	Articles for Hair-cut Improving one's Looks	62.59	36.40	46.73	58.39	74.78	102.14	129.7
# 理发美容用品	Articles for Hair-cut Improving one's Looks	2.14	0.93	0.51	1.09	2.16	6.64	158.5
美容化妆品	Cosmetics	57.84	34.70	45.46	54.08	69.05	90.27	129.5
旅游	Tourism	191.06	65.10	77.06	166.51	256.17	426.60	139.4
# 火车费	Train Fare	33.60	11.77	11.76	28.87	53.47	68.60	136.7
其他交通费	Other Fare for Transport	21.53	2.76	2.56	19.47	12.31	76.96	112.8
住宿费	Fare for Accmmodation	11.95	5.13	6.74	7.47	13.13	28.50	136.1
其 他	Others	111.45	37.69	49.50	101.82	160.73	227.72	145.7
服务费	Services	25.98	16.90	21.38	24.30	30.83	37.72	97.9
# 理发洗澡费 用	Fare for Hair-cut and Bath	17.86	13.99	13.66	16.63	21.28	24.39	118.3
美 容 费	Fare for Improving one's Looks	3.62	0.49	2.62	3.02	5.61	6.64	171.6
其他商品	Other Commodities	13.85	5.71	4.73	13.58	16.00	24.41	175.3
其他服务	Other Services	32.09	14.7	23.65	36.86	36.46	52.07	85.1

18-12 1000户居民家庭平均每人年主要食品购买量
ANNUAL PURCHASES OF MAJOR FOOD PER CAPITA OF THE 1000 URBAN HOUSEHOLDS

单位：公斤 (kg)

项目 Item		总平均 Average	低收入户 Low Income	中等偏下收入户 Medium-Low Income	中等收入户 Medium Income	中等偏上收入户 Medium-High Income	高收入户 High Income	1999年为1998年% 1999 as % of 1998
粮食	Food	79.27	81.87	81.64	77.26	77.54	75.77	96.3
植物油	Edible Vegetable Oil	10.03	10.38	9.26	9.36	9.24	10.71	103.4
鲜菜	Fresh Vegetable	199.27	162.90	177.77	197.19	220.04	238.56	114.8
猪肉	Pork	33.78	27.99	30.06	32.42	36.23	42.65	112.2
牛羊肉	Beef and Mutton	11.94	9.44	10.93	11.67	13.23	14.14	97.2
家禽	Poultry	10.23	7.87	9.10	9.92	11.13	13.44	108.1
蛋类	Eggs	19.89	16.17	17.37	19.81	22.71	22.80	119.1
水产品	Aquatic Products	12.59	9.55	11.15	12.03	14.22	16.41	98.4
食糖	Sugar	2.77	2.67	2.37	2.73	2.92	2.95	108.6
卷烟 (盒)	Cigarettes (case)	29.52	28.10	35.78	30.22	28.29	25.94	103.6
酒	Wine	14.31	11.59	14.02	15.66	15.88	13.43	99.0
茶叶	Tea	0.42	0.42	0.43	0.42	0.39	0.41	107.7
鲜瓜果	Fresh Melons and Fruits	67.14	58.44	61.81	66.64	74.30	76.31	99.9
糖果	Candy	0.70	0.47	0.63	0.73	0.80	0.94	118.6
糕点	Cake	5.69	4.65	5.66	5.94	6.51	6.10	99.8
鲜奶	Milk	20.25	14.43	19.11	17.85	23.22	27.99	119.7

18-13 1000户居民家庭平均每百人穿着商品购买量
PER 100 PERSONS ANNUAL PURCHASES OF DRESSING COMMODITIES OF THE 1000 URBAN HOUSEHOLDS

项目	Item	总平均 Average	低收入户 Low Income	中等偏下收入户 Medium-Low Income	中等收入户 Medium Income	中等偏上收入户 Medium-High Income	高收入户 High Income	1999年为1998年% 1999 as % of 1998
毛皮大衣 (件)	Fur coats (unit)	4.37	0.90	4.02	4.01	5.26	8.29	132.4
呢大衣 (件)	Woolen Coats (unit)	4.63	2.71	3.24	3.53	5.77	8.11	104.8
风雨衣 (件)	Raincoat (unit)	2.98	2.11	1.24	3.05	3.57	5.29	88.4
西服 (件)	Western-style Clothes (unit)	9.06	4.37	4.33	8.99	11.38	17.28	101.6
毛线衣 (件)	Sweater (unit)	56.41	31.02	50.21	54.74	63.67	85.88	113.7
各式童装 (件)	Children Wear (unit)	93.44	83.56	95.79	82.99	99.15	110.21	99.7
棉布 (米)	Cotton Cloth (m)	91.52	61.14	67.1	82.75	115.79	145.43	96.1
棉化纤混纺布 (米)	Cotton/Chemical Fabric Blend Cloth (m)	21.61	15.15	25.31	18.77	24.18	25.64	92.4
化纤布 (米)	Chemical Fabric Cloth (m)	43.80	33.34	37.25	24.87	56.08	71.79	66.2
呢绒 (米)	Woolen Fabric (m)	10.31	6.61	3.92	8.62	15.30	18.23	68.6
绸缎 (米)	Silk and Stain (m)	7.97	5.19	8.36	5.09	8.51	13.98	97.4
毛线 (公斤)	Knitting Wool (kg)	10.21	9.29	11.09	8.56	11.83	10.16	92.7
皮鞋 (双)	Leather Shoes (pair)	78.94	54.35	63.19	73.52	89.81	116.56	102.2
旅游鞋 (双)	Travel Shoes (pair)	18.55	14.76	18.54	20.55	19.19	19.40	104.8

18-14 1000户居民家庭平均每百户耐用消费品年购买量
PER 100 HOUSEHOLDS ANNUAL PURCHASES OF DURABLE CONSUMER GOODS OF THE 1000 URBAN HOUSEHOLDS

项目		Item		总平均 Average	低收入户 Low Income	中等偏下收入户 Medium-Low Income	中等收入户 Medium Income	中等偏上收入户 Medium-High Income	高收入户 High Income	1999年为1998年% 1999 as % of 1998
组合家具	(套)	Combined Furniture	(set)	1.9	1.0	1.5	0.5	1.5	5.0	86.4
沙发床	(个)	Bed with Mattress	(unit)	4.2	1.5	3.5	4.5	5.0	6.5	131.3
沙　发	(个)	Sofas	(unit)	7.7	4.5	0.5	5.0	9.0	18.5	120.3
摩托车	(辆)	Motorcyles	(unit)	0.3				0.5	1.0	150.0
自行车	(辆)	Bicycles	(unit)	15.9	12.0	13.5	15.5	18.0	20.5	95.8
家用汽车	(辆)	Cars	(unit)	0.2				0.5	0.5	
电风扇	(台)	Electric Fans	(set)	9.5	7.0	11.5	7.5	12.0	10.0	215.9
电冰箱	(台)	Refrigerators	(set)	4.7	3.0	4.0	4.5	5.5	6.0	94.0
洗衣机	(台)	Washing Machines	(set)	6.0	5.5	5.5	4.0	8.5	6.5	85.7
缝纫机	(台)	Sewing Machine	(set)	0.1			0.1			50.0
冰　柜	(台)	Freezers	(set)	0.3				1.0	0.5	75.0
微波炉	(台)	Microwave Stove	(set)	7.2	4.5	8.0	9.5	8.5	5.5	167.4
空调器	(台)	Air-Conditioners	(set)	9.4	2.0	4.5	12.0	9.5	18.5	134.3
电炊具	(台)	Electric Cooking Appliances	(set)	14.0	12.0	12.0	13.5	14.0	18.5	142.9
淋浴热水器	(个)	Showers	(set)	7.1	3.5	6.0	9.5	11.0	7.0	104.4
脱排油烟机	(台)	Range Hoods	(set)	4.3	2.5	4.5	6.5	4.0	3.5	134.4
吸尘器	(台)	Dust Catcher	(set)	0.4		0.5	1.0		0.5	200.0
彩　电	(台)	Color TV Sets	(set)	12.9	8.5	10.5	9.5	19.5	15.5	131.6
影碟机	(台)	Video CD	(set)	6.8	4.0	9.5	6.5	6.0	8.5	183.8
录放像机	(台)	Videorecorders	(set)	0.1		0.5				12.5
家用电脑	(台)	Game-Computers	(set)	4.9	0.5	5.0	5.5	6.0	7.5	204.2
组合音响	(套)	Hi-Fi Systems	(set)	2.2	1.5	1.0	1.5	2.5	4.5	550.0
录音机	(台)	Recorders	(set)	6.0	4.5	3.0	5.0	7.5	10.0	240.0
摄象机	(台)	Pickup Camera	(set)	0.5	0.5			1.0	1.0	
钢　琴	(台)	Piano	(set)							
其他中高档乐器	(件)	Secondary and Top Grade Musical Instrument	(unit)	1.1	0.5	1.5	1.0	0.5	2.0	550.0
照相机	(架)	Camera	(set)	2.6		2.0	3.5	1.5	5.5	130.0

18-15 1000户居民家庭平均每百户耐用消费品年拥有量 PER 100 HOUSEHOLDS ANNUAL POSSESSION OF DURABLE CONSUMER GOODS OF THE 1000 URBAN HOUSEHOLDS

项目		Item		总平均 Average	低收入户 Low Income	中等偏下收入户 Medium-Low Income	中等收入户 Medium Income	中等偏上收入户 Medium-High Income	高收入户 High Income	1999年为1998年% 1999 as % of 1998
组合家具	(套)	Combined Furniture	(set)	75.1	64.0	72.0	74.5	75.5	89.0	101.2
沙发床	(个)	Bed with Mattress	(unit)	77.3	57.0	60.0	84.0	92.0	93.0	106.8
沙发	(个)	Sofas	(unit)	153.5	122.0	131.5	134.5	166.5	212.0	92.5
摩托车	(辆)	Motorcycles	(unit)	6.0	6.5	3.0	5.5	7.0	8.0	157.9
自行车	(辆)	Bicycles	(unit)	220.1	215.5	224.0	218.0	218.5	223.5	99.6
家用汽车	(辆)	Cars	(unit)	2.5	3.0	2.5	2.5	1.0	3.5	250.0
电风扇	(台)	Electric Fans	(set)	145.4	131.0	140.5	139.5	155.5	157.5	100.3
电冰箱	(台)	Refrigerators	(set)	102.8	97.5	103.0	104.0	103.5	105.5	97.5
洗衣机	(台)	Washing Machines	(set)	99.6	94.0	100.5	96.5	102.0	104.5	97.5
健身器材	(件)	Health Equipment	(set)	10.0	6.5	6.5	9.0	10.5	16.0	156.3
冰柜	(台)	Freezers	(set)	17.1	12.5	16.0	13.0	23.5	20.5	109.6
微波炉	(台)	Microwave Stove	(set)	48.8	29.0	45.0	48.0	60.0	61.0	131.2
空调器	(台)	Air-Conditioners	(set)	49.9	31.0	43.0	42.5	58.0	74.5	146.8
电炊具	(台)	Electric Cooking Appliances	(set)	83.7	60.0	66.5	79.0	92.0	119.5	122.0
淋浴热水器	(个)	Showers	(set)	67.1	52.0	59.5	69.0	75.0	78.5	102.6
脱排油烟机	(台)	Range Hoods	(set)	62.9	43.0	55.5	65.0	70.5	78.5	105.9
吸尘器	(台)	Dust Catcher	(set)	23.1	13.5	15.0	20.0	31.0	35.5	98.7
彩电	(台)	Color TV Sets	(set)	141.4	123.0	138.0	131.0	151.0	162.5	106.2
影碟机	(台)	Video CD	(set)	38.2	23.5	37.5	38.5	42.5	48.5	185.4
录放像机	(台)	Videorecorders	(set)	54.1	40.0	50.5	55.0	57.0	66.5	90.5
家用电脑	(台)	Game-Computers	(set)	23.5	10.5	18.5	20.0	27.5	40.5	156.7
组合音响	(套)	Hi-Fi Systems	(set)	25.6	10.5	23.0	20.5	31.0	42.0	115.3
录音机	(台)	Recorders	(set)	69.9	66.5	64.0	67.5	70.5	80.0	96.0
摄像机	(台)	Pickup Camera	(set)	5.6	2.5	3.5	4.5	7.5	10.0	155.6
钢琴	(台)	Piano	(set)	2.9	1.5	0.5	2.5	5.5	4.5	96.7
其他中高档乐器	(件)	Secondary and Top Grade Musical Instrument	(unit)	12.2	6.5	11.5	12.0	13.0	18.0	92.4
照相机	(架)	Camera	(set)	95.0	67.5	87.0	95.5	98.5	125.5	99.8
移动电话	(台)	Mobilphone	(unit)	12.9	5.5	8.5	10.0	13.0	26.5	430.0

18-16 1000户居民家庭居住情况
HOUSING CONDITIONS OF THE 1000 URBAN HOUSEHOLDS

项　目		Item		1999	1998	1999年为1998年% 1999 as % of 1998
平均每户居室间数	(间)	Number of Rooms Per Household	(room)	2.14	2.14	100.0
平均每人使用面积	(平方米)	Per Capita Using Space	(sq.m)	13.04	12.83	101.6
平均每人居住面积	(平方米)	Per Capita Living Space	(sq.m)	9.01	8.88	101.5
平均每人辅助面积	(平方米)	Per Capita Auxiliary Space	(sq.m)	4.03	3.95	102.0
按居住面积分		**Grouped by Living Space**				
无房户	(户)	No House	(household)			
4平方米以下	(户)	below 4 sq.m	(household)	44	56	78.6
4-6平方米	(户)	4-6 sq.m	(household)	173	164	105.5
6-8平方米	(户)	6-8 sq.m	(household)	229	206	111.2
8-10平方米	(户)	8-10 sq.m	(household)	225	210	107.1
10-12平方米	(户)	10-12 sq.m	(household)	115	136	84.6
12-14平方米	(户)	12-14 sq.m	(household)	97	86	112.8
14平方米以上	(户)	above 14 sq.m	(household)	117	142	82.4
按自来水使用情况分		**Grouped by Using of Tap Water**				
无自来水	(户)	No Tap Water	(household)	3		
独用自来水	(户)	Using by oneself	(household)	751	778	96.5
公用自来水	(户)	Public Tap Water	(household)	246	222	110.8
按卫生设备拥有情况分		**Grouped by Possession of Sanitary Equipment**				
无卫生设备	(户)	No Sanitary Equipment	(household)	289	286	101.0
有浴室厕所	(户)	Having Bathroom and Lavatory	(household)	74	70	105.7
有厕所无浴室	(户)	Having Lavatory and No Bathroom	(household)	501	558	89.8
公用卫生设备	(户)	Public Sanitary Equipment	(household)	136	86	158.1
按取暖设备拥有情况		**Grouped by Possession of Heating Equipment**				
无取暖设备	(户)	No Heating Equipment	(household)	2	2	100.0
空调设备	(户)	Air Conditioner	(household)	15	2	750.0
暖　气	(户)	Central Heating	(household)	655	652	100.5
其　他	(户)	Others	(household)	328	344	95.3

18-16 续表 continued

单位：户 (household)

项 目	Item	1999	1998	1999 年为 1998 年% 1999 as % of 1998
按厨房使用情况分	**Grouped by Using of Kitchen**			
无厨房	No Kitchen	196	200	98.0
独用厨房	Using Kitchen by oneself	691	766	90.2
公用厨房	Public Kitchen	113	34	332.4
按房屋产权分	**Grouped by House Property Rights**			
公房	Public House	639	766	83.4
租赁私房	Rent Private House	17	20	85.0
自有房	Self-house	121	128	94.5
部分产权自有房	Self-house with Part Property Rights	221	74	298.6
其他	Others	2	12	16.7
按燃料使用情况分	**Grouped by Using of Fuel**			
管道煤气	Pipeline Gas	536	494	108.5
液化石油气	Liquefied Petroleum Gas	403	442	91.2
煤	Coal	39	42	92.9
其他	Others	22	22	100.0
按电话拥有情况分	**Grouped by Possession of Telephone**			
无电话	No Telephone	146	226	64.6
公费电话	Free Telephone	60	66	90.9
自费电话	Telephone at one's Own Expenses	786	680	115.6
公用电话	Public Telephone	8	28	28.6
按住房建筑式样分	**Grouped by Style of House Construction**			
家庭单栋配套楼房	Individual Storied Building of a Family	1		
单元式配套楼房	Storied Building on Unit Style	610	590	103.4
一居室	One-room	99	68	145.6
二居室	Two-room	358	352	101.7
三居室	Three-room	133	164	81.1
四局室以上	Four-room and above	20	6	333.3
普通楼房	Ordinary Storied Building	55	54	101.9
普通平房及其他	Ordinary Single-story Building	334	356	93.8

18-17 35 个大中城市居民人均收支对比
CONTRAST ON PER CAPITA INCOME AND EXPENDITURE OF URBAN RESIDENTS OF 35 LARGE AND MEDIUM CITIES

单位：元 (yuan)

城市	City	人均可支配收入 Discretionary Income Per Capita			人均消费性支出 Living Expenditure Per Capita		
		1999	1998	1999 年为 1998 年% 1999 as % of 1998	1999	1998	1999 年为 1998 年% 1999 as % of 1998
北京	Beijing	9182.8	8472.0	108.4	7498.5	6970.8	107.6
天津	Tianjin	7649.8	7110.5	107.6	5851.5	5471.0	107.0
石家庄	Shijiazhuang	6131.0	5952.5	103.0	5002.8	4723.2	105.9
太原	Taiyuan	5627.4	5391.2	104.4	4693.4	4473.1	104.9
呼和浩特	Huhehaote	5167.4	4738.8	109.0	4172.8	3673.5	113.6
沈阳	Shenyang	5364.3	4931.6	108.8	4652.2	4639.6	100.3
大连	Dalian	6274.0	6092.9	103.0	5530.3	5521.3	100.2
长春	Changchun	5110.2	4751.4	107.6	4571.2	4172.3	109.6
哈尔滨	Haerbin	5032.3	4449.5	113.1	4215.8	3844.0	109.7
上海	Shanghai	10931.6	8773.1	124.6	8247.7	6866.4	120.1
南京	Nanjing	7693.8	7018.2	109.6	6448.6	6056.0	106.5
杭州	Hangzhou	9084.5	8465.2	107.3	7423.7	7234.9	102.6
宁波	Ningbo	9491.7	9193.2	103.2	7493.3	7911.9	94.7
合肥	Hefei	5812.9	5524.5	105.2	4551.7	4290.5	106.1
福州	Fuzhou	7413.8	7363.1	100.7	5732.9	6258.2	91.6
厦门	Xiamen	9625.6	9179.3	104.9	7889.6	7478.3	105.5
南昌	Nanchang	5287.5	4870.7	108.6	4077.4	3839.8	106.2
济南	Jinan	7162.5	6757.1	106.0	6415.4	5440.2	117.9
青岛	Qingdao	7281.7	6554.4	111.1	5980.8	5565.2	107.5
郑州	Zhengzhou	6147.7	5720.7	107.5	5064.7	4776.9	106.0
武汉	Wuhan	6262.1	5912.5	105.9	5452.8	5264.5	103.6
长沙	Changsha	7297.1	6650.0	109.7	6538.3	5706.3	114.6
广州	Guangzhou	12326.0	11464.1	107.5	10272.3	9699.8	105.9
深圳	Shenzhen	20548.4	20245.3	101.5	15726.1	16011.7	98.2
南宁	Nanning	6846.4	6570.1	104.2	6320.5	5800.1	109.0
海口	Haikou	7058.9	6749.4	104.6	5569.3	5287.3	105.3
成都	Chengdu	7098.0	6446.4	110.1	5798.0	5482.3	105.8
重庆	Chongqing	5896.0	5466.6	107.9	5444.2	4977.3	109.4
贵阳	Guiyang	6082.2	5369.0	113.3	5327.1	5036.5	105.8
昆明	Kunming	7239.4	7054.8	102.6	6371.1	6021.5	105.8
西安	Xi'an	5998.8	5669.6	105.8	5361.0	4806.6	111.5
兰州	Lanzhou	5127.5	4553.9	112.6	4505.6	3567.2	126.3
西宁	Xining	4764.9	4245.0	112.2	3966.3	3698.3	107.2
银川	Yinchuan	5167.7	4821.1	107.2	4484.4	4398.4	102.0
乌鲁木齐	Wulumuqi	6676.0	6441.3	103.6	5183.6	4406.8	117.6

18-18 2240户农民家庭基本情况
SAMPLING STATISTICS FOR 2240 RURAL HOUSEHOLDS

项目 Item	总平均 Average	按人均年纯收入水平分组 Grouped by Annual Net Income Per Capita				1999年为1998年% 1999 as % of 1998
		2000元以下 Below 2000 yuan	2000~3500	3500~5000	5000元以上 above 5000 yuan	
调查户数 (户) Households Surveyed (household)	2240	331	659	530	720	101.8
常住人口 (人) Permanent Residents (person)	8104	1305	2504	1905	2390	101.4
平均每户 (人) Average Per Household (person)	3.62	3.94	3.8	3.59	3.32	99.7
整半劳动力 (个) Full-time and Part-time Labors (person)	5687	880	1726	1351	1730	102.7
平均每户 (个) Average Per Household (person)	2.54	2.66	2.62	2.55	2.4	100.8
平均每一劳动力负担人口 (人) Dependents Per Labor Force (person)	1.43	1.48	1.45	1.41	1.38	99.3
学龄前儿童人数 (人) Number of Preschool Children (person)	208	40	78	47	43	92.4
6~11岁人口 (人) Persons at Age 6-11 (person)	526	102	176	114	134	89.5
# 在校人口 (人) at School (person)	488	91	163	108	126	89.4
12~14岁人口 (人) Persons at Age 12-14 (person)	511	92	150	114	155	111.3
# 在校人口 (人) at School (person)	511	92	150	114	155	111.6
15~17岁人口 (人) Persons at Age 15-17 (person)	430	62	132	100	136	103.1
# 在校人口 (人) at School (person)	423	58	130	99	136	103.4
家庭经营耕地面积 (公顷) Cultivated Land Area Runned by Households (hectare)	508.7	77.5	132.1	173.0	126.1	120.1
家庭经营山地面积 (公顷) Mountain Land Area Runned by Households (hectare)	110.5	25.5	63.9	7.2	13.9	113.0
人均生产性固定资产原值 (元) Original Value of Productive Fixed Assets Per Capita (yuan)	1054.2	1086.5	797.8	792.7	1513.7	112.2
人均住房面积 (平方米) Per Capita Living Space (sq.m)	28.6	24.4	26.7	28.7	33.0	103.6
人均总收入 (元) Per Capita Total Revenue (yuan)	4950.3	1957.8	3262.6	4678.3	8582.8	108.2
# 现金收入 (元) Cash Income (yuan)	4666.8	1726.5	3018.2	4376.2	8231.1	110.9
人均纯收入 (元) Net Income Per Capita (yuan)	4316.4	1458.6	2756.4	4170.6	7627.3	107.1
人均生活消费支出 (元) Per Capita Annual Living Expenditures (yuan)	3132.5	1601.4	2301.3	3049.4	4905.4	106.3
# 现金支出 (元) Cash Expenditures (yuan)	2996.3	1450.1	2155.4	2906.9	4792.9	107.4
职工人数 (人) Staff and Workers (person)	693.0	59.0	167.0	173.0	294.0	95.3
乡村企业从业人数 (人) Employees of Village Enterprises (person)	1208.0	118.0	327.0	299.0	464.0	106.2
平均每个劳动力创造纯收入 (元) Average Net Income Per Labor Force (yuan)	5725.8	1997.2	3713.9	5553.5	9763.6	104.7

18-19 2240户农民家庭平均每人年纯收入
ANNUAL NET INCOME PER CAPITA OF THE 2240 RURAL HOUSEHOLDS

单位：元 (yuan)

项　目	Item	总平均 Average	按人均年纯收入水平分组 Grouped by Annual Net Income Per Capita 2000元以下 Below 2000 yuan	2000～3500	3500～5000	5000元以上 above 5000 yuan	1999年为1998年% 1999 as % of 1998
合　计	**Total**	**4316.4**	**1458.6**	**2756.4**	**4170.6**	**7627.3**	**107.1**
基本收入	**Basic Income**	**4018.0**	**1346.8**	**2560.0**	**3938.5**	**7067.4**	**106.1**
劳动者的报酬收入	Remuneration of Labors	2881.7	862.5	1781.8	2928.0	5099.5	104.2
在集体组织中劳动的报酬	from Collective Units	1113.8	332.4	688.5	1172.4	1939.4	96.8
在企业劳动得到的报酬	from Enterprises	1692.0	458.2	1032.5	1670.7	3073.6	107.9
在集体企业的劳动所得	Collective-owned	1044.4	275.1	619.0	989.2	1954.2	111.7
在个体企业的劳动所得	Individuals	151.9	87.1	115.6	144.9	230.8	97.6
在其他企业的劳动所得	Others	495.7	96.0	297.9	536.6	888.6	103.9
在其他单位劳动得到的报酬	from Other Units	75.9	71.9	60.8	84.9	86.5	164.1
家庭经营纯收入	Net Income from Family Business	1136.3	484.3	778.2	1010.5	1967.9	111.0
从第一产业得到	Primary Industry	736.4	375.6	602.0	764.0	1049.3	101.1
从第二产业得到	Secondary Industry	31.3	-1.7	27.1	20.4	62.6	119.7
从第三产业得到	Tertiary Industry	368.6	110.4	149.1	226.1	856.0	136.9
转移性和财产性收入	**Transfer and Property Income**	**298.4**	**111.8**	**196.4**	**232.1**	**559.9**	**124.0**
在外人口寄、带回	Transferring from Family Members	10.8	6.5	4.7	7.4	22.2	112.5
农村外部亲友赠送	Gifts from Relatives and Friends	15.4	5.1	14.5	14.0	23.0	114.9
奖励收入	Rewards	27.3	3.9	18.0	28.4	48.8	131.9
财产性收入	Property Income	102.7	20.7	37.8	52.0	256.0	103.5

18-20 2240 户农民家庭平均每人年生活费支出
ANNUAL LIVING EXPENDITURES PER CAPITA OF THE 2240 RURAL HOUSEHOLDS

单位：元 (yuan)

项目	Item	总平均 Average	按人均年纯收入水平分组 Grouped by Annual Net Income Per Capita				1999 年为 1998 年% 1999 as % of 1998
			2000 元以下 Below 2000 yuan	2000～3500	3500～5000	5000 元以上 above 5000 yuan	
合计	**Total**	**3132.5**	**1601.4**	**2301.3**	**3049.4**	**4905.4**	**106.3**
食品支出	**Food Expenditure**	**1253.5**	**792.6**	**1050.9**	**1244.9**	**1724.2**	**100.9**
#主食	Staple Food	263.3	242.5	256.0	259.8	285.1	92.0
副食	Non-Staple Food	512.3	324.0	436.3	520.5	688.0	96.9
其他食品	Others	336.5	182.8	260.7	317.9	514.5	108.1
衣着支出	**Clothing Expenditure**	**256.5**	**110.4**	**161.1**	**237.4**	**451.4**	**97.9**
#服装支出	Garments	127.1	46.1	67.7	111.4	246.2	101.0
居住支出	**Residence**	**416.3**	**191.6**	**290.5**	**376.3**	**702.8**	**99.6**
#住房	Housing	200.1	82.1	105.7	195.8	366.9	63.0
燃料	Fuel	104.4	61.0	92.4	108.1	137.7	104.3
家庭设备用品及服务支出	**Household Facilities, Articles and Services**	**263.2**	**85.7**	**168.3**	**237.0**	**480.5**	**116.6**
#耐用消费品	Durable Consumer Goods	144.2	28.8	78.2	123.9	292.7	127.7
家庭日用杂品	Daily Use Household Articles	96.4	46.9	71.1	94.4	151.3	106.6
医疗保健支出	**Medicines and Medical Services**	**223.0**	**103.0**	**165.2**	**233.2**	**341.0**	**127.7**
交通和通讯支出	**Transportation and Communications**	**165.5**	**53.1**	**105.5**	**125.9**	**321.4**	**112.0**
#交通工具	Transportation Means	69.3	16.3	43.1	41.7	147.7	122.4
交通费	Transportation	20.5	12.1	15.7	20.2	30.4	110.2
邮电费	Posts and Telecommunications	43.4	12.9	29.8	34.1	81.7	142.8
文教娱乐用品及服务支出	**Cultural,Education and Recreation Articles and Services**	**461.6**	**239.9**	**307.1**	**505.3**	**709.5**	**120.1**
#文娱用机电消费品	Mechanical and Electric Consumer Goods of Culture and Recreation	104.5	21.2	35.7	123.6	207.0	127.3
书报杂志	Books,Newspapers and Magazines	5.2	1.9	2.9	4.9	9.7	100.0
学杂费	Tuition and Incidentals	299.4	199.1	243.4	325.2	392.4	121.9
文娱费	Recreation	17.1	4.0	5.2	13.9	39.3	135.7
其他商品及服务支出	**Other Commodity and Services**	**92.9**	**25.1**	**52.7**	**89.4**	**174.6**	**102.0**
#商品性支出	Commodity Expenditures	19.0	3.5	8.2	18.4	39.4	105.6

18-21 2240户农民家庭平均每人年粮食收支存情况
BROUGHT IN, SENT OUT AND INVENTORY OF GRAIN PER CAPITA OF THE 2240 HOUSEHOLDS

单位：公斤 (kg)

项目	Item	总平均 Average	按人均年纯收入水平分组 Grouped by Annual Net Income Per Capita 2000元以下 Below 2000 yuan	2000～3500	3500～5000	5000元以上 above 5000 yuan	1999年为1998年% 1999 as % of 1998
年初粮食结存	**Grain Inventory (year-end)**	**208.8**	**203.3**	**234.5**	**221.4**	**174.8**	**101.9**
年内粮食收入	**Brought in within this Year**	**534.8**	**404.6**	**468.9**	**504.3**	**699.4**	**106.5**
从集体得到	From Collective	0.1			0.1	0.1	9.3
家庭经营生产	Household Production	432.1	331.8	384.1	419.2	547.6	104.6
购入	Purchasing	99.9	70.5	83.1	81.3	148.3	115.7
# 从集市购入	From Free Market	40.7	27.3	38.2	36.3	54.1	106.3
其他	Others	2.7	2.3	1.7	3.7	3.4	128.1
年内粮食支出	**Sent out within this Year**	**396.2**	**324.1**	**378.6**	**352.2**	**489.2**	**108.8**
生活用粮	Living Consumption	164.1	162.3	161.3	161.8	167.0	97.9
# 稻谷	Rice	33.8	26.2	32.6	33.0	39.8	100.6
小麦	Wheat	98.3	102.9	98.4	103.4	91.4	92.3
出售粮食	Selling	205.1	150.9	195.4	177.7	266.9	112.2
# 出售给国家	to Government	133.8	87.1	119.1	123.7	182.7	156.1
其他	Others	27.0	10.9	21.9	12.7	55.3	195.6
年末粮食结存	**Grain Inventory (year-end)**	**347.4**	**283.8**	**324.8**	**373.5**	**385.0**	**101.3**
# 口粮	Grain Ration	196.5	188.6	206.7	220.1	171.4	98.0
饲料	Forage	8.1	11.4	4.6	6.2	11.5	172.3
种籽	Seed	3.8	2.9	4.3	4.7	3.0	111.8

18-22 2240户农民家庭主要生活消费品平均每人消费量
CONSUMPTION OF MAJOR LIVING CONSUMER GOODS PER CAPITA OF THE 2240 RURAL HOUSEHOLDS

项目 Item				总平均 Average	按人均年纯收入水平分组 Grouped by Annual Net Income Per Capita				1999年为1998年% 1999 as % of 1998
					2000元以下 Below 2000 yuan	2000～3500	3500～5000	5000元以上 above 5000 yuan	
粮食	(公斤)	Grains	(kg)	164.13	162.29	161.30	161.77	169.98	97.9
豆制品	(公斤)	Bean Products	(kg)	3.85	2.29	4.19	3.80	4.38	104.6
蔬菜	(公斤)	Vegetables	(kg)	103.53	84.85	98.54	105.34	117.52	107.8
植物油	(公斤)	Vegetable Oil	(kg)	8.51	7.29	8.27	8.48	9.45	99.9
动物油	(公斤)	Animal Oil	(kg)	0.46	0.55	0.56	0.45	0.32	75.4
猪牛羊肉	(公斤)	Pork,Beef,Mutton	(kg)	14.65	9.39	12.51	16.48	18.28	109.4
家禽	(公斤)	Poultry	(kg)	1.86	0.62	1.34	1.46	3.38	125.7
蛋类	(公斤)	Eggs	(kg)	8.09	4.64	7.39	8.62	10.28	108.3
奶及奶制品	(公斤)	Milk and Diary Products	(kg)	3.45	1.10	2.44	3.12	6.07	128.2
水产品	(公斤)	Aquatic Products	(kg)	4.19	2.42	3.12	4.02	6.42	117.7
食糖	(公斤)	Sugar	(kg)	1.51	1.04	1.68	1.22	1.80	88.3
糖果	(公斤)	Candy	(kg)	0.26	0.13	0.20	0.25	0.39	89.7
酒类	(公斤)	Liquor	(kg)	17.07	12.81	15.37	17.23	21.06	106.4
茶叶	(公斤)	Tea	(kg)	1.04	0.87	1.07	0.96	1.17	273.7
糕点	(公斤)	Cake	(kg)	2.41	1.33	1.94	2.55	3.38	112.6
瓜果	(公斤)	Melons and Fruits	(kg)	37.15	21.26	28.86	39.55	52.61	112.9
棉布及其服装	(米)	Cotton Cloth and Related Clothing	(m)	0.82	0.54	0.71	0.82	1.08	103.8
化纤布及其服装	(米)	Chemical Fiber Cloth and Related Clothing	(m)	1.72	1.00	1.62	1.74	2.20	100.6
呢绒、绸缎及其服装	(米)	Woolen Febric,Silk and Stains and Related Clothing	(m)	0.06	0.02	0.03	0.09	0.11	85.7
毛线及其织品	(公斤)	Knitting Wool and Related Products	(kg)	0.26	0.12	0.21	0.25	0.39	104.0
针织衣裤	(件)	Knitwear	(piece)	0.65	0.36	0.51	0.66	0.94	106.6
# 尼龙衫裤	(件)	Nylonwear	(piece)	0.04	0.03	0.04	0.04	0.04	100.0
棉毛衫裤	(件)	Cotton/Woolen Wear	(unit)	0.32	0.15	0.26	0.34	0.48	106.7
卫生衫裤	(件)	Sweater	(piece)	0.28	0.18	0.21	0.28	0.42	103.7
皮鞋	(双)	Leather Shoes	(pair)	0.61	0.33	0.47	0.66	0.88	103.4
胶球鞋	(双)	Rubber Overshoes	(pair)	0.2	0.25	0.19	0.2	0.19	95.2
肥皂	(块)	Soup	(unit)	1.41	0.96	1.75	1.38	1.32	119.5
洗衣粉	(公斤)	Washing Powder	(kg)	3.54	1.86	4.55	3.6	3.35	160.2

18-23 2240户农民家庭平均每百户耐用消费品拥有量
DURABLE CONSUMER GOODS POSSESSION PER 100 HOUSEHOLDS OF THE 2240 HOUSEHOLDS

项目 Item				总平均 Average	按人均年纯收入水平分组 Grouped by Annual Net Income Per Capita				1999年为1998年% 1999 as % of 1998
					2000元以下 Below 2000 yuan	2000～3500	3500～5000	5000元以上 above 5000 yuan	
自行车	(辆)	Bicycles	(unit)	241	211	235	245	258	96.8
缝纫机	(架)	Sewing Machines	(unit)	69	65	71	73	65	98.6
钟	(只)	Clocks	(unit)	119	107	116	121	126	102.6
手　表	(只)	Wristwatches	(unit)	225	186	211	230	252	99.1
电风扇	(台)	Electric Fans	(set)	143	111	131	152	162	107.5
洗衣机	(台)	Washing Machines	(set)	86	72	84	88	94	101.2
电冰箱	(台)	Refrigerators	(set)	81	55	73	81	99	108.0
摩托车	(辆)	Motorcycles	(unit)	34	21	31	34	45	121.4
收音机	(台)	Radios	(set)	46	36	46	47	50	97.9
黑白电视机	(台)	Black and White TV Sets	(set)	34	38	40	32	27	87.2
彩色电视机	(台)	Color TV Sets	(set)	101	87	93	101	116	109.8
收录机	(台)	Recorders	(set)	59	50	57	60	65	101.7
照相机	(架)	Cameras	(set)	29	11	19	29	46	111.5
录相机	(台)	Videorecorders	(set)	15	5	10	12	25	100.0
抽油烟机	(台)	Range Hoods	(set)	17	8	10	18	28	113.3
吸尘器	(台)	Vacuum Cleaners	(set)	5	2	4	3	8	125.0
组合家具	(套)	Combined Furniture	(set)	52	41	48	52	61	106.1
沙　发	(个)	Sofas	(unit)	266	191	243	266	322	100.8
床	(个)	Beds	(unit)	207	165	200	215	226	103.0
大衣柜	(个)	Wardrobes	(unit)	105	93	103	107	110	101.9
写字台	(张)	Writing Desks	(unit)	105	95	100	105	113	101.9

主要统计指标解释

城镇居民家庭就业人口 指城镇居民从事社会劳动并取得劳动报酬或经营收入的人口。就业人口包括通过国家统筹规划和指导由劳动部门介绍就业，自愿组织起来就业和自谋职业等方式，在国有制、集体所有制、中外合资、中外合作、外资在华独资的企事业单位和私营企业单位工作或从事个体劳动的有固定性职业或临时性职业的人口。被聘用和留用的离退休人员也计入就业人口。本指标可以反映城镇居民的就业情况，是计算就业面、负担系数的重要资料。

城镇居民家庭全部收入 指被调查城镇居民家庭全部的实际现金收入，包括经常或固定的收入和一次性收入。不包括周转性收入，如提取银行存款、向亲友借入款、收回借出款以及其他各种暂收款。

城镇居民家庭可支配收入 指居民家庭在支付个人所得税后，所余下的实际收入。计算公式为：

可支配收入=实际收入－个人所得税－家庭副业生产支出－记帐补贴

城镇居民家庭消费性支出 指被调查的城镇居民家庭用于日常生活的全部支出，包括购买商品支出和文化生活、服务等非商品性支出。不包括罚没、丢失款和缴纳的各种税款（如个人所得税、牌照税、房产税等），也不包括个体劳动者经营过程中发生的各项费用。

农村居民家庭纯收入 指农村居民家庭总收入中，扣除从事生产和非生产经营费用支出、缴纳税款和上交承包集体任务金额以后剩余的，可直接用于进行生产性、非生产性建设投资、生活消费和积蓄的那一部分收入。它是反映农民家庭实际收入水平的综合性的主要指标。农民家庭纯收入，既包括从事生产性和非生产性的经营收入，又包括取自在外人口寄回带回和国家财政救济、各种补贴等非经营性收入；既包括货币收入，又包括自产自用的实物收入。但不包括向银行、信用社和向亲友借款等属于借贷性的收入。

农村居民家庭整半劳动力 指农村常住居民家庭成员中有劳动能力并经常参加实际劳动的人员。是生产的基本要素指标之一，是发展生产增加农民家庭收入的重要源泉。按规定，农村男18周岁至50周岁、女18周岁至45周岁为整劳动力；男16周岁至17周岁、51周岁到60周岁，女16周岁到17周岁、46周岁至55周岁为半劳动力。农民家庭整半劳动力既包括在上述规定劳动年龄内和在劳动年龄以外有劳动能力并经常参加实际劳动的男女整半劳动力；也包括农民家庭常住人员中属于职工的劳动力。但不包括在劳动年龄内已丧失劳动能力的人员。

农村居民家庭生活消费支出 指农村常住居民家庭年内用于日常生活的全部开支。它是用来反映和研究农民家庭实际生活消费水平高低的重要指标。农民家庭生活消费支出，包括用于吃、穿、住、烧、用等生活消费品开支和文化、生活服务费用开支两大部分。

Explanatory Notes On Main Statistical Indicators

Employed Population in Urban Households refers to urban residents engaged in certain work and receiving payment for their labor or income from their business operation, including those who work in state-owned or collective units, joint ventures, foreign-owned units and private units with permanent or temporary jobs, self-employed individuals and re-employed retirees. The indicator reflects the situation of urban employment and is the basic data for calculating employment rate and dependency ratio.

Total Income of Urban Households refers to the total actual cash income of the sample households, including regular or fixed income and occasional income, excluding temporary transferred income, such as withdrawal from bank deposits, borrowed money from relatives or friends, repayment of loans received and various temporary receipts of money.

Discretionary Income of Urban Households refers to the total actual income of households after individual income tax turned over.The formula:

Discretionary Income=Actual Income – Individual Income Tax – Expenditure of Sideline Production – Subsidies of Account

Expenditure on Consumption of Urban Households refers to total expenditure of the sample households on consumption in daily life, including expenditure on various commodities and non-commodity items, such as culture and service, etc., but excluding fines and confiscation, loss, tax payments (such as income tax, license tax, real estates tax, etc.) or various operating expenses in individual business.

Net Income of Rural Households refers to the total income of the permanent residents of the rural households with deduction of the operating expenses in productive and non-productive business, the tax payment and the payment to collective units for their contracted tasks. The net income can be used for investments in productive and non-productive construction, for consumption in daily life and for savings deposit. It is a comprehensive indicator to show the actual income level of the peasants' household, which includes not only the income from the productive and non-productive work, but also the transferred income, such as the money remitted or brought back by household members who are in other places, the government relief and various subsidies, not only the money income, but also the income in kind. But the money borrowed from banks, friends and relatives is excluded.

Full and half Labors of Rural Households refer to permanent residents of rural households who are able to work and actually engaged in social labor, which are factors of production and sources of rural household income. According to the relevant regulations, male aged 18-50 and female aged 18-45 are considered as full labors; male aged 16-17 and 51-60, female aged 16-17 and 46-55 are considered as half labors. Those who are not in the above age range but able to work and actually engaged in social labor are also considered as full or half labors.

Expenditure on Consumption of Rural Households refers to total expenditure of rural households on daily life , including expenses on food, clothing, housing , fuel, articles for daily use, and expenses on cultural life and services. This indicator is used to show the actual consumption level of peasants.

社会福利、政法及其他
SOCIAL WELFARE，POLITICS，LAW AND OTHERS

历届律师资格考试情况（1988-1999年）
Statistics for Lawyer Qualification Examination

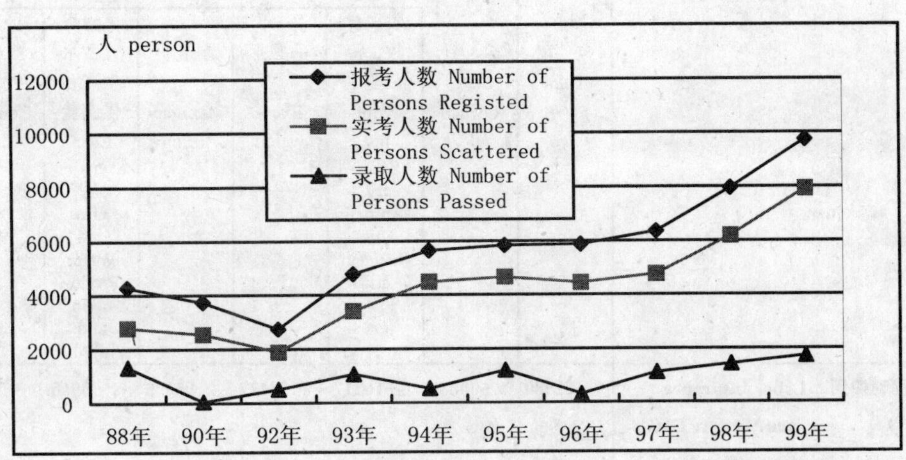

	1999年	1998年
离休、退休职工人数(人) Number of Retired and VCSR(person)	1685968	1555704
保险福利费用（万元） Labour Insurance and Welfare Funds(10000 yuan)		
在职职工 Staff and Workers at Posts	602080	545084
非在职职工 Staff and Workers off Posts	1690829	1411546

结 婚 登 记 情 况
Basic Statistics for Marriage Registrations (couple)

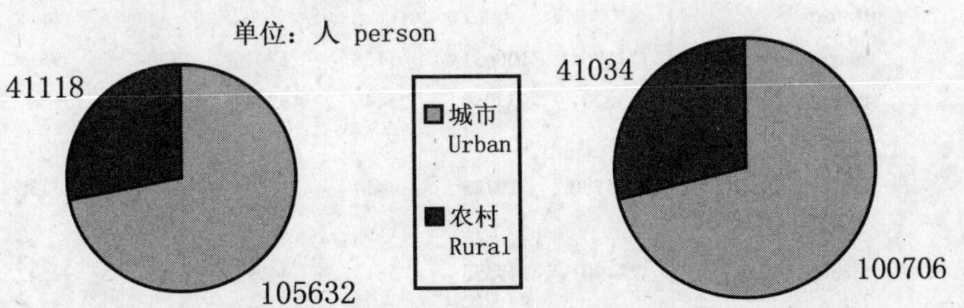

19-1 职工劳保福利费用

单位：万元

项目	Item	全市 Total	国有单位合计 State-Owned	农、林牧、渔业 Farming, Forestry, Animal Husbandry and Fishery	采掘业 Excavation	制造业 Manufacturing	电力煤气及水生产和供应业 Electricity, Gas and Water Production and Supply	建筑业 Construction	地质勘查业、水利管理业 Geological Prospecting and Water Conservancy
在职职工劳保福利费用	**Labor Insurance and Welfare Funds for Staff and Workers at Posts**	**602080**	**500885**	**10217**	**4427**	**95335**	**5968**	**36358**	**2622**
医疗卫生费	Medical Fare	407806	341410	6125	2826	69659	4896	24045	1829
集体福利设施费	Collective Welfare Facilities	57051	46864	747	423	7806	331	3503	265
文体宣传费	Expenses for Cultural Activities, Sports and Propaganda	19143	16838	231	262	2552	190	1531	104
丧葬、抚恤救济费	Funeral Expenses and Pensions for Family of the Deceased	5889	5223	99	338	1392	42	556	27
生活困难补助	Living Allowances	6170	5346	119	88	1054	40	425	20
计划生育补贴	Subsidies for Family Planning	8854	7459	134	34	1233	86	290	17
冬季取暖补贴	Heating Allowances	24725	19782	653	189	4277	103	1382	81
其他	Others	72442	57963	2109	267	7362	280	4626	279
非在职职工保险福利费用	**Insurance and Welfare Funds for Staff and Workers off Posts**	**1690829**	**1425656**	**34776**	**24977**	**500241**	**28808**	**150665**	**7664**
离休工资	Wages for VCSR	111764	106631	1168	1741	18204	951	5648	1001
退休金	Pensions for Retired	1155391	957059	25440	16738	378699	17246	100577	4247
退职生活费	Resignation Allowance	24780	10725	414	130	3254	313	1082	28
医疗卫生费	Medical Care	284903	248558	5813	4499	75887	9254	32785	1818
其他	Others	113991	102684	1941	1870	24197	1044	10574	569

LABOR INSURANCE AND WELFARE FUNDS FOR STAFF AND WORKERS

(10000 yuan)

交通运输仓储及邮电通信业 Transportation, Storage Post and Telecommunications	批发和零售贸易、餐饮业 Wholesale, Retail and Catering	金融、保险业 Banking and Insurance	房地产业 Real Estate	社会服务业 Social Services	卫生、体育和社会福利业 Health, Sports and Social Welfare	教育、文化艺术及广播电影电视业 Education, Culture, Arts, Radio Film and Television	科学研究和综合技术服务业 Scientific Research and Polytechnical Services	国家机关政党机关社会团体 Government Organs, Party Organs, and Social Bodies	其他行业 Others	集体所有制单位 Collective Owned	其他所有制单位 Others
58734	**54101**	**33162**	**9815**	**42863**	**14693**	**46493**	**40975**	**36772**	**8350**	**39022**	**62173**
42580	42036	19056	6908	29611	8597	30013	23548	25106	4575	28689	37708
5106	2450	2530	1021	3578	1560	3904	9950	2449	1241	1540	8647
2245	680	1012	247	1700	925	1310	2120	1453	276	722	1583
362	293	78	53	252	197	653	286	493	102	334	332
494	588	113	60	331	124	617	587	624	62	442	381
1054	692	994	106	558	268	612	554	635	192	684	712
1902	2353	591	283	1738	841	2585	493	1875	436	2512	2431
4991	5009	8788	1137	5095	2181	6799	3437	4137	1466	4099	10379
92461	**128177**	**14430**	**13217**	**69849**	**38657**	**108082**	**98712**	**99792**	**15148**	**228104**	**37069**
8463	6883	1407	364	5025	3874	13193	15876	21766	1065	4368	765
67386	82538	7145	7711	42211	25601	64731	61615	48750	6426	169812	28521
1129	1125	19	73	213	429	1402	304	722	89	13720	334
8765	31030	3761	3926	17748	5545	13805	14224	16382	3315	30713	5632
6718	6600	2099	1144	4652	3208	14951	6693	12172	4252	9490	1817

19-2 离休、退休职工人数
NUMBER OF RETIRED AND VCSR

单位：人 (person)

行业 Sector		1999			1998		
		合计 Total	# 退休职工 Retired	# 离休干部 VCSR	合计 Total	# 退休职工 Retired	# 离休干部 VCSR
总计	**Total**	**1685968**	**1544041**	**88253**	**1555704**	**1416383**	**91862**
按隶属关系分	**Grouped by Administrative Relationship**						
中央单位	Central Units	347952	295850	45586	322352	268865	48160
地方单位	Local Units	1338016	1248191	42667	1233352	1147518	43702
按登记注册类型分	**Grouped by Registered Type**						
国有经济	State-Owned	1334456	1227468	83651	1232955	1124985	86942
集体经济	Collective-Owned	310733	277314	3917	294555	264443	4229
其　他	Others	40779	39259	685	28194	26955	691
在国有经济中：	**Of State-Owned Economy**						
农、林、牧、渔业	Farming,Forestry,Animal Husbandry and Fishery	37190	35488	965	32059	30543	993
采 掘 业	Excavation	25074	23253	1501	24061	22231	1531
制 造 业	Manufacturing	511024	489447	14132	492608	470202	15058
电力、煤气及水的生产和供应业	Electricity,Gas and Water Production and Supply	25084	23466	846	22868	21412	883
建筑业	Construction	133107	126236	4381	109653	103810	3742
地质勘查业、水利管理业	Geological Prospecting and Water Conservancy	5015	4170	784	4491	3570	877
交通运输、仓储及邮电通信业	Transportation,Storage, Posts and Telecommunications	98800	89255	7467	100011	89898	8206
批发、零售贸易、餐饮业	Wholesale,Retail and Catering	132353	124140	5274	107799	99778	5591
金融、保险业	Banking and Insurance	10812	9669	1105	9289	8067	1195
房地产业	Real Estate	10997	10512	314	10425	9854	414
社会服务业	Social Services	66601	61416	4655	62764	57473	4842
卫生、体育和社会福利业	Health Care,Sports and Social Welfare	31959	28311	2793	28689	24790	3120
教育、文化艺术和广播电影电视业	Education,Culture,Arts, Radio,Film and Television	99443	85056	11616	94680	79590	12462
科学研究和综合技术服务业	Scientific Research and Polytechnical Services	66951	56346	10107	63282	52429	10465
国家机关、政党机关和社会团体	Government Organs,Party Organs and Social Bodies	70245	52067	16751	62430	44615	16577
其他行业	Others	9801	8636	960	7846	6723	985

19-3 优抚、救济对象得到抚恤、补助、救济情况
STATISTICS FOR SPECIAL PENSIONS,ALLOWANCES AND RELIEF FUNDS

项目	Item	人数（人）Number of Persons (person)	抚恤、补助、救济金额（千元）Amount of Pensions, Subsidies and Relief Funds (1000 yuan)
烈属牺牲病故军人家属抚恤	Pensions for Members of Revolutionary Martyr's Family,Armymen Sacrificed and Died of Illness	3481	14405
革命伤残人员抚恤	Pensions for Disabled Veterans	12168	6540
复退军人生活补助	Living Allowances for Demobilized Soldiers	18254	63833
农村五保户定期救济补助	Register Relief for Rural Households with Five-guarantees	3580	7699
农村贫困户救济	Relief for Rural Poor Households	12118	8832
城镇散居孤老残幼救济	Relief for Urban Scattered Orphans and Widows,Disabled,the Old and the Youth		
城镇贫困户定期救济	Register Relief for Urban Poor House-holds	43121	46427
精简退职老职工救济	Relief for Old Staff and Workers Redu-ced and Discharged	8477	13743
自然灾害救济 (人次)	Relief for Natural Calamity (person.time)	13.7	17354
临时救济困难户 (人次)	Temporary Relieves for Households with Living Difficulties (person.time)	77729	6571
离退休人员	VCSR and RRSW	30387	230932
# 离　休	VCSR	2666	41092

19-4 优抚及主要救济对象情况
STATISTICS FOR PERSONS RECEIVING SPECIAL PENSIONS AND RELIEF

单位：人　　(person)

项目	Item	人数 Number of Persons 1999	1998	1999年为1998年% 1999 as % of 1998
优抚对象合计	**Persons Receiving Special Pensions**	**278256**	**289034**	**96.3**
烈　属	Members of A Revolutionary Martyr's Family	14552	17353	83.9
牺牲、病故军人家属	Families of Soldiers Sacrificed or Died of Illness	2381	2711	87.8
现役军人家属	Servicemen's Families	124280	137883	90.1
革命伤残人员	Revolutionary Disabled	12168	12327	98.7
在乡复员军人	Demobilized Soldiers in Hometown	14405	15015	95.9
在乡退伍军人	Veterans in Hometown	110466	103742	106.5
在乡退伍军红军老战士	Demobilized Old Red Army Men in Hometown	4	3	133.3
主要救济对象	**Major Persons Receiving Special Relief**			
社会困难户人数	Households with Living Difficulties	70323	65476	**107.4**
社会散居孤老、残、幼	Scattered Orphans and Widows,Dis-abled the Old and the Youth	7037	6264	112.3
精简退职老职工	Old Staff and Workers Reduced and Discharged	8477	8250	102.7

19-5 社 会 福 利 事 业 情 况
BASIC STATISTICS FOR SOCIAL WELFARE PROJECTS

项目 Item				1999	1998	1999年为1998年% 1999 as % of 1998
建立社会保障网络的乡镇	(个)	Town and Townships with Social Security Network	(unit)	165	178	92.7
社会福利企业	(个)	Social Welfare Enterprises	(unit)	1987	2221	89.5
# 民政部门办	(个)	Under the Civil Administration Department	(unit)	187	185	101.1
职工人数	(人)	Staff and Workers	(person)	55055	62683	87.8
# 残疾职工	(人)	Disabled Persons	(person)	23397	26940	86.8
全年增加值	(万元)	Total Value Added	(10000 yuan)	1028624	1001630	102.7
城镇社区服务设施	(个)	Urban Welfare Facilities	(unit)	1051	1125	93.4

19-6 城 乡 各 种 福 利 院 情 况
STATISTICS FOR URBAN AND RURAL WELFARE HOMES

项目 Item				合计 Total	光荣院 Homes for Disabled Veterans	社会福利院 Social Welfare Homes	儿童福利院 Welfare Homes for Children	精神病院 Mental Homes	敬老院 Homes for Old People
福利院单位数	(个)	Welfare Homes	(unit)	226	10	5	2	2	207
职工人数	(人)	Staff and Workers	(person)	3108	232	620	336	257	1324
床位数	(张)	Beds	(bed)	11869	608	1150	480	596	9035
收养人数	(人)	Persons Adopted	(person)	8434	477	1082	470	547	5858
# 自费	(人)	at One's Own Expense	(person)	4457	21	749	17	288	3382
国家拨款	(千元)	Financial Allocation	(1000 yuan)	66758	12948	27500	13210	5047	8053

19-7 社会保险基金统筹情况
SOCIAL BLANKET INSURANCE FUNDS

项目 Item		退休(养老)基金统筹 Retirement Funds(Old-age)			失业保险基金统筹 Unemployment Insurance Funds		
		单位个数 (个) Number of Units (unit)	人数 (人) Number of Persons (person)	应缴金额 (万元) Amount Drawn (10000 yuan)	单位个数 (个) Number of Units (unit)	人数 (人) Number of Persons (person)	应缴金额 (万元) Amount Drawn (10000 yuan)
合计	**Total**	**20610**	**3790005**	**889721**	**25807**	**3062151**	**45323**
按登记注册类型分	**Grouped by Registered Type**						
国有	State-Owned	6893	1956739	642866	7738	1718053	28417
集体	Collective-Owned	2254	276042	64505	5133	270436	2889
其他	Others	11463	1557224	182350	12936	1073662	14017
按隶属关系划分	**Grouped by Administrative Relationship**						
# 中央单位	Central Units	1032	1605935	187452	2991	457056	8081
地方单位	Local Units	19578	2184070	702269	22816	2605095	37242

19-8 婚姻登记情况
BASIC STATISTICS FOR MARRIAGE REGISTRATIONS

项目		Item		1999	1998	1999年为1998年% 1999 as % of 1998
登记结婚对数	(对)	**Registered Marriages**	**(couple)**	**82464**	**84631**	**97.4**
初婚人数	(人)	First Marriages	(person)	141740	146750	96.6
城市	(人)	Urban	(person)	100706	105632	95.3
男初婚人数	(人)	Male	(person)	53028	54675	97.0
#22-24岁	(人)	Age 22-24	(person)	5513	6132	89.9
25岁以上	(人)	Age 25 and above	(person)	47515	48543	97.9
女初婚人数	(人)	Female	(person)	47678	50957	93.6
#20-22岁	(人)	Age 20-22	(person)	4238	4174	101.5
23岁以上	(人)	Age 23 and above	(person)	43440	46783	92.9
农村	(人)	Rural	(person)	41034	41118	99.8
男初婚人数	(人)	Male	(person)	17346	18121	95.7
#22-24岁	(人)	Age 22-24	(person)	8620	9272	93.0
25岁以上	(人)	Age 25 and above	(person)	8726	8849	98.6
女初婚人数	(人)	Female	(person)	23688	22997	103.0
#20-22岁	(人)	Age 20-22	(person)	8604	8153	105.5
23岁以上	(人)	Age 23 and above	(person)	15084	14844	101.6
再婚人数	(人)	Remarriages	(person)	23188	22512	103.0
男性	(人)	Male	(person)	11813	11835	99.8
女性	(人)	Female	(person)	11375	10677	106.5
登记离婚对数	(对)	**Registered Divorces**	**(couple)**	**23905**	**23683**	**100.9**

19-9 律师工作
STATISTICS FOR LAWYERS

项目		Item		1999	1998	1999年为1998年% 1999 as % of 1998
律师事务所	(个)	Law Offices	(unit)	319	294	108.5
律师工作人员	(人)	Lawyers	(person)	5017	4968	101.0
专职律师	(人)	Full-time Lawyers	(person)	2317	1915	121.0
兼职律师	(人)	Part-time Lawyers	(person)	1092	1122	97.3
特邀律师	(人)	Lawyers Specially Invited	(person)	270	312	86.5
其他	(人)	Others	(person)	1338	1619	82.6
聘请常年法律顾问的单位	(个)	Units with Permanent Legal Advisers	(unit)	4112	4876	84.3
民事代理	(件)	Civil Case	(case)	8971	7868	114.0
经济案件	(件)	Economic Case	(case)	8362	6854	122.0
行政案件	(件)	Administrative Case	(case)	169	162	104.3
刑事辩护	(件)	Criminal Defense	(case)	4320	4867	
非诉讼法律事务	(件)	Off-court Case	(case)	12489	12411	100.6

19-10 部分市属律师事务所主要业务情况
STATISTICS FOR MAJOR MUNICIPAL LAW OFFICES

律师事务所 Law Office	担任常年法律顾问(家) Acted as Permanent Legal Advisers (unit)	律协诉讼案件(件) Lawsuit Cases(case)			办理非诉讼法律事务(件) Off-court Case (case)
		刑 事 Criminal	民 事 Civil	经 济 Economic	
君 合	10		4	70	190
嘉 和	38	4	67	101	155
海 问				3	24
竞 天	12	4	22	75	234
北 斗	55	57	114	147	
金 杜	36		28	130	180
隆 安	43	7	30	87	33
中 伦	99	7	14	60	37
共 和	24	8	28	96	36
陆 通	20	5	18	19	9
国 浩	26			77	25
大 成	50	107	148	113	63
天 元	33	3		68	26
通 商	6				262
经 纬	15	2	23	85	29
正 见	7		16	14	52
尚 公	13	5	23	56	20
广 盛	21		2	25	22
浩 天	39		13	24	23

19-11 部分基层法律服务所主要工作情况
STATISTICS FOR MAJOR LAW SERVICE OFFICES AT BASIC-LEVEL

基层法律服务所 Basic-Level Law Service Office	担任常年法律顾问 (家) Acted as Permanent Legal Advisers (unit)	民事代理 (件) Civil Case (case)	代写法律文书 (份) Legal Document Written on Behalf of Client (unit)	协办公证 (件) Deal Notarization Jointly (case)	解答法律咨询 (人次) Legal Advisory Services (person.time)
景山	15	32	52	5	544
丰盛	25	200	198		1958
包诚	5	260	68		3221
天桥	15	30	18	4	475
天正	11	53	55	2	200
天成	15	194	603	2	1250
卢沟桥	15	52	170	1	345
广汇	11	92	236	12	582
东辛房	20	45	4		90
河北	20	82	189	38	688
永顺	35	131	189	21	888
温阳	5	37	65	4	1500
穆家峪	15	96	136		125
韩庄	14	64	88		720
小汤山	30	82	175	20	300
庞各庄	8	58	185		150
大孙各庄	20	40	30	21	78
永宁	15	36	150	5	280

19-12 历届律师资格考试情况
STATISTICS FOR LAWYER QUALIFICATION EXAMINATION

单位：人 (person)

项目 Item	报考人数 Number of Persons Registered	实考人数 Number of Persons Scattered	录取人数 Number of Persons Passed	录取人数占实考人数比例(%) Percentage of Passed in Persons Attended (%)
1988	4280	2782	1329	47.8
1990	3735	2549	46	1.8
1992	2732	1882	510	27.1
1993	4769	3400	1068	31.4
1994	5653	4480	533	11.9
1995	5842	4661	1204	25.8
1996	5873	4445	317	7.1
1997	6350	4760	1126	23.7
1998	7946	6188	1436	23.2
1999	9736	7911	1727	21.3

19-13 乡镇(街道)法律服务情况
STATISTICS FOR TOWNSHIP(URBAN SUBDISTRICT) LAW SERVICES

项目		Item		1999	1998	1999年为1998年% 1999 as % of 1998
法律服务所	(个)	Law Service Offices	(unit)	352	412	85.4
法律工作者	(人)	Law Personnel	(person)	2285	2347	97.4
调解纠纷	(件)	Disputes Mediated	(case)	6258	9487	66.0
协办公证	(件)	Deal Notarization Jointly	(case)	1726	2950	58.5
担任法律顾问	(家)	Act as Legal Advisers	(unit)	3479	3406	102.1
民事代理	(件)	Civil Cases	(case)	13531	15533	87.1

19-14 法院行政案件收、结案情况
STATISTICS FOR ADMINISTRATIVE CASES ACCEPTED AND CLOSED BY COURT

单位：件 (case)

项目	Item	收案 Cases Accepted	结案 Cases Closed	#维持 Affirm	#撤销 Recall	#撤诉 Withdraw
合计	**Total**	**680**	**683**	**229**	**75**	**225**
公安	Security	91	99	32	3	28
工商	Industry and Commerce	22	20	6	1	9
卫生	Health Care	5	5	2		1
土地	Land	81	82	24	7	45
税务	Tax	18	17	13	2	
城建	Urban Construction	259	260	89	43	90
环保	Environmental Protection	1	3	1		1
林业	Forestry	1	2	2		
专利	Patent	20	16	7	6	1
民政	Civil Affairs	1	2			1
其他	Others	181	177	53	13	49

19-15 刑事案件情况
STATISTICS FOR CRIMINAL CASES

单位：起 (case)

项目 Item		1999	1998	1999年为1998年% 1999 as % of 1998
刑事案件	**Criminal Cases**			
立案	Cases Registered	65750	72039	91.3
破案	Cases Solved	21285	16519	128.9
破案率	**Detection Rate**	**32.4**	**22.9**	**141.5**
# 重大案件	Important Cases			
立案	Cases Registered	43251	47446	91.2
破案	Cases Solved	10863	8753	124.1
破案率 (%)	Detection Rate (%)	25.1	18.4	136.4

19-16 法院刑事案件收、结案情况
STATISTICS FOR CRIMINAL CASES ACCEPTED AND CLOSED BY COURT

项目 Item		收案 (件) Cases Accepted (case)	结案 (件) Cases Closed (case)	排挤判决发生法律效力 Judgment with Legal Force	
				件数(件) Number of Cases (case)	人数(人) Number of Persons (person)
合计	**Total**	**11338**	**11358**	**10430**	**15338**
危害国家安全罪	Offense against State Security	10	7	5	11
危害公共安全罪	Offense against Public Security	713	713	657	715
破坏社会主义市场经济秩序罪	Offense against the Socialist Market Economic Order	590	586	532	825
侵犯公民人身权利、民主权利罪	Infringement of Civil Personal Rights and Democratic Rights	2910	2953	2504	3162
侵犯财产罪	Infringement Property	5453	5446	5142	8389
妨害社会管理秩序罪	Interference with Public Function	1447	1443	1431	2041
危害国防利益罪	Offense against National Defense Interest	6	6	6	12
贪污贿赂罪	Corruption and Bribery Crime	197	191	143	167
渎职罪	Malpractice Duty	12	13	10	16

19-17 法院民事案件收、结案情况
STATISTICS FOR CIVIL CASES ACCEPTED AND CLOSED BY COURT

单位：件 (case)

项目 Item		收案 Cases Accepted	结案 Cases Closed	# 调解 Mediation	# 判决 Judgment
合计	**Total**	**84766**	**85385**	**28011**	**30764**
离婚	Divorce	26058	26230	12783	5743
抚养	Foster	2389	2396	983	799
继承	Inherit	821	817	249	363
房屋	House	9918	10034	1551	4695
相邻关系	Relation of Neighborhood	1513	1507	267	645
赔偿	Compensation	9176	9284	2192	4782
债务	Debt	27972	28053	8302	10945
著作权	Copyright	173	168	16	67
人身权	Personal Right	267	274	24	137
其他	Others	6479	6622	1644	2588

19-18 法院经济纠纷案件收、结案情况
STATISTICS FOR ECONOMIC DISPUTE CASES ACCEPTED AND CLOSED BY COURT

单位：件 (case)

项目	Item	收案 Cases Accepted	结案 Cases Closed	#调解 Mediation	#判决 Judgment
合计	**Total**	**24919**	**25210**	**7146**	**8853**
购销合同	Purchases and Sales Contracts	9978	10124	3424	2911
加工承揽合同	Processing Contracts	1911	1999	669	608
借款合同	Debt Contracts	2766	2815	595	1611
企业承包经营合同	Contracts of Enterprises	901	926	169	242
联营合同	Joint Business Contracts	273	286	59	109
财产租赁合同	Property Leases Contracts	847	871	230	307
建筑工程承包合同	Construction Project Contracts	91	78	28	30
交通运输纠纷	Transportation Dispute	189	203	69	55
农村承包合同	Foreign,Hongkong,Macao and	250	261	72	97
其　他	Others	7713	7647	1831	2883

19-19 检察机关办理各类案件情况
STATISTICS FOR CASES HANDLED BY PROCURATORIAL ORGAN

项目	Item	受案(受理) Cases Accepted		审结案合计 Cases Closed		#重特大案 Important Cases
		件 Case	人 Person	件 Case	人 Person	人 Person
审查批捕	**Examine for Arrest**	**10867**	**15955**	**10372**	**15126**	
#批准逮捕	Approve			10001	14522	
不批准逮捕	Disapprove			371	574	
审查起、免诉	**Examine for Sue**	**12004**	**18300**	**11064**	**16536**	**2962**
#起诉	Sue	11998	18290	10928	16336	
不起诉	Immunity from Suit	6	10	136	200	
举报控告案件	**Prosecution Cases**	**8159**		**8319**		
申诉案件	**Appeal Cases**	**377**		**326**		
民事、行政检察	**Civil and Administrative Procuratorial Work**	**1272**		**1000**		
民事案	Civil Cases	950		767		
知识产权案	Intellectual Property	17		11		
经济纠纷案	Economic Disputes	168		102		
行政案	Administrative Cases	137		120		

19-20 检察机关自侦经济、法纪案件情况
CASES SELF-INVESTIGATION OF ECONOMY,LAW AND DISCIPLINE BY PROCURATORIAL ORGAN

项目		Item		自侦经济案件 Self-investigate Economic Cases					自侦法纪案件 Self-Investigate Law and Discipline Cases
				合计 Total	# 贪污 Corruption	# 受贿 Accepting Bribes	# 行贿 Bribe	#挪用公款 Misappropriate Public Funds	
受 案	**(件)**	**Cases Accepted**	**(case)**	**1150**	**608**	**269**	**16**	**257**	**90**
立 案	**(件)**	**Cases Registered**	**(case)**	**319**	**126**	**83**	**11**	**99**	**21**
# 重特大案		Important Cases							
5至10万元		50000-100000 Yuan		45	16	14	1	14	
10至50万元		100000-500000 Yuan		99	42	14	8	35	
50至100万元		500000-1000000 Yuan		5	7	2	1	15	
100万元以上		Over 1000000 Yuan		42	13	1		28	
结 案		**Cases Closed**							
件数	(件)	Number of Cases	(case)	240	94	66	7	73	9
人数	(人)	Number of Persons	(person)	263	106	66	9	82	12
# 移送起诉		Hand over to Suit							
件数	(件)	Number of Cases	(case)	225	91	59	6	69	7
人数	(人)	Number of Persons	(person)	244	100	59	7	78	10
挽回经济损失	**(万元)**	**Retrieve Pecuniary Losses**	**(10000 yuan)**	**6075.4**	**1724.4**	**712.3**	**5.4**	**3633.3**	**52**

19-21 查处治安案件情况
STATISTICS FOR INVESTIGATING AND HANDLING PUBLIC ORDER CASES

项目	Item	查处(起) Investigating and Handling (case)	构成(%) Composition (%)
合 计	**Total**	**101849**	**100**
扰乱工作、公共秩序	Disturb Working or Public Order	28495	28.0
结伙斗殴、寻衅滋事	Gang Fighting	1389	1.4
侮辱妇女及其他流氓活动	Insult Woman and Other Immoral Behavior	334	0.3
阻碍国家工作人员执行公务	Interference with Government Function	618	0.6
违反枪支管理规定	Violate Regulatory Regime for Firearms	178	0.2
违反爆炸物品管理规定	Violate Regulatory Regime for Explosive Goods	598	0.6
殴打他人	Beat up Others	9786	9.6
偷窃财物	Steal	8771	8.6
骗取、抢夺、敲诈勒索财物	Cheat,Rob and Extort Property	1935	1.9
哄抢公私财物	Rob Public Property	110	0.1
故意损坏公私财物	Damage Public and Private Properties Intentionally	323	0.3
伪造倒卖票券、证件	Forge,Resell Bill,Ticket and Credentials	608	0.6
利用迷信扰乱秩序或骗财	Disturb Public Order or Defraud sb.of His Belongings by Superstitions	231	0.2
卖淫、嫖娼	Prostitution,Visit Prostitution	1517	1.5
赌 博	Gambling	1193	1.2
违反户口、居民身份证管理	Violate Regulations for Residence Cards or ID	21952	21.5
其 他	Others	23811	23.4

19-22 调 解 工 作
MEDIATION

项 目 Item	1999	1998	1999年为1998年% 1999 as % of 1998
专职司法助理员 (人) Full-time Judicial Assistants (person)	646.0	645.0	100.2
人民调解委员会 (个) People's Mediation Committees (unit)	12517.0	12807.0	97.7
调解人员 (万人) Intermediators (10000 persons)	16.0	16.9	94.9
调解委员 (万人) Members of the Mediation Institution (10000 persons)	5.5	5.7	96.0
调解各类纠纷 (万件) Disputes Mediated (10000 cases)	12.1	13.5	89.4
防止民间纠纷激化 (件) Prevent Intensification of Civil Disputes (case)	2546.0	3160.0	80.6

19-23 公 证 工 作
NOTARIZATIONS

项 目 Item	1999	1998	1999年为1998年% 1999 as % of 1998
公证处 (个) Notary Offices (unit)	24	24	100.0
公证人员 (人) Notary Personnel (person)	237	249	95.2
办理国内民事公证 (件) Notarized Domestic Civil Affairs (case)	64325	51826	124.1
办理国内经济公证 (件) Notarized Domestic Economic Affairs (case)	34418	14045	245.1
办理涉外公证 (件) Notarized Foreign Affairs (case)	192503	163147	118.0

19-24 1999年全市公证办情况
STATISTICS FOR WORK OF NOTARY OFFICES

单位：件 (case)

区 县 District and County		总办证量 Notary Documents	# 国内民事 Domestic Civil Affairs	# 国内经济 Domestic Economic Affairs
东城区	Dongcheng	28952	12867	1310
西城区	Xicheng	14248	5086	16
崇文区	Chongwen	5913	2960	28
宣武区	Xuanwu	10674	7522	103
朝阳区	Chaoyang	10613	3907	141
海淀区	Haidian	65565	10362	430
丰台区	Fengtai	3655	1663	86
石景山区	Shijingshan	5080	1702	7
门头沟区	Mentougou	1379	1097	105
房山区	Fangshan	1142	267	491
通州区	Tongzhou	3100	2536	229
昌平区	Changping	1193	775	128
顺义区	Shunyi	1032	847	90
平谷县	Pinggu	493	170	323
怀柔县	Huairou	902	212	690
密云县	Miyun	1372	1248	98
延庆县	Yanqing	480	358	86
大兴县	Daxing	620	336	81

19-25 国内公证文书分类
CLASSIFIED STATISTICS FOR DOMESTIC NOTARY DOCUMENTS

单位：件 (case)

项目	Item	民事公证数 Civil Notarization
收养	Adoption	251
解除收养	Dissolution of Adoption	9
继承权	Rights of Inheritance	4185
遗嘱	Testaments	2279
产权	Property Rights	174
亲属关系	Kinship	148
死亡	Death Certificates	12
房屋买卖	House Purchase and Sale	738
房屋租赁	House Leases	87
留学协议	Agreements on Studying Abroad	638
遗赠扶养协议	Agreements on Bequeath and Fostering	85
委托书	Certificate of Entrustment	4820
赠与书	Deed of Gift	14275
声明书	Declarations	4390
现场监督	Spot Supervision	1686
签名印鉴属实	True Signature	4156
文本相符	Confirmation of Copies to the Original	1786
宅基地使用权	Using House Site Rights	7
证据保全	Evidence Preservation	876
拆迁协议	Dismantle,Move Agreement	598
计划生育	Family Planning Agreemen	426
赡养协议	Support Agreements	189
合伙协议	Partnership Agreements	5
夫妻财产协议	Agreements on Estates by the Entirety	162
其他民事协议	Other Civil Agreements	10459
其他	Others	11888
合计	**Total**	**64329**

项目	Item	经济公证数 Economic Notarization
购销	Purchases and Sales	11
联营	Joint Business	6
拍卖	Actions	6
贷款	Loans	271
担保	Guarantees	395
招标投标	Bidding	178
科技协作	Scientific and Technological Cooperation	619
供用电	Electricity Supply or Use	
劳务合同	Labor Contracts	2004
建筑工程承包	Construction Projects Contracts	14
工商服务业承包	Contracts of Industry,Commerce and Services	6
农林牧副渔业承包	Contract of Farming,Forestry,Animal Husbandry,Sideline and Fishery	375
乡镇企业承包	Contracts of Township Enterprises	99
财产租赁	Property Leases	282
企业租赁	Enterprise Leases	73
资产经营责任制	Asset Business Contracts	12
还款协议	Agreements on Paying off Loans	1271
土地使用权出让转让	Selling and Transferring of Land Using Right	37
其他经济合同	Other Economic Contracts	2007
法人(代表人)资格	Identification of Institutional Units(Agent)	44
法人委托书	Trust Deeds of Institutional Units	1437
公司章程	Corporation Constitutions	88
执行许可证明	Operating Permits	8
提存	Drawings	9138
抵押登记	Mortgage Registration	788
公司会议记录	Records of Corporation Conference	12434
其他	Others	2815
合计	**Total**	**34418**

19-26 消防建设情况
STATISTICS FOR FIRE FIGHTING

项目 Item		1999	1998	1997	1996	1995	1994
消防队数 (个)	Number of Fire Brigades (unit)	77	41	38	36	35	35
消防车辆 (辆)	Number of Fire Engines (unit)	236	210	190	180	180	180
义务消防团 (个)	Voluntary Fire Brigades (unit)				20	20	20
队数 (万个)	Fire Bridges (10000)				3.9	3.9	3.9
人数 (万人)	Persons (10000 persons)				77	77	77

19-27 火灾及损失
FIRE AND LOSSES

项目 Item		数量 Amount		直接经济损失(万元) Direct Pecuniary Loss (10000 yuan)	
		1999	1998	1999	1998
总计 (起)	**Total (unit)**	**5395**	**4763**	**3165**	**4221.3**
# 特大火灾	Extraordinarily Serious	1	2	1736	2477.2
重大火灾	Heavy	5	2	1808	130.0
起火原因	**Cause of Fire**				
# 电器	Electric Appliances	1216	1346	2254.8	2618.9
违反安全规定	Violate Safety Regulation	149	133	62.5	488.7
吸烟	Smoking	969	715	139.4	145.3
生活用火不慎	Careless	1354	1230	129.1	170.7
玩火	Play with Fire	191	178	21.9	13.7
伤人 (人)	**Injuries (person)**	**92**	**101**		
死人 (人)	**Deaths (person)**	**53**	**40**		

19-28 交通事故及损失
STATISTICS FOR TRAFFIC ACCIDENTS AND LOSSES

项目 Item		1999	1998	1999年为1998年% 1999 as % of 1998
总计 (起)	**Total (case)**	**32291**	**35778**	**90.3**
伤人 (人)	Injuries (person)	10607	8464	125.3
死亡 (人)	Deaths (person)	1502	1487	101.0
在总计中：机动车事故 (起)	**Of Total:Motor Vehicle Accident (case)**	**29923**	**33599**	**89.1**
伤人 (人)	Injuries (person)	8577	6770	126.7
死亡 (人)	Deaths (person)	1101	1031	106.8
直接经济损失 (万元)	**Direct Pecuniary Losses (10000 yuan)**	**15539.3**	**16454.6**	**94.4**
每万辆机动车死亡 (人)	Deaths Per 10000 Motor Vehicles (persons)	10.8	11.5	

19-29 妇联组织状况
STATISTICS FOR WOMAN FEDERATION ORGANIZATIONS

单位：个，人 (unit,person)

项目	Item	1999	1998
区妇联数	Number of District Women Organizations	13	12
区妇联干部数	Cadres in District Women Organization Cadres	161	178
县妇联数	Number of County Women Organizations	5	6
县妇联干部数	Cadres in County Women Organization Cadres	43	55
乡妇联组织数	Number of Township Women Organizations	240	273
街妇联组织数	Number of Street Women Organizations	116	107
乡、街妇联干部数	Cadres of Township and Street Women Organization	434	456
城市基层妇代会组织数	Number of Urban Basic Women Congress	4548	4988
农村基层妇代会组织数	Number of Rural Basic Women Congress	4332	4000
机关及事业单位妇委会组织数	Number of Women Committees in Organs and Institutions	2420	876
厂矿企业女职工委员会数	Number of Female Staff and Workers Committees in Industrial Enterprises	4433	7683
乡、镇企业妇委会组织数	Number of Women Committees in Township and Village Enterprises	1044	1044
各类妇女联谊组织数	Women Connection Organizations	19	14

19-30 各级工会情况
LABOR UNIONS

项目	Item	基层以上工会组织（个）Labor Union above Basic-level(unit)		工会专职干部人数（人）Full-time Cadre(person)	
		1999	1998	1999	1998
市总工会	Municipal Federation of Labor Union	1	1	163	174
区县级工会	Labor Union at District and County Level	18	18	407	396
产业及局总公司集团工会	Labor Union of Industry and General Company Group	89	90	553	553
二级公司工会	Labor Union of Second-level Company	514	589	1074	1352
乡镇级工会	Labor Union at Villiage-and -town Level	59	45	33	34
街道级工会	Labor Union at Subdistrict Level	76	84	103	112

19-31 工会组织建设情况
WORKERS CONGRESS BUILDING

项目 Item				国有经济 State-owned	集体经济 Collective-owned	股份有限公司 Share Holding Company	有限责任公司 Limited-Liability Company	股份合作企业 Share Holding Cooperative
基层工会组织	(个)	Workers Congress at Basic-level	(unit)	3432	1594	144	196	147
在岗职工人数	(人)	Staff and Workers at Posts	(person)	1253956	155204	61583	64013	20091
# 女职工	(人)	Female	(person)	474882	75763	27753	25195	10529
工会小组	(个)	Workers Congress Group	(unit)	94175	9258	3851	4126	1210
工会积极分子	(人)	Activist of Workers Congress	(person)	169292	20292	5822	8254	2091
工会专职干部	(人)	Full-time Cadre of Workers Congress	(person)	5522	752	157	320	70
取得上岗资格证书	(人)	Workers get Credentials for Work	(person)	2805	295	100	183	32

项目 Item				私营经济 Private Business	联营经济 Joint-owned	其他经济 Others	外商投资经济 Foreign Funded Business	港澳台商投资经济 HongKong,Macao and Taiwan Funded Business
基层工会组织	(个)	Workers Congress at Basic-level	(unit)	133	58	16	270	178
在岗职工人数	(人)	Staff and Workers at Posts	(person)	6821	11556	1742	83395	22357
# 女职工		Female		3098	5520	922	33571	9885
工会小组	(个)	Workers Congress Group	(unit)	445	695	55	4823	1010
工会积极分子	(人)	Activist of Workers Congress	(person)	813	1398	45	9135	2273
工会专职干部	(人)	Full-time Cadre of Workers Congress	(person)	25	60	4	253	64
取得上岗资格证书	(人)	Workers get Credentials for Work	(person)	6	29	3	132	27

19-32 职工民主管理情况
STATISTICS FOR WORKERS DEMOCRACY MANAGEMENT

项目		Item		国有经济 State-owned	集体经济 Collective-owned	股份有限公司 Share Holding Company	有限责任公司 Limited-Liability Company	股份合作企业 Share Holding Cooperative
建立职工代表大会制度的单位	(个)	Number of Units with Workers Congress	(unit)	2800	1188	129	141	114
建立女职工工作委员会的单位	(个)	Number of Units with Working Committee for Female Workers	(unit)	2699	1079	123	122	97
召开职工代表大会的单位	(个)	Number of Units Hold Workers Congress	(unit)	2752	1129	124	140	109
职工代表大会的职工代表人数	(人)	Number of Delegate to Workers Congress	(person)	117070	23537	7923	5543	2818
# 女职工代表	(人)	Female	(person)	39567	11259	2088	1849	1492
建立劳动法律监督组织的单位	(个)	Number of Units with Supervise Organization for Labor Law	(unit)	1757	773	94	91	60
开展民主评议企业领导的单位	(个)	Number of Enterprises Carry out Democratic Appraise Cadre	(unit)	2893	1167	125	144	108
民主评议后受到奖励的企业领导干部	(人)	Number of Cadre Encouraged after Democratic Appraise	(person)	2003	453	36	77	29
民主评议后受到处罚的企业领导干部	(人)	Number of Cadre Punished after Democratic Appraise	(person)	144	20	7	3	6

项目		Item		私营经济 Private Business	联营经济 Joint-owned	其他经济 Others	外商投资经济 Foreign Funded Business	港澳台商投资经济 HongKong,Macao and Taiwan Funded Business
建立职工代表大会的单位	(个)	Number of Units with Workers Congress	(unit)	40	37	12	129	86
建立女职工工作委员会的单位	(个)	Number of Units with Working Committee for Female Workers	(unit)	25	36	12	150	90
召开职工代表大会的单位	(个)	Number of Units Hold Workers Congress	(unit)	40	38	5	125	84
职工代表大会的职工代表人数	(人)	Number of Delegate to Workers Congress	(person)	420	1718	84	4920	2170
# 女职工代表	(人)	Female	(person)	210	666	44	2188	986
建立劳动法律监督组织的单位	(个)	Number of Units with Supervise Organization for Labor Law	(unit)	15	24	4	84	55
开展民主评议企业领导的单位	(个)	Number of Enterprises Carry out Democratic Appraise Cadre	(unit)	23	35	9	87	66
民主评议后受到奖励的企业领导干部	(人)	Number of Cadre Encouraged after Democratic Appraise	(person)	27	22		146	40
民主评议后受到处罚的企业领导干部	(人)	Number of Cadre Punished after Democratic Appraise	(person)	2			11	4

19-33 职工经济技术活动情况
ECONOMIC AND TECHNICAL ACTIVITIES OF STAFF AND WORKERS

项目		Item		国有经济 State-owned	集体经济 Collective-owned	股份有限公司 Share Holding Company	有限责任公司 Limited-Liability Company	股份合作企业 Share Holding Cooperative
开展合理化建议活动单位	(个)	Units Carry out Rationlization Proposal Activities	(unit)	2090	654	91	115	74
本年度提出合理化建议件数	(件)	Number of Rationlization Proposal Presented in this Year	(unit)	342366	12487	12803	6619	1376
本年度已实施的合理化建议件数	(件)	Number of Rationlization Proposal Carried out in this Year	(unit)	91949	4100	2277	1445	812
本年度已实施的合理化建议创造的经济效益	(万元)	Economic Benefits Created by Rationlization Proposal Carried out	(10000 yuan)	130067	2351	7156	31042	190
开展劳动竞赛活动的单位	(个)	Units Hold Labor Emulation	(unit)	2131	739	94	116	80
参加劳动竞赛活动的人数	(人)	Participants of Labor Emulation	(person)	2022967	57211	44217	33768	9798
劳动竞赛创造的可计算的经济效益	(万元)	Calculable Economic Benefits Created by Labor emulation	(10000 yuan)	346074	4329	11000	10450	585

项目		Item		私营经济 Private Business	联营经济 Joint-owned	其他经济 Others	外商投资经济 Foreign Funded Business	港澳台商投资经济 HongKong,Macao and Taiwan Funded Business
开展合理化建议活动单位	(个)	Units Carry out Rationlization Proposal Activities	(unit)	22	28	5	119	72
本年度提出合理化建议件数	(件)	Number of Rationlization Proposal Presented in this Year	(unit)	245	708	19	29331	2910
本年度已实施的合理化建议件数	(件)	Number of Rationlization Proposal Carried out in this Year	(unit)	103	235	11	2514	652
本年度已实施的合理化建议创造的经济效益	(万元)	Economic Benefits Created by Rationlization Proposal Carried out	(10000 yuan)	55	182	2	3069	584
开展劳动竞赛活动的单位	(个)	Units Hold Labor Emulation	(unit)	19	25	3	106	57
参加劳动竞赛活动的人数	(人)	Participants of Labor Emulation	(person)	1673	4627	161	38150	8724
劳动竞赛创造的可计算的经济效益	(万元)	Calculable Economic Benefits Created by Labor emulation	(10000 yuan)	107	888	2	18918	1331

19-34 参加社会保障的单位情况
STATISTICS FOR UNITS ATTEND SOCIAL SECURITY

单位：个 (unit)

项目	Item	国有经济 State-owned	集体经济 Collective-owned	股份有限公司 Share Holding Company	有限责任公司 Limited-Liability Company	股份合作企业 Share Holding Cooperative
建立劳动争议调解委员会的单位	Units Found Labor Dispute Mediation Committee	334	98	13	21	12
参加养老保险社会统筹的单位	Units Attend Social Overall Endowment Insurance	3331	1430	137	182	136
参加医疗保险的单位	Units Attend Medical Insurance	2864	1298	130	162	127
足额交纳养老保险金的单位	Units Pay Full Endowment Insurance Pension	3284	1413	133	180	136
足额交纳医疗保险金的单位	Units Pay Full Medical Insurance Pension	2762	1236	129	159	123
建立职工互助补充保险的单位	Units Build Mutual Aid and Supplementary Insurance	464	90	37	23	11
参加职工互助保险的人数 (人)	Persons Attend Mutual aid and Supplementary Insurance (person)	206884	5387	10008	4070	755

项目	Item	私营经济 Private Business	联营经济 Joint-owned	其他经济 Others	外商投资经济 Foreign Funded Business	港澳台商投资经济 HongKong,Macao and Taiwan Funded Business
建立劳动争议调解委员会的单位	Units Found Labor Dispute Mediation Committee	2	9		25	15
参加养老保险社会统筹的单位	Units Attend Social Overall Endowment Insurance	66	50	10	230	151
参加医疗保险的单位	Units Attend Medical Insurance	50	46	5	217	145
足额交纳养老保险金的单位	Units Pay Full Endowment Insurance Pension	72	47	9	221	144
足额交纳医疗保险金的单位	Units Pay Full Medical Insurance Pension	49	44	5	210	141
建立职工互助补充保险的单位	Units Build Mutual Aid and Supplementary Insurance	2	11		14	2
参加职工互助保险的人数 (人)	Persons Attend Mutual aid and Supplementary Insurance (person)	2	758		7836	108

19-35 《九十年代中国儿童发展规划纲要》监测统计资料(目标指标)
SUPERVISORY STATISTICS FOR 《PROGRAM OUTLINE OF CHINESE CHILDREN DEVELOPMENT IN 1990S》(OBJECT INDICATORS)

项目	Item	1990	1998	1999
婴儿死亡率 (‰)	Infant Death Rate (‰)	11.66	7.58	7.95
城市	Urban	11.15	9.07	7.78
农村	Rural	12.27	5.75	8.38
五岁以下儿童死亡率 (‰)	Death Rate of Children below 5-year-old (‰)	13.72	9.6	9.97
城市	Urban	13.06	11.08	9.64
农村	Rural	14.51	7.78	10.81
孕产妇死亡率 (1/10 万)	Death Rate of Pregnant Woman and Lying-in Woman (10/million)	24.99	10.46	17.53
城市	Urban	20.92	10.87	15.69
农村	Rural	29.89	9.97	22.06
五岁以下儿童中重度营养不良患病率 (%)	Rate of Heavy Malnutrition of Children below 5-year-old (%)	2.44	0.78	0.61
城市	Urban	1.04	0.75	0.62
农村	Rural	3.49	0.83	0.59
年龄别体重	Weight by Stages of Age	2.44	0.78	0.61
年龄别身高	Height by Stages of Age		1.02	0.79
身高别体重	Weight by Stages of Height		0.47	0.38
缺水地区农村饮用水受益人口 (万人)	Population Benefited from Drinking Water in Rural Water Deficient Area (10000 persons)	62	74	
城市污水处理率 (%)	Disposal Rate of Urban Sewage (%)	6.60	22.38	24.69
城市卫生厕所覆盖率 (%)	Covering Rate of Urban Toilet (%)	99.50	99.82	99.83
农村享有卫生厕所的人口比重 (%)	Rate of Rural Population Use Toilet (%)	8.54	71.20	75.79
学龄儿童入学率 (%)	Enrollment Rate of Children at School-age (%)	99.50	99.96	99.95
城市	Urban	99.70	99.97	99.96
农村	Rural	99.60	99.93	99.93
小学毕业率 (%)	Graduate Rate of Primary School (%)	99.20	99.81	100.05
小学巩固率 (%)	Stronging Rate of Primary School (%)	100.23	99.79	99.83
小学辍学率 (%)	Rate of Leaving off Study of Primary School (%)	-0.17	0.08	0.06
男	Male		0.13	0.07
女	Female		0.04	0.04
初中入学率 (%)	Enrollment Rate of Junior Middle School (%)	99.24	97.95	97.85
初中毕业率 (%)	Graduate Rate of Junior Middle School (%)	91.43	96.00	96.04
初中巩固率 (%)	Stronging Rate of Junior Middle School (%)	93.69	98.14	97.83
小学专任教师学历合格率 (%)	Qualified Rate of Educational Background of Full-time Teacher of Primary Schoo (%)	89.00	97.34	97.72
3-6 岁儿童入园率 (%)	Enrollment Rate of Kindergarten of Children at Age 3-6 (%)	71.20	81.90	80.80
城市	Urban	94.10		90.80
农村	Rural	50.80		71.10
青壮年文盲率 (%)	Illiteracy Rate of Young People (%)	1.60		
校外教育活动场所数 (个)	Number of Locations of After-school Education	1434	1554	1594
家长受教育率 (%)	Educated Rate of Parents (%)		97.30	97.30
科学育儿知识普及率 (%)	Spreading Rate of Raising Children with Scientific Method (%)	59.40	95.63	96.11
出生缺陷儿发生率 (‰)	Rate of Defect New-borns (‰)	7.36	9.53	10.60
城市	Urban	5.34	10.63	11.31
农村	Rural	6.34	8.52	9.88
婚前检查率 (%)	Rate of Pre-martial Check-up (%)	54.70	100.00	98.70
城市	Urban	77.00	101.82	99.77
农村	Rural	23.30	95.70	95.79
残疾儿童入学率 (%)	Enrollment Rate of Deformed Children (%)	64.15	97.24	99.00

19-36 《九十年代中国儿童发展规划纲要》监测统计资料(措施指标)

SUPERVISORY STATISTICS FOR 《PROGRAM OUTLINE OF CHINESE CHILDREN DEVELOPMENT IN 1990S》(MEASURE INDICATORS)

项目	Item	1990	1998	1999
人口自然增长率 (‰)	Natural Growth Rate of Population (‰)	6.62	0.7	0.9
节育手术并发症发生率 (1/万)	Rate of Complication from Birth Control Operation (1/ten thousand)	2.50	2.27	2.28
城市	Urban	3.50	2.68	2.34
农村	Rural	2.70	1.15	2.12
预算内卫生事业经费增长速度 (%)	Growth Rate of Budgetary Health Fund (%)		18.00	24.00
妇幼保健费增长速度(卫生局系统) (%)	Growth Rate of Maternal and Child Hygiene Subsidies(Health Bureau System) (%)		-5.00	-10.00
卫生防疫费增长速度(卫生局系统) (%)	Growth Rate of Epidemic Prevention Subsidies(Health Bureau System) (%)		8.00	1.00
新法接生率 (%)	Rate of Delivering Children with New Method (%)	99.70	100.00	99.68
城市	Urban	99.90	100.00	99.61
农村	Rural	99.60	100.00	99.84
孕产妇住院分娩率 (%)	Childbirth Rate of Pregnant Woman and Lying-in Woman in Hospital (%)	83.79	98.92	98.82
城市	Urban	99.90	99.22	99.09
农村	Rural	67.30	98.44	98.15
产后出血死亡率 (1/10 万)	Death Rate of Birth Hemorrhage (10/million)	9.28	2.99	3.19
孕妇缺铁性贫血患病率 (%)	Rate of Iron-deficiency Anemia of Pregnant Woman (%)		6.94	6.39
城市	Urban		8.24	6.78
农村	Rural		4.47	5.10
母乳喂养率(0-4 个月) (%)	Rate of Feeding on Mother Milk (0-4 months) (%)		90.30	90.99
城市	Urban	13.60	86.38	87.96
农村	Rural	67.00	95.46	95.37
七岁以下儿童保健复盖率 (%)	Health Protection Rate of Children below 7-year-old (%)	59.40	95.63	96.11
城市	Urban		96.60	97.62
农村	Rural	82.73	94.18	93.79
孕产妇保健复盖率 (%)	Covering Rate of Health Protection for Pregnant Woman and Lying-in Woman (%)		94.89	95.38
城市	Urban		94.78	96.75
农村	Rural		95.06	91.95
一岁以内儿童计划免疫"四苗"接种率 (%)	Inoculation Rate of Immunity Four-Vaccine of Children within 1-year-old (%)	98.73	99.76	91.60
卡介苗	BCG Vaccine	99.50	99.94	93.60
麻疹疫苗	Measles Vaccine	99.20	99.95	98.50
百白破三联制剂	Pertussis,Diphtheria and Tetanus Vaccine	99.10	99.87	98.70
脊髓灰质炎疫苗	Poliomyelitis Polio Vaccine	99.30	99.89	98.80
小儿脊髓灰质炎发病率 (1/10 万)	Rate of Poliomyelitis Polio of Children (10/million)	0.04		
新生儿破伤风发病率 (‰)	Rate of Tetanus of New-borns (‰)	0.04	0.00	0.00
新生儿破伤风死亡专率 (‰)	Death Rate of Tetanus of Newborns (‰)	0.5	0.00	0.00
麻疹死亡专率 (1/10 万)	Death Rate of Measles (10/million)			
麻疹发病率 (1/10 万)	Rate of Measles (10/million)	0.51	1.28	1.93
儿童腹泻发病率 (‰)	Rate of Diarrhea of Children (‰)		1.25	1.17
五岁以下儿童因腹泻死亡的人数比例 (1/10 万)	Proportion of Children below 5-year-old Died of Diarrhea (10/million)	4.46	1.78	3.69
急性呼吸道感染标准病例管理率 (%)	Managing Rate of Standard Case of Acute Infection of Respiratory Tract (%)		80.55	90.31
急性呼吸道感染临床管理率 (%)	Clinical Managing Rate of Acute Infection of Respiratory Tract (%)		93.69	99.31
五岁以下儿童因急性呼吸道感染死亡的人数 (人)	Number of Children below 5-year-old Died of Infection of Respiratory Tract (person)	92	45	39
地方性甲状腺肿大率 (%)	Rate of Local Goitre (%)	1.90		3.40
城市三岁以上儿童入园率 (%)	Enrollment Rate in Kindergarten of Urban Children over 3-year-old (%)		90.80	90.80
农村学前一年幼儿入园(班)率达 60% (%)	Enrollment Rate in Kindergarten of Rural Children at Age Preschool a Year Reaching 60% (%)		94.10	95.00

主要统计指标解释

社会福利事业单位 指为社会上丧失劳动能力、无依无靠、无生活来源的孤老残幼、家庭无力照管的老人、残疾儿童、精神病人和优抚对象、困难户、社区居民提供收养、帮助、服务的福利机构和福利设施。

社会福利企业 指以集中安置有一定劳动能力的残疾人就业为目的、带有社会福利性质的特殊企业的总称（残疾职工占生产人员 10%以上）。

社会收养单位 指国有优抚（休）疗养院、福利院以及集体所有制和其他所有制的光荣院、敬老院事业单位的总称。

收养人数 指优抚疗养院、福利院报告期末实际收养的优抚对象、社会“三无”对象和自费人员在院的总人数。

律师 指受聘参加律师事务所工作，提任法律顾问、刑（民）事代理人、刑事辩护人，办理非诉讼事件、解答法律询问，代写法律事务文书等主要从事律师业务的专职法律工作者和兼职律师。

公证人员 指在国家公证机关依法办理公证事务的司法人员。包括公证员、助理公证员和在公证处工作的其他人员。

办理公证文书 指公证处在一定时期内办结的公证文书件数。公证文书系按司法部规定或批准的格式制作。包括国内公证和涉外公证两部分。其中国内公证分为经济公证和民事法律关系公证两大类。

调解人员 指人民调解委员会担负调解民间一般民事纠纷和轻微违法行为所引起的纠纷的工作人员。包括调解委员会的委员和调解小组调解员。

调解民间纠纷 指调解委员会依照法律规定，根据自愿原则，用说服教育的方法调解民间发生的有关民事权利和义务的争执，促成当事双方达到协议和谅解，解决纠纷。包括婚姻家庭纠纷，财产权益纠纷等。不包括法院受理调解的民事案件数。

离休、退休、退职人员 指正式办理了离休、退休、退职手续，并享受相应的离休、退休、退职待遇的人员。

保险福利费用 指企业、事业、机关单位再工作以外实际支付给职工和离休、退休、退职人员个人以及用于集体的劳动保险和福利费用。

1. 职工保险福利费用具体包括：

（1）医疗卫生费 指实行公费医疗企业的职工及其供养的直系亲属的医疗费、医务经费、职工因工伤就医路费以及住院伙食补助费等；卫生部门开支的事业及机关单位职工的公费医疗经费；未参加公费医疗的企业、事业和机关单位职工的医疗费。

（2）丧葬抚恤救济费 指因职工死亡而支付的丧葬费、丧葬补助费和所遗供养直系亲属的抚恤费、救济费、生活补助费以及职工供养直系亲属死亡时的丧葬补助费等。

（3）生活困难补助 指对生活困难的职工实际支付的定期补助和临时性补助。

（4）文体宣传费 指企业、事业和机关单位实际支付的文体宣传费。不包括学习费。

（5）集体福利事业补贴费 指对职工浴室、理发室、洗衣房、哺乳室、托儿所等集体福利设施各项支出与收入相抵后的差额补助费。

（6）集体福利设施费 指按照国家规定开支的集体福利设施费用。如职工食堂炊事用具的购置费、修理费、职工宿舍的修缮费用。不包括由企业、事业和机关单位自筹经费开支的职工福利设施的基本建设费用。

（7）计划生育补贴　指发给职工独生子女的补贴费和保健营养费。

（8）其他　指上述费用以外，单位支付给职工的保险福利费。

2. 离休、退休、退职人员保险福利费用具体包括：

（1）离休金　指发给离休人员的工资和按 1982 年国务院发布的“关于老干部离职休养制度的几项规定”发给符合规定的离休干部相当于 1—2 个月标准工资的生活补贴和按有关文件规定提高离休人员的待遇所增加的费用及粮油价格补贴等。

（2）退休金　指按照国家有关规定发给退休人员的退休费和按有关文件规定提高退休人员的待遇所增加的费用及粮油价格补贴等。

（3）职工生活费　指按照 1978 年国务院《关于工人退休、退职的暂行办法》规定定期发给退职人员的生活费用和按有关文件规定提高退职人员的待遇所增加的费用及粮油价格补贴等。

（4）医疗卫生费　指离休、退休、退职人员的医疗费、住院费以及住院伙食补助等费用。

（5）护理费　指因工致残、饮食起居需人扶助的离休、退休人员的护理费以及因病不能自理的离休人员的护理费。

（6）生活补贴　指按照 1985 年国务院《关于发给离退休人员生活补贴费的通知》规定，发给离休、退休人员的生活补贴费。

（7）交通费补贴　指按月发给离休人员的交通费补贴。

（8）丧葬抚恤救济费　指离休、退休、退职人员死亡的丧葬费、丧葬补助费和所遗供养直系亲属的抚养费、救济费、生活补助费以及供养直系亲属死亡时的丧葬补助费等。

（9）其他　包括易地安置的离休、退休、退职人员的安家补助费；离休、退休、退职人员的生活困难补助费、书报费、洗理费、副食品价格补贴、房租价格补贴、水电补贴、少数民族补贴以及老干部活动经费开支的旅游费用等。

Explanatory Notes On Main Statistical Indicators

Social Welfare Institutions refer to institutions providing adoption,help and services to persons such as (1)those who have no kith and kin and can not support themselves, (2)the old,deformed children,mental patients with no cares of family (3)persons receiving special pensions or with living difficulties,etc.

Social Welfare Enterprises refer to special enterprises which centralized employing deformed man with ability to work （the proportion of deformed staff and workers to all production personnel above 10%）.

Adoption Units　including state-owned sanatoriums for persons receiving special pensions,social welfare homes, collective-owned and other ownership homes for disable veterans and old people.

Number of People Adopted by Social Welfare Institutions refers to the number of persons receiving special pensions,those who have no ability to work,no dependent and no living source and persons at one's expenses taken in by social welfare institutions at the end of reported period.

Lawyers include full or part-time lawyers and full-time legal workers employed by law office to act as law advisers, agents in criminal or civil lawsuits, defenders in criminal lawsuits, or to handle non-litigious legal affairs, to advise on legal matters, or to write legal papers for others.

Notary Personnel refer to judicial officials of the state notary offices handling notarization work according to law. They include notaries, assistant notaries, and other people working for notary offices.

Notarized Documents refer to the notary documents finished by notary offices in a year. The notary documents are drawn up in accordance with the regulations of the Ministry of Justice, including domestic documents and foreign-related documents.

Domestic documents are divided into two major categories: documents on economy and documents on civil legal relations.

Mediators refer to workers in people's mediation committees responsible for mediating in civil disputes and cases of slight infraction of the law, including members of the mediation committees and mediators in mediation groups.

Mediation of Civil Disputes refers to mediation committees' work in mediating of civil disputes concerning civil rights and responsibilities through persuasion and education in accordance with the provisions of law on a voluntary basis, so as to solve disputes by helping the parties involved come to an agreement and understanding . The disputes include divorce cases and disputes over property ownership , but exclude the civil cases to be handled by the court.

Retired or Resigned Personnel refers to the persons who have formally gone through the formalities for their retirement or quitting work and enjoy the corresponding treatments.

Insurance and Welfare Funds refers to labor insurance and welfare fund paid by enterprises, organizations and institutions to their staff and workers as well as retired and quitted persons in addition to their wages and salaries.

1. **Insurance and Welfare Funds for Staff and Workers** include:

(1) Medical Care Allowance includes cost of medical care of staff and workers and their dependent family members covered by the medical care system of enterprises, traveling expenses of injured employees to hospital and their food subsidies during hospitalization; the cost of medical care of employees covered by the medical care system of institutions and organizations; the cost of medicine of employees in enterprises, institutions and organizations not covered by the medical care system.

(2) Funeral Expenses and Pensions for Family of the Deceased refer to funeral expenses of staff and workers, pensions and allowance for their dependent family members, as well as subsidies to funeral expenses of staff and workers' dependent family members.

(3) Allowance for Living refers to regular or temporary allowance to staff and workers with difficulties in making living.

(4) Expenses on Recreation, Sports and Publicity Activities refer to actual payment made by enterprises and institutions in recreational , sports and publicity activities, excluding training cost .

(5) Subsidies to Collective Welfare refer to the expenditures on making up the loss of welfare operations, such as public bathrooms, barber shops, laundries, nurseries and kindergartens.

(6) Expenses on Collective Welfare Facilities refer to expenditures on collective welfare facilities in line with state regulations, such as the purchase and repair of cooking utensils for canteens, and repair of living quarters of staff and workers, but excluding the expenses on welfare projects financed with self-raised funds.

(7) Family Planning Subsidy refers to subsidy of health allowance paid to staff and workers in one-child family.

(8) Others refer to other insurance and welfare funds paid to staff and workers.

2. **Insurance and Welfare Funds for Retired and quitted Staff and Workers** include:

(1) Merit Retirement Pensions refer to pensions and other subsidies paid to merit retired in line with relevant government documents.

(2) Retirement Pensions refer to pensions and other subsidies paid to retired staff and workers in line with the relevant government documents.

(3) Quitted Allowances for Living refer to living allowances and subsidies paid to quitted staff and workers in line with relevant government instructions.

(4) Expenses for Medical Care refer to the costs for medical treatment, hospitalization and food subsidies in hospitals for merit retired, retired and quitted staff and workers.

(5) Nursing Cost refers to cost for nursing retired or quitted staff and workers without ability to take care of themselves and need the help of nurses.

(6) Living Subsidy refers to living subsidy paid to merit retired and retired employees in line with the instructions in a 1985 State Council document.

(7) Traffic Subsidy refers to the traffic subsidy paid monthly to merit retired staff.

(8) Funeral Expenses and Pensions for Family of the Deceased refer to the funeral expenses of merit retired, retired and quitted staff and workers, pensions and allowances for their dependent family members, as well as subsidies to funeral expenses of their dependent family members.

(9) Others refer to other expenses, including moving and settlement allowance, living allowance for difficult families, book and newspaper allowance, subsidy for non-staple foods, allowance for bath and haircut, housing subsidy, water and electricity subsidy, special allowance for staff and workers of national minorities, travelling cost for senior retired staff, etc.

服务业
SERVICE

固定资产原价构成

Composition of Original Value on Fixed Assets

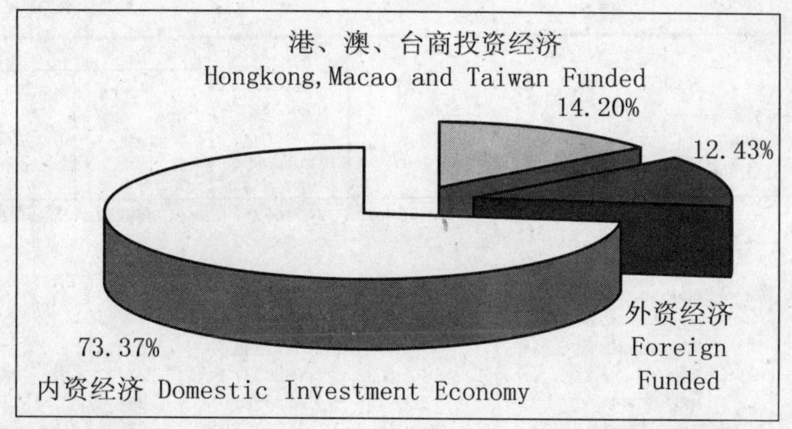

单位：亿元 100 million yuan	固定资产原价 Original Value of Fixed Assets	利润总额 Income Tax Payable	投资收益 Investment Income
总计 Total	1667.7	295.2	253.9
内资经济 Domestic Investment Economy	1223.7	329.1	249.6
外商投资经济 Foreign Funded	207.3	-12.9	2.2
港、澳、台商投资经济 Hongkong,Macao and Taiwan Funded	236.8	-21.0	2.1

主营业务收入构成

Composition of Revenue of Major Business

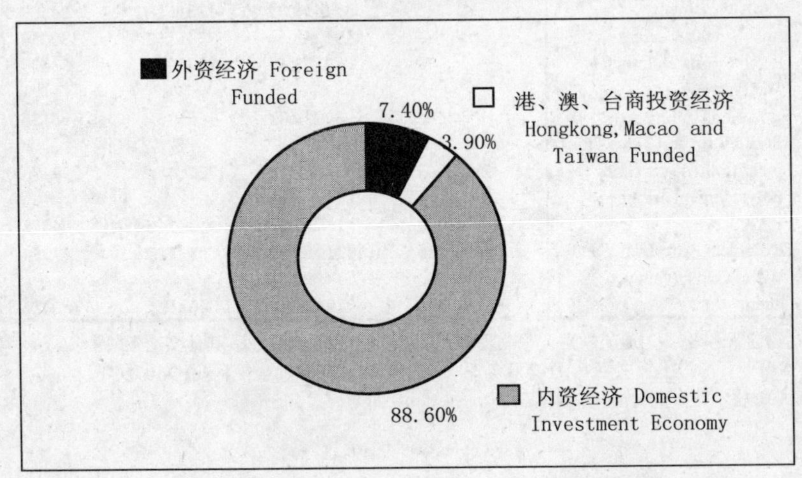

20-1 服务业企业财务状况

单位：万元

项目	Item	单位个数 Units (unit)	流动资产合计 Total Circulating Assets	#货币资金 Cash	#应收帐款 Accounts Receivable	#存货 Stock
合计	**Total**	**14605**	**165465957.5**	**19406152.2**	**4218044.8**	**22453724.1**
按登记注册类型分	**Grouped by Registered Type**					
内资经济	Domestic Investment Economy	13111	149723599.3	16938907.8	3569407.5	13964651.5
国有经济	State-owned	4534	116473735.1	10763274.4	2160698.9	7163968.6
集体经济	Collective-owned	2682	5889727.4	1250823.9	166573.7	3733976.9
联营经济	Joint Owned	259	550015.0	95140.0	65184.5	200822.2
私营经济	Private Owned	1572	638952.0	92190.6	47067.5	247931.1
股份合作企业	ShareHolding Cooperative	959	2761035.6	333925.6	70977.8	113540.7
股份有限公司	Share Holding Company	364	13286802.9	1136325.1	522477.0	674090.1
有限责任公司	Limited-Liability Company	2719	10102046.7	3266139.1	535548.7	1815446.3
其他	Others	22	21284.6	1089.1	879.4	14875.6
外商投资经济	Foreign Funded	829	6655454.3	1600194.3	502667.2	2341739.1
港澳台商投资经济	Hongkong,Macao and Taiwan Funded	665	9086903.9	867050.1	145970.1	6147333.5
按国民经济行业分	**Grouped by Sector**					
金融业	Banking	95	109774351.7	8557467.3	80063.8	3483807.3
保险业	Insurance	10	2706294.1	1172923.1		
房地产业	Real Estate	1301	26779996.2	2002842.6	126964.7	16503423.5
公共服务业	Public Services	689	785294.4	277074.8	106470.1	205497.9
居民服务业	Personal Services	781	123937.2	32386.3	18682.2	28794.2
旅馆业	Hotel	1066	1165456.3	535307.4	135339.6	130871.5
旅游业	Tourism	241	375286.3	96354.2	142814.2	4701.6
交通运输辅助业	Logistic Support for Transportation	142	216748.5	82398.8	51144.9	17700.5
仓储业	Storage	91	60825.8	11951.1	5847.5	5806.8
商业经纪与代理业	Commercial Brokerage and Agencies	50	1024038.6	414915.3	282140.7	46849.8
租赁服务业	Rental Services	171	429873.6	109789.1	145140.7	13799.4
计算机应用服务业	Computer Application Services	1369	1011643.3	251241.6	176971.0	202907.2
娱乐服务业	Entertainment Services	163	135205.5	31529.9	19581.4	6728.7
信息咨询服务业	Consulting Services	2632	2668134.6	825416.3	571681.6	124758.8
#广告业	Advertisement	515	371698.8	133061.1	74220.8	7231.7
其他社会服务业	Other Social Services	676	3191240.6	774511.8	330050.7	50518.0
卫生、体育和社会福利业	Health,Sports and Social Welfare	70	87175.6	34595.3	33437.6	7757.5
教育文化艺术和广播电影电视业	Education,Culture,Arts, Radio,Film and Television	565	937959.0	365606.4	96176.3	246005.7
科学研究和综合技术服务业	Scientific Research and Polytechnical Services	4063	6776071.4	1727645.7	1099403.0	928994.7
农林牧渔服务业	FFAF Services	91	16063.9	3254.5	4018.3	3939.6
地质勘察和水利管理业	Geological Prospecting and Water Conservancy	25	421012.6	58721.2	27094.7	20580.0
其他	Others	314	6779348.3	2040219.5	765021.8	420281.4

注：服务业企业包括 (1)农林牧渔服务业；(2)地质勘察、水利管理业；(3)交通运输辅助业、其他交通运输业；(4)仓储业；(5)商业经纪与代理业；(6)金融、保险业；(7)房地产业；(8)社会服务业；(9)卫生、体育和社会福利业；(10)教育、文化艺术及广播电影、电视业；(11)科学研究和综合技术服务业；(12)其他行业。

FINANCIAL INDICATORS FOR SERVICES ENTERPRISES

(10000 yuan)

长 期 投 资 Long-term Investment	固定资产 合 计 Total Fixed Assets	固定资产 原价合计 Original Value of Fixed Assets	# 生 产 经 营 用 for Production Use	累 计 折 旧 Accumulative Depreciation	#本 年 折 旧 of this Year	无形及 递延资产 合 计 Intangible and Deffered Assets	#无 形 资 产 Intangible	其 他 资 产 合 计 Other Assets
64294397.9	15066333.0	16677120.6	8970034.5	4716573.8	832202.3	2594176.2	1270075.7	107208815.4
62418003.1	11934712.6	12236630.5	6067683.5	3210367.6	560126.6	1623369.9	675111.4	105642567.0
57060369.3	9283678.8	9360481.2	4590796.1	2464179.8	378194.1	922017.5	379577.3	101544427.0
1252938.7	657756.4	838181.7	335075.6	283530.5	51555.2	171352.1	89528.0	656047.0
60391.8	137523.9	114562.1	49476.4	35696.2	5382.4	38081.7	21535.0	219.9
53039.5	98375.3	115101.9	63803.2	27293.5	10137.7	43055.3	13425.6	11372.3
201268.2	203887.0	218328.8	148727.1	77742.1	13451.1	42138.6	23510.3	12016.0
2449011.9	756633.4	755273.8	344533.6	176153.7	43229.9	216485.8	66082.5	2495076.6
1340587.5	795659.5	833019.2	534251.9	145192.5	58047.3	190101.2	81389.2	923070.7
396.2	1198.3	1681.8	1019.6	579.3	128.9	137.7	63.5	337.5
1493214.6	1511809.3	2072506.7	1368421.1	598360.8	147061.0	327275.0	188102.4	1155003.7
383180.2	1619811.1	2367983.4	1533929.9	907845.4	125014.7	643531.3	406861.9	411244.7
45871254.4	2528280.9	2197473.1	16829.7	562055.8	109026.9	523423.2	87566.6	101233048.1
202044.3	204396.1	161950.8		22091.1	7378.7	18139.7	1615.0	25989.5
1349283.7	2152795.5	2345867.4	1448712.5	461699.1	95478.7	755025.5	427648.6	850941.7
138499.5	1169167.6	1555365.2	866456.9	469599.2	70534.0	49845.3	37177.0	16104.5
14770.0	60082.3	70702.6	43408.7	22091.3	5959.2	14664.2	5502.5	4057.8
488857.2	2597100.5	3576249.6	2155586.7	1231212.9	182238.2	407483.4	237671.5	137749.1
224380.5	159054.2	163158.5	76239.5	38366.9	9787.3	17634.9	9115.3	18637.2
159718.5	200235.8	261154.7	78613.3	78736.3	16965.9	9544.9	3497.0	1133.0
10706.9	72131.6	92921.3	46225.4	27933.1	3678.7	12628.5	8007.7	1553.0
325122.2	129959.1	108849.8	52257.2	18635.8	4706.9	7650.8	4766.7	5709.2
36521.6	258869.3	315912.2	241785.0	67603.1	11293.4	94155.1	21112.4	408373.0
121977.4	215671.1	308583.8	199523.5	139409.4	29861.2	41060.8	26859.1	18648.1
12645.5	223490.5	299610.7	210162.9	96376.2	15288.9	59726.1	17445.0	29417.1
1213223.4	445197.1	514195.8	311368.9	150063.6	51176.6	62629.7	24592.0	190854.2
34731.0	57944.0	73555.9	55400.9	24130.3	6195.7	10133.3	7288.4	4558.2
3251664.8	576311.3	667215.8	534115.0	160123.0	34778.4	68469.3	43090.4	806323.3
3458.0	49102.1	60289.9	30346.8	12980.8	2482.9	7098.7	4267.5	1150.3
100371.9	609952.1	653863.3	450329.0	178278.7	37363.1	30147.8	18556.7	10342.7
2844159.6	1508660.8	1567435.4	1045028.1	433421.8	89251.0	334498.1	249957.9	846970.9
6392.2	16586.6	16828.8	7630.5	5699.3	1350.4	211.5	46.1	355.2
1871043.6	230423.2	405173.2	351459.1	184023.1	5936.3	5006.2	1835.1	142058.2
6048302.7	1658865.3	1334318.7	803955.8	356173.3	47665.6	75132.5	39745.6	2459399.3

Note: Service enterprises include(a)FFAF services, (b)geographical prospecting and water conservancy, (c)logistic support for transportation and other transportation, (d)storage, (e)commercial brokerage and agencies, (f)banking and insurance, (g)real estate, (h)social services, (i)health,sports and social welfares, (j)education, culture,arts,radio,film and television, (k)scientific research and polytechnical services, (l)other services.

20-1 续表 1 continued

单位：万元

项目 Item		资产合计 Total Assets	流动负债合计 Total Circulating Liability	# 短期借款 Short-term Loans	# 应付帐款 Accounts Payable	长期负债合计 Total Long-term Liability
合　计	**Total**	**355530852.9**	**185646453.1**	**57381341.2**	**3962282.2**	**108721878.5**
按登记注册类型分	**Grouped by Registered Type**					
内资经济	Domestic Investment Economy	331942920.0	173911856.1	53682535.0	3331835.6	103946810.3
国有经济	State-owned	285800896.3	143578101.9	51181822.3	2230017.4	95346151.2
集体经济	Collective-owned	8652312.2	6311321.7	328809.6	204576.5	1396459.6
联营经济	Joint Owned	787976.6	500684.1	96544.1	63514.7	78328.5
私营经济	Private Owned	846421.0	556303.7	105404.6	66334.7	34428.2
股份合作企业	Share Holding Cooperative	3233967.2	1933146.3	60509.1	50994.3	858339.0
股份有限公司	Share Holding Company	19225160.7	14099164.3	503170.0	304204.9	2702244.6
有限责任公司	Limited-Liability Company	13372831.7	6909993.9	1403732.1	410539.6	3530549.2
其　他	Others	23354.3	23140.2	2543.2	1653.5	310.0
外商投资经济	Foreign Funded	11290038.2	5330950.4	2267770.9	376565.5	2199677.3
港澳台商投资经济	Hongkong,Macao and Taiwan Funded	12297894.7	6403646.6	1431035.3	253881.1	2575390.9
按国民经济行业分	**Grouped by Sector**					
金融业	Banking	259930358.3	142206131.4	46577746.8	8862.5	90977176.8
保险业	Insurance	3156863.7	700779.0			2162392.1
房地产业	Real Estate	31984205.5	20475500.4	4495456.2	198119.4	4612189.7
公共服务业	Public Services	2171015.4	894967.1	193369.1	376855.1	127851.8
居民服务业	Personal Services	218807.9	106201.5	13579.1	21169.8	13047.1
旅馆业	Hotel	4880332.1	1823506.4	392728.5	193756.7	1333989.2
旅游业	Tourism	806621.2	355859.1	135231.2	106353.3	28609.9
交通运输辅助业	Logistic Support for Transportation	588394.0	201307.2	25878.2	101769.2	158310.0
仓储业	Storage	170178.0	87252.1	46269.9	4621.9	9687.6
商业经纪与代理业	Commercial Brokerage and Agencies	1494459.0	833273.2	186549.6	234188.0	91093.7
租赁服务业	Rental Services	1343186.2	414312.5	53912.8	136437.3	645015.0
计算机应用服务业	Computer Application Services	1420507.6	743423.7	143324.3	151192.0	60627.1
娱乐服务业	Entertainment Services	468533.7	271314.6	94527.2	28465.1	102295.1
信息咨询服务业	Consulting Services	4636644.7	2012108.5	407263.8	568178.0	731362.2
# 广告业	Advertisement	479969.1	323609.2	29127.1	125474.3	4825.5
其他社会服务业	Other Social Services	7942817.4	2317845.1	776350.3	253448.4	1651791.7
卫生、体育和社会福利业	Health,Sports and Social Welfare	150976.8	58738.6	3625.0	8164.4	4926.2
教育文化艺术和广播电影电视业	Education,Culture,Arts, Radio,Film and Television	1774407.1	582531.9	68840.7	163602.0	63509.7
科学研究和综合技术服务业	Scientific Research and Polytechnical Services	12343569.7	5124508.9	1163161.5	849378.2	1460839.7
农林牧渔服务业	FFAF Services	39610.4	18263.7	5857.7	4422.9	4738.9
地质勘察和水利管理业	Geological Prospecting and Water Conservancy	2678126.3	1032357.7	702914.9	13164.0	646215.4
其　他	Others	17331237.9	5386270.5	1894754.4	540134.0	3836209.6

20-1 续表 2 continued

(10000 yuan)

# 长期借款 Long-term Loans	负债合计 Total Liabili-ties	所有者权益合计 Ownership Interest	# 实收资本 Proceeds of Capital	#国家资本 State	#集体资本 Collective	#法人资本 Institutional Units	#个人资本 Individual	#港澳台资本 Hongkong, Macao and Taiwan
72781012.2	**294633483.8**	**60897369.1**	**41942957.4**	**24047766.0**	**595630.2**	**3281053.9**	**660390.9**	**855196.8**
69292717.8	278053424.3	53889495.7	34640635.1	23520901.4	553937.3	2793856.4	619911.7	22908.5
67900246.3	239047287.3	46753609.0	29370293.6	22518539.6	27521.3	1200950.2	96840.1	9953.5
105256.2	7738564.5	913747.7	688348.6	48695.9	362751.3	82650.9	23296.5	3128.0
62856.1	579868.1	208108.5	198727.4	73833.4	34010.1	62660.4	2108.3	
19641.2	591788.5	254632.5	230879.0	1219.0	3601.2	29266.5	106018.4	1063.9
17289.3	2795882.6	438084.6	314805.2	98506.7	18782.6	48010.9	62976.6	351.5
277076.2	16810768.5	2414392.2	1486753.2	335409.7	28590.9	349929.2	123105.1	411.8
910042.5	10465787.4	2907044.3	2347760.4	444552.1	78485.1	1019966.2	205139.9	7999.8
310.0	23477.4	-123.1	3067.7	145.0	194.8	422.1	426.8	
1538357.5	7560684.2	3729354.0	3694485.7	192755.8	27550.1	215399.0	2725.5	112995.2
1949936.9	9019375.3	3278519.4	3607836.6	334108.8	14142.8	271798.5	37753.7	719293.1
61014255.4	233183308.2	26747050.1	19352949.3	13026113.8		113241.0	5500.0	
30.4	2863171.1	293692.6	384185.9	190885.9				
3335165.5	25122534.5	6861671.0	5819531.9	1076676.9	33654.2	146876.9	26726.4	204067.8
78935.3	1097332.3	1073683.1	695359.8	457276.3	67531.0	127783.8	9497.4	31595.1
10544.7	119428.3	99379.6	114432.8	23078.0	19639.6	18798.6	40331.2	9378.1
1053446.2	3166276.7	1714055.4	1969986.1	961209.1	80628.1	447229.6	14804.5	284315.9
22104.5	385817.8	420803.4	258459.0	165569.6	4926.2	63637.6	13824.2	10319.0
82761.0	359835.3	228558.7	224747.8	100392.6	8769.7	18203.9	90992.6	2137.1
4407.1	101476.2	68701.8	58726.9	15756.5	7601.9	17225.2	149.4	13542.3
83122.2	924928.1	569530.9	347453.0	274608.9	420.0	44258.9	1781.0	
610217.3	1060193.7	282992.5	218758.2	138353.8	8129.8	35325.8	6705.5	7102.2
32300.6	820435.1	600072.5	502448.0	136797.9	23627.8	107460.6	71585.1	45842.0
66089.5	374054.3	94479.4	218921.2	39557.9	15868.3	40149.3	14730.2	42074.4
587008.8	2759223.6	1877421.1	1522414.8	367412.7	51338.5	450199.6	88410.1	30175.8
3218.9	340896.5	139072.6	118194.3	44668.1	8989.3	27043.7	24598.7	4239.6
1485224.1	3977046.6	3965770.8	2340886.2	1875034.4	47033.1	121601.3	15966.0	28758.9
1090.3	63899.1	87077.7	27520.4	10666.2	2220.5	2136.6	1109.5	845.4
51428.0	647313.1	1127094.0	454788.7	321820.6	17675.4	46841.3	6436.7	59783.0
1031734.8	6659545.2	5684024.5	3290333.0	1654499.1	158966.5	964095.8	195063.2	50308.2
3837.5	23036.5	16573.9	13373.8	3760.0	9002.2	486.7	124.9	
615506.0	1680335.5	997790.8	813483.5	810920.2	427.7	2135.6		
2611803.0	9244292.6	8086945.3	3314197.1	2397375.6	38169.7	513365.8	56653.0	34951.6

20-1 续表 3 continued

单位：万元

项　　目	Item	#外商资本 Foreign	主营业务收入 Revenue of Major Business	营业成本 Operating Cost	营业费用 Operating Expenses	营业税金及附加 Operating Tax and Extra Charges
合　计	**Total**	**1782738.7**	**31744328.6**	**11517047.5**	**1635574.7**	**869284.7**
按登记注册类型分	**Grouped by Registered Type**					
内资经济	Domestic Investment Economy	4855.2	28135463.4	9652875.0	1055151.4	735611.2
国有经济	State-owned	1472.9	21826676.8	6242982.7	585279.2	538735.5
集体经济	Collective-owned		955869.2	510463.6	114720.0	30910.7
联营经济	Joint Owned		182086.8	129423.1	19408.5	5839.6
私营经济	Private Owned	30.0	422926.4	263607.2	74733.0	11673.3
股份合作企业	Share Holding Cooperative	2183.5	524751.7	326047.7	28828.6	15844.5
股份有限公司	Share Holding Company		2229654.3	832573.3	55107.6	65875.3
有限责任公司	Limited-Liability Company	1168.8	1988251.4	1344048.3	176554.3	66666.9
其　他	Others		5246.8	3729.1	520.2	65.4
外商投资经济	Foreign Funded	1747875.4	2357841.3	1241025.6	315947.7	78412.1
港澳台商投资经济	Hongkong,Macao and Taiwan Funded	30008.1	1251023.9	623146.9	264475.6	55261.4
按国民经济行业分	**Grouped by Sector**					
金融业	Banking		13507823.7	15771.4	18643.8	374494.6
保险业	Insurance		1832807.5			27725.6
房地产业	Real Estate	22052.3	3166290.0	2520156.8	244039.8	176401.2
公共服务业	Public Services	1676.2	465104.9	401156.7	39651.5	26201.4
居民服务业	Personal Services	3207.3	100268.0	47404.8	31333.7	3429.4
旅馆业	Hotel	172489.9	1085114.0	167405.0	435058.2	55755.8
旅游业	Tourism	182.4	460567.2	418607.7	29316.2	4346.8
交通运输辅助业	Logistic Support for Transportation	4251.9	219285.2	144750.1	25649.2	11593.9
仓储业	Storage	4451.6	37863.4	16759.5	9162.2	1205.7
商业经纪与代理业	Commercial Brokerage and Agencies	26384.2	580130.1	522934.9	9487.2	1069.9
租赁服务业	Rental Services	23141.1	133074.0	57071.8	21434.5	5151.7
计算机应用服务业	Computer Application Services	117134.6	956423.6	658159.3	93190.8	13228.6
娱乐服务业	Entertainment Services	66541.1	87671.1	15917.7	40140.1	5719.6
信息咨询服务业	Consulting Services	534878.1	1489505.3	891664.9	179460.0	41593.1
# 广告业	Advertisement	8654.9	271137.1	160439.9	34556.0	11354.4
其他社会服务业	Other Social Services	252492.5	903300.2	616998.6	101618.6	20221.0
卫生、体育和社会福利业	Health,Sports and Social Welfare	10542.2	68600.3	39108.1	7894.9	372.4
教育文化艺术和广播电影电视业	Education,Culture,Arts, Radio,Film and Television	2231.7	867092.9	509644.1	87936.6	19576.9
科学研究和综合技术服务业	Scientific Research and Polytechnical Services	267400.2	4056413.6	3163477.1	214796.4	54923.2
农林牧渔服务业	FFAF Services		15806.8	11022.0	1681.3	156.2
地质勘察和水利管理业	Geological Prospecting and Water Conservancy		107276.9	90424.7	1233.2	1251.4
其　他	Others	273681.4	1603909.9	1208612.3	43846.5	24866.3

20-1 续表 4 continued

(10000 yuan)

经营利润 Business Profits	其他业务利润 Profits of Other Business	管理费用 Overhead Expense	# 税金 Taxes	#财产保险费 Premium of Property	# 劳动待业保险 Premium for Employment	财务费用 Financial Expense	# 利息支出 Interest Expenditure	营业利润 Operating Profits
2763870.8	**282239.1**	**2690238.9**	**143807.1**	**21655.1**	**86387.7**	**681139.0**	**834379.6**	**103050.9**
1830785.6	216364.2	1659529.2	105985.9	14551.8	81250.1	419742.9	583612.6	518767.7
1156783.3	121795.4	1068856.7	96775.3	8668.3	64192.0	336676.9	494866.3	490740.2
140046.5	10486.8	130411.4	2770.6	2745.0	3915.6	13046.4	12184.0	-74469.1
23335.1	5019.5	32715.9	289.5	161.0	409.4	5615.8	6134.2	-5896.6
69867.8	1832.8	70891.2	593.6	264.7	215.8	1533.2	1990.5	2321.3
48597.4	8535.5	42002.5	334.6	279.3	729.5	3834.1	3190.9	32906.7
131538.7	48197.0	95200.0	3044.3	1536.2	9659.9	21670.2	23261.1	38670.2
259680.2	20495.1	218630.6	2168.6	890.1	2118.1	37265.9	41877.2	34482.1
936.6	2.1	820.9	9.4	7.2	9.8	100.4	108.4	12.9
608208.6	49380.3	634693.5	22886.6	3238.4	3761.7	105432.5	92796.6	-171370.6
324876.6	16494.6	396016.2	14934.6	3864.9	1375.9	155963.6	157970.4	-244346.2
8461.5	3506.2	1343.1	68643.4	3240.1	26823.8	-14.9	45.0	408354.8
			947.5	478.6	877.2			-32413.0
164995.0	35850.3	435396.1	14217.0	3807.3	7992.0	283283.5	251583.5	-457137.1
-1904.7	-2216.9	128416.8	2330.4	1513.9	17717.1	4634.8	6193.0	-137173.2
18100.1	1443.5	21322.4	309.0	152.8	1267.6	776.1	1001.4	-2554.9
424575.6	4868.4	420112.5	19453.5	5608.3	8636.9	107563.3	133424.1	-95912.4
8296.5	39550.8	34241.2	527.9	241.2	492.4	6125.7	6246.7	7480.4
37292.0	873.1	24163.3	317.9	184.7	401.3	13851.9	13948.7	149.9
10736.0	3040.0	14886.0	354.2	271.5	276.8	2104.1	2197.2	-3214.1
46638.1	13267.2	30963.0	585.0	131.0	340.0	-47518.0	5220.8	76460.3
49416.0	1177.8	27063.6	5169.7	333.7	229.2	5477.1	5872.3	18053.1
191844.9	35397.1	173037.5	1002.8	316.0	1300.5	3365.1	4754.1	50839.4
25893.7	-384.3	41506.4	786.2	229.2	132.6	7918.0	3924.4	-23915.0
376787.3	27345.1	378350.7	14203.3	780.6	1235.6	-1114.8	13415.6	26896.5
64786.8	2028.1	45441.5	419.8	68.3	260.3	-215.7	554.5	21589.1
164462.0	29165.9	138556.5	2518.9	761.4	5601.9	122809.7	138139.6	-67738.3
21224.9	123.0	10564.6	349.0	10.4	5.1	-328.9	69.2	11112.2
249935.3	27617.5	150006.9	4498.5	707.5	6103.2	-2853.9	3533.8	130399.8
623216.9	36122.8	457012.2	4208.3	2075.4	4568.9	55811.5	36638.2	146516.0
2947.3	546.4	2503.2	35.0	20.6	31.1	544.5	437.2	446.0
14367.6	303.3	19985.5	246.3	24.9	147.6	6955.3	27217.9	-12269.9
326584.8	24641.9	180807.4	3103.3	766.0	2206.9	111748.9	180516.9	58670.4

20-1 续表 5 continued

单位：万元

项 目	Item	投资收益 Investment Income	补贴收入 Subsidy Income	营业外收入 Out-business Income	营业外支出 Out-business Expenditure	利润总额 Total Profits
合 计	**Total**	**2538980.7**	**236229.6**	**139462.4**	**83830.3**	**2952100.7**
按登记注册类型分	**Grouped by Registered Type**					
内资经济	Domestic Investment Economy	2496069.0	235619.6	82969.1	57921.2	3290843.3
国有经济	State-owned	2074370.1	230064.3	59008.1	40900.5	2831045.9
集体经济	Collective-owned	79541.8	866.6	9181.5	6129.8	8313.4
联营经济	Joint Owned	937.2	262.5	1436.2	434.7	-3303.2
私营经济	Private Owned	648.4	16.7	657.6	835.4	3169.6
股份合作企业	Share Holding Cooperative	9872.0	185.6	1235.8	1288.8	42940.9
股份有限公司	Share Holding Company	241582.4	1180.7	6157.3	4017.8	283089.3
有限责任公司	Limited-Liability Company	89117.1	3043.2	5275.5	4310.7	125560.9
其 他	Others			17.1	3.5	26.5
外商投资经济	Foreign Funded	22320.2	548.7	37876.2	19669.8	-128811.0
港澳台商投资经济	Hongkong,Macao and Taiwan Funded	20591.5	61.3	18617.1	6239.3	-209931.6
按国民经济行业分	**Grouped by Sector**					
金融业	Banking	1787712.4	24000.1	151.0	114.7	2222858.6
保险业	Insurance	107265.2	-1179.9			73794.8
房地产业	Real Estate	50042.8	3522.2	31099.4	10161.2	-383642.0
公共服务业	Public Services	5946.9	142512.8	12579.1	13490.1	10691.3
居民服务业	Personal Services	487.3	7.3	1196.3	1009.9	-1685.3
旅馆业	Hotel	17113.1	-408.5	30040.2	7372.3	-49292.9
旅游业	Tourism	12581.2	103.5	2914.4	1026.3	22352.0
交通运输辅助业	Logistic Support for Transportation	8002.1		1072.9	405.4	8899.6
仓储业	Storage	438.1	1007.2	151.4	336.1	-1818.8
商业经纪与代理业	Commercial Brokerage and Agencies	8498.6	45.0	1222.4	417.4	84586.3
租赁服务业	Rental Services	804.2	161.1	522.3	398.3	18751.7
计算机应用服务业	Computer Application Services	4637.0	979.3	7101.9	3248.1	61726.5
娱乐服务业	Entertainment Services	255.3	13.0	1195.0	728.9	-22751.0
信息咨询服务业	Consulting Services	44554.5	77.7	3203.5	12713.8	61088.2
# 广告业	Advertisement	5166.4		1167.8	799.5	26779.0
其他社会服务业	Other Social Services	196865.5	35494.8	4061.0	5600.2	164304.0
卫生、体育和社会福利业	Health,Sports and Social Welfare	5.8	228.5	308.2	528.6	10713.1
教育文化艺术和广播电影电视业	Education,Culture,Arts,Radio,Film and Television	13906.2	23176.3	10042.1	3568.8	173476.9
科学研究和综合技术服务业	Scientific Research and Polytechnical Services	80765.7	3364.6	20032.4	12558.6	243325.4
农林牧渔服务业	FFAF Services	64.8	25.1	507.4	303.2	756.9
地质勘察和水利管理业	Geological Prospecting and Water Conservancy	15402.9	23.0	1650.3	77.5	4734.5
其 他	Others	183631.1	3076.2	10411.2	9770.9	249230.9

20-1 续表 6 continued

(10000 yuan)

应交所得税 Income Tax Payable	转作奖金的利润 Profits Distributed as Bonus	提取盈余公积 Surplus Accumulation Funds Drawn	应付利润 Profits Payable	# 已分配股利 Divided Payment	未分配利润 Undistributed Profits	本年应付工资总额 Total Wages Payable in the Year	# 主营业务应付工资 Wage Payable of Major Business	本年应付福利费总额 Welfares Payable in the Year	# 主营业务应付福利费 of Major Business
497802.4	**11304.4**	**243262.2**	**134839.5**	**97927.0**	**-286663.2**	**1856799.8**	**1122691.1**	**291728.2**	**187480.8**
438736.1	10508.0	236774.6	91881.3	87357.3	488844.6	1405206.5	803382.2	175349.8	116967.7
316822.0	5596.4	187746.7	-21542.6	70505.9	364375.5	768933.4	489306.8	112370.0	76290.6
12653.9	3849.2	7227.6	11922.7	172.5	-17206.5	98667.0	65860.3	11933.7	8090.1
2647.1	26.1	1086.3	1625.7	6.2	1430.8	15509.4	11574.8	1968.0	1480.6
4415.6	270.2	2418.2	3595.7	787.2	2807.3	40877.4	32838.5	4221.0	3531.8
10375.3	14.8	1713.6	519.4	50.0	-4499.5	21693.4	17576.6	2995.7	2249.8
53036.0	20.2	19288.6	20709.8	5736.8	59471.2	217450.3	44470.8	18205.4	6066.2
38779.3	731.1	17127.1	75046.0	10098.7	82964.0	241671.5	141409.9	23604.4	19238.0
6.9		166.5	4.6		-498.2	404.1	344.5	51.6	20.6
34271.6	452.0	5426.7	31825.8	4107.8	-323584.3	317893.0	228333.6	65514.0	38805.4
24794.7	344.4	1060.9	11132.4	6461.9	-451923.5	133700.3	90975.3	50864.4	31707.7
191629.8	2517.1	1.4	-52662.9		4998.9	171735.0	2438.8	30437.0	564.0
391.3			14042.8			21174.3		4714.9	
62728.6	137.9	2195.4	25565.4	13.0	-284877.0	159057.7	58744.7	29217.5	11947.3
5267.3	156.9	4212.0	1608.1	773.7	8872.0	153625.3	104692.8	16711.9	14547.2
1400.2	134.5	1130.7	803.1	-44.2	-10724.1	20940.7	18038.7	2692.3	2143.7
13973.9	386.0	5908.2	12805.0	6201.5	-392843.2	190750.4	148852.5	52064.3	39802.9
3544.8	12.2	4501.5	448.1		14537.1	15098.1	11308.1	2233.2	1472.6
3109.5	16.2	1706.7	5869.0	2723.9	16011.5	18341.4	16277.5	2211.1	1988.2
373.3	17.8	116.4	54.3		-5828.8	7733.5	6178.1	1320.1	892.4
26766.3		13578.7	2931.8		58234.0	6897.5	5872.4	1397.4	1282.0
1055.6	17.0	414.2	997.1	-42.4	-7773.1	9608.4	8606.9	1959.2	1703.2
12561.7	1095.0	48903.0	10939.7	2015.6	-2600.7	185492.5	112432.3	20146.6	9551.2
1285.7	1.2	274.1	1374.9	1183.7	-42891.9	16077.1	13586.8	3446.2	2916.5
30390.5	686.5	12806.8	22017.0	12632.0	-28408.2	135827.0	121027.2	21756.5	19959.4
10802.4	145.9	2994.8	5126.5	1398.4	20631.8	19211.5	17893.4	3457.0	3055.1
24482.2	3009.0	26742.5	14490.3	2066.8	85896.6	173887.0	101514.6	28065.8	27248.6
123.2	12.7	5544.5	192.1	93.5	3290.0	6105.6	4633.2	571.4	512.6
61897.2	1323.3	39561.6	12312.6	30.5	177162.5	65083.4	51616.3	10050.8	6803.3
41787.6	921.8	42171.2	39253.2	11056.2	147348.6	412655.7	261665.5	49064.1	33582.8
22.7	185.1	240.7	100.9	2.6	75.5	1868.7	1396.0	182.9	135.0
44.8	96.3	809.8	3488.3	126.1	-800.6	4501.9	4125.1	760.1	724.0
14966.2	577.9	32442.8	18208.7	59094.8	-26342.3	80338.6	69683.6	12724.9	9703.9

区县资料

STATISTICS FOR DISTRICTS AND COUNTIES

21-1 东城区、西城区国民经济主要指标
MAIN NATIONAL ECONOMIC INDICATORS FOR DONGCHENG AND XICHENG DISTRICTS

项目 Item	东城区 Dongcheng			西城区 Xicheng		
	1999	1998	1999年为1998年% 1999 as % of 1998	1999	1998	1999年为1998年% 1999 as % of 1998
综合 General Survey						
国内生产总值 (万元) Gross Domestic Product (10000 yuan)	268175.6	234895.0	114.2	388605.0	353919.0	109.8
第一产业 Primary Industry						
第二产业 Secondary Industry	37675.0	27532.0	136.8	27842.0	26495.0	105.1
第三产业 Tertiary Industry	230500.6	207363.0	111.2	360763.0	327423.0	110.2
财政收入 (万元) Fiscal Revenue (10000 yuan)	115302.6	96318.0	119.7	136294.0	124571.0	109.4
#增值税 Increased Value Tax						
营业税 Operating Tax	49196.0	44737.0	110.0	65439.0	57404.0	114.0
个人所得税 Private Income Tax	18772.0	12728.0	147.5	16743.0	12219.0	137.0
企业所得税 Enterprise Income Tax	21860.0	16608.0	131.6	36557.0	41265.0	88.6
财政支出 (万元) Fiscal Expenditure (10000 yuan)	157666.0	118469.0	133.1	160983.0	139684.0	115.2
#基本建设支出 Capital Construction	11499.0	8390.0	137.1	16698.0	14444.0	115.6
支援农业生产支出 Supporting Agriculture						
文教卫生事业费 Culture,Education and Health	37523.0	34687.0	108.2	41271.0	40995.0	100.7
人口和劳动力 Population and Labor Force						
总人口 (人) Total Population (person)	709733.0	699752.0	101.4	859262.0	869006.0	98.9
常住户籍人口 (人) Permanent Registered Population (person)	628665.0	632533.0	99.4	787261.0	791595.0	99.5
#非农业人口 Non-agriculture	628665.0	632533.0	99.4	787259.0	791593.0	99.5
男 Male	313418.0	315550.0	99.3	394379.0	397054.0	99.3
女 Female	315247.0	316983.0	99.5	392880.0	394548.0	99.6
出生率 (‰) Birth Rate (‰)	4.2	4.0		4.1	3.9	
死亡率 (‰) Death Rate (‰)	6.0	7.2		5.5	7.1	
自然增长率 (‰) Natural Growth Rate (‰)	-1.9	-3.2		-1.4	-3.3	
从业人员 (人) Employment (person)	127268.0	120755.0	105.4	141323.0	132352.0	106.8
按职工非职工分 Grouped by Staff and Workers or Non-staff-and-worker						
职工人数 (人) Staff and Worker (person)	120096.0	115747.0	103.8	121904.0	113259.0	107.6
#国有单位 State-owned	56603.0	59085.0	95.8	63811.0	58230.0	109.6
集体单位 Collective-owned	25147.0	25891.0	97.1	20074.0	21018.0	95.5
城镇个体劳动者 Urban and Rural Individuals	24880.0	24119.0	103.2	15673.0	14388.0	108.9
劳动工资 Wages						
工资总额 (万元) Total Wages (10000 yuan)	147517.9	124190.1	118.8	160650.0	135431.0	118.6
#国有单位 State-owned	78778.8	71344.5	110.4	90127.0	75083.0	120.0
集体单位 Collective-owned	21325.1	19871.0	107.3	18016.0	18019.0	100.0
职工平均工资 (元) Average Wage (yuan)	12357.0	11265.0	109.7	14426.0	12592.0	114.6
固定资产投资 Investment in Fixed Assets						
全社会固定资产投资 (万元) Total Investment in Fixed Assets (10000 yuan)	446137.0	456580.0	97.7	434403.0	525194.0	82.7
按建设性质分 Grouped by Type of Construction						
#基本建设投资 Capital Construction	40828.0	33793.0	120.8	19589.0	47855.0	40.9
更新改造投资 Innovation and Replacement	28086.0	37207.0	75.5	54384.0	74514.0	73.0
按登记注册类型分 Grouped by Registered Type						
# 国有单位 (万元) State-owned (10000 yuan)	113755.0	149906.0	75.9	104428.0	175001.0	59.7
集体单位 (万元) Collective-owned (10000 yuan)	759.0	144.0	527.1		76.0	

21-1 续表 1 continued

项目	Item	东城区 Dongcheng 1999	1998	1999年为1998年% 1999 as % of 1998	西城区 Xicheng 1999	1998	1999年为1998年% 1999 as % of 1998
新增固定资产 (万元)	Incremental Fixed Assets (10000 yuan)	211790.0	286816.0	73.8	349130.0	389769.0	89.6
#国有单位	State-owned	103743.0	74767.0	138.8	51751.0	52050.0	99.4
集体单位	Collective-owned	623.0				76.0	
房屋施工面积 (万平方米)	Floor Space of Buildings Under Construction (10000 sq.m)	244.7	220.3	111.1	274.3	295.7	92.8
#国有单位	State-owned	60.3	77.4	77.9	39.6	78.4	50.5
集体单位	Collective-owned	1.5	0.2	1000.0			
房屋竣工面积 (万平方米)	Floor Space of Buildings Completed (10000 sq.m)	45.2	53.4	84.6	77.5	56.6	136.9
#国有单位	State-owned	24.1	27.6	87.3	11.6	13.1	88.5
#住宅	Residence	13.8	18.3	75.4	6.6	6.2	106.5
#集体单位	Collective-owned	0.2					
#住宅	Residence						
工业	**Industry**						
全部工业企业单位数 (个)	Number of Enterprises (unit)	266.0	218.0	122.0	319.0	353.0	90.4
国有	State-owned	55.0	56.0	98.2	78.0	118.0	66.1
集体	Collective-owned	98.0	92.0	106.5	107.0	117.0	91.5
其他	Others	113.0	70.0	161.4	134.0	118.0	113.6
全部工业总产值 (现价,万元)	Gross Output Value of Industry (at current prices,10000 yuan)	65700.0	60809.9	108.0	83385.0	75306.0	110.7
国有	State-owned	12377.9	12543.7	98.7	15088.0	15609.0	96.7
集体	Collective-owned	30321.0	26704.3	113.5	10194.0	8322.0	122.5
其他	Others	23001.1	21561.9	106.7	58103.0	51375.0	113.1
全部工业总产值 (1990年不变价,万元)	Gross Output Value of Industry (at constant prices of 1990,10000 yuan)	52181.0	42495.8	122.8	72418.0	64621.0	112.1
国有	State-owned	10825.5	9606.8	112.7	10784.0	10090.0	106.9
集体	Collective-owned	22544.6	19447.1	115.9	8979.0	7092.0	126.6
其他	Others	18810.9	13441.9	139.9	52655.0	47440.0	111.0
全部轻工业总产值 (现价,万元)	Gross Output Value of Light Industry (at current prices,10000yuan)	50754.9	46506.9	109.1	40731.0	45535.0	89.4
以农产品为原料	Using Farm Products as Raw Materials	40760.9	40464.1	100.7	27687.0	31591.0	87.6
以非农产品为原料	Using Non-farm Products as Raw Materials	9994.0	6042.8	165.4	13044.0	13944.0	93.5
全部重工业总产值 (现价,万元)	Gross Output Value of Heavy Industry (at current prices,10000yuan)	14945.1	14303.0	104.5	42654.0	29771.0	143.3
采掘工业	Excavation						
原料工业	Raw Materials Industry	51.5			1879.0	2154.0	87.2
制造工业	Manufacturing Industry	14893.6	14303.0	104.1	40775.0	27617.0	147.6
独立核算工业企业工业增加值 (万元)	Value Added of Enterprises with Independent Accounting system (10000 yuan)	21254.5	12526.4	169.7	31246.0	26651.0	117.2
独立核算工业企业平均职工人数 (人)	Average Number of Staff and Workers in Enterprises with Independent Accounting System (person)	12326.0	6383.0	193.1	12555.0	8292.0	151.4

21-1 续表 2 continued

项目 Item		东城区 Dongcheng 1999	东城区 Dongcheng 1998	东城区 Dongcheng 1999年为1998年% 1999 as % of 1998	西城区 Xicheng 1999	西城区 Xicheng 1998	西城区 Xicheng 1999年为1998年% 1999 as % of 1998
#国有	State-owned	2544.0	1652.0	154.0	3135.0	2934.0	106.9
集体	Collective-owned	7119.0	3121.0	228.1	2960.0	2852.0	103.8
独立核算工业企业总产值(现价,万元)	Gross Output Value of Enterprises with Independent Accounting System(at current prices, 10000 yuan)	65700.0	44909.6	146.3	83385.0	75306.0	110.7
#国有	State-owned	12377.9	12128.5	102.1	15088.0	15609.0	96.7
集体	Collective-owned	30321.0	11219.2	270.3	10194.0	8322.0	122.5
独立核算工业企业财务指标	Financial Indicators for Enterprises with Independent Accounting System						
产品销售收入 (万元)	Sales Revenue (10000yuan)	66666.3	45075.0	147.9	93912.0	82408.0	114.0
#国有	State-owned	10173.6	11184.7	91.0	14737.0	15092.0	97.6
产品销售成本 (万元)	Cost of Sales (10000yuan)	49740.8	33555.0	148.2	73841.0	61283.0	120.5
#国有	State-owned	7161.3	7990.3	89.6	11649.0	12310.0	94.6
固定资产原价 (万元)	Original Value of Fixed Assets (10000 yuan)	46883.2	20039.8	234.0	48105.0	32302.0	148.9
#国有	State-owned	9015.9	4382.8	205.7	13469.0	8819.0	152.7
固定资产净值 (万元)	Net Value of Fixed Assets (10000 yuan)	31217.8	13891.2	224.7	29544.0	22151.0	133.4
#国有	State-owned	6201.6	3235.2	191.7	9759.0	6416.0	152.1
全部流动资金年平均余额 (万元)	Annual Average Balance of Circulating Funds (10000 yuan)	75186.0	47329.9	158.9	114322.0	96475.0	118.5
#国有	State-owned	12878.5	9867.4	130.5	19438.0	16108.0	120.7
利润总额 (万元)	Total Profits (10000yuan)	936.3	442.5	211.6	-2266.0	2614.0	
#国有	State-owned	1119.3	1461.8	76.6	413.0	896.0	46.1
资金利税率 (%)	Ratio of Pre-tax Profits to Total Capital (%)	4.4	4.2		1.2	2.6	
产品销售率 (%)	Ratio of Sales Value to Gross Output Value (%)	96.1	97.5		95.8	92.9	
增加值率 (%)	Ratio of Added Value to Gross Output Value (%)	22.6	19.6		37.5	35.0	
独立核算工业企业全员劳动生产率 (元/人)	Overall Labor Productivity of Enterprises with Independent Accounting System (yuan/person)	17244.0	19625.0	87.9	66416.0	90817.0	73.1
#国有	State-owned	18683.0	31477.0	59.4	48128.0	53199.0	90.5
集体	Collective-owned	16929.0	9171.0	184.6	34439.0	29179.0	118.0
商业	**Commerce**						
社会消费品零售额 (万元)	Retail Sales of Consumer Goods (10000 yuan)	548189.0	526483.0	104.1	809619.0	693818.0	116.7
按登记注册类型分	Grouped by Registered Type						
国有	State-owned	143916.0	148538.0	96.9	348136.0	366336.0	95.0
集体	Collective-owned	70696.0	74603.0	94.8	37450.0	54118.0	69.2
其他	Others	333577.0	303342.0	110.0	424033.0	273364.0	155.1
按类别分	Grouped by Type of Goods						
吃的商品 (万元)	Food (10000 yuan)	240969.0	244638.0	98.5	194308.0	168598.0	115.2

21-1 续表 3 continued

项目		Item	东城区 Dongcheng 1999	1998	1999年为1998年% 1999 as % of 1998	西城区 Xicheng 1999	1998	1999年为1998年% 1999 as % of 1998
穿的商品	(万元)	Clothing (10000 yuan)	85410.0	69266.0	123.3	170020.0	164435.0	103.4
用的商品	(万元)	Daily Used Articles (10000 yuan)	217697.0	206796.0	105.3	445291.0	360785.1	123.4
烧的商品	(万元)	Fuel (10000 yuan)	4113.0	5783.0	71.1			
网点数	(个)	Number of Outlets (unit)	15637.0	14772.0	105.9	11042.0	12097.0	91.3
#商业		Wholesale and Retail	11395.0	10533.0	108.2	6952.0	7910.0	87.9
饮食业		Catering	2578.0	2591.0	99.5	2057.0	2213.0	93.0
服务业		Services	1664.0	1648.0	101.0	1963.0	1896.0	103.5
#宾馆、饭店		Hotels	133.0	112.0	118.8	67.0	78.0	85.9
营业人员	(人)	Personnel (person)	104737.0	94414.0	110.9	58635.0	65335.0	89.7
#商业		Wholesale and Retail	56389.0	50997.0	110.6	35158.0	41785.0	84.1
饮食业		Catering Service	17335.0	16201.0	107.0	10399.0	12080.0	86.1
服务业		Services	31013.0	27216.0	114.0	10265.0	8607.0	119.3
#宾馆、饭店		Hotels	4587.0	4684.0	97.9	3335.0	2863.0	116.5
外经、外贸		**Foreign Economy and Trade**						
出口商品交货额	(万元)	Delivery Value of Exports (10000 yuan)				2230.0	1731.0	128.8
利用外资签订协议(合同)数	(个)	Number of Signed Agreements and Contracts of Foreign Capital to be Utilized (unit)	43.0	33.0	130.3	41.0	47.0	87.2
利用外资签订协议(合同)金额	(万美元)	Amount of Foreign Capital to be Utilized through Agreements and Contracts (USD 10000)	5630.3	192997.0	2.9	2845.0	3274.1	86.9
实际利用外资	(万美元)	Amount of Foreign Capital Actually Used(USD 10000)	40584.8	54323.5	74.7	3516.0	15521.0	22.7
旅游人数	(万人)	Number of Tourists (10000 persons)	1212.1	917.5	132.1	2495.0	2368.0	105.4
教育		**Education**						
学校数	(个)	Number of Schools (unit)	113.0	113.0	100.0	134.0	140.0	95.7
小学		Primary Schools	64.0	66.0	97.0	77.0	81.0	95.1
普通中学		Regular Secondary Schools	33.0	33.0	100.0	52.0	54.0	96.3
中等专业教育		Specialized Secondary Schools	16.0	14.0	114.3	5.0	5.0	100.0
招生数	(人)	New Student Enrollment (person)	21966.0	23023.0	95.4	24356.0	23688.0	102.8
小学		Primary Schools	4689.0	4940.0	94.9	4865.0	5060.0	96.1
初级中等学校		Junior Secondary Schools	9511.0	9336.0	101.9	10529.0	9901.0	106.3
高级中等学校		Senior Secondary Schools	5372.0	5376.0	99.9	8795.0	8537.0	103.0
中等专业教育		Specialized Secondary Schools	2394.0	3371.0	71.0	167.0	190.0	87.9
在校学生	(人)	Student Enrollment (person)	92511.0	96553.0	95.8	99493.0	105859.0	94.0
小学		Primary Schools	38527.0	41837.0	92.1	42055.0	47202.0	89.1
初级中等学校		Junior Secondary Schools	28627.0	29572.0	96.8	30752.0	32097.0	95.8

21-1 续表 4 continued

项　　目 Item			东城区 Dongcheng 1999	1998	1999年为1998年% 1999 as % of 1998	西城区 Xicheng 1999	1998	1999年为1998年% 1999 as % of 1998
高级中等学校		Senior Secondary Schools	15660.0	14303.0	109.5	25564.0	25375.0	100.7
中等专业教育		Specialized Secondary Schools	9697.0	10841.0	89.4	1122.0	1185.0	94.7
毕业生	(人)	Graduates (person)	25898.0	26764.0	96.8	29920.0	29718.0	100.7
小学		Primary Schools	8796.0	8547.0	102.9	10329.0	9592.0	107.7
初级中等学校		Junior Secondary Schools	9769.0	10790.0	90.5	11352.0	12498.0	90.8
高级中等学校		Senior Secondary Schools	4049.0	4166.0	97.2	7891.0	7317.0	107.8
中等专业教育		Specialized Secondary Schools	3284.0	3261.0	100.7	348.0	311.0	111.9
达到"国家体育标准"学生数	(人)	Number of Students Come to the Standard for State Physical Training (person)	76023.0	74335.0	102.3	96152.0	88222.0	109.0
幼儿园、托儿所个数	(个)	Number of Kindergardens (unit)	66.0	71.0	93.0	82.0	98.0	83.7
幼儿入托数	(人)	New Enrollment (person)	10013.0	10314.0	97.1	13140.0	13861.0	94.8
文化		**Culture**						
文化馆、站	(个)	Cultural Centers (unit)	11.0	11.0	100.0	11.0	11.0	100.0
公共图书馆	(个)	Public Libraries (unit)	2.0	2.0	100.0	2.0	1.0	200.0
公共图书馆藏书	(万册)	Collection (10000 volume)	298.0	296.1	100.6	37.1	33.1	112.1
电影放映单位	(个)	Film Projection Units (unit)	8.0	6.0	133.3	13.0	15.0	86.7
区级以上重点文物保护单位	(个)	Cultural Relics Preserved at District Level and above (unit)	130.0	130.0	100.0	108.0	108.0	100.0
卫生		**Health**						
卫生机构数	(个)	Number of Health Institutions (unit)	86.0	84.0	102.4	603.0	747.0	80.7
#医院		Hospitals	30.0	30.0	100.0	24.0	26.0	92.3
卫生院		Clinics						
床位数	(张)	Number of Beds (unit)	6691.0	6878.0	97.3	7977.0	7733.0	103.2
#医院		Hospitals	6691.0	6878.0	97.3	7877.0	7633.0	103.2
卫生院		Clinics						
平均每千人拥有床位数	(张)	Average Number of Beds Per 1000 Persons (unit)	10.6	10.9	97.5	10.1	9.8	103.4
卫生技术人员	(人)	Medical Technical Personnel (person)	13945.0	14237.0	97.9	13322.0	15323.0	86.9
#医生		Doctors	5877.0	5985.0	98.2	5100.0	6703.0	76.1
公用设施		**Public Utilities**						
区级以上公园	(个)	Parks at District Level and above (unit)	7.0	7.0	100.0	10.0	10.0	100.0
体育场馆	(个)	Stadiums and Gymnasiums (unit)	9.0	9.0	100.0	217.0	217.0	100.0
道路长度	(公里)	Length of Roads (km)	98.0	97.0	101.0	243.0	240.2	101.2

21-2 崇文区、宣武区国民经济主要指标
MAIN NATIONAL ECONOMIC INDICATORS FOR DONGCHENG AND XICHENG DISTRICTS

项目		Item	崇文区 Chongwen 1999	1998	1999年为1998年% 1999 as % of 1998	宣武区 Xuanwu 1999	1998	1999年为1998年% 1999 as % of 1998
综合		**General Survey**						
国内生产总值	(万元)	Gross Domestic Product (10000 yuan)	128171.9	107668.6	119.0	165416.4	149151.2	110.9
第一产业		Primary Industry						
第二产业		Secondary Industry	27295.0	19595.6	139.3	41022.6	34865.3	117.7
第三产业		Tertiary Industry	100876.9	88073.0	114.5	124393.8	114285.9	108.8
财政收入	(万元)	Fiscal Revenue (10000 yuan)	49420.0	42168.8	117.2	97143.0	70750.0	137.3
#增值税		Increased Value Tax						
营业税		Operating Tax	18821.0	15418.0	122.1	57706.0	42144.0	136.9
个人所得税		Private Income Tax	6288.0	5230.0	120.2	10111.0	6224.0	162.5
企业所得税		Enterprise Income Tax	11897.0	9480.0	125.5	11786.0	10301.0	114.4
财政支出	(万元)	Fiscal Expenditure (10000 yuan)	52907.0	45303.0	116.8	109987.0	79842.0	137.8
#基本建设支出		Capital Construction	3437.0	1010.0	340.3	18408.0	6539.0	281.5
支援农业生产支出		Supporting Agriculture						
文教卫生事业费		Culture,Education and Health	17392.0	16080.0	108.2	23928.0	20395.0	117.3
人口和劳动力		**Population and Labor Force**						
总人口	(人)	Total Population (person)	463427.0	461743.0	100.4	595706.0	593397.0	100.4
常住户籍人口	(人)	Permanent Registered Population (person)	417247.0	420540.0	99.2	536813.0	538567.0	99.7
#非农业人口		Non-agriculture	417188.0	420475.0	99.2	536797.0	538551.0	99.7
男		Male	208598.0	210264.0	99.2	270990.0	272022.0	99.6
女		Female	208649.0	210276.0	99.2	265807.0	266529.0	99.7
出生率	(‰)	Birth Rate (‰)	3.3	3.3		3.6	3.6	
死亡率	(‰)	Death Rate (‰)	5.4	9.3		6.9	9.1	
自然增长率	(‰)	Natural Growth Rate (‰)	-2.1	-6.0		-3.3	-5.5	
从业人员	(人)	Employment (person)	71972.0	59311.0	121.3	87553.0	85463.0	102.4
按职工非职工分		Grouped by Staff and Workers or Non-staff-and-worker						
职工人数	(人)	Staff and Worker (person)	75804.0	56727.0	133.6	85310.0	82406.0	103.5
#国有单位		State-owned	35555.0	32611.0	109.0	37845.0	40878.0	92.6
集体单位		Collective-owned	19803.0	15484.0	127.9	26792.0	28738.0	93.2
城镇个体劳动者		Urban and Rural Individuals						
劳动工资		**Wages**						
工资总额	(万元)	Total Wages (10000 yuan)	78047.5	55952.4	139.5	93599.3	95187.8	98.3
#国有单位		State-owned	41967.3	36465.3	115.1	48279.5	55769.2	86.6
集体单位		Collective-owned	14591.9	10382.8	140.5	22716.6	24743.4	91.8
职工平均工资	(元)	Average Wage (yuan)	10296.0	9863.0	104.4	11102.0	10400.0	106.8
固定资产投资		**Investment in Fixed Assets**						
全社会固定资产投资	(万元)	Total Investment in Fixed Assets (10000 yuan)	141616.0	169038.0	83.8	201205.0	320939.0	62.7
按建设性质分		Grouped by Type of Construction						
#基本建设投资		Capital Construction	13227.0	24387.0	54.2	14870.0	9899.0	150.2
更新改造投资		Innovation and Replacement	28148.0	569.0	4946.9	51523.0	86200.0	59.8
按登记注册类型分		Grouped by Registered Type						
#国有单位	(万元)	State-owned (10000 yuan)	44856.0	32527.0	137.9	125508.0	159983.0	78.5

21-2 续表 1 continued

项目		Item	崇文区 Chongwen 1999	1998	1999年为1998年% 1999 as % of 1998	宣武区 Xuanwu 1999	1998	1999年为1998年% 1999 as % of 1998
集体单位	(万元)	Collective-owned (10000 yuan)	1577.0	1672.0	94.3	5678.0	7344.0	77.3
新增固定资产	(万元)	Incremental Fixed Assets (10000 yuan)	164373.0	217220.0	75.7	341393.0	133624.0	255.5
#国有单位		State-owned	46357.0	12106.0	382.9	216156.0	67971.0	318.0
集体单位		Collective-owned	2349.0	569.0	412.8	18591.0	3200.0	581.0
房屋施工面积	(万平方米)	Floor Space of Buildings Under Construction (10000 sq.m)	92.0	95.3	96.5	261.8	208.8	125.4
#国有单位		State-owned	26.2	29.6	88.5	160.6	110.1	145.9
集体单位		Collective-owned	2.9	3.9	74.4	19.4	17.9	108.4
房屋竣工面积	(万平方米)	Floor Space of Buildings Completed (10000 sq.m)	11.5	20.2	56.9	97.9	61.9	158.2
#国有单位		State-owned	7.2	3.4	211.8	45.1	27.6	163.4
#住宅		Residence	2.9	4.7	61.7	23.3	24.0	97.1
#集体单位		Collective-owned	1.0	3.8	26.3	13.4	2.9	462.1
#住宅		Residence	0.7	3.5	20.0	9.3	1.9	489.5
工业		**Industry**						
全部工业企业单位数	(个)	Number of Enterprises (unit)	184.0	170.0	108.2	257.0	230.0	111.7
国有		State-owned	30.0	31.0	96.8	46.0	50.0	92.0
集体		Collective-owned	96.0	87.0	110.3	118.0	103	114.6
其他		Others	58.0	52.0	111.5	93.0	77.0	120.8
全部工业总产值 (现价,万元)		Gross Output Value of Industry (at current prices,10000 yuan)	49716.7	39953.6	124.4	56097.3	42913.1	130.7
国有		State-owned	5732.0	4189.3	136.8	10468.0	5381.4	194.5
集体		Collective-owned	16710.5	13155.1	127.0	18436.5	9133.7	201.9
其他		Others	27274.2	22609.2	120.6	27192.4	28398	95.8
全部工业总产值 (1990年不变价,万元)		Gross Output Value of Industry (at constant prices of 1990,10000 yuan)	43521.2	32452.0	134.1	54619.7	42293	129.1
国有		State-owned	4440.2	3210.4	138.3	9747.5	5088.8	191.5
集体		Collective-owned	15336.7	10982.0	139.7	18474.4	9225.5	200.3
其他		Others	23744.3	18259.6	130.0	26397.8	27978.7	94.3
全部轻工业总产值 (现价,万元)		Gross Output Value of Light Industry at current prices,10000 yuan)	31999.6	30050.2	106.5	40238.8	37191.8	108.2
以农产品为原料		Using Farm Products as Raw Materials	19554.5	17608.1	111.1	22168.2	22884.3	96.9
以非农产品为原料		Using Non-farm Products as Raw Materials	12445.1	12442.1	100.0	18070.6	14307.5	126.3
全部重工业总产值 (现价,万元)		Gross Output Value of Heavy Industry at current prices,10000 yuan)	17717.1	9903.4	178.9	15858.5	5721.3	277.2
采掘工业		Excavation						
原料工业		Raw Materials Industry	1770.5	770.6	229.8	816.9	656.9	124.4
制造工业		Manufacturing Industry	15946.6	9132.8	174.6	15041.6	5064.4	297.0
独立核算工业企业工业增加值	(万元)	Value Added of Enterprises with Independent Accounting system (10000 yuan)	16113.4	14528.8	110.9	19346.0	13978.8	138.4
独立核算工业企业平均职工人数	(人)	Average Number of Staff and Workers in Enterprises with Independent Accounting System (person)	11275.0	6066.0	185.9	12245.0	5515	222.0

21-2 续表 2 continued

项目	Item	崇文区 Chongwen 1999	1998	1999年为1998年% 1999 as % of 1998	宣武区 Xuanwu 1999	1998	1999年为1998年% 1999 as % of 1998
#国有	State-owned	2523.0	784.0	321.8	2902.0	940.0	308.7
集体	Collective-owned	5904.0	3151.0	187.4	7054.0	2641.0	267.1
独立核算工业企业总产值 (现价,万元)	Gross Output Value of Enterprises with Independent Accounting System(at current prices, 10000 yuan)	49716.7	39953.6	124.4	56097.3	42853.6	130.9
#国有	State-owned	5732.0	4189.3	136.8	10468.4	5321.9	196.7
集体	Collective-owned	16710.5	13155.1	127.0	18436.5	9133.7	201.9
独立核算工业企业财务指标	Financial Indicators for Enterprises with Independent Accounting System						
产品销售收入 (万元)	Sales Revenue (10000yuan)	52511.2	36950.6	142.1	66918.3	48915.7	136.8
#国有	State-owned	7997.7	4150.6	192.7	10354.1	5074.1	204.1
产品销售成本 (万元)	Cost of Sales (10000yuan)	38781.1	28387.8	136.6	51787.9	32745.7	158.2
#国有	State-owned	5600.0	3227.0	173.5	8751.1	4121.7	212.3
固定资产原价 (万元)	Original Value of Fixed Assets (10000 yuan)	27578.4	11967.9	230.4	43620.4	16662.3	261.8
#国有	State-owned	8050.8	804.6	1000.6	12211.1	2125.5	574.5
固定资产净值 (万元)	Net Value of Fixed Assets (10000 yuan)	16400.3	6614.1	248.0	23399.5	10576.7	221.2
#国有	State-owned	5370.5	442.3	1214.2	7446.3	1275.4	583.8
全部流动资金年平均余额 (万元)	Annual Average Balance of Circulating Funds (10000 yuan)	61992.6	33319.5	186.1	90016.6	21189.8	424.8
#国有	State-owned	12424.9	4453.9	279.0	16932.9	4378.3	386.7
利润总额 (万元)	Total Profits (10000yuan)	748.7	1991.4	37.6	-1406.1	1832.2	
#国有	State-owned	-275.7	380.5		-128.2	396.2	
资金利税率 (%)	Ratio of Pre-tax Profits to Total Capital (%)	6.1	5.3		1.5	8.4	
产品销售率 (%)	Ratio of Sales Value to Gross Output Value (%)	97.5	98.3		103.6	100.0	
增加值率 (%)	Ratio of Added Value to Gross Output Value (%)	32.4	39.0		34.5	32.6	
独立核算工业企业全员劳动生产率 (元/人)	Overall Labor Productivity of Enterprises with Independent Accounting System (yuan/person)	14291.0	23951.0	59.7	16012.3	25346.8	63.2
#国有	State-owned	6418.0	18532.0	34.6	11649.9	19066.0	61.1
集体	Collective-owned	6238.0	15169.0	41.1	10223.8	9706.0	105.3
商业	**Commerce**						
社会消费品零售额 (万元)	Retail Sales of Consumer Goods (10000 yuan)	345431.0	331704.0	104.1	394507.0	359833.0	109.6
按登记注册类型分	Grouped by Registered Type						
国有	State-owned	103203.0	58563.0	176.2	72984.0	66411.0	109.9
集体	Collective-owned	25849.0	16999.0	152.1	113618.0	104403.0	108.8
其他	Others	216379.0	132459.0	163.4	207905.0	189019.0	110.0
按类别分	Grouped by Type of Goods						
吃的商品 (万元)	Food (10000 yuan)	170465.0	172902.0	98.6	156381.0	137626.0	113.6

21-2 续表 3 continued

项目	Item	崇文区 Chongwen 1999	崇文区 Chongwen 1998	1999年为1998年% 1999 as % of 1998	宣武区 Xuanwu 1999	宣武区 Xuanwu 1998	1999年为1998年% 1999 as % of 1998
穿的商品 (万元)	Clothing (10000 yuan)	66431.0	59200.0	112.2	44501.0	40942.0	108.7
用的商品 (万元)	Daily Used Articles (10000 yuan)	107078.0	97783.0	109.5	189985.0	178192.0	106.6
烧的商品 (万元)	Fuel (10000 yuan)	1457.0	1819.0	80.1	3640.0	3073.0	118.5
网点数 (个)	Number of Outlets (unit)	7364.0	7103.0	103.7	8602.0	10259.0	83.8
#商业	Wholesale and Retail	5404.0	5090.0	106.2	6872.0	7995.0	86.0
饮食业	Catering	717.0	708.0	101.3	1024.0	1588.0	64.5
服务业	Services	1243.0	1305.0	95.2	706.0	676.0	104.4
#宾馆、饭店	Hotels	19.0	27.0	70.4	133.0	127.0	104.7
营业人员 (人)	Personnel (person)	42789.0	46295.0	92.4	94405.0	71378.0	132.3
#商业	Wholesale and Retail	34479.0	34184.0	100.9	56776.0	38569.0	147.2
饮食业	Catering Service	4901.0	5141.0	95.3	11667.0	8186.0	142.5
服务业	Services	3409.0	6970.0	48.9	25962.0	24623	105.4
#宾馆、饭店	Hotels	2383.0	3125.0	76.3	5746.0	5531	103.9
外经、外贸	**Foreign Economy and Trade**						
出口商品交货额 (万元)	Delivery Value of Exports (10000 yuan)	6936.3	5718.7	121.3	149.5	197.1	75.8
利用外资签订协议(合同)数 (个)	Number of Signed Agreements and Contracts of Foreign Capital to be Utilized (unit)	10.0	15.0	66.7	6.0	11.0	54.5
利用外资签订协议(合同)金额 (万美元)	Amount of Foreign Capital to be Utilized through Agreements and Contracts (USD 10000)	19775.0	10114.2	195.5	…	107.7	
实际利用外资 (万美元)	Amount of Foreign Capital Actually Used (USD 10000)	13165.3	13009.7	101.2	968.0	639.0	151.5
旅游人数 (万人)	Number of Tourists (10000 persons)	1.6	2.0	80.0	2.9	3.6	80.6
教育	**Education**						
学校数 (个)	Number of Schools (unit)	78.0	79.0	98.7	94.0	101.0	93.1
小学	Primary Schools	44.0	43.0	102.3	54.0	58.0	93.1
普通中学	Regular Secondary Schools	25.0	27.0	92.6	30.0	32.0	93.8
中等专业教育	Specialized Secondary Schools	9.0	9.0	100.0	10.0	11.0	90.9
招生数 (人)	New Student Enrollment (person)	13739.0	13490.0	101.8	15639.0	15573.0	100.4
小学	Primary Schools	2734.0	2744.0	99.6	3298.0	3475.0	94.9
初级中等学校	Junior Secondary Schools	5994.0	5769.0	103.9	7273.0	6671.0	109.0
高级中等学校	Senior Secondary Schools	2592.0	2631.0	98.5	2958.0	2827.0	104.6
中等专业教育	Specialized Secondary Schools	2419.0	2346.0	103.1	2110.0	2600.0	81.2
在校学生 (人)	Student Enrollment (person)	57940.0	61916.0	93.6	67353.0	71283.0	94.5
小学	Primary Schools	24698.0	27750.0	89.0	29212.0	33011.0	88.5
初级中等学校	Junior Secondary Schools	17769.0	19145.0	92.8	21177.0	22175.0	95.5

21-2 续表 4 continued

项目	Item	崇文区 Chongwen 1999	1998	1999年为1998年% 1999 as % of 1998	宣武区 Xuanwu 1999	1998	1999年为1998年% 1999 as % of 1998
高级中等学校	Senior Secondary Schools	7797.0	7222.0	108.0	8603.0	7508.0	114.6
中等专业教育	Specialized Secondary Schools	7676.0	7799.0	98.4	8361.0	8589.0	97.3
毕业生 (人)	Graduates (person)	17583.0	18092.0	97.2	19349.0	19897.0	97.2
小学	Primary Schools	6036.0	5684.0	106.2	7268.0	6773.0	107.3
初级中等学校	Junior Secondary Schools	7107.0	8240.0	86.3	7894.0	9437.0	83.6
高级中等学校	Senior Secondary Schools	1944.0	2008.0	96.8	1872.0	1700.0	110.1
中等专业教育	Specialized Secondary Schools	2496.0	2160.0	115.6	2315.0	1987.0	116.5
达到"国家体育标准"学生数 (人)	Number of Students Come to the Standard for State Physical Training (person)	52789.0	55001.0	96.0	65199.0	56948.0	114.5
幼儿园、托儿所个数 (个)	Number of Kindergardens (unit)	38.0	40.0	95.0	50.0	50.0	100.0
幼儿入托数 (人)	New Enrollment (person)	6535.0	7072.0	92.4	7351.0	7525.0	97.7
文化	**Culture**						
文化馆、站 (个)	Cultural Centers (unit)	10.0	10.0	100.0	9.0	9.0	100.0
公共图书馆 (个)	Public Libraries (unit)	1.0	1.0	100.0	1.0	1.0	100.0
公共图书馆藏书 (万册)	Collection (10000 volume)	40.0	38.0	105.3	24.0	23.0	104.3
电影放映单位 (个)	Film Projection Units (unit)	2.0	2.0	100.0	4.0	6.0	66.7
区级以上重点文物保护单位 (个)	Cultural Relics Preserved at District Level and above (unit)	21.0	21.0	100.0	38.0	38.0	100.0
卫生	**Health**						
卫生机构数 (个)	Number of Health Institutions (unit)	20.0	20.0	100.0	366.0	366.0	100.0
#医院	Hospitals	11.0	11.0	100.0	20.0	19.0	105.3
卫生院	Clinics						
床位数 (张)	Number of Beds (unit)	1730.0	1730.0	100.0	3894.0	3981.0	97.8
#医院	Hospitals	1730.0	1730.0	100.0	3894.0	3981.0	97.8
卫生院	Clinics						
平均每千人拥有床位数 (张)	Average Number of Beds Per 1000 Persons (unit)	4.1	4.1	100.0	7.2	7.4	97.3
卫生技术人员 (人)	Medical Technical Personnel (person)	4442.0	4553.0	97.6	7658.0	7347.0	104.2
#医生	Doctors	1570.0	1517.0	103.5	3067.0	3102.0	98.9
公用设施	**Public Utilities**						
区级以上公园 (个)	Parks at District Level and above (unit)	4.0	4.0	100.0	4.0	4.0	100.0
体育场馆 (个)	Stadiums and Gymnasiums (unit)	6.0	6.0	100.0	2.0	2.0	100.0
道路长度 (公里)	Length of Roads (km)	176.4	176.4	100.0	116.4	113.9	102.2

21-3 朝阳区、丰台区国民经济主要指标
MAIN NATIONAL ECONOMIC INDICATORS FOR CHAOYANG AND FENGTAI DISTRICTS

项目		Item	朝阳区 Chaoyang			丰台区 Fengtai		
			1999	1998	1999年为1998年% 1999 as % of 1998	1999	1998	1999年为1998年% 1999 as % of 1998
综合		**General Survey**						
国内生产总值	(万元)	Gross Domestic Product (10000 yuan)	786066.9	703017.3	111.8	385424.0	346159.0	111.3
第一产业		Primary Industry	26977.9	28377.0	95.1	18469.0	16199.0	114.0
第二产业		Secondary Industry	191695.3	177705.3	107.9	125118.0	118255.0	105.8
第三产业		Tertiary Industry	567393.7	496935.0	114.2	241837.0	211705.0	114.2
财政收入	(万元)	Fiscal Revenue (10000 yuan)	201124.0	173196.0	116.1	77943.0	63799.0	122.2
#增值税		Increased Value Tax				54045.0	46676.0	115.8
营业税		Operating Tax	106965.0	95044.0	112.5	31029.0	25557.0	121.4
个人所得税		Private Income Tax	27212.0	22143.0	122.9	7732.0	5316.0	145.4
企业所得税		Enterprise Income Tax	29884.0	26756.0	111.7	9504.0	8725.0	108.9
财政支出	(万元)	Fiscal Expenditure (10000 yuan)	216414.0	190395.0	113.7	115047.0	87627.0	131.3
#基本建设支出		Capital Construction	14824.0	13550.0	109.4	7322.0	4960.0	147.6
支援农业生产支出		Supporting Agriculture	5764.0	8282.0	69.6	2009.0	853.0	235.5
文教卫生事业费		Culture,Education and Health	61322.0	61045.0	100.5	28549.0	24664.0	115.8
人口和劳动力		**Population and Labor Force**						
总人口	(人)	Total Population (person)	1860558.0	1761500.0	105.6	1059740.0	1007611.0	105.2
常住户籍人口	(人)	Permanent Registered Population (person)	1487650.0	1476931.0	100.7	809487.0	794675.0	101.9
#非农业人口		Non-agriculture	1300513.0	1280284.0	101.6	661870.0	646355.0	102.4
男		Male	757792.0	752833.0	100.7	412499.0	404393.0	102.0
女		Female	729858.0	724098.0	100.8	396988.0	390282.0	101.7
出生率	(‰)	Birth Rate (‰)	5.1	4.5		5.1	5.3	
死亡率	(‰)	Death Rate (‰)	5.3	4.8		5.8	8.5	
自然增长率	(‰)	Natural Growth Rate (‰)	-0.3	-0.3		-0.7	-3.2	
从业人员	(人)	Employment (person)	124076.0	121451.0	102.2	95566.0	86562.0	110.4
按产业分		Grouped by Industry						
第一产业		Primary Industry	188.0	391.0	48.1	70.0	35.0	200.0
第二产业		Secondary Industry	39575.0	36786.0	107.6	29778.0	23196.0	128.4
第三产业		Tertiary Industry	84313.0	84274.0	100.0	65718.0	63331.0	103.8
按职工非职工分		Grouped by Staff and Workers or Non-staff-and-worker						
职工人数		Staff and Worker	117411.0	118312.0	99.2	91883.0	82956.0	110.8
#国有单位		State-owned	72808.0	73128.0	99.6	42613.0	43549.0	97.9
集体单位		Collective-owned	39319.0	38315.0	102.6	19872.0	15266.0	130.2
城镇个体劳动者		Urban and Rural Individuals	38189.0	42337.0	90.2	11602.0	11568.0	100.3
劳动工资		**Wages**						
工资总额	(万元)	Total Wages (10000 yuan)	146285.8	137888.7	106.1	100937.0	83499.4	120.9
#国有单位		State-owned	111492.7	97992.0	113.8	55068.7	48532.3	113.5
集体单位		Collective-owned	27321.0	30672.0	89.1	12798.8	10299.0	124.3
职工平均工资	(元)	Average Wage (yuan)	12682.0	11421.0	111.0	11221.0	10220.0	109.8
固定资产投资		**Investment in Fixed Assets Assets (10000 yuan)**						
全社会固定资产投资	(万元)	Total Investment in Fixed Assets	384073.0	284536.0	135.0	166037.0	82391.0	201.5
按建设性质分		Grouped by Type of Construction						
#基本建设投资		Capital Construction		127804.0		37973.0	23683.0	160.3
更新改造投资		Innovation and Replacement	19415.0	559.0	3473.2	31357.0		

21-3 续表 1 continued

项目	Item	朝阳区 Chaoyang 1999	1998	1999年为1998年% 1999 as% of 1998	丰台区 Fengtai 1999	1998	1999年为1998年% 1999 as% of 1998
按登记注册类型分	Grouped by Registered Type						
#国有单位 (万元)	State-owned (10000 yuan)	186481.0	169681.0	109.9	94348.0	53373.0	176.8
集体单位 (万元)	Collective-owned (10000 yuan)	48440.0	4996.0	969.6	700.0		
新增固定资产 (万元)	Incremental Fixed Assets (10000 yuan)	295412.0	210342.0	140.4	161693.0	79109.0	204.4
#国有单位	State-owned	154821.0	26701.0	579.8	95845.0	47859.0	200.3
集体单位	Collective-owned	61757.0					
房屋施工面积 (万平方米)	Floor Space of Buildings Under Construction (10000 sq.m)	288.7	280.3	103.0	137.4	123.3	111.4
#国有单位	State-owned	96.0	108.2	88.7	61.9	98.5	62.8
集体单位	Collective-owned	58.4	2.2	2654.5	0.6		
房屋竣工面积 (万平方米)	Floor Space of Buildings Completed (10000 sq.m)	105.5	67.8	155.6	60.3	39.5	152.7
#国有单位	State-owned	47.8	30.4	157.2	23.9	26.5	90.2
#住宅	Residence	28.3	13.2	214.4	15.3	16.7	91.6
#集体单位	Collective-owned	32.6					
#住宅	Residence	30.7					
农村经济	**Rural Economy**						
农村劳动力 (人)	Labor Force (person)	90957.0	92651.0	98.2	71394.0	70258.0	101.6
种植业	Planting	14663.0	15629.0	93.8	15412.0	15603.0	98.8
林业	Forestry	764.0	580.0	131.7	1616.0	1700.0	95.1
牧业	Animal Husbandry	2058.0	1806.0	114.0	1083.0	1082.0	100.1
渔业	Fishery	947.0	874.0	108.4	192.0	181.0	106.1
农村工业	Rural Industry	29000.0	31209.0	92.9	26284.0	28941.0	90.8
农村建筑业	Rural Construction	4150.0	3669.0	113.1	2042.0	1813.0	112.6
农村运输业	Rural Transportation	9027.0	6332.0	142.6	4765.0	4764.0	100.0
农村商、饮食业、服务业	Commerce,Catering and Services	8712.0	8068.0	108.0	20000.0	16174.0	123.7
耕地面积 (公顷)	Area under Cultivation (hectare)	13656.4	13660.0	100.0	6105.9	6366.2	95.9
农业机械总动力 (千瓦)	Total Power of Agricultural Machinery (kw)	233852.0	261182.0	89.5	154763.0	171690.0	90.1
化肥施用实物量 (吨)	Consumption of Chemical Fertilizers (ton)	10879.0	13130.0	82.9	4828.0	5338.2	90.4
化肥施用折纯量 (吨)	Consumption of Chemical Fertilizers(100%) (ton)	4074.0	4311.0	94.5	1625.0	1742.8	93.2
农村用电量 (万千瓦时)	Consumption of Electricity (10000 kwh)	36210.1	32582.0	111.1	26304.8	25345.8	103.8
农村国内生产总值 (万元)	Rural Gross Domestic Product (10000 yuan)	291752.2	310902.1	93.8	165977.2	152127.2	109.1
第一产业	Primary Industry	26968.0	28311.3	95.3	18468.7	16552.3	111.6
第二产业	Secondary Industry	115725.5	116671.5	99.2	55101.4	57825.0	95.3
第三产业	Tertiary Industry	149058.7	165919.3	89.8	92407.1	77749.9	118.9
农业总产值 (万元)	Gross Output Value of Agriculture (10000 yuan)	37653.5	37147.7	101.4	27766.5	27608.9	100.6
种植业	Planting	19215.1	19365.3	99.2	21022.8	19162.5	109.7
林业	Forestry	646.1	432.6	149.4	402.9	220.6	182.6
牧业	Animal Husbandry	9684.2	12263.1	79.0	5901.8	7878.3	74.9
渔业	Fishery	7944.5	5086.8	156.2	439.0	347.6	126.3
农作物总播种面积 (万公顷)	Sown Area of Farm Crops (10000 hectare)	1.2	1.2	100.0	0.7	0.8	86.4
粮食作物	Grain	1.2	1.2	100.0	0.3	0.3	88.2
经济作物	Industrial Crops				0.4	0.5	85.1
其他作物	Other Crops						

21-3 续表 2 continued

项目		Item	朝阳区 Chaoyang 1999	1998	1999年为1998年% 1999 as% of 1998.	丰台区 Fengtai 1999	1998	1999年为1998年% 1999 as% of 1998
农副产品产量		Yield of Farm and Side-line Crops						
粮食	(万吨)	Grain (10000 tons)	6.6	7.6	86.8	1.1	1.5	71.9
蔬菜	(吨)	Vegetable (ton)	176573.0	182846.0	96.6	155205.0	190516.0	81.5
干鲜果	(吨)	Dry and Fresh Fruits (ton)	770.0	980.0	78.6	4926.0	5814.0	84.7
畜产品产量		Output of Livestock Products						
生猪出栏	(头)	Slaughtered Hogs (head)	262005.0	304187.0	86.1	86574.0	100712.0	86.0
商品猪	(头)	Commodity Hogs (head)				86574.0	100712.0	86.0
猪牛羊肉	(吨)	Pork,Beef and Mutton (ton)	17994.0	20756.0	86.7	5574.0	6470.0	86.2
#猪肉		Pork	17250.0	20165.0	85.5	5483.0	6402.0	85.6
禽肉		Meat of Poultry (ton)	176.0	359.0	49.0	750.0	1224.0	61.3
禽蛋		Poultry Eggs (ton)	753.0	1584.0	47.5	5181.0	8213.0	63.1
牲畜年底头数	(头)	Number of Livestock (year-end) (head)						
大牲畜		Large Animals	3010.0	3640.0	82.7	1468.0	1685.0	87.1
猪		Hogs	136908.0	178794.0	76.6	57305.0	60033.0	95.5
羊		Goats and Sheep	15766.0	17194.0	91.7	11128.0	7878.0	141.3
水产品产量	(吨)	Output of Aquatic Product (ton)	6079.0	6660.0	91.3	404.0	649.0	62.2
农村集体经济收入	(万元)	Rural Collective Economic Revenue (10000 yuan)	1230570.0	1128116.6	109.1	895380.0	843955.0	106.1
农村集体经济利润总额	(万元)	Total Profits of Rural Collective Economy 10000 yuan)	81594.0	76824.4	106.2	80231.0	76133.0	105.4
国家税金		State Taxes	39394.2	39847.3	98.9	22154.0	22497.5	98.5
集体积累		Collective Accumulation	57346.0	54001.0	106.2	32646.0	25337.0	128.8
劳动所得		Income from Work	130383.5	122514.3	106.4	92111.0	85079.0	108.3
乡镇企业单位数	(个)	Number of Township and Village Enterprise (unit)	1678.0	1914.0	87.7	2405.0	1469.0	163.7
乡镇企业人数	(人)	Number of Persons of Township and Village Enterprises (person)	84503.0	91638.0	92.2	64559.0	63843.0	101.1
乡镇企业纯利润	(万元)	Net Profit of Township and Village Enterprises (10000 yuan)	31140.2	25978.5	119.9	49681.0	40922.0	121.4
乡镇企业固定资产原价	(万元)	Original Value of Fixed Assets of Township and Village Enterprises (10000 yuan)	361348.3	331937.8	108.9	348019.0	341583.0	101.9
乡镇企业固定资产净值	(万元)	Net Value of Fixed Assets of Township and Village Enterprises (10000 yuan)	258426.7	239321.2	108.0	235905.0	234863.0	100.4
工业		**Industry**						
全部工业企业单位数	(个)	Number of Enterprises (unit)	2037.0	2544.0	80.1	1242.0	1223.0	101.6
国有		State-owned	148.0	215.0	68.8	86.0	94.0	91.5
集体		Collective-owned	1215.0	1787.0	68.0	517.0	577.0	89.6
其他		Others	674.0	542.0	124.4	639.0	552.0	115.8
全部工业总产值 (现价,万元)		Gross Output Value of Industry (at current prices,10000 yuan)	631750.2	549911.6	114.9	435865.6	383267.7	113.7
国有		State-owned	15012.8	18058.8	83.1	38067.8	29903.1	127.3
集体		Collective-owned	311327.2	304508.8	102.2	128870.0	137005.1	94.1
其他		Others	305410.2	227344.0	134.3	384910.8	216359.5	177.9

21-3 续表 3 continued

项 目	Item	朝阳区 Chaoyang 1999	1998	1999年为1998年% 1999 as % of 1998	丰台区 Fengtai 1999	1998	1999年为1998年% 1999 as % of 1998
全部工业总产值 (1990年不变价,万元)	Gross Output Value of Industry (at constant price of 1990,10000yuan)	575819.3	502409.5	114.6	401377.8	357076.5	112.4
国有	State-owned	11843.8	13727.8	86.3	35499.7	27743.9	128.0
集体	Collective-owned	283756.3	279827.3	101.4	121643.4	127152.1	95.7
其他	Others	280219.2	208854.4	134.2	244234.7	202180.5	120.8
全部轻工业总产值 (现价,万元)	Gross Output Value of Light Industry (at current prices,10000 yuan)	353784.3	294869.2	120.0	177367.8	151362.3	117.2
以农产品为原料	Using Farm Products as Raw Materials	271706.3	226430.8	120.0	107298.1	86109.5	124.6
以非农产品为原料	Using Non-farm Products as Raw Materials	82078.0	68438.4	119.9	70069.7	65252.8	107.4
全部重工业总产值 (现价,万元)	Gross Output Value of Heavy Industry (at current prices,10000 yuan)	277965.9	255042.4	109.0	258497.8	205714.2	125.7
采掘工业	Mining and Quarrying				3560.2	3792.4	93.9
原料工业	Raw Materials Industry	29186.4	26883.9	108.6	29314.1	26015.9	112.7
制造工业	Manufacturing Industry	248779.5	228158.5	109.0	225623.5	175905.9	128.3
独立核算工业企业平均职工人数 (人)	Average Number of Staff and Workers in Enterprises with Independent Accounting System (person)	87424.0	80625.0	108.4	46786.0	55200.0	84.8
#国有	State-owned	4728.0	3190.0	148.2	4290.0	5759.0	74.5
集体	Collective-owned	52350.0	56083.0	93.3	24356.0	32226.0	75.6
独立核算工业企业总产值 (现价,万元)	Gross Output Value of Enterprises with Independent Accounting System(at current prices, 10000 yuan)	631750.2	549911.6	114.9	415132.6	361876.0	114.7
#国有	State-owned	15012.8	18058.8	83.1	38067.8	29903.1	127.3
集体	Collective-owned	311327.2	304508.8	102.2	128870.0	137005.1	94.1
独立核算工业企业工业增加值 (万元)	Value Added of Enterprises with Independent Accounting system (10000 yuan)				136403.2	99157.3	137.6
独立核算工业企业财务指标	Financial Indicators for Enterprises with Independent Accounting System						
产品销售收入 (万元)	Sales Revenue (10000yuan)	600820.4	543324.5	110.6	398845	345455.3	115.5
#国有	State-owned	13430.6	16690.2	80.5	36852.7	25239.4	146.0
产品销售成本 (万元)	Cost of Sales (10000 yuan)	475343.5	430233.3	110.5	319531	286266.0	111.6
#国有	State-owned	11060.3	13160.0	84.0	30145.5	20465.9	147.3
固定资产原价 (万元)	Original Value of Fixed Assets (10000 yuan)				278687.2	220380.2	126.5
#国有	State-owned				15768.7	6661.9	236.7
固定资产净值 (万元)	Net Value of Fixed Assets (10000 yuan)	227110.1	205208.6	110.7	189605.0	147997.8	128.1
#国有	State-owned	5677.8	5194.6	109.3	9379.2	4243.3	221.0
全部流动资金年平均余额 (万元)	Annual Average Balance of Circulating Funds (10000 yuan)	500483.4	452755.7	110.5	396467.4	343776.7	115.3
#国有	State-owned	16515.9	14850.6	111.2	43492.0	40504.5	107.4
利润总额 (万元)	Total Profits (10000 yuan)	7155.0	6312.2	113.4	8410.2	-5800.4	
#国有	State-owned	2218.0	795.7	278.7	1592.1	-53.4	

21-3 续表 4 continued

项目	Item	朝阳区 Chaoyang 1999	1998	1999年为1998年% 1999 as% of 1998	丰台区 Fengtai 1999	1998	1999年为1998年% 1999 as% of 1998
资金利税率 (%)	Ratio of Pre-tax Profits to Total of Capital (%)				4.9	3.2	
产品销售率 (%)	Ratio of Sales Value to Gross Output Value (%)	94.5	93.0		97.0	96.6	
增加值率 (%)	Ratio of Added Value to Gross Output Value (%)	30.7	33.8		32.9	27.4	
独立核算工业企业全员劳动生产率 (元/人)	Overall Labor Productivity of Enterprises with Independent Accounting System (yuan/person)	22333.0	23050.0	96.9	23609.0	14659.0	161.1
#国有	State-owned	22341.8	23058.9	96.9	20081.0	13177.0	152.4
集体	Collective-owned	17259.6	17813.8	96.9	12307.0	8356.0	147.3
商业	**Commerce**						
社会消费品零售额 (万元)	Retail Sales of Consumer Goods (10000 yuan)	1281129.0	1158745.0	110.6	613137.0	549564.0	111.6
按登记注册类型分	Grouped by Registered Type						
国有	State-owned	382936.5	410196.0	93.4	78753.0	102489.0	76.8
集体	Collective-owned	120609.3	177288.0	68.0	86773.0	75037.0	115.6
其他	Others	777583.2	571261.0	136.1	447611.0	372038.0	120.3
按类别分	Grouped by Type of Goods						
吃的商品 (万元)	Food (10000 yuan)	421491.0	272305.0	154.8	283987.0	242772.0	117.0
穿的商品 (万元)	Clothing (10000 yuan)	175515.0	121668.0	144.3	64920.0	62122.0	104.5
用的商品 (万元)	Daily Used Articles (10000 yuan)	588038.0	665120.0	88.4	241656.0	223536.0	108.1
烧的商品 (万元)	Fuel (10000 yuan)	96085.0	44032.0	218.2	22574.0	21134.0	106.8
网点数 (个)	Number of Outlets (unit)	31444.0	33066.0	95.1	26339.0	25885.0	101.8
#商业	Wholesale and Retail	24832.0	26926.0	92.2	22408.0	21145.0	106.0
饮食业	Catering	2638.0	2758.0	95.6	2088.0	2065.0	101.1
服务业	Services	3974.0	3382.0	117.5	1843.0	2675.0	68.9
#宾馆、饭店	Hotels				68.0		
营业人员 (人)	Personnel (person)	181397.0	184708.0	98.2	66049.0	72941.0	90.6
#商业	Wholesale and Retail	94179.0	89469.0	105.3	46546.0	52498.0	88.7
饮食业	Catering	17905.0	21241.0	84.3	8258.0	10667.0	77.4
服务业	Services	69313.0	73998.0	93.7	11245.0	9776.0	115.0
#宾馆、饭店	Hotels				4258.0		
外经、外贸	**Foreign Economy and Trade**						
出口商品交货额 (万元)	Delivery Value of Exports (10000 yuan)	20092.0	22118.6	90.8	2977.3	2224.7	133.8
利用外资签订协议(合同)数 (个)	Number of Signed Agreements and Contracts of Foreign Capital to be Utilized (unit)	80.0	93.0	86.0	21.0	35.0	60.0
利用外资签订协议(合同)金额 (万美元)	Amount of Foreign Capital to be Utilized through Agreements and Contracts (USD 10000)	9338.9	9801.8	95.3	5153.0	8289.6	62.2
实际利用外资 (万美元)	Amount of Foreign Capital Actually Used (USD 10000)	7569.1	7764.6	97.5	3037.2	4496.8	67.5
旅游人数 (万人)	Number of Tourists (10000 persons)				295.0	270.6	109.0
教育	**Education**						
学校数 (个)	Number of Schools (unit)	320.0	324.0	98.8	178.0	186.0	95.7
小学	Primary Schools	216.0	220.0	98.2	115.0	122.0	94.3

21-3 续表 5 continued

项目 Item			朝阳区 Chaoyang 1999	1998	1999年为1998年% 1999 as % of 1998	丰台区 Fengtai 1999	1998	1999年为1998年% 1999 as % of 1998
普通中学		Regular Secondary School	78.0	76.0	102.6	62.0	63.0	98.4
中等专业教育		Specialized Secondary Schools	26.0	28.0	92.9	1.0	1.0	100.0
招生数	(人)	New Student Enrollment (person)	35439.0	34945.0	101.4	22345.0	22508.0	99.3
小学		Primary Schools	9822.0	10278.0	95.6	7215.0	7536.0	95.7
初级中等学校		Junior Secondary Schools	15728.0	13918.0	113.0	9939.0	8842.0	112.4
高级中等学校		Senior Secondary Schools	6041.0	5254.0	115.0	5191.0	6050.0	85.8
中等专业教育		Specialized Secondary Schools	3848.0	5495.0	70.0		80.0	
在校学生	(人)	Student Enrollment (person)	154970.0	163458.0	94.8	97622.0	101909.0	95.8
小学		Primary Schools	79751.0	88690.0	89.9	54815.0	58667.0	93.4
初级中等学校		Junior Secondary Schools	43977.0	44790.0	98.2	27382.0	27349.0	100.1
高级中等学校		Senior Secondary Schools	16345.0	14196.0	115.1	15228.0	15503.0	98.2
中等专业教育		Specialized Secondary Schools	14897.0	15782.0	94.4	197.0	390.0	50.5
毕业生	(人)	Graduates (person)	40923.0	41377.0	98.9	24495.0	24426.0	100.3
小学		Primary Schools	16934.0	15092.0	112.2	10686.0	9601.0	111.3
初级中等学校		Junior Secondary Schools	15797.0	18369.0	86.0	9005.0	10171.0	88.5
高级中等学校		Senior Secondary Schools	3677.0	3199.0	114.9	4611.0	4443.0	103.8
中等专业教育		Specialized Secondary Schools	4515.0	4717.0	95.7	193.0	211.0	91.5
达到"国家体育标准"学生数	(人)	Number of Students Come to the Standard for State Physical Training (person)	120707.0	101338.0	119.1	82344.0	80534.0	102.2
幼儿园、托儿所个数	(个)	Number of Kindergardens (unit)	220.0			136.0	145.0	93.8
幼儿入托数	(人)	New Enrollment (person)	10923.0			17539.0	16138.0	108.7
文化		**Culture**						
文化馆、站	(个)	Cultural Centers (unit)	44.0	43.0	102.3	17.0	17.0	100.0
公共图书馆	(个)	Public Libraries (unit)	1.0	1.0	100.0	1.0	1.0	100.0
公共图书馆藏书	(万册)	Collection (10000 volume)	46.5	44.0	105.7	22.0	20.0	110.0
电影放映单位	(个)	Film Projection Units (unit)	12.0	12.0	100.0	2.0	2.0	100.0
区级以上重点文物保护单位	(个)	Cultural Relics Preserved at District Level and above (unit)	13.0	13.0	100.0	20.0	17.0	117.6
卫生		**Health**						
卫生机构数	(个)	Number of Health Institutions (unit)	1112.0	1107.0	100.5	599.0	532.0	112.6
#医院		Hospitals	111.0	107.0	103.7	57.0	56.0	101.8
卫生院		Clinics						
床位数		Number of Beds (unit)	10504.0	10213.0	102.8	5475.0	5324.0	102.8
#医院		Hospitals	10398.0	10187.0	102.1	5475.0	5324.0	102.8
卫生院		Clinics						
平均每千人拥有床位数	(张)	Average Number of Beds Per 1000 Persons (unit)	7.1	6.9	102.9	6.8	6.8	100.0
卫生技术人员	(人)	Medical Technical Personnel (person)	18217.0	15012.0	121.3	9140.0	8896.0	102.7
#医生		Doctors (person)	8417.0	6430.0	130.9	3900.0	3869.0	100.8
公用设施		**Public Utilities**						
区级以上公园	(个)	Parks at District Level and above (unit)	21.0	20.0	105.0	7.0	6.0	116.7
体育场馆	(个)	Stadiums and Gymnasiums (unit)	9.0	9.0	100.0	6.0	6.0	100.0
道路长度	(公里)	Length of Roads (km)	263.5	263.5	100.0	214.0		

21-4 石景山区、海淀区国民经济主要指标
MAIN NATIONAL ECONOMIC INDICATORS FOR SHIJINGSHAN AND HAIDIAN DISTRICTS

项目	Item	石景山区 Shijingshan			海淀区 Haidian		
		1999	1998	1999年为1998年% 1999 as % of 1998	1999	1998	1999年为1998年% 1999 as % of 1998
综合	**General Survey**						
国内生产总值 (万元)	Gross Domestic Product (10000 yuan)	123219.5	98953.0	124.5	2192168.1	1857424.9	118.0
第一产业	Primary Industry	1937.1	1439.1	134.6	22049.9	21579.9	102.2
第二产业	Secondary Industry	25670.9	21289.8	120.6	1358219.2	1063595.0	127.7
第三产业	Tertiary Industry	95611.5	76224.1	125.4	811899.0	772250.0	105.1
财政收入 (万元)	Fiscal Revenue (10000 yuan)	32920.0	26316.0	125.1	219755.0	172214.0	127.6
#增值税	Increased Value Tax				7872.0	6576.0	119.7
营业税	Operating Tax	18820.0	15148.0	124.2	105990.0	86083.0	123.1
个人所得税	Private Income Tax	4692.0	3529.0	133.0	47645.0	31007.0	153.7
企业所得税	Enterprise Income Tax	7852.0	3821.0	205.5	28647.0	18720.0	153.0
财政支出 (万元)	Fiscal Expenditure (10000 yuan)	58946.0	48000.0	122.8	294428.0	259932.0	113.3
#基本建设支出	Capital Construction	9667.0	4348.0	222.3	52098.0	37313.0	139.6
支援农业生产支出	Supporting Agriculture	732.0	209.0	350.2	3545.0	4859.0	73.0
文教卫生事业费	Culture,Education and Health	17001.0	14391.0	118.1	58406.0	48035.0	121.6
人口和劳动力	**Population and Labor Force**						
总人口 (人)	Total Population (person)	404292.0	398541.0	101.4			
常住户籍人口 (人)	Permanent Registered Population (person)	326803.0	324230.0	100.8	1530773.0	1526111.0	100.3
#非农业人口	Non-agriculture	311153.0	308590.0	100.8	1443213.0	1395802.0	103.4
男	Male	165399.0	164194.0	100.7	749761.0	724393.0	103.5
女	Female	145754.0	144396.0	100.9	693452.0	671409.0	103.3
出生率 (‰)	Birth Rate (‰)	4.5	4.6		5.1	6.0	
死亡率 (‰)	Death Rate (‰)	4.8	7.0		4.1	5.0	
自然增长率 (‰)	Natural Growth Rate (‰)	-0.3	-2.4		1.0	1.2	
从业人员 (人)	Employment (person)	48114.0	39710.0	121.2	356886.0	329713.0	108.2
按产业分	Grouped by Industry						
第一产业	Primary Industry	1322.0			16779.0	12094.0	138.7
第二产业	Secondary Industry	11780.0	10317.0	114.2	101405.0	89464.0	113.3
第三产业	Tertiary Industry	35012.0	29393.0	119.1	238702.0	228155.0	104.6
按职工非职工分	Grouped by Staff and Workers or Non-staff-and-worker						
职工人数	Staff and Worker	43226.0	38057.0	113.6	272488.0	254383.0	107.1
#国有单位	State-owned	22178.0	23027.0	96.3	82279.0	90029.0	91.4
集体单位	Collective-owned	8323.0	8740.0	95.2	40931.0	47139.0	86.8
城镇个体劳动者	Urban and Rural Individuals				32526.0	30303.0	107.3
劳动工资	**Wages**						
工资总额 (万元)	Total Wages (10000 yuan)	49069.5	41277.0	118.9	410276.3	344468.8	119.1
#国有单位	State-owned	31170.0	28905.0	107.8	128324.1	133228.9	96.3
集体单位	Collective-owned	6106.6	6133.0	99.6	54963.5	60931.7	90.2
职工平均工资 (元)	Average Wage (yuan)	11331.0	10872.0	104.2	15164.0	13708.0	110.6
固定资产投资	**Investment in Fixed Assets**						
全社会固定资产投资 (万元)	Total Investment in Fixed Assets (10000 yuan)	70977.0	57890.0	122.6	484044.0	424955.0	113.9
按建设性质分	Grouped by Type of Construction						
#基本建设投资	Capital Construction	21218.0	22390.0	94.8	211951.0	292230.0	72.5
更新改造投资	Innovation and Replacement	6395.0	6613.0	96.7	14700.0		

21-4 续表 1 continued

项目	Item	石景山区 Shijingshan 1999	1998	1999年为1998年% 1999 as % of 1998	海淀区 Haidian 1999	1998	1999年为1998年% 1999 as % of 1998
按登记注册类型分	Grouped by Ownership						
#国有单位 (万元)	State-owned (10000 yuan)	65546.0	53989.0	121.4	267706.0	167505.0	159.8
集体单位 (万元)	Collective-owned (10000 yuan)		374.0		31348.0	42999.0	72.9
新增固定资产 (万元)	Incremental Fixed Assets (10000 yuan)	59547.0	84023.0	70.9	445716.0	288877.0	154.3
#国有单位	State-owned	55979.0	74461.0	75.2	271421.0	150996.0	179.8
集体单位	Collective-owned		4340.0		11674.0	48867.0	23.9
房屋施工面积 (万平方米)	Floor Space of Buildings Under Construction (10000 sq.m)	71.6	86.6	82.7	336.7	369.1	91.2
#国有单位	State-owned	66.3	78.4	84.6	141.5	159.0	89.0
集体单位	Collective-owned		2.7		30.7	25.4	120.9
房屋竣工面积 (万平方米)	Floor Space of Buildings Completed (10000 sq.m)	22.0	36.2	60.8	120.2	114.8	104.7
#国有单位	State-owned	21.2	30.7	69.1	55.1	53.5	103.0
#住宅	Residence	17.2	14.9	115.4	30.0	26.4	113.6
#集体单位	Collective-owned		2.7		7.1	12.5	56.8
#住宅	Residence		2.4		6.1	4.6	132.6
农村经济	**Rural Economy**						
农村劳动力 (人)	Labor Force (person)	7638.0	7729.0	98.8	61383.0	57154.0	107.4
种植业	Planting	859.0	736.0	116.7	12777.0	9375.0	136.3
林业	Forestry	222.0	120.0	185.0	909.0	458.0	198.5
牧业	Animal Husbandry	194.0	284.0	68.3	1389.0	1517.0	91.6
渔业	Fishery	6.0	11.0	54.5	224.0	229.0	97.8
农村工业	Rural Industry	3050.0	3249.0	93.9	21287.0	23879.0	89.1
农村建筑业	Rural Construction	127.0	97.0	130.9	3274.0	2522.0	129.8
农村运输业	Rural Transportation	303.0	390.0	77.7	2264.0	1991.0	113.7
农村商、饮食业、服务业	Commerce,Catering and Services	2877.0	2842.0	101.2	6819.0	5380.0	126.7
耕地面积 (公顷)	Area under Cultivation (hectare)	396.1	424.7	93.3	8624.4	8728.0	98.8
农业机械总动力 (千瓦)	Total Power of Agricultural Machinery (kw)	7075.0	46200.0	15.3	156000.0	155773.0	100.1
化肥施用实物量 (吨)	Consumption of Chemical Fertilizers (ton)	128.0	156.3	81.9	8738.0	8951.6	97.6
化肥施用折纯量 (吨)	Consumption of Chemical Fertilizers(100%) (ton)	46.0	46.2	99.6	2955.0	3071.8	96.2
农村用电量 (万千瓦时)	Consumption of Electricity (10000 kwh)	2244.0	1683.1	133.3	20477.9	14860.3	137.8
农村国内生产总值 (万元)	Rural Gross Domestic Product (10000 yuan)	19118.8	21099.7	90.6	169265.7	159532.4	106.1
第一产业	Primary Industry	1937.1	1920.7	100.9	22049.9	21579.9	102.2
第二产业	Secondary Industry	6867.2	7216.7	95.2	52058.6	52542.0	99.1
第三产业	Tertiary Industry	10314.5	11962.3	86.2	95157.2	85410.5	111.4
农业总产值 (万元)	Gross Output Value of Agriculture (10000 yuan)	4401.4	4913.4	89.6	45019.8	50993.2	88.3
种植业	Planting	902.4	1014.3	89.0	28251.0	22988.9	122.9
林业	Forestry	80.0	11.0	727.3	864.0	458.6	188.4
牧业	Animal Husbandry	3397.8	3856.1	88.1	11655.4	25610.6	45.5
渔业	Fishery	21.2	32.0	66.3	4249.4	1935.1	219.6
农作物总播种面积 (万公顷)	Sown Area of Farm Crops (10000 hectare)	0.1	0.1	100.0	1.0	1.0	100.0
粮食作物	Grain				0.5	0.5	100.0
经济作物	Industrial Crops	0.1	0.1	100.0			
其他作物	Other Crops				0.5	0.5	100.0

21-4 续表 2 continued

项目	Item	石景山区 Shijingshan 1999	1998	1999年为1998年% 1999 as % of 1998	海淀区 Haidian 1999	1998	1999年为1998年% 1999 as % of 1998
农副产品产量	Yield of Farm and Side-line Crops						
粮食 (万吨)	Grain (10000 tons)				3.5	3.5	100.0
蔬菜 (吨)	Vegetable (ton)	8825.0	9653.0	91.4	139312.0	157836.0	88.3
干鲜果 (吨)	Dry and Fresh Fruits (ton)	770.0	852.0	90.4	11112.0	14844.0	74.9
畜产品产量	Output of Livestock Products						
生猪出栏 (头)	Slaughtered Hogs (head)	37687.0	27558.0	136.8	5815.0	170924.0	3.4
商品猪 (头)	Commodity Hogs (head)	37687.0	27558.0	136.8	5815.0	170924.0	3.4
猪牛羊肉 (吨)	Pork,Beef and Mutton (ton)	2374.0	1820.0	130.4	6731.0	10477.0	64.2
#猪肉	Pork	2374.0	1820.0	130.4	6627.0	10410.0	63.7
禽肉	Meat of Poultry (ton)	74.0	283.0	26.1	1322.0	1775.0	74.5
禽蛋	Poultry Eggs (ton)	1540.0	2254.0	68.3	404.0	8419.0	4.8
牲畜年底头数 (头)	Number of Livestock (year-end) (head)	16814.0	11914.0	141.1			
大牲畜	Large Animals	523.0	540.0	96.9	1108.0	3559.0	31.1
猪	Hogs	16291.0	11374.0	143.2	40672.0	92448.0	44.0
羊	Goats and Sheep				8053.0	2543.0	316.7
水产品产量 (吨)	Output of Aquatic Product (ton)	40.0	40.0	100.0	2171.0	2584.5	84.0
农村集体经济收入 (万元)	Rural Collective Economic Revenue (10000 yuan)				769660.0	794818.0	96.8
农村集体经济利润总额 (万元)	Total Profits of Rural Collective Economy (10000 yuan)				69521.0	14778.0	470.4
国家税金	State Taxes				20317.0	20583.0	98.7
集体积累	Collective Accumulation				35881.0	36450.0	98.4
劳动所得	Income from Work				63859.0	63682.0	100.3
乡镇企业单位数 (个)	Number of Township and Village Enterprise (unit)	239.0	256.0	93.4	1231.0	1477.0	83.3
乡镇企业人数 (人)	Number of Persons of Township and Village Enterprises (person)	7975.0	9151.0	87.1	44104.0	53940.0	81.8
乡镇企业纯利润 (万元)	Net Profit of Township and Village Enterprises (10000 yuan)	1864.0	2545.0	73.2	23330.0	12236.0	190.7
乡镇企业固定资产原价 (万元)	Original Value of Fixed Assets of Township and Village Enterprises (10000 yuan)	37099.0	45403.0	81.7	204265.0	182153.0	112.1
乡镇企业固定资产净值 (万元)	Net Value of Fixed Assets of Township and Village Enterprises (10000 yuan)		32255.0		133580.0	118682.0	112.6
工业	**Industry**						
全部工业企业单位数 (个)	Number of Enterprises (unit)	366.0	288.0	127.1	1030.0	1149.0	89.6
国有	State-owned	45.0	45.0	100.0	161.0	174.0	92.5
集体	Collective-owned	166.0	150.0	110.7	544.0	629.0	86.5
其他	Others	155.0	93.0	166.7	325.0	346.0	93.9
全部工业总产值 (现价,万元)	Gross Output Value of Industry (at current prices,10000 yuan)	80272.5	73568.8	109.1	3958418.5	3324840.0	119.1
国有	State-owned	1837.8	1813.8	101.3	1946855.9	2110791.1	92.2
集体	Collective-owned	30474.8	32097.6	94.9	254272.5	264110.3	96.3
其他	Others	47959.9	39657.4	120.9	1757290.1	949938.6	185.0

21-4 续表 3 continued

项目	Item	石景山区 Shijingshan 1999	1998	1999年为1998年% 1999 as % of 1998	海淀区 Haidian 1999	1998	1999年为1998年% 1999 as % of 1998
全部工业总产值(1990年不变价,万元)	Gross Output Value of Industry (at constant price of 1990,10000yuan)	76728.0	68642.3	111.8	4889338.4	3254463.3	150.2
国有	State-owned	1829.6	1778.2	102.9	2517993.8	1657475.0	151.9
集体	Collective-owned	27422.9	30020.4	91.3	215383.6	175783.6	122.5
其他	Others	46475.5	36843.7	126.1	2155961.0	1421204.7	151.7
全部轻工业总产值(现价,万元)	Gross Output Value of Light Industry (at current prices,10000 yuan)	28422.9	23720.7	119.8	722679.8	445642.4	162.2
以农产品为原料	Using Farm Products as Raw Materials	20091.1	18330.1	109.6	439389.3	270755.0	162.3
以非农产品为原料	Using Non-farm Products as Raw Materials	7485.6	5390.6	138.9	283290.5	174887.4	162.0
全部重工业总产值(现价,万元)	Gross Output Value of Heavy Industry (at current prices,10000 yuan)	52695.8	44836.6	117.5	3235738.7	2879197.6	112.4
采掘工业	Mining and Quarrying	74.8	71.5	104.6	790.7	1099.0	71.9
原料工业	Raw Materials Industry	8512.6	6647.0	128.1	106779.4	93857.4	113.8
制造工业	Manufacturing Industry	44108.4	38158.1	115.6	3128168.6	2784331.2	112.3
独立核算工业企业平均职工人数 (人)	Average Number of Staff and Workers in Enterprises with Independent Accounting System (person)	12316.0	11237.0	109.6	134704.0	88605.0	152.0
#国有	State-owned	513.0	752.0	68.2	17396.0	21917.0	79.4
集体	Collective-owned	7423.0	7107.0	104.4	29234.0	34673.0	84.3
独立核算工业企业总产值(现价,万元)	Gross Output Value of Enterprises with Independent Accounting System(at current prices, 10000 yuan)	80272.5	73523.8	109.2	3958418.5	3324840.0	119.1
#国有	State-owned	1837.8	1813.8	101.3	1946855.9	2110791.1	92.2
集体	Collective-owned	30474.8	32052.6	95.1	254272.5	264110.3	96.3
独立核算工业企业工业增加值 (万元)	Value Added of Enterprises with Independent Accounting system (10000 yuan)	22473.6	27720.8	81.1	1223151.3	1045898.8	116.9
独立核算工业企业财务指标	Financial Indicators for Enterprises with Independent Accounting System						
产品销售收入 (万元)	Sales Revenue (10000yuan)	86289.1	74420.1	115.9	3297419.6	3238554.3	101.8
#国有	State-owned	1899.6	2084.6	91.1	1257879.1	2013811.7	62.5
产品销售成本 (万元)	Cost of Sales (10000 yuan)	68181.4	58174.2	117.2	2703579.7	2525529.6	107.1
#国有	State-owned	1487.1	1532.1	97.1	1058849.2	1526130.5	69.4
固定资产原价 (万元)	Original Value of Fixed Assets (10000 yuan)	67143.6	50569.6	132.8	823485.2	829599.0	99.3
#国有	State-owned	998.3	1712.6	58.3	188916.8	192741.1	98.0
固定资产净值 (万元)	Net Value of Fixed Assets (10000 yuan)	47663.0	36654.0	130.0	563993.9	597371.5	94.4
#国有	State-owned	602.8	1383.2	43.6	128723.5	143594.0	89.6
全部流动资金年平均余额 (万元)	Annual Average Balance of Circulating Funds (10000 yuan)	101703.9	74397.3	136.7	2441751.6	2741113.1	89.1
#国有	State-owned	1447.2	2120.1	68.3	599808.9	1047272.5	57.3
利润总额 (万元)	Total Profits (10000 yuan)	-2813.4	92.1		180920.8	158954.2	113.8
#国有	State-owned	76.5	-31.1		59282.0	89391.4	66.3

21-4 续表 4 continued

项目		Item	石景山区 Shijingshan 1999	1998	1999年为1998年% 1999 as % of 1998	海淀区 Haidian 1999	1998	1999年为1998年% 1999 as % of 1998
资金利税率	(%)	Ratio of Pre-tax Profits to Total of Capital (%)	-1.6	0.4		4.9	5.4	
产品销售率	(%)	Ratio of Sales Value to Gross Output Value (%)	98.1	96.3		95.6	96.0	
增加值率	(%)	Ratio of Added Value to Gross Output Value (%)	28.0	37.7		30.9	31.5	
独立核算工业企业全员劳动生产率	(元/人)	Overall Labor Productivity of Enterprises with Independent Accounting System (yuan/person)	18247.5	24669.0	74.0	90802.0	118041.0	76.9
#国有		State-owned	11333.0	9121.0	124.3	345814.0	310536.0	111.4
集体		Collective-owned	14241.0	11799.0	120.7	26876.0	23393.0	114.9
商业		**Commerce**						
社会消费品零售额	(万元)	Retail Sales of Consumer Goods (10000 yuan)	319603.1	306219.0	104.4	2400543.0	2273086.0	105.6
按登记注册类型分		Grouped by Registered Type						
国有		State-owned		53213.0		813844.0	794324.0	102.5
集体		Collective-owned		11848.0		367044.0	294548.0	124.6
其他		Others		241158.0		1219655.0	1184214.0	103.0
按类别分		Grouped by Type of Goods						
吃的商品	(万元)	Food (10000 yuan)	178753.0	160954.0	111.1	371857.0	401484.0	92.6
穿的商品	(万元)	Clothing (10000 yuan)	14076.0	14069.0	100.0	106660.0	107600.0	99.1
用的商品	(万元)	Daily Used Articles (10000 yuan)	121800.0	124027.0	98.2	1910316.0	1752361.0	109.0
烧的商品	(万元)	Fuel (10000 yuan)	4974.1	7169.0	69.4	11710.0	11641.0	100.6
网点数	(个)	Number of Outlets (unit)	11746.0	10583.0	111.0			
#商业		Wholesale and Retail	7534.0	7625.0	98.8	26545.0	31005.0	85.6
饮食业		Catering	1788.0	815.0	219.4	3730.0	3712.0	100.5
服务业		Services	2424.0	2143.0	113.1	5937.0	5446.0	109.0
#宾馆、饭店		Hotels				188.0	188.0	100.0
营业人员	(人)	Personnel (person)	48065.0	43175.0	111.3	137869.0	142971.0	96.4
#商业		Wholesale and Retail	22779.0	22317.0	102.1	72777.0	80598.0	90.3
饮食业		Catering	8944.0	3418.0	261.7	17098.0	20041.0	85.3
服务业		Services	16342.0	17440.0	93.7	47994.0	42332.0	113.4
#宾馆、饭店		Hotels				8525.0	7497.0	113.7
外经、外贸		**Foreign Economy and Trade**						
出口商品交货额	(万元)	Delivery Value of Exports (10000 yuan)	4971.9	5324.7	93.4	215847.0	189507.8	113.9
利用外资签订协议(合同)数	(个)	Number of Signed Agreements and Contracts of Foreign Capital to be Utilized (unit)	2.0	10.0	20.0	138.0	122.0	113.1
利用外资签订协议(合同)金额	(万美元)	Amount of Foreign Capital to be Utilized through Agreements and Contracts (USD 10000)	46.0	300.2	15.3	17005.0	19057.2	89.2
实际利用外资	(万美元)	Amount of Foreign Capital Actually Used (USD 10000)	782.4	815.0	96.0	9877.8	9077.6	108.8
旅游人数	(万人)	Number of Tourists (10000 persons)	281.6	281.8	99.9	1.3	1.7	76.5
教育		**Education**						
学校数	(个)	Number of Schools (unit)	77.0	81.0	95.1	250.0	254.0	98.4
小学		Primary Schools	44.0	48.0	91.7	142.0	144.0	98.6

21-4 续表 5 continued

项目 Item		石景山区 Shijingshan 1999	1998	1999年为1998年% 1999 as % of 1998	海淀区 Haidian 1999	1998	1999年为1998年% 1999 as % of 1998
普通中学	Regular Secondary School	28.0	28.0	100.0	86.0	88.0	97.7
中等专业教育	Specialized Secondary Schools	5.0	5.0	100.0			
招生数 (人)	New Student Enrollment (person)	9784.0	9130.0	107.2	47777.0	40962.0	116.6
小学	Primary Schools	2514.0	2556.0	98.4	14222.0	14146.0	100.5
初级中等学校	Junior Secondary Schools	4142.0	3625.0	114.3	18012.0	16199.0	111.2
高级中等学校	Senior Secondary Schools	1728.0	1261.0	137.0	15543.0	10617.0	146.4
中等专业教育	Specialized Secondary Schools	1400.0	1688.0	82.9			
在校学生 (人)	Student Enrollment (person)	40623.0	41485.0	97.9	199946.0	185919.0	107.5
小学	Primary Schools	19603.0	21367.0	91.7	100437.0	103746.0	96.8
初级中等学校	Junior Secondary Schools	11476.0	11622.0	98.7	51663.0	51377.0	100.6
高级中等学校	Senior Secondary Schools	4800.0	3589.0	133.7	47846.0	30796.0	155.4
中等专业教育	Specialized Secondary Schools	4744.0	4907.0	96.7			
毕业生 (人)	Graduates (person)	11185.0	11527.0	97.0	47033.0	45396.0	103.6
小学	Primary Schools	4204.0	3640.0	115.5	17788.0	16093.0	110.5
初级中等学校	Junior Secondary Schools	4229.0	5314.0	79.6	17225.0	20873.0	82.5
高级中等学校	Senior Secondary Schools	1134.0	983.0	115.4	12011.0	8430.0	142.5
中等专业教育	Specialized Secondary Schools	1528.0	1590.0	96.1			
达到"国家体育标准"学生数 (人)	Number of Students Come to the Standard for State Physical Training (person)				181072.0	182953.0	99.0
幼儿园、托儿所个数 (个)	Number of Kindergardens (unit)	75.0	53.0	141.5	215.0	233.0	92.3
幼儿入托数 (人)	New Enrollment (person)	2851.0	2617.0	108.9	40687.0	42449.0	95.8
文化	**Culture**						
文化馆、站 (个)	Cultural Centers (unit)	7.0	7.0	100.0	27.0	27.0	100.0
公共图书馆 (个)	Public Libraries (unit)	2.0	2.0	100.0	6.0	2.0	300.0
公共图书馆藏书 (万册)	Collection (10000 volume)	39.0	33.1	117.8	2026.0	2160.0	93.8
电影放映单位 (个)	Film Projection Units (unit)	1.0	1.0	100.0	3.0	3.0	100.0
区级以上重点文物保护单位 (个)	Cultural Relics Preserved at District Level and above (unit)	2.0	2.0	100.0	24.0	39.0	61.5
卫生	**Health**						
卫生机构数 (个)	Number of Health Institutions (unit)	209.0	205.0	102.0	163.0	165.0	98.8
#医院	Hospitals	22.0	21.0	104.8	88.0	87.0	101.1
卫生院	Clinics	1.0	1.0	100.0	8.0	8.0	100.0
床位数	Number of Beds (unit)	3746.0	3732.0	100.4	8863.0	9358.0	94.7
#医院	Hospitals	3026.0	3012.0	100.5	8633.0	8908.0	96.9
卫生院	Clinics	20.0	20.0	100.0	530.0	494.0	107.3
平均每千人拥有床位数 (张)	Average Number of Beds Per 1000 Persons (unit)	11.4	11.5	99.1	5.8	6.1	95.1
卫生技术人员 (人)	Medical Technical Personnel (person)	5170.0	5289.0	97.8	12753.0	12604.0	101.2
#医生	Doctors (person)	2231.0	2338.0	95.4	8109.0	7966.0	101.8
公用设施	**Public Utilities**						
区级以上公园 (个)	Parks at District Level and Above (unit)	10.0	10.0	100.0	6.0	6.0	100.0
体育场馆 (个)	Stadiums and Gymnasiums (unit)	4.0	4.0	100.0	3.0	2.0	150.0
道路长度 (公里)	Length of Roads (km)	177.9	177.9	100.0	672.9	595.0	113.1

21-5 门头沟区、房山区国民经济主要指标
MAIN NATIONAL ECONOMIC INDICATORS FOR MENTOUGOU AND FANGSHAN DISTRICTS

项目	Item	门头沟区 Mentougou 1999	1998	1999年为1998年% 1999 as % of 1998	房山区 Fanshan 1999	1998	1999年为1998年% 1999 as % of 1998
综合	**General Survey**						
国内生产总值 (万元)	Gross Domestic Product (10000 yuan)	173555.6	142372.6	121.9	751012.8	667719.2	112.5
第一产业	Primary Industry	4821.9	4716.3	102.2	73177.2	67713.2	108.1
第二产业	Secondary Industry	65861.3	63298.0	104.0	334833.6	314986.8	106.3
第三产业	Tertiary Industry	102872.4	74358.3	138.3	343002.0	285019.2	120.3
财政收入 (万元)	Fiscal Revenue (10000 yuan)	29041.0	14380.0	202.0	33576.0	28649.0	117.2
#增值税	Increased Value Tax	19768.0	12616.0	156.7			
营业税	Operating Tax	15207.0	9683.0	157.0	17740.0	13069.0	133.4
个人所得税	Private Income Tax	1403.0	912.0	153.8	2201.0	1946.0	113.1
企业所得税	Enterprise Income Tax	12120.0	7521.0	161.0	9153.0	6289.0	147.1
财政支出 (万元)	Fiscal Expenditure (10000 yuan)	65330.0	46490.0	140.5	68719.0	58734.0	117.0
#基本建设支出	Capital Construction	1036.0	1017.0	101.9	2330.0	2227.0	104.6
支援农业生产支出	Supporting Agriculture	4618.0	3496.0	132.1	6137.0	4915.0	124.9
文教卫生事业费	Culture,Education and Health	13041.0	11747.0	111.0	25600.0	20782.0	123.2
人口和劳动力	**Population and Labor Force**						
总人口 (人)	Total Population (person)	256203.0	259107.0	98.9	752185.0	749978.0	100.3
常住户籍人口 (人)	Permanent Registered Population (person)	235146.0	233088.0	100.9	752185.0	749978.0	100.3
#非农业人口	Non-agriculture	151853.0	148531.0	102.2	267403.0	262042.0	102.0
男	Male	122770.0	121740.0	100.8	378393.0	377884.0	100.1
女	Female	112376.0	111348.0	100.9	373792.0	372094.0	100.5
出生率 (‰)	Birth Rate (‰)	6.2	6.6		7.6	7.1	
死亡率 (‰)	Death Rate (‰)	8.4	10.1		6.4	6.8	
自然增长率 (‰)	Natural Growth Rate (‰)	-2.2	-3.5		1.2	0.3	
从业人员 (人)	Employment (person)	86613.0	91604.0	94.6	279863.0	280459.0	99.8
按产业分	Grouped by Industry						
第一产业	Primary Industry	11729.0	13529.0	86.7	78891.0	81787.0	96.5
第二产业	Secondary Industry	21804.0	25803.0	84.5	101856.0	94830.0	107.4
第三产业	Tertiary Industry	53080.0	52272.0	101.5	99116.0	103842.0	95.4
按职工非职工分	Grouped by Staff and Workers or Non-staff-and-worker						
职工人数	Staff and Worker	37603.0	41416.0	90.8	56444.0	49458.0	114.1
#国有单位	State-owned	20390.0	22178.0	91.9	45357.0	36399.0	124.6
集体单位	Collective-owned	5771.0	6631.0	87.0	18506.0	11167.0	165.7
城镇个体劳动者	Urban and Rural Individuals	6182.0	4658.0	132.7	10265.0	13500.0	76.0
劳动工资	**Wages**						
工资总额 (万元)	Total Wages (10000 yuan)	37067.9	34532.5	107.3	53486.0	43433.4	123.1
#国有单位	State-owned	24298.7	21351.5	113.8	49892.4	35073.9	142.2
集体单位	Collective-owned	4676.4	4537.7	103.1	13250.0	7057.3	187.8
职工平均工资 (元)	Average Wage (yuan)	10547.0	9146.0	115.3	9696.0	8708.0	111.3
固定资产投资	**Investment in Fixed Assets Assets (10000 yuan)**						
全社会固定资产投资 (万元)	Total Investment in Fixed Assets	23352.0	13018.0	179.4	165784.0	75346.0	220.0
按建设性质分	Grouped by Type of Construction						
#基本建设投资	Capital Construction	1449.6	9597.0	15.1	18431.0	10287.0	179.2
更新改造投资	Innovation and Replacement	320.0	756.0	42.3	3499.0	3578.0	97.8

21-5 续表 1 continued

项目 Item		门头沟区 Mentougou 1999	1998	1999年为1998年% 1999 as % of 1998	房山区 Fanshan 1999	1998	1999年为1998年% 1999 as % of 1998
按登记注册类型分	Grouped by Registered Type						
#国有单位 (万元)	State-owned (10000 yuan)	14955.0	10939.0	136.7	56479.2	13865.0	407.4
集体单位 (万元)	Collective-owned (10000 yuan)	1417.0	742.0	191.0	60849.3	31434.0	193.6
新增固定资产 (万元)	Incremental Fixed Assets (10000 yuan)	18092.0	17510.0	103.3	129677.4	32264.0	401.9
#国有单位	State-owned				58818.0	13865.0	424.2
集体单位	Collective-owned				52476.0	18399.0	285.2
房屋施工面积 (万平方米)	Floor Space of Buildings Under Construction (10000 sq.m)	31.4	25.5	123.1	129.3	54.1	239.0
#国有单位	State-owned				52.0	44.5	116.9
集体单位	Collective-owned				65.6	9.6	683.3
房屋竣工面积 (万平方米)	Floor Space of Buildings Completed (10000 sq.m)	18.9	14.0	134.9	85.5	18.5	462.2
#国有单位	State-owned				44.1	11.8	373.7
#住宅	Residence				27.1	9.3	291.4
#集体单位	Collective-owned				33.8	6.7	504.4
#住宅	Residence				20.0	2.2	909.1
农村经济	**Rural Economy**						
农村劳动力 (人)	Labor Force (person)	43210.0	45530.0	94.9	213154.0	217501.0	98.0
种植业	Planting	8284.0	10237.0	80.9	60215.0	68081.0	88.4
林业	Forestry	1547.0	1495.0	103.5	5766.0	4538.0	127.1
牧业	Animal Husbandry	1849.0	1767.0	104.6	11472.0	8094.0	141.7
渔业	Fishery	49.0	30.0	163.3	678.0	498.0	136.1
农村工业	Rural Industry	7723.0	9688.0	79.7	46018.0	47284.0	97.3
农村建筑业	Rural Construction	2304.0	2028.0	113.6	28585.0	28502.0	100.3
农村运输业	Rural Transportation	7159.0	6246.0	114.6	24489.0	22431.0	109.2
农村商、饮食业、服务业	Commerce,Catering and Services	4167.0	3653.0	114.1	35931.0	38073.0	94.4
耕地面积 (公顷)	Area under Cultivation (hectare)	2854.7	2917.5	97.8	41225.9	41238.5	100.0
农业机械总动力 (千瓦)	Total Power of Agricultural Machinery (kw)	120701.0	109365.0	110.4	637144.0	689000.0	92.5
化肥施用实物量 (吨)	Consumption of Chemical Fertilizers (ton)	1774.0	1972.1	90.0	49230.0	51932.7	94.8
化肥施用折纯量 (吨)	Consumption of Chemical Fertilizers(100%) (ton)	628.0	471.5	133.2	16940.0	15454.8	109.6
农村用电量 (万千瓦时)	Consumption of Electricity (10000 kwh)	5897.5	5072.1	116.3	27372.4	25778.8	106.2
农村国内生产总值 (万元)	Rural Gross Domestic Product (10000 yuan)	65396.1	55240.0	118.4	541464.4	472399.2	114.6
第一产业	Primary Industry	5015.0	4920.7	101.9	73177.2	67713.2	108.1
第二产业	Secondary Industry	26113.2	23566.2	110.8	250902.7	223907.2	112.1
第三产业	Tertiary Industry	34267.9	26753.1	128.1	217384.5	180778.8	120.2
农业总产值 (万元)	Gross Output Value of Agriculture (10000 yuan)	6663.7	5733.5	116.2	77774.9	69681.9	111.6
种植业	Planting	2478.5	2097.2	118.2	38098.0	41468.4	91.9
林业	Forestry	538.1	548.2	98.2	1432.8	1362.1	105.2
牧业	Animal Husbandry	3235.2	2900.6	111.5	37336.8	25968.4	143.8
渔业	Fishery	411.8	187.5	219.6	907.3	883.0	102.8
农作物总播种面积 (万公顷)	Sown Area of Farm Crops (10000 hectare)	0.5	0.5	102.5	5.7	5.8	98.3
粮食作物	Grain	0.4	0.4	100.0	5.3	5.4	98.3
经济作物	Industrial Crops				0.1	0.1	100.0
其他作物	Other Crops	0.1	0.1	100.0	0.3	0.3	100.0

21-5 续表 2 continued

项目		Item	门头沟区 Mentougou 1999	1998	1999年为1998年% 1999 as % of 1998	房山区 Fanshan 1999	1998	1999年为1998年% 1999 as % of 1998
农副产品产量		Yield of Farm and Sideline Crops						
粮食	(万吨)	Grain (10000 tons)	0.8	0.9	88.9	27.9	29.8	93.6
蔬菜	(吨)	Vegetable (ton)	22989.0	21293.8	108.0	206200.0	202449.0	101.9
干鲜果	(吨)	Dry and Fresh Fruits (ton)	5442.0	4886.0	111.4	51413.0	48027.0	107.1
畜产品产量		Output of Livestock Products						
生猪出栏	(头)	Slaughtered Hogs (head)	37959.0	38983.0	97.4	314223.0	276430.0	113.7
商品猪	(头)	Commodity Hogs (head)						
猪牛羊肉	(吨)	Pork,Beef and Mutton (ton)	3292.0	3269.0	100.7	26861.0	22844.0	117.6
#猪肉		Pork	2659.0	2697.0	98.6	23362.0	20079.0	116.4
禽肉		Meat of Poultry (ton)	254.0	187.0	135.8	8665.0	4406.0	196.7
禽蛋		Poultry Eggs (ton)	1339.0	1704.0	78.6	13645.0	12962.0	105.3
牲畜年底头数	(头)	Number of Livestock (year-end) (head)	90875.0	99945.0	90.9	480611.0	416554.0	115.4
大牲畜		Large Animals	2521.0	2540.0	99.3	11510.0	13579.0	84.8
猪		Hogs	21572.0	28215.0	76.5	201613.0	180056.0	112.0
羊		Goats and Sheep	66782.0	69190.0	96.5	263488.0	222919.0	118.2
水产品产量	(吨)	Output of Aquatic Product (ton)	400.0	350.0	114.3	2054.0	2027.4	101.3
农村集体经济收入	(万元)	Rural Collective Economic Revenue (10000 yuan)	125844.0	109424.0	115.0	735083.0	752213.7	97.7
农村集体经济利润总额	(万元)	Total Profits of Rural Collective Economy (10000 yuan)	8144.0	5925.0	137.5	41755.0	40109.4	104.1
国家税金		State Taxes	4888.0	4181.0	116.9	19920.0	23087.0	86.3
集体积累		Collective Accumulation	1640.0	1761.0	93.1	14316.0	10675.4	134.1
劳动所得		Income from Work		9342.0		51038.0	52775.0	96.7
乡镇企业单位数	(个)	Number of Township and Village Enterprise (unit)	7953.0	6720.0	118.3	30271.0	25728.0	117.7
乡镇企业人数	(人)	Number of Persons of Township and Village Enterprises (person)	31373.0	31316.0	100.2	173525.0	168502.0	103.0
乡镇企业纯利润	(万元)	Net Profit of Township and Village Enterprises (10000 yuan)	18413.0	15393.0	119.6	67653.4	85713.0	78.8
乡镇企业固定资产原价	(万元)	Original Value of Fixed Assets of Township and Village Enterprises (10000 yuan)	56289.0	54988.0	102.4	268983.0	249819.0	107.7
乡镇企业固定资产净值	(万元)	Net Value of Fixed Assets of Township and Village Enterprises (10000 yuan)	40962.0	39916.0	102.6	197993.0	187355.0	105.7
工业		**Industry**						
全部工业企业单位数	(个)	Number of Enterprises (unit)	880.0	928.0	94.8	3469.0	3074.0	112.8
国有		State-owned	23.0	29.0	79.3	20.0	20.0	100.0
集体		Collective-owned	315.0	442.0	71.3	1037.0	1211.0	85.6
其他		Others	542.0	457.0	118.6	2412.0	1843.0	130.9
全部工业总产值(现价,万元)		Gross Output Value of Industry (at current prices,10000 yuan)	162004.8	156054.3	103.8	586643.2	538898.8	108.9
国有		State-owned	11897.1	15878.0	74.9	19265.0	19452.7	99.0
集体		Collective-owned	50151.3	66046.2	75.9	375432.6	380664.1	98.6
其他		Others	99956.4	74130.1	134.8	191945.6	138782.0	138.3

21-5 续表 3 continued

项目 Item		门头沟区 Mentougou 1999	1998	1999年为1998年% 1999 as % of 1998	房山区 Fanshan 1999	1998	1999年为1998年% 1999 as % of 1998
全部工业总产值 (1990年不变价,万元)	Gross Output Value of Industry (at constant price of 1990,10000yuan)	148420.5	144661.3	102.6	538617.7	494227.1	109.0
国有	State-owned	11663.9	12634.2	92.3	14717.7	14480.5	101.6
集体	Collective-owned	57466.9	62899.8	91.4	342231.0	348109.7	98.3
其他	Others	79289.7	69127.3	114.7	181669.0	131636.9	138.0
全部轻工业总产值 (现价,万元)	Gross Output Value of Light Industry (at current prices,10000 yuan)	64862.7	61191.2	106.0	200976.1	188614.6	106.6
以农产品为原料	Using Farm Products as Raw Materials	44815.1	35127.8	127.6	130634.5	122599.5	106.6
以非农产品为原料	Using Non-farm Products as Raw Materials	20047.6	26063.4	76.9	70341.6	66015.1	106.6
全部重工业总产值 (现价,万元)	Gross Output Value of Heavy Industry (at current prices,10000 yuan)	83557.8	83470.1	100.1	385667.1	350284.2	110.0
采掘工业	Mining and Quarrying	21295.4	20002.0	106.5	71022.3	64506.4	110.1
原料工业	Raw Materials Industry	13403.6	14371.8	93.3	111005.8	100821.6	110.1
制造工业	Manufacturing Industry	48858.8	49096.3	99.5	203639.0	184956.2	110.1
独立核算工业企业平均职工人数 (人)	Average Number of Staff and Workers in Enterprises with Independent Accounting System (person)	12029.0	14908.0	80.7	51468.0	52416.0	98.2
#国有	State-owned	2361.0	2866.0	82.4	4912.0	4495.0	109.3
集体	Collective-owned	5196.0	6742.0	77.1	40590.0	43248.0	93.9
独立核算工业企业总产值 (现价,万元)	Gross Output Value of Enterprises with Independent Accounting System(at current prices, 10000 yuan)	106446.0	107513.3	99.0	258314.1	263167.9	98.2
#国有	State-owned	10951.5	10470.2	104.6	19265.0	20182.0	95.5
集体	Collective-owned	16917.9	27629.3	61.2	187683.1	200039.6	93.8
独立核算工业企业工业增加值 (万元)	Value Added of Enterprises with Independent Accounting system (10000 yuan)	34188.5	33490.8	102.1	80783.7	79953.0	101.0
独立核算工业企业财务指标	Financial Indicators for Enterprises with Independent Accounting System						
产品销售收入 (万元)	Sales Revenue (10000yuan)	89729.1	80164.3	111.9	230856.8	242572.9	95.2
#国有	State-owned	6562.3	7306.7	89.8	18253.3	18371.9	99.4
产品销售成本 (万元)	Cost of Sales (10000 yuan)	70999.6	64187.7	110.6	194950.0	205269.6	95.0
#国有	State-owned	5254.0	6168.9	85.2	14485.9	15496.4	93.5
固定资产原价 (万元)	Original Value of Fixed Assets (10000 yuan)	92682.4	100748.2	92.0	220187.2	204858.5	107.5
#国有	State-owned	17043.1	16162.6	105.4	30566.0	27534.6	111.0
固定资产净值 (万元)	Net Value of Fixed Assets (10000 yuan)	74433.8	82818.2	89.9	149718.6	140274.1	106.7
#国有	State-owned	13789.0	12733.4	108.3	18170.4	16254.5	111.8
全部流动资金年平均余额 (万元)	Annual Average Balance of Circulating Funds (10000 yuan)	104077.5	96868.7	107.4	189083.2	180586.4	104.8
#国有	State-owned	14223.5	13958.1	101.9	16235.2	15024.9	108.1
利润总额 (万元)	Total Profits (10000 yuan)	-2913.2	-3919.9		3947.7	3689.1	107.0
#国有	State-owned	-1703.1	-2032.7		-1019.7	-631.8	

21-5 续表 4 continued

项目	Item	门头沟区 Mentougou 1999	1998	1999年为1998年% 1999 as % of 1998	房山区 Fanshan 1999	1998	1999年为1998年% 1999 as % of 1998
资金利税率 (%)	Ratio of Pre-tax Profits to Total of Capital (%)	2.6	-1.5			6.5	
产品销售率 (%)	Ratio of Sales Value to Gross Output Value (%)	93.4	97.7		90.7	94.4	
增加值率 (%)	Ratio of Added Value to Gross Output Value (%)	37.3	38.4		31.3	32.6	
独立核算工业企业全员劳动生产率 (元/人)	Overall Labor Productivity of Enterprises with Independent Accounting System (yuan/person)	25642.0	16519.0	155.2	15696.0	13880.0	113.1
#国有	State-owned	26810.0	7967.0	336.5	10123.0	8786.0	115.2
集体	Collective-owned	20676.0	10892.0	189.8	15952.0	13335.0	119.6
商业	**Commerce**						
社会消费品零售额 (万元)	Retail Sales of Consumer Goods (10000 yuan)	161720.8	143717.0	112.5	454008.2	412074.7	110.2
按登记注册类型分	Grouped by Registered Type						
国有	State-owned	49177.0	22480.3	218.8	80269.2	73443.5	109.3
集体	Collective-owned	21380.9	35764.7	59.8	271621.2	248523.9	109.3
其他	Others	91162.9	85472.0	106.7	102117.8	90107.3	113.3
按类别分	Grouped by Type of Goods						
吃的商品 (万元)	Food (10000 yuan)	74626.7	63137.9	118.2	124578.3	107828.8	115.5
穿的商品 (万元)	Clothing (10000 yuan)	10971.7	4391.9	249.8	79058.8	67667.8	116.8
用的商品 (万元)	Daily Used Articles (10000 yuan)	70976.7	71346.6	99.5	205149.5	199008.0	103.1
烧的商品 (万元)	Fuel (10000 yuan)	5145.7	4840.6	106.3	45221.6	37570.1	120.4
网点数 (个)	Number of Outlets (unit)	8041.0	6007.0	133.9	10809.0	9088.0	118.9
#商业	Wholesale and Retail	6526.0	4750.0	137.4	7255.0	6518.0	111.3
饮食业	Catering	671.0	545.0	123.1	2387.0	1410.0	169.3
服务业	Services	530.0	395.0	134.2	1167.0	1150.0	101.5
#宾馆、饭店	Hotels	4.0	4.0	100.0	66.0	63.0	104.8
营业人员 (人)	Personnel (person)	26588.0	22431.0	118.5	29860.0	27290.0	109.4
#商业	Wholesale and Retail	17072.0	16272.0	104.9	22485.0	20435.0	110.0
饮食业	Catering	2257.0	1828.0	123.5	4099.0	3725.0	110.0
服务业	Services	6770.0	3891.0	174.0	3276.0	3130.0	104.7
#宾馆、饭店	Hotels	842.0	782.0	107.7	2726.0	2602.0	104.7
外经、外贸	**Foreign Economy and Trade**						
出口商品交货额 (万元)	Delivery Value of Exports (10000 yuan)	6236.6	7993.7	78.0	25785.5	32091.7	80.3
利用外资签订协议(合同)数 (个)	Number of Signed Agreements and Contracts of Foreign Capital to be Utilized (unit)	15.0	17.0	88.2	15.0	12.0	125.0
利用外资签订协议(合同)金额 (万美元)	Amount of Foreign Capital to be Utilized through Agreements and Contracts (USD 10000)	1200.9	1032.9	116.3	1201.9	2152.0	55.9
实际利用外资 (万美元)	Amount of Foreign Capital Actually Used (USD 10000)	453.3	403.2	112.4	2087.9	2061.0	101.3
旅游人数 (万人)	Number of Tourists (10000 persons)	300.6	261.5	115.0	271.2	250.3	108.3
教育	**Education**						
学校数 (个)	Number of Schools (unit)	109.0	115.0	94.8	346.0	380.0	91.1
小学	Primary Schools	79.0	85.0	92.9	275.0	307.0	89.6

21-5 续表 5 continued

项目 Item	门头沟区 Mentougou 1999	1998	1999年为1998年% 1999 as % of 1998	房山区 Fanshan 1999	1998	1999年为1998年% 1999 as % of 1998
普通中学 Regular Secondary School	24.0	24.0	100.0	67.0	65.0	103.1
中等专业教育 Specialized Secondary Schools	6.0	6.0	100.0	4.0	4.0	100.0
招生数 (人) New Student Enrollment (person)	7662.0	7651.0	100.1	25355.0	26204.0	96.8
小学 Primary Schools	2026.0	2266.0	89.4	7604.0	8596.0	85.5
初级中等学校 Junior Secondary Schools	3953.0	3751.0	105.4	14134.0	12923.0	109.4
高级中等学校 Senior Secondary Schools	937.0	775.0	120.9	3032.0	4003.0	75.7
中等专业教育 Specialized Secondary Schools	746.0	859.0	86.8	585.0	682.0	85.8
在校学生 (人) Student Enrollment (person)	32072.0	33303.0	96.3	132470.0	138962.0	95.3
小学 Primary Schools	16391.0	18421.0	89.0	77863.0	85373.0	91.2
初级中等学校 Junior Secondary Schools	11051.0	10802.0	102.3	40104.0	39553.0	101.4
高级中等学校 Senior Secondary Schools	2408.0	2011.0	119.7	11672.0	11118.0	105.0
中等专业教育 Specialized Secondary Schools	2222.0	2069.0	107.4	2831.0	2918.0	97.0
毕业生 (人) Graduates (person)	8572.0	8918.0	96.1	30764.0	30559.0	100.7
小学 Primary Schools	3984.0	3780.0	105.4	14709.0	13312.0	110.5
初级中等学校 Junior Secondary Schools	3489.0	4031.0	86.6	11994.0	12906.0	92.9
高级中等学校 Senior Secondary Schools	543.0	553.0	98.2	3273.0	3519.0	93.0
中等专业教育 Specialized Secondary Schools	556.0	554.0	100.4	788.0	822.0	95.9
达到"国家体育标准"学生数 (人) Number of Students Come to the Standard for State Physical Training (person)	26732.0	27912.0	95.8	121364.0	127634.0	95.1
幼儿园、托儿所个数 (个) Number of Kindergardens (unit)	20.0	20.0	100.0	176.0	331.0	53.2
幼儿入托数 (人) New Enrollment (person)	1882.0	1830.0	102.8	7986.0	8080.0	98.8
文化 Culture						
文化馆、站 (个) Cultural Centers (unit)	15.0	15.0	100.0	13.0	15.0	86.7
公共图书馆 (个) Public Libraries (unit)	1.0	1.0	100.0	1.0	1.0	100.0
公共图书馆藏书 (万册) Collection (10000 volume)	22.0	21.6	101.9	7.0	7.0	100.0
电影放映单位 (个) Film Projection Units (unit)	5.0	5.0	100.0	12.0	13.0	92.3
区级以上重点文物保护单位 (个) Cultural Relics Preserved at District Level and above (unit)	74.0	74.0	100.0	68.0	68.0	100.0
卫生 Health						
卫生机构数 (个) Number of Health Institutions (unit)	28.0	28.0	100.0	44.0	44.0	100.0
#医院 Hospitals	5.0	5.0	100.0	6.0	6.0	100.0
卫生院 Clinics	15.0	15.0	100.0	26.0	26.0	100.0
床位数 Number of Beds (unit)	736.0	724.0	101.7	1730.0	1702.0	101.6
#医院 Hospitals	623.0	621.0	100.3	1098.0	1101.0	99.7
卫生院 Clinics	93.0	103.0	90.3	596.0	565.0	105.5
平均每千人拥有床位数 (张) Average Number of Beds Per 1000 Persons (unit)	3.1	3.1	100.0	2.3	2.3	100.0
卫生技术人员 (人) Medical Technical Personnel (person)	1192.0	1179.0	101.1	2536.0	2539.0	99.9
#医生 Doctors (person)	599.0	581.0	103.1	1745.0	1638.0	106.5
公用设施 Public Utilities						
区级以上公园 (个) Parks at District Level and Above (unit)	4.0	4.0	100.0	4.0	4.0	100.0
体育场馆 (个) Stadiums and Gymnasiums (unit)	2.0	2.0	100.0	257.0	256.0	100.4
道路长度 (公里) Length of Roads (km)	452.3	448.5	100.8	1796.0	1769.1	101.5

21-6 昌平区、顺义区国民经济主要指标
MAIN NATIONAL ECONOMIC INDICATORS FOR CHANGPING AND SHUNYI DISTRICTS

项目	Item	昌平区 Changping			顺义区 Shunyi		
		1999	1998	1999年为1998年% 1999 as % of 1998	1999	1998	1999年为1998年% 1999 as % of 1998
综合	**General Survey**						
国内生产总值 (万元)	Gross Domestic Product (10000 yuan)	510631.1	455665.9	112.1	783554.2	690176.0	113.5
第一产业	Primary Industry	48281.9	45978.5	105.0	157252.4	147885.9	106.3
第二产业	Secondary Industry	194474.9	167855.2	115.9	346094.1	308607.7	112.1
第三产业	Tertiary Industry	267874.3	241823.2	110.8	280207.7	233682.4	119.9
财政收入 (万元)	Fiscal Revenue (10000 yuan)	25434.0	20377.0	124.8	44146.0	28423.0	155.3
#增值税	Increased Value Tax						
营业税	Operating Tax	12469.0	10654.0	117.0	16263.0	10711.0	151.8
个人所得税	Private Income Tax	2039.0	1523.0	133.9	5572.0	2997.0	185.9
企业所得税	Enterprise Income Tax	3740.0	3149.0	118.8	13845.0	12552.0	110.3
财政支出 (万元)	Fiscal Expenditure (10000 yuan)	54023.0	46541.0	116.1	85936.0	65375.0	131.5
#基本建设支出	Capital Construction	2170.0	861.0	252.0	4486.0	4628.0	96.9
支援农业生产支出	Supporting Agriculture	5141.0	4217.0	121.9	17613.0	10911.0	161.4
文教卫生事业费	Culture,Education and Health	15518.0	13583.0	114.2	24481.0	21606.0	113.3
人口和劳动力	**Population and Labor Force**						
总人口 (人)	Total Population (person)	475945.0	459379.0	103.6	540398.0	539973.0	100.1
常住户籍人口 (人)	Permanent Registered Population (person)	424919.0	418775.0	101.5	540398.0	536913.0	100.1
#非农业人口	Non-agriculture	173669.0	165566.0	104.9	109920.0	103695.0	106.0
男	Male	211780.0	208863.0	101.4	266275.0	265973.0	100.1
女	Female	213139.0	209909.0	101.5	274123.0	274000.0	100.0
出生率 (‰)	Birth Rate (‰)	7.3	7.1		9.9	7.6	
死亡率 (‰)	Death Rate (‰)	5.3	8.8		7.6	8.1	
自然增长率 (‰)	Natural Growth Rate (‰)	2.0	-1.7		2.2	-0.5	
从业人员 (人)	Employment (person)	199076.0	170361.0	116.9	271051.0	270655.0	100.1
按产业分	Grouped by Industry						
第一产业	Primary Industry	49182.0	42117.0	116.8	63765.0	61961.0	102.9
第二产业	Secondary Industry	54072.0	54279.0	99.6	97281.0	99441.0	97.8
第三产业	Tertiary Industry	95822.0	73965.0	129.6	110005.0	109253.0	100.7
按职工非职工分	Grouped by Staff and Workers or Non-staff-and-worker						
职工人数	Staff and Worker	65744.0	67728.0	97.1	63749.0	64387.0	99.0
#国有单位	State-owned	36848.0	39429.0	93.5	46040.0	45723.0	100.7
集体单位	Collective-owned	16382.0	17452.0	93.9	11073.0	13143.0	84.3
城镇个体劳动者	Urban and Rural Individuals	1545.0	1054.0	146.6	19916.0	19240.0	103.5
劳动工资	**Wages**						
工资总额 (万元)	Total Wages (10000 yuan)	62027.9	55616.8	111.5	68865.3	57775.4	119.2
#国有单位	State-owned	38175.1	33460.3	114.1	51634.1	43217.3	119.5
集体单位	Collective-owned	12264.1	12409.0	98.8	9059.4	9110.7	99.4
职工平均工资 (元)	Average Wage (yuan)	9406.0	8390.0	112.1	10674.0	8978.2	118.9
固定资产投资	**Investment in Fixed Assets Assets (10000 yuan)**						
全社会固定资产投资 (万元)	Total Investment in Fixed Assets	92691.2	84669.4	109.5	210000.0	208000.0	101.0
按建设性质分	Grouped by Type of Construction						
#基本建设投资	Capital Construction	74763.7	71988.9	103.9	140000.0	108160.0	129.4
更新改造投资	Innovation and Replacement	17927.5	12680.5	141.4	70000.0	99840.0	70.1

21-6 续表 1 continued

项目	Item	昌平区 Changping			顺义区 Shunyi		
		1999	1998	1999年为1998年% 1999 as % of 1998	1999	1998	1999年为1998年% 1999 as % of 1998
按登记注册类型分	Grouped by Registered Type						
#国有单位 (万元)	State-owned (10000 yuan)	39698.5	35565.0	111.6	105000.0	111000.0	94.6
集体单位 (万元)	Collective-owned (10000 yuan)	28488.2	34918.3	81.6	84000.0	74000.0	113.5
新增固定资产 (万元)	Incremental Fixed Assets (10000 yuan)	95466.0	57171.7	167.0	149000.0	137200.0	108.6
#国有单位	State-owned	45775.5	27666.4	165.5	55000.0	73260.0	75.1
集体单位	Collective-owned	24541.0	24935.6	98.4	16000.0	48840.0	32.8
房屋施工面积 (万平方米)	Floor Space of Buildings Under Construction (10000 sq.m)	92.2	107.3	85.9	120.0	159.0	75.5
#国有单位	State-owned	46.4	38.2	121.5	70.0	68.0	102.9
集体单位	Collective-owned	26.5	48.0	55.2	42.0	62.0	67.7
房屋竣工面积 (万平方米)	Floor Space of Buildings Completed (10000 sq.m)	52.0	38.6	134.7	88.7	89.0	99.7
#国有单位	State-owned	26.3	11.4	230.7	51.0	45.0	113.3
#住宅	Residence	21.2	8.8	240.9	37.5	35.0	107.1
#集体单位	Collective-owned	19.2	23.1	83.1	32.0	24.0	133.3
#住宅	Residence	7.2	13.7	52.6	10.5	14.0	75.0
农村经济	**Rural Economy**						
农村劳动力 (人)	Labor Force (person)	118142.0	102781.0	114.9	189018.0	187978.0	100.6
种植业	Planting	35370.0	32798.0	107.8	45398.0	45238.0	100.4
林业	Forestry	5690.0	3518.0	161.7	2185.0	2491.0	87.7
牧业	Animal Husbandry	5839.0	3999.0	146.0	13001.0	11262.0	115.4
渔业	Fishery	862.0	668.0	129.0	2204.0	1908.0	115.5
农村工业	Rural Industry	22491.0	20918.0	107.5	55423.0	57138.0	97.0
农村建筑业	Rural Construction	8057.0	6754.0	119.3	15476.0	14569.0	106.2
农村运输业	Rural Transportation	12414.0	9321.0	133.2	12311.0	11335.0	108.6
农村商、饮食业、服务业	Commerce,Catering and Services	7650.0	6462.0	118.4	11742.0	11370.0	103.3
耕地面积 (公顷)	Area under Cultivation (hectare)	24178.9	24456.9	98.9	50290.7	50650.0	99.3
农业机械总动力 (千瓦)	Total Power of Agricultural Machinery (kw)	206464.0	204000.0	101.2	537816.0	545438.0	98.6
化肥施用实物量 (吨)	Consumption of Chemical Fertilizers (ton)	25500.0	26907.0	94.8	88613.0	93033.4	95.2
化肥施用折纯量 (吨)	Consumption of Chemical Fertilizers(100%) (ton)	10339.0	9931.0	104.1	34484.0	34613.0	99.6
农村用电量 (万千瓦时)	Consumption of Electricity (10000 kwh)	24841.4	25584.0	97.1	34923.2	37779.5	92.4
农村国内生产总值 (万元)	Rural Gross Domestic Product (10000 yuan)	276095.9	242153.6	114.0	462727.0	408675.4	113.2
第一产业	Primary Industry	48281.9	45987.5	105.0	156083.2	146514.8	106.5
第二产业	Secondary Industry	88363.2	79006.1	111.8	165067.9	146136.6	113.0
第三产业	Tertiary Industry	139450.8	117160.0	119.0	141575.9	116024.0	122.0
农业总产值 (万元)	Gross Output Value of Agriculture (10000 yuan)	115565.9	109824.5	105.2	231542.8	204181.1	113.4
种植业	Planting	51295.1	46214.0	111.0	76253.3	75564.0	100.9
林业	Forestry	4292.2	2852.6	150.5	1342.4	1200.0	111.9
牧业	Animal Husbandry	53141.5	60303.6	88.1	143084.3	119372.9	119.9
渔业	Fishery	6483.1	6333.8	102.4	10862.8	8044.2	135.0
农作物总播种面积 (万公顷)	Sown Area of Farm Crops (10000 hectare)	3.6	3.7	97.3	9.2	9.3	98.9
粮食作物	Grain	3.2	3.4	94.1	7.7	7.8	98.7
经济作物	Industrial Crops		...			0.1	
其他作物	Other Crops	0.3	...		1.5	1.4	107.1

21-6 续表 2 continued

项目 Item		昌平区 Changping 1999	1998	1999年为1998年% 1999 as % of 1998	顺义区 Shunyi 1999	1998	1999年为1998年% 1999 as % of 1998
农副产品产量	Yield of Farm and Side-line Crops						
粮食 (万吨)	Grain (10000 tons)	16.3	17.1	95.3	37.8	44.4	85.1
蔬菜 (吨)	Vegetable (ton)	122148.0	104995.0	116.3	850208.0	839945.7	101.2
干鲜果 (吨)	Dry and Fresh Fruits (ton)	52805.0	50838.0	103.9	41968.0	41127.1	102.0
畜产品产量	Output of Livestock Products						
生猪出栏 (头)	Slaughtered Hogs (head)	250817.0	273996.0	91.5	1340344.0	1199115.0	111.8
商品猪 (头)	Commodity Hogs (head)				1340344.0	1199115.0	111.8
猪牛羊肉 (吨)	Pork,Beef and Mutton (ton)	14507.0	17374.0	83.5	123057.0	112454.6	109.4
#猪肉	Pork	12610.0	14955.0	84.3	108843.0	100199.6	108.6
禽肉	Meat of Poultry (ton)	16021.0	15727.0	101.9	72024.0	68141.3	105.7
禽蛋	Poultry Eggs (ton)	8122.0	13077.0	62.1	22408.0	22789.2	98.3
牲畜年底头数 (头)	Number of Livestock (year-end) (head)	207050.0	245588.0	84.3	974676.0	898948.0	108.4
大牲畜	Large Animals	13350.0	18039.0	74.0	30988.0	31277.0	99.1
猪	Hogs	124359.0	168038.0	74.0	824362.0	769870.0	107.1
羊	Goats and Sheep	69341.0	59511.0	116.5	119326.0	97801.0	122.0
水产品产量 (吨)	Output of Aquatic Product (ton)	8046.0	8002.0	100.5	16036.8	16140.0	99.4
农村集体经济收入 (万元)	Rural Collective Economic Revenue (10000 yuan)	346022.5	345414.0	100.2	1125968.0	1019446.0	110.4
农村集体经济利润总额 (万元)	Total Profits of Rural Collective Economy (10000 yuan)	27282.5	35302.0	77.3	296678.0	269349.0	110.1
国家税金	State Taxes	19591.1	18014.0	108.8	17683.0	14290.0	123.7
集体积累	Collective Accumulation	8852.1	12990.0	68.1	28405.0	22410.0	126.8
劳动所得	Income from Work	112642.4	101747.0	110.7	210707.0	193225.0	109.0
乡镇企业单位数 (个)	Number of Township and Village Enterprise (unit)	1078.0	1101.0	97.9	922.0	1007.0	91.6
乡镇企业人数 (人)	Number of Persons of Township and Village Enterprises (person)	43862.0	48067.0	91.3	82396.0	86325.0	95.4
乡镇企业纯利润 (万元)	Net Profit of Township and Village Enterprises (10000 yuan)	14826.0	15227.0	97.4	25964.0	20535.0	126.4
乡镇企业固定资产原价 (万元)	Original Value of Fixed Assets of Township and Village Enterprises (10000 yuan)	167890.0	148945.0	112.7	334505.0	303957.0	110.1
乡镇企业固定资产净值 (万元)	Net Value of Fixed Assets of Township and Village Enterprises (10000 yuan)	121758.0	107748.0	113.0	244103.0	222223.0	109.8
工业	**Industry**						
全部工业企业单位数 (个)	Number of Enterprises (unit)	1207.0	1083.0	111.4	2971.0	2660.0	111.7
国有	State-owned	57.0	47.0	121.3	60.0	83.0	72.3
集体	Collective-owned	793.0	780.0	101.7	624.0	673.0	92.7
其他	Others	357.0	256.0	139.5	2287.0	1904.0	120.1
全部工业总产值 (现价,万元)	Gross Output Value of Industry (at current prices,10000 yuan)	453914.9	376876.7	120.4	1154822.3	1094513.3	105.5
国有	State-owned	45879.2	34665.5	132.3	311883.4	297926.3	104.7
集体	Collective-owned	194083.8	195690.1	99.2	282013.5	323832.5	87.1
其他	Others	213951.9	146521.1	146.0	560925.4	472754.5	118.7

21-6 续表 3 continued

项目	Item	昌平区 Changping			顺义区 Shunyi		
		1999	1998	1999 年为 1998 年% 1999 as % of 1998	1999	1998	1999 年为 1998 年% 1999 as % of 1998
全部工业总产值 (1990 年不变价,万元)	Gross Output Value of Industry (at constant price of 1990,10000yuan)	440411.5	358170.6	123.0	1065147.4	962686.6	110.6
国有	State-owned	38000.0	27165.2	139.9	239046.3	205505.8	116.3
集体	Collective-owned	193410.0	190683.4	101.4	265390.8	298179.2	89.0
其他	Others	209001.5	140322.0	148.9	560710.3	459001.6	122.2
全部轻工业总产值 (现价,万元)	Gross Output Value of Light Industry (at current prices,10000 yuan)	230387.7	193996.9	118.8	780505.6	679840.7	114.8
以农产品为原料	Using Farm Products as Raw Materials	133032.7	113193.2	117.5	572521.2	497707.0	115.0
以非农产品为原料	Using Non-farm Products as Raw Materials	97355.0	80803.7	120.5	207984.4	182710.2	113.8
全部重工业总产值 (现价,万元)	Gross Output Value of Heavy Industry (at current prices,10000 yuan)	210023.8	164173.7	127.9	374316.7	334646.6	111.9
采掘工业	Mining and Quarrying	9830.5	6919.0	142.1	2710.7	2417.2	112.1
原料工业	Raw Materials Industry	15399.9	11948.8	128.9	81601.1	69926.8	116.7
制造工业	Manufacturing Industry	184793.4	145305.9	127.2	29004.9	263370.9	110.1
独立核算工业企业平均职工人数 (人)	Average Number of Staff and Workers in Enterprises with Independent Accounting System (person)	52315.0	53686.0	97.4	100654.0	104390.0	96.4
#国有	State-owned	3486.0	2447.0	142.5	19581.0	15464.0	126.6
集体	Collective-owned	32472.0	36962.0	87.9	49557.0	58977.0	84.0
独立核算工业企业总产值 (现价,万元)	Gross Output Value of Enterprises with Independent Accounting System(at current prices, 10000 yuan)	431737.3	360692.8	119.7	1070257.1	1020532.0	104.9
#国有	State-owned	24667.7	18972.6	130.0	311883.4	297926.3	104.7
集体	Collective-owned	191710.9	195199.1	98.2	282013.5	323832.5	87.1
独立核算工业企业工业增加值 (万元)	Value Added of Enterprises with Independent Accounting system (10000 yuan)	148898.8	123729.2	120.3	255111.6	224002.2	113.9
独立核算工业企业财务指标	Financial Indicators for Enterprises with Independent Accounting System						
产品销售收入 (万元)	Sales Revenue (10000yuan)	390318.6	319612.9	122.1	1026557.6	934105.4	109.9
#国有	State-owned	27878.2	21628.2	128.9	316974.0	282965.3	112.0
产品销售成本 (万元)	Cost of Sales (10000 yuan)	312673.9	257273.0	121.5	801995.2	739001.4	108.5
#国有	State-owned	21570.3	17653.9	122.2	210504.8	188900.1	111.4
固定资产原价 (万元)	Original Value of Fixed Assets (10000 yuan)	289388.7	259631.7	111.5	892364.6	714574.7	124.9
#国有	State-owned	21962.1	15535.6	141.4	339970.1	224361.7	151.5
固定资产净值 (万元)	Net Value of Fixed Assets (10000 yuan)	200725.7	180447.4	111.2	685640.1	532830.4	128.7
#国有	State-owned	13243.3	9969.4	132.8	267190.7	166255.8	160.7
全部流动资金年平均余额 (万元)	Annual Average Balance of Circulating Funds (10000 yuan)	336758.1	364520.8	92.4	700776.9	591836.6	118.4
#国有	State-owned	23734.8	17844.6	133.0	195229.5	157028.9	124.3
利润总额 (万元)	Total Profits (10000 yuan)	16375.4	4965.4	329.8	55797.8	47065.8	118.6
#国有	State-owned	-1606.1	-141.9		48328.0	44559.0	108.5

21-6 续表 4 continued

项目		Item	昌平区 Changping 1999	1998	1999年为1998年% 1999 as % of 1998	顺义区 Shunyi 1999	1998	1999年为1998年% 1999 as % of 1998
资金利税率	(%)	Ratio of Pre-tax Profits to Total of Capital (%)	6.5	3.8		10.0	9.9	
产品销售率	(%)	Ratio of Sales Value to Gross Output Value (%)	94.7	91.5		95.9	92.0	
增加值率	(%)	Ratio of Added Value to Gross Output Value (%)	34.5	34.3		24.5	23.6	
独立核算工业企业全员劳动生产率	(元/人)	Overall Labor Productivity of Enterprises with Independent Accounting System (yuan/person)	28461.0	23047.0	123.5	25345.4	21458.2	118.1
#国有		State-owned	22477.0	20587.0	109.2	68455.8	71355.7	95.9
集体		Collective-owned	20861.0	17589.0	118.6	11238.0	9603.4	117.0
商业		**Commerce**						
社会消费品零售额	(万元)	Retail Sales of Consumer Goods (10000 yuan)	180521.0	158686.0	113.8	323403.0	301749.0	107.2
按登记注册类型分		Grouped by Registered Type						
国有		State-owned	22545.0	25829.0	87.3	85797.0	85025.0	100.9
集体		Collective-owned	79020.0	66946.0	118.0	77875.0	78467.0	99.2
其他		Others	78956.0	66911.0	118.0	159731.0	138257.0	115.5
按类别分		Grouped by Type of Goods						
吃的商品	(万元)	Food (10000 yuan)	74798.0	62788.0	119.1	113191.0	112808.0	100.3
穿的商品	(万元)	Clothing (10000 yuan)	17871.0	17072.0	104.7	48510.0	45729.0	106.1
用的商品	(万元)	Daily Used Articles (10000 yuan)	76334.0	66214.0	115.3	129361.0	111827.0	115.7
烧的商品	(万元)	Fuel (10000 yuan)	11518.0	12612.0	91.3	32341.0	31385.0	103.0
网点数	(个)	Number of Outlets (unit)	9984.0	7504.0	133.0	5436.0	5381.0	101.0
#商业		Wholesale and Retail	6616.0	4810.0	137.5	3764.0	3743.0	100.6
饮食业		Catering	2638.0	869.0	303.6	630.0	633.0	99.5
服务业		Services	704.0	1791.0	39.3	1042.0	1005.0	103.7
#宾馆、饭店		Hotels	2.0	3.0	66.7	14.0	9.0	155.6
营业人员	(人)	Personnel (person)	28093.0	24748.0	113.5	33665.0	35109.0	95.9
#商业		Wholesale and Retail	18326.0	17677.0	103.7	21845.0	22311.0	97.9
饮食业		Catering	7091.0	4061.0	174.6	3633.0	3933.0	92.4
服务业		Services	2406.0	2740.0	87.8	8187.0	8865.0	92.4
#宾馆、饭店		Hotels	350.0	415.0	84.3	1701.0	2663.0	63.9
外经、外贸		**Foreign Economy and Trade**						
出口商品交货额	(万元)	Delivery Value of Exports (10000 yuan)	59642.2	39935.9	149.3	225353.6	189390.6	119.0
利用外资签订协议(合同)数	(个)	Number of Signed Agreements and Contracts of Foreign Capital to be Utilized (unit)	24.0	18.0	133.3	23.0	40.0	57.5
利用外资签订协议(合同)金额	(万美元)	Amount of Foreign Capital to be Utilized through Agreements and Contracts (USD 10000)	2453.4	6195.4	39.6	1792.7	6831.3	26.2
实际利用外资	(万美元)	Amount of Foreign Capital Actually Used (USD 10000)	2488.5	6741.4	36.9	10272.5	10257.6	100.1
旅游人数	(万人)	Number of Tourists (10000 persons)	1055.0	992.0	106.4	72.5	70.1	103.4
教育		**Education**						
学校数	(个)	Number of Schools (unit)	184.0	190.0	96.8	188.0	202.0	93.1
小学		Primary Schools	141.0	147.0	95.9	147.0	161.0	91.3

21-6 续表 5 continued

项目 Item		昌平区 Changping 1999	1998	1999年为1998年% 1999 as % of 1998	顺义区 Shunyi 1999	1998	1999年为1998年% 1999 as % of 1998
普通中学	Regular Secondary School	42.0	42.0	100.0	39.0	38.0	102.6
中等专业教育	Specialized Secondary Schools	1.0	1.0	100.0	2.0	3.0	66.7
招生数 (人)	New Student Enrollment (person)	13033.0	13882.0	93.9	22990.0	20693.0	111.1
小学	Primary Schools	3538.0	3659.0	96.7	5003.0	5833.0	85.8
初级中等学校	Junior Secondary Schools	6878.0	6692.0	102.8	13619.0	11008.0	123.7
高级中等学校	Senior Secondary Schools	2554.0	3369.0	75.8	2792.0	2262.0	123.4
中等专业教育	Specialized Secondary Schools	63.0	162.0	38.9	1576.0	1590.0	99.1
在校学生 (人)	Student Enrollment (person)	58690.0	62890.0	93.3	110209.0	113950.0	96.7
小学	Primary Schools	30019.0	33571.0	89.4	64810.0	72954.0	88.8
初级中等学校	Junior Secondary Schools	19652.0	19576.0	100.4	34134.0	29917.0	114.1
高级中等学校	Senior Secondary Schools	8588.0	9084.0	94.5	7720.0	7163.0	107.8
中等专业教育	Specialized Secondary Schools	431.0	659.0	65.4	3545.0	3916.0	90.5
毕业生 (人)	Graduates (person)	15992.0	16455.0	97.2	27188.0	24487.0	111.0
小学	Primary Schools	7043.0	6714.0	104.9	13749.0	11083.0	124.1
初级中等学校	Junior Secondary Schools	6055.0	6801.0	89.0	9613.0	9715.0	99.0
高级中等学校	Senior Secondary Schools	2603.0	3069.0	84.8	2236.0	2041.0	110.0
中等专业教育	Specialized Secondary Schools	291.0	339.0	85.8	1590.0	1648.0	96.5
达到"国家体育标准"学生数 (人)	Number of Students Come to the Standard for State Physical Training (person)	57931.0	60986.0	95.0	85645.0	73246.0	116.9
幼儿园、托儿所个数 (个)	Number of Kindergardens (unit)	183.0	184.0	99.5	113.0	134.0	84.3
幼儿入托数 (人)	New Enrollment (person)	10502.0	9950.0	105.5	9155.0	9159.0	100.0
文化	**Culture**						
文化馆、站 (个)	Cultural Centers (unit)	26.0	26.0	100.0	20.0	20.0	100.0
公共图书馆 (个)	Public Libraries (unit)	1.0	1.0	100.0	1.0	1.0	100.0
公共图书馆藏书 (万册)	Collection (10000 volume)	17.8	15.0	118.7	15.0	13.5	111.1
电影放映单位 (个)	Film Projection Units (unit)	41.0	50.0	82.0	30.0	28.0	107.1
区级以上重点文物保护单位 (个)	Cultural Relics Preserved at District Level and above (unit)	63.0	65.0	96.9	9.0	10.0	90.0
卫生	**Health**						
卫生机构数 (个)	Number of Health Institutions (unit)	57.0	59.0	96.6	47.0	46.0	102.2
#医院	Hospitals	18.0	15.0	120.0	14.0	11.0	127.3
卫生院	Clinics	26.0	26.0	100.0	23.0	26.0	88.5
床位数	Number of Beds (unit)	4398.0	4556.0	96.5	1901.0	1706.0	111.4
#医院	Hospitals	3759.0	3767.0	99.8	1498.0	1324.0	113.1
卫生院	Clinics	341.0	311.0	109.6	371.0	382.0	97.1
平均每千人拥有床位数 (张)	Average Number of Beds Per 1000 Persons (unit)	10.4	10.9	95.4	3.5	3.2	109.4
卫生技术人员 (人)	Medical Technical Personnel (person)	3696.0	4000.0	92.4	2879.0	2706.0	106.4
#医生	Doctors (person)	1509.0	1744.0	86.5	1533.0	1333.0	115.0
公用设施	**Public Utilities**						
区级以上公园 (个)	Parks at District Level and Above (unit)	8.0	8.0	100.0	3.0	3.0	100.0
体育场馆 (个)	Stadiums and Gymnasiums (unit)	2.0	2.0	100.0	4.0	4.0	100.0
道路长度 (公里)	Length of Roads (km)	1323.9	1292.5	102.4	1516.0	1493.0	101.5

21-7 通州区、大兴县国民经济主要指标
MAIN NATIONAL ECONOMIC INDICATORS FOR TONGZHOU DISTRICT AND DAXING COUNTY

项目		Item	通州区 Tongzhou 1999	1998	1999年为1998年% 1999 as % of 1998	大兴县 Daxing 1999	1998	1999年为1998年% 1999 as % of 1998
综合		**General Survey**						
国内生产总值	(万元)	Gross Domestic Product (10000 yuan)	500563.9	445273.8	111.3	448922.7	395423.8	113.5
第一产业		Primary Industry	100694.6	95698.0	90.1	106926.1	104575.3	102.2
第二产业		Secondary Industry	158136.5	139236.7	121.6	138131.5	117720.3	117.3
第三产业		Tertiary Industry	241732.8	210339.1	114.9	203865.1	173128.2	117.8
财政收入	(万元)	Fiscal Revenue (10000 yuan)	30319.0	23590.0		32186.0	21678.0	148.5
#增值税		Increased Value Tax						
营业税		Operating Tax	15314.0	10626.0	128.5	14122.0	9895.0	142.7
个人所得税		Private Income Tax	2444.0	1139.0	144.1	1861.0	1681.0	110.7
企业所得税		Enterprise Income Tax	6915.0	4597.0	214.6	8010.0	5089.0	157.4
财政支出	(万元)	Fiscal Expenditure (10000 yuan)	60740.0	45453.0	150.4	65975.0	47855.0	137.9
#基本建设支出		Capital Construction	1579.0	2403.0	67.7	4295.0	1480.0	290.2
支援农业生产支出		Supporting Agriculture	6417.0	5118.0	125.4	5445.0	3559.0	153.0
文教卫生事业费		Culture,Education and Health	15765.0	13534.0	116.5	20655.0	17314.0	119.3
人口和劳动力		**Population and Labor Force**						
总人口	(人)	TotalPopulation (person)	642139.0	626845.0	102.4	604800.0	601197.0	100.6
常住户籍人口	(人)	Permanent Registered Population (person)	597139.0	595890.0	100.2	523800.0	520858.0	100.6
#非农业人口		Non-agriculture	184977.0	175965.0	105.1	149240.0	143609.0	103.9
男		Male	294140.0	293806.0	100.1	82490.0	79810.0	103.4
女		Female	302999.0	301994.0	100.3	66750.0	63799.0	104.6
出生率	(‰)	BirthRate (‰)	5.4	5.6		6.2	6.7	
死亡率	(‰)	DeathRate (‰)	7.0	6.6		5.4	6.5	
自然增长率	(‰)	NaturalGrowth Rate (‰)	-1.6	-1.0		0.8	0.2	
从业人员	(人)	Employment (person)	243225.0	236243.0	103.0	253226.0	235496.0	107.5
按产业分		Grouped by Industry						
第一产业		Primary Industry	83900.0	82193.0	102.1	128073.0	124914.0	102.5
第二产业		Secondary Industry	78444.0	75495.0	103.9	53326.0	49807.0	107.1
第三产业		Tertiary Industry	80881.0	78555.0	103.0	71827.0	60775.0	118.2
按职工非职工分		Grouped by Staff and Workers or Non-staff-and-worker						
职工人数		Staff and Worker	53521.0	49320.0	108.5	60937.0	55931.0	109.0
#国有单位		State-owned	37287.0	35017.0	106.5	32576.0	35408.0	92.0
集体单位		Collective-owned	8950.0	10250.0	87.3	8826.0	9576.0	92.2
城镇个体劳动者		Urban and Rural Individuals	5101.0	3606.0	141.5	1089.0	1376.0	79.1
劳动工资		**Wages**						
工资总额	(万元)	Total Wages (10000 yuan)	51536.4	42815.0	120.4	58627.1	48963.0	119.7
#国有单位		State-owned	39481.2	31492.0	125.4	35376.8	32211.0	109.8
集体单位		Collective-owned	6025.5	6704.0	89.9	6423.1	6078.5	105.7
职工平均工资	(元)	AverageWage (yuan)	9468.0	8571.0	110.5	9659.0	8889.0	108.7
固定资产投资		**Investment in Fixed Assets (10000 yuan)**						
全社会固定资产投资	(万元)	Total Investment in Fixed Assets	61984.0	47957.1	129.2	77193.0	48979.0	157.6
按建设性质分		Grouped by Type of Construction						
#基本建设投资		Capital Construction	41747.0	34802.2	120.0	17630.0	10832.0	162.8
更新改造投资		Innovation and Replacement	20237.0	13154.9	153.8	2338.0	2753.0	84.9

21-7 续表 1 continued

项目	Item	通州区 Tongzhou 1999	1998	1999年为1998年% 1999as % of 1998	大兴县 Daxing 1999	1998	1999年为1998年% 1999 as% of 1998
按登记注册类型分	Grouped by Registered Type						
#国有单位 (万元)	State-owned (10000 yuan)	25022.0	24618.1	101.6	27267.0	37339.0	73.0
集体单位 (万元)	Collective-owned (10000 yuan)	10806.0	12644.1	85.5	2488.0	1145.0	217.3
新增固定资产 (万元)	Incremental Fixed Assets (10000 yuan)	52086.0	44085.1	118.1	63311.0	60638.0	104.4
#国有单位	State-owned	26988.0	26858.0	100.5	43305.0	44142.0	98.1
集体单位	Collective-owned	10762.0	13260.1	81.2	2038.0	1298.0	157.0
房屋施工面积 (万平方米)	Floor Space of Buildings Under Construction (10000 sq.m)	65.8	54.0	121.9	71.5	57.8	123.7
#国有单位	State-owned	28.9	29.5	98.0	38.8	35.0	110.9
集体单位	Collective-owned	9.0	16.0	66.3	2.6	1.0	260.0
房屋竣工面积 (万平方米)	Floor Space of Buildings Completed (10000 sq.m)	46.3	37.2	124.5	39.3	30.3	129.7
#国有单位	State-owned	22.6	18.0	125.6	27.6	22.3	123.8
#住宅	Residence	21.2	14.3	148.3	20.0	18.0	111.1
#集体单位	Collective-owned	8.9	13.2	67.4	2.0	1.0	200.0
#住宅	Residence	0.7	5.4	13.0	1.6	1.0	160.0
农村经济	**Rural Economy**						
农村劳动力 (人)	LaborForce (person)	184599.0	183317.0	100.7	191692.0	179112.0	107.0
种植业	Planting	69844.0	70083.0	99.7	112834.0	114804.0	98.3
林业	Forestry	2111.0	1908.0	110.6	5943.0	4387.0	135.5
牧业	Animal Husbandry	8544.0	6928.0	123.3	8105.0	4635.0	174.9
渔业	Fishery	2353.0	2233.0	105.4	539.0	507.0	106.3
农村工业	Rural Industry	44452.0	48739.0	91.2	20833.0	21621.0	96.4
农村建筑业	Rural Construction	14875.0	13114.0	113.4	6220.0	5790.0	107.4
农村运输业	Rural Transportation	12751.0	9847.0	129.5	7417.0	6112.0	121.4
农村商业、饮食业、服务业	Commerce,Catering and Services	29669.0	30465.0	97.4	7880.0	5603.0	140.6
耕地面积 (公顷)	Area under Cultivation (hectare)	4986.7	50907.7	98.0	52308.3	52435.6	99.8
农业机械总动力 (千瓦)	Total Power of Agricul-turalMachinery (kw)	381362.0	406506.0	93.8	581800.0	582000.0	100.0
化肥施用实物量 (吨)	Consumption of Chemical Fertilizers (ton)	99244.0	106457.4	93.2	109350.0	111965.3	97.7
化肥施用折纯量 (吨)	Consumption of Chemical Fertilizers(100%) (ton)	34862.0	37544.8	92.9	31870.0	34273.0	93.0
农村用电量 (万千瓦时)	Consumption of Electri-city (10000 kwh)	23762.0	19697.0	120.6	28034.2	25449.3	110.2
农村国内生产总值 (万元)	Rural Gross Domestic Pro-duct (10000 yuan)	339030.0	296195.9	114.5	334352.1	284403.2	117.6
第一产业	Primary Industry	100694.6	95698.0	105.2	106569.1	105361.6	101.1
第二产业	Secondary Industry	135203.0	116776.4	115.8	100264.3	92562.7	108.3
第三产业	Tertiary Industry	130132.5	83721.5	155.4	127518.7	84338.5	151.2
农业总产值 (万元)	Gross Output Value of Agriculture (10000 yuan)	111278.7	107585.0	103.4	141717.7	137273.6	103.2
种植业	Planting	69132.8	68137.0	101.5	97909.7	97884.1	100.0
林业	Forestry	756.1	653.0	115.8	1397.7	1314.1	106.4
牧业	Animal Husbandry	33328.4	31560.0	105.8	40476.4	36124.0	112.0
渔业	Fishery	7711.4	7235.0	106.6	1933.9	1951.4	99.1
农作物总播种面积 (万公顷)	Sown Area of Farm Crops (10000 hectare)	9.2	9.4	97.9	8.5	8.6	98.6
粮食作物	Grain	7.3	7.7	94.8	5.4	5.7	94.9
经济作物	Industrial Crops	0.2	0.2	100.0	0.4	0.4	102.6
其他作物	Other Crops	1.7	1.5	11.3	2.6	2.6	102.0

21-7 续表 2 continued

项目 Item	通州区 Tongzhou 1999	1998	1999年为1998年% 1999as % of 1998	大兴县 Daxing 1999	1998	1999年为1998年% 1999 as % of 1998
农副产品产量 Yield of Farm and Side-line Crops						
粮食 (万吨) Grain (10000 tons)	38.3	50.0	76.6	28.3	33.3	85.0
蔬菜 (吨) Vegetable (ton)	756107.0	753073.3	100.4	984891.0	928986.0	106.0
干鲜果 (吨) Dry and Fresh Fruits(ton	33065.0	30963.0	106.8	85106.0	83413.0	102.0
畜产品产量 Output of Livestock Products						
生猪出栏 (头) Slaughtered Hogs (head)	426598.0	394745.0	108.1	382075.0	354929.0	107.6
商品猪 (头) Commodity Hogs (head)		...				
猪牛羊肉 (吨) Pork,Beef and Mutton(ton)	34996.0	31102.0	112.4	28051.0	25602.0	109.6
#猪肉 Pork	31098.0	27866.0	111.6	24140.0	22371.0	107.9
禽肉 Meat of Poultry (ton)	9345.0	7191.0	130.0	15137.0	8153.0	185.7
禽蛋 PoultryEggs (ton)	14795.0	14116.0	104.8	28419.0	29220.0	97.3
牲畜年底头数 (头) Number of Livestock (year-end) (head)	352577.0	348964.0	101.0	385585.0	394363.0	97.8
大牲畜 Large Animals	14552.0	18509.0	78.6	14031.0	14353.0	97.8
猪 Hogs	245650.0	237755.0	103.3	231538.0	236121.0	98.1
羊 Goats and Sheep	92375.0	92700.0	99.6	140016.0	143889.0	97.3
水产品产量 (吨) Output of Aquatic Product (ton)	13460.0	11500.0	117.0	4634.0	4655.0	99.5
农村集体经济收入 (万元) Rural Collective Economic Revenue (10000 yuan)	444857.0	390403.0	113.9	567122.0	476974.5	118.9
农村集体经济利润总额 (万元) Total Profits of Rural Collective Economy (10000 yuan)	33010.0	27504.0	120.0	46077.7	41333.1	111.5
国家税金 State Taxes	20914.0	18246.0	114.6	19331.4	16983.4	113.8
集体积累 Collective Accumulation	15668.0	15559.0	100.7	23738.3	23017.5	103.1
劳动所得 Income from Work	45974.0	46118.0	99.7	37685.5	36772.8	102.5
乡镇企业单位数 (个) Number of Township and Village Enterprise (unit)	1920.0	2832.0	67.8	1291.0	1427.0	90.5
乡镇企业人数 (人) Number of Persons of Township and Village Enterprises (person)	91122.0	80252.0	101.8	51663.0	50457.0	102.4
乡镇企业纯利润 (万元) Net Profit of Township and Village Enterprises (10000 yuan)	17937.0	21824.0	82.2	29055.0	26842.0	108.2
乡镇企业固定资产原价 (万元) Original Value of Fixed Assets of Township and Village Enterprises (10000 yuan)	316624.0	301056.0	105.2	291097.0	206102.0	141.2
乡镇企业固定资产净值 (万元) Net Value of Fixed Assets of Township a nd Village Enterprises (10000 yuan)	224479.0	221505.0	101.3	231530.0	158248.0	146.3
工业 Industry						
全部工业企业单位数 (个) Number of Enterprises (unit)	2794.0	2507.0	111.4	2292.0	2125.0	107.9
国有 State-owned	26.0	27.0	96.3	213.0	224.0	95.1
集体 Collective-owned	2405.0	2155.0	111.6	944.0	989.0	95.4
其他 Others	363.0	325.0	111.7	1135.0	912.0	124.5
全部工业总产值 (现价,万元) Gross Output Value of Industry (at current prices, (10000 yuan)	542952.4	490163.0	110.8	577266.5	501339.9	115.1
国有 State-owned	26379.5	30840.7	85.5	38211.8	67558.8	56.6
集体 Collective-owned	379977.0	312531.0	121.6	177315.9	199660.6	88.8
其他 Others	136595.9	146791.3	93.1	361738.8	234120.5	154.5

21-7 续表 3 continued

项目	Item	通州区 Tongzhou 1999	1998	1999年为1998年% 1999 as % of 1998	大兴县 Daxing 1999	1998	1999年为1998年% 1999 as % of 1998
全部工业总产值(1990年不变价,万元)	Gross Output Value of Industry (at constant priceof 1990,10000 yuan)	529043.7	475220.0	111.3	556802.5	475030.8	117.2
国有	State-owned	21205.6	23531.4	90.1	35173.4	52625.6	66.8
集体	Collective-owned	378764.8	311451.6	121.6	177090.0	196756.7	90.0
其他	Others	129073.3	140237.0	92.0	344539.1	225648.5	152.7
全部轻工业总产值(现价,万元)	Gross Output Value of Light Industry (at current prices,10000 yuan)	321118.3	267893.5	119.9	349038.6	280854.0	124.3
以农产品为原料	Using Farm Products as Raw Materials	200413.4	167195.2	119.9	161631.1	163469.7	98.9
以非农产品为原料	Using Non-farm Products as Raw Materials	120704.9	100698.3	119.9	187407.5	117384.3	159.7
全部重工业总产值(现价,万元)	Gross Output Value of Heavy Industry (at current prices,10000 yuan)	221834.1	222269.4	99.8	228227.9	220485.9	103.5
采掘工业	Mining and Quarrying				569.0		
原料工业	Raw Materials Industry	41271.5	41352.5	99.8	45584.3	37922.0	120.2
制造工业	Manufacturing Industry	180562.6	180916.9	99.8	182074.6	181508.1	100.3
独立核算工业企业平均职工人数(人)	Average Number of Staff and Workers in Enterprises with Independent Accounting System (person)	31390.0	28184.0	111.4	55710.0	52737.0	105.6
#国有	State-owned	4300.0	5235.0	82.1	7614.0	10075.0	75.6
集体	Collective-owned	16719.0	14831.0	112.7	22927.0	24695.0	92.8
独立核算工业企业总产值(现价,万元)	Gross Output Value of Enterprises with Independent Accounting System(at current prices, 10000 yuan)	177592.3	164891.2	107.7	537739.6	493415.2	109.0
#国有	State-owned	26379.5	30840.7	85.5	38211.8	60957.3	62.7
集体	Collective-owned	66689.5	65870.4	101.2	177657.9	194409.1	91.4
独立核算工业企业工业增加值(万元)	Value Added of Enterprises with Independent Accounting system (10000 yuan)				115781.5		
独立核算工业企业财务指标	Financial Indicatorsfor Enterprises with Indepe n-dent Accounting System						
产品销售收入(万元)	SalesRevenue(10000yuan)	141736.4	134141.8	105.7	504759.6	443925.2	113.7
#国有	State-owned	19054.8	22457.3	84.8	34328.9	57839.4	59.4
产品销售成本(万元)	Cost of Sales(10000 yuan)	12583.8	106816.1	117.8	404743.1	354109.1	114.3
#国有	State-owned	23107.6	17866.6	129.3	27588.1	48096.7	57.4
固定资产原价(万元)	Original Value of Fixed Assets (10000 yuan)	162421.2	155592.7	104.4	308586.8	296713.7	104.0
#国有	State-owned	34759.3	41801.8	83.2	46586.1	66683.3	69.9
固定资产净值(万元)	Net Value of Fixed Assets (10000 yuan)	101597.1	108566.0	93.6	221878.6	227289.7	97.6
#国有	State-owned	21587.2	29624.2	72.9	22821.7	51577.6	44.2
全部流动资金年平均余额(万元)	Annual Average Balance of Circulating Funds (10000 yuan)	146913.3	154314.9	95.2	342543.6	327202.0	104.7
#国有	State-owned	25541.1	28161.1	90.7	37927.0	52205.1	72.6
利润总额(万元)	Total Profits (10000 yuan)	-6170.3	476.2		23717.6	14932.7	158.8
#国有	State-owned	-834.5	-15.0		803.1	-105.1	

21-7 续表 4 continued

项目 Item		通州区 Tongzhou 1999	1998	1999年为1998年% 1999as % of 1998	大兴县 Daxing 1999	1998	1999年为1998年% 1999 as % of 1998
资金利税率 (%)	Ratio of Pre-tax Profits to Total of Capital (%)	1.9	2.4		8.7	5.9	
产品销售率 (%)	Ratio of Sales Value to Gross Output Value (%)	105.5	90.7		93.6	91.5	
增加值率 (%)	Ratio of Added Value to Gross Output Value (%)	21.2	39.1		18.9	14.2	
独立核算工业企业全员劳动生产率 (元/人)	Overall Labor Productivity of Enterprises with Independent Accounting System (yuan/person)	14835.9	15973.0	92.9	20782.7	18130.0	114.6
#国有	State-owned	12981.1	13976.0	92.9			
集体	Collective-owned	14486.7	15597.0	92.9			
商业	**Commerce**						
社会消费品零售额 (万元)	Retail Sales of Consumer Goods (10000 yuan)	330069.0	319921.0	103.2	263515.0	242154.0	108.8
按登记注册类型分	Grouped by Registered Type						
国有	State-owned	30002.7	30728.0	97.6	64845.0	59111.0	109.7
集体	Collective-owned	44011.0	43089.0	102.1	36384.0	34612.0	105.1
其他	Others	256055.3	246104.0	104.0	162286.0	148431.0	109.3
按类别分	Grouped by Type of Goods						
吃的商品 (万元)	Food (10000 yuan)	166025.0	161165.0	103.0	122959.0	119370.0	103.0
穿的商品 (万元)	Clothing (10000 yuan)	23765.0	22900.0	103.8	27666.0	27244.0	101.5
用的商品 (万元)	Daily Used Articles (10000 yuan)	134008.0	129971.0	103.1	86329.0	76544.0	112.8
烧的商品 (万元)	Fuel (10000 yuan)	6271.0	5885.0	106.6	19212.0	14015.0	137.1
网点数 (个)	NumberoOutlets (unit)	12924.0	11709.0	110.4	13119.0	14329.0	91.6
#商业	Wholesale and Retail	9839.0	8322.0	118.2	9757.0	11531.0	84.6
饮食业	Catering	1658.0	1528.0	108.2	1565.0	1498.0	104.5
服务业	Services	674.0	727.0	92.7	1797.0	1300.0	138.2
#宾馆、饭店	Hotels	2.0	2.0	100.0	2.0	2.0	100.0
营业人员 (人)	Personnel (person)	26362.0	24921.0	105.8	25755.0	27355.0	94.2
#商业	Wholesale and Retail	19089.0	17818.0	107.1	19034.0	20634.0	92.2
饮食业	Catering	4013.0	3975.0	101.0	4076.0	4273.0	95.4
服务业	Services	1519.0	1438.0	105.6	2645.0	2448.0	108.0
#宾馆、饭店	Hotels	622.0	612.0	101.6	564.0	564.0	100.0
外经、外贸	**Foreign Economy and Trade**						
出口商品交货额 (万元)	Delivery Value of Exports (10000 yuan)	60400.3	50612.4	119.3	62948.6	46317.5	135.9
利用外资签订协议(合同)数 (个)	Number of Signed Agreements and Contracts of Foreign Capital to be Utilized (unit)	28.0	34.0	82.4	35.0	34.0	102.9
利用外资签订协议(合同)金额 (万美元)	Amount of Foreign Capital to be Utilized through Agreements and Contracts (USD 10000)	1954.2	2026.9	96.4	1918.6	1297.8	147.8
实际利用外资 (万美元)	Amount of Foreign Capital Actually Used (USD 10000)	4503.0	4123.1	109.2	2948.4	2303.5	128.0
旅游人数 (万人)	Number of Tourists (10000 persons)	133.5	158.2	84.4	71.0	63.9	111.1
教育	**Education**						
学校数 (个)	NumberofSchools (unit)	208.0	222.0	93.7	192.0	256.0	75.0
小学	Primary Schools	162.0	175.0	92.6	192.0	205.0	93.7

21-7 续表 5 continued

项目 Item		通州区 Tongzhou 1999	1998	1999年为1998年% 1999 as % of 1998	大兴县 Daxing 1999	1998	1999年为1998年% 1999 as % of 1998
普通中学	Regular Secondary School	42.0	43.0	97.7	52.0	51.0	102.0
中等专业教育	Specialized Secondary Schools	4.0	4.0	100.0	1.0	1.0	100.0
招生数 (人)	New Student Enrollment (person)	19551.0	18718.0	104.5	22468.0	21702.0	103.5
小学	Primary Schools	5959.0	6805.0	87.6	5839.0	6469.0	90.3
初级中等学校	Junior Secondary Schools	10524.0	8882.0	118.5	12827.0	10400.0	123.3
高级中等学校	Senior Secondary Schools	2276.0	1923.0	118.4	3621.0	4280.0	84.6
中等专业教育	Specialized Secondary Schools	792.0	1108.0	71.5	181.0	553.0	32.7
在校学生 (人)	Student Enrollment (person)	96553.0	100928.0	95.7	102842.0	106833.0	96.3
小学	Primary Schools	60650.0	65806.0	92.2	58805.0	66082.0	89.0
初级中等学校	Junior Secondary Schools	27533.0	27481.0	100.2	31851.0	28433.0	112.0
高级中等学校	Senior Secondary Schools	5840.0	5042.0	115.8	11271.0	10828.0	104.1
中等专业教育	Specialized Secondary Schools	2530.0	2599.0	97.3	915.0	1490.0	61.4
毕业生 (人)	Graduates (person)	23373.0	23468.0	99.6	24242.0	22446.0	108.0
小学	Primary Schools	11014.0	9219.0	119.5	13020.0	10734.0	121.3
初级中等学校	Junior Secondary Schools	9975.0	11910.0	83.8	8176.0	8620.0	94.8
高级中等学校	Senior Secondary Schools	1537.0	1492.0	103.0	2775.0	2554.0	108.7
中等专业教育	Specialized Secondary Schools	847.0	847.0	100.0	271.0	538.0	50.4
达到"国家体育标准"学生数 (人)	Number of Students Come to the Standard for State Physical Training (person)	98509.0	100456.0	98.1			
幼儿园、托儿所个数 (个)	Number of Kindergartens (unit)	141.0	189.0	74.6	222.0	207.0	107.2
幼儿入托数 (人)	NewEnrollment (person)	16478.0	20598.0	80.0	4635.0	6357.0	72.9
文化	**Culture**						
文化馆、站 (个)	CulturalCenters (unit)	23.0	19.0	121.0	22.0	22.0	100.0
公共图书馆 (个)	PublicLibraries (unit)	1.0	1.0	100.0	1.0	1.0	100.0
公共图书馆藏书 (万册)	Collection (10000 volume)	15.0	15.0	100.0	10.9	11.0	99.1
电影放映单位 (个)	Film Projection Units (unit)	19.0	26.0	73.1	21.0	21.0	100.0
区级以上重点文物保护单位 (个)	Cultural Relics Preserved at District Level and above (unit)	28.0	25.0	112.0	15.0	15.0	100.0
卫生	**Health**						
卫生机构数 (个)	Number of Health Institutions (unit)	171.0	149.0	114.8	45.0	46.0	97.8
#医院	Hospitals	11.0	11.0	100.0	11.0	11.0	100.0
卫生院	Clinics	16.0	16.0	100.0	27.0	28.0	96.4
床位数	NumberofBeds (unit)	1987.0	1920.0	103.5	2077.0	1942.0	107.0
#医院	Hospitals	1603.0	1526.0	105.0	1410.0	1306.0	108.0
卫生院	Clinics	365.0	375.0	97.3	647.0	616.0	105.0
平均每千人拥有床位数 (张)	Average Number of Beds Per1000Persons (unit)	3.3	3.2	103.1	4.0	3.7	108.1
卫生技术人员 (人)	Medical Technical Personnel (person)	2954.0	2883.0	102.5	2495.0	2450.0	101.8
#医生	Doctors (person)	1467.0	1421.0	103.2	1236.0	951.0	130.0
公用设施	**Public Utilities**						
区级以上公园 (个)	Parks at District Level andAbove (unit)	1.0	1.0	100.0	2.0	2.0	100.0
体育场馆 (个)	Stadiums and Gymnasiums (unit)	1.0	1.0	100.0	2.0	2.0	100.0
道路长度 (公里)	LengthofRoads (km)	1722.7	1719.4	100.2	1390.0	1370.0	101.5

21-8 平谷县、怀柔县国民经济主要指标
MAIN NATIONAL ECONOMIC INDICATORS FOR PINGGU AND HUAIROU COUNTIES

项目	Item	平谷县 Pinggu 1999	1998	1999年为1998年% 1999 as % of 1998	怀柔县 Huairou 1999	1998	1999年为1998年% 1999 as % of 1998
综合	**General Survey**						
国内生产总值 (万元)	Gross Domestic Product (10000 yuan)	299446.6	269820.4	111.0	339925.3	295864.3	114.9
第一产业	Primary Industry	75616.0	75290.8	100.4	37609.0	36680.5	102.5
第二产业	Secondary Industry	119049.7	98445.9	120.9	185608.8	153884.5	120.6
第三产业	Tertiary Industry	104780.9	96083.7	109.1	116707.5	105299.3	110.8
财政收入 (万元)	Fiscal Revenue (10000 yuan)	17625.0	10711.0	164.6	24232.0	17334.0	139.8
#增值税	Increased Value Tax						
营业税	Operating Tax	13408.0	6533.0	205.2	14532.0	8573.0	169.5
个人所得税	Private Income Tax	1301.0	777.0	167.4	1889.0	1398.0	135.1
企业所得税	Enterprise Income Tax	14313.0	6962.0	205.6	4469.0	3917.0	114.1
财政支出 (万元)	Fiscal Expenditure (10000 yuan)	66489.0	50102.0	132.7	81827.0	64911.0	126.1
#基本建设支出	Capital Construction	3153.0	2146.0	146.9	4036.0	2560.0	157.7
支援农业生产支出	Supporting Agriculture	4475.0	4503.0	99.4	7901.0	6552.0	120.6
文教卫生事业费	Culture,Education and Health	14896.0	13084.0	113.8	16393.0	13345.0	122.8
人口和劳动力	**Population and Labor Force**						
总人口 (人)	Total Population (person)	398565.0	395967.0	100.7	265215.0	264539.0	100.3
常住户籍人口 (人)	Permanent Registered Population (person)	389092.0	388767.0	100.1	262699.0	262222.0	100.2
#非农业人口	Non-agriculture	92981.0	89162.0	104.3	78160.0	75320.0	103.8
男	Male	48740.0	47005.0	103.7	133225.0	134570.0	99.0
女	Female	44241.0	42157.0	104.9	129474.0	127652.0	101.4
出生率 (‰)	Birth Rate (‰)	6.1	5.6		7.1	7.4	
死亡率 (‰)	Death Rate (‰)	4.8	5.6		6.1	8.5	
自然增长率 (‰)	Natural Growth Rate (‰)	1.3	0.1		1.0	-1.1	
从业人员 (人)	Employment (person)	202063.0	193881.0	104.2	140403.0	139774.0	100.5
按产业分	Grouped by Industry						
第一产业	Primary Industry	80395.0	71816.0	111.9	36860.0	35540.0	103.7
第二产业	Secondary Industry	66621.0	66025.0	100.9	52080.0	53804.0	96.8
第三产业	Tertiary Industry	55047.0	56040.0	98.2	51463.0	50430.0	102.0
按职工非职工分	Grouped by Staff and Workers or Non-staff-and-worker						
职工人数	Staff and Worker	47013.0	47370.0	99.2	34597.0	39872.0	86.8
#国有单位	State-owned	37017.0	38023.0	97.4	19896.0	20291.0	98.1
集体单位	Collective-owned	3327.0	2650.0	125.5	5562.0	8962.0	62.1
城镇个体劳动者	Urban and Rural Individuals	9745.0	9409.0	103.6	16600.0	14328.0	115.9
劳动工资	**Wages**						
工资总额 (万元)	Total Wages (10000 yuan)	42106.1	39321.7	107.1	40014.2	39463.3	101.4
#国有单位	State-owned	35213.7	33122.2	106.3	22916.5	20267.0	113.1
集体单位	Collective-owned	1015.4	853.4	119.0	4747.0	6642.3	71.5
职工平均工资 (元)	Average Wage (yuan)	8889.0	8134.0	109.3	11472.0	9710.0	118.1
固定资产投资	**Investment in Fixed Assets Assets (10000 yuan)**						
全社会固定资产投资 (万元)	Total Investment in Fixed Assets	38895.0	34124.0	114.0	94688.0	100649.0	94.1
按建设性质分	Grouped by Type of Construction						
#基本建设投资	Capital Construction	12931.0	25878.0	50.0	31450.0	89623.0	35.1
更新改造投资	Innovation and Replacement	7092.0	1530.0	463.5	37362.0	8540.0	437.5

21-8 续表 1 continued

项目 Item		平谷县 Pinggu 1999	1998	1999年为1998年% 1999 as % of 1998	怀柔县 Huairou 1999	1998	1999年为1998年% 1999 as % of 1998
按登记注册类型分	Grouped by Registered Type						
#国有单位 (万元)	State-owned (10000 yuan)	15991.0	11585.0	138.0	24464.0	21766.0	112.4
集体单位 (万元)	Collective-owned (10000 yuan)	18172.0	11273.0	161.2	29600.0	40876.0	72.4
新增固定资产 (万元)	Incremental Fixed Assets (10000 yuan)	34854.0	29870.0	116.7	72584.0	64799.0	112.0
#国有单位	State-owned	13723.0	15206.0	90.2	24649.0	22636.0	108.9
集体单位	Collective-owned	17099.0	10572.0	161.7	36051.0	36487.0	98.8
房屋施工面积 (万平方米)	Floor Space of Buildings Under Construction (10000 sq.m)	53.8	43.6	123.4	67.9	64.1	105.9
#国有单位	State-owned	20.3	20.0	101.5	26.9	19.6	137.2
集体单位	Collective-owned	15.5	13.0	119.2	29.1	37.0	78.6
房屋竣工面积 (万平方米)	Floor Space of Buildings Completed (10000 sq.m)	39.2	34.6	113.3	41.1	32.6	126.1
#国有单位	State-owned	8.6	16.0	53.8	15.6	11.9	131.1
#住宅	Residence	5.4	13.0	41.5	7.8	8.2	95.1
#集体单位	Collective-owned	12.8	9.0	142.2	18.9	19.2	98.4
#住宅	Residence	5.7	5.0	114.0	12.2	9.7	125.8
农村经济	**Rural Economy**						
农村劳动力 (人)	Labor Force (person)	149169.0	139513.0	106.9	81752.0	81135.0	100.8
种植业	Planting	67947.0	62818.0	108.2	25445.0	24636.0	103.3
林业	Forestry	2717.0	2034.0	133.6	7796.0	7215.0	108.1
牧业	Animal Husbandry	6310.0	4372.0	144.3	2759.0	2892.0	95.4
渔业	Fishery	2261.0	1963.0	115.2	330.0	349.0	94.6
农村工业	Rural Industry	32263.0	32182.0	100.3	11938.0	13121.0	91.0
农村建筑业	Rural Construction	13427.0	11987.0	112.0	5950.0	5949.0	100.0
农村运输业	Rural Transportation	6099.0	4620.0	132.0	5659.0	5310.0	106.6
农村商、饮食业、服务业	Commerce,Catering and Services	18145.0	19537.0	92.9	5470.0	5070.0	107.9
耕地面积 (公顷)	Area under Cultivation (hectare)	19063.1	19117.3	99.7	15101.9	15403.4	98.0
农业机械总动力 (千瓦)	Total Power of Agricultural Machinery (kw)	336108.0	341630.0	98.4	211088.0	210753.0	100.2
化肥施用实物量 (吨)	Consumption of Chemical Fertilizers (ton)	63298.0	60500.0	104.6	20650.0	21937.4	94.1
化肥施用折纯量 (吨)	Consumption of Chemical Fertilizers(100%) (ton)	19340.0	19108.0	101.2	8330.0	8861.2	94.0
农村用电量 (万千瓦时)	Consumption of Electricity (10000 kwh)	18240.5	17821.4	102.4	14919.9	14416.7	103.5
农村国内生产总值 (万元)	Rural Gross Domestic Product (10000 yuan)	197358.5	165541.6	119.2	210774.0	190303.7	110.8
第一产业	Primary Industry	58828.5	61365.0	95.9	37609.0	36680.5	102.5
第二产业	Secondary Industry	88214.8	58017.1	152.0	107150.7	92355.1	116.0
第三产业	Tertiary Industry	50315.2	46159.5	109.0	66014.3	61268.1	107.7
农业总产值 (万元)	Gross Output Value of Agriculture (10000 yuan)	84212.4	81502.7	103.3	46048.0	43602.9	105.6
种植业	Planting	47653.2	44808.8	106.3	21223.3	21355.7	99.4
林业	Forestry	1167.5	1371.8	85.1	3910.8	3885.7	100.6
牧业	Animal Husbandry	28012.6	28236.1	99.2	18059.0	17086.5	105.7
渔业	Fishery	7379.1	7086.0	104.1	2854.9	1275.0	223.9
农作物总播种面积 (万公顷)	Sown Area of Farm Crops (10000 hectare)	3.4	3.5	97.1	2.3	2.4	97.9
粮食作物	Grain	2.6	2.7	96.3	2.0	2.1	95.7
经济作物	Industrial Crops	0.1	0.1	100.0	0.1	0.1	142.9
其他作物	Other Crops	0.7	0.7	100.0	0.2	0.2	105.3

21-8 续表 2 continued

项目 Item		平谷县 Pinggu 1999	1998	1999年为1998年% 1999 as % of 1998	怀柔县 Huairou 1999	1998	1999年为1998年% 1999 as % of 1998
农副产品产量	Yield of Farm and Sideline Crops						
粮食 (万吨)	Grain (10000 tons)	10.9	15.6	69.9	11.3	13.3	85.0
蔬菜 (吨)	Vegetable (ton)	330697.0	296576.0	111.5	51183.0	50341.0	101.7
干鲜果 (吨)	Dry and Fresh Fruits (ton)	146911.0	146147.0	100.5	47915.0	46178.9	103.8
畜产品产量	Output of Livestock Products						
生猪出栏 (头)	Slaughtered Hogs (head)	248650.0	228547.0	108.8	192760.0	192098.0	100.3
商品猪 (头)	Commodity Hogs (head)				188900.0	176730.0	106.9
猪牛羊肉 (吨)	Pork,Beef and Mutton (ton)	18182.0	17173.0	105.9	15089.0	15725.0	96.0
#猪肉	Pork	15681.0	14550.0	107.8	13425.0	14152.0	94.9
禽肉	Meat of Poultry (ton)	6811.0	5777.0	117.9	6283.0	4805.0	130.8
禽蛋	Poultry Eggs (ton)	20953.0	28423.0	73.7	6749.0	8625.0	78.2
牲畜年底头数 (头)	Number of Livestock (year-end) (head)	223678.0	222042.0	100.7	159536.0	176516.0	90.4
大牲畜	Large Animals	9775.0	11089.0	88.2	15006.0	15111.0	99.3
猪	Hogs	165904.0	161681.0	102.6	109864.0	123481.0	89.0
羊	Goats and Sheep	47999.0	49272.0	97.4	34666.0	37924.0	91.4
水产品产量 (吨)	Output of Aquatic Product (ton)	13997.0	15449.0	90.6	2004.0	1602.0	125.1
农村集体经济收入 (万元)	Rural Collective Economic Revenue (10000 yuan)	388082.0	288232.4	134.6	564756.0	538575.0	104.9
农村集体经济利润总额 (万元)	Total Profits of Rural Collective Economy (10000 yuan)	25504.0	12102.8	210.7	34764.0	30495.0	114.0
国家税金	State Taxes	21375.0	13797.3	154.9	28304.0	25108.0	112.7
集体积累	Collective Accumulation	9303.0	4470.4	208.1	12387.0	13033.0	95.0
劳动所得	Income from Work	20116.3	21309.6	94.4	79091.0	71882.0	110.0
乡镇企业单位数 (个)	Number of Township and Village Enterprise (unit)	818.0	798.0	102.5	731.0	730.0	100.1
乡镇企业人数 (人)	Number of Persons of Township and Village Enterprises (person)	49933.0	50848.0	98.2	42203.0	39553.0	106.7
乡镇企业纯利润 (万元)	Net Profit of Township and Village Enterprises (10000 yuan)	25217.0	12846.0	196.3	35859.0	27900.0	128.5
乡镇企业固定资产原价 (万元)	Original Value of Fixed Assets of Township and Village Enterprises (10000 yuan)	186814.0	163041.0	114.6	183204.0	171430.0	106.9
乡镇企业固定资产净值 (万元)	Net Value of Fixed Assets of Township and Village Enterprises (10000 yuan)	121257.0	124882.0	97.1	145524.0	139661.0	104.2
工业	**Industry**						
全部工业企业单位数 (个)	Number of Enterprises (unit)	523.0	520.0	100.6	652.0	679.0	96.0
国有	State-owned	65.0	68.0	95.6	57.0	55.0	103.6
集体	Collective-owned	357.0	360.0	99.2	426.0	464.0	91.8
其他	Others	101.0	92.0	109.8	169.0	160.0	105.6
全部工业总产值 (现价,万元)	Gross Output Value of Industry (at current prices,10000 yuan)	428418.1	354763.5	120.8	874521.0	815513.7	107.2
国有	State-owned	45284.4	52114.1	86.9	41976.0	42896.6	97.9
集体	Collective-owned	142105.9	127341.1	111.6	211291.0	361774.8	58.4
其他	Others	241027.8	175308.3	137.5	521254.0	410842.3	126.9

21-8 续表 3 continued

项目 Item		平谷县 Pinggu 1999	1998	1999年为1998年% 1999 as % of 1998	怀柔县 Huairou 1999	1998	1999年为1998年% 1999 as % of 1998
全部工业总产值(1990年不变价,万元)	Gross Output Value of Industry (at constant price of 1990,10000yuan)	430112.0	345031.9	124.7	890122.0	832997.7	106.9
国有	State-owned	58300.6	58064.2	100.4	43899.0	44642.0	98.3
集体	Collective-owned	140757.0	125124.2	112.5	269396.0	351073.8	76.7
其他	Others	231054.4	161843.5	142.8	576827.0	437281.9	131.9
全部轻工业总产值(现价,万元)	Gross Output Value of Light Industry (at current prices,10000 yuan)	295947.3	218513.2	135.4	549344.0	542605.2	101.2
以农产品为原料	Using Farm Products as Raw Materials	179397.9	181586.5	98.8	358762.0	366797.2	97.8
以非农产品为原料	Using Non-farm Products as Raw Materials	116549.4	36926.7	315.6	190582.0	175808.0	108.4
全部重工业总产值(现价,万元)	Gross Output Value of Heavy Industry (at current prices,10000 yuan)	132470.8	136250.3	97.2	340778.0	270885.8	125.8
采掘工业	Mining and Quarrying	1305.2	4114.2	31.7	20567.0	25167.4	81.7
原料工业	Raw Materials Industry	14817.9	14512.8	102.1	38974.0	36229.0	107.6
制造工业	Manufacturing Industry	116347.7	117623.3	98.9	281237.0	209912.1	134.0
独立核算工业企业平均职工人数 (人)	Average Number of Staff and Workers in Enterprises with Independent Accounting System (person)	45248.0	47126.0	96.0	38038.0	42738.0	89.0
#国有	State-owned	5593.0	6340.0	88.2	3296.0	4344.0	75.9
集体	Collective-owned	23727.0	23048.0	102.9	23932.0	23923.0	100.0
独立核算工业企业总产值(现价,万元)	Gross Output Value of Enterprises with Independent Accounting System(at current prices, 10000 yuan)	427133.9	349342.7	122.3	869521.0	808513.7	107.5
#国有	State-owned	44295.0	47338.5	93.6	41976.0	35896.6	116.9
集体	Collective-owned	141879.1	126695.9	112.0	309291.0	361774.8	85.5
独立核算工业企业工业增加值 (万元)	Value Added of Enterprises with Independent Accounting system (10000 yuan)	115906.7	105161.4	110.2	151520.2	121597.2	124.6
独立核算工业企业财务指标	Financial Indicators for Enterprises with Independent Accounting System						
产品销售收入 (万元)	Sales Revenue (10000yuan)	364933.7	296550.1	123.1	771836.4	711525.3	108.5
#国有	State-owned	37997.8	38947.2	97.6	29565.8	28454.9	103.9
产品销售成本 (万元)	Cost of Sales (10000 yuan)	290865.0	239318.7	121.5	61593.0	572783.8	10.8
#国有	State-owned	32290.4	30579.6	105.6	27192.6	29173.1	93.2
固定资产原价 (万元)	Original Value of Fixed Assets (10000 yuan)	295045.6	292280.3	100.9	329419.5	332268.4	99.1
#国有	State-owned	27999.6	35624.4	78.6	27292.4	24880.7	109.7
固定资产净值 (万元)	Net Value of Fixed Assets (10000 yuan)	229436.6	232576.4	98.6	302736.3	305385.0	99.1
#国有	State-owned	18136.3	23354.0	77.7	21201.4	20392.1	104.0
全部流动资金年平均余额 (万元)	Annual Average Balance of Circulating Funds (10000 yuan)	258437.6	237237.3	108.9	391469.5	383435.2	102.1
#国有	State-owned	28435.2	34093.6	83.4	27921.0	29260.5	95.4
利润总额 (万元)	Total Profits (10000 yuan)	20847.3	10746.4	194.0	33967.5	17831.8	190.5
#国有	State-owned	700.0	1809.7	38.7	348.1	-1096.6	

21-8 续表 4 continued

项目	Item	平谷县 Pinggu 1999	1998	1999年为1998年% 1999 as % of 1998	怀柔县 Huairou 1999	1998	1999年为1998年% 1999 as % of 1998
资金利税率 (%)	Ratio of Pre-tax Profits to Total of Capital (%)	8.0	5.6		11.6	7.1	
产品销售率 (%)	Ratio of Sales Value to Gross Output Value (%)	90.3	93.6		97.6	96.8	
增加值率 (%)	Ratio of Added Value to Gross Output Value (%)	26.2	29.1		16.3	15.0	
独立核算工业企业全员劳动生产率 (元/人)	Overall Labor Productivity of Enterprises with Independent Accounting System (yuan/person)	25616.0	22315.0	114.8	234009.0	191555.0	122.2
#国有	State-owned	27223.0	29198.0	93.2	158537.0	111105.4	142.7
集体	Collective-owned	12132.0	14389.0	84.3	142515.0	143006.0	99.7
商业	**Commerce**						
社会消费品零售额 (万元)	Retail Sales of Consumer Goods (10000 yuan)	128418.0	121958.9	105.3	137223.0	128162.0	107.1
按登记注册类型分	Grouped by Registered Type						
国有	State-owned	37241.0	35915.2	103.7	31073.0	32345.0	96.1
集体	Collective-owned	17979.0	16950.7	106.1	45044.0	39959.0	112.7
其他	Others	73198.0	69093.0	105.9	61106.0	55858.0	109.4
按类别分	Grouped by Type of Goods						
吃的商品 (万元)	Food (10000 yuan)	44004.0	39911.4	110.3	49861.0	35962.0	138.6
穿的商品 (万元)	Clothing (10000 yuan)	23629.0	30855.6	76.6	23915.0	23407.0	102.2
用的商品 (万元)	Daily Used Articles (10000 yuan)	49099.0	40288.7	121.9	61265.0	63162.0	97.0
烧的商品 (万元)	Fuel (10000 yuan)	11686.0	10903.2	107.2	2182.0	5631.0	38.7
网点数 (个)	Number of Outlets (unit)	7595.0	7286.0	104.2	9335.0	8065.0	115.7
#商业	Wholesale and Retail	4277.0	3897.0	109.8	6531.0	5824.0	112.1
饮食业	Catering	462.0	706.0	65.4	1354.0	788.0	171.8
服务业	Services	1033.0	710.0	145.5	1450.0	1453.0	99.8
#宾馆、饭店	Hotels	23.0	21.0	109.5	30.0	31.0	96.8
营业人员 (人)	Personnel (person)	14869.0	14898.0	99.8	18207.0	18050.0	100.9
#商业	Wholesale and Retail	8783.0	8349.0	105.2	12882.0	12659.0	101.8
饮食业	Catering	1500.0	1186.0	126.5	3215.0	2722.0	118.1
服务业	Services	1431.0	999.0	143.2	2110.0	2669.0	79.1
#宾馆、饭店	Hotels	1383.0	1340.0	103.2	984.0	801.0	122.8
外经、外贸	**Foreign Economy and Trade**						
出口商品交货额 (万元)	Delivery Value of Exports (10000 yuan)	76470.4	75668.8	101.1	37120.6	32266.8	115.0
利用外资签订协议(合同)数 (个)	Number of Signed Agreements and Contracts of Foreign Capital to be Utilized (unit)	27.0	21.0	128.6	20.0	6.0	333.3
利用外资签订协议(合同)金额 (万美元)	Amount of Foreign Capital to be Utilized through Agreements and Contracts (USD 10000)	2781.8	2177.1	127.8	1622.0	3200.0	50.7
实际利用外资 (万美元)	Amount of Foreign Capital Actually Used (USD 10000)	246.5	2725.0	9.0	3075.4	1486.5	206.9
旅游人数 (万人)	Number of Tourists (10000 persons)	281.0	261.6	107.4	554.2	500.2	110.8
教育	**Education**						
学校数 (个)	Number of Schools (unit)	208.0	221.0	94.1	123.0	145.0	84.8
小学	Primary Schools	172.0	186.0	92.5	97.0	109.0	89.0

21-8 续表 5 continued

项目	Item	平谷县 Pinggu 1999	平谷县 Pinggu 1998	平谷县 Pinggu 1999年为1998年% 1999 as % of 1998	怀柔县 Huairou 1999	怀柔县 Huairou 1998	怀柔县 Huairou 1999年为1998年% 1999 as % of 1998
普通中学	Regular Secondary School	35.0	34.0	102.9	21.0	30.0	70.0
中等专业教育	Specialized Secondary Schools	1.0	1.0	100.0	1.0	1.0	100.0
招生数 (人)	New Student Enrollment (person)	17977.0	16107.0	111.6	11141.0	10798.0	103.2
小学	Primary Schools	4804.0	5043.0	95.3	3139.0	3304.0	95.0
初级中等学校	Junior Secondary Schools	10572.0	8443.0	125.2	5010.0	4749.0	105.5
高级中等学校	Senior Secondary Schools	2601.0	2541.0	102.4	1147.0	1174.0	97.7
中等专业教育	Specialized Secondary Schools		80.0		40.0	30.0	133.3
在校学生 (人)	Student Enrollment (person)	80458.0	83449.0	96.4	45809.0	45792.0	100.0
小学	Primary Schools	47575.0	53924.0	88.2	23781.0	25191.0	94.4
初级中等学校	Junior Secondary Schools	25343.0	22487.0	112.7	14020.0	13280.0	105.6
高级中等学校	Senior Secondary Schools	7350.0	6688.0	109.9	3434.0	3226.0	106.4
中等专业教育	Specialized Secondary Schools	190.0	350.0	54.3	113.0	158.0	71.5
毕业生 (人)	Graduates (person)	20378.0	18387.0	110.8	11716.0	11823.0	99.1
小学	Primary Schools	10862.0	8575.0	126.7	5070.0	4827.0	105.0
初级中等学校	Junior Secondary Schools	7260.0	7473.0	97.1	4151.0	4857.0	85.5
高级中等学校	Senior Secondary Schools	2096.0	2177.0	96.3	929.0	874.0	106.3
中等专业教育	Specialized Secondary Schools	160.0	162.0	98.8	39.0	175.0	22.3
达到"国家体育标准"学生数 (人)	Number of Students Come to the Standard for State Physical Training (person)	76218.0	61442.0	124.0	43749.0	33476.0	130.7
幼儿园、托儿所个数 (个)	Number of Kindergardens (unit)	211.0	320.0	65.9	100.0	138.0	72.5
幼儿入托数 (人)	New Enrollment (person)	11656.0	12019.0	97.0	5456.0	5791.0	94.2
文化	**Culture**						
文化馆、站 (个)	Cultural Centers (unit)	22.0	22.0	100.0	15.0	15.0	100.0
公共图书馆 (个)	Public Libraries (unit)	1.0	1.0	100.0	1.0	1.0	100.0
公共图书馆藏书 (万册)	Collection (10000 volume)	12.0	13.4	89.6	11.0	11.0	100.0
电影放映单位 (个)	Film Projection Units (unit)	12.0	11.0	109.1	30.0	51.0	58.8
区级以上重点文物保护单位 (个)	Cultural Relics Preserved at District Level and above (unit)	18.0	20.0	90.0	14.0	14.0	100.0
卫生	**Health**						
卫生机构数 (个)	Number of Health Institutions (unit)	76.0	75.0	101.3	440.0	429.0	102.6
#医院	Hospitals	6.0	5.0	120.0	9.0	9.0	100.0
卫生院	Clinics	20.0	20.0	100.0	11.0	11.0	100.0
床位数	Number of Beds (unit)	960.0	1029.0	93.3	1034.0	893.0	115.8
#医院	Hospitals	676.0	670.0	100.9	961.0	844.0	113.9
卫生院	Clinics	259.0	279.0	92.8	73.0	49.0	149.0
平均每千人拥有床位数 (张)	Average Number of Beds Per 1000 Persons (unit)	2.5	2.6	96.2	3.9	3.4	114.7
卫生技术人员 (人)	Medical Technical Personnel (person)	1804.0	1801.0	100.2	1441.0	1671.0	86.2
#医生	Doctors (person)	910.0	865.0	105.2	774.0	753.0	102.8
公用设施	**Public Utilities**						
区级以上公园 (个)	Parks at District Level and Above (unit)	1.0	1.0	100.0	8.0	8.0	100.0
体育场馆 (个)	Stadiums and Gymnasiums (unit)	1.0	1.0	100.0	4.0	4.0	100.0
道路长度 (公里)	Length of Roads (km)	841.1	830.5	101.3	1153.8	1152.0	100.2

21-9 密云县、延庆县国民经济主要指标
MAIN NATIONAL ECONOMIC INDICATORS FOR MIYUN AND YANQING COUNTIES

项目		Item	密云县 Miyun 1999	1998	1999年为1998年% 1999 as % of 1998	延庆县 Yanqing 1999	1998	1999年为1998年% 1999 as % of 1998
综合		**General Survey**						
国内生产总值	(万元)	Gross Domestic Product (10000 yuan)	290550.4	259975.9	111.8	197936.7	166680.8	118.7
第一产业		Primary Industry	60704.9	60308.2	100.7	72968.4	69688.7	104.7
第二产业		Secondary Industry	126224.6	90581.4	139.3	60417.5	43029.9	140.4
第三产业		Tertiary Industry	103620.9	109086.3	95.0	64550.8	53962.2	119.6
财政收入	(万元)	Fiscal Revenue (10000 yuan)	19083.0	10480.0	182.1	19401.0	14990.0	129.4
#增值税		Increased Value Tax				11903.0	9335.0	127.5
营业税		Operating Tax	10262.0	6416.0	159.9	6785.0	4696.0	144.5
个人所得税		Private Income Tax	1280.0	525.0	243.8	923.0	462.0	199.8
企业所得税		Enterprise Income Tax	9503.0	2525.0	376.4	5457.0	2681.0	204.0
财政支出	(万元)	Fiscal Expenditure (10000 yuan)	84148.0	48768.0	172.5	52688.0	41678.0	126.4
#基本建设支出		Capital Construction	2151.0	1449.0	148.4	1070.0	1231.0	86.9
支援农业生产支出		Supporting Agriculture	10082.0	5993.0	168.2	3365.0	3074.0	109.5
文教卫生事业费		Culture,Education and Health	17091.0	14145.0	120.8	14704.0	12410.0	118.5
人口和劳动力		**Population and Labor Force**						
总人口	(人)	Total Population (person)	430711.0	431654.0	99.8	271790.0	272017.0	99.9
常住户籍人口	(人)	Permanent Registered Population (person)	425495.0	425476.0	100.0	269252.0	269327.0	99.9
#非农业人口		Non-agriculture	96609.0	89216.0	108.3	57836.0	56143.0	103.0
男		Male	214232.0	214351.0	99.9	138040.0	138435.0	99.7
女		Female	211263.0	211125.0	101.5	133750.0	133582.0	100.1
出生率	(‰)	Birth Rate (‰)	8.8	8.4		14.0	13.4	
死亡率	(‰)	Death Rate (‰)	7.7	3.9		7.0	7.0	
自然增长率	(‰)	Natural Growth Rate (‰)	1.1	4.5		7.0	6.3	
从业人员	(人)	Employment (person)	213025.0	210987.0	101.0	129851.0	121446.0	106.6
按产业分		Grouped by Industry						
第一产业		Primary Industry	80096.0	72087.0	111.1	52660.0	47689.0	110.4
第二产业		Secondary Industry	61380.0	59200.0	103.7	25193.0	24739.0	101.8
第三产业		Tertiary Industry	71549.0	79700.0	89.8	51998.0	73757.0	106.0
按职工非职工分		Grouped by Staff and Workers or Non-staff-and-worker						
职工人数		Staff and Worker	43483.0	43572.0	99.8	32463.0	32217.0	100.8
#国有单位		State-owned	29926.0	31862.0	93.9	25578.0	24137.0	105.9
集体单位		Collective-owned	4328.0	3379.0	128.1	3587.0	6069.0	59.1
城镇个体劳动者		Urban and Rural Individuals	3846.0	3428.0	112.2	7584.0	10168.0	74.5
劳动工资		Wages						
工资总额	(万元)	Total Wages (10000 yuan)	42996.5	38218.0	112.5	31334.4	30151.9	103.9
#国有单位		State-owned	32515.1	30050.0	108.2	26661.3	23918.5	111.5
集体单位		Collective-owned	2650.4	1947.0	136.1	2281.7	4448.6	51.3
职工平均工资	(元)	Average Wage (yuan)	9846.0	8765.0	112.3	9652.0	8980.0	107.5
固定资产投资		**Investment in Fixed Assets Assets (10000 yuan)**						
全社会固定资产投资	(万元)	Total Investment in Fixed Assets	66065.0	60345.0	109.5	43499.0	19746.0	220.2
按建设性质分		Grouped by Type of Construction						
#基本建设投资		Capital Construction	24422.0	11556.0	211.3	43499.0	19471.0	223.4
更新改造投资		Innovation and Replacement	2879.0	100.0	2879.0		275.0	

21-9 续表 1 continued

项目	Item	密云县 Miyun 1999	1998	1999年为1998年% 1999 as % of 1998	延庆县 Yanqing 1999	1998	1999年为1998年% 1999 as % of 1998
按登记注册类型分	Grouped by Registered Type						
#国有单位 (万元)	State-owned (10000 yuan)	35381.0	40683.0	87.0	29209.0	15291.0	191.0
集体单位 (万元)	Collective-owned (10000 yuan)	19688.0	6386.0	308.3	9014.0	4180.0	215.6
新增固定资产 (万元)	Incremental Fixed Assets (10000 yuan)	87986.0	53390.0	164.8	28932.0	12236.0	236.4
#国有单位	State-owned	38565.0	36688.0	105.1	24517.0	8643.0	283.6
集体单位	Collective-owned	22111.0	6256.0	353.4	3651.0	3593.0	101.6
房屋施工面积 (万平方米)	Floor Space of Buildings Under Construction (10000 sq.m)	79.4	73.0	108.8	38.7	21.7	178.3
#国有单位	State-owned	35.5	47.7	74.4	27.9	15.8	176.5
集体单位	Collective-owned	21.5	10.0	215.0	10.8	5.9	183.1
房屋竣工面积 (万平方米)	Floor Space of Buildings Completed (10000 sq.m)	57.2	50.8	112.6	19.1	13.2	144.7
#国有单位	State-owned	26.8	27.5	97.5	10.4	8.3	125.3
#住宅	Residence	19.3	22.2	86.9	8.0	3.1	258.0
#集体单位	Collective-owned	21.9	8.4	260.7	3.9	4.9	79.6
#住宅	Residence	19.1	8.3	230.1	3.9	4.4	88.6
农村经济	**Rural Economy**						
农村劳动力 (人)	Labor Force (person)	156183.0	156927.0	99.5	97388.0	88671.0	109.8
种植业	Planting	59103.0	54679.0	108.1	43890.0	40176.0	109.2
林业	Forestry	8206.0	7618.0	107.7	3512.0	2721.0	129.1
牧业	Animal Husbandry	10356.0	8277.0	125.1	4818.0	4036.0	119.3
渔业	Fishery	939.0	991.0	94.8	448.0	216.0	207.4
农村工业	Rural Industry	20084.0	20432.0	98.3	7734.0	7946.0	97.3
农村建筑业	Rural Construction	11489.0	10912.0	105.3	11294.0	10038.0	112.5
农村运输业	Rural Transportation	8862.0	8188.0	108.2	5277.0	4685.0	112.6
农村商、饮食业、服务业	Commerce,Catering and Services	7004.0	6045.0	115.9	20415.0	18853.0	108.2
耕地面积 (公顷)	Area under Cultivation (hectare)	23503.7	23532.3	99.9	32607.8	32649.3	99.8
农业机械总动力 (千瓦)	Total Power of Agricultural Machinery (kw)	316279.0	292641.0	108.1	230025.0	191410.0	120.1
化肥施用实物量 (吨)	Consumption of Chemical Fertilizers (ton)	48517.0	45177.0	107.4	39858.0	39329.0	101.3
化肥施用折纯量 (吨)	Consumption of Chemical Fertilizers(100%) (ton)	12219.0	11400.0	107.2	12082.0	12042.1	100.3
农村用电量 (万千瓦时)	Consumption of Electricity (10000 kwh)	10467.8	9062.5	115.5	6800.6	5157.5	131.8
农村国内生产总值 (万元)	Rural Gross Domestic Product (10000 yuan)	167566.6	158072.2	106.0	140571.4	123894.9	113.4
第一产业	Primary Industry	45736.4	54016.5	84.7	72968.4	69688.7	104.7
第二产业	Secondary Industry	55373.1	50833.8	108.9	33670.1	27544.7	122.2
第三产业	Tertiary Industry	66457.1	53221.9	124.9	33932.9	26661.9	127.2
农业总产值 (万元)	Gross Output Value of Agriculture (10000 yuan)	59848.0	59650.9	100.3	59257.2	54712.2	108.3
种植业	Planting	21206.0	26216.0	80.9	29133.2	33620.3	86.6
林业	Forestry	1854.3	2128.2	87.1	2753.6	1388.2	198.3
牧业	Animal Husbandry	34951.5	29776.9	117.4	22219.3	18340.2	121.1
渔业	Fishery	1836.2	1529.8	120.0	1383.1	1363.5	101.4
农作物总播种面积 (万公顷)	Sown Area of Farm Crops (10000 hectare)	3.2	3.2	100.0	3.1	3.1	100.0
粮食作物	Grain	2.5	2.5	100.0	2.4	2.5	96.0
经济作物	Industrial Crops	0.4	0.4	100.0	0.6	0.6	100.0
其他作物	Other Crops	0.3	0.3	100.0	0.1		

21-9 续表 2 continued

项目	Item	密云县 Miyun 1999	密云县 Miyun 1998	1999年为1998年% 1999 as % of 1998	延庆县 Yanqing 1999	延庆县 Yanqing 1998	1999年为1998年% 1999 as % of 1998
农副产品产量	Yield of Farm and Side-line Crops						
粮食 (万吨)	Grain (10000 tons)	9.8	13.0	75.4	14.0	17.7	79.1
蔬菜 (吨)	Vegetable (ton)	159061.0	161349.0	98.6	423024.0	360962.0	117.2
干鲜果 (吨)	Dry and Fresh Fruits (ton)	38000.0	55000.0	69.1	40677.0	32712.0	124.3
畜产品产量	Output of Livestock Products						
生猪出栏 (头)	Slaughtered Hogs (head)	308285.0	304893.0	101.1	146492.0	132106.0	110.9
商品猪 (头)	Commodity Hogs (head)				146492.0	132106.0	110.9
猪牛羊肉 (吨)	Pork,Beef and Mutton (ton)	24164.0	24021.0	100.6	13656.0	11661.0	117.1
#猪肉	Pork	20844.0	21197.0	98.3	11406.0	9925.0	114.9
禽肉	Meat of Poultry (ton)	14140.0	11643.0	121.4	10904.0	5031.0	216.7
禽蛋	Poultry Eggs (ton)	16653.0	16267.0	102.4	12198.0	11179.0	109.1
牲畜年底头数 (头)	Number of Livestock (year-end) (head)				155649.0	152961.0	101.8
大牲畜	Large Animals	21674.0	23354.0	92.8	21653.0	22012.0	98.3
猪	Hogs	201071.0	212425.0	94.7	77200.0	82366.0	93.7
羊	Goats and Sheep	104785.0	108919.0	96.2	56796.0	48583.0	116.9
水产品产量 (吨)	Output of Aquatic Product (ton)	4114.0	3550.0	115.9	2716.2	2609.0	104.1
农村集体经济收入 (万元)	Rural Collective Economic Revenue (10000 yuan)	449370.0	428017.0	105.0	183923.0	136292.0	134.9
农村集体经济利润总额 (万元)	Total Profits of Rural Collective Economy (10000 yuan)	9291.9	1694.5	548.4	11649.0	7430.8	156.8
国家税金	State Taxes	9224.3	11160.7	82.6	10792.0	7701.0	140.1
集体积累	Collective Accumulation				4702.0	2954.0	159.2
劳动所得	Income from Work	99902.8	98059.9	101.9	80842.0	70747.0	114.3
乡镇企业单位数 (个)	Number of Township and Village Enterprise (unit)	9544.0	8187.0	116.6	4121.0	2293.0	179.7
乡镇企业人数 (人)	Number of Persons of Township and Village Enterprises (person)	56749.0	52191.0	108.7	34202.0	30244.0	113.1
乡镇企业纯利润 (万元)	Net Profit of Township and Village Enterprises (10000 yuan)	13568.0	11995.0	113.1	8691.0	4438.0	195.8
乡镇企业固定资产原价 (万元)	Original Value of Fixed Assets of Township and Village Enterprises (10000 yuan)	144606.0	113347.0	127.6	62541.0	54687.0	114.4
乡镇企业固定资产净值 (万元)	Net Value of Fixed Assets of Township and Village Enterprises (10000 yuan)	110189.0	83259.0	132.3	47557.0	41575.0	114.4
工业	**Industry**						
全部工业企业单位数 (个)	Number of Enterprises (unit)	1354.0	1356.0	99.9	223.0	214.0	104.2
国有	State-owned	21.0	22.0	95.5	22.0	24.0	91.7
集体	Collective-owned	239.0	312.0	76.6	32.0	145.0	22.1
其他	Others	1094.0	1022.0	107.0	169.0	47.0	359.5
全部工业总产值 (现价,万元)	Gross Output Value of Industry (at current prices,10000 yuan)	401314.2	302851.3	132.5	152084.6	121374.6	125.3
国有	State-owned	32431.9	41375.4	78.4	11813.1	11628.0	101.6
集体	Collective-owned	84363.7	100565.2	83.9	40264.0	29953.8	134.4
其他	Others	284518.6	160910.7	176.8	100007.5	79792.8	125.3

21-9 续表 3 continued

项目	Item	密云县 Miyun			延庆县 Yanqing		
		1999	1998	1999年为1998年% 1999 as % of 1998	1999	1998	1999年为1998年% 1999 as % of 1998
全部工业总产值(1990年不变价,万元)	Gross Output Value of Industry (at constant price of 1990,10000yuan)	378963.5	269491.7	140.6	145170.3	115522.1	125.7
国有	State-owned	21619.6	27319.6	79.1	8757.8	7892.9	110.9
集体	Collective-owned	78486.3	90421.8	86.8	37823.7	28676.7	131.9
其他	Others	278857.6	151750.3	183.8	98588.8	78952.5	124.9
全部轻工业总产值(现价,万元)	Gross Output Value of Light Industry (at current prices,10000 yuan)	155408.7	148110.2	104.9	127429.2	74301.7	171.5
以农产品为原料	Using Farm Products as Raw Materials	139675.3	133035.0	105.0	107286.2	61667.2	173.9
以非农产品为原料	Using Non-farm Products as Raw Materials	15733.4	15075.2	104.4	20143.0	12634.5	159.4
全部重工业总产值(现价,万元)	Gross Output Value of Heavy Industry (at current prices,10000 yuan)	196283.2	69275.4	283.3	24655.4	41220.4	59.8
采掘工业	Mining and Quarrying	54810.2	21404.7	256.1	501.0	408.0	122.8
原料工业	Raw Materials Industry	29331.3	9065.5	323.5	6123.0	5932.0	103.2
制造工业	Manufacturing Industry	111141.7	38805.2	286.4	18031.4	34880.4	51.7
独立核算工业企业平均职工人数(人)	Average Number of Staff and Workers in Enterprises with Independent Accounting System (person)	39029.0	42293.0	92.3	13015.0	14221.0	91.5
#国有	State-owned	6498.0	7048.0	92.2	1724.0	2538.0	67.9
集体	Collective-owned	18409.0	23043.0	79.9	5809.0	6945.0	83.6
独立核算工业企业总产值(现价,万元)	Gross Output Value of Enterprises with Independent Accounting System(at current prices, 10000 yuan)	263604.6	217385.6	121.3	63535.4	58701.0	108.2
#国有	State-owned	32431.9	42022.9	77.2	14505.0	11628.0	124.7
集体	Collective-owned	49417.4	94936.5	52.1	26372.0	29953.8	88.0
独立核算工业企业工业增加值(万元)	Value Added of Enterprises with Independent Accounting system (10000 yuan)	86639.6	66208.4	130.9	16389.6	22206.5	73.8
独立核算工业企业财务指标	Financial Indicators for Enterprises with Independent Accounting System						
产品销售收入(万元)	Sales Revenue (10000yuan)	309562.4	189093.5	163.7	65582.0	52007.7	126.1
#国有	State-owned	36098.8	38931.1	92.7	10212.4	9693.3	105.3
产品销售成本(万元)	Cost of Sales (10000 yuan)	242700.7	153290.1	158.3	53946.4	43256.5	124.7
#国有	State-owned	28375.2	31524.8	90.0	7547.8	7762.1	97.2
固定资产原价(万元)	Original Value of Fixed Assets (10000 yuan)	205694.1	198019.9	103.9	54122.4	54519.6	99.3
#国有	State-owned	55108.8	50238.1	109.7	13333.0	14529.1	91.8
固定资产净值(万元)	Net Value of Fixed Assets (10000 yuan)	135096.6	138090.8	97.8	38229.9	38467.4	99.4
#国有	State-owned	35484.5	31292.7	113.4	8927.2	9825.3	90.9
全部流动资金年平均余额(万元)	Annual Average Balance of Circulating Funds (10000 yuan)	210494.7	184941.9	113.8	56709.1	54236.7	104.5
#国有	State-owned	39625.0	45051.7	88.0	11836.4	11383.7	103.9
利润总额(万元)	Total Profits (10000 yuan)	14890.4	-10923.5		-939.8	-1820.0	
#国有	State-owned	-837.5	-2145.3		-1002.0	-1107.8	

21-9 续表 4 continued

项目 Item			密云县 Miyun			延庆县 Yanqing		
			1999	1998	1999年为1998年% 1999 as % of 1998	1999	1998	1999年为1998年% 1999 as % of 1998
资金利税率	(%)	Ratio of Pre-tax Profits to Total of Capital (%)	5.9	0.5		4.3	3.0	
产品销售率	(%)	Ratio of Sales Value to Gross Output Value (%)	99.0	94.1		94.9	83.2	
增加值率	(%)	Ratio of Added Value to Gross Output Value (%)	29.2	30.0		25.4	17.0	
独立核算工业企业全员劳动生产率	(元/人)	Overall Labor Productivity of Enterprises with Independent Accounting System (yuan/person)	67541.0	51400.0	131.4	48817.0	41426.0	117.8
#国有		State-owned	49911.0	59624.0	83.7	84135.0	31098.0	270.5
集体		Collective-owned	26844.0	41200.0	65.2	45398.0	41291.0	109.9
商业		**Commerce**						
社会消费品零售额	(万元)	Retail Sales of Consumer Goods (10000 yuan)	148629.0	135258.0	109.9	192332.0	155695.0	123.5
按登记注册类型分		Grouped by Registered Type						
国有		State-owned	21527.0	19590.0	109.9	45146.0	41569.0	108.6
集体		Collective-owned	12602.0	13437.0	93.8	49370.0	30429.0	162.2
其他		Others	114500.0	102231.0	112.0	97816.0	83697.0	116.9
按类别分		Grouped by Type of Goods						
吃的商品	(万元)	Food (10000 yuan)	82078.0	74889.0	109.6	81064.0	61698.0	131.8
穿的商品	(万元)	Clothing (10000 yuan)	16551.0	16082.0	102.9	40922.0	32840.0	124.6
用的商品	(万元)	Daily Used Articles (10000 yuan)	41616.0	38226.0	108.9	62385.0	55041.0	113.3
烧的商品	(万元)	Fuel (10000 yuan)	8384.0	6061.0	137.7	7961.0	6116.0	130.2
网点数	(个)	Number of Outlets (unit)	8293.0	8658.0	95.8	5761.0	5501.0	104.7
#商业		Wholesale and Retail	5435.0	6079.0	89.4	3974.0	3678.0	108.0
饮食业		Catering	1139.0	872.0	130.6	1080.0	970.0	111.3
服务业		Services	1719.0	1707.0	100.7	707.0	853.0	82.9
#宾馆、饭店		Hotels	130.0	115.0	113.0	16.0	14.0	114.3
营业人员	(人)	Personnel (person)	18890.0	18801.0	100.5	13309.0	12205.0	109.0
#商业		Wholesale and Retail	13283.0	13617.0	97.5	6491.0	6090.0	106.6
饮食业		Catering	2055.0	1686.0	121.9	3788.0	3861.0	98.1
服务业		Services	3552.0	3498.0	101.5	3030.0	2254.0	134.4
#宾馆、饭店		Hotels	1920.0	1695.0	113.3	1258.0	1150.0	109.4
外经、外贸		**Foreign Economy and Trade**						
出口商品交货额	(万元)	Delivery Value of Exports (10000 yuan)	38086.8	41048.9	92.8	26412.2	13524.8	195.3
利用外资签订协议(合同)数	(个)	Number of Signed Agreements and Contracts of Foreign Capital to be Utilized (unit)	20.0	16.0	125.0	6.0	6.0	100.0
利用外资签订协议(合同)金额	(万美元)	Amount of Foreign Capital to be Utilized through Agreements and Contracts (USD 10000)	1578.8	2665.9	59.2	443.1	1301.3	34.1
实际利用外资	(万美元)	Amount of Foreign Capital Actually Used (USD 10000)	152.0	1260.3	12.1	47.5	92.0	51.1
旅游人数	(万人)	Number of Tourists (10000 persons)	359.7	360.0	99.9	672.9	624.6	107.7
教育		**Education**						
学校数	(个)	Number of Schools (unit)	226.0	227.0	99.6	201.0	217.0	92.6
小学		Primary Schools	174.0	178.0	97.8	161.0	176.0	91.5

21-9 续表 5 continued

项目		Item	密云县 Miyun 1999	密云县 Miyun 1998	1999年为1998年% 1999 as % of 1998	延庆县 Yanqing 1999	延庆县 Yanqing 1998	1999年为1998年% 1999 as % of 1998
普通中学		Regular Secondary School	38.0	39.0	97.4	32.0	33.0	97.0
中等专业教育		Specialized Secondary Schools	6.0	2.0	300.0	8.0	8.0	100.0
招生数	(人)	New Student Enrollment (person)	14212.0	13628.0	104.3	10847.0	11021.0	98.4
小学		Primary Schools	4240.0	4545.0	93.3	2939.0	3041.0	96.6
初级中等学校		Junior Secondary Schools	7952.0	6852.0	116.1	5975.0	5860.0	101.9
高级中等学校		Senior Secondary Schools	1219.0	1099.0	110.9	1088.0	1019.0	106.8
中等专业教育		Specialized Secondary Schools	512.0	431.0	118.8	845.0	1101.0	76.7
在校学生	(人)	Student Enrollment (person)	65905.0	70132.0	94.0	50003.0	50726.0	98.6
小学		Primary Schools	39314.0	43465.0	90.4	28259.0	31366.0	90.1
初级中等学校		Junior Secondary Schools	20584.0	19688.0	104.6	16092.0	14096.0	114.6
高级中等学校		Senior Secondary Schools	3370.0	3261.0	103.3	2934.0	2767.0	106.0
中等专业教育		Specialized Secondary Schools	1139.0	1557.0	73.2	2718.0	2497.0	108.9
毕业生	(人)	Graduates (person)	17139.0	17130.0	100.1	11080.0	11089.0	99.9
小学		Primary Schools	8148.0	6986.0	116.6	5994.0	5879.0	101.9
初级中等学校		Junior Secondary Schools	6566.0	7583.0	86.6	3667.0	3736.0	98.2
高级中等学校		Senior Secondary Schools	1070.0	892.0	120.0	855.0	868.0	98.5
中等专业教育		Specialized Secondary Schools	444.0	818.0	54.3	564.0	606.0	93.1
达到"国家体育标准"学生数	(人)	Number of Students Come to the Standard for State Physical Training (person)	67700.0	69474.0	97.4	38261.0	48403.0	79.0
幼儿园、托儿所个数	(个)	Number of Kindergardens (unit)	223.0	245.0	91.0	53.0	61.0	86.9
幼儿入托数	(人)	New Enrollment (person)	10207.0	10018.0	101.9	5092.0	5354.0	95.1
文化		**Culture**						
文化馆、站	(个)	Cultural Centers (unit)	20.0	20.0	100.0	19.0	19.0	100.0
公共图书馆	(个)	Public Libraries (unit)	1.0	1.0	100.0	1.0	1.0	100.0
公共图书馆藏书	(万册)	Collection (10000 volume)	17.0	16.0	106.3	12.8	12.6	101.6
电影放映单位	(个)	Film Projection Units (unit)	22.0	22.0	100.0	12.0	15.0	80.0
区级以上重点文物保护单位	(个)	Cultural Relics Preserved at District Level and above (unit)	30.0	30.0	100.0	106.0	92.0	115.2
卫生		**Health**						
卫生机构数	(个)	Number of Health Institutions (unit)	82.0	32.0	256.3	32.0	32.0	100.0
#医院		Hospitals	10.0	8.0	125.0	6.0	6.0	100.0
卫生院		Clinics	17.0	17.0	100.0	17.0	17.0	100.0
床位数		Number of Beds (unit)	1015.0	974.0	104.2	795.0	765.0	103.9
#医院		Hospitals	778.0	705.0	110.4	655.0	665.0	98.5
卫生院		Clinics	186.0	269.0	69.1	100.0	100.0	100.0
平均每千人拥有床位数	(张)	Average Number of Beds Per 1000 Persons (unit)	2.4	2.3	104.3	2.9	2.8	103.6
卫生技术人员	(人)	Medical Technical Personnel (person)	1782.0	1773.0	100.5	1243.0	1220.0	101.9
#医生		Doctors (person)	909.0	872.0	104.2	582.0	586.0	99.3
公用设施		**Public Utilities**						
区级以上公园	(个)	Parks at District Level and Above (unit)	2.0	1.0	200.0	2.0	1.0	200.0
体育场馆	(个)	Stadiums and Gymnasiums (unit)	1.0	1.0	100.0	1.0	1.0	100.0
道路长度	(公里)	Length of Roads (km)	1173.0	1173.0	100.0	918.4	914.0	100.4

主要统计指标解释

国内生产总值 为区县及以下单位创造的国内生产总值。不包括民航、铁路、及中央属、市属单位。

财政收入、财政支出 为区县财政局提供的地方财政收支数字。

人口：为公安局户籍人口按地域范围统计的数据。

从业人员：为在区县及以下各单位中工作人员，包括在岗职工、聘用留用的离退休人员、外方和港澳台方人员以及人事档案关系保留在原单位的人员以及农村劳动力和城镇个体。

职工人数 为区县及以下各单位职工人数，即在岗职工和不在岗职工。

工资总额 与“职工人数”同口径。

全社会固定资产投资 为区县及以下各单位基本建设、更新改造、城镇集体单位投资及商品房投资。

工业增加值 为区县及以下各独立核算工业企业进行的工业经济活动，不包括中央和市属各工业企业的经济活动。

轻、重工业总产值 与“工业增加值”同口径。

商业 为区县及以下各商业活动单位数据。

外经、外贸 为各区县外经委数据。

教育 用区县教育局数据，不包括成人教育。其中高级中学包括普通高中和职业高中，中等专业教育含师范学校。

文化 按地域统计。海淀区图书馆数和藏书应包括北京图书馆、东城区应包括首都图书馆。

卫生 为各区县卫生局地域统计数据。

公园 按地域统计。

体育场馆 指专门用于体育训练、比赛和健身活动，有专人管理和一定投资的体育建筑设施。用于经营性和非经营性比赛训练和健身锻炼、长期闲置和临时被占用的体育场地均予统计，按地域统计。

道路长度 为市政管理系统道路长度和公路局系统公路长度之和。

旅游人数 按地域统计（包括海外旅游者及国内旅游者）。

Explanatory Notes On Main Statistical Indicators

Gross Domestic Product refers to that created by units at district and county level and below, exclude units of civil aviation, railway and central , municipal units.

Fiscal Revenue or Expenditure refers to local fiscal revenue or expenditure provided by Bureau of Finance of district and county.

Population refers to registered statistics counted according to scope of region by Public Security Bureau.

Employment refers to those worked in units at district and county level and below, include staff and workers at their posts, retired and VCSR engaged and kept on, foreign, Hongkong, Macao and Taiwan employee and personnel who organizational affiliation reserved in reformer units and rural labor force, urban individuals.

Staff and Workers refers to those at and off their posts in units at district and county level and below.

Total Wages the same account as "staff and workers".

Total Investment in Fixed Assets include investment in capital construction, innovation, real estate and urban collective-owned investment of units at district and county level and below.

Value Added of Industry refers to that created by enterprises with independent accounting system at district and county level, exclude central and municipal industrial enterprises.

Gross Output Value of Light or Heavy Industry: the same account as "Value Added of Industry".

Commerce refers to data of commercial units at district and county level and below.

Foreign Economy and Trade refers to data provide by Committee of Foreign Economics and Trade.

Education refers to data provided by Bureau of Education of district and county, exclude adult education. And senior middle school include regular secondary school and vocational school, special secondary school include teacher training school.

Culture refers to data counted according to scope of region. Libraries and collections of Haidian District include Beijing Library, and those of Dongcheng District include Capital Library.

Health refers to data counted according to scope of region by Health Bureau of district and county.

Parks refers to data counted according to scope of region.

Stadiums and Gymnasiums refers to data counted according to scope of region, include physical construction with special management and some investment specially used in training, match and body-building, also include long-time idle and temporarily occupied places used in managing or non-managing training, match and body-building.

Length of Roads refers to the sum of length of roads of Municipal Management System and Highway Bureau System.

Tourists refers to data counted according to scope of region, include foreign and domestic tourists.

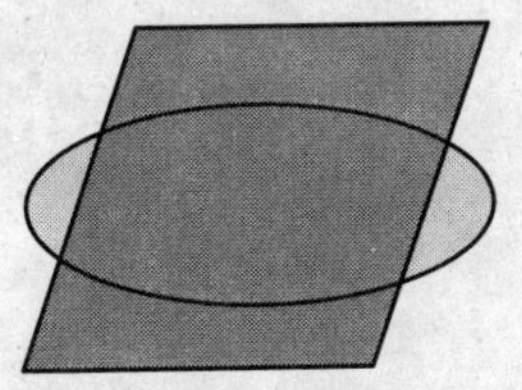

附 录
APPENDIX

附录 1：历史资料
APPENDIX 1：HISTORICAL STATISTICS
附 1-1 人 口 状 况
POPULATION

年 份 Year	年底总人口(万人) Total Population (10000 persons)	按性别分 By Sex		按农业、非农业分 By Agriculture and Non-agriculture		人口出生率(‰) Birth Rate (‰)	人口死亡率(‰) Death Rate (‰)	人口自然增长率(‰) Natural Growth Rate (‰)
		男 Male	女 Female	农业人口 Agriculture	非农业人口 Non-agriculture			
1978	872	443	429	393	479	12.93	6.12	6.81
1979	897	455	442	387	510	13.67	5.92	7.75
1980	904	458	446	383	521	15.56	6.30	9.26
1981	919	466	453	386	533	16.93	6.02	10.91
1982	935	474	461	391	544	20.04	5.68	14.36
1983	950	483	467	393	557	15.63	5.49	10.14
1984	965	491	474	395	570	16.74	5.53	11.21
1985	981	500	481	395	586	15.45	5.75	9.70
1986	1028	524	504	407	621	15.82	4.47	11.35
1987	1047	525	522	410	637	17.29	5.40	11.89
1988	1061	534	527	411	650	14.43	5.08	9.35
1989	1075	538	537	431	664	12.84	5.53	7.49
1990	1086	545	541	413	673	13.04	5.75	7.23
1991	1094	547	547	411	683	8.03	5.82	2.21
1992	1102	554	548	410	692	9.22	6.11	3.11
1993	1112	559	553	405	707	9.35	6.16	3.19
1994	1125	564	561	400	725	8.96	5.76	3.20
1995	1251	627	624	436	815	7.92	5.12	2.80
1996	1259	639	620	430	829	8.02	5.34	2.68
1997	1240	629	611	414	826	7.91	6.02	1.89
1998	1246	631	615	408	838	6.00	5.30	0.70
1999	1257	636	621	403	854	6.50	5.60	0.90

注：1982-1989 年数据是根据 1982、1990 年两年人口普查数据调整的，1990 年以后数据是人口变动抽样调查数,其余年份数据为户籍统计数。

Note：Data from 1982 to 1989 were obtained from adjustment of cencus of 1982 and 1990,data after 1990 were those from sample survey of population changes,and data of other years were those of registered permanent population.

附 1-2 按城乡分从业人员(年底数)
EMPLOYEE BY URBAN AND RURAL AREA(YEAR-END)

单位：万人 (10000 persons)

年份 Year	合计 Total	城镇 Urban	#国有经济单位 State-Owned	#集体经济单位 Collective-Owned	#联营经济单位 Joint Owned	#股份制经济单位 Share Holding	#外商投资经济单位 Foreign Funded	# 港澳台投资经济单位 Hongkong, Macao and Taiwan Funded	# 个体 Individuals	乡村 Rural
1978	444.1	291.6	240.9	50.7						152.5
1979	470.5	312.0	254.2	57.8						158.6
1980	484.2	326.8	269.4	57.1					0.3	157.4
1981	511.7	345.2	283.1	61.3					0.8	166.5
1982	535.2	361.1	293.0	67.1					1.0	174.1
1983	552.0	373.8	303.4	68.5					1.9	178.2
1984	556.2	377.6	302.5	71.6			1.3		2.2	178.6
1985	558.7	384.8	308.1	72.6			1.6		2.5	173.9
1986	572.7	400.5	324.4	71.1			2.4		2.6	172.2
1987	580.3	408.4	331.8	70.7			2.8		3.1	171.9
1988	603.1	413.9	336.4	69.9	0.2		3.4		3.5	189.2
1989	593.9	424.0	343.8	67.4	3.4		3.7		5.6	169.9
1990	627.1	461.2	357.9	86.8	5.1		4.6		6.3	165.9
1991	634.0	477.2	367.8	89.0	0.5		7.7	0.2	7.2	156.8
1992	649.3	490.6	371.5	90.5	0.4		11.4	0.2	14.0	158.7
1993	627.8	481.4	362.3	79.7	2.8		11.0	6.4	14.0	146.4
1994	664.3	492.7	363.5	73.3	3.5	6.3	15.0	9.4	20.9	171.6
1995	665.3	492.7	358.1	72.1	3.7	8.0	17.4	10.4	21.9	172.6
1996	660.2	495.7	355.1	68.6	3.4	14.8	20.7	10.1	22.9	164.5
1997	655.8	498.8	354.7	68.5	3.2	19.3	21.2	10.2	21.2	157.1
1998	622.2	463.2	308.1	51.0	5.2	44.5	21.2	13.1	20.1	158.9
1999	618.6	456.1	287.6	49.7	4.8	24.9	20.6	13.5	23.7	162.5

附 1-3 从业人员和职工人数(年底数)
NUMBER OF EMPLOYEE,STAFF AND WORKERS(YEAR-END)

单位：万人 (10000 persons)

年份 Year	从业人员 Employee	第一产业 Primary Industry	第二产业 Secondary Industry	第三产业 Tertiary Industry	职工人数 Staff and Workers	国有经济单位 State-Owned	城镇集体经济单位 Urban Collective Owned	其他经济单位 Others
1978	444.1	125.9	177.9	140.3	291.6	240.9	50.7	
1979	470.5	121.4	195.2	153.9	311.9	254.2	57.7	
1980	484.2	118.0	207.3	158.9	326.5	269.4	57.1	
1981	511.7	117.2	220.4	174.1	344.4	283.1	61.3	
1982	535.2	115.1	228.6	191.5	360.1	293.0	67.1	
1983	552.0	117.1	240.2	194.7	371.9	303.4	68.5	
1984	566.5	106.7	246.5	213.3	375.4	302.5	71.6	1.3
1985	574.8	97.1	254.3	223.4	382.3	308.1	72.6	1.6
1986	590.0	93.3	260.8	235.9	397.9	324.4	71.1	2.4
1987	598.2	91.8	264.1	242.3	405.2	331.8	70.7	2.7
1988	584.1	88.4	267.6	228.1	410.4	336.4	69.9	4.1
1989	593.9	91.0	266.3	236.6	418.4	343.8	67.4	7.2
1990	627.1	90.7	281.6	254.8	454.9	357.9	86.8	10.2
1991	634.0	90.8	279.7	263.5	470.0	367.8	89.0	13.2
1992	649.3	84.5	281.6	283.2	476.6	371.5	90.5	14.6
1993	627.8	65.1	279.4	283.3	467.3	362.3	79.6	25.4
1994	664.3	73.2	272.2	318.9	471.8	363.5	73.4	34.9
1995	665.3	70.6	271.0	323.7	470.9	358.2	72.1	40.6
1996	660.2	72.5	260.1	327.6	460.6	349.0	64.8	46.8
1997	655.8	71.0	257.6	328.1	465.3	348.7	65.0	51.6
1998	622.2	71.5	226.0	324.7	450.1	321.7	50.8	77.6
1999	618.6	74.5	216.2	327.9	438.0	303.0	49.6	85.4

附 1-4 国 民 生 产 总 值
GROSS NATIONAL PRODUCT

单位：亿元 (100 million yuan)

年 份 Year	国民生产总值 Gross National	国内生产总值 Gross Domestic Product	第一产业 Primary Industry	第二产业 Secondary Industry	# 工 业 Industry	# 建筑业 Constru-ction	第三产业 Tertiary Industry	#运输邮电业 Transporta-tion,Post and Teleco-mmunication	# 商业 Commerce	人均国内生产总值 (元) Per Capita Gross Domes-tic Product (yuan)
1978	108.84	108.84	5.63	77.43	70.22	7.21	25.78	7.00	8.28	1290
1979	120.11	120.11	5.17	85.18	77.37	7.81	29.76	6.55	8.79	1396
1980	139.07	139.07	6.07	95.79	86.94	8.85	37.21	6.96	11.01	1584
1981--1985	**950.95**	**950.95**	**62.46**	**589.30**	**515.41**	**73.89**	**299.19**	**48.08**	**80.80**	
1981	139.15	139.15	6.61	92.52	82.71	9.81	40.02	7.60	11.86	1558
1982	154.94	154.94	10.34	99.79	89.30	10.49	44.81	8.25	11.05	1704
1983	183.13	183.13	12.85	112.65	98.76	13.89	57.63	9.06	13.63	1979
1984	216.61	216.61	14.85	130.68	113.99	16.69	71.08	10.43	18.37	2306
1985	257.12	257.12	17.81	153.66	130.65	23.01	85.65	12.74	25.89	2702
1986--1990	**1978.58**	**1978.68**	**162.93**	**1084.23**	**917.29**	**166.94**	**731.52**	**94.39**	**172.89**	
1986	284.86	284.86	19.14	165.75	141.17	24.58	99.97	14.98	27.99	2953
1987	326.82	326.82	24.31	182.59	154.54	28.05	119.92	17.70	27,21	3336
1988	410.22	410.22	37.07	221.27	189.48	31.79	151.88	19.03	39.07	4124
1989	455.96	455.96	38.53	252.23	212.83	39.40	165.20	18.72	34.77	4509
1990	500.72	500.82	43.88	262.39	219.27	43.12	194.55	23.96	43.85	4878
1991--1995	**4650.47**	**4650.44**	**303.97**	**2167.24**	**1791.38**	**375.86**	**2179.23**	**247.74**	**586.26**	
1991	598.79	598.89	45.52	291.53	255.59	35.94	261.84	29.61	65.65	5782
1992	709.00	709.10	48.67	345.91	292.97	52.94	314.52	35.49	85.41	6804
1993	863.23	863.53	53.57	414.79	334.00	80.79	395.17	37.58	113.88	8239
1994	1084.33	1084.03	74.77	499.84	405.11	94.73	509.42	61.51	146.62	10261
1995	1395.12	1394.89	81.44	615.17	503.71	111.46	698.28	83.55	174.70	13085
1996	1616.03	1615.73	83.46	683.14	541.41	141.73	849.13	113.78	187.59	15044
1997	1810.49	1810.09	84.85	738.56	588.36	150.20	986.68	135.79	202.45	16735
1998	2011.77	2011.31	86.56	786.85	610.66	176.19	1137.90	154.45	207.33	18478
1999	2174.97	2174.46	87.48	840.23	649.34	190.89	1246.75	167.54	210.43	19846

注：本表按当年价格计算。

Note: Data of this table is calculated at current prices.

附 1-5 国民生产总值指数(1978=100)
INDEX OF GROSS NATIONAL PRODUCT(1978=100)

年 份 Year	国民生产总值 Gross National	国内生产总值 Gross Domestic Product	第一产业 Primary Industry	第二产业 Secondary Industry	# 工业 Industry	# 建筑业 Construction	第三产业 Tertiary Industry	#运输邮电业 Transportation,Post and Telecommunication	# 商业 Commerce	人均国内生产总值(元) Per Capita Gross Domestic Product (yuan)
1978	100	100	100	100	100	100	100	100	100	100
1979	109.7	109.7	105	109.2	110.1	108.4	113.2	93.5	104.3	107.6
1980	122.6	122.6	114.8	120.2	121.2	119.6	134.1	96.7	124.5	117.8
1981	120.8	120.8	139.0	113.4	119.2	127.2	142.3	104.1	132.3	115.1
1982	129.7	129.7	157.6	116.9	123.0	141.3	167.5	117.5	151.7	121.4
1983	150.2	150.2	169.4	134.9	137.1	187.0	199.3	113.9	159.1	138.1
1984	176.7	176.5	180.9	157.8	158.6	222.1	242.4	130.1	210.5	159.9
1985	191.9	191.7	192.2	174.6	173.4	277.0	252.8	149.2	249.7	171.4
1986	209.0	208.8	192.4	178.9	178.2	278.1	320.3	152.1	255.4	184.3
1987	229.0	228.8	217.9	187.5	186.3	295.6	379.6	168.2	227.8	198.8
1988	258.3	258.1	242.3	213.0	210.5	314.9	424.0	166.7	268.9	220.9
1989	269.7	269.5	245.0	228.8	228.2	353.3	421.9	227.2	204.6	226.9
1990	284.3	284.0	253.3	231.1	232.5	337.7	480.9	241.3	244.9	235.5
1991	311.3	311.0	262.5	248.8	261.8	275.6	543.5	313.4	239.0	257.8
1992	347.4	347.1	270.3	279.0	288.8	346.4	611.4	344.4	283.5	286.0
1993	389.4	389.1	278.7	314.9	319.1	445.1	689.1	379.2	328.0	318.8
1994	442.0	441.6	286.0	360.9	362.2	537.7	783.5	471.0	359.5	359.0
1995	497.2	496.4	262.2	388.4	390.0	578.6	947.2	658.9	422.0	399.9
1996	543.0	542.0	254.4	417.1	413.8	659.0	1063.7	783.4	444.8	433.5
1997	595.1	594.1	256.9	450.9	449.8	692.6	1189.2	883.7	468.0	471.7
1998	653.4	652.3	260.8	494.2	488.9	790.9	1317.6	972.1	486.7	533.0
1999	720.0	718.8	267.3	553.5	551.5	854.2	1437.5	1058.6	499.8	583.6

注：本表按可比价格计算。

Note：Data of this table are calculated at constant prices.

附 1-6 国民生产总值指数(上年=100)
INDEX OF GROSS NATIONAL PRODUCT(PRECEDING YEAR=100)

年 份 Year	国民生产总值 Gross National	国内生产总值 Gross Domestic Product	第一产业 Primary Industry	第二产业 Secondary Industry	# 工业 Industry	# 建筑业 Constru-ction	第三产业 Tertiary Industry	#运输邮电业 Transporta-tion,Post and Teleco-mmunication	# 商业 Commerce	人均国内生产总值(元) Per Capita Gross Domes-tic Product (yuan)
1979	109.7	109.7	105.0	109.2	110.1	108.4	113.2	93.5	104.3	107.6
1980	111.8	111.8	109.3	110.1	110.1	110.3	118.5	103.4	119.4	109.5
1981	98.5	98.5	121.1	94.3	98.3	106.4	106.1	107.7	106.2	97.7
1982	107.4	107.4	113.4	103.1	103.2	111.1	117.7	112.8	114.7	105.5
1983	115.8	115.8	107.5	115.4	111.5	132.3	119.0	97.0	104.9	113.7
1984	117.6	117.5	106.8	117.0	115.7	118.8	121.6	114.2	132.3	115.8
1985	108.6	108.6	106.2	110.6	109.3	124.7	104.3	114.7	118.6	107.2
1986	108.9	108.9	100.1	102.5	102.8	100.4	126.7	101.9	102.3	107.5
1987	109.6	109.6	113.3	104.8	104.5	106.3	118.5	110.6	89.2	107.9
1988	112.8	112.8	111.2	113.6	113.0	106.5	111.7	99.1	118.0	111.1
1989	104.4	104.4	101.1	107.4	108.4	112.2	99.5	136.3	76.1	102.7
1990	105.4	105.4	103.4	101.0	101.9	95.6	114.0	106.2	119.7	103.8
1991	109.5	109.5	103.6	107.7	112.6	81.6	113.0	129.9	97.6	109.5
1992	111.6	111.6	103.0	112.1	110.3	125.7	112.5	109.9	118.6	110.9
1993	112.1	112.1	103.1	112.9	110.5	128.5	112.7	110.1	115.7	111.5
1994	113.5	113.5	102.6	114.6	113.5	120.8	113.7	124.2	109.6	112.6
1995	112.5	112.4	91.7	107.6	107.7	107.6	120.9	139.9	117.4	111.4
1996	109.2	109.2	97.0	107.4	106.1	113.9	112.3	118.9	105.4	108.4
1997	109.6	109.6	101.0	108.1	108.7	105.1	111.8	112.8	105.2	108.8
1998	109.8	109.8	101.5	109.6	108.7	114.2	110.8	110.0	104.0	113.0
1999	110.2	110.2	102.5	112.0	112.8	108.0	109.1	108.9	102.7	109.5

注：本表按可比价格计算。

Note：Data of this table are calculated at constant prices.

附 1-7 国 内 支 出 总 额
GROSS DOMESTIC EXPENDITURE

单位：亿元 (100 million yuan)

年 份 Year	国内支出总额 Gross Domes-tic Expendi-ture	最终消费 Final Consump-tion	居民消费 Residen-tial Con-sumption	农民 Peasant	非农业居民 Non-Peasant	政府消费 Government Consump-tion	资本形成总额 Total Capital Formation	固定资产 Fixed Assets	存货 Stock
1978	108.84	40.98	30.47	7.32	23.15	10.51	31.67	24.84	6.83
1979	102.11	49.34	36.24	8.63	27.61	13.10	37.40	29.76	7.64
1980	139.07	57.44	44.35	10.53	33.82	13.09	43.69	35.63	8.06
1981--1985	**950.95**	**424.69**	**306.14**	**87.83**	**218.31**	**118.55**	**343.04**	**271.97**	**71.07**
1981	139.15	63.72	47.66	11.98	35.68	16.06	38.85	29.53	9.32
1982	154.94	71.22	51.24	13.64	37.60	19.98	34.43	26.10	8.33
1983	183.13	81.31	56.45	16.57	39.88	24.86	54.76	49.04	5.72
1984	216.61	96.14	67.65	21.05	46.60	28.49	78.57	68.60	9.97
1985	257.12	112.30	83.14	24.59	58.55	29.16	136.43	98.70	37.73
1986--1990	**1978.68**	**880.15**	**640.93**	**188.47**	**452.46**	**239.22**	**1218.96**	**925.87**	**293.09**
1986	284.86	125.16	92.40	26.10	66.30	32.76	156.33	129.75	26.58
1987	326.82	147.87	107.73	29.12	78.61	40.14	208.33	170.12	38.21
1988	410.22	178.49	131.98	37.25	94.73	46.51	250.01	197.79	52.22
1989	455.96	197.67	138.99	46.78	92.21	58.68	297.00	200.26	96.74
1990	500.82	230.96	169.83	49.22	120.61	61.13	307.29	227.95	79.34
1991--1995	**5274.68**	**1701.59**	**1177.92**	**276.13**	**901.79**	**523.87**	**3530.54**	**2119.49**	**1411.05**
1991	560.21	225.47	153.62	37.59	116.03	71.85	322.77	184.37	138.40
1992	681.43	262.97	177.08	40.11	136.97	85.89	423.71	200.98	222.73
1993	1019.55	310.28	207.21	52.95	154.26	103.07	625.15	326.82	298.33
1994	1318.60	396.29	264.55	66.95	197.60	131.74	902.63	519.01	383.62
1995	1694.89	506.58	375.46	78.53	296.93	131.32	1256.28	888.31	367.97
1996	1678.52	617.85	451.96	92.89	359.07	165.89	1107.06	922.48	184.58
1997	1870.93	703.36	492.88	97.25	395.63	210.48	1228.65	1001.73	226.92
1998	2046.31	809.82	563.62	109.26	454.36	246.20	1396.40	1171.90	224.50
1999	2174.46	954.14	633.76	112.52	521.24	320.38	1526.16	1233.46	292.70

注：本表按当年价格计算。

Note：Data of this table is calculated at current prices.

附 1-8 全社会固定资产投资
TOTAL INVESTMENT IN FIXED ASSETS

单位：亿元 (100 million yuan)

年 份 Year	合计 Total	国有经济单位 State-Owned	#基本建设 Capital Construction	#更新改造 Innovation	集体经济单位 Collective Owned	#农 村 Rural	其他经济单位 Others	私营个体经济 Private and Individual	#农 村 Rural
1985	94.0	73.6	50.7	21.7	16.2	10.8		4.2	3.8
1986--1990	**724.1**	**609.6**	**378.2**	**201.3**	**83.1**	**49.1**		**31.4**	**27.5**
1986	106.2	88.7	54.2	33.4	13.3	6.4		4.2	4.0
1987	136.2	115.8	71.7	43.1	15.2	8.3		5.2	4.5
1988	163.0	133.2	87.7	43.6	21.4	13.7		8.4	7.6
1989	139.5	117.7	79.8	36.5	15.1	9.0		6.7	5.7
1990	179.2	154.2	84.8	44.7	18.1	11.7		6.9	5.7
1991--1995	**2358.7**	**1764.2**	**808.7**	**567.9**	**188.7**	**134.8**	**381.0**	**24.8**	**19.3**
1991	192.0	165.0	86.8	52.4	20.2	14.6		6.8	6.4
1992	266.0	230.1	114.9	79.2	27.3	19.8		8.6	7.4
1993	410.4	340.1	157.1	116.1	37.4	28.8	30.9	2.0	1.2
1994	648.8	514.8	229.2	179.2	44.6	33.7	86.3	3.1	2.0
1995	841.5	514.2	220.7	141.0	59.2	37.9	263.8	4.3	2.3
1996	876.9	545.7	241.8	156.4	57.6	41.1	268.8	4.8	2.5
1997	961.2	605.7	294.1	174.4	54.7	38.5	296.8	4.0	2.1
1998	1155.6	727.9	369.1	196.5	48.7	24.3	349	30.0	17.5
1999	1170.6	735.7	389.0	164.6	55.8	25.7	344.3	34.8	23.4

年份 Year	固定资产投资来源 Source of Investment in Fixed Assets					固 定 资 产 投 资 Investment in Fixed Assets					
	国家预算内投资 State Budgetary Investment	国内贷款 Domestic Loan	利用外资 Foreign Capital	自筹投资 Self-raised investment	其他投资 Other Investment	第一产业 Primary Industry	第二产业 Secondary Industry	#工 业 Industry	#能源工业 Energy	第三产业 Tertiary Industry	#运输邮电业 Transportation,Post and Telecommunications
1985	30.4	11.5	5.1	26.4	4.4	1.6	32.4	28.8	4.4	43.8	5.3
1986--1990	**184.9**	**90.3**	**69.1**	**245.6**	**39.5**	**9.4**	**218.8**	**209.1**	**43.1**	**384.2**	**47.7**
1986	33.0	17.0	4.6	37.4	2.5	1.5	41.4	38.8	5.5	51.6	6.6
1987	43.1	19.5	8.8	49.1	5.7	1.6	46.9	44.3	10.0	72.9	9.7
1988	37.4	18.2	22.3	62.3	9.2	2.0	48.8	47.2	9.9	87.9	7.8
1989	35.6	12.8	18.2	44.5	12.0	1.9	38.4	37.0	8.5	81.9	10.0
1990	35.8	22.8	15.2	52.3	10.1	2.4	43.3	41.8	9.2	89.9	13.6
1991--1995	**254.5**	**274.8**	**189.6**	**888.4**	**127.3**	**15.5**	**624.1**	**585.1**	**154.8**	**973.5**	**256.2**
1991	35.5	28.2	13.9	65.5	8.0	2.7	51.3	49.3	11.8	90.4	13.0
1992	42.2	40.1	14.9	109.9	9.6	3.9	82.9	80.2	22.0	114.2	28.4
1993	46.4	71.0	28.0	168.9	35.9	2.1	150.4	134.6	28.2	165.7	51.7
1994	62.5	70.9	87.8	283.7	44.8	3.7	185.8	175.9	40.2	318.4	81.2
1995	67.9	64.6	45.0	260.4	29.0	3.1	153.7	145.1	52.6	284.8	81.9
1996	73.1	71.1	53.8	265.7	39.8	2.8	174.9	167.3	69.8	319.7	99.5
1997	82.8	89.7	51.3	322.4	41.3	0.9	201.1	192.1	93.3	380.1	113.4
1998	93.9	108.4	41.2	382.9	43.0	1.5	201.7	192.6	96.2	479.7	169.8
1999	135.7	96.9	34.5	359.1	31.4	1.7	179.4	166.6	85.1	470.4	108.2

注：1.全社会固定资产投资来源中,1985 和 1986 年为固定资产投资完成额资金来源分组。
2.按资金来源和三次产业划分的固定资产投资不含房地产开发投资。

a) In source of total investment of fixed assets,data of 1985 and 1986 are grouped by source of investment completed.
b) Data of investment grouped by source of funds and three industry excluded real estate development.

附 1-9 基本建设投资额
INVESTMENT IN CAPITAL CONSTRUCTION

年 份 Year	基本建设投资额 (万元) Investment (10000 yuan)	按隶属关系分 Grouped by Administrative Relationship		按建设性质分 Grouped by Type of Construction			新增固定资产 (万元) Incremental Fixed Assets (10000 yuan)	固定资产交付使用率 (%) Rate of Fixed Assets Put into Operation (%)
		中央 Central	地方 Local	新建 Newly-built	扩建、改建 Expanding, Replacement	其他 Others		
1978	198908	90498	108410				169148	85.0
1979	234741	124132	110609	107611	105561	21569	212111	90.4
1980	265185	139843	125342	123520	135064	6601	231715	87.4
1981--1985	**1672352**	**926161**	**746191**	**670739**	**827830**	**173783**	**1421535**	**85.0**
1981	238693	130589	108104	111150	121431	6112	309203	129.5
1982	259866	121116	138750	119196	130002	10668	199313	76.7
1983	271126	141087	130039	93471	172287	5368	236816	87.3
1984	360756	210516	150240	136480	161372	62904	360997	100.1
1985	541911	322853	219058	210442	242738	88731	315206	58.2
1986--1990	**4000931**	**2506444**	**1494487**	**1888490**	**1641503**	**470938**	**2662712**	**66.6**
1986	587030	358562	228468	249512	254774	82744	354264	60.3
1987	763286	494817	268469	297042	359192	107052	463887	60.8
1988	926549	590549	336000	454766	365721	106062	455230	49.1
1989	835661	521340	314321	419002	323336	93323	512484	61.3
1990	888405	541176	347229	468168	338480	81757	876847	98.7
1991--1995	**9314619**	**5081070**	**4233549**	**3940498**	**4651510**	**722611**	**5263959**	**56.5**
1991	902052	481844	420208	390091	412787	99174	779764	86.4
1992	1185313	646031	539282	458089	618029	109195	726984	61.3
1993	1726260	934439	791821	640690	962772	122798	805405	46.7
1994	2851219	1329286	1521933	1340373	1306164	204682	1386866	48.6
1995	2649775	1689470	960305	1111255	1351758	186762	1564940	59.1
1996	3138456	1892321	1246135	1213019	1675846	249591	2625211	83.6
1997	3743212	2233708	1509504	1250778	2124370	368064	2639688	70.5
1998	4295514	2506556	1788958	1337033	2559533	398948	3000077	69.8
1999	4327251	2420060	1907191	1294950	2481402	550899	3569318	82.5

附 1-10 国有单位基本建设投资额
INVESTMENT IN CAPITAL CONSTRUCTION OF STATE-OWNED UNITS

年 份 Year	基本建设投资额 (亿元) Investment (100 million yuan)	按隶属关系分 Grouped by Administrative Relationship		按建设性质分 Grouped by Type of Construction			新增固定资产 (亿元) Incremental Fixed Assets (100 million yuan)	固定资产交付使用率 (%) Rate of Fixed Assets Put into Operation (%)
		中央 Central	地方 Local	新建 Newly-built	扩建、改建 Expanding, Replacement	其他 Others		
1981--1985	**160.2**						**132.6**	**82.8**
1981	23.4						24.9	106.4
1982	25.0	12.1	12.9				19.4	77.6
1983	26.4	14.1	12.3				23.2	87.9
1984	34.7	21.0	13.7	13.0	15.9	5.8	35.0	100.9
1985	50.7	32.3	18.4	18.8	23.9	8.0	30.1	59.4
1986--1990	**378.2**	**250.4**	**127.8**	**177.6**	**160.6**	**40.0**	**251.2**	**66.4**
1986	54.2	35.8	18.4	22.7	24.6	6.9	32.9	60.7
1987	71.7	49.5	22.2	26.8	35.5	9.4	43.7	60.9
1988	87.7	58.9	28.8	42.4	36.0	9.3	42.3	48.2
1989	79.8	52.1	27.7	40.1	31.7	8.0	48.3	60.5
1990	84.8	54.1	30.7	45.6	32.8	6.4	84.0	99.1
1991--1995	**808.7**	**480.8**	**327.9**				**457.9**	**56.6**
1991	86.8	48.2	38.6	38.1	40.4	8.3	75.6	87.1
1992	114.9	64.6	50.3	45.2	60.1	9.6	67.4	58.7
1993	157.1	89.7	67.4				53.5	34.1
1994	229.2	125.6	103.6				124.3	54.2
1995	220.7	152.7	68.0				137.1	62.1
1996	241.8	165.8	76.0				229.8	95.0
1997	294.1	193.0	101.1	64.5	194.0	35.6	221.0	75.1
1998	369.1	224.5	144.6	93.3	237.3	38.5	207.5	56.2
1999	389.0	218.7	170.3	98.8	235.9	54.3	308.8	79.4

附 1-11 更新改造投资额
INVESTMENT IN INNOVATIONS

年 份 Year	更新改造投资额(万元) Investment (10000 yuan)	按隶属关系分 Grouped by Administrative Relationship		按建设性质分 Grouped by Type of Construction			新增固定资产(万元) Incremental Fixed Assets (10000 yuan)	固定资产交付使用率(%) Rate of Fixed Assets Put into Operation (%)
		中央 Central	地方 Local	新建 Newly-built	扩建、改建 Expanding, Replacement	其他 Others		
1980	66542						48089	72.3
1981--1985	**671784**						**479560**	**71.4**
1981	75545						56527	74.8
1982	84818	16044	68774				63785	75.2
1983	114327	26087	88240				88582	77.5
1984	161276	35069	126207	3354	138963	18959	110265	68.4
1985	235818	44706	191112	14281	208010	13527	160401	68.0
1986--1990	**2123897**	**331964**	**1791933**	**133715**	**1710681**	**279501**	**1511075**	**71.1**
1986	358357	57582	300775	26619	289075	42663	230940	64.4
1987	450629	79105	371524	11550	386744	52335	335159	74.4
1988	460025	66340	393685	29480	366311	64234	317796	69.1
1989	386827	58418	328409	26969	307067	52791	283194	73.2
1990	468059	70519	397540	39097	361484	67478	343986	73.5
1991--1995	**6178916**	**1888982**	**4289934**	**237180**	**5256320**	**685416**	**4378783**	**70.9**
1991	541624	86149	455475	11578	460759	69287	448861	82.9
1992	824518	169979	654539	17901	731095	75522	600487	72.8
1993	1218170	367869	850301	33269	1092674	92227	687026	56.4
1994	2022193	669408	1352785	36723	1855312	130158	1625303	80.4
1995	1572441	595577	976834	137709	1283375	151327	1017106	64.7
1996	1680479	636918	1043561	222645	1318904	138930	1553521	92.4
1997	1911525	894052	1017473	180134	1550027	181364	1301241	68.1
1998	2114549	1003398	1111151	27792	1822482	264275	1412362	66.8
1999	1752093	646454	1105639	10618	1536248	205227	1990395	113.6

附 1-12 国有单位更新改造投资额
INVESTMENT IN INNOVATIONS OF STATE-OWNED UNITS

年 份 Year	更新改造投资额 (亿 元) Investment (100 million yuan)	按隶属关系分 Grouped by Administrative Relationship		按建设性质分 Grouped by Type of Construction			新增固定资产 (亿 元) Incremental Fixed Assets (100 million yuan)	固定资产交付使用率 (%) Rate of Fixed Assets Put into Operation (%)
		中央 Central	地方 Local	新建 Newly-built	扩建、改建 Expanding, Replacement	其他 Others		
1981--1985	**62.5**						**44.7**	**71.5**
1981	6.8						5.3	77.9
1982	7.9	1.6	6.3				5.9	74.7
1983	10.8	2.6	8.2				8.1	75.0
1984	15.3	3.5	11.8	0.3	13.2	1.8	10.3	67.3
1985	21.7	4.5	17.2	1.3	19.3	1.1	15.1	69.6
1986--1990	**201.3**	**33.2**	**168.1**	**12.8**	**163.1**	**25.4**	**143.2**	**71.1**
1986	33.4	5.7	27.7	2.4	27.1	3.9	21.9	65.6
1987	43.1	7.9	35.2	1.1	37.1	4.9	32.1	74.5
1988	43.6	6.6	37.0	2.8	34.9	5.9	29.5	67.7
1989	36.5	5.9	30.6	2.6	29.2	4.7	26.8	73.4
1990	44.7	7.1	37.6	3.9	34.8	6.0	32.9	73.6
1991--1995	**567.9**	**185.1**	**382.8**				**418.3**	**73.7**
1991	52.4	8.6	43.8	1.2	44.9	6.3	43.1	82.3
1992	79.2	17.0	62.2	1.8	70.5	6.9	57.8	73.0
1993	116.1	36.3	79.8				66.7	57.5
1994	179.2	65.9	113.3				154.9	86.4
1995	141.0	57.3	83.7				95.8	67.9
1996	156.4	61.8	94.6				138.4	88.5
1997	174.4	87.8	86.6	10.1	112.8	51.5	123.6	70.9
1998	196.5	98.9	97.6	8.5	172.2	15.8	131.7	67.0
1999	164.6	63.8	100.8	0.4	144.4	19.8	181.8	110.4

附 1-13 房 地 产 投 资 额
INVESTMENT IN REAL ESTATE DEVELOPMENT

年 份 Year	投 资 总 额 (亿元) Total Investment (100 million yuan)	商品房屋施工面积 (万平方米) Floor Space of Commodity Buildings under Construction (10000 sq.m)	# 本年新开工面积 Construction of this Year	商品房屋竣工面积 (万平方米) Floor Space of Commodity Buildings under Construction (10000 sq.m)	商品房销售建筑面积 (万平方米) Floor Space of Commodity Buildings Sales (10000 sq.m)
1990	22.5	774.0	249.1	271.6	142.2
1991--1995	**568.4**	**7501.6**	**3022.6**	**2061.7**	**855.6**
1991	24.0	815.1	317.6	275.2	154.0
1992	33.7	1021.1	508.6	331.4	159.1
1993	58.4	1262.0	524.8	356.4	182.0
1994	99.5	1593.2	659.4	445.7	168.6
1995	352.8	2810.2	1012.2	653.0	191.9
1996	328.2	2824.6	578.7	663.4	215.3
1997	330.3	2869.6	848.4	682.3	290.9
1998	377.4	3499.1	1193.4	842.8	409.2
1999	421.5	3784.0	1061.8	1208.5	544.4

附1-14 地方财政收支
LOCAL FINANCIAL REVENUE AND EXPENDITURE

单位：亿元 (100 million yuan)

年份 Year	地方财政收入 Local Financial Revenue	#各项税收 Taxes	地方财政支出 Local Financial Expenditure	#基本建设 Capital Construction	#农业生产和农业事业费 Agricultural Production and Operating Expenses	#文教科卫事业费 Culture,Education,Science and Health Expenses	#教育事业费 Education	#科学事业费 Scientific Research
1978	50.46	18.25	20.38	10.89	0.84	2.43	1.46	0.22
1979	47.75	19.41	20.06	10.07	0.86	2.94	1.77	0.24
1980	51.29	21.22	14.87	5.65	0.75	3.22	1.93	0.26
1981--1985	**234.27**	**149.21**	**111.40**	**39.75**	**4.69**	**24.82**	**14.04**	**1.64**
1981	49.12	22.47	14.85	5.95	0.71	3.65	2.15	0.29
1982	47.25	24.40	16.80	6.44	0.80	4.17	2.37	0.27
1983	39.84	26.45	19.61	6.47	0.83	4.63	2.65	0.36
1984	45.62	31.49	27.15	10.06	1.12	5.53	3.00	0.37
1985	52.44	44.40	32.99	10.83	1.23	6.84	3.87	0.37
1986--1990	**337.13**	**335.42**	**272.89**	**55.78**	**12.72**	**59.36**	**30.48**	**2.99**
1986	60.34	49.82	44.27	11.22	1.57	8.20	4.45	0.49
1987	63.62	55.16	49.67	10.47	1.91	9.21	4.79	0.58
1988	68.11	67.27	52.93	10.53	2.88	11.46	6.04	0.58
1989	71.05	79.30	59.50	11.70	3.15	13.67	7.00	0.57
1990	74.01	83.87	66.52	11.86	3.21	16.82	8.20	0.76
1991--1995	**456.48**	**586.35**	**473.64**	**51.07**	**22.74**	**131.86**	**73.30**	**7.36**
1991	77.02	92.02	67.98	9.35	3.67	17.58	9.41	1.01
1992	80.25	104.14	71.74	8.57	3.98	19.72	10.56	1.10
1993	84.10	136.77	80.99	10.35	4.33	24.08	13.10	1.30
1994	99.85	107.48	98.53	9.37	4.93	29.81	17.22	1.62
1995	115.26	145.94	154.40	13.43	5.83	40.67	23.01	2.34
1996	150.90	203.07	187.45	21.66	7.42	51.66	29.57	2.94
1997	209.91	239.13	262.20	24.89	9.85	63.83	35.97	3.74
1998	265.61	272.23	316.84	32.50	10.70	72.79	41.31	4.11
1999	320.45	319.90	410.19	58.37	13.13	84.6	49.24	4.91

注：1.1978-1998 年地方财政收支数为决算数，1999 年为初步统计数。

2.1996-1999 年各项税收中含企业所得税。

(a) Data from 1978 to 1998 is the final one, while that of 1999 is the preliminary one.

(b) Taxes from 1996 to 1999 include those from enterprise income.

附 1-15 北京市各银行各项存款年末余额
YEAR-END BALANCE OF DEPOSITS OF BANKS OF BEIJING

单位：万元 (10000 yuan)

年份 Year	合计 Total	企业存款 Enterprises	财政存款 Financial	机关团体、部队存款 Government Organs Bodies and Army	城镇储蓄存款 Urban Saving Deposits	农村存款 Rural
1978	1146580	527922	40273	389409	88991	46749
1979	1390517	649013	49342	463723	104400	57357
1980	1679891	834102	71486	566547	133310	67679
1981	2204737	1131870	65544	750606	157369	89070
1982	2792318	1432034	87904	974105	191882	105168
1983	3212851	1660027	85297	1087862	251065	128364
1984	3755220	2254153	129052	927955	321447	122081
1985	4109535	2454797	182064	890667	422447	137390
1986	5087562	3116297	165906	1027730	556249	179889
1987	6107619	3555956	150093	1335385	751854	205995
1988	6099142	3328559	97147	1180338	905519	295712
1989	7176132	3709770	259761	1218831	1337629	317000
1990	8689227	4293690	290365	1503878	1879081	297212
1991	11060952	5484293	333025	1879611	2498786	367665
1992	13095965	7005468	112779	1422621	3282099	534536
1993	16492164	8351199	142235	1551093	4824810	804791
1994	23111169	10377956	227561	2004247	7414350	932779
1995	30541198	16074288	359667	2116841	11034549	184283
1996	37818707	19705705	483317	2364532	15060889	199136
1997	51036605	29211539	381652	3303945	17709062	252358
1998	63691737	36289291	970772	5134092	20631876	266550
1999	79068543	44475637	1968641	7252845	24290306	271969

注：1997-1999 年存款合计中含代理财政存款。

Note: Deposits from 1997 to 1999 include agent financial deposits.

附 1-16 北京市各银行各项贷款年末余额
YEAR-END BALANCE OF LOANS OF BANKS BEIJING

单位：万元 (10000 yuan)

年 份 Year	合 计 Total	工业生产企业贷款 Industrial Production	商 业企业贷款 Commerce	建 筑企业贷款 Construc-tion	农业贷款 Agricul-ture	固定资产贷 款 Fixed Assets	短 期贷 款 Short-term	中长期贷 款 Mid,Long-term
1978	539078	214352	319239		5484	3		
1979	742332	216791	475507		6133	43901		
1980	873420	252528	495423	2198	7442	110685		
1981	912591	265718	517190	3624	8642	102540		
1982	1090686	346081	522596	10508	9479	178107		
1983	1494770	687371	552268	21486	14350	189486		
1984	1933724	774286	646218	76085	55606	304220		
1985	2534647	926420	697008	90789	61870	428020		
1986	3127010	1126873	814253	109423	96030	528287		
1987	3623937	1237457	896170	120812	126462	608207		
1988	4157237	1401628	1133718	162539	72292	753177	2777141	
1989	4870606	1740436	1407018	175324	99980	776477		
1990	5526782	2113813	1613340	187509	147878	946906	4159282	946906
1991	6326887	2407065	1810436	201089	193636	1159300	4724335	1159300
1992	7304636	2662278	2091350	218154	232829	1473004	5325684	1473004
1993	9715379	3372431	2519224	262157	271067	2344437	6713712	2344437
1994	10703251	3887403	1954192	284100	274209	3124624	7155394	3124624
1995	15605875	4643921	3592487	358327	339788	3563697	10159790	3563697
1996	18096848	5747916	4327060	483578	386784	3918864	12463119	3918864
1997	25444738	7412815	5632541	1000396	477519	5524730	18353500	5524730
1998	31269744	8919232	5892568	1383505	530789	7281840	20993880	7281840
1999	37612521	9917578	6722679	1967942	505578	8229492	25601364	8229492

附 1-17 各种物价总指数
AGGREGATE PRICE INDICES

年份 Year	商品零售价格总指数(上年=100) Aggregate Retail Price Index (preceding year=100)	居民消费价格总指数(上年=100) Aggregate Consumer Price Index (preceding year=100)	农副产品收购价格总指数(上年=100) Purchasing Price Index of Farm and Sideline Products (preceding year=100)	农业生产资料价格指数(上年=100) Price Index of Agricultural Capital Goods (preceding year=100)	商品零售价格总指数(1978=100) Aggregate Retail Price Index (1978=100)	居民消费价格总指数(1978=100) Aggregate Consumer Price Index (1978=100)	农副产品收购价格总指数(1978=100) Purchasing Price Index of Farm and Sideline Products (1978=100)	农业生产资料价格指数(1978=100) Price Index of Agricultural Capital Goods (1978=100)
1978	100.6	100.6					100.0	100.0
1979	101.8	101.8	109.5	100.0	101.8	101.8	109.5	100
1980	106.7	106.0	105.5	100.2	108.6	107.9	115.5	100.3
1981	101.4	101.3	109.4	100.1	110.2	109.2	126.4	100.3
1982	102.0	101.8	101.9	100.1	112.3	111.2	128.7	100.4
1983	100.6	100.5	101.8	101.6	113.0	111.8	131.0	102.0
1984	102.1	102.2	102.3	109.7	115.4	114.2	133.9	111.9
1985	118.6	117.6	117.6	100.9	136.8	134.4	157.5	112.9
1986	106.7	106.8	108.1	102.7	145.9	143.5	170.3	115.9
1987	108.7	108.6	116.1	110.8	158.6	155.8	197.6	128.4
1988	121.9	120.4	123.2	117.6	193.3	187.6	243.4	151.0
1989	118.5	117.2	106.8	121.5	229.1	219.9	260.0	183.5
1990	104.1	105.4	101.9	102.1	238.5	231.8	264.9	187.4
1991	108.5	111.9	101.7	102.5	258.8	259.4	269.4	192.1
1992	108.3	109.9	102.4	103.6	280.3	285.1	275.9	199.0
1993	116.9	119.0	107.0	109.1	327.7	339.3	295.2	217.1
1994	117.9	124.9	133.4	120.1	386.4	423.8	393.8	260.7
1995	112.6	117.3	130.6	133.2	435.1	497.1	514.3	347.3
1996	107.3	111.6	101.5	106.8	466.9	554.8	522.0	370.9
1997	103.8	105.3	92.8	100.4	484.6	584.2	484.4	372.2
1998	98.3	102.4	93.6	102.6	476.4	598.2	484.4	372.2
1999	98.8	100.6	97.5	94.2	470.7	601.8	442.1	359.7

附 1-18 职工工资总额和保险福利费
TOTAL WAGES,INSURANCE AND WELFARES OF STAFF AND WORKERS

年份 Year	职工工资总额(亿元) Total Wages (100 million yuan)	国有经济单位 State-Owned	城镇集体经济单位 Urban Collective Owned	其他经济单位 Others	职工保险福利费用总额(亿元) Total Insurance and Welfares (100 million yuan)	国有经济单位 State-Owned	城镇集体经济单位 Urban Collective Owned	其他经济单位 Others
1978	18.7	16.2	2.5		2.6	2.6		
1979	22.4	19.4	3.0		3.1	3.1		
1980	26.9	23.3	3.6		4.3	4.3		
1981--1985	**183.7**	**153.7**	**29.6**	**0.4**	**39.5**	**39.5**		
1981	28.3	24.2	4.1		5.2	5.2		
1982	30.5	25.9	4.6		5.8	5.8		
1983	33.8	28.5	5.3		7.7	7.7		
1984	40.4	33.7	6.6	0.1	9.3	9.3		
1985	50.7	41.4	9.0	0.3	11.5	11.5		
1986--1990	**421.1**	**349.7**	**64.4**	**7.0**	**95.7**	**91.5**	**3.6**	**0.6**
1986	58.0	48.5	9.1	0.4	13.9	13.9		
1987	66.7	56.0	10.1	0.6	17.0	17.0		
1988	81.2	68.1	12.1	1.0	24.3	24.3		
1989	96.3	81.0	13.4	1.9	19.5	17.4	1.8	0.3
1990	118.9	96.1	19.7	3.1	21.0	18.9	1.8	0.3
1991--1995	**1198.1**	**950.3**	**156.6**	**91.2**	**156.0**	**138.9**	**10.9**	**6.2**
1991	132.2	106.1	21.5	4.6	25.3	22.6	2.1	0.6
1992	158.5	128.6	23.9	6.0	30.6	27.4	2.4	0.8
1993	218.9	176.6	28.5	13.8	36.0	32.2	2.5	1.3
1994	306.5	243.4	36.2	26.9	30.4	27.0	1.9	1.5
1995	382.0	295.6	46.5	39.9	33.7	29.7	2.0	2.0
1996	442.4	339.4	46.2	56.8	37.3	31.7	2.8	2.8
1997	514.8	383.6	53.8	77.4	48.1	41.6	2.8	3.7
1998	558.2	391.9	45.0	121.3	54.5	47.5	3.0	4.0
1999	614.5	420.0	44.8	149.7	60.2	50.1	4.0	6.2

附 1-19 职工平均工资及指数
AVERAGE WAGE AND INDEX OF STAFF AND WORKERS

年份 Year	职工平均工资(元) Average Wage (yuan)	国有经济单位 State-Owned	城镇集体经济单位 Urban Collective Owned	其他经济单位 Others	职工实际工资指数(1978=100) Index of Actual Wage	国有经济单位 State-Owned	城镇集体经济单位 Urban Collective Owned	其他经济单位 Others
1978	673	703	471		100	100	100	100
1979	742	778	556		108.3	108.7	116.0	
1980	848	889	635		116.8	117.3	125.0	
1981	837	880	685		113.9	114.6	133.1	
1982	863	896	715		115.3	114.6	136.5	
1983	931	964	785		123.7	122.6	149.0	
1984	1086	1127	946	1170	141.3	140.3	175.8	
1985	1343	1367	1231	1768	148.5	144.7	194.5	112.5
1986	1488	1530	1287	2080	154.1	151.7	190.4	123.9
1987	1670	1712	1449	2267	159.3	156.3	197.5	124.4
1988	2000	2048	1738	2661	158.4	155.3	196.7	121.2
1989	2312	2366	1992	2761	156.2	153.1	192.3	107.3
1990	2653	2713	2334	3243	170.1	166.5	213.8	119.6
1991	2877	2937	2504	3713	164.8	161.1	205.0	122.3
1992	3402	3500	2828	4289	177.3	174.6	210.6	128.6
1993	4780	4920	3834	5469	209.3	206.3	239.9	137.8
1994	6540	6695	5009	8179	229.3	224.7	250.9	165.0
1995	8144	8237	6516	10278	243.4	235.7	278.3	176.7
1996	9579	9645	7133	13851	256.5	247.3	273.0	213.4
1997	11019	10917	8259	15370	280.2	265.6	300.2	224.9
1998	12285	11971	8800	15989	306.1	285.5	313.3	229.1
1999	13778	13483	8928	17748	335.2	314.0	310.3	248.4

附1-20 居民生活
PEOPLE'S LIVELIHOOD

年份 Year	城镇居民家庭平均每人每年(元) Annual Per Capita of Urban Households(yuan)					农村居民家庭平均每人每年(元) Annual Per Capita of Rural Households(yuan)				
	全部收入 Total Income	可支配收入 Discretionary Income	可支配收入指数(1978=100) Index of Discretionary Income (1978=100)	生活消费支出 Living Expenditures	#食品 Food	纯收入 Net Income	纯收入指数(1978=100) Index of Net Income (1978=100)	总支出 Total Expenditures	生活消费支出 Living Expenditures	#食品 Food
1978	450.2	365.4	100.0	359.9	211.2	224.8	100.0	219.0	185.4	116.7
1979	491.5	415.0	111.6	408.7	236.7	250.0	110.9	235.0	204.7	131.1
1980	599.4	501.4	127.2	490.4	271.0	308.1	135.4	290.0	256.8	140.2
1981	619.6	514.1	128.8	511.4	295.1	361.4	158.5	351.0	307.2	160.6
1982	668.1	561.1	138.0	534.8	317.6	430.2	186.1	411.0	345.5	181.1
1983	716.6	590.5	144.5	574.1	337.7	519.5	225.1	499.0	384.4	193.8
1984	837.7	693.7	166.1	666.8	379.1	664.2	282.9	559.0	435.0	222.5
1985	1158.8	907.7	134.8	923.3	466.9	775.1	324.0	726.0	510.0	240.5
1986	1317.3	1067.5	203.5	1067.4	543.4	823.1	335.6	857.0	645.3	292.4
1987	1413.2	1181.9	207.5	1147.6	605.0	916.4	357.4	943.0	705.5	340.9
1988	1767.7	1437.0	209.3	1455.6	743.4	1062.6	368.8	1246.0	883.3	407.9
1989	1899.6	1597.1	198.5	1520.4	841.3	1230.7	376.8	1356.0	976.3	484.3
1990	2067.3	1787.1	210.8	1646.1	892.2	1297.1	384.8	1372.0	980.7	496.8
1991	2359.9	2040.4	215.3	1860.2	1016.8	1422.3	391.3	1585.0	1100.1	537.0
1992	2813.1	2363.7	226.9	2134.7	1126.3	1568.8	399.4	1684.0	1179.0	573.8
1993	3935.4	3296.0	265.9	2939.6	1404.7	1854.8	419.8	1714.0	1308.9	611.7
1994	5585.9	4731.2	305.5	4134.1	1919.0	2422.1	457.8	2175.0	1676.5	824.8
1995	6748.7	5868.4	322.9	5019.8	2346.5	3208.5	486.3	3080.0	2433.0	1206.0
1996	7945.8	6885.5	378.9	5729.5	2671.5	3562.7	509.8	3272.0	2655.5	1233.1
1997	8741.7	7813.1	365.9	6531.8	2854.4	3762.4	535.8	3379.0	2795.4	1248.4
1998	10098.2	8472.0	387.6	6970.8	2865.7	4028.9	571.7	3617.0	2945.5	1241.9
1999	10654.8	9182.8	417.6	7498.5	2959.2	4316.4	612.9	3938.0	3132.5	1253.5

年份 Year	每一城镇就业者负担人数(人) Dependents Per Urban Employee (person)	每一农村劳动力负担人数(人) Dependents Per Rural Labor Force (person)	城市人均居住面积(平方米) Urban Per Capita Living Space (sq.m)	农村人均住房面积(平方米) Rural Per Capita Living Space (sq.m)	城乡储蓄存款余额(亿元) Balance of Saving Deposits (100 million yuan)	城镇储蓄 Urban	农户储蓄 Rural	人均储蓄(元) Per Capita Saving Deposits (yuan)
1978	1.86	2.15	4.55	9.25	9.33	8.90	0.43	107.09
1979	1.83	2.16	4.57	9.67	11.07	10.44	0.63	123.04
1980	1.80	2.13	4.79	10.09	14.39	13.33	1.06	159.20
1981	1.72	2.13	5.08	12.35	17.39	15.74	1.65	189.23
1982	1.66	1.97	5.38	13.01	21.77	19.19	2.58	232.55
1983	1.65	1.82	5.68	14.09	29.81	25.11	4.70	312.49
1984	1.63	1.79	5.92	14.08	38.82	32.14	6.67	401.42
1985	1.66	1.64	6.17	16.37	51.70	42.24	9.45	522.7
1986	1.66	1.66	6.46	17.17	68.58	55.62	12.95	664.52
1987	1.65	1.64	6.82	18.38	92.98	75.19	17.79	871.38
1988	1.71	1.63	7.17	19.23	111.64	90.55	21.09	1032.98
1989	1.52	1.62	7.45	20.09	162.01	133.75	28.26	1597.76
1990	1.52	1.61	7.72	20.62	226.62	188.03	38.59	2208.73
1991	1.47	1.59	8.01	21.92	298.18	249.88	48.30	2878.21
1992	1.43	1.58	8.31	22.67	387.82	328.21	59.61	3721.93
1993	1.42	1.51	8.51	23.7	560.66	482.48	78.18	5349.78
1994	1.41	1.49	8.73	24.42	853.21	745.88	107.33	8079.62
1995	1.41	1.47	8.87	24.74	1253.95	1111.50	142.46	11757.61
1996	1.41	1.45	9.17	25.74	1706.98	1528.41	178.56	15839.09
1997	1.43	1.48	9.49	27.39	1975.23	1770.90	204.36	18196.80
1998	1.40	1.44	9.87	27.64	2287.19	2063.19	224.00	20954.54
1999	1.41	1.43	10.43	28.65	2680.67	2429.03	251.63	24374.11

附 1-21 城镇居民家庭平均每百户主要耐用消费品拥有量
POSSESSION OF MAIN DURABLE CONSUMER GOODS OF PER 100 URBAN HOUSEHOLDS

年 份 Year	自行车 (辆) Bicycles (unit)	录放像机 (台) Videocorders (set)	淋 浴 热水器 (台) Showers (unit)	洗衣机 (台) Washing Machines (unit)	彩 色 电视机 (台) Color TV Sets (set)	黑 白 电视机 (台) Black and White (set)	收录机 (台) Recorders (set)	电冰箱 (台) Refrige-rators (unit)	照相机 (架) Cameras (set)
1978	135.8					19.2	0.6		7.5
1979	145.7			0.1		41.8	2.4		9.8
1980	150.9			1.9		65.8	9.5	0.3	11.4
1981	153.8			12.3	1.7	80.0	20.0	1.7	13.3
1982	166.5			18.8	1.7	84.8	28.0	2.7	17.2
1983	175.8			28.7	4.3	86.6	40.5	7.0	20.6
1984	183.0			42.2	8.0	86.5	51.5	15.3	29.1
1985	177.0			57.5	32.2	80.7	70.3	41.9	34.6
1986	193.9			75.9	50.9	69.2	80.1	61.5	47.4
1987	210.2			82.6	57.5	70.5	87.0	71.8	55.5
1988	193.7			86.0	69.7	57.8	91.8	81.2	59.6
1989	233.0	10.1		89.7	80.5	55.4	95.5	89.4	62.2
1990	228.3	19.9		93.2	90.9	51.2	99.6	96.4	66.5
1991	233.8	28.4		93.0	97.1	44.0	100.0	101.7	72.7
1992	229.2	41.7	17.0	96.1	101.4	39.5	104.1	101.3	77.2
1993	243.2	45.6	23.2	99.8	107.2	39.2	113.0	100.8	82.4
1994	246.8	49.8	38.8	102.8	111.8	37.4	107.8	104.4	85.4
1995	243.6	54.2	45.4	100.4	113.6	33.8	110.2	104.4	86.8
1996	249.0	57.8	52.0	101.4	119.2	30.8	113.8	105.4	87.2
1997	209.4	56.0	58.4	100.6	123.8		65.0	104.2	88.2
1998	221.0	59.8	65.4	102.2	133.2			105.4	95.2
1999	220.1	54.1	67.1	99.6	141.4		69.9	102.8	95.0

附 1-22 农民家庭平均每百户主要耐用消费品拥有量
POSSESSION OF MAIN DURABLE CONSUMER GOODS OF PER 100 RURAL HOUSEHOLDS

年 份 Year	自行车 (辆) Bicycles (unit)	缝纫机 (架) Sewing Machines (set)	手 表 (只) Watches (unit)	黑 白 电视机 (台) Black and White TV Sets (set)	彩 色 电视机 (台) Color TV Sets (set)	录音机 (台) Recorders (set)	照相机 (架) Cameras (set)	电风扇 (台) Electric Fans (unit)	洗衣机 (台) Washing Machines (unit)	电冰箱 (台) Refrige-rators (unit)
1978	109	36	46							
1979	98	32	67	1						
1980	123	39	103	5						
1981	135	46	136	14						
1982	141	50	169	33		2		11	2	
1983	167	55	192	41		7		17	6	
1984	187	58	211	57		14		28	15	1
1985	182	57	201	53	7	21	2	32	23	2
1986	191	56	211	59	12	28	4	42	39	5
1987	204	60	226	63	15	34	5	52	48	9
1988	218	61	231	66	20	41	7	61	56	14
1989	224	63	232	66	25	47	8	67	61	19
1990	235	65	243	65	29	47	8	73	63	23
1991	232	63	217	58	42	48	11	84	69	36
1992	245	64	229	60	46	50	14	92	73	40
1993	249	68	223	56	56	53	15	98	76	47
1994	254	69	239	54	65	59	17	109	80	53
1995	251	67	214	46	74	56	21	115	81	63
1996	250	68	217	44	79	58	21	117	83	67
1997	248	68	221	43	85	58	25	127	84	72
1998	249	70	227	39	92	58	26	133	85	75
1999	241	69	225	34	101	59	29	143	86	81

附 1-23 农业基本情况
BASIC STATISTICS FOR AGRICULTURE

年份 Year	农林牧渔业从业人员（万人） Labors Force of Farming,Freostry Animal Husbandry and Fishery (10000 persons)	年末实有耕地面积（万公顷） Cultivated Area (year-end) (10000 hectare)	当年减少耕地面积（万公顷） Decresae of Cultivated Area of this Year (10000 hectare)	播种面积（万公顷） Sown Area (10000 hectare)	# 粮食作物 Grain Crops	# 经济作物 Cash Crops	造林面积（万公顷） Afforestation Area (10000 hectare)	受灾面积（万公顷） Disaster Area (10000 hectare)	成灾面积（万公顷） Infested Area (10000 hectare)
1978	117.7	42.9	0.3	69.1	56.1	4.9	1.4		
1979	115.5	42.7	0.2	67.7	56	3.7	1.6		
1980	113.3	42.6	0.1	65.7	54.9	3.3	2.4		
1981	112.6	42.5	0.1	64.3	53.0	3.2	2.7		
1982	110.1	42.4	0.1	64.2	52.7	2.9	2.8		
1983	112.2	42.3	0.1	63.8	53.0	2.8	3.3	16.2	8.9
1984	101.1	42.2	0.1	63.3	52.3	2.7	3.2	18.0	14.0
1985	90.3	42.1	0.1	61.8	51.1	2.9	3.0	14.0	8.0
1986	86.1	41.9	0.2	60.5	49.9	2.4	1.4	7.0	3.0
1987	84.6	41.8	0.1	59.8	49.5	2.0	2.0	3.0	1.0
1988	80.9	41.6	0.2	59.5	48.8	1.9	1.6	11.0	5.0
1989	83.4	41.4	0.2	58.9	48.3	1.6	0.8	21.0	9.0
1990	82.5	41.3	0.1	59	48.4	1.6	4.1	17.8	8.7
1991	80.3	41.1	0.2	59.0	48.3	1.7	1.5	16.9	7.7
1992	74.6	40.9	0.2	58.6	47.7	1.7	1.5	3.8	0.8
1993	72.5	40.6	0.3	56.5	45.6	1.8	4.8	11.9	5.3
1994	68.7	40.2	0.4	55.1	43.0	1.7	5.5	19.3	4.6
1995	65.5	39.9	0.3	55.3	43.4	1.5	4.7	12.1	3.7
1996	66.9	39.9	0.3	53.8	42.7	1.4	4.0	12.3	5.0
1997	65.3	34.2	0.3	53.6	42.5	1.2	3.8	14.3	9.7
1998	67.7	34.1	0.3	53.5	42.3	1.2	3.7	7.8	3.9
1999	71.1	33.8	0.3	52.7	41.0	1.3	3.0		

注：1995、1996、1997 年耕地面积由市土地局提供。

Note：Data of cultivated area of 1995 and 1996 are provided by Municipal Land Bureau.

附1-24 农业生产条件
PRODUCTIVE CONDITIONS OF AGRICULTURE

年份 Year	农用机械总动力 (万千瓦) Total Power of Agricultural Machinery (10000kw)	农用大中型拖拉机 (台) Large Medium Tractors (unit)	小型拖拉机 (台) Mini-Tractors (unit)	灌溉面积 (千公顷) Irrigated Area (1000 hectare)	化肥施用量 (万吨) Consumption of Chemical Fertilizers (10000 tons)	农村用电量 (万千瓦小时) Rural Electricity Consumption (10000 kwh)	农村居民家庭每户生产性固定资产 (元) Productive Fixed Assets Per Rural Households (yuan)	每公顷面积产量(公斤) Yield Per Hectare(kg) 粮食 Grain	棉花 Cotton	油料 Oilbearing Crops
1978	189.4	5568	23412	341.7	1.2	58802	5.0	3315	255	788
1979	212.2	6496	24724	340.8	1.1	59531	6.5	3090	278	855
1980	234.6	7705	24952	340.3	1.2	76753	8.0	3390	443	1118
1981	244.8	8284	23465	341.3	1.1	91843	10.9	3413	338	810
1982	242.2	9032	22843	339.3	1.2	96960	22.3	3518	503	953
1983	262.1	9855	22652	343.3	1.2	104608	95.3	3803	593	1065
1984	291.3	10859	26563	342.7	1.1	119287	163.0	4155	900	1500
1985	320.4	11319	35051	338.4	8.2	126830	394.3	4298	848	1928
1986	345.5	11664	37023	337.9	9.1	180640	419.2	4335	735	1530
1987	388.4	12170	37319	337.9	10.0	159450	444.0	4590	908	2085
1988	399.7	12596	45013	338.1	10.6	163986	549.7	4800	810	2055
1989	423.9	12344	47546	338.4	11.8	128414	543.3	4950	960	2220
1990	416.2	12844	47020	335.1	14.4	122711	595.6	5460	1035	2565
1991	384.8	12906	44610	328.7	14.4	111347	700.4	5787	885	2685
1992	399.8	12752	44525	331.1	14.4	143963	844.9	5907	1051	2760
1993	450.5	12701	44200	314.7	14.9	169911	951.6	6236	1043	3009
1994	459.2	12475	44500	323.4	19.8	172042	2194.6	6420	910	3051
1995	468.1	12228	42100	292.4	18.8	201731	2776.5	5985	825	2794
1996	468.4	12272	38200	301.9	18.9	275871	2394.2	5659	924	2741
1997	433.2	12088	30000	323.3	19.7	301655	2818.9	5594	1040	2736
1998	415.5	12032	30000	323.7	19.3	290859	3411.8	5661	854	2941
1999	410.4	11852	27295	322.1	19.0	330069	3814.0	4905	1016	2647

注：1.化肥施用量为折纯量。

2.农村居民家庭每户生产性固定资产为抽样调查数。

a) Consumption of chemical fertilizers are those converted into pure.

b) Data of productive fixed assets per rural household refers to those from sample survey.

附 1-25 农林牧渔业总产值和指数
GROSS OUTPUT VALUE OF FARMING,FORESTRY,ANIMAL HUSBANDRY FISHERY AND THEIR INDEX

年份 Year	农林牧渔业总产值(亿元) Gross Output Value of Farming,Forestry, Animal Husbandry and Fishery (100 million yuan)	农业 Farming	林业 Forestry	牧业 Animal Husbandry	渔业 Fishery	农林牧渔业总产值指数(1978=100) Index of Gross Output Value of FFAF (1978=100)	农业 Farming	林业 Forestry	牧业 Animal Husbandry	渔业 Fishery
1978	11.5	8.9	0.2	2.4	0.01	100.0	100.0	100.0	100.0	100.0
1979	12.3	8.8	0.2	3.3	0.02	99.1	95.8	87.5	108.5	200.0
1980	14.2	9.7	0.5	3.9	0.05	101.2	92.9	137.5	122.0	200.0
1981--1985	**98.2**	**63.0**	**4.2**	**30.1**	**0.80**					
1981	14.9	10.1	0.7	4.1	0.05	100.6	92.1	137.5	120.7	200.0
1982	16.7	11.2	0.7	4.7	0.05	108.5	96.3	137.5	140.2	200.0
1983	19.4	12.5	0.8	6.0	0.10	123.6	107.1	150.0	168.3	400.0
1984	22.2	14.4	0.9	6.7	0.20	137.6	120.0	150.0	182.9	600.0
1985	25.9	16.1	0.8	8.6	0.40	146.4	126.3	137.5	198.8	1200.0
1986--1990	**242.4**	**138.8**	**4.1**	**91.6**	**7.9**					
1986	28.1	17.2	0.8	9.4	0.7	147.0	125.0	125.0	202.4	1464.4
1987	34.4	20.3	0.8	12.3	1.0	160.0	134.2	137.5	224.4	2185.4
1988	52.6	31.4	0.9	18.6	1.7	179.4	140.8	125.0	278.0	2907.4
1989	60.4	34.2	0.7	23.3	2.2	198.2	151.3	112.5	324.4	3236.8
1990	70.2	39.0	0.9	28.0	2.3	210.3	154.2	125.0	348.8	3622.8
1991--1995	**567.9**	**291.0**	**11.2**	**244.6**	**21.1**					
1991	76.4	39.5	1.5	32.8	2.6	229.1	164.6	162.5	395.1	4211.4
1992	84.5	43.2	1.6	36.3	3.4	244.5	172.5	150.0	431.7	5092.8
1993	100.4	51.1	2.3	42.7	4.3	257.3	183.3	162.5	443.9	5887.7
1994	144.3	72.5	3.1	64.0	4.7	276.7	193.8	187.5	487.8	6131.4
1995	164.4	86.8	2.7	68.8	6.1	273.9	195.4	200.0	462.2	7500.8
1996	168.9	89.2	2.8	71.1	5.8	271.5	190.0	212.5	473.2	7000.0
1997	170.9	87.0	2.9	74.8	6.2	273.8	199.7	226.9	466.2	6522.4
1998	176.6	89.2	3.2	76.6	7.6	283.0	201.5	202.3	484.4	7374.0
1999	184.3	91.2	4.25	81.1	7.8	301.8	204.6	225.0	529.3	9502.0

注：绝对数按现价计算，指数按可比价计算。

Note：Value are calculated at current prices and index are calculated at constant prices.

附 1-26 主要农业产品产量
OUTPUT OF MAJOR AGRICULTURAL PRODUCTS

年份 Year	粮食 (万吨) Grain (10000 tons)	# 谷物 Cereal	棉花 (万吨) Cotton (10000 tons)	油料 (万吨) Oilbearing Crops (10000 tons)	猪牛羊肉 (万吨) Pork,Beef and Mutton (10000 tons)	禽蛋 (万吨) Poultry Eggs (10000 tons)	水产品 (万吨) Aquatic Products (10000 tons)	大牲畜年底头数 (万头) Large Animals (year-end) (10000 heads)	# 役畜 Draught Animals	猪年底头数 (万头) Hogs (year-end) (10000 heads)
1978	186.0	180.4	0.3	2.6	11.9	0.5	0.2	30.4	21.5	248.3
1979	172.8	168.4	0.1	2.6	13.2	1.0	0.3	29.2	20.4	246.7
1980	186.0	182.2	0.1	3.1	15.1	3.4	0.4	27.9	19.3	232.5
1981--1985	**1004.8**	**984.1**	**1.4**	**13.1**	**70.7**	**44.3**	**4.0**	**119.5**	**89.7**	**927.0**
1981	180.7	177.7	0.1	2.2	14.3	3.7	0.4	26.3	19.2	210.9
1982	185.5	182.5	0.1	2.3	14.1	5.4	0.4	24.9	18.2	206.4
1983	201.5	198.3	0.2	2.1	14.9	8.9	0.6	24.3	18.1	190.3
1984	217.4	211.5	0.6	2.6	13.9	12.2	1.0	22.8	17.6	161.8
1985	219.7	214.1	0.4	3.9	13.5	14.1	1.6	21.2	16.6	157.6
1986--1990	**1181.9**	**1154.1**	**1.4**	**15.2**	**77.3**	**103.8**	**18.8**	**115.2**	**82.7**	**805.0**
1986	216.5	211.2	0.2	3.0	13.3	14.7	2.2	21.9	16.6	145.6
1987	227.0	220.9	0.3	3.3	13.0	16.8	3.0	23.1	16.9	120.4
1988	234.6	229.2	0.3	3.0	13.4	21.8	3.9	23.1	16.3	145.3
1989	239.2	233.7	0.3	2.8	17.2	24.7	4.6	23.8	16.6	187.7
1990	264.6	259.1	0.3	3.1	20.4	25.8	5.1	23.3	16.3	206.0
1991--1995	**1381.6**	**1349.3**	**1.9**	**17.6**	**138.0**	**139.3**	**34.7**	**130.6**	**61.3**	**1276.5**
1991	279.7	274.7	0.3	3.3	24.8	25.0	5.6	27.9	15.0	241.7
1992	281.9	276.7	0.5	3.4	27.3	26.5	6.4	26.9	13.6	269.1
1993	284.1	278.2	0.4	3.8	28.2	28.1	7.0	26.2	12.8	252.2
1994	249.2	267.0	0.4	3.8	30.7	31.2	7.6	26.7	10.9	260.1
1995	259.8	252.7	0.3	3.3	27.0	28.5	8.1	22.9	9.0	253.4
1996	237.4	231.8	0.3	3.0	27.6	24.7	7.8	20.5	7.4	240.0
1997	237.5	232.3	0.2	2.7	27.9	23.8	7.7	19.7	6.0	241.0
1998	239.2	234.0	0.2	2.8	31.2	17.9	7.6	18.5	5.3	254.5
1999	201.0	196.1	0.2	2.8	32.3	15.8	7.6	19.0	4.1	248.3

附 1-27 每一农林牧渔业从业者农业生产量

PRODUCTION VOLUME PER EMPLOYEE OF FARMING,FORESTRY, ANIMAL HUSBANDRY AND FISHERY

年 份 Year	农林牧渔业总产值(元) Gross Output Value of Farming,Forestry, Animal Husbandry and Fishery (yuan)	粮 食 (公斤) Grain (kg)	# 谷物 Cereal	棉 花 (公斤) Cotton (kg)	油 料 (公斤) Oilbearing Crops (kg)	猪牛羊肉 (公斤) Pork,Beef and Mutton (kg)	禽 蛋 (公斤) Poultry Eggs (kg)	水产品 (公斤) Aquatic Products (kg)
1978	977.9	1580.1	1529.3	2.9	22.2	101.1	4.6	1.5
1979	1066.7	1496.2	1458.3	0.6	22.2	114.0	8.5	2.4
1980	1248.9	1641.7	1608.1	0.8	27.3	133.2	29.6	3.6
1981	1318.8	1604.4	1577.7	0.6	19.8	127.1	32.7	3.8
1982	1512.3	1684.6	1657.5	0.9	20.7	128.3	51.1	3.4
1983	1729.1	1795.8	1767.1	1.8	18.3	132.6	79.2	4.9
1984	2146.4	2150.0	2092.4	5.6	26.2	137.5	120.9	10.0
1985	2823.9	2432.5	2370.5	4.8	43.6	149.3	156.1	17.6
1986	3228.8	2514.2	2453.3	2.5	35.4	155.0	170.6	25.6
1987	3995.3	2683.3	2610.9	3.1	38.7	153.1	198.4	35.5
1988	6415.3	2900.0	2833.6	3.4	37.0	166.0	269.1	48.2
1989	7146.3	2868.5	2801.6	3.1	34.1	205.8	296.3	55.2
1990	8400.0	3207.5	3140.5	4.2	37.5	247.0	312.4	61.9
1991	9402.2	3483.3	3421.0	4.3	40.9	309.1	311.5	69.4
1992	11166.2	3779.2	3708.9	6.5	45.6	366.5	355.1	86.0
1993	13848.3	3917.4	3837.8	5.9	52.2	389.1	387.7	96.9
1994	21004.4	4019.6	3886.2	5.4	55.2	447.4	453.8	111.1
1995	25099.2	3965.8	3858.3	4.2	50.2	412.0	435.7	122.9
1996	25232.6	3545.7	3465.4	3.8	44.0	411.6	368.8	117.0
1997	26152.0	3634.8	3556.1	3.4	41.8	426.8	363.9	117.3
1998	26077.0	3532.4	3454.0	2.7	41.9	460.8	264.0	129.1
1999	25919.0	2827.0	2758.1	2.6	39.4	454.3	222.2	106.9

附1-28 工业总产值
GROSS OUTPUT VALUE OF INDUSTRY

单位：亿元 (100 million yuan)

年份 Year	工业总产值 Gross Output Value	# 国有工业 State-owned	# 集体工业 Collective-owned	# 乡及乡以上 at Township Level and above	轻工业 Light Industry	重工业 Heavy Industry	# 大中型工业 Large and Medium Industry
1984	276.20	217.27	54.14	276.20	117.99	158.22	178.66
1985	324.19	248.48	69.43	324.19	135.75	188.44	213.73
1986--1990	**2618.45**	**1491.40**	**516.39**	**2521.45**	**1070.73**	**1450.73**	**1741.65**
1986	344.95	268.20	68.80	344.95	144.34	200.61	237.43
1987	399.09	305.99	81.08	399.09	164.80	234.29	280.16
1988	508.69		104.06	508.69	218.16	290.53	354.45
1989	622.37	450.88	134.46	622.37	272.66	349.71	421.68
1990	743.35	466.33	127.99	646.35	270.77	375.59	447.93
1991--1995	**6866.31**	**3737.35**	**1139.43**	**5862.75**	**1952.32**	**3910.41**	**3799.15**
1991	880.79	527.78	146.53	757.05	309.08	447.96	526.02
1992	1085.37	627.84	170.07	915.50	326.31	589.19	625.27
1993	1513.59	797.13	227.78	1242.56	385.44	857.12	796.27
1994	1721.13	906.56	243.61	1456.85	460.06	996.79	915.45
1995	1665.43	878.04	351.44	1490.79	471.43	1019.35	936.14
1996	1853.34	887.00	277.38	1632.17	522.43	1109.74	987.48
1997	1963.83	960.04	179.76	1744.98	554.07	1190.91	958.61
1998	2027.02	863.46	301.14	1991.96	612.02	1379.94	1084.25
1999	2190.26	769.54	263.17	2144.61	610.68	1533.93	1071.44

注：总产值按现价计算，乡及乡以上工业总产值从1998年开始调整为不含个体工业企业口径。（以下乡及乡以上口径变化与此相同）

Note: Gross output value is calculated at current prices, that at township level and above changed to that of enterprises except individual industry from 1998.(the followings have the same change)

附 1-29 工业总产值指数(1978=100)
INDEX OF GROSS OUTPUT VALUE OF INDUSTRY(1978=100)

年份 Year	工业总产值 Gross Output Value	# 国有工业 State-owned	# 集体工业 Collective-owned	# 乡及乡以上 at Township Level and above	轻工业 Light Industry	重工业 Heavy Industry	# 大中型工业 Large and Medium Industry
1978	100.0	100.0	100.0	100.0	100.0	100.0	100.0
1979	110.5	110.1	112.1	121.3	113.1	109.1	110.9
1980	121.3	118.6	134.3	122.0	134.9	113.9	118.5
1981--1985							
1981	112.1	119.5	139.8	123.3	154.5	106.4	121.2
1982	118.4	125.9	147.9	130.2	159.6	114.5	134.7
1983	129.7	136.3	170.4	142.7	171.9	127.2	151.4
1984	145.9	148.7	204.2	160.4	188.5	146.0	175.3
1985	159.2	158.4	240.2	175.1	204.7	159.9	199.1
1986--1990							
1986	166.6	167.0	242.4	183.2	214.9	166.9	212.1
1987	184.9	182.6	278.0	203.4	233.5	188.4	239.0
1988	216.6	207.0	337.9	238.2	280.5	216.3	274.8
1989	232.2	215.7	373.2	255.3	301.2	231.6	286.4
1990	257.0	215.7	396.3	268.3	312.2	245.9	297.7
1991--1995							
1991	398.1	230.3	447.2	299.1	340.9	278.3	329.7
1992	454.8	252.2	514.5	341.8	353.8	338.2	365.1
1993	516.1	277.9	651.4	413.8	418.4	415.0	381.0
1994	532.2	269.0	657.1	444.6	447.8	446.9	393.3
1995	569.5	290.6	665.9	494.1	432.3	533.6	472.6
1996	624.7	290.6	771.5	512.1	443.3	559.4	470.0
1997	694.0	325.9	485.9	574.1	487.0	628.5	442.3
1998	819.4	353.2	475.7	679.7	497.7	792.6	633.2
1999	936.6	290.7	460.0	774.9	513.1	940.0	695.1

注：指数按可比价计算。

Note：Index are calculated at constant prices.(the following table is the same)

附 1-30 工业总产值指数(上年=100)
INDEX OF GROSS OUTPUT VALUE OF INDUSTRY(PRECEDING YEAR=100)

年份 Year	工业总产值 Gross Output Value	# 国有工业 State-owned	# 集体工业 Collective-owned	# 乡及乡以上 at Township Level and above	轻工业 Light Industry	重工业 Heavy Industry	# 大中型工业 LargeandMedium Industry
1978	111.5	114.5	112.5	114.2	110.8	116.1	100.0
1979	111.2	110.1	112.1	110.5	113.1	109.1	110.9
1980	110.4	107.7	119.7	109.8	119.3	104.5	106.9
1981--1985							
1981	101.8	100.8	104.2	101.7	114.5	93.4	102.7
1982	106.1	105.4	105.8	105.6	103.3	107.6	111.2
1983	111.0	108.3	115.2	109.6	107.7	111.2	112.4
1984	113.8	109.1	119.9	112.4	109.6	114.7	115.7
1985	110.8	106.5	117.6	109.2	108.6	109.6	113.6
1986--1990							
1986	105.9	105.5	100.9	104.6	104.9	104.4	106.5
1987	113.4	109.3	114.7	111.0	108.7	112.8	112.7
1988	121.1	113.3	121.6	117.1	120.1	114.8	114.9
1989	109.0	104.2	110.4	107.2	107.4	107.1	104.2
1990	106.1	100.0	106.2	105.1	103.7	106.2	104.0
1991--1995							
1991	113.5	106.8	112.9	111.5	109.2	113.2	110.7
1992	118.0	109.5	115.0	114.3	103.8	121.5	110.7
1993	122.3	110.2	126.6	121.1	118.3	122.7	104.4
1994	104.2	96.8	100.9	107.4	107.0	107.7	103.2
1995	107.0	107.9	101.3	111.1	96.5	119.4	120.2
1996	109.7	103.8	126.1	109.2	109.7	109.7	102.5
1997	111.1	112.1	63.0	112.1	109.9	112.4	94.1
1998	118.1	108.4	97.9	118.4	102.2	126.1	142.4
1999	114.3	82.3	96.7	114.0	103.1	118.6	109.8

附 1-31 独立核算工业企业主要指标
MAIN INDICATORS FOR INDUSTRIAL ENTERPRISES WITH INDEPENDENT ACCOUNTING SYSTEM

年 份 Year	平均职工人数 (万人) Average Number of Staff and Workers (10000 persons)	总产值 (万元) Gross Output Value (10000 yuan)	固定资产原价 (万元) Original Value of Fixed Assets (10000 yuan)	产品销售收入 (万元) Sales Revenue (10000 yuan)	利税总额 (万元) Total Pre-tax Profits (10000 yuan)	国有工业 State-owned Industry 平均职工人数 (万人) Average Number of Staff and Workers (10000 persons)	总产值 (万元) Gross Output Value (10000 yuan)	固定资产原价 (万元) Original Value of Fixed Assets (10000 yuan)	产品销售收入 (万元) Sales Revenue (10000 yuan)	利税总额 (万元) Total Pre-tax Profits (10000 yuan)
1978	114.79	1654593	1305271	1098279		89.0	1397086	1211739	919313	435095
1979	116.79	1843056	1371335	1186497		92.3	1543621	1262408	984888	
1980	140.91	2061664	1495083	1987967	604241	95.3	1694298	1366890	1647908	520978
1981--1985		**12511777**	**9642045**	**12561630**	**3383077**		**9940322**	**8614039**	**10117128**	**2852798**
1981	152.90	2105591	1622035	2054862	599452	103.7	1716072	1474519	1693086	518716
1982	158.70	2205469	1750727	2183458	604372	107.6	1794192	1581902	1796342	521452
1983	161.98	2389253	1886857	2408893	642437	109.3	1918673	1693586	1961803	545140
1984	165.50	2702857	2045344	2728866	707360	109.4	2117273	1812660	2179349	589607
1985	165.63	3108607	2337082	3185551	829456	110.1	2394112	2051372	2486548	677883
1986--1990		**24483553**	**17321757**	**24054442**	**4825016**		**18108076**	**14798805**	**18384654**	**3925489**
1986	169.85	3365481	2627346	3385055	813979	111.5	2601751	2281006	2659067	676895
1987	170.52	3875977	3008917	3935004	885303	112.6	2970928	2604582	3065446	732447
1988	170.54	4956478	3412765	5032042	1081370	112.8	3695388	2949027	3835082	882479
1989		6026646	3890267	5597829	1087017		4352862	3294245	4258859	885038
1990	173.46	6258971	4382462	6104512	957347	115.4	4487147	3669945	4566200	748630
1991--1995		**57607603**	**44341698**	**57731437**	**8051832**		**35547109**	**35600600**	**37861701**	**5876833**
1991	172.39	7302060	5052285	7271529	1106009	112.2	5080426	4210383	5274088	837566
1992	175.48	8600195	5754181	8526860	1347058	116.3	5834134	4757957	6054470	1027279
1993	167.90	11666047	9986886	12822058	1811556	114.6	7598865	8471018	8977254	1379167
1994	179.50	15536585	9648050	13207344	1857476	109.9	8599364	7493956	7815491	1224709
1995	176.16	14502716	13900296	15903646	1929733	107.3	8434320	10667286	9740398	1408112
1996	166.63	15222854	16319878	15801389	1225314	97.7	8366714	12273744	9303959	762024
1997	157.52	17161951	18503218	17070867	1405499	91.2	9355501	14106270	9570024	878170
1998	167.11	19886587	22213387	20345380	1617338	70.3	8615543	13621321	9532486	823114
1999	161.10	21446119	23121446	22186280	1846310	62.4	5920611	13276604	8423097	873620

注：利税总额包括增值税。

Note：Total pre-tax profits included added value tax.

附1-32 独立核算工业企业效益指标
BENEFICIAL INDICATORS FOR INDUSTRIAL ENTERPRISES WITH INDEPENDENT ACCOUNTING SYSTEM

年份 Year	百元固定资产实现利税(元) Pre-tax Profits/Fixed Assets (yuan)	资金利税率(%) Pre-tax Profits/Total Assets (%)	产值利税率(%) Pre-tax Profits/Gross Output Value (%)	百元销售收入实现利润(元) After-tax Profits/Sales Revenue (yuan)	增加值劳动生产率(元/人) Labor Productivity at Value Added (yuan/person)	国有工业 State-owned Industry				
						百元固定资产实现利税(元) Pre-tax Profits/Fixed Assets (yuan)	资金利税率(%) Pre-tax Profits/Total Assets (%)	产值利税率(%) Pre-tax Profits/Gross Output Value (%)	百元销售收入实现利润(元) After-tax Profits/Sales Revenue (yuan)	增加值劳动生产率(元/人) Labor Productivity at Value Added (yuan/person)
1978				33.76		35.91		31.14	34.71	
1979				34.92					36.24	
1980	40.42	38.50	29.31	22.79		38.11	38.00	20.75	23.65	
1981	36.96	34.70	28.47	21.45		35.18	34.40	30.23	22.53	
1982	34.52	32.60	27.40	20.15		32.96	32.50	29.06	21.16	
1983	34.05	34.80	26.89	19.48		32.19	34.70	28.41	20.27	
1984	34.58	35.30	26.17	18.51		32.53	35.33	27.85	19.24	
1985	35.49	35.47	26.68	17.30		33.05	35.34	28.31	17.68	
1986	30.98	28.13	24.19	15.48		29.68	30.79	26.02	16.11	
1987	29.42	29.98	22.84	14.50		28.12	28.85	24.65	15.21	
1988	31.69		21.82	13.94		29.92	30.38	23.88	14.64	
1989	27.94	25.03	18.04	11.40		26.87	25.95	20.33	11.79	
1990	21.84	19.21	15.30	8.02		20.40	19.33	16.68	7.72	
1991	21.89	19.50	15.15	8.02		19.89	19.07	16.49	7.70	
1992	23.41	16.46	15.66	8.77		21.59	16.98	17.61	8.92	
1993	18.14	12.37	15.53	8.54	24364	16.28	12.10	18.15	9.26	20197
1994	19.25	13.05	11.96	7.28	31294	16.34	12.78	14.24	7.73	25144
1995	13.89	9.92	13.31	5.36	26068	13.20	10.95	16.70	6.32	27241
1996	9.30	5.41	8.05	2.09	23445	7.88	5.19	9.11	1.82	19571
1997	9.36	5.44	8.19	2.37	28220	7.80	5.39	9.39	2.40	27534
1998	9.15	4.99	8.13	2.38	35033	7.69	5.10	9.55	2.31	36926
1999	10.15	5.65	8.61	3.15	36437	8.49	5.57	11.35	3.11	33567

注：增加值劳动生产率按现价工业增加值计算。

Note: Labor productivity at value added is calculated by value added at current prices of industry.

附 1-33 工 业 产 品 产 量
OUTPUT OF INDUSTRIAL PRODUCTS

年 份 Year	布 (万米) Cloth (10000 m)	纱 (万吨) Yarn (10000 m)	机制纸及纸板 (万吨) Machine-made Paper and Paperboard (10000 tons)	合成洗涤剂 (万吨) Synthetic Detergents (10000 tons)	饮料酒 (万吨) Soft Drinking (10000 tons)	家用电冰箱 (万台) Household Refrige-rators (10000)	家用洗衣机 (万台) Household Washing Machines (10000)	电视机 (万台) TV Sets (10000)	# 彩色 Color TV Sets
1978	25436.0	5.4	12.1	2.1	8.4			3.9	0.0
1979	27297.0	5.8	13.9	2.2	9.9	2.0	0.7	12.5	0.3
1980	28940.0	6.5	14.0	2.4	11.6	2.6	5.8	28.0	1.2
1981--1985	**142080.0**	**34.5**	**86.9**	**18.9**	**87.3**	**41.6**	**211.7**	**262.3**	**79.5**
1981	28635.0	6.8	14.5	2.4	13.4	3.1	18.7	43.0	7.2
1982	29758.0	6.9	15.8	3.0	14.9	4.5	32.1	43.4	8.0
1983	30068.0	6.9	17.1	3.7	17.4	6.4	44.3	41.4	10.3
1984	27621.0	7.1	18.9	4.8	20.3	10.3	51.4	59.1	15.5
1985	25998.0	6.9	20.6	5.1	21.3	17.3	65.2	75.4	38.5
1986--1990	**153032.0**	**38.8**	**120.5**	**29.6**	**131.4**	**96.4**	**237.4**	**410.5**	**248.8**
1986	27503.0	7.4	21.9	5.8	21.5	18.1	70.0	67.5	34.2
1987	29738.0	7.7	24.1	5.4	22.7	19.4	57.7	85.1	48.5
1988	32262.0	8.1	23.3	5.7	23.9	23.6	58.0	92.9	57.9
1989	32271.0	7.9	25.8	6.4	28.7	24.7	31.9	88.9	57.6
1990	31258.0	7.7	25.4	6.4	34.6	10.7	19.7	76.1	50.7
1991--1995	**133994.0**	**38.6**	**116.5**	**38.1**	**347.3**	**27.0**	**81.7**	**369.9**	**299.4**
1991	31497.0	7.7	27.2	5.7	43.8	7.1	21.9	91.6	58.2
1992	29717.0	8.0	22.6	6.6	56.6	9.1	14.7	64.1	64.1
1993	26816.0	8.7	19.1	7.9	72.6	4.2	14.1	56.9	56.9
1994	21440.0	6.9	21.0	7.3	83.1	6.6	20.0	90.0	70.0
1995	24524.0	7.4	26.6	10.7	91.2		11.0	67.4	50.2
1996	22585.0	6.8	15.3	9.3	102.2	6.3	13.1	37.2	31.2
1997	25185.0	6.4	18.1	9.5	...	...	12.0	40.8	38.2
1998	21299.0	6.1	13.1	6.3		0.3	6.4	12.1	11.1
1999	14753.0	4.7	13.0	5.8	148.8	5.8	20.0	11.7	11.7

年 份 Year	原 煤 (万吨) Coal (10000 tons)	发电量 (万千瓦时) Electricity (10000 kwh)	钢 (万吨) Steel (10000 tons)	成品钢材 (万吨) Rolled-steel (10000 tons)	水 泥 (万吨) Cement (10000 tons)	硫 酸 (万吨) Sulphuric Acid (10000 tons)	烧 碱 (万吨) Caustic Soda (10000 tons)	化 肥 (万吨) Chemical Fertilizer (10000 tons)	化学农药 (万吨) Chemical Pesticide
1978	818.7	990750.0	191.0	116.8	191.5	14.95	5.47	10.70	1.28
1979	711.1	1042870.0	196.5	137.5	196.9	14.05	6.68	12.01	1.08
1980	791.0	1065060.0	200.9	152.1	217.4	13.01	8.13	12.41	0.93
1981--1985	**4269.1**	**5101356.0**	**1114.2**	**907.9**	**1355.7**	**61.85**	**42.56**	**57.68**	**2.32**
1981	788.7	993071.0	190.3	149.5	225.7	13.02	7.81	12.19	0.76
1982	811.3	1003446.0	200.4	159.4	249.1	12.64	8.24	12.00	0.60
1983	840.5	1028826.0	214.1	177.9	270.8	15.20	8.41	13.04	0.41
1984	884.3	1038842.0	241.7	200.1	291.6	13.24	8.92	12.36	0.42
1985	944.3	1037171.0	267.7	221.0	318.5	7.75	9.18	8.09	0.13
1986--1990	**4745.3**	**5656282.0**	**1837.8**	**1556.7**	**1649.3**	**50.49**	**51.89**	**45.77**	**0.10**
1986	917.2	1043208.0	303.6	255.5	310.5	7.87	9.25	8.26	0.04
1987	899.8	1057493.0	335.5	283.4	319.6	11.86	9.61	9.02	
1988	906.0	1110758.0	369.0	314.9	334.3	13.07	11.04	9.53	0.02
1989	1016.8	1191269.0	386.0	327.9	345.9	10.64	11.26	9.74	0.02
1990	1005.5	1253554.0	443.7	375.0	339.0	7.05	10.73	9.22	0.02
1991--1995	**4851.0**	**6772732.0**	**3411.0**	**2613.9**	**2364.7**	**38.57**	**55.69**	**46.41**	**0.43**
1991	996.5	1318000.0	499.7	402.9	377.6	7.12	11.00	6.94	0.05
1992	1015.2	1423000.0	575.0	438.3	403.0	8.23	11.38	9.70	0.11
1993	835.4	1410900.0	702.7	525.3	477.9	3.96	11.23	9.61	0.14
1994	1008.5	1298718.0	828.7	617.6	531.7	9.29	10.76	9.57	0.10
1995	995.4	1322114.0	804.9	629.8	574.2	9.97	11.32	10.59	0.03
1996	1013.7	1415555.0	794.7	654.3	666.0	10.85		12.72	0.14
1997	1011.7	1464302.0	801.7	652.4	700.9	9.26	11.36	11.92	
1998	989.5	1566621.0	803.2	676.1	762.0	7.75	10.28	11.25	
1999	792.1	1431772.0	734.5	663.8	803.0	8.42	11.74	8.79	

附 1-34 独立核算建筑业企业基本情况
BASIC STATISTICS FOR CONSTRUCTION ENTERPRISES WITH INDEPENDENT ACCOUNTING SYSTEM

年份 Year	建筑施工企业单位数 (个) Construction Enterprises (unit)	建筑施工企业从业人员 (万人) Employee (10000 persons)	建筑施工企业总产值 (亿元) Gross Output Value (100 million yuan)	建筑施工企业全员劳动生产率 (元/人) Overall Labor Productivity (yuan/person)	建筑施工企业工程优良品率 (%) Rate of High Quality Projects (%)	建筑施工企业利润总额 (万元) Total Profits (10000 yuan)
1978	64	25.4	10.5	4397	72.9	7017
1979	70	26.4	12.7	4680	67.9	9256
1980	71	27.8	14.7	5249	65.5	14543
1981	71	27.0	14.5	5264	65.9	15778
1982	91	30.7	17.3	5404	81.2	17169
1983	116	37.2	22.6	6128	68.3	25489
1984	2765	53.0	33.4	6345	45.3	32342
1985	2549	62.8	43.9	7197	31.8	39277
1986	2361	61.3	51.3	8702	56.3	33084
1987	2292	64.4	67.0	10832	61.3	41202
1988	1659	64.2	81.6	12992	58.2	38679
1989	1545	60.0	89.0	14539	53.8	38189
1990	994	60.2	94.7	16340	54.5	33762
1991	922	60.3	99.6	17031	47.7	27690
1992	976	62.7	122.6	19786	25.0	30984
1993	1098	75.9	210.7	27739	21.9	61432
1994	1259	73.4	301.5	41099	26.7	94385
1995	1332	82.6	370.7	44852	23.3	77857
1996	1292	82.5	468.1	56750	17.5	88896
1997	1297	80.3	519.2	64633	19.8	104320
1998	1482	75.6	624.7	73644	21.4	123744
1999	1588	82.6	681.4	82465	18.7	135595

注：(1) 1994 年以后从业人员为计算劳产率的年平均人数；1996 年以后全部指标不包括建筑业活动单位及四级以下施工企业。

(2) 工程优良品率按单位工程个数计算。

(a) Data of number of employment after 1994 refers to annual average number for calculating labor productivity; indicators after 1996 exclude construction units and enterprises below fourth grade.

(b) Rate of high quality project is calculated by number of unit-project.

附 1-35 运输邮电业基本情况
TRANSPORTATON,POSTS AND TELECOMMUNICATIONS

年 份 Year	铁路里程 (公里) Railway Operating Length (km)	公路里程 (公里) Highway Operating Length (km)	客运量 (万人) Passenger Traffic (10000 persons)	#铁 路 Railway	#公 路 Highway	# 民 航 Civil Aviation	货运量 (万吨) Freight Traffic	# 铁 路 Railway	# 公 路 Highway
1978	699	6562		2264		46.5	7394.4	3370	4023
1979	700	7278		2504		53.2	7763.7	3485	4277
1980	707	7339		2762		58.4	7571.0	3356	4213
1981--1985				**17688**		**544.0**	**37500.1**	**15425**	**22061**
1981	858	7427		2982		70.7	6895.1	3046	3847
1982	858	7543		3205		78.8	7379.2	3065	4312
1983	860	2906		3546		78.3	7639.6	3152	4485
1984	864	8131		3877		169.1	7897.2	3133	4761
1985	876	8487		4078		147.1	7689.0	3029	4656
1986--1990			**38861.7**	**21290**	**16560**	**1011.7**	**74886.0**	**15522**	**59324**
1986	876	8849	7336.7	4106	3059	171.7	7994.3	3030	4958
1987	876	8956	7763.4	4418	3117	228.4	7985.0	3125	4852
1988	876	9124	8491.4	4782	3460	249.4	7598.1	3168	4421
1989	876	9218	7834.1	4214	3434	186.1	24918.8	3144	21767
1990	876	9648	7436.1	3770	3490	176.1	26389.8	3055	23326
1991--1995			**41315.9**	**21787**	**17370**	**2158.9**	**118991.4**	**15062**	**103852**
1991	876	10259	7649.2	4036	3378	235.2	26391.4	3051	23326
1992	875	10827	8158.0	4196	3593	369.0	26733.2	2983	23739
1993	875	11242	6887.2	4374	2141	372.2	3063.7	3048	26730
1994	875	11532	8537.5	3993	4008	536.5	30725.1	3006	27700
1995	875	11532	10084.0	5188	4250	646.0	32078.0	2974	29087
1996	922.0	11682	9798.9	4736.0	4395	668.0	32905.6	2851	29960
1997	923.5	12306	10383.8	4828.8	4902	653.0	32349.7	2883	29360
1998	923.5	12498	11227.7	3761.6	6704	762.1	30126.5	2562.5	27490
1999	997.1	12825	14866.4	4200.5	9878	787.7	28274.8	2582.8	25635

附 1-35 续表 1 continued

年 份 Year	# 民 航 Civil Aviation	旅 客 周转量 (万人公里) Passenger-Kilometers (10000 passenger-km)	# 铁 路 Railway	# 公路 Highway	# 民航 Civil Aviation	货 物 周转量 (万吨公里) Freight Ton-Kilometers (10000 ton-km)	# 铁 路 Railway	# 公 路 Highway	# 民 航 Civil Aviation
1978	1.4			59367				92247	
1979	1.7			64033				97616	
1980	2.0			73692				93899	
1981--1985	**14.1**							**437318**	
1981	2.1			81879				93254	
1982	2.2			90092				106767	24173
1983	2.6			103742				110118	26713
1984	3.2			113871				113871	20896
1985	4.0	1187072	473328	109184	604560	2128868	1992247	109184	27437
1986--1990	**40.0**	**6333894**	**2608550**	**629210**	**3076133**	**13732367**	**1007906**	**2496086**	**191715**
1986	6.3	1133620	496288	119065	518267	2579647	2133836	405645	28281
1987	8.0	1281763	534720	113735	613308	2802099	2282106	471393	37966
1988	9.1	1503508	588947	141625	772936	2896715	2344684	498391	42612
1989	7.8	1216981	521263	122435	573283	2765660	2179878	546022	38194
1990	8.8	1198022	467332	132350	598339	2688246	2067402	574635	44662
1991--1995	**77.4**	**8690002**	**2645880**	**842807**	**5201313**	**14180124**	**1382191**	**2797933**	**346841**
1991	14.4	1383465	506431	139041	737993	2938658	2230406	642200	65614
1992	11.2	1666810	531574	161735	973501	2799742	2153176	591187	54929
1993	15.7	1656130	551392	127461	977277	2458751	2303265	767790	73216
1994	19.1	1906718	547488	180030	1179199	3107722	2301941	725740	78142
1995	17.0	2076879	508995	234540	1333343	3231034	2393403	762027	74940
1996	17.0	2107834	459514	250488	1397832	3174846	2311011	784888	78595
1997	19.0	2154186	477538	261204	1415444	3127394	2263274	769190	94500
1998	22.4	2419787	505554	304592	1609641	2846652	1952602	783237	110470
1999	29.9	2701470.8	579759	400597	1721115	2838856.6	1929269	754264	155171

附 1-35 续表 2 continued

年份 Year	民用汽车拥有量（辆）Possession of Civil Motor Vehicles (unit)	# 公路部门 Highway Department	# 私人 Individuals	邮电局所（处）Post and Telecommunications Offices (unit)	邮电业务总量（万元）Revenue of Post and Telecommunications (10000 yuan)	市话交换机容量（万门）City Switchboards Capacity (10000)	电话机拥有量（部）Possession of Telephones (unit)	城市 Urban	农村 Rural
1978	77059			415	9050.6	26.2	87428	75597	11831
1979	89447			418	9986.8	31.5	93012	80365	12647
1980	103826			427	11403.7	35.0	99104	86057	13047
1981--1985									
1981	116360			427	12781.7	39.0	107310	94415	12895
1982	130332			437	13986.5	43.3	114908	101163	13745
1983	139756			450	15724.0	46.4	124907	111048	13859
1984	167028			472	18357.4	53.1	136481	123137	13344
1985	224272			479	22413.3	62.1	151861	138130	13731
1986--1990									
1986	266706			476	25347.7	69.6	178527	163377	15150
1987	272290	5983	7148	478	29282.3	83.8	209294	193865	15929
1988	312174			475	35478.5	101.6	238122	236389	1733
1989	353315	6195	24029	470	43922.3	119.9	277967	276234	1733
1990	384451			479	77205.6	136.2	332946	331188	1758
1991--1995									
1991				484	157417.7	165.0	394837	393046	1791
1992	341015	5813	48643	494	215768.9	193.9	479937	478024	1913
1993	416047	5298	66883	507	311251.3	226.2	664676	662449	2227
1994	481279	5280	85474	536	418773.9	303.5	1890224		
1995	577214	5237	127568	633	561296.4	369.3	2417207		
1996	614021		351835	681	729022.4	442.0	2923042		
1997	775946		540564	701	930136.7	546.4	3577825		
1998	890141		697707	728	1290966.5	686.8	5225253		
1999	948506		762361	750	1566110.3	748.3	6545155		

注：1.公路货运量 1988 年以前和 1993 年为交通运输部门数据。

2.铁路是北京市辖范围。

a) Data of freight traffic of highway before 1988 and 1993 were provided by transport department.

b) Railway refers to that within the jurisdiction of Beijing.

附 1-36 社会消费品零售额
TOTAL RETAIL SALES OF CONSUMER GOODS

单位：亿元 (100 million yuan)

年份 Year	社会消费品零售额 Retail Sales of Consumer Goods	按地区分 By Region			按经济类型分 By Ownership				
		市 City	县 County	县以下 Below County Level	国有经济 State-Owned	集体经济 Collective Owned	合营经济 Joint Owned	个体经济 Individuals	其他经济 Others
1978	44.2	34.5	5.3	4.4	37.2	7.0			
1979	52.2	41.6	5.8	4.8	44.2	7.9		0.1	
1980	61.3	49.3	6.6	5.4	49.1	11.8		0.4	
1981--1985	**455.3**	**364.0**	**48.3**	**43.0**	**301.7**	**143.5**	**1.0**	**9.1**	
1981	68.8	55.6	7.3	5.9	48.7	19.2	0.2	0.7	
1982	73.3	58.6	8.1	6.6	51.0	21.2	0.2	0.9	
1983	83.6	66.6	9.3	7.7	56.0	26.1	0.1	1.4	
1984	101.7	81.1	10.4	10.2	67.7	32.1	0.2	1.7	
1985	127.9	102.1	13.2	12.6	78.3	44.9	0.3	4.4	
1986--1990	**1131.8**	**943.0**	**103.4**	**85.5**	**617.7**	**401.1**	**6.4**	**106.7**	
1986	146.5	121.7	12.1	12.7	84.5	51.0	0.4	10.6	
1987	176.6	145.7	16.2	14.7	97.1	64.5	0.6	14.5	
1988	234.3	195.0	21.2	18.1	129.4	84.5	0.6	19.7	
1989	266.7	221.5	25.0	20.2	143.8	92.2	2.6	28.2	
1990	307.7	259.1	28.9	19.7	162.9	108.9	2.2	33.7	
1991--1995	**2813.6**	**2215.9**	**373.6**	**224.1**	**1332.7**	**792.6**	**76.3**	**530.3**	**81.7**
1991	357.8	301.2	33.4	23.2	191.8	122.9	2.6	40.5	
1992	430.0	360.2	41.1	28.7	230.6	139.6	3.3	56.5	
1993	531.8	430.9	60.6	40.3	273.0	162.5	8.1	88.2	
1994	667.0	525.1	90.6	51.3	299.3	171.2	23.1	152.3	21.1
1995	827.0	598.5	147.9	80.6	338.0	196.4	39.2	192.8	60.6
1996	923.7	664.5	95.6	163.6	314.8	217.3	70.5	241.8	79.3
1997	1051.5	808.3	88.2	155.0	368.8	247.9	83.4	236.5	114.9
1998	1195.2	952.5	77.0	165.7	344.8	231.5	114.3	243.0	261.6
1999	1313.3	1037.7	84.0	191.6					

年份 Year	按行业分 By Sector				按类别分 By Category				农业生产资料零售额 Retail Sales of Agricultural Capital Goods	集市贸易成交额 Value of Country Fair Trade
	批发零售贸易业 Wholesale and Retail Sales	餐饮业 Catering	制造业 Manufacturing	其他行业 Others	食品类 Food	衣着类 Clothing	日用品类 Daily Use Articles	燃料类 Fuels		
1978	40.7	1.7	1.2	0.6	18.0	8.9	12.4	1.3	3.6	
1979	47.3	2.1	2.1	0.7	20.4	11.1	15.7	1.5	3.5	0.2
1980	53.5	2.7	3.5	1.6	24.4	12.9	18.8	1.6	3.6	0.7
1981--1985	**381.7**	**21.9**	**34.0**	**17.7**	**174.3**	**82.0**	**161.3**	**10.3**	**27.4**	**8.2**
1981	57.8	3.5	5.1	2.4	27.2	14.1	21.9	1.7	3.9	0.9
1982	61.4	3.7	5.5	2.7	28.9	13.3	24.2	1.7	5.2	1.1
1983	70.4	4.0	6.0	3.2	32.9	15.2	27.9	1.9	5.7	1.3
1984	85.6	4.7	7.8	3.6	38.1	18.0	37.0	2.2	6.4	1.5
1985	106.5	6.0	9.6	5.8	47.2	21.4	50.3	2.8	6.2	3.4
1986--1990	**906.7**	**70.7**	**64.5**	**89.9**	**451.8**	**152.4**	**447.9**	**24.1**	**55.6**	**71.1**
1986	119.3	8.1	8.9	10.2	57.4	21.6	57.1	3.3	7.1	6.4
1987	140.2	10.7	12.0	13.7	72.4	25.6	67.3	3.7	7.6	8.5
1988	186.4	16.1	13.9	17.9	92.0	33.0	93.9	4.1	11.3	14.1
1989	213.1	16.5	15.4	21.7	108.0	31.6	106.3	5.8	14.9	18.4
1990	247.7	19.3	14.3	26.4	122.0	40.6	123.3	7.2	14.6	23.6
1991--1995	**2079.3**	**215.5**	**119.8**	**399.0**	**1095.5**	**418.1**	**1195.0**	**64.9**	**83.4**	**514.9**
1991	286.2	22.9	16.8	31.9	138.6	47.1	146.6	7.7	17.8	31.0
1992	333.7	30.8	19.4	46.1	165.5	57.2	174.8	10.3	22.2	55.3
1993	393.0	44.6	28.7	65.5	192.0	84.0	241.5	14.3	17.6	83.4
1994	481.5	54.2	25.3	106.0	246.4	109.0	294.6	17.0	12.4	150.1
1995	584.9	63.0	29.6	149.5	353.0	120.9	337.5	15.6	13.4	195.1
1996	657.1	68.4	38.1	160.1	372.0	132.7	401.8	17.2	11.6	250.8
1997	709.4	72.5	56.3	213.3	389.7	140.6	492.2	29.1	9.5	285.3
1998	865.7	81.8	63.8	183.9	347.9	145.5	664.9	36.9	10.5	323.8
1999	926.2	81.3	79.8	226.0	374.5	155.6	742.1	41.1	6.4	307.0

注：1993 年以前是社会商品零售总额，从 1993 年起为社会消费品零售总额。

Note：Data before 1993 refers to total retail sales of commodity and data since 1993 refers to total retail sales of consumer goods.

附 1-37 北京市对外经济贸易和国际旅游
FOREIGN ECONOMICS,TRADE AND TOURISM

年份 Year	进出口总额(万美元) Total Value of Imports and Exports (USD 10000)	# 出口 Exports	签订利用外资协议项目(个) Contracts Signed of Foreign Capital Utilization (unit)	# 对外借款 Foreign Loans	# 外商直接投资 Direct Foreign Investment	签订利用外资协议金额(万美元) Contracted Foreign Capital (USD10000)	对外借款 Foreign Loans	外商直接投资 Direct Foreign Investment	外商其他投资 Other Foreign Investment
1978	29751	28524							
1979	45036	41757							
1980	66280	59277							
1981--1985	**382296**	**308276**							
1981	70091	63230							
1982	68921	61339							
1983	69621	59009							
1984	76303	62623	55	2	31	13826	1600	11660	566
1985	97360	62075	108	1	83	40788	130	39649	1009
1986--1990	**940420**	**457112**	**853**	**58**	**709**	**171046**	**26952**	**138628**	**5467**
1986	166847	65252	85	2	63	55888	9700	41952	4236
1987	154470	78239	97	6	72	66515	3322	62414	779
1988	198846	99121	193	21	148	18533	4144	14202	187
1989	205162	102336	209	10	185	14252	5731	8372	149
1990	215095	112164	269	19	241	15859	4055	11688	116
1991--1995	**1999096**	**836561**	**10987**	**67**	**10911**	**1699801**	**168840**	**1530412**	**549**
1991	258632	123987	735	8	724	47995	19431	28488	76
1992	320171	152555	2231	23	2208	177274	30079	147195	
1993	420029	137056	3765	13	3752	664911	36987	627924	
1994	469339	195936	2688	13	2675	505300	52000	453300	
1995	530925	227027	1568	10	1552	304321	30344	273505	472
1996	539201	208624	868		868	179029		179029	
1997	557576	246503	798	8	790	171532	3429	168103	
1998	650536	282896	656	5	651	410567	890	409677	
1999	844212	326101	647	2	645	182649	964	181685	

年份 Year	实际利用外资金额(万美元) Foreign Capital Actually Used (USD10000)	对外借款 Foreign Loans	外商直接投资 Direct Foreign Investment	外商其他投资 Other Foreign Investment	对外承包工程和劳务合作 Constructed Projects and Labor Services Cooperation with Foreign Countries: 合同数(份) Contracts (unit)	合同金额(万美元) Contracted (USD 10000)	完成营业额(万美元) Fulfiled Value (USD 10000)	旅游外汇收入总额(万美元) Tourism Foreign Exchange Earnings (USD 10000)
1978								10000
1979								9000
1980								12000
1981--1985								**94000**
1981								12000
1982								13000
1983					9	218.5	837.1	14000
1984					9	2801.5	1843.2	23000
1985					14	852.8	2083.1	32000
1986--1990					**331**	**7733.7**	**5108.9**	**280901**
1986					30	445.3	1535.5	46000
1987	17725.4	7146.6	9534.0	1044.8	37	548.6	697.6	55000
1988	61943.8	11524.4	50277.9	141.5	46	884.9	802.4	67000
1989	49506.8	17491.0	31845.9	169.9	113	2099.4	1017.5	47195
1990	40641.4	12743.5	27695.5	202.4	105	3755.5	1055.9	65706
1991--1995	**579524.3**	**168401.4**	**410896.0**	**226.9**	**586**	**79267.8**	**48984.0**	**735519**
1991	36798.1	12303.8	24481.8	12.5	114	3202.2	1896.8	85001
1992	52711.9	17710.8	34984.2	16.9	130	8887.6	3299.6	107286
1993	97619.8	30729.3	66693	197.5	117	36854.0	11442.0	124128
1994	194740.2	50280.2	144460		109	15521.0	18671.0	200904
1995	197654.3	57377.3	140277		116	15613.0	12789.0	218200
1996	225842.3	70552.3	155290.0		116	67688.0	43057.0	225200
1997	259161.8	73330.4	159286.4	26545.0	107	35640.0	29629.0	224800
1998	286973.4	57194.5	206414.9	23364.0	184	28520.0	45812.0	238400
1999	293681.6	89823.8	223123.8	26612.3	90	25229.0	26165.0	249600

注：进出口总额 1986 年以前为外贸部门口径，从 1986 年开始为海关口径。

Note: Data of total value of imports and exports refers to customs from 1986, while that before 1986 was provided from foreign trade department.

附1-38 教育基本情况
BASIC STATISTICS FOR EDUCATION

年份 Year	在校学生数(万人) Students Enrollment (10000 persons)				升学率(%) Rate of Entering Higher Grade Schools(%)		学龄儿童入学率(%) Enrollment Rate of Children at School-Age (%)	平均一专任教师负担学生数(人) Average Number of Students Instructed by a Professional Teacher(person)		
	合计 Total	高等学校 Institutions of Higher Education	普通中学 Regular Secondary Schools	小学 Primary Schools	初中毕业生 Graduates of Junior Middle Schools	小学毕业生 Graduates of Primary Schools		高等学校 Institutions of Higher Education	普通中学 Regular Secondary Schools	小学 Primary Schools
1978	208.1	4.9	109.5	93.7	79.7	102.6	99.0	2.4	19.9	20.7
1979	186.1	5.5	83.7	96.9	63.0	99.6	98.4	2.3	16.1	21.3
1980	173.5	6.4	71.9	95.2	80.3	99.5	98.7	2.6	14.5	21.7
1981	157.5	7.7	59.8	90.0	57.3	98.8	98.9	3.8	13.4	19.7
1982	144.6	7.2	51.9	85.5	58.6	97.0	98.9	3.2	12.3	19.5
1983	139.1	8.1	47.2	83.8	60.1	97.8	99.0	3.0	11.5	19.6
1984	137.4	9.1	52.0	76.3	61.2	98.7	99.3	3.3	13.2	18.2
1985	139.6	12.0	54.2	73.4	72.6	98.3	99.1	3.6	13.9	17.4
1986	156.0	13.0	56.5	74.9	77.1	97.8	99.49	3.6	13.9	17.4
1987	157.2	13.6	52.3	77.8	65.1	98.6	99.46	3.7	12.8	16.8
1988	160.3	14.5	46.9	85.1	64.3	98.5	99.50	4.0	11.4	17.6
1989	166.0	14.1	43.4	93.5	80.5	99.1	98.97	3.8	11.0	19.1
1990	168.7	14.0	40.9	99.6	81.8	99.3	99.47	3.9	10.1	18.6
1991	171.8	13.7	43.2	101.3	86.4	98.8	99.72	3.1	10.2	18.0
1992	176.2	14.0	47.6	100.2	88.5	99.6	99.65	4.0	11.3	17.4
1993	186.3	15.9	52.3	102.2	93.5	98.7	99.88	4.6	12.1	17.4
1994	196.1	17.5	58.4	102.4	86.7	99.4	99.92	4.9	13.1	16.9
1995	202.8	18.2	62.8	100.7	87.3	99.5	99.93	5.0	13.6	16.5
1996	207.9	19.0	64.9	100.0	88.1	99.3	99.93	5.2	13.7	16.1
1997	207.3	19.6	62.6	97.7	92.3	98.6	99.95	5.4	13.2	15.7
1998	204.7	21.3	61.0	92.0	92.2	98.7	99.96	5.8	12.8	14.9
1999	201.6	23.4	63.5	83.7	94.7	98.3	99.95	6.7	13.2	13.7

附 1-39 卫生情况和离退休退职人数
HEALTH AND NUMBER OF VCSR AND RRSW

年 份 Year	医院数 (个) Hospital (unit)	医生数 (人) Doctors (person)	医 院 床位数 (万张) Beds (10000)	每千人 拥 有 医生数 (人) Doctors Per 1000 Persons (person)	每千人 拥 有 医院床位 (张) Beds Per 1000 Persons (bed)	离退休、退职人数 (万人) Number of VCSR and RRSW(10000 persons)	国有单位 State-Owned	城镇集体单位 Urban Collective Owned	其他单位 Others	在职职工与离退休退职人员之比 Ratio of Staff and Workers on Their Posts to VCSR and RRSW
1978	389	28435	26432	3.35	3.11					
1979	387	31842	26808	3.66	3.08					
1980	393	34365	28495	3.88	3.22					
1981	406	37886	29783	4.21	3.31					
1982	413	39385	30940	4.29	3.37					
1983	412	41216	32242	4.42	3.46					
1984	423	42112	34602	4.46	3.66					
1985	376	42498	38180	4.44	3.99					
1986	371	43403	40903	4.47	4.21					
1987	398	46007	44407	4.66	4.49					
1988	445	48216	48711	4.82	4.87					
1989	470	49361	51877	4.83	5.08	75.9	58.4	17.3	0.2	5.3
1990	512	50934	55474	4.93	5.37	81.9	64.2	17.5	0.2	5.3
1991	525	52309	58747	5.03	5.65	87.7	70.0	17.6	0.2	5.2
1992	535	53254	59833	5.10	5.73	94.1	75.8	18.1	0.2	5.1
1993	548	53906	62340	5.13	5.93	100.8	82.1	17.9	0.8	4.5
1994	629	53865	64416	5.07	6.07	110.5	86.6	23.0	0.9	4.3
1995	629	54114	64211	5.06	6.00	120.7	93.6	25.2	1.9	3.9
1996	405	54091	60997	5.02	6.02	133.0	103.5	27.1	2.4	3.5
1997	435	54909	61865	5.06	6.06	144.3	113.2	28.6	2.5	3.2
1998	449	51902	63144	4.76	6.13	155.6	123.3	29.5	2.8	2.9
1999	460	52646	63660	4.79	6.15	168.6	133.4	31.1	4.1	2.6

注：1.最后一列以离退休、退职人数为 1。

2.1996 年起，医院数仅指县及县以上医院和其他医院，乡镇卫生院不再做为医院统计。

a) Data of last line are caculated according to number of VCSR and RRSW=1.

b) From 1996, number of hospitals included hospitals at county level and above and other hospitals, township hospitals were not calculated as hospitals any more.

附录 2：各类开发区资料

APPENDIX 2：VARIOUS DEVELOPMENT ZONES

附 2-1 各类开发区基本情况

BASIC STATISTICS FOR DEVELOPMENT ZONES

项目		Item		合计 Total	国家级 Of State	市级 Of City
开发区个数	(个)	Number of Development Zones	(unit)	30	5	25
累计完成征用土地面积	(平方公里)	Accumulative Area of Requisitions Realized	(sq.km)	46.4	11.9	34.5
累计"七通一平"土地开发面积	(平方公里)	Accumulative Area of Began Seven-through-One-Flat	(sq.km)	36.6	9.9	26.7
累计完成"七通一平"土地开发面积	(平方公里)	Accumulative Area of Seven-through-One-Flat Realized	(sq.km)	32.7	9.8	22.9
累计招商占用土地面积	(平方公里)	Accumulative Area Spared for Business	(sq.km)	21.1	5.0	16.1
# 三资企业占用	(平方公里)	Foreign Funded Enterprises	(sq.km)	7.4	1.8	5.6
累计建成区土地面积	(平方公里)	Accumulative Completed Area	(sq.km)	27.2	10.1	17.1
# 工业用地	(平方公里)	For Industrial Use	(sq.km)	14.8	3.7	11.1
累计招商个数	(个)	Accumulative Number of Hirer Leaseholder	(unit)	5733	2317	3416
累计项目总投资	(亿元)	Accumulative Investment	(100 million yuan)	957.3	272.9	684.4
累计注册资本	(亿元)	Accumulative Registered Capital	(100 million yuan)	468.3	185.5	282.8
# 外方	(亿元)	Foreign Partner	(100 million yuan)	295.5	113.1	182.4
累计协议外资金额	(亿美元)	Accumulative Contracted Foreign Capital	(USD 100 million)	57.3	11.3	46
外商累计入资	(亿美元)	Accumulative Foreign Capital Inflow	(USD 100 million)	31.9	8.7	23.2

说明：1.累计完成征用土地面积中包括原建成区面积。

2.表内"七通"指：上水、下水、煤气、热力、电力、通讯和道路通；"一平"指：场地自然平整。

3.表内"累计"指自开始至 1999 年末的累计数。

a) Accumulative requisition area of included original completed area.

b) Seven-through refers to water,drainage,gas,heat,electricity,communications and transportation,and one-flat refers to flat ground.

c) Accumulative data of this table refers to that from the beginning to the end of 1999.

附 2-2 各类开发区主要指标完成情况
STATISTICS FOR FULFILLMENT OF MAJOR INDICATORS OF DEVELOPMENT ZONES

项目		Item	1999	1998	1999 年为 1998 年% 1999 as % of 1998
完成固定资产投资	(亿元)	Investment in Fixed Assets Completed (100 million yuan)	84.1	65.9	127.6
新增固定资产	(亿元)	Incremental Fixed Assets (100 million yuan)	31.3	26.3	119.0
房屋建筑施工面积	(万平方米)	Floor Space of Buildings under Construction (10000 sq.m)	407.4	390.3	104.4
房屋建筑竣工面积	(万平方米)	Floor Space of Buildings Completed (10000 sq.m)	143.1	108.2	132.3
完成增加值	(亿元)	Value Added Completed (100 million yuan)	281.5	207.4	135.7
实现销售收入	(亿元)	Sales Revenue Completed (100 million yuan)	1173.3	801.1	146.5
实现利润总额	(亿元)	Total Profits Completed (100 million yuan)	66.5	35.5	187.3
应缴税金总额	(亿元)	Total Taxes Turned over (100 million yuan)	53.6	37.3	143.7

附 2-3 各类开发区一览表
DEVELOPMENT ZONES LIST

名称 Name	通讯地址 Address	主要负责人 Chairman	邮编 Post Code	电话 Telephone
北京经济技术开发区	北京经济技术开发区万源街 4 号	李凤玲	100076	67681207
北京市王府井地区开发建设办公室	王府井大街 99 号世纪大厦 A608 室	刘晓晨	100006	65129999
北京西三旗高新建材城	海淀区西三旗	蒋卫平	100096	82910873
北京市朝阳望京工业区	朝阳区东湖渠甲 3 号	佟克克	100015	64374723
朝阳东部旅游经济开发区	朝阳区农展南路 9 号	田锦籼	100026	65940942
中关村科技园区海淀园	海淀白石桥路甲 7 号海淀科技大厦	马　林	100080	62569636
中关村科技园区丰台园	丰台科学城海鹰路 2 号	汪　洪	100070	63725608
北京八大处高科技园区	石景山苹果园北路海特花园实兴大厦	韩振北	100041	68863653
北京市门头沟区石龙工业区	门头沟区石龙南路 6 号	韩立宝	102308	69843664
北京良乡卫星城工业开发区	房山凯旋大街金光路 2 号	李建民	102488	69351867
北京市燕山东流水工业区	北京市燕山东流水工业区管委会	黄祖团	102500	69347332
北京大兴工业开发区	北京大兴工业开发区广茂大街 9 号	蔡连军	102600	69244179
北京埝坛工业区	大兴县黄村镇念坛村	刘中铁	102600	69245165
通州工业开发区	通州区张家湾镇	唐　钰	101113	69541700
北京永乐经济开发区	通州区永乐店小甸屯村南	刘洪刚	101105	80511459
北京次渠工业区	通州区次渠工业区	杨　顺	101111	69502049
中关村科技园区昌平园	昌平城区镇超前路 9 号	洪起忠	102200	69709140
北京雁栖工业开发区	怀柔县雁栖工业开发区	崔玉明	101407	61668124
北京凤翔科技开发区	怀柔县杨宋镇	线继文	101400	61679488
北京怀柔农业经济开发区	怀柔县富乐小区北里 26 号	唐爱民	101400	69641848
北京中国乡镇企业城	海淀复兴路甲 23 号城乡华懋商厦 14 层	曹　林	101400	68298317
怀柔民营经济开发区	怀柔龙山宾馆北二楼万通公司	许　立	101400	60693701
平谷县滨河工业开发区	平谷县府前西大街 22 号	王新海	101200	69963791
平谷县兴谷经济开发区	平谷县乐园西小区 7 号	李宝峰	101200	69964071
北京市密云县工业开发区	密云工业开发区	李永军	101500	69041550
北京林河工业开发区	顺义区林河工业区	张东生	101300	89493610
北京天竺空港工业区	顺义区天竺镇	李友生	101312	64565745
北京市延庆经济技术开发区	延庆县城东外大街 15 号	张德福	102100	69142562
北京八达岭经济开发区	延庆县西大街 2 号	李志民	102100	69141563
北京电子城科技园	北京朝阳区酒仙桥路 12 号北门	鲍玉桐	100016	64377993

附2-4 各类开发区招商、入资情况
STATISTICS ON HIRER LEASEHOLDER AND CAPITAL INFLOW OF DEVELOPMENT ZONES

名称 Name	自开始至报告期累计 Accumulative Number from Beginning					
	招商个数(个) Number of Hirer Leaseholder (unit)	项目总投资(万元) Total Investment (10000 yuan)	注册资本(万元) Registered Capital (10000 yuan)	# 外方 Foreign Partner	协议外资金额(万美元) Contracted Foreign Capital(USD 10000)	外商实际投资(万美元) Foreign Actual Investment (USD 10000)
北京经济技术开发区	492	1763285	1164673	874040	94959	72555
王府井商业区	26	2852288	806250	773001	315849	130496
北京西三旗高新建材城	22	144810	98437	92177	9104	8710
望京工业区	35	242476	54816	18922	1985	1985
东部旅游经济开发区	6	210903	75032	75032	6191	4121
中关村科技园区海淀园						
中关村科技园区丰台园	1169	369186	362305	97138	4800	5351
八大处高科技园区	527	190877	179606	45025	4733	3407
北京石龙工业区	916	402350	344729	99647	7875	7656
良乡卫星城工业开发区	130	155595	28915	6702	317	769
燕山东流水工业区	13	2677	1389	570	100	20
北京大兴工业开发区	206	181302	100196	43958	2936	2541
北京念坛工业区						
通州工业开发区	38	82208	55233	31656	3840	3192
永乐工业开发区	13	42111	22584	10880	3980	1165
北京次渠工业区	9	143200	67113	5344	193	193
中关村科技园区昌平园	656	596000	327948	159901	13408	9586
雁栖工业开发区	90	221660	116790	109934	18000	18000
凤翔科技开发区	199	68527	35102	14880	2930	2350
怀柔农业经济开发区	26	12997	11022	4532	498	498
中国乡镇企业城	34	82493	58057	24600	5290	3500
怀柔民营经济开发区	40	86275	86275			
滨河工业区	234	108082	72664	20679	1724	1724
兴谷经济开发区	140	204113	93243	81883	14808	12538
密云县工业开发区	78	460000	35700	21000	9000	3200
顺义林河工业开发区	36	95815	37325	24243	2218	1598
天竺空港工业区	79	705550	352168	301763	47300	23400
延庆经济技术开发区	267	73136	53197	17979	600	600
八达岭经济开发区	252	74873	42536			
北京电子城科技园						

附 2-5 各类开发区投资、生产情况
INVESTMENT AND PRODUCTION OF DEVELOPMENT ZONES

单位：平方米、万元 (sq.m,10000 yuan)

名称 Name	自年初累计 Accumulative Number from Year-beginning					
	完成固定资产投资 Investment in Fixed Assets	新增固定资产 Incremental Fixed Assets	房屋建筑施工面积 Floor Space of Buildings under Construction	房屋建筑竣工面积 Floor Space of Buildings Completed	完成产值 Gross Output Value Completed	完成销售收入 Sales Revenue Completed
北京经济技术开发区	98252	4886	518041	61914	420000	500000
王府井商业区	266818	35629	399170	40851		53834
北京西三旗高新建材城	6830	10988	86963	46104	40194	41272
望京工业区	25853	88017	1153279	495789	21255	21883
东部旅游经济开发区	500		13700			37559
中关村科技园区海淀园	64815	51982	637357	239009	4408200	6373200
中关村科技园区丰台园	8983	16375	131768	62201	190000	366000
八大处高科技园区	12167	8667	163478	58379	27230	179460
北京石龙工业区	6795		47806	8279	186672	433341
良乡卫星城工业开发区	2040	720	30944	30944	77625	135000
燕山东流水工业区	2258	136	7439	7439	2998	2374
北京大兴工业开发区	10094	18643	138034	109954	39148	62841
北京念坛工业区						
通州工业开发区	1065	75	13360	7460	6271	20500
永乐工业开发区	1578	92	7788	450	3	3
北京次渠工业区	29400		95593		12084	12203
中关村科技园区昌平园	11813	8584	173636	45317	180476	201942
雁栖工业开发区	450	500	2000	2000	56000	54000
凤翔科技开发区	8000	600	5000	5000	58000	83000
怀柔农业经济开发区					1214	361
中国乡镇企业城	1586	1586			56265	34987
怀柔民营经济开发区					4200	898
滨河工业区	360	360			23940	21591
兴谷经济开发区	4500	4500	8000	3000	65739	57416
密云县工业开发区	220000	30000	100000	65000	104936	101263
顺义林河工业开发区	5284	1420	57401	9940	15999	18053
天竺空港工业区	15201	5900	127300	18800	804326	872095
延庆经济技术开发区	4129		31965	31965	62463	85420
八达岭经济开发区	6798		27792	3567	29158	437225
北京电子城科技园	25000	23000	96000	78000	1451606	1524799

附录 3：各类市场情况 APPENDIX 3：VARIOUS MARKETS

附 3-1 房产交易情况
HOUSE PROPERTY BUSINESS

项目	Item	起 Case	建筑面积 (万平方米) Floor Space (10000 sq.m)	# 楼房 Storied Building	立契价 (万元) Contracted Price (10000 yuan)
合计	**Total**	**182258**	**2185.3**	**2175.6**	**2628488.1**
市房屋交易所	**Municipal Transaction Department of Houses**	**1669**	**49.0**	**47.8**	**472215.3**
区县交易所	**Transaction Department of District and County**	**180589**	**2136.3**	**2127.8**	**2156272.8**
东城区	Dongcheng	12054	94.4	93.3	131899.6
西城区	Xicheng	14717	96.4	95.8	59204.1
崇文区	Chongwen	3912	29.4	29.1	40800.0
宣武区	Xuanwu	5399	37.8	37.7	56790.3
朝阳区	Chaoyang	49125	1059.0	1059.0	755909.6
丰台区	Fengtai	11480	100.3	100.2	199137.7
石景山区	Shijingshan	15768	112.3	112.3	89485.4
海淀区	Haidian	29275	279.0	278.9	517920.5
门头沟区	Mentougou	3245	20.1	18.6	11853.2
房山区	Fangshan	2665	19.6	19.6	14021.0
通州区	Tongzhou	10356	84.1	82.9	78093.6
昌平区	Changping	4809	39.5	39.6	29817.1
顺义区	Shunyi	2509	18.7	18.7	11836.1
大兴县	Daxing	7428	72.3	72.0	95806.4
平谷县	Pinggu	1570	18.2	17.8	11620.2
怀柔县	Huairou	3962	33.8	33.7	37537.7
密云县	Miyun	747	7.4	6.3	5517.0
延庆县	Yanqing	1568	14.0	12.5	9023.3

附 3-2 城乡集贸市场基本情况
URBAN AND RURAL FREE MARKET

单位：个 (unit)

项目	Item	全市 Total	城市 Urban	农村 Rural
集贸市场总数	**Number of Free Market**	**929**	**845**	**84**
消费品综合市场	Mixed Markets of Consumer Goods	417	359	58
农副产品市场	Markets of Farm and Sideline Products	317	295	22
农副产品综合市场	Multiple Markets	281	260	21
农副产品专业市场	Specialized Markets	36	35	1
工业消费品市场	Markets of Industrial Consumer Goods	162	159	3
工业消费品综合市场	Multiple Markets	98	96	2
工业消费品专业市场	Specialized Markets	64	63	1
其他	Others	33	32	1

附 3-3 集市贸易成交额(按商品类别分)
TRANSACTION VALUE OF FREE MARKET(BY CATEGORY OF COMMODITY)

单位：万元 (10000 yuan)

项目	Item	全市 Total	城市 Urban	农村 Rural
成交总额	**Total Transaction Value**	**3070274**	**2878663**	**191611**
粮食类	Grain	190359	180377	9982
油脂油料类	Edible Vegetable Oil	238613	228942	9671
棉烟麻类	Cotton,Tobacco and Hemp Crops	835	571	264
肉食禽蛋类	Meat,Poultry and Eggs	444143	407450	36693
水产品类	Aquatic Products	206066	195819	10247
蔬菜类	Vegetables	715185	673829	41356
干鲜果类	Dried and Fresh Fruits	288778	261047	27731
大牲畜类	Large Domestic Animals	410	113	297
家禽幼禽类	Young Poultry	9006	8685	321
工业品类	Industrial Products	815064	783152	31912
其他	Others	161815	138678	23137

附 3-4 集市贸易成交额(按市场类型分)
TRANSACTION VALUE OF FREE MARKET(BY TYPE OF MARKET)

单位：万元 (10000 yuan)

项目	Item	全市 Total	城市 Urban	农村 Rural
成交总额	**Total Transaction Value**	**3070274**	**2878663**	**191611**
综合市场	Mixed Markets	1197186	1090631	106555
农副产品市场	Markets of Farm and Sideline Products	1092425	1009568	82857
工业消费品市场	Markets of Industrial Consumer Goods	656103	653910	2193
其他	Others	124560	124554	6

附 3-5 集 市 贸 易 成 交 量
TRANSACTION VOLUME OF FREE MARKET

单位：吨 (ton)

项　目	Item	全　市 Total	城　市 Urban	农　村 Rural
粮　食	Grain	601029	551647	49382
#大　米	Rice	343182	324409	18773
玉　米	Corn	13992	13774	218
油脂油料类	Edible Vegetable Oil	206948	193677	13271
棉烟麻	Cotton,Tobacco and Hemp Crops	557	291	286
猪　肉	Pork	158778	143176	15602
牛　肉	Beef	57578	52989	4589
羊　肉	Mutton	48330	43598	4732
鲜　蛋	Poultry Eggs	83365	73113	10252
家　禽	Poultry	30839	29186	1653
水产品	Aquatic Products	191068	178712	12356
蔬　菜	Vegetables	4111849	3830581	281268
干鲜果	Dried and Fresh Fruits	1256210	1187799	68411
家禽幼禽	Young Poultry	9344	8772	572

附 3-6 集市贸易成交量占社会销售量比重
THE PROPORTION OF FREE MARKET VOLUME IN TOTAL SOCIAL SALES

单位：吨 (ton)

项　目	Item	成 交 量 Transaction Volume	社会销售量 Total Sales Volume	成交量占社会销售量比重（%） Proportion(%)
粮　食	Grain	601029	1739420	34.6
油脂油料类	Edible Vegetable Oil	206948	342092	60.5
猪　肉	Pork	158778	320540	49.5
牛　肉	Beef	57578	100791	57.1
羊　肉	Mutton	48330	102907	47.0
鲜　蛋	Poultry Eggs	83365	117530	70.9
家　禽	Poultry	30839	175422	17.6
水产品	Aquatic Products	191068	228178	83.7

附 3-7 生产资料市场成交情况
STATISTICS FOR TRANSACTION IN CAPITAL GOODS MARKETS

项　目	Item	1999	1998	1999 年为 1998 年% 1999 as % of 1998
成 交 额　(万元)	**Transaction Value　(10000 yuan)**	**1037397**	**1462783**	**70.9**
成 交 量	**Transaction Volume**			
新、旧汽车　(辆)	New and Old Automobiles　(unit)	78757	123432	63.8
钢　材　(吨)	Rolled Steel　(ton)	293982	153509	191.5
木　材　(立方米)	Timber　(cu.m)	367954	249434	147.5
煤　炭　(吨)	Coal　(ton)	2235	5861	38.1

附 3-8 消 费 者 投 诉 与 处 理
CONSUMER'S LAWSUITS AND HANDLING

单位：件 (case)

项目 Item		1999 受理投诉件数 Cases Accepted	1999 构成(%) Composition(%)	1998 受理投诉件数 Cases Accepted	1998 构成(%) Composition(%)
总　计	**Total**	**15379**	**100**	**13448**	**100**
按行业分	**By Sector**				
家用电器类	Household Appliances	1451	9.4	1299	9.7
# 电视机	TV Sets	186	12.8	204	15.7
电冰箱	Refrigerators	75	5.2	98	7.5
洗衣机	Washing Machines	32	2.2	27	2.1
收录机	Recorders	71	4.9	85	6.5
家用机械类	Household Machines	745	4.8	750	5.6
# 照相机	Cameras	35	4.7	32	4.3
自行车	Bicycles	118	15.8	113	15.1
摩托车	Motorcycles	158	21.2	194	25.9
钟　表	Clocks and Watches	100	13.4	103	13.7
日用百货类	Articles of Daily Use	5454	35.5	4688	34.9
# 家　具	Furniture	548	10.1	614	13.1
服　装	Garments	1634	30.0	1255	26.8
鞋	Shoes	2482	45.5	2151	45.8
化妆品	Cosmetics	131	2.4	167	3.6
食　品	Food	2481	16.1	1979	14.7
药　品	Medicine	102	0.7	78	0.6
服　务	Services	2773	18.0	2710	20.1
农用资料	Materials for Agricultural Use	207	1.4	137	1.0
邮　购	Mail-order	543	3.5	527	3.9
其　他	Others	1623	10.6	1280	9.5
按内容分	**By Content**				
质　量	Quality	10698	70	9540	71
价　格	Price	631	4.1	584	4.3
虚假广告	False Advertisements	93	0.6	64	0.5
假冒伪劣商品	Counterfeit Goods	151	0.9	194	1.4
计　量	Measure	1175	7.6	895	6.6
欺诈骗销	Cheating Sales	132	0.8	126	0.9
其　他	Others	2499	16.0	2045	15.3

注：总解决率为 99.2 %。

Note：Total rate of settlement is 99.2%.

附录4：企业及企业集团资料

附4-1 建立现代企业制度企业主要经济指标(1999年)

单位：万元

项目	Item	单位数（个）Number of Enterprises (unit)	资产总计 Total Assets
总计	**Total**	**195**	**167698644.9**
国家重点联系企业	**Key Enterprises in Contact with State**		
按确定企业改制的主管部门划分	**By Department Responsible for Enterprise Restructure**		
国家经贸委	State Economic and Trade Commission	10	5147699.5
国家体改委	State Commission for Restructuring Economy	7	3961252.0
市经贸委	Municipal Economic and Trade Commission	10	5241990.6
市体改委	Municipal Commission for Restructuring Economy	88	10822394.7
企业主管部门	Departments in Charge of Enterprises	25	9645715.1
其他	Other	55	132879593.0
按登记注册类型划分	**By Registered Type**		
国有企业	State-owned	88	125419141.1
国有独资公司	Exclusive State-owned	50	31247667.0
其他有限责任公司	Other State-owned	16	8556169.7
股份有限公司	Joint Share Limited Companies	35	2374559.2
其他	Others	6	101108.0
按控股情况划分	**By Share Holding**		
国有绝对控股	State-owned Absolute Holding Enterprises	167	166656464.7
国有相对控股	State-owned Relative Holding Enterprises	9	396007.6
集体绝对控股	Collective-owned Absolute Holding Enterprises	9	200155.4
集体相对控股	Collective-owned Relative Holding Enterprises	3	77707.0
其他	Others	7	368310.2
按企业规模划分	**By Size**		
特大型	Oversized	43	131548773.2
大型	Large-sized	109	26471483.6
中型	Medium-sized	26	661054.5
小型	Small-sized	10	224017.2
其他	Others	7	8793316.4
按行业划分	**By Sector**		
农、林、牧、渔业	Farming,Forestry,Animal Husbandry and Fishery	4	1175154.2
采掘业	Excavation	5	7732421.3
制造业	Manufacturing	84	19983749.9
电力、煤气及水的生产和供应业	Electricity,Gas,Water Production and Supply	5	92122027.0
建筑业	Construction	11	7374116.0
运输邮电业	Transportation,Posts and Telecommunications	7	18885297.8
批发零售贸易餐饮业	Wholesale,Retail and Catering	58	11161526.9
金融保险业	Banking and Insurance	1	881.0
房地产业	Real Estate	2	1111537.0
其他	Others	18	8151933.9

注：按企业规模划分的"其他"指没有划分标准的非工业企业。(附4-7表同)

APPENDIX 4：STATISTICS FOR ENTERPRISE AND ENTERPRISES GROUP
MAIN ECONOMIC INDICATORS OF ENTERPRISES WITH MODERN ENTERPRISE SYSTEM（1999）

(10000 yuan)

固定资产 原　值 Original Value of Fixed Assets	流动资产 平均余额 Average Balance of Circulating Funds	负债合计 Total Liabilities	主营收入 Major Business Revenue	利润总额 Total Profits	从业人员 （人） Number of Employees (person)	从业人员 报　酬 Payment for Employees
81461265.0	**53601816.4**	**95419555.2**	**59737863.2**	**2063376.1**	**2060544**	**3298660.9**
2691991.8	1909772.3	2393378.0	2244134.8	105655.0	62571	114791.7
1608194.9	1622237.9	3183125.7	1288353.7	29941.7	70384	94259.5
2758343.3	1734777.6	2668095.5	2413334.2	43184.4	95203	141766.6
4103659.3	5755596.1	6397559.1	5207451.3	135510.2	273858	384844.4
4815107.4	4077167.9	7415901.0	2554176.4	-25309.9	160361	249351.3
65483968.2	38502264.6	73361496.0	46030412.9	1774394.7	1398167	2313647.4
66405118.4	37330992.9	68717248.3	45347961.0	1431202.5	1304830	2181111.4
9952984.2	12047304.9	19415880.5	9595622.7	282021.5	534989	770252.5
4075378.4	3083431.6	6190655.1	3242796.3	258555.6	150392	267517.5
978649.3	1091528.7	1012495.9	1520334.1	94625.5	63645	73559.6
49134.8	48558.2	83275.4	31149.1	-3029.0	6688	6220.0
81177267.3	53160566.6	94856264.4	59181814.2	2055316.3	2031808	3268840.5
85965.8	185901.7	205940.8	189302.1	-4026.8	9644	11011.8
48418.6	107635.4	122237.6	165347.5	7531.2	5824	5041.9
26639.0	21055.0	53271.0	44066.0	-7990.0	3224	2887.0
122974.3	126657.7	181841.4	157333.4	12545.4	10044	10879.8
71353032.5	37609371.2	73821337.2	45421460.0	1431718.8	1536718	2503471.1
5604615.1	12286151.4	14803591.6	11137006.1	390481.1	355620	540965.0
214001.8	370840.9	476503.4	414216.8	-2651.6	27451	25937.8
49762.6	157319.3	188256.5	121137.0	-2218.9	4789	4868.5
4239853.0	3178133.6	6129866.6	2644043.3	246046.8	135966	223418.5
376333.5	719859.9	886620.5	485740.3	1174.7	43614	55403.3
2097634.8	1630957.6	4315681.7	1815050.4	289288.6	79707	122931.0
9419823.0	8506277.3	11607603.0	12005948.0	400424.5	417262	603447.4
58629677.0	27274036.0	47355992.0	29854862.0	927868.0	1011303	1729597.6
1116250.6	5261679.5	5990877.2	4257863.6	59591.4	253280	354020.2
7435074.5	1975622.7	13977282.3	6915736.0	192021.3	103576	197669.0
1425582.6	5661507.8	7059729.8	3510554.3	86886.4	57070	100043.7
39.0	428.0	355.0	337.0	9.9	7	6.7
9550.0	1038098.0	929673.0	192306.0	5471.0	1555	4085.5
951300.1	1533349.6	3295740.7	699465.7	100640.3	93170	131456.6

Note: In groups for size, "others" refers to non-industry enterprises which having no classfied standard.(appendix 4-7 is the same)

附 4-2 北京市国有大中型骨干企业主要经济指标（1999 年）

单位：万元

项　目 Item		单位数（个）Number of Enterprises (unit)	# 改制企业 Repacking Enterprises	资产总计 Total Assets	# 改制企业 Repacking Enterprises	固定资产原值 Original Value of FixedAssets	# 改制企业 Repacking Enterprises
总　计	**Total**	**189**	**105**	**23874271.5**	**18035988.1**	**10127755.4**	**8117623.4**
按确定企业改制的主管部门划分	**By Department Responsible for Enterprise Restructure**						
经委系统	Economy Committee System	57	34	9595335.0	8475603.9	5294479.3	4718774.9
商委系统	Commerce Committee System	64	37	1547325.5	995178.3	527137.1	330519.2
建委系统	Build Committee System	14	9	7868991.9	5624970.1	684038.7	639802.3
市政管委系统	MunicipalAdministrationCommitteeSystem	21	7	3523466.8	2057476.6	3066051.9	2020738.4
农口系统	Agriculture System	18	8	812534.2	455582.0	316157.1	202459.2
经贸委系统	EconomicandTrade Commission System	5	3	251181.2	190328.2	32111.2	24279.2
旅游系统	Tourism System	10	7	275437.0	236849.0	207780.2	181050.2
按登记注册类型划分	**By Registered Type**						
国有企业	State-owned	81		5731549.1		1980665.7	
国有独资公司	Exclusive State-owned	20	20	10690358.7	10690358.7	5405687.7	5405687.7
其他有限责任公司	Other State-owned	43	41	2241725.7	2178210.7	768225.2	750211.2
股份有限公司	Joint Share Limited Companies	37	37	4935325.3	4935325.3	1859846.3	1859846.3
中外合资	Joint Venture	6	6	231418.4	231418.4	101279.2	101279.2
其　他	Others	2	1	43894.3	675.0	12051.3	599.0
按控股情况划分	**By Share Holding**						
国有绝对控股	State-owned Absolute Holding Enterprises	163	84	22746800.2	17069568.4	9684075.2	7717640.4
国有相对控股	State-owned Relative Holding Enterprises	17	13	757842.8	619847.2	305360.7	277718.5
集体绝对控股	Collective-owned Absolute Holding Enterprises	2	1	24804.0	1748.0	17047.0	992.0
其　他	Others	7	7	344824.5	344824.5	121272.5	121272.5
按企业规模划分	**By Size**						
特大型	Oversized	4	4	6241917.9	6241917.9	3747370.3	3747370.3
大　型	Large-sized	110	67	14395341.6	11389551.9	5837018.4	4168174.1
中　型	Medium-sized	54	26	754936.0	274948.9	290716.8	127681.2
小　型	Small-sized	3	1	14813.0	624.0	5672.0	176.0
其　他	Others	18	7	2467263.0	128945.4	246977.9	74221.8
按行业划分	**By Sector**						
农、林、牧、渔业	Farming,Forestry,Animal Husbandry and Fishery	6	2	278169.6	62578.6	138874.8	42117.0
采掘业	Excavation	1		290396.0		168400.0	
制造业	Manufacturing	65	41	9557692.2	8707112.9	5214483.0	4798978.5
电力、煤气及水的生产和供应业	Electricity,Gas,Water Production and Supply	5	4	1660612.1	1162110.1	1742537.8	1234158.8
建筑业	Construction	12	4	4257468.4	3766505.6	540992.2	502329.3
运输邮电业	Transportation,Postsand Telecommunications	5		132607.6		99312.3	
批发零售贸易餐饮业	Wholesale,Retail and Catering	65	37	2007671.4	1340642.5	651018.1	436118.4
金融保险业	Banking and Insurance	1		2357.0		1946.0	
房地产业	Real Estate	6	1	3327302.0	1107246.0	62807.0	23616.0
其　他	Others	23	16	2359995.2	1889792.4	1507384.2	1080305.4

注：1 户被兼并，实报数为 189 户。

MAIN ECONOMIC INDICATORS OF STATE-OWNED LARGE AND MEDIUM ENTERPRISES(1999)

(10000 yuan)

流动资产平均余额 Average Balance ofirculating Enterprises	# 改制企业 Recapping Enterprises	负债合计 Total Liabilities	# 改制企业 Recapping Enterprises	主营业务收入 Major Business Revenue	# 改制企业 Recapping	利润总额 Total Profits	# 改制企业 Recapping Enterprises	从业人员(人) Number of Employees (person)	# 改制企业 Recapping Enterprises	从业人员报酬 Payment for Employees	# 改制企业 Recapping Enterprises
12155094.6	**8241832.4**	**14629197.9**	**10625818.6**	**9223300.0**	**7367023.1**	**262292.2**	**217467.9**	**593014**	**423861**	**865587.6**	**654290.4**
3289076.6	2642565.6	5267195.5	4574239.6	3594008.6	3201512.2	144740.6	127037.3	221194	156066	302761.8	230092.6
752289.3	448798.2	914907.4	514848.9	1693310.7	1021996.7	36531.9	25516.0	76002	40086	98459.4	54448.3
6425049.4	4266525.3	6473732.9	4484818.5	2295726.8	2115976.9	72375.8	56260.9	117974	111919	227786.5	216702.8
854536.8	337625.5	1113482.4	534454.5	899458.7	495992.2	-15123.3	-12189.9	136326	90220	190461.5	123361.6
539040.5	311793.8	488293.1	215388.6	424034.9	309925.8	21994.8	20545.3	26613	13544	28236.1	15259.0
192653.0	149939.0	222730.5	172208.5	182395.9	115860.9	-2995.0	-3776.0	1719	1088	3571.5	2224.3
102449.0	84585.0	148856.1	129860.1	134364.4	105758.4	4767.5	4074.5	13186	10938	14310.8	12201.8
3839689.1		3929320.8		1833318.4		44324.4		166130		208441.6	
4238183.0	4238183.0	6361719.2	6361719.2	3276975.4	3276975.4	54450.3	54450.3	186329	186329	310775.1	310775.1
1333101.1	1286970.1	1655673.0	1610874.0	1527305.7	1510231.7	18195.4	17887.4	69538	67736	117474.6	115516.4
2612854.7	2612854.7	2536552.1	2536552.1	2380331.0	2380331.0	137908.4	137908.4	159211	159211	216947.1	216947.1
103611.7	103611.7	115946.4	115946.4	199076.1	199076.1	7311.9	7311.9	10518	10518	11028.8	11028.8
27655.1	213.0	29986.5	727.0	6293.5	409.0	101.9	-90.0	1288	67	920.4	23.0
11680180.8	7879966.1	14056612.6	10162583.8	8550065.2	6748840.2	229172.5	186921.3	565563	402345	831463.8	626489.9
349729.0	248397.5	387264.3	286733.8	371312.3	321094.4	21492.5	19119.4	16069	11517	20469.4	15301.3
12212.0	496.0	9461.0	641.0	8567.0	3733.0	-61.0	-261.0	1489	106	1274.2	119.0
112972.8	112972.8	175860.0	175860.0	293355.5	293355.5	11688.2	11688.2	9893	9893	12380.2	12380.2
1604351.3	1604351.3	3389969.6	3389969.6	2094031.8	2094031.8	52537.5	52537.5	143044	143044	223651.1	223651.1
7981927.9	6414769.5	8640591.1	6954101.4	6113175.4	4822937.1	167069.2	155544.8	385879	259042	563372.7	406250.1
430676.9	141833.2	522621.8	192327.9	688452.2	390650.0	17230.0	2667.6	40880	17916	45078.0	18374.1
4580.0	45.0	10023.0	130.0	9918.0	1239.0	-195.0	128.0	1380	132	1809.0	174.0
2133558.5	80833.4	2065992.4	89289.7	317722.6	58165.3	25650.5	6590.1	21831	3727	31676.8	5841.1
135603.3	24432.2	201497.8	52633.2	173160.7	114146.5	775.8	-475.0	15182	5377	13430.3	4569.0
163778.0		182310.0		92825.0		3535.0		26615		29196.0	
3235291.1	2737467.5	5238642.8	4711246.0	3621753.3	3315317.0	145573.0	131375.0	206047	166492	286625.2	242380.8
238092.6	166957.6	247313.7	180154.7	330617.0	250444.0	-35893.0	-25856.0	17724	13346	25696.5	19602.9
3374405.5	2943499.9	3650538.7	3197402.7	1811563.2	1642171.1	47829.5	46441.9	110025	92080	205314.1	179666.1
55628.3		78326.4		93700.4		1032.4		11628		14439.6	
1118426.6	779021.2	1185824.4	699091.4	2022886.5	1218858.6	46478.4	35190.9	73683	38809	100072.2	56384.6
682.0		600.0		1308.0		-200.0		372		336.0	
3121283.0	1018536.0	2894259.0	931704.0	332974.0	193390.0	21053.0	5361.0	11274	5443	20963.2	11756.0
711903.2	571918.0	949885.1	853586.7	742511.9	632695.9	32108.2	25430.2	120464	102314	169514.5	139931.0

Note: Because one enterprise has been annexed, the actual reported number of enterprises is 189.

附 4-3 企业集团主要经济指标（1999 年）

单位：万元

项目	Item	集团个数（个）Number of Groups (unit)	所属企业数（个）Number of Enterprises Belonged to (unit)	资产总计 Total Assets
总　计	**Total**	**91**	**1394**	**64178137.8**
按审批部门划分	**By Departments Responsible for Approval**			
国务院	The State Council	1	40	26817696.0
国务院主管部门	Competent Authorities of the State Council	40	631	17322047.5
省级政府	Municipal Government	40	620	16494648.1
省级政府主管部门	Competent Authorities of Municipal Government	8	95	3044486.5
其　他	Others	2	8	499259.8
按登记注册类型划分	**By Registered Type**			
国有企业	State-owned	42	613	16639358.1
国有独资公司	Exclusive State-owned	32	625	43536235.5
其他有限责任公司	Other State-owned	6	63	2347911.7
股份有限公司	Joint Share Limited Companies	6	43	1475860.8
其　他	Others	5	50	178771.8
按控股情况划分	**By Share Holding**			
国有绝对控股	State-owned Absolute Holding Enterprises	81	1310	63491460.1
国有相对控股	State-owned Relative Holding Enterprises	3	33	309920.5
集体绝对控股	Collective-owned Absolute Holding Enterprises	2	10	48973.7
其　他	Others	5	41	327783.5
按行业划分	**By Sector**			
农、林、牧、渔业	Farming,Forestry,Animal Husbandry and Fishery	2	39	204504.6
采掘业	Excavation	1	12	100716.0
制造业	Manufacturing	34	444	8999149.6
建筑业	Construction	7	127	5194769.0
运输邮电业	Transportation,Posts and Telecommunications	1	14	24604.3
批发零售贸易餐饮业	Wholesale,Retail and Catering	22	281	7264888.6
金融保险业	Banking and Insurance	1	40	26817696.0
房地产业	Real Estate	3	110	2697570.2
其　他	Others	20	327	12874239.6
按隶属关系划分	**By Administrative Relationship**			
中　央	Central	41	671	44139743.5
地　方	Local	50	723	20038394.3

MAIN ECONOMIC INDICATORS OF BUSINESS GROUP（1999）

(10000 yuan)

固定资产净值 Net Value of Fixed Assets	流动资产平均余额 Average Balance of Circulating Funds	负债合计 Total Liabilities	所有者权益 Ownership Interest	主营收入 Major Business Revenue	利润总额 Total Profits	从业人员（人） Number of Employees (person)	从业人员报酬 Payment for Employees	研究开发费用 Research and Exploit Expenses
13372810.5	**35991799.7**	**48284417.3**	**14682053.9**	**17762576.1**	**628716.1**	**865400**	**1163988.7**	**136769.6**
2432866.0	14693742.0	22735773.0	3673854.0	2866552.0	253269.0	51729	94071.0	4991.0
4339437.6	10868610.8	11713472.7	4993425.3	8355482.9	160142.6	330736	451613.6	97563.3
5880723.7	7969277.5	11399164.6	4933707.2	5915374.9	136741.0	432745	560626.5	26543.2
434232.5	2326935.1	2300776.0	720381.8	424432.0	40414.6	37068	43108.4	3811.7
285550.8	133234.3	135231.1	360685.6	200734.4	38149.0	13122	14569.1	3860.4
4113762.2	10199926.6	11724868.9	4622302.5	6699165.9	100551.2	298345	367473.5	51439.5
7767121.4	23984903.5	34410575.9	8264943.9	9405544.6	402605.5	469036	649204.7	58154.4
933753.0	1087089.0	1417995.0	924368.7	828818.0	49586.0	62354	94596.2	2084.0
490503.2	618701.5	596212.1	830613.5	746644.0	78923.0	26964	44473.4	24315.1
67670.8	101179.0	134765.5	39825.3	82403.6	-2949.5	8701	8240.8	776.6
13234745.5	35673636.5	47957343.6	14350568.7	17472866.0	612427.4	854588	1149316.1	128276.3
43268.4	169093.9	142137.9	164955.6	147974.4	90.7	4918	6032.5	182.6
25654.0	24344.0	21079.0	27894.7	12265.0	526.0	1835	1540.6	
69142.7	124725.3	163856.9	138634.9	129470.7	15672.1	4059	7099.5	8310.7
79103.0	118927.1	145521.4	57866.2	110024.0	3754.1	10059	12486.0	
60006.0	46544.0	76929.0	23787.0	26438.0	153.0	7518	5310.0	528.0
4435226.2	3434777.9	5715316.8	3090278.5	3453244.7	111600.5	251814	305333.5	78218.8
855877.7	3946928.3	4333288.0	812751.0	2303957.5	35756.6	123644	201405.7	1373.0
8521.2	16571.5	14249.9	10354.4	26660.0	986.3	1276	1413.2	550.0
1426863.4	4788396.8	5544513.2	1679156.4	4084058.1	52550.4	155181	208505.9	516.0
2432866.0	14693742.0	22735773.0	3673854.0	2866552.0	253269.0	51729	94071.0	4991.0
237285.3	2367422.4	2302774.2	387030.0	231918.4	18223.7	7545	11473.3	
3837061.7	6578489.6	7416051.9	4946976.4	4659723.4	152422.6	256634	323989.9	50592.8
6772303.6	25562352.8	34449245.7	8667279.3	11222034.9	413411.6	382465	545684.6	102554.3
6600506.9	10429446.9	13835171.6	6014774.6	6540541.2	215304.5	482935	618304.0	34215.3

附4-4 北京市国有大中型骨干企业主要经济指标（1998年）

单位：万元

项目	Item	单位数（个） Numberof Enterprises (unit)	# 改制企业 Repacking Enterprises	资产总计 Total Assets	# 改制企业 Repacking Enterprises	固定资产净值 Net Value of Fixed Assets	# 改制企业 Repacking Enterprises
总　计	**Total**	**185**	**68**	**20112602.4**	**13553759.0**	**5624328.5**	**4006562.3**
按确定企业改制的主管部门划分	**By Department Responsible for Enterprise Restructure**						
市体改委	Commission For Economic System Reform of Beijing Municipality	185	68	20112602.4	13553759.0	5624328.5	4006562.3
按登记注册类型划分	**By Registered Type**						
国有企业	State-owned	112		4571754.6		1581319.4	
国有独资公司	Exclusive State-owned	23	22	12496372.9	10599460.9	3088941.0	3065045.0
其他有限责任公司	Other State-owned	19	16	484261.8	439913.8	213196.3	208228.3
股份有限公司	Joint Share Limited Companies	25	25	2300419.7	2300419.7	676571.0	676571.0
其　他	Others	6	5	259793.5	213964.7	64300.7	56718.0
按控股情况划分	**By Share Holding**						
国有绝对控股	State-ownedAbsolute Holding Enterprises	160	55	19121559.8	12944829.0	5301155.8	3753156.6
国有相对控股	State-owned Relative Holding Enterprises	11	6	560845.7	441898.6	200818.7	182387.1
集体绝对控股	Collective-owned Absolute Holding Enterprises	1	1	609.0	609.0	76.0	76.0
集体相对控股	Collective-owned Relative Holding Enterprises	1		4693.0		21.0	
其　他	Others	12	6	424894.9	166422.4	122257.0	70942.6
按企业规模划分	**By Size**						
特大型	Oversized	4	4	5092873.3	5092873.3	1841166.0	1841166.0
大　型	Large-sized	116	49	11639153.3	8187297.0	3455414.6	2094033.6
中　型	Medium-sized	50	13	752811.0	267554.3	185498.5	66830.8
小　型	Small-sized	3	1	5421.0	609.0	1081.0	76.0
其　他	Others	12	1	2622343.7	5425.4	141168.3	4455.9
按行业划分	**By Sector**						
农业	Agriculture	4	1	266596.4	58479.0	96932.1	27971.0
工业	Industry	66	28	8919208.8	6953180.6	3593869.6	2793031.7
建筑业	Construction	12	3	3445583.8	2959217.0	297023.1	262962.0
运输邮电业	Transportation,Posts and Telecommunications	6	1	259629.4	144541.0	181269.1	128921.0
批发零售贸易餐饮业	Wholesale,Retail and Catering	68	28	1996702.6	1053691.0	568174.3	277829.0
金融保险业	Banking and Insurance						
房地产业	Real Estate	6	2	3813760.0	1604305.0	78276.0	51030.0
其　他	Others	23	5	1411121.5	780345.4	808784.3	464817.6

注：因兼并、合并等原因，实报户数为185户。

MAIN ECONOMIC INDICATORS OF STATE-OWNED LARGE AND MEDIUM ENTERPRISES(1998)

(10000 yuan)

流动资产 平均余额 Average Balance of Circulating Funds	# 改制 企业 Recapping Enterprises	负 债 合 计 Total Liabilities	# 改制 企业 Recapping Enterprises	主营业务 收 入 Major Business Revenue	# 改制 企业 Recapping Enterprises	利 润 总 额 Total Profits	# 改制 企业 Recapping Enterprises	从业人员 (人) Number of Employees (person)	# 改制 企业 Recapping Enterprises	从业人员 报 酬 Payment for Employees	# 改制 企业 Recapping Enterprises
10289742.1	**6448457.4**	**12210601.1**	**7656381.7**	**7949486.6**	**5409697.1**	**302019.1**	**260771.4**	**596463**	**365048**	**801967.2**	**529156.8**
10289742.1	6448457.4	12210601.1	7656381.7	7949486.6	5409697.1	302019.1	260771.4	596463	365048	801967.2	529156.8
2182195.6		2815089.2		2357017.1		43117.0		225057		264447.6	
6816023.7	5226232.7	8066519.2	6393597.2	3675081.7	3518596.7	131514.0	133922.0	288634	285296	445199.4	439705.4
192951.6	152800.6	315702.0	281793.0	359012.2	338696.2	10634.0	10446.0	13776	12115	16658.0	14936.8
980431.1	980431.1	874103.5	874106.5	1414941.5	1414941.5	111412.9	111412.9	59729	59729	66937.4	66937.4
118140.1	88993.0	139187.2	106888.1	143434.2	137462.7	5341.3	4990.5	9267	7908	8724.9	7577.3
9856884.2	6254479.2	11653741.9	7376086.2	7527013.5	5161631.6	274818.9	238732.5	563091	351192	765532.1	515382.4
205170.5	117195.9	258613.8	169526.2	160030.8	120230.2	21493.0	21047.9	11297	7467	11805.4	7711.4
520.0	520.0	108.0	108.0	1309.0	1309.0	204.0	204.0	151	151	186.0	186.0
2456.0		3693.0		34480.0		3.0		1250		1795.5	
224711.4	76262.3	294444.3	110661.3	226653.4	126526.3	5500.3	787.0	20674	6238	22648.3	5877.0
1458983.6	1458983.6	2512285.2	2512285.2	1849575.9	1849575.9	106538.7	106538.7	155398	155398	213629.1	213629.1
6314900.2	4859300.4	6918492.6	4969932.3	5141736.4	3265883.9	184876.4	152791.1	376040	196852	517850.6	302917.2
421274.9	128532.4	526275.5	170762.3	632844.3	290873.4	7968.2	900.7	39869	12142	44998.7	12006.5
3828.0	520.0	3964.0	108.0	2800.0	1309.0	-159.0	204.0	397	151	407.0	186.0
2090755.4	1121.0	2249583.7	3293.9	322530.1	2054.9	2794.9	337.0	24759	505	25081.8	418.0
134430.5	27153.0	192514.7	49039.0	128735.8	82799.0	-2674.8	-3860.0	15222	2817	11592.7	1962.0
2887413.0	2128028.2	4177630.3	3078904.9	3436245.5	2764360.8	168471.1	155300.0	248836	148982	303400.7	190614.4
2767384.6	2404487.0	2986931.0	2543515.0	1448024.2	1250359.0	39456.6	37231.0	119039	97343	213147.5	183668.6
47182.2	6685.0	124666.6	59592.0	71153.9	18152.0	4667.0	5811.0	15757	402	12835.2	283.0
1010332.3	515673.9	1162791.8	507121.5	2142701.1	927659.0	60048.5	39630.9	77148	27839	95654.0	36396.5
3049447.6	1181352.0	3112566.9	1148801.0	333958.3	143547.0	12102.4	13060.0	10913	4916	17639.8	8825.9
393551.8	185078.3	453499.8	269408.3	388667.9	222820.3	19948.4	13598.6	109548	82749	147697.4	107406.4

Note: Enterprises actually counted are 185 because of annexation and amalgamation.

附 4-5 地方企业集团按销售收入排序
ARRANGING IN SALES REVENUE ORDER OF LOCAL BUSINESS GROUP

序 号 No.	企 业 名 称	Enterprises
1	北京汽车工业集团	BEIJING AUTOMOTIVE INDUSTRY CORP
2	北京化学工业集团有限责任公司	BEIJING CHEMICAL INDUSTRY GROUP CO.,LTD.
3	北京建工集团	BEIJING CONSTRUCTION ENGINEERING GROUP CO.,LTD..
4	北京二商集团有限责任公司	BEIJING ERSHANG （GROUP）CO.,LTD.
5	北京旅游集团有限责任公司	BEIJING TOURISM GROUP CO.LTD.
6	北京建筑材料集团有限责任公司	BEIJING BUILDING MATERIALS GROUP
7	北京住宅开发建设集团总公司	BEIJING ZHUZONG GROUP CO.,LTD.
8	北京一商集团有限责任公司	BEIJING YI SHANG GROUP CO.LTD.
9	北京首都创业集团	CAPITAL GROUP
10	北京北辰实业集团公司	BEIJING NORTH STAR INDUSTRIAL GROUP
11	北京燕莎集团有限责任公司	BEIJING YANSHA GROUP CO.,LTD..
12	北京西单友谊集团	BEIJING XIDAN MARKET GROUP
13	北京燕京啤酒集团公司	BEIJING YANJING BEER GROUP CORPORATION
14	北京城市开发集团有限责任公司	BEIJING URBAN DEVELOPMENT GROUP CO.,LTD.
15	北京东安集团公司	BEIJING DONGAN GROUP CO.,LTD.
16	北京一轻集团有限责任公司	BEIJING YIQING GROUP CO.,LTD.
17	北京王府井百货（集团）股份有限公司	BEIJING WANGFUJING DEPARTMENT STORE （GROUP）CO.,LTD.
18	北京城乡建设集团有限责任公司	BEIJING URBAN & RURAL CONSTRUCTION GROUP CO.,LTD.
19	北京天鸿集团公司	BEIJING TIANHONG GROUP CORPORATION
20	北内集团	BEIJING GROUP CORPORATION
21	北京牡丹电子集团公司	BEIJING PEONY ELECTRONIC GROUP CO.
22	北京外企服务集团有限责任公司	BEIJING FOREIGN ENTERPRISE SERVICE GROUP CO.,LTD.
23	北京东方电子集团股份有限公司	BEIJING ORIENT ELECTRONICS GROUP CO.,LTD.
24	北京华都集团有限责任公司	BEIJING HUADU GROUP CO.,LTD.
25	北京雪花电器集团公司	BEIJING SNOWFLAKE ELECTRIC APPLIANCE GROUP CROP
26	首汽集团	SHOUQI GROUP
27	北人集团	BEIREN GROUP CORPORATION
28	北京市针棉织品进出口集团公司	BEIJING KNITWEAR IMP. & EXP. GROUP CORPORATION
29	北京粮食集团有限责任公司	BEIJING GRAIN GROUP CO.,LTD.
30	北京市三环毛纺针织集团公司	BEIJING SANHUAN WOOLLEN SPINNING AND KNITTING GROUP
31	北京兆维电子（集团）有限责任公司	BEIJING C&W ELECTRONICS (GROUP)CO.,LTD.
32	北京印刷集团有限责任公司	BEIJING PRINTING GROUP CO.,LTD.
33	中国北京全聚德集团有限责任公司	CHINA BEIJING QUANJUDE GROUP CO.LTD.
34	北京华讯集团	BEIJING HUAXUN GROUP
35	北京饮食服务集团有限责任公司	BEIJING CATERING & SERVICES GROUP CO.LTD.
36	北京用友软件股份有限公司	BEIJING UFSOFT CO.,LTD.
37	北京飞达电子集团公司	BEIJING FEIDA ELECTRONICS GROUP COMPANY
38	北京轻联包装印刷集团	BEIJINGTHEUNITOFLIGHTINDUSTRYPACKINGPRINTINGGROUPCORPORATION
39	北京青年实业集团公司	BEIJING YOUTH INDUSTRIAL(GROUP)CO.
40	北京北奥有限责任公司	BEIJING BEI AO INCORATION
41	北京厨房设备集团公司	BEIJING KITCHEN EQUIPMENT GROUP CORPORATION
42	北京百花集团	BEIJING BAIHUA GROUP
43	北京五洲染织集团公司	BEIJING WUZHOU DYEING AND WEAVING GROUP CORPORATION
44	北京标准件工业集团公司	BEIJING STANDARD FASTENERS INDUSTRIAL GROUP CO.
45	北京市京工服装工业集团公司	BEIJING JING GONG GARMENT INDUSTRY GROUP CORPORATION
46	北京章光 101 集团公司	BEIJING ZHANG GUANG 101 GROUP CORP.
47	北京轻联皮革集团公司	BEIJING QING LIAN LEATHER GROUP CORPORATION
48	北京太上企业发展集团公司	BEIJING TASON ENTERPRISE GROUP CORP
49	北京首都科技集团有限责任公司	BEIJING CAPITAL SCIENCE TECHNOLOGY GROUP CO.,LTD.
50	北京市九达纺织集团公司	BEIJING JIU DA TEXTILE GROUP CORP.

附 4-6 地方企业集团按利润总额排序
ARRANGING IN TOTAL PROFITS OF LOCAL BUSINESS GROUP

序号 No.	企业名称	Enterprises
1	北京旅游集团有限责任公司	BEIJING TOURISM GROUP CO.LTD.
2	北京燕京啤酒集团公司	BEIJING YANJING BEER GROUP CORPORATION
3	北京首都创业集团	CAPITAL GROUP
4	北京天鸿集团公司	BEIJING TIANHONG GROUP CORPORATION
5	北京燕莎集团有限责任公司	BEIJING YANSHA GROUP CO.,LTD..
6	北京住宅开发建设集团总公司	BEIJING ZHUZONG GROUP CO.,LTD.
7	北京东方电子集团股份有限公司	BEIJING ORIENT ELECTRONICS GROUP CO.,LTD.
8	北京西单友谊集团	BEIJING XIDAN MARKET GROUP
9	北人集团	BEIREN GROUP CORPORATION
10	北京建工集团	BEIJING CONSTRUCTION ENGINEERING GROUP CO.,LTD..
11	北京建筑材料集团有限责任公司	BEIJING BUILDING MATERIALS GROUP
12	北京城市开发集团有限责任公司	BEIJING URBAN DEVELOPMENT GROUP CO.,LTD.
13	北京用友软件股份有限公司	BEIJING UFSOFT CO.,LTD.
14	北京市九达纺织集团公司	BEIJING JIU DA TEXTILE GROUP CORP.
15	北京兆维电子（集团）有限责任公司	BEIJING C&W ELECTRONICS (GROUP)CO.,LTD.
16	北京一轻集团有限责任公司	BEIJING YIQING GROUP CO.,LTD.
17	北京北辰实业集团公司	BEIJING NORTH STAR INDUSTRIAL GROUP
18	中国北京全聚德集团有限责任公司	CHINA BEIJING QUANJUDE GROUP CO.LTD.
19	北京城乡建设集团有限责任公司	BEIJING URBAN & RURAL CONSTRUCTION GROUP CO.,LTD.
20	北京外企服务集团有限责任公司	BEIJING FOREIGN ENTERPRISE SERVICE GROUP CO.,LTD.
21	首汽集团	SHOUQI GROUP
22	北京华都集团有限责任公司	BEIJING HUADU GROUP CO.,LTD.
23	北京华讯集团	BEIJING HUAXUN GROUP
24	北京雪花电器集团公司	BEIJING SNOWFLAKE ELECTRIC APPLIANCE GROUP CROP
25	北京东安集团公司	BEIJING DONGAN GROUP CO.,LTD.
26	北京汽车工业集团	BEIJING AUTOMOTIVE INDUSTRY CORP
27	北京五洲染织集团公司	BEIJING WUZHOU DYEING AND WEAVING GROUP CORPORATION
28	北京轻联包装印刷集团	BEIJINGTHEUNITOFLIGHTINDUSTRYPACKINGPRINTINGGROUPCORPORATION
29	北京一商集团有限责任公司	BEIJING YI SHANG GROUP CO.LTD.
30	北京北奥有限责任公司	BEIJING BEI AO INCORATION
31	北京王府井百货（集团）股份有限公司	BEIJING WANGFUJING DEPARTMENT STORE （GROUP）CO.,LTD.
32	北京百花集团	BEIJING BAIHUA GROUP
33	北京印刷集团有限责任公司	BEIJING PRINTING GROUP CO.,LTD.
34	北京饮食服务集团有限责任公司	BEIJING CATERING & SERVICES GROUP CO.LTD.
35	北京市京工服装工业集团公司	BEIJING JING GONG GARMENT INDUSTRY GROUP CORPORATION
36	北京标准件工业集团公司	BEIJING STANDARD FASTENERS INDUSTRIAL GROUP CO.
37	北京首都科技集团有限责任公司	BEIJING CAPITAL SCIENCE TECHNOLOGY GROUP CO.,LTD.
38	北京轻联皮革集团公司	BEIJING QING LIAN LEATHER GROUP CORPORATION
39	北京青年实业集团公司	BEIJING YOUTH INDUSTRIAL(GROUP)CO.
40	北京太上企业发展集团公司	BEIJING TASON ENTERPRISE GROUP CORP
41	北京厨房设备集团公司	BEIJING KITCHEN EQUIPMENT GROUP CORPORATION
42	北京章光 101 集团公司	BEIJING ZHANG GUANG 101 GROUP CORP.
43	北京飞达电子集团公司	BEIJING FEIDA ELECTRONICS GROUP COMPANY
44	北京市针棉织品进出口集团公司	BEIJING KNITWEAR IMP. & EXP. GROUP CORPORATION
45	北内集团	BEIJING GROUP CORPORATION
46	北京二商集团有限责任公司	BEIJING ERSHANG （GROUP）CO.,LTD.
47	北京市三环毛纺针织集团公司	BEIJING SANHUAN WOOLEN SPINNING AND KNITTING GROUP
48	北京粮食集团有限责任公司	BEIJING GRAIN GROUP CO.,LTD.
49	北京化学工业集团有限责任公司	BEIJING CHEMICAL INDUSTRY GROUP CO.,LTD.
50	北京牡丹电子集团公司	BEIJING PEONY ELECTRONIC GROUP CO.

附 4-7 地方企业集团按资产总额排序
ARRANGINGIN TOTAL ASSETS OF LOCAL BUSINESS GROUP

序号 No.	企业名称	Name of Enterprises
1	北京化学工业集团有限责任公司	BEIJING CHEMICAL INDUSTRY GROUP CO.,LTD.
2	北京天鸿集团公司	BEIJING TIANHONG GROUP CORPORATION
3	北京首都创业集团	CAPITAL GROUP
4	北京建工集团	BEIJING CONSTRUCTION ENGINEERING GROUP CO.,LTD..
5	北京汽车工业集团	BEIJING AUTOMOTIVE INDUSTRY CORP
6	北京旅游集团有限责任公司	BEIJING TOURISM GROUP CO.LTD.
7	北京住宅开发建设集团总公司	BEIJING ZHUZONG GROUP CO.,LTD.
8	北京建筑材料集团有限责任公司	BEIJING BUILDING MATERIALS GROUP
9	北京城市开发集团有限责任公司	BEIJING URBAN DEVELOPMENT GROUP CO.,LTD.
10	北京一轻集团有限责任公司	BEIJING YIQING GROUP CO.,LTD.
11	北京北辰实业集团公司	BEIJING NORTH STAR INDUSTRIAL GROUP
12	北内集团	BEIJING GROUP CORPORATION
13	北京二商集团有限责任公司	BEIJING ERSHANG （GROUP）CO.,LTD.
14	北京燕京啤酒集团公司	BEIJING YANJING BEER GROUP CORPORATION
15	北京一商集团有限责任公司	BEIJING YI SHANG GROUP CO.LTD.
16	北京城乡建设集团有限责任公司	BEIJING URBAN & RURAL CONSTRUCTION GROUP CO.,LTD.
17	北京王府井百货（集团）股份有限公司	BEIJING WANGFUJING DEPARTMENT STORE （GROUP）CO.,LTD.
18	北人集团	BEIREN GROUP CORPORATION
19	北京粮食集团有限责任公司	BEIJING GRAIN GROUP CO.,LTD.
20	北京西单友谊集团	BEIJING XIDAN MARKET GROUP
21	北京燕莎集团有限责任公司	BEIJING YANSHA GROUP CO.,LTD..
22	北京东方电子集团股份有限公司	BEIJING ORIENT ELECTRONICS GROUP CO.,LTD.
23	北京外企服务集团有限责任公司	BEIJING FOREIGN ENTERPRISE SERVICE GROUP CO.,LTD.
24	北京牡丹电子集团公司	BEIJING PEONY ELECTRONIC GROUP CO.
25	北京兆维电子（集团）有限责任公司	BEIJING C&W ELECTRONICS (GROUP)CO.,LTD.
26	首汽集团	SHOUQI GROUP
27	北京雪花电器集团公司	BEIJING SNOWFLAKE ELECTRIC APPLIANCE GROUP CROP
28	北京东安集团公司	BEIJING DONGAN GROUP CO.,LTD.
29	北京华都集团有限责任公司	BEIJING HUADU GROUP CO.,LTD.
30	北京市针棉织品进出口集团公司	BEIJING KNITWEAR IMP. & EXP. GROUP CORPORATION
31	北京印刷集团有限责任公司	BEIJING PRINTING GROUP CO.,LTD.
32	北京饮食服务集团有限责任公司	BEIJING CATERING & SERVICES GROUP CO.LTD.
33	北京市三环毛纺针织集团公司	BEIJING SANHUAN WOOLEN SPINNING AND KNITTING GROUP
34	北京市九达纺织集团公司	BEIJING JIU DA TEXTILE GROUP CORP.
35	北京飞达电子集团公司	BEIJING FEIDA ELECTRONICS GROUP COMPANY
36	中国北京全聚德集团有限责任公司	CHINA BEIJING QUANJUDE GROUP CO.LTD.
37	北京五洲染织集团公司	BEIJING WUZHOU DYEING AND WEAVING GROUP CORPORATION
38	北京青年实业集团公司	BEIJING YOUTH INDUSTRIAL(GROUP)CO.
39	北京轻联包装印刷集团	BEIJINGTHEUNITOFLIGHTINDUSTRYPACKINGPRINTINGGROUPCORPORATION
40	北京标准件工业集团公司	BEIJING STANDARD FASTENERS INDUSTRIAL GROUP CO.
41	北京北奥有限责任公司	BEIJING BEI AO INCORATION
42	北京轻联皮革集团公司	BEIJING QING LIAN LEATHER GROUP CORPORATION
43	北京厨房设备集团公司	BEIJING KITCHEN EQUIPMENT GROUP CORPORATION
44	北京百花集团	BEIJING BAIHUA GROUP
45	北京华讯集团	BEIJING HUAXUN GROUP
46	北京市京工服装工业集团公司	BEIJING JING GONG GARMENT INDUSTRY GROUP CORPORATION
47	北京用友软件股份有限公司	BEIJING UFSOFT CO.,LTD.
48	北京太上企业发展集团公司	BEIJING TASON ENTERPRISE GROUP CORP
49	北京章光 101 集团公司	BEIJING ZHANG GUANG 101 GROUP CORP.
50	北京首都科技集团有限责任公司	BEIJING CAPITAL SCIENCE TECHNOLOGY GROUP CO.,LTD.

附录 5：世界主要国家和地区统计资料

APPENDIX 5: STATISTICS OF MAJOR COUNTRIES AND TERRITORIES

附 5-1 1998 年世界主要国家和地区人均国民生产总值

GROSS NATIONAL PRODUCT(GNP) PER CAPITA IN MAIN COUNTRIES AND TERRITORIES OF 1998

国家和地区 Country or Territory		人均国民生产总值 GNP Per Capita		购买力平价法计算的 GNP GNP Calculated in Purchasing-power-parity way	
		人均值（美元）Per Capita (US$)	年增长率（%）Growth Rate (%)	总额（10 亿美元）Total (US$ 1 billion)	人均值（美元）Per Capita (US$)
中国	China	750.0	6.5	3983.6	3220.0
美国	United States	29340.0	2.8	7922.6	29340.0
日本	Japan	32380.0	-2.8	2928.4	23180.0
德国	Germany	25850.0	-0.4	1708.5	20810.0
英国	United Kingdom	21400.0	1.9	1218.6	20640.0
法国	France	24940.0	2.9	1312.0	22320.0
意大利	Italy	20250.0	2.2	11634.0	20200.0
加拿大	Canada	20020.0	5.1	735.6	24050.0
澳大利亚	Australia	20300.0	2.6	3775.0	20130.0
波兰	Poland	3900.0	5.4	260.7	6740.0
罗马尼亚	Romania	1390.0	-5.3	89.3	3970.0
保加利亚	Bulgaria	1230.0			
印度	India	430.0	4.2	1660.9	1700.0
印度尼西亚	Indonesia	680.0	-16.2	568.9	2790.0
巴基斯坦	Pakistan	480.0	2.5	204.9	1560.0
泰国	Thailand	2200.0	-8.5	357.1	5840.0
菲律宾	Philippines	1050.0	-2.1	265.6	3540.0
马来西亚	Malaysia	3600.0	-8.4	155.1	6990.0
韩国	Korea Rep.	7970.0	-7.1	569.3	12270.0
尼日利亚	Nigeria	300.0	-1.7	99.7	820.0
巴西	Brazil	4570.0	-1.4	10214.0	6160.0
墨西哥	Mexico	3970.0	3.0	785.8	8190.0
阿根廷	Argentina	8970.0	2.7	3685.0	10200.0
孟加拉国	Bangladesh	350.0	3.4	137.7	1100.0
新加坡	Singapore	30060.0	-0.4	90.5	28620.0
越南	Viet Nam	330.0	2.8	131.0	1690.0
阿尔及利亚	Algeria	1550.0	5.0	131.4	4380.0
南非	South Africa Rep.	2880.0	-1.2	288.7	6990.0
新西兰	New Zealand	14700.0	0.5	60.1	15840.0

资料来源：世界银行《1999/2000 年世界发展指标》。

Source: 1999/2000 World Development Indicator of World Bank.

附 5-2 世界主要国家和地区经济增长率

GROWTH RATE OF ECONOMY IN MAIN COUNTRIES AND TERRITORIES

单位：% (%)

国家和地区 Country or Territory		1996	1997	1998	1999 *
中国	China	9.6	8.8	7.8	6.6
美国	United States	3.4	3.9	3.9	3.7
日本	Japan	3.9	1.4	-2.8	1.0
德国	Germany	1.3	1.8	2.3	1.4
英国	United Kingdom	2.2	3.5	2.2	1.1
法国	France	1.6	2.3	3.2	2.5
意大利	Italy	0.7	1.5	1.3	1.2
加拿大	Canada	1.2	4.0	3.1	3.6
澳大利亚	Australia	3.7	3.9	5.1	4.0
波兰	Poland	6.1	6.8	4.8	3.7
匈牙利	Hungary	1.3	4.6	5.1	3.7
罗马尼亚	Romania	3.9	-6.9	-7.3	-3.5
印度	India	7.5	5.5	5.8	5.7
印度尼西亚	Indonesia	8.0	4.7	-13.7	-0.8
巴基斯坦	Pakistan	5.2	1.2	3.3	3.1
泰国	Thailand	5.5	-1.3	-9.4	4.0
菲律宾	Philippines	5.7	5.2	-0.5	2.2
马来西亚	Malaysia	8.6	7.7	-6.7	2.4
韩国	Korea Rep.	7.1	5.0	-5.8	6.5
埃及	Egypt	4.3	5.0	5.4	6.0
巴西	Brazil	2.8	3.7	0.1	-1.0
墨西哥	Mexico	5.2	7.0	4.6	3.0
阿根廷	Argentina	4.8	8.1	3.9	-3.0
新加坡	Singapore	6.9	9.0	0.3	4.5
阿尔及利亚	Algeria	3.8	1.1	4.7	4.6
南非	South Africa Rep.	3.2	2.5	0.5	0.7
新西兰	New Zealand	3.1	2.1	-0.3	2.6

注：*为预测数。

资料来源：1999 年《世界经济展望》。

Note: * indicates the predetermined data.

Source: 1999 Prospects for the World Economy.

附 5-3 世界主要国家和地区通货膨胀率
INFLATION RATE OF MAIN COUNTRIES AND TERRITORIES

单位：% (%)

国家和地区	Country or Territory	1996	1997	1998	1999 *
中国	China	8.4	2.8	-0.8	-1.5
美国	United States	1.9	2.3	1.6	2.2
日本	Japan	-0.5	1.7	0.6	-0.4
德国	Germany	1.0	1.5	0.6	0.4
英国	United Kingdom	3.1	2.8	2.7	2.3
法国	France	1.2	1.3	0.7	0.5
意大利	Italy	5.0	1.7	1.7	1.5
加拿大	Canada	1.4	1.4	1.0	1.5
澳大利亚	Australia	2.2	1.7	1.6	1.8
波兰	Poland	19.9	15.0	12.0	7.0
匈牙利	Hungary	23.5	18.0	14.0	9.0
罗马尼亚	Romania	38.8	155.0	59.0	40.0
印度	India	6.9	7.2	13.0	6.5
印度尼西亚	Indonesia	7.9	6.6	59.6	22.7
巴基斯坦	Pakistan	10.3	12.5	7.8	6.1
泰国	Thailand	5.9	5.6	8.1	0.5
菲律宾	Philippines	8.4	6.0	9.7	8.5
马来西亚	Malaysia	3.5	2.7	5.3	3.0
韩国	Korea Rep.	3.4	4.4	7.5	0.7
埃及	Egypt	7.2	6.2	3.8	3.7
巴西	Brazil	11.1	6.0	3.8	4.6
墨西哥	Mexico	34.4	20.6	16.7	17.1
阿根廷	Argentina	0.2	0.8	0.9	-0.8
新加坡	Singapore	1.4	2.0	-0.3	0.2
阿尔及利亚	Algeria	18.7	6.8	6.2	5.3
南非	South Africa Rep.	7.4	8.6	6.9	6.5
新西兰	New Zealand	2.0	1.7	1.5	1.3

注：*为预测数。

资料来源：1999 年《世界经济展望》。

Note: * indicates the predetermined data.

Source: 1999 Prospects for the World Economy.

附 5-4 1998 年世界主要国家和地区投资率
INVESTMENT RATE IN MAIN COUNTRIES AND TERRITORIES OF 1998

单位：%　　　　(%)

国家和地区	Country or Territory	1980	1995	1996	1997	1998
世界	World	25.0	21.8	22.0	22.0	20.0
中国	China	35.0	40.8	39.2	35.0	39.0
美国	United States	20.0	17.7	18.0	18.0	18.0
日本	Japan	32.0	28.5	29.0	29.0	
德国	Germany		22.5	23.0	23.0	21.0
英国	United Kingdom	17.0	16.0	16.0		16.0
法国	France	24.0	18.2	18.0	18.0	17.0
意大利	Italy	27.0	18.1	18.0	18.0	17.0
加拿大	Canada	23.0	18.4	18.0	18.0	18.0
澳大利亚	Australia	25.0	21.5	21.0	21.0	20.0
波兰	Poland	26.0	18.0	20.4	22.0	24.0
俄罗斯	Russia		23.2	22.2	22.0	20.0
罗马尼亚	Romania	40.0	25.6	25.4	25.0	20.0
保加利亚	Bulgaria	34.0	15.7	14.1	14.0	12.0
印度	India	20.0	26.2	26.5	25.0	23.0
印度尼西亚	Indonesia	24.0	31.1	31.8	31.0	31.0
巴基斯坦	Pakistan	18.0	18.7	18.6	19.0	17.0
泰国	Thailand	29.0	42.3	41.0	41.0	35.0
菲律宾	Philippines	29.0	22.2	24.2	25.0	25.0
马来西亚	Malaysia	30.0	40.6	41.2	43.0	32.0
韩国	Korea Rep.	32.0	37.0	38.2	35.0	35.0
尼日利亚	Nigeria	21.0	18.5	18.7	18.0	20.0
埃及	Egypt	28.0	16.7	16.6	18.0	19.0
巴西	Brazil	23.0	21.9	19.5	20.0	21.0
墨西哥	Mexico	27.0	19.6	20.9	21.0	26.0
阿根廷	Argentina	25.0	18.3	18.5	19.0	22.0
孟加拉国	Bangladesh	22.0	16.6	17.0	17.0	21.0
新加坡	Singapore	46.0	33.1	35.1	37.0	37.0
阿尔及利亚	Algeria	39.0	32.0	27.0	27.0	27.0
南非	South Africa Rep.	28.0	18.6	17.5	16.0	20.0
新西兰	New Zealand	21.0	21.9	22.0	22.0	22.0

资料来源：世界银行《1999/2000 年世界发展指标》。
Source: 1999/2000 World Development Indicator of World Bank.

附 5-5 1998 年世界主要国家和地区储蓄率
SAVING DEPOSITS RATE IN MAIN COUNTRIES AND TERRITORIES OF 1998

单位：% (%)

国家和地区	Country or Territory	1980	1995	1996	1997	1998
世界	World	24.0	22.1	22.0	22.0	21.0
中国	China	35.0	42.0	44.0	40.0	43.0
美国	United States	19.0	16.2	16.0	16.0	16.0
日本	Japan	31.0	30.0	30.0	30.0	
德国	Germany		23.4	23.0	23.0	22.0
英国	United Kingdom	19.0	15.0	15.0		15.0
法国	France	23.0	20.5	21.0	21.0	20.0
意大利	Italy	24.0	22.3	22.0	22.0	22.0
加拿大	Canada	25.0	20.9	21.0	21.0	21.0
澳大利亚	Australia	24.0	21.3	21.0	21.0	21.0
波兰	Poland	23.0	19.4	17.6	18.0	20.0
俄罗斯	Russia		26.8	25.4	25.0	24.0
罗马尼亚	Romania	35.0	21.1	18.9	19.0	13.0
保加利亚	Bulgaria	39.0	17.9	16.7	17.0	17.0
印度	India	17.0	22.7	23.9	22.0	18.0
印度尼西亚	Indonesia	38.0	32.3	33.2	31.0	31.0
巴基斯坦	Pakistan	7.0	15.7	14.2	14.0	13.0
泰国	Thailand	23.0	36.2	35.3	35.0	36.0
菲律宾	Philippines	24.0	14.4	14.4	16.0	15.0
马来西亚	Malaysia	33.0	37.2	41.9	44.0	47.0
韩国	Korea Rep.	24.0	36.0	34.2	34.0	34.0
尼日利亚	Nigeria	31.0	20.9	24.4	24.0	12.0
埃及	Egypt	15.0	12.1	12.1	12.0	10.0
巴西	Brazil	21.0	21.1	18.2	18.0	19.0
墨西哥	Mexico	25.0	22.5	23.4	23.0	24.0
阿根廷	Argentina	24.0	18.4	18.2	18.0	19.0
孟加拉国	Bangladesh	13.0	8.3	7.2	10.0	15.0
新加坡	Singapore	38.0	50.8	50.5	51.0	51.0
阿尔及利亚	Algeria	39.0	29.0	34.0	27.0	27.0
南非	South Africa Rep.	36.0	18.7	18.3	17.0	17.0
新西兰	New Zealand	20.0	22.9	23.0	23.0	22.0

资料来源：世界银行《1999/2000 年世界发展指标》。
Source: 1999/2000 World Development Indicator of World Bank.

附 5-6 1998 年世界主要国家和地区消费率
CONSUMPTION RATE IN MAIN COUNTRIES AND TERRITORIES OF 1998

单位：%　　　　(%)

国家和地区	Country or Territory	1980	1995	1996	1997	1998
世界	World	76.0	77.9	79.0	78.0	79.0
中国	China	66.0	59.0	58.6	60.0	57.0
美国	United States	81.0	83.8	84.0	84.0	84.0
日本	Japan	69.0	70.0	70.0	70.0	
德国	Germany		76.6	77.0	77.0	78.0
英国	United Kingdom	81.0	85.0	85.0	21.0	85.0
法国	France	77.0	79.5	79.0	79.0	80.0
意大利	Italy	76.0	77.7	77.0	77.0	77.0
加拿大	Canada	75.0	79.1	80.0	80.0	79.0
澳大利亚	Australia	77.0	78.7	79.0	79.0	80.0
波兰	Poland	76.0	80.6	82.4	82.0	81.0
俄罗斯	Russia		73.2	74.6	74.0	77.0
罗马尼亚	Romania	65.0	78.9	81.1	81.0	87.0
保加利亚	Bulgaria	61.0	82.1	83.3	83.0	82.0
印度	India	83.0	77.3	76.1	78.0	82.0
印度尼西亚	Indonesia	62.0	67.7	66.8	70.0	70.0
巴基斯坦	Pakistan	93.0	84.3	85.8	85.0	87.0
泰国	Thailand	77.0	63.8	64.7	65.0	64.0
菲律宾	Philippines	76.0	85.6	85.6	85.0	86.0
马来西亚	Malaysia	68.0	62.8	58.1	56.0	53.0
韩国	Korea Rep.	76.0	64.0	65.8	66.0	66.0
尼日利亚	Nigeria	68.0	79.1	75.6	82.0	88.0
埃及	Egypt	85.0	87.9	87.9	88.0	90.0
巴西	Brazil	79.0	78.9	81.8	82.0	81.0
墨西哥	Mexico	75.0	77.5	76.6	76.0	76.0
阿根廷	Argentina	76.0	81.6	81.8	82.0	81.0
孟加拉国	Bangladesh	88.0	91.7	92.8	91.0	84.0
新加坡	Singapore	63.0	49.2	49.5	48.0	49.0
阿尔及利亚	Algeria	61.0	71.0	66.0	73.0	73.0
南非	South Africa Rep.	63.0	81.3	81.7	83.0	83.0
新西兰	New Zealand	80.0	77.1	77.0	77.0	77.0

资料来源：世界银行《1999/2000 年世界发展指标》。
Source: 1999/2000 World Development Indicator of World Bank.

附 5-7 世界主要国家和地区中央政府收入占 GDP 比重
COMPOSITION OF REVENUE OF CENTRAL GOVERNMENT IN GDP OF MAIN COUNTRIES AND TERRITORIES

单位：%　　(%)

国家和地区 Country or Territory		税收 Tax		非税收 Non-tax	
		1980	1997	1980	1997
中国	China		4.9		0.6
美国	United States	18.5	19.8	1.7	1.5
日本	Japan	11.0		0.6	
英国	United Kingdom	30.6	33.4	4.6	2.8
法国	France	36.7	39.2	2.9	2.6
意大利	Italy	29.3	42.2	2.5	2.5
加拿大	Canada	16.0		2.5	
澳大利亚	Australia	19.5	23.2	2.2	1.9
波兰	Poland		35.2		3.4
西班牙	Spanish	22.1	28.3	1.9	2.0
俄罗斯	Russia		17.9		1.1
罗马尼亚	Romania	10.1	24.4	35.2	2.1
保加利亚	Bulgaria		25.2		6.8
印度	India	9.0	10.8	1.8	3.3
印度尼西亚	Indonesia	20.2	14.7	1.0	2.3
巴基斯坦	Pakistan	13.3	12.9	2.9	3.1
泰国	Thailand	13.2	16.1	1.2	1.9
菲律宾	Philippines	12.5	17.0	1.5	2.0
马来西亚	Malaysia	23.5	19.4	2.8	4.2
韩国	Korea Rep.	15.5	18.6	2.2	2.9
埃及	Egypt	28.8	21.5	15.2	13.9
巴西	Brazil	17.8		4.8	
墨西哥	Mexico	13.9	12.8	1.1	2.5
阿根廷	Argentina	10.4	11.2	5.2	1.1
蒙古	Mongolia		17.0		4.8
孟加拉国	Bangladesh	5.7		2.7	
新加坡	Singapore	17.5	15.9	7.8	8.3
南非	South Africa Rep.	20.5	27.5	3.0	2.0
芬兰	Finland	25.1	28.4	2.1	5.1
新西兰	New Zealand	30.7	31.2	3.5	2.7

资料来源：世界银行《1999/2000 年世界发展指标》。
Source: 1999/2000 World Development Indicator of World Bank.

附 5-8 世界主要国家和地区中央政府支出占 GDP 比重
COMPOSITION OF EXPENDITURE OF CENTRAL GOVERNMENT IN GDP OF MAIN COUNTRIES AND TERRITORIES

单位：% (%)

国家和地区 Country or Territory		经常项目支出 Current Expenditure		资本支出 Capital Expenditure	
		1980	1997	1980	1997
美国	United States	20.7	21.0	1.3	0.7
日本	Japan	14.8		3.6	
英国	United Kingdom	36.4	39.6	1.8	2.1
法国	France	37.4	44.6	2.1	2.0
意大利	Italy	37.8	45.4	2.2	2.5
加拿大	Canada	20.8		0.2	
澳大利亚	Australia	21.1	25.3	1.5	0.9
波兰	Poland		39.3		1.9
西班牙	Spanish	23.6	34.9	2.9	1.9
罗马尼亚	Romania	29.8	29.1	15.0	2.9
保加利亚	Bulgaria		30.9		2.6
印度	India	10.8	14.7	1.4	1.7
印度尼西亚	Indonesia	11.7	8.7	10.4	6.0
巴基斯坦	Pakistan	14.5	19.9	3.1	2.8
泰国	Thailand	14.4	11.0	4.4	7.7
菲律宾	Philippines	9.9	16.3	3.4	2.2
马来西亚	Malaysia	19.2	15.5	9.9	4.6
韩国	Korea Rep.	14.8	14.7	2.4	4.1
埃及	Egypt	39.5	27.7	10.8	6.6
巴西	Brazil	18.6		1.6	
墨西哥	Mexico	11.7	13.7	5.0	1.9
阿根廷	Argentina	18.2	12.7	0.0	1.1
蒙古	Mongolia		16.0		3.7
新加坡	Singapore	15.6	11.6	4.5	5.0
南非	South Africa Rep.	19.1	32.5	3.0	1.3
芬兰	Finland	25.2	38.5	3.0	1.6
新西兰	New Zealand	35.9	31.4	2.4	0.9

资料来源：世界银行《1999/2000 年世界发展指标》。
Source: 1999/2000 World Development Indicator of World Bank.

附 5-9 世界主要国家和地区人文发展指数
HUMANE DEVELOPMENT INDEX IN MAIN COUNTRIES AND TERRITORIES

国家和地区	Country or Territory	出生时的预期寿命（岁）Anticipated Age When Born (year)	成人识字率（%）Literacy Rate of Adult (%)	初等、中等和高等教育综合入学率（%）Entrance Rate of Primary,Secondary and Higher Education (%)	实际人均GDP（PPP$）Actual GDP Per Capita（PPP$）	人文发展指数 Humane Development Index
		1997	1997	1997	1997	1997
中国	China	69.8	82.9	69.0	3130.0	0.701
美国	United States	76.7	99.0	94.0	29010.0	0.927
日本	Japan	80.0	99.0	85.0	24070.0	0.924
德国	Germany	77.2	99.0	88.0	21260.0	0.906
英国	United Kingdom	77.2	99.0	100.0	20730.0	0.918
法国	France	78.1	99.0	92.0	22030.0	0.918
意大利	Italy	78.2	98.3	82.0	20290.0	0.900
加拿大	Canada	79.0	99.0	99.0	22480.0	0.932
澳大利亚	Australia	78.2	99.0	100.0	20210.0	0.922
波兰	Poland	72.5	99.0	77.0	6520.0	0.802
罗马尼亚	Romania	69.9	97.8	68.0	4310.0	0.752
保加利亚	Bulgaria	71.1	98.2	70.0	4010.0	0.758
印度	India	62.6	53.5	55.0	1670.0	0.545
印度尼西亚	Indonesia	65.1	85.0	64.0	3490.0	0.681
巴基斯坦	Pakistan	64.0	40.9	43.0	1560.0	0.508
泰国	Thailand	68.8	94.7	59.0	6690.0	0.753
菲律宾	Philippines	68.3	94.6	82.0	3520.0	0.740
马来西亚	Malaysia	72.0	85.7	65.0	8140.0	0.768
韩国	Korea Rep.	72.4	97.2	90.0	13590.0	0.852
尼日利亚	Nigeria	50.1	59.5	54.0	920.0	0.456
巴西	Brazil	66.8	84.0	80.0	6480.0	0.739
墨西哥	Mexico	72.2	90.1	70.0	8370.0	0.786
阿根廷	Argentina	72.9	96.5	79.0	10300.0	0.827
孟加拉国	Bangladesh	58.1	38.9	35.0	1050.0	0.440
新加坡	Singapore	77.1	91.4	73.0	28460.0	0.888
越南	Viet Nam	67.4	91.9	62.0	1630.0	0.664
阿尔及利亚	Algeria	68.9	60.3	68.0	4460.0	0.665
南非	South Africa Rep.	54.7	84.0	93.0	7380.0	0.695
新西兰	New Zealand	76.9	99.0	95.0	17410.0	0.901

资料来源：联合国《1999 年人文发展报告》。
Source: 1999 Humane Development Report of the United .Nations

附 5-10 世界主要国家和地区医疗卫生指标统计
MEDICAL AND HEALTH INDICATORS IN MAIN COUNTRIES AND TERRITORIES

国家和地区 Country or Territory		对医疗卫生的公共开支占 GDP 的% Composition of Public Expenditure for Medical and Health in GDP	获得安全饮用水的人口占总人口的% Composition of Population Get Health Drinking Water in Total Population		获得卫生设施的人口占总人口的% Composition of Population Get Health Facilities in Total Population		婴儿死亡率（每千例活产婴儿在一岁以下死亡人数）Death Rate of Infant (Death Number below 1-year-old of 1000 Live Infants)		总和生育率（每位妇女的生育个数）Fertility Rate (Fertility Number of Per Woman)	
		1990-1995	1980	1995	1980	1995	1980	1996	1980	1996
中国	China	2.1		90.0		21.0	42.0	33.0	2.5	1.9
美国	United States	6.6		90.0	98.0	85.0	13.0	7.0	1.8	2.1
日本	Japan	5.7				85.0	8.0	4.0	1.8	1.4
德国	Germany	8.2				100.0	12.0	5.0	1.4	1.3
英国	United Kingdom	5.8		100.0		96.0	12.0	6.0	1.9	1.7
法国	France	8.0		100.0	85.0	96.0	10.0	5.0	1.9	1.7
意大利	Italy	5.4	99.0		99.0	100.0	15.0	6.0	1.6	1.2
加拿大	Canada	6.8	97.0	100.0	60.0	85.0	10.0	6.0	1.7	1.7
澳大利亚	Australia	6.0	99.0	95.0	99.0	90.0	11.0	6.0	1.9	1.8
波兰	Poland	4.8	67.0		50.0	100.0	21.0	12.0	2.3	1.6
罗马尼亚	Romania	3.6	77.0		50.0	49.0	29.0	22.0	2.4	1.3
保加利亚	Bulgaria	4.0	96.0			99.0	20.0	16.0	2.0	1.2
印度	India	0.7		81.0		29.0	116.0	65.0	5.0	3.1
印度尼西亚	Indonesia	0.7		62.0		51.0	90.0	49.0	4.3	2.6
巴基斯坦	Pakistan	0.8	38.0	60.0	16.0	30.0	124.0	88.0	7.0	5.1
泰国	Thailand	1.4		81.0		70.0	49.0	34.0	3.5	1.8
菲律宾	Philippines	1.3					52.0	37.0	4.8	3.6
马来西亚	Malaysia	1.4		88.0	75.0	91.0	30.0	11.0	4.2	3.4
韩国	Korea Rep.	1.8		89.0		100.0	26.0	9.0	2.6	1.7
尼日利亚	Nigeria	0.3		39.0		36.0	99.0	78.0	6.9	5.4
巴西	Brazil	2.7		72.0		41.0	67.0	36.0	3.9	2.4
墨西哥	Mexico	2.8		83.0		66.0	51.0	32.0	4.5	2.9
阿根廷	Argentina	4.3		64.0		89.0	35.0	22.0	3.3	2.7
孟加拉国	Bangladesh	1.2		79.0		35.0	132.0	77.0	6.1	3.4
新加坡	Singapore	1.3	100.0	100.0		97.0	12.0	4.0	1.7	1.7
越南	Viet Nam	1.1		36.0		21.0	57.0	40.0	5.0	3.0
阿尔及利亚	Algeria	3.3	77.0				98.0	32.0	6.7	3.4
南非	South Africa Rep.	3.6		70.0		46.0	67.0	49.0	4.6	2.9
新西兰	New Zealand	5.7	87.0				13.0	6.0	2.0	2.0

资料来源：世界银行《1999/2000 年世界发展指标》。

Source: 1999/2000 World Development Indicator of World Bank.

附录 6：香港特别行政区主要社会经济指标
APPENDIX 6：MAIN SOCIAL AND ECONOMIC INDICATORS OF HONG KONG

项目 Item				1995	1997	1998	1999
年中人口数	（万人）	Mid-year Population	(10000 persons)	615.6	650.2	668.7	684.3
出生率	（‰）	Birth Rate	(‰)	11.2	9.1	7.9	7.5
死亡率	（‰）	Death Rate	(‰)	5.1	4.9	4.9	4.8
自然增长率	（‰）	Natural Growth Rate	(‰)	6.1	3.0	2.8	2.5
平均期望寿命	（岁）	Life Expectancy at Birth	(year)				
男		Male		76.0	76.8	77.2	77.2
女		Female		81.5	82.2	82.6	82.6
劳动力总人数	（万人）	Active Population Total	(10000 persons)	300.1	333.0	343.4	352.9
男		Male		184.1	201.6	207.8	211.6
女		Female		116.0	131.4	135.6	141.3
失业人数	（万人）	Unemployed	(10000 persons)	9.6	7.7	20.1	22.0
失业率	（%）	Unemployment Rate	(%)	3.2	2.2	5.7	6.0
国内生产总值		Gross Domestic Product					
以当时市价计算	（亿港元）	At Current Market Prices	(HK$100 million)	10771.0	13239.0	12668.0	
以固定（1990）市价计算	（亿港元）	At Constant(1990) Market Prices	(HK$100 million)	7558.0	8290.0	7864.0	
人均国内生产总值		Per Capita GDP					
以当时市价计算	（港元）	At Current Market Prices	(HK$)	174972.0	203605.0	189443.0	
以固定(1990)市价计算	（港元）	At Constant(1990) Market Prices	(HK$)	122778.0	128533.0	119833.0	
国内生产总值部门构成	(%)	Composition of GDP by Kind of Activity	(%)				
农业和渔业		Agriculture and Fishery		0.1	0.1	0.1	
采矿业		Mining and Quarrying					
制造业		Manufacturing		8.3	6.5	6.2	
电、煤气、水		Electricity,Gas and Water		2.3	2.4	2.8	
建筑业		Construction		5.4	5.8	6.1	
商业、饭店、旅馆		Whole Sale,Retail Sale and Hotels		26.6	25.4	24.0	
运输、仓储、通信		Transport,Storage and Co-mmunications		10.1	9.2	9.3	
金融、保险、不动产和产业服务		Financing,Insurance, Real Estate and Business Services		24.4	26.2	25.6	
房屋所有权		Ownership of Premises		13.3	13.9	14.5	
社会团体和个人服务		Community,Social and Personal Services		17.3	17.9	19.9	
非直接计算的金融中介服务调整		Banking Medium Services Adjust-ment Indirectly Calculated		-7.8	-7.3	-8.5	
制造业生产指数		Indices of Manufacturing Production Industry		126.2	120.6	110.1	101.6
商品进出口贸易总额	（亿港元）	Total Imports and Exports	(HK$100 million)	28352.5	30710.0	27768.0	27417.0
商品进口额		Imports		14911.2	16151.0	14291.0	13927.0
商品出口额		Domestic Exports		2316.6	2114.0	1885.0	1706.0
商品转口额		Re-exports		11124.7	12445.0	11592.0	11784.0

附录 6 续表 continued

项目	Item	1995	1997	1998	1999
政府财政收支（十亿港元）	Government Revenue and Expenditure (HK$1 billion)				
总收入	Total Revenue	153.2	208.4	281.2	216.1
总支出	Total Expenditure	155.9	173.6	194.2	218.8
消费者物价指数 (%)	Consumer Price Indices (%)	101.8	105.8	102.8	96.0
电力耗用（兆焦耳）	Electricity Consumption (terajoules)				
住宅	Domestic		28937	32793	31400
商业	Commercial		67849	73857	76028
工业	Industrial		18965	18489	17547
街灯	Street lighting		322	307	301
出口往中国内地	Export to the mainland of China		2014	2197	2279
总计	Total		118088	127643	127555
抵港及离港旅客人数（千人次）	Number of Passengers (1000 person.times)				
抵港	to Hongkong		52780	57742	64560
离港	off Hongkong		52764	57745	64475
公共道路长度（公里）	Length of Roads (km)		1831	1865	1885
公共交通乘客人数（百万人次）	Number of Passengers of Public Traffic (1 million person.times)		3963	3865	3888
按种类划分的领牌车辆数字（千辆）	Vehicles grouped by Type (1000)				
私家车	Individuals		315	318	322
电单车（包括机动三轮车）	Motorcycles		24	23	24
的士	Taxi		18	18	18
公共及私家巴士	Public and Private Mini-bus		11	12	12
公共及私家小型巴士	Public and Private Bus		7	7	6
货车	Trucks		118	115	114
特别用途车辆（*少于 0.5）	Special-use(*<0.5)		*	*	*
政府车辆	of Government		8	7	7
总计	Total		500	501	5.4
按主要死亡原因划分的死亡人数及死亡率	Number Deaths and Death Rate by Death Cause				
恶性肿瘤死亡人数（人）	Malignant Tumour (person)		10373	10691	10922
死亡率（人/每十万名人口）	Death Rate (1/100 thousand persons)		159.5	159.9	159.6
心脏病死亡人数（人）	Heart Trouble (person)		4806	5060	5169
死亡率（人/每十万名人口）	Death Rate (1/100 thousand persons)		73.9	75.7	75.5
肺炎死亡人数（人）	Pneumonia (person)		4100	3691	3771
死亡率（人/每十万名人口）	Death Rate (1/100 thousand persons)		63.1	55.2	55.1
脑血管疾病死亡人数（人）	Cerebrovasular disease (person)		3026	3297	3368
死亡率（人/每十万名人口）	Death Rate (1/100 thousand persons)		46.5	49.3	49.2
受伤及中毒死亡人数（人）	Injured and Poisoned (person)		1908	1910	1951
死亡率（人/每十万名人口）	Death Rate (1/100 thousand persons)		29.3	28.6	28.5
婴儿死亡率（按每千名出生登记活产婴儿计算）（‰）	Death Rate of New-borns (according to 1000 New-borns registered) (‰)		4.0	3.2	3.2

附录 7：澳门地区主要社会经济指标
Appendix 7：MAIN SOCIAL AND ECONOMIC INDICATORS OF MACAO

项目 Item				1995	1997	1998	1999 *
年中人口数	(万人)	Mid-year Population	(10000 persons)	40.9	41.9	42.5	43.5
失业率	(%)	Unemployment Rate	(%)	3.4	3.2	4.6	6.6
国内生产总值	(百万美元)	Gross Domestic Product	(US$ 1 million)	7441.4	7349.2	6344.2	
人均国内生产总值	(美元)	GDP Per Capita	($)	18181.0	17545.0	16055.0	
实质本地增长率	(%)	Real Local Growth Rate	(%)	3.6	-0.1	-4.0	
通胀率	(%)	Inflation Rate	(%)	8.6	3.5	0.2	-3.2
对外贸易	(百万元澳门币)	Foreign Trade	(1 million MDP)				
出口总值(离岸价格)		Export Value(FOB)		16259.9	17129.2	17083.6	17760.4
本地产品出口		Local Products			15048.1	14903.8	15181.2
再出口		Re-export			2081.0	2179.8	2579.2
进口总值(到岸价格)		Import Value(CIF)		16506.0	16603.4	15596.4	16323.1
贸易差额		Balance of Trade Value		-246.1	525.8	1487.2	1437.3
出口/进口	(%)	Export/Import	(%)	98.5	103.2	109.5	108.8
旅游指标		Tourism					
入境旅客	(千人)	Foreign Tourists	(1000 persons)	7752.5	7000.4	6948.5	7455.7
酒店住客数目	(千人)	Visitors in Hotels	(1000 persons)	2400.9	2124.9	2080.8	2191.1
留宿时间	(晚数)	Staying Time	(night)	1.3	1.3	1.4	1.4
房间入住率	(%)	Living Rate of Rooms	(%)	60.1	52.1	53.1	54.2
五星、四星及三星酒店		5,4 and 3 stars		63.6	55.7	56.8	58.2
酒店客房供应数目	(房间)	Number of Guest Rooms	(room)	7796.0	8324.0	8320.0	8245.0
五星、四星及三星酒店		5,4 and 3 stars		6641.0	7231.0	7232.0	7217.0
能源指标		Energy					
电力		Electricity					
本地净生产电量	(百万千瓦小时)	Local Net Production	(1 million kwh)	1119.5	1248.1	1377.0	1374.2
供应电量	(百万千瓦小时)	Supply	(1 million kwh)	1261.8	1404.9	1514.7	1513.2
平均价格	(澳门币/千瓦小时)	Average Price	(MDP/kwh)	0.98	1.09	1.08	1.07
进口燃料价值	(百万澳门币)	Fuels Value Imported	(1 million MDP)	690.7	911.4	826.4	835.5
占进口总值%	(%)	the Proportion in Import	(%)	4.2	5.5	5.3	5.2

注：*为初步估计数（下表同）。

Note: * indicate the estimated data.(the following is the same)

附录 7 续表 continued

项　目	Item	1995	1997	1998	1999 *
消费物价指数 (%)	Consumer Price Indices (%)	94.8	102.8	103.0	99.7
（九五年七月至九六年六月=100）	(July,1995--June,1996 =100)				
粮食及不含酒精饮品	Grain and Soft Drink	95.8	103.7	104.3	99.7
衣履	Clothing	93.1	100.4	101.4	99.2
维修及住屋开支	Repairs and Residence	95.6	107.8	109.2	107.0
烟酒	Tabacco and Liquor	96.7	102.0	105.5	105.3
家居用品	Daily Use Articles	96.7	99.9	98.9	96.3
药物及医疗	Medicines and Medical Services	99.1	107.5	109.2	106.5
交通及通讯	Transportation and Co-mmunications	100.1	103.1	100.0	97.9
教育文化及休闲	Education,Culture and Recreation	89.3	102.4	104.7	101.9
其他物品及服务	Others	90.6	97.6	94.5	91.6
中央政府收支状况 （百万元澳门币）	Revenue and Expenditure of Central Government (1 million MDP)				
总收益	Total Revenue		15000.6	10723.1	10476.5
总支出	Total Expenditure		14240.7	10680.4	9943.5
财政结余	Balance		759.9	42.7	533.0
货币汇率	Exchange Rate				
（每百外币兑澳门元）	(Patacas to 100 unit of foreign currency)				
美元	US$	796.8	797.5	797.9	799.1
马克	DEM	557.0	460.6	454.2	438.1
英镑	GBP	1257.7	1306.9	1322.4	1293.1
法国法郎	FEF	159.9	136.8	135.5	130.6
欧洲货币单位	ECU	1031.0	901.9	896.1	822.6
日元	JPY	8.5	6.6	6.1	7.0
人民币	RMB	95.4	96.2	96.4	96.5
综合货币概况(期末数值） (百万元澳门币)	Currency (1 million MDP)				
货币供应（M2）	Supply(M2)	69284.0	78354.0	86210.0	91038.0
流通货币	Circulation	1280.0	1518.0	1548.0	1647.0
活期及储蓄存款	Current and Saving Deposits	17730.0	17435.0	18617.0	20704.0
预先通知及定期存款	Advance Noticed and Fixed Deposits	50274.0	59401.0	66045.0	68687.0
本地信贷	Local Credit	41613.0	48738.0	48000.0	45888.0
公共	Public	141.0	115.0	139.0	180.0
机构及私人	Institutions and Individuals	41472.0	48622.0	47862.0	45708.0
净对外资产	Net Foreign Assets	39257.0	42820.0	52882.0	60920.0
货币及汇兑监理署	Monetary authority	17978.0	20223.0	19657.0	22271.0
其他金融机构	Other Banking Institutions	21278.0	22598.0	33225.0	38689.0

中国统计出版社最新资料书目

(京)新登字 041 号

图书在版编目（CIP）数据

北京统计年鉴，2000/北京市统计局编.-北京：中国统计出版社，2000.6
ISBN 7-5037-3202-4/C·1713
Ⅰ.北… Ⅱ.北… Ⅲ.社会经济统计-统计资料-北京-2000-年鉴 Ⅳ.C832.1-54
中国版本图书馆 CIP 数据核字（2000）第 27974 号

北京统计年鉴-2000

出版发行/中国统计出版社
通信地址/北京市西城区三里河月坛南街 75 号　中国统计出版社
电　　话/（010）63262295
印　　刷/北京理工大学印刷厂
开　　本/787×1092 毫米/16 开本
字　　数/200 万字
印　　张/43.5 印张　　彩插/1 印张
印　　数/0001-2000 册
版　　别/2000 年 6 月第 1 版
版　　次/2000 年 6 月第 1 次印刷
书　　号/ISBN 7-5037-3202-4/C·1713
定　　价/280.00 元